OPCW:
The Legal Texts

3rd Edition

Working together for a world free of chemical weapons

ORGANISATION FOR THE
PROHIBITION OF CHEMICAL WEAPONS

OPCW:
The Legal Texts

3rd Edition

compiled and edited by
THE OFFICE OF THE LEGAL ADVISER

 ASSER PRESS

 Springer

ORGANISATION FOR THE PROHIBITION OF CHEMICAL WEAPONS
Johan de Wittlaan 32
2517 JR The Hague
The Netherlands
Tel.: +31 70 416 3300
Fax: +31 70 306 3535
Website: www.opcw.org

Materials of the United Nations have been reprinted with the permission of the United Nations.

ISBN 978-94-6265-043-5 (Hardcover)   ISBN 978-94-6265-044-2 (ebook)

ISBN 978-94-6265-046-6 (Softcover)

© OPCW, The Hague, The Netherlands, 1999, 2009, 2014

Published by T·M·C·ASSER PRESS, The Hague, The Netherlands www.asserpress.nl

Produced and distributed for T·M·C·ASSER PRESS by Springer-Verlag Berlin Heidelberg

All rights reserved. No part of this work may be reproduced, stored in a retrieval system, or transmitted in any form or by any means, electronic, mechanical, photocopying, microfilming, recording or otherwise, without written permission from the copyright owner, with the exception of any material supplied specifically for the purpose of being entered and executed on a computer system, for exclusive use by the purchaser of the work. The use of general descriptive names, registered names, trademarks, etc. in this publication does not imply, even in the absence of a specific statement, that such names are exempt from the relevant protective laws and regulations and therefore free for general use.

Printed on acid-free paper

Springer is part of Springer Science+Business Media (www.springer.com)

FOREWORD

The entry into force of the Chemical Weapons Convention on 29 April 1997 signalled the beginning of an era in which chemical weapons were to be eliminated forever.

To succeed in achieving its ambitious goals, the implementation of the Convention by the Organisation for the Prohibition of Chemical Weapons requires the active participation of all its States Parties and the Technical Secretariat.

After seventeen years of operation, the Chemical Weapons Convention—under which the OPCW has verified the destruction of over 80% of all declared chemical weapons—is a cornerstone in the construction of a world free of an entire category of weapons of mass destruction. Its success is due, to a considerable extent, to the continuous development of new rules, decisions, and guidelines making the text—arduously negotiated during the final years of the Cold War—a living instrument aimed at solving the challenges of chemical weapons disarmament and non-proliferation in the twenty first century.

OPCW: The Legal Texts was originally published in April 1999. At that time, the book provided a clear picture of the significant developments registered in the implementation of the Chemicals Weapons Convention during the early years of its life. The book was revised and republished in 2009 to encompass further major developments and to shed light on the overall implementation of the Chemical Weapons Convention more than ten years after its entry into force. Both of the compilations were well received both by practitioners and academics alike, who found in it a useful tool for understanding the institutions and organs tasked with the interpretation and implementation of the Convention.

The decision-making process that characterises the OPCW is relevant not only for the number of decisions adopted, but also for the balance achieved between the innovation and stability that mark the evolution of a truly multilateral agreement. With the activities conducted by the OPCW in the last several years to implement the Convention and establish a comprehensive regime for total chemical disarmament, it was considered that a new edition of the book was necessary. This new edition includes decisions adopted by the policy-making organs, reports, and other texts that testify to the level of activity of the Technical Secretariat and the commitment of States Parties and other stakeholders to work towards the achievement of the goals of the Convention. The texts also demonstrate how the priorities of the international community have evolved over the last seventeen years. Thus, for example, texts included in this volume address the global counter-terrorism efforts, industry participation in the multilateral process, and efforts to achieve universal adherence to the Convention. Documents pertaining to particular cases and missions have generally not been included, as the aim of the book is to make available decisions and interpretative instruments that can provide general guidance in a variety of areas relevant to the work of the Organisation and its States Parties. Some of the documents have been replaced with updated versions.

In this spirit, it is hoped that the book will provide ready assistance to academicians and practitioners engaged in the work of the OPCW as well as the work of universities or other international organisations and provide insights into the successful operation of a multilateral instrument. The book is also intended to serve as a source of technical information and guidance for those charged with the verification and destruction of chemical weapons.

The Hague, July 2014

AMBASSADOR AHMET ÜZÜMCÜ
Director-General

TABLE OF CONTENTS

Implementation

TABLE OF ABBREVIATIONS

ABAF	Advisory Body on Administrative and Financial Matters
ACAT	Assistance Coordination and Assessment Team
ACC	American Chemistry Council
ACW	abandoned chemical weapon
ADPA	Annual Declaration on Past Activities
ADR	European Agreement on the International Carriage of Dangerous Goods by Road
AND	aggregate national data
ATP	European Agreement on the International Carriage of Perishable Foodstuffs
BOD	beginning of destruction
CA	Confidentiality Annex
CA name	Chemical Abstract Index Guide name
CAS	Chemical Abstracts Service
CBO	chemical of biological origin
CEFIC	European Chemical Industry Council
CI	chemical ionisation
CW	chemical weapon
CWC	Chemical Weapons Convention
CWDF	Chemical Weapons Destruction Facility
CWPF	Chemical Weapons Production Facility
CWSF	Chemical Weapons Storage Facility
DFI	Detailed Facility Information
DOC	Discrete Organic Chemical
EC	Executive Council
EI	electron ionisation
EIF	entry into force
EU	European Union
FA	facility agreement
GC	gas chromatography
GC/MS	gas chromatography/mass spectrometry
GPS	global positioning system
GRULAC	Group of Latin America and Caribbean Countries
GTS	General Training Scheme
HCM	Hydrogen Concentration Measurement
IAEA	International Atomic Energy Agency
IATA	International Air Transport Association
ICCA	International Council of Chemical Associations
ICSC	International Civil Service Commission
IMS	information management system
IR	infrared
IRFA	issues requiring further attention
IPSAS	International Public Sector Accounting Standards
ISO	International Standards Organisation
ISP	Inspected State Party
IT	Inspection Team
IUPAC	International Union for Pure and Applied Chemistry
MCP	Manual of Confidentiality Procedure
MFA	Ministry of Foreign Affairs
MOT	means of transmission
MOU	Memorandum of Understanding
MS	mass spectrometry
NDE	Non-Destructive Evaluation
NGO	non-governmental organisation
NMR	nuclear magnetic resonance

OACW	old and abandoned chemical weapons
OCAD	OPCW Central Analytical Database
OECD	Organisation for Economic Cooperation and Development
OFPP	other facility for protective purposes
OFRMPhP	other Schedule 1 facilities for research, medical, or pharmaceutical purposes
OCPF	other chemical production facilities
OCS	Office of the Confidentiality and Security in the Technical Secretariat
OCW	old chemical weapon
OPCW	Organisation for the Prohibition of Chemical Weapons
OPOC	OPCW Policy on Confidentiality
PC	Preparatory Commission for the OPCW
POC	point of contact
POE	Point of Entry/Point of Exit
POI	Programme of Instruction
PR	Permanent Representative
PrepCom	Preparatory Commission for the OPCW
PSF	phosphorus, sulfur, fluorine
PTS	Provisional Technical Secretariat of the Preparatory Commission
QA/QC	quality assurance/quality control
RBM	results-based management
ROM	read only memory
ROP	Recommended Operating Procedure
SAB	Scientific Advisory Board
SCBA	Self contained breathing apparatus
SCN	Secure Critical Network
SIPRI	Stockholm International Peace Research Institute
SITC	Standard International Trade Classification
SOP	Standard Operating Procedure
SP	State Party
SSSF	single small-scale facility
TIC	total ion chromatogram
TNO	Netherlands Organisation for Applied Scientific Research
TS	Technical Secretariat of the OPCW
TVA	transitional verification arrangement
UN	United Nations
UNITAR	United Nations Training and Research Institute
UNSCOM	UN Special Commission on Iraq
VA	Verification Annex
VIS	Verification Information System
WEOG	Western European and Others Group
WHO	World Health Organization

TABLE OF DECISIONS

DECISIONS ADOPTED BY THE CONFERENCE AT ITS REGULAR SESSIONS

DECISIONS ADOPTED BY THE CONFERENCE AT ITS SPECIAL SESSIONS

DECISIONS ADOPTED BY THE COUNCIL AT ITS REGULAR SESSIONS

DECISIONS ADOPTED BY THE COUNCIL AT ITS MEETINGS

TABLE OF OTHER MATERIALS

PRE-OPCW MATERIALS

OPCW MATERIALS

The Conference

The Council

The Administrative Body on Administrative and Financial Matters

The Director-General

Chemical Weapons Convention

Chemical Weapons Convention

1. TEXT OF THE CONVENTION

(corrected version)

BACKGROUND NOTE

The draft Convention on the Prohibition of the Development, Production, Stockpiling and Use of Chemical Weapons and on Their Destruction (as contained in the Appendix to the Report of the Ad Hoc Committee on Chemical Weapons to the Conference on Disarmament, document CD/1170, dated 26 August 1992) was adopted in Geneva on 3 September 1992 by the Conference on Disarmament and transmitted to the Forty-Seventh Session of the United Nations General Assembly (Report of the Conference on Disarmament, OFFICIAL RECORDS OF THE GENERAL ASSEMBLY, 47th Session, Supplement no. 27 (A/47/27), paragraphs 73-74). The General Assembly commended the Convention on 30 November 1992 and requested the United Nations Secretary-General, as Depositary, to open it for signature in Paris on 13 January 1993 (General Assembly resolution 47/39, document A/RES/47/39, dated 16 December 1992). The Convention was open for signature in Paris from 13 to 15 January 1993 and thereafter at United Nations Headquarters, New York, until 29 April 1997. By that date the Convention had received 165 signatures. States which did not sign the Convention before entry into force may accede to it at any time.

The Convention entered into force on 29 April 1997. At entry into force there were 87 States Parties. As of July 2014, there were 190 States Parties to the Convention.

The corrected text of the Convention consists of the Appendix to Conference on Disarmament document CD/1170, dated 26 August 1992, corrected by Depositary Notifications C.N.246.1994. TREATIES-5 of 31 August 1994 (procès-verbal of rectification of the original of the Convention: Arabic, Chinese, English, French, Russian and Spanish texts); C.N.359.1994.TREATIES-8 of 27 January 1995 (procès-verbal of rectification of the original of the Convention: Spanish text); C.N.454.1995.TREATIES-12 of 2 February 1996 (procès-verbal of rectification of the original of the Convention: Arabic and Russian texts); C.N.916.1999.TREATIES-7 of 8 October 1999 (acceptance of amendment for a change to Section B of Part VI of the Annex on Implementation and Verification ("Verification Annex"), effective 31 October 1999); and C.N.157.2000.TREATIES-1 of 13 March 2000 (acceptance of corrections to the amendments, effective 9 March 2000) and C.N.610.2005.TREATIES-4 of 29 July 2005 [Approval of changes to Part V of the Annex on Implementation and Verification ("Verification Annex")]

CONVENTION ON THE PROHIBITION OF THE DEVELOPMENT, PRODUCTION, STOCKPILING AND USE OF CHEMICAL WEAPONS AND ON THEIR DESTRUCTION

PREAMBLE

The States Parties to this Convention,

DETERMINED to act with a view to achieving effective progress towards general and complete disarmament under strict and effective international control, including the prohibition and elimination of all types of weapons of mass destruction,

DESIRING to contribute to the realization of the purposes and principles of the Charter of the United Nations,

RECALLING that the General Assembly of the United Nations has repeatedly condemned all actions contrary to the principles and objectives of the Protocol for the Prohibition of the Use in War of Asphyxiating, Poisonous or Other Gases, and of Bacteriological Methods of Warfare, signed at Geneva on 17 June 1925 (the Geneva Protocol of 1925),

RECOGNISING that this Convention reaffirms principles and objectives of and obligations assumed under the Geneva Protocol of 1925, and the Convention on the Prohibition of the Development, Production and Stockpiling of Bacteriological (Biological) and Toxin Weapons and on their Destruction signed at London, Moscow and Washington on 10 April 1972,

BEARING IN MIND the objective contained in Article IX of the Convention on the Prohibition of the Development, Production and Stockpiling of Bacteriological (Biological) and Toxin Weapons and on their Destruction,

DETERMINED for the sake of all mankind, to exclude completely the possibility of the use of chemical weapons, through the implementation of the provisions of this Convention, thereby complementing the obligations assumed under the Geneva Protocol of 1925,

RECOGNISING the prohibition, embodied in the pertinent agreements and relevant principles of international law, of the use of herbicides as a method of warfare,

CONSIDERING that achievements in the field of chemistry should be used exclusively for the benefit of mankind,

DESIRING to promote free trade in chemicals as well as international cooperation and exchange of scientific and technical information in the field of chemical activities for purposes not prohibited under this Convention in order to enhance the economic and technological development of all States Parties,

CONVINCED that the complete and effective prohibition of the development, production, acquisition, stockpiling, retention, transfer and use of chemical weapons, and their destruction, represent a necessary step towards the achievement of these common objectives,

HAVE AGREED as follows:

ARTICLE I
GENERAL OBLIGATIONS

1. Each State Party to this Convention undertakes never under any circumstances:
    (a) To develop, produce, otherwise acquire, stockpile or retain chemical weapons, or transfer, directly or indirectly, chemical weapons to anyone;
    (b) To use chemical weapons;
    (c) To engage in any military preparations to use chemical weapons;
    (d) To assist, encourage or induce, in any way, anyone to engage in any activity prohibited to a State Party under this Convention.
2. Each State Party undertakes to destroy chemical weapons it owns or possesses, or that are located in any place under its jurisdiction or control, in accordance with the provisions of this Convention.

3. Each State Party undertakes to destroy all chemical weapons it abandoned on the territory of another State Party, in accordance with the provisions of this Convention.
4. Each State Party undertakes to destroy any chemical weapons production facilities it owns or possesses, or that are located in any place under its jurisdiction or control, in accordance with the provisions of this Convention.
5. Each State Party undertakes not to use riot control agents as a method of warfare.

ARTICLE II
DEFINITIONS AND CRITERIA

For the purposes of this Convention:
1. "Chemical Weapons" means the following, together or separately:
    (a) Toxic chemicals and their precursors, except where intended for purposes not prohibited under this Convention, as long as the types and quantities are consistent with such purposes;
    (b) Munitions and devices, specifically designed to cause death or other harm through the toxic properties of those toxic chemicals specified in subparagraph (a), which would be released as a result of the employment of such munitions and devices;
    (c) Any equipment specifically designed for use directly in connection with the employment of munitions and devices specified in subparagraph (b).
2. "Toxic Chemical" means:
    Any chemical which through its chemical action on life processes can cause death, temporary incapacitation or permanent harm to humans or animals. This includes all such chemicals, regardless of their origin or of their method of production, and regardless of whether they are produced in facilities, in munitions or elsewhere.
    (For the purpose of implementing this Convention, toxic chemicals which have been identified for the application of verification measures are listed in Schedules contained in the Annex on Chemicals.)
3. "Precursor" means:
    Any chemical reactant which takes part at any stage in the production by whatever method of a toxic chemical. This includes any key component of a binary or multicomponent chemical system.
    (For the purpose of implementing this Convention, precursors which have been identified for the application of verification measures are listed in Schedules contained in the Annex on Chemicals.)
4. "Key Component of Binary or Multicomponent Chemical Systems" (hereinafter referred to as "key component") means:
    The precursor which plays the most important role in determining the toxic properties of the final product and reacts rapidly with other chemicals in the binary or multicomponent system.
5. "Old Chemical Weapons" means:
    (a) Chemical weapons which were produced before 1925; or
    (b) Chemical weapons produced in the period between 1925 and 1946 that have deteriorated to such extent that they can no longer be used as chemical weapons.
6. "Abandoned Chemical Weapons" means:
    Chemical weapons, including old chemical weapons, abandoned by a State after 1 January 1925 on the territory of another State without the consent of the latter.
7. "Riot Control Agent" means:
    Any chemical not listed in a Schedule, which can produce rapidly in humans sensory irritation or disabling physical effects which disappear within a short time following termination of exposure.

8. "Chemical Weapons Production Facility":
    (a) Means any equipment, as well as any building housing such equipment, that was designed, constructed or used at any time since 1 January 1946:
        (i) As part of the stage in the production of chemicals ("final technological stage") where the material flows would contain, when the equipment is in operation:
            (1) Any chemical listed in Schedule 1 in the Annex on Chemicals; or
            (2) Any other chemical that has no use, above 1 tonne per year on the territory of a State Party or in any other place under the jurisdiction or control of a State Party, for purposes not prohibited under this Convention, but can be used for chemical weapons purposes;
        or
        (ii) For filling chemical weapons, including, *inter alia*, the filling of chemicals listed in Schedule 1 into munitions, devices or bulk storage containers; the filling of chemicals into containers that form part of assembled binary munitions and devices or into chemical submunitions that form part of assembled unitary munitions and devices, and the loading of the containers and chemical submunitions into the respective munitions and devices;
    (b) Does not mean:
        (i) Any facility having a production capacity for synthesis of chemicals specified in subparagraph (a) (i) that is less than 1 tonne;
        (ii) Any facility in which a chemical specified in subparagraph (a) (i) is or was produced as an unavoidable by-product of activities for purposes not prohibited under this Convention, provided that the chemical does not exceed 3 per cent of the total product and that the facility is subject to declaration and inspection under the Annex on Implementation and Verification (hereinafter referred to as "Verification Annex"); or
        (iii) The single small-scale facility for production of chemicals listed in Schedule 1 for purposes not prohibited under this Convention as referred to in Part VI of the Verification Annex.
9. "Purposes Not Prohibited Under this Convention" means:
    (a) Industrial, agricultural, research, medical, pharmaceutical or other peaceful purposes;
    (b) Protective purposes, namely those purposes directly related to protection against toxic chemicals and to protection against chemical weapons;
    (c) Military purposes not connected with the use of chemical weapons and not dependent on the use of the toxic properties of chemicals as a method of warfare;
    (d) Law enforcement including domestic riot control purposes.
10. "Production Capacity" means:
    The annual quantitative potential for manufacturing a specific chemical based on the technological process actually used or, if the process is not yet operational, planned to be used at the relevant facility. It shall be deemed to be equal to the nameplate capacity or, if the nameplate capacity is not available, to the design capacity. The nameplate capacity is the product output under conditions optimized for maximum quantity for the production facility, as demonstrated by one or more test-runs. The design capacity is the corresponding theoretically calculated product output.
11. "Organization" means the Organization for the Prohibition of Chemical Weapons established pursuant to Article VIII of this Convention.
12. For the purposes of Article VI:
    (a) "Production" of a chemical means its formation through chemical reaction;
    (b) "Processing" of a chemical means a physical process, such as formulation, extraction and purification, in which a chemical is not converted into another chemical;
    (c) "Consumption" of a chemical means its conversion into another chemical via a chemical reaction.

ARTICLE III
DECLARATIONS

1. Each State Party shall submit to the Organization, not later than 30 days after this Convention enters into force for it, the following declarations, in which it shall:
    (a) With respect to chemical weapons:
        (i) Declare whether it owns or possesses any chemical weapons, or whether there are any chemical weapons located in any place under its jurisdiction or control;
        (ii) Specify the precise location, aggregate quantity and detailed inventory of chemical weapons it owns or possesses, or that are located in any place under its jurisdiction or control, in accordance with Part IV (A), paragraphs 1 to 3, of the Verification Annex, except for those chemical weapons referred to in sub-subparagraph (iii);
        (iii) Report any chemical weapons on its territory that are owned and possessed by another State and located in any place under the jurisdiction or control of another State, in accordance with Part IV (A), paragraph 4, of the Verification Annex;
        (iv) Declare whether it has transferred or received, directly or indirectly, any chemical weapons since 1 January 1946 and specify the transfer or receipt of such weapons, in accordance with Part IV (A), paragraph 5, of the Verification Annex;
        (v) Provide its general plan for destruction of chemical weapons that it owns or possesses, or that are located in any place under its jurisdiction or control, in accordance with Part IV (A), paragraph 6, of the Verification Annex;
    (b) With respect to old chemical weapons and abandoned chemical weapons:
        (i) Declare whether it has on its territory old chemical weapons and provide all available information in accordance with Part IV (B), paragraph 3, of the Verification Annex;
        (ii) Declare whether there are abandoned chemical weapons on its territory and provide all available information in accordance with Part IV (B), paragraph 8, of the Verification Annex;
        (iii) Declare whether it has abandoned chemical weapons on the territory of other States and provide all available information in accordance with Part IV (B), paragraph 10, of the Verification Annex;
    (c) With respect to chemical weapons production facilities:
        (i) Declare whether it has or has had any chemical weapons production facility under its ownership or possession, or that is or has been located in any place under its jurisdiction or control at any time since 1 January 1946;
        (ii) Specify any chemical weapons production facility it has or has had under its ownership or possession or that is or has been located in any place under its jurisdiction or control at any time since 1 January 1946, in accordance with Part V, paragraph 1, of the Verification Annex, except for those facilities referred to in sub-subparagraph (iii);
        (iii) Report any chemical weapons production facility on its territory that another State has or has had under its ownership and possession and that is or has been located in any place under the jurisdiction or control of another State at any time since 1 January 1946, in accordance with Part V, paragraph 2, of the Verification Annex;
        (iv) Declare whether it has transferred or received, directly or indirectly, any equipment for the production of chemical weapons since 1 January 1946 and specify the transfer or receipt of such equipment, in accordance with Part V, paragraphs 3 to 5, of the Verification Annex;
        (v) Provide its general plan for destruction of any chemical weapons production facility it owns or possesses, or that is located in any place under its jurisdiction or control, in accordance with Part V, paragraph 6, of the Verification Annex;

    (vi) Specify actions to be taken for closure of any chemical weapons production facility it owns or possesses, or that is located in any place under its jurisdiction or control, in accordance with Part V, paragraph 1 (i), of the Verification Annex;

    (vii) Provide its general plan for any temporary conversion of any chemical weapons production facility it owns or possesses, or that is located in any place under its jurisdiction or control, into a chemical weapons destruction facility, in accordance with Part V, paragraph 7, of the Verification Annex;

(d) With respect to other facilities:

    Specify the precise location, nature and general scope of activities of any facility or establishment under its ownership or possession, or located in any place under its jurisdiction or control, and that has been designed, constructed or used since 1 January 1946 primarily for development of chemical weapons. Such declaration shall include, *inter alia*, laboratories and test and evaluation sites;

(e) With respect to riot control agents: Specify the chemical name, structural formula and Chemical Abstracts Service (CAS) registry number, if assigned, of each chemical it holds for riot control purposes. This declaration shall be updated not later than 30 days after any change becomes effective.

2. The provisions of this Article and the relevant provisions of Part IV of the Verification Annex shall not, at the discretion of a State Party, apply to chemical weapons buried on its territory before 1 January 1977 and which remain buried, or which had been dumped at sea before 1 January 1985.

ARTICLE IV
CHEMICAL WEAPONS

1. The provisions of this Article and the detailed procedures for its implementation shall apply to all chemical weapons owned or possessed by a State Party, or that are located in any place under its jurisdiction or control, except old chemical weapons and abandoned chemical weapons to which Part IV (B) of the Verification Annex applies.

2. Detailed procedures for the implementation of this Article are set forth in the Verification Annex.

3. All locations at which chemical weapons specified in paragraph 1 are stored or destroyed shall be subject to systematic verification through on-site inspection and monitoring with on-site instruments, in accordance with Part IV (A) of the Verification Annex.

4. Each State Party shall, immediately after the declaration under Article III, paragraph 1 (a), has been submitted, provide access to chemical weapons specified in paragraph 1 for the purpose of systematic verification of the declaration through on-site inspection. Thereafter, each State Party shall not remove any of these chemical weapons, except to a chemical weapons destruction facility. It shall provide access to such chemical weapons, for the purpose of systematic on-site verification.

5. Each State Party shall provide access to any chemical weapons destruction facilities and their storage areas, that it owns or possesses, or that are located in any place under its jurisdiction or control, for the purpose of systematic verification through on-site inspection and monitoring with on-site instruments.

6. Each State Party shall destroy all chemical weapons specified in paragraph 1 pursuant to the Verification Annex and in accordance with the agreed rate and sequence of destruction (hereinafter referred to as "order of destruction"). Such destruction shall begin not later than two years after this Convention enters into force for it and shall finish not later than 10 years after entry into force of this Convention. A State Party is not precluded from destroying such chemical weapons at a faster rate.

7. Each State Party shall:
   (a) Submit detailed plans for the destruction of chemical weapons specified in paragraph 1 not later than 60 days before each annual destruction period begins, in accordance with Part IV (A), paragraph 29, of the Verification Annex; the detailed plans shall encompass all stocks to be destroyed during the next annual destruction period;
   (b) Submit declarations annually regarding the implementation of its plans for destruction of chemical weapons specified in paragraph 1, not later than 60 days after the end of each annual destruction period; and
   (c) Certify, not later than 30 days after the destruction process has been completed, that all chemical weapons specified in paragraph 1 have been destroyed.
8. If a State ratifies or accedes to this Convention after the 10-year period for destruction set forth in paragraph 6, it shall destroy chemical weapons specified in paragraph 1 as soon as possible. The order of destruction and procedures for stringent verification for such a State Party shall be determined by the Executive Council.
9. Any chemical weapons discovered by a State Party after the initial declaration of chemical weapons shall be reported, secured and destroyed in accordance with Part IV (A) of the Verification Annex.
10. Each State Party, during transportation, sampling, storage and destruction of chemical weapons, shall assign the highest priority to ensuring the safety of people and to protecting the environment. Each State Party shall transport, sample, store and destroy chemical weapons in accordance with its national standards for safety and emissions.
11. Any State Party which has on its territory chemical weapons that are owned or possessed by another State, or that are located in any place under the jurisdiction or control of another State, shall make the fullest efforts to ensure that these chemical weapons are removed from its territory not later than one year after this Convention enters into force for it. If they are not removed within one year, the State Party may request the Organization and other States Parties to provide assistance in the destruction of these chemical weapons.
12. Each State Party undertakes to cooperate with other States Parties that request information or assistance on a bilateral basis or through the Technical Secretariat regarding methods and technologies for the safe and efficient destruction of chemical weapons.
13. In carrying out verification activities pursuant to this Article and Part IV (A) of the Verification Annex, the Organization shall consider measures to avoid unnecessary duplication of bilateral or multilateral agreements on verification of chemical weapons storage and their destruction among States Parties.

   To this end, the Executive Council shall decide to limit verification to measures complementary to those undertaken pursuant to such a bilateral or multilateral agreement, if it considers that:
   (a) Verification provisions of such an agreement are consistent with the verification provisions of this Article and Part IV (A) of the Verification Annex;
   (b) Implementation of such an agreement provides for sufficient assurance of compliance with the relevant provisions of this Convention; and
   (c) Parties to the bilateral or multilateral agreement keep the Organization fully informed about their verification activities.
14. If the Executive Council takes a decision pursuant to paragraph 13, the Organization shall have the right to monitor the implementation of the bilateral or multilateral agreement.
15. Nothing in paragraphs 13 and 14 shall affect the obligation of a State Party to provide declarations pursuant to Article III, this Article and Part IV (A) of the Verification Annex.
16. Each State Party shall meet the costs of destruction of chemical weapons it is obliged to destroy. It shall also meet the costs of verification of storage and destruction of these chemical weapons unless the Executive Council decides otherwise. If the Executive Council decides to limit verification measures of the Organization pursuant to paragraph 13, the costs of com-

plementary verification and monitoring by the Organization shall be paid in accordance with the United Nations scale of assessment, as specified in Article VIII, paragraph 7.

17. The provisions of this Article and the relevant provisions of Part IV of the Verification Annex shall not, at the discretion of a State Party, apply to chemical weapons buried on its territory before 1 January 1977 and which remain buried, or which had been dumped at sea before 1 January 1985.

ARTICLE V
CHEMICAL WEAPONS PRODUCTION FACILITIES

1. The provisions of this Article and the detailed procedures for its implementation shall apply to any and all chemical weapons production facilities owned or possessed by a State Party, or that are located in any place under its jurisdiction or control.

2. Detailed procedures for the implementation of this Article are set forth in the Verification Annex.

3. All chemical weapons production facilities specified in paragraph 1 shall be subject to systematic verification through on-site inspection and monitoring with on-site instruments in accordance with Part V of the Verification Annex.

4. Each State Party shall cease immediately all activity at chemical weapons production facilities specified in paragraph 1, except activity required for closure.

5. No State Party shall construct any new chemical weapons production facilities or modify any existing facilities for the purpose of chemical weapons production or for any other activity prohibited under this Convention.

6. Each State Party shall, immediately after the declaration under Article III, paragraph 1 (c), has been submitted, provide access to chemical weapons production facilities specified in paragraph 1, for the purpose of systematic verification of the declaration through on-site inspection.

7. Each State Party shall:
   (a) Close, not later than 90 days after this Convention enters into force for it, all chemical weapons production facilities specified in paragraph 1, in accordance with Part V of the Verification Annex, and give notice thereof; and
   (b) Provide access to chemical weapons production facilities specified in paragraph 1, subsequent to closure, for the purpose of systematic verification through on-site inspection and monitoring with on-site instruments in order to ensure that the facility remains closed and is subsequently destroyed.

8. Each State Party shall destroy all chemical weapons production facilities specified in paragraph 1 and related facilities and equipment, pursuant to the Verification Annex and in accordance with an agreed rate and sequence of destruction (hereinafter referred to as "order of destruction"). Such destruction shall begin not later than one year after this Convention enters into force for it, and shall finish not later than 10 years after entry into force of this Convention. A State Party is not precluded from destroying such facilities at a faster rate.

9. Each State Party shall:
   (a) Submit detailed plans for destruction of chemical weapons production facilities specified in paragraph 1, not later than 180 days before the destruction of each facility begins;
   (b) Submit declarations annually regarding the implementation of its plans for the destruction of all chemical weapons production facilities specified in paragraph 1, not later than 90 days after the end of each annual destruction period; and
   (c) Certify, not later than 30 days after the destruction process has been completed, that all chemical weapons production facilities specified in paragraph 1 have been destroyed.

10. If a State ratifies or accedes to this Convention after the 10-year period for destruction set forth in paragraph 8, it shall destroy chemical weapons production facilities specified in para-

graph 1 as soon as possible. The order of destruction and procedures for stringent verification for such a State Party shall be determined by the Executive Council.

11. Each State Party, during the destruction of chemical weapons production facilities, shall assign the highest priority to ensuring the safety of people and to protecting the environment. Each State Party shall destroy chemical weapons production facilities in accordance with its national standards for safety and emissions.

12. Chemical weapons production facilities specified in paragraph 1 may be temporarily converted for destruction of chemical weapons in accordance with Part V, paragraphs 18 to 25, of the Verification Annex. Such a converted facility must be destroyed as soon as it is no longer in use for destruction of chemical weapons but, in any case, not later than 10 years after entry into force of this Convention.

13. A State Party may request, in exceptional cases of compelling need, permission to use a chemical weapons production facility specified in paragraph 1 for purposes not prohibited under this Convention. Upon the recommendation of the Executive Council, the Conference of the States Parties shall decide whether or not to approve the request and shall establish the conditions upon which approval is contingent in accordance with Part V, Section D, of the Verification Annex.

14. The chemical weapons production facility shall be converted in such a manner that the converted facility is not more capable of being reconverted into a chemical weapons production facility than any other facility used for industrial, agricultural, research, medical, pharmaceutical or other peaceful purposes not involving chemicals listed in Schedule 1.

15. All converted facilities shall be subject to systematic verification through on-site inspection and monitoring with on-site instruments in accordance with Part V, Section D, of the Verification Annex.

16. In carrying out verification activities pursuant to this Article and Part V of the Verification Annex, the Organization shall consider measures to avoid unnecessary duplication of bilateral or multilateral agreements on verification of chemical weapons production facilities and their destruction among States Parties.

   To this end, the Executive Council shall decide to limit the verification to measures complementary to those undertaken pursuant to such a bilateral or multilateral agreement, if it considers that:

   (a) Verification provisions of such an agreement are consistent with the verification provisions of this Article and Part V of the Verification Annex;

   (b) Implementation of the agreement provides for sufficient assurance of compliance with the relevant provisions of this Convention; and

   (c) Parties to the bilateral or multilateral agreement keep the Organization fully informed about their verification activities.

17. If the Executive Council takes a decision pursuant to paragraph 16, the Organization shall have the right to monitor the implementation of the bilateral or multilateral agreement.

18. Nothing in paragraphs 16 and 17 shall affect the obligation of a State Party to make declarations pursuant to Article III, this Article and Part V of the Verification Annex.

19. Each State Party shall meet the costs of destruction of chemical weapons production facilities it is obliged to destroy. It shall also meet the costs of verification under this Article unless the Executive Council decides otherwise. If the Executive Council decides to limit verification measures of the Organization pursuant to paragraph 16, the costs of complementary verification and monitoring by the Organization shall be paid in accordance with the United Nations scale of assessment, as specified in Article VIII, paragraph 7.

ARTICLE VI
ACTIVITIES NOT PROHIBITED UNDER THIS CONVENTION

1. Each State Party has the right, subject to the provisions of this Convention, to develop, produce, otherwise acquire, retain, transfer and use toxic chemicals and their precursors for purposes not prohibited under this Convention.

2. Each State Party shall adopt the necessary measures to ensure that toxic chemicals and their precursors are only developed, produced, otherwise acquired, retained, transferred, or used within its territory or in any other place under its jurisdiction or control for purposes not prohibited under this Convention. To this end, and in order to verify that activities are in accordance with obligations under this Convention, each State Party shall subject toxic chemicals and their precursors listed in Schedules 1, 2 and 3 of the Annex on Chemicals, facilities related to such chemicals, and other facilities as specified in the Verification Annex, that are located on its territory or in any other place under its jurisdiction or control, to verification measures as provided in the Verification Annex.

3. Each State Party shall subject chemicals listed in Schedule 1 (hereinafter referred to as "Schedule 1 chemicals") to the prohibitions on production, acquisition, retention, transfer and use as specified in Part VI of the Verification Annex. It shall subject Schedule 1 chemicals and facilities specified in Part VI of the Verification Annex to systematic verification through on-site inspection and monitoring with on-site instruments in accordance with that Part of the Verification Annex.

4. Each State Party shall subject chemicals listed in Schedule 2 (hereinafter referred to as "Schedule 2 chemicals") and facilities specified in Part VII of the Verification Annex to data monitoring and on-site verification in accordance with that Part of the Verification Annex.

5. Each State Party shall subject chemicals listed in Schedule 3 (hereinafter referred to as "Schedule 3 chemicals") and facilities specified in Part VIII of the Verification Annex to data monitoring and on-site verification in accordance with that Part of the Verification Annex.

6. Each State Party shall subject facilities specified in Part IX of the Verification Annex to data monitoring and eventual on-site verification in accordance with that Part of the Verification Annex unless decided otherwise by the Conference of the States Parties pursuant to Part IX, paragraph 22, of the Verification Annex.

7. Not later than 30 days after this Convention enters into force for it, each State Party shall make an initial declaration on relevant chemicals and facilities in accordance with the Verification Annex.

8. Each State Party shall make annual declarations regarding the relevant chemicals and facilities in accordance with the Verification Annex.

9. For the purpose of on-site verification, each State Party shall grant to the inspectors access to facilities as required in the Verification Annex.

10. In conducting verification activities, the Technical Secretariat shall avoid undue intrusion into the State Party's chemical activities for purposes not prohibited under this Convention and, in particular, abide by the provisions set forth in the Annex on the Protection of Confidential Information (hereinafter referred to as "Confidentiality Annex").

11. The provisions of this Article shall be implemented in a manner which avoids hampering the economic or technological development of States Parties, and international cooperation in the field of chemical activities for purposes not prohibited under this Convention including the international exchange of scientific and technical information and chemicals and equipment for the production, processing or use of chemicals for purposes not prohibited under this Convention.

ARTICLE VII
NATIONAL IMPLEMENTATION MEASURES

GENERAL UNDERTAKINGS

1. Each State Party shall, in accordance with its constitutional processes, adopt the necessary measures to implement its obligations under this Convention. In particular, it shall:
    (a) Prohibit natural and legal persons anywhere on its territory or in any other place under its jurisdiction as recognized by international law from undertaking any activity prohibited to a State Party under this Convention, including enacting penal legislation with respect to such activity;
    (b) Not permit in any place under its control any activity prohibited to a State Party under this Convention; and
    (c) Extend its penal legislation enacted under subparagraph (a) to any activity prohibited to a State Party under this Convention undertaken anywhere by natural persons, possessing its nationality, in conformity with international law.
2. Each State Party shall cooperate with other States Parties and afford the appropriate form of legal assistance to facilitate the implementation of the obligations under paragraph 1.
3. Each State Party, during the implementation of its obligations under this Convention, shall assign the highest priority to ensuring the safety of people and to protecting the environment, and shall cooperate as appropriate with other States Parties in this regard.

RELATIONS BETWEEN THE STATE PARTY AND THE ORGANIZATION

4. In order to fulfil its obligations under this Convention, each State Party shall designate or establish a National Authority to serve as the national focal point for effective liaison with the Organization and other States Parties. Each State Party shall notify the Organization of its National Authority at the time that this Convention enters into force for it.
5. Each State Party shall inform the Organization of the legislative and administrative measures taken to implement this Convention.
6. Each State Party shall treat as confidential and afford special handling to information and data that it receives in confidence from the Organization in connection with the implementation of this Convention.

    It shall treat such information and data exclusively in connection with its rights and obligations under this Convention and in accordance with the provisions set forth in the Confidentiality Annex.
7. Each State Party undertakes to cooperate with the Organization in the exercise of all its functions and in particular to provide assistance to the Technical Secretariat.

ARTICLE VIII
THE ORGANIZATION

A. GENERAL PROVISIONS

1. The States Parties to this Convention hereby establish the Organization for the Prohibition of Chemical Weapons to achieve the object and purpose of this Convention, to ensure the implementation of its provisions, including those for international verification of compliance with it, and to provide a forum for consultation and cooperation among States Parties.
2. All States Parties to this Convention shall be members of the Organization. A State Party shall not be deprived of its membership in the Organization.
3. The seat of the Headquarters of the Organization shall be The Hague, Kingdom of the Netherlands.

4. There are hereby established as the organs of the Organization: the Conference of the States Parties, the Executive Council, and the Technical Secretariat.
5. The Organization shall conduct its verification activities provided for under this Convention in the least intrusive manner possible consistent with the timely and efficient accomplishment of their objectives. It shall request only the information and data necessary to fulfil its responsibilities under this Convention. It shall take every precaution to protect the confidentiality of information on civil and military activities and facilities coming to its knowledge in the implementation of this Convention and, in particular, shall abide by the provisions set forth in the Confidentiality Annex.
6. In undertaking its verification activities the Organization shall consider measures to make use of advances in science and technology.
7. The costs of the Organization's activities shall be paid by States Parties in accordance with the United Nations scale of assessment adjusted to take into account differences in membership between the United Nations and this Organization, and subject to the provisions of Articles IV and V. Financial contributions of States Parties to the Preparatory Commission shall be deducted in an appropriate way from their contributions to the regular budget. The budget of the Organization shall comprise two separate chapters, one relating to administrative and other costs, and one relating to verification costs.
8. A member of the Organization which is in arrears in the payment of its financial contribution to the Organization shall have no vote in the Organization if the amount of its arrears equals or exceeds the amount of the contribution due from it for the preceding two full years. The Conference of the States Parties may, nevertheless, permit such a member to vote if it is satisfied that the failure to pay is due to conditions beyond the control of the member.

B. THE CONFERENCE OF THE STATES PARTIES

COMPOSITION, PROCEDURES AND DECISION-MAKING

9. The Conference of the States Parties (hereinafter referred to as "the Conference") shall be composed of all members of this Organization. Each member shall have one representative in the Conference, who may be accompanied by alternates and advisers.
10. The first session of the Conference shall be convened by the depositary not later than 30 days after the entry into force of this Convention.
11. The Conference shall meet in regular sessions which shall be held annually unless it decides otherwise.
12. Special sessions of the Conference shall be convened:
    (a) When decided by the Conference;
    (b) When requested by the Executive Council;
    (c) When requested by any member and supported by one third of the members; or
    (d) In accordance with paragraph 22 to undertake reviews of the operation of this Convention.
    Except in the case of subparagraph (d), the special session shall be convened not later than 30 days after receipt of the request by the Director-General of the Technical Secretariat, unless specified otherwise in the request.
13. The Conference shall also be convened in the form of an Amendment Conference in accordance with Article XV, paragraph 2.
14. Sessions of the Conference shall take place at the seat of the Organization unless the Conference decides otherwise.
15. The Conference shall adopt its rules of procedure. At the beginning of each regular session, it shall elect its Chairman and such other officers as may be required. They shall hold office until a new Chairman and other officers are elected at the next regular session.
16. A majority of the members of the Organization shall constitute a quorum for the Conference.

17. Each member of the Organization shall have one vote in the Conference.

18. The Conference shall take decisions on questions of procedure by a simple majority of the members present and voting. Decisions on matters of substance should be taken as far as possible by consensus. If consensus is not attainable when an issue comes up for decision, the Chairman shall defer any vote for 24 hours and during this period of deferment shall make every effort to facilitate achievement of consensus, and shall report to the Conference before the end of this period. If consensus is not possible at the end of 24 hours, the Conference shall take the decision by a two-thirds majority of members present and voting unless specified otherwise in this Convention. When the issue arises as to whether the question is one of substance or not, that question shall be treated as a matter of substance unless otherwise decided by the Conference by the majority required for decisions on matters of substance.

POWERS AND FUNCTIONS

19. The Conference shall be the principal organ of the Organization. It shall consider any questions, matters or issues within the scope of this Convention, including those relating to the powers and functions of the Executive Council and the Technical Secretariat. It may make recommendations and take decisions on any questions, matters or issues related to this Convention raised by a State Party or brought to its attention by the Executive Council.

20. The Conference shall oversee the implementation of this Convention, and act in order to promote its object and purpose. The Conference shall review compliance with this Convention. It shall also oversee the activities of the Executive Council and the Technical Secretariat and may issue guidelines in accordance with this Convention to either of them in the exercise of their functions.

21. The Conference shall:
    (a) Consider and adopt at its regular sessions the report, programme and budget of the Organization, submitted by the Executive Council, as well as consider other reports;
    (b) Decide on the scale of financial contributions to be paid by States Parties in accordance with paragraph 7;
    (c) Elect the members of the Executive Council;
    (d) Appoint the Director-General of the Technical Secretariat (hereinafter referred to as "the Director-General");
    (e) Approve the rules of procedure of the Executive Council submitted by the latter;
    (f) Establish such subsidiary organs as it finds necessary for the exercise of its functions in accordance with this Convention;
    (g) Foster international cooperation for peaceful purposes in the field of chemical activities;
    (h) Review scientific and technological developments that could affect the operation of this Convention and, in this context, direct the Director-General to establish a Scientific Advisory Board to enable him, in the performance of his functions, to render specialized advice in areas of science and technology relevant to this Convention, to the Conference, the Executive Council or States Parties. The Scientific Advisory Board shall be composed of independent experts appointed in accordance with terms of reference adopted by the Conference;
    (i) Consider and approve at its first session any draft agreements, provisions and guidelines developed by the Preparatory Commission;
    (j) Establish at its first session the voluntary fund for assistance in accordance with Article X;
    (k) Take the necessary measures to ensure compliance with this Convention and to redress and remedy any situation which contravenes the provisions of this Convention, in accordance with Article XII.

22. The Conference shall not later than one year after the expiry of the fifth and the tenth year after the entry into force of this Convention, and at such other times within that time period

as may be decided upon, convene in special sessions to undertake reviews of the operation of this Convention. Such reviews shall take into account any relevant scientific and technological developments. At intervals of five years thereafter, unless otherwise decided upon, further sessions of the Conference shall be convened with the same objective.

C. THE EXECUTIVE COUNCIL

COMPOSITION, PROCEDURE AND DECISION-MAKING

23. The Executive Council shall consist of 41 members. Each State Party shall have the right, in accordance with the principle of rotation, to serve on the Executive Council. The members of the Executive Council shall be elected by the Conference for a term of two years. In order to ensure the effective functioning of this Convention, due regard being specially paid to equitable geographical distribution, to the importance of chemical industry, as well as to political and security interests, the Executive Council shall be composed as follows:

(a) Nine States Parties from Africa to be designated by States Parties located in this region. As a basis for this designation it is understood that, out of these nine States Parties, three members shall, as a rule, be the States Parties with the most significant national chemical industry in the region as determined by internationally reported and published data; in addition, the regional group shall agree also to take into account other regional factors in designating these three members;

(b) Nine States Parties from Asia to be designated by States Parties located in this region. As a basis for this designation it is understood that, out of these nine States Parties, four members shall, as a rule, be the States Parties with the most significant national chemical industry in the region as determined by internationally reported and published data; in addition, the regional group shall agree also to take into account other regional factors in designating these four members;

(c) Five States Parties from Eastern Europe to be designated by States Parties located in this region. As a basis for this designation it is understood that, out of these five States Parties, one member shall, as a rule, be the State Party with the most significant national chemical industry in the region as determined by internationally reported and published data; in addition, the regional group shall agree also to take into account other regional factors in designating this one member;

(d) Seven States Parties from Latin America and the Caribbean to be designated by States Parties located in this region. As a basis for this designation it is understood that, out of these seven States Parties, three members shall, as a rule, be the States Parties with the most significant national chemical industry in the region as determined by internationally reported and published data; in addition, the regional group shall agree also to take into account other regional factors in designating these three members;

(e) Ten States Parties from among Western European and other States to be designated by States Parties located in this region. As a basis for this designation it is understood that, out of these 10 States Parties, 5 members shall, as a rule, be the States Parties with the most significant national chemical industry in the region as determined by internationally reported and published data; in addition, the regional group shall agree also to take into account other regional factors in designating these five members;

(f) One further State Party to be designated consecutively by States Parties located in the regions of Asia and Latin America and the Caribbean. As a basis for this designation it is understood that this State Party shall be a rotating member from these regions.

24. For the first election of the Executive Council 20 members shall be elected for a term of one year, due regard being paid to the established numerical proportions as described in paragraph 23.

25. After the full implementation of Articles IV and V the Conference may, upon the request of a

majority of the members of the Executive Council, review the composition of the Executive Council taking into account developments related to the principles specified in paragraph 23 that are governing its composition.

26. The Executive Council shall elaborate its rules of procedure and submit them to the Conference for approval.

27. The Executive Council shall elect its Chairman from among its members.

28. The Executive Council shall meet for regular sessions. Between regular sessions it shall meet as often as may be required for the fulfilment of its powers and functions.

29. Each member of the Executive Council shall have one vote. Unless otherwise specified in this Convention, the Executive Council shall take decisions on matters of substance by a two-thirds majority of all its members. The Executive Council shall take decisions on questions of procedure by a simple majority of all its members. When the issue arises as to whether the question is one of substance or not, that question shall be treated as a matter of substance unless otherwise decided by the Executive Council by the majority required for decisions on matters of substance.

POWERS AND FUNCTIONS

30. The Executive Council shall be the executive organ of the Organization. It shall be responsible to the Conference. The Executive Council shall carry out the powers and functions entrusted to it under this Convention, as well as those functions delegated to it by the Conference. In so doing, it shall act in conformity with the recommendations, decisions and guidelines of the Conference and assure their proper and continuous implementation.

31. The Executive Council shall promote the effective implementation of, and compliance with, this Convention. It shall supervise the activities of the Technical Secretariat, cooperate with the National Authority of each State Party and facilitate consultations and cooperation among States Parties at their request.

32. The Executive Council shall:
    (a) Consider and submit to the Conference the draft programme and budget of the Organization;
    (b) Consider and submit to the Conference the draft report of the Organization on the implementation of this Convention, the report on the performance of its own activities and such special reports as it deems necessary or which the Conference may request;
    (c) Make arrangements for the sessions of the Conference including the preparation of the draft agenda.

33. The Executive Council may request the convening of a special session of the Conference.

34. The Executive Council shall:
    (a) Conclude agreements or arrangements with States and international organizations on behalf of the Organization, subject to prior approval by the Conference;
    (b) Conclude agreements with States Parties on behalf of the Organization in connection with Article X and supervise the voluntary fund referred to in Article X;
    (c) Approve agreements or arrangements relating to the implementation of verification activities, negotiated by the Technical Secretariat with States Parties.

35. The Executive Council shall consider any issue or matter within its competence affecting this Convention and its implementation, including concerns regarding compliance, and cases of non-compliance, and, as appropriate, inform States Parties and bring the issue or matter to the attention of the Conference.

36. In its consideration of doubts or concerns regarding compliance and cases of non-compliance, including, *inter alia*, abuse of the rights provided for under this Convention, the Executive Council shall consult with the States Parties involved and, as appropriate, request the State Party to take measures to redress the situation within a specified time. To the extent that the Executive Council considers further action to be necessary, it shall take, *inter alia*, one or

more of the following measures:

(a) Inform all States Parties of the issue or matter;

(b) Bring the issue or matter to the attention of the Conference;

(c) Make recommendations to the Conference regarding measures to redress the situation and to ensure compliance.

The Executive Council shall, in cases of particular gravity and urgency, bring the issue or matter, including relevant information and conclusions, directly to the attention of the United Nations General Assembly and the United Nations Security Council. It shall at the same time inform all States Parties of this step.

D. THE TECHNICAL SECRETARIAT

37. The Technical Secretariat shall assist the Conference and the Executive Council in the performance of their functions. The Technical Secretariat shall carry out the verification measures provided for in this Convention. It shall carry out the other functions entrusted to it under this Convention as well as those functions delegated to it by the Conference and the Executive Council.

38. The Technical Secretariat shall:

(a) Prepare and submit to the Executive Council the draft programme and budget of the Organization;

(b) Prepare and submit to the Executive Council the draft report of the Organization on the implementation of this Convention and such other reports as the Conference or the Executive Council may request;

(c) Provide administrative and technical support to the Conference, the Executive Council and subsidiary organs;

(d) Address and receive communications on behalf of the Organization to and from States Parties on matters pertaining to the implementation of this Convention;

(e) Provide technical assistance and technical evaluation to States Parties in the implementation of the provisions of this Convention, including evaluation of scheduled and unscheduled chemicals.

39. The Technical Secretariat shall:

(a) Negotiate agreements or arrangements relating to the implementation of verification activities with States Parties, subject to approval by the Executive Council;

(b) Not later than 180 days after entry into force of this Convention, coordinate the establishment and maintenance of permanent stockpiles of emergency and humanitarian assistance by States Parties in accordance with Article X, paragraphs 7 (b) and (c). The Technical Secretariat may inspect the items maintained for serviceability. Lists of items to be stockpiled shall be considered and approved by the Conference pursuant to paragraph 21 (i) above;

(c) Administer the voluntary fund referred to in Article X, compile declarations made by the States Parties and register, when requested, bilateral agreements concluded between States Parties or between a State Party and the Organization for the purposes of Article X.

40. The Technical Secretariat shall inform the Executive Council of any problem that has arisen with regard to the discharge of its functions, including doubts, ambiguities or uncertainties about compliance with this Convention that have come to its notice in the performance of its verification activities and that it has been unable to resolve or clarify through its consultations with the State Party concerned.

41. The Technical Secretariat shall comprise a Director-General, who shall be its head and chief administrative officer, inspectors and such scientific, technical and other personnel as may be required.

42. The Inspectorate shall be a unit of the Technical Secretariat and shall act under the supervision of the Director-General.

43. The Director-General shall be appointed by the Conference upon the recommendation of the Executive Council for a term of four years, renewable for one further term, but not thereafter.

44. The Director-General shall be responsible to the Conference and the Executive Council for the appointment of the staff and the organization and functioning of the Technical Secretariat. The paramount consideration in the employment of the staff and in the determination of the conditions of service shall be the necessity of securing the highest standards of efficiency, competence and integrity. Only citizens of States Parties shall serve as the Director-General, as inspectors or as other members of the professional and clerical staff. Due regard shall be paid to the importance of recruiting the staff on as wide a geographical basis as possible. Recruitment shall be guided by the principle that the staff shall be kept to a minimum necessary for the proper discharge of the responsibilities of the Technical Secretariat.

45. The Director-General shall be responsible for the organization and functioning of the Scientific Advisory Board referred to in paragraph 21 (h). The Director-General shall, in consultation with States Parties, appoint members of the Scientific Advisory Board, who shall serve in their individual capacity. The members of the Board shall be appointed on the basis of their expertise in the particular scientific fields relevant to the implementation of this Convention. The Director-General may also, as appropriate, in consultation with members of the Board, establish temporary working groups of scientific experts to provide recommendations on specific issues. In regard to the above, States Parties may submit lists of experts to the Director-General.

46. In the performance of their duties, the Director-General, the inspectors and the other members of the staff shall not seek or receive instructions from any Government or from any other source external to the Organization. They shall refrain from any action that might reflect on their positions as international officers responsible only to the Conference and the Executive Council.

47. Each State Party shall respect the exclusively international character of the responsibilities of the Director-General, the inspectors and the other members of the staff and not seek to influence them in the discharge of their responsibilities.

E. PRIVILEGES AND IMMUNITIES

48. The Organization shall enjoy on the territory and in any other place under the jurisdiction or control of a State Party such legal capacity and such privileges and immunities as are necessary for the exercise of its functions.

49. Delegates of States Parties, together with their alternates and advisers, representatives appointed to the Executive Council together with their alternates and advisers, the Director-General and the staff of the Organization shall enjoy such privileges and immunities as are necessary in the independent exercise of their functions in connection with the Organization.

50. The legal capacity, privileges, and immunities referred to in this Article shall be defined in agreements between the Organization and the States Parties as well as in an agreement between the Organization and the State in which the headquarters of the Organization is seated. These agreements shall be considered and approved by the Conference pursuant to paragraph 21 (i).

51. Notwithstanding paragraphs 48 and 49, the privileges and immunities enjoyed by the Director-General and the staff of the Technical Secretariat during the conduct of verification activities shall be those set forth in Part II, Section B, of the Verification Annex.

ARTICLE IX
CONSULTATIONS, COOPERATION AND FACT-FINDING

1. States Parties shall consult and cooperate, directly among themselves, or through the Organization or other appropriate international procedures, including procedures within the framework of the United Nations and in accordance with its Charter, on any matter which may be raised relating to the object and purpose, or the implementation of the provisions, of this Convention.

2. Without prejudice to the right of any State Party to request a challenge inspection, States Parties should, whenever possible, first make every effort to clarify and resolve, through exchange of information and consultations among themselves, any matter which may cause doubt about compliance with this Convention, or which gives rise to concerns about a related matter which may be considered ambiguous. A State Party which receives a request from another State Party for clarification of any matter which the requesting State Party believes causes such a doubt or concern shall provide the requesting State Party as soon as possible, but in any case not later than 10 days after the request, with information sufficient to answer the doubt or concern raised along with an explanation of how the information provided resolves the matter. Nothing in this Convention shall affect the right of any two or more States Parties to arrange by mutual consent for inspections or any other procedures among themselves to clarify and resolve any matter which may cause doubt about compliance or gives rise to a concern about a related matter which may be considered ambiguous. Such arrangements shall not affect the rights and obligations of any State Party under other provisions of this Convention.

PROCEDURE FOR REQUESTING CLARIFICATION

3. A State Party shall have the right to request the Executive Council to assist in clarifying any situation which may be considered ambiguous or which gives rise to a concern about the possible non-compliance of another State Party with this Convention. The Executive Council shall provide appropriate information in its possession relevant to such a concern.

4. A State Party shall have the right to request the Executive Council to obtain clarification from another State Party on any situation which may be considered ambiguous or which gives rise to a concern about its possible non-compliance with this Convention. In such a case, the following shall apply:

   (a) The Executive Council shall forward the request for clarification to the State Party concerned through the Director-General not later than 24 hours after its receipt;

   (b) The requested State Party shall provide the clarification to the Executive Council as soon as possible, but in any case not later than 10 days after the receipt of the request;

   (c) The Executive Council shall take note of the clarification and forward it to the requesting State Party not later than 24 hours after its receipt;

   (d) If the requesting State Party deems the clarification to be inadequate, it shall have the right to request the Executive Council to obtain from the requested State Party further clarification;

   (e) For the purpose of obtaining further clarification requested under subparagraph (d), the Executive Council may call on the Director-General to establish a group of experts from the Technical Secretariat, or if appropriate staff are not available in the Technical Secretariat, from elsewhere, to examine all available information and data relevant to the situation causing the concern. The group of experts shall submit a factual report to the Executive Council on its findings;

   (f) If the requesting State Party considers the clarification obtained under subparagraphs (d) and (e) to be unsatisfactory, it shall have the right to request a special session of the Executive Council in which States Parties involved that are not members of the Executive

Council shall be entitled to take part. In such a special session, the Executive Council shall consider the matter and may recommend any measure it deems appropriate to resolve the situation.

5. A State Party shall also have the right to request the Executive Council to clarify any situation which has been considered ambiguous or has given rise to a concern about its possible non-compliance with this Convention. The Executive Council shall respond by providing such assistance as appropriate.

6. The Executive Council shall inform the States Parties about any request for clarification provided in this Article.

7. If the doubt or concern of a State Party about a possible non-compliance has not been resolved within 60 days after the submission of the request for clarification to the Executive Council, or it believes its doubts warrant urgent consideration, notwithstanding its right to request a challenge inspection, it may request a special session of the Conference in accordance with Article VIII, paragraph 12 (c). At such a special session, the Conference shall consider the matter and may recommend any measure it deems appropriate to resolve the situation.

PROCEDURES FOR CHALLENGE INSPECTIONS

8. Each State Party has the right to request an on-site challenge inspection of any facility or location in the territory or in any other place under the jurisdiction or control of any other State Party for the sole purpose of clarifying and resolving any questions concerning possible non-compliance with the provisions of this Convention, and to have this inspection conducted anywhere without delay by an inspection team designated by the Director-General and in accordance with the Verification Annex.

9. Each State Party is under the obligation to keep the inspection request within the scope of this Convention and to provide in the inspection request all appropriate information on the basis of which a concern has arisen regarding possible non-compliance with this Convention as specified in the Verification Annex. Each State Party shall refrain from unfounded inspection requests, care being taken to avoid abuse. The challenge inspection shall be carried out for the sole purpose of determining facts relating to the possible non-compliance.

10. For the purpose of verifying compliance with the provisions of this Convention, each State Party shall permit the Technical Secretariat to conduct the on-site challenge inspection pursuant to paragraph 8.

11. Pursuant to a request for a challenge inspection of a facility or location, and in accordance with the procedures provided for in the Verification Annex, the inspected State Party shall have:

    (a) The right and the obligation to make every reasonable effort to demonstrate its compliance with this Convention and, to this end, to enable the inspection team to fulfil its mandate;

    (b) The obligation to provide access within the requested site for the sole purpose of establishing facts relevant to the concern regarding possible non-compliance; and

    (c) The right to take measures to protect sensitive installations, and to prevent disclosure of confidential information and data, not related to this Convention.

12. With regard to an observer, the following shall apply:

    (a) The requesting State Party may, subject to the agreement of the inspected State Party, send a representative who may be a national either of the requesting State Party or of a third State Party, to observe the conduct of the challenge inspection.

    (b) The inspected State Party shall then grant access to the observer in accordance with the Verification Annex.

    (c) The inspected State Party shall, as a rule, accept the proposed observer, but if the inspected State Party exercises a refusal, that fact shall be recorded in the final report.

13. The requesting State Party shall present an inspection request for an on-site challenge inspection to the Executive Council and at the same time to the Director-General for immediate processing.

14. The Director-General shall immediately ascertain that the inspection request meets the requirements specified in Part X, paragraph 4, of the Verification Annex, and, if necessary, assist the requesting State Party in filing the inspection request accordingly. When the inspection request fulfils the requirements, preparations for the challenge inspection shall begin.

15. The Director-General shall transmit the inspection request to the inspected State Party not less than 12 hours before the planned arrival of the inspection team at the point of entry.

16. After having received the inspection request, the Executive Council shall take cognizance of the Director-General's actions on the request and shall keep the case under its consideration throughout the inspection procedure. However, its deliberations shall not delay the inspection process.

17. The Executive Council may, not later than 12 hours after having received the inspection request, decide by a three-quarter majority of all its members against carrying out the challenge inspection, if it considers the inspection request to be frivolous, abusive or clearly beyond the scope of this Convention as described in paragraph 8. Neither the requesting nor the inspected State Party shall participate in such a decision. If the Executive Council decides against the challenge inspection, preparations shall be stopped, no further action on the inspection request shall be taken, and the States Parties concerned shall be informed accordingly.

18. The Director-General shall issue an inspection mandate for the conduct of the challenge inspection. The inspection mandate shall be the inspection request referred to in paragraphs 8 and 9 put into operational terms, and shall conform with the inspection request.

19. The challenge inspection shall be conducted in accordance with Part X or, in the case of alleged use, in accordance with Part XI of the Verification Annex. The inspection team shall be guided by the principle of conducting the challenge inspection in the least intrusive manner possible, consistent with the effective and timely accomplishment of its mission.

20. The inspected State Party shall assist the inspection team throughout the challenge inspection and facilitate its task. If the inspected State Party proposes, pursuant to Part X, Section C, of the Verification Annex, arrangements to demonstrate compliance with this Convention, alternative to full and comprehensive access, it shall make every reasonable effort, through consultations with the inspection team, to reach agreement on the modalities for establishing the facts with the aim of demonstrating its compliance.

21. The final report shall contain the factual findings as well as an assessment by the inspection team of the degree and nature of access and cooperation granted for the satisfactory implementation of the challenge inspection. The Director-General shall promptly transmit the final report of the inspection team to the requesting State Party, to the inspected State Party, to the Executive Council and to all other States Parties. The Director-General shall further transmit promptly to the Executive Council the assessments of the requesting and of the inspected States Parties, as well as the views of other States Parties which may be conveyed to the Director-General for that purpose, and then provide them to all States Parties.

22. The Executive Council shall, in accordance with its powers and functions, review the final report of the inspection team as soon as it is presented, and address any concerns as to:
    (a) Whether any non-compliance has occurred;
    (b) Whether the request had been within the scope of this Convention; and
    (c) Whether the right to request a challenge inspection had been abused.

23. If the Executive Council reaches the conclusion, in keeping with its powers and functions, that further action may be necessary with regard to paragraph 22, it shall take the appropriate measures to redress the situation and to ensure compliance with this Convention, including specific recommendations to the Conference. In the case of abuse, the Executive Council

shall examine whether the requesting State Party should bear any of the financial implications of the challenge inspection.

24. The requesting State Party and the inspected State Party shall have the right to participate in the review process. The Executive Council shall inform the States Parties and the next session of the Conference of the outcome of the process.

25. If the Executive Council has made specific recommendations to the Conference, the Conference shall consider action in accordance with Article XII.

ARTICLE X
ASSISTANCE AND PROTECTION AGAINST CHEMICAL WEAPONS

1. For the purposes of this Article, "Assistance" means the coordination and delivery to States Parties of protection against chemical weapons, including, *inter alia*, the following: detection equipment and alarm systems; protective equipment; decontamination equipment and decontaminants; medical antidotes and treatments; and advice on any of these protective measures.

2. Nothing in this Convention shall be interpreted as impeding the right of any State Party to conduct research into, develop, produce, acquire, transfer or use means of protection against chemical weapons, for purposes not prohibited under this Convention.

3. Each State Party undertakes to facilitate, and shall have the right to participate in, the fullest possible exchange of equipment, material and scientific and technological information concerning means of protection against chemical weapons.

4. For the purposes of increasing the transparency of national programmes related to protective purposes, each State Party shall provide annually to the Technical Secretariat information on its programme, in accordance with procedures to be considered and approved by the Conference pursuant to Article VIII, paragraph 21 (i).

5. The Technical Secretariat shall establish, not later than 180 days after entry into force of this Convention and maintain, for the use of any requesting State Party, a data bank containing freely available information concerning various means of protection against chemical weapons as well as such information as may be provided by States Parties.

   The Technical Secretariat shall also, within the resources available to it, and at the request of a State Party, provide expert advice and assist the State Party in identifying how its programmes for the development and improvement of a protective capacity against chemical weapons could be implemented.

6. Nothing in this Convention shall be interpreted as impeding the right of States Parties to request and provide assistance bilaterally and to conclude individual agreements with other States Parties concerning the emergency procurement of assistance.

7. Each State Party undertakes to provide assistance through the Organization and to this end to elect to take one or more of the following measures:
   (a) To contribute to the voluntary fund for assistance to be established by the Conference at its first session;
   (b) To conclude, if possible not later than 180 days after this Convention enters into force for it, agreements with the Organization concerning the procurement, upon demand, of assistance;
   (c) To declare, not later than 180 days after this Convention enters into force for it, the kind of assistance it might provide in response to an appeal by the Organization. If, however, a State Party subsequently is unable to provide the assistance envisaged in its declaration, it is still under the obligation to provide assistance in accordance with this paragraph.

8. Each State Party has the right to request and, subject to the procedures set forth in paragraphs 9, 10 and 11, to receive assistance and protection against the use or threat of use of chemical weapons if it considers that:
   (a) Chemical weapons have been used against it;

(b) Riot control agents have been used against it as a method of warfare; or

(c) It is threatened by actions or activities of any State that are prohibited for States Parties by Article I.

9. The request, substantiated by relevant information, shall be submitted to the Director-General, who shall transmit it immediately to the Executive Council and to all States Parties. The Director-General shall immediately forward the request to States Parties which have volunteered, in accordance with paragraphs 7 (b) and (c), to dispatch emergency assistance in case of use of chemical weapons or use of riot control agents as a method of warfare, or humanitarian assistance in case of serious threat of use of chemical weapons or serious threat of use of riot control agents as a method of warfare to the State Party concerned not later than 12 hours after receipt of the request. The Director-General shall initiate, not later than 24 hours after receipt of the request, an investigation in order to provide foundation for further action. He shall complete the investigation within 72 hours and forward a report to the Executive Council. If additional time is required for completion of the investigation, an interim report shall be submitted within the same time-frame. The additional time required for investigation shall not exceed 72 hours. It may, however, be further extended by similar periods. Reports at the end of each additional period shall be submitted to the Executive Council. The investigation shall, as appropriate and in conformity with the request and the information accompanying the request, establish relevant facts related to the request as well as the type and scope of supplementary assistance and protection needed.

10. The Executive Council shall meet not later than 24 hours after receiving an investigation report to consider the situation and shall take a decision by simple majority within the following 24 hours on whether to instruct the Technical Secretariat to provide supplementary assistance. The Technical Secretariat shall immediately transmit to all States Parties and relevant international organizations the investigation report and the decision taken by the Executive Council. When so decided by the Executive Council, the Director-General shall provide assistance immediately. For this purpose, the Director-General may cooperate with the requesting State Party, other States Parties and relevant international organizations. The States Parties shall make the fullest possible efforts to provide assistance.

11. If the information available from the ongoing investigation or other reliable sources would give sufficient proof that there are victims of use of chemical weapons and immediate action is indispensable, the Director-General shall notify all States Parties and shall take emergency measures of assistance, using the resources the Conference has placed at his disposal for such contingencies. The Director-General shall keep the Executive Council informed of actions undertaken pursuant to this paragraph.

ARTICLE XI
ECONOMIC AND TECHNOLOGICAL DEVELOPMENT

1. The provisions of this Convention shall be implemented in a manner which avoids hampering the economic or technological development of States Parties, and international cooperation in the field of chemical activities for purposes not prohibited under this Convention including the international exchange of scientific and technical information and chemicals and equipment for the production, processing or use of chemicals for purposes not prohibited under this Convention.

2. Subject to the provisions of this Convention and without prejudice to the principles and applicable rules of international law, the States Parties shall:

(a) Have the right, individually or collectively, to conduct research with, to develop, produce, acquire, retain, transfer, and use chemicals;

(b) Undertake to facilitate, and have the right to participate in, the fullest possible exchange of chemicals, equipment and scientific and technical information relating to the development and application of chemistry for purposes not prohibited under this Convention;

(c) Not maintain among themselves any restrictions, including those in any international agreements, incompatible with the obligations undertaken under this Convention, which would restrict or impede trade and the development and promotion of scientific and technological knowledge in the field of chemistry for industrial, agricultural, research, medical, pharmaceutical or other peaceful purposes;

(d) Not use this Convention as grounds for applying any measures other than those provided for, or permitted, under this Convention nor use any other international agreement for pursuing an objective inconsistent with this Convention;

(e) Undertake to review their existing national regulations in the field of trade in chemicals in order to render them consistent with the object and purpose of this Convention.

ARTICLE XII
MEASURES TO REDRESS A SITUATION AND TO ENSURE COMPLIANCE, INCLUDING SANCTIONS

1. The Conference shall take the necessary measures, as set forth in paragraphs 2, 3 and 4, to ensure compliance with this Convention and to redress and remedy any situation which contravenes the provisions of this Convention. In considering action pursuant to this paragraph, the Conference shall take into account all information and recommendations on the issues submitted by the Executive Council.

2. In cases where a State Party has been requested by the Executive Council to take measures to redress a situation raising problems with regard to its compliance, and where the State Party fails to fulfil the request within the specified time, the Conference may, *inter alia*, upon the recommendation of the Executive Council, restrict or suspend the State Party's rights and privileges under this Convention until it undertakes the necessary action to conform with its obligations under this Convention.

3. In cases where serious damage to the object and purpose of this Convention may result from activities prohibited under this Convention, in particular by Article I, the Conference may recommend collective measures to States Parties in conformity with international law.

4. The Conference shall, in cases of particular gravity, bring the issue, including relevant information and conclusions, to the attention of the United Nations General Assembly and the United Nations Security Council.

ARTICLE XIII
RELATION TO OTHER INTERNATIONAL AGREEMENTS

Nothing in this Convention shall be interpreted as in any way limiting or detracting from the obligations assumed by any State under the Protocol for the Prohibition of the Use in War of Asphyxiating, Poisonous or Other Gases, and of Bacteriological Methods of Warfare, signed at Geneva on 17 June 1925, and under the Convention on the Prohibition of the Development, Production and Stockpiling of Bacteriological (Biological) and Toxin Weapons and on Their Destruction, signed at London, Moscow and Washington on 10 April 1972.

ARTICLE XIV
SETTLEMENT OF DISPUTES

1. Disputes that may arise concerning the application or the interpretation of this Convention shall be settled in accordance with the relevant provisions of this Convention and in conformity with the provisions of the Charter of the United Nations.

2. When a dispute arises between two or more States Parties, or between one or more States Parties and the Organization, relating to the interpretation or application of this Convention,

the parties concerned shall consult together with a view to the expeditious settlement of the dispute by negotiation or by other peaceful means of the parties' choice, including recourse to appropriate organs of this Convention and, by mutual consent, referral to the International Court of Justice in conformity with the Statute of the Court. The States Parties involved shall keep the Executive Council informed of actions being taken.

3. The Executive Council may contribute to the settlement of a dispute by whatever means it deems appropriate, including offering its good offices, calling upon the States Parties to a dispute to start the settlement process of their choice and recommending a time-limit for any agreed procedure.

4. The Conference shall consider questions related to disputes raised by States Parties or brought to its attention by the Executive Council. The Conference shall, as it finds necessary, establish or entrust organs with tasks related to the settlement of these disputes in conformity with Article VIII, paragraph 21 (f).

5. The Conference and the Executive Council are separately empowered, subject to authorization from the General Assembly of the United Nations, to request the International Court of Justice to give an advisory opinion on any legal question arising within the scope of the activities of the Organization. An agreement between the Organization and the United Nations shall be concluded for this purpose in accordance with Article VIII, paragraph 34 (a).

6. This Article is without prejudice to Article IX or to the provisions on measures to redress a situation and to ensure compliance, including sanctions.

ARTICLE XV
AMENDMENTS

1. Any State Party may propose amendments to this Convention. Any State Party may also propose changes, as specified in paragraph 4, to the Annexes of this Convention. Proposals for amendments shall be subject to the procedures in paragraphs 2 and 3. Proposals for changes, as specified in paragraph 4, shall be subject to the procedures in paragraph 5.

2. The text of a proposed amendment shall be submitted to the Director-General for circulation to all States Parties and to the Depositary. The proposed amendment shall be considered only by an Amendment Conference. Such an Amendment Conference shall be convened if one third or more of the States Parties notify the Director-General not later than 30 days after its circulation that they support further consideration of the proposal. The Amendment Conference shall be held immediately following a regular session of the Conference unless the requesting States Parties ask for an earlier meeting. In no case shall an Amendment Conference be held less than 60 days after the circulation of the proposed amendment.

3. Amendments shall enter into force for all States Parties 30 days after deposit of the instruments of ratification or acceptance by all the States Parties referred to under subparagraph (b) below:

    (a) When adopted by the Amendment Conference by a positive vote of a majority of all States Parties with no State Party casting a negative vote; and

    (b) Ratified or accepted by all those States Parties casting a positive vote at the Amendment Conference.

4. In order to ensure the viability and the effectiveness of this Convention, provisions in the Annexes shall be subject to changes in accordance with paragraph 5, if proposed changes are related only to matters of an administrative or technical nature. All changes to the Annex on Chemicals shall be made in accordance with paragraph 5. Sections A and C of the Confidentiality Annex, Part X of the Verification Annex, and those definitions in Part I of the Verification Annex which relate exclusively to challenge inspections, shall not be subject to changes in accordance with paragraph 5.

5. Proposed changes referred to in paragraph 4 shall be made in accordance with the following procedures:

(a) The text of the proposed changes shall be transmitted together with the necessary information to the Director-General. Additional information for the evaluation of the proposal may be provided by any State Party and the Director-General. The Director-General shall promptly communicate any such proposals and information to all States Parties, the Executive Council and the Depositary;

(b) Not later than 60 days after its receipt, the Director-General shall evaluate the proposal to determine all its possible consequences for the provisions of this Convention and its implementation and shall communicate any such information to all States Parties and the Executive Council;

(c) The Executive Council shall examine the proposal in the light of all information available to it, including whether the proposal fulfils the requirements of paragraph 4. Not later than 90 days after its receipt, the Executive Council shall notify its recommendation, with appropriate explanations, to all States Parties for consideration. States Parties shall acknowledge receipt within 10 days;

(d) If the Executive Council recommends to all States Parties that the proposal be adopted, it shall be considered approved if no State Party objects to it within 90 days after receipt of the recommendation. If the Executive Council recommends that the proposal be rejected, it shall be considered rejected if no State Party objects to the rejection within 90 days after receipt of the recommendation;

(e) If a recommendation of the Executive Council does not meet with the acceptance required under subparagraph (d), a decision on the proposal, including whether it fulfils the requirements of paragraph 4, shall be taken as a matter of substance by the Conference at its next session;

(f) The Director-General shall notify all States Parties and the Depositary of any decision under this paragraph;

(g) Changes approved under this procedure shall enter into force for all States Parties 180 days after the date of notification by the Director-General of their approval unless another time period is recommended by the Executive Council or decided by the Conference.

ARTICLE XVI
DURATION AND WITHDRAWAL

1. This Convention shall be of unlimited duration.
2. Each State Party shall, in exercising its national sovereignty, have the right to withdraw from this Convention if it decides that extraordinary events, related to the subject-matter of this Convention, have jeopardized the supreme interests of its country. It shall give notice of such withdrawal 90 days in advance to all other States Parties, the Executive Council, the Depositary and the United Nations Security Council. Such notice shall include a statement of the extraordinary events it regards as having jeopardized its supreme interests.
3. The withdrawal of a State Party from this Convention shall not in any way affect the duty of States to continue fulfilling the obligations assumed under any relevant rules of international law, particularly the Geneva Protocol of 1925.

ARTICLE XVII
STATUS OF THE ANNEXES

The Annexes form an integral part of this Convention. Any reference to this Convention includes the Annexes.

ARTICLE XVIII
SIGNATURE

This Convention shall be open for signature for all States before its entry into force.

ARTICLE XIX
RATIFICATION

This Convention shall be subject to ratification by States Signatories according to their respective constitutional processes.

ARTICLE XX
ACCESSION

Any State which does not sign this Convention before its entry into force may accede to it at any time thereafter.

ARTICLE XXI
ENTRY INTO FORCE

1. This Convention shall enter into force 180 days after the date of the deposit of the 65th instrument of ratification, but in no case earlier than two years after its opening for signature.
2. For States whose instruments of ratification or accession are deposited subsequent to the entry into force of this Convention, it shall enter into force on the 30th day following the date of deposit of their instrument of ratification or accession.

ARTICLE XXII
RESERVATIONS

The Articles of this Convention shall not be subject to reservations. The Annexes of this Convention shall not be subject to reservations incompatible with its object and purpose.

ARTICLE XXIII
DEPOSITARY

The Secretary-General of the United Nations is hereby designated as the Depositary of this Convention and shall, *inter alia*:

(a) Promptly inform all signatory and acceding States of the date of each signature, the date of deposit of each instrument of ratification or accession and the date of the entry into force of this Convention, and of the receipt of other notices;

(b) Transmit duly certified copies of this Convention to the Governments of all signatory and acceding States; and

(c) Register this Convention pursuant to Article 102 of the Charter of the United Nations.

ARTICLE XXIV
AUTHENTIC TEXTS

This Convention, of which the Arabic, Chinese, English, French, Russian and Spanish texts are equally authentic, shall be deposited with the Secretary-General of the United Nations.

IN WITNESS WHEREOF the undersigned, being duly authorized to that effect, have signed this Convention.

Done at Paris on the thirteenth day of January, one thousand nine hundred and ninety-three.

ANNEX ON CHEMICALS

A. GUIDELINES FOR SCHEDULES OF CHEMICALS

GUIDELINES FOR SCHEDULE 1

1. The following criteria shall be taken into account in considering whether a toxic chemical or precursor should be included in Schedule 1:
   (a) It has been developed, produced, stockpiled or used as a chemical weapon as defined in Article II;
   (b) It poses otherwise a high risk to the object and purpose of this Convention by virtue of its high potential for use in activities prohibited under this Convention because one or more of the following conditions are met:
      (i) It possesses a chemical structure closely related to that of other toxic chemicals listed in Schedule 1, and has, or can be expected to have, comparable properties;
      (ii) It possesses such lethal or incapacitating toxicity as well as other properties that would enable it to be used as a chemical weapon;
      (iii) It may be used as a precursor in the final single technological stage of production of a toxic chemical listed in Schedule 1, regardless of whether this stage takes place in facilities, in munitions or elsewhere;
   (c) It has little or no use for purposes not prohibited under this Convention.

GUIDELINES FOR SCHEDULE 2

2. The following criteria shall be taken into account in considering whether a toxic chemical not listed in Schedule 1 or a precursor to a Schedule 1 chemical or to a chemical listed in Schedule 2, part A, should be included in Schedule 2:
   (a) It poses a significant risk to the object and purpose of this Convention because it possesses such lethal or incapacitating toxicity as well as other properties that could enable it to be used as a chemical weapon;
   (b) It may be used as a precursor in one of the chemical reactions at the final stage of formation of a chemical listed in Schedule 1 or Schedule 2, part A;
   (c) It poses a significant risk to the object and purpose of this Convention by virtue of its importance in the production of a chemical listed in Schedule 1 or Schedule 2, part A;
   (d) It is not produced in large commercial quantities for purposes not prohibited under this Convention.

GUIDELINES FOR SCHEDULE 3

3. The following criteria shall be taken into account in considering whether a toxic chemical or precursor, not listed in other Schedules, should be included in Schedule 3:
   (a) It has been produced, stockpiled or used as a chemical weapon;
   (b) It poses otherwise a risk to the object and purpose of this Convention because it possesses such lethal or incapacitating toxicity as well as other properties that might enable it to be used as a chemical weapon;
   (c) It poses a risk to the object and purpose of this Convention by virtue of its importance in the production of one or more chemicals listed in Schedule 1 or Schedule 2, part B;
   (d) It may be produced in large commercial quantities for purposes not prohibited under this Convention.

B. SCHEDULES OF CHEMICALS

The following Schedules list toxic chemicals and their precursors. For the purpose of implementing this Convention, these Schedules identify chemicals for the application of verification measures according to the provisions of the Verification Annex. Pursuant to Article II, subparagraph 1 (a), these Schedules do not constitute a definition of chemical weapons.

(Whenever reference is made to groups of dialkylated chemicals, followed by a list of alkyl groups in parentheses, all chemicals possible by all possible combinations of alkyl groups listed in the parentheses are considered as listed in the respective Schedule as long as they are not explicitly exempted. A chemical marked "*" on Schedule 2, part A, is subject to special thresholds for declaration and verification, as specified in Part VII of the Verification Annex.)

SCHEDULE 1   (CAS registry number)

A. TOXIC CHEMICALS:

(1) O-Alkyl ($\leq C_{10}$, incl. cycloalkyl) alkyl
     (Me, Et, n-Pr or i-Pr)-phosphonofluoridates
     e.g. Sarin: O-Isopropyl methylphosphonofluoridate   (107-44-8)
           Soman: O-Pinacolyl methylphosphonofluoridate   (96-64-0)

(2) O-Alkyl ($\leq C_{10}$, incl. cycloalkyl) N,N-dialkyl
     (Me, Et, n-Pr or i-Pr) phosphoramidocyanidates
     e.g. Tabun: O-Ethyl N,N-dimethyl
                           phosphoramidocyanidate   (77-81-6)

(3) O-Alkyl (H or $\leq C_{10}$, incl. cycloalkyl) S-2-dialkyl
     (Me, Et, n-Pr or i-Pr)-aminoethyl alkyl
     (Me, Et, n-Pr or i-Pr) phosphonothiolates and
     corresponding alkylated or protonated salts
     e.g. VX: O-Ethyl S-2-diisopropylaminoethyl
                           methyl phosphonothiolate   (50782-69-9)

(4) Sulfur mustards:
     2-Chloroethylchloromethylsulfide   (2625-76-5)
     Mustard gas: Bis(2-chloroethyl)sulfide   (505-60-2)
     Bis(2-chloroethylthio)methane   (63869-13-6)
     Sesquimustard: 1,2-Bis(2-chloroethylthio)ethane   (3563-36-8)
     1,3-Bis(2-chloroethylthio)-n-propane   (63905-10-2)
     1,4-Bis(2-chloroethylthio)-n-butane   (142868-93-7)
     1,5-Bis(2-chloroethylthio)-n-pentane   (142868-94-8)
     Bis(2-chloroethylthiomethyl)ether   (63918-90-1)
     O-Mustard: Bis(2-chloroethylthioethyl)ether   (63918-89-8)

(5) Lewisites:
     Lewisite 1: 2-Chlorovinyldichloroarsine   (541-25-3)
     Lewisite 2: Bis(2-chlorovinyl)chloroarsine   (40334-69-8)
     Lewisite 3: Tris(2-chlorovinyl)arsine   (40334-70-1)

(6) Nitrogen mustards:
     HN1: Bis(2-chloroethyl)ethylamine   (538-07-8)
     HN2: Bis(2-chloroethyl)methylamine   (51-75-2)
     HN3: Tris(2-chloroethyl)amine   (555-77-1)

(7)   Saxitoxin   (35523-89-8)

(8)   Ricin   (9009-86-3)

B.   PRECURSORS:

(9)   Alkyl (Me, Et, n-Pr or i-Pr) phosphonyldifluorides
      e.g. DF: Methylphosphonyldifluoride   (676-99-3)

(10) O-Alkyl (H or $\leq C_{10}$, incl. cycloalkyl) O-2-dialkyl
      (Me, Et, n-Pr or i-Pr)-aminoethyl alkyl
      (Me, Et, n-Pr or i-Pr) phosphonites and
      corresponding alkylated or protonated salts
      e.g. QL: O-Ethyl O-2-diisopropylaminoethyl
                                  methylphosphonite   (57856-11-8)

(11) Chlorosarin: O-Isopropyl methylphosphonochloridate (1445-76-7)

(12) Chlorosoman: O-Pinacolyl methylphosphonochloridate (7040-57-5)

SCHEDULE 2

A.   TOXIC CHEMICALS:

(1)   Amiton: O,O-Diethyl S-[2-(diethylamino)ethyl]
      phosphorothiolate   (78-53-5)
      and corresponding alkylated or protonated salts

(2)   PFIB: 1,1,3,3,3-Pentafluoro-2-(trifluoromethyl)-1-propene   (382-21-8)

(3)   BZ: 3-Quinuclidinyl benzilate (*)   (6581-06-2)

B.   PRECURSORS:

(4)   Chemicals, except for those listed in Schedule 1,
      containing a phosphorus atom to which is bonded
      one methyl, ethyl or propyl (normal or iso) group
      but not further carbon atoms,
      e.g. Methylphosphonyl dichloride   (676-97-1)
            Dimethyl methylphosphonate   (756-79-6)

      Exemption: Fonofos: O-Ethyl S-phenyl
                                 ethylphosphonothiolothionate   (944-22-9)

(5)   N,N-Dialkyl (Me, Et, n-Pr or i-Pr) phosphoramidic dihalides

(6)   Dialkyl (Me, Et, n-Pr or i-Pr) N,N-dialkyl
      (Me, Et, n-Pr or i-Pr)-phosphoramidates

(7)   Arsenic trichloride   (7784-34-1)

(8)   2,2-Diphenyl-2-hydroxyacetic acid   (76-93-7)

(9)   Quinuclidin-3-ol   (1619-34-7)

(10) N,N-Dialkyl (Me, Et, n-Pr or i-Pr) aminoethyl-2-chlorides
      and corresponding protonated salts

(11) N,N-Dialkyl (Me, Et, n-Pr or i-Pr) aminoethane-2-ols
      and corresponding protonated salts

      Exemptions: N,N-Dimethylaminoethanol   (108-01-0)
                               and corresponding protonated salts
                               N,N-Diethylaminoethanol   (100-37-8)
                               and corresponding protonated salts

(12) N,N-Dialkyl (Me, Et, n-Pr or i-Pr) aminoethane-2-thiols
      and corresponding protonated salts

(13) Thiodiglycol: Bis(2-hydroxyethyl)sulfide   (111-48-8)

(14) Pinacolyl alcohol: 3,3-Dimethylbutan-2-ol   (464-07-3)

SCHEDULE 3

A.   TOXIC CHEMICALS:

(1)   Phosgene: Carbonyl dichloride   (75-44-5)

(2)   Cyanogen chloride   (506-77-4)

(3)   Hydrogen cyanide   (74-90-8)

(4)   Chloropicrin: Trichloronitromethane   (76-06-2)

B.   PRECURSORS:

(5)   Phosphorus oxychloride   (10025-87-3)

(6)   Phosphorus trichloride   (7719-12-2)

(7)   Phosphorus pentachloride   (10026-13-8)

(8)   Trimethyl phosphite   (121-45-9)

(9)   Triethyl phosphite   (122-52-1)

(10) Dimethyl phosphite   (868-85-9)

(11) Diethyl phosphite   (762-04-9)

(12) Sulfur monochloride (10025-67-9)

(13) Sulfur dichloride (10545-99-0)

(14) Thionyl chloride (7719-09-7)

(15) Ethyldiethanolamine (139-87-7)

(16) Methyldiethanolamine (105-59-9)

(17) Triethanolamine (102-71-6)

ANNEX ON IMPLEMENTATION AND VERIFICATION
("VERIFICATION ANNEX")

PART I
DEFINITIONS

1. "Approved Equipment" means the devices and instruments necessary for the performance of the inspection team's duties that have been certified by the Technical Secretariat in accordance with regulations prepared by the Technical Secretariat pursuant to Part II, paragraph 27 of this Annex. Such equipment may also refer to the administrative supplies or recording materials that would be used by the inspection team.

2. "Building" as referred to in the definition of chemical weapons production facility in Article II comprises specialized buildings and standard buildings.

    (a) "Specialized Building" means:

        (i)   Any building, including underground structures, containing specialized equipment in a production or filling configuration;

        (ii) Any building, including underground structures, which has distinctive features which distinguish it from buildings normally used for chemical production or filling activities not prohibited under this Convention.

    (b) "Standard Building" means any building, including underground structures, constructed to prevailing industry standards for facilities not producing any chemical specified in Article II, paragraph 8 (a) (i), or corrosive chemicals.

3. "Challenge Inspection" means the inspection of any facility or location in the territory or in any other place under the jurisdiction or control of a State Party requested by another State Party pursuant to Article IX, paragraphs 8 to 25.

4. "Discrete Organic Chemical" means any chemical belonging to the class of chemical compounds consisting of all compounds of carbon except for its oxides, sulfides and metal carbonates, identifiable by chemical name, by structural formula, if known, and by Chemical Abstracts Service registry number, if assigned.

5. "Equipment" as referred to in the definition of chemical weapons production facility in Article II comprises specialized equipment and standard equipment.

    (a) "Specialized Equipment" means:

        (i)   The main production train, including any reactor or equipment for product synthesis, separation or purification, any equipment used directly for heat transfer in the final technological stage, such as in reactors or in product separation, as well as any other equipment which has been in contact with any chemical specified in Article II, paragraph 8 (a) (i), or would be in contact with such a chemical if the facility were operated;

        (ii) Any chemical weapon filling machines;

        (iii) Any other equipment specially designed, built or installed for the operation of the facility as a chemical weapons production facility, as distinct from a facility constructed according to prevailing commercial industry standards for facilities not producing any chemical specified in Article II, paragraph 8 (a) (i), or corrosive chemicals, such as: equipment made of high-nickel alloys or other special corrosion-resistant material; special equipment for waste control, waste treatment, air filtering, or solvent recovery; special containment enclosures and safety shields; non-standard laboratory equipment used to analyse toxic chemicals for chemical weapons purposes; custom-designed process control panels; or dedicated spares for specialized equipment.

    (b) "Standard Equipment" means:

        (i)   Production equipment which is generally used in the chemical industry and is not included in the types of specialized equipment;

    (ii) Other equipment commonly used in the chemical industry, such as: fire-fighting equipment; guard and security/safety surveillance equipment; medical facilities, laboratory facilities; or communications equipment.

6. "Facility" in the context of Article VI means any of the industrial sites as defined below ("plant site", "plant" and "unit").

    (a) "Plant Site" (Works, Factory) means the local integration of one or more plants, with any intermediate administrative levels, which are under one operational control, and includes common infrastructure, such as:

        (i)   Administration and other offices;

        (ii) Repair and maintenance shops;

        (iii) Medical centre;

        (iv) Utilities;

        (v)   Central analytical laboratory;

        (vi) Research and development laboratories;

        (vii) Central effluent and waste treatment area; and

        (viii)Warehouse storage.

    (b) "Plant" (Production facility, Workshop) means a relatively self-contained area, structure or building containing one or more units with auxiliary and associated infrastructure, such as:

        (i)   Small administrative section;

        (ii) Storage/handling areas for feedstock and products;

        (iii) Effluent/waste handling/treatment area;

        (iv) Control/analytical laboratory;

        (v)   First aid service/related medical section; and

        (vi) Records associated with the movement into, around and from the site, of declared chemicals and their feedstock or product chemicals formed from them, as appropriate.

    (c) "Unit" (Production unit, Process unit) means the combination of those items of equipment, including vessels and vessel set up, necessary for the production, processing or consumption of a chemical.

7. "Facility Agreement" means an agreement or arrangement between a State Party and the Organization relating to a specific facility subject to on-site verification pursuant to Articles IV, V and VI.

8. "Host State" means the State on whose territory lie facilities or areas of another State, Party to this Convention, which are subject to inspection under this Convention.

9. "In-Country Escort" means individuals specified by the inspected State Party and, if appropriate, by the Host State, if they so wish, to accompany and assist the inspection team during the in-country period.

10. "In-Country Period" means the period from the arrival of the inspection team at a point of entry until its departure from the State at a point of entry.

11. "Initial Inspection" means the first on-site inspection of facilities to verify declarations submitted pursuant to Articles III, IV, V and VI and this Annex.

12. "Inspected State Party" means the State Party on whose territory or in any other place under its jurisdiction or control an inspection pursuant to this Convention takes place, or the State Party whose facility or area on the territory of a Host State is subject to such an inspection; it does not, however, include the State Party specified in Part II, paragraph 21 of this Annex.

13. "Inspection Assistant" means an individual designated by the Technical Secretariat as set forth in Part II, Section A, of this Annex to assist inspectors in an inspection or visit, such as medical, security and administrative personnel and interpreters.

14. "Inspection Mandate" means the instructions issued by the Director-General to the inspection

team for the conduct of a particular inspection.

15. "Inspection Manual" means the compilation of additional procedures for the conduct of inspections developed by the Technical Secretariat.

16. "Inspection Site" means any facility or area at which an inspection is carried out and which is specifically defined in the respective facility agreement or inspection request or mandate or inspection request as expanded by the alternative or final perimeter.

17. "Inspection Team" means the group of inspectors and inspection assistants assigned by the Director-General to conduct a particular inspection.

18. "Inspector" means an individual designated by the Technical Secretariat according to the procedures as set forth in Part II, Section A, of this Annex, to carry out an inspection or visit in accordance with this Convention.

19. "Model Agreement" means a document specifying the general form and content for an agreement concluded between a State Party and the Organization for fulfilling the verification provisions specified in this Annex.

20. "Observer" means a representative of a requesting State Party or a third State Party to observe a challenge inspection.

21. "Perimeter" in case of challenge inspection means the external boundary of the inspection site, defined by either geographic coordinates or description on a map.

   (a) "Requested Perimeter" means the inspection site perimeter as specified in conformity with Part X, paragraph 8, of this Annex;

   (b) "Alternative Perimeter" means the inspection site perimeter as specified, alternatively to the requested perimeter, by the inspected State Party; it shall conform to the requirements specified in Part X, paragraph 17, of this Annex;

   (c) "Final Perimeter" means the final inspection site perimeter as agreed in negotiations between the inspection team and the inspected State Party, in accordance with Part X, paragraphs 16 to 21, of this Annex;

   (d) "Declared Perimeter" means the external boundary of the facility declared pursuant to Articles III, IV, V and VI.

22. "Period of Inspection", for the purposes of Article IX, means the period of time from provision of access to the inspection team to the inspection site until its departure from the inspection site, exclusive of time spent on briefings before and after the verification activities.

23. "Period of Inspection", for the purposes of Articles IV, V and VI, means the period of time from arrival of the inspection team at the inspection site until its departure from the inspection site, exclusive of time spent on briefings before and after the verification activities.

24. "Point of Entry"/"Point of Exit" means a location designated for the in-country arrival of inspection teams for inspections pursuant to this Convention or for their departure after completion of their mission.

25. "Requesting State Party" means a State Party which has requested a challenge inspection pursuant to Article IX.

26. "Tonne" means metric ton, i.e. 1,000 kg.

PART II
GENERAL RULES OF VERIFICATION

A. DESIGNATION OF INSPECTORS AND INSPECTION ASSISTANTS

1. Not later than 30 days after entry into force of this Convention the Technical Secretariat shall communicate, in writing, to all States Parties the names, nationalities and ranks of the inspectors and inspection assistants proposed for designation, as well as a description of their qualifications and professional experiences.

2. Each State Party shall immediately acknowledge receipt of the list of inspectors and inspec-

tion assistants, proposed for designation communicated to it. The State Party shall inform the Technical Secretariat in writing of its acceptance of each inspector and inspection assistant, not later than 30 days after acknowledgement of receipt of the list. Any inspector and inspection assistant included in this list shall be regarded as designated unless a State Party, not later than 30 days after acknowledgement of receipt of the list, declares its non-acceptance in writing. The State Party may include the reason for the objection.

In the case of non-acceptance, the proposed inspector or inspection assistant shall not undertake or participate in verification activities on the territory or in any other place under the jurisdiction or control of the State Party which has declared its non-acceptance. The Technical Secretariat shall, as necessary, submit further proposals in addition to the original list.

3.   Verification activities under this Convention shall only be performed by designated inspectors and inspection assistants.

4.   Subject to the provisions of paragraph 5, a State Party has the right at any time to object to an inspector or inspection assistant who has already been designated. It shall notify the Technical Secretariat of its objection in writing and may include the reason for the objection. Such objection shall come into effect 30 days after receipt by the Technical Secretariat. The Technical Secretariat shall immediately inform the State Party concerned of the withdrawal of the designation of the inspector or inspection assistant.

5.   A State Party that has been notified of an inspection shall not seek to have removed from the inspection team for that inspection any of the designated inspectors or inspection assistants named in the inspection team list.

6.   The number of inspectors or inspection assistants accepted by and designated to a State Party must be sufficient to allow for availability and rotation of appropriate numbers of inspectors and inspection assistants.

7.   If, in the opinion of the Director-General, the non-acceptance of proposed inspectors or inspection assistants impedes the designation of a sufficient number of inspectors or inspection assistants or otherwise hampers the effective fulfilment of the tasks of the Technical Secretariat, the Director-General shall refer the issue to the Executive Council.

8.   Whenever amendments to the above-mentioned lists of inspectors and inspection assistants are necessary or requested, replacement inspectors and inspection assistants shall be designated in the same manner as set forth with respect to the initial list.

9.   The members of the inspection team carrying out an inspection of a facility of a State Party located on the territory of another State Party shall be designated in accordance with the procedures set forth in this Annex as applied both to the inspected State Party and the Host State Party.

B.   PRIVILEGES AND IMMUNITIES

10.   Each State Party shall, not later than 30 days after acknowledgement of receipt of the list of inspectors and inspection assistants or of changes thereto, provide multiple entry/exit and/ or transit visas and other such documents to enable each inspector or inspection assistant to enter and to remain on the territory of that State Party for the purpose of carrying out inspection activities. These documents shall be valid for at least two years after their provision to the Technical Secretariat.

11.   To exercise their functions effectively, inspectors and inspection assistants shall be accorded privileges and immunities as set forth in subparagraphs (a) to (i). Privileges and immunities shall be granted to members of the inspection team for the sake of this Convention and not for the personal benefit of the individuals themselves. Such privileges and immunities shall be accorded to them for the entire period between arrival on and departure from the territory of the inspected State Party or Host State, and thereafter with respect to acts previously performed in the exercise of their official functions.

(a) The members of the inspection team shall be accorded the inviolability enjoyed by diplomatic agents pursuant to Article 29 of the Vienna Convention on Diplomatic Relations of 18 April 1961.

(b) The living quarters and office premises occupied by the inspection team carrying out inspection activities pursuant to this Convention shall be accorded the inviolability and protection accorded to the premises of diplomatic agents pursuant to Article 30, paragraph 1, of the Vienna Convention on Diplomatic Relations.

(c) The papers and correspondence, including records, of the inspection team shall enjoy the inviolability accorded to all papers and correspondence of diplomatic agents pursuant to Article 30, paragraph 2, of the Vienna Convention on Diplomatic Relations. The inspection team shall have the right to use codes for their communications with the Technical Secretariat.

(d) Samples and approved equipment carried by members of the inspection team shall be inviolable subject to provisions contained in this Convention and exempt from all customs duties. Hazardous samples shall be transported in accordance with relevant regulations.

(e) The members of the inspection team shall be accorded the immunities accorded to diplomatic agents pursuant to Article 31, paragraphs 1, 2 and 3, of the Vienna Convention on Diplomatic Relations.

(f) The members of the inspection team carrying out prescribed activities pursuant to this Convention shall be accorded the exemption from dues and taxes accorded to diplomatic agents pursuant to Article 34 of the Vienna Convention on Diplomatic Relations.

(g) The members of the inspection team shall be permitted to bring into the territory of the inspected State Party or Host State Party, without payment of any customs duties or related charges, articles for personal use, with the exception of articles the import or export of which is prohibited by law or controlled by quarantine regulations.

(h) The members of the inspection team shall be accorded the same currency and exchange facilities as are accorded to representatives of foreign Governments on temporary official missions.

(i) The members of the inspection team shall not engage in any professional or commercial activity for personal profit on the territory of the inspected State Party or the Host State.

12. When transiting the territory of non-inspected States Parties, the members of the inspection team shall be accorded the privileges and immunities enjoyed by diplomatic agents pursuant to Article 40, paragraph 1, of the Vienna Convention on Diplomatic Relations. Papers and correspondence, including records, and samples and approved equipment, carried by them, shall be accorded the privileges and immunities set forth in paragraph 11 (c) and (d).

13. Without prejudice to their privileges and immunities the members of the inspection team shall be obliged to respect the laws and regulations of the inspected State Party or Host State and, to the extent that is consistent with the inspection mandate, shall be obliged not to interfere in the internal affairs of that State. If the inspected State Party or Host State Party considers that there has been an abuse of privileges and immunities specified in this Annex, consultations shall be held between the State Party and the Director-General to determine whether such an abuse has occurred and, if so determined, to prevent a repetition of such an abuse.

14. The immunity from jurisdiction of members of the inspection team may be waived by the Director-General in those cases when the Director-General is of the opinion that immunity would impede the course of justice and that it can be waived without prejudice to the implementation of the provisions of this Convention. Waiver must always be express.

15. Observers shall be accorded the same privileges and immunities accorded to inspectors pursuant to this section, except for those accorded pursuant to paragraph 11 (d).

C. STANDING ARRANGEMENTS

POINTS OF ENTRY

16. Each State Party shall designate the points of entry and shall supply the required information to the Technical Secretariat not later than 30 days after this Convention enters into force for it. These points of entry shall be such that the inspection team can reach any inspection site from at least one point of entry within 12 hours. Locations of points of entry shall be provided to all States Parties by the Technical Secretariat.

17. Each State Party may change the points of entry by giving notice of such change to the Technical Secretariat. Changes shall become effective 30 days after the Technical Secretariat receives such notification to allow appropriate notification to all States Parties.

18. If the Technical Secretariat considers that there are insufficient points of entry for the timely conduct of inspections or that changes to the points of entry proposed by a State Party would hamper such timely conduct of inspections, it shall enter into consultations with the State Party concerned to resolve the problem.

19. In cases where facilities or areas of an inspected State Party are located on the territory of a Host State Party or where the access from the point of entry to the facilities or areas subject to inspection requires transit through the territory of another State Party, the inspected State Party shall exercise the rights and fulfil the obligations concerning such inspections in accordance with this Annex. The Host State Party shall facilitate the inspection of those facilities or areas and shall provide for the necessary support to enable the inspection team to carry out its tasks in a timely and effective manner. States Parties through whose territory transit is required to inspect facilities or areas of an inspected State Party shall facilitate such transit.

20. In cases where facilities or areas of an inspected State Party are located on the territory of a State not Party to this Convention, the inspected State Party shall take all necessary measures to ensure that inspections of those facilities or areas can be carried out in accordance with the provisions of this Annex. A State Party that has one or more facilities or areas on the territory of a State not Party to this Convention shall take all necessary measures to ensure acceptance by the Host State of inspectors and inspection assistants designated to that State Party. If an inspected State Party is unable to ensure access, it shall demonstrate that it took all necessary measures to ensure access.

21. In cases where the facilities or areas sought to be inspected are located on the territory of a State Party, but in a place under the jurisdiction or control of a State not Party to this Convention, the State Party shall take all necessary measures as would be required of an inspected State Party and a Host State Party to ensure that inspections of such facilities or areas can be carried out in accordance with the provisions of this Annex. If the State Party is unable to ensure access to those facilities or areas, it shall demonstrate that it took all necessary measures to ensure access. This paragraph shall not apply where the facilities or areas sought to be inspected are those of the State Party.

ARRANGEMENTS FOR USE OF NON-SCHEDULED AIRCRAFT

22. For inspections pursuant to Article IX and for other inspections where timely travel is not feasible using scheduled commercial transport, an inspection team may need to utilize aircraft owned or chartered by the Technical Secretariat. Not later than 30 days after this Convention enters into force for it, each State Party shall inform the Technical Secretariat of the standing diplomatic clearance number for non-scheduled aircraft transporting inspection teams and equipment necessary for inspection into and out of the territory in which an inspection site is located. Aircraft routings to and from the designated point of entry shall be along established international airways that are agreed upon between the States Parties and the Technical Secretariat as the basis for such diplomatic clearance.

23. When a non-scheduled aircraft is used, the Technical Secretariat shall provide the inspected State Party with a flight plan, through the National Authority, for the aircraft's flight from the

last airfield prior to entering the airspace of the State in which the inspection site is located to the point of entry, not less than six hours before the scheduled departure time from that airfield. Such a plan shall be filed in accordance with the procedures of the International Civil Aviation Organization applicable to civil aircraft. For its owned or chartered flights, the Technical Secretariat shall include in the remarks section of each flight plan the standing diplomatic clearance number and the appropriate notation identifying the aircraft as an inspection aircraft.

24. Not less than three hours before the scheduled departure of the inspection team from the last airfield prior to entering the airspace of the State in which the inspection is to take place, the inspected State Party or Host State Party shall ensure that the flight plan filed in accordance with paragraph 23 is approved so that the inspection team may arrive at the point of entry by the estimated arrival time.

25. The inspected State Party shall provide parking, security protection, servicing and fuel as required by the Technical Secretariat for the aircraft of the inspection team at the point of entry when such aircraft is owned or chartered by the Technical Secretariat. Such aircraft shall not be liable for landing fees, departure tax, and similar charges. The Technical Secretariat shall bear the cost of such fuel, security protection and servicing.

ADMINISTRATIVE ARRANGEMENTS

26. The inspected State Party shall provide or arrange for the amenities necessary for the inspection team such as communication means, interpretation services to the extent necessary for the performance of interviewing and other tasks, transportation, working space, lodging, meals and medical care. In this regard, the inspected State Party shall be reimbursed by the Organization for such costs incurred by the inspection team.

APPROVED EQUIPMENT

27. Subject to paragraph 29, there shall be no restriction by the inspected State Party on the inspection team bringing onto the inspection site such equipment, approved in accordance with paragraph 28, which the Technical Secretariat has determined to be necessary to fulfil the inspection requirements. The Technical Secretariat shall prepare and, as appropriate, update a list of approved equipment, which may be needed for the purposes described above, and regulations governing such equipment which shall be in accordance with this Annex. In establishing the list of approved equipment and these regulations, the Technical Secretariat shall ensure that safety considerations for all the types of facilities at which such equipment is likely to be used, are taken fully into account. A list of approved equipment shall be considered and approved by the Conference pursuant to Article VIII, paragraph 21 (i).

28. The equipment shall be in the custody of the Technical Secretariat and be designated, calibrated and approved by the Technical Secretariat. The Technical Secretariat shall, to the extent possible, select that equipment which is specifically designed for the specific kind of inspection required. Designated and approved equipment shall be specifically protected against unauthorized alteration.

29. The inspected State Party shall have the right, without prejudice to the prescribed time-frames, to inspect the equipment in the presence of inspection team members at the point of entry, i.e., to check the identity of the equipment brought in or removed from the territory of the inspected State Party or the Host State. To facilitate such identification, the Technical Secretariat shall attach documents and devices to authenticate its designation and approval of the equipment. The inspection of the equipment shall also ascertain to the satisfaction of the inspected State Party that the equipment meets the description of the approved equipment for the particular type of inspection. The inspected State Party may exclude equipment not meeting that description or equipment without the above-mentioned authentication documents and devices. Procedures for the inspection of equipment shall be considered and approved by the Conference pursuant to Article VIII, paragraph 21 (i).

30. In cases where the inspection team finds it necessary to use equipment available on site not belonging to the Technical Secretariat and requests the inspected State Party to enable the team to use such equipment, the inspected State Party shall comply with the request to the extent it can.

D.   PRE-INSPECTION ACTIVITIES

NOTIFICATION

31. The Director-General shall notify the State Party before the planned arrival of the inspection team at the point of entry and within the prescribed time-frames, where specified, of its intention to carry out an inspection.
32. Notifications made by the Director-General shall include the following information:
    (a) The type of inspection;
    (b) The point of entry;
    (c) The date and estimated time of arrival at the point of entry;
    (d) The means of arrival at the point of entry;
    (e) The site to be inspected;
    (f) The names of inspectors and inspection assistants;
    (g) If appropriate, aircraft clearance for special flights.
33. The inspected State Party shall acknowledge the receipt of a notification by the Technical Secretariat of an intention to conduct an inspection, not later than one hour after receipt of such notification.
34. In the case of an inspection of a facility of a State Party located on the territory of another State Party, both States Parties shall be simultaneously notified in accordance with paragraphs 31 and 32.

ENTRY INTO THE TERRITORY OF THE INSPECTED STATE PARTY OR HOST STATE AND TRANSFER TO THE INSPECTION SITE

35. The inspected State Party or Host State Party which has been notified of the arrival of an inspection team, shall ensure its immediate entry into the territory and shall through an in-country escort or by other means do everything in its power to ensure the safe conduct of the inspection team and its equipment and supplies, from its point of entry to the inspection site(s) and to a point of exit.
36. The inspected State Party or Host State Party shall, as necessary, assist the inspection team in reaching the inspection site not later than 12 hours after the arrival at the point of entry.

PRE-INSPECTION BRIEFING

37. Upon arrival at the inspection site and before the commencement of the inspection, the inspection team shall be briefed by facility representatives, with the aid of maps and other documentation as appropriate, on the facility, the activities carried out there, safety measures and administrative and logistic arrangements necessary for the inspection. The time spent for the briefing shall be limited to the minimum necessary and in any event not exceed three hours.

E.   CONDUCT OF INSPECTIONS

GENERAL RULES

38. The members of the inspection team shall discharge their functions in accordance with the provisions of this Convention, as well as rules established by the Director-General and facility agreements concluded between States Parties and the Organization.
39. The inspection team shall strictly observe the inspection mandate issued by the Director-General. It shall refrain from activities going beyond this mandate.

40. The activities of the inspection team shall be so arranged as to ensure the timely and effective discharge of its functions and the least possible inconvenience to the inspected State Party or Host State and disturbance to the facility or area inspected. The inspection team shall avoid unnecessarily hampering or delaying the operation of a facility and avoid affecting its safety. In particular, the inspection team shall not operate any facility. If inspectors consider that, to fulfil their mandate, particular operations should be carried out in a facility, they shall request the designated representative of the inspected facility to have them performed. The representative shall carry out the request to the extent possible.

41. In the performance of their duties on the territory of an inspected State Party or Host State, the members of the inspection team shall, if the inspected State Party so requests, be accompanied by representatives of the inspected State Party, but the inspection team must not thereby be delayed or otherwise hindered in the exercise of its functions.

42. Detailed procedures for the conduct of inspections shall be developed for inclusion in the inspection manual by the Technical Secretariat, taking into account guidelines to be considered and approved by the Conference pursuant to Article VIII, paragraph 21 (i).

SAFETY

43. In carrying out their activities, inspectors and inspection assistants shall observe safety regulations established at the inspection site, including those for the protection of controlled environments within a facility and for personal safety. In order to implement these requirements, appropriate detailed procedures shall be considered and approved by the Conference pursuant to Article VIII, paragraph 21 (i).

COMMUNICATIONS

44. Inspectors shall have the right throughout the in-country period to communicate with the Headquarters of the Technical Secretariat. For this purpose they may use their own, duly certified, approved equipment and may request that the inspected State Party or Host State Party provide them with access to other telecommunications. The inspection team shall have the right to use its own two-way system of radio communications between personnel patrolling the perimeter and other members of the inspection team.

INSPECTION TEAM AND INSPECTED STATE PARTY RIGHTS

45. The inspection team shall, in accordance with the relevant Articles and Annexes of this Convention as well as with facility agreements and procedures set forth in the inspection manual, have the right to unimpeded access to the inspection site. The items to be inspected will be chosen by the inspectors.

46. Inspectors shall have the right to interview any facility personnel in the presence of representatives of the inspected State Party with the purpose of establishing relevant facts. Inspectors shall only request information and data which are necessary for the conduct of the inspection, and the inspected State Party shall furnish such information upon request. The inspected State Party shall have the right to object to questions posed to the facility personnel if those questions are deemed not relevant to the inspection. If the head of the inspection team objects and states their relevance, the questions shall be provided in writing to the inspected State Party for reply. The inspection team may note any refusal to permit interviews or to allow questions to be answered and any explanations given, in that part of the inspection report that deals with the cooperation of the inspected State Party.

47. Inspectors shall have the right to inspect documentation and records they deem relevant to the conduct of their mission.

48. Inspectors shall have the right to have photographs taken at their request by representatives of the inspected State Party or of the inspected facility. The capability to take instant development photographic prints shall be available. The inspection team shall determine whether

photographs conform to those requested and, if not, repeat photographs shall be taken. The inspection team and the inspected State Party shall each retain one copy of every photograph.

49. The representatives of the inspected State Party shall have the right to observe all verification activities carried out by the inspection team.

50. The inspected State Party shall receive copies, at its request, of the information and data gathered about its facility(ies) by the Technical Secretariat.

51. Inspectors shall have the right to request clarifications in connection with ambiguities that arise during an inspection. Such requests shall be made promptly through the representative of the inspected State Party. The representative of the inspected State Party shall provide the inspection team, during the inspection, with such clarification as may be necessary to remove the ambiguity. If questions relating to an object or a building located within the inspection site are not resolved, the object or building shall, if requested, be photographed for the purpose of clarifying its nature and function. If the ambiguity cannot be removed during the inspection, the inspectors shall notify the Technical Secretariat immediately. The inspectors shall include in the inspection report any such unresolved question, relevant clarifications, and a copy of any photographs taken.

COLLECTION, HANDLING AND ANALYSIS OF SAMPLES

52. Representatives of the inspected State Party or of the inspected facility shall take samples at the request of the inspection team in the presence of inspectors. If so agreed in advance with the representatives of the inspected State Party or of the inspected facility, the inspection team may take samples itself.

53. Where possible, the analysis of samples shall be performed on-site. The inspection team shall have the right to perform on-site analysis of samples using approved equipment brought by it. At the request of the inspection team, the inspected State Party shall, in accordance with agreed procedures, provide assistance for the analysis of samples on-site. Alternatively, the inspection team may request that appropriate analysis on-site be performed in its presence.

54. The inspected State Party has the right to retain portions of all samples taken or take duplicate samples and be present when samples are analysed on-site.

55. The inspection team shall, if it deems it necessary, transfer samples for analysis off-site at laboratories designated by the Organization.

56. The Director-General shall have the primary responsibility for the security, integrity and preservation of samples and for ensuring that the confidentiality of samples transferred for analysis off-site is protected. The Director-General shall do so in accordance with procedures, to be considered and approved by the Conference pursuant to Article VIII, paragraph 21 (i), for inclusion in the inspection manual. He shall:

    (a) Establish a stringent regime governing the collection, handling, transport and analysis of samples;

    (b) Certify the laboratories designated to perform different types of analysis;

    (c) Oversee the standardization of equipment and procedures at these designated laboratories, mobile analytical equipment and procedures, and monitor quality control and overall standards in relation to the certification of these laboratories, mobile equipment and procedures; and

    (d) Select from among the designated laboratories those which shall perform analytical or other functions in relation to specific investigations.

57. When off-site analysis is to be performed, samples shall be analysed in at least two designated laboratories. The Technical Secretariat shall ensure the expeditious processing of the analysis. The samples shall be accounted for by the Technical Secretariat and any unused samples or portions thereof shall be returned to the Technical Secretariat.

58. The Technical Secretariat shall compile the results of the laboratory analysis of samples relevant to compliance with this Convention and include them in the final inspection report. The

Technical Secretariat shall include in the report detailed information concerning the equipment and methodology employed by the designated laboratories.

EXTENSION OF INSPECTION DURATION

59. Periods of inspection may be extended by agreement with the representative of the inspected State Party.

DEBRIEFING

60. Upon completion of an inspection the inspection team shall meet with representatives of the inspected State Party and the personnel responsible for the inspection site to review the preliminary findings of the inspection team and to clarify any ambiguities. The inspection team shall provide to the representatives of the inspected State Party its preliminary findings in written form according to a standardized format, together with a list of any samples and copies of written information and data gathered and other material to be taken off-site. The document shall be signed by the head of the inspection team. In order to indicate that he has taken notice of the contents of the document, the representative of the inspected State Party shall countersign the document. This meeting shall be completed not later than 24 hours after the completion of the inspection.

F.   DEPARTURE

61. Upon completion of the post-inspection procedures, the inspection team shall leave, as soon as possible, the territory of the inspected State Party or the Host State.

G.   REPORTS

62. Not later than 10 days after the inspection, the inspectors shall prepare a factual, final report on the activities conducted by them and on their findings. It shall only contain facts relevant to compliance with this Convention, as provided for under the inspection mandate. The report shall also provide information as to the manner in which the State Party inspected cooperated with the inspection team. Differing observations made by inspectors may be attached to the report. The report shall be kept confidential.

63. The final report shall immediately be submitted to the inspected State Party. Any written comments, which the inspected State Party may immediately make on its findings shall be annexed to it. The final report together with annexed comments made by the inspected State Party shall be submitted to the Director-General not later than 30 days after the inspection.

64. Should the report contain uncertainties, or should cooperation between the National Authority and the inspectors not measure up to the standards required, the Director-General shall approach the State Party for clarification.

65. If the uncertainties cannot be removed or the facts established are of a nature to suggest that obligations undertaken under this Convention have not been met, the Director-General shall inform the Executive Council without delay.

H.   APPLICATION OF GENERAL PROVISIONS

66. The provisions of this Part shall apply to all inspections conducted pursuant to this Convention, except where the provisions of this Part differ from the provisions set forth for specific types of inspections in Parts III to XI of this Annex, in which case the latter provisions shall take precedence.

PART III
GENERAL PROVISIONS FOR VERIFICATION MEASURES PURSUANT TO ARTICLES IV, V AND VI, PARAGRAPH 3

A. INITIAL INSPECTIONS AND FACILITY AGREEMENTS

1. Each declared facility subject to on-site inspection pursuant to Articles IV, V, and VI, paragraph 3, shall receive an initial inspection promptly after the facility is declared. The purpose of this inspection of the facility shall be to verify information provided and to obtain any additional information needed for planning future verification activities at the facility, including on-site inspections and continuous monitoring with on-site instruments, and to work on the facility agreements.

2. States Parties shall ensure that the verification of declarations and the initiation of the systematic verification measures can be accomplished by the Technical Secretariat at all facilities within the established time-frames after this Convention enters into force for them.

3. Each State Party shall conclude a facility agreement with the Organization for each facility declared and subject to on-site inspection pursuant to Articles IV, V, and VI, paragraph 3.

4. Facility agreements shall be completed not later than 180 days after this Convention enters into force for the State Party or after the facility has been declared for the first time, except for a chemical weapons destruction facility to which paragraphs 5 to 7 shall apply.

5. In the case of a chemical weapons destruction facility that begins operations more than one year after this Convention enters into force for the State Party, the facility agreement shall be completed not less than 180 days before the facility begins operation.

6. In the case of a chemical weapons destruction facility that is in operation when this Convention enters into force for the State Party, or begins operation not later than one year thereafter, the facility agreement shall be completed not later than 210 days after this Convention enters into force for the State Party, except that the Executive Council may decide that transitional verification arrangements, approved in accordance with Part IV (A), paragraph 51, of this Annex and including a transitional facility agreement, provisions for verification through on-site inspection and monitoring with on-site instruments, and the time-frame for application of the arrangements, are sufficient.

7. In the case of a facility, referred to in paragraph 6, that will cease operations not later than two years after this Convention enters into force for the State Party, the Executive Council may decide that transitional verification arrangements, approved in accordance with Part IV (A), paragraph 51, of this Annex and including a transitional facility agreement, provisions for verification through on-site inspection and monitoring with on-site instruments, and the time-frame for application of the arrangements, are sufficient.

8. Facility agreements shall be based on models for such agreements and provide for detailed arrangements which shall govern inspections at each facility. The model agreements shall include provisions to take into account future technological developments and shall be considered and approved by the Conference pursuant to Article VIII, paragraph 21 (i).

9. The Technical Secretariat may retain at each site a sealed container for photographs, plans and other information that it may wish to refer to in the course of subsequent inspections.

B. STANDING ARRANGEMENTS

10. Where applicable, the Technical Secretariat shall have the right to have continuous monitoring instruments and systems and seals installed and to use them, in conformity with the relevant provisions in this Convention and the facility agreements between States Parties and the Organization.

11. The inspected State Party shall, in accordance with agreed procedures, have the right to in-

spect any instrument used or installed by the inspection team and to have it tested in the presence of representatives of the inspected State Party. The inspection team shall have the right to use the instruments that were installed by the inspected State Party for its own monitoring of the technological process of the destruction of chemical weapons. To this end, the inspection team shall have the right to inspect those instruments that it intends to use for purposes of verification of the destruction of chemical weapons and to have them tested in its presence.

12. The inspected State Party shall provide the necessary preparation and support for the establishment of continuous monitoring instruments and systems.

13. In order to implement paragraphs 11 and 12, appropriate detailed procedures shall be considered and approved by the Conference pursuant to Article VIII, paragraph 21 (i).

14. The inspected State Party shall immediately notify the Technical Secretariat if an event occurs or may occur at a facility where monitoring instruments are installed, which may have an impact on the monitoring system. The inspected State Party shall coordinate subsequent actions with the Technical Secretariat with a view to restoring the operation of the monitoring system and establishing interim measures, if necessary, as soon as possible.

15. The inspection team shall verify during each inspection that the monitoring system functions correctly and that emplaced seals have not been tampered with. In addition, visits to service the monitoring system may be required to perform any necessary maintenance or replacement of equipment, or to adjust the coverage of the monitoring system as required.

16. If the monitoring system indicates any anomaly, the Technical Secretariat shall immediately take action to determine whether this resulted from equipment malfunction or activities at the facility. If, after this examination, the problem remains unresolved, the Technical Secretariat shall immediately ascertain the actual situation, including through immediate on-site inspection of, or visit to, the facility if necessary. The Technical Secretariat shall report any such problem immediately after its detection to the inspected State Party which shall assist in its resolution.

C.   PRE-INSPECTION ACTIVITIES

17. The inspected State Party shall, except as specified in paragraph 18, be notified of inspections not less than 24 hours in advance of the planned arrival of the inspection team at the point of entry.

18. The inspected State Party shall be notified of initial inspections not less than 72 hours in advance of the estimated time of arrival of the inspection team at the point of entry.

PART IV (A)
DESTRUCTION OF CHEMICAL WEAPONS AND ITS VERIFICATION PURSUANT TO ARTICLE IV

A.   DECLARATIONS

CHEMICAL WEAPONS
1.   The declaration of chemical weapons by a State Party pursuant to Article III, paragraph 1 (a) (ii), shall include the following:
(a) The aggregate quantity of each chemical declared;
(b) The precise location of each chemical weapons storage facility, expressed by:
     (i)   Name;
     (ii) Geographical coordinates; and
     (iii) A detailed site diagram, including a boundary map and the location of bunkers/storage areas within the facility.
(c) The detailed inventory for each chemical weapons storage facility including:

    (i)   Chemicals defined as chemical weapons in accordance with Article II;

    (ii)   Unfilled munitions, sub-munitions, devices and equipment defined as chemical weapons;

    (iii) Equipment specially designed for use directly in connection with the employment of munitions, sub-munitions, devices or equipment specified in sub-subparagraph (ii);

    (iv) Chemicals specifically designed for use directly in connection with the employment of munitions, sub-munitions, devices or equipment specified in sub-subparagraph (ii).

2.   For the declaration of chemicals referred to in paragraph 1 (c) (i) the following shall apply:

    (a)   Chemicals shall be declared in accordance with the Schedules specified in the Annex on Chemicals;

    (b)   For a chemical not listed in the Schedules in the Annex on Chemicals the information required for possible assignment of the chemical to the appropriate Schedule shall be provided, including the toxicity of the pure compound. For a precursor, the toxicity and identity of the principal final reaction product(s) shall be provided;

    (c)   Chemicals shall be identified by chemical name in accordance with current International Union of Pure and Applied Chemistry (IUPAC) nomenclature, structural formula and Chemical Abstracts Service registry number, if assigned. For a precursor, the toxicity and identity of the principal final reaction product(s) shall be provided;

    (d)   In cases involving mixtures of two or more chemicals, each chemical shall be identified and the percentage of each shall be provided, and the mixture shall be declared under the category of the most toxic chemical. If a component of a binary chemical weapon consists of a mixture of two or more chemicals, each chemical shall be identified and the percentage of each provided;

    (e)   Binary chemical weapons shall be declared under the relevant end product within the framework of the categories of chemical weapons referred to in paragraph 16. The following supplementary information shall be provided for each type of binary chemical munition/device:

        (i)   The chemical name of the toxic end-product;

        (ii)   The chemical composition and quantity of each component;

        (iii) The actual weight ratio between the components;

        (iv) Which component is considered the key component;

        (v)   The projected quantity of the toxic end-product calculated on a stoichiometric basis from the key component, assuming 100 per cent yield. A declared quantity (in tonnes) of the key component intended for a specific toxic end-product shall be considered equivalent to the quantity (in tonnes) of this toxic end-product calculated on a stoichiometric basis assuming 100 per cent yield.

    (f)   For multicomponent chemical weapons, the declaration shall be analogous to that envisaged for binary chemical weapons;

    (g)   For each chemical the form of storage, i.e. munitions, sub-munitions, devices, equipment or bulk containers and other containers shall be declared. For each form of storage the following shall be listed:

        (i)   Type;

        (ii)   Size or calibre;

        (iii) Number of items; and

        (iv) Nominal weight of chemical fill per item.

    (h)   For each chemical the total weight present at the storage facility shall be declared;

    (i)   In addition, for chemicals stored in bulk, the percentage purity shall be declared, if known.

3. For each type of unfilled munitions, sub-munitions, devices or equipment, referred to in paragraph 1 (c) (ii), the information shall include:
    (a) The number of items;
    (b) The nominal fill volume per item;
    (c) The intended chemical fill.

DECLARATIONS OF CHEMICAL WEAPONS PURSUANT TO ARTICLE III, PARAGRAPH 1 (A) (III)

4. The declaration of chemical weapons pursuant to Article III, paragraph 1 (a) (iii), shall contain all information specified in paragraphs 1 to 3 above. It is the responsibility of the State Party on whose territory the chemical weapons are located to make appropriate arrangements with the other State to ensure that the declarations are made. If the State Party on whose territory the chemical weapons are located is not able to fulfil its obligations under this paragraph, it shall state the reasons therefor.

DECLARATIONS OF PAST TRANSFERS AND RECEIPTS

5. A State Party that has transferred or received chemical weapons since 1 January 1946 shall declare these transfers or receipts pursuant to Article III, paragraph 1 (a) (iv), provided the amount transferred or received exceeded 1 tonne per chemical per year in bulk and/or munition form. This declaration shall be made according to the inventory format specified in paragraphs 1 and 2. This declaration shall also indicate the supplier and recipient countries, the dates of the transfers or receipts and, as precisely as possible, the current location of the transferred items. When not all the specified information is available for transfers or receipts of chemical weapons for the period between 1 January 1946 and 1 January 1970, the State Party shall declare whatever information is still available to it and provide an explanation as to why it cannot submit a full declaration.

SUBMISSION OF THE GENERAL PLAN FOR DESTRUCTION OF CHEMICAL WEAPONS

6. The general plan for destruction of chemical weapons submitted pursuant to Article III, paragraph 1 (a) (v), shall provide an overview of the entire national chemical weapons destruction programme of the State Party and information on the efforts of the State Party to fulfil the destruction requirements contained in this Convention. The plan shall specify:
    (a) A general schedule for destruction, giving types and approximate quantities of chemical weapons planned to be destroyed in each annual destruction period for each existing chemical weapons destruction facility and, if possible, for each planned chemical weapons destruction facility;
    (b) The number of chemical weapons destruction facilities existing or planned to be operated over the destruction period;
    (c) For each existing or planned chemical weapons destruction facility:
        (i)   Name and location; and
        (ii) The types and approximate quantities of chemical weapons, and the type (for example, nerve agent or blister agent) and approximate quantity of chemical fill, to be destroyed;
    (d) The plans and programmes for training personnel for the operation of destruction facilities;
    (e) The national standards for safety and emissions that the destruction facilities must satisfy;
    (f) Information on the development of new methods for destruction of chemical weapons and on the improvement of existing methods;
    (g) The cost estimates for destroying the chemical weapons; and
    (h) Any issues which could adversely impact on the national destruction programme.

B. MEASURES TO SECURE THE STORAGE FACILITY AND STORAGE FACILITY PREPARATION

7. Not later than when submitting its declaration of chemical weapons, a State Party shall take such measures as it considers appropriate to secure its storage facilities and shall prevent any movement of its chemical weapons out of the facilities, except their removal for destruction.

8. A State Party shall ensure that chemical weapons at its storage facilities are configured to allow ready access for verification in accordance with paragraphs 37 to 49.

9. While a storage facility remains closed for any movement of chemical weapons out of the facility other than their removal for destruction, a State Party may continue at the facility standard maintenance activities, including standard maintenance of chemical weapons; safety monitoring and physical security activities; and preparation of chemical weapons for destruction.

10. Maintenance activities of chemical weapons shall not include:
    (a) Replacement of agent or of munition bodies;
    (b) Modification of the original characteristics of munitions, or parts or components thereof.

11. All maintenance activities shall be subject to monitoring by the Technical Secretariat.

C. DESTRUCTION

PRINCIPLES AND METHODS FOR DESTRUCTION OF CHEMICAL WEAPONS

12. "Destruction of chemical weapons" means a process by which chemicals are converted in an essentially irreversible way to a form unsuitable for production of chemical weapons, and which in an irreversible manner renders munitions and other devices unusable as such.

13. Each State Party shall determine how it shall destroy chemical weapons, except that the following processes may not be used: dumping in any body of water, land burial or open-pit burning. It shall destroy chemical weapons only at specifically designated and appropriately designed and equipped facilities.

14. Each State Party shall ensure that its chemical weapons destruction facilities are constructed and operated in a manner to ensure the destruction of the chemical weapons; and that the destruction process can be verified under the provisions of this Convention.

ORDER OF DESTRUCTION

15. The order of destruction of chemical weapons is based on the obligations specified in Article I and the other Articles, including obligations regarding systematic on-site verification. It takes into account interests of States Parties for undiminished security during the destruction period; confidence-building in the early part of the destruction stage; gradual acquisition of experience in the course of destroying chemical weapons; and applicability irrespective of the actual composition of the stockpiles and the methods chosen for the destruction of the chemical weapons. The order of destruction is based on the principle of levelling out.

16. For the purpose of destruction, chemical weapons declared by each State Party shall be divided into three categories:

    Category 1: Chemical weapons on the basis of Schedule 1 chemicals and their parts and components;

    Category 2: Chemical weapons on the basis of all other chemicals and their parts and components;

    Category 3: Unfilled munitions and devices, and equipment specifically designed for use directly in connection with employment of chemical weapons.

17. A State Party shall start:
    (a) The destruction of Category 1 chemical weapons not later than two years after this Convention enters into force for it, and shall complete the destruction not later than 10 years after entry into force of this Convention. A State Party shall destroy chemical weapons

in accordance with the following destruction deadlines:

   (i)   Phase 1: Not later than two years after entry into force of this Convention, testing of its first destruction facility shall be completed. Not less than 1 per cent of the Category 1 chemical weapons shall be destroyed not later than three years after the entry into force of this Convention;

   (ii)   Phase 2: Not less than 20 per cent of the Category 1 chemical weapons shall be destroyed not later than five years after the entry into force of this Convention;

   (iii)   Phase 3: Not less than 45 per cent of the Category 1 chemical weapons shall be destroyed not later than seven years after the entry into force of this Convention;

   (iv)   Phase 4: All Category 1 chemical weapons shall be destroyed not later than 10 years after the entry into force of this Convention.

(b)   The destruction of Category 2 chemical weapons not later than one year after this Convention enters into force for it and shall complete the destruction not later than five years after the entry into force of this Convention. Category 2 chemical weapons shall be destroyed in equal annual increments throughout the destruction period. The comparison factor for such weapons is the weight of the chemicals within Category 2; and

(c)   The destruction of Category 3 chemical weapons not later than one year after this Convention enters into force for it, and shall complete the destruction not later than five years after the entry into force of this Convention. Category 3 chemical weapons shall be destroyed in equal annual increments throughout the destruction period. The comparison factor for unfilled munitions and devices is expressed in nominal fill volume (m3) and for equipment in number of items.

18.   For the destruction of binary chemical weapons the following shall apply:

(a)   For the purposes of the order of destruction, a declared quantity (in tonnes) of the key component intended for a specific toxic end-product shall be considered equivalent to the quantity (in tonnes) of this toxic end-product calculated on a stoichiometric basis assuming 100 per cent yield.

(b)   A requirement to destroy a given quantity of the key component shall entail a requirement to destroy a corresponding quantity of the other component, calculated from the actual weight ratio of the components in the relevant type of binary chemical munition/device.

(c)   If more of the other component is declared than is needed, based on the actual weight ratio between components, the excess shall be destroyed over the first two years after destruction operations begin.

(d)   At the end of each subsequent operational year a State Party may retain an amount of the other declared component that is determined on the basis of the actual weight ratio of the components in the relevant type of binary chemical munition/device.

19.   For multicomponent chemical weapons the order of destruction shall be analogous to that envisaged for binary chemical weapons.

MODIFICATION OF INTERMEDIATE DESTRUCTION DEADLINES

20.   The Executive Council shall review the general plans for destruction of chemical weapons, submitted pursuant to Article III, paragraph 1 (a) (v), and in accordance with paragraph 6, *inter alia*, to assess their conformity with the order of destruction set forth in paragraphs 15 to 19. The Executive Council shall consult with any State Party whose plan does not conform, with the objective of bringing the plan into conformity.

21.   If a State Party, due to exceptional circumstances beyond its control, believes that it cannot achieve the level of destruction specified for Phase 1, Phase 2 or Phase 3 of the order of destruction of Category 1 chemical weapons, it may propose changes in those levels. Such a proposal must be made not later than 120 days after the entry into force of this Convention and shall contain a detailed explanation of the reasons for the proposal.

22. Each State Party shall take all necessary measures to ensure destruction of Category 1 chemical weapons in accordance with the destruction deadlines set forth in paragraph 17 (a) as changed pursuant to paragraph 21. However, if a State Party believes that it will be unable to ensure the destruction of the percentage of Category 1 chemical weapons required by an intermediate destruction deadline, it may request the Executive Council to recommend to the Conference to grant an extension of its obligation to meet that deadline. Such a request must be made not less than 180 days before the intermediate destruction deadline and shall contain a detailed explanation of the reasons for the request and the plans of the State Party for ensuring that it will be able to fulfil its obligation to meet the next intermediate destruction deadline.

23. If an extension is granted, the State Party shall still be under the obligation to meet the cumulative destruction requirements set forth for the next destruction deadline. Extensions granted pursuant to this Section shall not, in any way, modify the obligation of the State Party to destroy all Category 1 chemical weapons not later than 10 years after the entry into force of this Convention.

EXTENSION OF THE DEADLINE FOR COMPLETION OF DESTRUCTION

24. If a State Party believes that it will be unable to ensure the destruction of all Category 1 chemical weapons not later than 10 years after the entry into force of this Convention, it may submit a request to the Executive Council for an extension of the deadline for completing the destruction of such chemical weapons. Such a request must be made not later than nine years after the entry into force of this Convention.

25. The request shall contain:
    (a) The duration of the proposed extension;
    (b) A detailed explanation of the reasons for the proposed extension; and
    (c) A detailed plan for destruction during the proposed extension and the remaining portion of the original 10-year period for destruction.

26. A decision on the request shall be taken by the Conference at its next session, on the recommendation of the Executive Council. Any extension shall be the minimum necessary, but in no case shall the deadline for a State Party to complete its destruction of all chemical weapons be extended beyond 15 years after the entry into force of this Convention. The Executive Council shall set conditions for the granting of the extension, including the specific verification measures deemed necessary as well as specific actions to be taken by the State Party to overcome problems in its destruction programme. Costs of verification during the extension period shall be allocated in accordance with Article IV, paragraph 16.

27. If an extension is granted, the State Party shall take appropriate measures to meet all subsequent deadlines.

28. The State Party shall continue to submit detailed annual plans for destruction in accordance with paragraph 29 and annual reports on the destruction of Category 1 chemical weapons in accordance with paragraph 36, until all Category 1 chemical weapons are destroyed. In addition, not later than at the end of each 90 days of the extension period, the State Party shall report to the Executive Council on its destruction activity. The Executive Council shall review progress towards completion of destruction and take the necessary measures to document this progress. All information concerning the destruction activities during the extension period shall be provided by the Executive Council to States Parties, upon request.

DETAILED ANNUAL PLANS FOR DESTRUCTION

29. The detailed annual plans for destruction shall be submitted to the Technical Secretariat not less than 60 days before each annual destruction period begins pursuant to Article IV, paragraph 7 (a), and shall specify:
    (a) The quantity of each specific type of chemical weapon to be destroyed at each destruc-

tion facility and the inclusive dates when the destruction of each specific type of chemical weapon will be accomplished;

(b) The detailed site diagram for each chemical weapons destruction facility and any changes to previously submitted diagrams; and

(c) The detailed schedule of activities for each chemical weapons destruction facility for
the upcoming year, identifying time required for design, construction or modification
of the facility, installation of equipment, equipment check-out and operator training,
destruction operations for each specific type of chemical weapon, and scheduled periods
of inactivity.

30. A State Party shall provide, for each of its chemical weapons destruction facilities, detailed
facility information to assist the Technical Secretariat in developing preliminary inspection
procedures for use at the facility.

31. The detailed facility information for each destruction facility shall include the following information:

(a) Name, address and location;

(b) Detailed, annotated facility drawings;

(c) Facility design drawings, process drawings, and piping and instrumentation design
drawings;

(d) Detailed technical descriptions, including design drawings and instrument specifications, for the equipment required for: removing the chemical fill from the munitions,
devices, and containers; temporarily storing the drained chemical fill; destroying the
chemical agent; and destroying the munitions, devices, and containers;

(e) Detailed technical descriptions of the destruction process, including material flow rates,
temperatures and pressures, and designed destruction efficiency;

(f) Design capacity for each specific type of chemical weapon;

(g) A detailed description of the products of destruction and the method of their ultimate
disposal;

(h) A detailed technical description of measures to facilitate inspections in accordance with
this Convention;

(i) A detailed description of any temporary holding area at the destruction facility that will
be used to provide chemical weapons directly to the destruction facility, including site
and facility drawings and information on the storage capacity for each specific type of
chemical weapon to be destroyed at the facility;

(j) A detailed description of the safety and medical measures in force at the facility;

(k) A detailed description of the living quarters and working premises for the inspectors; and

(l) Suggested measures for international verification.

32. A State Party shall provide, for each of its chemical weapons destruction facilities, the plant
operations manuals, the safety and medical plans, the laboratory operations and quality assurance and control manuals, and the environmental permits that have been obtained, except
that this shall not include material previously provided.

33. A State Party shall promptly notify the Technical Secretariat of any developments that could
affect inspection activities at its destruction facilities.

34. Deadlines for submission of the information specified in paragraphs 30 to 32 shall be considered and approved by the Conference pursuant to Article VIII, paragraph 21 (i).

35. After a review of the detailed facility information for each destruction facility, the Technical
Secretariat, if the need arises, shall enter into consultation with the State Party concerned
in order to ensure that its chemical weapons destruction facilities are designed to assure the
destruction of chemical weapons, to allow advanced planning on how verification measures
may be applied and to ensure that the application of verification measures is consistent with
proper facility operation, and that the facility operation allows appropriate verification.

ANNUAL REPORTS ON DESTRUCTION

36. Information regarding the implementation of plans for destruction of chemical weapons shall be submitted to the Technical Secretariat pursuant to Article IV, paragraph 7 (b), not later than 60 days after the end of each annual destruction period and shall specify the actual amounts of chemical weapons which were destroyed during the previous year at each destruction facility. If appropriate, reasons for not meeting destruction goals should be stated.

D. VERIFICATION

VERIFICATION OF DECLARATIONS OF CHEMICAL WEAPONS THROUGH ON-SITE INSPECTION

37. The purpose of the verification of declarations of chemical weapons shall be to confirm through on-site inspection the accuracy of the relevant declarations made pursuant to Article III.
38. The inspectors shall conduct this verification promptly after a declaration is submitted. They shall, *inter alia*, verify the quantity and identity of chemicals, types and number of munitions, devices and other equipment.
39. The inspectors shall employ, as appropriate, agreed seals, markers or other inventory control procedures to facilitate an accurate inventory of the chemical weapons at each storage facility.
40. As the inventory progresses, inspectors shall install such agreed seals as may be necessary to clearly indicate if any stocks are removed, and to ensure the securing of the storage facility during the inventory. After completion of the inventory, such seals will be removed unless otherwise agreed.

SYSTEMATIC VERIFICATION OF STORAGE FACILITIES

41. The purpose of the systematic verification of storage facilities shall be to ensure that no undetected removal of chemical weapons from such facilities takes place.
42. The systematic verification shall be initiated as soon as possible after the declaration of chemical weapons is submitted and shall continue until all chemical weapons have been removed from the storage facility. It shall in accordance with the facility agreement, combine on-site inspection and monitoring with on-site instruments.
43. When all chemical weapons have been removed from the storage facility, the Technical Secretariat shall confirm the declaration of the State Party to that effect. After this confirmation, the Technical Secretariat shall terminate the systematic verification of the storage facility and shall promptly remove any monitoring instruments installed by the inspectors.

INSPECTIONS AND VISITS

44. The particular storage facility to be inspected shall be chosen by the Technical Secretariat in such a way as to preclude the prediction of precisely when the facility is to be inspected. The guidelines for determining the frequency of systematic on-site inspections shall be elaborated by the Technical Secretariat, taking into account the recommendations to be considered and approved by the Conference pursuant to Article VIII, paragraph 21 (i).
45. The Technical Secretariat shall notify the inspected State Party of its decision to inspect or visit the storage facility 48 hours before the planned arrival of the inspection team at the facility for systematic inspections or visits. In cases of inspections or visits to resolve urgent problems, this period may be shortened. The Technical Secretariat shall specify the purpose of the inspection or visit.
46. The inspected State Party shall make any necessary preparations for the arrival of the inspectors and shall ensure their expeditious transportation from their point of entry to the storage facility. The facility agreement will specify administrative arrangements for inspectors.
47. The inspected State Party shall provide the inspection team upon its arrival at the chemical weapons storage facility to carry out an inspection, with the following data on the facility:

(a) The number of storage buildings and storage locations;

(b) For each storage building and storage location, the type and the identification number or designation, shown on the site diagram; and

(c) For each storage building and storage location at the facility, the number of items of each specific type of chemical weapon, and, for containers that are not part of binary munitions, the actual quantity of chemical fill in each container.

48. In carrying out an inventory, within the time available, inspectors shall have the right:

(a) To use any of the following inspection techniques:

(i) inventory all the chemical weapons stored at the facility;

(ii) inventory all the chemical weapons stored in specific buildings or locations at the facility, as chosen by the inspectors; or

(iii) inventory all the chemical weapons of one or more specific types stored at the facility, as chosen by the inspectors; and

(b) To check all items inventoried against agreed records.

49. Inspectors shall, in accordance with facility agreements:

(a) Have unimpeded access to all parts of the storage facilities including any munitions, devices, bulk containers, or other containers therein. While conducting their activity, inspectors shall comply with the safety regulations at the facility. The items to be inspected will be chosen by the inspectors; and

(b) Have the right, during the first and any subsequent inspection of each chemical weapons storage facility, to designate munitions, devices, and containers from which samples are to be taken, and to affix to such munitions, devices, and containers a unique tag that will indicate an attempt to remove or alter the tag. A sample shall be taken from a tagged item at a chemical weapons storage facility or a chemical weapons destruction facility as soon as it is practically possible in accordance with the corresponding destruction programmes, and, in any case, not later than by the end of the destruction operations.

SYSTEMATIC VERIFICATION OF THE DESTRUCTION OF CHEMICAL WEAPONS

50. The purpose of verification of destruction of chemical weapons shall be:

(a) To confirm the identity and quantity of the chemical weapons stocks to be destroyed; and

(b) To confirm that these stocks have been destroyed.

51. Chemical weapons destruction operations during the first 390 days after the entry into force of this Convention shall be governed by transitional verification arrangements. Such arrangements, including a transitional facility agreement, provisions for verification through on-site inspection and monitoring with on-site instruments, and the time-frame for application of the arrangements, shall be agreed between the Organization and the inspected State Party. These arrangements shall be approved by the Executive Council not later than 60 days after this Convention enters into force for the State Party, taking into account the recommendations of the Technical Secretariat, which shall be based on an evaluation of the detailed facility information provided in accordance with paragraph 31 and a visit to the facility. The Executive Council shall, at its first session, establish the guidelines for such transitional verification arrangements, based on recommendations to be considered and approved by the Conference pursuant to Article VIII, paragraph 21 (i). The transitional verification arrangements shall be designed to verify, throughout the entire transitional period, the destruction of chemical weapons in accordance with the purposes set forth in paragraph 50, and to avoid hampering ongoing destruction operations.

52. The provisions of paragraphs 53 to 61 shall apply to chemical weapons destruction operations that are to begin not earlier than 390 days after the entry into force of this Convention.

53. On the basis of this Convention and the detailed destruction facility information, and as the case may be, on experience from previous inspections, the Technical Secretariat shall prepare a draft plan for inspecting the destruction of chemical weapons at each destruction facility.

The plan shall be completed and provided to the inspected State Party for comment not less than 270 days before the facility begins destruction operations pursuant to this Convention. Any differences between the Technical Secretariat and the inspected State Party should be resolved through consultations. Any unresolved matter shall be forwarded to the Executive Council for appropriate action with a view to facilitating the full implementation of this Convention.

54. The Technical Secretariat shall conduct an initial visit to each chemical weapons destruction facility of the inspected State Party not less than 240 days before each facility begins destruction operations pursuant to this Convention, to allow it to familiarize itself with the facility and assess the adequacy of the inspection plan.

55. In the case of an existing facility where chemical weapons destruction operations have already been initiated, the inspected State Party shall not be required to decontaminate the facility before the Technical Secretariat conducts an initial visit. The duration of the visit shall not exceed five days and the number of visiting personnel shall not exceed 15.

56. The agreed detailed plans for verification, with an appropriate recommendation by the Technical Secretariat, shall be forwarded to the Executive Council for review. The Executive Council shall review the plans with a view to approving them, consistent with verification objectives and obligations under this Convention. It should also confirm that verification schemes for destruction are consistent with verification aims and are efficient and practical. This review should be completed not less than 180 days before the destruction period begins.

57. Each member of the Executive Council may consult with the Technical Secretariat on any issues regarding the adequacy of the plan for verification. If there are no objections by any member of the Executive Council, the plan shall be put into action.

58. If there are any difficulties, the Executive Council shall enter into consultations with the State Party to reconcile them. If any difficulties remain unresolved they shall be referred to the Conference.

59. The detailed facility agreements for chemical weapons destruction facilities shall specify, taking into account the specific characteristics of the destruction facility and its mode of operation:

    (a) Detailed on-site inspection procedures; and

    (b) Provisions for verification through continuous monitoring with on-site instruments and physical presence of inspectors.

60. Inspectors shall be granted access to each chemical weapons destruction facility not less than 60 days before the commencement of the destruction, pursuant to this Convention, at the facility. Such access shall be for the purpose of supervising the installation of the inspection equipment, inspecting this equipment and testing its operation, as well as for the purpose of carrying out a final engineering review of the facility. In the case of an existing facility where chemical weapons destruction operations have already been initiated, destruction operations shall be stopped for the minimum amount of time required, not to exceed 60 days, for installation and testing of the inspection equipment. Depending on the results of the testing and review, the State Party and the Technical Secretariat may agree on additions or changes to the detailed facility agreement for the facility.

61. The inspected State Party shall notify, in writing, the inspection team leader at a chemical weapons destruction facility not less than four hours before the departure of each shipment of chemical weapons from a chemical weapons storage facility to that destruction facility. This notification shall specify the name of the storage facility, the estimated times of departure and arrival, the specific types and quantities of chemical weapons being transported, whether any tagged items are being moved, and the method of transportation. This notification may include notification of more than one shipment. The inspection team leader shall be promptly notified, in writing, of any changes in this information.

CHEMICAL WEAPONS STORAGE FACILITIES AT CHEMICAL WEAPONS DESTRUCTION FACILITIES

62. The inspectors shall verify the arrival of the chemical weapons at the destruction facility and the storing of these chemical weapons. The inspectors shall verify the inventory of each shipment, using agreed procedures consistent with facility safety regulations, prior to the destruction of the chemical weapons. They shall employ, as appropriate, agreed seals, markers or other inventory control procedures to facilitate an accurate inventory of the chemical weapons prior to destruction.

63. As soon and as long as chemical weapons are stored at chemical weapons storage facilities located at chemical weapons destruction facilities, these storage facilities shall be subject to systematic verification in conformity with the relevant facility agreements.

64. At the end of an active destruction phase, inspectors shall make an inventory of the chemical weapons, that have been removed from the storage facility, to be destroyed. They shall verify the accuracy of the inventory of the chemical weapons remaining, employing inventory control procedures as referred to in paragraph 62.

SYSTEMATIC ON-SITE VERIFICATION MEASURES AT CHEMICAL WEAPONS DESTRUCTION FACILITIES

65. The inspectors shall be granted access to conduct their activities at the chemical weapons destruction facilities and the chemical weapons storage facilities located at such facilities during the entire active phase of destruction.

66. At each chemical weapons destruction facility, to provide assurance that no chemical weapons are diverted and that the destruction process has been completed, inspectors shall have the right to verify through their physical presence and monitoring with on-site instruments:
    (a) The receipt of chemical weapons at the facility;
    (b) The temporary holding area for chemical weapons and the specific type and quantity of chemical weapons stored in that area;
    (c) The specific type and quantity of chemical weapons being destroyed;
    (d) The process of destruction;
    (e) The end-product of destruction;
    (f) The mutilation of metal parts; and
    (g) The integrity of the destruction process and of the facility as a whole.

67. Inspectors shall have the right to tag, for sampling, munitions, devices, or containers located in the temporary holding areas at the chemical weapons destruction facilities.

68. To the extent that it meets inspection requirements, information from routine facility operations, with appropriate data authentication, shall be used for inspection purposes.

69. After the completion of each period of destruction, the Technical Secretariat shall confirm the declaration of the State Party, reporting the completion of destruction of the designated quantity of chemical weapons.

70. Inspectors shall, in accordance with facility agreements:
    (a) Have unimpeded access to all parts of the chemical weapons destruction facilities and the chemical weapons storage facilities located at such facilities, including any munitions, devices, bulk containers, or other containers, therein. The items to be inspected shall be chosen by the inspectors in accordance with the verification plan that has been agreed to by the inspected State Party and approved by the Executive Council;
    (b) Monitor the systematic on-site analysis of samples during the destruction process; and
    (c) Receive, if necessary, samples taken at their request from any devices, bulk containers and other containers at the destruction facility or the storage facility thereat.

PART IV (B)
OLD CHEMICAL WEAPONS AND
ABANDONED CHEMICAL WEAPONS

A. GENERAL

1. Old chemical weapons shall be destroyed as provided for in Section B.
2. Abandoned chemical weapons, including those which also meet the definition of Article II, paragraph 5 (b), shall be destroyed as provided for in Section C.

B. REGIME FOR OLD CHEMICAL WEAPONS

3. A State Party which has on its territory old chemical weapons as defined in Article II, paragraph 5 (a), shall, not later than 30 days after this Convention enters into force for it, submit to the Technical Secretariat all available relevant information, including, to the extent possible, the location, type, quantity and the present condition of these old chemical weapons.

    In the case of old chemical weapons as defined in Article II, paragraph 5 (b), the State Party shall submit to the Technical Secretariat a declaration pursuant to Article III, paragraph 1 (b) (i), including, to the extent possible, the information specified in Part IV (A), paragraphs 1 to 3, of this Annex.

4. A State Party which discovers old chemical weapons after this Convention enters into force for it shall submit to the Technical Secretariat the information specified in paragraph 3 not later than 180 days after the discovery of the old chemical weapons.

5. The Technical Secretariat shall conduct an initial inspection, and any further inspections as may be necessary, in order to verify the information submitted pursuant to paragraphs 3 and 4 and in particular to determine whether the chemical weapons meet the definition of old chemical weapons as specified in Article II, paragraph 5. Guidelines to determine the usability of chemical weapons produced between 1925 and 1946 shall be considered and approved by the Conference pursuant to Article VIII, paragraph 21 (i).

6. A State Party shall treat old chemical weapons that have been confirmed by the Technical Secretariat as meeting the definition in Article II, paragraph 5 (a), as toxic waste. It shall inform the Technical Secretariat of the steps being taken to destroy or otherwise dispose of such old chemical weapons as toxic waste in accordance with its national legislation.

7. Subject to paragraphs 3 to 5, a State Party shall destroy old chemical weapons that have been confirmed by the Technical Secretariat as meeting the definition in Article II, paragraph 5 (b), in accordance with Article IV and Part IV (A) of this Annex. Upon request of a State Party, the Executive Council may, however, modify the provisions on time-limit and order of destruction of these old chemical weapons, if it determines that doing so would not pose a risk to the object and purpose of this Convention. The request shall contain specific proposals for modification of the provisions and a detailed explanation of the reasons for the proposed modification.

C. REGIME FOR ABANDONED CHEMICAL WEAPONS

8. A State Party on whose territory there are abandoned chemical weapons (hereinafter referred to as the "Territorial State Party") shall, not later than 30 days after this Convention enters into force for it, submit to the Technical Secretariat all available relevant information concerning the abandoned chemical weapons. This information shall include, to the extent possible, the location, type, quantity and the present condition of the abandoned chemical weapons as well as information on the abandonment.

9. A State Party which discovers abandoned chemical weapons after this Convention enters

into force for it shall, not later than 180 days after the discovery, submit to the Technical Secretariat all available relevant information concerning the discovered abandoned chemical weapons. This information shall include, to the extent possible, the location, type, quantity and the present condition of the abandoned chemical weapons as well as information on the abandonment.

10. A State Party which has abandoned chemical weapons on the territory of another State Party (hereinafter referred to as the "Abandoning State Party") shall, not later than 30 days after this Convention enters into force for it, submit to the Technical Secretariat all available relevant information concerning the abandoned chemical weapons. This information shall include, to the extent possible, the location, type, quantity as well as information on the abandonment, and the condition of the abandoned chemical weapons.

11. The Technical Secretariat shall conduct an initial inspection, and any further inspections as may be necessary, in order to verify all available relevant information submitted pursuant to paragraphs 8 to 10 and determine whether systematic verification in accordance with Part IV (A), paragraphs 41 to 43, of this Annex is required. It shall, if necessary, verify the origin of the abandoned chemical weapons and establish evidence concerning the abandonment and the identity of the Abandoning State.

12. The report of the Technical Secretariat shall be submitted to the Executive Council, the Territorial State Party, and to the Abandoning State Party or the State Party declared by the Territorial State Party or identified by the Technical Secretariat as having abandoned the chemical weapons. If one of the States Parties directly concerned is not satisfied with the report it shall have the right to settle the matter in accordance with provisions of this Convention or bring the issue to the Executive Council with a view to settling the matter expeditiously.

13. Pursuant to Article I, paragraph 3, the Territorial State Party shall have the right to request the State Party which has been established as the Abandoning State Party pursuant to paragraphs 8 to 12 to enter into consultations for the purpose of destroying the abandoned chemical weapons in cooperation with the Territorial State Party. It shall immediately inform the Technical Secretariat of this request.

14. Consultations between the Territorial State Party and the Abandoning State Party with a view to establishing a mutually agreed plan for destruction shall begin not later than 30 days after the Technical Secretariat has been informed of the request referred to in paragraph 13. The mutually agreed plan for destruction shall be transmitted to the Technical Secretariat not later than 180 days after the Technical Secretariat has been informed of the request referred to in paragraph 13. Upon the request of the Abandoning State Party and the Territorial State Party, the Executive Council may extend the time-limit for transmission of the mutually agreed plan for destruction.

15. For the purpose of destroying abandoned chemical weapons, the Abandoning State Party shall provide all necessary financial, technical, expert, facility as well as other resources. The Territorial State Party shall provide appropriate cooperation.

16. If the Abandoning State cannot be identified or is not a State Party, the Territorial State Party, in order to ensure the destruction of these abandoned chemical weapons, may request the Organization and other States Parties to provide assistance in the destruction of these abandoned chemical weapons.

17. Subject to paragraphs 8 to 16, Article IV and Part IV (A) of this Annex shall also apply to the destruction of abandoned chemical weapons. In the case of abandoned chemical weapons which also meet the definition of old chemical weapons in Article II, paragraph 5 (b), the Executive Council, upon the request of the Territorial State Party, individually or together with the Abandoning State Party, may modify or in exceptional cases suspend the application of provisions on destruction, if it determines that doing so would not pose a risk to the object and purpose of this Convention. In the case of abandoned chemical weapons which do not meet the definition of old chemical weapons in Article II, paragraph 5 (b), the Execu-

tive Council, upon the request of the Territorial State Party, individually or together with the Abandoning State Party, may in exceptional circumstances modify the provisions on the time-limit and the order of destruction, if it determines that doing so would not pose a risk to the object and purpose of this Convention. Any request as referred to in this paragraph shall contain specific proposals for modification of the provisions and a detailed explanation of the reasons for the proposed modification.

18. States Parties may conclude between themselves agreements or arrangements concerning the destruction of abandoned chemical weapons. The Executive Council may, upon request of the Territorial State Party, individually or together with the Abandoning State Party, decide that selected provisions of such agreements or arrangements take precedence over provisions of this Section, if it determines that the agreement or arrangement ensures the destruction of the abandoned chemical weapons in accordance with paragraph 17.

PART V
DESTRUCTION OF CHEMICAL WEAPONS PRODUCTION FACILITIES AND ITS VERIFICATION PURSUANT TO ARTICLE V

A. DECLARATIONS

DECLARATIONS OF CHEMICAL WEAPONS PRODUCTION FACILITIES

1. The declaration of chemical weapons production facilities by a State Party pursuant to Article III, paragraph 1 (c) (ii), shall contain for each facility:
   (a) The name of the facility, the names of the owners, and the names of the companies or enterprises operating the facility since 1 January 1946;
   (b) The precise location of the facility, including the address, location of the complex, location of the facility within the complex including the specific building and structure number, if any;
   (c) A statement whether it is a facility for the manufacture of chemicals that are defined as chemical weapons or whether it is a facility for the filling of chemical weapons, or both;
   (d) The date when the construction of the facility was completed and the periods during which any modifications to the facility were made, including the installation of new or modified equipment, that significantly changed the production process characteristics of the facility;
   (e) Information on the chemicals defined as chemical weapons that were manufactured at the facility; the munitions, devices, and containers that were filled at the facility; and the dates of the beginning and cessation of such manufacture or filling:
      (i) For chemicals defined as chemical weapons that were manufactured at the facility, such information shall be expressed in terms of the specific types of chemicals manufactured, indicating the chemical name in accordance with the current International Union of Pure and Applied Chemistry (IUPAC) nomenclature, structural formula, and the Chemical Abstracts Service registry number, if assigned, and in terms of the amount of each chemical expressed by weight of chemical in tonnes;
      (ii) For munitions, devices and containers that were filled at the facility, such information shall be expressed in terms of the specific type of chemical weapons filled and the weight of the chemical fill per unit;
   (f) The production capacity of the chemical weapons production facility:
      (i) For a facility where chemical weapons were manufactured, production capacity shall be expressed in terms of the annual quantitative potential for manufacturing a specific substance on the basis of the technological process actually used or, in the case of processes not actually used, planned to be used at the facility;
      (ii) For a facility where chemical weapons were filled, production capacity shall be

expressed in terms of the quantity of chemical that the facility can fill into each specific type of chemical weapon a year;

(g) For each chemical weapons production facility that has not been destroyed, a description of the facility including:

    (i) A site diagram;

    (ii) A process flow diagram of the facility; and

    (iii) An inventory of buildings at the facility, and specialized equipment at the facility and of any spare parts for such equipment;

(h) The present status of the facility, stating:

    (i) The date when chemical weapons were last produced at the facility;

    (ii) Whether the facility has been destroyed, including the date and manner of its destruction; and

    (iii) Whether the facility has been used or modified before entry into force of this Convention for an activity not related to the production of chemical weapons, and if so, information on what modifications have been made, the date such non-chemical weapons related activity began and the nature of such activity, indicating, if applicable, the kind of product;

(i) A specification of the measures that have been taken by the State Party for closure of, and a description of the measures that have been or will be taken by the State Party to inactivate the facility;

(j) A description of the normal pattern of activity for safety and security at the inactivated facility; and

(k) A statement as to whether the facility will be converted for the destruction of chemical weapons and, if so, the dates for such conversions.

DECLARATIONS OF CHEMICAL WEAPONS PRODUCTION FACILITIES PURSUANT TO ARTICLE III, PARA-GRAPH 1 (C) (III)

2.   The declaration of chemical weapons production facilities pursuant to Article III, paragraph 1 (c) (iii), shall contain all information specified in paragraph 1 above. It is the responsibility of the State Party on whose territory the facility is or has been located to make appropriate arrangements with the other State to ensure that the declarations are made. If the State Party on whose territory the facility is or has been located is not able to fulfil this obligation, it shall state the reasons therefor.

DECLARATIONS OF PAST TRANSFERS AND RECEIPTS

3.   A State Party that has transferred or received chemical weapons production equipment since 1 January 1946 shall declare these transfers and receipts pursuant to Article III, paragraph 1 (c) (iv), and in accordance with paragraph 5 below. When not all the specified information is available for transfer and receipt of such equipment for the period between 1 January 1946 and 1 January 1970, the State Party shall declare whatever information is still available to it and provide an explanation as to why it cannot submit a full declaration.

4.   Chemical weapons production equipment referred to in paragraph 3 means:

(a) Specialized equipment;

(b) Equipment for the production of equipment specifically designed for use directly in connection with chemical weapons employment; and

(c) Equipment designed or used exclusively for producing non-chemical parts for chemical munitions.

5.   The declaration concerning transfer and receipt of chemical weapons production equipment shall specify:

(a) Who received/transferred the chemical weapons production equipment;

(b) The identity of such equipment;

    (c) The date of transfer or receipt;

    (d) Whether the equipment was destroyed, if known; and

    (e) Current disposition, if known.

SUBMISSION OF GENERAL PLANS FOR DESTRUCTION

6. For each chemical weapons production facility, a State Party shall supply the following information:

    (a) Envisaged time-frame for measures to be taken; and

    (b) Methods of destruction.

7. For each chemical weapons production facility that a State Party intends to convert temporarily into a chemical weapons destruction facility, the State Party shall supply the following information:

    (a) Envisaged time-frame for conversion into a destruction facility;

    (b) Envisaged time-frame for utilizing the facility as a chemical weapons destruction facility;

    (c) Description of the new facility;

    (d) Method of destruction of special equipment;

    (e) Time-frame for destruction of the converted facility after it has been utilized to destroy chemical weapons; and

    (f) Method of destruction of the converted facility.

SUBMISSION OF ANNUAL PLANS FOR DESTRUCTION AND ANNUAL REPORTS ON DESTRUCTION

8. The State Party shall submit an annual plan for destruction not less than 90 days before the beginning of the coming destruction year. The annual plan shall specify:

    (a) Capacity to be destroyed;

    (b) Name and location of the facilities where destruction will take place;

    (c) List of buildings and equipment that will be destroyed at each facility; and

    (d) Planned method(s) of destruction.

9. A State Party shall submit an annual report on destruction not later than 90 days after the end of the previous destruction year. The annual report shall specify:

    (a) Capacity destroyed;

    (b) Name and location of each facility where destruction took place;

    (c) List of buildings and equipment that were destroyed at each facility;

    (d) Methods of destruction.

10. For a chemical weapons production facility declared pursuant to Article III, paragraph 1 (c) (iii), it is the responsibility of the State Party on whose territory the facility is or has been located to make appropriate arrangements to ensure that the declarations specified in paragraphs 6 to 9 above are made. If the State Party on whose territory the facility is or has been located is not able to fulfil this obligation, it shall state the reasons therefor.

B. DESTRUCTION

GENERAL PRINCIPLES FOR DESTRUCTION OF CHEMICAL WEAPONS PRODUCTION FACILITIES

11. Each State Party shall decide on methods to be applied for the destruction of chemical weapons production facilities, according to the principles laid down in Article V and in this Part.

PRINCIPLES AND METHODS FOR CLOSURE OF A CHEMICAL WEAPONS PRODUCTION FACILITY

12. The purpose of the closure of a chemical weapons production facility is to render it inactive.

13. Agreed measures for closure shall be taken by a State Party with due regard to the specific characteristics of each facility. Such measures shall include, *inter alia*:

    (a) Prohibition of occupation of the specialized buildings and standard buildings of the facility except for agreed activities;

(b) Disconnection of equipment directly related to the production of chemical weapons, including, *inter alia*, process control equipment and utilities;

(c) Decommissioning of protective installations and equipment used exclusively for the safety of operations of the chemical weapons production facility;

(d) Installation of blind flanges and other devices to prevent the addition of chemicals to, or the removal of chemicals from, any specialized process equipment for synthesis, separation or purification of chemicals defined as a chemical weapon, any storage tank, or any machine for filling chemical weapons, the heating, cooling, or supply of electrical or other forms of power to such equipment, storage tanks, or machines; and

(e) Interruption of rail, road and other access routes for heavy transport to the chemical weapons production facility except those required for agreed activities.

14. While the chemical weapons production facility remains closed, a State Party may continue safety and physical security activities at the facility.

TECHNICAL MAINTENANCE OF CHEMICAL WEAPONS PRODUCTION FACILITIES PRIOR TO THEIR DESTRUCTION

15. A State Party may carry out standard maintenance activities at chemical weapons production facilities only for safety reasons, including visual inspection, preventive maintenance, and routine repairs.

16. All planned maintenance activities shall be specified in the general and detailed plans for destruction. Maintenance activities shall not include:

(a) Replacement of any process equipment;

(b) Modification of the characteristics of the chemical process equipment;

(c) Production of chemicals of any type.

17. All maintenance activities shall be subject to monitoring by the Technical Secretariat.

PRINCIPLES AND METHODS FOR TEMPORARY CONVERSION OF CHEMICAL WEAPONS PRODUCTION FACILITIES INTO CHEMICAL WEAPONS DESTRUCTION FACILITIES

18. Measures pertaining to the temporary conversion of chemical weapons production facilities into chemical weapons destruction facilities shall ensure that the regime for the temporarily converted facilities is at least as stringent as the regime for chemical weapons production facilities that have not been converted.

19. Chemical weapons production facilities converted into chemical weapons destruction facilities before entry into force of this Convention shall be declared under the category of chemical weapons production facilities.

They shall be subject to an initial visit by inspectors, who shall confirm the correctness of the information about these facilities. Verification that the conversion of these facilities was performed in such a manner as to render them inoperable as chemical weapons production facilities shall also be required, and shall fall within the framework of measures provided for the facilities that are to be rendered inoperable not later than 90 days after entry into force of this Convention.

20. A State Party that intends to carry out a conversion of chemical weapons production facilities shall submit to the Technical Secretariat, not later than 30 days after this Convention enters into force for it, or not later than 30 days after a decision has been taken for temporary conversion, a general facility conversion plan, and subsequently shall submit annual plans.

21. Should a State Party have the need to convert to a chemical weapons destruction facility an additional chemical weapons production facility that had been closed after this Convention entered into force for it, it shall inform the Technical Secretariat thereof not less than 150 days before conversion. The Technical Secretariat, in conjunction with the State Party, shall make sure that the necessary measures are taken to render that facility, after its conversion, inoperable as a chemical weapons production facility.

22. A facility converted for the destruction of chemical weapons shall not be more fit for resuming chemical weapons production than a chemical weapons production facility which has been closed and is under maintenance. Its reactivation shall require no less time than that required for a chemical weapons production facility that has been closed and is under maintenance.

23. Converted chemical weapons production facilities shall be destroyed not later than 10 years after entry into force of this Convention.

24. Any measures for the conversion of any given chemical weapons production facility shall be facility-specific and shall depend upon its individual characteristics.

25. The set of measures carried out for the purpose of converting a chemical weapons production facility into a chemical weapons destruction facility shall not be less than that which is provided for the disabling of other chemical weapons production facilities to be carried out not later than 90 days after this Convention enters into force for the State Party.

PRINCIPLES AND METHODS RELATED TO DESTRUCTION OF A CHEMICAL WEAPONS PRODUCTION FACILITY

26. A State Party shall destroy equipment and buildings covered by the definition of a chemical weapons production facility as follows:
    (a) All specialized equipment and standard equipment shall be physically destroyed;
    (b) All specialized buildings and standard buildings shall be physically destroyed.

27. A State Party shall destroy facilities for producing unfilled chemical munitions and equipment for chemical weapons employment as follows:
    (a) Facilities used exclusively for production of non-chemical parts for chemical munitions or equipment specifically designed for use directly in connection with chemical weapons employment, shall be declared and destroyed. The destruction process and its verification shall be conducted according to the provisions of Article V and this Part of this Annex that govern destruction of chemical weapons production facilities;
    (b) All equipment designed or used exclusively for producing non-chemical parts for chemical munitions shall be physically destroyed. Such equipment, which includes specially designed moulds and metal-forming dies, may be brought to a special location for destruction;
    (c) All buildings and standard equipment used for such production activities shall be destroyed or converted for purposes not prohibited under this Convention, with confirmation, as necessary, through consultations and inspections as provided for under Article IX;
    (d) Activities for purposes not prohibited under this Convention may continue while destruction or conversion proceeds.

ORDER OF DESTRUCTION

28. The order of destruction of chemical weapons production facilities is based on the obligations specified in Article I and the other Articles of this Convention, including obligations regarding systematic on-site verification. It takes into account interests of States Parties for undiminished security during the destruction period; confidence- building in the early part of the destruction stage; gradual acquisition of experience in the course of destroying chemical weapons production facilities; and applicability irrespective of the actual characteristics of the facilities and the methods chosen for their destruction. The order of destruction is based on the principle of levelling out.

29. A State Party shall, for each destruction period, determine which chemical weapons production facilities are to be destroyed and carry out the destruction in such a way that not more than what is specified in paragraphs 30 and 31 remains at the end of each destruction period. A State Party is not precluded from destroying its facilities at a faster pace.

30. The following provisions shall apply to chemical weapons production facilities that produce Schedule 1 chemicals:
    (a) A State Party shall start the destruction of such facilities not later than one year after this Convention enters into force for it, and shall complete it not later than 10 years after entry into force of this Convention. For a State which is a Party at the entry into force of this Convention, this overall period shall be divided into three separate destruction periods, namely, years 2-5, years 6-8, and years 9-10. For States which become a Party after entry into force of this Convention, the destruction periods shall be adapted, taking into account paragraphs 28 and 29;
    (b) Production capacity shall be used as the comparison factor for such facilities. It shall be expressed in agent tonnes, taking into account the rules specified for binary chemical weapons;
    (c) Appropriate agreed levels of production capacity shall be established for the end of the eighth year after entry into force of this Convention. Production capacity that exceeds the relevant level shall be destroyed in equal increments during the first two destruction periods;
    (d) A requirement to destroy a given amount of capacity shall entail a requirement to destroy any other chemical weapons production facility that supplied the Schedule 1 facility or filled the Schedule 1 chemical produced there into munitions or devices;
    (e) Chemical weapons production facilities that have been converted temporarily for destruction of chemical weapons shall continue to be subject to the obligation to destroy capacity according to the provisions of this paragraph.
31. A State Party shall start the destruction of chemical weapons production facilities not covered in paragraph 30 not later than one year after this Convention enters into force for it, and complete it not later than five years after entry into force of this Convention.

DETAILED PLANS FOR DESTRUCTION
32. Not less than 180 days before the destruction of a chemical weapons production facility starts, a State Party shall provide to the Technical Secretariat the detailed plans for destruction of the facility, including proposed measures for verification of destruction referred to in paragraph 33 (f), with respect to, *inter alia*:
    (a) Timing of the presence of the inspectors at the facility to be destroyed; and
    (b) Procedures for verification of measures to be applied to each item on the declared inventory.
33. The detailed plans for destruction of each chemical weapons production facility shall contain:
    (a) Detailed time schedule of the destruction process;
    (b) Layout of the facility;
    (c) Process flow diagram;
    (d) Detailed inventory of equipment, buildings and other items to be destroyed;
    (e) Measures to be applied to each item on the inventory;
    (f) Proposed measures for verification;
    (g) Security/safety measures to be observed during the destruction of the facility; and
    (h) Working and living conditions to be provided for inspectors.
34. If a State Party intends to convert temporarily a chemical weapons production facility into a chemical weapons destruction facility, it shall notify the Technical Secretariat not less than 150 days before undertaking any conversion activities. The notification shall:
    (a) Specify the name, address, and location of the facility;
    (b) Provide a site diagram indicating all structures and areas that will be involved in the destruction of chemical weapons and also identify all structures of the chemical weapons production facility that are to be temporarily converted;
    (c) Specify the types of chemical weapons, and the type and quantity of chemical fill to be destroyed;

    (d) Specify the destruction method;

    (e) Provide a process flow diagram, indicating which portions of the production process and specialized equipment will be converted for the destruction of chemical weapons;

    (f) Specify the seals and inspection equipment potentially affected by the conversion, if applicable; and

    (g) Provide a schedule identifying: The time allocated to design, temporary conversion of the facility, installation of equipment, equipment check-out, destruction operations, and closure.

35. In relation to the destruction of a facility that was temporarily converted for destruction of chemical weapons, information shall be provided in accordance with paragraphs 32 and 33.

REVIEW OF DETAILED PLANS

36. On the basis of the detailed plan for destruction and proposed measures for verification submitted by the State Party, and on experience from previous inspections, the Technical Secretariat shall prepare a plan for verifying the destruction of the facility, consulting closely with the State Party. Any differences between the Technical Secretariat and the State Party concerning appropriate measures should be resolved through consultations. Any unresolved matters shall be forwarded to the Executive Council for appropriate action with a view to facilitating the full implementation of this Convention.

37. To ensure that the provisions of Article V and this Part are fulfilled, the combined plans for destruction and verification shall be agreed upon between the Executive Council and the State Party. This agreement should be completed, not less than 60 days before the planned initiation of destruction.

38. Each member of the Executive Council may consult with the Technical Secretariat on any issues regarding the adequacy of the combined plan for destruction and verification. If there are no objections by any member of the Executive Council, the plan shall be put into action.

39. If there are any difficulties, the Executive Council shall enter into consultations with the State Party to reconcile them. If any difficulties remain unresolved they shall be referred to the Conference. The resolution of any differences over methods of destruction shall not delay the execution of other parts of the destruction plan that are acceptable.

40. If agreement is not reached with the Executive Council on aspects of verification, or if the approved verification plan cannot be put into action, verification of destruction shall proceed through continuous monitoring with on-site instruments and physical presence of inspectors.

41. Destruction and verification shall proceed according to the agreed plan. The verification shall not unduly interfere with the destruction process and shall be conducted through the presence of inspectors on-site to witness the destruction.

42. If required verification or destruction actions are not taken as planned, all States Parties shall be so informed.

C. VERIFICATION

VERIFICATION OF DECLARATIONS OF CHEMICAL WEAPONS PRODUCTION FACILITIES THROUGH ON-SITE INSPECTION

43. The Technical Secretariat shall conduct an initial inspection of each chemical weapons production facility in the period between 90 and 120 days after this Convention enters into force for the State Party.

44. The purposes of the initial inspection shall be:

    (a) To confirm that the production of chemical weapons has ceased and that the facility has been inactivated in accordance with this Convention;

    (b) To permit the Technical Secretariat to familiarize itself with the measures that have been taken to cease production of chemical weapons at the facility;

(c) To permit the inspectors to install temporary seals;

(d) To permit the inspectors to confirm the inventory of buildings and specialized equipment;

(e) To obtain information necessary for planning inspection activities at the facility, including use of tamper-indicating seals and other agreed equipment, which shall be installed pursuant to the detailed facility agreement for the facility; and

(f) To conduct preliminary discussions regarding a detailed agreement on inspection procedures at the facility.

45. Inspectors shall employ, as appropriate, agreed seals, markers or other inventory control procedures to facilitate an accurate inventory of the declared items at each chemical weapons production facility.

46. Inspectors shall install such agreed devices as may be necessary to indicate if any resumption of production of chemical weapons occurs or if any declared item is removed. They shall take the necessary precaution not to hinder closure activities by the inspected State Party. Inspectors may return to maintain and verify the integrity of the devices.

47. If, on the basis of the initial inspection, the Director-General believes that additional measures are necessary to inactivate the facility in accordance with this Convention, the Director-General may request, not later than 135 days after this Convention enters into force for a State Party, that such measures be implemented by the inspected State Party not later than 180 days after this Convention enters into force for it. At its discretion, the inspected State Party may satisfy the request. If it does not satisfy the request, the inspected State Party and the Director-General shall consult to resolve the matter.

SYSTEMATIC VERIFICATION OF CHEMICAL WEAPONS PRODUCTION FACILITIES AND CESSATION OF THEIR ACTIVITIES

48. The purpose of the systematic verification of a chemical weapons production facility shall be to ensure that any resumption of production of chemical weapons or removal of declared items will be detected at this facility.

49. The detailed facility agreement for each chemical weapons production facility shall specify:

(a) Detailed on-site inspection procedures, which may include:

(i) Visual examinations;

(ii) Checking and servicing of seals and other agreed devices; and

(iii) Obtaining and analysing samples;

(b) Procedures for using tamper-indicating seals and other agreed equipment to prevent the undetected reactivation of the facility, which shall specify:

(i) The type, placement, and arrangements for installation; and

(ii) The maintenance of such seals and equipment; and

(c) Other agreed measures.

50. The seals or other approved equipment provided for in a detailed agreement on inspection measures for that facility shall be placed not later than 240 days after this Convention enters into force for a State Party. Inspectors shall be permitted to visit each chemical weapons production facility for the installation of such seals or equipment.

51. During each calendar year, the Technical Secretariat shall be permitted to conduct up to four inspections of each chemical weapons production facility.

52. The Director-General shall notify the inspected State Party of his decision to inspect or visit a chemical weapons production facility 48 hours before the planned arrival of the inspection team at the facility for systematic inspections or visits. In the case of inspections or visits to resolve urgent problems, this period may be shortened. The Director-General shall specify the purpose of the inspection or visit.

53. Inspectors shall, in accordance with the facility agreements, have unimpeded access to all parts of the chemical weapons production facilities. The items on the declared inventory to

be inspected shall be chosen by the inspectors.

54. The guidelines for determining the frequency of systematic on-site inspections shall be considered and approved by the Conference pursuant to Article VIII, paragraph 21 (i). The particular production facility to be inspected shall be chosen by the Technical Secretariat in such a way as to preclude the prediction of precisely when the facility is to be inspected.

VERIFICATION OF DESTRUCTION OF CHEMICAL WEAPONS PRODUCTION FACILITIES

55. The purpose of systematic verification of the destruction of chemical weapons production facilities shall be to confirm that the facility is destroyed in accordance with the obligations under this Convention and that each item on the declared inventory is destroyed in accordance with the agreed detailed plan for destruction.

56. When all items on the declared inventory have been destroyed, the Technical Secretariat shall confirm the declaration of the State Party to that effect. After this confirmation, the Technical Secretariat shall terminate the systematic verification of the chemical weapons production facility and shall promptly remove all devices and monitoring instruments installed by the inspectors.

57. After this confirmation, the State Party shall make the declaration that the facility has been destroyed.

VERIFICATION OF TEMPORARY CONVERSION OF A CHEMICAL WEAPONS PRODUCTION FACILITY INTO A CHEMICAL WEAPONS DESTRUCTION FACILITY

58. Not later than 90 days after receiving the initial notification of the intent to convert temporarily a production facility, the inspectors shall have the right to visit the facility to familiarize themselves with the proposed temporary conversion and to study possible inspection measures that will be required during the conversion.

59. Not later than 60 days after such a visit, the Technical Secretariat and the inspected State Party shall conclude a transition agreement containing additional inspection measures for the temporary conversion period. The transition agreement shall specify inspection procedures, including the use of seals, monitoring equipment, and inspections, that will provide confidence that no chemical weapons production takes place during the conversion process. This agreement shall remain in force from the beginning of the temporary conversion activity until the facility begins operation as a chemical weapons destruction facility.

60. The inspected State Party shall not remove or convert any portion of the facility, or remove or modify any seal or other agreed inspection equipment that may have been installed pursuant to this Convention until the transition agreement has been concluded.

61. Once the facility begins operation as a chemical weapons destruction facility, it shall be subject to the provisions of Part IV (A) of this Annex applicable to chemical weapons destruction facilities. Arrangements for the pre-operation period shall be governed by the transition agreement.

62. During destruction operations the inspectors shall have access to all portions of the temporarily converted chemical weapons production facilities, including those that are not directly involved with the destruction of chemical weapons.

63. Before the commencement of work at the facility to convert it temporarily for chemical weapons destruction purposes and after the facility has ceased to function as a facility for chemical weapons destruction, the facility shall be subject to the provisions of this Part applicable to chemical weapons production facilities.

D. CONVERSION OF CHEMICAL WEAPONS PRODUCTION FACILITIES TO PURPOSES NOT PROHIBITED UNDER THIS CONVENTION

PROCEDURES FOR REQUESTING CONVERSION

64. A request to use a chemical weapons production facility for purposes not prohibited under

this Convention may be made for any facility that a State Party is already using for such purposes before this Convention enters into force for it, or that it plans to use for such purposes.

65. For a chemical weapons production facility that is being used for purposes not prohibited under this Convention when this Convention enters into force for the State Party, the request shall be submitted to the Director-General not later than 30 days after this Convention enters into force for the State Party. The request shall contain, in addition to data submitted in accordance with paragraph 1 (h) (iii), the following information:

(a) A detailed justification for the request;

(b) A general facility conversion plan that specifies:

    (i)   The nature of the activity to be conducted at the facility;

    (ii)   If the planned activity involves production, processing, or consumption of chemicals: the name of each of the chemicals, the flow diagram of the facility, and the quantities planned to be produced, processed, or consumed annually;

    (iii) Which buildings or structures are proposed to be used and what modifications are proposed, if any;

    (iv) Which buildings or structures have been destroyed or are proposed to be destroyed and the plans for destruction;

    (v)   What equipment is to be used in the facility;

    (vi) What equipment has been removed and destroyed and what equipment is proposed to be removed and destroyed and the plans for its destruction;

    (vii) The proposed schedule for conversion, if applicable; and

    (viii) The nature of the activity of each other facility operating at the site; and

(c) A detailed explanation of how measures set forth in subparagraph (b), as well as any other measures proposed by the State Party, will ensure the prevention of standby chemical weapons production capability at the facility.

66. For a chemical weapons production facility that is not being used for purposes not prohibited under this Convention when this Convention enters into force for the State Party, the request shall be submitted to the Director-General not later than 30 days after the decision to convert, but in no case later than four years after this Convention enters into force for the State Party. The request shall contain the following information:

(a) A detailed justification for the request, including its economic needs;

(b) A general facility conversion plan that specifies:

    (i)   The nature of the activity planned to be conducted at the facility;

    (ii)   If the planned activity involves production, processing, or consumption of chemicals: the name of each of the chemicals, the flow diagram of the facility, and the quantities planned to be produced, processed, or consumed annually;

    (iii) Which buildings or structures are proposed to be retained and what modifications are proposed, if any;

    (iv) Which buildings or structures have been destroyed or are proposed to be destroyed and the plans for destruction;

    (v)   What equipment is proposed for use in the facility;

    (vi) What equipment is proposed to be removed and destroyed and the plans for its destruction;

    (vii) The proposed schedule for conversion; and

    (viii) The nature of the activity of each other facility operating at the site; and

(c) A detailed explanation of how the measures set forth in subparagraph (b), as well as any other measures proposed by the State Party, will ensure the prevention of standby chemical weapons production capability at the facility.

67. The State Party may propose in its request any other measures it deems appropriate to build confidence.

ACTIONS PENDING A DECISION

68. Pending a decision of the Conference, a State Party may continue to use for purposes not prohibited under this Convention a facility that was being used for such purposes before this Convention enters into force for it, but only if the State Party certifies in its request that no specialized equipment and no specialized buildings are being used and that the specialized equipment and specialized buildings have been rendered inactive using the methods specified in paragraph 13.

69. If the facility, for which the request was made, was not being used for purposes not prohibited under this Convention before this Convention enters into force for the State Party, or if the certification required in paragraph 68 is not made, the State Party shall cease immediately all activity pursuant to Article V, paragraph 4. The State Party shall close the facility in accordance with paragraph 13 not later than 90 days after this Convention enters into force for it.

CONDITIONS FOR CONVERSION

70. As a condition for conversion of a chemical weapons production facility for purposes not prohibited under this Convention, all specialized equipment at the facility must be destroyed and all special features of buildings and structures that distinguish them from buildings and structures normally used for purposes not prohibited under this Convention and not involving Schedule 1 chemicals must be eliminated.

71. A converted facility shall not be used:

    (a) For any activity involving production, processing, or consumption of a Schedule 1 chemical or a Schedule 2 chemical; or

    (b) For the production of any highly toxic chemical, including any highly toxic organophosphorus chemical, or for any other activity that would require special equipment for handling highly toxic or highly corrosive chemicals, unless the Executive Council decides that such production or activity would pose no risk to the object and purpose of this Convention, taking into account criteria for toxicity, corrosiveness and, if applicable, other technical factors, to be considered and approved by the Conference pursuant to Article VIII, paragraph 21 (i).

72. Conversion of a chemical weapons production facility shall be completed not later than six years after entry into force of this Convention.

72bis If a State ratifies or accedes to this Convention after the six-year period for conversion set forth in paragraph 72, the Executive Council shall, at its second subsequent regular session, set a deadline for submission of any request to convert a chemical weapons production facility for purposes not prohibited under this Convention. A decision by the Conference to approve such a request, pursuant to paragraph 75, shall establish the earliest practicable deadline for completion of the conversion. Conversion shall be completed as soon as possible, but in no case later than six years after this Convention enters into force for the State Party. Except as modified in this paragraph, all provisions in Section D of this Part of this Annex shall apply.

DECISIONS BY THE EXECUTIVE COUNCIL AND THE CONFERENCE

73. Not later than 90 days after receipt of the request by the Director-General, an initial inspection of the facility shall be conducted by the Technical Secretariat. The purpose of this inspection shall be to determine the accuracy of the information provided in the request, to obtain information on the technical characteristics of the proposed converted facility, and to assess the conditions under which use for purposes not prohibited under this Convention may be permitted. The Director-General shall promptly submit a report to the Executive Council, the Conference, and all States Parties containing his recommendations on the measures necessary to convert the facility to purposes not prohibited under this Convention and to provide

assurance that the converted facility will be used only for purposes not prohibited under this Convention.

74. If the facility has been used for purposes not prohibited under this Convention before this Convention enters into force for the State Party, and is continuing to be in operation, but the measures required to be certified under paragraph 68 have not been taken, the Director-General shall immediately inform the Executive Council, which may require implementation of measures it deems appropriate, *inter alia*, shut-down of the facility and removal of specialized equipment and modification of buildings or structures. The Executive Council shall stipulate the deadline for implementation of these measures and shall suspend consideration of the request pending their satisfactory completion. The facility shall be inspected promptly after the expiration of the deadline to determine whether the measures have been implemented. If not, the State Party shall be required to shut down completely all facility operations.

75. As soon as possible after receiving the report of the Director-General, the Conference, upon recommendation of the Executive Council, shall decide, taking into account the report and any views expressed by States Parties, whether to approve the request, and shall establish the conditions upon which approval is contingent. If any State Party objects to approval of the request and the associated conditions, consultations shall be undertaken among interested States Parties for up to 90 days to seek a mutually acceptable solution. A decision on the request and associated conditions, along with any proposed modifications thereto, shall be taken, as a matter of substance, as soon as possible after the end of the consultation period.

76. If the request is approved, a facility agreement shall be completed not later than 90 days after such a decision is taken. The facility agreement shall contain the conditions under which the conversion and use of the facility is permitted, including measures for verification. Conversion shall not begin before the facility agreement is concluded.

DETAILED PLANS FOR CONVERSION

77. Not less than 180 days before conversion of a chemical weapons production facility is planned to begin, the State Party shall provide the Technical Secretariat with the detailed plans for conversion of the facility, including proposed measures for verification of conversion, with respect to, *inter alia*:
    (a) Timing of the presence of the inspectors at the facility to be converted; and
    (b) Procedures for verification of measures to be applied to each item on the declared inventory.

78. The detailed plan for conversion of each chemical weapons production facility shall contain:
    (a) Detailed time schedule of the conversion process;
    (b) Layout of the facility before and after conversion;
    (c) Process flow diagram of the facility before, and as appropriate, after the conversion;
    (d) Detailed inventory of equipment, buildings and structures and other items to be destroyed and of the buildings and structures to be modified;
    (e) Measures to be applied to each item on the inventory, if any;
    (f) Proposed measures for verification;
    (g) Security/safety measures to be observed during the conversion of the facility; and
    (h) Working and living conditions to be provided for inspectors.

REVIEW OF DETAILED PLANS

79. On the basis of the detailed plan for conversion and proposed measures for verification submitted by the State Party, and on experience from previous inspections, the Technical Secretariat shall prepare a plan for verifying the conversion of the facility, consulting closely with the State Party. Any differences between the Technical Secretariat and the State Party concerning appropriate measures shall be resolved through consultations. Any unresolved matters shall be forwarded to the Executive Council for appropriate action with a view to

facilitate the full implementation of this Convention.

80. To ensure that the provisions of Article V and this Part are fulfilled, the combined plans for conversion and verification shall be agreed upon between the Executive Council and the State Party. This agreement shall be completed not less than 60 days before conversion is planned to begin.

81. Each member of the Executive Council may consult with the Technical Secretariat on any issue regarding the adequacy of the combined plan for conversion and verification. If there are no objections by any member of the Executive Council, the plan shall be put into action.

82. If there are any difficulties, the Executive Council should enter into consultations with the State Party to reconcile them. If any difficulties remain unresolved, they should be referred to the Conference. The resolution of any differences over methods of conversion should not delay the execution of other parts of the conversion plan that are acceptable.

83. If agreement is not reached with the Executive Council on aspects of verification, or if the approved verification plan cannot be put into action, verification of conversion shall proceed through continuous monitoring with on-site instruments and physical presence of inspectors.

84. Conversion and verification shall proceed according to the agreed plan. The verification shall not unduly interfere with the conversion process and shall be conducted through the presence of inspectors to confirm the conversion.

85. For the 10 years after the Director-General certifies that conversion is complete, the State Party shall provide to inspectors unimpeded access to the facility at any time. The inspectors shall have the right to observe all areas, all activities, and all items of equipment at the facility. The inspectors shall have the right to verify that the activities at the facility are consistent with any conditions established under this Section, by the Executive Council and the Conference. The inspectors shall also have the right, in accordance with provisions of Part II, Section E, of this Annex to receive samples from any area of the facility and to analyse them to verify the absence of Schedule 1 chemicals, their stable by-products and decomposition products and of Schedule 2 chemicals and to verify that the activities at the facility are consistent with any other conditions on chemical activities established under this Section, by the Executive Council and the Conference. The inspectors shall also have the right to managed access, in accordance with Part X, Section C, of this Annex, to the plant site at which the facility is located. During the 10-year period, the State Party shall report annually on the activities at the converted facility. Upon completion of the 10-year period, the Executive Council, taking into account recommendations of the Technical Secretariat, shall decide on the nature of continued verification measures.

86. Costs of verification of the converted facility shall be allocated in accordance with Article V, paragraph 19.

PART VI
ACTIVITIES NOT PROHIBITED UNDER THIS CONVENTION IN ACCORDANCE WITH ARTICLE VI

REGIME FOR SCHEDULE 1 CHEMICALS AND FACILITIES RELATED TO SUCH CHEMICALS

A. GENERAL PROVISIONS

1. A State Party shall not produce, acquire, retain or use Schedule 1 chemicals outside the territories of States Parties and shall not transfer such chemicals outside its territory except to another State Party.

2. A State Party shall not produce, acquire, retain, transfer or use Schedule 1 chemicals unless:
    (a) The chemicals are applied to research, medical, pharmaceutical or protective purposes; and

    (b)   The types and quantities of chemicals are strictly limited to those which can be justified for such purposes; and

    (c)   The aggregate amount of such chemicals at any given time for such purposes is equal to or less than 1 tonne; and

    (d)   The aggregate amount for such purposes acquired by a State Party in any year through production, withdrawal from chemical weapons stocks and transfer is equal to or less than 1 tonne.

B. TRANSFERS

3.   A State Party may transfer Schedule 1 chemicals outside its territory only to another State Party and only for research, medical, pharmaceutical or protective purposes in accordance with paragraph 2.

4.   Chemicals transferred shall not be retransferred to a third State.

5.   Not less than 30 days before any transfer to another State Party both States Parties shall notify the Technical Secretariat of the transfer.

5bis For quantities of 5 milligrams or less, the Schedule 1 chemical saxitoxin shall not be subject to the notification period in paragraph 5 if the transfer is for medical/diagnostic purposes. In such cases, the notification shall be made by the time of transfer.

6.   Each State Party shall make a detailed annual declaration regarding transfers during the previous year. The declaration shall be submitted not later than 90 days after the end of that year and shall for each Schedule 1 chemical that has been transferred include the following information:

    (a)   The chemical name, structural formula and Chemical Abstracts Service registry number, if assigned;

    (b)   The quantity acquired from other States or transferred to other States Parties. For each transfer the quantity, recipient and purpose shall be included.

C. PRODUCTION

GENERAL PRINCIPLES FOR PRODUCTION

7.   Each State Party, during production under paragraphs 8 to 12, shall assign the highest priority to ensuring the safety of people and to protecting the environment. Each State Party shall conduct such production in accordance with its national standards for safety and emissions.

SINGLE SMALL-SCALE FACILITY

8.   Each State Party that produces Schedule 1 chemicals for research, medical, pharmaceutical or protective purposes shall carry out the production at a single small-scale facility approved by the State Party, except as set forth in paragraphs 10, 11 and 12.

9.   The production at a single small-scale facility shall be carried out in reaction vessels in production lines not configured for continuous operation. The volume of such a reaction vessel shall not exceed 100 litres, and the total volume of all reaction vessels with a volume exceeding 5 litres shall not be more than 500 litres.

OTHER FACILITIES

10. Production of Schedule 1 chemicals in aggregate quantities not exceeding 10 kg per year may be carried out for protective purposes at one facility outside a single small-scale facility. This facility shall be approved by the State Party.

11. Production of Schedule 1 chemicals in quantities of more than 100 g per year may be carried out for research, medical or pharmaceutical purposes outside a single small-scale facility in aggregate quantities not exceeding 10 kg per year per facility. These facilities shall be approved by the State Party.

12. Synthesis of Schedule 1 chemicals for research, medical or pharmaceutical purposes, but not for protective purposes, may be carried out at laboratories in aggregate quantities less than 100 g per year per facility. These facilities shall not be subject to any obligation relating to declaration and verification as specified in Sections D and E.

D. DECLARATIONS

SINGLE SMALL-SCALE FACILITY

13. Each State Party that plans to operate a single small-scale facility shall provide the Technical Secretariat with the precise location and a detailed technical description of the facility, including an inventory of equipment and detailed diagrams. For existing facilities, this initial declaration shall be provided not later than 30 days after this Convention enters into force for the State Party. Initial declarations on new facilities shall be provided not less than 180 days before operations are to begin.

14. Each State Party shall give advance notification to the Technical Secretariat of planned changes related to the initial declaration. The notification shall be submitted not less than 180 days before the changes are to take place.

15. A State Party producing Schedule 1 chemicals at a single small-scale facility shall make a detailed annual declaration regarding the activities of the facility for the previous year. The declaration shall be submitted not later than 90 days after the end of that year and shall include:

    (a) Identification of the facility;

    (b) For each Schedule 1 chemical produced, acquired, consumed or stored at the facility, the following information:

        (i) The chemical name, structural formula and Chemical Abstracts Service registry number, if assigned;

        (ii) The methods employed and quantity produced;

        (iii) The name and quantity of precursors listed in Schedules 1, 2, or 3 used for production of Schedule 1 chemicals;

        (iv) The quantity consumed at the facility and the purpose(s) of the consumption;

        (v) The quantity received from or shipped to other facilities in the State Party. For each shipment the quantity, recipient and purpose should be included;

        (vi) The maximum quantity stored at any time during the year; and

        (vii) The quantity stored at the end of the year; and

    (c) Information on any changes at the facility during the year compared to previously submitted detailed technical descriptions of the facility including inventories of equipment and detailed diagrams.

16. Each State Party producing Schedule 1 chemicals at a single small-scale facility shall make a detailed annual declaration regarding the projected activities and the anticipated production at the facility for the coming year. The declaration shall be submitted not less than 90 days before the beginning of that year and shall include:

    (a) Identification of the facility;

    (b) For each Schedule 1 chemical anticipated to be produced, consumed or stored at the facility, the following information:

        (i) The chemical name, structural formula and Chemical Abstracts Service registry number, if assigned;

        (ii) The quantity anticipated to be produced and the purpose of the production; and

    (c) Information on any anticipated changes at the facility during the year compared to previously submitted detailed technical descriptions of the facility including inventories of equipment and detailed diagrams.

OTHER FACILITIES REFERRED TO IN PARAGRAPHS 10 AND 11

17. For each facility, a State Party shall provide the Technical Secretariat with the name, location and a detailed technical description of the facility or its relevant part(s) as requested by the Technical Secretariat. The facility producing Schedule 1 chemicals for protective purposes shall be specifically identified. For existing facilities, this initial declaration shall be provided not later than 30 days after this Convention enters into force for the State Party. Initial declarations on new facilities shall be provided not less than 180 days before operations are to begin.

18. Each State Party shall give advance notification to the Technical Secretariat of planned changes related to the initial declaration. The notification shall be submitted not less than 180 days before the changes are to take place.

19. Each State Party shall, for each facility, make a detailed annual declaration regarding the activities of the facility for the previous year. The declaration shall be submitted not later than 90 days after the end of that year and shall include:

    (a) Identification of the facility;

    (b) For each Schedule 1 chemical the following information:

        (i) The chemical name, structural formula and Chemical Abstracts Service registry number, if assigned;

        (ii) The quantity produced and, in case of production for protective purposes, methods employed;

        (iii) The name and quantity of precursors listed in Schedules 1, 2, or 3, used for production of Schedule 1 chemicals;

        (iv) The quantity consumed at the facility and the purpose of the consumption;

        (v) The quantity transferred to other facilities within the State Party. For each transfer the quantity, recipient and purpose should be included;

        (vi) The maximum quantity stored at any time during the year; and

        (vii) The quantity stored at the end of the year; and

    (c) Information on any changes at the facility or its relevant parts during the year compared to previously submitted detailed technical description of the facility.

20. Each State Party shall, for each facility, make a detailed annual declaration regarding the projected activities and the anticipated production at the facility for the coming year. The declaration shall be submitted not less than 90 days before the beginning of that year and shall include:

    (a) Identification of the facility;

    (b) For each Schedule 1 chemical the following information:

        (i) The chemical name, structural formula and Chemical Abstracts Service registry number, if assigned; and

        (ii) The quantity anticipated to be produced, the time periods when the production is anticipated to take place and the purposes of the production; and

    (c) Information on any anticipated changes at the facility or its relevant parts, during the year compared to previously submitted detailed technical descriptions of the facility.

E. VERIFICATION

SINGLE SMALL-SCALE FACILITY

21. The aim of verification activities at the single small-scale facility shall be to verify that the quantities of Schedule 1 chemicals produced are correctly declared and, in particular, that their aggregate amount does not exceed 1 tonne.

22. The facility shall be subject to systematic verification through on-site inspection and monitoring with on-site instruments.

23. The number, intensity, duration, timing and mode of inspections for a particular facility shall

be based on the risk to the object and purpose of this Convention posed by the relevant chemicals, the characteristics of the facility and the nature of the activities carried out there. Appropriate guidelines shall be considered and approved by the Conference pursuant to Article VIII, paragraph 21 (i).

24. The purpose of the initial inspection shall be to verify information provided concerning the facility, including verification of the limits on reaction vessels set forth in paragraph 9.

25. Not later than 180 days after this Convention enters into force for a State Party, it shall conclude a facility agreement, based on a model agreement, with the Organization, covering detailed inspection procedures for the facility.

26. Each State Party planning to establish a single small-scale facility after this Convention enters into force for it shall conclude a facility agreement, based on a model agreement, with the Organization, covering detailed inspection procedures for the facility before it begins operation or is used.

27. A model for agreements shall be considered and approved by the Conference pursuant to Article VIII, paragraph 21 (i).

OTHER FACILITIES REFERRED TO IN PARAGRAPHS 10 AND 11

28. The aim of verification activities at any facility referred to in paragraphs 10 and 11 shall be to verify that:

    (a) The facility is not used to produce any Schedule 1 chemical, except for the declared chemicals;

    (b) The quantities of Schedule 1 chemicals produced, processed or consumed are correctly declared and consistent with needs for the declared purpose; and

    (c) The Schedule 1 chemical is not diverted or used for other purposes.

29. The facility shall be subject to systematic verification through on-site inspection and monitoring with on-site instruments.

30. The number, intensity, duration, timing and mode of inspections for a particular facility shall be based on the risk to the object and purpose of this Convention posed by the quantities of chemicals produced, the characteristics of the facility and the nature of the activities carried out there. Appropriate guidelines shall be considered and approved by the Conference pursuant to Article VIII, paragraph 21 (i).

31. Not later than 180 days after this Convention enters into force for a State Party, it shall conclude facility agreements with the Organization, based on a model agreement covering detailed inspection procedures for each facility.

32. Each State Party planning to establish such a facility after entry into force of this Convention shall conclude a facility agreement with the Organization before the facility begins operation or is used.

PART VII
ACTIVITIES NOT PROHIBITED UNDER THIS CONVENTION IN ACCORDANCE WITH ARTICLE VI

REGIME FOR SCHEDULE 2 CHEMICALS AND FACILITIES RELATED TO SUCH CHEMICALS

A. DECLARATIONS

DECLARATIONS OF AGGREGATE NATIONAL DATA

1. The initial and annual declarations to be provided by each State Party pursuant to Article VI, paragraphs 7 and 8, shall include aggregate national data for the previous calendar year on the quantities produced, processed, consumed, imported and exported of each Schedule 2 chemical, as well as a quantitative specification of import and export for each country involved.

2.   Each State Party shall submit:
     (a) Initial declarations pursuant to paragraph 1 not later than 30 days after this Convention enters into force for it; and, starting in the following calendar year,
     (b) Annual declarations not later than 90 days after the end of the previous calendar year.

DECLARATIONS OF PLANT SITES PRODUCING, PROCESSING OR CONSUMING SCHEDULE 2 CHEMICALS

3.   Initial and annual declarations are required for all plant sites that comprise one or more plant(s) which produced, processed or consumed during any of the previous three calendar years or is anticipated to produce, process or consume in the next calendar year more than:
     (a) 1 kg of a chemical designated "*" in Schedule 2, part A;
     (b) 100 kg of any other chemical listed in Schedule 2, part A; or
     (c) 1 tonne of a chemical listed in Schedule 2, part B.

4.   Each State Party shall submit:
     (a) Initial declarations pursuant to paragraph 3 not later than 30 days after this Convention enters into force for it; and, starting in the following calendar year;
     (b) Annual declarations on past activities not later than 90 days after the end of the previous calendar year;
     (c) Annual declarations on anticipated activities not later than 60 days before the beginning of the following calendar year. Any such activity additionally planned after the annual declaration has been submitted shall be declared not later than five days before this activity begins.

5.   Declarations pursuant to paragraph 3 are generally not required for mixtures containing a low concentration of a Schedule 2 chemical. They are only required, in accordance with guidelines, in cases where the ease of recovery from the mixture of the Schedule 2 chemical and its total weight are deemed to pose a risk to the object and purpose of this Convention. These guidelines shall be considered and approved by the Conference pursuant to Article VIII, paragraph 21 (i).

6.   Declarations of a plant site pursuant to paragraph 3 shall include:
     (a) The name of the plant site and the name of the owner, company, or enterprise operating it;
     (b) Its precise location including the address; and
     (c) The number of plants within the plant site which are declared pursuant to Part VIII of this Annex.

7.   Declarations of a plant site pursuant to paragraph 3 shall also include, for each plant which is located within the plant site and which falls under the specifications set forth in paragraph 3, the following information:
     (a) The name of the plant and the name of the owner, company, or enterprise operating it;
     (b) Its precise location within the plant site including the specific building or structure number, if any;
     (c) Its main activities;
     (d) Whether the plant:
          (i)   Produces, processes, or consumes the declared Schedule 2 chemical(s);
          (ii) Is dedicated to such activities or multi-purpose; and
          (iii) Performs other activities with regard to the declared Schedule 2 chemical(s), including a specification of that other activity (e.g. storage); and
     (e) The production capacity of the plant for each declared Schedule 2 chemical.

8.   Declarations of a plant site pursuant to paragraph 3 shall also include the following information on each Schedule 2 chemical above the declaration threshold:
     (a) The chemical name, common or trade name used by the facility, structural formula, and Chemical Abstracts Service registry number, if assigned;
     (b) In the case of the initial declaration: the total amount produced, processed, consumed,

imported and exported by the plant site in each of the three previous calendar years;

(c) In the case of the annual declaration on past activities: the total amount produced, processed, consumed, imported and exported by the plant site in the previous calendar year;

(d) In the case of the annual declaration on anticipated activities: the total amount anticipated to be produced, processed or consumed by the plant site in the following calendar year, including the anticipated time periods for production, processing or consumption; and

(e) The purposes for which the chemical was or will be produced, processed or consumed:

   (i) Processing and consumption on site with a specification of the product types;

   (ii) Sale or transfer within the territory or to any other place under the jurisdiction or control of the State Party, with a specification whether to other industry, trader or other destination and, if possible, of final product types;

   (iii) Direct export, with a specification of the States involved; or

   (iv) Other, including a specification of these other purposes.

DECLARATIONS ON PAST PRODUCTION OF SCHEDULE 2 CHEMICALS FOR CHEMICAL WEAPONS PURPOSES

9. Each State Party shall, not later than 30 days after this Convention enters into force for it, declare all plant sites comprising plants that produced at any time since 1 January 1946 a Schedule 2 chemical for chemical weapons purposes.

10. Declarations of a plant site pursuant to paragraph 9 shall include:

(a) The name of the plant site and the name of the owner, company, or enterprise operating it;

(b) Its precise location including the address;

(c) For each plant which is located within the plant site, and which falls under the specifications set forth in paragraph 9, the same information as required under paragraph 7, subparagraphs (a) to (e); and

(d) For each Schedule 2 chemical produced for chemical weapons purposes:

   (i) The chemical name, common or trade name used by the plant site for chemical weapons production purposes, structural formula, and Chemical Abstracts Service registry number, if assigned;

   (ii) The dates when the chemical was produced and the quantity produced; and

   (iii) The location to which the chemical was delivered and the final product produced there, if known.

INFORMATION TO STATES PARTIES

11. A list of plant sites declared under this Section together with the information provided under paragraphs 6, 7 (a), 7 (c), 7 (d) (i), 7 (d) (iii), 8 (a) and 10 shall be transmitted by the Technical Secretariat to States Parties upon request.

B.　VERIFICATION

GENERAL

12. Verification provided for in Article VI, paragraph 4, shall be carried out through on-site inspection at those of the declared plant sites that comprise one or more plants which produced, processed or consumed during any of the previous three calendar years or are anticipated to produce, process or consume in the next calendar year more than:

(a) 10 kg of a chemical designated "*" in Schedule 2, part A;

(b) 1 tonne of any other chemical listed in Schedule 2, part A; or

(c) 10 tonnes of a chemical listed in Schedule 2, part B.

13. The programme and budget of the Organization to be adopted by the Conference pursuant to Article VIII, paragraph 21 (a) shall contain, as a separate item, a programme and budget for verification under this Section. In the allocation of resources made available for verification

under Article VI, the Technical Secretariat shall, during the first three years after the entry into force of this Convention, give priority to the initial inspections of plant sites declared under Section A. The allocation shall thereafter be reviewed on the basis of the experience gained.

14. The Technical Secretariat shall conduct initial inspections and subsequent inspections in accordance with paragraphs 15 to 22.

INSPECTION AIMS

15. The general aim of inspections shall be to verify that activities are in accordance with obligations under this Convention and consistent with the information to be provided in declarations. Particular aims of inspections at plant sites declared under Section A shall include verification of:
   (a) The absence of any Schedule 1 chemical, especially its production, except if in accordance with Part VI of this Annex;
   (b) Consistency with declarations of levels of production, processing or consumption of Schedule 2 chemicals; and
   (c) Non-diversion of Schedule 2 chemicals for activities prohibited under this Convention.

INITIAL INSPECTIONS

16. Each plant site to be inspected pursuant to paragraph 12 shall receive an initial inspection as soon as possible but preferably not later than three years after entry into force of this Convention. Plant sites declared after this period shall receive an initial inspection not later than one year after production, processing or consumption is first declared. Selection of plant sites for initial inspections shall be made by the Technical Secretariat in such a way as to preclude the prediction of precisely when the plant site is to be inspected.

17. During the initial inspection, a draft facility agreement for the plant site shall be prepared unless the inspected State Party and the Technical Secretariat agree that it is not needed.

18. With regard to frequency and intensity of subsequent inspections, inspectors shall during the initial inspection assess the risk to the object and purpose of this Convention posed by the relevant chemicals, the characteristics of the plant site and the nature of the activities carried out there, taking into account, *inter alia*, the following criteria:
   (a) The toxicity of the scheduled chemicals and of the end-products produced with it, if any;
   (b) The quantity of the scheduled chemicals typically stored at the inspected site;
   (c) The quantity of feedstock chemicals for the scheduled chemicals typically stored at the inspected site;
   (d) The production capacity of the Schedule 2 plants; and
   (e) The capability and convertibility for initiating production, storage and filling of toxic chemicals at the inspected site.

INSPECTIONS

19. Having received the initial inspection, each plant site to be inspected pursuant to paragraph 12 shall be subject to subsequent inspections.

20. In selecting particular plant sites for inspection and in deciding on the frequency and intensity of inspections, the Technical Secretariat shall give due consideration to the risk to the object and purpose of this Convention posed by the relevant chemical, the characteristics of the plant site and the nature of the activities carried out there, taking into account the respective facility agreement as well as the results of the initial inspections and subsequent inspections.

21. The Technical Secretariat shall choose a particular plant site to be inspected in such a way as to preclude the prediction of exactly when it will be inspected.

22. No plant site shall receive more than two inspections per calendar year under the provisions of this Section. This, however, shall not limit inspections pursuant to Article IX.

INSPECTION PROCEDURES

23. In addition to agreed guidelines, other relevant provisions of this Annex and the Confidentiality Annex, paragraphs 24 to 30 below shall apply.

24. A facility agreement for the declared plant site shall be concluded not later than 90 days after completion of the initial inspection between the inspected State Party and the Organization unless the inspected State Party and the Technical Secretariat agree that it is not needed. It shall be based on a model agreement and govern the conduct of inspections at the declared plant site. The agreement shall specify the frequency and intensity of inspections as well as detailed inspection procedures, consistent with paragraphs 25 to 29.

25. The focus of the inspection shall be the declared Schedule 2 plant(s) within the declared plant site. If the inspection team requests access to other parts of the plant site, access to these areas shall be granted in accordance with the obligation to provide clarification pursuant to Part II, paragraph 51, of this Annex and in accordance with the facility agreement, or, in the absence of a facility agreement, in accordance with the rules of managed access as specified in Part X, Section C, of this Annex.

26. Access to records shall be provided, as appropriate, to provide assurance that there has been no diversion of the declared chemical and that production has been consistent with declarations.

27. Sampling and analysis shall be undertaken to check for the absence of undeclared scheduled chemicals.

28. Areas to be inspected may include:

    (a) Areas where feed chemicals (reactants) are delivered or stored;
    (b) Areas where manipulative processes are performed upon the reactants prior to addition to the reaction vessels;
    (c) Feed lines as appropriate from the areas referred to in subparagraph (a) or subparagraph (b) to the reaction vessels together with any associated valves, flow meters, etc.;
    (d) The external aspect of the reaction vessels and ancillary equipment;
    (e) Lines from the reaction vessels leading to long- or short-term storage or to equipment further processing the declared Schedule 2 chemicals;
    (f) Control equipment associated with any of the items under subparagraphs (a) to (e);
    (g) Equipment and areas for waste and effluent handling;
    (h) Equipment and areas for disposition of chemicals not up to specification.

29. The period of inspection shall not last more than 96 hours; however, extensions may be agreed between the inspection team and the inspected State Party.

NOTIFICATION OF INSPECTION

30. A State Party shall be notified by the Technical Secretariat of the inspection not less than 48 hours before the arrival of the inspection team at the plant site to be inspected.

C.   TRANSFERS TO STATES NOT PARTY TO THIS CONVENTION

31. Schedule 2 chemicals shall only be transferred to or received from States Parties. This obligation shall take effect three years after entry into force of this Convention.

32. During this interim three-year period, each State Party shall require an end-use certificate, as specified below, for transfers of Schedule 2 chemicals to States not Party to this Convention. For such transfers, each State Party shall adopt the necessary measures to ensure that the transferred chemicals shall only be used for purposes not prohibited under this Convention. *Inter alia*, the State Party shall require from the recipient State a certificate stating, in relation to the transferred chemicals:

    (a) That they will only be used for purposes not prohibited under this Convention;
    (b) That they will not be re-transferred;
    (c) Their types and quantities;

(d) Their end-use(s); and

(e) The name(s) and address(es) of the end-user(s).

PART VIII
ACTIVITIES NOT PROHIBITED UNDER THIS CONVENTION IN ACCORDANCE WITH ARTICLE VI

REGIME FOR SCHEDULE 3 CHEMICALS AND FACILITIES RELATED TO SUCH CHEMICALS

A. DECLARATIONS

DECLARATIONS OF AGGREGATE NATIONAL DATA

1. The initial and annual declarations to be provided by a State Party pursuant to Article VI, paragraphs 7 and 8, shall include aggregate national data for the previous calendar year on the quantities produced, imported and exported of each Schedule 3 chemical, as well as a quantitative specification of import and export for each country involved.

2. Each State Party shall submit:

    (a) Initial declarations pursuant to paragraph 1 not later than 30 days after this Convention enters into force for it; and, starting in the following calendar year,

    (b) Annual declarations not later than 90 days after the end of the previous calendar year.

DECLARATIONS OF PLANT SITES PRODUCING SCHEDULE 3 CHEMICALS

3. Initial and annual declarations are required for all plant sites that comprise one or more plants which produced during the previous calendar year or are anticipated to produce in the next calendar year more than 30 tonnes of a Schedule 3 chemical.

4. Each State Party shall submit:

    (a) Initial declarations pursuant to paragraph 3 not later than 30 days after this Convention enters into force for it; and, starting in the following calendar year;

    (b) Annual declarations on past activities not later than 90 days after the end of the previous calendar year;

    (c) Annual declarations on anticipated activities not later than 60 days before the beginning of the following calendar year. Any such activity additionally planned after the annual declaration has been submitted shall be declared not later than five days before this activity begins.

5. Declarations pursuant to paragraph 3 are generally not required for mixtures containing a low concentration of a Schedule 3 chemical. They are only required, in accordance with guidelines, in such cases where the ease of recovery from the mixture of the Schedule 3 chemical and its total weight are deemed to pose a risk to the object and purpose of this Convention. These guidelines shall be considered and approved by the Conference pursuant to Article VIII, paragraph 21 (i).

6. Declarations of a plant site pursuant to paragraph 3 shall include:

    (a) The name of the plant site and the name of the owner, company, or enterprise operating it;

    (b) Its precise location including the address; and

    (c) The number of plants within the plant site which are declared pursuant to Part VII of this Annex.

7. Declarations of a plant site pursuant to paragraph 3 shall also include, for each plant which is located within the plant site and which falls under the specifications set forth in paragraph 3, the following information:

    (a) The name of the plant and the name of the owner, company, or enterprise operating it;

    (b) Its precise location within the plant site, including the specific building or structure number, if any;

    (c) Its main activities.

8.   Declarations of a plant site pursuant to paragraph 3 shall also include the following information on each Schedule 3 chemical above the declaration threshold:

    (a) The chemical name, common or trade name used by the facility, structural formula, and Chemical Abstracts Service registry number, if assigned;

    (b) The approximate amount of production of the chemical in the previous calendar year, or, in case of declarations on anticipated activities, anticipated for the next calendar year, expressed in the ranges: 30 to 200 tonnes, 200 to 1,000 tonnes, 1,000 to 10,000 tonnes, 10,000 to 100,000 tonnes, and above 100,000 tonnes; and

    (c) The purposes for which the chemical was or will be produced.

DECLARATIONS ON PAST PRODUCTION OF SCHEDULE 3 CHEMICALS FOR CHEMICAL WEAPONS PURPOSES

9.   Each State Party shall, not later than 30 days after this Convention enters into force for it, declare all plant sites comprising plants that produced at any time since 1 January 1946 a Schedule 3 chemical for chemical weapons purposes.

10. Declarations of a plant site pursuant to paragraph 9 shall include:

    (a) The name of the plant site and the name of the owner, company, or enterprise operating it;

    (b) Its precise location including the address;

    (c) For each plant which is located within the plant site, and which falls under the specifications set forth in paragraph 9, the same information as required under paragraph 7, subparagraphs (a) to (c); and

    (d) For each Schedule 3 chemical produced for chemical weapons purposes:

        (i) The chemical name, common or trade name used by the plant site for chemical weapons production purposes, structural formula, and Chemical Abstracts Service registry number, if assigned;

        (ii) The dates when the chemical was produced and the quantity produced; and

        (iii) The location to which the chemical was delivered and the final product produced there, if known.

INFORMATION TO STATES PARTIES

11. A list of plant sites declared under this Section together with the information provided under paragraphs 6, 7 (a), 7 (c), 8 (a) and 10 shall be transmitted by the Technical Secretariat to States Parties upon request.

B. VERIFICATION

GENERAL

12. Verification provided for in paragraph 5 of Article VI shall be carried out through on-site inspections at those declared plant sites which produced during the previous calendar year or are anticipated to produce in the next calendar year in excess of 200 tonnes aggregate of any Schedule 3 chemical above the declaration threshold of 30 tonnes.

13. The programme and budget of the Organization to be adopted by the Conference pursuant to Article VIII, paragraph 21 (a), shall contain, as a separate item, a programme and budget for verification under this Section taking into account Part VII, paragraph 13, of this Annex.

14. Under this Section, the Technical Secretariat shall randomly select plant sites for inspection through appropriate mechanisms, such as the use of specially designed computer software, on the basis of the following weighting factors:

    (a) Equitable geographical distribution of inspections; and

    (b) The information on the declared plant sites available to the Technical Secretariat, related to the relevant chemical, the characteristics of the plant site and the nature of the activities carried out there.

15. No plant site shall receive more than two inspections per year under the provisions of this Section. This, however, shall not limit inspections pursuant to Article IX.

16. In selecting plant sites for inspection under this Section, the Technical Secretariat shall observe the following limitation for the combined number of inspections to be received by a State Party per calendar year under this Part and Part IX of this Annex: the combined number of inspections shall not exceed three plus 5 per cent of the total number of plant sites declared by a State Party under both this Part and Part IX of this Annex, or 20 inspections, whichever of these two figures is lower.

INSPECTION AIMS

17. At plant sites declared under Section A, the general aim of inspections shall be to verify that activities are consistent with the information to be provided in declarations. The particular aim of inspections shall be the verification of the absence of any Schedule 1 chemical, especially its production, except if in accordance with Part VI of this Annex.

INSPECTION PROCEDURES

18. In addition to agreed guidelines, other relevant provisions of this Annex and the Confidentiality Annex, paragraphs 19 to 25 below shall apply.

19. There shall be no facility agreement, unless requested by the inspected State Party.

20. The focus of the inspections shall be the declared Schedule 3 plant(s) within the declared plant site. If the inspection team, in accordance with Part II, paragraph 51, of this Annex, requests access to other parts of the plant site for clarification of ambiguities, the extent of such access shall be agreed between the inspection team and the inspected State Party.

21. The inspection team may have access to records in situations in which the inspection team and the inspected State Party agree that such access will assist in achieving the objectives of the inspection.

22. Sampling and on-site analysis may be undertaken to check for the absence of undeclared scheduled chemicals. In case of unresolved ambiguities, samples may be analysed in a designated off-site laboratory, subject to the inspected State Party's agreement.

23. Areas to be inspected may include:
    (a) Areas where feed chemicals (reactants) are delivered or stored;
    (b) Areas where manipulative processes are performed upon the reactants prior to addition to the reaction vessel;
    (c) Feed lines as appropriate from the areas referred to in subparagraph (a) or subparagraph (b) to the reaction vessel together with any associated valves, flow meters, etc.;
    (d) The external aspect of the reaction vessels and ancillary equipment;
    (e) Lines from the reaction vessels leading to long- or short-term storage or to equipment further processing the declared Schedule 3 chemicals;
    (f) Control equipment associated with any of the items under subparagraphs (a) to (e);
    (g) Equipment and areas for waste and effluent handling;
    (h) Equipment and areas for disposition of chemicals not up to specification.

24. The period of inspection shall not last more than 24 hours; however, extensions may be agreed between the inspection team and the inspected State Party.

NOTIFICATION OF INSPECTION

25. A State Party shall be notified by the Technical Secretariat of the inspection not less than 120 hours before the arrival of the inspection team at the plant site to be inspected.

C.   TRANSFERS TO STATES NOT PARTY TO THIS CONVENTION

26.   When transferring Schedule 3 chemicals to States not Party to this Convention, each State Party shall adopt the necessary measures to ensure that the transferred chemicals shall only be used for purposes not prohibited under this Convention. *Inter alia*, the State Party shall require from the recipient State a certificate stating, in relation to the transferred chemicals:
      (a)   That they will only be used for purposes not prohibited under this Convention;
      (b)   That they will not be re-transferred;
      (c)   Their types and quantities;
      (d)   Their end-use(s); and
      (e)   The name(s) and address(es) of the end-user(s).
27.   Five years after entry into force of this Convention, the Conference shall consider the need to establish other measures regarding transfers of Schedule 3 chemicals to States not Party to this Convention.

PART IX
ACTIVITIES NOT PROHIBITED UNDER THIS CONVENTION IN ACCORDANCE WITH ARTICLE VI

REGIME FOR OTHER CHEMICAL PRODUCTION FACILITIES

A.   DECLARATIONS

LIST OF OTHER CHEMICAL PRODUCTION FACILITIES
1.   The initial declaration to be provided by each State Party pursuant to Article VI, paragraph 7, shall include a list of all plant sites that:
      (a)   Produced by synthesis during the previous calendar year more than 200 tonnes of unscheduled discrete organic chemicals; or
      (b)   Comprise one or more plants which produced by synthesis during the previous calendar year more than 30 tonnes of an unscheduled discrete organic chemical containing the elements phosphorus, sulfur or fluorine (hereinafter referred to as "PSF-plants" and "PSF-chemical").
2.   The list of other chemical production facilities to be submitted pursuant to paragraph 1 shall not include plant sites that exclusively produced explosives or hydrocarbons.
3.   Each State Party shall submit its list of other chemical production facilities pursuant to paragraph 1 as part of its initial declaration not later than 30 days after this Convention enters into force for it. Each State Party shall, not later than 90 days after the beginning of each following calendar year, provide annually the information necessary to update the list.
4.   The list of other chemical production facilities to be submitted pursuant to paragraph 1 shall include the following information on each plant site:
      (a)   The name of the plant site and the name of the owner, company, or enterprise operating it;
      (b)   The precise location of the plant site including its address;
      (c)   Its main activities; and
      (d)   The approximate number of plants producing the chemicals specified in paragraph 1 in the plant site.
5.   With regard to plant sites listed pursuant to paragraph 1 (a), the list shall also include information on the approximate aggregate amount of production of the unscheduled discrete organic chemicals in the previous calendar year expressed in the ranges: under 1,000 tonnes, 1,000 to 10,000 tonnes and above 10,000 tonnes.
6.   With regard to plant sites listed pursuant to paragraph 1 (b), the list shall also specify the number of PSF-plants within the plant site and include information on the approximate ag-

gregate amount of production of PSF-chemicals produced by each PSF-plant in the previous calendar year expressed in the ranges: under 200 tonnes, 200 to 1,000 tonnes, 1,000 to 10,000 tonnes and above 10,000 tonnes.

ASSISTANCE BY THE TECHNICAL SECRETARIAT
7. If a State Party, for administrative reasons, deems it necessary to ask for assistance in compiling its list of chemical production facilities pursuant to paragraph 1, it may request the Technical Secretariat to provide such assistance. Questions as to the completeness of the list shall then be resolved through consultations between the State Party and the Technical Secretariat.

INFORMATION TO STATES PARTIES
8. The lists of other chemical production facilities submitted pursuant to paragraph 1, including the information provided under paragraph 4, shall be transmitted by the Technical Secretariat to States Parties upon request.

B. VERIFICATION

GENERAL
9. Subject to the provisions of Section C, verification as provided for in Article VI, paragraph 6, shall be carried out through on-site inspection at:
    (a) Plant sites listed pursuant to paragraph 1 (a); and
    (b) Plant sites listed pursuant to paragraph 1 (b) that comprise one or more PSF-plants which produced during the previous calendar year more than 200 tonnes of a PSF-chemical.
10. The programme and budget of the Organization to be adopted by the Conference pursuant to Article VIII, paragraph 21 (a), shall contain, as a separate item, a programme and budget for verification under this Section after its implementation has started.
11. Under this Section, the Technical Secretariat shall randomly select plant sites for inspection through appropriate mechanisms, such as the use of specially designed computer software, on the basis of the following weighting factors:
    (a) Equitable geographical distribution of inspections;
    (b) The information on the listed plant sites available to the Technical Secretariat, related to the characteristics of the plant site and the activities carried out there; and
    (c) Proposals by States Parties on a basis to be agreed upon in accordance with paragraph 25.
12. No plant site shall receive more than two inspections per year under the provisions of this Section. This, however, shall not limit inspections pursuant to Article IX.
13. In selecting plant sites for inspection under this Section, the Technical Secretariat shall observe the following limitation for the combined number of inspections to be received by a State Party per calendar year under this Part and Part VIII of this Annex: the combined number of inspections shall not exceed three plus 5 per cent of the total number of plant sites declared by a State Party under both this Part and Part VIII of this Annex, or 20 inspections, whichever of these two figures is lower.

INSPECTION AIMS
14. At plant sites listed under Section A, the general aim of inspections shall be to verify that activities are consistent with the information to be provided in declarations. The particular aim of inspections shall be the verification of the absence of any Schedule 1 chemical, especially its production, except if in accordance with Part VI of this Annex.

INSPECTION PROCEDURES

15. In addition to agreed guidelines, other relevant provisions of this Annex and the Confidentiality Annex, paragraphs 16 to 20 below shall apply.

16. There shall be no facility agreement, unless requested by the inspected State Party.

17. The focus of inspection at a plant site selected for inspection shall be the plant(s) producing the chemicals specified in paragraph 1, in particular the PSF-plants listed pursuant to paragraph 1 (b). The inspected State Party shall have the right to manage access to these plants in accordance with the rules of managed access as specified in Part X, Section C, of this Annex. If the inspection team, in accordance with Part II, paragraph 51, of this Annex, requests access to other parts of the plant site for clarification of ambiguities, the extent of such access shall be agreed between the inspection team and the inspected State Party.

18. The inspection team may have access to records in situations in which the inspection team and the inspected State Party agree that such access will assist in achieving the objectives of the inspection.

19. Sampling and on-site analysis may be undertaken to check for the absence of undeclared scheduled chemicals. In cases of unresolved ambiguities, samples may be analysed in a designated off-site laboratory, subject to the inspected State Party's agreement.

20. The period of inspection shall not last more than 24 hours; however, extensions may be agreed between the inspection team and the inspected State Party.

NOTIFICATION OF INSPECTION

21. A State Party shall be notified by the Technical Secretariat of the inspection not less than 120 hours before the arrival of the inspection team at the plant site to be inspected.

C. IMPLEMENTATION AND REVIEW OF SECTION B

IMPLEMENTATION

22. The implementation of Section B shall start at the beginning of the fourth year after entry into force of this Convention unless the Conference, at its regular session in the third year after entry into force of this Convention, decides otherwise.

23. The Director-General shall, for the regular session of the Conference in the third year after entry into force of this Convention, prepare a report which outlines the experience of the Technical Secretariat in implementing the provisions of Parts VII and VIII of this Annex as well as of Section A of this Part.

24. At its regular session in the third year after entry into force of this Convention, the Conference, on the basis of a report of the Director-General, may also decide on the distribution of resources available for verification under Section B between "PSF-plants" and other chemical production facilities. Otherwise, this distribution shall be left to the expertise of the Technical Secretariat and be added to the weighting factors in paragraph 11.

25. At its regular session in the third year after entry into force of this Convention, the Conference, upon advice of the Executive Council, shall decide on which basis (e.g. regional) proposals by States Parties for inspections should be presented to be taken into account as a weighting factor in the selection process specified in paragraph 11.

REVIEW

26. At the first special session of the Conference convened pursuant to Article VIII, paragraph 22, the provisions of this Part of the Verification Annex shall be re-examined in the light of a comprehensive review of the overall verification regime for the chemical industry (Article VI, Parts VII to IX of this Annex) on the basis of the experience gained. The Conference shall then make recommendations so as to improve the effectiveness of the verification regime.

PART X
CHALLENGE INSPECTIONS PURSUANT TO ARTICLE IX

A. DESIGNATION AND SELECTION OF INSPECTORS AND INSPECTION ASSISTANTS

1. Challenge inspections pursuant to Article IX shall only be performed by inspectors and inspection assistants especially designated for this function. In order to designate inspectors and inspection assistants for challenge inspections pursuant to Article IX, the Director-General shall, by selecting inspectors and inspection assistants from among the inspectors and inspection assistants for routine inspection activities, establish a list of proposed inspectors and inspection assistants. It shall comprise a sufficiently large number of inspectors and inspection assistants having the necessary qualification, experience, skill and training, to allow for flexibility in the selection of the inspectors, taking into account their availability, and the need for rotation. Due regard shall be paid also to the importance of selecting inspectors and inspection assistants on as wide a geographical basis as possible. The designation of inspectors and inspection assistants shall follow the procedures provided for under Part II, Section A, of this Annex.

2. The Director-General shall determine the size of the inspection team and select its members taking into account the circumstances of a particular request. The size of the inspection team shall be kept to a minimum necessary for the proper fulfilment of the inspection mandate. No national of the requesting State Party or the inspected State Party shall be a member of the inspection team.

B. PRE-INSPECTION ACTIVITIES

3. Before submitting the inspection request for a challenge inspection, the State Party may seek confirmation from the Director-General that the Technical Secretariat is in a position to take immediate action on the request. If the Director-General cannot provide such confirmation immediately, he shall do so at the earliest opportunity, in keeping with the order of requests for confirmation. He shall also keep the State Party informed of when it is likely that immediate action can be taken. Should the Director-General reach the conclusion that timely action on requests can no longer be taken, he may ask the Executive Council to take appropriate action to improve the situation in the future.

NOTIFICATION
4. The inspection request for a challenge inspection to be submitted to the Executive Council and the Director-General shall contain at least the following information:
    (a) The State Party to be inspected and, if applicable, the Host State;
    (b) The point of entry to be used;
    (c) The size and type of the inspection site;
    (d) The concern regarding possible non-compliance with this Convention including a specification of the relevant provisions of this Convention about which the concern has arisen, and of the nature and circumstances of the possible non-compliance as well as all appropriate information on the basis of which the concern has arisen; and
    (e) The name of the observer of the requesting State Party.
    The requesting State Party may submit any additional information it deems necessary.
5. The Director-General shall within one hour acknowledge to the requesting State Party receipt of its request.
6. The requesting State Party shall notify the Director-General of the location of the inspection site in due time for the Director-General to be able to provide this information to the

inspected State Party not less than 12 hours before the planned arrival of the inspection team at the point of entry.

7. The inspection site shall be designated by the requesting State Party as specifically as possible by providing a site diagram related to a reference point with geographic coordinates, specified to the nearest second if possible. If possible, the requesting State Party shall also provide a map with a general indication of the inspection site and a diagram specifying as precisely as possible the requested perimeter of the site to be inspected.

8. The requested perimeter shall:
   (a) Run at least a 10 metre distance outside any buildings or other structures;
   (b) Not cut through existing security enclosures; and
   (c) Run at least a 10 metre distance outside any existing security enclosures that the requesting State Party intends to include within the requested perimeter.

9. If the requested perimeter does not conform with the specifications of paragraph 8, it shall be redrawn by the inspection team so as to conform with that provision.

10. The Director-General shall, not less than 12 hours before the planned arrival of the inspection team at the point of entry, inform the Executive Council about the location of the inspection site as specified in paragraph 7.

11. Contemporaneously with informing the Executive Council according to paragraph 10, the Director-General shall transmit the inspection request to the inspected State Party including the location of the inspection site as specified in paragraph 7. This notification shall also include the information specified in Part II, paragraph 32, of this Annex.

12. Upon arrival of the inspection team at the point of entry, the inspected State Party shall be informed by the inspection team of the inspection mandate.

Entry into the territory of the inspected State Party or the Host State

13. The Director-General shall, in accordance with Article IX, paragraphs 13 to 18, dispatch an inspection team as soon as possible after an inspection request has been received. The inspection team shall arrive at the point of entry specified in the request in the minimum time possible, consistent with the provisions of paragraphs 10 and 11.

14. If the requested perimeter is acceptable to the inspected State Party, it shall be designated as the final perimeter as early as possible, but in no case later than 24 hours after the arrival of the inspection team at the point of entry. The inspected State Party shall transport the inspection team to the final perimeter of the inspection site. If the inspected State Party deems it necessary, such transportation may begin up to 12 hours before the expiry of the time period specified in this paragraph for the designation of the final perimeter. Transportation shall, in any case, be completed not later than 36 hours after the arrival of the inspection team at the point of entry.

15. For all declared facilities, the procedures in subparagraphs (a) and (b) shall apply. (For the purposes of this Part, "declared facility" means all facilities declared pursuant to Articles III, IV, and V. With regard to Article VI, "declared facility" means only facilities declared pursuant to Part VI of this Annex, as well as declared plants specified by declarations pursuant to Part VII, paragraphs 7 and 10 (c), and Part VIII, paragraphs 7 and 10 (c), of this Annex.)
   (a) If the requested perimeter is contained within or conforms with the declared perimeter, the declared perimeter shall be considered the final perimeter. The final perimeter may, however, if agreed by the inspected State Party, be made smaller in order to conform with the perimeter requested by the requesting State Party.
   (b) The inspected State Party shall transport the inspection team to the final perimeter as soon as practicable, but in any case shall ensure their arrival at the perimeter not later than 24 hours after the arrival of the inspection team at the point of entry.

ALTERNATIVE DETERMINATION OF FINAL PERIMETER

16. At the point of entry, if the inspected State Party cannot accept the requested perimeter, it shall propose an alternative perimeter as soon as possible, but in any case not later than 24 hours after the arrival of the inspection team at the point of entry. In case of differences of opinion, the inspected State Party and the inspection team shall engage in negotiations with the aim of reaching agreement on a final perimeter.

17. The alternative perimeter should be designated as specifically as possible in accordance with paragraph 8. It shall include the whole of the requested perimeter and should, as a rule, bear a close relationship to the latter, taking into account natural terrain features and man-made boundaries. It should normally run close to the surrounding security barrier if such a barrier exists. The inspected State Party should seek to establish such a relationship between the perimeters by a combination of at least two of the following means:

   (a) An alternative perimeter that does not extend to an area significantly greater than that of the requested perimeter;

   (b) An alternative perimeter that is a short, uniform distance from the requested perimeter;

   (c) At least part of the requested perimeter is visible from the alternative perimeter.

18. If the alternative perimeter is acceptable to the inspection team, it shall become the final perimeter and the inspection team shall be transported from the point of entry to that perimeter. If the inspected State Party deems it necessary, such transportation may begin up to 12 hours before the expiry of the time period specified in paragraph 16 for proposing an alternative perimeter. Transportation shall, in any case, be completed not later than 36 hours after the arrival of the inspection team at the point of entry.

19. If a final perimeter is not agreed, the perimeter negotiations shall be concluded as early as possible, but in no case shall they continue more than 24 hours after the arrival of the inspection team at the point of entry. If no agreement is reached, the inspected State Party shall transport the inspection team to a location at the alternative perimeter. If the inspected State Party deems it necessary, such transportation may begin up to 12 hours before the expiry of the time period specified in paragraph 16 for proposing an alternative perimeter. Transportation shall, in any case, be completed not later than 36 hours after the arrival of the inspection team at the point of entry.

20. Once at the location, the inspected State Party shall provide the inspection team with prompt access to the alternative perimeter to facilitate negotiations and agreement on the final perimeter and access within the final perimeter.

21. If no agreement is reached within 72 hours after the arrival of the inspection team at the location, the alternative perimeter shall be designated the final perimeter.

VERIFICATION OF LOCATION

22. To help establish that the inspection site to which the inspection team has been transported corresponds to the inspection site specified by the requesting State Party, the inspection team shall have the right to use approved location-finding equipment and have such equipment installed according to its directions. The inspection team may verify its location by reference to local landmarks identified from maps. The inspected State Party shall assist the inspection team in this task.

SECURING THE SITE, EXIT MONITORING

23. Not later than 12 hours after the arrival of the inspection team at the point of entry, the inspected State Party shall begin collecting factual information of all vehicular exit activity from all exit points for all land, air, and water vehicles of the requested perimeter. It shall provide this information to the inspection team upon its arrival at the alternative or final perimeter, whichever occurs first.

24. This obligation may be met by collecting factual information in the form of traffic logs,

photographs, video recordings, or data from chemical evidence equipment provided by the inspection team to monitor such exit activity. Alternatively, the inspected State Party may also meet this obligation by allowing one or more members of the inspection team independently to maintain traffic logs, take photographs, make video recordings of exit traffic, or use chemical evidence equipment, and conduct other activities as may be agreed between the inspected State Party and the inspection team.

25. Upon the inspection team's arrival at the alternative perimeter or final perimeter, whichever occurs first, securing the site, which means exit monitoring procedures by the inspection team, shall begin.

26. Such procedures shall include: the identification of vehicular exits, the making of traffic logs, the taking of photographs, and the making of video recordings by the inspection team of exits and exit traffic. The inspection team has the right to go, under escort, to any other part of the perimeter to check that there is no other exit activity.

27. Additional procedures for exit monitoring activities as agreed upon by the inspection team and the inspected State Party may include, *inter alia*:

    (a) Use of sensors;
    (b) Random selective access;
    (c) Sample analysis.

28. All activities for securing the site and exit monitoring shall take place within a band around the outside of the perimeter, not exceeding 50 metres in width, measured outward.

29. The inspection team has the right to inspect on a managed access basis vehicular traffic exiting the site. The inspected State Party shall make every reasonable effort to demonstrate to the inspection team that any vehicle, subject to inspection, to which the inspection team is not granted full access, is not being used for purposes related to the possible non-compliance concerns raised in the inspection request.

30. Personnel and vehicles entering and personnel and personal passenger vehicles exiting the site are not subject to inspection.

31. The application of the above procedures may continue for the duration of the inspection, but may not unreasonably hamper or delay the normal operation of the facility.

PRE-INSPECTION BRIEFING AND INSPECTION PLAN

32. To facilitate development of an inspection plan, the inspected State Party shall provide a safety and logistical briefing to the inspection team prior to access.

33. The pre-inspection briefing shall be held in accordance with Part II, paragraph 37, of this Annex. In the course of the pre-inspection briefing, the inspected State Party may indicate to the inspection team the equipment, documentation, or areas it considers sensitive and not related to the purpose of the challenge inspection. In addition, personnel responsible for the site shall brief the inspection team on the physical layout and other relevant characteristics of the site. The inspection team shall be provided with a map or sketch drawn to scale showing all structures and significant geographic features at the site. The inspection team shall also be briefed on the availability of facility personnel and records.

34. After the pre-inspection briefing, the inspection team shall prepare, on the basis of the information available and appropriate to it, an initial inspection plan which specifies the activities to be carried out by the inspection team, including the specific areas of the site to which access is desired. The inspection plan shall also specify whether the inspection team will be divided into subgroups. The inspection plan shall be made available to the representatives of the inspected State Party and the inspection site. Its implementation shall be consistent with the provisions of Section C, including those related to access and activities.

PERIMETER ACTIVITIES

35. Upon the inspection team's arrival at the final or alternative perimeter, whichever occurs first,

the team shall have the right to commence immediately perimeter activities in accordance with the procedures set forth under this Section, and to continue these activities until the completion of the challenge inspection.

36. In conducting the perimeter activities, the inspection team shall have the right to:
    (a) Use monitoring instruments in accordance with Part II, paragraphs 27 to 30, of this Annex;
    (b) Take wipes, air, soil or effluent samples; and
    (c) Conduct any additional activities which may be agreed between the inspection team and the inspected State Party.

37. The perimeter activities of the inspection team may be conducted within a band around the outside of the perimeter up to 50 metres in width measured outward from the perimeter. If the inspected State Party agrees, the inspection team may also have access to any building or structure within the perimeter band. All directional monitoring shall be oriented inward. For declared facilities, at the discretion of the inspected State Party, the band could run inside, outside, or on both sides of the declared perimeter.

C. CONDUCT OF INSPECTIONS

GENERAL RULES

38. The inspected State Party shall provide access within the requested perimeter as well as, if different, the final perimeter. The extent and nature of access to a particular place or places within these perimeters shall be negotiated between the inspection team and the inspected State Party on a managed access basis.

39. The inspected State Party shall provide access within the requested perimeter as soon as possible, but in any case not later than 108 hours after the arrival of the inspection team at the point of entry in order to clarify the concern regarding possible non-compliance with this Convention raised in the inspection request.

40. Upon the request of the inspection team, the inspected State Party may provide aerial access to the inspection site.

41. In meeting the requirement to provide access as specified in paragraph 38, the inspected State Party shall be under the obligation to allow the greatest degree of access taking into account any constitutional obligations it may have with regard to proprietary rights or searches and seizures. The inspected State Party has the right under managed access to take such measures as are necessary to protect national security. The provisions in this paragraph may not be invoked by the inspected State Party to conceal evasion of its obligations not to engage in activities prohibited under this Convention.

42. If the inspected State Party provides less than full access to places, activities, or information, it shall be under the obligation to make every reasonable effort to provide alternative means to clarify the possible non-compliance concern that generated the challenge inspection.

43. Upon arrival at the final perimeter of facilities declared pursuant to Articles IV, V and VI, access shall be granted following the pre-inspection briefing and discussion of the inspection plan which shall be limited to the minimum necessary and in any event shall not exceed three hours. For facilities declared pursuant to Article III, paragraph 1 (d), negotiations shall be conducted and managed access commenced not later than 12 hours after arrival at the final perimeter.

44. In carrying out the challenge inspection in accordance with the inspection request, the inspection team shall use only those methods necessary to provide sufficient relevant facts to clarify the concern about possible non-compliance with the provisions of this Convention, and shall refrain from activities not relevant thereto. It shall collect and document such facts as are related to the possible non-compliance with this Convention by the inspected State Party, but shall neither seek nor document information which is clearly not related thereto, unless the

inspected State Party expressly requests it to do so. Any material collected and subsequently found not to be relevant shall not be retained.

45. The inspection team shall be guided by the principle of conducting the challenge inspection in the least intrusive manner possible, consistent with the effective and timely accomplishment of its mission. Wherever possible, it shall begin with the least intrusive procedures it deems acceptable and proceed to more intrusive procedures only as it deems necessary.

MANAGED ACCESS

46. The inspection team shall take into consideration suggested modifications of the inspection plan and proposals which may be made by the inspected State Party, at whatever stage of the inspection including the pre-inspection briefing, to ensure that sensitive equipment, information or areas, not related to chemical weapons, are protected.

47. The inspected State Party shall designate the perimeter entry/exit points to be used for access. The inspection team and the inspected State Party shall negotiate: the extent of access to any particular place or places within the final and requested perimeters as provided in paragraph 48; the particular inspection activities, including sampling, to be conducted by the inspection team; the performance of particular activities by the inspected State Party; and the provision of particular information by the inspected State Party.

48. In conformity with the relevant provisions in the Confidentiality Annex the inspected State Party shall have the right to take measures to protect sensitive installations and prevent disclosure of confidential information and data not related to chemical weapons. Such measures may include, *inter alia*:

    (a) Removal of sensitive papers from office spaces;

    (b) Shrouding of sensitive displays, stores, and equipment;

    (c) Shrouding of sensitive pieces of equipment, such as computer or electronic systems;

    (d) Logging off of computer systems and turning off of data indicating devices;

    (e) Restriction of sample analysis to presence or absence of chemicals listed in Schedules 1, 2 and 3 or appropriate degradation products;

    (f) Using random selective access techniques whereby the inspectors are requested to select a given percentage or number of buildings of their choice to inspect; the same principle can apply to the interior and content of sensitive buildings;

    (g) In exceptional cases, giving only individual inspectors access to certain parts of the inspection site.

49. The inspected State Party shall make every reasonable effort to demonstrate to the inspection team that any object, building, structure, container or vehicle to which the inspection team has not had full access, or which has been protected in accordance with paragraph 48, is not used for purposes related to the possible non-compliance concerns raised in the inspection request.

50. This may be accomplished by means of, *inter alia*, the partial removal of a shroud or environmental protection cover, at the discretion of the inspected State Party, by means of a visual inspection of the interior of an enclosed space from its entrance, or by other methods.

51. In the case of facilities declared pursuant to Articles IV, V and VI, the following shall apply:

    (a) For facilities with facility agreements, access and activities within the final perimeter shall be unimpeded within the boundaries established by the agreements;

    (b) For facilities without facility agreements, negotiation of access and activities shall be governed by the applicable general inspection guidelines established under this Convention;

    (c) Access beyond that granted for inspections under Articles IV, V and VI shall be managed in accordance with procedures of this section.

52. In the case of facilities declared pursuant to Article III, paragraph 1 (d), the following shall apply: if the inspected State Party, using procedures of paragraphs 47 and 48, has not granted

full access to areas or structures not related to chemical weapons, it shall make every reasonable effort to demonstrate to the inspection team that such areas or structures are not used for purposes related to the possible non-compliance concerns raised in the inspection request.

OBSERVER

53. In accordance with the provisions of Article IX, paragraph 12, on the participation of an observer in the challenge inspection, the requesting State Party shall liaise with the Technical Secretariat to coordinate the arrival of the observer at the same point of entry as the inspection team within a reasonable period of the inspection team's arrival.

54. The observer shall have the right throughout the period of inspection to be in communication with the embassy of the requesting State Party located in the inspected State Party or in the Host State or, in the case of absence of an embassy, with the requesting State Party itself. The inspected State Party shall provide means of communication to the observer.

55. The observer shall have the right to arrive at the alternative or final perimeter of the inspection site, wherever the inspection team arrives first, and to have access to the inspection site as granted by the inspected State Party. The observer shall have the right to make recommendations to the inspection team, which the team shall take into account to the extent it deems appropriate. Throughout the inspection, the inspection team shall keep the observer informed about the conduct of the inspection and the findings.

56. Throughout the in-country period, the inspected State Party shall provide or arrange for the amenities necessary for the observer such as communication means, interpretation services, transportation, working space, lodging, meals and medical care. All the costs in connection with the stay of the observer on the territory of the inspected State Party or the Host State shall be borne by the requesting State Party.

DURATION OF INSPECTION

57. The period of inspection shall not exceed 84 hours, unless extended by agreement with the inspected State Party.

D.   POST-INSPECTION ACTIVITIES

DEPARTURE

58. Upon completion of the post-inspection procedures at the inspection site, the inspection team and the observer of the requesting State Party shall proceed promptly to a point of entry and shall then leave the territory of the inspected State Party in the minimum time possible.

REPORTS

59. The inspection report shall summarize in a general way the activities conducted by the inspection team and the factual findings of the inspection team, particularly with regard to the concerns regarding possible non-compliance with this Convention cited in the request for the challenge inspection, and shall be limited to information directly related to this Convention. It shall also include an assessment by the inspection team of the degree and nature of access and cooperation granted to the inspectors and the extent to which this enabled them to fulfil the inspection mandate. Detailed information relating to the concerns regarding possible non-compliance with this Convention cited in the request for the challenge inspection shall be submitted as an Appendix to the final report and be retained within the Technical Secretariat under appropriate safeguards to protect sensitive information.

60. The inspection team shall, not later than 72 hours after its return to its primary work location, submit a preliminary inspection report, having taken into account, *inter alia*, paragraph 17 of the Confidentiality Annex, to the Director-General. The Director-General shall promptly transmit the preliminary inspection report to the requesting State Party, the inspected State Party and to the Executive Council.

61. A draft final inspection report shall be made available to the inspected State Party not later than 20 days after the completion of the challenge inspection. The inspected State Party has the right to identify any information and data not related to chemical weapons which should, in its view, due to its confidential character, not be circulated outside the Technical Secretariat. The Technical Secretariat shall consider proposals for changes to the draft final inspection report made by the inspected State Party and, using its own discretion, wherever possible, adopt them. The final report shall then be submitted not later than 30 days after the completion of the challenge inspection to the Director-General for further distribution and consideration in accordance with Article IX, paragraphs 21 to 25.

PART XI
INVESTIGATIONS IN CASES OF
ALLEGED USE OF CHEMICAL WEAPONS

A. GENERAL

1. Investigations of alleged use of chemical weapons, or of alleged use of riot control agents as a method of warfare, initiated pursuant to Articles IX or X, shall be conducted in accordance with this Annex and detailed procedures to be established by the Director-General.

2. The following additional provisions address specific procedures required in cases of alleged use of chemical weapons.

B. PRE-INSPECTION ACTIVITIES

REQUEST FOR AN INVESTIGATION

3. The request for an investigation of an alleged use of chemical weapons to be submitted to the Director-General, to the extent possible, should include the following information:
   (a) The State Party on whose territory use of chemical weapons is alleged to have taken place;
   (b) The point of entry or other suggested safe routes of access;
   (c) Location and characteristics of the areas where chemical weapons are alleged to have been used;
   (d) When chemical weapons are alleged to have been used;
   (e) Types of chemical weapons believed to have been used;
   (f) Extent of alleged use;
   (g) Characteristics of the possible toxic chemicals;
   (h) Effects on humans, animals and vegetation;
   (i) Request for specific assistance, if applicable.

4. The State Party which has requested an investigation may submit at any time any additional information it deems necessary.

NOTIFICATION

5. The Director-General shall immediately acknowledge receipt to the requesting State Party of its request and inform the Executive Council and all States Parties.

6. If applicable, the Director-General shall notify the State Party on whose territory an investigation has been requested. The Director-General shall also notify other States Parties if access to their territories might be required during the investigation.

ASSIGNMENT OF INSPECTION TEAM

7. The Director-General shall prepare a list of qualified experts whose particular field of expertise could be required in an investigation of alleged use of chemical weapons and constantly keep this list updated. This list shall be communicated, in writing, to each State Party not later than 30 days after entry into force of this Convention and after each change to the list. Any qualified expert included in this list shall be regarded as designated unless a State Party, not

later than 30 days after its receipt of the list, declares its non-acceptance in writing.

8. The Director-General shall select the leader and members of an inspection team from the inspectors and inspection assistants already designated for challenge inspections taking into account the circumstances and specific nature of a particular request. In addition, members of the inspection team may be selected from the list of qualified experts when, in the view of the Director-General, expertise not available among inspectors already designated is required for the proper conduct of a particular investigation.

9. When briefing the inspection team, the Director-General shall include any additional information provided by the requesting State Party, or any other sources, to ensure that the inspection can be carried out in the most effective and expedient manner.

DISPATCH OF INSPECTION TEAM

10. Immediately upon the receipt of a request for an investigation of alleged use of chemical weapons the Director-General shall, through contacts with the relevant States Parties, request and confirm arrangements for the safe reception of the team.

11. The Director-General shall dispatch the team at the earliest opportunity, taking into account the safety of the team.

12. If the inspection team has not been dispatched within 24 hours from the receipt of the request, the Director-General shall inform the Executive Council and the States Parties concerned about the reasons for the delay.

BRIEFINGS

13. The inspection team shall have the right to be briefed by representatives of the inspected State Party upon arrival and at any time during the inspection.

14. Before the commencement of the inspection the inspection team shall prepare an inspection plan to serve, *inter alia*, as a basis for logistic and safety arrangements. The inspection plan shall be updated as need arises.

C. CONDUCT OF INSPECTIONS

ACCESS

15. The inspection team shall have the right of access to any and all areas which could be affected by the alleged use of chemical weapons. It shall also have the right of access to hospitals, refugee camps and other locations it deems relevant to the effective investigation of the alleged use of chemical weapons. For such access, the inspection team shall consult with the inspected State Party.

SAMPLING

16. The inspection team shall have the right to collect samples of types, and in quantities it considers necessary. If the inspection team deems it necessary, and if so requested by it, the inspected State Party shall assist in the collection of samples under the supervision of inspectors or inspection assistants. The inspected State Party shall also permit and cooperate in the collection of appropriate control samples from areas neighbouring the site of the alleged use and from other areas as requested by the inspection team.

17. Samples of importance in the investigation of alleged use include toxic chemicals, munitions and devices, remnants of munitions and devices, environmental samples (air, soil, vegetation, water, snow, etc.) and biomedical samples from human or animal sources (blood, urine, excreta, tissue etc.).

18. If duplicate samples cannot be taken and the analysis is performed at off-site laboratories, any remaining sample shall, if so requested, be returned to the inspected State Party after the completion of the analysis.

EXTENSION OF INSPECTION SITE

19. If the inspection team during an inspection deems it necessary to extend the investigation into a neighbouring State Party, the Director-General shall notify that State Party about the need for access to its territory and request and confirm arrangements for the safe reception of the team.

EXTENSION OF INSPECTION DURATION

20. If the inspection team deems that safe access to a specific area relevant to the investigation is not possible, the requesting State Party shall be informed immediately. If necessary, the period of inspection shall be extended until safe access can be provided and the inspection team will have concluded its mission.

INTERVIEWS

21. The inspection team shall have the right to interview and examine persons who may have been affected by the alleged use of chemical weapons. It shall also have the right to interview eyewitnesses of the alleged use of chemical weapons and medical personnel, and other persons who have treated or have come into contact with persons who may have been affected by the alleged use of chemical weapons. The inspection team shall have access to medical histories, if available, and be permitted to participate in autopsies, as appropriate, of persons who may have been affected by the alleged use of chemical weapons.

D. REPORTS

PROCEDURES

22. The inspection team shall, not later than 24 hours after its arrival on the territory of the inspected State Party, send a situation report to the Director-General. It shall further throughout the investigation send progress reports as necessary.

23. The inspection team shall, not later than 72 hours after its return to its primary work location, submit a preliminary report to the Director-General. The final report shall be submitted to the Director-General not later than 30 days after its return to its primary work location. The Director-General shall promptly transmit the preliminary and final reports to the Executive Council and to all States Parties.

CONTENTS

24. The situation report shall indicate any urgent need for assistance and any other relevant information. The progress reports shall indicate any further need for assistance that might be identified during the course of the investigation.

25. The final report shall summarize the factual findings of the inspection, particularly with regard to the alleged use cited in the request. In addition, a report of an investigation of an alleged use shall include a description of the investigation process, tracing its various stages, with special reference to:

    (a) The locations and time of sampling and on-site analyses; and

    (b) Supporting evidence, such as the records of interviews, the results of medical examinations and scientific analyses, and the documents examined by the inspection team.

26. If the inspection team collects through, *inter alia*, identification of any impurities or other substances during laboratory analysis of samples taken, any information in the course of its investigation that might serve to identify the origin of any chemical weapons used, that information shall be included in the report.

E. STATES NOT PARTY TO THIS CONVENTION

27. In the case of alleged use of chemical weapons involving a State not Party to this Convention or in territory not controlled by a State Party, the Organization shall closely cooperate with the Secretary-General of the United Nations. If so requested, the Organization shall put its resources at the disposal of the Secretary-General of the United Nations.

ANNEX ON THE PROTECTION OF CONFIDENTIAL INFORMATION ("CONFIDENTIALITY ANNEX")

A. GENERAL PRINCIPLES FOR THE HANDLING OF CONFIDENTIAL INFORMATION

1. The obligation to protect confidential information shall pertain to the verification of both civil and military activities and facilities. Pursuant to the general obligations set forth in Article VIII, the Organization shall:
    (a) Require only the minimum amount of information and data necessary for the timely and efficient carrying out of its responsibilities under this Convention;
    (b) Take the necessary measures to ensure that inspectors and other staff members of the Technical Secretariat meet the highest standards of efficiency, competence, and integrity;
    (c) Develop agreements and regulations to implement the provisions of this Convention and shall specify as precisely as possible the information to which the Organization shall be given access by a State Party.
2. The Director-General shall have the primary responsibility for ensuring the protection of confidential information. The Director-General shall establish a stringent regime governing the handling of confidential information by the Technical Secretariat, and in doing so, shall observe the following guidelines:
    (a) Information shall be considered confidential if:
        (i) It is so designated by the State Party from which the information was obtained and to which the information refers; or
        (ii) In the judgement of the Director-General, its unauthorized disclosure could reasonably be expected to cause damage to the State Party to which it refers or to the mechanisms for implementation of this Convention;
    (b) All data and documents obtained by the Technical Secretariat shall be evaluated by the appropriate unit of the Technical Secretariat in order to establish whether they contain confidential information. Data required by States Parties to be assured of the continued compliance with this Convention by other States Parties shall be routinely provided to them. Such data shall encompass:
        (i) The initial and annual reports and declarations provided by States Parties under Articles III, IV, V and VI, in accordance with the provisions set forth in the Verification Annex;
        (ii) General reports on the results and effectiveness of verification activities; and
        (iii) Information to be supplied to all States Parties in accordance with the provisions of this Convention;
    (c) No information obtained by the Organization in connection with the implementation of this Convention shall be published or otherwise released, except, as follows:
        (i) General information on the implementation of this Convention may be compiled and released publicly in accordance with the decisions of the Conference or the Executive Council;
        (ii) Any information may be released with the express consent of the State Party to which the information refers;
        (iii) Information classified as confidential shall be released by the Organization only through procedures which ensure that the release of information only occurs in strict conformity with the needs of this Convention. Such procedures shall be considered and approved by the Conference pursuant to Article VIII, paragraph 21 (i);
    (d) The level of sensitivity of confidential data or documents shall be established, based on criteria to be applied uniformly in order to ensure their appropriate handling and protection. For this purpose, a classification system shall be introduced, which by taking

account of relevant work undertaken in the preparation of this Convention shall provide for clear criteria ensuring the inclusion of information into appropriate categories of confidentiality and the justified durability of the confidential nature of information. While providing for the necessary flexibility in its implementation the classification system shall protect the rights of States Parties providing confidential information. A classification system shall be considered and approved by the Conference pursuant to Article VIII, paragraph 21 (i);

(e) Confidential information shall be stored securely at the premises of the Organization. Some data or documents may also be stored with the National Authority of a State Party. Sensitive information, including, *inter alia*, photographs, plans and other documents required only for the inspection of a specific facility may be kept under lock and key at this facility;

(f) To the greatest extent consistent with the effective implementation of the verification provisions of this Convention, information shall be handled and stored by the Technical Secretariat in a form that precludes direct identification of the facility to which it pertains;

(g) The amount of confidential information removed from a facility shall be kept to the minimum necessary for the timely and effective implementation of the verification provisions of this Convention; and

(h) Access to confidential information shall be regulated in accordance with its classification. The dissemination of confidential information within the Organization shall be strictly on a need-to-know basis.

3. The Director-General shall report annually to the Conference on the implementation of the regime governing the handling of confidential information by the Technical Secretariat.

4. Each State Party shall treat information which it receives from the Organization in accordance with the level of confidentiality established for that information. Upon request, a State Party shall provide details on the handling of information provided to it by the Organization.

B. EMPLOYMENT AND CONDUCT OF PERSONNEL IN THE TECHNICAL SECRETARIAT

5. Conditions of staff employment shall be such as to ensure that access to and handling of confidential information shall be in conformity with the procedures established by the Director-General in accordance with Section A.

6. Each position in the Technical Secretariat shall be governed by a formal position description that specifies the scope of access to confidential information, if any, needed in that position.

7. The Director-General, the inspectors and the other members of the staff shall not disclose even after termination of their functions to any unauthorized persons any confidential information coming to their knowledge in the performance of their official duties. They shall not communicate to any State, organization or person outside the Technical Secretariat any information to which they have access in connection with their activities in relation to any State Party.

8. In the discharge of their functions inspectors shall only request the information and data which are necessary to fulfil their mandate. They shall not make any records of information collected incidentally and not related to verification of compliance with this Convention.

9. The staff shall enter into individual secrecy agreements with the Technical Secretariat covering their period of employment and a period of five years after it is terminated.

10. In order to avoid improper disclosures, inspectors and staff members shall be appropriately advised and reminded about security considerations and of the possible penalties that they would incur in the event of improper disclosure.

11. Not less than 30 days before an employee is given clearance for access to confidential infor-

mation that refers to activities on the territory or in any other place under the jurisdiction or control of a State Party, the State Party concerned shall be notified of the proposed clearance. For inspectors the notification of a proposed designation shall fulfil this requirement.

12. In evaluating the performance of inspectors and any other employees of the Technical Secretariat, specific attention shall be given to the employee's record regarding protection of confidential information.

C. MEASURES TO PROTECT SENSITIVE INSTALLATIONS AND PREVENT DISCLOSURE OF CONFIDENTIAL DATA IN THE COURSE OF ON-SITE VERIFICATION ACTIVITIES

13. States Parties may take such measures as they deem necessary to protect confidentiality, provided that they fulfil their obligations to demonstrate compliance in accordance with the relevant Articles and the Verification Annex. When receiving an inspection, the State Party may indicate to the inspection team the equipment, documentation or areas that it considers sensitive and not related to the purpose of the inspection.

14. Inspection teams shall be guided by the principle of conducting on-site inspections in the least intrusive manner possible consistent with the effective and timely accomplishment of their mission. They shall take into consideration proposals which may be made by the State Party receiving the inspection, at whatever stage of the inspection, to ensure that sensitive equipment or information, not related to chemical weapons, is protected.

15. Inspection teams shall strictly abide by the provisions set forth in the relevant Articles and Annexes governing the conduct of inspections. They shall fully respect the procedures designed to protect sensitive installations and to prevent the disclosure of confidential data.

16. In the elaboration of arrangements and facility agreements, due regard shall be paid to the requirement of protecting confidential information. Agreements on inspection procedures for individual facilities shall also include specific and detailed arrangements with regard to the determination of those areas of the facility to which inspectors are granted access, the storage of confidential information on-site, the scope of the inspection effort in agreed areas, the taking of samples and their analysis, the access to records and the use of instruments and continuous monitoring equipment.

17. The report to be prepared after each inspection shall only contain facts relevant to compliance with this Convention. The report shall be handled in accordance with the regulations established by the Organization governing the handling of confidential information. If necessary, the information contained in the report shall be processed into less sensitive forms before it is transmitted outside the Technical Secretariat and the inspected State Party.

D. PROCEDURES IN CASE OF BREACHES OR ALLEGED BREACHES OF CONFIDENTIALITY

18. The Director-General shall establish necessary procedures to be followed in case of breaches or alleged breaches of confidentiality, taking into account recommendations to be considered and approved by the Conference pursuant to Article VIII, paragraph 21 (i).

19. The Director-General shall oversee the implementation of individual secrecy agreements. The Director-General shall promptly initiate an investigation if, in his judgement, there is sufficient indication that obligations concerning the protection of confidential information have been violated. The Director-General shall also promptly initiate an investigation if an allegation concerning a breach of confidentiality is made by a State Party.

20. The Director-General shall impose appropriate punitive and disciplinary measures on staff members who have violated their obligations to protect confidential information. In cases of serious breaches, the immunity from jurisdiction may be waived by the Director-General.

21. States Parties shall, to the extent possible, cooperate and support the Director-General in

investigating any breach or alleged breach of confidentiality and in taking appropriate action in case a breach has been established.

22. The Organization shall not be held liable for any breach of confidentiality committed by members of the Technical Secretariat.

23. For breaches involving both a State Party and the Organization, a "Commission for the settlement of disputes related to confidentiality", set up as a subsidiary organ of the Conference, shall consider the case. This Commission shall be appointed by the Conference. Rules governing its composition and operating procedures shall be adopted by the Conference at its first session.

2. DECLARATIONS AND STATEMENTS MADE[1] UPON SIGNATURE, RATIFICATION, OR ACCESSION[2]

AUSTRIA

Declaration made upon ratification:
"As a Member State of the European Community, the Government of Austria will implement the provisions of the Convention on the Prohibition of Chemical Weapons, in accordance with its obligations arising from the rules of the Treaties establishing the European Communities to the extent that such rules are applicable."

BELGIUM

Declaration made upon signature and confirmed upon ratification:
"As a Member State of the European Community, the Government of Belgium will implement the provisions of the Convention on the Prohibition of Chemical Weapons, in accordance with its obligations arising from the rules of the Treaties establishing the European Communities to the extent that such rules are applicable."

CHINA

Declaration made upon signature:
"*I. China has consistently stood for the complete prohibition and thorough destruction of all chemical weapons and their production facilities. The Convention constitutes the legal basis for the realization of this goal. China therefore supports the object and purpose and principles of the Convention.*

II. The object and purpose and principles of the Convention should be strictly abided by. The relevant provisions on challenge inspection should not be abused to the detriment of the security interests of States Parties unrelated to chemical weapons. Otherwise, the universality of the Convention is bound to be adversely affected.

III. States Parties that have abandoned chemical weapons on the territories of other States Parties should implement in earnest the relevant provisions of the Convention and undertake the obligation to destroy the abandoned chemical weapons.

IV. The Convention should effectively facilitate trade, scientific and technological exchanges and cooperation in the field of chemistry for peaceful purposes. All export controls inconsistent with the Convention should be abolished."

Declarations made upon ratification:
"*1. China has always stood for complete prohibition and thorough destruction of chemical weapons. As CWC has laid an international legal foundation for the realization of this goal, China supports the purposes, objectives and principles of CWC.*

2. China calls upon the countries with the largest chemical weapons arsenals to ratify CWC without delay with a view to attaining its purposes and objectives at an early date.

3. The purposes, objectives and principles of CWC should be strictly observed. The provisions concerning challenge inspection shall not be abused and the national security interests of

---

[1] This compilation was made based upon the notifications issued by the Secretary-General of the United Nations in his capacity as Depositary of the Chemical Weapons Convention as of July 2014. Unless otherwise indicated, the declarations were made on ratification, acceptance, accession or succession.

[2] Article XXII of the Convention provides as follows:
Article XXII. Reservations
The Articles of this Convention shall not be subject to reservations. The Annexes of this Convention shall not be subject to reservations incompatible with its object and purpose.

States Parties not related to chemical weapons shall not be compromised. China is firmly opposed to any act of abusing the verification provisions which endangers its sovereignty and security.

4. Any country which has abandoned chemical weapons on the territory of another country should effectively implement the relevant CWC provisions, undertake the obligations to destroy those chemical weapons and ensure the earliest complete destruction of all the chemical weapons it has abandoned on another state's territory.

5. CWC should play a sound role in promoting international trade, scientific and technological exchanges and cooperation for peaceful purposes in the field of chemical industry. It should become the effective legal basis for regulating trade and exchange among the States Parties in the field of chemical industry."

CUBA

Declarations made upon ratification:
"The Government of the Republic of Cuba declares, in conformity with article III(1)(a)(iii) of the Convention, that there is a colonial enclave in its territory - the Guantanamo Naval Base - a part of Cuban national territory over which the Cuban State does not exercise its rightful jurisdiction, owing to its illegal occupation by the United States of America by reason of a deceitful and fraudulent Treaty.

Consequently, for the purposes of the Convention, the Government of the Republic of Cuba does not assume any responsibility with respect to the aforesaid territory, since it does not know whether or not the United States has installed, possesses, maintains or intends to possess chemical weapons in the part of Cuban territory that it illegally occupies.

The Government of the Republic of Cuba also considers that it has the right to require that the entry of any inspection group mandated by the Organization for the Prohibition of Chemical Weapons, to carry out in the territory of Guantanamo Naval Base the verification activities provided for in the Convention, should be effected through a point of entry in Cuban national territory to be determined by the Cuban Government.

The Government of the Republic of Cuba considers that, under the provisions of article XI of the Convention, the unilateral application by a State party to the Convention against another State party of any restriction which would restrict or impede trade and the development and promotion of scientific and technological knowledge in the field of chemistry for industrial, agricultural, research, medical, pharmaceutical or other purposes not prohibited under the Convention, would be incompatible with the object and purpose of the Convention.

The Government of Cuba designates the Ministry of Science, Technology and Environment, in its capacity as the national authority of the Republic of Cuba for the Convention on the Prohibition of the Development, Production, Stockpiling and Use of Chemical Weapons and on Their Destruction, as the body of the central administration of the State responsible for organizing, directing, monitoring and supervising the activities aimed at preparing the Republic of Cuba to fulfil the obligations it is assuming as a State party to the aforementioned Convention."

DENMARK

Declaration made upon signature:
"As a Member State of the European Community, Denmark will implement the provisions of the Convention on the Prohibition of Chemical Weapons, in accordance with its obligations arising from the rules of the Treaties establishing the European Communities to the extent that such rules are applicable."

FRANCE

Declaration made upon signature:
"As a Member State of the European Community, France will implement the provisions of the

Convention on the Prohibition of Chemical Weapons, in accordance with its obligations arising from the rules of the Treaties establishing the European Communities to the extent that such rules are applicable."

GERMANY

Declaration made upon signature and confirmed upon ratification:
"As a Member State of the European Community, the Federal Republic of Germany will implement the provisions of the Convention on the Prohibition of Chemical Weapons, in accordance with its obligations arising from the rules of the Treaties establishing the European Communities to the extent that such rules are applicable."

GREECE

Declaration made upon signature and confirmed upon ratification:
"As a Member State of the European Community, the Government of Greece will implement the provisions of the Convention on the Prohibition of Chemical Weapons, in accordance with its obligations arising from the rules of the Treaties establishing the European Communities to the extent that such rules are applicable."

HOLY SEE

Declaration made upon ratification:
"By ratifying the 'Convention on the Prohibition of the Development, Production, Stockpiling and Use of Chemical Weapons," which was adopted in Paris on 13 January 1993, signed by the Holy See on 14 January 1993 and which came into force on 29 April 1997, the Holy See, in conformity with the nature and particular condition of Vatican City State, intends to renew its encouragement to the International Community to continue on the path towards a situation of general and complete disarmament, capable of promoting peace and cooperation at world level.
Dialogue and multilateral negotiation are essential values in this process. Through the instruments of international law, they facilitate the peaceful resolution of controversies and help better mutual understanding. In this way they promote the effective affirmation of the culture of life and peace. While not possessing chemical weapons of any kind, the Holy See accedes to the solemn act of ratification of the Convention in order to lend its moral support to this important area of international relations which seeks to ban weapons which are particularly cruel and inhuman and aimed at producing long-term traumatic effects among the defenceless civilian population."

IRAN (ISLAMIC REPUBLIC OF)

Declaration made upon ratification:
"The Islamic Republic of Iran, on the basis of the Islamic principles and beliefs, considers chemical weapons inhuman, and has consistently been on the vanguard of the international efforts to abolish these weapons and prevent their use.

1. **The Islamic Consultative Assembly (the Parliament) of the Islamic Republic of Iran approved the bill presented by the Government to join the Convention on the Prohibition of the Development, Production, Stockpiling and Use of Chemical Weapons and on Their Destruction (CWC) on 27 July 1997, and the Guardian Council found the legislation compatible with the Constitution and the Islamic Tenets on 30 July 1997, in accordance with its required Constitutional process. The Islamic Consultative Assembly decided that:**

    The Government is hereby authorized, at an appropriate time, to accede to the Convention on the Prohibition of the Development, Production, Stockpiling and Use of Chemical Weapons and on Their Destruction - which was opened for signature in Paris on January 13,

1993 - as annexed to this legislation and to deposit its relevant instrument.

The Ministry of Foreign Affairs must pursue in all negotiations and within the framework of the Organization of the Convention, the full and indiscriminate implementation of the Convention, particularly in the areas of inspection and transfer of technology and chemicals for peaceful purposes. In case the aforementioned requirements are not materialized, upon the recommendation of the Cabinet and approval of the Supreme National Security Council, steps aimed at withdrawing from the Convention will be put in motion.

2. **The Islamic Republic of Iran attaches vital significance to the full, unconditional and indiscriminate implementation of all provisions of the Convention. It reserves the right to withdraw from the Convention under the following circumstances:**
    - non-compliance with the principle of equal treatment of all States Parties in implementation of all relevant provisions of the Convention;
    - disclosure of its confidential information contrary to the provisions of the Convention;
    - imposition of restrictions incompatible with the obligations under the Convention.

3. As stipulated in Article XI, exclusive and non-transparent regimes impeding free international trade in chemicals and chemical technology for peaceful purposes should be disbanded. The Islamic Republic of Iran rejects any chemical export control mechanism not envisaged in the Convention.

4. The Organization for Prohibition of Chemical Weapons (OPCW) is the sole international authority to determine the compliance of States Parties regarding chemical weapons. Accusations by States Parties against other States Parties in the absence of a determination of non-compliance by OPCW will seriously undermine the Convention and its repetition may make the Convention meaningless.

5. One of the objectives of the Convention as stipulated in its preamble is to 'promote free trade in chemicals as well as international cooperation and exchange of scientific and technical information in the field of chemical activities for purposes not prohibited under the Convention in order to enhance the economic and technological development of all States Parties.' This fundamental objective of the Convention should be respected and embraced by all States Parties to the Convention. Any form of undermining, either in words or in action, of this overriding objective is considered by the Islamic Republic of Iran a grave breach of the provisions of the Convention.

6. **In line with the provisions of the Convention regarding non-discriminatory treatment of States Parties:**
    - inspection equipment should be commercially available to all States Parties without condition or limitation.
    - the OPCW should maintain its international character by ensuring fair and balanced geographical distribution of the personnel of its Technical Secretariat, provision of assistance to and cooperation with States Parties, and equitable membership of States Parties in subsidiary organs of the Organization.

7. The implementation of the Convention should contribute to international peace and security and should not in any way diminish or harm national security or territorial integrity of the States Parties."

IRELAND

Declaration made upon signature and confirmed upon ratification:
"As a Member State of the European Community, Ireland will implement the provisions of the Convention on the Prohibition of Chemical Weapons, in accordance with its obligations arising from the rules of the Treaties establishing the European Communities to the extent that such rules are applicable."

ITALY

Declaration made upon signature and confirmed upon ratification:
"As a Member State of the European Community, Italy will implement the provisions of the Convention on the Prohibition of Chemical Weapons, in accordance with its obligations arising from the rules of the Treaties establishing the European Communities to the extent that such rules are applicable."

LUXEMBOURG

Declaration made upon signature and confirmed upon ratification:
 "As a Member State of the European Community, Luxembourg will implement the provisions of the Convention on the Prohibition of Chemical Weapons, in accordance with its obligations arising from the rules of the Treaties establishing the European Communities to the extent that such rules are applicable."

THE NETHERLANDS

Declaration made upon signature:
"As a Member State of the European Community, the Netherlands will implement the provisions of the Convention on the Prohibition of Chemical Weapons, in accordance with its obligations arising from the rules of the Treaties establishing the European Communities to the extent that such rules are applicable."

PAKISTAN

Declaration made upon ratification:
"1. Pakistan has consistently stood for the complete prohibition and thorough destruction of all chemical weapons and their production facilities. The Convention constitutes an international legal framework for the realization of this goal. Pakistan, therefore, supports the objectives and purposes of the Convention.
2.   The objectives and purposes of the Convention must be strictly adhered to by all states. The relevant provisions on Challenge Inspections must not be abused to the detriment of the economic and security interests of the States Parties unrelated to chemical weapons. Otherwise, the universality and effectiveness of the Convention is bound to be jeopardized.
3.   Abuse of the verification provisions of the Convention, for purposes unrelated to the Convention, will not be acceptable. Pakistan will never allow its sovereignty and national security to be compromised.
4.   The Convention should effectively facilitate trade, scientific and technological exchanges and cooperation in the field of chemistry for peaceful purposes. All export control regimes inconsistent with the Convention must be abolished."

PORTUGAL

Declaration made upon ratification:
"As a Member State of the European Community, Portugal will implement the provisions of the Convention on the Prohibition of Chemical Weapons, in accordance with its obligations arising from the rules of the Treaties establishing the European Communities to the extent that such rules are applicable."

SPAIN

Declaration made upon signature:
"As a Member State of the European Community, Spain will implement the provisions of the

Convention on the Prohibition of Chemical Weapons, in accordance with its obligations arising from the rules of the Treaties establishing the European Communities to the extent that such rules are applicable."

SUDAN

Declaration made upon accession:
"Firstly, the unilateral application by a State Party to the Convention, runs counter to the objectives and purposes of the Convention.
Secondly, the Convention must be fully and indiscriminately implemented particularly in the areas of inspection and transfer of technology for peaceful purposes.
Thirdly, no restrictions incompatible with the obligations under the Convention shall be imposed.
Fourthly, the Organisation for the Prohibition of Chemical Weapons (OPCW), is the sole international authority to determine the compliance of States Parties with the provisions of the Convention."

SYRIAN ARAB REPUBLIC

Declaration made upon accession:
"[The Government of the Syrian Arab Republic] shall comply with the stipulations contained [in the Convention] and observe them faithfully and sincerely, applying the Convention provisionally pending its entry into force for the Syrian Arab Republic. [The Government of the Syrian Arab Republic] also affirms the following:
The accession of the Syrian Arab Republic to the Convention shall not in any sense imply recognition of Israel, and shall not entail entering into any relations with Israel in the matters governed by the provisions thereof."

UNITED KINGDOM OF GREAT BRITAIN AND NORTHERN IRELAND

Declaration made upon signature:
"As a Member State of the European Community, the United Kingdom of Great Britain and Northern Ireland will implement the provisions of the Convention on the Prohibition of Chemical Weapons, in accordance with its obligations arising from the rules of the Treaties establishing the European Communities to the extent that such rules are applicable."

UNITED STATES OF AMERICA

Statement made upon ratification:
" … [the] ratification of the Convention, with Annexes, [is] subject to the condition which relates to the Annex on Implementation and Verification, that no sample collected in the United States pursuant to the Convention will be transferred for analysis to any laboratory outside the territory of the United States."

Interpretation

3. CHEMICAL WEAPON (CW) ISSUES

3.1 Understanding on what is considered a CW under Article II 1(b) and (c)

C-III/DEC.13 adopted by the Conference of the States Parties at its Third Session on 20 November 1998 entitled "Understanding of what is considered a chemical weapon, in particular in relation to Article II, subparagraphs 1(b) and 1(c) (on the basis of the comments provided in relation to Section D of the draft Declaration Handbook)"

The Conference

Having considered the meaning of the terms "munitions and devices" and "equipment" as defined in subparagraphs 1(b) and 1(c) of Article II of the Convention;

Taking into account the work of the Preparatory Commission on this issue;

Noting in particular that subparagraphs 1(b) and 1(c) of Article II were incorporated into the draft of Section D, Declarations on Chemical Weapons (Declarations due under Part IV(A) of the Verification Annex) of the various versions of the Draft Declaration Handbook, and that most States Parties which have made declarations on chemical weapons due under Part IV(A) of the Verification Annex have, for this purpose, made use of the forms contained in these drafts of Section D of the Draft Declaration Handbook;

Recognising the right of States Parties to approach the Technical Secretariat for advice on any matter related to the definition of a chemical weapon for declaration purposes;

Noting that the issue was referred to the Committee of the Whole by the Conference of the States Parties (hereinafter the "Conference") at its First Session (C-I/2, dated 12 May 1997);

Having received from the Committee of the Whole during the Third Session of the Conference the report containing a recommendation to adopt the decision below:

Hereby:

1. Decides that, in relation to the terms "munitions and devices" and "equipment" as contained in subparagraphs 1(b) and 1(c) of Article II of the Convention, the Technical Secretariat be tasked to make an analysis of declarations submitted, and to compile a list of illustrative, non-exhaustive examples of chemical weapons meeting the definitions contained in subparagraphs 1(b) and 1(c) of Article II;

2. Decides that, on the basis of the above-mentioned analysis, the Director-General shall report[1] to the Fourth Session of the Conference on this compilation with a view to resolving the issue; and

3. Agrees to remove from the list of unresolved issues the issue of "the understanding of what is considered a chemical weapon in particular in relation to Article II, subparagraphs 1(b) and 1(c) (on the basis of the comments provided in relation to Section D of the Draft Declaration Handbook)".

---

[1] Contained in C-8/DG.2, dated 10 April 2003. The Note of the Director-General was noted by the Conference of the States Parties on 24 October 2013 (C-8/7, paragraph 9.3).

3.2 Declaration requirements for CWs and the determination of how States Parties report CWs on their territory which are owned by another State

EC-XIV/DEC.3 adopted by the Executive Council at its Fourteenth Session on 4 February 1999 and entitled "The declaration requirements for chemical weapons and the determination of how States Parties report chemical weapons on their territory which are owned by another State". This decision was confirmed by decision C-IV/DEC.10 adopted by the Conference of the States Parties at its Fourth Session on 29 June 1999.

The Executive Council

Having considered the issue of the declaration requirements for chemical weapons and the determination of how States Parties report chemical weapons on their own territory;

Noting that the declaration requirements for chemical weapons are set out in the Convention, under paragraphs 1-3 of Part IV(A) of the Verification Annex;

Noting further that the requirements for reporting of chemical weapons on the territory of a State Party which are owned or possessed by another State are set out in paragraph 4 of Part IV(A) of the Verification Annex;

Taking into account the work of the Preparatory Commission on this issue;

Noting that the issue was referred by the Conference of the States Parties to the Committee of the Whole (C-I/2, dated 12 May 1997);

Recalling the decision of the Conference of the States Parties on the procedure for addressing unresolved issues during the third intersessional period (C-III/DEC.11, dated 20 November 1998);

Having received the report from the Chairman of the Committee of the Whole containing a recommendation to adopt the decision below;

Hereby:
1. Requests the Technical Secretariat to review the declarations submitted by States Parties under Part IV(A) of the Verification Annex and on that basis to revise the draft declaration forms for declarations under that Part, taking also into account that the formats for reporting on the progress in the destruction should be compatible with these declaration forms;
2. Recommends that States Parties use these revised forms as from the date of this decision for any declarations due under Part IV(A) of the Verification Annex, otherwise using the various versions of Section D, Declarations on Chemical Weapons (declarations due under Part IV(A) of the Verification Annex), of the Draft Declaration Handbook available from the work of the Preparatory Commission as guidance.

    These revised forms should be used for:
    (a) declarations of chemical weapons which are owned or possessed by the declaring State Party, or which are located in any place under its jurisdiction or control; including
    (b) declarations of chemical weapons on the territory of a State Party which are owned by another State.
3. Recommends that the Conference of the States Parties confirm this decision at its Fourth Session and remove the issues of "the declaration requirements for chemical weapons" and "the determination of how States Parties report chemical weapons on their territory which are owned by another State" from the list of unresolved issues.

3.3 CWs buried after 1976 or dumped at sea after 1984

3.3.1 Declaration requirements for CWs buried after 1976 or dumped at sea after 1984

C-I/DEC.30 adopted by the Conference of the States Parties at its First Session on 16 May 1997 and entitled "Declaration requirements for chemical weapons buried by a State Party on its territory after 1976 or dumped at sea after 1984"

The Conference

Recalling that the Commission, in its PC-XVI/36. paragraph 10.2, adopted the understanding with respect to the declaration requirements for chemical weapons buried by a State Party on its territory after 1976 or dumped at sea after 1984,

Bearing in mind that the Commission recommended in paragraph 49.4.2 of its Final Report that the Conference adopt the above mentioned understanding,

Hereby:
1. Adopts the understanding with respect to the declaration requirements for chemical weapons buried by a State Party on its territory after 1976 or dumped at sea after 1984, annexed hereto.

ANNEX
DECLARATION REQUIREMENTS [2]

1. If a State Party buried chemical weapons on its territory after 1976, that State Party is obliged to include this fact in its declaration. A State Party is also obliged to declare the sea dumping of chemical weapons after 1984.
2. Article III subparagraph 1(a) and the relevant provisions of Part IV(A) of the Verification Annex should be the basis for declarations related to the issues of chemical weapons buried by a State Party on its territory after 1976 and of chemical weapons dumped at sea after 1984.
3. The declaration could include any additional information, if available, that could facilitate the Technical Secretariat's evaluation of the information, *inter alia*:
   (a) the exact date when the chemical weapons were buried or dumped;
   (b) how the chemical weapons were buried or dumped, e.g. inside crates, individual items, etc.;
   (c) the present condition of the buried and dumped chemical weapons; and
   (d) possible environmental risks posed.

3.3.2 Understanding with respect to the terms "buried by a State Party on its territory" and "dumped at sea"

C-I/DEC.31 adopted by the Conference of the States Parties at its First Session on 16 May 1997 and entitled "Understanding with respect to the terms "buried by a state party on its territory" and "dumped at sea"

The Conference

Recalling that the Commission, in its PC-XVI/36, paragraph 10.2, adopted the understanding

---

[2] Contained in PC-XVI/B/WP.4, Annex 2.

with respect to the terms "buried on its territory" and "dumped at sea",

Bearing in mind that the Commission recommended in paragraph 49.4.2 of its Final Report that the Conference adopt the above mentioned understanding,

Hereby:
1. Adopts the understanding with respect to the terms "buried on its territory" and "dumped at sea", annexed hereto.

ANNEX

UNDERSTANDING ON THE TERMS "BURIED BY A STATE PARTY
ON ITS TERRITORY" AND "DUMPED AT SEA" [3]

For the purposes of the Convention on the Prohibition of Chemical Weapons:
(a) the term "buried by a State Party on its territory" in Article III, paragraph 2 and Article IV, paragraph 17, shall be understood to cover chemical weapons buried on the land territory of a State Party and in its internal waters;
(b) the term "dumped at sea" in the same paragraphs shall be understood to cover chemical weapons dumped at all parts of sea, including territorial sea of a State Party;
(c) for the practical purpose of the implementation of Article III, paragraph 2 and Article IV, paragraph 17 of the Convention, the border between the territorial sea of a State Party and its land territory and internal waters shall be determined in accordance with the relevant rules of international maritime law; and
(d) if chemical weapons were dumped in archipelagic waters, such chemical weapons should be considered as "dumped at sea".

3.3.3 Aspects of the issue of CWs buried after 1976 or dumped at sea after 1984, including a possible challenge inspection

C-III/DEC.12 adopted by the Conference of the States Parties at its Third Session on 20 November 1998 and entitled "All aspects of the issue of chemical weapons buried by a State Party on its territory after 1976 or dumped at sea after 1984, including a possible challenge inspection, and its implications for the Technical Secretariat's responsibilities"

The Conference

Having considered the issue of chemical weapons buried by a State Party on its territory after 1976 or dumped at sea after 1984, including a possible challenge inspection, and its implications for the Technical Secretariat's responsibilities and other Expert Groups' tasks in this regard;

Taking into account the work of the Preparatory Commission on these issues;

Noting that the following decisions were taken at the First Session of the Conference of the States Parties:

C-I/DEC.31, dated 16 May 1997: "Understanding with Respect to the Terms 'Buried by a State Party on its Territory' and 'Dumped at Sea'",

C-I/DEC.30, also dated 16 May 1997: "Declaration Requirements for Chemical Weapons Buried by a State Party on its Territory after 1976 or Dumped at Sea after 1984";

Noting that the issue was referred by the Conference of the States Parties at its First Session to the Committee of the Whole (C-I/2, dated 12 May 1997);

Reaffirming that verification should be conducted in a cost-effective manner, taking due regard of safety aspects;

---

[3] Contained in PC-XVI/B/WP.4, Annex 1.

Noting also that the challenge inspection procedures of the Convention, in accordance with the provisions of Article IX, also apply to such chemical weapons;

Having received the report from the Committee of the Whole during the Third Session of the Conference of the States Parties containing a recommendation to adopt the decision below;

Hereby:
1. Decides that the Technical Secretariat shall inspect chemical weapons buried on the territory of a State Party after 1976 or dumped at sea after 1984 on the basis of declarations submitted to this effect, taking into consideration that such weapons have to be accessible in terms of the identification thereof as required in Article IV and the relevant provisions of Part IV of the Verification Annex; and
2. Agrees to remove the issue of "all aspects of the issue of chemical weapons buried by a State Party at its territory after 1976 or dumped at sea after 1984, including a possible challenge inspection, and its implication for the Technical Secretariat's responsibilities" from the list of unresolved issues.

3.4 Declaration of Riot Control Agents

S/1177/2014 containing a Note by the Technical Secretariat dated 1 May 2014 and entitled "Declaration of Riot Control Agents: Advice from the Scientific Advisory Board"

1. In accordance with subparagraph 1(e) of Article III of the Chemical Weapons Convention (hereinafter "the Convention"), States Parties are required to declare riot control agents (RCAs), which are defined in paragraph 7 of Article II of the Convention.
2. At its Twentieth Session, the Scientific Advisory Board (SAB) was requested by the Director-General (Annex 4 of SAB-20/1, dated 14 June 2013) to provide technical advice on an initial list of RCAs that had been declared by States Parties, researched, or were commercially available.
3. The SAB has advised the Director-General that the following 17 chemicals correspond to an RCA as defined by paragraph 7 of Article II of the Convention:
   (a) 2-Chloroacetophenone (CN) [CAS[4] 532-27-4];
   (b) 2-Chlorobenzylidenemalonitrile (CS) [CAS 2698-41-1];
   (c) Dibenzo[b,f][1,4]oxazepine (CR) [CAS 257-07-8];
   (d) Oleoresin capsicum (OC) [CAS 8023-77-6];
   (e) 8-Methyl-N-vanillyl-trans-6-nonenamide (capsaicin) [CAS 404-86-4];
   (f) 8-Methyl-N-vanillylnonamide (dihydrocapsaicin) [CAS 19408-84-5];
   (g) N-Vanillylnonamide (pseudocapsaicin, PAVA) [CAS 2444-46-4];
   (h) N-Vanillyl-9-methyldec-7-(E)-enamide (homocapsaicin) [CAS 58493-48-4];
   (i) N-Vanillyl-9-methyldecanamide (homodihydrocapsaicin) [CAS 20279-06-5];
   (j) N-Vanillyl-7-methyloctanamide (nordihydrocapsaicin) [CAS 28789-35-7];
   (k) 4-Nonanolylmorpholine (MPA) [CAS 5299-64-9];
   (l) 2'-Chloroacetophenone [CAS 2142-68-9];
   (m) 3'-Chloroacetophenone [CAS 99-02-5];
   (n) α-Chlorobenzylidenemalononitrile [CAS 18270-61-6];
   (o) Cis-4-acetylaminodicyclohexylmethane [CAS 37794-87-9];
   (p) N,N'-Bis(isopropyl)ethylenediimine [CAS E,E 28227-41-0; Z,Z 185245-09-4]; and
   (q) N,N'-Bis(tert-butyl)ethylenediimine [CAS 30834-74-3; E,E 28227-42-1].

---

[4] CAS = Chemical Abstracts Service

3.5 Destroyed CW munitions retained for display or training purposes

C-I/DEC.26 adopted by the Conference of the States Parties at its First Session on 16 May 1997 and entitled "Destroyed chemical weapons munitions retained for display or training purposes"

The Conference

Recalling that the Commission, in its PC-VI/22, subparagraph 6.8(h), adopted the concept concerning destroyed chemical weapons munitions retained for display or training purposes,

Bearing in mind that the Commission recommended in paragraph 49.2.5 of its Final Report that the Conference adopt the above mentioned concept,

Hereby:
1. Adopts the concept concerning destroyed chemical weapons munitions retained for display or training purposes, annexed hereto.

ANNEX

CONDITIONS UNDER WHICH UNFILLED CHEMICAL MUNITIONS WHICH A STATE PARTY WISHES TO RETAIN FOR DISPLAY OR TRAINING PURPOSES ARE CONSIDERED DESTROYED

1. As there are no specific provisions within the text of the Convention covering the destruction of unfilled chemical munitions which a State Party may wish to retain for display or training purposes, it follows that the ordinary provisions for destruction shall apply.
2. However, a State Party may wish to destroy unfilled chemical munitions using, on a case by case basis, a destruction process that meets the requirements of the Convention but does not preclude their use for either display or training purposes.
3. In such situations the State Party should inform the Secretariat well in advance of its intentions. One method of doing this would be to use the declaration format for detailed annual plans for destruction.
4. The criteria to be used by inspectors in assessing the destruction of such chemical munitions are, according to Part IV(A), paragraph 12, as follows:
    (a) irreversibility of the destruction; and
    (b) unusability of the munitions.
5. To be accepted as destroyed the chemical munitions shall meet the above criteria to ensure that they have been rendered harmless and pose no risk to the object and purpose of the Convention.
6. Note should be taken of the destruction processes identified in paragraph 19 of PC-V/B/WP.17.

3.6 Understanding on the costs of verification under Articles IV and V [1997 and 1998]

Extract of the Annex to C-I/DEC.74* (for 1997) adopted by the Conference of the States Parties at its First Session on 23 May 1997 and entitled "Programme and Budget and Working Capital Fund", pp. 59 - 61

ANNEX

COSTS OF VERIFICATION UNDERSTANDING FOR IMPLEMENTATION OF ARTICLE IV AND ARTICLE V

Article IV, paragraph 16 of the Convention states that "Each State Party shall meet the costs of destruction of chemical weapons it is obliged to destroy. It shall also meet the costs of verification of storage and destruction of these chemical weapons unless the Executive Council decides otherwise. If the Executive Council decides to limit verification measures of the Organisation pursuant to paragraph 13, the costs of complementary verification and monitoring by the Organisation shall be paid in accordance with the United Nations scale of assessment, as specified in Article VIII, paragraph 7."

Article V, paragraph 19 of the Convention states that "Each State Party shall meet the costs of destruction of chemical weapons production facilities it is obliged to destroy. It shall also meet the costs of verification under this Article unless the Executive Council decides otherwise. If the Executive Council decides to limit verification measures of the Organisation pursuant to paragraph 16, the costs of complementary verification and monitoring by the Organisation shall be paid in accordance with the United Nations scale of assessment, as specified in Article VIII, paragraph 7."

The principle is accepted that without prejudice to the prerogatives of the Executive Council, the basic approach to implementing Article IV, paragraph 16 and Article V paragraph 19 of the Convention should be to derive costs in a consistent manner for all Member States subject to the provisions of these paragraphs. It is accepted that, in implementing Article IV, paragraph 16 and Article V, paragraph 19 for the inaugural pro-rated OPCW budget in 1997, the verification costs to be borne (or goods or services to be provided) by such Member States shall cover the following costs, if incurred:

1. ON-SITE ACTIVITIES
   (a) Conduct of inspections
      (i) Installation and maintenance of continuous monitoring instruments and systems and seals
      (ii) Consumable items of inspection equipment, protection and safety equipment, medical supplies and equipment used during the inspection
      (iii) Service, maintenance and operating costs directly related to the use in a particular inspection
      (iv) Collection and analysis of samples on-site
      (v) Decontamination of equipment/supplies
   (b) Continuous monitoring equipment left on-site
   (c) Local transportation

2. IN-COUNTRY PERIOD
   (a) Amenities
      (i) Official Inspection-related Communications
      (ii) Interpretation services
      (iii) Working space

           (iv) Lodging
           (v) Meals
           (vi) Medical care directly related to inspections
    (b) In-country transportation for inspections
           (i) Inspectors
           (ii) Equipment
           (iii) Samples
    (c) Inspectors
           (i) Daily Subsistence Allowance
           (ii) Salaries

3.   TRANSPORTATION TO AND FROM THE HAGUE TO THE POINT OF ENTRY (POE)
    (a) Inspectors:
           (i) international travel;
           (ii) Daily Subsistence Allowance
           (iii) Salaries during transit
    (b) Equipment
    (c) Samples

VISITS

Costs incurred in relation to visits pursuant to implementation of Article IV paragraph 16 and Article V paragraph 19 shall be treated under items 1, 2 and 3 above in the same manner as inspection costs.

COST ELEMENTS TO BE FURTHER EVALUATED

The following inspection related items will continue to be evaluated in relation to assessing costs relevant to inspections under Article IV paragraph 16 and Article V paragraph 19 of the Convention.

4.   HEADQUARTERS ACTIVITIES, SUCH AS
    *   Generation of Inspection Reports
    *   Analysis of Samples
    *   Inspection planning
    *   Negotiation of Facility Agreements
    *   Processing of relevant declarations (specific site)
To the extent that the costs for such activities, including salaries, can be attributed to Member States' obligations under Article IV, paragraph 16 or Article V, paragraph 19.

5.   OTHER OPCW EQUIPMENT COSTS
    (a) Purchase and replacement
    (b) Additional servicing and calibration
    (c) Purchase of spares
    (d) Storage
    (e) Cost of OPCW laboratory
    (f) Depreciation of durable OPCW equipment for time spent in-country
To the extent that the costs for such activities can be attributed to Member States' obligations under Article IV, paragraph 16 or Article V paragraph 19.

6.   RECRUITMENT AND TRAINING
Recruitment and training (both initial and subsequent) of inspectors to the extent that the costs for such activities, including salaries, can be attributed to Member States' obligations under Article IV, paragraph 16 or Article V paragraph 19.

UNDERSTANDINGS

It is understood that this arrangement is purely for the purposes of the inaugural (1997) OPCW budget, and is without prejudice to and sets no precedent for the costs elements which will be developed in the 1998 OPCW budget. In particular, given that the amount of clearly predictable staff costs attributable to the destruction of chemical weapons and chemical weapon production facilities arising in 1997, beyond those identified above, is likely to be minimal, the Conference did not take a decision on the attribution of these costs. Member States will consider this issue at the next Conference of States Parties with a view to determining what proportions of these staff costs, if any, will be borne by Member States with obligations under article IV, paragraph 16 or article V, paragraph 19 as well as the apportionment of the costs of verification of these provisions in general.

The issue of the attribution of costs related to inspections of old and abandoned chemical weapons remains unresolved.

To facilitate decisions on the various outstanding questions pertaining to the costs of verification, the Technical Secretariat shall document by category and Member State all costs incurred related to inspections under Articles IV and V. For transparency purposes an initial report on this documentation will be made available to all Member States when the draft 1998 budget is taken up by the Executive Council. These records will be used to reconcile the final 1997 budget and to develop the 1998 budget once the issues concerning cost attribution are resolved.

Further to this objective, the Technical Secretariat shall prepare a report to the Executive Council addressing the feasibility of accurately accounting for headquarters activity costs for cost of verification purposes, including a description of any additional resources required.

Extract of C-II/DEC.17* adopted by the Conference of the States Parties at its Second Session on 5 December 1997 and entitled "Programme and Budget for 1998 and Working Capital Fund"

The Conference

Hereby: ...

2. As regards the Article IV and V reimbursement criteria, in the absence of a finally agreed solution, the Conference agrees, for the 1998 budget:

    (a) that, as recommended by the Executive Council at its Seventh Session in subparagraph 3.3 of EC-VII/2, Member States should apply the Article IV and V reimbursement criteria contained in C-I/DEC.74*, dated 23 May 1997, except as provided for in subparagraphs 2(b) and 2(c) below;

    (b) that the issues with respect to "salary" and "the attribution of costs related to inspections of old and abandoned chemical weapons" be further addressed and resolved, after appropriate preparation in the first six months of 1998, at the Executive Council's session in June 1998, and that the solution reached be applied to the 1998 OPCW budget, on the basis of more definitive details gathered by the Technical Secretariat;

    (c) that interpretation services shall be reimbursed in respect of such services between a language which is not one of the six languages of the Convention and a language which is one of the six languages of the Convention;

3.7 Costs of verification under Articles IV and V [commencing 1999]

C-III/DEC.8 adopted by the Conference of the States Parties at its Third Special Session on 17 November 1998 and entitled "Costs of verification under Articles IV and V"[5]

The Conference

Recalling paragraph 2 of decision C-II/DEC.17*, dated 5 December 1997, of the Conference of the States Parties at its Second Session;

Recalling the Article IV and V reimbursement criteria contained in decision C-I/DEC.74*, dated 23 May 1997, of the Conference of the States Parties at its First Session, as modified by the Conference of the States Parties at its Second Session;

Taking note of the deliberations on the above subject at the Tenth and Eleventh Sessions of the Executive Council;

Further taking note of comments by the States Parties (EC-X/NAT.4, dated 19 June 1998, EC-X/NAT.8, also dated 19 June 1998, EC-XI/NAT.1, dated 29 July 1998, and EC-XI/NAT.2, dated 7 August 1998) and of documentation provided by the Technical Secretariat (EC-XI/DG.5, dated 3 August 1998, and Corr.1 and Corr.2, dated 13 August 1998 and 1 September 1998 respectively), addressing the issue of reducing the financial burden of the inspected States Parties where possible;

Recognising that the efforts by the Technical Secretariat in cooperation with the States Parties have already led to substantial savings for verification, and requesting the Technical Secretariat to continue such efforts in cooperation with the States Parties, while safeguarding effective verification under the Convention;

Noting decision EC-XI/DEC.1,[6] dated 4 September 1998, of the Executive Council adopted *ad referendum* at its Eleventh Session (paragraph 12 of EC-XI/2, dated 4 September 1998) and confirmed at it its Twelfth Session (subparagraph 16.5 of EC-XII/3, dated 9 October 1998) and the recommendations to the Conference at its Third Session contained therein;

Hereby:

Decides to apply the reimbursement criteria for 1998 as contained in the section entitled "Costs of verification. Understanding for implementation of Article IV and Article V" of the decision C-I/DEC.74* and subparagraph 2(c) of decision C-II/DEC.17* and, with respect to "salary",

---

[5] Extract from the Report of the Third Session of the Conference of the States Parties (subparagraph 12.2(e) of C-III/4): "In accordance with the decision of the Conference at its Second Session on the Programme and Budget for 1998 and Working Capital Fund (C-II/DEC.17*, dated 5 December 1997), and with the decision taken ad referendum by the Council at its Eleventh Session and confirmed by the Council at its Twelfth Session (EC-XI/DEC.1, dated 4 September 1998), the Conference considered and adopted the decision on the costs of verification under Articles IV and V (C-III/DEC.8, dated 17 November 1998). The Conference took note of the cost-saving methods contained in Council decision EC-XI/DEC.1, dated 4 September 1998, and reiterated the request made by the Council to the Technical Secretariat concerning cost-saving methods for Article IV and V inspections."

[6] Extract from EC-XI/DEC.1:

" ... Further taking note of comments by the States Parties (EC-X/NAT.4, dated 19 June 1998, EC-X/NAT.8, also dated 19 June 1998, EC-XI/NAT.1, dated 29 July 1998, and EC-XI/NAT.2, dated 7 August 1998) and of documentation provided by the Technical Secretariat (EC-XI/DG.5, dated 3 August 1998, and Corr.1 and Corr.2, dated 13 August 1998 and 1 September 1998 respectively), addressing the issue of reducing the financial burden of the inspected States Parties where possible;

Recognising that the efforts by the Technical Secretariat in cooperation with the States Parties have already led to substantial savings for verification, and requesting the Technical Secretariat to continue such efforts in cooperation with the States Parties, while safeguarding effective verification under the Convention; ... ."

as contained in EC-XI/DEC.1, (see footnote [7] below) also for future budgets, starting with the 1999 OPCW budget;

Decides, with respect to "Cost Elements to be further evaluated" as contained in chapter 2 of C-I/DEC.74*, section entitled "Costs of verification. Understanding for implementation of Article IV and Article V", paragraphs 4, 5, and 6:

(a) to include reimbursement for the involvement of members of an inspection team in inspection planning before and in inspection report generation after an inspection on the following basis:

   (i)   for CW storage and production facilities: for inspection planning - a three-day planning period for two inspection team members prior to departure, and for inspection report generation - two days for two inspection team members; and

   (ii) for CW destruction facilities: for inspection planning - a two-day planning period for two inspection team members prior to departure, and for inspection report generation - two days for two inspection team members;

(b) not to consider further other such cost elements;

Decides that the use of on-site monitoring instruments at CW facilities, in particular in CWDFs, to reduce the costs of verification, could be applied, where consistent with the requirements for effective verification.

3.8 Costs of inspections of abandoned CWs

C-IV/DEC.5 adopted by the Conference of the States Parties at its Fourth Session on 29 June 1999 and entitled "Costs of inspections of abandoned chemical weapons"

The Conference

Recalling that the Executive Council had been requested by the Conference of the States Parties at its Third Session to continue addressing the issue of the attribution of the costs related to inspections of old and abandoned chemical weapons, with a view to making appropriate recommendations for a decision to be taken on these matters by the Conference at its Fourth Session;

Recalling the decision of the Executive Council at its Fourteenth Session on the costs of inspections of abandoned chemical weapons (EC-XIV/DEC.2, and subparagraph 4.6 of EC XIV/2);

Bearing in mind that, pursuant to paragraph 11 of Part IV(B) of the Verification Annex, the Technical Secretariat shall conduct an initial inspection, and any further inspections as may be necessary, in order to verify all available information submitted pursuant to paragraphs 8 to 10 and determine whether systematic verification in accordance with Part IV(A), paragraphs 41 to 43, of that Annex is required;

Taking into account that the Technical Secretariat shall, if necessary, verify the origin of the

---

[7] For reimbursement under Articles IV and V in 1998:

(a) a daily salary will be calculated by dividing an annual base salary by 365 days;

(b) the costs for the actual inspection team members participating in the inspection will be calculated and reimbursed on the basis of an average inspector salary.

Annual base salary means:

(a) for inspection team members in the professional category net salary plus post adjustment; and

(b) for inspection team members in the general service category net salary plus 25% allowance for overtime.

An average inspector salary is calculated by adding up individual annual base salaries for an average inspection team and then dividing that total by the number of inspection team members in such an average team. For the purposes of the 1998 OPCW budget the average inspection team consists of seven persons: one P-5 team leader, two P-4, three P-3 inspectors and one GS-PL inspection assistant. The average inspection team composition will be subject to annual review and adjustment, as appropriate [footnote in original].

abandoned chemical weapons and establish evidence concerning the abandonment and the identity of the abandoning State;

Considering that, pursuant to paragraph 15 of Part IV(B), for the purpose of destroying abandoned chemical weapons, the abandoning State Party shall provide all necessary financial, technical, expert, facility as well as other resources and the territorial State Party shall provide appropriate cooperation;

Considering also that, pursuant to paragraph 17 of Part IV(B), Article IV and Part IV(A) shall apply to the destruction of abandoned chemical weapons, taking into account the risk posed to the object and purpose of the Convention and the determination by the Technical Secretariat whether they also meet the definition of old chemical weapons in Article II, paragraph 5(b);

Without prejudice to decisions on other unresolved issues related to old and abandoned chemical weapons;

Hereby:

Decides, with effect from 1 January 1999:

(a) that the costs related to verification measures, including initial inspections and any further inspections as provided in paragraph 11 of Part IV(B) of the Verification Annex, for abandoned chemical weapons which have been confirmed by the Technical Secretariat as not meeting the definition of old chemical weapons in Article II, paragraph 5(b), will be attributed to the abandoning State Party;

(b) that, with regard to abandoned chemical weapons that have been confirmed by the Technical Secretariat as meeting the definition of old chemical weapons in Article II, paragraph 5(b), the costs related to initial inspections and any further inspections as provided in paragraph 11 of Part IV(B) of the Verification Annex will be attributed to the Organisation; the costs of further required verification measures will be attributed to the abandoning State Party; and

(c) to request the Technical Secretariat to apply, for reimbursement purposes, the criteria contained in the decision of the Conference C-III/DEC.8, dated 17 November 1998.

3.9 Visits by representatives of the Executive Council

C-11/DEC.20 adopted by the Conference of the States Parties at its Eleventh Session on 8 December 2006 and entitled "Visits by representatives of the Executive Council"

The Conference

Recalling that, pursuant to Article 1, paragraph 2 of the Chemical Weapons Convention (hereinafter the "Convention"), each State Party undertakes to destroy chemical weapons it owns or possesses in accordance with the provisions of the Convention;

Recalling also that, according to Article IV, paragraph 6 of the Convention each State Party shall destroy all chemical weapons specified in paragraph 1 of that Article pursuant to the Verification Annex to the Convention (hereinafter the "Verification Annex") and in accordance with the agreed rate and sequence of destruction;

Bearing in mind the stipulations in Part IV (A), paragraph 26 of the Verification Annex that any extension shall be the minimum necessary, and that in no case shall the deadline for a State Party to complete its destruction of all chemical weapons be extended beyond 15 years after the entry into force of the Convention (29 April 2012);

Bearing in mind also the stipulation in the same paragraph that the Executive Council (hereinafter the "Council") shall set conditions for the granting of the extension, including the specific verification measures deemed necessary, as well as specific actions to be taken by the State Party to overcome problems in its destruction programme;

Noting the progress already made in, and the present status of, the destruction of chemical weapons;

Also noting that States Parties have requested the extension of the deadline to complete the destruction of all their chemical weapons up to 15 years after entry into force of the Convention (29 April 2012) and the need to consider the progress and efforts to achieve complete destruction in accordance with the provisions of the Convention;

Taking into account the problems that States Parties face in the destruction of their chemical weapons stockpiles;

Stressing the need for States Parties to take measures to overcome the problems in their chemical weapons destruction programmes;

Welcoming the proposal for visits by the Council Chairperson and representatives of Council members to Chemical Weapons Destruction Facilities and/or CWDF construction sites to further consider progress and efforts towards achieving complete destruction in accordance with the provisions of the Convention, and any measures being taken to overcome possible problems in a destruction programme in accordance with Part IV (A), paragraph 26 of the Verification Annex;

Noting that such visits to consider progress and efforts to meet an extended deadline established in accordance with the provisions of the Convention, if offered voluntarily by a State Party possessing chemical weapons stockpiles, in the context of achieving complete destruction of its Category 1 chemical weapons in accordance with the provisions of the Convention, could be a useful additional transparency and confidence building measure;

Welcoming the understanding of both the United States and the Russian Federation that each will host such visits periodically, starting no later than 2008 and preferably with each relevant facility being visited at least once during the extension period; and

Bearing in mind the recommendations the Council has made on this matter at its Twenty-Sixth Meeting;

Hereby:

Agrees that such visits shall take place, as a means of addressing questions or concerns about a State Party's programme for fulfilling its obligations on chemical weapons destruction within its extended deadline;

Requests the Chairperson of the Council to work out with the State Party concerned the tentative arrangements for each specific visit (including the facility or facilities to be visited, timing, schedule, itinerary, composition of the visiting group, and safety requirements), and to consult the members of the Council on those arrangements before finalizing them;

Determines that the visits should be carried out without disruption to the destruction activities and with full observance of the destruction facilities' safety procedures;

Decides that the visiting groups should comprise: the Chairperson (or a Vice-Chairperson) of the Council; a representative from each of the other regional groups; one representative from other States Parties hosting such visits; the Director General of the Technical Secretariat (hereinafter "the Secretariat") (or his representative); and, if necessary, a Secretariat interpreter;

Agrees that each visit should include discussions with senior representatives of relevant government authorities as identified by the State Party hosting the visit;

Decides that the Secretariat, by internally establishing efficiencies and priorities to the extent necessary, shall cover the costs of its own staff and the Chairperson (or a Vice-Chairperson) of the Council, and that all other participants shall meet their own costs;

Requests the Council Chairperson (or a Vice-Chairperson) to coordinate preparation by the group of their draft factual report on the particular visit, taking into account the aims of such visits;

Decides that the State Party hosting the visit shall have an opportunity to review and comment on the draft report, prior to its submission to the Council, and to attach to it any additional factual information for the Council's consideration;

Decides that the Council will consider the report of the visiting group at its next regular Session following the visit; and

Agrees that nothing in this decision shall in any way affect the obligation of possessor States Parties to destroy all of their Category 1 chemical weapons by the extended deadlines under the terms of the Convention.

3.10 Practice on CW issues since entry into force of the Convention

Extract of RC-2/S/1* containing a Note by the Technical Secretariat dated 31 March 2008 and entitled "Review of the Operation of the Chemical Weapons Convention since the First Review Conference"

...

3.88 Initial declarations under Article III remain the very first requirement to eliminating chemical weapons stockpiles and former CWPFs. Their timely and accurate submission is an important condition for the functioning of the Convention's verification system. Since the First Review Conference, one additional State Party, the Libyan Arab Jamahiriya, has declared the possession of chemical weapons and of former CWPFs.

3.89 Completing the destruction of chemical weapons by the established deadlines constitutes a solemn legal obligation for the possessor States Parties. Significant progress towards the achievement of this key objective has been made by the States Parties since the First Review Conference.

3.90 Major steps have been taken towards eliminating CWPFs. The last remaining former CWPFs are currently undergoing conversion, one is temporarily used for chemical weapons destruction and will be destroyed thereafter. The verification measures applied by the OPCW are tailored to ensure that these production capacities are either rendered for peaceful purposes or destroyed in accordance with the Convention's requirements. All converted facilities remain under systematic verification. An issue that needs to be addressed is the scope of the verification measures to be applied past the 10-year period after former CWPFs have been certified by the OPCW as converted.

3.91 Extensions of the deadline for completing the destruction of Category 1 chemical weapons beyond the original 10-year period of destruction stipulated by the Convention were granted by the Conference at its Eleventh Session for five of the six States Parties that have declared possession of chemical weapons stockpiles. In accordance with paragraph 28 of Part IV(A) of the Verification Annex , these States Parties are required to report to the Council on the progress of their destruction activities "not later than at the end of each 90 days of the extension period". This more stringent declaration regime will allow the Secretariat and the Council to better review and document progress towards the completion of destruction and the complete elimination of chemical weapons stockpiles within the extended deadline stipulated by the Convention (that is, before 29 April 2012). In this regard, the Director General issued a Note to the Council at its Forty-Ninth Session (EC-49/DG.1, dated 8 March 2007) regarding modalities for implementing this obligation.

3.92 On 11 July 2007, Albania became the first possessor State Party to have finished the destruction of its chemical weapons stockpile. Chemical weapons continue to be destroyed in four of the current five possessor States Parties. Having declared 24 metric tonnes of Category 1 and 1,414 metric tonnes of Category 2 chemical weapons, the Libyan Arab Jamahiriya has destroyed all of its Category 3 chemical weapons and 39%, of its Category 2 chemical weapons. It has been granted an extension to 31 December 2010 of the deadline for the destruction of all of its Category 1 chemical weapons stockpiles and to 31 December 2011 to complete the destruction of its Category 2 chemical weapons. The Libyan Arab Jamahiriya has submitted to the Secretariat detailed facility information for the Rabta Toxic Chemical Disposal Facility, which has been designated to destroy both the chemical weapons agent and the remaining precursors that this State Party has declared.

3.93 According to the destruction plans presented by States Parties, the peak of destruction activities is expected to be reached in 2010. The increasing number of CWDFs represents great challenges (primarily financial and technological) for States Parties, and similarly, since 2002 the OPCW has faced a similar challenge in meeting the corresponding increase in verification requirements.

3.94 Some Member States have been assisting the efforts of possessor States Parties in eliminating their chemical weapons stockpiles. Such assistance remains of paramount importance and there is an expectation that it will continue to be forthcoming in the future.

3.95 Chemical weapons stockpiles continue to be inspected according to the verification measures applied by the OPCW to confirm declarations and remaining chemical weapons holdings. Past issues related to the identity and quantity of declared agents have been resolved by practical approaches. Since most storage facilities do not cater for sampling and analysis of chemical weapons on a routine basis, the identity of agents is established at the chemical weapons destruction facility. Similarly, precise measurements of chemical weapons quantities are carried out as part of the process of verifying chemical weapons destruction.

3.96 Progress in destruction activities has already led to a significant decrease in the number of chemical weapons storage facilities. Improvements in stockpile configuration and enhanced cooperation between the Secretariat and possessor States Parties have led to a more efficient, thus cost-saving conduct of inspections.

3.97 As regards old and abandoned chemical weapons, since the First Review Conference, three additional States Parties (Austria, the Russian Federation, and the Solomon Islands) have declared OCWs, thus increasing to 13 the number of States Parties that have declared OCWs. In this regard, one declaration-related issue deserves special attention. It concerns the declaration of new discoveries of OCWs, after the 29 April 2007 deadline, especially those produced between 1925 and 1946. Although all States Parties that have declared OCWs produced between 1925 and 1946 have completed their destruction (with the exception of Italy, which was granted an extension to 29 April 2012), the fact remains that new OCW discoveries are still likely to take place. Noting the expectation that recovery of pre-1946 chemical weapons will continue for decades at varying rates in different regions and that declarations, destruction, and verification procedures have remained unchanged, with the affected States Parties giving the Secretariat their full support and cooperation, the Secretariat leaves it to the policy-making organs to determine the practicality of whether a deadline for destruction of new recoveries of pre-1946 chemical weapons should be established.

3.98 In relation to OCWs, the issue of guidelines to determine the usability of chemical weapons produced between 1925 and 1946 remains outstanding (paragraph 5 of Part IV(B) of the Verification Annex). A facilitator had been assigned to work on this issue until 2004, but consultations on this matter were, in fact, discontinued in 2002. In 2000, pending guidance from States Parties and cognisant of the need to undertake the required verification, the Secretariat issued a paper on "Proposed Verification Measures for Old Chemical Weapons Produced between 1925 and 1946" (S/166/2000, dated 15 February 2000). While this has had no serious practical impact on the verification of declarations and the implementation of destruction to date, an agreement of the States Parties on these guidelines would still be beneficial. In addition, the attribution of costs related to OCW inspections also awaits clarification.

3.99 During the Forty-Sixth Session of the Council in July 2006, China and Japan were granted a five-year extension on their obligation to complete the destruction of the ACWs left by Japan in China. Both parties continue to discuss practical preparations for the destruction of ACWs in China. These meetings have produced progress and understanding in the areas of ACW recovery, temporary storage, transport, environmental and public safety, as well as the technical aspects of ACW destruction. These States Parties have also announced a decision to introduce a mobile destruction system to accelerate the destruction of ACWs. Implementation of the ACW destruction programmes will contribute to the goals of the Convention.

3.100 Possessor States Parties continue to implement changes/upgrades in their destruction technologies. The OPCW is working closely with these Member States to ensure that CWDFs are constructed and operated in a manner that complies with verification requirements. Complementary to this, the Secretariat constantly seeks to improve its own inspection procedures and equipment by introducing upgrades.

3.101 The importance of the comprehensive application of Article IV verification measures remains undiminished. To consolidate the credibility of the entire verification process, all steps in the destruction process need to be monitored by inspectors and/or appropriate technical means, regardless of any set agreements on accountability.

3.102 The Secretariat is constantly reviewing its verification approach and, together with possessor States Parties, further optimising activities in the field during the systematic quality-assurance visits. In parallel with this, on Article VI inspections, the introduction of sequential inspections has proven to be a powerful cost-saving tool and, pending agreement with Member States, is increasingly being implemented.

3.11 Deadline for the destruction of CWs

C-11/DEC.12 adopted by the Conference of the States Parties at its Eleventh Session on 8 December 2006 and entitled "Request by a State Party for an Extension of the Final Deadline for Destroying All of Its Category 1 Chemical Weapons"

The Conference of the States Parties,

Having considered the decision by the Executive Council (hereinafter "the Council") at its Forty-Fourth Session (EC-44/DEC.8, dated 15 March 2006) regarding a request by A State Party for an extension of the deadline by which it must destroy all of its Category 1 chemical weapons stockpiles;

Hereby:
1.   Grants an extension of the deadline by which this State Party must destroy all of its Category 1 chemical weapons stockpiles, subject to the following conditions:
    (a)   that the State Party shall complete the destruction of its Category 1 chemical weapons no later than 31 December 2008;
    (b)   that, in addition, it shall report to the Council on its destruction activity not later than at the end of each 90 days of the extension period; and
    (c)   that, until all of its Category 1 chemical weapons have been destroyed, it shall continue to submit to the Technical Secretariat:
        (i)   detailed annual plans for destruction in accordance with paragraph 29 of Part IV(A) of the Verification Annex; and
        (ii)   annual reports on the destruction of its Category 1 chemical weapons in accordance with paragraph 36 of that part;

2.   Requests that the Director-General report periodically to the Council on the progress made by the State Party in completing the destruction of its chemical weapons;

3.   Also requests that the Chairperson of the Council, in the exercise of his or her competencies and in cooperation with the Director-General, report periodically to the Council on these matters; and

4.   Further requests that the Council review the progress made by the State Party in destroying all of its Category 1 chemical weapons, take the necessary measures to document this progress, and provide to States Parties, on request, all information concerning the destruction activities of this State Party during the extension period.

C-11/DEC.14 adopted by the Conference of the States Parties at its Eleventh Session on 8 December 2006 and entitled "Proposal for a Date for the Completion of Phase 3 of the Destruction by the Russian Federation of Its Category 1 Chemical Weapons"

The Conference of the States Parties,

Having considered a recommendation by the Executive Council at its Forty-Fourth Session (EC-44/DEC.9, dated 17 March 2006) regarding a proposal by the Russian Federation for a date for the completion of the destruction of 45% of its Category 1 chemical weapons,

Hereby:

Sets 31 December 2009 as the date for completion of the destruction by the Russian Federation of 45% of its Category 1 chemical weapons stockpiles.

C-11/DEC.15 adopted by the Conference of the States Parties at its Eleventh Session on 8 December 2006 and entitled "Proposal by the Libyan Arab Jamahiriya for the Establishment of Specific Dates for Intermediate Destruction Deadlines, and Its Request for an Extension of the Final Deadline for the Destruction of Its Category 1 Chemical Weapons"

The Conference of the States Parties,

Having considered the decision by the Executive Council (hereinafter "the Council") at its Forty-Sixth Session on a proposal by the Libyan Arab Jamahiriya for the establishment of specific dates for its intermediate destruction deadlines, and on its request for an extension of the final deadline for the destruction of its category 1 chemical weapons (EC-46/DEC.2, dated 4 July 2006);

Hereby:

1.   Grants an extension, to 31 December 2010, of the deadline by which the Libyan Arab Jamahiriya must destroy all of its Category 1 chemical weapons stockpiles, on the understanding that:

(a)   the Libyan Arab Jamahiriya will report to the Council on its destruction activities no later than at the end of each 90 days of the extension period, in accordance with Part IV(A), paragraph 28, of the Verification Annex;

(b)   the Director-General will report periodically to the Council on the progress made by the Libyan Arab Jamahiriya in completing the destruction of its chemical weapons; and

(c)   the Chairperson of the Council, in the exercise of his or her competencies and in cooperation with the Director-General, will periodically report to the Council on these matters;

2.   Establishes the following dates for the intermediate deadlines for the destruction by the

Libyan Arab Jamahiriya of its Category 1 chemical weapons stockpiles: phase 1 (1%), to be completed by 1 May 2010; phase 2 (20%), to be completed by 1 July 2010; and phase 3 (45%), to be completed by 1 November 2010, on the understanding that, up until 29 April 2007, the Libyan Arab Jamahiriya shall keep the Council informed, at each alternate regular session and with supporting documentation, of the status of its plans to implement its destruction obligations; and

3.   Calls upon the Libyan Arab Jamahiriya to complete the destruction of its Category 2 chemical weapons as soon as possible, but in any case no later than 31 December 2011.

C-11/DEC.16 adopted by the Conference of the States Parties at its Eleventh Session on 8 December 2006 and entitled "Request by India for an Extension of the Deadline for Destroying All of Its Category 1 Chemical Weapons"

The Conference of the States Parties,

Having considered the recommendations that the Executive Council (hereinafter "the Council") made in the decision it adopted at its Forty-Fifth Session on a request by India for an extension of the deadline for destroying all of its Category 1 chemical weapons (EC-45/DEC.5, dated 17 May 2006);

Hereby:
1.   Grants an extension of the deadline by which India must destroy all of its Category 1 chemical weapons stockpiles, subject to the following conditions:
   (a) that India shall complete the destruction of its Category 1 chemical weapons no later than 28 April 2009;
   (b) that, in addition, it shall report to the Council on its destruction activities not later than at the end of each 90 days of the extension period; and
   (c) that, until all of its Category 1 chemical weapons have been destroyed, it shall continue to submit to the Technical Secretariat:
      (i)   detailed annual plans for destruction in accordance with paragraph 29 of Part IV(A) of the Verification Annex; and
      (ii) annual reports on the destruction of its Category 1 chemical weapons in accordance with paragraph 36 of that Part;
2.   Requests that the Director-General report periodically to the Council on the progress made by India in completing the destruction of its chemical weapons;
3.   Also requests that the Chairperson of the Council, in the exercise of his or her competencies and in cooperation with the Director-General, report periodically to the Council on these matters; and
4.   Further requests that the Council review the progress made by India in destroying all of its Category 1 chemical weapons, take the necessary measures to document this progress, and provide to States Parties, on request, all information concerning the destruction activities of this State Party during the extension period.

C-11/DEC.17 adopted by the Conference of the States Parties at its Eleventh Session on 8 December 2006 and entitled "Request by the United States of America for Establishment of a Revised Date for the Final Deadline for Destroying All of Its Category 1 Chemical Weapons"

The Conference of the States Parties,

Recalling that, pursuant to Article 1, paragraph 2 of the Chemical Weapons Convention (hereinafter the "Convention"), each State Party undertakes to destroy chemical weapons it owns or possesses in accordance with the provisions of the Convention;

Recalling also that, according to Article IV, paragraph 6, of the Convention, each State Party shall destroy all chemical weapons specified in paragraph 1 of that Article pursuant to the Verification Annex to the Convention (hereinafter "the Verification Annex") and in accordance with the agreed rate and sequence of destruction;

Recalling further that, according to Part IV (A), paragraph 24, of the Verification Annex, if a State Party believes that it will be unable to ensure the destruction of all of its Category 1 chemical weapons not later than 10 years after the entry into force of the Convention, it may submit a request to the Executive Council (hereinafter the "Council") for an extension of the deadline for completing the destruction of such chemical weapons, and that, according to paragraph 26 of that Part, a decision on the request shall be taken by the Conference of the States Parties (hereinafter the "Conference") at its next session, on the recommendation of the Council;

Bearing in mind the stipulations in the same paragraph that any extension shall be the minimum necessary, and that in no case shall the deadline for a State Party to complete the destruction of its chemical weapons be extended beyond 15 years after the entry into force of the Convention, in other words, 29 April 2012;

Bearing in mind further that, at its Eighth Session, it granted the United States of America, in principle, an extension of the final deadline for completing the destruction of its Category 1 chemical weapons (C-8/DEC.15, dated 24 October 2003);

Noting that the United States of America requested the establishment of 29 April 2012 as the revised date for the final deadline for completing destruction of all of its Category 1 chemical weapons stockpiles;

Recognising the United States of America's obligation to destroy all of its Category 1 chemical weapons not later than 29 April 2012; and

Also bearing in mind the recommendation that the Council at its Twenty-Sixth Meeting has made on this matter (EC-M-26/DEC.7, dated 8 December 2006);

Hereby:
1. Establishes 29 April 2012 as the date by which the United States of America must destroy all of its Category 1 chemical weapons, subject to the following conditions:
   (a) that nothing in this decision shall in any way affect the obligation of the United States of America under the terms of the Convention to destroy all of its Category 1 chemical weapons not later than 15 years after the entry into force of the Convention;
   (b) that the United States of America shall report to the Council on its destruction activity not later than at the end of each 90 days of the extension period, in accordance with Part IV(A), paragraph 28, of the Verification Annex; and
   (c) that, until all of its Category 1 chemical weapons have been destroyed, it shall continue to submit to the Technical Secretariat:
      (i) detailed annual plans for destruction in accordance with Part IV(A), paragraph 29, of the Verification Annex; and
      (ii) annual reports on the destruction of its Category 1 chemical weapons in accordance with paragraph 36 of that part; and
2. Requests that the Director-General report periodically to the Council on the progress made by the United States of America in completing destruction of its chemical weapons;
3. Requests that the Chairperson of the Council, in the exercise of the Chair's competencies and in cooperation with the Director-General, report periodically to the Council on these matters; and
4. Requests that the Council review the progress made by the United States of America in destroying all of its Category 1 chemical weapons, take the necessary measures to document this progress, provide to States Parties, on request, all information concerning the destruction activities of this State Party during the extension period.

C-11/DEC.18 adopted by the Conference of the States Parties at its Eleventh Session on 8 December 2006 and entitled "Proposal by the Russian Federation on Setting a Specific Date for Completion of the Destruction of Its Stockpiles of Category 1 Chemical Weapons"

The Conference of the States Parties,

Recalling that at its Eighth Session it granted the Russian Federation, in principle, an extension of the intermediate deadline for the destruction of 45% of its Category 1 chemical weapons stockpiles, and of the final deadline for destruction, on the understanding that this would not prejudice any of the Russian Federation's obligations under the Chemical Weapons Convention (hereinafter "the Convention"), including, with respect to the final deadline, Part IV(A), paragraph 28, of the Verification Annex to the Convention (hereinafter "the Verification Annex") (C-8/DEC.13, dated 24 October 2003);

Taking into account that the Russian Federation submitted to the Executive Council (hereinafter "the Council") a request for an extension of the deadline for completion of the destruction of its Category 1 chemical weapons by 29 April 2012 (EC-XXVII/DG.1, dated 26 October 2001);

Bearing in mind that it has set 31 December 2009 as the date for completion of the destruction by the Russian Federation of 45% of its Category 1 chemical weapons stockpiles (C-11/DEC.14, dated 8 December 2006);

Noting the economic and financial efforts undertaken by the Russian Federation for the purpose of implementing its National Programme for the Destruction of Chemical Weapons in the Russian Federation;

Noting also the substantial contribution of international assistance to that Programme;

Noting further the importance of planned, coordinated, targeted, and effectively utilised international assistance for the safe and secure destruction by the Russian Federation of its chemical weapons in accordance with the Convention;

Having considered the information submitted by the Russian Federation on the adjustment of the general plan for the destruction of chemical weapons (EC-45/NAT.4, dated 26 April 2006, and Corr.1, dated 17 May 2006), which, jointly with EC-XXVII/DG.1, dated 26 October 2001, fully meets the requirements of Part IV(A), paragraph 25, of the Verification Annex, and constitutes a proposal to set a specific date for completion of the destruction of chemical weapons in the Russian Federation;

Welcoming the commitment of the Russian Federation to the task of destroying its Category 1 chemical weapons as soon as possible but in no case later than 15 years after the entry into force of the Convention, and the efforts it has already made to achieve that goal; and

Also bearing in mind the recommendation that the Council at its Twenty-Sixth Meeting has made on this matter (EC-M-26/DEC.6, dated 8 December 2006);

Hereby:

Sets 29 April 2012 as the date for completion of the destruction by the Russian Federation of 100% of its chemical weapons stockpiles.

C-14/DEC.3 adopted by the Conference of the States Parties at its Fourteenth Session on 2 December 2009 and entitled "Extension of the Intermediate and Final Deadlines for the Destruction by the Libyan Arab Jamahiriya of its Category 1 Chemical Weapons"

The Conference of the States Parties,

Having considered the decision by the Executive Council (hereinafter "the Council") at its Fifty-Eighth Session on the request by the Libyan Arab Jamahiriya for the extension of the intermediate and final deadlines for the destruction of its Category 1 chemical weapons (EC-58/DEC.1, dated 15 October 2009);

Hereby:

1. Amends its decision (C-11/DEC.15, dated 8 December 2006) and grants an extension, to 15 May 2011, of the deadline by which the Libyan Arab Jamahiriya must destroy all of its Category 1 chemical weapons stockpiles, on the understanding that:

   (a) the Libyan Arab Jamahiriya will report to the Council on its destruction activities no later than at the end of each 90 days of the extension period, in accordance with paragraph 28 of Part IV(A) of the Verification Annex to the Chemical Weapons Convention;

   (b) the Director-General will report periodically to the Council on the progress made by the Libyan Arab Jamahiriya in completing the destruction of its chemical weapons; and

   (c) the Chairperson of the Council, in the exercise of his or her competencies and in cooperation with the Director-General, will periodically report to the Council on these matters; and

2. Grants extensions of the intermediate deadlines for the destruction by the Libyan Arab Jamahiriya of its Category 1 chemical weapons stockpiles, and establishes the following new intermediate deadlines: phase 1 (1%), to be completed by 1 November 2010; phase 2 (20%), to be completed by 15 December 2010; and phase 3 (45%), to be completed by 31 January 2011, on the understanding that the Libyan Arab Jamahiriya shall keep the Council informed, at each alternate regular session and with supporting documentation, of the status of its plans to implement its destruction obligations.

…

C-16/DEC.3 adopted by the Conference of the States Parties at its Sixteenth Session on 29 November 2011 and entitled "Extension of the Final Deadline for the Destruction by Libya of its Category 1 Chemical Weapons"

The Conference of the States Parties,
Having considered the decision by the Executive Council (hereinafter "the Council") at its Thirtieth Meeting (on 13, 20, and 30 May 2011) on the request by Libya concerning the completion of the destruction of its Category 1 and Category 2 chemical weapons (EC-M-30/DEC.1, dated 30 May 2011);

Hereby:

1. Amends its decision (C-14/DEC.3, dated 2 December 2009) and grants an extension, to 29 April 2012, of the deadline by which Libya, in accordance with the provisions of the Chemical Weapons Convention (hereinafter "the Convention"), must destroy all of its Category 1 chemical weapons stockpiles, on the understanding that:

   (a) Libya will keep the Council informed, at each regular session, of the status of its plans to implement its destruction obligations;

   (b) Libya will report to the Council on its destruction activities, no later than at the end of each 90 days of the extension period, in accordance with paragraph 28 of Part IV(A) of the Verification Annex to the Convention; and

   (c) the Director-General will report periodically to the Council on the progress made by Libya in completing the destruction of its chemical weapons; and

2. Calls upon Libya to complete the destruction of its Category 2 chemical weapons as soon as possible, but in any case, by no later than 29 April 2012.

C-16/DEC.11 adopted by the Conference of the States Parties at its Sixteenth Session on 1 December 2011 and entitled "Final Extended Deadline of 29 April 2012"

The Conference of the States Parties,
  Recalling the Obligation under Article 1 of the Convention on the Prohibition of the Develop-

ment, Production, Stockpiling and Use of Chemical Weapons and on Their Destruction (hereinafter referred to as the "Convention") in terms of which "Each State Party undertakes to destroy chemical weapons it owns or possesses, or that are located in any place under its jurisdiction or control, in accordance with the provisions of this Convention";

Recalling further that the Convention determines under Article IV that for each State Party "Such destruction shall begin not later than two years after this Convention enters into force for it and shall finish not later than 10 years after entry into force of this Convention" and that an extension of the deadline for destruction can be requested under Part IV (A) of the Convention's Annex on Implementation and Verification (hereinafter referred to as the "Verification Annex") "but in no case shall the deadline for a State Party to complete its destruction be extended beyond 15 years after the entry into force of this Convention";

Recalling and again welcoming the completion of the full destruction of the chemical weapons that had been owned, or possessed, by Albania, India, and a State Party, in accordance with the provisions of the Convention;

Recalling that Libya, the Russian Federation, and the United States of America (hereinafter referred to as the "possessor State concerned" or "possessor States concerned") were granted an extension of the deadline for the destruction of their chemical weapons by the Conference of the States Parties to the Convention (hereinafter referred to as the "Conference") in terms of decisions C-11/DEC.17 and C-11/DEC.18 dated 8 December 2006;

Recalling further that the final extended deadline for the destruction of chemical weapons by the possessor States concerned that was established by the Conference in accordance with Part IV (A) of the Convention's Verification Annex is 29 April 2012 and that further extensions of the deadline beyond this date are not possible;

Recalling further that the Executive Council of the Organisation for the Prohibition of Chemical Weapons (hereinafter referred to respectively as the "Executive Council" and the "Organisation") as reported in EC-64/5 dated 3 May 2011 has already been addressing the concern in accordance with Paragraph 36 of Article VIII of the Convention that the final extended deadline of 29 April 2012 may not be fully met and that the matter has also been brought to the attention of the Conference;

Recalling further that the Conference at its Fifteenth Session:

(a) "Considered and noted a report by the Director-General on the progress made by those States Parties that have been granted extensions of deadlines for the destruction of their Category 1 chemical weapons (C-15/DG.13, dated 11 November 2010)."

(b) "Reaffirmed the obligation of possessor States Parties to destroy their chemical weapons within the extended deadlines, in accordance with the relevant decisions by the Conference at its Eleventh Session, and to that end emphasised the timely commencement of destruction activities at all chemical weapons destruction facilities."

(c) "Noted with concern that the final extended deadline of 29 April 2012 may not be fully met (and) ... urged all possessor States Parties to take every necessary measure with a view to ensuring their compliance with the final extended destruction deadline."

(d) "Stressed in this regard that no action should be undertaken that would undermine the Convention or that would raise questions about the commitment of States Parties, or lead to the rewriting of or reinterpreting of Convention's provisions."

(e) "Further stressed that issues in this regard should be dealt with faithfully in accordance with the relevant provisions of the Convention."

Recalling further that the "Second Review Conference reaffirmed that complete destruction of chemical weapons, and conversion or complete destruction of CWPFs, is essential for the realisation of the object and purpose of the Convention. The Second Review Conference also reaffirmed the importance of the obligation of the possessor States Parties to complete the destruction of their chemical weapons stockpiles within the final extended deadlines as established by the Conference at its Eleventh Session."

Noting the statements by Libya, the Russian Federation, and the United States of America underlining their unequivocal commitment to their Obligations under Articles I and IV of the Convention for the destruction of their remaining chemical weapons in accordance with the provisions of this Convention and taking note that the inability to fully meet the final extended deadline of 29 April 2012 would come about due to reasons that are unrelated to the commitment of these States Parties to the General Obligations for the destruction of chemical weapons established under Article I of the Convention;

On the basis of the powers and functions of the Conference to take specific actions to promote the object and purpose of the Convention, to oversee implementation, or to ensure compliance with the Convention's provisions, and underlining that, in the event that the final extended deadline is not fully met, the destruction of the remaining chemical weapons of the possessor States concerned shall continue in accordance with the provisions of the Convention and its Annex on Implementation and Verification ("Verification Annex"), and with the application of the measures contained in this decision;

Hereby:
1. Decides that the Sixty-Eighth Session of the Executive Council shall be held immediately after the expiry of the final extended deadline of 29 April 2012 for the destruction of chemical weapons;
2. Requests the Director-General of the Organisation's Technical Secretariat (hereinafter referred to as the "Director-General") to report to the Sixty-Eighth Session of the Executive Council whether or not the final extended deadline has been fully met. The report to be submitted is to include information on the quantities of chemical weapons that have been fully destroyed and that remain to be destroyed by each of the possessor States concerned;
3. Decides that, if the Director-General reports that the final extended deadline has not been fully met, the following measures are to be implemented by the Organisation and the possessor States concerned:
   (a) The destruction of the remaining chemical weapons in the possessor States concerned shall be completed in the shortest time possible in accordance with the provisions of the Convention and its Verification Annex and under the verification of the Technical Secretariat of the Organisation as prescribed under the Convention and its Verification Annex.
   (b) The costs for the continued destruction of the chemical weapons by the possessor States concerned and the verification of their destruction shall continue to be met in accordance with Paragraph 16 of Article IV of the Convention;
   (c) Each possessor State concerned is to submit a detailed plan for the destruction of its remaining chemical weapons, which are to be destroyed in the shortest time possible, to the Sixty-Eighth Session of the Executive Council. The plan submitted by each possessor State, which is to also be considered and noted by the Council at its Sixty-Eighth Session, is to specify the planned completion date by which the destruction of its remaining chemical weapons is to be completed (hereinafter referred to as the "planned completion date"). The possessor States concerned are to take appropriate measures to meet the planned completion date. The detailed plan is to inter alia specify:
      (i) A schedule for destruction, giving types and approximate quantities of chemical weapons planned to be destroyed in each annual destruction period until completion for each existing destruction facility and, if possible, for each planned destruction facility.
      (ii) The number of destruction facilities existing or planned to be operated over the destruction period until completion.
      (iii) For each existing and planned chemical weapons destruction facility:
         a. Name and location;
         b. The types and approximate quantities of chemical weapons, and the type (for

example, nerve agent or blister agent) and approximate quantity of chemical fill, to be destroyed.

The submission of this detailed plan for destruction does not alter, modify or cancel any other requirements contained in the Convention and its Verification Annex for the submission of other destruction plans.

(d) Each possessor State concerned is to report, and provide a briefing in a closed meeting, at each regular session of the Executive Council on the progress achieved towards the complete destruction of remaining stockpiles, including information on measures to accelerate such progress, and identifying progress made since the last briefing in order to meet the planned completion date. These reports and briefings are to also include reporting on any specific measures undertaken to overcome problems in the destruction programme.

(e) The Director-General is to provide a written report at each regular session of the Executive Council on the overall destruction progress by the possessor States concerned that is based on the independent information that is received by the Technical Secretariat from the Organisation's inspectors undertaking verification in accordance with Part IV (A) D of the Verification Annex and that is to include information on:
   (i) The progress achieved to meet the planned completion date(s).
   (ii) The effectiveness of any specific measures that have been undertaken to overcome problems in the destruction programmes.

(f) The Conference of the States Parties is to undertake an annual review of the implementation of this decision at a specially designated meeting(s) of the Conference. At the annual Conference of the States Parties in 2017 an extra day is to be added for a specially designated meeting(s) for this purpose, unless otherwise decided at the Conference of the States Parties in 2016. Each possessor State concerned is to provide an annual report to the Conference of the States Parties, and provide an annual briefing at a closed meeting of the Conference of the States Parties, on the progress in the destruction of its remaining stockpiles of chemical weapons and identifying progress made since the last briefing in order to meet planned completion date. These reports, and briefings, are to also include:
   (i) Reporting on any specific measures undertaken to overcome problems in the destruction programmes.
   (ii) Information on the projected schedule for destruction activities to meet the planned completion date.

(g) The Director-General is to provide an annual written report to the Conference of the States Parties on the overall destruction progress by the possessor States concerned that is based on the independent information that is received by the Technical Secretariat from the Organisation's inspectors undertaking verification in accordance with Part IV (A) D of the Verification Annex and that is to include information on:
   (i) The progress achieved to meet the planned completion date(s).
   (ii) The effectiveness of any specific measures that have been undertaken to overcome problems in the destruction programmes.

(h) The Review Conference is to conduct a comprehensive review on the implementation of this decision at a specially designated meeting(s) of the Conference. This review is to be based on:
   (i) Reports by the possessor States concerned on the progress achieved to meet the planned completion date. These reports are to also include:
        a. Reporting on any specific measures undertaken to overcome problems in the destruction programmes.
        b. Information on the projected schedule for destruction activities to meet the planned destruction date.
   (ii) A written report by the Director-General of the Technical Secretariat that is based on the independent information that is received by the Technical Secretariat from the

Organisation's inspectors undertaking verification in accordance with Part IV (A) D of the Verification Annex and that is to include information on:

    a.   The progress achieved to meet the planned completion date(s).

    b.   The effectiveness of any specific measures that have been undertaken to overcome problems in the destruction programmes.

(i)   The submission of the reports under operative paragraphs 3 (d), (f) and (h)i of this decision do not alter, modify or cancel any other requirements contained in the Convention and its Verification Annex for the submission of other reports.

(j)   The possessor States concerned are to invite the Chairperson of the Executive Council, the Director-General and a delegation representing the Executive Council to undertake visits to obtain an overview of the destruction programmes being undertaken. These visits are to inter alia include visits to destruction facilities as well as meetings with parliamentarians, if possible, and government officials in capitals as a formal part of the visits. Invitations are to also be extended to observers to participate in the Executive Council delegation. The visits are to take place annually on the basis of biennial visits to the major possessor States concerned consecutively. Visits would also take place to Libya on a biennial basis.

4.   Notes that the Director-General has reported to the First Committee of the 66th Session of the United Nations General Assembly on the steps that have been undertaken by the Organisation in the event that the final extended deadline for the destruction of chemical weapons of the possessor States concerned is not met and that the Director-General will also address this issue when he reports to the 67th Session of the United Nations General Assembly.

C-16/5 containing the Report of the Sixteenth Session of the Conference of the States Parties, 28 November – 2 December 2011, adopted on 2 December 2011, Subparagraphs 9.4 to 9.7

Subitem 9(d):   **Issues related to meeting the final extended deadline and other destruction-related issues**

9.4   Pursuant to a recommendation by the Executive Council (hereinafter "the Council") at its Thirty-First Meeting, the Conference considered and adopted, by voting, the decision regarding the final extended deadline of 29 April 2012 (C-16/DEC.11, dated 1 December 2011), with the voting result of 101 for and one against the decision.

9.5   In this context, the Conference recalls paragraph 3.2 of the report of Thirty-First Meeting of the Council (EC-M-31/3, dated 2 December 2011), which reads as follows:

"Having considered the Draft Decision of the Conference regarding the final extended deadline of 29 April 2012 submitted by the Chairperson of the Council (EC-M-31/DEC/CRP.2, dated 22 November 2011; hereinafter referred to as the "Draft Decision"), the Council, underlining the unequivocal commitment by Libya, the Russian Federation and the United States of America to their obligations under Articles I and IV of the Convention for the complete destruction of their remaining chemical weapons in accordance with the provisions of the Convention and with the application of the measures contained in the Draft Decision; emphasising that the Draft Decision is to be adopted on the basis of the powers and functions of the Conference to promote the object and purpose of the Convention, to oversee implementation, or to ensure compliance with the Convention's provisions; emphasising that the Draft Decision does not provide for an open-ended timeline for the destruction of the remaining chemical weapons, and emphasising further that the plan submitted by each possessor State, which is to also be considered and noted by the Council at its Sixty-Eighth Session, is to specify the planned completion date by which the destruction of its remaining chemical weapons is to be completed, approved the Draft Decision and decided, pursuant to Rule 42 of its Rules of Procedure[8], to transmit the Draft Decision to the Conference at its Sixteenth Session, together with its recommendation that the Draft Decision be adopted by the Conference (EC-M-31/DEC.3, dated 24 November 2011). In accordance with Rule 44 of the Rules of Procedure of the Council, after the vote, a number of representatives explained their votes."

9.6   The report by the Director-General on financial, administrative, and programme and budget implications of the final extended deadline of 29 April 2012 (EC-M-31/DG.2 C-16/DG.17, dated 28 November 2011) had been circulated to the Member States.

9.7   The delegation of China referred to the destruction-related issue of particular interest to it on the territory of China.
       The delegation of Japan stressed the particular role of the Council on this issue.

EC-68/3 containing the Report of the Sixty-Eighth Session of the Executive Council adopted on 4 May 2012, Subparagraphs 6.1 to 6.15

Subitem 6(a):   Reports by the Director-General on destruction/deadline related issues

6.1   The Council recalled that, at its Sixteenth Session, the Conference of the States Parties (hereinafter "the Conference") adopted a decision on the final extended deadline of 29 April 2012 (C-16/DEC.11, dated 1 December 2011). The Council expressed its concern regarding the Director-General's statement in his report, provided in accordance with paragraph 2 of C-16/DEC.11, that "the three possessor States Parties, namely Libya, the Russian Federation, and the United States of America, have been unable to fully meet the final extended deadline of 29 April 2012 for the destruction of their chemical weapons stockpiles" (EC-68/DG.9, dated 1 May 2012).

6.2   The Council noted a Note by the Director-General on the status of implementation of the final extended deadline of 29 April 2012 (EC-68/DG.7, dated 1 May 2012), submitted pursuant to the decision by the Conference at its Sixteenth Session on the final extended deadline of 29 April 2012 (C-16/DEC.11).

6.3   The Council noted the Director-General's statement in his re report, provided in accordance with paragraph 4 of EC-67/DEC.6 (dated 15 February 2012), that "the deadline for the destruction of ACWs as established by the Council at its Forty-Sixth Session has not been fully met" (EC-68/DG.9). The Council also recalled that it had adopted a decision at its previous session entitled "The Deadline of 29 April 2012 and Future Destruction of Chemical Weapons Abandoned by Japan in the People's Republic of China" (EC-67/DEC.6).

6.4   The Council recalled the decision that was adopted at its previous session on the request by Italy for modification of decision EC-48/DEC.2, dated 13 March 2007, concerning the destruction of all its old chemical weapons (EC-67/DEC.8, dated 17 February 2012).

6.5   The Council recalled the commitments by these States Parties in these situations to complete the destruction of all the chemical weapons in accordance with the provisions of the Chemical Weapons Convention (hereinafter "the Convention") and its Verification Annex and also in accordance with the relevant decisions that have been adopted.

6.6   The Council considered and noted a status report by the Director-General on the progress

---

[8] The Draft Decision was approved with 39 votes for (Albania, Algeria, Argentina, Brazil, Cameroon, Canada, China, Colombia, Costa Rica, Croatia, Cuba, Denmark, Ecuador, France, Germany, Hungary, India, Iraq, Italy, Japan, Kenya, Libya, Luxembourg, Malaysia, Mexico, Morocco, Nigeria, Pakistan, Republic of Korea, Romania, Russian Federation, Rwanda, Saudi Arabia, South Africa, Spain, Sri Lanka, Turkey, United Kingdom of Great Britain and Northern Ireland, United States of America), and one vote against (Islamic Republic of Iran). One delegation was absent (Namibia) [footnote in original].

made by those States Parties that have been granted extensions of deadlines for the destruction of their chemical weapons (EC-68/DG.4, dated 20 April 2012 and Corr.1, dated 1 May 2012).

6.7 The Council considered and noted a Note by the Director-General (EC-68/DG.5, dated 26 April 2012) on information provided as per the request of the Council at its Fifty-Ninth Session (paragraph 5.8 of EC-59/4, dated 26 February 2010).

6.8 Further to a decision by the Council at its Sixty-Seventh Session entitled "The Deadline of 29 April 2012 and Future Destruction of the Chemical Weapons Abandoned by Japan in the People's Republic of China" (EC-67/DEC.6), the Council noted a report by the Director-General on the overall progress of the destruction of abandoned chemical weapons (EC-68/DG.6, dated 26 April 2012).

Subitem 6(b):   Implementation of the Conference of the States Parties and Executive Council decisions on destruction/deadline related issues

6.9 The Council recalled that, at its Sixteenth Session, the Conference decided that, if the final extended deadline had not been fully met, "The destruction of the remaining chemical weapons in the possessor States concerned shall be completed in the shortest time possible in accordance with the provisions of the Convention and its Verification Annex and under the verification of the Technical Secretariat of the Organisation as prescribed under the Convention and its Verification Annex." (C-16/DEC.11).

6.10 The Council recalled also that the Conference had further decided that "Each possessor State concerned is to submit a detailed plan for the destruction of its remaining chemical weapons, which are to be destroyed in the shortest time possible, to the Sixty-Eighth Session of the Executive Council. The plan submitted by each possessor State, which is to also be considered and noted by the Council at its Sixty-Eighth Session, is to specify the planned completion date by which the destruction of its remaining chemical weapons is to be completed (hereinafter referred to as the "planned completion date"). The possessor States concerned are to take appropriate measures to meet the planned completion date."

6.11 Pursuant to a decision by the Conference at its Sixteenth Session (C-16/DEC.11), the Council considered and noted a detailed plan by the Russian Federation for the destruction of remaining chemical weapons (EC-68/P/NAT.1, dated 11 April 2012).

6.12 Pursuant to the same decision by the Conference at its Sixteenth Session (C-16/DEC.11), the Council considered and noted a detailed plan by the United States of America for the destruction of remaining chemical weapons (EC-68/NAT.2, dated 13 April 2012).

6.13 Pursuant to the same decision by the Conference at its Sixteenth Session (C-16/DEC.11), the Council considered and noted a detailed plan by Libya for the destruction of remaining chemical weapons (EC-68/NAT.4, dated 18 April 2012).

6.14 The Council also reaffirmed that it had adopted a decision at its previous session entitled "The Deadline of 29 April 2012 and Future Destruction of Chemical Weapons Abandoned by Japan in the People's Republic of China" (EC-67/DEC.6).

6.15 The Council considered and noted the report of the visit by the Chairperson of the Council and representatives of the Council to the Kizner chemical weapons destruction facility in the Russian Federation from 19 to 23 March 2012 (EC-68/2, dated 24 April 2012).

4. CHEMICAL WEAPONS STORAGE FACILITY (CWSF) ISSUES

4.1 References to munitions in VA IV(A) 1(c)(iii) and (iv)

C-I/DEC.14 adopted by the Conference of the States Parties at its First Session on 16 May 1997 and entitled "References to munitions in the Verification Annex, Part IV(A), Section A, paragraphs 1(c)(iii) and 1(c)(iv)"

The Conference

Recalling that the Commission, in its PC-IV/23, paragraph 6.3.1, approved the understanding that the references to munitions in the Verification Annex, Part IV(A), Section A, paragraphs 1(c)(iii) and 1(c)(iv) apply to both filled and unfilled munitions,

Bearing in mind that the Commission recommended in paragraph 49.1.9 of its Final Report that the Conference adopt the above mentioned understanding,

Hereby:
1. Adopts the understanding that the references to munitions in the Verification Annex, Part IV(A), Section A, paragraphs 1(c)(iii) and 1(c)(iv) apply to both filled and unfilled munitions.

4.2 Precision of declarations of national aggregate quantities of toxic chemicals and their precursors defined as CW and of individual munitions and container items

C-I/DEC.15 adopted by the Conference of the States Parties at its First Session on 16 May 1997 and entitled "Precision of declaration of national aggregate quantities of toxic chemicals and their precursors defined as chemical weapons and of individual munitions and container items"

The Conference

Recalling that the Commission, in its PC-IV/23, paragraph 6.3.2, considered and approved the understanding that the precision of the declarations of national aggregate quantities of toxic chemicals and their precursors defined as chemical weapons should be rounded up to the nearest one tonne,

Recalling that the Commission also approved the understanding that the individual munitions and container items should be declared by nominal weight in kilograms,

Bearing in mind that the Commission recommended in paragraph 49.1.9 of its Final Report that the Conference adopt the above mentioned understanding,

Hereby:
1. Adopts the understanding regarding the precision of the declarations of national aggregate quantities of toxic chemicals and their precursors defined as chemical weapons and of the individual munitions and container items.

4.3 Simulant filled munitions for testing chemical munitions destruction procedures

C-I/DEC.16 adopted by the Conference of the States Parties at its First Session on 16 May 1997 and entitled "Simulant filled munitions for testing chemical munitions destruction procedures"

The Conference

Recalling that the Commission, in its PC-IV/23, paragraph 6.3.3, confirmed the understanding that simulant filled munitions intended for testing chemical weapons destruction procedures should be incorporated into national declarations,

Bearing in mind that the Commission recommended in paragraph 49.1.9 of its Final Report that the Conference adopt the above mentioned understanding,

Hereby:
1. Adopts the understanding that simulant filled munitions intended for testing chemical weapons destruction procedures should be incorporated into national declarations.

4.4 Declaration of CW locations and their detailed inventories

C-I/DEC.17 adopted by the Conference of the States Parties at its First Session on 16 May 1997 and entitled "Declaration of chemical weapons locations and their detailed inventories"

The Conference

Recalling that the Commission, in its PC-V/12, subparagraph 6.6(a), adopted the recommendation that, in declaring chemical weapons, all locations must be specified,

Recalling the understanding that these locations include CW storage facilities, CW storage facilities at CW destruction facilities and temporary holding areas at CW destruction facilities,

Recalling that the Commission recommended that all these locations and their detailed inventories should be declared using the illustrative formats developed by the Commission,

Bearing in mind that the Commission recommended in paragraph 49.1.9 of its Final Report that the Conference adopt the above mentioned recommendation,

Hereby:
1. Adopts the recommendation that, in declaring chemical weapons, all locations must be specified.

4.5 Declarations for CW storage locations and national aggregate declarations

C-I/DEC.18 adopted by the Conference of the States Parties at its First Session on 16 May 1997 and entitled "Declarations for chemical weapons storage locations and national aggregate declarations"

The Conference

Recalling that the Commission, in its PC-V/12, subparagraph 6.6(b), adopted the recommendation that declarations for each chemical weapons storage location and national aggregate declarations should each be submitted as complete documents containing appropriate chemical declaration forms as attachments,

Bearing in mind that the Commission recommended in paragraph 49.1.9 of its Final Report that the Conference adopt the above mentioned recommendation,

Hereby:
1. Adopts the recommendation regarding the submission of declarations for each chemical weapons storage location and national aggregate declarations.

4.6 Verification activities at a temporary holding area within a CWDF

C-I/DEC.19 adopted by the Conference of the States Parties at its First Session on 16 May 1997 and entitled "Verification activities at a temporary holding area within a CW destruction facility"

The Conference
Recalling that the Commission, in its PC-V/12, subparagraph 6.6(d), adopted the recommendation that CW stored in a temporary holding area at a CW destruction facility would not normally be subject to inspection by a CW storage facility inspection team,
Recalling that the Commission recommended that these verification activities would be the responsibility of a CW destruction facility inspection team,
Recalling the understanding that CW stored in a CW storage facility at a CW destruction facility should be inspected by CW storage facility inspection teams,
Recalling, also, the understanding that subsequent inspections at these CW storage facilities could be done either by CW storage facility inspection teams or by CW destruction inspection teams, as will be agreed in appropriate facility agreements,
Bearing in mind that the Commission recommended in paragraph 49.1.9 of its Final Report that the Conference adopt the above-mentioned recommendation,

Hereby:
1. Adopts the recommendation regarding verification activities at a temporary holding area within a CW destruction facility.

4.7 Recommendations for determining the frequency of systematic on-site inspections of storage facilities

C-I/DEC.10 adopted by the Conference of the States Parties at its First Session on 14 May 1997 and entitled "Recommendations for determining the frequency of systematic on-site inspections of storage facilities, in accordance with Part IV(A), paragraph 44, of the Verification Annex (Paris Resolution, subparagraph 12(l))"

The Conference
Recalling that the Commission in its PC-VII/8, paragraph 6.12, adopted the criteria for the determination of the frequency of inspections developed by the Expert Group on Chemical Weapons Storage Facilities and outlined in paragraph 9 of the Annex to PC-V/B/WP.13, and in Appendix B to the same Report,
Bearing in mind that the Commission recommended in paragraph 42.2 of its Final Report that the Conference adopt the above mentioned recommendations,

Hereby:
1. Adopts the criteria for the determination of the frequency of systematic on-site inspections of chemical weapons storage facilities, annexed hereto.

ANNEX

Once facility declarations have been received by the OPCW, a determination should be made as to which facilities should be inspected first. Once all initial inspections are complete and facility agreements finalised, the OPCW should then decide on the frequency of inspection of each facility. In determining the frequency of inspections at a particular CW storage facility, due regard should be given to any Executive Council decision to avoid duplication of adequate bilateral or multilateral verification regimes already applied to the facility. Possible criteria that could be used by the Technical Secretariat to determine the priority and frequency of inspection of a CW storage facility are at Annex B. These criteria are purposely qualitative and do not represent an exhaustive listing. The Conference wished to include these criteria which the Technical Secretariat may, on receipt of declarations and inspection reports, make more quantitative in nature.[1]

POSSIBLE CRITERIA FOR DETERMINATION OF FREQUENCY OF [2] INSPECTIONS

The criteria below could be considered when determining the frequency of inspection for each facility.

CRITERIA[3]	HIGHER FREQUENCY	LOWER FREQUENCY
Quantity of chemicals defined as CW[4]	Larger quantity	Lower quantity
Readiness of CW for use	a. CW is weaponized b. Binary components are collocated c. CW can be used immediately	a. CW is not weaponized b. Binary components are in separate CW storage facilities that are not in close proximity to each other [5] c. CW can be used only after substantial preparation or modification
Quantity of unfilled munitions, sub-munitions, devices or equipment	Larger quantity	Lower quantity
Results of previous inspections	Inconsistencies with requirements of the Convention or unresolved ambiguities reported	No substantial inconsistencies or unresolved ambiguities reported

---

[1] Contained in PC-V/B/WP.13, Annex, paragraph 9.

[2] Contained in PC-V/B/WP.13, Annex, Appendix B.

[3] The expressions under 'higher frequency' and 'lower frequency' for each of the possible criteria would include a variety of situations not expressed in this table. They should be interpreted as the potential higher and lower limits of a continuum [footnote in original].

[4] The terms 'larger quantity' and 'lower quantity' reflect the understanding of the Group that as of the time of writing, the potential quantities of chemicals in any possible CW storage facility is unknown. Thus the quantities are relative. Once storage facilities have been declared and verified, the Technical Secretariat may wish to assign more quantitative criteria, but at present they should remain relative only [footnote in original].

[5] 'Close proximity' may be State Party dependent. It may be affected by transportation availability, ease of dispensing agent from containers, degree of weaponization, etc [footnote in original].

4.8 Guidelines with respect to the applicability of bilateral/multilateral verification procedures

C-I/DEC.21 adopted by the Conference of the States Parties at its First Session on 16 May 1997 and entitled "Guidelines with respect to the applicability of bilateral/multilateral verification procedures"

The Conference

Recalling that the Commission, in its PC-VI/22, subparagraphs 6.6(a) - (d), adopted the guidelines with respect to the applicability of bilateral/multilateral verification procedures,

Bearing in mind that the Commission recommended in paragraph 49.1.9 of its Final Report that the Conference adopt the above mentioned guidelines,

Hereby:
1. Adopts the guidelines with respect to the applicability of bilateral/multilateral verification procedures, annexed hereto.

ANNEX
GUIDELINES WITH RESPECT TO THE APPLICABILITY OF
BILATERAL/MULTILATERAL VERIFICATION PROCEDURES

(a) the applicability of any bilateral or multilateral verification agreements be assessed against the criteria of consistency, comprehensives, and effectiveness in accordance with the principles and provisions noted in the Chairman's Paper to PC-VI/B/WP.9;

(b) if complementary verification measures related to any bilateral/multilateral agreement have been implemented by the Executive Council, the Director-General should report to the Executive Council on the verification activities taken by the parties to the bilateral/multilateral agreement and on the complementary measures. This should include an assessment of their effectiveness;

(c) should the Director-General have uncertainties at any time about the effectiveness of any bilateral/multilateral inspection regime he shall approach the States Parties concerned for clarification. If the uncertainties cannot be removed or if the facts established are of a nature to suggest that obligations undertaken under the Convention have not been met, the Director-General shall inform the Executive Council without delay; and

(d) if the Executive Council finds reason to doubt the effectiveness of any bilateral/multilateral agreement, it should consider directing the implementation of the Organisation's verification regime for the States Parties concerned. The Executive Council should take appropriate measures aimed at clarifying the issues prior to directing such action.

5. CHEMICAL WEAPONS DESTRUCTION FACILITY (CWDF) ISSUES

5.1 Recommendations for guidelines for Transitional Verification Arrangements and understanding in relation thereto

C-I/DEC.11 adopted by the Conference of the States Parties at its First Session on 14 May 1997 and entitled "Recommendations for guidelines for transitional verification arrangements, in accordance with Part IV(A), paragraph 51, of the Verification Annex (Paris Resolution, subparagraph 12(m))"

The Conference

Recalling that the Commission in its PC-VI/22, subparagraph 6.8(d) and Corr.1, adopted the concept and guidelines on transitional verification arrangements developed by the Expert Group,

Recalling that the Commission in its PC-XV/25, paragraph 8.2, decided to delete the task "Finalise recommendations for guidelines for transitional verification arrangements, in accordance with Part IV(A), paragraph 51 of the Verification Annex (subparagraph 12(m) of the Paris Resolution)" from its list of tasks. This deletion was on the understanding that the above task has been fully addressed by Section III and Appendix 1 of the Chairman's Paper annexed to the Third Report of the Expert Group on Chemical Weapons Destruction Facilities (PC-VI/B/WP.14) and by Table 1 of the same Group's Interim Report (PC-V/B/WP.17),

Bearing in mind that the Commission recommended in paragraph 43.3 of its Final Report that the Conference adopt the above mentioned recommendations,

Hereby:

1. Adopts the recommendations for guidelines to be established by the Executive Council for the assessment and approval of transitional verification arrangements, annexed hereto.

ANNEX
TRANSITIONAL VERIFICATION ARRANGEMENTS [TVAs][1]

1. Per Part III, paragraph 6, and Part IV(A), paragraph 51, the Convention provides the following:
    (a) TVAs which include a transitional facility agreement, provisions for verification through on-site inspection, and monitoring with on-site instruments apply for two types of chemical weapons destruction facilities (CWDFs) during the transitional period:
        (i)   those in operation at entry into force for the State Party (EIF/SP);
        (ii) those starting operation less than one year after EIF/SP;
    (b) TVAs are in force in the time frame from EIF/SP+60 to EIF+390. As a consequence, the minimum time frame would be 30, the maximum 330 days;
    (c) the permanent facility agreement shall be completed not later than EIF/SP+210, to replace the transitional facility agreement at EIF+390;
    (d) whilst the facility agreement may be completed before the end of the transitional period it will not enter into force until the end of this period, unless mutually agreed;
    (e) for the two sets of facilities under 5(a) the same timelines basically apply, but will depend on the actual start of operations. Therefore, a differentiating treatment may be required to accommodate, in practical terms, this factor;
    (f) in accordance with Part IV(A), paragraph 55, the initial visit shall not exceed 5 days.
2. In addition to the existing monitoring equipment installed at the site by the inspected State

---

[1] Contained in PC-VI/B/WP.14, Annex, Section 3.

Party, inspectors may use the agreed inspection equipment in a complementary manner, to fulfil inspection requirements.

3.   For original States Parties, the transitional period may last 330 days. However, for States Parties that ratify after entry into force (EIF) the transitional period will be shorter. A transitional facility agreement is primarily meant to provide a provisional basis for the early presence of inspectors at the destruction facility. However, given the time constraints, the agreement should be negotiated from the very beginning in the context of its transition into a permanent facility agreement within a relatively short period of time. The latter would enforce the systematic verification activity as required for a chemical weapons destruction facility starting operation one year after EIF.

4.   Table 1 in the Attachment is applicable for use in the transitional period.

5.   The factors listed in paragraph 41 of PC-V/B/WP.17 are also relevant in the context of a transitional facility agreement.

6.   The guidelines for inspection activities at a chemical weapons destruction facility operational at EIF or within one year after EIF will be very similar to those adopted for the conduct of inspection of chemical weapons destruction facilities (C-I/DEC.6) and will differ only in minor details.

7.   Guidelines to be established by the Executive Council for the assessment and approval of transitional verification arrangements are set out in the Attachment to this Paper.

ATTACHMENT

GUIDELINES TO BE ESTABLISHED BY THE EXECUTIVE COUNCIL FOR THE ASSESSMENT AND APPROVAL OF TRANSITIONAL VERIFICATION ARRANGEMENTS[2]

In accordance with Part III, paragraph 6 and Part IV(A), paragraph 51, guidelines are to be established by the Executive Council at its First Session for the assessment and approval of transitional verification arrangements. For these guidelines the following should be taken into account:

(a)   according to the Verification Annex Part IV(A), paragraph 50 the Secretariat shall, during the transitional period, verify the destruction of chemical weapons by:
    (i)   confirming the identity and quantity of the chemical weapons stocks to be destroyed; and
    (ii)   confirming that these stocks have been destroyed;

(b)   verification through on-site inspection and monitoring with on-site instruments according to a transitional facility agreement and a time frame for the application of the arrangements (Verification Annex Part III, paragraph 6, and Part IV(A), paragraph 51);

(c)   the Group recommended that the following guidelines be used by the Executive Council for the approval of a transitional facility agreement and of transitional verification arrangements:
    (i)   avoidance of any hampering of ongoing destruction operations; and
    (ii)   sufficiency with regard to consistency and comprehensiveness for the transitional facility agreement and verification arrangements, to enable verification as described above to apply within the facility which is described by the detailed facility information provided and by the report on the initial visit to this facility.

---

[2]   Contained in PC-VI/B/WP.14, Annex, Appendix 1.

DEADLINES FOR SUBMISSION OF DETAILED FACILITY INFORMATION AND ACTIVITIES PRIOR TO THE BEGINNING OF SYSTEMATIC ON-SITE VERIFICATION[3]

Table 1 – For Destruction Facilities Operational at EIF

ACTIVITY	MILESTONES	BASIS OR CWC REFERENCE
Provide Detailed Facility Information to the TS Initial/Final Submission by State Party	EIF + 30[4]	Based on Article III, 1(a)(v)
Initial Visit to the destruction facility by TS	EIF + 40	
Complete Transitional Verification Agreement	EIF + 60	Part IV(A), 51
Begin Transitional on-site presence by TS	EIF + 90	Based on Part III, 1&2
Draft Inspection Plan submitted by the TS	no later than EIF + 120	Based on Part IV(A), 54 & 56
Complete Routine Inspection Plan (TS) and Facility Agreement (TS and State Party)	EIF + 210	Part III, 6
Begin systematic on-site verification by TS	EIF + 390	Part IV(A), 51

5.2 Guidelines for the assessment and approval of Transitional Verification Arrangements for CWDFs operational during the first 390 days after EIF

EC-I/DEC.2 adopted by the Executive Council at its First Session on 21 May 1997 and entitled "Guidelines for the assessment and approval of transitional verification arrangements for chemical weapons destruction facilities operational during the first 390 days after EIF"

"Prior to their implementation, transitional verification arrangements (TVAs), agreed between the Organisation and a State Party, governing the verification of a chemical weapons destruction facility (CWDF) during the first 390 days after the entry into force of the Convention are, in accordance with paragraph 51 of Part IV(A) of the Verification Annex, subject to approval by the Executive Council. The Executive Council shall base its approval on the following guidelines:

(a) TVAs shall as a minimum address the matters contained in paragraphs 62 - 70 of Part IV(A) of the Verification Annex;

(b) the TVA shall provide for the on-site presence of inspectors from the Technical Secretariat and shall facilitate their work to confirm:
  (i)   the identity and quantity of the chemical weapons stocks to be destroyed; and
  (ii) that these stocks have been destroyed;

(c) the terms of the TVA shall be consistent with the OPCW Health and Safety Policy, the OPCW Policy on Confidentiality, the OPCW Media and Public Affairs Policy, the OPCW Financial Regulations and Rules, and the OPCW Staff Regulations and Rules;

(d) the TVA shall enable the Technical Secretariat to carry out its task in an efficient and cost-effective manner with the minimum interruption to ongoing destruction operations; and

(e) the TVA shall, to the extent possible, take into account the proposals for a model facility agreement for chemical weapons destruction facilities."

---

[3] Contained in PC-V/B/WP.17, Annex, Table 1.
[4] Time in days after EIF.

5.3 Deadlines for submission of information specified in VA IV(A) 30 to 32

C-I/DEC.9 adopted by the Conference of the States Parties on 14 May 1997 and entitled "Deadlines for submission of the information specified in Part IV(A), paragraphs 30 to 32 of the Verification Annex, in accordance with paragraph 34 of that Part (Paris Resolution, subparagraph 12(k))"

The Conference

Recalling that the Commission in its PC-VI/22, subparagraph 6.8(e), adopted the guidelines for the provision of the detailed facility information required in accordance with Part IV(A), paragraph 31, contained in Appendix 2 of the Chairman's Paper annexed to PC-VI/B/WP.14,

Recalling that the Commission in its PC-VI/22, subparagraph 6.8(f), adopted the deadlines for the above detailed facility information in respect to Category 2 and 3 chemical weapons, as elaborated in Charts 1 and 2 of the Chairman's Paper and the further recommendation on this issue contained in paragraph 18 of the Chairman's Paper annexed to PC-VI/B/WP.14,

Bearing in mind that the Commission recommended in paragraph 41.1 of its Final Report that the Conference adopt the above mentioned guidelines and deadlines,

Hereby:

1. Adopts the guidelines for the provision of the detailed facility information required in accordance with Part IV(A), paragraph 31, of the Verification Annex and the deadlines for the above detailed facility information in respect to Category 2 and 3 chemical weapons, annexed hereto.

ANNEX[5]

The deadlines are contained in Chart 2. A summary of the situation with respect to all possible situations and all categories of chemical weapons is given in Chart 1. Chart 2 for Category 2 and 3 chemical weapons should be used for all three categories of chemical weapons - Category 1, Category 2 and Category 3.

Chart 1 – Deadlines for the Submission of Detailed Facility Information

FACILITY OPERATIONAL	CATEGORY 1	CATEGORY 2 OR 3
At EIF/SP	EIF/SP + 30	EIF/SP + 30
< 360 days after EIF/SP	EIF/SP + 30	EIF/SP + 30
> 360 days after EIF/SP	BOD minus 360	Not Applicable

---

[5] Contained in PC-VI/B/WP.14.

Chart 2 – Deadlines for the Submission of Detailed Information and for Activities Prior to the Beginning of Systematic On-site Verification for Category 2 and 3 Chemical Weapons Destruction Facilities Operational at EIF or Beginning Operation no later than One Year after EIF for the State Party

ACTIVITY	MILESTONES OPERATIONAL AT OR BEFORE		BASIS OR CWC REFERENCE
	EIF/SP[6]	(EIF/SP +360)	
Provide detailed facility information to the Technical Secretariat (TS) Initial/Final submission by State Party	EIF/SP + 30[7]	EIF/SP + 30	Based on Article III,1(a)(v)
Initial visit to the destruction facility by TS	EIF/SP+ 40	the later of BOD minus 110 EIF/SP+ 40	
Complete transitional verification arrangement	EIF/SP + 60	the later of BOD minus 90 EIF/SP + 60	Part IV(A), 51
Begin transitional on-site presence to verify destruction by TS	EIF/SP + 90	the later of BOD minus 60 EIF/SP + 90	Based on Part III, 1& 2
Draft inspection plan submitted by the TS	no later than EIF/SP + 120	no later than EIF/SP + 120	Based on Part IV(A), 54 & 56
Complete routine inspection plan (TS) and facility agreement (TS and State Party)	EIF/SP + 210	EIF/SP + 210	Part III,6
Change to systematic on-site verification of destruction by TS	EIF + 390	EIF + 390	Part IV(A), 51

DETAILED FACILITY INFORMATION FOR A DESTRUCTION FACILITY[8]

REQUIREMENT No.	PARA No.	INFORMATION REQUESTED	INFORMATION RECOMMENDED FOR SUBMISSION
1	31(a)	Name, address, and location	1. Name 2. Mailing address 3.Geographic co-ordinates to the nearest second for the centre of the structure housing the destruction process
2	31(b)	Detailed, annotated facility drawings	Annotated plan of facility showing boundaries, location of buildings and major items of equipment/plant
3	31(c)	Facility design drawings, process drawings and piping and instrumentation design drawings	Design drawings showing sufficient detail to enable the Secretariat to make a proper assessment of the destruction process

---

[6] EIF for a State Party.

[7] Time in days after EIF.

[8] Contained in PC-VI/B/WP.14, Annex, Appendix 2.

Requirement No.	Para No.	Information Requested	Information Recommended for Submission
4	31(d)	Detailed technical descriptions for the equipment required for the destruction process	Design drawings and instrument specifications for the major items of equipment used in the draining, chemical destruction and munition destruction processes. The detail should be sufficient to enable the Secretariat to make a proper assessment of the destruction process
5	31(e)	Detailed technical description of the destruction process	To include flow diagrams, showing flow rates of the principal materials, pressures and temperatures throughout the system and details of the destruction efficiency
6	31(f)	Design capacity of facility for each specific type of chemical weapon	Number or quantity of chemical weapons which can be processed per hour/day
7	31(g)	Detailed description of the products of destruction and the method of their ultimate disposal	For each product chemical name, structural formula, Chemical Abstract Service (CAS) No., fraction (%) of total waste stream and details of proposed final disposal method
8	31(h)	Detailed technical description of methods adopted to facilitate inspections	E.g. location of sampling points, instrumentation, surveillance cameras, etc.
9	31(i)	Detailed description of any temporary holding area at the facility	Plan showing exact location within the facility. Details of function, capacity, storage methods, specialised features, e.g. ventilation, monitoring, etc.
10	31(j)	Detailed description of the safety and medical measures in force at the facility	Provide copies of the relevant parts of the facility's health and safety regulations and procedures
11	31(k)	Detailed description of the living quarters and working premises for the inspectors	Provide annotated floor plan showing size and functions of rooms. Provide brief description of facilities and services available
12	31(l)	Suggested measures for international verification	Provide details of any site plans or provisions aimed at enabling the facility readily to demonstrate compliance with the Convention
13	32	Plant operating manuals, safety and medical plans, laboratory operations, quality assurance and control manuals and environmental permits	Plant operating manuals, safety and medical plans, laboratory operations, quality assurance and control manuals and environmental permits

5.4 Verification activities at a temporary holding area within a CWDF

C-I/DEC.19 adopted by the Conference of the States Parties at its First Session on 16 May 1997 and entitled "Verification activities at a temporary holding area within a CW destruction facility"

The Conference

Recalling that the Commission, in its PC-V/12, subparagraph 6.6(d), adopted the recommendation that CW stored in a temporary holding area at a CW destruction facility would not normally be subject to inspection by a CW storage facility inspection team,

Recalling that the Commission recommended that these verification activities would be the responsibility of a CW destruction facility inspection team,

Recalling the understanding that CW stored in a CW storage facility at a CW destruction facility should be inspected by CW storage facility inspection teams,

Recalling, also, the understanding that subsequent inspections at these CW storage facilities could be done either by CW storage facility inspection teams or by CW destruction inspection teams, as will be agreed in appropriate facility agreements,

Bearing in mind that the Commission recommended in paragraph 49.1.9 of its Final Report that the Conference adopt the above-mentioned recommendation,

Hereby:
1. Adopts the recommendation regarding verification activities at a temporary holding area within a CW destruction facility.

5.5 Temporary holding areas at CWDFs

C-I/DEC.27 adopted by the Conference of the States Parties at its First Session on 16 May 1997 and entitled "Temporary holding areas at chemical weapons destruction facilities"

The Conference

Recalling that the Commission, in its PC-V/12, subparagraph 6.6(c), adopted the recommendation that temporary holding areas at chemical weapons destruction facilities be defined as locations within the declared perimeter of a chemical weapons destruction facility,

Recalling that the Commission also adopted the recommendation that these holding areas should contain at any time no more than one week's amount of agent or material, based on the declared design capacity of the destruction facility,

Bearing in mind that the Commission recommended in paragraph 49.2.5 of its Final Report that the Conference adopt the above mentioned recommendation,

Hereby:
1. Adopts the recommendation with respect to temporary holding areas at chemical weapons destruction facilities.

5.6 Guidelines on detailed procedures for verification and for the conduct of inspections at CWDFs

C-I/DEC.6 adopted by the Conference of the States Parties at its First Session on 14 May 1997 and entitled "Guidelines on detailed procedures for verification and for the conduct of inspections at chemical weapons destruction facilities, in accordance with, *inter alia*, Part II, paragraph 42, of the Verification Annex"

The Conference

Recalling that the Commission adopted the four sets of guidelines for inspection activities at chemical weapons destruction facilities in its PC-VI/22, paragraph 6.8(g),

Bearing in mind that the Commission recommended in paragraph 36.2.2 of its Final Report that the Conference adopt the above mentioned guidelines,

Hereby:
1. Adopts the four sets of guidelines for inspection activities at chemical weapons destruction facilities annexed hereto.

ANNEX

The following is a list of activities that may be carried out by the Secretariat's inspectors. It is not intended that these activities shall be carried out in any particular order or that all of them shall be applied in every case.[9]

PART I

DRAFT GUIDELINES FOR THE INITIAL VISIT TO A CHEMICAL WEAPONS DESTRUCTION FACILITY NOT OPERATIONAL WITHIN ONE YEAR AFTER EIF/SP

A. ACTIVITIES PRIOR TO THE DEPARTURE OF THE INSPECTORS TO THE STATE PARTY

Activity 1   Review documentation, available data and other information on the facility to be visited
Activity 1.1   Review the State Party's general and annual destruction plans
Activity 1.2   Review the detailed facility information submitted by the State Party
Activity 1.3   Review draft plans for verification prepared by the Secretariat
Activity 1.4   Prepare a preliminary list of logistical requirements for the support of systematic verification
Activity 1.5   Prepare a preliminary plan for the visit

B. ACTIVITIES AT THE VISITED FACILITY

Activity 2   Receive initial briefing
                 The team will receive a pre-visit briefing, at which the visited party will provide information, with the aid of maps and other documentation as appropriate, on:
                 (a) the facility;
                 (b) the activities to be carried out there;
                 (c) supplementary data (such as descriptions, diagrams, photos) and other relevant detailed information on the facility that has not previously been provided to the Technical Secretariat;
                 (d) security regulations;
                 (e) safety regulations, including a briefing on any hazards likely to be encountered; and
                 (f) the administrative and logistical arrangements that are relevant for the conduct of the visit.
Activity 3   Revise plan for initial visit as necessary and brief the visited State Party On the basis of the information provided in the initial briefing the team may modify its preliminary plan, as required, to accomplish the objectives of the visit.
Activity 4   Confirm the location of the visited facility
                 Inspectors will verify that the facility's location is as declared. This can be accomplished by utilising visual and map reconnaissance, a declared site diagram, and position locating equipment such as a global positioning system (GPS).
Activity 5   Assess the destruction facility
Activity 5.1   Confirm that the design of the destruction facility conforms to the detailed facility information provided
Activity 5.2   Assess, to the extent practicable, the proposed chemical destruction process
Activity 5.2.1   Assess the design of the destruction process
Activity 5.2.2   Confirm the integrity of the destruction process

---

[9] Contained in PC-VI/B/WP.14, Annex, Appendix 3.

Activity 5.2.3	Confirm the integrity of the chemical transfer system
Activity 5.2.4	Discuss the normal operating conditions
Activity 5.2.5	Assess the key destruction parameters
Activity 5.2.6	Discuss the location of sample points and the procedures for the collection and analysis of samples from the destruction process
Activity 5.2.7	Assess the capability of the process to meet the proposed end-point of the destruction
Activity 5.2.8	Discuss the procedures for the collection and analysis of samples from the destruction process effluent
Activity 5.2.9	Discuss the options and procedures for process observation (if necessary with closed-circuit television)
Activity 5.2.10	Discuss the maintenance of monitoring and verification equipment
Activity 5.2.11	Assess the procedures for the destruction of metal parts (if necessary with closed-circuit television)
Activity 5.3	Discuss the extent to which the installed process monitoring system can be used to assist the verification process
Activity 5.4	Assess the provisions for workplace exposure monitoring
Activity 5.4.1	Check the location or proposed location for workplace monitoring instrumentation
Activity 5.4.2	Discuss the procedures for workplace environmental sample-taking and analysis
Activity 6	Review the on-site analytical facilities and equipment
Activity 6.1	Discuss the availability to the inspection teams of on-site analytical facilities and equipment
Activity 6.2	Assess the capability of the on-site analytical facilities and equipment
Activity 7	Visit and assess, where appropriate, the temporary munition holding area7
Activity 7.1	Assess that the size and design of the holding area is consistent with the agreed definition for a holding area, i.e. that the amount of chemical weapons stored in such an area shall be limited to that capable of being destroyed during one week's normal operation of the facility
Activity 7.2	Discuss the procedures for inventorying munitions to be stored in this area
Activity 7.3	Discuss the procedures to be adopted for the tagging of chemical weapons for analysis
Activity 7.4	Discuss the procedures and methods for the analysis of samples collected from tagged munitions, sub-munitions, devices, containers, bulk and other equipment and agents
Activity 7.5	Discuss the provision of monitoring and verification equipment
Activity 8	Review the procedures to be used to confirm the destruction of CW munitions, sub-munitions, devices, bulk and other containers, equipment and agents destroyed
Activity 8.1	Discuss the proposed shipping/transfer documents
Activity 8.2	Discuss the procedures for inventory of the destroyed items (CW munitions, sub-munitions, devices, bulk and other containers, equipment and agents)
Activity 8.3	Discuss the procedures for determining the specific type and quantity of chemical weapons to be destroyed
Activity 8.4	Discuss the procedures for verifying the quantity of agent being destroyed during the destruction process
Activity 8.5	Discuss the procedures for confirming the destruction of CW munitions, sub-munitions, devices, bulk and other containers, equipment and agents
Activity 8.6	Agree on procedures for the preparation of samples for analysis
Activity 9	Initiate discussions on the facility agreement
Activity 10	Record findings for inclusion in the visit report and debrief the visited State Party

Activity 10.1 Provide the State Party with a copy of the preliminary visit report
Activity 10.2 Discuss and attempt to resolve any outstanding issues
Activity 10.3 Agree on target dates for further actions required by either the Secretariat or the
State Party, or by both parties

C. ACTIVITIES AFTER RETURN OF THE INSPECTORS TO THE OPCW

Activity 11   Complete and file the visit report with the Technical Secretariat

PART II
DRAFT GUIDELINES FOR VERIFICATION PROCEDURES OF A CHEMICAL WEAPONS
DESTRUCTION FACILITY FOR THE PERIOD COVERING (BOD minus 60 DAYS)
TO BOD

A. ACTIVITIES PRIOR TO ARRIVAL OF THE INSPECTION TEAM

Activity 1   Review documentation, available data and other information on the facility to be
inspected
Activity 1.1   Review the inspected State Party's general and annual destruction plans
Activity 1.2   Review detailed facility information submitted by inspected State Party, and
Activity 1.3   Review facility agreement including verification plan
Activity 2   Review and, if applicable, update logistical requirements
Activity 3   Prepare and verify inspection equipment (check authentication)

B. ACTIVITIES AT THE INSPECTED FACILITY

Activity 4   Upon arrival at the facility:
Activity 4.1   Receive pre-inspection briefing (updating of the pre-inspection briefing related to
the initial visit)
Activity 4.2   Walk through the destruction facility
Activity 4.3   Update documentation and data (to include health and safety documentation) as
appropriate, and
Activity 4.4   Review and discuss verification activities with the inspected State Party, amend
proposed verification activities as necessary
Activity 5   Activities during the 60-day period before BOD

DESTRUCTION PROCESS
Activity 5.1   Confirm the conformity of the design of the destruction process with the updated
information provided
Activity 5.2   Assess, to the extent practicable, the destruction process
Activity 5.3   Assess whether the proposed time frame for BOD is realistic

ON-SITE MONITORING
Activity 5.4   Discuss, review and update, if applicable, monitoring equipment installed for the
confirmation of destruction of CW
Activity 5.5   Confirm that the equipment operates in a satisfactory manner
Activity 5.6   Stipulate, if applicable, the requirement for additional equipment
Activity 5.7   If appropriate, update the arrangements for the verification and maintenance of
installed monitoring equipment

SAMPLING AND ANALYSIS
Activity 5.8   Confirm the location of sampling locations and, if applicable, update the
procedures and equipment to be used

Activity 5.9   Verify the presence and confirm the suitability of analytical equipment and amend requirements as necessary

Activity 5.10   Check the arrangements for the calibration of analytical equipment and undertake calibration as necessary

Activity 5.11   Review and, if necessary, update analytical procedures

Activity 5.12   Periodically walk through facility and check progress of operations

Activity 6   Activities related to CW holding area (if and when applicable)

Activity 6.1   Review and update documentation on CW stored at the CW destruction facility

Activity 6.2   Inspect and inventory CW holding area (identification and quantity)

Activity 6.3   When applicable update the inventory

Activity 6.4   Tag the CW for analysis (when appropriate)

Activity 6.5   Periodically walk through the holding area

Activity 7   Activities immediately preceding BOD

Activity 7.1   If appropriate, review and update any document

Activity 7.2   Verify inspection equipment and installed monitoring equipment

Activity 7.3   Perform a general review of the destruction process including the key parameters

Activity 7.4   Participate in any training activities related to the destruction in accordance with the model facility agreement and verification plan

PART III

DRAFT GUIDELINES FOR VERIFICATION PROCEDURES OF
A CHEMICAL WEAPONS DESTRUCTION FACILITY FOR THE PERIOD
COVERING BOD TO ROUTINE OPERATION

A.   ACTIVITIES PRIOR TO THE ARRIVAL OF THE INSPECTION TEAM

Activity 1   Review updated documentation, available data and other information on the facility to be inspected to include:
                (a) the inspected State Party's general and annual destruction plans;
                (b) the detailed facility information submitted by the inspected State Party;
                (c) the logistical requirements for the support of systematic verification;
                (d) the facility agreement (to include the verification plan).

B.   ACTIVITIES AT THE INSPECTED FACILITY

Activity 2   Receive initial briefing

Activity 3   Confirm and, if necessary, update the verification activities with the inspected State Party (at any time) and facility agreement (to include health and safety aspects)

Activity 4   Confirm the functionality of the facility and the destruction process(es) during the commissioning of the destruction facilities

Activity 4.1   Confirm the following:
                (a) the design of the destruction process;
                (b) the chemical transfer systems;
                (c) the operating conditions;
                (d) the key destruction parameters.

Activity 4.2   Assess the adequacy of the facility to meet the destruction time frames proposed by the State Party and/or imposed by the Convention

Activity 5   Confirm the adequacy of sampling locations, equipment and procedures for the collection and analysis of samples from the destruction process and destruction process effluent

Activity 6	Confirm the adequacy of procedures for process observation and monitoring in confirming the destruction of CW
Activity 7	Confirm and verify the effectiveness of the destruction (capability to meet the destruction end-point)
Activity 8	Confirm and verify the effectiveness of the destruction of metal parts
Activity 9	Confirm and, when applicable, improve the maintenance of monitoring and verification equipment
Activity 10	Visit the temporary holding area and confirm procedures to check transfer of CW
Activity 10.1	inventory of CW temporary holding area
Activity 10.2	tagging of CW for analysis
Activity 10.3	verify shipping/transfer documents
Activity 11	Verify the specific type and quantity of CW destroyed
Activity 12	Record findings for inclusion in periodic reports and/or the final report
Activity 13	Discuss and attempt to resolve any outstanding issues

PART IV

DRAFT HEADLINES TO ESTABLISH GUIDELINES FOR VERIFICATION PROCEDURES
FOR A CW DESTRUCTION FACILITY DURING SYSTEMATIC VERIFICATION

A.   ACTIVITIES PRIOR TO THE ARRIVAL OF THE INSPECTION TEAM

Activity 1	Review updated documentation and available data and other information on the facility to be inspected, to include: (a) the inspected State Party's general and annual destruction plans; (b) the detailed facility information submitted by the inspected State Party; (c) the facility agreement, to include the verification plan.
Activity 2	Review the logistical requirements and the schedule of delivery of supplies (qualitative, quantitative, time frame)
Activity 3	Review former visit or inspection reports
Activity 4	Prepare and verify inspection equipment (check authentication)
Activity 5	Prepare a draft plan for personnel turn-over

B.   ACTIVITIES AT THE INSPECTED FACILITY TO BE CONDUCTED IMMEDIATELY
     AFTER ARRIVAL

Activity 6	On arrival at the facility receive a pre-inspection briefing (to include updated information)
Activity 7	As appropriate, review the health and safety regulations, procedures and requirements of the OPCW and the inspected State Party with the State Party
Activity 8	Walk through the inspected facility
Activity 9	Discuss any outstanding issues concerning future activities. Review and, if appropriate, update the verification activities with the inspected State Party

C.   ACTIVITIES DURING SYSTEMATIC VERIFICATION

Activity 10	Confirm the destruction process
Activity 10.1	Confirm the chemical destruction process
Activity 10.1.1	Monitor the destruction process, to include: (a) the integrity of the destruction process; (b) the integrity of the chemical transfer system; (c) the current operating conditions; (d) the key destruction parameters; (e) the destruction end-point.

Activity 10.1.2	Observe the destruction process: (a) with monitoring equipment such as closed- circuit television; (b) periodically walk through the facility.
Activity 10.1.3	Control or ensure sampling and analysis collection and analysis of samples from the destruction process and destruction process effluents following agreed procedures (*cf.* Part I, Activity 8.6 of this Appendix) for the preparation of samples for analysis
Activity 10.2	Confirm the destruction of the metal parts of chemical weapons
Activity 10.2.1	Monitor and observe the destruction of metal parts
Activity 10.2.2	Confirm the destruction of these items in accordance with the facility agreement
Activity 10.2.3	Periodically walk through the facility
Activity 11	Inspect and inventory the temporary holding area for CW
Activity 11.1	Inventory the CW holding area
Activity 11.1.1	Inspect the stored items and conduct an inventory of them
Activity 11.1.2	When appropriate, tag chemical weapons for analysis
Activity 11.2	Inspect the shipping/transfer documents
Activity 11.3	Where and when appropriate, control or ensure sampling and analysis
Activity 12	Confirm destruction
Activity 12.1	Confirm the destruction of CW munitions, sub-munitions, devices, bulk and other containers, equipment and agents destroyed
Activity 12.2	Inventory destroyed items to include determining the precise quantity of agent destroyed
Activity 13	If applicable, verify environmental monitoring
Activity 14	Verify and check the maintenance of installed equipment for monitoring and verification of destruction
Activity 15	Discuss anomalies to obtain clarification from the inspected State Party
Activity 16	If necessary, request appropriate adjustments of the destruction process and/or any documents

D.   ADMINISTRATIVE ACTIVITIES

Activity 17	Compose periodic/final report
Activity 18	Prepare for the inspection team turnover and, when applicable, the briefing/debriefing of personnel

5.7 Guidelines with respect to the applicability of bilateral/multilateral verification procedures

C-I/DEC.21 adopted by the Conference of the States Parties at its First Session on 16 May 1997 and entitled "Guidelines with respect to the applicability of bilateral/multilateral verification procedures". For text of the decision, see Section 4.8.

5.8 Criteria for the applicability and sufficiency of bilateral/multilateral verification procedures

C-I/DEC.25 adopted by the Conference of the States Parties at its First Session on 16 May 1997 and entitled "Criteria for the applicability and sufficiency of bilateral/multilateral verification procedures"

The Conference

Recalling that the Commission, in its PC-VI/22, subparagraph 6.8(i), adopted the criteria for the applicability and sufficiency of bilateral/multilateral verification procedures,

Bearing in mind that the Commission recommended in paragraph 49.2.5 of its Final Report that the Conference adopt the above mentioned criteria,

Hereby:
1. Adopts the criteria for the applicability and sufficiency of bilateral/multilateral verification procedure, annexed hereto.

ANNEX

GENERIC APPLICABILITY OF BILATERAL/MULTILATERAL VERIFICATION PROCEDURES

1. In accordance with paragraphs 13 and 16 of Article IV, the OPCW shall consider measures to avoid the unnecessary duplication of bilateral and multilateral agreements on the verification of chemical weapons destruction between States Parties when:
    (a) the verification provisions of such an agreement are consistent with the verification provisions of Article IV, paragraph 13 and Part IV(A);
    (b) the implementation of such an agreement provides sufficient assurance of compliance with the relevant provisions of the Convention;
    (c) parties to the bilateral or multilateral agreement keep the OPCW fully informed about their verification activities.
2. The Executive Council shall decide to limit the OPCW's verification to measures complementary to those undertaken pursuant to such a bilateral or multilateral agreement by assessing it and its implementation against the following criteria:
    (a) consistency;
    (b) comprehensiveness; and
    (c) effectiveness.
3. The following should be evaluated against the above criteria when relevant or appropriate:
    (a) the definition of chemical weapons: the definition of chemical weapons in relation to a bilateral or multilateral agreement must be consistent with the definition of chemical weapons in the CWC;
    (b) declarations: there should be provisions in a bilateral or multilateral treaty for the declaration of the general plan for destruction, detailed annual plans for destruction, and annual reports on destruction of chemical weapons and detailed facility information, in a form that is compatible with the OPCW's declaration formats;
    (c) inspection regimes: there should be provision for an initial visit and for subsequent systematic on-site monitoring of chemical weapons destruction facilities to verify both the declarations referred to in 3(b) above and the destruction process and these should reflect an effectiveness sufficient to satisfy the requirements of the Convention. The burden of proof of the effectiveness of the bilateral/multilateral inspection regime lies with the parties to the bilateral/multilateral agreements. Indicators of bilateral/multilateral verifi-

cation effectiveness might include, *inter alia*, the frequency of inspections, notification timelines, and the intensity of inspections of equivalent facilities that are conducted by the OPCW;

(d) facility agreements: there should be an agreement mechanism which meets the requirements of the Convention for a facility agreement for each declared chemical weapons destruction facility. The facility agreements should be consistent with the facility agreements employed by the OPCW;

(e) provision of information: the following information shall be provided to the OPCW by the States involved in bilateral or multilateral agreements:

    (i) inspection reports, to be available to the Director-General within a time frame comparable to the submission of reports of inspections conducted by the OPCW;

    (ii) facility agreements or appropriate mechanisms as noted in 3(d) above; and

    (iii) notifications that could trigger multilateral monitoring activities, e.g. intent to conduct an inspection; and

    (iv) copies of declarations exchanged between parties to the bilateral/multilateral agreement. Such copies of declarations should provide information additional to that required by the OPCW's declaration formats that is relevant to the aims of the Convention.

4. The Executive Council should assess the sufficiency of bilateral/multilateral verification agreements against the criteria of consistency, comprehensiveness and effectiveness to determine whether the complementary measures or provisions of the verification regime shall apply.

5. If complementary measures have been implemented by the Executive Council, the Director-General should report to the Executive Council on the verification activities taken by the parties to bilateral/multilateral agreements and on the complementary measures. This should include an assessment of their effectiveness.

6. Should the Director-General at any time have uncertainties about the effectiveness of any bilateral/multilateral inspection regime, he shall approach the States Parties for clarification. If the uncertainties cannot be removed or if the facts established suggest that obligations undertaken under this Convention have not been met, the Director-General shall inform the Executive Council without delay.

7. If the Executive Council finds reason to doubt the effectiveness of any bilateral/multilateral agreement, it should consider directing the implementation of the OPCW's verification regime. The Executive Council should take appropriate measures aimed at clarifying the issue prior to directing such action.

8. In accordance with paragraph 16 of Article IV of the Convention, if the Executive Council decides to limit the OPCW's verification measures to complementary measures, the costs of these measures shall be paid in accordance with the United Nations scale of assessment as specified in paragraph 7 of Article VIII of the Convention.

6. CHEMICAL WEAPONS PRODUCTION FACILITY (CWPF) ISSUES

6.1 Understanding on the procedures for the closure/inactivation of a CWPF

C-I/DEC.24 adopted by the Conference of the States Parties at its First Session on 16 May 1997 and entitled "Procedures for the closure/inactivation of a CWPF"

The Conference

Recalling that the Commission, in its PC-V/12, subparagraph 6.2(a), adopted the understanding that the set of procedures identified as being necessary for the closure/inactivation of CWPFs in the context of their subsequent destruction or, pending a final decision, their temporary conversion to chemical weapons destruction facilities or possible conversion for purposes not prohibited by the Convention, should apply in all of the above three cases,

Bearing in mind that the Commission recommended in paragraph 49.3.5 of its Final Report that the Conference adopt the above mentioned procedures and understanding,

Hereby:

1. Adopts the procedures necessary for the closure/inactivation of CWPFs in the context of their subsequent destruction or, pending a final decision, their temporary conversion to chemical weapons destruction facilities or possible conversion for purposes not prohibited by the Convention, annexed hereto, as well as the understanding that the above mentioned procedures should apply in all of the three cases.[1]

ANNEX

CHART 1	GUIDELINES FOR CLOSURE/INACTIVATION OF CWPFS	
Requirements under paragraph 13 of Part V	Illustrative examples of minimum closure activities	Recommended additional measures to reduce the risk of the facility
13 (a) Prohibition of the occupation of specialised buildings and standard buildings of the facility except for agreed activities.	(a) Disconnect, seal off and shutdown utility connections except for agreed activities as appropriate; (b) Seal all doors except those required to undertake agreed activities. Establish control and logging procedures for all unsealed doors.	(i) Disconnect, seal off and shut down all utility connections (except for safety and environmental purposes)
13 (b) Disconnection of equipment directly related to the production of chemical weapons, *inter alia*, process control equipment and utilities	(a) Disconnect all utility connections to specialised equipment; (b) Disconnect and seal off all inlets and outlets connected to specialised equipment; (c) Disconnect, seal off and shutdown all utilities connections to standard equipment; (d) Disconnect and seal off all inlets and outlets connected to standard equipment; (e) Disconnect control circuits to any power operated valves and sensors to measure technological parameters. (f) Use physical and tamper resistant seals	(i) Remove all specialised equipment from production area, store in a declared secure location;[1] (ii) Remove all connecting piping from standard equipment
13(c) Decommissioning of protective installations and equipment used exclusively for the safety of operations of the CWPF.	(a) Render inoperable specialised features of the building unless required for safety during destruction/conversion of the facility.	(i) Remove some or all of the specialised features of the building unless required for safety during destruction of the facility. Store in a secure location.

---

[1] The Delegation of the Islamic Republic of Iran made a reservation on the issue of a declared secure location. In its view "secure location" should be defined in order to minimise the misuse of dismantled specialised equipment between EIF and the initial inspection by the Technical Secretariat [footnote in original].

CHART 1	GUIDELINES FOR CLOSURE/INACTIVATION OF CWPFs	
13 (d) Installation of blind flanges and other devices to prevent the addition of chemicals to, or the removal of chemicals from, any specialised process equipment for synthesis, separation or purification of chemicals defined as a chemical weapon, any storage tank, or any machine for filling chemical weapons, the heating, cooling, or supply of electrical or other forms of power to such equipment, storage tanks, or machines	(a) Drain and undertake primary decontamination of CW process equipment and filling machines. Insert blind flanges. (b) Drain heating and cooling liquids and insert blind flanges. (c) Empty storage tanks and cylinders, e.g. liquid, compressed air or gases exclusively used for the production of chemical weapons and insert blind flanges. (d) Disconnect, seal off and shut down external water, electric, sewage, steam and piped natural gas connections, etc. to the extent that this will not preclude agreed activities from being undertaken.	
13 (e) Interruption of rail, road and other access routes for heavy transport to the chemical weapons production facility except those required for agreed activities	(a) Disconnect and seal off material pipelines leading from facility except those required for disposal or destruction of waste; (b) Interrupt rail, road and other heavy transport access routes except as required for agreed activities; (c) Render pipeline connections to facility inactive (e.g., using seals and blind flanges); (d) disconnect swing-lines or pipe bridges except as required for agreed activities (e) Adjust security measures to that appropriate with a closed/inactivated CWPF.	(i) Disconnect, dismantle and seal off material pipelines from facility except as required for destruction/conversion; (See paragraph 8 of Chairman's paper); (ii) Dismantle rail, road and other heavy transport access routes except as required for agreed activities.

6.2 Understanding regarding primary decontamination of CWPFs

C-I/DEC.23 adopted by the Conference of the States Parties at its First Session on 16 May 1997 and entitled "Primary decontamination of the chemical weapons production facility"

The Conference

Recalling that the Commission, in its PC-V/12, subparagraph 6.2(b), adopted the understanding that, in order to ensure the safe conduct of on-site inspections, a State Party should be encouraged to complete the primary decontamination of the CWPF as part of its closure and inactivation measures,

Recalling the understanding that some limited decontamination capability may be required after closure and inactivation to ensure the safety of inspectors and personnel,

Recalling also the understanding that a decontamination capability may also be required to provide safe conditions for dismantling and destroying the plant and to avoid potential environmental contamination,

Recalling that the Commission noted that, in connection with these decontamination requirements, a limited amount of safety equipment will be required,

Bearing in mind that the Commission recommended in paragraph 49.3.5 of its Final Report that the Conference adopt the above mentioned understanding,

Hereby:

1.   Adopts the understanding regarding primary decontamination of the chemical weapons production facilities.

6.3 Temporary conversion of CWPFs to CWDFs

C-I/DEC.28 C adopted by the Conference of the States Parties at its First Session on 16 May 1997 and entitled "Temporary conversion of chemical weapons production facilities to chemical weapons destruction facilities"

The Conference

Recalling that the Commission, in its PC-VII/8, subparagraph 6.10, adopted the understandings in relation to the temporary conversion of chemical weapons production facilities to chemical weapons destruction facilities,

Bearing in mind that the Commission recommended in paragraph 49.3.5 of its Final Report that the Conference adopt the above mentioned understandings,

Hereby:
1. Adopts the understandings in relation to the temporary conversion of chemical weapons production facilities to chemical weapons destruction facilities, annexed hereto.

ANNEX

TEMPORARY CONVERSION OF CHEMICAL WEAPONS PRODUCTION FACILITIES TO CHEMICAL WEAPONS DESTRUCTION FACILITIES

1. A State Party intending to convert temporarily a chemical weapons production facility for use in the destruction of chemical weapons shall notify the Technical Secretariat not later than 30 days after the Convention enters into force for the State Party or no later than 30 days after its decision to convert temporarily the facility for purposes of destruction;
2. In the absence of clear provisions within the Convention concerning the precise contents of such a notification the following information shall be provided:
   2.1 the name, address, and precise location of the facility;
   2.2 a site diagram indicating all the structures and areas that will be involved in the destruction of chemical weapons and which also identifies all structures of the chemical weapons production facility that is to be temporarily converted;
   2.3 the types of chemical weapons, and the type and quantity of chemical fill to be destroyed at the temporarily converted facility;
   2.4 the destruction method(s);
   2.5 a process flow diagram indicating which parts of the production process and which items of specialised equipment will be converted for the destruction of chemical weapons;
   2.6 the seals and inspection equipment potentially affected by the conversion; and
   2.7 a schedule identifying the time allocated to each of the following operations:
      (a) process design,
      (b) temporary conversion of the facility,
      (c) installation of equipment,
      (d) process commissioning,
      (e) chemical weapon destruction operations,
      (f) closure.
3. After the initial notification, the State Party shall document the status of the temporary conversion of the chemical weapons production facility in the plans that it provides pursuant to paragraphs 6 and 29 of Part IV(A) of the Verification Annex.
4. The State Party shall provide to the Secretariat detailed facility information pursuant to paragraphs 30, 31, 32 and 33 of Part IV(A) not less than twelve months prior to the start of destruction operations in order to assist in the development of preliminary inspection proce-

dures for use at the facility.

5. No later than 90 days after receiving the initial notification of the intent to convert temporarily a chemical weapons production facility, the Technical Secretariat shall have the right to visit the facility to familiarise itself with the proposed temporary conversion and to study possible inspection measures that will be required during the conversion.

6. No later than 60 days after such a visit, the State Party shall conclude a transitional facility agreement with the Technical Secretariat containing additional inspection measures covering the temporary conversion period. This agreement shall specify procedures for inspections, including the use of seals and monitoring equipment, to ensure that no chemical weapons production takes place during the temporary conversion process. It shall remain in force from the beginning of the temporary conversion until the converted facility begins operation as a chemical weapons destruction facility.

7. The inspected State Party shall not remove or convert any part of the facility, or remove or modify any seal or other agreed item of inspection equipment that may have been installed before concluding the transitional facility agreement.

8. Arrangements for the commissioning phase shall be governed by the transitional facility agreement. Once the facility begins operation as a chemical weapons destruction facility, it shall be subject to systematic verification as provided for under Part IV(A)(c).

9. During destruction, the inspectors shall have access to all parts of the temporarily converted production facility, including those that are not directly involved with the destruction of chemical weapons.

10. Prior to the commencement of work at the facility to convert it temporarily for chemical weapons destruction purposes and after the facility has ceased to function as a facility for chemical weapons destruction, the facility shall be subject to the provisions of Part V.

6.4 Agreed guidelines for "levelling out" in the destruction of CWPFs

C-I/DEC.29 adopted by the Conference of the States Parties at its First Session on 16 May 1997 and entitled "Destruction of chemical weapons production facilities"

The Conference

Recalling that the Commission, in its PC-XIV/29, subparagraph 9.2, adopted the document entitled "Destruction of chemical weapons production facilities", which is annexed to PC-XIV/B/WP.2,

Bearing in mind that the Commission recommended in paragraph 49.3.5 of its Final Report that the Conference adopt the above mentioned document,

Hereby:

1. Adopts the document entitled "Destruction of chemical weapons production facilities", annexed hereto.

ANNEX
DESTRUCTION OF CHEMICAL WEAPONS PRODUCTION FACILITIES

INTRODUCTION

1. This document presents the agreed guidelines for "levelling out" in the destruction of CWPFs.

2. In accordance with Part V, subparagraph 30(d) of the Verification Annex both chemical weapons production facilities supplying chemicals to the Schedule 1 facility and any associated Schedule 1 filling facilities will be destroyed at the same time as the Schedule 1 production facility.

3. In accordance with Part V, paragraph 31, for facilities not covered by Part V, paragraph 30 including, *inter alia*, those facilities referred to in Part V, paragraph 27, destruction will begin not later than one year after entry into force for the State Party and will be completed not later than five years after the entry into force of the Convention. The schedule for destruction will be agreed between the Organisation and the State Party.

RESIDUAL PRODUCTION CAPACITY

4. In accordance with Part V of the Verification Annex (VA), subparagraphs 30(a) to (c), the maximum permitted residual production capacity of Schedule 1 CWPFs at the end of the eighth year after entry into force (EIF) would be 20% of the original; and that the permitted residual production capacity at the end of the three destruction periods would be as follows:

End of year 5	60%.	Destruction in initial period	40%
End of year 8	20%.	Destruction in second period	40%
End of Year 10	Zero.	Destruction in final period	20%.

5. The residual capacity at the end of each destruction period shall be based upon the aggregate percentage for all CWPFs within a State Party in accordance with VA, Part V, paragraph 29. This is to enable States Parties to proceed with the destruction in the most economic and efficient manner.
6. In accordance with VA, Part V, paragraph 26 all equipment and buildings, both standard and specialised, must be physically destroyed for a CWPF to be considered destroyed.

LEVELLING OUT OF PRODUCTION CAPACITY

7. In determining what has to be destroyed VA, Part V, paragraphs 8 and 9 indicate that production capacity and buildings/equipment will need to be taken into account and included into the annual destruction plan. The relative weighting to be given to these factors is shown in Table 1 below.
8. Table 2 below provides guidance on the weighting factors to be associated with the destruction of groups of items to be destroyed in manufacturing and/or filling facilities as comparison factors for the levelling out of production capacity. These items and their configuration may differ from facility to facility. This being so, the percentage values and items assigned to them which are proposed in Tables 2(a) to (c) may need to be interpreted for specific cases. Weighting factors are provided for three types of facility. Those where:
    a. manufacture and filling have taken place;
    b. manufacture only has taken place; and
    c. filling only has taken place.
    It should be noted that in order to qualify for the given percentage reduction indicated in Tables 2(a) to (c), all items within a given group must be destroyed.
9. The percentage values in Tables 2(a) to (c) (which add up to 100%) comprise the 75% associated with the items of specialised equipment to be destroyed in Table 1 below.
10. The Technical Secretariat (TS) will verify which of the items have been destroyed and that these items have been destroyed. If the percentages referred to in paragraph 4 of this Annex are not reached by the State Party or if the actual progress of destruction of a CWPF does not correspond to the agreed plan for the destruction of this CWPF, the TS will follow the procedures outlined in Part II of the Verification Annex, paragraphs 64 and 65.

Table 1 – Destruction of chemical weapons production facilities

ITEMS TO BE DESTROYED	ASSIGNED VALUE
Specialised equipment	75%
Standard equipment	4%
Specialised buildings	16%
Standard Buildings	5%

Table 2(a) – Manufacturing and filling facilities

ITEMS TO BE DESTROYED	VALUE
The main production train, including any reactor or equipment for product synthesis, any equipment used directly for heat transfer in the final technological stage: this includes, but is not restricted to, mixers, integral process control equipment, pumps, valves and piping, as well as to any other equipment which has been in contact with any chemical specified in Article II, subparagraph 8(a)(i), or would be in contact with such a chemical if the facility were operated.	35%
Chemical weapons filling machines and loading equipment	35%
The main production train, including any specialised purification and separation equipment: this includes, but is not restricted to, distillation, extraction, crystallisation, filtration and centrifugation equipment, as well as any other equipment which has been in contact with any chemical specified in Article II, subparagraph 8(a)(i), or would be in contact with such a chemical if the facility were operated.	15%
Other equipment specifically designed, built or installed for the operation of the facility as a chemical weapons production facility, as distinct from a facility constructed according to prevailing commercial industry standards for facilities not producing any chemical specified in Article II, subparagraph 8(a)(i) or corrosive chemicals, such as: equipment made of high nickel alloys or other special corrosion resistant material; special equipment for waste control, waste treatment, air filtering, or solvent recovery; special containment enclosures and safety shields; non-standard laboratory equipment used to analyse toxic chemicals for CW purposes; custom designed process control panels; or dedicated spares for specialised equipment.	15%

Table 2(b) – Manufacturing facilities

ITEMS TO BE DESTROYED	VALUE
The main production train, including any reactor or equipment for product synthesis, any equipment used directly for heat transfer in the final technological stage: this includes, but is not restricted to, mixers, integral process control equipment, pumps, valves and piping, as well as any other equipment which has been in contact with any chemical specified in Article II, subparagraph 8(a)(i), or would be in contact with such a chemical if the facility were operated.	70%
The main production train, including any specialised purification and separation equipment: this includes, but is not restricted to, distillation, extraction, crystallisation, filtration and centrifugation equipment, as well as any other equipment which has been in contact with any chemical specified in Article II, subparagraph 8(a)(i), or would be in contact with such a chemical if the facility were operated.	15%
Other equipment specifically designed, built or installed for the operation of the facility as a chemical weapons production facility, as distinct from a facility constructed according to prevailing commercial industry standards for facilities not producing any chemical specified in Article II, subparagraph 8(a)(i) or corrosive chemicals, such as: equipment made of high nickel alloys or other special corrosion resistant material; special equipment for waste control, waste treatment, air filtering, or solvent recovery; special containment enclosures and safety shields; non-standard laboratory equipment used to analyse toxic chemicals for CW purposes; custom designed process control panels; or dedicated spares for specialised equipment.	15%

Table 2(c) – Filling facilities

ITEMS TO BE DESTROYED	VALUE
Chemical weapons filling machines and loading equipment	85%
Other equipment specifically designed, built or installed for the operation of the facility as a chemical weapons production facility, as distinct from a facility constructed according to prevailing commercial industry standards such as equipment made of high nickel alloys or other special corrosion resistant material; special equipment for waste control, waste treatment or air filtering; special containment enclosures and safety shields; non-standard laboratory equipment used to analyse toxic chemicals for CW purposes; custom designed process control panels; or dedicated spares for specialised equipment.	15%

6.5 Changes in equipment or plans at a facility converted for purposes not prohibited under the Convention

C-IV/DEC.8 adopted by the Conference of the States Parties at its Fourth Session on 29 June 1999 and entitled "Changes in chemical process equipment or plans for new types of chemical products at a facility converted for purposes not prohibited under this Convention"

The Conference

Recalling the decision of the Executive Council contained in EC-MIV/DEC.2, dated 26 March 1999;

Hereby:

Confirms that if new chemical process equipment is to be installed by a State Party in a converted facility, or if new types of chemical products are planned for production at a converted facility, the State Party shall notify the Technical Secretariat not later than 90 days before the changes are to take place. The Technical Secretariat shall forward this notification, along with its evaluation as to whether the changes in the converted facility have met the requirements under paragraph 71 of Part V of the Verification Annex, to members of the Executive Council for consideration not later than 60 days before the changes are to take place. If an objection is raised by any member of the Executive Council within 30 days of receipt of the notification and evaluation, the Executive Council shall promptly consider the issue and shall forward its recommendation to the Conference of the States Parties for appropriate action, if necessary.

7. ARTICLE VI ISSUES (ACTIVITIES NOT PROHIBITED)

7.1 Understandings and generally applicable clarifications

7.1.1 The scope of the term "alkyl" in the Schedules of chemicals

C-I/DEC.35 adopted by the Conference of the States Parties at its First Session on 16 May 1997 and entitled "Scope of the term 'alkyl' in the Schedules of chemicals"

The Conference

Recalling that the Commission, in its PC-VII/8, paragraph 6.6, adopted an understanding on the scope of the term "alkyl" in the Schedules of Chemicals (paragraph 3.1 of PC-VII/B/WP.7),

Bearing in mind that the Commission recommended in paragraph 50.4 of its Final Report that the Conference adopt the above mentioned understanding,

Hereby:

Adopts the following understanding:

In relation to the groups of chemicals ("families") listed in the Schedules of Chemicals, the terms 'alkyl', 'cycloalkyl', 'alkylated' or 'Me' (methyl), 'Et' (ethyl), 'n-Pr' (n-propyl) or 'i-Pr' (isopropyl) are to be understood literally, i.e. as not including any substituted alkyl, methyl, ethyl, etc.

7.1.2 The meaning of "production" for the purposes of Article VI

C-II/DEC.6 adopted by the Conference of the States Parties at its Second Session on 5 December 1997 and entitled "Meaning of 'production' as defined in Article II, subparagraph 12(a)"

The Conference

Having considered the issue of the meaning of the term "production" as used in Article II, subparagraph 12(a) of the Convention;

Taking note of the work of the Preparatory Commission on this issue;

Hereby:

Decides that the term "production" as used in subparagraph 12(a) of Article II should be understood to include a scheduled chemical (i.e. a Schedule 1, Schedule 2 or Schedule 3 chemical) produced by a biochemical or biologically mediated reaction.

7.1.3 Declarations

C-I/DEC.38 adopted by the Conference of the States Parties at its First Session on 16 May 1997 and entitled "Changes to annual declarations"

The Conference

Recalling that the Commission, in its PC-VII/8, paragraph 6.6, adopted an understanding on changes to annual in relation to industrial declarations,

Bearing in mind that the Commission recommended in paragraph 50.4 of its Final Report that the Conference adopt the above mentioned understanding,

Hereby:
1.   Adopts the understanding on changes to annual declarations.

ANNEX
CHANGES TO ANNUAL DECLARATIONS[1]

1.   It is understood that any change to those parts of the annual declaration that would not normally be expected to change from year to year, such as the name, address and location, should be communicated to the Technical Secretariat on the next occasion upon which a declaration is due.
2.   It is also understood that, even where there is no change to the substance of a declaration compared to a previous one, the information required under that later declaration shall be provided in full.
3.   In regard to the declaration of additional activities required in accordance with paragraphs 4(c) of Parts VII and VIII, the following was understood in regard to which changes need to be declared:
    (a) any change during the year that involves:
        (i)   an additional Schedule 2 plant or Schedule 3 plant;
        (ii) an additional Schedule 2 chemical or Schedule 3 chemical;
        (iii) an additional type of activity related to a Schedule 2 chemical (production, processing, consumption, direct export, or sale or transfer);
        (iv) any other non-quantitative change in relation to the anticipatory declarations, except for those to which paragraph 9 of PC-V/B/WP.15 applies;
    (b) any quantitative upward change that changes the status of a plant (crossing of the declaration or verification threshold);
    (c) any Schedule 3 plant which increases production above the range given in the anticipatory declaration;
    (d) any additional time period when a declarable activity in relation to a Schedule 2 chemical takes place;
    (e) any increase in the declared anticipated annual production/processing/ consumption figure for a Schedule 2 chemical.[2]
4.   In regard to subparagraph 3(d) above, it was understood that the declaration of time periods when declared activities are anticipated to occur should be as precise as possible, but should in any case be accurate to within a 3 month period. The declaration requirement in relation to these time periods does not necessarily mean that individual planned production (processing, consumption) campaigns need to be declared. Such an understanding, it was considered, might provide a flexible framework for industrial declarations and might reduce the frequency of declarations of additional activities in regard to time periods of production, and the processing or consumption of Schedule 2 chemicals.
5.   It was further agreed that it may also be useful if States Parties, on a voluntary basis, would inform the Technical Secretariat of cases when plants or plant sites which have been declared to undertake activities in relation to Schedule 2 or Schedule 3 chemicals cease to do so.

---

[1] As contained in paragraph 3.4 of PC-VII/B/WP.7.
[2] It is likely that plant sites, and hence State Parties, may show a tendency to include a certain margin in their anticipatory declaration [footnote in original].

C-I/DEC.36 adopted by the Conference of the States Parties at its First Session on 16 May 1997 and entitled "Sub-distribution and packaging"

The Conference

Recalling that the Commission, in its PC-VII/8, paragraph 6.6, adopted an understanding on sub-distribution and packaging in relation to processing of scheduled chemicals (paragraph 3.2 of PC-VII/B/WP.7),

Bearing in mind that the Commission recommended in paragraph 50.4 of its Final Report that the Conference adopt the above mentioned understanding,

Hereby:

Adopts the following understanding:

It is understood that the activities of sub-distribution and packaging are not to be considered as processing of scheduled chemicals and are therefore not subject to declaration.

EC-XIX/DEC.5 adopted by the Executive Council at its Nineteenth Session on 7 April 2000 and entitled "Rounding rule in relation to declarations of scheduled chemicals"

The Executive Council

Noting that some States Parties have expressed concern at the perceived lack of consistency in the application of rounding rules to declarations of scheduled chemicals;

Noting also that any decision on the rounding rule shall not prejudge any future decision on the methodology for collecting and declaring aggregate national data (AND);

Further noting that plant site declarations for Schedule 3 chemicals are made in ranges as prescribed by the Convention;

Bearing in mind that this rounding rule does not apply to notification and detailed annual declaration of transfers of Schedule 1 chemicals.

Hereby:

Decides to adopt the following rounding rule in relation to the declaration of scheduled chemicals, where applicable:

Quantities will be declared to three figures:

- quantities with more than three figures are to be rounded to three;
- quantities having fewer than three figures are to be extended to three by the addition of zeros; and
- zeros in front of the first non-zero digit are not counted.

Qualifiers:

(a) Quantities may be declared in the following units only:

picogramme	pg	10^{-12} g
nanogramme	ng	10^{-9} g
microgrammes	μg	10^{-6} g
milligrammes	mg	10^{-3} g
grammes	g	g
kilogrammes	kg	10^{3} g
tonnes	t	10^{6} g
kilotonnes	kt	10^{9} g

(b) Plant site/facility data for Schedule 1, 2 and 3 chemicals should be declared in the units that relate to the declaration threshold in the appropriate Part of the Verification Annex for the scheduled chemical being declared, e.g.:

Schedule	Unit
1	g/kg
2A*	kg/t
2A	kg/t
2B	t/kt
3	t (declared in ranges)

(c) For States Parties which include only quantities above declaration thresholds in their AND declarations, these same units may be used for AND.

(d) For States Parties which also include quantities below declaration thresholds in AND, smaller units may be appropriate.

(e) For States Parties which declare actual transfers of Schedule 3 chemicals in AND, t/kt units should be used.

(f) Examples of the application of this rounding rule are provided in the next table.

EXAMPLES OF THE ROUNDING RULE

FIGURE PROVIDED TO NATIONAL AUTHORITY	MAIN ROUNDING RULE OPTIONS
0.004 mg	0.00400 mg/4.00 µg
0.3 mg	0.300 mg/300 µg
0.8388 mg	0.839 mg/839 µg
1.674 mg	1.67 mg
1.677 mg	1.68 mg
5 mg	5.00 mg
0.002 g	0.00200 g/2.00 mg
100.5 g	101 g/0.101 kg
0.068 kg	0.0680 kg/68.0 g
266.6 kg	267 kg/0.267 t
1.66 t	1.66 t
104.4 t	104 t/0.104 kt
1004.5 t	1.00 kt
10539 t	10.5 kt

EC-36/DEC.7 adopted by the Executive Council at its Thirty-Sixth Session on 26 March 2004 and entitled "Clarification of declarations"

The Executive Council

Considering that clarification requests help the Technical Secretariat (hereinafter "the Secretariat") to effectively carry out its functions under the Chemical Weapons Convention (hereinafter "the Convention");

Further considering that timely responses by States Parties to such requests for clarification promote the effective and efficient implementation of the verification regime of the Convention;

Affirming the need for States Parties to improve implementation by pledging to respond to such requests as fully and as expeditiously as possible;

Specifying that nothing in this decision prejudices existing obligations under the Convention or creates additional ones;

Recalling the requirements under Article VIII, paragraph 40 of the Convention; and

Recognising the need to continue work on this issue, in particular on the issue of clarification of transfer discrepancies, and on the need for the Secretariat to continue to explore how it can best exchange confidential information with States Parties in accordance with the confidentiality procedures of the Convention;

Hereby:

Urges all States Parties to expedite responses to requests for clarification of their declarations, when these declarations do not involve other States Parties (i.e. transfer discrepancies), as follows: to send an initial response within 90 days after the official transmittal of the Secretariat's request which either responds fully to the request or indicates what steps they are taking to develop and communicate a full response; and

Recommends that, when the Secretariat issues a clarification request regarding possible errors or missing information in a submitted declaration that preclude the Secretariat from determining the facility's inspectability and receives no response from the State Party concerned within 90 days after the official transmittal of the Secretariat's request, the Secretariat inform the Council about the specific request in advance of its next regular session. The Secretariat will provide, 60 days following the issuance of the clarification request, a reminder to the State Party concerned.

EC-51/DEC.1 adopted by the Executive Council at its Fifty-First Session on 27 November 2007 and entitled "Timely Submission by States Parties of declarations under Article VI of the Convention"

The Executive Council

Bearing in mind that paragraphs 7 and 8 of Article VI of the Chemical Weapons Convention (hereinafter "the Convention"); and paragraphs 6, 13, 15, 16, 17, 19, and 20 of Part VI; paragraphs 1, 2, and 4 of Part VII; paragraphs 1, 2, and 4 of Part VIII; and paragraph 3 of Part IX of the Verification Annex to the Convention (hereinafter "the Verification Annex") require each State Party to submit the following:

(a) an initial declaration on relevant chemicals and facilities;

(b) annual declarations for relevant scheduled chemicals and related facilities; and

(c) any necessary updates to their lists of other chemical production facilities in accordance with the corresponding deadlines specified in the Convention;

Noting that the Conference of the States Parties (hereinafter "the Conference"), in its report of its Third Session (C-III/4, dated 20 November 1998), "expressed its serious concern at the significant number of States Parties to the Convention which have submitted no initial declarations or initial declarations in part only", urged States Parties that had failed to submit their initial declarations on time to do so without further delay, and also urged States Parties that had "submitted declarations in part only, particularly in the context of . . . paragraph 7 of Article VI, to submit without further delay the necessary additional parts of declarations or data required for their initial declarations to be complete";

Noting also that efforts by the Technical Secretariat (hereinafter "the Secretariat") and by the Conference after its Third Session resulted in significant progress being made in the submission of initial declarations, and with the expectation that similar success would ensue consequent to this decision;

Recalling that, at the First Special Session of the Conference of the States Parties to Review the Operation of the Chemical Weapons Convention, States Parties reaffirmed "their commitment to comply with all their obligations under all the provisions of the Convention, and their commitment to implement them fully, effectively, and in a manner which is non discriminatory and which further enhances confidence among the States Parties and between the States Parties and the Technical Secretariat of the Organisation for the Prohibition of Chemical Weapons (OPCW)" (RC-1/3, dated 9 May 2003);

Noting that the Executive Council (hereinafter "the Council"), at its Thirty-Eighth (EC-38/2, dated 15 October 2004) and Thirty-Ninth Sessions (EC-39/2, dated 14 December 2004), urged all States Parties to meet their obligations regarding annual declarations in a timely manner;

Noting also that the Council, at its Forty-Fourth Session, stressed anew that the submission of these declarations by States Parties is important both to the object and purpose of the Convention and to the non-discriminatory treatment of all States Parties, and also underscored the need to continue consultations on the matter within the corresponding cluster during the intersessional period (paragraph 5.21 of EC-44/2, dated 17 March 2006);

Acknowledging the important role that timely and accurate declarations play in allowing the Secretariat to efficiently and effectively carry out its verification activities;

Hereby requests:
1.   All States Parties that have yet to do so to adopt the necessary measures to ensure that their declarations are submitted in accordance with the deadlines provided for in the Convention;
2.   States Parties to adopt the necessary measures to implement the following obligations, specifically that:
     (a)   each State Party that has not yet submitted its initial declaration in accordance with the requirements of paragraph 7 of Article VI of the Convention, or that has submitted this initial declaration in part only, submit its initial declaration or complete it without further delay;
     (b)   each State Party that has indicated in its initial declaration that it does not have any declarable activities under Article VI of the Convention, but which now finds that it has declarable activities taking place within its territory, to submit the relevant annual declarations no later than 30 March 2008 and, in subsequent years, by the appropriate deadlines; and
     (c)   each State Party that has indicated in its initial declaration that it does have declarable activities under any of Parts VI, VII, VIII, and IX of the Verification Annex, but has not provided the relevant annual declarations, to submit these declarations no later than 30 March 2008, and by the appropriate deadlines in subsequent years;
3.   The States Parties referred to in paragraph 2 of this decision to inform the Secretariat by 30 March 2008 of the circumstances for not meeting these obligations and whether they would welcome assistance from the Secretariat in order to meet these obligations without further delay;
4.   States Parties that anticipate difficulties in regard to the timely submission of their declarations in accordance with the deadlines in the Convention to inform the Secretariat at the earliest possible date of the circumstances of such difficulties and whether they would welcome assistance from the Secretariat in order to meet their obligations on time;
5.   The Secretariat to:
     (a)   advise all States Parties of this decision and to make its requirements known at regional meetings and at any other venues that the Secretariat deems effective; and
     (b)   bring this decision to the particular attention of those States Parties affected by subparagraphs 2(a), 2(b), and 2(c) above;
6.   The Secretariat to prepare status reports for the Council on the implementation of this decision, particularly the submission of initial and annual declarations under Article VI and the ongoing efforts to assist States Parties in meeting their obligations under this decision, as well as the difficulties being encountered by States Parties pursuant to paragraphs 3 and 4 above,

in order to better facilitate assistance between States Parties on establishing declaration and submittal processes; and

7. The Council to keep under consideration the implementation of this decision and to take, if necessary, any appropriate measures to ensure the timely submission of declarations.

7.1.4 The frequency, duration, and intensity of inspection of industrial facilities

C-I/DEC.33 adopted by the Conference of the States Parties at its First Session on 16 May 1997 and entitled "Frequency, duration, and intensity of inspection of industrial facilities"

The Conference

Recalling that the Commission, in its PC-VI/22, sub-paragraph 6.2(a), adopted the understandings on the frequency, duration and intensity of inspection of industrial facilities,

Bearing in mind that the Commission recommended in paragraph 50.4 of its Final Report that the Conference adopt the above mentioned understanding,

Hereby:

1. Adopts the understandings on the frequency, duration, and intensity of inspection of industrial facilities annexed hereto.

ANNEX
FREQUENCY, DURATION, AND INTENSITY OF INSPECTION OF INDUSTRIAL FACILITIES[3]

The Executive Council will supervise the implementation of the verification activities undertaken by the Technical Secretariat. A decision on which industrial facilities to inspect and when will be a decision for the Technical Secretariat, based on the risk assessment. The number of inspections conducted by the Technical Secretariat at a particular facility will fall within the provisions of the Verification Annex in regard to the maximum number of inspections per plant site and per State Party, and in regard to conducting initial inspections at Schedule 2 plant sites as soon as possible, but preferably during the first three years after EIF, but will be dictated by a wide range of factors including the results of the risk assessment for the facility undertaken in accordance with paragraph 18 of Part VII, the number of other facilities to be inspected, and the number of inspectors available as inspection timetables are worked out.

7.1.5 Mixed plants

C-I/DEC.40 adopted by the Conference of the States Parties at its First Session on 16 May 1997 and entitled "Mixed plants"

The Conference

Recalling that the Commission, in its PC-VII/8, paragraph 6.6, adopted an understanding on mixed plants,

Bearing in mind that the Commission recommended in paragraph 50.4 of its Final Report that the Conference adopt the above mentioned understanding,

---

[3] As contained in paragraph 19 of the Chairman's Paper annexed to PC/VI/B/WP.5.

Hereby:

1. Adopts the understanding on mixed plants.

ANNEX
MIXED PLANTS[4]

1. "Mixed plants" are plants which are individually covered under more than one Part of the Verification Annex related to Article VI. The term covers, for example, a multipurpose plant that manufactures, in the same process line but at different points in time or parallel in several process lines, Schedule 2 and Schedule 3 chemicals (and/or DOCs). However, the term does not relate either to a case where a plant produces a Schedule 3 chemical in a multiple-step reaction involving the production of a DOC in the initial steps, or to a case when, during the production of a Schedule 3 chemical, a low concentration of a Schedule 2 chemical is simultaneously produced (this would be classified as either a Schedule 3 or a Schedule 2 plant depending on the applicable rules for low concentrations).

2. "Mixed plants" will be declared in accordance with all the appropriate Parts of the Verification Annex related to Article VI.

3. "Mixed plants" will be inspected according to the particular Part of the Verification Annex under which the inspection was mandated and will be limited to the provisions of that Part of the Verification Annex. In particular:

    (a) notification of an inspection of the plant site where a mixed plant is located will have to be timed in accordance with the applicable provision of the Part under which the inspection is initiated;

    (b) access within a "mixed plant" that is being inspected will be governed by the inspection provisions of the Part under which the inspection is initiated (Section E of Part VI, paragraphs 23 to 29 of Part VII, paragraphs 18 to 24 of Part VIII or paragraphs 15 to 20 of Part IX);

    (c) inspections at a "mixed plant" are counted separately for the different Parts of the Verification Annex. Each inspection at a "mixed plant" is consequently counted under the Part under which it is initiated.

4. It was understood that if it were possible for different parts of a plant to be configured in such a way that they could be inspected separately under the different procedures without overlap, these parts would be considered as separate plants and would be declared as such. In such cases, the concept of "mixed plants" would therefore not apply.

C-I/DEC.34 adopted by the Conference of the States Parties at its First Session on 16 May 1997 and entitled "Verification at mixed plant sites"

The Conference

Recalling that the Commission, in its PC-VI/22, sub-paragraph 6.2(a), adopted the understandings on verification at mixed plant sites,

Bearing in mind that the Commission recommended in paragraph 50.4 of its Final Report that the Conference adopt the above mentioned understanding,

Hereby:

1. Adopts the understandings on verification at mixed plant sites annexed hereto.

---

[4] As contained in paragraph 3.6 of PC-VII/B/WP.7.

ANNEX

VERIFICATION AT MIXED PLANT SITES[5]

1. "Mixed plant sites" are those plant sites which contain:
   (a) one or more plant(s) individually covered under more than one Part of the Verification Annex related to Article VI ("mixed plants"); or
   (b) different plants covered by different Parts of the Verification Annex related to Article VI.

2. As a general principle governing the rules for inspections at mixed plant sites, it is understood that an inspection will count under the relevant Part of the Verification Annex it was initiated under and will be limited to the provisions of that Part. If an inspection mission was to be conducted under two (or more) Parts of the Verification Annex, that mission would count as two (or more) sequential or simultaneous inspections and the provisions of the respective Parts, including those on notification times, would apply.

3. During inspections at mixed plant sites, the following rules will apply:
   (a) access to plants liable for inspection under another Part of the Verification Annex related to Article VI will be governed by:
       (i) in case of an inspection pursuant to Part VI of the Verification Annex, paragraph 51 of Part II and any additional provisions contained in the facility agreement;
       (ii) in case of an inspection pursuant to Part VII of the Verification Annex, paragraph 25 of Part VII;
       (iii) in case of an inspection pursuant to Part VIII of the Verification Annex, paragraph 20 of Part VIII;
       (iv) in case of an inspection pursuant to Part IX of the Verification Annex, paragraph 17 of Part IX;
   (b) access to parts of the common infrastructure of the plant site that are shared between plants covered under different Parts of the Verification Annex would not be considered access to that other plant;
   (c) access to shared records would have to be provided according to the same rule as that for physical access for inspectors as contained in sub-paragraph (b) above;
   (d) the maximum number of inspections at a mixed plant site is the accumulation of the maximum number of inspections possible under the different Parts related to Article VI;
   (e) an inspection pursuant to one Part of the Verification Annex during which the inspection team is, on a voluntary basis, granted access to a plant covered by another Part related to Article VI is counted as one inspection under the Part it was initiated under. Passage through the plant site to a plant that is the focus of inspection does not count as access to another plant, covered under another Part related to Article VI;
   (f) separate facility agreements will have to be negotiated for inspections to be conducted under the different Parts of the Verification Annex related to Article VI.

---

[5] As contained in paragraphs 21 to 24 of the Chairman's paper annexed to PC-VI/B/WP.2.

7.1.6 Operation of provisions on activities not prohibited since entry into force of the Convention

Extract of RC-2/S/1* containing a Note by the Technical Secretariat dated 31 March 2008 and entitled "Review of the Operation of the Chemical Weapons Convention since the First Review Conference". The annexes referred to in this Note are not reproduced in this volume.

...

ACTIVITIES NOT PROHIBITED UNDER THE CHEMICAL WEAPONS CONVENTION

COOPERATION OF THE CHEMICAL INDUSTRY

3.103 As a key player in the negotiation phase of the Convention, the involvement and support of the chemical industry was critical in drafting the non-proliferation provisions of the Convention. This high level of support has continued since EIF and is a major factor in the successful implementation of the Convention. By the end of 2007, over 1300 industry inspections had been conducted in 77 different countries with the full cooperation of the chemical industry.

DECLARATIONS UNDER ARTICLE VI

LATE SUBMISSIONS

3.104 Late declarations have a significant impact on the verification activities. Beginning in 2004, the Secretariat began reporting on the status of submissions of annual declarations (most recently in S/662/2007, dated 15 November 2007). The Secretariat's reports have been noted by the Council (EC-44/2, dated 17 March 2006). At its Fifty-First Session the Council adopted a decision in which, *inter alia*, it called upon States Parties that had yet to do so to take the necessary measures to ensure that their declarations were submitted in accordance with the deadlines provided for in the Convention, and requested States Parties that anticipated difficulties in regard to timely submission of their declarations to inform the Secretariat of the circumstances of such difficulties (EC-51/DEC.1, dated 27 November 2007). In accordance with this decision the Secretariat will prepare regular status reports to the Council on the implementation of this decision, the first of which will be submitted to the Council at its Fifty-Third Session. Detailed statistics on submissions from 2002 to 2006 are provided in Annex 1.

FACILITY AND PLANT-SITE DECLARATIONS

3.105 The numbers of Schedule 1 facilities and Schedule 2 and 3 plant sites declared have remained relatively constant in the period since the First Review Conference (see Annex 2). The number of OCPFs declared, and the number of States Parties making such declarations, increased steadily after the First Review Conference until 2006 (see Annex 2). The decrease seen in 2007 (based on ADPAs for 2006) was primarily due to several States Parties removing large numbers of OCPFs from their declared lists, following an initiative by the Secretariat to highlight the need for States Parties to review their lists of declared OCPFs and remove those that were no longer declarable.

ESTABLISHMENT OF COMMON STANDARDS OF DECLARATION

3.106 Following the First Review Conference, work has continued on establishing common standards of declaration to ensure a "level playing field" in the implementation of Article VI between different States Parties. Decisions have been taken by the Conference, setting out understandings on declarations of the captive-use production of Schedule 1 chemicals (C-10/DEC.12, dated 10 November 2005) and of Schedule 2 and 3 chemicals (C-9/DEC.6, dated 30 November 2004), as well as on clarifying the definition of "production" (C-8/DEC.7, dated 23 October 2003). However, in several areas, no agreement on common standards has been reached, including:

(a) guidelines on low concentration limits for mixtures containing Schedule 2A and 2A* chemicals;

(b) declaration of salts of scheduled chemicals (especially of Schedule 1 chemicals); and

(c) the scope of the definition of "production by synthesis" under Part IX of the Verification Annex.

3.107 Although the impact of some of these outstanding issues on the verification regime is arguably limited, implementation of the Convention will remain uneven without agreement by the policy-making organs on these issues.

3.108 Of particular importance is the lack of common standards for declaring aggregate national data (AND), which forms a key element of the data-monitoring component of the verification regime. Data monitoring is the only means available to the Secretariat to verify chemical activities for purposes not prohibited under the Convention in those States Parties that have no inspectable facilities (which at present is over half of all States Parties). The declaration of AND is stipulated in paragraph 1 of Part VII and paragraph 1 of Part VIII of the Verification Annex. The import and export data submitted under these provisions are the sole source of information that the Secretariat can use for monitoring data for States Parties without declarable facilities under Parts VII and VIII of the Verification Annex. They are also the Secretariat's only source of information in relation to transfers of scheduled chemicals to States not Party. The Secretariat has noted that the information declared by the exporting and importing States Parties often does not match and has reported this issue to the Council ("Declarations of Imports and Exports of Schedule 2/3 chemicals"; EC-XXIII/S.1, dated 12 January 2001).

3.109 Although guidelines for reporting AND were agreed upon at the Seventh Session of the Conference (C-7/DEC.14, dated 10 October 2002), the problem remains and during the Thirty-Fourth Session of the Council, the Secretariat distributed a discussion paper on the factors that contribute to discrepancies (EC-34/S/1, dated 3 September 2003; Add.1, dated 3 December 2003; and Corr.1, dated 12 September 2003). The discrepancies between transfers declared by States Parties are of such magnitude (as much as 75% of the import/export data declared in each of the last five years – see Annex 3) that effective data monitoring for non-proliferation purposes is very difficult for the Secretariat to achieve. Hence, the Secretariat believes that this issue should have a high priority.

3.110 The issue is currently being discussed during consultations under the cluster of chemical-industry and other Article VI issues. The focus of the consultations is on the development of an understanding on the meaning of the terms "import" and "export" for the purposes of making AND declarations under paragraph 1 of Part VII, and paragraph 1 of Part VIII, of the Verification Annex, and of declaring imports and exports from declared Schedule 2 plant sites (paragraph 8 of Part VII of the Verification Annex). In addition, a Secretariat proposal to adopt new criteria for discrepancies, which would focus on those that are most significant, was discussed in the consultations and was implemented for the evaluation of annual declarations of past activities for the year 2005.

3.111 The issue of whether States Parties should be required to inform the Secretariat when Schedule 2 and 3 plant sites stop activities related to Schedule 2 and 3 chemicals was raised at the First Review Conference. From the point of view of the Secretariat, timely information on plant-site activity, which can affect whether a particular facility is inspectable or not, greatly facilitates inspection planning. The First Session of the Conference urged States Parties to inform the Secretariat, on a voluntary basis, of cases when plants or plant sites that have been declared as undertaking activities in relation to Schedule 2 or Schedule 3 chemicals cease to do so (C-I/DEC.38, dated 16 May 1997). This recommendation was reiterated by the First Review Conference, which also requested the Council to consider whether to make such submissions from States Parties a formal requirement. Although some States Parties are implementing this recommendation, in some cases the Secretariat is left with no clear idea as to whether or not a site is inspectable, resulting in the need for clarification.

IMPROVEMENTS IN THE SUBMISSION AND HANDLING OF DECLARATIONS

3.112 A key advance in the submission and handling of declarations in the period since the First Review Conference has been the implementation of the first phase of the VIS. As at December 2007, the modules for document management of all verification-related information and for analysis of Article VI-related declarations are operational, and work is underway on the module for planning Article VI inspections. Modules dealing with chemical weapons data are currently being planned.

3.113 It is anticipated that, by merging the 23 different Microsoft Access databases that were previously used into one centrally managed, easy-to-use system, the VIS will significantly improve the quality and reliability of data held by the Secretariat. The VIS will also greatly enhance the ability of the Secretariat to analyse declarations and carry out data monitoring.

3.114 The VIS makes it possible to receive declarations from States Parties in electronic format, which greatly facilitates the work of the Secretariat by eliminating the need for the labour-intensive and error-prone process of manual data entry. Similarly, declaration data stored in the VIS can be provided to States Parties in electronic form, facilitating their own data-analysis processes.

3.115 The reduction in the manual handling and processing of Article VI declaration data due to the introduction of the VIS will allow Secretariat personnel to carry out more in-depth analysis of declaration data. It should be noted that although the VIS allows electronic submission of declaration data, it is not expected that all States Parties will use this capability. In addition, amendments to declaration data will still have to be carried out manually. Furthermore, following data entry, all declaration data entered into the VIS will be validated. Consequently, although over time, the overall workload will be reduced with the introduction of electronic Article VI declarations, the Secretariat will have to retain the ability to carry out manual data-entry processes and validation of declarations in all six official languages.

3.116 The First Review Conference (subparagraph 7.71(b) of RC-1/5) encouraged the Council to improve the submission and handling of industry declarations (including common criteria and standards, simplified declaration forms, and the submission of declaration data in electronic form). Initial consultations on this issue focussed on preparing an improved version of the Handbook on Chemicals as an aid to States Parties; a new version was released in 2005. In addition to these improvements, there are a number of minor interpretive issues that could be discussed, with any understandings reached to be reflected in future versions of the Declarations Handbook, thereby leading to greater consistency and accuracy in declarations submitted by States Parties.

3.117 The slow pace of clarification of ambiguities in declarations was highlighted at the First Review Conference (paragraph 4.14 of RC-1/DG.1, dated 17 April 2003). This issue was addressed by a decision by the Council at its Thirty-Sixth Session (EC-36/DEC.7, dated 26 March 2004), which urged States Parties to expedite their responses to requests for clarification and recommended that the Secretariat inform the Council in cases where ambiguities in a declaration precluded the Secretariat from determining the inspectability of a facility, with no response within 90 days of transmittal of a request for clarification. The Secretariat has put procedures in place for identifying such cases – and the follow-up action necessary – in time for analysis of the annual declaration of past activities for the year 2005. Since that date, there has been a marked improvement in the time taken for initial responses to such inspectability-related requests for clarification, and in no case has the 90-day deadline for an initial response been exceeded.

3.118 In the period since the First Review Conference, four cases of transfers of Schedule 2 chemicals (amounting to a total of 298 tonnes) to States not Party, in breach of the ban on such transfers, have been brought to the attention of the Secretariat by the States Parties from which the chemicals were exported. The States Parties concerned have indicated that the companies involved have either been prosecuted or are under investigation.

3.119 Paragraph 27 of Part VIII of the Verification Annex provides that five years after EIF, the Conference shall consider the need to establish other measures regarding transfers of Schedule 3 chemicals to States not Party to the Convention. The First Review Conference particularly requested the Council to continue working towards an early resolution of this issue and to submit a recommendation to the next regular Session of the Conference (paragraph 7.73 of RC-1/5). At its Forty-Seventh Session, the Council adopted a decision calling upon States Parties to adopt the necessary measures to ensure that Schedule 3 chemicals transferred by them to States not Party are used only for purposes not prohibited by the Convention, and recommending that the Second Review Conference review the implementation of measures regarding such transfers and consider the need to establish other measures (EC-47/DEC.8, dated 8 November 2006). It is anticipated that the issue will be addressed during the Second Review Conference. Statistics on the transfers of Schedule 3 chemicals to States not Party are provided in Annex 4.

SCHEDULE 1 CHEMICALS AND RELATED FACILITIES

GENERAL PROVISIONS OF THE CONVENTION

3.120 Schedule 1 chemicals are considered to pose the highest risk to the object and purpose of the Convention. Chemicals have been selected for inclusion in this list according to three main criteria:

(a) *history*: used as chemical weapons in the past;
(b) *potential for use as chemical weapons*: high toxicity, similar physical properties and/or chemical structure, close precursor to any of the Schedule 1 chemicals used as chemical weapons in the past; and
(c) *purpose*: little or no use for purposes not prohibited by the Convention.

3.121 Comprehensive, detailed declarations for each Schedule 1 chemical produced, acquired, consumed, or stored (only when such action takes place at facilities producing Schedule 1 chemicals, as declared under paragraphs 10 and 11 of Part VI of the Verification Annex), as well as its transfer(s) are required. The number and the capability of production facilities (as well as quantities produced) are strictly limited based on the assumption that only bigger quantities of chemicals can pose a potential military threat. Frequent, regular monitoring of declared activities and limitation of production capabilities are the main tools for implementation.

3.122 The need to produce a chemical listed in Schedule 1 can only be justified by its use for any of the *following purposes*: research, medical, pharmaceutical, or protective. This criterion is further linked to another restriction, which requires that the type and quantities are appropriate for the declared purpose.

3.123 An upper annual limit for aggregate amounts of up to 1 tonne of Schedule 1 chemicals per year and per country has been defined (paragraph 2 of Part VI of the Verification Annex). Furthermore, approval by the State Party is required for each facility declared under the provisions of paragraphs 8, 10, and 11 of Part VI of the Verification Annex.

3.124 The production capacity is limited by restrictions imposed on the following:
(a) the number of facilities one State Party can possess: only one single small-scale facility (SSSF) and one other facility for protective purposes (OFPP);

(b) the amount that these facilities can produce: one tonne per year for SSSFs (similar to a pilot plant in industry) and 10 kg for other facilities (lab scale);

(c) the size of the equipment permitted: in SSSFs the volume of any reaction vessel shall not exceed 100 litres and the total volume of vessels exceeding five litres shall not be more than 500 litres; and

(d) the configuration of the equipment: for SSSFs, the reaction vessels shall not be configured for continuous operation.

RISK ASSESSMENT OF SCHEDULE 1 FACILITIES: BACKGROUND

3.125 According to the Convention, all Schedule 1 facilities shall be subject to systematic verification through on-site inspection and monitoring with on-site instruments (paragraphs 22 and 29 of Part VI of the Verification Annex), although the Secretariat has never contemplated the idea of using on-site monitoring instruments because of the nature of the facilities and the activities carried out there. The Convention further stipulates that the number, intensity, duration, and mode of inspection shall be risk-based, taking into account the *chemicals produced*, the *characteristics of the facility*, and the *nature of the activities carried out there* (paragraphs 23 and 30 of Part VI of the Verification Annex).

3.126 The Conference has yet to take a decision on the risk assessment and frequency of inspections for Schedule 1 facilities, as required by paragraphs 23 and 30 of Part VI of the Verification Annex. A draft decision developed by the Preparatory Commission prior to EIF included a set of guidelines that classified Schedule 1 facilities into five risk categories. This served as a basis for consultations shortly after EIF. These guidelines had been provisionally adopted at the Expert Group level but were not considered for final adoption.

3.127 Since EIF, through conducting inspections, the Secretariat has gained a wealth of experience in assessing the risk at Schedule 1 facilities and has issued a number of papers that describe the relative risk of Schedule 1 facilities, including a paper issued at the time of the First Review Conference in 2003. The general risk groupings are outlined in the next section.

CHARACTERISTICS OF FACILITIES DECLARED AND INSPECTED

3.128 There are at present 28 declared and inspectable Schedule 1 facilities in 22 States Parties:

(a) eight single small-scale facilities (SSSFs);

(b) eighteen "other Schedule 1 facilities" (OFPPs), producing for protective purposes; and

(c) two "other Schedule 1 facilities for research, medical, or pharmaceutical purposes" (OFRM-PhPs).

3.129 Among the 28 Schedule 1 facilities declared, the eight SSSFs represented greater relevance, and four of these SSSFs were of particular relevance to the object and purpose of the Convention, based on the key risk elements: the relevant chemicals, the characteristics of the facility and the nature of the activities carried out at the facility. The other 20 Schedule 1 facilities were found to present a lower risk to the object and purpose of the Convention, based on the amounts and numbers of different chemicals produced as well as the characteristics and capabilities of the facilities themselves (many of them are producing less than 100g per year of aggregate Schedule 1 chemicals).

3.130 Furthermore, an analysis of the Schedule 1 chemicals produced from 1997 to the end of 2006, based on the annual declaration of past activities submitted by the declaring States Parties, indicates that an aggregate amount of only one tonne was produced in all the Schedule 1 facilities of all Member States, of which about 620 kg was produced in SSSFs. In addition, the analysis of the annual declarations on past activities for 2006 shows that almost one-third of these facilities had little (a few grams only) or no production at all. (Actually, three OFPPs have not declared production of any Schedule 1 chemical since EIF; however, these facilities were subject to systematic verification and have jointly received 17 inspections since EIF.) The overall low level of production at Schedule 1 facilities over an extended period of time (since EIF) is an important factor when refining the assessment of risk related to the nature of their activities.

IMPLEMENTATION EXPERIENCE

3.131 All these elements clearly demonstrate that, while before EIF Schedule 1 facilities were perceived to pose the highest risk to the object and purpose of the Convention, the evaluation of the actual risk after 10 years of inspection experience has indicated otherwise. In addition, the strict declaration and verification requirements have allowed the Secretariat to effectively monitor all facilities producing Schedule 1 chemicals.

3.132 Through 31 December 2007, 182 Schedule 1 inspections have been undertaken by the Secretariat since EIF. Of this number, 75 have been undertaken since the First Review Conference. Of the current 28 declared facilities, one has been inspected nine times, four have been inspected eight times, and a further six have been inspected seven times since EIF. One facility which was first declared in December 2007 had not been inspected by 31 December 2007.

3.133 The results of these inspections indicate that of the 75 inspections that have taken place since the First Review Conference, only five have recorded issues requiring further attention (IRFAs). No "Uncertainty" has ever been reported in Schedule 1 inspections.

3.134 The most frequently reported issues are those related to discrepancies between the declared quantities of Schedule 1 chemicals handled by the facility and the verified figures. Other issues have involved changes in the delineation of the facility, removal of equipment without updating the relevant declaration, and undeclared Schedule 1 chemicals.

FUTURE CONSIDERATIONS
Frequency of inspections at Schedule 1 facilities
3.135 The Convention stipulates that the number, intensity, duration, timing, and mode of Schedule 1 inspections for a particular facility shall be based on the "risk to the object and purpose of this Convention posed by the relevant chemicals, the characteristics of the facility and the nature of activities carried out there" (paragraphs 23 and 30 of Part VI of the Verification Annex). It states that the Conference shall consider and approve guidelines for such risk assessment. In the early years of the OPCW, the Secretariat made a number of proposals for such guidelines (EC-XII/TS.2*, dated 8 October 1998, and EC-XVI/TS.3*, dated 3 September 1999; Rev.1, dated 1 December 1999; and Corr.1, dated 14 September 1999); however, no consensus was reached. The issue was raised again in the context of the First Review Conference, which requested that the Council, assisted by the Secretariat, prepare these guidelines for consideration and adoption as early as possible (paragraph 7.66 of RC-1/5).

3.136 Although since 1999, there have been no substantive discussions on the frequency of inspections, the Secretariat has had no difficulties establishing the frequency of inspections, and these are reviewed by the Council and the Conference through the budget process. The Secretariat notes, however, that appropriate guidelines with regard to the number, intensity, duration, timing, and mode of inspections at Schedule 1 facilities have to be considered by the Conference, as required by the Convention (paragraphs 23 and 30 of Part VI of the Verification Annex).

SCHEDULE 2 CHEMICALS AND RELATED FACILITIES

GENERAL PROVISIONS OF THE CONVENTION
3.137 As defined in paragraph 2 of Section A of the Annex on Chemicals, Schedule 2 chemicals are either toxic chemicals possessing lethal or incapacitating toxicity (as well as other properties that could enable them to be used as a chemical weapon) or precursor chemicals at the final stage

of the formation of a chemical listed in Schedule 1 or Schedule 2, Part A. Consequently, these chemicals are considered to pose a significant risk to the object and purpose of the Convention.

3.138 Furthermore, in accordance with paragraphs 16, 18, and 20 of Section B of Part VII of the Verification Annex, each plant site that produces, processes, or consumes Schedule 2 chemicals above a specific threshold shall receive an initial inspection as soon as possible, but preferably not later than three years after EIF. Those plant sites declared after this period shall be subject to an initial inspection no later than one year after being first declared and to subsequent inspections thereafter, with a frequency and intensity derived from the assessment of the risk posed to the object and purpose of the Convention, taking into account the respective facility agreement as well as the results of the initial and subsequent inspections. The risk to the object and purpose relates to the *relevant chemicals*, the *characteristics of the plant site*, and the *nature of the activities* carried out there. Paragraph 18 of Part VII of the Verification Annex lists the following criteria, which have been further detailed by the Conference in its decision on risk assessment for Schedule 2 facilities (C-I/DEC.32, dated 16 May 1997):

(a) the *toxicity* of scheduled chemicals and end products produced, if any;
(b) the *quantity* of scheduled chemicals typically *stored*;
(c) the *quantity of feedstock* chemicals for the scheduled chemical(s);
(d) the *production capacity* of the Schedule 2 plants; and
(e) the *capability and convertibility* for initiating production, storage, and filling of toxic chemicals at the inspected site.

RISK ASSESSMENT AND SELECTION OF FACILITIES FOR INSPECTION
3.139 The Secretariat continued to assess risks and to plan subsequent Schedule 2 inspections during the period that has elapsed since the First Review Conference by using the methodology described in EC-XXII/TS.1, dated 6 October 2000 (Corr.1, dated 19 October 2000; and Corr.2, dated 7 December 2000). This methodology takes into account the nature of the activities carried out at the plant site (production, processing, and/or consumption), the relevant chemicals at the plant site (2A/2A*, or 2B chemicals), and the related quantities, as outlined in the Conference decision (C-I/DEC.32, dated 16 May 1997) in order to assess the risk posed by a Schedule 2 plant site to the object and purpose of the Convention.

3.140 Three main groups were identified as follows: **Group 1 (low risk)**: plant sites processing and/or consuming up to 100 tonnes of Schedule B chemicals per year; **Group 2 (medium risk)**: plant sites processing and/or consuming more than 100 tonnes/year and/or producing up to 500 tonnes of Schedule B chemicals per year; and **Group 3 (high risk)**: plant sites producing more than 500 tonnes of Schedule B chemicals per year and/or producing Schedule 2A/ 2A* chemicals.

3.141 For the low-risk category (Group 1), a frequency of three inspections (including the initial inspection) over a 10-year period was recommended by the Secretariat in a paper submitted in 2000 (EC-XXII/TS.1, Corr.1, and Corr.2). No recommendation was made for the medium-risk (Group 2) and the high-risk (Group 3) categories, pending further discussion with Member States. In the absence of any agreement between States Parties vis-à-vis the frequency of inspections for the medium- and high-risk categories, the Secretariat has essentially applied the same frequency of inspections it has for Schedule 2 plant sites in the low-risk group (averaging three inspections over 10 years, including the initial inspection) for the medium-risk group and a slightly higher frequency for the high-risk group. This was further constrained by the requirement to make initial inspections a priority and by the number of Schedule 2 inspections approved in the annual OPCW Programme and Budget.

CHARACTERISTICS OF THE FACILITIES DECLARED AND INSPECTED
3.142 The number of inspectable plant sites also varied from 153 in 21 States Parties in 2003 to 165 in 22 States Parties by December 2007.

3.143 There are seven States Parties that have 10 or more inspectable plant sites, which comprises 75% of all inspectable plant sites. It should be noted, however, that there has been a significant turnover in Schedule 2 plant sites since EIF, with many of the sites inspected in the years 1997 to 1999 dropping below declaration thresholds, shutting down operations completely, switching to non-scheduled chemicals, or becoming not declarable as a result of the Conference decision on the low concentration limit for Schedule 2B chemicals. Other plant sites from this category, although still declared, remained below verification thresholds after initial inspection and therefore were never subject to subsequent inspections. At the same time, new plants sites have been added that more than make up for the number of sites that have dropped off the inspectable list.

3.144 With regard to the characteristics of the Schedule 2 plant sites inspected, the Secretariat has noticed a wide range of equipment configurations. Based on the list of inspectable Schedule 2 plant sites, 60% are multipurpose-batch, 27% are dedicated-batch, and 13% are dedicated-continuous. The equipment in the multipurpose-batch configurations normally have greater flexibility to produce, process, or consume a wider range of chemicals.

3.145 A large number of the sites are involved in processing and/or consumption activities involving Schedule 2B4 and 2B13 chemicals. Some of these plant sites have been found to possess similar simple process configurations and basic safety features, while some others have an equipment setup with more flexibility. All these plant sites typically consume or process the Schedule 2B chemicals used as flame retardants for construction materials, paper, and textiles.

3.146 There are currently 15 plant sites declared to be involved in activities related to 3-quinuclidinyl benzilate (*) (BZ) and PFIB (Schedule 2A* and 2A chemicals, respectively). These plant sites are considered to pose the highest risk to the object and purpose of the Convention, not necessarily because of their intrinsic characteristics but because of the chemicals involved. The plant sites that produce and consume PFIB typically have dedicated production equipment. PFIB is generated as an unwanted, unavoidable by-product that is incinerated after being produced (either on-site or off-site). BZ is an intermediate chemical in the production of pharmaceutical products. Plant sites that produce and consume BZ have multipurpose-batch equipment arrangements. No plant site producing, processing, or consuming Schedule 2A amiton has ever been declared.

MAIN SCHEDULE 2 CHEMICALS PRODUCED, PROCESSED, AND CONSUMED
3.147 Based on information declared to the Secretariat, trends in the production and consumption of Schedule 2 chemicals have changed since the First Review Conference. The total amount of Schedule 2 chemicals produced and consumed rose steadily after 2003, from 16,500 tonnes to 24,000 tonnes in 2006. This increase was basically caused by four chemicals: PFIB, methylphosphinic acid, butyl methylphosphinate, and methylphosphonous dichloride. The total amount produced for these four chemicals, compared to the total amount of Schedule 2 chemicals produced, increased from 47.6% in 2003 to 59% in 2006, when the production of these four compounds represented 10.4%, 11.1%, 18.7%, and 18.9%, respectively, of the total Schedule 2 chemicals produced. The amounts of dimethyl methylphosphonate and thiodyglycol produced have also increased since 2003, while the amount of diethyl ethylphosphonate has decreased from 1,800 tonnes to 1,000 tonnes. The amounts of the remaining Schedule 2 chemicals produced have basically been constant since 1997.

3.148 The total amount of Schedule 2 chemicals consumed follows the same trend as their production, rising from 13,400 tonnes in 2003 to 19,500 tonnes in 2006, with the increase being due to the same four chemicals mentioned above. This represents 81% of the total Schedule 2 chemicals produced each year.

3.149 The difference between the amounts produced and consumed corresponds approximately to the quantities processed. The amount processed, however, decreased from 4,700 tonnes (29% of the total amount produced in 2003) to 3,300 tonnes (14% of the total amount produced in 2006).

IMPLEMENTATION EXPERIENCE

3.150 A total of 405 Schedule 2 inspections (which includes 244 initial inspections) has been carried out in 22 States Parties since EIF (through December 2007). From the 42 Schedule 2 inspections made in 2007, 16 (or 38%) were initial inspections. This is very similar to the proportion of 35% initial Schedule 2 inspections carried out in 2006, and represents an increase compared to the 7% initial inspections recorded for 2005 and 17% recorded for 2004. The situation presented during the First Review Conference (covering the period from EIF through 2002) was characterised by 92% initial inspections and 8% subsequent inspections, while during the period from 2003 through 2007 (up to the Second Review Conference), the situation was 30% initial and 70% subsequent inspections.

3.151 The analysis of the final inspection reports for a total of 207 Schedule 2 inspections, conducted from 2003 until the end of December 2007, indicates that 14 inspections have recorded IRFAs, and in two of them, uncertainties were reported. These IRFAs are mainly related to discrepancies between declared and verified figures for production, processing, consumption, or transfers of Schedule 2 chemicals. The two uncertainties were both related to a lack of sufficient records to allow verification that these chemicals were not diverted for purposes prohibited by the Convention. The situation is substantially different from the period from 1997 to 2002, where, out of a total number of 198 Schedule 2 inspections conducted, 149 recorded IRFAs, with uncertainties identified in 14 of them. This significant decrease in the number of inspections recording IRFAs is due to a variety of reasons. One important point contributing to this reduction is that Member States, as well as the Secretariat, have gained more experience and practice in implementing the requirements of the Schedule 2 regime.

3.152 There has been a wealth of experience gained from conducting these inspections, which has reinforced the Secretariat's view that Schedule 2 verification is very comprehensive in nature and is a very effective regime under Article VI of the Convention. The Schedule 2 regime allows the collection, evaluation, and reporting of key information on the site of the declared Schedule 2 plants (including process, equipment configuration, and material-balance record-keeping over a three-year period prior to inspection) in order to ensure compliance with the Convention.

SAMPLING AND ANALYSIS

3.153 The Convention provides for sampling and analysis as a routine verification tool in Article VI inspections (paragraph 52 of Part II and paragraph 27 of Part VII of the Verification Annex). In December of 2005, the Director-General indicated that the Secretariat would begin a start-up period of one and one-half years, during which sampling and analysis will be used on a limited basis and only in subsequent Schedule 2 inspections, which would provide an additional safeguard in the implementation of the regime. Up to the end of December 2007, sampling and analysis was conducted effectively at 11 plant sites in 11 different countries, with two of the missions being conducted in 2006 and nine missions being conducted in 2007. Although sampling and analysis is still in the start-up period, from the findings gathered, the use of sampling and analysis in Schedule 2 subsequent inspections resulted in additional confidence with regard to the absence of undeclared scheduled chemicals, in particular, the absence of Schedule 1 production.

FUTURE CONSIDERATIONS
Frequency of inspections at Schedule 2 plants
3.154 The First Review Conference has already acknowledged the time and effort that have been spent by both States Parties and the Secretariat in developing an acceptable methodology for conducting the risk assessment of Schedule 2 plant sites. While the aim of this methodology is to provide a basis for determining the appropriate frequency of inspections, no consensus has been reached thus far.

3.155 As indicated in the Director-General's letter (L/ODG/121431/07, dated 6 February 2007) to the Chairperson of the Council, regarding future industry inspections, the Secretariat has finalised an analysis of inspectable Schedule 2 plant sites that have been subject to an initial inspection. The aim of this analysis was to update the data related to their corresponding risk assessments and to propose a new approach for the resolution of the issue of determining the appropriate frequency of inspections. The results of this analysis, as well as a more detailed explanation of a proposed new statistical method, are included in a paper entitled "Risk assessment for Schedule 2 plant sites and frequency of inspection", dated 28 May 2007. In this paper, the Secretariat proposed a new, simplified algorithm for risk assessment and also recommended the frequency of inspections for the three risk groups. Further discussion with Member States is anticipated as this remains an outstanding issue in the Council and one which has been referred to the Industry Cluster consultations (EC-XVI/INF.3, dated 22 September 1999).

SCHEDULE 3 CHEMICALS AND RELATED FACILITIES

GENERAL PROVISIONS OF THE CONVENTION

3.156 Paragraph 5 of Article VI of the Convention requires each State Party to subject the chemicals listed in Schedule 3 and related facilities specified in Part VIII of the Verification Annex to data monitoring and on-site verification.

3.157 Part VIII of the Verification Annex establishes that the initial and annual declarations to be provided by a State Party shall include aggregate national data for the previous calendar year on the quantities produced, imported, and exported of each Schedule 3 chemical. Also required are declarations of plant sites that comprise one or more plants that, during the previous calendar year, have produced more than 30 tonnes of a Schedule 3 chemical, or which are anticipated to produce more than 30 tonnes of a Schedule 3 chemical in the next calendar year.

SELECTION OF SCHEDULE 3 FACILITIES FOR INSPECTION

3.158 According to paragraph 14 of Part VIII of the Verification Annex, the Secretariat shall randomly select Schedule 3 plant sites for inspection by using specially designed computer software on the basis of two weighting factors: (a) equitable geographical distribution of inspections and (b) the information available to the Secretariat related to the relevant chemical, the characteristics of the plant site, and the nature of activities carried out there. Two additional constraints have to be observed by the Secretariat when selecting Schedule 3 plant sites for inspection: first, that no plant site will receive more than two inspections per year, under the provisions of paragraph 15 of Part VIII of the Verification Annex, and second, that the combined number of inspections that a State Party can receive per calendar year, under Part VIII and Part IX of the Verification Annex, shall not exceed three plus 5% of the total number of sites declared under both Part VIII and Part IX—or 20 inspections—whichever of these two figures is lower (paragraph 16 of Part VIII of the Verification Annex).

3.159 The Council considered and approved a mechanism to be applied in the selection of Schedule 3 plant sites (EC-XVII/DEC.7, dated 1 December 1999). This decision put in place a selection methodology that is based on a two-step random-selection process. In the first step, the State Party is selected according to the probability of its being inspected, calculated with a formula that takes into account the total number of Schedule 3 plant sites that are verifiable in that State Party. In the second step, a plant site within the selected State Party is selected by using the weighting factors detailed in subparagraph 14(b) of Part VIII of the Verification Annex.

CHARACTERISTICS OF THE FACILITIES DECLARED AND INSPECTED

3.160 In most cases, the plants producing Schedule 3 chemicals are dedicated and are usually in continuous operation. The majority of them produce large volumes of chemicals. For example, the annual production for phosgene plants normally ranges from 10,000 to 100,000 tonnes/year, and even higher in some cases. Only five of the 57 plants producing phosgene that have been inspected have declared a smaller range of production. Similarly, for hydrogen cyanide production, between 10,000 and 100,000 tonnes per year have been declared by 25 inspected plant sites out of the 39 sites that are still inspectable. Phosgene and hydrogen cyanide plants are normally integrated with other process streams involved in the production of other organic chemicals that are the final products of the plant site. Triethanolamine is another Schedule 3 chemical typically produced in large quantities: between 1,000 and 10,000 tonnes per year, but higher in some cases. Phosphorus trichloride is also produced in large quantities and is one of the most widely used chlorinating agents in the chemical industry worldwide. The remaining 13 Schedule 3 chemicals are typically produced in lower annual volumes.

3.161 Given the large production capacities involved and the fact that most of the Schedule 3 plants are dedicated to the production of these chemicals, the analysis of the inspection results indicates that the Schedule 3 plants lack flexibility in terms of their ability to be converted to the production of other scheduled chemicals.

3.162 Schedule 3 inspections were initiated late in 1998, more than one year after EIF. This was influenced by the need to satisfy other, more stringent, requirements of the Convention, such as the need to conclude a facility agreement for each declared Schedule 1 facility within 180 days after EIF (paragraphs 25 and 31 of Part VI of the Verification Annex) and to inspect all verifiable Schedule 2 plant sites "preferably not later than three years after entry into force" (paragraph 16 of Part VII of the Verification Annex). Between 31 December 2002 and 31 December 2007, the Secretariat conducted 118 Schedule 3 inspections in 34 States Parties, of which five were subsequent Schedule 3 inspections. These latter inspections were initiated in 2004 with one re-inspection being carried out each year since then, except for 2005 when two such inspections were conducted. The distribution of Schedule 3 inspections among the regional groups compared to the number of Schedule 3 inspectable plant sites is depicted in the two tables below.

TABLE 1: DISTRIBUTION OF SCHEDULE 3 INSPECTIONS (2003 THROUGH 31 DECEMBER 2007)

REGION	INSPECTIONS
Asia	62
Africa	0
Eastern Europe	8
GRULAC	7
WEOG	41

TABLE 2: DISTRIBUTION OF SCHEDULE 3 INSPECTABLE SITES

REGION	INSPECTABLE SITES
Asia	300
Africa	1
Eastern Europe	20
GRULAC	10
WEOG	103

Note: Data as at 31 December 2007.

IMPLEMENTATION EXPERIENCE
3.163 This analysis shows that the methodology approved by the Council in 1999 for the selection of Schedule 3 plant sites has appropriately ensured the equitable geographical distribution of

inspections (as specified in paragraph 14(a) of Part VII of the Verification Annex). Moreover, it confirms that the weighting factors used in the selection of Schedule 3 plant sites (i.e., the relevant chemicals, their number, and the nature of activities carried out at the inspected plant sites) have also had the desired result. As an example, plant sites that are producing the four toxic Schedule 3 chemicals (phosgene, cyanogen chloride, hydrogen cyanide, and chloropicrin) account for more than 65% of all inspected plant sites, compared with the rest of the Schedule 3 chemicals that are listed as precursors.

3.164 The results of the Schedule 3 inspections carried out prior to the First Review Conference indicate a significant number of inspections recording IRFAs (32 out of 113 inspections) and one that had recorded an "Uncertainty".

3.165 By comparison, the results of the Schedule 3 inspections carried out between the First and the Second Review Conference show that only IRFAs have been recorded—in just two inspections. One inspection recorded an issue related to the inspectability of the site, while the second one recorded an issue related to the delineation of the plant site. However, discrepancies between declared and verified information have been identified in a significant number of inspections. These discrepancies were in relation to the name, address, owner/operator of the plant site, number of plants, the product-group codes describing the main activities of the plant site, the product-group codes describing the purpose of production, and the range of production.

OTHER CHEMICAL PRODUCTION FACILITIES

GENERAL PROVISIONS OF THE CONVENTION

3.166 Discrete organic chemicals (DOCs), as defined in Part I of the Verification Annex, include "any chemical belonging to the class of chemical compounds consisting of all compounds of carbon except for its oxides, sulfides and metal carbonates, identifiable by chemical name, by structural formula, if known, and by Chemical Abstracts Service registry number, if assigned" (paragraph 4 of Part I of the Verification Annex). A further understanding of this definition was adopted by the First Session of the Conference (see C-I/DEC.39, dated 16 May 1997 for details). DOCs, either toxic or non-toxic, have legitimate applications in many parts of the chemical industry. The Convention does not restrict their production in OCPFs, and the States Parties have the right to develop, produce, acquire, retain, transfer, and use these chemicals for purposes not prohibited under the Convention (paragraph 1 of Article VI). The verification of these activities is done through on-site inspections as set out in Part IX of the Verification Annex.

3.167 According to Part IX of the Verification Annex, those facilities that, in a calendar year, produce by synthesis in excess of an aggregate of 200 tonnes of unscheduled DOCs, or that have at least one plant producing in excess of 30 tonnes of a DOC containing phosphorus, sulphur, or fluorine (PSF chemicals) shall be included in the initial declaration provided by each State Party. (Plant sites that exclusively produce explosives or hydrocarbons are not required to be included in the initial declaration.) Annual updates of the information related to these declared plant sites shall be provided no later than 90 days after the beginning of each year. No annual declaration of anticipated activities is required for OCPFs.

3.168 The information for each OCPF shall include the name of the plant site and the owner (operator), the precise location, its main activities, the approximate number of plants producing DOCs (including PSF chemicals), and the number of plants producing PSF chemicals (including data on their aggregate production, expressed in ranges), as well as the aggregate production of DOCs for the entire plant site, expressed in ranges.

3.169 During the initial three years after EIF (1997–2000), OCPFs were subject to declarations only. The implementation of on-site inspections started at the beginning of the fourth year after EIF (May 2000) as per the provisions of paragraph 22 of Part IX of the Verification Annex.

SELECTION OF OCPFs FOR INSPECTION
3.170 The selection of OCPFs for on-site inspections shall be done randomly using specially designed computer software on the basis of the weighting factors defined in paragraph 11 of Part IX of the Verification Annex: (a) equitable geographical distribution of inspections and (b) information on the listed plant sites available to the Secretariat, related to the characteristics of the plant site, and activities carried out there, and (c) proposals by States Parties on a basis to be agreed upon by the Conference.

3.171 In selecting OCPFs for inspection, the Secretariat has to observe two specific limitations, as stated in Part IX of the Verification Annex:
(a) No plant site shall receive more than two inspections per year under paragraph 12 of Part IX of the Verification Annex; and
(b) The combined number of inspections to be received by a State Party per calendar year shall not exceed three plus 5% of the total number of plant sites declared by a State Party as Schedule 3 and OCPF, or 20 inspections, whichever of these two figures is lower (paragraph 13).

CHARACTERISTICS OF THE OCPFs DECLARED AND INSPECTED: GENERAL REMARKS
3.172 Although scheduled chemicals are not generally handled in OCPFs, many of these facilities have the capability to produce and handle highly toxic chemicals. The convertibility of their processing equipment, coupled with their production, were used to define selection algorithms and to assess the effectiveness of the on-site verification process.

3.173 In the following section, the technical characteristics of the OCPFs inspected between 2000 and 2006 are presented. (Unless otherwise indicated, the statistics used in this section are based on inspections carried out by the Secretariat during this time.) It is worth mentioning that, out of the 390 plant sites inspected, 24 were found not to be inspectable for various reasons, leading to 366 inspections for this period.

3.174 Two main criteria have been used for qualitative evaluation of OCPFs: (a) the types of chemicals produced and (b) their characteristics in relation to the processes and equipment used.

Characterisation of OCPFs in relation to the chemical(s) produced
3.175 The category of PSF plant sites includes all the OCPFs that contain at least one declarable PSF plant. They can be further classified as follows:
(a) high-relevance plant sites: plant sites producing pesticides, herbicides, fungicides, and pharmaceuticals;
(b) medium-relevance plant sites: plant sites producing PSF chemicals, such as dyes, pigments, and flotation agents for the mining industry; and
(c) low-relevance plant sites: plant sites producing linear alkyl benzene sulfonates (LABS) or other tensioactive agents containing sulphur and/or phosphorus.

3.176 Based on these criteria, the distribution of PSF plant sites inspected is summarised in Table 3 (from inspection data beginning in April 2000 through 31 December 2006).

TABLE 3: DISTRIBUTION OF PSF FACILITIES ACCORDING TO THE CHEMICALS PRODUCED

CATEGORY OF PSFs	NO OF FACILITIES	%
Pesticides/Herbicides/Pharmaceuticals (high relevance)	111	51
General PSFs (medium relevance)	89	41
Detergents (LABS) (low relevance)	18	8
Total	218	100

3.177 The category of non-PSF plant sites includes all the OCPFs that do not contain any declarable PSF plant. They can be further classified as follows:

(a) high-relevance plant sites: pharmaceuticals and food ingredients;

(b) medium-relevance plant sites: other DOC production sites; and

(c) low-relevance plant sites: bulk chemicals (such as methanol, urea, formaldehyde, vinyl chloride, and methyl tertiary-butyl ether (MTBE)).

3.178 Table 4 summarises the distribution of non-PSF plant sites inspected in relation to the chemicals produced (from inspection data beginning in April 2000 through 31 December 2006).

TABLE 4: DISTRIBUTION OF NON-PSF DOC FACILITIES ACCORDING TO THE CHEMICALS PRODUCED

CATEGORY OF NON-PSF DOCS	NO OF FACILITIES	%
Pharmaceuticals and food ingredients (high relevance)	18	12
Other DOCs (medium relevance)	54	37
High-volume bulk chemicals (urea, methanol, MTBE, formaldehydes)	76	51
Total	148	100

Characterisation of OCPF plant sites in relation to process characteristics and hardware

3.179 Two main criteria, based on the type of process (batch or continuous) and on the flexibility of the technology (dedicated or multipurpose) can be used for subdividing the OCPFs further:

(a) high-relevance plant sites: batch and multipurpose. Several chemicals can be obtained on the same production line in these plant sites. They possess at least one plant operating in the batch mode. Sometimes the equipment and connections are flexible, allowing several configurations. They use corrosion-resistant equipment and are capable of switching rapidly between different products;

(b) medium-relevance plant sites: batch and dedicated or continuous and multipurpose. Examples of batch and dedicated sites are plant sites producing high volumes of pharmaceuticals or biologically active chemicals. An example of continuous and multipurpose production would be the production of organic esters (such as butyl acetate and iso-butyl acetate) in the same continuous plant; and

(c) low-relevance plant sites: continuous and dedicated. A single product is produced in a continuous mode, often in high-capacity plants. Typical examples are urea, methanol, formaldehyde, or MTBE plants.

3.180 Again using the criteria presented above, and the two main sub-divisions of OCPFs (producing PSF or non-PSF DOCs), the inspections can be summarised as presented in Tables 5 and 6 below (from inspection data beginning in April 2000 through 31 December 2006):

TABLE 5: DISTRIBUTION OF PSF FACILITIES ACCORDING TO THEIR ENGINEERING FEATURES

CATEGORY OF PSFS	NO. OF FACILITIES	%
Batch/Multipurpose (high relevance)	128	59
Dedicated/Batch and multipurpose/continuous (medium relevance)	59	27
Dedicated continuous (low relevance)	31	14
Total	218	100

TABLE 6: DISTRIBUTION OF NON-PSF DOC FACILITIES ACCORDING TO THEIR ENGINEERING FEATURES

CATEGORY OF NON-PSF DOCS	NO. OF FACILITIES	%
Batch/Multipurpose (high relevance)	21	14
Dedicated/Batch and multipurpose/continuous (medium relevance)	45	31
Dedicated continuous (low relevance)	82	55
Total	148	100

IMPLEMENTATION EXPERIENCE

3.181 In the first two years of on-site OCPF inspections (2000 and 2001), a two-step selection methodology was applied (EC-XIX/DEC/CRP.11, dated 4 April 2000). In the first step, the State Party was selected. In the second step, the plant site within the State Party was selected, based on its range of production (irrespective of whether it contained PSF plants or not) and whether it had already been inspected in the past. During the first year of implementation, the State Party was selected with a probability proportional to the cube root of the number of its declared inspectable facilities. From November 2001 onward, the Secretariat attempted to broaden the geographic distribution of inspections by selecting with equal probability the States Parties to be inspected.

3.182 This selection methodology led to broader geographical distribution, but it also resulted in the selection of a large proportion of sites that were deemed to be of low relevance to the object and purpose of the Convention. That was mainly due to the fact that the highest probability of being selected was assigned to plant sites declaring the highest range of production (a declaration of a production range code of B 33, which is equivalent to more than 10,000 tonnes/year of DOC being produced by synthesis). As a consequence, more than 50% of the plant sites inspected in this period of time were found to involve dedicated production of large volumes of bulk chemicals, such as formaldehyde, methanol, and urea, with little flexibility in their engineering features and equipment-train capabilities.

3.183 In order to increase the effectiveness of the verification process, the Secretariat later developed a new selection algorithm (the so-called "A14 method"), which was meant to increase the probability of selecting OCPFs of greater relevance to the object and purpose of the Convention. Based on the information provided in declarations, the A14 method is similar to the previous algorithm. It takes into account the number of DOC plants, the production range (with a higher probability attributed to medium-range production facilities), the presence of PSF plants, and the standard international trade classification (SITC) product-group codes. Using these characteristics, the A14 algorithm assigns a numerical value that quantifies the relevance of individual plant sites.

3.184 This methodology was recognised by the Council as an improvement over the previously used selection mechanism, and the Council commended the Secretariat for its ongoing efforts to improve and refine the selection process. The relevance of selected plant sites improved considerably because the new algorithm resulted in a proportional increase in the number of selected plant sites with advanced engineering features and process capabilities.

3.185 However, the selection mechanism still incorporated a strong probability for equal selection of States Parties. This had a significant side effect: 17 States Parties with relatively small chemical industries had 100% of their inspectable OCPFs inspected as of 31 December 2006. An additional 19 States Parties had at least 50% of their inspectable OCPFs inspected. Cumulatively, 36 States Parties (49%) out of 73 with inspectable facilities have had at least 50% of their declared chemical industries inspected under this regime, even though these countries have declared fewer than 4% of the total number of inspectable sites. In contrast, the five countries with the largest number of inspectable OCPFs, representing about 67% of the total worldwide number of inspectable OCPF sites (as at December 2006), have had only 1.1% of their plant sites inspected.

3.186 The methodology for the random selection of OCPF plant sites and the weighting factors used were subjected to extensive examination and discussion in the Industry Cluster. There has been emerging consensus on how to implement the provisions of subparagraphs 11(a) and 11(b) of Part IX of the Verification Annex. While nearly all Member States agree that the OCPF selection methodology has to be modified in order to ensure more equitable geographic distribution and to increase the effectiveness of the verification process, the implementation of subparagraph 11(c) is still an ongoing issue, with divergent views among Member States.

3.187 As directed by the Director-General, a number of OCPF inspections (calculated as 5% of the total number budgeted for each year) shall take place at previously inspected plant sites as a means of ensuring a reasonable level of confidence that activities prohibited by the Convention do not occur in previously inspected OCPFs. This practice was started in 2005 and is ongoing.

FUTURE CONSIDERATIONS

3.188 Considering the significant number of declared OCPFs, there is a need to improve the selection process to target the more relevant plant sites. This can be accomplished in two steps: by improving geographical distribution and by improving targeting to select more-relevant plant sites.

Improve equitable geographical distribution

3.189 The Director-General has informed the States Parties about his initiative to modify the methodology for selecting OCPF plant sites for inspection (see S/641/2007, dated 25 May, 2007 and Corr.1, dated 4 June 2007). The modification does not introduce a new criterion for selection, but it helps make the selection of sites more equitable and ensures that inspections are adequately focussed. In following this methodology, the Secretariat will of course ensure that the total number of OCPF inspections received by a State Party stays within the maximum set by Part IX of the Verification Annex. The modified methodology is being used for selecting the plant sites that are subject to inspection since 1 January 2008.

Improve targeting to select more-relevant plant sites

3.190 The second step is further improvement in targeting so that more-relevant plant sites are selected: fine-tuning the A14 algorithm could focus the inspection of OCPF plant sites more on what are considered to be the most relevant facilities. However, considering that the existing algorithm is already using the key plant-site information provided in declarations, the impact of these changes will be limited. States Parties would have to agree on the need to submit more specific information on declared plant sites so that this could be worked into the selection methodology.

3.191 There have been extensive consultations in the Industry Cluster on the methodology for selecting OCPF sites; however, no decision has yet been taken with respect to subparagraph 11(c) of Part IX of the Verification Annex, which covers proposals from States Parties on the process of selecting OCPF plant sites. Consultations on this issue are expected to continue, but the resolution is overdue and should be addressed by the Second Review Conference.

…

7.2 Regime for Schedule 1 chemicals and facilities related to such chemicals

7.2.1 "Production" in the context of Schedule 1 production facilities

C-I/DEC.43 adopted by the Conference of the States Parties at its First Session on 16 May 1997 and entitled "The meaning of 'production' in the context of Schedule 1 production facilities covered under Article VI"

The Conference

Recalling that the Commission, in its PC-IX/11, paragraph 7.2, adopted an understanding on the meaning of "production" in the context of Schedule 1 production facilities covered under Article VI,

Bearing in mind that the Commission recommended in paragraph 50.4 of its Final Report that the Conference adopt the above mentioned understanding,

Hereby:

1.   Adopts the understanding on the meaning of "production" in the context of Schedule 1 pro-
     duction facilities covered under Article VI.

ANNEX

THE MEANING OF "PRODUCTION" IN THE CONTEXT OF SCHEDULE 1 PRODUC-
TION FACILITIES COVERED UNDER ARTICLE VI [6]

It is understood that:

(a) the "acquisition" of Schedule 1 chemicals, as referred to in paragraphs 1 and 2 of Part VI of
     the Verification Annex, includes their extraction from natural sources;

(b) for Schedule 1 chemicals that are normally not produced in the terms of the Convention but
     are isolated by processing (e.g. toxins), extraction and isolation of Schedule 1 chemicals
     above the declaration threshold shall be undertaken only in declared Schedule 1 facilities;
     and

(c) any facility that produces Schedule 1 chemicals above the declaration threshold through
     chemical synthesis or extraction/isolation will have to be declared and verified under Part VI
     of the Verification Annex.

**C-V/DEC.17 adopted by the Conference of the States Parties at its Fifth Session on 18 May
2000 and entitled "Reporting of Ricin Production"**

The Conference

     Having considered the issue of the reporting of ricin production;

     Taking into account the work of the Preparatory Commission on this issue;

     Recalling that the issue of the reporting of ricin production was referred to the Scientific
Advisory Board (Conference decision C-II/DEC.5, dated 5 December 1997), and that advice was
received from the Scientific Advisory Board in this respect (SAB-II/1, dated 23 April 1999);

     Recalling further that the Director-General was invited by the Conference to further study
the issue, to convene a meeting of experts to analyse all its aspects, and to convey the findings of
that meeting to the Executive Council (Conference decision C-IV/DEC.20, dated 2 July 1999);

     Recalling also that the Executive Council was requested to consider this issue with a view to
preparing a recommendation to the Conference for consideration and adoption at its Fifth Session
(Conference decision C-IV/DEC.20, dated 2 July 1999);

     Noting that the issue was considered in a meeting of experts, and that the results of this meet-
ing were submitted by the Director-General to the Executive Council for consideration during its
Nineteenth Session (EC-XIX/DG.4, dated 14 March 2000);

     Cognisant that the Executive Council noted that the annex to the above-mentioned Note by
the Director General to the Executive Council at its Nineteenth Session containing the report of
the chairman of the expert meeting was considered to contain the substance of the report required
for the Conference at its Fifth Session (subparagraph 13.1 of EC-XIX/6, dated 3 May 2000);

Hereby:

1.   Decides that castor oil processing plants should not be subject to the Convention's reporting
     procedures under Schedule 1; and

2.   Agrees to remove from the list of unresolved issues the reporting of ricin production as it
     relates to castor oil processing plants.

---

[6] As contained in paragraph 2.3 of PC-VIII/B/WP.10.

C-10/DEC.12 adopted by the Conference of the States Parties at its Tenth Session on 10 November 2005 and entitled "Understanding relating to the concept of 'Captive Use' in connection with declarations of production and consumption under Part VI of the Verification Annex to the Convention"

The Conference

Recalling that, according to paragraph 3 of Article VI of the Chemical Weapons Convention (hereinafter "the Convention"), "Each State Party shall subject chemicals listed in Schedule 1... to the prohibitions on production, acquisition, retention, transfer and use as specified in Part VI of the Verification Annex. It shall subject Schedule 1 chemicals and facilities specified in Part VI of the Verification Annex to systematic verification through on site inspection and monitoring with on site instruments in accordance with that Part of the Verification Annex";

Recalling also that, according to Article VI, paragraph 11, the provisions of that Article shall be implemented in a manner that avoids hampering the economic or technological development of States Parties;

Recalling further that Part VI of the Verification Annex to the Chemical Weapons Convention (hereinafter "the Verification Annex") requires declarations of the production of Schedule 1 chemicals for research, medical, pharmaceutical, or protective purposes at a single small-scale facility; of the production of Schedule 1 chemicals in aggregate quantities not exceeding 10kg per year for protective purposes at one facility outside a single small-scale facility; and of the production of Schedule 1 chemicals in quantities of more than 100g per year for research, medical, or pharmaceutical purposes outside a single small-scale facility in aggregate quantities not exceeding 10kg per year per facility;

Recalling further the decision it took at its Ninth Session on the understanding of the concept of "captive use" in connection with declarations of production and consumption under Parts VII and VIII of the Verification Annex (C-9/DEC.6, dated 30 November 2004);

Noting the advice from the Scientific Advisory Board that it is not aware of any current examples of the captive use of Schedule 1 chemicals (S/528/2005, dated 1 November 2005);

Recognising nevertheless that certain chemical processes may result in the future in the production of Schedule 1 chemicals that are consumed within those processes without being isolated, and that this situation may result in an uneven application of the Convention and be inconsistent with its object and purpose;

Recognising further that the production limits specified in Part VI of the Verification Annex, when applied to Schedule 1 chemicals that are produced and consumed without being isolated, might in the future have a negative impact on production of such chemicals for research, medical, pharmaceutical, or protective purposes by limiting the quantities that can be produced and held for purposes not prohibited under the Convention;

Recalling further that a document on the issue of the captive use of Schedule 1 chemicals was among the materials transmitted to the Preparatory Commission for the OPCW by the Conference on Disarmament (A/47/27, dated 23 September 1992);

Bearing in mind that the destruction of chemical weapons can give rise to the production of Schedule 1 chemicals, and that such production and the destruction of such chemicals are already subject to verification under Part IV(A) of the Verification Annex;

Having considered that a standardised approach to declarations of production is necessary both in order to assist the States Parties in fulfilling their declaration obligations in a uniform manner, and in order to provide better information to the OPCW;

Cognisant of the economic and administrative implications of such guidelines for the States Parties; and

Noting the recommendation made on this matter by the Executive Council (hereinafter "the Council") at its Twenty-Fifth Meeting (EC-M-25/DEC.4, dated 9 November 2005);

Hereby:

Decides as follows:

(a) that the production of a Schedule 1 chemical is understood, for declaration purposes, to include intermediates, by-products, or waste products that are produced and consumed within a defined chemical manufacturing sequence, where such intermediates, by-products, or waste products are chemically stable and therefore exist for a sufficient time to make isolation from the manufacturing stream possible, but where, under normal or design operating conditions, isolation does not occur;

(b) to request States Parties to take the necessary measures to implement their obligations under Article VII, paragraph 1, of the Convention in respect of this decision as soon as possible; and

(c) to request the Council to examine and take action no later than at its second regular session following receipt of a request for an amendment to the production limits in Part VI of the Verification Annex that may be made in the future with respect to production, in a captive-use situation as defined in subparagraph (a) above, of a specific Schedule 1 chemical for purposes not prohibited by the Convention.

7.2.2 Transfers of Schedule 1 chemicals[7]

C-I/DEC.41 adopted by the Conference of the States Parties at its First Session on 16 May 1997 and entitled "Transfer of Schedule 1 chemicals"

The Conference

Recalling that the Commission, in its PC-VII/8, paragraph 6.6, adopted an understanding on the transfer of Schedule 1 chemicals (paragraph 3.7 of PC-VII/B/WP.7),

Bearing in mind that the Commission recommended in paragraph 50.4 of its Final Report that the Conference adopt the above mentioned understanding,

Hereby:

Adopts the following understanding:

The provisions on transfers and receipts of Schedule 1 chemicals contained in Section B of Part VI of the Verification Annex apply to all such transfers and receipts.

7.2.3 Guidelines for the number, intensity, duration, timing, and mode of inspections at Schedule 1 Single Small-Scale Facilities and at other Schedule 1 facilities

C-17/DEC.8 adopted by the Conference of the States Parties at its Seventeenth Session on 16 May 1997 and entitled "Guidelines for the Number, Intensity, Duration, Timing and Mode of Inspections at Schedule 1 Single Small-Scale Facilities and at Other Schedule 1 Facilities"

The Conference of the States Parties,

Recalling that paragraph 3 of Article VI of the Chemical Weapons Convention (hereinafter

---

[7] On 13 November 1998, in accordance with paragraphs 4 and 5 of Article XV of the Convention, Canada submitted to the Director-General a proposal for a change with respect to transfers of the Schedule 1 chemical, Saxitoxin, for medical/diagnostic purposes. This change, adding a new paragraph 5bis to Section B of Part VI of the Verification Annex, entered into effect on 31 October 1999.

"the Convention") requires that Schedule 1 facilities specified in Part VI of the Verification Annex to the Convention (hereinafter "the Verification Annex") shall be subjected to systematic verification through on-site inspection and monitoring with on-site instruments in accordance with that Part of the Verification Annex;

Recalling further that paragraph 23 of Part VI of the Verification Annex, relating to verification at Schedule 1 single small-scale facilities (SSSFs), as defined in paragraphs 8 and 9 of Part VI of the Verification Annex, provides that the "number, intensity, duration, timing and mode of inspections for a particular facility shall be based on the risk to the object and purpose of this Convention posed by the relevant chemicals, the characteristics of the facility and the nature of activities carried out there", and that "[a]ppropriate guidelines shall be considered and approved by the Conference";

Recalling also that paragraph 30 of Part VI of the Verification Annex, relating to verification at other facilities referred to in paragraphs 10 and 11 of Part VI of the Verification Annex (hereinafter "other Schedule 1 facilities"), provides that the "number, intensity, duration, timing and mode of inspections for a particular facility shall be based on the risk to the object and purpose of this Convention posed by the quantities of chemicals produced, the characteristics of the facility and the nature of the activities carried out there", and that "[a]ppropriate guidelines shall be considered and approved by the Conference";

Bearing in mind that facility agreements covering detailed inspection procedures at each facility have been concluded for all Schedule 1 facilities declared so far, in accordance with paragraphs 26 and 31 of Part VI of the Verification Annex;

Recalling moreover that, at its Sixty-Second Session, the Executive Council (hereinafter "the Council") noted the "Report of the Vice-Chairman of the Cluster on Chemical Industry and Other Article VI issues on the Status of Outstanding Industry Issues on the Agenda of the Executive Council since the Second Review Conference Prepared on the Basis of the Background Information Provided by the Technical Secretariat" (EC-62/4, dated 5 October 2010), and concurred with the proposal contained therein that the guidelines for the number, intensity, duration, timing, and mode of inspections at Schedule 1 SSSFs should be considered in conjunction with the issue of the guidelines for inspections at other Schedule 1 facilities (paragraph 16.5 of EC-62/6, dated 8 October 2010);

Having considered that there are currently 27 declared and inspectable Schedule 1 facilities in 22 States Parties, namely: eight SSSFs, 17 other Schedule 1 facilities for protective purposes, and two other Schedule 1 facilities for research, medical, or pharmaceutical purposes, and that, since entry into force of the Convention, all currently declared Schedule 1 facilities have been inspected with an average of 7.9 inspections per facility, with some of them having been inspected up to 11 times;

Noting that the level of the risk they pose to the object and purpose of the Convention is related to the Schedule 1 chemicals present at these facilities, their design and characteristics, as well as to their actual handling capabilities (production and storage);

Taking into account that, pending the adoption by the Conference of the States Parties (hereinafter "the Conference) of guidelines on this matter, the Technical Secretariat (hereinafter "the Secretariat") has been relying on previous inspection reports, declarations and official correspondence, as well as on the relevant facility agreements to select the facilities and plan the number, intensity, duration, and timing of inspections of those facilities;

Recalling that the number of inspections at Schedule 1 facilities is continuously adjusted, in line with the requirements of the Convention and decisions taken by the States Parties, that special consideration in selecting facilities to be inspected is given to the facilities that reported significant production activities and/or changes in the installation or in the delineation of these facilities, and that any newly-declared Schedule 1 facility shall be subject to an initial inspection;

Recalling further that, since 2007, inspections at Schedule 1 facilities have been carried out at the rate of 11 per year; and

Noting the recommendations of the Council in its decision EC-70/DEC.4, dated 28 September 2012;

Hereby:

1. Decides that, when planning the number, intensity, duration, timing, and mode of inspections of Schedule 1 facilities, based on the risk to the object and purpose of this Convention posed by the relevant chemicals at SSSFs or quantities of chemicals produced thereof at other Schedule 1 facilities, the characteristics of the facility and the nature of activities carried out there, the Secretariat should take into account the relevant approved facility agreement; relevant declarations and inspection findings; and any relevant decisions of the Council or the Conference;

2. Reaffirms its right, taking into account the advice of the Secretariat, to review the factors indicated in paragraph 1 above, should the circumstances so require, at the request of a State Party or the Council;

3. Considers the issues of guidelines on the number, intensity, duration, timing, and mode of inspections at Schedule 1 single small-scale facilities and at other Schedule 1 facilities as closed and not requiring further consideration; and

4. Calls upon the Secretariat to develop procedures for implementing these guidelines and to inform States Parties of these procedures, upon request.

7.3 Regime for Schedule 2 and 3 chemicals and facilities related to such chemicals

7.3.1 Declarations

C-I/DEC.37 adopted by the Conference of the States Parties at its First Session on 16 May 1997 and entitled "Waste disposal"

The Conference

Recalling that the Commission, in its PC-VII/8, paragraph 6.6, adopted an understanding on waste disposal in relation to scheduled chemicals (paragraph 3.3 of PC-VII/B/WP.7),

Bearing in mind that the Commission recommended in paragraph 50.4 of its Final Report that the Conference adopt the above mentioned understanding,

Hereby:

Adopts the following understanding:

It is understood that a plant site containing a plant in which a Schedule 2 chemical is consumed in a waste management or disposal system in quantities above the threshold for that chemical will declare this consumption in accordance with Part VII, paragraph 8.

C-I/DEC.42 adopted by the Conference of the States Parties at its First Session on 16 May 1997 and entitled "Recycled Schedule 2 chemicals"

The Conference

Recalling that the Commission, in its PC-IX/11, paragraph 7.2, adopted an understanding on recycled Schedule 2 chemicals,

Bearing in mind that the Commission recommended in paragraph 50.4 of its Final Report that the Conference adopt the above mentioned understanding,

Hereby:

1. Adopts the understanding on recycled Schedule 2 chemicals.

ANNEX

RECYCLED SCHEDULE 2 CHEMICALS [8]

1. A "recycled Schedule 2 chemical" is a chemical that is partly converted or consumed in a process and then recovered and re-introduced into the process upstream for another cycle of conversion or consumption followed by recovery. Any loss of Schedule 2 chemical from the process cycle through incomplete recovery will be compensated for by make-up quantities (net loss).

2. It is understood that a plant site containing a plant in which a Schedule 2 chemical undergoes a cycle of consumption and regeneration will, in accordance with Part VII, paragraph 8, make a declaration if, in total, $(X+Y)$ exceeds the declaration threshold where:

    X, expressed in the same unit as the declaration threshold, equals:

    (a) for batch processes, the total amount of the Schedule 2 chemical charged (then consumed, regenerated and subsequently recovered in a separate process step); or

    (b) for continuous processes, the total amount present in the reaction vessels and process streams; and

    Y, expressed in the same units as the declaration threshold, equals the aggregate annual compensation for the net loss of that chemical.

    It is further understood that the regeneration process is not required to be declared as a production of a Schedule 2 chemical in the cycle.

S/101/99 containing a Note by the Director-General dated 8 April 1999 and entitled "Understanding of 'main activities of the plant or plant site' to be provided in declarations under Parts VII, VIII and IX of the Verification Annex"

BACKGROUND

1. During the process of implementing the verification regime under Part VII of the Verification Annex, the Technical Secretariat (hereinafter the 'Secretariat') was requested by some States Parties to re-examine the understanding of the requirement to provide details of the 'main activities of the plant or plant site' in the declaration forms. This requirement, which is reflected in forms 2.3/3.3 and 4.1 of Section B of the Declaration Handbook (Industrial Declarations), calls for main activity codes (Appendix 3 of the Declaration Handbook) to be combined with product group codes (Appendix 4 of the Declaration Handbook) in order to identify the main activities of each plant or plant site.

THE SECRETARIAT'S UNDERSTANDING

2. The Secretariat has reviewed its understanding in relation to declarations of the "main activities of the plant or plant site" required under Parts VII, VIII and IX of the Verification Annex, and interprets the requirement as follows:

    (a) in forms 2.3/3.3 and 4.1 of Section B of the Declaration Handbook, no reference is to be made to the main activity codes listed in Appendix 3. This change is reflected in the modified forms 2.3/3.3 and 4.1 attached in annex 1 to this Note; and

    (b) the product group codes (Standard International Trade Classification (SITC) codes) listed in Appendix 4 (see annex 2 to this Note) are to be used to describe the kind of ultimate products manufactured at the plant or plant site. For example, in the case of a plant

---

[8] As contained in paragraphs 2.1 and 2.2 of PC-VIII/B/WP.10.

producing, consuming or processing a Schedule 2 chemical, its main activities may be identified as 'manufacturing' of chemicals or products that fall within the product group code '582' identified in Appendix 4 as 'plates, sheets, film, foil and strip, of plastics'.
[Annexes 1 and 2 not reproduced in this volume]

C-V/DEC.19 adopted by the Conference of the States Parties at its Fifth Session on 19 May 2000 and entitled "Guidelines regarding low concentration limits for declarations of Schedule 2 and 3 chemicals"

The Conference

Recalling the decision at its Fourth Session on guidelines for provisions regarding scheduled chemicals in low concentrations, including in mixtures, in accordance with paragraphs 5 of Parts VII and VIII of the Verification Annex (C-IV/DEC.16, dated 1 July 1999);

Determined to seek the harmonisation of provisions regarding Schedule 2 and Schedule 3 chemicals in low concentrations, consistent with the non-discriminatory and effective implementation of the Convention;

Cognisant of the economic and administrative implications of the implementation of such guidelines for States Parties;

Noting the decision by the Executive Council at its Tenth Meeting recommending that the Conference of the States Parties consider and adopt this decision at its Fifth Session;

Hereby:
1. Decides, with regard to the applicable concentration limits for declarations under Parts VII and VIII of the Verification Annex, that:
     (i)   declarations are not required for mixtures of chemicals containing 30 percent or less of a Schedule 2B or a Schedule 3 chemical; and
     (ii) States Parties are requested to take measures in accordance with Article VII, paragraph 1, to implement these guidelines by 1 January 2002; and
2. Requests the Director-General to task the Scientific Advisory Board to study all relevant aspects of the applicable concentration limits for mixtures of chemicals containing Schedule 2A and 2A* chemicals and to report the results to the Council for consideration with a view to a decision being submitted for the consideration of States Parties at the Sixth Session of the Conference of the States Parties.

C-8/DEC.7 adopted by the Conference of the States Parties at its Eighth Session on 23 October 2003 and entitled "Understandings regarding declarations under Article VI and Part VII and Part VIII of the Verification Annex to the Chemical Weapons Convention"

The Conference

Recalling that subparagraphs 12(a), 12(b), and 12(c) of Article II of the Chemical Weapons Convention (hereinafter the "Convention") state respectively that, for the purposes of Article VI, "production" of a chemical means its formation through chemical reaction; "processing" of a chemical means a physical process, such as formulation, extraction and purification, in which a chemical is not converted into another chemical; and "consumption" of a chemical means its conversion into another chemical via a chemical reaction;

Recalling further that subparagraph 6(a) of Part I of the Verification Annex to the Convention (hereinafter the "Verification Annex") states that "plant site" (works, factory) means the local integration of one or more plants, with any intermediate administrative levels, which are under one operational control, and includes common infrastructure, such as those components listed in subparagraphs 6(a)(i-viii);

Recalling further that subparagraph 6(b) of Part I of the Verification Annex states that "plant" (production facility, workshop) means a relatively self-contained area, structure or building containing one or more units with auxiliary and associated infrastructure, such as those components listed in subparagraphs 6(b)(i-vi);

Recalling further that subparagraph 6(c) of Part I of the Verification Annex states that "unit" (production unit, process unit) means the combination of those items of equipment, including vessels and vessel set up, necessary for the production, processing or consumption of a chemical;

Recalling further that paragraph 3 of Part VII of the Verification Annex states that declarations are required for all plant sites that comprise one or more plant(s) which produced, processed or consumed during any of the previous three calendar years or is anticipated to produce, process, or consume in the next calendar year more than 1 kg of a chemical designated "*" in Schedule 2, Part A; 100 kg of any other chemical listed in Schedule 2, Part A; or 1 tonne of a chemical listed in Schedule 2, Part B;

Recalling further that paragraph 3 of Part VIII of the Verification Annex states that declarations are required for all plant sites that comprise one or more plants which produced during the previous calendar year or are anticipated to produce in the next calendar year more than 30 tonnes of a Schedule 3 chemical;

Recalling further the decision that a plant site containing a plant in which a Schedule 2 chemical is consumed in a waste management or disposal system in quantities above the threshold for that chemical will declare this consumption in accordance with paragraph 8 of Part VII of the Verification Annex, contained in the relevant decision of the Conference of States Parties (hereinafter the "Conference") at its First Session (C-I/DEC.37, dated 16 May 1997);

Recalling further the guidelines regarding low concentration limits for the declaration of Schedule 2B and Schedule 3 chemicals contained in the relevant decision of the Conference at its Fifth Session (C-V/DEC.19, dated 19 May 2000);

Recalling further the rounding rules in relation to the declaration of scheduled chemicals, contained in the relevant decision of the Executive Council (EC-XIX/DEC.5, dated 7 April 2000);

Recognising that certain chemical processes may result in the production of Schedule 2 and Schedule 3 chemicals in concentrations below the threshold established by the Conference at its Fifth Session (C-V/DEC.19), which are then processed to a concentration above the threshold within the same plant, and that this situation may result in an uneven application of the Convention, and may be inconsistent with the object and purpose of the Convention;

Noting that any clarification of the definition of production in Article II of the Convention applies to Schedule 2 and Schedule 3 declarations;

Having considered that a standardised approach to declarations of production, processing, or consumption, as appropriate, is necessary in order to assist the States Parties in fulfilling their declaration obligations in a uniform manner, and in order to provide better information for use by the Organisation for the Prohibition of Chemical Weapons;

Cognisant of the economic and administrative implications of such guidelines for the States Parties;

Recognising the need to continue to work to resolve this issue, particularly in relation to captive use and the mechanism for determining low concentrations; and

Bearing in mind the recommendations that the Executive Council at its Thirty-First Session adopted on this matter (EC-31/DEC.7, dated 11 November 2002);

Hereby decides:
1. that the production of a Schedule 2 or Schedule 3 chemical is understood, for declaration purposes, to include all steps in the production of a chemical in any units within the same plant through chemical reaction, including any associated processes (e.g. purification, separation, extraction, distillation, or refining) in which the chemical is not converted into another chemical. The exact nature of any associated process (e.g. purification, etc.) is not required to be declared;

2. that declarations are required for all plant sites that comprise one or more plant(s) which produce, process, or consume a Schedule 2 chemical above the relevant declaration threshold quantity and in a concentration above the relevant low concentration limit. The processing steps which are part of declared production shall not be declared separately as processing;

3. that declarations are required for all plant sites that comprise one or more plants which produce a Schedule 3 chemical above the declaration threshold quantity and in a concentration above the low concentration limit;

4. that, for declaration purposes, concentration of a declarable Schedule 2 or Schedule 3 chemical may be measured directly or indirectly (including a measurement derived from the chemical process, a material balance, or other available plant data);

5. that "transient intermediates" are understood to mean chemicals which are produced in a chemical process but, because they are in a transition state in terms of thermodynamics and kinetics, exist only for a very short period of time, and cannot be isolated, even by modifying or dismantling the plant, or by altering process operating conditions, or by stopping the process altogether, and that the declaration requirements do not, therefore, apply to "transient intermediates"; and

6. to request States Parties to take any necessary measures in accordance with Article VII, paragraph 1, for implementation as soon as possible, and in any event no later than 1 January 2005.

C-9/DEC.6 adopted by the Conference of the States Parties at its Ninth Session on 30 November 2004 and entitled "Understanding of the concept of 'captive use' in connection with declarations of production and consumption under Parts VII and VIII of the Verification Annex to the Chemical Weapons Convention"

The Conference

Recalling the decision it took at its Eighth Session on understandings regarding declarations under Article VI of the Chemical Weapons Convention (hereinafter "the Convention") and Parts VII and VIII of the Verification Annex to the Convention (hereinafter "the Verification Annex") (C-8/DEC.7, dated 23 October 2003);

Recalling also that paragraph 3 of Part VII of the Verification Annex states that "declarations are required for all plant sites that comprise one or more plant(s) which produced, processed or consumed during any of the previous three calendar years or is anticipated to produce, process or consume in the next calendar year more than:

(a) 1 kg of a chemical designated "*" in Schedule 2, Part A;

(b) 100 kg of any other chemical listed in Schedule 2, Part A; or

(c) 1 tonne of a chemical listed in Schedule 2, Part B";

Recalling further that paragraph 3 of Part VIII of the Verification Annex states that "declarations are required for all plant sites that comprise one or more plants which produced during the previous calendar year or are anticipated to produce in the next calendar year more than 30 tonnes of a Schedule 3 chemical";

Keeping in mind the decision it took at its First Session (C-I/DEC.37, dated 16 May 1997), whereby it adopted the understanding that a plant site containing a plant in which a Schedule 2 chemical is consumed in a waste management or disposal system in quantities above the threshold for that chemical will declare this consumption in accordance with paragraph 8 of Part VII of the Verification Annex;

Also keeping in mind the guidelines in the decision it took at its Fifth Session (C-V/DEC.19, dated 19 May 2000) regarding low concentration limits for the declaration of Schedule 2B and Schedule 3 chemicals;

Recognising that certain chemical processes may result in the production of Schedule 2 and

Schedule 3 chemicals that are consumed within those processes, and that this situation may result in an uneven application of the Convention and be inconsistent with its object and purpose;

Noting that any clarification of the definition of production in Article II of the Convention applies to Schedule 2 and Schedule 3 declarations;

Having considered that a standardised approach to declarations of production, processing, or consumption, as appropriate, is necessary both in order to assist the States Parties in fulfilling their declaration obligations in a uniform manner, and for the provision of better information to the OPCW;

Cognisant of the economic and administrative implications of such guidelines for the States Parties; and

Recognising also the need to continue to work to resolve this issue, particularly in relation to the mechanism for determining low concentrations;

Hereby:

Decides as follows:

(a) that the production of a Schedule 2 or Schedule 3 chemical is understood, for declaration purposes, to include intermediates, by-products, or waste products that are produced and consumed within a defined chemical manufacturing sequence, where such intermediates, by-products, or waste products are chemically stable and therefore exist for a sufficient time to make isolation from the manufacturing stream possible, but where, under normal or design operating conditions, isolation does not occur; and

(b) to request States Parties to take the necessary measures to implement their obligations under Article VII, paragraph 1, of the Convention as soon as possible and in any event no later than 1 January 2005 in respect of Schedule 2 chemicals and 1 January 2006 in respect of Schedule 3 chemicals.

C-7/DEC.14 adopted by the Conference of the States Parties at its Seventh Session on 10 October 2002 and entitled "Guidelines regarding declarations of aggregate national data for Schedule 2 chemical production, processing, consumption, import and export and Schedule 3 import and export"

The Conference

Recalling that the Chemical Weapons Convention (hereinafter the "Convention") requires States Parties to make declarations of Schedule 2 and Schedule 3 aggregate national data (AND) under the provisions of paragraph 1 of Part VII and paragraph 1 of Part VIII of the Verification Annex of the Chemical Weapons Convention (hereinafter the "Verification Annex");

Recalling also that the Conference of the States Parties (hereinafter the "Conference") at its Second Session in C-II/DEC.8, dated 5 December 1997, and the Executive Council (hereinafter the "Council"), in EC-VIII/DEC.2, dated 30 January 1998, and EC-IX/DEC.10*, dated 24 April 1998, also requested States Parties to provide the basis on which Schedule 2 and Schedule 3 chemicals are to be declared; and recalling also the reports by the Technical Secretariat (hereinafter the "Secretariat") on information provided by States Parties in this regard;

Recalling further the guidelines on low concentration limits for the declaration of Schedule 2 and Schedule 3 chemicals adopted by the Conference at its Fifth Session (C-V/DEC.19, dated 19 May 2000);

Having considered that a standardised approach to declaration obligations is necessary for National Authorities to report AND and relevant plant site import and export data in a uniform and harmonised manner, and to provide more meaningful and comparable information for use by the Organisation in illustrating normal patterns of trade, and in identifying any trends important to the object and purpose of the Convention;

Cognisant of the financial and administrative implications of the implementation of such guidelines by States Parties, and the desirability of a simple, practical approach;

Noting the decision by the Council at its Thirtieth Session (EC-30/DEC.14, dated 13 September 2002) recommending that the Conference consider and adopt this decision at its Seventh Session;

Decides on the following:
1. that import and export data aggregated by each State Party in fulfilment of the declaration obligations of paragraph 1 of Part VII and paragraph 1 of Part VIII of the Verification Annex shall include activity by natural and legal persons transferring a declarable chemical between the territory of the declaring State Party and the territory of other States, as specified below;
2. that declarations by States Parties under paragraph 1 of Part VII of the Verification Annex shall include, using the relevant low concentration limit, production, processing, consumption, import, and export quantities of a given Schedule 2 chemical if the total for the year for that activity is more than the threshold specified for that chemical in subparagraphs 3(a), 3(b), or 3(c) of Part VII of the Verification Annex;
3. that declarations by States Parties under paragraph 1 of Part VIII of the Verification Annex shall include, using the relevant low concentration limit, import and export quantities of a Schedule 3 chemical if the total for the year for that activity is more than the threshold specified in paragraph 3 of Part VIII of the Verification Annex;
4. that, in addition, where declarations by States Parties under paragraph 1 of Part VII and paragraph 1 of Part VIII of the Verification Annex have reported the import or export of a Schedule 2 or Schedule 3 chemical in accordance with operative paragraphs 2 or 3 above, separate declarations shall also include, using the relevant low concentration limit, the aggregate quantities of each chemical imported from, or exported to, each given sending or receiving State, which shall be specified. When a quantity reported in this particular declaration is less than the threshold specified for that chemical in paragraph 3 of Part VII or paragraph 3 of Part VIII of the Verification Annex, the quantity should be expressed as "<(relevant threshold quantity)";
5. that States Parties are requested to take measures in accordance with paragraph 1 of Article VII of the Convention to implement these guidelines as soon as practicable, and in advance of 1 January 2004;
6. that although this decision does not dictate how and on what basis States Parties should collect data, but rather how data collected should be reported by States Parties to the Secretariat, States Parties shall review this, and the implementation of these guidelines in general, on the basis of the Secretariat's analysis of the first three years of harmonised AND submissions; and further
7. that the Council shall be tasked to continue work towards harmonising the reporting of Schedule 3 production AND.

C-13/DEC.4 adopted by the Conference of the States Parties at its Thirteenth Session on 3 December 2008 and entitled "Guidelines regarding declaration of import and export data for Schedule 2 and 3 chemicals"

The Conference

Recalling that the Chemical Weapons Convention (hereinafter "the Convention") requires, in accordance with paragraph 2 of Article VI, that each State Party shall adopt the necessary measures to ensure that toxic chemicals and their precursors are only developed, produced, otherwise acquired, retained, transferred, or used within its territory or in any other place under its jurisdiction or control for purposes not prohibited under the Convention;

Recalling further that the Convention also requires States Parties to include in their annual declarations aggregate national data (AND) on the quantities imported and exported of each Schedule 2 and Schedule 3 chemical under the provisions of paragraph 1 of Part VII and paragraph 1 of Part VIII of the Verification Annex to the Convention (hereinafter "the Verification Annex");

Recalling further that, in addition, for declared Schedule 2 plant sites, the Convention requires States Parties to provide data on the quantities imported and exported of each Schedule 2 chemical produced, processed, or consumed above the declaration threshold at the declared plant site under the provisions of paragraphs 8(b) and 8(c) of Part VII of the Verification Annex;

Recalling further the guidelines regarding declarations of AND for Schedule 2 chemical production, processing, consumption, import and export and Schedule 3 import and export adopted by the Conference of the States Parties at its Seventh Session (C-7/DEC.14, dated 10 October 2002) require that import and export data aggregated by each State Party in fulfilment of the declaration obligations of paragraph 1 of Part VII and paragraph 1 of Part VIII of the Verification Annex shall include activity by natural and legal persons transferring a declarable chemical between the territory of the declaring State Party and the territory of other States;

Recalling further that reporting AND and relevant plant site import and export data in a uniform manner will help to reduce discrepancies;

Recalling further that the criterion being used by the Technical Secretariat (hereinafter "the Secretariat") to identify discrepancies, is whether the difference between the quantities declared by the importing and exporting States Parties is more than the relevant threshold specified for that chemical in paragraph 3 of Part VII or paragraph 3 of Part VIII of the Verification Annex;

Having considered that while "production", "processing", and "consumption" are defined in paragraph 12 of Article II of the Convention, for the purposes of Article VI, there are no agreed understandings on the meaning of "import" and "export";

Cognisant of the financial and administrative implications of the implementation of such guidelines by States Parties, and the desirability of a simple, practical approach;

Noting that these guidelines are voluntary and hence do not dictate how and on what basis State Parties should collect data, but rather help to clarify what data should be reported for the purposes of declarations; and

Noting further that these guidelines are without prejudice to the relevant provisions of the Convention;

Hereby decides:

1. that, solely for the purposes of submitting declarations under paragraphs 1, 8(b) and 8(c) of Part VII and paragraph 1 of Part VIII of the Verification Annex, the term "import" shall be understood to mean the physical movement of scheduled chemicals into the territory or any other place under the jurisdiction or control of a State Party from the territory or any other place under the jurisdiction or control of another State, excluding transit operations; and the term "export" shall be understood to mean the physical movement of scheduled chemicals out of the territory or any other place under the jurisdiction or control of a State Party into the territory or any other place under the jurisdiction or control of another State, excluding transit operations;

2. that transit operations referred to in paragraph 1 above shall mean the physical movements in which scheduled chemicals pass through the territory of a State on the way to their intended State of destination. Transit operations include changes in the means of transport, including temporary storage only for that purpose;

3. that, for the purposes of declaring imports under paragraphs 1, 8(b) and 8(c) of Part VII and paragraph 1 of Part VIII of the Verification Annex, the declaring State Party shall specify the State from which the scheduled chemicals were dispatched, excluding the States through which the scheduled chemicals transited and regardless of the State in which the scheduled chemicals were produced;

4. that, for the purposes of declaring exports under paragraphs 1, 8(b) and 8(c) of Part VII and paragraph 1 of Part VIII of the Verification Annex, the declaring State Party shall specify the intended State of destination, excluding the States through which the scheduled chemicals transited;

5. to recommend that States Parties adopt the necessary measures, in accordance with the relevant provisions of the Convention, to utilise these guidelines as soon as practicable; and further

6. to request the Secretariat to report in three years on the progress achieved through the implementation of this decision for consideration by the Executive Council.

C-14/DEC.4 adopted by the Conference of the States Parties at its Fourteenth Session on 2 December 2009 and entitled "Guidelines Regarding Low Concentration Limits for Declarations of Schedule 2A and 2A* Chemicals"

The Conference of the States Parties,

Recalling that paragraph 5 of Part VII of the Verification Annex to the Chemical Weapons Convention (hereinafter "the Verification Annex") states that declarations are required for mixtures containing low concentrations of Schedule 2 chemicals, in accordance with guidelines, in cases where the ease of recovery from the mixture of a Schedule 2 chemical and its total weight are deemed to pose a risk to the object and purpose of the Chemical Weapons Convention (hereinafter "the Convention");

Taking into account the enhancement of the transparency that will result from the provision of such information in relation to the implementation of the Convention;

Recognising that these guidelines would enable the uniform implementation of the Convention with regard to declarations and inspections of facilities;

Stressing the desirability of adopting a common approach with respect to low concentration guidelines, consistent with the non-discriminatory and effective implementation of the Convention;

Recalling that declarations of plant sites in accordance with paragraph 5 of Part VII and paragraph 5 of Part VIII of the Verification Annex are triggered by the amount of a Schedule 2 or Schedule 3 chemical contained in a mixture, as well as its concentration (C-IV/DEC.16, dated 1 July 1999);

Recalling the decision of the Conference of the States Parties on guidelines regarding low-concentration limits for declarations of Schedule 2B and 3 chemicals (C-V/DEC.19, dated 19 May 2000) and bearing in mind the risks to the object and purpose of the Convention represented by Schedule 2A and 2A* chemicals;

Having considered the Note by the Director-General on the report of the Fourth Session of the Scientific Advisory Board (SAB) (EC-XXIV/DG.2, dated 9 March 2001), as well as the technical considerations of the SAB on the relevant aspects of the applicable concentration limits for mixtures of chemicals containing Schedule 2A and 2A* chemicals (SAB-IV/1, dated 6 February 2001);

Taking into account the understanding of the concept of "captive use" in connection with the declarations of production and consumption under Parts VII and VIII of the Verification Annex (C-9/DEC.6, dated 30 November 2004);

Recalling that the Second Special Session of the Conference of the States Parties to Review the Operation of the Chemical Weapons Convention "noted with concern that the issue of low concentrations in relation to Schedule 2A and 2A* chemicals has not yet been resolved", and urged the Executive Council (hereinafter "the Council") "to resume work promptly, with the support of the Secretariat, towards the earliest resolution of the issue" (paragraph 9.63 of RC-2/4, dated 18 April 2008); and

Cognisant of the economic and administrative implications of the implementation of such guidelines for States Parties;

Hereby decides that:
1. Declarations are not required under Part VII of the Verification Annex for:
    (a) mixtures of chemicals containing one percent (1%) or less of a Schedule 2A or 2A* chemical;
    (b) mixtures of chemicals containing more than 1% but less than or equal to 10% of a Schedule 2A or 2A* chemical, provided that the annual amount produced, processed, or consumed is less than the relevant verification thresholds specified in paragraph 12 of Part VII of the Verification Annex;
2. States Parties, in accordance with their constitutional processes, implement these guidelines as soon as practicable;
3. The Technical Secretariat report in detail annually to the Council in the Verification Implementation Report on the progress that States Parties have made in implementing this decision, beginning not later than 1 January 2012; and
4. The Third Special Session of the Conference of the States Parties to Review the Operation of the Chemical Weapons Convention review progress in carrying out this decision, with a view to ensuring its effective implementation.

7.3.2 Inspections

C-I/DEC.32 adopted by the Conference of the States Parties at its First Session on 16 May 1997 and entitled "Assessment of the risk posed by a Schedule 2 facility to the object and purpose of the Convention"

The Conference
Recalling that the Commission, in its PC-VI/22, sub-paragraph 6.2(a), adopted the understandings on the risk assessment of a Schedule 2 plant site,
Bearing in mind that the Commission recommended in paragraph 50.4 of its Final Report that the Conference adopt the above mentioned understanding,

Hereby:
1. Adopts the understandings on the assessment of the risk posed by a Schedule 2 plant site to the object and purpose of the Convention annexed hereto.

ANNEX[9]
ASSESSMENT OF THE RISK POSED BY A SCHEDULE 2 PLANT SITE
TO THE OBJECT AND PURPOSE OF THE CONVENTION

1. When assessing the risk a facility poses to the object and purpose of the Convention, several factors have to be taken into consideration, realising that these factors may not necessarily be inclusive. Relying solely on set factors to determine the frequency and intensity of subsequent inspections may be inadequate. The Technical Secretariat/Inspectorate will have to consider that each inspected party will have varying technology bases/resources, achieved different levels of production expertise, and may have dramatically different safety standards/measures required.

---

[9] As contained in paragraph 18 of the Chairman's Paper annexed to PC-VI/B/WP.2 in conjunction with Appendix B of PC-IV/B/WP.5.

2. Part VII, paragraphs 18 and 20 of the Verification Annex state that the Technical Secretariat should consider the risk posed by the relevant chemical, the characteristics of the plant site, and the nature of the activities carried out at the facility. It may also be necessary to consider the facility agreement, as well as the results of initial and subsequent inspections. It may be helpful to look at these categories separately.

3. In assessing the risk posed by <u>relevant chemicals at the plant sites</u>, the following may be considered:
    –   the toxicity of the scheduled toxic chemical(s), or, for scheduled precursor chemicals, of the end-products produced with them, if any (Part VII, paragraph 18 of the Verification Annex);
    –   the quantity of the scheduled chemicals typically stored at the inspected site (Part VII, paragraph 18 of the Verification Annex);
    –   the quantity of feed stock chemicals for the scheduled chemicals typically stored at the inspected site (Part VII, paragraph 18 of the Verification Annex);
    –   the chemical structure, to determine how closely it is related to that of toxic chemicals listed in Schedule 1, and to determine whether it has, or can be expected to have, comparable properties (Annex on Chemicals, Guidelines for Schedules of Chemicals);
    –   such lethal or incapacitating toxicity as well as other properties that would enable it to be used as a chemical weapon (Annex on Chemicals, Guidelines for Schedules of Chemicals);
    –   whether it may be used as a precursor of the final single technological stage of production of a toxic chemical listed in Schedule 1, regardless of whether this stage takes place in facilities, in munitions, or elsewhere (Annex on Chemicals, Guidelines for Schedules of Chemicals).

4. In assessing the risk posed by the <u>characteristics of the plant site</u>, the following may be considered:
    –   the characteristics of the process area, including:
        –   production capacity of the plant (Part VII, paragraph 18);
        –   the presence of process equipment, capable of handling highly toxic and corrosive materials, to include:
        –   high alloy, corrosive resistant equipment;
        –   welded pipelines;
        –   double/triple pipes;
        –   canned pumps;
        –   special seals on pumps or valves;
        –   the presence of individual items of process equipment that are enclosed or have hoods over them; and
        –   the physical layout, to include:
        –   air locks;
        –   large capacity ventilation systems, sufficient to maintain negative pressure,
        –   alarms designed to indicate the loss of negative pressure;
        –   air treatment systems (cyclones, charcoal filters, and scrubbers on the ventilation systems);
        –   enclosed process areas;
        –   isolated control rooms;
        –   air monitoring systems;
        –   laboratory suitable for toxic work;
        –   hoods over items of equipment;
    –   personnel considerations, including:
        –   background; and
        –   experience;

- consistency of security measures in force, with the declared activities, including:
    - high security or double fences;
    - intrusion detection devices;
    - excessive restrictions of access during the inspection to raw material storage areas or waste/treatment areas;
    - excessive restrictions of access during the inspection to records;
    - restricted contact for inspectors with operating personnel;
    - armed security;
    - military presence
    - specifics related to the location of the facility, such as unique location, isolation, or proximity to military facilities;
- safety equipment/procedures:
    - workers wearing impregnable clothing or carrying a protective mask;
    - workers wearing colour change badges or air samplers;
    - presence of full protective suits and self contained breathing apparatus (SCBA);
    - presence of mobile or portable decontamination equipment;
    - presence of special first aid kits containing antidotes;
    - signs warning of toxic chemicals;
    - alarm systems for evacuation of surrounding work areas;
    - emergency vehicles within close proximity;
    - isolated clothing change areas;
    - clinic/dispensary with patient wash down area and chemical emergency treatment area.
- based on the above indicators, assessments of the capability and convertibility for initiating production and storage of toxic chemicals (Part VII, paragraph 18 of the Verification Annex);
- potential for filling of toxic chemicals (Part VII, paragraph 18 of the Verification Annex);
- whether the facility is a dedicated or multi-purpose facility.

5. In assessing the risk posed by the nature of the activities carried out at the facility:
    - whether the scheduled chemicals are produced, processed or consumed, or whether such activities take place in combination;
    - which activities, not directly involving the declared Schedule 2 chemicals, take place at the plant site.

6. The presence of any one or any combination of these factors does not necessarily indicate that there is ongoing prohibited activities contrary to object and purpose of the Convention. However, these factors observed by the inspectors must be integrated with other information available to the Technical Secretariat in determining the frequency and intensity of inspections for that facility.

7. In applying the criteria in paragraph 18 of Part VII and the factors above, the Technical Secretariat will have to take into account the consistency of features encountered during the initial inspection with the framework the inspected plant site operates in. In order that specific features of a facility are not misinterpreted, due regard should be given to those factors - including climatic and other environmental factors, national legislation or accepted industrial practices, safety and environmental protection standards and regulations, plant site specific regulations and customs, and the location of the plant site in relation to populated areas - that would affect the way the plant site and the plants located therein are designed.

8. The risk assessment conducted during the initial inspection will form the point of departure for the Technical Secretariat in deciding on inspection frequency. Over time, additional factors will also have to be considered such as the track record of the plant site in relation to declaration and verification activities.

9. The factors listed above are not to be considered all-inclusive. Neither are they to be consid-

ered information that the plant site would be obliged to provide to the inspection team. The inspection is to be conducted in the least intrusive manner consistent with the effective and timely conduct of verification.

Extract of EC-XV/TS.2 containing a Note by the Director-General dated 22 April 1999 and entitled "Understanding on inspection of records during initial Schedule 2 inspections"

6.   ... Pending clear guidance from the Executive Council and the Conference of the States Parties on this issue, the Secretariat will continue to adopt the following approach to the verification of records during initial inspections of declared Schedule 2 plant sites.

7.   Inspection teams have been instructed initially to seek access to records of production, processing or consumption activities that were declared in the three calendar years prior to the year in which the initial inspection takes place. Only if such records show inconsistencies in the levels of production, processing or consumption will the inspection team seek access to records of production, processing or consumption activities that were declared for years prior to the three-year period before the year of the initial inspection in question.

8.   Inability to access these records in such situations will be considered for inclusion in the section on "pending issues" in the preliminary factual findings and in the section on "issues requiring further attention" in the final inspection reports.

9.   Any decision to be taken in this regard by the States Parties will be applied retroactively to any particular inspections in which the issue has arisen.

EC-XVII/DEC.7 adopted by the Executive Council at its Seventeenth Session on 1 December 1999 and entitled "Methodology for selecting Schedule 3 plant sites for inspection"

The Executive Council

Considering the provisions of paragraph 14 of Part VIII of the Verification Annex concerning the selection of Schedule 3 plant sites for inspection;

Recalling that, at its Sixteenth Session, the Executive Council took note of the Note by the Technical Secretariat on the comparison of methodologies for selecting Schedule 3 plant sites for inspection (EC-XVI/TS.4, dated 6 September 1999, and Corr.1, dated 21 September 1999), and decided to continue to deliberate this issue during the intersessional period, requesting the Technical Secretariat to develop further its analysis in this area;

Taking into account the background paper provided by the Secretariat, as requested by the Executive Council at its Sixteenth Session;

Hereby:

1.   Decides that Schedule 3 plant sites shall be selected each calendar year for inspection using the methodology described in the annex hereto; and

2.   Further decides to review this methodology on the basis of the results of the selection in the fourth year after the beginning of its implementation.

ANNEX
METHODOLOGY FOR SELECTING SCHEDULE 3 PLANT SITES
FOR INSPECTION

1.   The selection of Schedule 3 plant sites for inspection will be done randomly, as required by the provisions of paragraph 14 of Part VIII of the Verification Annex. This will be accomplished by a sequence of a two-step random selection.

2. In the first step, the State Party is selected according to its probability of being inspected, derived from the weighting factor f(x), which is calculated using the following relationship:

$$f(x) = 0.5x^{1/2} + 1 \quad \text{(see footnote }^{10})$$

where x represents the number of Schedule 3 plant sites in a given State Party which are verifiable according to the provisions of paragraph 12 of Part VIII of the Verification Annex, and 0.5 and 1 are the values of the coefficients which were introduced in order to ensure an equitable geographical distribution, as required by the provisions of Part VIII of the Verification Annex.

3. The second step consists of a random selection of plant sites within the already selected State Party, which will take into consideration the information available to the Secretariat, related to the relevant chemical, the characteristics of the plant site, and the nature of the activities carried out there, in accordance with the requirements of paragraph 14 of Part VIII of the Verification Annex.

7.3.3 Transfers

C-III/DEC.6 adopted by the Conference of the States Parties at its Third Session on 17 November 1998 and entitled "Paragraph 32 of Part VII and paragraph 26 of part VIII of the Verification Annex of the Convention"

The Conference

Having considered the issue of the information to be included in the end-use certificates in the case of transfers of Schedule 2 and 3 chemicals to traders/trading houses in States not party to the Chemical Weapons Convention;

Bearing in mind the decision of the Executive Council on end-use certificates for transfers of Schedule 2 and 3 chemicals to States not party to the Convention in accordance with paragraph 32 of Part VII and paragraph 26 of Part VIII of the Verification Annex (EC-VIII/DEC.3, dated 30 January 1998);

Bearing in mind that the Executive Council recommended, in its decision EC-IX/DEC.11, dated 24 April 1998, that the Conference adopt the agreement on the above-mentioned issue;

Hereby:

Decides that the terms "(d) Their end-use(s); and (e) The name(s) and address(es) of the end-user(s)", in cases of transfers to importers in States not party to this Convention who are not the actual end-users (e.g. trading firms), shall be understood to mean that, in these cases, before authorising transfers, a statement of the importer, in a manner consistent with paragraph 32 of Part VII and paragraph 26 of Part VIII of the Verification Annex of the Convention, and of national legislation and practices, shall be obtained, whereby the importer will be obliged to specify name(s) and address(es) of the end-user(s).

C-III/DEC.7 adopted by the Conference of the States Parties at its Third Session on 17 November 1998 and entitled "End-use certificates for transfers of Schedule 2 and 3 chemicals to States not party to the Convention in accordance with paragraph 32 of Part VII and paragraph 26 of Part VIII of the Verification Annex"

The Conference

---

[10] $x \frac{1}{2}$ is equal to $\sqrt{x}$, or the square of x [footnote in original].

Having considered the issue of the meaning of the term "shall require from the recipient State a certificate", as used in paragraph 32 of Part VII and in paragraph 26 of Part VIII of the Verification Annex;

Taking note of the opinion of the Legal Adviser on end-use certificates (EC-VII/TS.1, dated 14 November 1997) on this issue;

Bearing in mind that the Executive Council recommended, in its decision EC-VIII/DEC.3, dated 30 January 1998, that the Conference adopt the above-mentioned understanding;

Hereby:

Decides that the term "shall require from the recipient State a certificate", as used in paragraph 32 of Part VII and in paragraph 26 of Part VIII of the Verification Annex, shall be understood to mean "end-use certificates issued by the competent government authority of States not party to this Convention", and shall contain all the requisites established in subparagraphs (a) to (e) of the paragraphs referred to above.

C-V/DEC.16 adopted by the Conference of the States Parties at its Fifth Session on 17 May 2000 and entitled "Implementation of restrictions on transfers of Schedule 2 and Schedule 3 chemicals to and from States not party to the Convention"

The Conference

Recalling the decision of the Conference of the States Parties at its Fourth Session on guidelines for provisions regarding scheduled chemicals in low concentrations, including in mixtures, in accordance with paragraphs 5 of Parts VII and VIII of the Verification Annex (C-IV/DEC.16, dated 1 July 1999);

Bearing in mind the special responsibility of States Parties with regard to transfers of Schedule 2 or Schedule 3 chemicals to States not party to the Convention, and recalling in this respect the obligation under paragraph 31 of Part VII of the Verification Annex, which came into effect on 29 April 2000, that Schedule 2 chemicals shall only be transferred to or received from States Parties;

Recalling further that, with regard to transfers of Schedule 3 chemicals, five years after the entry into force of the Convention (29 April 2002) the Conference shall consider the need to establish other measures;

Recognising the need to ensure that the transfer provisions regarding Schedule 2 or Schedule 3 chemicals do not encompass impurities and consumer goods;

Noting that transfers of the products under consideration in this decision shall only be for purposes not prohibited under the Convention, and recognising the desire of States Parties in relation to this decision, to keep under review technical and possible security aspects of transfers of products as defined in the operative subparagraphs 1(a) and (b) below;

Noting further the recommendation to the Conference adopted by the Executive Council at its Nineteenth Session (EC-XIX/DEC.11, dated 2 May 2000);

Hereby:

1. Decides that, with regard to the application of the provisions on transfers of Schedule 2 chemicals to and from States not party to the Convention, paragraph 31 of Part VII of the Verification Annex shall not apply to:
   (a) products containing one percent or less of a Schedule 2A or 2A* chemical;
   (b) products containing 10 percent or less of a Schedule 2B chemical; and
   (c) products identified as consumer goods packaged for retail sale for personal use or packaged for individual use; and
2. Further requests, with regard to the application of the provisions on transfers of Schedule 3

chemicals, the Executive Council to prepare a recommendation to be considered by the Conference at its Sixth Session.

C-VI/DEC.10 adopted by the Conference of the States Parties at its Sixth Session on 17 May 2001 and entitled "Provisions on transfers of Schedule 3 chemicals to States not party to the Convention"

The Conference of the States Parties,

Recalling the decision of the Conference of the States Parties (hereinafter the "Conference") at its Fifth Session on the implementation of restrictions on transfers of Schedule 2 and Schedule 3 chemicals to and from States not party to the Convention (C-V/DEC.16, dated 17 May 2000);

Recalling further the decision of the Conference at its Fifth Session on national implementation measures (C-V/DEC.20, dated 19 May 2000);

Recalling in particular the decision by the Executive Council (hereinafter the "Council) at its Twelfth Meeting to refer to the Conference, at its Sixth Session, its recommendation for approval of the provisions on transfers of Schedule 3 chemicals to States not party to the Convention (EC-M-XII/DEC.1, dated 4 May 2001);

Bearing in mind the special responsibility of States Parties with regard to transfers of Schedule 3 chemicals to States not party to the Convention, and recalling in this respect the obligation under paragraph 26 of Part VIII of the Verification Annex, to adopt the necessary measures to ensure that the transferred chemicals shall only be used for purposes not prohibited under this Convention;

Recalling further that, in accordance with paragraph 27 of Part VIII of the Verification Annex, five years after the entry into force of the Convention, i.e. by 29 April 2002, the Conference shall consider the need to establish other measures regarding transfers of Schedule 3 chemicals to States not party to the Convention;

Considering the effective contribution of such measures to preventing the proliferation of chemical weapons and promoting universal adherence to the Convention;

Hereby:
1. Calls to the attention of States Parties their obligation, when transferring Schedule 3 chemicals to States not party to the Convention, to require from the recipient State an end-use certificate in accordance with paragraph 26 of Part VIII of the Verification Annex and with Conference decisions C-III/DEC.6 and C-III/DEC.7, both dated 17 November 1998;
2. Decides, with regard to the application of the obligation to require an end-use certificate for transfers of Schedule 3 chemicals to States not party to the Convention, and without prejudice to the right of any State Party to adopt a more restrictive approach, that end-use certificates are not required for:
    (i)   products containing 30 percent or less of a Schedule 3 chemical;
    (ii) products identified as consumer goods packaged for retail sale for personal use, or packaged for individual use;
3. Urges States Parties to adopt national legislative and administrative measures, as appropriate, to implement the provisions on transfers of Schedule 3 chemicals to States not party to the Convention, and, in accordance with paragraph 5 of Article VII of the Convention, to inform the Organisation concerning the measures taken;
4. Requests the Technical Secretariat to include in its regular reports on the implementation of the Convention the information provided by States Parties on the implementation of paragraph 26 of Part VIII of the Verification Annex on transfers of Schedule 3 chemicals to States not party to the Convention;
5. Requests the Council to consider the need to establish other measures regarding transfers of

Schedule 3 chemicals under paragraph 27 of Part VIII of the Verification Annex and to report the results of its consideration to the Conference at its Seventh Session; and

6. Recommends that five years after the implementation of this decision the concentration limits contained in operative paragraph 2 above may be reviewed upon a recommendation of the Council.

EC-47/DEC.8 adopted by the Executive Council at its Forty-Seventh Session on 8 November 2006 and entitled "Measures regarding the transfer of Schedule 3 chemicals to States not party to the Convention"

The Executive Council

Recalling that Part VIII, paragraph 26, of the Verification Annex to the Chemical Weapons Convention (hereinafter "the Verification Annex") prescribes the necessary measures, regarding transfers of Schedule 3 chemicals to States not Party to the Chemical Weapons Convention (hereinafter "the Convention"), *inter alia* the requirement of an end-use certificate from the recipient State;

Recalling also that paragraph 27 of the same Part requires that the Conference of the States Parties (hereinafter "the Conference") consider the need to establish other measures regarding transfers of Schedule 3 chemicals to States not Party;

Noting the decisions adopted by the Conference on transfers of Schedule 3 chemicals to States not Party (C-III/DEC.6, dated 17 November 1998; C-III/DEC.7, dated 17 November 1998; and C-VI/DEC.10, dated 17 May 2001);

Bearing in mind that, in paragraph 7.73 of its report (RC-1/5, dated 9 May 2003), the First Special Session of the Conference of the States Parties to Review the Operation of the Chemical Weapons Convention concluded that all States Parties should take the necessary measures to ensure full implementation of the Convention's requirement for end-use certification by recipient States not Party, and requested the Executive Council to submit a recommendation on this matter to the Conference at its Tenth Session;

Recalling further that the Conference at its Tenth Session, in a decision on the universality of the Convention (C-10/DEC.11, dated 10 November 2005), called upon all States not Party the non-adherence of which is a cause for serious concern to join the Convention without delay, reaffirming that States not Party cannot benefit from the same provisions under the Convention as States Parties including those related to transfers of Schedule 3 chemicals, and noting also that the Convention includes provisions for transfers to States not Party, and that these provisions contribute both to non-proliferation benefits and to the goal of the universality of the Convention;

Noting with concern the deficiencies in the implementation of legislative and administrative measures regarding transfers of Schedule 3 chemicals to States not Party deficiencies that can be observed through responses that have been provided by States Parties to the legislation questionnaires S/194/2000, dated 8 June 2000, and S/317/2002, dated 18 September 2002;

Hereby:

1. Calls upon all States Parties, and in particular those that have yet to do so, to adopt the necessary measures to ensure that Schedule 3 chemicals transferred by them to States not Party, the non-adherence of which is a cause for serious concern, are used only for purposes not prohibited under the Convention, and *inter alia*, to require an end-use certificate from the recipient State, as stipulated in Part VIII, paragraph 26, of the Verification Annex and in Conference decisions C-III/DEC.6 and C-III/DEC.7;

2. Recommends that the Second Special Session of the Conference of the States Parties to Review the Operation of the Chemical Weapons Convention review the implementation of measures regarding transfers of Schedule 3 chemicals to States not Party as stipulated in Part

VIII, paragraph 26, of the Verification Annex, and consider the need to establish other measures in this regard; and
3.   Decides to remain seized of this issue to review it further in accordance with Part VIII, paragraph 27, of the Verification Annex.

7.4 Regime for other chemical production facilities

C-I/DEC.39 adopted by the Conference of the States Parties at its First Session on 16 May 1997 and entitled "Understandings in relation to Part IX of the Verification Annex"

The Conference

Recalling that the Commission, in its PC-VII/8, paragraph 6.6, adopted understandings in relation to Part IX of the Verification Annex,

Bearing in mind that the Commission recommended in paragraph 50.4 of its Final Report that the Conference adopt the above mentioned understanding,

Hereby:
1.   Adopts the understandings in relation to Part IX of the Verification Annex.

ANNEX
UNDERSTANDINGS IN RELATION TO PART IX OF THE VERIFICATION ANNEX[11]

1.   The term "unscheduled discrete organic chemical" referred to in paragraph 1(a) of Part IX of the Verification Annex and the term "PSF chemical" referred to in paragraph 1(b) of the same Part do not cover:
      (a) oligomers and polymers, whether or not containing phosphorus, sulfur or fluorine[12];
      (b) chemicals only containing carbon and metal.
2.   The term "oxides of carbon" in the definition of unscheduled discrete organic chemicals (DOCs) refers to carbon monoxide and carbon dioxide. The term "sulfides of carbon" in the same definition refers to carbon disulfide. Both terms refer to carbonyl sulfide.
3.   In calculating the "approximate aggregate amount of production of unscheduled discrete organic chemicals" at the plant site pursuant to paragraph 1(a) of Part IX of the Verification Annex, the production data should be aggregated in a way that includes:
      (a) in the case of the production of two or more unscheduled DOCs at the same plant, the aggregate of all of these unscheduled DOCs;
      (b) in the case of multistep processes, only the quantity of the final product if it is an unscheduled DOC, or the quantity of the last intermediate in the multistep synthesis that meets the definition of an unscheduled DOC;
      (c) in the case of intermediates meeting the definition of an unscheduled DOC and being used by another plant at the site to produce an unscheduled DOC, the amount of the intermediate and of the product manufactured from it at that other plant.
4.   The term "hydrocarbon", referring to production which is excluded from the coverage of Part IX, includes all hydrocarbons (i.e. chemicals containing only carbon and hydrogen), irrespective of the number of carbon atoms in the compound.

---

[11] As contained in paragraph 3.5 of PC-VII/B/WP.7.
[12] The production of the monomers, however, is covered by the term, provided that the monomer otherwise meets the definition of a DOC [footnote in original].

8. CHALLENGE INSPECTION ISSUES[1]

8.1 Common understandings on the Notification Formats in challenge inspection

C-I/DEC.44 adopted by the Conference of the States Parties at its First Session on 16 May 1997 and entitled "Notification Formats in Challenge Inspection, illustrative examples of the type of information which might be included under "all appropriate information on the basis of which the concern (of possible non-compliance) has arisen", in the context of Format 1, common understandings on these Notification Formats, and Format of an Inspection Mandate for the Conduct of a Challenge Inspection"

The Conference

Recalling that the Commission, in its PC-XII/17, paragraph 8.2, adopted the Notification Formats 1-7 in Challenge Inspection together with the illustrative examples of the type of information which might be included under 'all appropriate information on the basis of which the concern (of possible non-compliance) has arisen', in the context of Format 1, the common understandings on these Notification Formats, and the Format of an Inspection Mandate for the Conduct of a Challenge Inspection,

Bearing in mind that the Commission recommended in paragraph 51.3 of its Final Report that the Conference adopt the above mentioned understanding,

Hereby:

1. Adopts the Notification Formats 1-7 in Challenge Inspection together with the illustrative examples of the type of information which might be included under "all appropriate information on the basis of which the concern (of possible non-compliance) has arisen", in the context of Format 1, the common understandings on these Notification Formats and the Format of an Inspection Mandate for the Conduct of a Challenge Inspection.

ANNEX [Extract]
NOTIFICATION FORMATS IN CHALLENGE INSPECTION, ILLUSTRATIVE
EXAMPLES OF THE TYPE OF INFORMATION WHICH MIGHT BE INCLUDED
UNDER "ALL APPROPRIATE INFORMATION ON THE BASIS OF WHICH THE
CONCERN (OF POSSIBLE NON-COMPLIANCE) HAS ARISEN", IN THE CONTEXT
OF FORMAT 1, COMMON UNDERSTANDINGS ON THESE NOTIFICATION
FORMATS, AND FORMAT OF AN INSPECTION MANDATE FOR THE CONDUCT
OF A CHALLENGE INSPECTION[2]

2. Notification Formats in Challenge Inspection
    Format 1:   Challenge Inspection Request format (Verification Annex, Part X,
                       Section B, paragraph 4)

---

[1] The First Special Session of the Conference of the States Parties to Review the Operation of the Chemical Weapons Convention requested the Technical Secretariat "to continue maintaining a high standard of readiness to conduct a challenge inspection in accordance with the provisions of the Convention, to keep the Council informed about its readiness, and to report any problems that may arise in relation to maintaining the necessary level of readiness to conduct a challenge inspection" (see paragraph 7.91 of the Report of the First Special Session, document RC-1/5, set out in Section 21.1). Pursuant to this direction, Notes by the Director-General are regularly submitted to the Executive Council reporting on "Readiness to Conduct a Challenge Inspection".

[2] As contained in Appendices 1 to 7 of the Annex to PC-IV/B/WP.10; paragraph 5 of the Annex to PC-IV/B/WP.10 as amended by PC-XIII/18, paragraph 7.4; and Annexes 1 and 2 of PC-XII/B/WP.3.

Format 2: Acknowledgement of Challenge Inspection Request Format (Verification Annex, Part X, Section B, paragraph 5)

Format 3: Format for Implementation of Article IX, paragraph 14

Format 4: Challenge Inspection Format for Notification of the Location of the Inspection Site (Verification Annex, Part X, Section B, paragraphs 6 and 7)

Format 4A: Challenge Inspection: Notification on Requesting State Party's Observer (Article IX, paragraph 12; Verification Annex, Part X, Section B, paragraph 4 and Section C, paragraphs 53 and 56)

Format 5: Format for the Transmission of Information from the Director-General to the Executive Council about the Location of the Inspection Site (Verification Annex, Part X, Section B, paragraph 10)

Format 6: Format for Transmission of the Inspection Request to the Inspected State Party Including Location of the Inspection Site and Information Specified in Verification Annex, Part II, paragraph 32 (Verification Annex, Part X, Section B, paragraph 11)

Format 7: Format for Acknowledgement of Receipt of Notification of Intent to Conduct a Challenge Inspection (Verification Annex, Part II, Section D, paragraph 33)

3. ILLUSTRATIVE EXAMPLES OF THE TYPE OF INFORMATION WHICH MIGHT BE INCLUDED UNDER "ALL APPROPRIATE INFORMATION ON THE BASIS OF WHICH THE CONCERN (OF POSSIBLE NON-COMPLIANCE) HAS ARISEN", IN THE CONTEXT OF FORMAT 1

Paragraph 9 of Article IX obliges the requesting State Party to "keep the inspection request within the scope of the Convention" and to provide "all appropriate information on the basis of which a concern has arisen regarding possible non-compliance with the Convention as specified in the Verification Annex". The following are illustrative examples, neither comprehensive nor prescriptive, of the type of such information which the requesting State Party could provide:

1. The nature of the suspected non-compliance, such as, <u>inter alia</u>:
   (a) development of chemical weapons;
   (b) production transfer/acquisition/stockpiling/retention of chemical weapons;
   (c) use of chemical weapons; use of riot control agents as a method of warfare;
   (d) assisting, encouraging or inducing anyone to engage in an activity prohibited under the Convention;
   (e) production/processing/consumption of scheduled chemicals except as permitted under the Convention;
   (f) omission of declarations, or submission of inaccurate declarations, due under the Convention.
2. The types and amounts, as appropriate, of chemicals, munitions, devices, or specifically designed equipment suspected to have been involved.
3. The period within which the activities are suspected to have been carried out.
4. The type of facility(ies)/installation(s)/building(s)/area(s) suspected to have been involved.
5. The possible extent of the activities and the ways and means used.
6. Specific chemical signatures emanating from the facility(ies).

8.2 *Understanding on the objective indicators of whether the right to request a challenge inspection has been abused*

C-I/DEC.45 adopted by the Conference of the States Parties at its First Session on 16 May 1997 and entitled "Illustrative list of objective indicators to facilitate the Executive Council in addressing any concern, in accordance with paragraph 22 of Article IX, whether the right to request a challenge inspection has been abused"

The Conference

Recalling that the Commission, in its PC-XIII/18, paragraph 7.4, adopted the illustrative list of objective indicators to facilitate the Executive Council in addressing any concern, in accordance with paragraph 22 of Article IX, whether the right to request a challenge inspection has been abused,

Bearing in mind that the Commission recommended in paragraph 51.3 of its Final Report that the Conference adopt the above mentioned understanding,

Hereby:

1. Adopts the illustrative list of objective indicators to facilitate the Executive Council in addressing any concern, in accordance with paragraph 22 of Article IX, whether the right to request a challenge inspection has been abused.

ANNEX

ILLUSTRATIVE LIST OF OBJECTIVE INDICATORS [3] TO FACILITATE THE
EXECUTIVE COUNCIL IN ADDRESSING ANY CONCERN, IN ACCORDANCE WITH
PARAGRAPH 22 OF ARTICLE IX, WHETHER THE RIGHT TO REQUEST
A CHALLENGE INSPECTION HAS BEEN ABUSED [4]

Paragraph 22 of Article IX authorises the Executive Council, as part of its review of the final report of the inspection team, to address any concerns as to "whether the right to request a Challenge Inspection had been abused." Such concerns would not arise in the event of an Executive Council conclusion in accordance with paragraph 23 of Article IX that concerns about possible non-compliance necessitated further action to redress the situation and to ensure compliance with the Convention. In addressing any such concerns, one or more of the following objective indicators are for the Executive Council to take into consideration when relevant. This list is not intended to be comprehensive or prescriptive.

(a) The result, if any, of the Executive Council having addressed, in accordance with paragraph 22(b) of Article IX, any concerns as to whether the request had been within the scope of the Convention.

(b) Information relating to the inspected site available prior to the inspection request (the authenticity and reliability of any information would need to be carefully assessed).

(c) Whether any of the information submitted as part of the inspection request, was shown to be false.

(d) The results, if available, of any efforts by the requesting State Party to seek to clarify or resolve any doubts concerning compliance, if that State Party elected to exercise its options in accordance with paragraphs 1 through 7 of Article IX.

---

[3] It is understood that these indicators may also, where relevant, facilitate any decision-making by the Executive Council under paragraph 17 of Article IX [footnote in original].

[4] As contained in the Annex to PC-XIII/B/WP.4.

(e) Whether the conduct of the observer, if any, named by the requesting State Party in accordance with the provisions of paragraph 12 of Article IX, was cause for concern, including on matters relating to confidentiality (e.g. as reflected or assessed in any comments in the preliminary or final inspection report).

(f) Whether challenge inspection requests, not resulting in Executive Council conclusions in accordance with paragraph 23 of Article IX on a need for further action to redress a compliance concern, had previously been made by the same requesting State Party vis-à-vis the same inspected site, and if so, their number and frequency.

9. INVESTIGATIONS OF ALLEGED USE

9.1 Director-General's obligation to inform the Executive Council of requests for investigations of alleged use

EC-70/5 containing the Report of the Seventieth Session of the Executive Council adopted on 28 September 2012, Subparagraph 3.3

...

3.3 The Council requested that, in case the provisions of paragraph 27 of Part XI of the Verification Annex to the Chemical Weapons Convention (hereinafter "the Verification Annex") or any other document related thereto and concluded between the OPCW and the United Nations are invoked, the Director-General will promptly inform the Council and all States Parties of the request and of the actions that the Technical Secretariat (hereinafter "the Secretariat") is undertaking to respond to the request.

...

9.2 Understanding on the status of "qualified experts" in the context of investigations of alleged use

C-I/DEC.46 adopted by the Conference of the States Parties at its First Session on 16 May 1997 and entitled "Understanding on the status of 'qualified experts' in the context of investigations of alleged use"

The Conference

Recalling that the Commission, in its PC-XII/17, subparagraph 8.6(b), adopted an understanding on the status of "qualified experts" in the context of investigations of alleged use,

Bearing in mind that the Commission recommended in paragraph 52.3 of its Final Report that the Conference adopt the above mentioned understanding,

Hereby:
1. Adopts the understanding on the status of "qualified experts" in the context of investigations of alleged use.

ANNEX
UNDERSTANDING ON THE STATUS OF "QUALIFIED EXPERTS"
IN THE CONTEXT OF INVESTIGATIONS OF ALLEGED USE [1]

1. "Qualified experts" will be designated in accordance with the provisions of paragraph 7 of Part XI of the Verification Annex, supplemented, as appropriate, by the second part of paragraph 2, and paragraphs 3 through 9 of Part II of the Verification Annex, and will become members of an inspection team in accordance with paragraph 8 of Part XI of the Verification Annex.

2. As members of an inspection team, the qualified experts are subject to the obligations of inspectors. The most conspicuous of these obligations are those in relation to the protection of confidentiality and the observance of safety regulations. However, the extent of the tasks which the qualified experts will be called upon to fulfil will define their involvement in the

---

[1] As contained in Annex 5 to PC-XII/B/WP.6.

team work, and their access to confidential information, as well as their terms of employment. It is important to note that qualified experts will join an inspection team for a specific purpose, and that their activities will be limited in accordance with that purpose and the instructions of the team leader. In this connection it is also assumed that each of the qualified experts will enter into a contract of employment (probably on a short-term basis) and into the Organisation's individual secrecy agreement.

3. Within the framework of their duties, the qualified experts may use only the approved inspection equipment designated, calibrated and approved by the Technical Secretariat for that investigation. Any additional equipment a qualified expert might bring to the point of entry, in coordination with the Technical Secretariat, can be brought onto the inspection site only with the express consent of and under conditions set by the State Party on whose territory the investigation takes place.

9.3 Sampling and analysis during investigations of alleged use

C-I/DEC.47 adopted by the Conference of the States Parties at its First Session on 16 May 1997 and entitled "Sampling and analysis during investigations of alleged use of chemical weapons"

The Conference

Recalling that the Commission, in its PC-XII/17, subparagraph 8.6(b), adopted a document on "sampling and analysis during investigations of alleged use of chemical weapons",

Recalling that the Commission, when adopting the above document, took note of an understanding recorded in subparagraph 6.1 of PC-XII/B/WP.6,[2]

Bearing in mind that the Commission recommended in paragraph 52.3 of its Final Report that the Conference adopt the above mentioned document,

Hereby:

1. Adopts the document on "sampling and analysis during investigations of alleged use of chemical weapons".

---

[2] Subparagraph 6.1 of PC-XII/B/WP.6, Preparatory Commission document dated 2 November 1995 entitled, "Report of the Expert Group on Inspection Procedures." The relevant extract from that Report is as follows:

"6.1 The Group reviewed and slightly revised the understanding on the status of "qualified experts" in the context of investigations of alleged use (subparagraph 8.3 of PC-XI/B/W.P.5) and the "Sampling and Analysis During Investigations of Alleged Use of Chemical Weapons" (provisionally approved on 25 October 1994, see subparagraph 7.3 of PC-IX/B/W.P.3). The Group agreed to recommend both documents, through Working Group B, for adoption by the Commission (Annexes 5 and 6 to this Report). The Group agreed that nothing in Annex 6 shall be considered as constituting any interpretation of provisions of the Convention. It is therefore understood that Annex 6 cannot be used to justify measures other than provided for, or permitted under, the Convention. In this context, the Group understood that no sampling on humans in accordance with the provisions of the Convention may be performed without the explicit consent of the individual(s) involved, following the provision of exhaustive information on all related aspects and potential consequences of such sampling. This agreement from the individual(s) shall be recorded taking due care that no external pressure has been exerted on the individual(s) to comply with the sampling request. The sample shall be taken solely for the purpose identified under the Convention, and no other use shall be authorised. In the case of an unconscious or dead person, the explicit consent, if possible, should be obtained from the family in accordance with the above procedures."

ANNEX
SAMPLING AND ANALYSIS DURING INVESTIGATIONS OF
ALLEGED USE OF CHEMICAL WEAPONS [3, 4]

I.   THE TIME FACTOR

1.   Investigation teams would rarely if ever be expected to arrive at a site earlier than three to five days after the alleged use. This will be of importance for the sample-taking as well as for the analyses:
      –   evidence of original chemical weapon component(s) is of importance;
      –   absorbing substrates will be of special importance;
      –   low concentrations might be expected due to evaporation and degradation;
      –   only involatile degradation products might remain in environmental samples;
      –   degradation products might depend on the nature of the substrate;
      –   only metabolic degradation products might remain in biological samples;
      –   stable by-products may be an important factor in the identification process of the origin of any chemical weapons used.

II.   SELECTION OF SAMPLES

2.   Initial chemical agent monitoring of the area under investigation will be necessary in order to establish the safety precautions required for the sampling operation. Such monitoring can at the same time be used to assist in the selection of promising sampling positions. Nevertheless, due to the anticipated levels of chemicals (trace levels) present in the samples, this may be a rather difficult task.

3.   A number of features related specifically to cases of alleged use will also need to be taken into consideration. Some examples are:
      (a)   on-site analysis, where considered safe, possible and advisable, can support off-site analysis, due to possible decomposition of agents during transportation to designated laboratories;
      (b)   analysis for the presence of trace chemicals may be required;
      (c)   the possible use of unscheduled chemicals must be considered;
      (d)   non-standard or special analytical procedures may need to be developed; and
      (e)   there will need to be high confidence that any positive detections are genuine, which might be difficult to accomplish if the chemical is unknown as stated in (c), and/or if different results are obtained by designated laboratories, which performed the analysis.

4.   Sample-taking of biological/medical samples from persons allegedly exposed to chemical weapons requires special attention:
      –   informed consent from the persons is required;
      –   sample-taking only by the investigation team's own medical personnel;
      –   the person's name and medical history should be recorded and confidentiality of that data guaranteed.

---

[3] As contained in Annex 6 of PC-XII/B/WP.6 in conjunction with subparagraph 6.1 of PC-XII/B/WP.6.

[4] Nothing in this document shall be considered as constituting any interpretation of provisions of the Convention. It is therefore understood that this document cannot be used to justify measures other than provided for, or permitted under, the Convention. In this context, it is understood that no sampling on humans in accordance with the provisions of the Convention may be performed without the explicit consent of the individual(s) involved, following the provision of exhaustive information on all related aspects and potential consequences of such sampling. This agreement from the individual(s) shall be recorded taking due care that no external pressure has been exerted on the individual(s) to comply with the sampling request. The sample shall be taken solely for the purpose identified under the Convention, and no other use shall be authorised. In the case of an unconscious or dead person, the explicit consent, if possible, should be obtained from the family in accordance with the above procedures [footnote in original].

5. Blank samples are essential, both for baseline determinations and for the preparation of spiked control samples. Blank samples should:
    –   as closely as possible resemble the actual samples taken;
    –   be taken in several areas close to the site of the alleged use but still not contaminated (it is essential for the designated laboratory performing the analysis, to ascertain that this has been achieved);
    –   be taken with extreme care in order to avoid cross-contamination, especially if the team just visited contaminated areas;
    –   in case of biological/medical samples (blood, urine, etc.), blank samples should be requested from unexposed local individuals forming an appropriate control group as uniform as possible under the circumstances.

III. SAMPLE PRESERVATION AND TRANSPORTATION
6. The preservation of a chain of custody is essential. This includes eliminating the risk for any cross-contamination during the continued handling. Such cross-contamination could arise, e.g. :
    –   during packaging of samples;
    –   during transportation through contaminated areas, including contamination present in the vapour phase;
    –   through contact with insufficiently decontaminated personal protective equipment;
    –   during the opening of the sample packages in a laboratory.
7. Samples and blanks must be kept under conditions to minimise the continued degradation of any chemicals present. This might involve, e.g.:
    –   preservation at low temperature;
    –   preservation under inert atmosphere, nitrogen only, under normal pressure;
    –   preservation in darkness.
8. Samples will usually have to be shipped via a commercial air carrier, using an approved transportation system. This means that very strict regulations will apply to packaging, and thus the investigation team will have to bring suitable packaging material and an approved transportation system.

IV. SAMPLE PREPARATION AND SAMPLE SPLITTING
9. Generally, it would be expected that the OPCW would handle the initial sample preparation and splitting. This might involve:
    –   preparation of split samples;
    –   preparation of blanks;
    –   preparation of blanks, spiked with known chemicals and/or their degradation products;
    –   labelling of samples, blanks and spiked blanks in such a way as to preclude laboratories which will perform the analysis from knowing which labels correspond to what.
10. If the sample size permits, a reference sample should be preserved in the OPCW custody until the investigation has been completed and the results have been studied by the States Parties.

V. DETAILED CHEMICAL ANALYSIS OFF-SITE
11. Only designated laboratories will be used for the detailed chemical analysis off-site. Up to three laboratories should analyse each set of samples simultaneously. In the case of discrepancy in the results of their analyses further analyses should be performed.
12. The decision on what to analyse a sample for is a critical one. The investigation team should suggest groups of chemicals, if they are sure. In addition, if available, information related to the battlefield should be included. The OPCW Laboratory could add to this list on the basis of, e.g., observations during the sample preparations. The designated laboratories should be given sufficient background information on the samples, to include results of on-site analysis,

if any, to allow also them to add to the list of groups of chemicals. The number of groups of chemicals to analyse for may be restricted by, e.g.:
– sample size;
– timing requirements for the final report.

13. The designated laboratories should report their results only to the Director-General. They should not be informed of which labels corresponded to which samples, blanks or spiked blanks until the investigation has been completed and the results have been studied by the States Parties.

9.4 List of items to be stockpiled for emergency and humanitarian assistance

C-I/DEC.12 adopted by the Conference of the States Parties at its First Session on 16 May 1997 and entitled "Lists of items to be stockpiled for emergency and humanitarian assistance in accordance with Article VIII(39)(b) (Paris Resolution, subparagraph 12(b))". For text of the decision, see Section 18.6.

10. GENERAL RULES OF VERIFICATION

10.1 Visa procedures for OPCW inspectors and inspection assistants

C-I/DEC.56 adopted by the Conference of the States Parties at its First Session on 16 May 1997 and entitled "Visa procedures for OPCW inspectors and inspection assistants"

The Conference

Recalling that the Commission, in PC-XIV/29, paragraph 8.3, approved the visa procedures for OPCW inspectors and inspection assistants annexed to PC-XIV/A/WP.7, as amended in sub-paragraph 5.2 of PC-XIV/A/3,

Bearing in mind that the Commission recommended in paragraph 47.2 of its Final Report that the Conference adopt the above-mentioned visa procedures for OPCW inspectors and inspection assistants,

Hereby:

Decides that, in respect of visa procedures for OPCW inspectors and inspection assistants, the process of visa issuance should reflect the clearance given by a State Party to inspectors and inspection assistants, and should be considered a logical consequence of that clearance. The preliminary list of potential inspectors and inspection assistants containing the information required in accordance with paragraph 1 of Part II A of the Verification Annex, as well as the national visa application form, would be provided to the States Parties at entry into force (EIF) of the Convention. It is understood that this activity is undertaken to facilitate the process of visa issuance and is separate from the procedures that are obligatory under paragraph 1 of Part II A of the Verification Annex. Since the issuance of visas for those inspectors and inspection assistants of the OPCW accepted by the State Party is an obligation articulated by the Convention, each State Party should instruct its relevant authorities to process visas in accordance with paragraph 10, Part II B of the Verification Annex, within 30 days after receipt of the list of inspectors and inspection assistants has been acknowledged.

10.2 The meaning of "interpretation"

C-II/DEC.9 adopted by the Conference of the States Parties at its Second Session on 5 December 1997 and entitled "Paragraph 26[1] of Part II of the Verification Annex of the Convention"

The Conference decides that the term "interpretation" in paragraph 26[1] of Part II of the Verification Annex of the Convention shall be understood to mean "interpretation between the language used by the inspection team and the language or languages used at the inspected site".

---

[1] The text of paragraph 26 is as follows:

"Administrative arrangements. The inspected State Party shall provide or arrange for the amenities necessary for the inspection team such as communication means, interpretation services to the extent necessary for the performance of interviewing and other tasks, transportation, working space, lodging, meals and medical care. In this regard, the inspected State Party shall be reimbursed by the Organization for such costs incurred by the inspection team." [footnote in original].

10.3 Health and Safety Regulations

C-I/DEC.8 adopted by the Conference of the States Parties at its First Session on 14 May 1997 and entitled "Procedures concerning the implementation of safety requirements for activities of inspectors and inspection assistants, in accordance with Part II, paragraph 43, of the Verification Annex"

The Conference

Recalling that the Commission approved the revised draft Health and Safety Policy, Appendix 1 to the Chairman's Paper to PC-VI/B/WP.10, with the addition of the following sentence to paragraph 3.3.3(c): "This is without prejudice to the obligations of a State Party to provide access to an inspected facility for the purpose of carrying out inspection activities, in accordance with the Convention" (PC-VI/22, paragraph 6.7),

Recalling that the Commission in its PC-XIII/18, paragraph 7.2, considered and adopted the Draft OPCW Health and Safety Regulations annexed to PC-XIII/B/WP.2,

Recalling that Working Group B in its PC-XIII/B/6, paragraph 2.2, considered the Draft OPCW Health and Safety Regulations annexed to PC-XIII/B/WP.2, took note of the understanding recorded in paragraph 3.2 of PC-XIII/B/WP.2, recommended that these Regulations be adopted by the Commission,

Bearing in mind that the Commission recommended in paragraph 40.5 of its Final Report that the Conference adopt the above mentioned draft OPCW Health and Safety Policy and the draft OPCW Health and Safety Regulations,

Hereby:

1. Adopts the OPCW Health and Safety Policy and the OPCW Health and Safety Regulations and takes note of the understanding recorded in paragraph 3.2 of PC-XIII/B/WP.2 annexed hereto.

ANNEX [extract from page 27 of C-I/DEC.8]
UNDERSTANDING CONTAINED IN PARAGRAPH 3.2 OF PC-XIII/B/WP.2

The Group understood that subparagraph 4.2 of the Draft OPCW Health and Safety Regulations does not prejudice the obligation of inspected States Parties to provide available data based on detection and monitoring, to an agreed extent necessary to satisfy concerns that may exist regarding the health and safety of the inspection team. In cases where detection and monitoring, as referred to in subparagraph 5.2.2 of the Draft OPCW Health and Safety Policy (PC-IX/B/WP.5) cannot be carried out, alternative risk assessment data or information will be provided by the inspected State Party, as provided for in subparagraph 5.1.1 of the Draft OPCW Health and Safety Policy.

10.4 Adoption and revision of the list of approved equipment

C-I/DEC.71 adopted by the Conference of the States Parties at its First Session on 23 May 1997 and entitled "List of approved equipment with operational requirements and technical specifications"

The Conference

Recalling that the Commission, in its PC-VIII/18, paragraph 6.15, approved the list of equipment as specified in table 3.8 of the Annex to PC-VIII/A/WP.7, for budgetary purposes; and decided, authorised or approved the addition of the following items to the list:

- Boots (reusable) (PC-IX/11, paragraph 6.4);
- Team Decontamination Kit (PC-XI/17, paragraph 7.4);
- Non-Destructive Evaluation (NDE) Hydrogen Concentration Measurement (HCM) Equipment (PC-XIV/29, paragraph 9.3);
- Individual Heat Stress Monitor (PC-XV/25, paragraph 8.3); and
- Portable Acetylcholinesterase Activity Monitor (PC-XV/25, paragraph 8.3),

Recalling that the Commission and, as appropriate, Working Group B adopted or noted operational requirements and technical specifications of inspection equipment in several meetings,

Bearing in mind that the Commission recommended in paragraph 38.8 of its PC-XVI/37 that the Conference adopt several of the above mentioned recommendations on the inclusion of certain items of equipment pending resolution of the issue of the list of approved equipment,

Hereby:
1. Adopts the list of inspection equipment with operational requirements, technical specifications and common evaluation criteria annexed hereto.

ANNEX [extract from pages 3-12 of C-I/DEC.71]
LIST OF APPROVED EQUIPMENT

The Conference adopted the list of approved equipment in the understanding that:
(a) the issues contained in paragraphs 118 and 119 of the Final Report of the Preparatory Commission remain unresolved for the time being. In accordance with paragraph 29 of Part II of the Verification Annex, "The inspection of the equipment shall also ascertain to the satisfaction of the inspected State Party that the equipment meets the description of the approved equipment for the particular type of inspection. The inspected State Party may exclude equipment not meeting that description or equipment without the above-mentioned authentication documents and devices";
(b) paragraph 13 of the Confidentiality Annex stipulates that "States Parties may take such measures as they deem necessary to protect confidentiality, provided that they fulfill their obligation to demonstrate compliance with the relevant Articles and the Verification Annex. When receiving an inspection, the State Party may indicate to the inspection team the equipment, documentation or areas that it considers sensitive and not related to the purpose of the inspection." This provision has further been specified in the OPCW Confidentiality Policy. These measures may include restrictions on the use of certain items of inspection equipment, which may be stipulated in facility agreements when applicable;
(c) in accordance with paragraph 43 of Part II of the Verification Annex, and in accordance with the OPCW Health and Safety Policy and Regulations, the inspected State Party may adopt procedures including restrictions on the use of certain equipment, which may be stipulated in facility agreements when applicable. In such a case an alternative inspection procedure should be adopted in consultation with the ISP in order to accomplish the inspection goals (OPCW Health and Safety Policy, subparagraph 4.3(a));
(d) the National Authority of each State Party should be able to access - in order to satisfy the inspected State Party and to enable it to familiarise itself with all the operational characteristics concerned - each item of equipment contained in the List of Approved Equipment and its use sufficiently prior to its use on the territory of the inspected State Party to ensure familiarity. In case any State Party finds that it is denied such access to any item of equipment approved for inspection purposes, it has the right to deny permission of that equipment for use on its national territory. The Director-General is requested to establish an appropriate mechanism to assist the National Authorities in their familiarisation with the approved equipment and its use.

LIST OF INSPECTION EQUIPMENT

[The list is not reproduced in the present volume. The full text of this decision, including the list of inspection equipment, may be downloaded from the OPCW website (http://www.opcw.org/). The list has, from time to time, been subject to revision by the Executive Council pursuant to the procedures set forth in the relevant decisions adopted by the Conference of States Parties.]

C-7/DEC.20 adopted by the Conference of the States Parties at its Seventh Session on 11 October 2002 and entitled "Procedures for updating the list of approved equipment"

The Conference

Recalling that, during its Fifteenth Session in April 1999, the Executive Council (hereinafter the "Council") had received a proposal on the need to establish procedures for the procurement of inspection equipment;

Further recalling that, at its First Session, the Conference of the States Parties (hereinafter the "Conference") adopted the list of approved equipment with operational requirements, technical specifications and common evaluation criteria (C-I/DEC.71, dated 23 May 1997);

Recognising that the Convention on the Prohibition of the Development, Production, Stockpiling and Use of Chemical Weapons and on Their Destruction (hereinafter the "Convention") requires the Conference to review scientific and technological developments that could affect the operation of the Convention;

Understanding that paragraph 27 of Part II of the Verification Annex to the Convention (hereinafter the "Verification Annex") requires the Technical Secretariat (hereinafter the "Secretariat") to prepare and, as appropriate, update a list of approved equipment for consideration and approval by the Conference;

Also understanding that the experience gained by the Organisation during the conduct of on-site inspections has provided, and will continue to provide, insight into the needs of inspectors, which may require the revision of the list of approved equipment;

Reaffirming that the Secretariat procures equipment using a transparent process, open to all States Parties according to the applicable Financial Regulations and Procurement Directives; and

Recognising that existing approved inspection equipment shall not be discarded before its full life is exhausted, or until it is unable to fulfil the requirements of conducting verification activities, or unless technological developments would enable more cost effective inspection operations;

Hereby:

Adopts the following procedures for updating the list of approved equipment:

1. the Director-General, on the basis of substantive and documented analysis (see the annex to this decision), shall recommend the revision of the list of approved equipment in order to demonstrably improve verification, to increase the efficiency of inspection teams, to protect health, to improve safety, or to directly reduce the operating costs of the Organisation. The items proposed for inclusion in the list shall be accompanied by requirements as specified by the annex to this decision, and shall be in accordance with the general and specific operational requirements. Items meeting these requirements shall be commercially available to States Parties to the Convention;
2. any such recommendations, together with the relevant analysis, shall be provided to States Parties and consultations shall be arranged amongst both experts designated by States Parties and representatives of the Secretariat in order to discuss the improvements, increased efficiencies, and/or reduced costs in question;
3. revisions of the list of approved equipment that are based on scientific and technological developments shall also be accompanied by observations from the Scientific Advisory Board;

4. this process shall be completed in an expeditious manner; and
5. the Director-General shall provide his/her recommendations, an accompanying analysis, and the results of review and consultations amongst experts designated by States Parties and representatives of the Secretariat to the Council for consideration and appropriate recommendation to the Conference for approval.

ANNEX

OUTLINE OF REQUIREMENTS FOR NEW ITEMS OF APPROVED EQUIPMENT

Item of equipment: Identification and description of the item being considered.

Justification of need: Statement of the specified inspection verification aim(s) to be accomplished, or of the efficiency, health and safety, and any cost savings and operational benefits which the item of equipment is intended to address.

Requirement: Description of the required capabilities of the item.

Technical Specifications: Technical specifications needed to meet the required capabilities.

Life Cycle Costs: Detailed breakdown of the estimated life cycle costs of the item, including:

(a) the number of items to be procured;
(b) the estimated cost of each item;
(c) the number of years of expected serviceable life;
(d) the annual support costs (supplies, maintenance, replacement parts and components, etc.).

Alternatives: Analysis of potential alternatives, including changes in inspector training or procedures and the use of inspected State Party equipment, which could satisfy the need.

Value Added: Analysis of the gain in verification effectiveness versus the cost involved and the potential alternatives.

C-8/DEC.3 adopted by the Conference of the States Parties at its Eighth Session on 22 October 2003 and entitled "Procedures for revising the technical specifications for approved equipment"

The Conference

Recalling that at its Seventh Session it forwarded a draft decision on the procedures for revising the technical specifications for approved equipment (EC-28/DEC/CRP.4, dated 15 February 2002) to the Executive Council (hereinafter "the Council") for approval, and for provisional application by the Technical Secretariat (hereinafter "the Secretariat") (C-7/5, dated 11 October 2002);

Also recalling that at the same Session it required that the decision to be adopted by the Council be submitted to the Eighth Session of the Conference of the States Parties (hereinafter "the Conference") for final consideration and approval;

Recalling further that the Council at its Thirty-First Session approved the procedures set out in subparagraphs (a) to (e) below for provisional application, and recommended that at its Eighth Session the Conference approve them (EC-31/DEC.8, dated 12 December 2002);

Understanding that developing and publishing technical specifications for the procurement of approved equipment ensures transparency, provides guidance for acquisition management, and ensures that States Parties are given an opportunity to understand the operational characteristics and capabilities of such equipment;

Also understanding that the technical specifications for approved equipment may need to be updated;

Recalling that States Parties have the right to familiarise themselves with all equipment procured by the OPCW and included in the list of approved equipment;

Reaffirming that, in procuring and acquiring equipment, the Secretariat uses a transparent process open to all States Parties according to the applicable financial regulations and procurement directives;

Recognising that existing approved equipment shall not be discarded before its full life is exhausted, or until it is unable to fulfil the requirements of conducting verification activities, or unless technological developments enable more-cost-effective inspection operations;

Hereby:

Approves the following procedures for revising the technical specifications for approved equipment:

(a)   the Director-General shall develop technical specifications for all items of approved equipment to be procured and acquired for the Organisation by the Secretariat, which shall be in accordance with the general and specific operational requirements. These technical specifications for approved equipment, whether procured or acquired, shall be such that equipment meeting these specifications is commercially available to States Parties to the Chemical Weapons Convention;

(b)   the technical specifications shall outline the required characteristics and capabilities of the item, and where necessary, the characteristics of its parts, components, and accessories, and shall outline the benefits given by these revised specifications from a technical point of view. The technical specifications shall seek to maximise the item's applicability to the Convention's verification regime and resources;

(c)   the Director-General shall distribute the proposed list of revisions to the technical specifications to States Parties for review, shall consider any comments received within 60 days and shall submit proposed technical specifications together with the results of the review to the Council for approval;

(d)   after each item from the list of revised technical specifications has been approved by the Council, the Director-General shall ensure that the Secretariat only procures and acquires approved equipment which complies with the approved technical specifications;

(e)   informal consultations shall be arranged in order to discuss the items not approved. The entire process shall be completed in an expeditious manner.

10.5 Procedures for the inspection of equipment

C-I/DEC.7 adopted by the Conference of the States Parties at its First Session on 14 May 1997 and entitled "Procedures for the inspection of equipment, in accordance with Part II, paragraph 29, of the Verification Annex (Paris Resolution, subparagraph 12(f))"

The Conference

Recalling that the Commission in its PC-VIII/18, paragraph 7.2, adopted Attachment 2 to PC-VIII/B/WP.2 entitled "Procedures for the Inspection by the Inspected State Party at the Point of Entry/Point of Exit (POE) of Approved Equipment Carried by the Inspection Team",

Bearing in mind that the Commission recommended in paragraph 39.2 of its Final Report that the Conference adopt the above mentioned procedures,

Hereby:

1.   Adopts the procedures for the inspection by the inspected State Party at the point of entry/ point of exit (POE) of approved equipment carried by the inspection team, annexed hereto.

PROCEDURES FOR THE INSPECTION BY THE INSPECTED STATE PARTY AT THE POINT OF ENTRY/POINT OF EXIT (POE) OF APPROVED EQUIPMENT CARRIED BY THE INSPECTION TEAM

1. GENERAL PROVISIONS
1.1 In accordance with paragraph 29 of Part II of the Verification Annex, the inspected State Party has the right to inspect the approved equipment in the presence of inspection team members at the point of entry/point of exit, i.e. to check the identity of the approved equipment brought in or removed from the territory of the inspected State Party or Host State by the inspection team. To facilitate such identification, the Technical Secretariat (TS) shall attach documents and devices to authenticate its designation and approval of the equipment. These authentication documents would include, *inter alia*, the description, the technical specifications and the operational requirements of the equipment and a description of the procedures used by the Technical Secretariat for the designation, calibration and approval of the approved equipment. The inspection of the inspection team's equipment shall also ascertain to the satisfaction of the inspected State Party that the inspection team's equipment meets the description of the approved equipment for the particular type of inspection. Approved equipment is the equipment from the list of equipment approved by the Conference of the States Parties in accordance with paragraph 21(i) of Article VIII; the Technical Secretariat shall, to the extent possible, select that equipment which is specifically designed for the specific kind of inspection.
1.2 If the inspection of the approved equipment by the inspected State Party indicates that the equipment meets the description of the approved equipment for the particular type of inspection, there shall be no restriction by the inspected State Party, apart from those pursuant to the provisions of Article IX and Part X of the Verification Annex, on the inspection team bringing onto the inspection site the approved equipment which the Technical Secretariat, in accordance with paragraph 28 of Part II of the Verification Annex, has determined to be necessary to fulfil the inspection requirements. This is without prejudice to the provisions in relation to the use of the equipment by the inspection team.

2. ROLE OF THE INSPECTED STATE PARTY
2.1 The inspected State Party has the right to inspect each individual item of approved equipment carried by the inspection team. This is without prejudice to paragraph 11(d) of Part II of the Verification Annex on the inviolability of approved equipment. In executing this right, the inspected State Party may use any appropriate procedure consistent with paragraph 4 below. The inspected State Party has the right to exclude equipment that does not meet the description of the approved equipment for the particular type of inspection or that lacks the authentication documents and devices issued by the TS.
2.2 The representative of the inspected State Party shall take into account any suggestions which the inspection team leader may have in relation to the application of a specific procedure for inspecting the approved equipment, in accordance with paragraph 3.2 below.

3. ROLE OF THE INSPECTION TEAM
3.1 Inspection team personnel shall be present during the inspection of the approved equipment at all times, shall observe fully the inspection, and shall discharge this responsibility without unnecessary delay.
3.2 If by virtue of the particular procedure chosen by the inspected State Party, the inspection team leader concludes that the inspection of approved equipment by the inspected State Party may render that equipment inoperable or interfere in any way with its function(s), the inspection team leader shall so inform the representative of the inspected State Party.

4. INSPECTION OF APPROVED EQUIPMENT

Pursuant to paragraph 1.1 above, subject to paragraphs 4.2 and 4.3 below, and within a period that will enable the inspection team and the inspected State Party to conduct the in-country activities within the times prescribed by the Convention for the particular type of inspection, the inspection of the approved equipment by the inspected State Party shall follow the principles set out below:

4.1 No inspection procedure chosen by the inspected State Party shall render the approved equipment inoperable or interfere, in any way, with its function(s).

4.2 The inspection of the approved equipment by the inspected State Party may, *inter alia*, include:

(a) inspection of the certificates, authentication documents and devices provided by the TS for each item of approved equipment;

(b) without compromising the functionality of the approved equipment, visual inspection and other non-destructive tests and checks suitable to establish that the equipment meets the description of the approved equipment for the particular type of inspection, which may include the utilisation of the procedures used by the Technical Secretariat for designation, calibration and approval of the equipment as specified in the documents attached to the equipment by the Technical Secretariat.

4.3 Both the hardware and software of approved equipment may be inspected in accordance with paragraphs 4.1 and 4.2 above. Such inspection shall not alter any data which is stored in the approved equipment and which is necessary for its proper performance.

5. RESOLUTION AFTER EXCLUSION OR POSSIBLE MISUSE OF EQUIPMENT, IF ANY

5.1 Any equipment that has been excluded by the inspected State Party at the POE in accordance with paragraph 29 of Part II of the Verification Annex shall be retained at the POE under joint control or joint seal and returned to the inspection team upon its departure from the point of exit.

5.2 In a case where the inspected State Party has demonstrated during the post-inspection activities that the equipment has been modified or used for purposes not in accordance with those which the Technical Secretariat has determined to be necessary to fulfil the inspection requirements and the matter cannot be resolved in consultations between the representative of the inspected State Party and the inspection team leader, the equipment shall be retained at the point of exit under joint control or joint seal until the matter can be resolved in the presence of a representative of the Technical Secretariat.

6. RECORDING OF THE INSPECTION OF APPROVED EQUIPMENT AT THE POE IN THE INSPECTION REPORT

The procedures and measures undertaken at the POE during the inspection of the approved equipment carried by the inspection team shall be duly recorded in the inspection report, to include, *inter alia*:

(a) the exclusions of equipment, if any, and the reasons provided for this by the inspected State Party;

(b) a reference to any discussion between the inspection team personnel and the inspected State Party on a method to inspect the equipment, or the scope of that inspection; and

(c) a reference to any other incidents in relation to the inspection of the approved equipment by the inspected State Party.

10.6 Use of approved equipment during on-site inspections

C-I/DEC.50 adopted by the Conference of the States Parties at its First Session on 16 May 1997 and entitled "The use of approved equipment during on-site inspections"

The Conference

Recalling that The Commission in its PC-VIII/18, paragraph 7.3, adopted Attachment 3 to PC-VIII/B/WP.2 entitled "The Use of Approved Equipment During On-Site Inspections",

Bearing in mind that the Commission recommended in paragraph 56.3 of its Final Report that the Conference adopt the above mentioned document,

Hereby:
1. Adopts the document entitled "The Use of Approved Equipment During On-Site Inspections", annexed hereto.

ANNEX

THE USE OF APPROVED EQUIPMENT DURING ON-SITE INSPECTIONS[2]

1. Subject to the following provisions, inspection teams will have the right during an inspection to use approved equipment brought onto the inspection site:
   (a) paragraphs 11(d), 27 to 30, and Section E of Part II of the Verification Annex;
   (b) the appropriate paragraphs of the applicable other Parts of the Verification Annex;
   (c) the Confidentiality Annex, the OPCW Confidentiality Policy and the applicable related regulations;
   (d) the OPCW Health and Safety Policy and the applicable related regulations; and
   (e) the provisions stipulated in the facility agreement, if any.
2. Subject to paragraph 1 above, the approved equipment shall be operated in accordance with the regulations established by the Technical Secretariat.
3. The use of approved equipment by the inspection team in challenge inspection will be restricted, at the perimeter of the inspection site, only by considerations in paragraph 1 above, in particular those contained in Part X of the Verification Annex, and by the provisions contained in Article IX. The use of approved equipment by the inspection team in challenge inspection under managed access will be subject to negotiation and agreement between the inspected State Party and the inspection team. Subject to the provisions of Article IX and Part X of the Verification Annex, the negotiation will, *inter alia*, relate to:
   (a) the types of approved equipment that the inspection team may use, if any;
   (b) the mode of use of the approved equipment;
   (c) any limitations on the use of the approved equipment in relation to specific areas, structures or buildings;
   (d) other limitations on the use of the approved equipment, such as time limits for its use.
4. The inspected State Party shall have the right to take note of any information collected, or to receive copies of such information. That will not apply to systems software and other OPCW data, provided that they are located in a ROM or on media that prevent the possibility of recording information, and that are sealed and certified by the Technical Secretariat.

---

[2] Contained in PC-VIII/B/WP.2, Attachment 3.

10.7 Measures in relation to approved equipment following completion of inspection activities

C-I/DEC.51 adopted by the Conference of the States Parties at its First Session on 16 May 1997 and entitled "Measures in relation to approved equipment following completion of inspection activities"

The Conference

Recalling that the Commission in its PC-X/23, paragraph 7.3, adopted the document entitled "Measures in Relation to Approved Equipment Following Inspection Activities" (Annex 1 to PC-X/B/WP.9) as amended by Working Group B (subparagraph 3.6 of PC-X/B/5),

Bearing in mind that the Commission recommended in paragraph 56.3 of its Final Report that the Conference adopt the above mentioned document,

Hereby:

1. Adopts the document entitled "Measures in Relation to Approved Equipment Following Completion of Inspection Activities", annexed hereto.

ANNEX

MEASURES IN RELATION TO APPROVED EQUIPMENT
FOLLOWING COMPLETION OF INSPECTION ACTIVITIES [3, 4]

1. GENERAL

1.1 Approved equipment that was brought onto the inspection site or, in the case of a challenge inspection, was used in the perimeter activities, may in addition to any previously conducted operational decontamination have to undergo additional measures of decontamination upon completion of the inspection activities. Such measures may include:

(a) decontamination or disposal of equipment for health and safety purposes; and

(b) removal by the inspection team of any traces of matter which may contain information unrelated to the purpose of the inspection.

These measures are without prejudice to the procedures for the inspection of the approved equipment by the inspected State Party at the point of exit (POE) and do not replace these procedures.

1.2 In cases when the inspected State Party elects to have the measures pursuant to subparagraph 1.1 above take place at the inspection site, the period of inspection, if necessary and pursuant to paragraph 59 of Part II of the Verification Annex, will be extended so as to allow completion of these measures.

1.3 Measures pursuant to subparagraph 1.1 above may be initiated if deemed necessary by the inspection team leader or by the representative of the inspected State Party.

1.4 Measures pursuant to subparagraph 1.1 above will be taken in accordance with methods agreed between the inspection team leader and the representative of the inspected State Party, on a case by case basis, consistent with State Party or local safety regulations, the OPCW Health and Safety Policy, related OPCW regulations and operating procedures, and/or the OPCW Confidentiality Policy.

---

[3] These measures will also apply in cases when, upon agreement between the TS and the inspected State Party, OPCW equipment other than approved equipment as defined in paragraph 1 of Part I of the Verification Annex is brought onto an inspection site [footnote in original].

[4] Contained in PC-X/B/WP.9, Annex 1, as amended by Working Group B (subparagraph 3.6 of PC-X/B/5).

2. MEASURES IN CASES WHERE DECONTAMINATION FOR HEALTH AND SAFETY PURPOSES IS NOT FEASIBLE

2.1 If, following the inspection activities, items of approved equipment cannot be appropriately decontaminated on-site, for health and safety purposes, to the satisfaction of the inspection team or the representative of the inspected State Party, they may be left on-site for any further decontamination as necessary. Such further decontamination will be carried out under conditions to be agreed between the Technical Secretariat and the inspected State Party, including the time limit of such activity and an agreement on the attribution of any costs so incurred. As a general rule, the party initiating the further decontamination will support the cost so incurred. When the equipment is decontaminated to the satisfaction of the side insisting on such decontamination, that side will transport such equipment back to the OPCW premises.

2.2 If, in the opinion of the inspection team leader and the representative of the inspected State Party, decontamination is not a feasible or a cost-efficient option, it may become necessary to dispose of equipment items at the inspection site or elsewhere:

(a) when applicable, subject to negotiation with the representative of the inspected State Party and further to a clear agreement on the attribution of any costs so incurred, this disposal will be performed in a safe manner at the inspection site or at a waste disposal location elsewhere on the territory of the inspected State Party; or

(b) when the provision in subparagraph 2.2(a) above is not applicable, upon the request of or subject to the approval of the representative of the inspected State Party the equipment will be removed for safe disposal by the Organisation, subject to a clear agreement on the attribution of any costs so incurred.

2.3 The provisions contained in subparagraphs 2.1 and 2.2 above are without prejudice to the provisions contained in paragraph 3 below.

3. REMOVAL OF INFORMATION UNRELATED TO THE PURPOSE OF THE INSPECTION

In accordance with the provisions of the Convention and with the OPCW Policy on Confidentiality, Section VI, subsection 3.4.3, paragraphs 3, 4 and 5, the following technical measures relate to situations where, after the selection of information relevant to the purpose of the inspection by the inspection team for inclusion in its preliminary findings, information not relevant to the purpose of the inspection has to be removed before the inspection team leaves the site. Any fact of application of these technical measures will be recorded in the preliminary findings. It should be kept in mind that in many cases the inspection team may request the inspected State Party to dispose of detachable or consumable parts of equipment when contaminated or used.

3.1 *Treatment of equipment for confidentiality reasons*

3.1.1 If the representative of the inspected State Party has reasons to believe that, as a result of the use of approved equipment, information unrelated to the purpose of the inspection is retained thereon, he/she will request the inspection team leader to undertake removal of the information unrelated to the purpose of the inspection from the equipment in order to remove the object of the particular concern.

3.1.2 If removal of the information unrelated to the purpose of the inspection from the equipment as mentioned in subparagraph 3.1.1 above is not possible, or successful, or when after full consultation no agreement can be reached on the specific removal techniques to be applied, the inspection team and the inspected State Party may instead agree to transfer the affected equipment, under joint seal, to the Technical Secretariat for removal of the information unrelated to the purpose of the inspection under the supervision, if requested, of a representative of the inspected State Party. After the arrival of such equipment at the premises of the OPCW it will be unsealed in the presence of the representative of the inspected State Party, if the inspected State Party decides to send such a representative, who will monitor that the information unrelated to the purpose of the inspection is removed from the equipment to his/her satisfaction, including the final disposal of any resulting waste. If the inspected State Party elects not to send such a representative, the information unrelated to the purpose of the inspection will be removed in accordance with standard OPCW procedures. All due care will be exercised, during the removal operation, to avoid disclosure of the information not related to the purpose of the inspection during which it was collected.

3.1.3   In an exceptional case, alternative to the provisions in subparagraph 3.1.2 above, the inspected State Party may choose to retain detachable parts of the equipment on-site, if applicable. In such a case the inspected State Party will replace them with identical parts acceptable to the Technical Secretariat and without altering in any way the operational and technical capabilities of the approved equipment (such reconstituted equipment shall be considered as approved equipment for the purposes of departure through the point of exit (POE)). If that is not feasible, the inspected State Party shall reimburse them in accordance with the conditions set out in subparagraph 3.3.

3.1.4   If no agreement can be reached on the application of the measures set out in subparagraphs 3.1.2 or 3.1.3 above, the inspected State Party may in very exceptional cases retain the equipment on-site, subject to its replacement with identical items of equipment acceptable to the Technical Secretariat or, if that is not feasible, reimbursement will be provided in accordance with the conditions set out in subparagraph 3.3 below.

3.2   *Information from recording media*

3.2.1   The Convention's requirement for the inspection team to provide, in accordance with paragraph 60 of Part II of the Verification Annex, to the representative of the inspected State Party its preliminary findings, including a list of any samples and copies of written information or data gathered and other material to be taken off-site, shall be implemented, in relation to recording media, by providing to the representative of the inspected State Party an identical copy of the recorded information.

The Inspection Manual will provide specific instructions for the preparation of copies under this paragraph.

3.2.2   These requirements do not relate to system software or to other OPCW data provided that they are:
(a)   located on a ROM or on a medium that inherently prevents the recording of information by the inspection team; and
(b)   sealed and certified by the Technical Secretariat.

3.2.3   In the case of equipment for the collection, preparation or analysis of samples, the inspection team will retain only data relevant to the purpose of the inspection. It is understood that in the case of negative results of the analysis in terms of the presence of chemicals searched for in accordance with the provisions of the Convention, the respective sample, computer file and any print-outs will be considered not relevant in the terms of the inspection mandate. This is without prejudice to both the right of the inspection team to transfer a sample for off-site analysis and the rights of a State Party in the case of a challenge inspection.

3.2.4   If the representative of the inspected State Party has reasons to believe that information not related to the purpose of the inspection has been recorded, that information will be removed by the inspection team from the recording media in the presence of the representative of the inspected State Party. To that end, and if technically feasible, the representative of the inspected State Party will supervise, either on-site or at another place as agreed, the extraction or transfer of the information relevant to the purpose of the inspection to a recording or retention medium acceptable both to the inspection team leader and to the representative of the inspected State Party. Thereafter the original item containing information not related to the purpose of the inspection should be processed as provided for in subparagraphs 3.1.2, 3.1.3, and 3.1.4 above.

3.2.5   In the exceptional case when the procedure under subparagraphs 3.2.3 to 3.2.4 above cannot be followed, the recording media will be retained on-site and replaced with equivalent recording media without altering in any way the operational and technical capabilities of the approved equipment or, if that is not feasible, reimbursed in accordance with the conditions set out in subparagraph 3.3 below.

3.3   *Conditions for the retention by a State Party of equipment or pieces of equipment*
         The conditions will be:
         (a)   immediate replacement or reimbursement in convertible currency at full immediate replacement cost by the inspected State Party before the inspection team leaves the POE, or in any case no later than 7 days after the departure of the inspection team from the POE; and
         (b)   disposal to the satisfaction of the inspection team of retained equipment or pieces of equipment before the team leaves the inspection site.

10.8 Sequential inspections

In the interest of reducing the costs and resources needed for inspections, a number of States Parties have requested, or have indicated their willingness to permit, sequential inspections on their territory or successively in their territory and in the territory of other States Parties.

Sequential inspections were not foreseen in the Convention and the consequences of consecutively inspecting a number of sites upon Convention-stipulated time frames or procedures need to be arranged between the Secretariat and the State Party concerned.

Such arrangements have covered: notification of the intent to conduct a sequential inspection followed by separate notifications for each facility within the Convention time frames; provision of separate mandates and conduct of separate equipment inspections at each consecutive facility; protection of confidential information retained by the inspection team; adjustment, when necessary, of time frames for transportation between inspection sites, depending upon whether the sites are served by the same POE or not; and total duration of the in-country period. Additional arrangements have been necessary for sequential inspections of a number of facilities located at one site by a single team for the delivery of preliminary findings prior to commencement of the next inspection. Agreement has also been reached to use the inspection team carrying out continuous monitoring of destruction activities to monitor non-continuous destruction operations at other locations.

11. DESIGNATED LABORATORIES

11.1 Criteria for the conduct of proficiency testing

C-I/DEC.65 adopted by the Conference of the States Parties at its First Session on 22 May 1997 and entitled "Criteria for the conduct of OPCW/PTS proficiency testing"

The Conference

Recalling that the Commission, in its PC-XIII/18, paragraph 7.5, adopted the "Criteria for the Conduct of OPCW/PTS Proficiency Testing",

Bearing in mind that the Commission recommended in paragraph 54.9 of its Final Report that the Conference adopt "Criteria for the Conduct of OPCW/PTS Proficiency Testing",

Hereby:
1. Adopts the "Criteria for the Conduct of OPCW/PTS Proficiency Testing".

ANNEX
CRITERIA FOR THE CONDUCT OF OPCW/PTS PROFICIENCY TESTING

1. INTRODUCTION

One of the criteria for laboratories seeking designation for the analysis of authentic samples is that those laboratories should regularly participate and perform successfully in inter-laboratory proficiency tests (PC-VI/B/WP.4). Criteria for acceptable performance of laboratories in a single proficiency test have been established (PC-XI/B/WP.6, Annex 1) and adopted by the Commission.

Proficiency testing is conducted by the Secretariat. In this process the Secretariat may be assisted by laboratories preparing the test samples and evaluating the results in accordance with the following standard operating procedures (SOPs):
(a) "Standard Operating Procedure (SOP) for Preparation of Test Samples for OPCW/PTS Proficiency Tests"; and
(b) "Standard Operating Procedure (SOP) for Evaluation of Results of OPCW/PTS Proficiency Tests".

As these assisting laboratories may be seeking designation for the analysis of authentic samples, their position in respect of their intention to become an OPCW designated laboratory needs to be considered.

In relation to the conduct of proficiency testing this paper addresses the following:
(a) the role of the Secretariat;
(b) the number of tests to be performed before applying for designation;
(c) the evaluation of laboratories for a series of tests; and
(d) considerations for laboratories preparing the test samples and evaluating the results.

2. THE ROLE OF THE SECRETARIAT

The Secretariat shall inform the proficiency test participants before the test of the purpose and the scenario of the test. After completion of the test by the participating laboratories, the Secretariat has the responsibility for evaluating the results of the proficiency test.

Prior to drawing any conclusions on the performance of individual laboratories participating in the proficiency test, the Secretariat shall make:
(a) an assessment of the stability, quality and validity of the test samples to assess the applicability of the test; and

(b) an assessment of the evaluation of the results of the test .

Then the Secretariat shall make a preliminary evaluation based on the "Criteria for Acceptable Performance of Laboratories in Proficiency Testing":

(a) evaluation of whether each of the participating laboratories fulfils all performance criteria; and

(b) scoring of the performance of those laboratories fulfilling all performance criteria in accordance with the scoring rules.

The Secretariat shall prepare a preliminary test report based on all above-mentioned data and shall thereafter inform the participants of their performance and shall request comments. The participants shall be given a minimum of one week to inform the Secretariat whether they accept the performance evaluation. The Secretariat shall inform the evaluating laboratory about the comments received concerning the evaluation of analytical data to allow it to take corrective measures if needed and to finalise its report. The Secretariat will finalise its test report on the basis of these results.

3. NUMBER OF PROFICIENCY TESTS TO BE PERFORMED BEFORE APPLYING FOR DESIGNATION

Applications by laboratories seeking designation for the analysis of authentic samples must be based on participation in at least three proficiency tests, and must take into account the following:

(a) laboratories must have participated in at least three out of the last five proficiency tests; and

(b) laboratories must have performed successfully in their last three consecutive proficiency tests.

4. THE EVALUATION OF LABORATORIES FOR A SERIES OF PROFICIENCY TESTS

Since test scenarios, number of spiking chemicals, samples and matrices vary between proficiency tests, a straightforward addition of scores achieved from different tests will not lead to fair or meaningful assessment of participating laboratories. The evaluation of laboratories over a series of proficiency tests shall be carried out as follows:

(a) once all the performance criteria have been fulfilled, the scoring rules as presented in "Criteria for Acceptable Performance of Laboratories in Proficiency Testing" shall be applied separately for each proficiency test for measuring the performance in an individual test (see table below);

(b) the performance of laboratories in an individual test shall be rated as presented in the table below to allow for a comparison of performance in a number of different proficiency tests in a simple and unambiguous way;

(c) the performance rating for three individual tests shall be combined and shall form the technical basis on which the Director-General may grant designation for the analysis of authentic samples provided that other criteria (quality assurance, accreditation) have been fulfilled; and

(d) the combined rating shall be used as a basis on which the Director-General shall classify laboratories consistent with their capabilities to support the analytical needs of the Convention.

Table: Method of evaluating laboratory performance

PERFORMANCE CRITERIA FULFILLED[1]	IDENTIFICATION OF CHEMICALS	PERFORMANCE SCORING[2]	PERFORMANCE RATING
Yes	Laboratory identifies all chemicals	Maximum score	A
Yes	Laboratory identifies all chemicals except one	Maximum score minus two	B
Yes	Laboratory identifies more than half of the chemicals	Score between zero and maximum minus two	C
Yes	Laboratory misses more chemicals than it identifies	Negative score	D
No		No score	Failure

5. CONSIDERATION FOR LABORATORIES PREPARING THE TEST SAMPLES AND EVALUATING THE RESULTS

The Secretariat shall consider the laboratories assisting it in preparing the samples or evaluating the analytical results and which are also in the process of seeking designation for the analysis of authentic samples as follows:

(a) laboratories preparing the samples shall be credited with a maximum performance rating of A (see table) for one proficiency test if the test samples meet the requirements of the "Standard Operating Procedure (SOP) for Preparation of Test Samples for OPCW/PTS Proficiency Tests";

(b) laboratories evaluating the analytical results shall be credited with a maximum performance rating of A (see table) for one proficiency test if the evaluation meets the requirements of the "Standard Operating Procedure (SOP) for Evaluation of Results of OPCW/PTS Proficiency Tests";

(c) laboratories cannot use performance rating for preparing the samples or evaluating the analytical results of more than one of their last three consecutive proficiency tests (i.e. laboratories must participate in at least two of the three tests as regular participants); and

(d) laboratories preparing the samples or evaluating the analytical results cannot participate as regular participants in a given test. However, such laboratories must analyse the samples.

11.2 Conditions in relation to proficiency tests

C-I/DEC.66 adopted by the Conference of the States Parties at its First Session on 22 May 1997 and entitled "Conditions in relation to future proficiency tests"

The Conference

Recalling that the Commission, in its PC-XV/25, paragraph 8.3(d), approved the understanding reached by the Expert Group of Inspection Procedures that, in relation to proficiency tests following the first test, the conditions set out in subparagraphs 4.1(b)(i) to (viii) of PC-XV/B/WP.9 shall apply,

Bearing in mind that the Commission recommended in paragraph 54.9 of its Final Report that

---

[1] See PC XI/B/WP.6 Annex 1, paragraph 2.

[2] For practical application of the scoring rules reference is made to the Note by the Executive Secretary on the Results of the Third Commission Inter-Laboratory Comparison Test: Trial Proficiency Test (PC XII/B/3) [footnote in original].

the Conference adopt the above mentioned understanding,

Hereby:
1. Approves the understanding reached by the Expert Group of Inspection Procedures that, in relation to proficiency tests following the first test, the conditions set out in subparagraphs 4.1(b)(i) to (viii) of PC-XV/B/WP.9 shall apply, annexed hereto.

ANNEX
CONDITIONS IN RELATION TO PROFICIENCY TESTS FOLLOWING
THE FIRST TEST[3]

In relation to the second and future official proficiency tests:
(i)   the participants receiving samples should inform the Secretariat that they have received the samples in order to trace possible problems in sample delivery;
(ii)   each measurement performed by each analytical technique should be backed up by the evidence of the analysis of the blank samples, if appropriate;
(iii) the IR spectrum should be compared to a reference spectrum arising from an authentic chemical or library, and should be compared with spectra recorded under spectroscopically comparable conditions;
(iv)   interpretation of mass or NMR spectral data of chemicals whose reference spectra are not available should be supported by the spectral information derived from closely related chemicals with a specific indication of the methods used;
(v)   the data required for EI are as follows:
    –   blank TIC;
    –   sample TIC;
    –   EI spectrum from sample; and
    –   EI spectrum from reference (authentic/library) or spectral interpretation;
(vi)   the data required for CI, when used as a supportive technique for EI, are as follows:
    –   blank TIC;
    –   sample TIC;
    –   CI spectrum from sample with pseudo molecular ion (M+1) indication or spectrum interpretation;
(vii) the data required for NMR in similar conditions:
    –   blank spectrum;
    –   sample spectrum; and
    –   spectrum of compound (authentic/library) or spectral interpretation; and
(viii) the data required for chromatographic techniques and capillary electrophoresis:
    –   blank chromatogram/electroferogram;
    –   sample chromatogram/electroferogram; and
    –   chromatogram/electroferogram of an authentic compound; and
    –   retention times, or retention indexes.

11.3 Proficiency testing leading to certification of designated laboratories

C-I/DEC.60 adopted by the Conference of the States Parties at its First Session on 22 May 1997 and entitled "Proficiency testing leading to certification of designated laboratories"

The Conference

---

[3] Contained in subparagraphs 4.1(b) (i) to (viii) of PC-XV/B/WP.9.

Recalling that the Commission, in its PC-IX/11, paragraph 7.3, adopted the document "Proficiency Testing Leading to Certification of Designated Laboratories",

Bearing in mind that the Commission recommended in paragraph 54.9 of its Final Report that the Conference adopt the above mentioned document "Proficiency Testing Leading to Certification of Designated Laboratories",

Hereby:
1. Adopts the "Proficiency Testing Leading to Certification of Designated Laboratories", annexed hereto.

ANNEX

PROFICIENCY TESTING LEADING TO CERTIFICATION OF "DESIGNATED LABORATORIES"

1. Tests will be open to all laboratories in Member States seeking to become a designated laboratory. The criteria for laboratories to be designated by the Organisation adopted by the Commission at its Sixth Session (PC-VI/22, paragraph 6.4) stipulate that such laboratories should:
    (a) have established an internationally recognised quality assurance system;
    (b) have obtained accreditation by an internationally recognised accreditation body for tasks for which they are seeking designation; and
    (c) regularly participate and perform successfully in inter-laboratory proficiency tests.
2. Laboratories may opt to participate either on a self-assessment basis or be actively seeking designation. Prior to each test participating laboratories will be asked on which basis they wish to participate.
3. In accordance with the Commission's 1995 Budget (Annex to PC-VIII/A/WP.7) the cost of participation, to include sample analysis, as well as, where applicable, the costs of sample preparation and evaluation of test results, will be borne by the participating laboratory or its Member State. The Secretariat may be able to offer some financial assistance in this regard in 1995, but it will be extremely limited. Test samples preparation and evaluation of test results will be the responsibility of the Secretariat, but may either be contracted out or provided by a Member State on a cost-free basis. If the sample preparation and the evaluation of test results are contracted out or are provided by a Member State, the relationship between the participating laboratories and the laboratories preparing samples and carrying out the evaluation of results should be open and transparent.
4. Proficiency testing evaluation will be carried out on the basis of the criteria to be developed and agreed to by the Expert Group on Inspection Procedures. These criteria will be reviewed based on the results of the first proficiency test. It will be the objective of the Secretariat, as is mentioned in the Commission's 1995 Budget (paragraph 3.4.7 of the Annex to PC-VIII/A/WP.7), to carry out proficiency testing on a quarterly basis during 1995. However, the number of proficiency tests may subsequently decrease, depending on the above-mentioned criteria.
5. The first of these tests will be a "Trial Proficiency Test" to:
    (a) evaluate the process;
    (b) provide a means for familiarising new participants with the Commission's requirements;
    (c) begin the process of establishing minimum performance criteria for "designated laboratories"; and
    (d) give participants an opportunity for self-evaluation.
6. A possible model for proficiency testing, including the trial proficiency test, is:
    (a) the Secretariat announces the test schedule for the following quarter;
    (b) the Secretariat has samples prepared:
    (c) coded samples are distributed to participating laboratories by registered carrier with evidence of receipt;

(d) there will be two options for the analysis period:
    (i) for laboratories seeking designation, 2 weeks are allowed for analysis and final reporting of the results, beginning from the date of the receipt of samples; or
    (ii) for laboratories participating on a self-assessment basis, 4 weeks for analysis and initial report plus an additional 2 weeks for the final reporting of results, beginning from the agreed date for the commencement of analysis;
(e) sample analysis by technique selected by the participant or from the Recommended Operating Procedures for Sampling and Analysis in the Verification of Chemical Disarmament (1994 Edition of the "Finnish Blue Books") may be used at participants' discretion;
(f) the results are reported to the Secretariat, and
(g) the results are analysed by the Secretariat. For laboratories seeking designation the results will be circulated to all Member States. Laboratories opting to participate on a self-assessment basis will be provided with their results in confidence.

11.4 Criteria for acceptable performance of laboratories in proficiency testing

C-I/DEC.62 adopted by the Conference of the States Parties at its First Session on 22 May 1997 and entitled "Criteria for acceptable performance of laboratories in proficiency testing"

The Conference

Recalling that the Commission, in its PC-XI/17, paragraph 7.2, adopted the document "Criteria for Acceptable Performance of Laboratories in Proficiency Testing",

Bearing in mind that the Commission recommended in paragraph 54.9 of its Final Report that the Conference adopt the above "Criteria for Acceptable Performance of Laboratories in proficiency Testing",

Hereby:
1. Adopts the "Criteria for Acceptable Performance of Laboratories in Proficiency Testing", annexed hereto.

ANNEX
CRITERIA FOR ACCEPTABLE PERFORMANCE OF LABORATORIES
IN PROFICIENCY TESTING [4]

1. INTRODUCTION

The following criteria are designed solely for the purpose of determining performance of laboratories in proficiency testing. Results from these tests will be used by the Director-General for designating laboratories. No such criteria shall be considered as constituting any interpretation of, or precedent for, related provisions of the Convention.

Verification analysis of samples in designated laboratories is primarily qualitative. Therefore performance criteria for proficiency testing as developed by international bodies can not be applied as such since they are based on quantitative results.

The Secretariat should inform the laboratories of the purpose of the test and the test scenario upon the arrival of the test samples in the same way as it will inform the laboratories in case of analyses of authentic samples.

The participating laboratories should report identified chemicals relevant to the test. Quantitation and an indication of the detection levels of the used analytical procedures are appreci-

---

[4] Contained in PC-XI/B/WP.6 and Corr.1, Annex 1.

ated but not required. These analytical procedures may help during the evaluation of the test and for follow-up actions. Laboratories must strive for high performance: if they perform unsatisfactorily in the tests, they must be prepared to take remedial action.

The following performance criteria have been proposed on the basis that the test samples are spiked with chemicals relevant to the aim of the test at a level of 1-10 ppm or higher.

2.   PERFORMANCE CRITERIA
   (a)   Analysis of test samples and reporting of test results should be carried out within the set time frame (15 calendar days starting from the day when the samples arrive at a laboratory site).*
   (b)   Identification of chemicals should be based on at least two different analysis techniques, preferably by two different spectrometric (e.g. EI-MS, CI-MS, LC-MS, IR, NMR) analysis techniques, when available, giving consistent results.
   (c)   All analytical data supporting the identifications made (chromatographic and spectrometric data) must be annexed to the report.
   (d)   The laboratory must indicate on which basis the chemicals are identified (comparison with data on standard chemicals, data in analytical databases or interpretation of spectra).
   (e)   The laboratory must describe sample preparation and analytical methods in detail or must make reference to Recommended Operating Procedures (ROPs), or Standard Operating procedures (SOPs) or to the validated procedures according to the quality assurance/quality control (QA/QC) regime of the laboratory. All deviations from the procedures will have to be described in detail.
   (f)   The identified chemicals must be reported with sufficient structural information, including at least the structural formula, CAS registry number (if available) and chemical name, and preferably the CWC Schedule-, IUPAC- or CA name. If IUPAC or CA names are not available, a name from which the structure can be derived should be included.
   (g)   Only chemicals relevant to the aims of the test should be reported.
   (h)   False positive results must not occur. Any chemical that is not contained in or that could not be formed in the sample matrix will constitute a false positive result. Reporting any false positive result will constitute failure of the Proficiency Test.

3.   SCORING OF THE PERFORMANCE
   The present scoring rules should be considered separately for each test and used as a basis for measuring performance in a specific test. Before establishing the final scoring, the Secretariat will check the consistency of material received in coordination with the laboratory which provided it. If the criteria contained in paragraph 2 of this Annex are met, the result of the laboratory will be scored as follows:
   (a)   Each correct identification will be positively scored (+1 point).
   (b)   Identification of a degradation product(s) instead of the spiking chemical will be positively scored (+1 point), if the original spiking chemical is no longer present.
   (c)   Identification of nerve agents in Schedule 1A and nerve agent precursors and degradation products in Schedule 1B and 2B shall be considered correct (+1 point) without specific identification of the locations of alkyl groups in the O-alkyl or O-cycloalkyl side chains. However, the side chain of the P-C bond must be fully identified.
   (d)   Identification of minor constituents of the spiking chemical(s) will be considered correct, but will not add to the score.

---

   * The results of the test must be faxed to the Secretariat within 15 days, and the full report must be despatched to the Secretariat by the end of the same period with a suitably validated date [footnote in original].

(e) False negative results arising from not finding a spiking chemical or its degradation product will be scored negatively (-1 point).

4. FOLLOW-UP ACTIONS

In case of errors (false positives and negatives) the Secretariat will report to the laboratory in question. The laboratory, after taking immediate action, should submit a full report stating the cause of the problem and any remedial actions taken to the Secretariat before the next test. If the laboratory fails to submit the report of any remedial actions taken the laboratory will not be allowed to participate in the new test. If the remedial actions taken by the laboratory prove to be ineffective, the Director-General may wish to reconsider the certification of the laboratory for performing this type of analysis (see paragraph 56(b) of the Verification Annex).

Any laboratory that fails to return the results of a Proficiency Test will fail that test unless the laboratory informs the Secretariat of its intention to withdraw before the end of the test and also provides a satisfactory explanation.

11.5 Criteria for the designation of laboratories by the OPCW

C-I/DEC.61 adopted by the Conference of the States Parties at its First Session on 22 May 1997 and entitled "Criteria for the designation of laboratories by the OPCW"

The Conference

Recalling that the Commission, in its PC-VI/22, paragraph 6.4, adopted the following criteria for the designation of laboratories by the OPCW. Such laboratories should:

(a) have established an internationally recognised quality assurance system;
(b) have obtained accreditation by an internationally recognised accreditation body for tasks for which they are seeking designation; and
(c) regularly participate and perform successfully in inter-laboratory proficiency tests. Analytical laboratories should obtain satisfactory results analysing control samples distributed by the OPCW.

Bearing in mind that the Commission recommended in paragraph 54.9 of its Final Report that the Conference adopt the above mentioned criteria for the designation of laboratories,

Hereby:

1. Adopts the criteria for the designation of laboratories as contained above.

11.6 Guidelines on the designation of laboratories for the analysis of authentic samples

EC-XX/DEC.3 adopted by the Executive Council at its Twentieth Session on 28 June 2000 and entitled "Guidelines on the designation of laboratories for the analysis of authentic samples"

The Executive Council

Recalling that at its First Session the Conference of the States Parties adopted the "Criteria for the designation of laboratories by the OPCW" (C-I/DEC.61), the "Criteria for acceptable performance of laboratories in proficiency testing" (C-I/DEC.62), and the "Criteria for the conduct of OPCW/PTS proficiency testing" (C-I/DEC.65, all dated 22 May 1997);

Reaffirming the need to maintain the high level of proficiency required of laboratories designated for the analysis of authentic samples transferred off-site in accordance with the relevant provisions of the Convention;

Recognising that, pursuant to subparagraph 56(b) of Part II of the Verification Annex, the Director-General has the responsibility to certify the laboratories designated to perform different types of analysis;

Recalling the criteria for the designation of laboratories for the analysis of authentic samples and the retention of designated status, laid down in the Note by the Director-General (S/86/98, dated 17 November 1998, and Corr.1, dated 18 November 1998);

Recalling further that, at its Fifth Session, the Conference mandated the Council to take a decision on this issue;

Hereby:

Decides that, in relation to the designation of laboratories for the analysis of authentic samples, the Director-General will take into account the guidelines annexed hereto.

ANNEX

GUIDELINES ON THE DESIGNATION OF LABORATORIES FOR THE ANALYSIS OF AUTHENTIC SAMPLES

1. Any laboratory that qualifies for designation will be designated by the Director General accordingly. When designating laboratories for the analysis of authentic samples, in accordance with C-I/DEC.61 and C-I/DEC.65, both dated 22 May 1997, the Director-General will take into account the following:
    (a) the validity of the laboratory's quality system and accreditation (C-I/DEC.61), considering the quality system and standards used (ISO/IEC Guide 25, EN 45001, or equivalent), as well as the accreditation body, the accreditation validity period, and the scope of the accreditation. A proper quality system must be in place, and the scope of the accreditation must be relevant to the analysis of chemical warfare agents and related compounds, i.e. the laboratory has been accredited for the tasks for which it is seeking designation[5]; and
    (b) the laboratory's successful performance in the OPCW's proficiency testing programme. A laboratory must participate at least once per calendar year. A combined rating of a laboratory's three most recent consecutive maximum scores (three A's, or two A's and one B) shall be regarded as successful performance (see subparagraph 4(d) of C-I/DEC.65).
2. Starting from 1 January 2000, for those laboratories that have been designated for the analysis of authentic samples, the Technical Secretariat (hereinafter the "Secretariat") will apply the following guidelines for assessing whether those laboratories may retain their designated status:
    (a) the criteria for determining whether a laboratory may retain its status as a designated laboratory are essentially the same as those that are applicable to laboratories seeking designation. A designated laboratory must inform the Secretariat of any changes in its accreditation status; and
    (b) in order to retain its designation, each designated laboratory will have to demonstrate once per calendar year that it has maintained its capabilities in proficiency tests organised by the Secretariat. Once per calendar year a laboratory must either participate in these tests as a regular participant, or support the Secretariat in preparing the test samples or in evaluating the test results[6]. The criteria for assessing the performance of

---

[5] See C-1/DEC.61, "Criteria for the designation of laboratories by the OPCW", and C-I/DEC.67, "Scope of activities of designated laboratories and the role and status of other laboratories" [footnote in original].

[6] Provided that they fulfil the requirements of subparagraph 5(c) of C-I/DEC.65: "laboratories cannot use performance rating for preparing the samples or evaluating the analytical results of more than one of

laboratories in proficiency tests are specified in C-I/DEC.62, dated 22 May 1997. It is the intention of the Secretariat to organise two proficiency tests per year, with the support of two laboratories in preparing the test samples or evaluating the test results. Such work could be performed by reputable commercial laboratories on a contractual basis, or by laboratories that fulfil the requirements set out in C-I/DEC.65.

3.   Should a designated laboratory perform unsuccessfully in a proficiency test, this will result in its temporary suspension. In this situation the laboratory will remain designated but will no longer be selected by the Director-General to receive and analyse authentic samples from the OPCW. However, it may perform other tasks as defined in C-I/DEC.67, dated 22 May 1997. Unsuccessful performance resulting in temporary suspension includes:
   (a)   unsatisfactory performance, as determined by the Director-General on the basis of C-I/DEC.65, in preparing the test samples or evaluating the results; or
   (b)   a rating of C, D or Failure (other than a false positive identification) in a single test; or
   (c)   two B's in its last three consecutive tests.
   A temporarily suspended designated laboratory may regain its full status once it has again achieved successful performance, as defined in subparagraph 1(b).
4.   The designation of a laboratory will be withdrawn should there be either a substantial change in its accreditation status, or a deterioration in its performance, such as in the following cases:
   (a)   the laboratory loses its accreditation for the analysis of chemical warfare agents and related compounds;
   (b)   the laboratory does not participate once per calendar year in a proficiency test organised by the Secretariat (see paragraph 2 above);
   (c)   the laboratory fails to regain the full status of designation while being temporarily suspended;
   (d)   false positive identification in a single proficiency test; and/or
   (e)   the laboratory's performance in the analysis of control samples distributed alongside authentic samples by the OPCW is unsatisfactory. In the off-site analysis of control samples, any false positive identification and/or failure to identify the chemicals present shall be regarded as unsatisfactory performance.
5.   Any designated laboratory whose designation has been withdrawn may regain its designated status once it demonstrates that it again fulfils the criteria set out in paragraph 1 above.

11.7 Scope of activities of designated laboratories and the role and status of other laboratories

C-I/DEC.67 adopted by the Conference of the States Parties at its First Session on 22 May 1997 and entitled "Scope of Activities of Designated Laboratories, and the Role and Status of Other Laboratories"

The Conference
   Recalling that the Commission, in its PC-XVI/36, paragraph 10.3, adopted the "Scope of Activities of Designated Laboratories, and the Role and Status of Other Laboratories",
   Bearing in mind that the Commission recommended in paragraph 54.9 of its Final Report that the Conference adopt the above mentioned understanding,

Hereby:
1.   Adopts the "Scope of Activities of Designated Laboratories, and the Role and Status of Other Laboratories" annexed hereto.

---

their last three consecutive proficiency tests (i.e. laboratories must participate in at least two of the three tests as regular participants)" [footnote in original].

Annex
SCOPE OF ACTIVITIES OF DESIGNATED LABORATORIES AND THE ROLE
AND STATUS OF OTHER LABORATORIES [7]

1. Only the designated laboratories shall perform the analysis of authentic samples. Designated
    laboratories may perform, *inter alia*, the following tasks:
    (a) the development and validation of analytical and other methods, to include analytical
         methods for use on-site;
    (b) the recording and validation of reference data;
    (c) the preparation and validation of reference compounds;
    (d) the preparation, validation and distribution of analytical standards;
    (e) internal quality assurance;
    (f) the development and validation of procedures for the certification, maintenance and stor-
         age of inspection equipment, to include protective means; and
    (g) the technical training of OPCW inspection personnel.
2. Other laboratories with an appropriate quality assurance programme comparable to interna-
    tionally recognised standards may perform, *inter alia*, the following tasks:
    (a) the development of analytical and other methods, to include analytical methods for use
         on-site;
    (b) the recording of reference data;
    (c) the preparation of reference compounds;
    (d) the preparation and distribution of analytical standards;
    (e) internal quality assurance;
    (f) the development of procedures for the maintenance and storage of inspection equipment,
         to include protective means; and
    (g) the technical training of OPCW inspection personnel.
3. In addition, designated and other laboratories with an appropriate quality assurance pro-
    gramme comparable to internationally recognised standards and fulfilling the requirements
    as set forth in the Secretariat's standard operating procedures, may perform the following
    tasks:
    (a) preparing samples for OPCW/TS proficiency tests (PC-XI/B/WP.6 and Corr.1, Annex
         2); and
    (b) assisting the Secretariat in the evaluation of results for OPCW/TS proficiency tests (PC-
         XIII/B/WP.5, Annex 1).
4. Designated laboratories and other laboratories shall be only from the States Parties, with the
    widest geographical diversity assured to the extent possible.
5. Any employment of other laboratories' services shall be specifically approved by the Direc-
    tor-General.
6. Except for the analysis of authentic samples, any other contracted services to be provided by
    designated laboratories as well as by other laboratories shall be subject to all OPCW financial
    rules and regulations, as well as to the provisions of OPCW procurement rules on competitive
    bids.

---

[7] Annex 1 to PC-XV/B/WP.6.

12. CENTRAL OPCW ANALYTICAL DATABASE

12.1 Content of the Central OPCW Analytical Database

C-I/DEC.64 adopted by the Conference of the States Parties at its First Session on 22 May 1997 and entitled "OPCW Central Analytical Database". The lists of validated analytical data for inclusion in the database have been subject to frequent updates, as reflected in numerous decisions adopted by the Executive Council.[1]

The Conference

Recalling that the Commission, in its PC-XV/25, subparagraph 8.3(b), approved the "The Results of the Evaluation of the GC data" and, in its PC-XVI/36, paragraph 10.3 approved the results of the evaluation of the GC data of analytical derivatives of scheduled chemicals,

Recalling that the Commission, in its PC-XVI/36, paragraph 10.3, removed the GC data of four chemicals from the results of the evaluation of the GC data,

Recalling that the Commission in its PC-XV/25, paragraph 8.3(c), approved the inclusion of analytical data in the OPCW Analytical Database for the test chemicals, as contained in the "Recommended Operating Procedure for On-Site Analysis by Gas Chromatography/Mass Spectrometry (GC/MS)" (PC-XIV/B/WP.5, Annex 5) on the understanding that the test samples will not contain scheduled chemicals and that, therefore, the use of the above data, during on-site analysis, will be restricted to GC/MS performance tests and that analytical procedures which prevent cross contamination of the test chemicals are applied, as appropriate,

Recalling that the Commission, in its PC-XVI/36, paragraph 10.3, approved the inclusion of analytical derivatives of scheduled chemicals using the reagents BSTFA and 3,4-dimercaptotoluene,

Bearing in mind that the Commission recommended in paragraph 54.9 of its Final Report that the Conference adopt the above mentioned inclusions into the OPCW Central Analytical Database,

Further bearing in mind that Working Group B noted the results of the evaluation of the spectra (MS, IR, NMR) of the scheduled chemicals (Annex 5 to PC-X/B/WP.9, see PC-X/B/5, subparagraph 3.9), the results of the evaluation of Infrared (IR) spectra (Annex 3 to PC-XI/B/WP.6, see PC-XI/B/12, subparagraph 3.5(ii)), the results of the evaluation of the MS and IR Spectra (Annex 3 to PC-XII/B/WP.6, see PC-XII/B/7, subparagraph 5.2(b)) and the results of the evaluation of the NMR and MS spectra (Annex 3 to PC-XIII/B/WP.5, see PC-XIII/B/6, subparagraph 5.3(b)).

---

[1] The amendments to the list have been effected by the following decisions adopted by the Executive Council: EC-XVI/DEC.3, dated 24/09/1999; EC-XVIII/DEC.1, dated 16/02/2000; EC-XIX/DEC.4, dated 06/04/2000; EC-XXI/DEC.3, dated 05/10/2000; EC-XXIII/DEC.3, dated 21/02/2001; EC-XXVII/DEC.1, dated 05/12/2001; EC-XXVII/DEC.2, dated 05/12/2001; EC-29/DEC.3, dated 28/06/2002; EC-29/DEC.4, dated 28/06/2002; EC-31/DEC.2, dated 15/01/2003; EC-32/DEC.1, dated 18/03/2003; EC-33/DEC.2, dated 24/06/2003; EC-32/DEC.1/Corr.1, dated 05/08/2003; EC-35/DEC.1, dated 03/12/2003; EC-36/DEC.3, dated 23/03/2004; EC-37/DEC.4, dated 29/06/2004; EC-38/DEC.10, dated 13/10/2004; EC-40/DEC.10, dated 16/03/2005; EC-40/DEC.9, dated 16/03/2005; EC-42/DEC.1, dated 29/09/2005; EC-45/DEC.7, dated 18/05/2006; EC-45/DEC.6, dated 18/05/2006; EC-46/DEC.5, dated 05/07/2006; EC-49/DEC.4, dated 27/06/2007; EC-51/DEC.3, dated 27/11/2007; EC-51/DEC.2, dated 27/11/2007; EC-53/DEC.13, dated 25/06/2008; EC-53/DEC.14, dated 25/06/2008; EC-54/DEC.4, dated 14/10/2008; EC-55/DEC.1, dated 14/10/2008; EC-56/DEC.1, dated 14/10/2008; EC-55/DEC.1, dated 18/02/2009; EC-56/DEC.1, dated 21/04/2009; EC-57/DEC.5, dated 16/07/2009; EC-59/DEC.1, dated 23/02/2010; EC-61/DEC.8, dated 02/07/2010; EC-63/DEC.2, dated 16/02/2011; EC-63/DEC.3, dated 16/02/2011; EC-65/DEC.1, dated 13/07/2011; EC-65/DEC.2, dated 13/07/2011; EC-67/DEC.1, dated 15/02/2012; EC-69/DEC.1, dated 11/07/2012; EC-71/DEC.6, dated 20/02/2013; EC-71/DEC.7, dated 20/02/2013; EC-73/DEC.2, dated 18/07/2013 and EC-76/DEC.4, dated 10 July 2014.

Hereby:
1. Adopts the content of the OPCW Central Analytical Database as attached hereto (Annexes 1 through 8),
2. Requests the Director-General to establish a consultative mechanism for updating the OPCW Central Analytical Database to enable the Executive Council to recommend proposed inclusions to the Conference for adoption.
[Annexes 1 to 8 not reproduced in this volume]

12.2 Consultative mechanism for updating
the Central OPCW Analytical Database

C-II/8 containing the Report of the Second Session of the Conference of the States Parties adopted on 5 December 1997, Subparagraph 11.2(c)

(c) PROPOSED MECHANISM FOR UPDATING THE OPCW CENTRAL ANALYTICAL DATABASE
In accordance with the recommendation of the Executive Council at its Fourth Session, the Conference adopted the decision on the "Proposed Mechanism for Updating the OPCW Central Analytical Database" (EC-IV/DEC.2, dated 5 September 1997). To allow Member States an opportunity to review spectra proposed for inclusion in the OPCW Central Analytical Database, the Conference decided to extend for sixty days the period for comment. The Conference was informed by the Secretariat that it had received an objection to the inclusion of certain spectra into the OPCW Central Analytical Database (infrared spectra 2-1-92 and 2-1-94, as well as mass spectra 5-2-107, 5-2-108, 5-2-109, 5-2-111, 5-2-117, 5-2-118, and 5-2-119). Provided that no objections from Member States received by the Secretariat are outstanding by 2 February 1998, the Conference decided to adopt the spectra referred to in paragraph 4 of [decision EC-IV/DEC.2] and to approve their incorporation into the OPCW Central Analytical Database with effect from that date. However, if there are outstanding objections to any particular spectra on the date, these spectra will not be included in the OPCW Central Analytical Database and the Director-General may undertake to provide further information to the Executive Council addressing the concerns expressed. The Conference also approved the consultative mechanism for updating the OPCW Central Analytical Database as outlined in paragraphs 1 to 3 of [that] decision.

EC-IV/DEC.2 adopted by the Executive Council at its Fourth Session on 5 September 1997 and entitled "Proposed mechanism for updating the OPCW Central Analytical Database"

The First Session of the Conference of the States Parties requested the Director-General to establish a consultative mechanism for updating the OPCW Central Analytical Database to enable the Executive Council to recommend proposed inclusions to the Conference for adoption (C-I/DEC.64, dated 22 May 1997).

The Executive Council proposes that a consultative mechanism be established by the Second Session of the Conference of the States Parties to enable approved validated spectra to be placed on the OPCW Central Analytical Database. The consultative mechanism should be implemented in the following manner:
1. the Secretariat will request States Parties to produce or to provide additional spectra on a mutually agreed basis in the most cost-efficient way. The Secretariat will seek the most cost-efficient solution, comparing offers from several States Parties. If specific spectra cannot be obtained in this manner, the Secretariat will contract "other laboratories" for this purpose;
2. spectra so obtained will be validated before they are proposed for incorporation into the database. To that end, an open-ended validation group, consisting of experts of recognised stand-

ing in the field of analytical chemistry, will be established. These experts shall be provided by States Parties at no cost to the Organisation. Before a particular spectrum will be presented to the Executive Council for approval, the validation group shall agree on the technical validity of the spectrum. The Council will review the operation of the validation group from time to time, with a view towards this group working in close association with the Scientific Advisory Board;

3. once a batch of spectra has been technically validated, it will be necessary to obtain approval from the States Parties for the incorporation of these spectra into the OPCW Central Analytical Database by implementing the following procedures:

    – the Director-General will present a list of newly validated spectra to the Executive Council at regular intervals;
    – any such proposal will be submitted to members of the Executive Council not later than 30 days before the opening of the session of the Council which is requested to consider its inclusion;
    – the list will also be distributed to all other States Parties 30 days in advance of the session in order to give them an opportunity to communicate to the Council any concerns which they may have in relation to the inclusion of the proposed spectra;
    – the Director-General will request the Executive Council to approve the inclusion of spectra into the OPCW Central Analytical Database;
    – the Executive Council will include in its report to the Conference of the States Parties a list of the spectra which have been approved by the Executive Council for inclusion into the OPCW Central Analytical Database;
    – should the Executive Council decide not to approve individual spectra presented to it, the Director-General may undertake to provide further information to the Executive Council addressing the concerns expressed.

4. In the interim, with respect to spectra already validated by the Specialist Task Force on the Analytical Database during the Preparatory Commission of the OPCW, but not brought to the First Session of the Conference of the States Parties for approval, the following approach is recommended:

    – copies of the spectra will be submitted to all Member States at least 60 days before the Second Session of the Conference with the request to communicate to the Executive Council or to the Secretariat any concerns they may have in relation to the inclusion of the proposed spectra. The Executive Council should consider the inclusion of the issue in its agenda if requested;
    – the Second Session of the Conference of the States Parties will consider the adoption of these spectra and approval of their incorporation into the Central OPCW Analytical Database.

5. The Executive Council recommends to the Second Session of the Conference of the States Parties that it consider adopting the spectra referred to in paragraph 4 above and approve their incorporation into the OPCW Central Analytical Database.

6. The Executive Council recommends to the Second Session of the Conference of the States Parties that the consultative mechanism for updating the OPCW Central Analytical Database, outlined in paragraphs 1 to 3 above, be approved by the Conference.

Implementation

13. POLICY

13.1 OPCW Policy on Confidentiality[1]

C-I/DEC.13/Rev.1 first adopted by the Conference of the States Parties at its First Session on 6 May 1997 and reviewed at its Eleventh Session on 5-8 December 2006

The Conference

Recalling that the Preparatory Commission developed a Draft OPCW Policy on Confidentiality (OPOC) that includes the above mentioned issues as well as rules governing the composition and operating procedures of the Commission for the Settlement of Disputes Related to Confidentiality (hereinafter "the Confidentiality Commission") as required by paragraph 23 the Confidentiality Annex to the Chemical Weapons Convention (hereinafter the "the Confidentiality Annex"), in a combined manner;

Recalling also that the Preparatory Commission adopted the draft OPOC, as annexed to PC-XI/B/WP.8, dated 23 June 1995, and as amended by Working Group B, and decided to apply the provisions of this draft OPOC, *mutatis mutandis*, to the work of the Preparatory Commission. (paragraph 7.7 of PC-XI/17, dated 27 July 1995; Corr.1 dated 14 August 1995; and Corr.2, dated 12 September 1995);

Recalling further that the Preparatory Commission decided to correct the clerical error in the second-to-last line of subparagraph 6.2 of Part VI of the Draft OPOC by replacing the word "should" with "shall". (paragraph 8.7 of PC-XII/17, dated 14 December 1995);

Bearing in mind that the Preparatory Commission recommended, in paragraph 45.4 of its final report that the Conference of State Parties (hereinafter "the Conference") adopt the above mentioned OPOC, as corrected.

Hereby:

1.   Adopts the above-mentioned OPOC, which is annexed hereto, as corrected.

---

[1] The revised version of the OPCW Policy on Confidentiality annexed hereto contains three sets of changes – those that were made in C-1/DEC.13/Corr.1, removing references to the draft OPOC submitted by the Preparatory Commission, those that were made in C-II/DEC.14 paragraph 3, amending Rule 1.4 of Part IX.2 of the Policy (Rules Governing the Confidentiality Commission) and those from C-10/DEC.9 which contained amendments to the OPCW Policy on Confidentiality [footnote in original].

Annex
OPCW POLICY ON CONFIDENTIALITY[2]

CONTENTS

PART I. INTRODUCTION

1. This document sets out the basis of the Organisation's policy for protecting confidentiality throughout activities related to the implementation of the Convention, for classifying and handling confidential information, and for dealing with breaches of confidentiality.
2. A policy for confidential information is essential to the work of the Organisation because of the intrusive verification measures which are aimed at promoting confidence in compliance with the Convention while respecting States Parties' legitimate concerns about the possible disclosure of sensitive information. Credible verification entails receptiveness on the part of States Parties and a level of intrusiveness in verification activities. The need for disclosure of appropriate information to demonstrate compliance with the Convention should be matched by credible reassurances for States Parties that proper measures are taken to prevent disclosure of information not relevant to the Convention and that any confidential information, once disclosed, will be appropriately protected.

---

[2] The original version of the OPOC was prefaced by the following note: [footnote in original]

"The Draft OPCW Policy on Confidentiality was developed by the Expert Group on Confidentiality (Annex to PC-XI/B/WP.8) and was adopted as amended by the Preparatory Commission at its Eleventh Session (PC-XI/17, subparagraph 7.7 and PC-XI/B/12, subparagraph 7.2). The Draft OPCW Media and Public Affairs Policy was developed by the Formal Consultations on OPCW Media and Public Affairs Policy (Attachment to PC-X/A/WP.5) and was provisionally approved as amended by the Preparatory Commission at its Tenth Session (PC-X/23, subparagraph 6.11 and PC-X/A/3, subparagraph 6.4), pending the adoption of other relevant documents including the Draft OPCW Policy on Confidentiality.

The Preparatory Commission also decided that the Draft OPCW Policy on Confidentiality and the Draft OPCW Media and Public Affairs Policy would apply, mutatis mutandis, to the work of the Preparatory Commission (PC-XI/17, subparagraph 7.7 and PC-X/23, subparagraph 6.12 respectively).

Ian R Kenyon
Executive Secretary"

3. Consequently, in defining States Parties' rights and obligations, the Convention embodies a balance between that disclosure necessary to enhance confidence in compliance with the Convention, and the prevention of disclosure of information not relevant to the Convention, in order to protect national security and proprietary rights, taking into account constitutional obligations. These two objectives are not necessarily in conflict; on the contrary, a credible and effective process of verification can be achieved which actively and integrally protects confidentiality. The Convention text provides practical assurances that all confidential information will be appropriately protected; and that verification procedures will seek to prevent the disclosure of information not related to verification of compliance with the Convention.

PART II. GENERAL POLICY

1. Paragraph 5 of Article VIII of the Convention provides the basis of the obligations of the Organisation to respect confidentiality:
    "The Organisation shall conduct its verification activities provided for under this Convention in the least intrusive manner possible consistent with the timely and efficient accomplishment of their objectives. It shall request only information and data necessary to fulfil its responsibilities under this Convention. It shall take every precaution to protect the confidentiality of information on civil and military activities and facilities coming to its knowledge in the implementation of this Convention and, in particular, shall abide by the provisions set forth in the Confidentiality Annex."
2. Paragraph 6 of Article VII of the Convention establishes the obligation on each State Party to:
    "treat as confidential and afford special handling to information and data that it receives in confidence from the Organisation in connection with the implementation of this Convention. It shall treat such information and data exclusively in connection with its rights and obligations under this Convention and in accordance with the provisions set forth in the Confidentiality Annex."
3. These basic requirements are elaborated in a number of other provisions of the Convention, especially in the Confidentiality Annex and in the provisions detailing verification procedures (e.g. paragraph 10 of Article VI; paragraphs 56 and 62, Part II of the Verification Annex and paragraph 48, Part X of the Verification Annex). From this basis, the fundamental elements of the Organisation's Policy on Confidentiality are:
    (a) only that information necessary for the timely and efficient carrying out of its responsibilities under the Convention shall be sought and required; and requirements for information to which the Organisation shall be given access by a State Party shall be specified as precisely as possible;
    (b) verification activities shall be designed, planned and carried out so as to avoid unnecessary disclosure of confidential information and so as to seek to prevent disclosure of such information not related to compliance with the Convention, consistent with effective and timely discharge of verification obligations under the Convention;
    (c) confidential information not relevant to the Convention shall not be sought, recorded or retained in the course of verification or other activities, without prejudice to an inspected State Party's right to request such a disclosure in accordance with the Convention. Once disclosed, it shall be protected, shall not be further disseminated, and shall be appropriately disposed of;
    (d) systematic procedures for limiting the dissemination of and access to information after information is collected and classified as confidential shall be established, monitored, and adhered to;
    (e) information obtained in connection with the implementation of the Convention shall not be published or otherwise released unless with explicit authority and in accordance with the release procedures outlined in Part VII of this policy; and

(f)   staff selection and training, and staffing policy and regulations, shall take into account the need to ensure that all staff members of the Secretariat meet the highest standards of efficiency, competence and integrity.

PART III. INFORMATION AND CONFIDENTIALITY

1.   This Part sets out guidelines for developing a practical understanding of the scope of the terms 'information', 'confidential information' and 'confidentiality'. The Convention sets out no definitive account of how these terms are to be applied, and it is clear that they are to be determined in an operational context consistent with the implementation of the Organisation's and States Parties' various responsibilities under the Convention.

2.   The Organisation will carry out its responsibilities greatly depending on the information obtained through its verification activities and provided by States Parties. Thus, information will be coming into the Organisation's possession or to a staff member of the Organisation in a continuous input-output pattern of acquiring, processing and producing further necessary information.

3.   In view of the integral role of confidentiality in all the Organisation's activities, information can generally be considered in operational terms, covering its characteristics, its means of acquisition and storage, and media for its processing and transmission.

SCOPE OF 'INFORMATION'

4.   The term 'information' must be understood in a very broad sense. Information is recognised by its capacity or potential to provide, either directly or indirectly, data or any knowledge, regardless of its physical or intangible character or make-up.

5.   It further applies to any means of acquiring, transmitting or retaining knowledge or data which may be perceived, acquired, derived or retained by any individual or by the Organisation including by its personnel or equipment in the implementation of the Convention.

6.   The term 'data' appears in several contexts in the Convention. Generally, 'data' carries the implication of information in a particular structure or format, such as the information embodied in a national declaration. However, in construing the text from the point of view of confidentiality, there is no substantial distinction between 'information' and 'data.' Hence, for the purposes of this policy, the term 'information' will be considered to subsume any references to 'data.' 'Information' or 'data' may include information which is incorrect, false or inaccurate.

7.   To illustrate the scope of its application, 'information' includes, but is not limited to:
   –   documents with graphic, schematic, numerical, symbolic, pictorial, digital, analogue, photographic or written information ;
   –   the products of photography, imagery, inspection, observation, data processing, sampling and analysis;
   –   data stored or displayed on electronic, magnetic or any other physical medium;
   –   information expressed in relative or absolute terms; and
   –   samples and other bodies of chemicals including chemicals carried by earth, dust, filters and sampling, and equipment including sampling, analysis and safety equipment. Samples contain information, and through sample analysis can provide further information.
Information can be acquired or transmitted through any medium of communications or human sense. Information can be obtained and transmitted due to the mere presence of persons on site or through access granted to them. Thus, equipment, objects, clothes and other personal belongings could become sources of information.

OPERATIONAL DEFINITIONS OF SOME FORMS OF INFORMATION

8.   The following operational definitions, which cover only some forms of information, apply

for the purpose of guidelines for handling and protection of information under this Policy. It is to be understood that the following definitions are flexible enough to ensure that handling guidelines can be applied effectively and practically:

- 'Document' could extend to a variety of physical items displaying information or data;
- 'Computer material' includes any computer storage and processing medium, such as disks, tapes and diskettes. This term also covers portable computers, which may be used to record information during an on-site inspection;
- 'Audio-visual material' includes audio and video tapes, developed and undeveloped photographic films including the negatives of still photographs and the positives. (Positive prints of still photographs may be considered also as documents); and
- 'Sample' includes a sample's collection medium and any further information acquired or derived from analysis.

In the application of general operating guidelines to particular items of information falling under these definitions, there may be overlapping reference (for instance, a transparency for overhead projection may be handled as a document or as audio-visual material, and a computer printout may be handled as a document or as computer material).

CONFIDENTIALITY OF INFORMATION UNDER THE CONVENTION

9. A basic principle on confidentiality, set down in subparagraph 2(c) of the Confidentiality Annex, is that no information obtained by the Organisation in connection with the implementation of the Convention shall be published or otherwise released, except as specifically provided for.

10. Specific procedural guidelines in subparagraph 2(a) of the Confidentiality Annex provide that information shall be considered confidential if:

 (a) it is so designated by the State Party from which the information was obtained and to which the information refers; or

 (b) in the judgement of the Director-General, its unauthorised disclosure could reasonably be expected to cause damage to the State Party to which it refers or to the mechanisms for implementation of the Convention.

11. The following factors shall be weighed and carefully balanced by the Director-General or his* delegate in determining confidentiality of information:

- the potential of its disclosure causing damage to a State Party, any other body of a State Party, including a commercial firm, any national of a State Party, or to the Convention or the Organisation;
- the potential of its disclosure offering particular or selective advantage to an individual, a State, or any other body, including a commercial firm;
- the basic requirement for effective verification of compliance; and
- benefits stemming from the dissemination of general information regarding the implementation of the Convention, in order to promote its acceptance and credibility.

12. In determining whether the information it is providing to the Organisation contains confidential information, a State Party could also consider the above factors. The designation of information as confidential shall not undermine the obligation for a State Party to demonstrate compliance with the Convention and shall not be used by a State Party to conceal non-compliance. Furthermore, a State Party cannot prevent the dissemination of information which in accordance with the Convention shall be transmitted in a specified manner to States Parties upon request or routinely.

13. Once information has been determined to contain confidential information, it will be neces-

---

* Throughout the English version of this Policy, the personal and possessive pronouns 'he' and 'his' refer without distinction to both the female and the male genders [footnote in original].

sary to specify the level of sensitivity and scope of access to it. This will be normally done through a system of classification which is set out in Part V of this Policy.

RELATIONSHIP OF INFORMATION TO THE CONVENTION

14. The relationship of information to the purposes of the Convention can have implications for how confidentiality measures will apply to that information. Three significant distinctions can be discerned in the implementation of the Convention:
    – information pertinent to the Organisation to fulfil its responsibilities under the Convention or provided by States Parties to fulfil their obligations under the Convention;
    – information not related to the aims of the Convention, to which an inspected State Party grants access to demonstrate compliance with the Convention, or which it incidentally discloses in the course of verification activities; and
    – information, including sensitive information, which is not related to the aims of the Convention, and to which an inspected State Party denies access consistent with its rights and obligations under the Convention.

15. Verification procedures and activities need to be guided by these distinctions. However, a judgement as to the relationship of information to the purposes of the Convention could be determined operationally, as the characterisation of information in this way is greatly dependant on individual contexts and circumstances. Obligations to protect confidentiality will be set in relation to information described under each of these distinctions.

PART IV. BASIC RESPONSIBILITIES ON CONFIDENTIALITY

1.   OVERALL RESPONSIBILITIES OF THE ORGANISATION

1.1   The OPCW will receive a great deal of confidential information from States Parties and may be exposed to or acquire more confidential information, often of a more sensitive nature, in the course of verification activities. The OPCW's internal processes will generate further confidential information. This Organisation including its constituent elements therefore must abide by certain obligations to respect confidentiality, in particular:
      (a) not to publish or otherwise release information obtained in connection with the implementation of the Convention unless in accordance with the information release procedures as set out in Part VII of this Policy;
      (b) to design, plan and carry out verification activities in the least intrusive manner possible, so as avoid disclosure of non-relevant information and to minimise disclosure of confidential information, where this is consistent with effective and timely verification;
      (c) to seek and require only the disclosure of information necessary to serve the aims of the Convention, and to specify informational requirements as precisely as possible;
      (d) to minimise accessibility of, to protect, and to prevent further dissemination of confidential information not relevant to the Convention which may be incidentally disclosed in the course of verification activities, consistent with effective and timely verification; and
      (e) to establish, follow and monitor systematic procedures for limiting the dissemination of and access to information classified as confidential.

1.2   RESPONSIBILITIES OF THE DIRECTOR-GENERAL

1.2.1 The Director-General is specifically tasked with primary responsibility for the protection of confidential information. The Director-General must establish the regime for handling confidential information within the Secretariat in accordance with the guidelines laid down in the Convention including the Confidentiality Annex and this Policy.

1.2.2 The Director-General is responsible for supervising adherence to the confidentiality regime within the Secretariat, and must report annually on the implementation of the regime.

1.2.3 The Director-General has a central role in dealing with breaches and alleged breaches of confidentiality. This includes the establishment of procedures to be followed and the conduct of investigations in accordance with the Breach Procedures[3], and the imposition of punitive and disciplinary actions in accordance with the Staff Rules and Regulations. The procedures to be followed should be based on any determinations by the Conference on this subject.

1.2.4 The Director-General may initiate requests for States Parties to provide "details on the handling of information provided by the Organisation" (CA, (A)4), and consult with States Parties on the form and timing of such requests in accordance with any guidelines set by the Conference. The Director-General could, for instance, request regular reports from all States Parties on their handing of confidential OPCW information.

1.3 RESPONSIBILITIES OF THE SECRETARIAT

1.3.1 The basic responsibilities of the Secretariat concerning confidentiality derive essentially from the responsibilities of the Organisation and of the Director-General. However, in the practical implementation of the Convention, the definition, conduct and monitoring of the responsibilities of Secretariat staff to safeguard confidentiality are of crucial importance. Particular obligations apply to staff of the Secretariat through their involvement in verification activities and their consequent access to confidential information, both civil and military, which will include information disclosed by a State Party in pursuance of CWC obligations, as well as sensitive information not relevant to the aims of the Convention in the event that such sensitive information is disclosed.

1.3.2 In addition to the broader obligations already outlined, the Secretariat has the following specific responsibilities:
   (a) through the appropriate unit, to evaluate all data and documents it obtains to determine whether confidential information is included;
   (b) to establish within a formal position description a specification of the scope of access to confidential information needed for each staff position;
   (c) to undertake secrecy agreements with each staff member and to undertake secrecy agreements with authorised bodies outside the Organisation, as necessary;
   (d) to maintain a continuing programme of training and awareness for all staff on confidentiality issues, and to monitor each employee's record on protecting confidential information as an explicit element of performance evaluation;
   (e) to advise a State Party of a proposed clearance of an employee for access to confidential information that refers to activities on the territory or in any other place under the jurisdiction and control of that State Party, not less than thirty days before access is granted; and
   (f) to handle and store confidential information in a form that precludes direct identification with the facility it refers to, as far as this can be done consistent with effective verification.

1.3.3 The responsibilities of individual staff members are further defined by a secrecy agreement which must be executed by each employee.

1.4 RESPONSIBILITIES OF THE INSPECTION TEAM

1.4.1 Particular responsibilities of members of an inspection team stem from the following:
   (a) inspectors on site may have access to confidential information;
   (b) the inspection team must negotiate with the inspected State Party on certain matters

---

[3] Set out in Part IX below [footnote in original].

related to confidentiality that require agreement;[4] and

(c) the inspection team is guided by its mandate, draws up an inspection plan, and must decide on specific measures to be employed during the inspection.

1.4.2 Inspection teams shall therefore:

(a) conduct inspections in the least intrusive manner possible consistent with the effective and timely accomplishment of their mission;

(b) plan the inspection and take into consideration proposals which may be made by the State Party receiving an inspection, at whatever stage of the inspection, to ensure that sensitive equipment or information, not related to chemical weapons, is protected;

(c) fully respect the procedures designed to protect sensitive installations and to prevent the unauthorised disclosure of confidential data;

(d) request only the information and data which are necessary to fulfil the inspection mandate;

(e) prepare an inspection report which only contains facts relevant to compliance with the Convention;

(f) protect and prevent further dissemination of confidential information not relevant to the Convention to which inspection teams have access in the course of on-site inspections; and

(g) respect an inspected State Party's denial of access to sensitive information consistent with the State Party's rights and obligations.

2.1 RESPONSIBILITIES OF THE STATES PARTIES

2.1.1 States Parties must treat information received from the Organisation in accordance with its level of sensitivity as expressed in its classification category. The way this obligation is carried out will naturally differ between States Parties, but as a rule this information should be given at least the same level of protection as that afforded to information with comparable national classification or comparable confidentiality under national legal systems. States Parties shall establish or adapt suitable means of handling and protection of OPCW confidential information in a manner consistent with the principles set out in Part VI of this Policy.

2.1.2 Each State Party must provide on request details on the handling of information provided to it by the Organisation. This procedure is aimed at promoting general reassurance among States Parties that confidentiality is effectively safeguarded. The responses of States Parties to such requests should at least confirm that standards for handling information are in accordance with subparagraph 2.1.1 above.

2.1.3 In safeguarding confidentiality of information, States Parties must adhere to the essential obligation to demonstrate compliance with the Convention in accordance with its verification provisions.

2.1.4 Each State Party must cooperate with and support, to the extent possible, the Director-General in investigating breaches or alleged breaches of confidentiality, and in taking appropriate action in accordance with the elaborated breach procedures should an investigation determine that a breach has occurred. This obligation may include provision of details on the handling of information provided to the State Party by the Organisation and, if necessary, the State Party's participation as one of the disputing parties before the "Commission for the settlement of disputes related to confidentiality" in the event of the breach going before that body.

---

[4] For instance in accordance with paragraph 46 of Part X of the Verification Annex and with paragraph 14 of the Confidentiality Annex [footnote in original].

2.2   RESPONSIBILITY OF OBSERVERS

2.2.1 When, in the course of a challenge inspection, the inspected State Party agrees to grant access to an observer in accordance with paragraph 55 of Part X of the Verification Annex, the observer may have access to some confidential information and will accordingly incur particular responsibilities in relation to its handling and protection. Thus the handling and protection of confidential information by the observer must be fully consistent with all relevant provisions of the Convention, including the Confidentiality Annex, and with this Policy, particularly the detailed handling provisions of Part VI of this Policy. As Article IX, subparagraph 12(a) of the Convention indicates that the observer is a "representative" of the requesting State Party, such information is also subject to the provisions of Article VII, paragraph 6, in respect of both the requesting State Party and the observer as its representative in particular, and hence shall be treated as confidential and afforded special handling.

2.2.2 Hence the requesting State Party shall be fully responsible for and shall take all necessary measures to ensure that the observer complies with and is individually bound by all relevant provisions of this Policy, as well as to ensure that effective legal remedies and penalties are available in the event of the observer breaching confidentiality, comparable to the measures taken in the event of an official of that State Party breaching confidentiality. Once any confidential information is disclosed to or acquired by the observer, in addition to and without diminishing the observer's own individual responsibility, the requesting State Party also becomes responsible for the handling and protection of that information in accordance with the Convention and with this Policy. For his part, the observer is to adhere to and be bound by all provisions of this Policy relating to the protection of confidential information, and shall not take any unauthorised action in this regard.

PART V. OPCW CLASSIFICATION SYSTEM FOR CONFIDENTIAL INFORMATION

1.   CATEGORIES OF CONFIDENTIAL INFORMATION

1.1   All information acquired or produced by the Organisation and its constituent elements which is determined to be confidential must be given a classification, based on established categories which correspond to the level of sensitivity of confidential information. In its application, the classification system will not impair the requirement for effective verification of compliance with the Convention, and it should be capable of providing, as necessary, for the release of general information, in adequately desensitised form, regarding the implementation of the Convention, in order to promote its acceptance and credibility.

1.2   The essential factors to be considered in determining the level of sensitivity of an item of information are as follows:
       (a) the degree of potential damage which its disclosure could cause to a State Party, any other body of a State Party, including a commercial firm, or to any national of a State Party, or to the Convention or the Organisation; and
       (b) the degree of potential particular or selective advantage its disclosure could offer to an individual, a State, or any other body, including a commercial firm.
       These factors correspond to the factors used in determining the confidentiality of information.

1.3   Based on these guiding factors, and the specific classification criteria set out below, confidential information shall be classified according to the following categories, in increasing order of sensitivity:
       − OPCW restricted
       − OPCW protected

– OPCW highly protected

The prefix 'OPCW' in the names of these categories is used purely to facilitate handling of classified material, in clearly identifying classifications as being those applied by the Organisation and in avoiding any conflict or misunderstanding with distinct national classification systems. The use of this prefix does not imply any particular scope of dissemination.

1.4 There is a distinction between a classification category (which is based on the sensitivity of information) and the scope of dissemination of information (which is based, for instance, on the subject matter, the need-to-know principle, and the particular purpose for which the information is to be used). Level of classification will not prevent the dissemination of information as specifically required by the Convention, including under subparagraph 2(b) of the Confidentiality Annex.

1.5 Information not falling into any of the above-mentioned categories shall be considered not classified and may be marked appropriately. Information which is not classified will be subject to appropriate protection from release by the Organisation and by States Parties, unless specifically cleared for release in accordance with the separately defined release procedures.

1.6 The level of protection afforded to confidential information shall be linked to the level of sensitivity as indicated by its classification category. Each State Party and the Organisation shall protect OPCW classified information originating both from within the Organisation and from States Parties in accordance with its level of sensitivity as expressed by its classification category.

CLASSIFICATION CATEGORY: OPCW RESTRICTED

CRITERION:

1.7 This category comprises information of which the unauthorised disclosure would be prejudicial to the effectiveness or credibility of the Convention, or prejudicial to the interests of a State Party or of a commercial or governmental body or of a national of a State Party.

EXAMPLES:

1.8 Unless specified otherwise, due to the greater or lesser sensitivity of the data in question, the following forms of information might be classified OPCW RESTRICTED when they are acquired or generated by any means by the Organisation:

(a) the initial and annual reports and declarations provided by States Parties under Articles III, IV, V and VI and in accordance with the Verification Annex, where these documents are considered by originating States Parties as being of this level of sensitivity;

(b) general reports on the results and effectiveness of verification activities; and

(c) information to be supplied to all States Parties in accordance with other provisions of the Convention.

1.9 Other information to be classified and handled as OPCW RESTRICTED may include: routine confidential correspondence between States Parties and the Secretariat, and internal working documents of the Organisation which are not of particular sensitivity. This may also include information relating to the internal processes and decision-making of the Secretariat, and other managerial or administrative information, where open disclosure of the information might hamper the Organisation's effectiveness in implementing the Convention.

DISSEMINATION:

1.10   OPCW RESTRICTED information that must be routinely provided to States Parties in accordance with subparagraph 2(b) of the Confidentiality Annex shall be disseminated accordingly.

CLASSIFICATION CATEGORY: OPCW PROTECTED

CRITERION:

1.11   This category comprises information of which the unauthorised disclosure may cause substantial damage to the effectiveness or credibility of the Convention, or to the interests of a State Party or of a commercial or governmental body or of a national of a State Party.

EXAMPLES:

1.12   Unless specified otherwise in accordance with greater or lesser sensitivity, the following forms of information might be classified as OPCW PROTECTED when they are acquired or generated by any means by the Organisation:

(a)   the initial and annual reports and declarations provided by States Parties under Articles III, IV, V and VI and in accordance with the Verification Annex, where these documents are considered by the originating States Parties as being of this level of sensitivity;

(b)   unpublished technological information about production processes and facilities, and technical information about industrial products;

(c)   less sensitive or more general information related to commercial transactions and the cost factors of industrial processes and production;

(d)   detailed initial reporting on an inspection, including information on anomalies or incidents at facilities, and inspection reports;

(e)   data and information regarding inspection planning of the Secretariat and the inspection goals for a specific facility;

(f)   facility agreements and any attachments thereto; and

(g)   information regarding the validation and evaluation of information contained in declarations, facility agreements and inspection reports.

Where such information is not considered relevant to verification of compliance, it will normally be treated initially as OPCW HIGHLY PROTECTED, even before any formal classification is determined, as specified in subparagraph 1.17 of this Part.

DISSEMINATION:

1.13   OPCW PROTECTED information that must be routinely provided to States Parties in accordance with subparagraph 2(b) of the Confidentiality Annex shall be disseminated accordingly.

CLASSIFICATION CATEGORY: OPCW HIGHLY PROTECTED

CRITERION:

1.14   This category comprises sensitive confidential information of which the unauthorised disclosure would cause serious damage to the effectiveness or credibility of the Convention, or its aims and purpose, or cause serious damage from the point of view of national security or commercial secrecy to the interests of a State Party or of a commercial or governmental body or national of a State Party.

EXAMPLES:

1.15   Unless specified otherwise in accordance with lesser sensitivity, the following forms of information might be classified as OPCW HIGHLY PROTECTED when they are acquired or generated by any means by the Organisation:

(a) the initial and annual reports and declarations provided by States Parties under Articles III, IV, V and VI and in accordance with the Verification Annex, where these documents are considered by originating States Parties as being of this level of sensitivity;

(b) samples taken from inspected sites and returned samples from designated laboratories, and results from analysis of samples;

(c) especially sensitive confidential information especially provided by a State Party; and

(d) confidential information for which access is normally only required, or voluntarily or incidentally provided, during the actual conduct of an on-site inspection, such as:
– process flow diagrams;
– photographs, plans and diagrams of the site;
– specific data related to technological processes and their parameters;
– analytical data of samples taken on site and analysed on site;
– commercially sensitive market information, such as a detailed list of customers, and individual quantities sold to them; and
– other detailed, highly specific technical, commercial or national security information.

Where such information is not considered relevant to the verification of compliance, it will normally be treated initially as opcw highly protected, even before any formal classification is determined, as specified in subparagraph 1.17 below.

1.16 In most inspection scenarios, the highly sensitive information specified in subparagraph 1.15(d) above, that may or may not have a national confidential classification, may be kept at the inspected facility and shall only be made available for on-site use during the inspection. When such information is not taken off site and access to it is limited, there will accordingly be no application of the OPCW classification process within the Secretariat. Even so, during inspection activities the inspection team will give this information at least the level of protection afforded to information as OPCW HIGHLY PROTECTED. The classification category of such information should be specified to the extent possible in facility agreements.

1.17 Sensitive confidential information not related to the verification of compliance which is incidentally revealed or collected by any member of an inspection team shall not be recorded in any form, and shall not be further disseminated. When access is afforded to such sensitive information during inspection activities, any member of the inspection team must give it at least the level of protection afforded to information classified as OPCW HIGHLY PROTECTED, until or unless the inspected State Party specifies particular handling or level of sensitivity. In such a case the inspected State Party may designate (as provided in subparagraph 2.5 of this Part) an initial classification of such information during the inspection process or in a facility agreement. In the event that such sensitive information is taken to the Secretariat inadvertently or by agreement with the inspected State Party, it shall be classified as OPCW HIGHLY PROTECTED, and protected accordingly, unless the inspected State Party specifies otherwise.

DISSEMINATION:

1.18 OPCW HIGHLY PROTECTED information that must be routinely provided to States Parties in accordance with subparagraph 2(b) of the Confidentiality Annex shall be disseminated accordingly.

2.   CLASSIFICATION AUTHORITY

2.1   For information which has been determined to be classified and which is transmitted to or generated by the Secretariat, it is mandatory for a classification regime to be applied in accordance with the above categories and guidelines under the direct authority of the Director-General. This regime will include an internal procedure for maintaining consistency of classification for documents generated within the Secretariat, and for consulting on and, if necessary, authorising such classification.

2.2   The classification of such information is to be established by the following authorities:

(a)   in the case of confidential information provided by a State Party, that State Party has the authority to designate its initial classification category;

– if a State Party provides information which appears to be confidential without indicating a level of sensitivity, the Director-General or his delegate will be responsible for applying a provisional classification category and treat the information accordingly. He* will have the responsibility for consulting promptly with the originating State Party in order to confirm, amend or remove this provisional classification; and

(b)   in the case of confidential information generated by the Secretariat, the originator of the information shall be responsible for assigning a provisional classification. The Director-General or his delegate has the authority and responsibility to apply a definitive classification to the information.

2.3   Any document being generated within the Organisation which contains confidential information should provisionally be classified by its originator. In establishing a classification category for a new document that is being generated within the Organisation, due regard should be paid by the originator to the level of sensitivity already established for documents and/or information held by the Organisation and which is pertinent to this new document.

2.4   States Parties, in designating a classification category for confidential information, should take into account its level of sensitivity and the corresponding criteria established for each category described in subparagraphs 1.7, 1.11 and 1.14 above. The illustrative indications, set out above, of the forms of information which may be classified under each category do not prejudice the primary authority of a State Party to establish the classification of confidential information it provides.

CLASSIFICATION AUTHORITY IN THE COURSE OF INSPECTIONS

2.5   During the course of an inspection, or in the formulation of a facility agreement, an inspected State Party may designate an initial classification for confidential information, taking into account the level of sensitivity and the corresponding classification criteria. This initial classification will have immediate effect during the conduct of an inspection and in the transmission of confidential information to the Secretariat on completion of the inspection. In cases when the inspected State Party discloses to any member of the inspection team sensitive confidential information without establishing a formal classification for it, or when such information is revealed to any member of the inspection team, this member will bear the responsibility of treating this information as OPCW HIGHLY PROTECTED, unless the inspected State Party specifies otherwise.

3.   DURATION OF CLASSIFICATION

3.1   As a rule, the classification determined for a particular item of information will continue to apply until it is specifically altered or removed in accordance with the guidelines established for reclassification and declassification. When providing confidential information, a State Party may indicate the duration of classification that is to apply to the information. If no indication is given, the duration will be assumed to be unlimited.

---

* Throughout the English version of this Policy, the personal and possessive pronouns 'he' and 'his' refer without distinction to both the female and male genders.

3.2   To maintain viable and effective protection of confidential information, to enhance effective verification of compliance and understanding of the whole verification system, and to reduce the archival holdings of formerly sensitive material, States Parties, the Director-General and other originators of such documents within the Organisation may need, *inter alia*, to keep under review the designation of confidentiality, and the continuing application of classification categories, with a view to either declassification, reduction of classification, or release.

3.3   Classification of information and its duration may be reviewed in particular in the context of a programme for the disposal of records of the Organisation. In carrying out such a programme, the Director-General may from time to time seek the written consent of the originating States Parties in the declassification of records in accordance with agreed procedures. For confidential information generated by the Secretariat, the Director-General shall from time to time review the assigned classifications for holdings of confidential information. If the information refers to any State Party, that State Party will need to provide its written consent before the termination of the duration of the classification. In this respect, an internal review procedure will be established.

4.   CHANGE OF CLASSIFICATION CATEGORY

RECLASSIFICATION OF CONFIDENTIAL INFORMATION

4.1   The authority to change the classification of an item of confidential information will be the same as that specified in subparagraphs 2.2(a) and 2.2(b) of this Part for determination of the original classification of that information. In particular, an item of information supplied by a State Party shall not be reclassified without the written consent of that State Party. This rule will also apply to such items of information contained in documents which had originated within the Organisation.

4.2   States Parties which have originated or received an item of OPCW classified information, and senior Secretariat staff (Branch Heads and above) making use of an item of such information, may request a change in the classification category for that item. Such a request should be based on a clear operational need, and should be acted upon in accordance with the following provisions.

4.3   When the State Party which originated an item of OPCW classified information requests a change of classification, that request will be carried out. Before confirming the change, the Director-General may consult with that State Party on the consequences of the proposed change.

4.4   When there is a request, in accordance with subparagraph 4.2 above, for a change in the classification category of confidential information which was generated by the Secretariat, the Director-General or his delegate shall, in making a determination, abide by the criteria established for the application of classification categories with reference to the stated operational need.

4.5   Reclassification of Secretariat-generated information may be required when the information is amended, supplemented or revised so as to create a substantial difference in sensitivity. For instance, a draft report on compliance may have greater sensitivity than the final version, or sensitive material may be omitted in a revised version of an inspection report intended for wider distribution. The principles set out above will be applied in undertaking reclassification, unless the Convention specifies otherwise.

DECLASSIFICATION OF CONFIDENTIAL INFORMATION

4.6   The provisions specified above for reclassification of confidential information shall also apply to its declassification. In particular, an item of information supplied by a State Party shall not be declassified without the written consent of that State Party. The following guidelines shall additionally be followed in deciding on the declassification of confidential information:

(a) if declassification is proposed for confidential information originating in the Secretariat and referring to a State Party in a way that influenced its original classification, the Director-General shall obtain the express written consent of the State Party for the declassification; and

(b) for confidential information generated by the Secretariat, the Director-General (or his delegate) shall consider at least the same aspects that he took into account when he designated the information as confidential.

4.7 The declassification of confidential information does not imply that it is, ipso facto, available for public release. Release beyond the Organisation of any information, including formerly confidential information which has been declassified, will require a separate process of consultation and approval in accordance with Part VII of this Policy. This will also apply to information provided to States Parties by the Organisation under an OPCW classification.

PART VI. GENERAL PRINCIPLES FOR HANDLING AND PROTECTION
OF CONFIDENTIAL INFORMATION

1. INTRODUCTION

1.1 This Part sets out the principles governing the Organisation's provision of access to and regular dissemination of information determined to be confidential, and governing the associated procedures for handling and protection of confidential information. This covers the transmission of confidential information within the Organisation (including its constituent elements), and the transmission of confidential information to authorised representatives of States Parties. Guidelines for public or other release of information beyond the Organisation and States Parties are set out in Part VII.

1.2 These principles are to be applied in the detailed elaboration of all procedures relating to the handling of confidential information, including in the OPCW Inspection Manual, the Declaration Handbook, and the Manual of Confidentiality Procedure (MCP). Further practical procedures shall be set out on the basis of these principles in administrative directives issued by the Director-General. The principles contained in this Part shall apply to all operations of the Organisation, within the Secretariat and other organs of the Organisation, as well as in their dealings with States Parties. States Parties which receive confidential information from the Organisation are required to protect it in accordance with obligations under paragraph 6 of Article VII and paragraph 4 of the Confidentiality Annex. States Parties should therefore establish or adapt suitable means of handling and protection for OPCW confidential information in a manner consistent with these principles.

1.3 The Confidentiality Annex (CA) sets out the two principles governing access to and the dissemination of confidential information within the Organisation:

– access to confidential information shall be regulated in accordance with its classification; and

– the dissemination of confidential information within the Organisation shall be strictly on a need-to-know basis (CA, subparagraph 2(h)).

1.4 It follows from these fundamental principles firstly that the level of sensitivity of confidential information will govern the procedures by which it is made available to its recipients and the means employed to protect it; and secondly that the authorised recipients of confidential information will be determined in accordance with their demonstrated need, related to the purposes of the Convention. An important consideration in managing the dissemination of confidential information is the scope of access afforded to States

Parties: in this context, a primary and unconditional need to know is established by the requirement for data to be provided to all States Parties for them to be assured of continued compliance with the Convention by other States Parties (CA, subparagraph 2(b)). Access to the relevant confidential information defined by this provision must therefore be provided to serve the vital aim of due transparency and enhanced mutual confidence between States Parties.

1.5   The actual scope of access associated with a certain item of confidential information shall be specifically determined, rather than implicitly assumed, and specific practical steps shall be undertaken in order to protect it against illegitimate or unauthorised access. The rigour of the determination of scope of authorised access and the required level and intensity of protection against unauthorised access shall be regulated in accordance with the classification of that confidential information. However, level of classification does not in itself determine the scope of access to classified information, but simply the manner in which it is to be handled and protected against unauthorised disclosure.

2.   ACCESS, DISSEMINATION AND PROTECTION

2.1   The scope of access to confidential information is the full set of possible recipients authorised to acquire or retain that information; dissemination is the process of actively passing that information to its authorised recipients. Accordingly, the notion of 'access' to information entails permitting an individual to acquire or retain that information. Dissemination of confidential information is made possible by the application of protection measures applied in accordance with the level of sensitivity of information, so that it is disseminated to the extent required for the implementation of the Convention without unnecessary or unauthorised disclosure. Accordingly, dissemination of confidential information to all authorised recipients within the Organisation must take place, irrespective of level of classification, with the appropriate protection measures being taken. In this connection, it is notable that States Parties have an obligation under Article VII, paragraph 6, to apply special handling to confidential information received in accordance with the Convention.

2.2   Detailed protection procedures and measures are therefore to be elaborated to permit access to confidential information by an individual Secretariat staff member or by a State Party in accordance with a functional need to know or a specific provision of the Convention, while impeding all other access with a rigour and level of effort linked to the sensitivity of the information as established by its classification. The provision of confidential information to the Conference and to the Executive Council shall be based on the general principles for the dissemination of confidential information.

NEED-TO-KNOW PRINCIPLE

2.3   The need-to-know principle is the governing principle for determination of the scope of access and the recipients of dissemination of information. There is no absolute right within the Organisation to receive confidential information: no individual staff member of the Secretariat and no member of any organ of the Organisation is entitled by virtue of status or level alone to have access to any items of OPCW confidential information.

2.4   Access to confidential information shall normally be granted both on a case-by-case basis and in accordance with the determination of the functional need to know. There is, however, an unconditional requirement for access to certain information by States Parties in accordance with subparagraph 2(b) of the Confidentiality Annex, and this and related provisions should be viewed as establishing an unquestionable need to know for each State Party, so as to be ensured of the continued compliance of other States Parties with the Convention.

2.5   Within the Secretariat, the specific function or tasks defined for a staff member shall, within practical bounds, be the principal determinant of that individual's need to know and of the consequent scope of authorised access to confidential information.

2.6   The Director-General has the primary responsibility for ensuring the protection of confidential information (CA, paragraph 2). Hence, subject to the provisions of the Convention, the Director-General shall be the final arbiter in the determination of the need to know in relation to any particular items of confidential information.

ADMINISTRATION OF DISSEMINATION AND HANDLING PROCEDURES

2.7   The Office of Confidentiality and Security (OCS) shall be charged by the Director-General with the overall supervision of the administration of confidentiality provisions. The Director-General may decide to delegate specific issues related to confidentiality to the Head of the OCS. Ultimate responsibility for confidentiality remains with the Director-General.

2.8   Once the scope of authorised access to confidential information has been determined on the basis of the need-to-know principle, access shall be granted by means of detailed handling procedures established for the Organisation, to ensure that the manner of access and the level of protection provided are linked to the classification which applies. Each access by a staff member of the Secretariat to a physical medium holding confidential information shall be controlled on a need-to-know basis and shall be recorded, and this record shall be retained. In the event that such access is through an electronic data system, a log-on and log-out procedure shall be established and followed by authorised staff members to ensure that no individual can gain access in the name of another staff member. The OCS will supervise the routine operation of these handling procedures.

DETERMINATION OF SCOPE OF ACCESS AND DISSEMINATION OF CONFIDENTIAL INFORMATION TO STATES PARTIES

2.9   There are various circumstances when the Secretariat will need to determine authorised scope of access and consequently to disseminate confidential information to States Parties. In all cases, the governing principle is that established in subparagraph 2(b) of the Confidentiality Annex, and procedures shall be established to ensure that the requirements of this provision are met. Hence, data required by States Parties to be assured of the continued compliance with this Convention by other States Parties shall be routinely provided to them. In particular, information management and clearance procedures shall be followed to ensure that the information which must be provided to all States Parties, in accordance with subparagraph 2(b) of the Confidentiality Annex, is duly provided without further need for consultation and approval within the Secretariat.

2.10   In the case of the provision of certain confidential information to a State Party for a particular purpose, when it is not the application of a specific requirement under the Convention for dissemination, but is related to a more specific need to know (such as in the course of clarifications under Article IX, paragraphs 3 - 7, or in the settlement of disputes under Article XIV), the general rule is that the Director-General or a single senior official to whom this authority is specifically delegated under the primary responsibility of the Director-General shall be consulted and shall give specific clearance for the proposed access, after confirming the need to know, with the agreement of any State Party to which the information refers and/or which has provided the information. The Director-General shall at all times be kept informed of any exercise of such authority.

2.11   The method of provision of confidential information to a State Party by the Organisation shall be based on the need for continuity of protection, at a level linked to the sensitivity of the information. The receiving State Party is obliged in turn to afford such confidential information the special handling appropriate to its level of sensitivity, and shall provide, upon request, details on the handling of information provided to it by the Organisation.

GRANTING OF ACCESS TO OTHER AUTHORISED RECIPIENTS ASSOCIATED WITH THE
ORGANISATION

2.12   It may be necessary to disseminate OPCW confidential information to certain authorised
        entities or individuals that are outside the Secretariat but are integral to the Organisa-
        tion's implementation of particular functions specified in the Convention. The Director-
        General shall establish a stringent regime to govern such access and, in accordance with
        the Confidentiality Annex, paragraph 2, will retain primary responsibility for any access
        approved under this regime. Any such proposed access must be specifically authorised
        by the Director-General or the single senior official specifically delegated this authority
        under the regime and under the direct responsibility of the Director-General, and then
        only after a functional need to know has been clearly established for the proposed re-
        cipient. The Director-General shall at all times be kept informed of any exercise of such
        authority.

        –   The Secretariat shall notify a State Party of any such access of those authorised
            entities or individuals to confidential information in relation to the territory of the
            State Party or any other place under the jurisdiction or control of the State Party.
            A specific secrecy agreement providing for protection of confidentiality shall be
            required as a condition for such access, and this agreement shall be binding on each
            individual it designates as an authorised recipient. An assessment of the level of
            protection provided to confidential information by the proposed recipient may be
            undertaken as a preliminary measure.

        –   The above principle applies to the transfer of samples to designated laboratories
            under the regime established under paragraph 56 of Part II of the Verification An-
            nex. It may also apply, *inter alia*, to any access to OPCW confidential information
            required by an authorised expert (such as may be appointed under subparagraph
            4(e) of Article IX or paragraph 8 of Part XI of the Verification Annex) in order to
            discharge an official function.

        –   In case of access to confidential information by authorised entities and individuals
            outside the Secretariat, such access shall be strictly limited to the minimum neces-
            sary for carrying out functions integral to the Convention's implementation.

2.13   Each person who has been granted access to OPCW confidential information in accord-
        ance with this provision shall be responsible for ensuring that any individual beyond the
        Secretariat to whom he subsequently discloses such information has a functional need
        to know and also has written authorisation from the Director-General or the delegate (as
        specified in subparagraph 2.12 above) granting the necessary access.

DETERMINATION OF SCOPE OF ACCESS TO CONFIDENTIAL INFORMATION WITHIN THE
SECRETARIAT

2.14   Access to OPCW confidential information within the Secretariat shall be granted only to
        those for whom such access is necessary for the fulfilment of designated professional du-
        ties. In determining need to know within the Secretariat, close attention shall be paid to a
        staff member's formal position description and specified scope of access to confidential
        information. An explicit reference to a staff member's particular professional functions
        is required in permitting access to OPCW PROTECTED and OPCW HIGHLY PROTECTED in-
        formation. The authorised scope of access to confidential information classified OPCW
        HIGHLY PROTECTED shall be expressed in writing on a case-by-case basis.

2.15   A register shall be kept of those staff members whose professional duties entail regular
        access to confidential information relating to each State Party. The Secretariat shall in-
        form a State Party of proposals to accord to an individual staff member access to confi-
        dential information in relation to the territory of that State Party or any other place under
        its jurisdiction or control. The State Party concerned shall be informed not less than

thirty days before access is confirmed. Any staffing appointments or changes in personnel structure or functions that will lead to access to confidential information relating to States Parties must be advised to the States Parties concerned not less than thirty days in advance.

2.16   Only certain senior executive staff members shall be authorised to grant access to confidential information to other staff members under their supervision. An administrative directive shall be established by the Director-General which determines the respective criteria according to strict need to know. The granting of access is in each case contingent on a determination that the subject matter is of direct relevance to the proposed recipient's specified duties, with such access always subject to review by the Director-General. In cases of uncertainty about the functional or task-specific need-to-know status of a proposed recipient, a senior staff member with a supervisory responsibility over the recipient must be consulted.

3.   PRINCIPLES FOR HANDLING AND DISSEMINATION

DISSEMINATION OF CONFIDENTIAL INFORMATION

3.1   The dissemination of confidential information needs to be distinguished from the process of release of information by the Organisation. In general terms, the dissemination of confidential information refers to the authorised disclosure of such information within the Organisation including all its organs and to the governments of States Parties, including governmental organisations and authorised entities or individuals within States Parties concerned with the operation of the Convention, when this disclosure is essential for specific professional tasks or is in accord with the provisions of the Convention for the furnishing of information to States Parties. With regard to the "release" of information by the Organisation[5], this process, and its precise scope of application, are defined in Part VII of this Policy.

ACQUISITION, COLLECTION AND GENERATION OF CONFIDENTIAL INFORMATION

3.2   Specific handling and protective procedures shall be applied on a continuous basis from the first acquisition, collection or generation of confidential information by the Organisation, and to all subsequent activities during its dissemination. Information[6] that may be confidential is acquired, collected and generated by the Organisation in several ways:
   (a) information is provided to the Organisation by States Parties:
        –   in conformity with their declaration obligations and reporting requirements specified under the Convention;
        –   in the course of a formal procedure established under the Convention, such as those included in Article IX; and
        –   in passing on other information pertinent to implementation of the Convention;
   (b) other information pertinent to implementation of the Convention in a State Party may be passed to the Secretariat by that State Party;
   (c) information may be passed to the Secretariat or any other organ of the Organisation by a representative of a State Party in the course of a formal procedure established under the Convention, such as those included in Article IX;
   (d) information is acquired or collected by an inspection team in the course of an on-site inspection;

---

[5] "Release" of information refers to the approved disclosure of information beyond the Organisation itself (including all its constituent elements) and beyond the governments of States Parties (specifically, beyond governmental organisations and authorised entities or individuals within States Parties concerned with the operation of the Convention (subparagraph 1.1 of Part VII of this Policy)) [footnote in original].

[6] As defined in Part III of this Policy [footnote in original].

(e) information is generated by Secretariat staff members through the synthesis or other processing of other information, for instance in the course of analysing samples or compiling inspection reports. Generated information may draw on or duplicate information initially provided by States Parties, or may only use information from within the Secretariat. The synthesis of information or the conduct of analysis may produce confidential information which is of a higher level of sensitivity than its original sources.

3.3   When information is received by the Organisation from any of these sources, specific obligations are incurred to protect and handle it appropriately. In particular, the initial recipient or the originator of the information is obliged to ensure that the confidentiality content is clearly determined, and that the correct classification has been applied, in consultation where necessary with the OCS. Confidential information which is compiled or synthesised by Secretariat staff members, and which draws on confidential information originating from States Parties shall, as a rule, bear at a minimum the classification designated by the State Party, unless the level of the sensitivity of the information has been reduced with the consent of the originating State Party, or the level of sensitivity is determined to be higher. Any deviation from this rule shall be authorized by the Director-General or by a member of staff authorised by him to do so. The Director-General has authorised the Head of OCS to do so.

3.4   Information generated within the Secretariat (such as analytical or other reports, policy papers, profiles, letters, memoranda) which contains confidential information shall be initially classified and so labelled by its originator in accordance with its sensitivity, at a level at least as high as the most sensitive classification of the source material from which it was derived or which was used in the synthesis. Where the level of sensitivity has consequently increased above that of the original source material, a higher level of classification shall be applied.

3.5   Information, including that designated as confidential, which is passed to the Organisation by a State Party must be provided by an official representative of that State Party. The Secretariat will establish and follow a registry process to record the receipt and the official source of such material.

3.6   The classification of information provided by a State Party to the Secretariat would in most cases have already been specified by that State Party, in view of its primary authority for classification. In doing so, the State Party should take into account the level of sensitivity and the corresponding criteria established for each classification category in Part V of this Policy. If a State Party provides the Secretariat with information which appears to be confidential, but without indicating a level of sensitivity, a provisional classification category shall be implemented as provided under subparagraph 2.2 of Part V of this Policy.

3.7   The overall obligation to protect and appropriately handle information upon first disclosure to the Organisation is especially important when information is collected during the course of on-site inspections, such as the collection of site-specific observations or the taking of samples. Particular principles for the handling and protection of confidential information during inspections are accordingly set out in paragraph 6 of this Part.

HANDLING PROCEDURES FOR THE PROTECTION OF CONFIDENTIAL INFORMATION

GENERAL GUIDELINES ON HANDLING AND PROTECTION

3.8   Individuals shall not discuss or disclose confidential matters in any circumstances when they do not have control over the security of the information and its environment. The Director-General shall establish in an administrative directive specific procedures to prevent unauthorised access and disclosure in conversation or through telecommunication media, with the level of physical or other protective measures linked to the level of sensitivity of the information as expressed in its classification. Actual recourse to the approved use of telecommunications for transmission of confidential information shall be limited to cases of clear operational necessity.

3.9   Subject to the obligation to preclude unauthorised access, Secretariat staff members may disclose confidential information to, or discuss it with:

(a) authorised Secretariat staff members with an established need to know;

(b) persons, who are not staff members and, to whom access has been granted under the provisions of subparagraphs 2.12 and 2.13 of this Part, such as authorised experts or authorised personnel of a designated laboratory who are individually bound by secrecy agreements; in such a case the amount of information disclosed shall be kept to a minimum and any such information shall be provided on a need-to-know basis, yet should be sufficient to facilitate the task for which the access was granted; and

(c) authorised representatives of a State Party to which the information pertains, which has the clear entitlement to such disclosure as explicitly established by a provision of the Convention, or for which any other authorisation and need to know have been established.

3.10   The Director-General shall issue and the OCS shall supervise the implementation of administrative directives setting out detailed practical handling procedures for the following categories of physical media, to ensure the protection of confidential information each such medium carries during all handling and storage operations:

– documents, including papers and paper files;
– computer material;
– audio-visual material; and
– samples.

These administrative directives shall aim at establishing practical mechanisms for ensuring that all the principles established in this document are met.

3.11   For confidential information which relates specifically to inspected or declared facilities, a coding system and associated storage shall be applied to preclude direct identification of any facility to which it pertains, to the greatest extent consistent with effective verification.

4.   SPECIFIC HANDLING PROCEDURES FOR CONFIDENTIAL INFORMATION

MARKING OF CONFIDENTIAL INFORMATION

4.1   In order to ensure the proper handling of OPCW confidential information, all documents and media for information storage shall be clearly marked in accordance with the marking instructions set out in an administrative directive issued by the Director-General and supervised by the OCS. The basis of the markings will be the three classification categories, one of which should be clearly applied to any medium carrying information determined to be confidential:

– OPCW restricted
– OPCW protected
– OPCW highly protected

4.2   Each individual document must be clearly marked according to the highest level of sensitivity of the material it contains. Where this may facilitate subsequent release or dissemination of less sensitive portions of a document, the principle of portion (paragraph) marking may be applied so that classification indications are given of the particular levels of sensitivity of sections within a document, the overall document being clearly marked as bearing the highest level of sensitivity. Alternatively, all confidential information may be contained in a confidential annex to an otherwise unclassified document, the overall document to be clearly marked as bearing the highest level of sensitivity.

4.3   The Confidentiality Annex stipulates that all data and documents obtained by the Secretariat shall first be evaluated for confidentiality content (subparagraph 2(b)) and that, if confidential, such data and documents shall then be classified (subparagraph 2(d)); this process shall accord with the right of any State Party to designate information it provides as confidential. The unit of the Secretariat that receives a given document will be the appropriate unit for this task and, when it deems it necessary, will therefore implement procedures, with the assistance of the OCS, to ensure that all information with possible confidentiality content which has been acquired from outside the Secretariat is evaluated and any necessary classification is clearly marked. The determination of the classification to be applied and the authority to classify must be in accordance with the OPCW Classification System. In cases where information appears to be confidential but is initially not clearly marked by the originator, appropriate marking shall be carried out by the unit, with the determination of a provisional classification category if necessary. Any provisional classification so applied should be promptly confirmed, amended or removed following consultations with the originator of the information.

4.4   All confidential information generated in the Secretariat is required to be clearly marked by its originator in accordance with a provisional classification category relevant to its sensitivity. The level of this classification must be determined in accordance with the OPCW Classification System. Branch heads must supervise the proper marking of internally generated confidential material, under the overall coordination and authority of the OCS.

4.5   Information generated by inspectors on the basis of information provided by an inspected State Party, such as inspection reports or parts thereof, shall be marked with the classification which accords with the level of sensitivity indicated by the State Party. In cases where the level of sensitivity of such information is unclear, the information shall be treated as OPCW HIGHLY PROTECTED until the level of sensitivity has been clarified through consultations with the inspected State Party.

FILING AND RECORD-KEEPING

4.6   Filing and record-keeping procedures to ensure that the internal routing and filing of confidential information are registered shall be established by the Secretariat in accordance with an administrative directive issued by the Director-General and supervised by the OCS. These procedures shall record the provision of any such confidential information to any individual, agency or body within and beyond the Secretariat, including to representatives of States Parties.

4.7   All confidential information should be stored and internally distributed in a manner that records each staff member who has had access to it, and the date and time of access. The Secretariat shall also establish additional record-keeping procedures to ensure the continuous monitoring of OPCW HIGHLY PROTECTED information, and to determine who has had or currently has such information in his possession.

COPYING OF CONFIDENTIAL INFORMATION

4.8   Copying information entails its replication in a way that generates potential or possible additional access to the information. When copying confidential information, the number of copies made should be kept to a minimum and shall be linked to the approved scope of access and consequent dissemination. The staff member responsible for copying the information must ensure that all copies of a copied document clearly have the appropriate markings.

4.9   Classified information shall be copied only under disciplined and auditable conditions.

OPCW HIGHLY PROTECTED information can be copied only after obtaining the registered consent of an authorised senior staff member other than the staff member who will be copying the information, or in terms of a specific standing order. Such consent may specify that the copying must be done under the supervision of another staff member. The number of copies taken must be recorded, and each copy numbered. Copies should be distributed to any approved recipients, with this transmission recorded. Any surplus copies, or copies no longer in use shall be returned to the filing clerk, who shall either file or destroy them, recording this action.

4.10   Information to be provided to States Parties in accordance with subparagraph 2(b) of the Confidentiality Annex, but which is confidential, shall be copied and disseminated routinely in accordance with the requests of States Parties and in accordance with an administrative directive issued by the Director-General. In the case of OPCW PROTECTED and OPCW HIGHLY PROTECTED information, a record should be kept of the number of copies taken and the recipient(s) of each of the copies.

DISPOSAL AND DESTRUCTION OF CONFIDENTIAL INFORMATION

4.11   An administrative directive issued by the Director-General shall establish handling procedures for the Secretariat to ensure the secure disposal and destruction of material containing confidential information. These procedures shall cover:
   –   technical methods of destruction or disposal for all categories of media;
   –   registration of destroyed or disposed material;
   –   witness procedures during destruction and disposal; and
   –   reporting requirements for highly classified material provided by States Parties.

TRANSMISSION OF CONFIDENTIAL INFORMATION

4.12   Transmission of confidential information, in hard copy and electronic format, to and from the Secretariat shall occur in conformity with the level of sensitivity of the information and shall be bound by strict procedures set out in an administrative directive issued by the Director-General. These procedures shall include:
   –   guidelines for secure mailing or manual transmission, and the safe-hand carriage, of confidential information; and
   –   procedures for secure transmission by telephone, telefacsimile and other telecommunications systems.

4.13   These rules must ensure that for each item of confidential information disseminated:
   –   the item is received at its intended destination;
   –   only authorised users have access to any transmitted data; and
   –   the recipient of a message can verify that the sender is an authorised person.

4.14   An administrative directive issued by the Director-General will describe the standards set down for the secure communications system established for the IMS, and this will be applied in the inspection manual.

SAFEGUARDING OF CONFIDENTIAL INFORMATION

4.15   Staff members and other personnel authorised in accordance with paragraphs 2.12 and 2.13 above, who are using confidential information or are responsible for its safe-keeping must take every precaution to prevent deliberate or accidental access to such information by unauthorised persons. This involves at a minimum following all the procedures and meeting the standards established within the Organisation for handling and protecting confidential information, and ensuring the continuity of protection during dissemination.

4.16   Confidential information must not be used or placed so that it is exposed or made accessible to individuals not authorised to have access to such information. The Director-General has designated the OCS to establish procedures to ensure that confidential information is properly handled by Secretariat staff members, and the Director-General shall ensure that these procedures are fully carried out, that any violations are detected and reported, and that appropriate disciplinary sanctions are imposed in accordance with Part IX of this Policy .

PHYSICAL PROTECTION AND STORAGE

4.17   The Director-General shall set out, in an administrative directive, physical security measures for offices, laboratories, information storage areas, computer media and audio-visual material classified as confidential, as well as standards for physical storage facilities within the Secretariat, including locks and security of secure areas, filing cabinets and sealed containers. These measures shall include procedures for restricting access to OPCW buildings and other sites, and for registering the presence of visitors and staff members during and after working hours. The procedures shall include special access arrangements for especially sensitive areas within the OPCW building(s) and other sites, such as storage areas for confidential information, office areas working with the processing and validation of declarations and inspection reports, the operations centre, and the OPCW Laboratory.

4.18   Confidential information shall be stored securely at the premises of the Organisation. Some data or documents may also be stored with the National Authority of a State Party. Sensitive information, including, *inter alia*, photographs, plans and other documents required only for the inspection of a specific facility may be kept under lock and key at this facility (CA, subparagraph 2(e)).

4.19   To the extent practicable, storage of OPCW confidential information at the National Authority of a State Party or at an inspected facility should accord with the minimum standards applied by the Secretariat.

REMOVAL OF CONFIDENTIAL INFORMATION FROM OPCW PREMISES

4.20   Handling procedures shall be established in an administrative directive issued by the Director-General to cover the carriage of confidential information from the premises of the Organisation, between inspected sites and the Organisation, and between the Organisation and representatives of States Parties. Any such removal shall occur only for purposes related to the implementation of the Convention, and only to the minimal extent necessary for the performance of authorised professional functions.

LOSS OF CONFIDENTIAL INFORMATION

4.21   Procedures shall be set out in an administrative directive issued by the Director-General to cover the eventuality of a loss or suspected loss of OPCW confidential information, including loss by an inspector, by a staff member of the Secretariat or by a representative of a State Party, as well as loss in transit. Such procedures shall include requirements for reporting, investigations, and consulting with States Parties concerned. As the loss or suspected loss indicates a possible breach of confidentiality, the procedures for dealing with breaches or alleged breaches of confidentiality must be invoked.

5.   HANDLING PROCEDURES FOR PARTICULAR INFORMATION MEDIA

5.1   The handling procedures for confidential information set out in paragraph 4 above apply to all confidential information, regardless of the medium on which it is stored; the following additional procedures relate to information carried on particular forms of media.

AUDIO-VISUAL MATERIAL

5.2   An administrative directive shall set out procedures for the handling of audio-visual material containing confidential information, specifying levels of protection in accordance with classification categories, and following closely the procedures specified for handling documents containing confidential information.

CONFIDENTIAL INFORMATION IN COMPUTERS AND COMPUTER MATERIAL

5.3   Access to all sites of the OPCW and key components of the IMS, such as the servers and mass storage devices, must be controlled. All hardware in the confidential part of the IMS and especially workstations, servers and user terminals shall be protected, not only from theft or criminal damage, but also from unauthorised physical access and tampering attempts. In addition, maintenance and repair activities on IMS hardware shall be supervised and recorded. Access to such hardware items as servers, printers, back-up devices, as well as other output devices, shall be limited to staff members with appropriate clearances.

5.4   Procedures for the protection of data stored within the confidential part of the IMS and any other electronic data-processing system or storage device shall incorporate the following elements:
   –   access control measures against unauthorised users or any unauthorised external access;
   –   separation of the files and data of the various users; and
   –   audit on user activities including access to the databases and changes made to operating system parameters and system files. In particular, any access by individual staff to computer files containing confidential information shall be recorded and regular audits conducted of these records.

5.5   The data, document and information computer security procedures shall provide detailed guidelines for protecting confidentiality while creating, handling, marking, backing up and destroying all forms of computer files, computer documents and other documents relevant for tasks such as system administration and computer security management and operations.

5.6   Computer material (including portable storage media such as diskettes) and confidential information stored in the OPCW IMS must be handled and protected in accordance with handling and storage procedures supported by detailed technical specifications set out in an administrative directive by the Director-General.

SAMPLES FROM ON-SITE INSPECTIONS

5.7   Paragraph 55 of Part II of the Verification Annex provides for the transfer of samples taken during inspections off-site for analysis at designated laboratories. The process of sampling is inherently relevant to the verification of compliance with the Convention, but such samples may also incidentally carry and potentially yield other information which is itself not directly relevant to verification. For this reason, the inspection manual shall include procedures for ensuring the protection of the confidentiality of samples transferred for off-site analysis at designated laboratories.

5.8   Development and implementation of the regime established under paragraph 56 of Part II of the Verification Annex for the collection, handling, transport and analysis of samples shall be founded on the requirement for the protection of confidentiality during the transfer to and storage by designated laboratories. This regime shall address the particular concern that further confidential information not related to compliance might be yielded during the process of compliance-related analysis. Further confidentiality concerns shall be addressed by the sample accounting procedures established under paragraph 57 of Part II of the Verification Annex, and associated procedures for informing the inspected State Party that designated laboratories have destroyed samples or have returned them to the Secretariat after the completion of analysis for appropriate final handling. Designated laboratories shall be required to enter specific secrecy agreements confirming obligations established under the regime governing the sampling and analysis process.

6.   HANDLING AND PROTECTION OF CONFIDENTIAL INFORMATION DURING ON-SITE VERIFICATION ACTIVITIES

INSPECTION PROCEDURES

6.1   The Confidentiality Annex and earlier sections of this Policy establish fundamental principles for the handling and protection of confidential information during inspections, both the information acquired or collected during the verification of compliance, and other information not relevant to the aims of the Convention which may be disclosed in the course of inspection activities. The OPCW inspection manual is to establish detailed procedures founded on these principles, including the necessary procedures for the use, protection and scope of access of data, documents and files during the conduct of inspections, consistent with the requirements of the Confidentiality Annex and the functional requirements for inspectors in the field. These must take into account functional requirements for the protection of data stored in portable devices, and the general procedures established for the carriage and storage of confidential information.

6.2   The key practical elements for the protection of confidential information in the course of inspections are the inspection procedures, the use of equipment, and the process of consultation within the inspection team and with representatives of the inspected State Party. Inspection procedures shall stipulate a clear hierarchical line of communication within the inspection team to allow consultations on issues that arise in relation to confidentiality, and the use to be made of confidential information. In accordance with this structure, there shall be consultations during facility agreement negotiations, pre-inspection briefings, and during the conduct of initial and subsequent inspections, between representatives of the inspected State Party, the inspected facility and the inspection team, to establish clearly the level of access to be granted to each inspection team member and the treatment to be afforded to confidential information disclosed or collected. In the case of a challenge inspection, an observer is obliged to respect fully the confidentiality of any information to which access is provided in accordance with the Convention's challenge inspection provisions, and shall treat such information accordingly.

EVALUATION AND CLASSIFICATION OF CONFIDENTIAL INFORMATION

6.3   The classification procedure set out in subparagraph 2.5 of Part V of this Policy shall be applied to information collected during the course of inspection. In accordance with this procedure, such information shall be promptly evaluated for confidentiality, and shall thereupon be given an initial classification and due protection in accordance with its sensitivity, with close reference to any facility agreement and in agreement with representatives of the inspected State Party. Where there is no relevant agreement in place prior to the inspection, the inspected State Party should be encouraged by the inspection team to nominate whenever possible the classification category of any confidential information disclosed during the course of inspection. In the event that sensitive confidential information is disclosed or revealed to any member of the inspection team without any indication of its classification category, the classification system requires that it be handled and protected as OPCW HIGHLY PROTECTED unless the inspected State Party provides otherwise. In general, where there is doubt or uncertainty, handling and protection afforded to confidential information should be at the most stringent level applicable, and consultations on further disclosure and dissemination even within the inspection team must fully heed the need-to-know principle for determining scope of access. If collected information includes confidential information not relevant to the Convention, it will require particular handling as discussed in the relevant paragraph below.

ON-SITE VERIFICATION: PROTECTION OF NON-RELEVANT CONFIDENTIAL INFORMATION

6.4   This Policy sets out clear principles governing the protection of confidential informa-
       tion not relevant to compliance with the Convention, and the particular responsibilities
       in this regard.[7] Hence verification activities must be designed, planned and carried out
       so as to avoid unnecessary disclosure of confidential information and so as to seek to
       prevent disclosure of such information not related to compliance with the Convention in
       the terms of any inspection mandate, consistent with effective and timely discharge of
       verification obligations. These principles also require that confidential information not
       relevant to compliance with the Convention shall not be sought, recorded or retained: in
       the course of any inspection, it is a basic responsibility of each member of the inspection
       team, and especially of its leader, to ensure that this does not occur. However, it is rec-
       ognised that in the course of inspection activities, it might occur that other confidential
       information which is itself not relevant to the purpose of the inspection is collected or re-
       corded in various forms (as are set out in the definition of "information" in Part III of this
       Policy)[8], by means of items such as approved inspection equipment, inspectors' cloth-
       ing, and personal articles. In the event that such information is disclosed in the course
       of inspection activities, it shall not be further disseminated in any form, even within the
       inspection team, and shall be returned to the inspected State Party or destroyed under its
       supervision.

6.5   In the course of inspection activities, the Confidentiality Annex specifies that States
       Parties "may take such measures as they deem necessary to protect confidentiality, pro-
       vided that they fulfil their obligations to demonstrate compliance in accordance with
       the relevant Articles and the Verification Annex"[9]. Inspection teams are obliged, among
       other things, "to take into consideration proposals which may be made by the State Party
       receiving the inspection, at whatever stage of the inspection, to ensure that sensitive
       equipment or information, not related to chemical weapons, is protected". [10] "Inspection
       teams shall strictly abide by the provisions set forth in the relevant Articles and Annexes
       governing the conduct of inspections. They shall fully respect the procedures designed
       to protect sensitive installations and to prevent the disclosure of confidential data."[11]

6.6   Subject to a full consultation process with the inspected State Party both during and
       after an inspection (such as is established for challenge inspections in subparagraph 61
       of Part X of the Verification Annex), the Organisation is responsible for confirming to
       the inspected State Party that information gathered in accordance with the provisions of
       the Convention in the course of inspection activities is relevant to compliance with the
       Convention in the terms of the inspection mandate. The inspection team must protect
       any information gathered during the inspection in accordance with the classification
       level which the inspected State Party prescribes for it. The inspected State Party may not,
       within the framework of existing obligations in relation to demonstration of compliance
       with the Convention, object to inclusion of information in the preliminary inspection
       findings, if following full consultations the inspection team maintains that it is relevant
       to compliance with the Convention in the terms of the inspection mandate.

6.7   Any information gathered in the course of inspection but not included in the listed and
       copied material provided to the inspected State Party is presumed not to be relevant to
       the inspection mandate, and must be treated as specified in subparagraph 6.4 above. The
       principle is recognised that limitations on access and dissemination, such as those agreed

---

[7] Set out in Part IV, subparagraph 1.4 of this Policy.
[8] Set out in Part III of this Policy, under the heading "Scope of information".
[9] Confidentiality Annex, paragraph 13.
[10] Confidentiality Annex, paragraph 14.
[11] Confidentiality Annex, paragraph 15.

as part of managed access in the case of a challenge inspection, shall be complied with by inspection team members and that no information a State Party views as confidential but of which it has not received a copy will leave the inspection site without its consent. Without prejudice to the obligation for a State Party to demonstrate compliance, procedures to implement the above principles include, *inter alia*:

- additional cleaning of inspection equipment;
- changing of clothes before or after a particular inspection activity;
- leaving personal articles behind before entrance to a particular area;
- the transfer of affected equipment under joint seal to the Secretariat for decontamination under the supervision, if requested, of a representative of the inspected State Party;
- the retention on site of detachable parts carrying confidential information unrelated to the Convention; or
- after exploring all other possibilities, including the above, the retention of equipment on site.

These procedures shall not be abused and shall be implemented, where relevant, in accordance with a legal framework respecting the immunity established under subparagraph 11(d) of Part II of the Verification Annex.

6.8   None of the procedures followed in accordance with these principles shall impede or delay verification activities conducted under the inspection mandate and in accordance with the provisions of the Convention.

PART VII. PROCEDURES FOR THE RELEASE OF INFORMATION BY THE OPCW

1.   GENERAL
1.1   This Part of this Policy sets out the principles governing the procedures which the Organisation is to follow concerning the release of any information which it holds in connection with the implementation of the Convention. 'Release' of information by the Organisation refers to the approved disclosure of information beyond the Organisation itself (including all its constituent elements) and beyond the governments of States Parties (specifically, beyond governmental organisations and authorised entities or individuals within States Parties concerned with the operation of the Convention). Accordingly, these principles govern the release of OPCW information to any other international organisation, to the government of a State not party to the Convention, to private or governmental organisations unrelated to the implementation of the Convention, or to any individual who is neither employed or contracted by the Organisation nor authorised by a State Party in relation to implementation of the Convention.

1.2   In the course of the implementation of the Convention, there will be cases in which the Organisation needs to release information in order to comply with its obligations. The release may be fully public, or may be limited in scope according to particular circumstances. The need to release information may arise for both unclassified and classified information. No information obtained or generated by the Organisation in connection with the implementation of the Convention shall be published or otherwise released, except in accordance with the following guidelines.

2.   PUBLIC RELEASE OF INFORMATION
2.1   The Director-General may publicly release information that is not designated as confidential (including formerly confidential information which has been declassified in accordance with subparagraphs 4.6 and 4.7 of Part V of this Policy) and that falls into one of the following categories:
       (a) general information on the course of the implementation of the Convention which

does not contain material relating specifically to any State Party. This excludes specific information about inspection activities being conducted in or planned for a State Party. The types of information which may be released publicly under this provision will be set out in a list approved by the Conference; this list could include details of declaration requirements and forms, generic or model documentation, summary information about the overall verification programme, and verification technology and methodology applied in on-site inspections;

(b) factual organisational information about the Organisation, except for information that relates to the security of the Organisation, or to personnel matters and the privacy of staff of the Secretariat; or

(c) information referring to a State Party, which is unclassified and which that State Party has specifically requested or consented to be publicly released.

2.2   The Director-General shall consider and decide upon individual requests for the public release of information, provided that it falls within the terms of the preceding paragraph. Requests going beyond these parameters shall be referred to the Executive Council or the Conference for decision.

2.3   All contacts between Secretariat staff members and the media shall be subject to this Policy, in particular, Part VII of this Policy (including these procedures established for the public release of information) and the OPCW Media and Public Affairs Policy. The Director-General shall issue an administrative directive governing media policy, in accordance with these public release policy guidelines.

3.   LIMITED OR NON-PUBLIC RELEASE OF INFORMATION

3.1   There may be cases where it is necessary[12] to release information beyond the Organisation in a manner that is short of full public release. This may include release to an international organisation or governmental organisation for official use only, and subject to certain conditions. Such non-public release may apply to confidential information bearing an OPCW classification, or to declassified as well as to unclassified information. Confidential information bearing an OPCW classification shall be released only if the Director-General confirms that adequate protection and control can be maintained in the recipient organisation. The Director-General shall conclude an agreement or agreed arrangements with potential recipient organisations on the handling and protection of classified information.

3.2   Limited or non-public release of information might take place:

(a) when the Executive Council decides to bring an issue or matter directly to the attention of the United Nations General Assembly and the United Nations Security Council in accordance with paragraph 36 of Article VIII;

(b) when the Conference decides to bring an issue to the attention of the United Nations General Assembly and the United Nations Security Council in accordance with paragraph 4 of Article XII; or

(c) when the Conference or the Executive Council decides to request the opinion of the International Court of Justice with the authorisation of the General Assembly of the United Nations in accordance with paragraph 5 of Article XIV.

3.3   The limited or non-public release of information which does not bear an OPCW classification can be authorised by the Director-General provided that the information falls within the categories set out in subparagraph 2.1 of this Part. Requests for the release of information not bearing an OPCW classification but going beyond these parameters shall be referred to the Executive Council or the Conference for decision.

3.4   When limited or non-public release is proposed for confidential information, the scope

---

[12] In accordance with subparagraph 2(c) of the Confidentiality Annex.

and conditions for such release shall be in strict conformity with the needs of the implementation of the Convention. The need-to-know principle governing dissemination of information must still apply.

3.5   If confidential information refers to a particular State Party, and that State Party expressly requests or consents to its release, then the release may proceed without further consultation. In all other cases, a decision of the Conference or the Executive Council is required for the release of confidential information beyond the Organisation. While a request for a decision on such a release can be put to either organ, such a request will normally be part of a general policy decision by the Conference or Executive Council to refer a related issue to an external body in accordance with the Convention, and so the decision on release would be taken by the same organ considering the general policy question.

3.6   A decision to approve such a release should be based upon:
       (a) an explicit determination that the intended recipient has a clear need to know in accordance with the recipient's role in the implementation of the Convention; and
       (b) a determination that the intended release conforms with the needs of the Convention.

3.7   When an apparent need arises for release of confidential information, the Director-General shall prepare a draft proposal for release for consultation and review by the parties concerned. The factors for determining confidentiality and the classification of the information are required to be fully addressed in the formulation of the proposed release. When applicable, the information proposed for release shall be processed into less sensitive forms so that disclosure of confidential information not relevant to the purpose of the release is avoided. In this case the processes for declassification or reclassification should be applied. If the confidential information was obtained from or refers to a State Party, the Director-General or a delegate authorised for this function is required to obtain the written consent of that State Party for the proposed release. The withholding of such consent shall not be used to avoid a State Party's obligations under the Convention.

3.8   In preparing a release proposal, the Director-General may propose specific conditions or limitations on the scope to be associated with the release, with the aim of ensuring that the release is focused on its particular purpose connected with the implementation of the Convention. Some of the limitations of scope or conditions that may apply are:
       (a) access to the confidential information only on a temporary basis, such as for the duration of a meeting or for the duration of a consultancy;
       (b) specification that the information is for official use only;
       (c) request for particular handling, such as a request to destroy or return the information after a specified period;
       (d) specific controls on some sensitive parts of the confidential information; and
       (e) visual display of the confidential information, such as projection during the course of a meeting.

3.9   After consultation with the parties concerned, the proposal for release will then be put to the Executive Council or the Conference for decision.

PART VIII. ADMINISTRATION

THE DIRECTOR-GENERAL

1.   The Director-General shall establish and supervise the implementation and auditing of the regime for the protection and handling of confidential information within the Organisation in accordance with the principles set out in the Confidentiality Annex and this Policy. To this end, the Director-General shall issue and supervise the implementation of administrative directives required by this Policy.

2. The Director-General shall have the primary responsibility for the enforcement of this regime and will charge appropriate units in the Secretariat with particular tasks for the implementation of the regime in accordance with this Policy. In exceptional cases, the Director-General may delegate specific authority in relation to implementation of the confidentiality regime to a limited number of senior Secretariat staff members, subject to specific limitations set out in this Policy[13]. The Director-General shall also personally supervise the conduct of those units and shall remain personally responsible for actions taken by his delegates in exercising his authority.

ADMINISTRATION OF THE CONFIDENTIALITY REGIME IN THE SECRETARIAT

3. The confidentiality regime shall apply to the operations of all elements of the Secretariat. The OCS shall assist the receiving Secretariat units in reviewing data and documents obtained by the Secretariat, to establish whether they contain confidential information, applying the guidelines set out in subparagraph 2(a) of the Confidentiality Annex and paragraph 11 of Part III of this Policy. Auditing of the operation of the confidentiality regime shall be conducted by the Office of Internal Oversight in the exercise of its confidentiality-audit function, and shall be kept functionally distinct from any unit tasked with its implementation.

4. Under the Director-General's supervision, the Secretariat shall ensure that its staff members are properly advised and reminded about their obligation to protect confidential information and to abide by the confidentiality regime, as well as about the principles of this Policy and the procedures required to implement it, the principles and procedures relating to security, and the possible penalties that they would incur in the event of unauthorised disclosure of confidential information. Training requirements shall also be taken into account following any change in the organisational structure of the Secretariat that affects personnel handling confidential material. In such cases, these additional training requirements shall be met preferably within three months, but in any event as soon as possible after the introduction of the structural change in question.

PART IX. BREACH PROCEDURES

IX.1: BREACH INVESTIGATION PROCEDURES

1. INVESTIGATIONS INTO BREACHES AND ALLEGED BREACHES OF CONFIDENTIALITY AND VIOLATIONS OF CONFIDENTIALITY OBLIGATIONS

   On the basis of the provisions of the Confidentiality Annex (paragraph 19), this Part of the Policy outlines the procedure for investigations by the Director-General in relation to breaches and alleged breaches of confidentiality and violations of related obligations to protect confidential information.

   Step 1: Investigation by the Director-General
   Step 2: Interim action
   Step 3: Report of investigations
   Step 4: Action in response to an investigation report
        4a: Disciplinary sanctions against serving Secretariat staff
        4b: Sanctions against former Secretariat staff
        4c: Action taken in relation to waiver of immunity
        4d: Other legal action within national jurisdiction
        4e: Action taken when a State Party appears responsible
        4f: Action to reform or enhance the confidentiality regime

---

[13] Refer in particular to subparagraphs 2.10 and 2.12 of Part VI of this Policy.

2. DEFINITIONS

A breach of the obligation to protect confidentiality ('a breach of confidentiality') includes any unauthorised disclosure of OPCW information to any individual, or government or private entity, regardless of the intention or the consequences of the disclosure. A breach of confidentiality can also be associated with misuse of information to gain a personal advantage or to benefit or damage the interests of a third party. A violation of obligations concerning the protection of confidential information is deemed to have taken place if there has been non-compliance with the specified procedures for the handling, protection, release and dissemination of confidential information so as to create a clear risk of unauthorised disclosure, with or without such disclosure actually occurring. In practical terms, there is considerable overlap between a breach of confidentiality and a violation of obligations to protect confidential information.

3.   STEP 1: INVESTIGATION BY THE DIRECTOR-GENERAL

3.1 As required in the terms of the Confidentiality Annex, the Director-General shall promptly initiate an investigation:

(a) following 'sufficient indication' that there has been a violation of an obligation to protect confidential information on the part of a staff member of the Secretariat, another authorised individual or entity beyond the Secretariat , or an agent or official of a State Party; or

(b) when a State Party has lodged an allegation concerning a breach of confidentiality.

3.2 In particular, the Director-General shall initiate an investigation if he becomes aware that there is a reasonable possibility, or clear risk, of unauthorised disclosure of confidential information occurring, *inter alia*, in a manner:

(a) which violates the policy or guidelines of the Organisation established for the handling, protection, release and dissemination of confidential information; or

(b) which could adversely affect the object and purpose of the Convention or the interests of the Organisation, a State Party, or a commercial or governmental body or a national of a State Party, or could offer particular or selective advantage to an individual, a State, or any other body, including a commercial firm.

3.3 The Director-General is obliged to investigate any allegation by a State Party that a breach of confidentiality has occurred. Such an allegation should be made in writing to the Director-General, and should to the extent possible provide supporting information. An allegation should, if possible, state the nature of the information involved, the time and location at which the breach is alleged to have occurred, and the actual or possible future damage believed to affect relevant interests.

3.4 When a decision has been taken by the Director-General to proceed with an investigation, the decision should be made known immediately to any States Parties and any Secretariat staff member involved in the alleged breach or suspected violation.

3.5 The aim of the investigation is to establish whether there has been a breach of confidentiality or a violation of the handling, protection, dissemination or release procedures for confidential information, and the severity of any breach including the degree and nature of any damage caused. The investigation should also consider ways of enhancing the confidentiality regime so as to prevent any recurrence of a breach or violation of procedures.

3.6 The Director-General shall be directly responsible for the investigation, and will direct it personally, but may designate a senior staff member to conduct investigatory work. The investigation should commence with a preliminary review of the circumstances surrounding the allegation or indication of a violation, and a consideration of any evidence or supporting information. The Director-General at this stage may find that a *prima facie* case does not exist; if so, he may, at his discretion, either consult with a State Party that has made an allegation, or he may conclude the investigation and report a finding that no *prima facie* case was established. Following the establishment of a *prima facie* case of a breach affecting the interests of a State Party, the Director-General shall notify the Executive Council that an investigation into a breach is in progress and, with the consent of that State Party, may present specific information about the investigation, if requested.

3.7   The investigation procedure following the establishment of a *prima facie* case may include the following activities:

(a)   the collection and examination of evidence within the OPCW or its constituent organs;

(b)   the examination of further material supplied by States Parties as evidence;

(c)   confidential interviews with staff members of the Secretariat;

(d)   consultations with States Parties concerned, including with representatives of industry or private entities concerned nominated by States Parties; and/or

(e)   a request for a State Party to provide details on the handling of information provided to it by the Organisation.

3.8   The proceedings of the investigation will remain confidential, and will be subject to the strict application of the need-to-know principle. Particular care should be given to the possible damaging effects of disclosures about such an investigation to Secretariat staff members as well as to the interests of States Parties. The investigation should be conducted on the basis of objectivity and due process, and there should be no use of coercion to elicit information from any individual concerned. Every effort should be made to conclude the investigation and take appropriate action in response to its findings as quickly as is possible and consistent with proper procedure.

3.9   All States Parties concerned and all staff members of the Secretariat involved shall cooperate with and support the investigation to the extent possible. For States Parties, this may entail providing details of internal investigations conducted, furnishing evidence, advising on national judicial proceedings in relation to the same matter, and advising on the degree and nature of damage caused by a breach. Staff members are required to provide any factual information relating to the aims of the investigation and their professional responsibilities.

4.   STEP 2: INTERIM ACTION

4.1   If a *prima facie* case is established which apparently implicates a currently serving member of the Secretariat:

(a)   procedures will be initiated in accordance with the Staff Regulations and Rules to impose interim restrictive measures for the duration of the investigation, such as withdrawal from certain functions or denial of access to certain information, or, if the case appears serious, temporary suspension in accordance with the OPCW Staff Regulations and Rules;

(b)   the Director-General shall consider and may propose immediate action, if necessary in consultation with the Executive Council, to protect all legitimate interests which could be prejudiced by the breach or alleged breach of confidentiality, including the interests of a State Party or of the Organisation; and

(c)   if the investigation is at the request of a State Party, then the Director-General shall inform this State Party of any such interim action taken.

4.2   An employee suspected of involvement in a breach should be informed by registered letter of the decision to take such interim action, stating the basis of this action and advising of any recourse available.

4.3   If the preliminary stage of the investigation discloses *prima facie* indications that a State Party may have been responsible for a breach, or may have otherwise been involved, the Director-General shall consider and may propose immediate action for decision of the Executive Council, to protect all legitimate interests which could be prejudiced by the breach of confidentiality, including the interests of any other State Party or of the Organisation. The Director-General may request that State Party to provide details on the handling of information provided to it by the Organisation.

4.4   If the preliminary stage of the investigation discloses *prima facie* indications that a natural or legal person in a State Party's jurisdiction may have been responsible for a breach, or may have otherwise been involved, the Director-General may consult with and request support from that State Party, if necessary following Executive Council approval, on possible action to protect all legitimate interests which could be prejudiced by the breach of confidentiality.

5.   STEP 3: REPORT OF INVESTIGATIONS

5.1   The Director-General shall prepare a report of the investigation which will state whether there has been a breach of confidentiality or a violation of the handling, protection, dissemination or release procedures for confidential information. The report will be prepared in two forms, a full form which sets out the facts determined in detail, and a modified form from which specific confidential material has been removed to ensure that confidential information connected with a breach is not further disclosed beyond its authorised scope of access, and to respect those elements of the privacy of individual staff members not relevant to the case.

5.2   The full report shall be treated as confidential, to be classified and handled according to its sensitivity. It should be made available only to all those who are directly involved in the investigation, including any individual staff members implicated in a breach or alleged breach, and any State Party making an allegation of a breach. In its modified form, the report may be made available to any State Party upon request and it shall be summarised in the annual report of the Director-General to the Conference concerning confidentiality as required under paragraph 3 of the Confidentiality Annex. Where possible, the report should, in both forms, contain concrete proposals for the enhancement of the confidentiality regime. If the Director-General requested the Executive Council to approve interim action in accordance with subparagraphs 4.1, 4.3 or 4.4 of this Part, then he should report directly to the Executive Council on the implementation of interim action.

5.3   When the report finds that there has been a breach of confidentiality, there should be an account of the degree of severity of the breach, with reference to the following factors:
        (a) whether the breach occurred through deliberate or accidental steps, or through negligent omission;
        (b) whether the breach involved a violation of obligations under this Policy and associated administrative directives, or of specific agreements such as a staff secrecy agreement or a facility agreement;
        (c) the degree of actual or potential damage, if any, to the interests of any party concerned; and
        (d) the degree of any private advantage gained through the unauthorised disclosure or consequent misuse of information, in particular promoting self-interest, competitive advantage, the benefit of a third party, or an intention to damage a third party's interest.

5.4   If the State Party requesting an investigation is not satisfied with the report issued by the Director-General following an investigation, and after all reasonable attempts have been made to resolve the issue through consultations, that State Party has the right to request that the Confidentiality Commission be convened to consider the case.

5.5   If the investigation has not been completed within three months of the initial decision to proceed, the Director-General should make an interim progress report to those who receive the final report. This report should set out the steps taken to that date, and any obstacles or reasons for delay in completing the investigation. If, after consultations, it subsequently appears that these obstacles or delays can not be expediently overcome, the Director-General may conclude the investigation and in his report request that the Confidentiality Commission be convened to consider the case in accordance with paragraph 23 of the Confidentiality Annex.

5.6   If, on conclusion of the investigation, it is determined that a breach or violation has not occurred, the Director-General's report should include a statement exonerating the accused Secretariat staff member or State Party.

6.   STEP 4: ACTION IN RESPONSE TO AN INVESTIGATION REPORT
        An investigation and report which finds that there has been a breach or violation may lead to four broad categories of possible response:
        (a) disciplinary actions internal to the Organisation and covering current staff of the Secretariat, and sanctions covering former staff members;
        (b) legal proceedings conducted under the national jurisdiction of a State Party, following the waiver, when relevant, of any immunity from jurisdiction;
        (c) reform or enhancement of the OPCW confidentiality regime; and
        (d) other action when a State Party appears responsible.

7.   STEP 4A: DISCIPLINARY SANCTIONS AGAINST SERVING SECRETARIAT STAFF
7.1   If, on conclusion of the investigation, it is determined that a breach or violation has been committed by a Secretariat staff member, the Director-General shall apply proper disciplinary measures in accordance with the OPCW Staff Regulations and Rules.
7.2   The severity of the breach and the degree of individual responsibility should be weighed in determining which measures should apply to a staff member.
7.3   The decision of the Director-General concerning disciplinary action may be subject to review or appeal, in accordance with procedures established under the OPCW Staff Regulations and Rules.

8.   STEP 4B: SANCTIONS AGAINST FORMER SECRETARIAT STAFF
        If a breach or violation is determined within the report to have been committed by a former member of staff of the Secretariat, the Director-General may decide on the application of whatever measures may still be applied within the terms of the OPCW Staff Regulations and Rules. This may include the loss of financial or other entitlements, such as those related to the OPCW Provident Fund.

9.   STEP 4C: ACTION TAKEN IN RELATION TO WAIVER OF IMMUNITY
9.1   Separate from these disciplinary measures, the Director-General may decide to waive immunity from prosecution. This applies both to currently serving Secretariat staff members of the Secretariat, and to former staff members who may retain immunity relating to actions taken during their term of service with the Secretariat. Waiver of immunity is to be considered only in the event of a serious breach, when individual responsibility has been established and damage has been suffered as a result thereof, and should ensue in conjunction with confidential consultations as to the possibilities of relevant national jurisdiction being applied. The individual secrecy agreement signed by the staff member should also be reviewed for its possible use in legal action.
9.2   Any decision to waive immunity may be subject to review or appeal in accordance with the procedures established under the OPCW Staff Regulations and Rules.
9.3   States Parties shall take appropriate legal action, to the extent possible, in making an appropriate response to the waiver of immunity. The action to be taken will be in accord-

ance with Part IX.3 of this Policy below including possible legal proceedings that may apply to the present or former staff member whose immunity is waived. If the present or former staff member responsible for a breach is residing or is otherwise within the jurisdiction of a State not Party to the Convention, the Director-General may seek the authority of the Executive Council or the Conference to undertake consultations with the aim of encouraging that State to initiate or facilitate appropriate action to support legal processes resulting from the breach.

10.   STEP 4D: OTHER LEGAL ACTION WITHIN NATIONAL JURISDICTION

10.1   If the investigation by the Director-General determines that a natural or legal person (including a commercial entity) under the jurisdiction of a State Party appears to have been responsible for a breach of confidentiality, has derived particular advantage from a breach of confidentiality, or has otherwise been involved in a breach of confidentiality, that State Party may be required to take appropriate legal action in accordance with Part IX.3 of this Policy below.

10.2   If a legal or natural person found responsible for a breach is residing or is otherwise within the jurisdiction of a State not Party to the Convention, the Director-General may seek the authority of the Executive Council or the Conference to undertake consultations with the aim of encouraging that State to initiate or facilitate appropriate action to support legal processes resulting from the breach.

11.   STEP 4E: ACTION TAKEN WHEN A STATE PARTY APPEARS RESPONSIBLE

11.1   If the investigation by the Director-General determines that a State Party, including an official of a State Party, appears to have been responsible for a breach of confidentiality:

   (a)   that State Party shall assist the Director-General to resolve the matter, to the extent possible, including providing full details of its handling and protection of confidential information supplied by the Organisation;

   (b)   that State Party shall take appropriate legal action in accordance with Part IX.3 of this Policy below; and

   (c)   the Director-General may raise the matter with the Executive Council and request further action in response to the investigation report.

11.2   A State Party's possible responsibility is to be assessed in the light of its obligations under the Convention, particularly paragraph 6 of Article VII and paragraph 4 of the Confidentiality Annex.

11.3   If an investigation finds that a State Party appears responsible for a breach, the Confidentiality Commission may be convened in case of disputes to consider the case in accordance with paragraph 23 of the Confidentiality Annex and the detailed procedures established for the Confidentiality Commission.

11.4   Where the investigation discloses a breach of confidentiality involving the interests and actions of States Parties only, the Director-General shall inform the States Parties concerned of such an outcome.

12.   STEP 4F: ACTION TO REFORM OR ENHANCE THE CONFIDENTIALITY REGIME

12.1   The report of the investigation should contain concrete proposals for the reform or enhancement of the protection of confidential information within the Organisation, both specifically to prevent the recurrence of any breach or violation established by the investigation, and on the basis of other observations about the general protection of confidentiality which may emerge from the investigation.

12.2   The Director-General should recommend to the Conference for adoption at its next meeting any proposals for reform or enhancement of this Policy or other basic policy documents that emerge from the investigation.

12.3   If the investigation demonstrates a need for improved handling and protection proce-
         dures, or any other alteration of the working procedures of the Secretariat, the Director-
         General shall issue appropriate administrative directives to implement these changes
         without delay.

IX.2:   RULES GOVERNING THE COMMISSION FOR THE SETTLEMENT OF DIS-
         PUTES RELATED TO CONFIDENTIALITY ("THE CONFIDENTIALITY COM-
         MISSION")

1.   RULES GOVERNING THE COMPOSITION OF THE CONFIDENTIALITY COMMISSION
1.1   The Confidentiality Commission as a whole will be made up of persons appointed in a
         personal capacity from a list of nominees put forward by States Parties to the Conven-
         tion. Each State Party may nominate one of its citizens who is available and qualified
         to serve on the Confidentiality Commission. This list of nominees will be submitted to
         the Conference and 20 persons shall be appointed from it to serve on the Confidentiality
         Commission for an initial two-year term.
1.2   The 20 appointees are to be determined through a process of consultation with regional
         groups under the direction of the Chair of the Conference: these consultations shall
         take into account the principle of rotation and the need for a comprehensive spread of
         relevant fields of expertise, to result in the designation of four nominees from each of
         the five regions defined in paragraph 23 of Article VIII of the Convention by the States
         Parties belonging to the respective regions. Due appointment of these nominees to the
         Confidentiality Commission shall then be taken by the Conference as a decision on a
         matter of substance, in accordance with Article VIII, paragraph 18 of the Convention.
1.3   Nominees should be proposed by States Parties on the basis of individual competence,
         integrity and background in one or more fields relevant to the work of the Confidenti-
         ality Commission, such as dispute resolution of various types; the confidentiality and
         verification provisions of the Convention; the chemical industry; military security; data
         security; international law; and national legal systems.
1.4[14] The Confidentiality Commission as a whole shall meet for an inaugural meeting during
         the course of the first Conference at which it shall, by consensus, elect its Chair from
         amongst its members to serve for an initial term of one year. Thereafter, the Confiden-
         tiality Commission shall hold a regular annual meeting, within reasonable time prior to
         the regular annual session of the Conference, during which the Confidentiality Commis-
         sion will elect its Chair ('the Chair') for the coming year in accordance with the operat-
         ing procedures approved by the Conference.

2.   DISPUTES THE CONFIDENTIALITY COMMISSION MAY DEAL WITH
         The Confidentiality Commission may be called upon to deal with disputes in the follow-
         ing circumstances:
         (a) when invoked to consider disputes arising from a breach or breaches of confidenti-
              ality involving both a State Party and the Organisation;
         (b) when, in accordance with Article XIV, paragraph 4, of the Convention, the Confer-
              ence of the States Parties entrusts it with a dispute relating to confidentiality other
              than a dispute such as those identified in subparagraph 2.(a) above; or
         (c) when chosen by two States Parties in dispute over a matter of confidentiality as a
              means of resolving their dispute pursuant to Article XIV, paragraph 2 of the Con-
              vention.

---

[14] Amended by paragraph 3 of Conference decision C-II/DEC.14.

3.   RULES GOVERNING THE OPERATING PROCEDURES OF THE CONFIDENTIALITY COMMISSION
      These rules were approved by the Third Session of the Conference and govern the de-
      tailed operating Procedures for the Confidentiality Commission.

      COMMENCEMENT OF THE DISPUTE RESOLUTION PROCESS
3.1   In the event of the Confidentiality Commission being called upon to deal with a dispute
      in the circumstances set out in paragraph 2 above, the matter will immediately be for-
      warded to the Chair, who shall in turn immediately inform all members of the Confiden-
      tiality Commission about the case. The Chair shall then consult with all members of the
      Confidentiality Commission on the timing and process for resolving the dispute, includ-
      ing convening meetings as necessary, in accordance with procedural guidelines in the
      operating procedures which take into account such factors as indications of gravity or
      urgency on the part of a disputing party, the complexity of substantive issues involved,
      the scale of alleged loss or damage, and the need for minimising the scope of further ac-
      cess to confidential information. At the conclusion of these preliminary steps, the Chair
      shall obtain the agreement of the Confidentiality Commission on a proposed timetable
      and a process for resolution for the dispute.

      SEEKING A MUTUALLY AGREEABLE RESOLUTION
3.2   The Confidentiality Commission shall initially aim at clarifying the basis of the dispute
      and at resolving the dispute in a manner that is acceptable to the disputing parties and
      that is consistent with the rights and obligations of States Parties and the Organisation
      under the Convention. In making every effort to encourage disputing parties towards a
      mutually satisfactory outcome, the Confidentiality Commission should adopt a means
      of dispute resolution appropriate to the case, which takes account of any common pref-
      erence of the disputing parties: for instance, the initial means adopted would prefer-
      ably comprise a mediation process practically geared to reaching an agreed settlement
      through negotiation.
3.3   To this end, the Confidentiality Commission may form an advisory committee to un-
      dertake informal mediation consultations; normally this advisory committee should be
      composed of five Confidentiality Commission members, one from each region, unless
      the disputing parties agree to request a similar, modified structure which they believe
      would serve better to reach a mediated resolution. Any such committee must report to
      the Confidentiality Commission on the progress and result of any consultations, and any
      possible mediated resolution derived from this process must be put to the Confidentiality
      Commission to be certified.
3.4   If, by any appropriate means, the Confidentiality Commission reaches a mediated reso-
      lution of the dispute acceptable to the disputing parties, this outcome shall be certified
      by the Confidentiality Commission and a factual statement on the outcome shall be
      provided to the disputing parties for their agreement to be recorded.

      ABSENCE OF MUTUALLY ACCEPTABLE RESOLUTION
3.5   If no such outcome can be reached, the Confidentiality Commission shall prepare a
      report outlining the basic facts of the dispute, commenting objectively upon the dispute
      and recommending further action that might be taken to resolve it, by the disputing par-
      ties themselves, by the Confidentiality Commission, by the Conference, or by another
      organ of the Organisation, in accordance with a specific mandate from the Conference.
      This report shall be passed by the Confidentiality Commission to the disputing parties.
      The report and recommendations of the Confidentiality Commission shall not be binding
      on the disputing parties, but may provide a basis or rationale for further action on the
      part of the disputing parties or competent organs of the Organisation: in particular, the

Confidentiality Commission may refer the matter to the Conference, or to another organ of the Organisation in accordance with a specific mandate from the Conference and if the disputing parties concur that this is necessary due to the urgency of the case.

3.6   If two disputing States Parties agree as a condition of referring a dispute to the Confidentiality Commission, the Confidentiality Commission may, with the explicit consent of the disputing parties, decide on an arbitrated resolution to the dispute which is binding on the disputing parties.

3.7   In preparing its reports and recommendations, the Confidentiality Commission shall take into account the need-to-know principle governing access to confidential information and the specific procedures adopted by the Confidentiality Commission to ensure that confidentiality remains protected in the exercise of its functions. Confidentiality Commission members shall themselves be bound by all obligations under the Convention and this Policy in relation to handling and protection of confidential information.

REPORTING TO THE CONFERENCE

3.8   The Confidentiality Commission shall remain responsible to the Conference, and shall report on its activities in the preceding year at every regular session of the Conference. This report shall include the number of mediated and arbitrated resolutions reached, the categories of disputes considered, the outcomes reached, and details of the outcomes consistent with the continuing protection of confidentiality. The Confidentiality Commission shall also report on its general operations, as well as on its effectiveness and efficiency, and may make proposals or recommendations for its improvement.

RESPONSIBILITIES OF CONFIDENTIALITY COMMISSION MEMBERS

3.9   The Confidentiality Commission, and its members individually, shall act without interference or direction from either the Secretariat or other organs of the Organisation, but must follow any mandate of the Conference. The Chair may, however, seek and receive conference and logistical support and assistance from the Secretariat in the exercise of his functions. Confidentiality Commission members with a conflict of interest in relation to a particular dispute shall refrain from dealing with that dispute; it is the responsibility of individual Confidentiality Commission members to declare any conflict of interest as soon as any dispute is notified. Confidentiality Commission members shall neither exercise any other office within the Organisation or its organs, nor maintain any legal or financial relationship or interest linked to the Organisation.

MEETINGS OF THE CONFIDENTIALITY COMMISSION

3.10   The Confidentiality Commission shall meet initially and in conjunction with regular sessions of the Conference in accordance with subparagraph 1.4 of this Part, and shall also meet as necessary to consider disputes brought before it.

3.11   At its initial and subsequent annual meetings, the Confidentiality Commission shall:
   (a) choose by consensus a Chair to serve for the forthcoming year taking into account the principle of rotation among the regions designated in paragraph 23 of Article VIII of the Convention;
   (b) consider and adopt a report to the Conference as to the outcome of disputes handled by the Confidentiality Commission during the previous year;
   (c) consider and adopt a report to the Conference on the operation, effectiveness and efficiency of the Confidentiality Commission and consider any recommendations or proposals made by the Chair in this regard;
   (d) as necessary, review and recommend any amendment to its operating procedures;
   (e) issue such guidelines to or make such requests of the Chair as it sees fit; and
   (f) make such further recommendations or proposals to the Conference as it sees fit.

PREPARATION OF OPERATING PROCEDURES

3.12   The Conference shall approve detailed operating procedures for the Confidentiality Commission, setting out, *inter alia*:

(a) by what formal process meetings of the Confidentiality Commission are to be convened;

(b) how disputes are to be immediately forwarded to the Chair, and how the Chair is to inform all Confidentiality Commission members immediately;

(c) how the Confidentiality Commission is to decide on the timing and process of dispute resolution in accordance with subparagraph 3.1 of this Part;

(d) how the Confidentiality Commission is to certify a mutually agreed resolution of a dispute, and how the agreement of disputing parties to such resolution of a dispute is to be registered;

(e) procedures for preparation and submission of reports and recommendations by the Confidentiality Commission to disputing parties and to the Conference or to another organ of the Organisation in accordance with the Conference's authority;

(f) a procedure to ensure that confidentiality remains protected in the exercise by the Confidentiality Commission of its functions, consistent with the Confidentiality Annex, the OPCW Policy on Confidentiality and the need-to-know principle governing access to confidential information;

(g) a procedure for the imposition of time-limits within which Confidentiality Commission functions must be exercised;

(h) procedures for the election of successive Chairs, for the election of successive members to the Confidentiality Commission, and for the filling of any casual vacancies taking into account the principles established in subparagraphs 1.1, 1.2 and 1.3 of this Part;

(i) in respect of those Confidentiality Commission members currently considering a particular dispute, a mechanism for facilitating continuity of their service throughout the dispute resolution process, consistent with and subordinate to the principles of the rules governing composition set out in paragraph 1 of this Part;

(j) a procedure by which the Confidentiality Commission's efficiency shall be monitored; and

(k) a procedure for amendment of these operating procedures.

DECISION-MAKING PROCEDURE

3.13   The Chair shall seek consensus on any decision or recommendation before the Confidentiality Commission as a whole but, in the event that consensus cannot be reached on a particular decision, the Confidentiality Commission may resolve the matter by two-thirds majority of all its members.

IX.3:   THE ROLE OF STATES PARTIES IN RELATION TO BREACH PROCEDURES

1.   INTRODUCTION: RELEVANT CONVENTION OBLIGATIONS

1.1   Provisions of the Convention which specifically relate to States Parties' involvement in the protection of confidentiality include the obligations on individual States Parties to:

(a) to the extent possible, cooperate with and support the Director-General in investigating any breach or alleged breach of confidentiality and in taking appropriate action in case a breach has been established (paragraph 21, Confidentiality Annex);

(b) treat as confidential and afford special handling to information and data received in confidence from the Organisation in connection with the implementation of the Convention, and to treat such information and data exclusively in connection with rights and obligations under the Convention, and in accordance with the provisions of the Confidentiality Annex (Article VII, 6);

   (c)   treat information received from the Organisation in accordance with the level of confidentiality established for it (Confidentiality Annex, paragraph 4); and

   (d)   provide upon request details on the handling of confidential information provided to them by the Organisation (Confidentiality Annex, paragraph 4).

1.2   In addition, implementation of the provision for waiver of immunity established in paragraph 20 of the Confidentiality Annex would mean that a relevant national jurisdiction would need to apply in the event that a Secretariat staff member committed a serious breach of confidentiality.

1.3   As this Policy deals with the operations of the Organisation itself and its relationship with States Parties, this Part does not establish or prescribe specific internal State Party measures that may be undertaken in pursuance of the objectives of the Convention in relation to confidentiality, or for the implementation of specific States Parties' responsibilities in this regard such as the application of national jurisdiction or the provision of compensation in the event of a breach. If necessary or desirable in particular cases, such specific internal State Party measures or specific responsibilities of States Parties might also be referred to and further developed in bilateral agreements or other implementation arrangements between the Organisation and States Parties.

2.   POSSIBLE SCENARIOS

A State Party's obligations concerning confidentiality could arise in a number of practical scenarios, in particular in relation to:

   (a)   an OPCW investigation into a breach or alleged breach of confidentiality;

   (b)   the waiver of immunity by the OPCW Director-General in the event of a serious breach of confidentiality;

   (c)   a breach of confidentiality for which a State Party is directly responsible; or

   (d)   a breach of confidentiality by a legal or natural person in the jurisdiction of a State Party.

3.   INVESTIGATION OF BREACHES OF CONFIDENTIALITY

In addition to the general requirement under Article VII, paragraph 7 of the Convention to provide assistance to the Secretariat, each State Party has a particular obligation in relation to the investigation by the Director-General of a breach or alleged breach of confidentiality (as noted in subparagraph 1.1(a) of this Part). Within the framework of these obligations, the nature of support and cooperation by States Parties in relation to any particular investigation is to be determined on a case-by-case basis.

4.   WAIVER OF IMMUNITY IN THE CASE OF A SERIOUS BREACH OF CONFIDENTIALITY

4.1   The Convention (Confidentiality Annex, paragraphs 20 and 21) presumes that jurisdiction should apply in the event of immunity from jurisdiction being waived in respect of a staff member of the Technical Secretariat who has committed a serious breach of confidentiality. If the Director-General decides to waive immunity in such a case, legal proceedings under an applicable jurisdiction of a State Party should be instituted against such a staff member on the basis of the request of the Director-General or a State Party affected by the serious breach. States Parties should take any appropriate administrative and legal measures to ensure that this mechanism can be effectively implemented.

4.2   It will remain the primary responsibility of States Parties to determine the applicability of national jurisdiction on a case-by-case basis. The Conference may also consider proposals for an arrangement that would ensure a consistent and comprehensive response to any serious breach of confidentiality obligations by Secretariat staff members.

5.   BREACHES IMPUTED TO A STATE PARTY
         If information provided in confidence by the Organisation to a State Party is disclosed to
         unauthorised recipients or if confidentiality is otherwise abused by that State Party, then
         this would run contrary to the obligations upon States Parties established under Article
         VII, paragraph 6 of the Convention and under the Confidentiality Annex, paragraph 4.
         Treatment as confidential of information received in confidence is, moreover, an essen-
         tial part of the effective operation of the Convention as a whole. In such a case, a breach
         of confidentiality may be imputed to the State Party in question, as contravening these
         obligations. This may arise as a finding of an investigation by the Director-General into
         a breach or alleged breach [15], in which case the matter would be subject to the Conven-
         tion's dispute resolution mechanisms, and in particular to the Confidentiality Commis-
         sion[16] under the authority of the Conference.

6.   OTHER APPLICATION OF NATIONAL JURISDICTION
         As noted in paragraph 5 above, a State Party's disclosure of information, having been
         provided by the Organisation in confidence, in such a way as to breach its confidentiality
         would run contrary to the obligations upon States Parties established under Article VII,
         paragraph 6 of the Convention and under the Confidentiality Annex, paragraph 4. States
         Parties are therefore required to take appropriate administrative and legal measures they
         judge to be necessary to ensure that these obligations are effectively met, including by
         any agents acting with their authority or sponsorship.

PART X. ANNUAL REPORT ON THE IMPLEMENTATION OF THE REGIME GOVERN-
ING THE HANDLING OF CONFIDENTIAL INFORMATION BY THE SECRETARIAT

1.   The Director-General is required to report annually to the Conference on the implementation
     of the regime governing the handling of confidential information by the Secretariat (Confi-
     dentiality Annex, paragraph 3). The points identified below should be covered in the report,
     but in such a way as to preclude any diminution of the confidentiality of any confidential
     information disclosed to, handled by or held in the Secretariat, and governed by the principles
     of this Policy.
2.   The Director-General shall focus in his report on practical details of the handling of confiden-
     tial information by staff members of the Secretariat (CA, paragraph 3) in the preceding year,
     including:
     2.1 resource requirements for implementing the confidentiality regime, including an esti-
          mate of the volume of confidential information handled by the Secretariat;
     2.2 important actions taken to implement the confidentiality regime, including significant
          changes in procedures or personnel, and staff training and awareness programmes to
          ensure compliance of Secretariat staff with the regime;
     2.3 breaches or alleged breaches and the actions taken to investigate and redress them; and
     2.4 problems or policy issues that have arisen with respect to the confidentiality regime.
3.   While not limiting the scope of the report, it should in particular cover the following detailed
     elements:
     3.1 the estimated number of items of confidential information received, generated, stored
          and disseminated by the Secretariat;
     3.2 the number, recipients and description of release[17] of items of confidential information

---

[15] In accordance with Step 4e of the breach investigation procedures in Part IX.1 [footnote in original].

[16] See Part IX. 2 [footnote in original].

[17] "Release" of information refers to the approved disclosure of information beyond the Organisation
itself (including all its constituent elements) and beyond the governments of States Parties (specifically, beyond governmental organisations and authorised entities or individuals within States Parties concerned with
the operation of the Convention (subparagraph 1.1 of Part VII of this Policy)) [footnote in original].

made during the previous year, and access granted to authorised recipients associated with the Organisation[18];

3.3 the number of clearances granted for access to confidential information in accordance with paragraph 11 of the Confidentiality Annex, and any changes in senior staff positions concerned with the implementation of the confidentiality regime;

3.4 resource and operational requirements and general policy issues arising from confidentiality procedures in the course of verification activities and in the IMS;

3.5 any changes that have been made in administrative directives established to implement this Policy, including any changes to administrative directives that have been made necessary by the Conference's approval of amendments to this Policy;

3.6 any reported loss of confidential information;

3.7 any breaches or alleged breaches involving staff members of the Secretariat, breach investigations conducted by the Director-General, and consequent actions taken;

3.8 any changes in the IMS which have substantial implications for the security of confidential information contained in the system;

3.9 the conduct of staff training and awareness programmes about the obligation to protect confidential information and to abide by the confidentiality regime, and the provision of instruction, advice and regular reminders to all staff members of the Secretariat about the principles of this Policy and the procedures required to implement it, as well as about the principles and procedures relating to security, and the possible penalties that staff members would incur in the event of improper disclosure of confidential information; and

3.10 the number of items of confidential information to which authorised recipients associated with the Organisation were granted access in accordance with the principles set out in subparagraph 2.12 of Part VI of this Policy.

PART XI. AMENDMENT PROCEDURE

1. Any State Party or the Director-General may propose amendments to this Policy. Any proposed amendments shall be forwarded by the Director-General, through the Executive Council, to the Conference of the States Parties for its consideration and approval in accordance with its rules of procedure.

2. The Director-General shall, without delay, issue any changes to administrative directives that are made necessary by the Conference's approval of amendments to this Policy, and shall report on any such changes to the Executive Council and to the Conference in the annual report on the confidentiality regime. The Director-General shall ensure that all staff employed by the Organisation are informed of such changes immediately and receive related training, preferably within three months, but in any event as soon as possible after their introduction.

GLOSSARY

'The Convention': The Convention on the Prohibition of the Development, Production, Stockpiling and Use of Chemical Weapons and on their Destruction

'The Confidentiality Annex' or 'CA': The Annex on the Protection of Confidential Information, annexed to the Convention

'The Organisation' or 'The OPCW': The Organisation for the Prohibition of Chemical Weapons, established under Article VIII, paragraph 1 of the Convention

---

[18] In accordance with the principles set out in subparagraph 2.12 of Part VI of this Policy [footnote in original].

'The Conference': The Conference of the States Parties established under Article VIII, paragraph 4 of the Convention

'The Secretariat': The Technical Secretariat established under Article VIII, paragraph 4 of the Convention

'The Confidentiality Commission': The Commission for the settlement of disputes related to confidentiality cited in paragraph 23 of the Confidentiality Annex

MCP: Manual of Confidentiality Procedure

OCS: Office of Confidentiality and Security in the Technical Secretariat

13.2 OPCW Media and Public Affairs Policy

C-I/DEC.55 adopted by the Conference of the States Parties at its First Session on 6 May 1997 and entitled "OPCW Media and Public Affairs Policy"

The Conference

Recalling that the Commission, in PC-X/23, paragraph 6.11, provisionally approved the Draft OPCW Media and Public Affairs Policy, as attached to PC-X/A/WP.5 and amended by Working Group A in PC-X/A/3, paragraph 6.2, including the "Indicative List of Areas Where Information may be Routinely Provided by the OPCW to the News Media and the General Public," annexed to the attachment to PC-X/A/WP.5, pending the adoption of other relevant documents including the Draft OPCW Policy on Confidentiality,

Recalling further that the Commission, in PC-XI/17, paragraph 7.7, adopted the Draft OPCW Policy on Confidentiality, as annexed to PC-XI/B/WP.8 and amended by Working Group B in PC-XI/B/12, paragraph 7.2,

Bearing in mind that the Commission recommended in paragraph 46.4 of its Final Report that the Conference adopt the above-mentioned Draft OPCW Media and Public Affairs Policy, including the "Indicative List of Areas Where Information may be Routinely Provided by the OPCW to the News Media and the General Public,"

Hereby:

1. Adopts the OPCW Media and Public Affairs Policy, including the "Indicative List of Areas Where Information may be Routinely Provided by the OPCW to the News Media and the General Public," annexed hereto.

ANNEX
OPCW MEDIA AND PUBLIC AFFAIRS POLICY

1. INTRODUCTION

This document, which sets out the OPCW Media and Public Affairs Policy (hereinafter referred to as "the Media Policy") for all OPCW organs, OPCW personnel and their activities, will apply to contacts with the news media or with any individual who is not employed or contracted by the Organisation nor authorised by a State Party in relation to implementation of the Convention. It will cover oral, written, electronic or any other communications.

The implementation of the Media Policy shall be consistent with the OPCW Policy on Confidentiality.

2. PRINCIPLES AND OBJECTIVES

To the extent needed to facilitate the achievement of the object and the purpose of the Convention, the implementation of the Media Policy shall assist the news media and the general public in understanding the tasks and the activities of the Organisation. It shall promote the image of the OPCW as an accessible international organisation which provides balanced, timely and objective information. It will not be overly promotional and active, but will avoid being merely reactive.

3.   RESPONSIBILITIES
The Director-General shall be responsible for ensuring that the Media Policy is implemented at all levels of the Organisation. The Director-General shall issue appropriate administrative directives and shall take other necessary measures for the proper implementation of that policy by the OPCW personnel.

4.   OPCW CONTACTS

4.1   OPENNESS
The OPCW will endeavour to be as open and accessible as possible in providing factual information on its activities and shall conduct an effective Public Affairs Programme with respect to the news media and the general public. An indicative list of areas in which information may be routinely provided by the Organisation for these purposes, is set out in the Annex to this Media Policy. Such information shall not be related to a specific State Party or site.

4.2   HEADQUARTERS ACTIVITIES
(a) The Director-General and, under his responsibility and acting in consultation with the relevant units of the OPCW Technical Secretariat {the appropriate unit responsible for administering the OPCW Media and Public Affairs Policy},[19] shall have the authority to handle routinely all dealings of the OPCW Technical Secretariat with the news media and the general public.
(b) The Director-General may release to the news media or the general public information specifically related to a State Party only at the request of or with the express consent of the State Party to which this information refers.

4.3   INSPECTION ACTIVITIES

4.3.1   INSPECTION TEAMS
(a) The inspection team leader shall be responsible for ensuring strict adherence to the Media Policy by all members of the inspection team, including, when present, qualified experts designated by the Director-General under paragraph 7, Part XI of the Verification Annex. Members of the inspection team shall be fully conversant with the Media Policy and the relevant administrative directives of the Director-General.
(b) Members of the inspection teams shall neither initiate contacts with, nor comment on, any aspect of a specific inspection activity in a State Party for the benefit of the news media or the general public. If required, without prejudice to the provision of paragraph 2(c)(ii) of the Annex on Confidentiality and after prior authorisation by the Director-General, the inspection team leader may make statements to the news media or the general public. Any such statement should be in conformity with standard press guidelines on the general verification and inspection programme, which will be developed by the Organisation. The inspected State Party shall be

---

[19] The brackets {} indicate that the bracketed text will be replaced by the name of the respective OPCW TS unit after a decision is taken on the final TS structure.

consulted, prior to contact with the news media, on the advisability of establishing such contacts and of making such statements.

4.3.2   OBSERVER
The requesting State Party shall be fully responsible for and shall take all necessary measures to ensure that the Observer complies with all relevant provisions of the Media Policy. For his/her part, the Observer therefore is to adhere to and be bound by the same provisions of the Media Policy that apply to members of the inspection team and is not to take any independent action in this regard.

4.3.3   INSPECTED STATE PARTY
(a) The inspected State Party shall ensure that the inspection team is not subjected to attention from the news media of a type which could impair the inspection team activities during the In-Country Period.
(b) When the inspected State Party considers it desirable, for a better public under-standing of the background to the verification activities, to arrange contacts with the news media with the participation of the inspection team leader, the Representa-tive of the inspected State Party and the inspection team leader will consult, prior to contact with the news media, in accordance with the provisions of subparagraph 4.3.1(b) above.

ANNEX [to the policy]
INDICATIVE LIST OF AREAS IN WHICH INFORMATION MAY BE ROUTINELY PROVIDED BY THE OPCW TO THE NEWS MEDIA AND THE GENERAL PUBLIC

1.   GENERAL INFORMATION ON:
(a) OPCW structure, offices, budget, technical support and staffing policy and patterns;
(b) activities of the OPCW, including its cooperation with States Parties;
(c) OPCW cooperation with the United Nations and other intergovernmental organisa-tions;
(d) contacts with scientific and research institutions and support received from other institutions for the purpose of the Convention;
(e) chemical industries, promotion of trade in chemicals and related equipment, and scientific and technological developments in the chemical field;
(f) national bodies concerned with the implementation of the Convention, including National Authorities, chemical industry associations etc.;
(g) progress towards the destruction of chemical weapons, old chemical weapons and abandoned chemical weapons; and
(h) verification activities, including technology and methodology applied in on-site in-spections.

2.   OTHER MATERIALS BASED ON:
(a) the contents of the Convention and its implementation procedures, e.g. declaration forms, model agreements and inspection procedures;
(b) non-confidential reports or parts of reports of the Organisation on the implementa-tion of the Convention, as envisaged in Article VIII (paragraph 38(b)), taking into account possible decisions of the Conference, the Executive Council or the Director General not to make such reports or certain parts of them public; and
(c) publicly-available materials provided by States Parties concerning their respective policies having a bearing on the implementation of the Convention.

13.3 OPCW Health and Safety Policy and Regulations

C-I/DEC.8 adopted by the Conference of the States Parties at its First Session on 6 May 1997 and entitled "Procedures concerning the implementation of safety requirements for activities of inspectors and inspection assistants, in accordance with Part II, paragraph 43, of the Verification Annex"

The Conference

Recalling that the Commission approved the revised draft Health and Safety Policy, Appendix 1 to the Chairman's Paper to PC-VI/B/WP.10, with the addition of the following sentence to paragraph 3.3.3(c): "This is without prejudice to the obligations of a State Party to provide access to an inspected facility for the purpose of carrying out inspection activities, in accordance with the Convention" (PC-VI/22, paragraph 6.7),

Recalling that the Commission in its PC-XIII/18, paragraph 7.2, considered and adopted the Draft OPCW Health and Safety Regulations annexed to PC-XIII/B/WP.2,

Recalling that Working Group B in its PC-XIII/B/6, paragraph 2.2, considered the Draft OPCW Health and Safety Regulations annexed to PC-XIII/B/WP.2, took note of the understanding recorded in paragraph 3.2 of PC-XIII/B/WP.2, recommended that these Regulations be adopted by the Commission,

Bearing in mind that the Commission recommended in paragraph 40.5 of its Final Report that the Conference adopt the above mentioned draft OPCW Health and Safety Policy and the draft OPCW Health and Safety Regulations,

Hereby:

1. Adopts the OPCW Health and Safety Policy and the OPCW Health and Safety Regulations and takes note of the understanding recorded in paragraph 3.2 of PC-XIII/B/WP.2 annexed hereto.

ANNEX
OPCW HEALTH AND SAFETY POLICY

TABLE OF CONTENTS

1.   HEALTH AND SAFETY POLICY STATEMENT
          The OPCW attaches great importance to health and safety. The health and safety of
          all personnel who may be involved in or affected by its operations is paramount. All
          operations involving OPCW personnel will be accomplished in a manner which to the
          extent possible minimises exposure, affords reasonable safety to personnel, minimises
          operational risk and encourages good health. The Director-General of the OPCW will
          ensure that the policy on health and safety is implemented at all levels of the Organisa-
          tion. The Director-General will review this policy and complementary health and safety
          documents at regular intervals and will take appropriate actions to amend them where
          necessary.

                                                                        [Name]
                                                        Director-General of the OPCW
                                                                        [Date]

2.   INTRODUCTION

          This document sets out the OPCW policy for health and safety for all OPCW person-
          nel, operations, including inspections, and OPCW premises. The means by which this
          policy will be implemented is contained in the OPCW Health and Safety Regulations
          document. Guidance for implementation is contained in the OPCW Health and Safety
          Guidelines document. The general principles on health and safety set down in this docu-
          ment are mandatory.

3.   RESPONSIBILITIES

3.1   *OPCW*

3.1.1   The Director-General is responsible for the health and safety of OPCW personnel. The
          Director-General shall establish within the Organisation a Health and Safety Office,
          headed and staffed by appropriately qualified personnel, to ensure that the Health and

Safety Policy and Regulations approved by the Conference of the States Parties are strictly adhered to. The Director-General shall issue and maintain OPCW Health and Safety Guidelines.

3.1.2 All OPCW personnel are required to abide by the Organisation's Health and Safety Policy and its associated Regulations. They shall also take reasonable care to protect their own health and safety, and that of other persons who might be affected by their acts.

3.1.3 The Head of the Health and Safety Office shall:

(a) develop guidelines and establish procedures in line with the approved OPCW Health and Safety Policy to ensure the health and safety of OPCW personnel;

(b) implement procedures for the screening, hiring, training, certification and re-evaluation of OPCW personnel as required in the areas of health and safety;

(c) have the power to delegate health and safety functions to suitably qualified members of inspection teams or other groups according to the requirements of the particular situation;

(d) when appropriate, request additional, suitably qualified personnel where unusually hazardous conditions prevail;

(e) monitor and regularly report to the Director-General on the implementation of the Health and Safety Policy and Regulations throughout the OPCW and on any incident or failure and recommend corrective action where necessary;

(f) seek cooperation, assistance and technical information from States Parties on health and safety issues; and

(g) advise on the procurement of health and safety equipment for the OPCW.

3.2 *OPCW INSPECTION TEAMS*

3.2.1 The inspection team leader is responsible for the health and safety of inspection personnel while engaged in an inspection. The team leader shall be assisted and advised by appropriately qualified health and safety personnel, as required, to ensure that all OPCW Health and Safety Policy and Regulations are properly implemented in the light of prevailing conditions in order to minimise health and safety risks. All inspection team personnel must be fully conversant with all OPCW health and safety requirements. The inspection teams will be provided with safety and medical staff as appropriate.

3.2.2 In carrying out their activities, inspectors and inspection assistants shall observe safety regulations established at the inspection site, including those for the protection of controlled environments within a facility and for personal safety without prejudice to the need also to comply with OPCW Health and Safety Regulations.

3.2.3 If at any time the inspection team cannot comply with OPCW Regulations the inspection activities will cease until such time as a waiver is granted in accordance with paragraph 7 below. In the case of difficulties, the provisions of paragraph 3.3.3 below shall apply.

3.2.4 Inspection team personnel are also responsible for their own safety and shall comply with advice from OPCW health and safety representatives at all times. At hazardous sites, inspection team personnel must remain constantly aware of their personal environment and must be alert to the activities of others in the immediate area. All members of an inspection team are required to comply with the OPCW Health and Safety Policy and Regulations and also with the inspected State Party national and site-specific health and safety policies and regulations, and, where appropriate, also with those of a relevant Host State.

3.3 *INSPECTED STATES PARTIES*

3.3.1 Inspected States Parties (or, where applicable, Host States) shall assign the highest priority to the health and safety of people and the protection of the environment. To this end, information on national safety and health standards, local health and safety requirements, disclosure of relevant known hazards, and the availability of on-site support shall, where reasonably practicable, be provided to the Technical Secretariat in advance of inspections. Where this is not practicable the appropriate health and safety information shall be included in the initial inspection team briefing.

3.3.2   An inspected State Party shall be responsible for ensuring that the health and safety risks are minimised and shall facilitate the conduct of the inspection in a safe manner. When, despite a high level of safety measures, a risk remains, the inspected State Party shall inform the inspection team leader of the level of risk.

3.3.3   An inspected State Party shall have the right to ensure compliance by all inspection team personnel with its national health and safety policy and regulations and with local, or site-specific requirements and regulations giving consideration to the need to protect national or site confidentiality and in this regard:

(a)   whenever a national or site specific requirement is more stringent than the OPCW provisions or conforms with them, the inspected State Party shall either provide the resources needed to meet its standards or waive their enforcement;

(b)   whenever an OPCW requirement is more stringent than the national or site-specific (Host State's) provisions, the inspection team leader shall have the right to require all OPCW inspection team members to conform to OPCW Policy and Regulations, as long as it does not infringe upon site-specific health, safety and confidentiality requirements. The team leader may also encourage all other personnel to comply with them as far as is reasonably practicable; and

(c)   differences in the interpretation of the applicable health and safety policy and regulations that cannot be resolved on-site will be referred by the inspection team leader to the Director-General for resolution, taking due note of the requirement for confidentiality. In situations where the Director-General authorises the team leader to proceed, and the inspected State Party concurs, a clear division of responsibility shall be agreed, in respect to any incident or accident that might result. However, in order to ensure the control of the level of risk for the inspection team members and for the inspected site the inspection will not proceed unless the State Party has concurred. This is without prejudice to the obligations of a State Party to provide access to an inspected facility for the purpose of carrying out inspection activities, in accordance with the Convention.

4.   ORGANISATION AND ADMINISTRATION

4.1   The efficient implementation of the OPCW Health and Safety Policy will require an in-house safety and medical capability. This shall take the form of a Health and Safety Office within the Organisation, with the right, when necessary and appropriate, of direct access to the Director-General in matters pertaining to the health and safety of OPCW personnel.

4.2   The Health and Safety Office's size and structure shall be sufficient to ensure that the OPCW Health and Safety Policy and Regulations can be fully implemented, both at the OPCW premises and in the field. The resources required will be related to the size, the location of the facilities and the composition of the Technical Secretariat, particularly the Inspectorate.

4.3   In the event of an internal dispute within the OPCW over health and safety issues which cannot be resolved in any other way, the Head of the Health and Safety Office shall refer the matter to the Director-General for resolution, taking due note of the requirement for confidentiality.

5.   GENERAL PRINCIPLES
The Health and Safety Office will adopt a mode of operation based on the assessment and management of risk.

5.1   *RISK ASSESSMENT*

5.1.1   GENERAL CONSIDERATIONS ON RISK ASSESSMENT
A risk assessment will be conducted as part of inspection and activity planning in order to minimise health and safety risks. This assessment shall include, *inter alia*, an evaluation of environmental, structural, physical and chemical hazards as well as radiation, endemic diseases and appropriate ways of managing them. Where this evaluation implies undue knowledge of issues protected by confidentiality restrictions, the relevant components of the risk assessment in terms of level and measures to be adopted shall be provided by the inspected State Party. Risk assessments will be updated during inspections as appropriate. Risk assessment procedures will be standardised throughout the OPCW.

5.1.2   CHEMICAL HAZARD DATA
The Health and Safety Office will maintain comprehensive chemical hazard data for scheduled chemicals and other hazardous chemicals.

5.1.3   NON-CHEMICAL HAZARDS
The OPCW Health and Safety Office will give attention not only to chemical hazards, but to any hazard which a working environment may present to OPCW personnel. The dangers of explosives in working areas, including unexploded ordnance, may be a particular hazard to OPCW personnel, and must receive attention in the health and safety plan for any activity. Attention will also be given to aspects such as radiation, noise, dust, mechanical, electrical and environmental hazards, the use of pressure vessels and lasers, etc.

5.2   *RISK MANAGEMENT*

5.2.1   GENERAL CONSIDERATIONS ON RISK MANAGEMENT
The fundamental principle to be observed in any location or operation involving hazardous environments (such as hazardous chemicals or explosives) is to limit the potential exposure to a minimum number of personnel, for a minimum period of time, and to a minimum amount of the hazardous material consistent with safe and efficient operations.

5.2.2   DETECTION AND MONITORING
Monitoring of the environment for the presence of hazards will be undertaken whenever possible, both before and during any operation. Monitoring shall be subject to national, site-specific and, when relevant, OPCW Regulations, as well as confidentiality. Approved monitors for Schedule 1 chemicals, preferably with alarms or, when appropriate, suitable, approved and agreed industrial equipment will be used at the inspection site to monitor the presence of hazardous chemical substances. When selecting monitoring devices, consideration must be given to national and, when relevant, OPCW standards.

5.2.3   PROTECTION
(a) The use of protective clothing and equipment is the least desirable method of preventing exposure of personnel to hazardous chemicals. Efforts must be made to reduce dependence upon protective clothing and equipment in hazardous environ-

ments through the reasonable use of engineering and administrative controls such as ventilation, isolation, and elimination of all non-essential entries into hazardous areas. The appropriate risk assessment must demonstrate that such alternatives have been explored.

(b) In addition to the initial risk assessment based on available information on possible hazards, the selection and use of protective clothing and equipment will also be based on monitoring results and operational requirements, bearing in mind the physiological limitations imposed by certain environments.

(c) Keeping in mind that inspection teams will have to perform their duties in a wide range of locations and environments, the procurement of an appropriate range of safety and protective equipment is required. No OPCW personnel shall be in a toxic industrial or Schedule 1 chemical operating area without being issued with appropriate safety and ocular/cutaneous/respiratory protection equipment. Consideration must be given as required to other protective requirements (e.g. hard hats or safety shoes).

(d) All protective clothing and equipment used by OPCW personnel must be approved by the Director-General or his designated representative on the advice of the Health and Safety Office of the OPCW. Such approval shall be based upon appropriate tests and procedures for certification and the provision of certificates of approval. During an inspection any specific protective clothing and equipment used by OPCW personnel must be approved by the Director-General or his designated representative on the advice of the Health and Safety Office of the OPCW.

5.2.4   CONTAMINATION CONTROL

All operations must be conducted with the objective of avoiding contamination, or limiting the spread of contamination where it already exists. If contamination is unavoidable, appropriate decontamination equipment and procedures will be used, as identified in the health and safety plan for the operation in accordance with standards approved by the Director-General.

5.2.5   EQUIPMENT

(a) During the equipment procurement process by the OPCW, due consideration shall be given to the provisions contained in this Policy and complementary OPCW health and safety documents. Equipment with the least amount of hazard to the operator that is consistent with specific inspection requirements shall be selected.

(b) All OPCW equipment (not covered by paragraph 5.2.3 (d)) for use in hazardous environments must be approved by the Health and Safety Office. Only equipment that sufficiently ensures the health and safety of OPCW personnel, in accordance with OPCW requirements, will be selected.

5.3   *HEALTH AND SAFETY REQUIREMENTS*

5.3.1   OPCW STANDARDS

The means by which this policy will be implemented is contained in the OPCW Health and Safety Regulations. Guidance for the application of these Regulations is contained in the OPCW Health and Safety Guidelines document.

5.3.2   NATIONAL HEALTH AND SAFETY STANDARDS

(a) Considerable variation exists in national health and safety standards. The Head of the Health and Safety Office shall ensure that due regard is given to meet these standards by the OPCW during the planning and conduct of activities. The Health and Safety Office shall establish and maintain a database of the relevant, principal health and safety regulations of Member States. Subject to the approval of relevant national or local authorities, on the basis of inspected site safety and confidentiality, additional health and safety measures may need to be provided or arranged as appropriate to comply with OPCW standards.

(b) States Parties are obligated to render all possible agreed assistance to OPCW personnel in medical, health or safety-related issues. Where national health and safety standards are different from those adopted by the OPCW, the provisions of paragraphs 3.3 and 5.5.1 will apply.

(c) Inspections will be preceded by the preparation and adoption of a written health and safety plan that will include provision for compliance with required OPCW and, where appropriate, national health and safety standards. Decisions on the need to include health and safety personnel and equipment on the inspection will be based on the type of inspection and its location. Compliance with national standards and site regulations during all types of inspections, particularly in the absence of prior relevant agreement (e.g. challenge inspections or alleged use) will require discussion with representatives of the inspected State Party and the possible modification of the health and safety plan at the POE or at the site.

5.3.3   LOCAL HEALTH AND SAFETY CONSIDERATIONS

(a) OPCW personnel engaged in inspection activities in various parts of the world will encounter varying degrees of health and safety risk. The Head of the Health and Safety Office must ensure that due regard is given to such variations during the planning and conduct of activities, and must also ensure that appropriate measures are contained in the written health and safety plan.

(b) Health and safety planning must take account of the unique requirements presented by specific types of OPCW inspections or other activities.

5.3.4   PACKAGING AND TRANSPORTATION OF HAZARDOUS CHEMICALS

The overall objective of packaging and labelling is to ensure that materials can withstand the risks of handling, the shocks of transportation, and can be correctly identified. Adequate packaging and labelling must be accomplished prior to any movement of hazardous substances or environmental samples, and must be in accordance with the relevant national or international codes or regulations.

5.4   *HEALTH AND SAFETY WITHIN THE OPCW*

5.4.1   MEDICAL SUPPORT

(a) A comprehensive medical and health plan must be developed for the OPCW by the Health and Safety Office, and must take account of the health requirements for the OPCW as a whole. Its basic elements would include provision for preventive medicine measures, a protective programme, and up-to-date medical care/treatment/rehabilitation aspects. Effective procedures must be developed for emergency medical evacuation from deployment sites.

(b) A medical surveillance programme must be implemented, including pre-employment, periodic, episodic and termination examinations as appropriate for the job description of individual persons. The plan shall also contain procedures for the co-ordination of the efforts, rights and obligations of the medical service of the inspected State Party (or Host State) and of the medical representatives of an inspection team.

(c) A medical documentation system will be adopted that makes appropriate provision for the proper maintenance of personal medical records. Records will be maintained of cumulative exposures and monitoring/surveillance results during deployments, and a medical summary record will be compiled to accompany deployments for all personnel. Non-confidential statistical data on accidents, illness, etc. will be collected and provided to the management of the Technical Secretariat at regular intervals. All data concerning an inspector's health, including the dynamics of its changes, as well as information about acute and cumulative effects should be placed in a specially designed database.

(d) Medical support for OPCW operations will include provision for health maintenance based on local conditions, medical response to toxic exposures, and medical treatment and evacuation after accidents, trauma, and serious illness. A heat-illness prevention programme will be developed and implemented during all operations using protective clothing.

5.4.2 GENERAL OPCW BUILDING AND OFFICE SAFETY
The OPCW Health and Safety Office will consider the health and safety of all OPCW personnel in all working environments. This extends from hazardous inspection locations to administrative offices. The Health and Safety Office will implement a comprehensive OPCW Building safety plan.

5.4.3 LABORATORY SAFETY
Hazardous chemical operations and storage which are performed in the OPCW Laboratory will be subject to the OPCW Health and Safety Regulations. When operating in other national laboratories, the provisions of para. 3.3 above will apply. Regarding the OPCW Laboratory, due regard must be given to safe design features, access control, and good laboratory practice.

5.5 *HEALTH AND SAFETY PRINCIPLES DURING INSPECTIONS*

5.5.1 INSPECTION TEAM MEMBERS
To ensure the health and safety of inspection team members and of the inspected site without impairing confidentiality during all inspections, particularly challenge inspections, and subject to the provisions of the Convention, the following procedures shall apply whenever the inspected State Party deems appropriate:

(a) the use of any safety equipment shall be subject to agreement before the inspection begins. The agreement (e.g. facility agreement, managed access rules) shall be subject to the need to meet site-specific safety and confidentiality considerations in accordance with site safety rules and regulations, particularly when pertaining to sensitive areas of an inspected site;

(b) after reaching agreement on the use of health and safety equipment the inspected State Party will provide the health and safety equipment, including, *inter alia*, personal monitors, protective clothing and masks, provided the equipment meets OPCW standards and Regulations, as applicable; and

(c) at the end of an inspection, if the inspected State Party so requests, any piece of health and safety equipment involved in the inspection activities will be left on the site of the inspected State Party in order to comply with Health and Safety Regulations and/or in order to prevent the disclosure of confidential information. Where this provision is invoked, the inspected State Party shall make arrangements for the immediate replacement of the OPCW equipment. In the particular case of a challenge inspection, any replacement of health and safety equipment could be subject to the provisions of Article IX, para. 23.

5.5.2   HEALTH AND SAFETY CONSIDERATIONS FOR OBSERVERS

(a) Due to the unique situation of the observer participating in a challenge inspection, including the lack of control over health and safety background and training,
neither the OPCW nor the inspected State Party can take full responsibility for the
observer's health and safety. However, where reasonable and practical, the OPCW
and the inspected State Party will provide the observer with medical care, assistance
and information to ensure compliance with the OPCW health and safety plan for
the inspection and any relevant national or site-specific regulations, as the inspected
State Party deems appropriate. Costs so incurred shall be borne by the requesting
State Party.

(b) The requesting State Party shall take all necessary measures prior to departure to
prepare the observer within the area of health and safety, according to the identified or anticipated level of risk to be encountered during the challenge inspection.
Documentation of such preparation (e.g. medical and training records, etc.) in the
format specified in the OPCW Health and Safety Regulations shall be provided by
the observer to the inspected State Party prior to the commencement of inspection
activities. The inspected State Party shall provide the observer with, as appropriate,
the same health and safety information as provided to the inspection team.

(c) The observer, with the guidance of the inspection team leader, shall at all times
comply with the relevant provisions of the OPCW health and safety plan, as well
as with any national or site-specific regulations. The observer cannot take any independent actions during inspections.

6.   TRAINING

6.1   Training is the single most important tool available to the OPCW to enable individuals
to take responsibility for their own health and safety and to make optimum use of the
equipment and procedures provided by the OPCW.

6.2   The Director-General of the OPCW is responsible for ensuring that health and safety
protection issues are adequately covered in training programmes, and that re-training/
update courses occur on a regular and adequate basis. Standards of training in safety-
related subjects must be monitored by the Health and Safety Office of the OPCW, wherever such training may occur. The Director-General is responsible for the safety of training methods used by the OPCW, which must be approved by the Director-General or his
designated representative on the advice of the Head of the Health and Safety Office.

6.3   Training in all safety-related procedures must be practically oriented, with an adequate
theoretical background. For those personnel that need certification for the use of protective clothing and equipment, training must include test exposures to a challenge agent
(using 2-Chlorobenzal malanonitrile [CS] or other suitable training agents). There must
be emphasis on the development of equipment familiarity and confidence.

6.4   The OPCW shall provide specialist training modules for the training and qualification of
OPCW health and safety personnel.

6.5   Safety-related training must be followed by assessment and qualification of personnel.

6.6   It is essential that minimum proficiency standards for key safety-related activities are
specified, achieved, and maintained. The range of activities for which an individual will
be expected to maintain proficiency will depend on the duties assigned, and will be
specified in the relevant post description. The Head of the Health and Safety Office will
be responsible for ensuring that proficiency standards are met and maintained.

7.   WAIVERS

7.1   A fundamental principle of the OPCW is strict adherence to its Health and Safety Policy and Regulations and the Health and Safety Guidelines, and the avoidance of all waivers.

7.2   In situations where it is necessary to deviate from strict compliance with the OPCW Health and Safety Regulations in order fully to meet the object and purpose of the Convention, a team leader may seek a temporary release from the Regulations. Any such release would have to be fully evaluated and justified in a formal request for the granting of a waiver by the Director-General on the advice of the Head of the Health and Safety Office.

7.3   Waivers may be granted only by the Director-General of the OPCW, who:
         (a) will ensure the existence of compelling operational reasons for the granting of a waiver;
         (b) will ensure that adequate compensatory or complementary measures are in effect, when applicable; and
         (c) will take note of an inspected State Party's right to protect sensitive installations, and to prevent the disclosure of confidential information and data, not related to the Convention.

7.4   The Director-General may delegate waiver authority to a designated representative if he believes it to be necessary for operational reasons or to meet specific provisions of the Convention.

8.   AMENDMENTS

8.1   Proposed amendments to the OPCW Health and Safety Policy shall be submitted by the Director-General to the Conference of States Parties for formal approval.

8.2   Proposed amendments to the OPCW Health and Safety Regulations shall be submitted to the Executive Council for approval pending confirmation by the next meeting of the Conference of State Parties.

8.3   Amendments to OPCW Health and Safety Guidelines, in line with the approved Policy and Regulations, shall be approved and implemented by the Director-General.

8.4   Once approved, amendments shall be implemented by the Director-General as soon as practicable, or in any case within 30 days.

OPCW HEALTH AND SAFETY REGULATIONS[20]

TABLE OF CONTENTS

[20] Contained in PC XIII/B/WP.2, Annex.

1. INTRODUCTION

    (a) The OPCW Health and Safety Regulations, hereinafter referred to as "OPCW Regulations", set out the means by which the OPCW Health and Safety Policy, hereinafter referred to as "OPCW Policy", is implemented. The OPCW Regulations form a consistent basis for the development of the OPCW Health and Safety Technical Guidelines, hereinafter referred to as "OPCW Guidelines".
    (b) Risk Assessment and Risk Management principles will contribute to ensure the health and safety of OPCW personnel in their activities.

2. RISK ASSESSMENT AND RISK MANAGEMENT
    A risk is characterised by the probability of an occurrence of an event and the level of expected damage associated with this event should it occur.

2.1 *INTRODUCTION*
    (a) This section contains a purely technical description of the risk assessment and risk management processes. These processes shall not be interpreted as a requirement for the Inspected State Party (ISP) to provide more information than is required under the terms of the Convention.
    (b) The general principles of risk assessment and risk management are based on the following methodological process:
        (i) taking into account the potential hazards relevant to health and safety;
        (ii) assessment of the risks associated with such significant hazards (level of damage, probability of occurrence) and a decision on the acceptability of such risks;

(iii) management of the risks by using technical and organisational measures of prevention and protection;

(iv) recording the assessment and deciding upon the frequency of review.

(c) Adequate training of personnel will greatly contribute to minimising risks.

2.2   *RISK ASSESSMENT*

(a) Risk assessment provides a tool for estimating the risks, both initial and after considering the existing or proposed measures aimed at minimising those risks. The potential for and the consequences of hazards have to be carefully considered on the basis of available data before undertaking any activity.

(b) In cases where, by the nature of the operation, occurrence of a hazard is expected (such as in emergency destruction, training, or certain preventive maintenance operations), its consequences are to be determined and hence the measures defined, in order to ensure that personnel, objects, and the environment are either protected or not subject to exposure.

(c) Risk assessment will be based upon available data on hazards. If the probability of occurrence of a hazard or its associated level of damage cannot be appropriately assessed, the risk assessment may have to consider the most credible worst-case scenario.

2.3   *RISK MANAGEMENT*

(a) Risk management consists of applying technical, medical, organisational and administrative procedures to safeguard health and safety. It is aimed at reducing the risks to acceptable levels. The number of individuals exposed to risks, and the exposure period, shall be minimised.

(b) If the risk involved with a specific activity is considered to be unacceptable, the activity shall be modified until the risk falls within acceptable limits or, if that is not possible, the activity shall not be performed,

(c) Risk management measures to be taken as a result of the risk assessment can be divided into two different categories:

(i) preventive measures;

(ii) protective measures.

(d) Technical, medical, organisational and administrative measures may be applied in combination or separately. Potential interaction between such measures, and combinations of their effect on the situation, must be considered.

(e) Action should continuously be undertaken to ensure that the residual risks are contained within acceptable limits. If, for any reason, the risk exceeds acceptable limits, corrective measures must be undertaken to bring the risk back within its acceptable limits.

(f) Preventive and/or protective measures shall be adjusted according to the evolution of the risk.

3.   HEALTH AND SAFETY WITHIN THE OPCW PREMISES

3.1   *HEALTH AND SAFETY PLAN*

(a) The Health and Safety Office will prepare a health and safety plan for each building. While preparing and implementing this plan the principles of the risk assessment and risk management processes will be implemented. This plan will cover the following topics:

(i) Nomination of staff responsible for implementation and monitoring of the plan. This will involve the appointment of area/divisional representatives;

  (ii) Requirements for compliance with host state, national and/or local regulations, rules and guidelines. To this purpose workplace standards are important and must include as a minimum:

   (aa) work at visual display units;
   (bb) manual handling of loads (lifting practices);
   (cc) environmental comfort;
   (dd) lighting standards;
   (ee) electricity supplies, fittings and cables; and
   (ff) maintenance of the building and equipment.

  (iii) Induction and maintenance training of OPCW personnel regarding the health and safety aspects of office work;
  (iv) Provisions for fire prevention, first aid and emergency procedures;
  (v) Safety of visitors and contractors; and
  (vi) Consideration of special hazards.

(b) The health and safety plan will be distributed to and acknowledged by all employees and contractors.

(c) The Health and Safety Office will carry out a full health and safety inspection at least annually, sending a report to the Director-General.

(d) The Health and Safety Plan must be regularly updated according to results of inspections and changing requirements.

3.2 *EMERGENCY PROVISIONS*

(a) Plans must be established to deal with emergency situations.

(b) The requirements of local and national fire regulations must be met.

3.3 *OPCW PREMISES*

(a) In OPCW buildings the Occupational Hygienist will be responsible for conducting the necessary environmental monitoring. The Senior Medical Officer will be responsible for conducting the biological monitoring, if any.

(b) The Occupational Hygienist will be responsible for overseeing the cleaning, daily maintenance and periodical upkeep of the equipment to be used for office detection and monitoring purposes.

(c) If inspection equipment brought back to OPCW premises from inspection sites is contaminated, contamination control procedures are essential. Detailed procedures regarding decontamination of equipment, and safe disposal of toxic chemicals, contaminated clothing and equipment are described in the OPCW Guidelines.

(d) Laboratory activities will be in accordance with ISO Guide 25 and will also be based on Good Laboratory Practices, if applicable.

(e) The application of the Dutch Law and OPCW Regulations to health and safety within the OPCW Premises shall be in accordance with the provisions of the OPCW Headquarters Agreement.

(f) Safety regarding laboratory activities not covered by the provisions of ISO Guide 25, Good Laboratory Practices or applicable Dutch Law are detailed in the OPCW Guidelines.

3.4 *HEALTH AND SAFETY AUDITS*

(a) The Health and Safety Plan must be audited on a regular basis. The auditing procedures are detailed in the OPCW Guidelines.

(b) Audits must assess the organisational and the technical elements of the health and safety plan and its application by OPCW personnel.

4.   HEALTH AND SAFETY PRINCIPLES DURING INSPECTIONS

4.1   *BASIC PRINCIPLES*
         Inspectors shall comply with the ISP national and site-specific health and safety policy
         and regulations, and OPCW Policy and Regulations.
         (a) Activities during inspections shall be performed in accordance with para. 43 of Part
              II of the Verification Annex.
         (b) Some variation from the strict implementation of the OPCW Regulations may be
              necessary to comply with specific requirements under provision of para. 43 of Part
              II of the Verification Annex or of the Confidentiality Annex.
         (c) Such variations do not constitute a waiver situation since they are consistent with
              the OPCW Policy. Any such variations shall be reported in writing.
         (d) In accordance with the OPCW Policy, the inspection team should aim to maintain
              the health and safety procedures to be applied as close as possible to the procedures
              as detailed in the OPCW Guidelines.
         (e) No activity should involve a health and safety risk unacceptable to the inspection
              team or the ISP.
         (f) In the context of the implementation at an inspection site of the Risk Assessment
              and Risk Management principles described in section 2, the specific measures taken
              subject to the consent of and in close co-ordination with the ISP, shall not prejudice
              the relevant provisions of the Convention. However, Risk Management provides
              for flexibility for accommodating all relevant requirements.

4.2   *DETECTION AND MONITORING*
         Should the inspection team consider detection and monitoring a necessity for health and
         safety purposes, it will consult with the ISP on that necessity. If the ISP gives its consent
         to such detection and monitoring, it will generally perform these activities. The ISP may
         also suggest that these activities are carried out by the inspection team. If agreement is
         reached, the following may be involved, singly or in combination, to satisfy the concerns
         of the inspection team.
         (a) Provision of data by the State Party.
         (b) Detection and monitoring performed by the State Party, using its own equipment.
         (c) Detection and monitoring performed by the inspection team in the least intrusive
              manner, e.g. using equipment on alarm mode.

4.3   *MODIFICATION OF INSPECTION ACTIVITIES FOR HEALTH AND/OR SAFETY*
         REASONS
         (a) The inspection team leader, after consultation with the ISP, may consider that a
              particular activity cannot be carried out or completed in the planned way for health
              and safety reasons, or for reasons related to the implementation of paragraph 43 of
              part II of the Verification Annex. In such a case an alternative inspection procedure
              should be adopted in consultation with the ISP in order to accomplish the inspec-
              tion goals. A higher level of protection, or alternative preventive and corrective
              measures may be used for this purpose. It is the responsibility of the inspection team
              leader, only after the agreement of the ISP, to decide whether or not to change the
              inspection procedure after having reviewed the alternative inspection scenarios.
         (b) The causes of an accident must be determined, and, where necessary, the risk as-
              sessment, health and safety procedures and inspection activities must be reviewed
              before the affected inspection activities resume. Such review, and possible changes
              to inspection procedures, should be agreed with the ISP.

5. MEDICAL REQUIREMENTS

5.1 *FITNESS FOR WORK*

(a) All OPCW job descriptions shall include a section which sets out the physical and mental requirements of the position.

(b) All personnel must undergo a medical examination prior to commencing employment with the OPCW. Criteria for establishing the fitness of all inspectors and the OPCW requirements for initial and periodic medical examinations are contained in the OPCW Guidelines. The examination will normally be performed in a candidate's country of recruitment by an OPCW approved Physician. The results of the examination will be reviewed by the Senior Medical Officer of the OPCW, or a delegated medical officer, to determine a candidate's fitness to work with the OPCW.

(c) Withholding of medical information required for the pre-employment medical examination could result in an employee's subsequent dismissal from the OPCW.

(d) Staff members will have periodic medical examinations in order to ensure that their fitness to work is maintained, and as a preventative health measure. The frequency of such medical examinations depends on the staff member's job and his age. Inspectors, particularly those with the potential to be exposed to hazardous chemicals, will undergo additional specific periodical examinations. Details appear in the OPCW Guidelines.

(e) Where a staff member becomes permanently unfit to perform his duties as a result of injury or illness, it will be attempted to further employ him/her in an alternative post. If this is not possible, the Head of the Health and Safety Office may recommend to the Director-General that the staff member's contract be terminated on medical grounds.

(f) If in accordance with paragraph 43 of Part II of the Verification Annex, the ISP requests specific medical information in regard to the health and safety regulations on-site related to the fitness of an inspector, the inspection team leader will consult with ISP representatives on the ways to obtain such information. In case of divergences between the ISP and the inspection team, this shall be resolved in accordance with paragraph 3.3.3 (c) of the OPCW Policy.

5.2 *MEDICAL TREATMENT*

(a) The OPCW has the responsibility to provide, or to oversee medical treatment relating to occupational illness and injury. Staff members must obtain medical treatment for non-occupational illness or injury via their family doctor, or other local medical service. Details of the provisions of medical treatment, including that during travel, are contained in the OPCW Guidelines.

(b) Wherever possible, religious and cultural considerations will be taken into account in the provision of medical treatment.

5.3 *MEDICAL TREATMENT DURING OFFICIAL TRAVEL*

(a) Obtaining treatment on official travel unrelated to inspection or training activities will be the responsibility of the OPCW staff member concerned. In the event of injury or illness abroad, the advice of the Health and Safety Office can be sought. The Health and Safety Office will provide staff members with information relevant to health needs when travelling.

(b) Provisions for medical treatment during inspector training will be negotiated and recorded in an agreement to be concluded between the OPCW and the involved parties.

(c) During travel with inspection teams:

     (i)   Basic first aid will be provided by the Paramedic or Medical Officer on the team, or, in teams without either, by the team member with secondary health and safety duties.

     (ii) Where inspection teams include medical personnel medical treatment should only be provided by qualified personnel. In other circumstances treatment will be sought from local medical officers.

     (iii) In cases requiring hospitalisation, the OPCW Senior Medical Officer or his delegate must be promptly notified.

     (iv) Assistance may be requested from the inspected State Party. When appropriate, such assistance will be provided in accordance with the facility agreement.

     (v) Where medical evacuation of a patient is required, the inspected State Party will assist, to the extent possible, at all stages, including transportation of the patient to a departure point. Maximum effort shall be made to transport a patient to a suitable medical facility as soon as possible.

     (vi) While it is not normally the policy of the OPCW that its health and safety personnel should provide treatment for non-OPCW personnel, in an emergency situation where no local health personnel are present, or when non-OPCW personnel are injured by an inspection related activity, emergency first aid will be rendered.

(d)   Requests under Article X of the Convention for medical treatment of suspected chemical casualties will normally be met by medical personnel from assisting State Parties. Health and safety personnel from inspection teams will not normally render such treatment, unless instructed otherwise by the Director-General of the OPCW.

5.4   *MEDICAL RECORDS AND ACCIDENT/INJURY REPORTING*

(a)   The Health and Safety Office will keep records of all employees' known exposures to hazardous substances, reflecting any relevant clinical, laboratory, or monitoring results, as well as records of pre-employment or periodic medical examinations. Such records will be kept indefinitely. Relevant aspects of these records will be summarised in a standardised format and shall be brought onto the inspected site for each inspector. Records of general medical conditions occurring during duty travel, or occupational illness or injury, must be maintained in the facility where the employee is treated, and transmitted to the OPCW in summarised form. All medical records are confidential.

(b)   All incidents causing, or nearly causing, injuries or death during duty in all places will be reported to the Senior Safety Officer. An investigation will be carried out by the Senior Safety Officer and supervisor of the personnel concerned. Reporting and investigating details can be found in the OPCW Guidelines.

5.5   *CLEAN AIR POLICY*

All employees have the right to a smoke-free workplace. The OPCW recognises the hazard to health of active and passive smoking and discourages staff members from smoking. The OPCW will establish a clean air policy to be developed in co-operation with staff.

5.6   *MEDICAL ASPECTS OF STAFF REGULATIONS*

(a)   Medical disability pensions shall be established by the OPCW only in cases where damage to health of a staff member has been causally linked to activities undertaken for and on behalf of the OPCW. The extent of disability shall be determined by examination in suitable OPCW approved medical institutions. Injuries sustained in the course of OPCW missions shall be compensated by the OPCW.

(b) The OPCW shall provide medical insurance for inspectors for the period of their training, and shall agree with a State Party providing training and an insurance company of that country or an international insurance company on the procedures for medical assistance in cases of serious illness or injury.

(c) Negligence or misconduct of Health and Safety Office staff in implementing the provisions of the OPCW Policy and Regulations shall be deemed as professional inadequacy and could result in termination of employment.

6.   HEALTH AND SAFETY TRAINING

6.1   *INTRODUCTION*
Adequate attention to the training and education of individuals in Risk Assessment/Management in relation to their work enables them to take personal responsibility for their safety.

6.2   *RESPONSIBILITIES*
In addition to the responsibilities for health and safety training set out in paragraph 6.2 of the OPCW Policy, the following apply.

(a) The Senior Safety Officer must identify and update on the basis of experience general and specialist safety training needs in consultation with employees' immediate supervisors who will advise the Head of the Health and Safety Office of any such requirement.

(b) The appropriate training authority will be responsible for arranging and recording all necessary safety training.

6.3   *NEW EMPLOYEES*
All new staff will receive basic safety instruction by the Health and Safety Office.

6.4   *HEALTH AND SAFETY TRAINING CONTENT*
Syllabuses of all Health and Safety training courses will be developed, evaluated, and updated by the appropriate training authority in conjunction with the Health and Safety Office, and are detailed in the OPCW Guidelines.

7.   WAIVERS AND EXEMPTIONS

(a) The goal of the OPCW is the avoidance of all waivers and exemptions from and strict adherence to OPCW Policy and Regulations.

(b) Variations from standard OPCW Regulations and Guidelines made in order to comply with paragraph 43 of Part II of the Verification Annex, do not constitute waiver situations since they are consistent with the OPCW Policy.

(c) On the rare occasion that a waiver may be required, the procedure is contained in the OPCW Guidelines.

7.1   *REQUESTS FOR WAIVERS*
When compliance with the OPCW Policy and Regulations cannot be achieved, a request for waiver should be submitted through the Head of the Health and Safety Office to the Director-General or an Authorised Official.

7.2   *GRANTING OF WAIVERS*
(a) Waivers may be granted by the Director-General or an Authorised Official.
(b) A request for amendment will be initiated when factors or circumstances requir-

ing a change to the original waiver are identified and must also be granted by the Director-General or an Authorised Official.

7.3 *EXEMPTIONS*

Requests for exemptions will be submitted to the Director-General.

UNDERSTANDING CONTAINED IN PARAGRAPH 3.2 OF PC-XIII/B/WP.2

"The Group understood that subparagraph 4.2 of the Draft OPCW Health and Safety Regulations does not prejudice the obligation of inspected States Parties to provide available data based on detection and monitoring, to an agreed extent necessary to satisfy concerns that may exist regarding the health and safety of the inspection team. In cases where detection and monitoring, as referred to in subparagraph 5.2.2 of the Draft OPCW Health and Safety Policy (PC-IX/B/WP.5) cannot be carried out, alternative risk assessment data or information will be provided by the inspected State Party, as provided for in subparagraph 5.1.1 of the Draft OPCW Health and Safety Policy."

14. FACILITY AGREEMENTS
(ARTICLES IV, V, AND VI(3))

14.1 Model for Schedule 1 facilities

C-III/DEC.14 adopted by the Conference of the States Parties at its Third Session on 20 November 1998 and entitled "Model Facility Agreement for Schedule 1 facilities"

The Conference

Recalling that, in accordance with paragraphs 27 and 31 of Part VI of the Verification Annex, the Conference shall consider and approve model agreements for single small-scale facilities as well as for other Schedule 1 facilities;

Bearing in mind subparagraphs 12(i) and (r) of the Paris Resolution;

Recalling that the issue of a model for facility agreements, in accordance with paragraphs 27 and 31 of Part VI of the Verification Annex, was referred by the Conference to the Committee of the Whole (C-I/2, dated 12 May 1997);

Further Recalling its decision on the procedure for addressing unresolved issues during the second intersessional period (C-II/DEC.3, dated 5 December 1997);

Taking note of the decision taken by the Executive Council on the model agreement for Schedule 1 facilities (EC-XII/DEC.1, dated 9 October 1998)·

Taking note of the report submitted to it by the Chairman of the Committee of the Whole on the results of the work on unresolved issues during the second intersessional period (C-III/CoW.2, dated 16 November 1998);

Hereby:
1. Decides to adopt the model agreement for Schedule 1 facilities as contained in the annex to this decision;
2. Further decides to remove the issue of the model agreement for Schedule 1 facilities from the list of unresolved issues.

ANNEX

MODEL FOR FACILITY AGREEMENTS FOR SCHEDULE 1 FACILITIES

The Organisation for the Prohibition of Chemical Weapons, hereinafter referred to as the "Organisation",

and the Government of _____, hereinafter referred to as "the inspected State Party", both constituting the Parties to this Agreement,

have agreed on the following arrangements in relation to the conduct of inspections pursuant to paragraph 3 of Article VI of the Convention on the Prohibition of the Development, Production, Stockpiling and Use of Chemical Weapons and on Their Destruction, hereinafter referred to as "the Convention",

at _____ (insert name of the facility, its precise location, including the address), declared under paragraphs 7 and 8 of Article VI, hereinafter referred to as "the facility":

SECTION 1. GENERAL PROVISIONS

1. The purpose of this Agreement is to facilitate the implementation of the provisions of the Convention in relation to inspections conducted at the facility pursuant to paragraph 3 of

Article VI of the Convention and in accordance with the obligations of the inspected State Party and the Organisation under the Convention.

2. Nothing in this Agreement shall be applied or interpreted in a way that is contradictory to the provisions of the Convention. In case of inconsistency between this Agreement and the Convention, the Convention shall prevail.

3. The Parties have agreed to apply for planning purposes the general factors contained in Attachment 1.

4. The frequency and intensity of inspections at the facility are given in Part B of Attachment 1 and reflect the risk assessment of the Organisation conducted pursuant to paragraphs 23 or 30 of Part VI of the Verification Annex, whichever applies.

5. The inspection team shall consist of no more than _____ persons.

6. The language(s) for communication between the inspection team and the inspected State Party during inspections shall be _____ (insert one or more of the languages of the Convention).

SECTION 2. HEALTH AND SAFETY

1. Health and safety matters are governed by the Convention, the OPCW Health and Safety Policy and Regulations and applicable national, local and facility safety and environmental regulations. The specific arrangements for implementing the relevant provisions of the Convention and the OPCW Health and Safety Policy in relation to inspections at the facility are contained in Attachment 2.

2. All applicable health and safety regulations relevant to the conduct of the inspection at the facility are listed in Attachment 2 and shall be made available for use by the inspection team at the facility.

3. In the course of the pre-inspection briefing the inspection team shall be briefed by the representatives of the facility on all health and safety matters which, in the view of those representatives, are relevant to the conduct of the inspection at the facility, including:

   (a) the health and safety measures at the Schedule 1 facilities to be inspected and the likely risks that may be encountered during the inspection;

   (b) any additional health and safety measures or regulations that need to be observed at the facility;

   (c) procedures to be followed in case of an accident or in case of other emergencies, including a briefing on emergency signals, routes and exits, and the location of emergency meeting points and facilities; and

   (d) specific inspection activities which must be limited within particular areas at the facility, and in particular within those Schedule 1 facilities to be inspected under the inspection mandate, for reasons of health and safety.

   Upon request, the inspection team shall certify receipt of any such information if it is provided in written form.

4. During the course of the inspection, the inspection team shall refrain from any action which by its nature could endanger the safety of the team, the facility or its personnel or could cause harm to the environment. Should the inspected State Party refuse certain inspection activities, it may explain the circumstances and safety considerations involved, and shall provide alternative means for conducting the inspection activities.

5. In the case of emergency situations or accidents involving inspection team members while at the facility, the inspection team shall comply with the facility emergency procedures and the inspected State Party shall to the extent possible provide medical and other assistance in a timely and effective manner with due regard to the rules of medical ethics if medical assistance is requested. Information on medical services and facilities to be used for this purpose is contained in Part D of Attachment 2. If the Organisation undertakes other measures for

medical support in regard to inspection team members involved in emergency situations or accidents, the inspected State Party will render assistance to such measures to the extent possible. The Organisation will be responsible for the consequences of such measures.

6. In accordance with the OPCW Health and Safety Policy, the inspected State Party may provide available data based on detection and monitoring, to the agreed extent necessary to satisfy concerns that may exist regarding the health and safety of the inspection team.

SECTION 3. CONFIDENTIALITY

1. Matters related to confidentiality are governed by the Convention, including its Confidentiality Annex, and the OPCW Policy on Confidentiality. The specific arrangements for implementing the provisions of the Convention and the OPCW Policy on Confidentiality in relation to the protection of confidential information at the facility are contained in Attachment 3.

SECTION 4. MEDIA AND PUBLIC RELATIONS

1. Media and public relations are governed by the OPCW Media and Public Relations Policy. The specific arrangements for the inspection team's contacts with the media or the public, if any, in relation to inspections of the facility are contained in Attachment 4.

SECTION 5. INSPECTION EQUIPMENT

1. As agreed between the inspected State Party and the Organisation, the approved equipment listed in Part A of Attachment 5 will, at the discretion of the Organisation and on a routine basis, be used specifically for the Schedule 1 inspection. The equipment will be used in accordance with the Convention, the relevant decisions taken by the Conference of the States Parties, and any agreed procedures contained in Attachment 5.

2. The provisions of paragraph 1 above are without prejudice to paragraphs 27 to 29 of Part II of the Verification Annex.

3. The items of equipment available on-site, not belonging to the Organisation which the inspected State Party has volunteered to provide to the inspection team upon its request for use on-site during the conduct of inspections together with any procedures for the use of such equipment, if required, any requested support which can be provided and conditions for the provision of equipment are listed in Part B of Attachment 5. Prior to any use of such equipment the inspection team may confirm that the performance characteristics of such equipment are consistent with those for similar OPCW approved equipment, or – with respect to items of equipment which are not on the list of OPCW approved equipment – are consistent with the intended purpose for using such equipment.

4. Requests from the inspection team for the inspected State Party during the inspection to provide equipment mentioned in paragraph 3 above, shall be made in writing by an authorised member of the inspection team using the form contained in Attachment 5. The same procedure will also apply to other requests of the inspection team in accordance with paragraph 30 of Part II of the Verification Annex.

5. Agreed procedures for the decontamination of any equipment are contained in Part C of Attachment 5.

6. For the purpose of verification, the list of agreed on-site monitoring instruments, if any, as well as agreed conditions, procedures for use, maintenance, repair, modification, replacement and provisions for the inspected State Party's support, if required, installation points, and security measures to prevent tampering with such on-site monitoring instruments are contained in Part D of Attachment 5.

SECTION 6. PRE-INSPECTION ACTIVITIES

1. The inspection team shall be given a pre-inspection briefing by the representatives of the facility in accordance with Part II, paragraph 37 of the Verification Annex. The pre-inspection briefing shall include:
    (a) information on the facility as described in Attachment 6;
    (b) health and safety specifications described in section 2 above and detailed in Attachment 2; and
    (c) any changes to the above-mentioned information since the last inspection.
2. Any information about the facility that the inspected State Party has volunteered to provide to the inspection team during the pre-inspection briefing with indications as to which information may be transferred off-site is referenced in Part B of Attachment 6.

SECTION 7. CONDUCT OF THE INSPECTION

7.1 STANDING ARRANGEMENTS
1. The inspection period shall begin immediately upon completion of the pre-inspection briefing, unless agreed otherwise. Upon completion of the pre-inspection briefing, the inspected State Party may on a voluntary basis provide a site tour at the request of the inspection team. Arrangements for the conduct of a site tour, if any, are contained in Attachment 7.
2. Before commencement of inspection activities, the inspection team leader shall inform the representative of the inspected State Party about the initial steps to be taken in implementing the inspection plan. The plan will be adjusted by the inspection team as circumstances warrant throughout the inspection process in consultation with the inspected State Party as to its implementability in regard to paragraph 40 of Part II of the Verification Annex.
3. The activities of the inspection team shall be so arranged as to ensure the timely and effective discharge of its functions and the least possible inconvenience to the inspected State Party and disturbance to the facility inspected. The inspection team shall avoid unnecessarily hampering or delaying the operation of the facility and avoid affecting safety. In particular, the inspection team shall not operate the facility. If the inspection team considers that, to fulfil the mandate, particular operations should be carried out in the facility, it shall request the designated representative of the facility to have them performed.
4. The inspection team shall, upon the request of the inspected State Party, communicate with the personnel of the facility only in the presence of or through a representative of the inspected State Party.
5. The inspected State Party shall, upon request, provide a securable workspace for the inspection team, including adequate space for the storage of equipment. The inspection team shall have the right to seal its workspace.
7.2 ACCESS TO THE DECLARED FACILITY
    The object of the inspection shall be the declared Schedule 1 facility as referenced in Attachment 6.
7.3 ACCESS TO AND INSPECTION OF DOCUMENTATION AND RECORDS
    The agreed list of the documentation and records to be routinely made available for inspection purposes to the inspection team by the inspected State Party during an inspection, as well as arrangements with regard to access to such records for the purpose of protecting confidential information, are contained in Attachment 8. Such documentation and records will be provided to the inspection team upon request.
7.4 SAMPLING AND ANALYSIS
    Without prejudice to paragraphs 52 to 58 of Part II of the Verification Annex, procedures for sampling and analysis for verification purposes are contained in Attachment 9.

7.5 INVENTORY CONTROL DEVICES (FOR SSSF ONLY)

The inspectors may employ, as appropriate, agreed markers or other inventory control devices to facilitate the verification of inventories of equipment as well as chemicals at the facility. Agreed markers or other inventory control devices are contained in Part A of Attachment 5 of this Agreement and inventory control procedures, including procedures for the use of inventory control devices, are contained in Attachment 8 of this Agreement. Such inventory control devices shall be removed upon completion of the inspection.

SECTION 8. VISITS

1. This section applies to visits conducted pursuant to paragraphs 15 and 16 of Part III of the Verification Annex.
2. The size of a team on such a visit shall be kept to the minimum number of personnel necessary to perform the specific tasks for which the visit is being conducted and shall in any case not exceed the size of inspection team referenced in paragraph 5 of Section 1.
3. The duration of the visit pursuant to this Section shall be limited to the minimum time required to perform the specific tasks relating to monitoring systems for which the visit is being conducted and in any case shall not exceed the estimated period of inspection referenced in Part B of Attachment 1 of this Agreement.
4. Access provided to the monitoring systems during the visit shall be limited to that required to perform the specific tasks for which the visit is being conducted, unless otherwise agreed to with the inspected State Party.
5. General arrangements and notifications for a visit shall be the same as for the conduct of an inspection.

SECTION 9. DEBRIEFING AND PRELIMINARY FINDINGS

1. In accordance with paragraph 60 of Part II of the Verification Annex, upon completion of an inspection the inspection team shall meet with representatives of the inspected State Party and the personnel responsible for the inspection site to review the preliminary findings of the inspection team and to clarify any ambiguities. The inspection team shall provide to the representatives of the inspected State Party its preliminary findings in written form according to a standardised format, together with a list of any samples and copies of written information and data gathered and other material to be taken off-site. The document shall be signed by the head of the inspection team. In order to indicate that he has taken notice of the contents of the document, the representative of the inspected State Party shall countersign the document. This meeting shall be completed not later than 24 hours after the completion of the inspection.
2. The document on preliminary findings shall also include, *inter alia*, the list of results of analysis, if conducted on site, records of seals, results of inventories, copies of photographs to be retained by the inspection team, and results of specified measurements. It will be prepared in accordance with the preliminary findings format referenced in Annex 5. Any substantive changes to this format will be made only after consultation with the inspected State Party.
3. Before the conclusion of the debriefing, the inspected State Party may provide comments and clarifications to the inspection team on any issue related to the conduct of the inspection. The inspection team shall provide to the representative of the inspected State Party its preliminary findings in written form sufficiently prior to the conclusion of the debriefing to permit the inspected State Party to prepare any comments and clarifications. The inspected State Party's written comments and clarifications shall be attached to the document on preliminary findings.

SECTION 10. ADMINISTRATIVE ARRANGEMENTS

1. The inspected State Party shall provide or arrange for the provision of the amenities listed in detail in Attachment 10 to the inspection team throughout the duration of the inspection. The inspected State Party shall be reimbursed by the Organisation for such costs incurred by the inspection team, unless agreed otherwise.
2. Requests from the inspection team for the inspected State Party to provide or arrange amenities shall be made in writing by an authorised member of the inspection team[1] using the form contained in Annex 5. Requests shall be made as soon as the need for amenities has been identified. The provision of such requested amenities shall be certified in writing by the authorised member of the inspection team. Copies of all such certified requests shall be kept by both Parties.
3. The inspection team has the right to refuse extra amenities that in its view are not needed for the conduct of the inspection.

SECTION 11. LIABILITIES

1. Any claim by the inspected State Party against the Organisation or by the Organisation against the inspected State Party in respect of any alleged damage or injury resulting from inspections at the facility in accordance with this Agreement, without prejudice to paragraph 22 of the Confidentiality Annex, shall be settled in accordance with international law and, as appropriate, with the provisions of Article XIV of the Convention.

SECTION 12. STATUS OF ATTACHMENTS

1. The Attachments form an integral part of this Agreement. Any reference to the Agreement includes the Attachments. However, in case of any inconsistency between this Agreement and any Attachment, the sections of the Agreement shall prevail.

SECTION 13. AMENDMENTS, MODIFICATIONS AND UPDATES

1. Amendments to the sections of this Agreement may be proposed by either Party and shall be agreed to and enter into force under the same conditions as provided for under paragraph 1 of Section 15.
2. Modifications to the Attachments of this Agreement, other than Attachment 1 and Part B of Attachment 5 may be agreed upon at any time between the representative of the Organisation and the representative of the inspected State Party, each being specifically authorised to do so. The Director-General shall inform the Executive Council about any such modifications. Each Party to this Agreement may revoke its consent to a modification not later than four weeks after it had been agreed upon. After this time period the modification shall take effect.
3. The inspected State Party will update Part A of Attachment 1 and Part B of Attachment 5 as necessary for the effective conduct of inspections. The Organisation will update Part B of Attachment 1 as necessary for the effective conduct of inspections.

SECTION 14. SETTLEMENT OF DISPUTES

1. Any dispute between the Parties that may arise out of the application or interpretation of this

---

[1] The name of the authorised member(s) of the inspection team should be communicated to the inspected State Party no later than at the Point of Entry [footnote in original].

Agreement shall be settled in accordance with Article XIV of the Convention.

SECTION 15. ENTRY INTO FORCE

1. This Agreement shall enter into force upon approval by the Executive Council and signature by the two Parties. If the inspected State Party has additional internal requirements, it shall so notify the Organisation in writing by the date of signature. In such cases, this Agreement shall enter into force on the date that the inspected State Party gives the Organisation written notification that its internal requirements for entry into force have been met.

SECTION 16. DURATION AND TERMINATION

1. This Agreement shall cease to be in force when, as determined by the Executive Council, the provisions of paragraphs 3 and 8 of Article VI and Part VI of the Verification Annex no longer apply to this facility.

Done at _____ in ___ copies, in _____ language(s), each being equally authentic.

ATTACHMENTS
The following attachments shall be completed where applicable:

Attachment 1.   General factors for the conduct of inspections
Attachment 2.   Health and safety requirements and procedures
Attachment 3.   Specific arrangements in relation to the protection of confidential information at the facility
Attachment 4.   Arrangements for the inspection team's contacts with the media or the public
Attachment 5.   Inspection equipment
Attachment 6.   Information on the facility provided in accordance with Section 6
Attachment 7.   Arrangements for site tour
Attachment 8.   Records routinely made available to the inspection team at the facility
Attachment 9.   Sampling and analysis for verification purposes
Attachment 10. Administrative arrangements

ATTACHMENT 1. GENERAL FACTORS FOR THE CONDUCT OF INSPECTIONS

PART A. TO BE PROVIDED AND UPDATED BY THE INSPECTED STATE PARTY:
(a)   Schedule 1 facility(s) working hours, if applicable: ____hrs to____ hrs (days)
(b)   working days:
(c)   holidays or other non-working days:
(d)   inspection activities which could/could not[2] be supported during non-working hours with notation of times and activities:
(e)   any other factors that could adversely effect the effective conduct of inspections:

PART B. TO BE PROVIDED AND UPDATED BY THE ORGANISATION:
Inspection Frequency:
(a)   inspection frequency:

Inspection Intensity:
(b)   maximum estimated period of inspection (for planning purposes):

---
[2] Choose one option [footnote in original].

(c)   approximate inspection team size:

(d)   estimated volume and weight of equipment to be brought on-site

ATTACHMENT 2. HEALTH AND SAFETY REQUIREMENTS AND PROCEDURES

A.   BASIC PRINCIPLES

1.   Applicable health and safety regulations of the OPCW, with agreed variations from strict implementation, if any:

2.   Health and safety regulations applicable at the facility:

3.   Health and safety requirements and regulations agreed between the inspected State Party and the Organisation:

B.   DETECTION AND MONITORING

1.   Applicable specific safety standards for workspace chemical exposure limits and/or concentrations which should be observed during the inspection, if any:

2.   Procedures for detection and monitoring in accordance with the OPCW Health and Safety Policy, including data to be collected by, or provided to, the inspection team:

C.   PROTECTION

1.   Protective equipment to be provided by the OPCW and agreed procedures for equipment certification and use, if required:

2.   Protective equipment to be provided by the inspected State Party, and agreed procedures, personnel training, and personnel qualification tests and certification required; and agreed procedures for use of the equipment:

D.   MEDICAL REQUIREMENTS

1.   Applicable medical standards of the inspected State Party and, in particular, the inspected facility:

2.   Medical screening procedures for members of the inspection team:

3.   Agreed medical assistance to be provided by the inspected State Party:

4.   Emergency medical evacuation procedures:

5.   Agreed additional medical measures to be taken by the inspection team:

6.   Procedures for emergency response to chemical casualties of the inspection team:

E.   MODIFICATION OF INSPECTION ACTIVITIES DUE TO HEALTH AND SAFETY REASONS, AND AGREED ALTERNATIVES TO ACCOMPLISH THE INSPECTION GOALS:

ATTACHMENT 3. SPECIFIC ARRANGEMENTS IN RELATION TO THE PROTECTION OF CONFIDENTIAL INFORMATION AT THE FACILITY

1.   Designation of the classification of the inspected State Party's documents provided to the inspection team:

2.   Specific procedures for access by the inspection team to confidential areas or materials:

3.   Procedures in relation to the certification by the inspection team of the receipt of any documents provided by the inspected facility:

4.   Storage of confidential documents at the inspected facility (including, if applicable, procedures in relation to the use of a dual control container on site):

5.   Procedures for the removal off site of any written information, data and other material gathered by the inspection team:

6.   Procedures for providing the representatives of the inspected State Party with copies of writ-

ten information, inspector's notebooks, data and other material gathered by the inspection team:

7.   Other arrangements, if any:

ATTACHMENT 4. ARRANGEMENTS FOR THE INSPECTION TEAM'S CONTACTS WITH THE MEDIA OR THE PUBLIC

ATTACHMENT 5. INSPECTION EQUIPMENT

PART A. LIST OF EQUIPMENT:

Item of approved inspection equipment	Nature of restriction(s) (location, time periods, etc.), if any	Indication of reason(s) (safety, confidentiality, etc.)	Alternative for meeting inspection requirement(s), if so required by the inspection team

PART B. EQUIPMENT WHICH THE INSPECTED STATE PARTY HAS VOLUNTEERED TO PROVIDE:

Item of equipment	Procedures for use	Support to be provided, if required	Conditions (timing; cost, if any)

PART C. PROCEDURES FOR THE DECONTAMINATION OF EQUIPMENT:

PART D. AGREED ON-SITE MONITORING INSTRUMENTS

REQUEST FOR AND CERTIFICATION OF EQUIPMENT AVAILABLE ON SITE TO BE PROVIDED IN ACCORDANCE WITH PARAGRAPH 3 OF SECTION 5

Date:

Facility:

Inspection number:

Name of the authorised member of the inspection team:

Type and number of item(s) of equipment requested:

Approval of the request by inspected State Party:

Comments on the request by the inspected State Party:

Indication of the costs , if any, for the use of the equipment requested/volunteered:

Certification of the authorised member of the inspection team that the requested item(s) of equipment have been provided:

Comments, if any, by the authorised member of the inspection team in regard to the equipment provided:

Name and signature of the authorised member of the inspection team:

Name and signature of the representative of the inspected State Party:

ATTACHMENT 6. INFORMATION ON THE FACILITY

PART A. TOPICS OF INFORMATION FOR THE PRE-INSPECTION BRIEFING:

(a) specification of the elements constituting the declared facility, including their physical location(s), with indications as to which information may be transferred off-site:

(b) procedures for the unimpeded access within the declared facility

(c) other:

PART B. ANY INFORMATION ABOUT THE FACILITY THAT THE INSPECTED STATE PARTY VOLUNTEERS TO PROVIDE TO THE INSPECTION TEAM DURING THE PRE-INSPECTION BRIEFING WITH INDICATIONS AS TO WHICH MAY BE TRANSFERRED OFF-SITE:

ATTACHMENT 7. ARRANGEMENTS FOR SITE TOUR

The inspected State Party may provide a site tour at the request of the inspection team. The inspected State Party may provide explanations to the inspection team during the site tour.

ATTACHMENT 8. RECORDS ROUTINELY MADE AVAILABLE TO THE INSPECTION TEAM AT THE FACILITY

ATTACHMENT 9. SAMPLING AND ANALYSIS FOR VERIFICATION PURPOSES

PART A. AGREED SAMPLING POINTS CHOSEN WITH DUE CONSIDERATION TO EXISTING SAMPLING POINTS USED BY THE FACILITY(S) OPERATOR(S):
PART B. PROCEDURES FOR TAKING SAMPLES:
PART C. PROCEDURES FOR SAMPLE HANDLING AND SAMPLE SPLITTING:
PART D. PROCEDURES FOR ON-SITE SAMPLE ANALYSIS, IF ANY:
PART E. PROCEDURES FOR OFF-SITE ANALYSIS, IF ANY:
PART F. ARRANGEMENTS IN REGARD TO THE PAYMENT OF COSTS ASSOCIATED WITH THE DISPOSAL OR REMOVAL BY THE INSPECTED STATE PARTY OF HAZARDOUS WASTE GENERATED DURING SAMPLING AND ON-SITE ANALYSIS DURING THE INSPECTION:

ATTACHMENT 10. ADMINISTRATIVE ARRANGEMENTS

PART A. THE AMENITIES DETAILED BELOW SHALL BE PROVIDED TO THE INSPECTION TEAM BY THE INSPECTED STATE PARTY, SUBJECT TO PAYMENT AS INDICATED IN PART B BELOW:
1. International and local official communication (telephone, fax), including calls/faxes between site and headquarters:
2. Vehicles:
3. Working room, including adequate space for the storage of equipment:
4. Lodging:
5. Meals:
6. Medical care:
7. Interpretation services:
   (a) Number of interpreters:
   (b) Estimated interpretation time:
   (c) Languages:
8. Other:

PART B. DISTRIBUTION OF COSTS FOR PROVISIONS OF AMENITIES BY THE INSPECTED STATE PARTY (TICK ONE OPTION FOR EACH AMENITY PROVIDED, AS APPROPRIATE)

Paragraphs 1 to 8 in Part A above	To be paid directly by the OPCW after the inspection	To be paid by the inspection team on behalf of the OPCW during the in-country period	To be paid by the inspected State Party and subsequently reimbursed by the OPCW	To be paid voluntarily by the inspected State Party

PART C. OTHER ARRANGEMENTS:

1. Number of sub-teams (consisting of no less than two inspectors per sub-team) to be accommodated.

REQUEST FOR AND CERTIFICATION OF AMENITIES TO BE PROVIDED
OR ARRANGED

Date:
Facility:
Inspection number:
Category of amenities requested:
Description of amenities requested:
Approval of the request by inspected State Party:
Comments on the request by the inspected State Party:
Indication of the costs for the amenities requested:
Certification of the authorised member of the inspection team that the requested amenities have been provided:
Comments by the authorised member of the inspection team in regard to the quality of the amenities provided:
Name and signature of the authorised member of the inspection team:
Name and signature of the representative of the inspected State Party:

ANNEXES
Note: These annexes, *inter alia*, can be attached if requested by the inspected State Party.

Annex 1 OPCW Media and Public Relations Policy
Annex 2 OPCW Health and Safety Policy and Regulations
Annex 3 OPCW Policy on Confidentiality
Annex 4 Facility Declaration
Annex 5 Preliminary and Final Inspection Report Formats

14.2 Model for Schedule 2 plant sites

C-III/DEC.15 adopted by the Conference of the States Parties at its Third Session on 20 November 1998 and entitled "Model Facility Agreement for Schedule 2 plant sites"

The Conference

Recalling that, in accordance with paragraph 24 of Part VII of the Verification Annex, facility agreements for Schedule 2 plant sites shall be based on a model agreement;

Further Recalling that the issue of a model for facility agreements, in accordance with paragraph 24 of Part VII of the Verification Annex, was referred by the Conference to the Committee of the Whole (C-I/2, dated 12 May 1997);

Further Recalling its decision on the procedure for addressing unresolved issues during the second intersessional period (C-II/DEC.3, dated 5 December 1997);

Taking note of the decision taken by the Executive Council on the model agreement for Schedule 2 plant sites (EC-XI/DEC.4, dated 4 September 1998);

Taking note of the report submitted to it by the Chairman of the Committee of the Whole on the results of the work on unresolved issues during the second intersessional period (C-III/CoW.1, dated 9 May 1998);

Hereby:
1. Decides to adopt the model agreement for Schedule 2 plant sites as contained in the annex to this decision;
2. Further decides to remove the issue of the model agreement for Schedule 2 plant sites from the list of unresolved issues.

ANNEX

MODEL FOR FACILITY AGREEMENTS FOR SCHEDULE 2 PLANT SITES

The Organisation for the Prohibition of Chemical Weapons, hereinafter referred to as the "Organisation",

and the Government of _____, hereinafter referred to as "the inspected State Party", both constituting the Parties to this Agreement,

have agreed on the following arrangements in relation to the conduct of inspections pursuant to paragraph 4 of Article VI of the Convention on the Prohibition of the Development, Production, Stockpiling and Use of Chemical Weapons and on their Destruction, hereinafter referred to as "the Convention",

at _____ (insert name of the plant site, its precise location, including the address), declared under paragraphs 7 and 8 of Article VI, hereinafter referred to as "the plant site":

SECTION 1. GENERAL PROVISIONS

1. The purpose of this Agreement is to facilitate the implementation of the provisions of the Convention in relation to inspections conducted at the plant site pursuant to paragraph 4 of Article VI of the Convention and in accordance with the obligations of the inspected State Party and the Organisation under the Convention.
2. Nothing in this Agreement shall be applied or interpreted in a way that is contradictory to the provisions of the Convention. In case of inconsistency between this Agreement and the Convention, the Convention shall prevail.
3. The Parties have agreed to apply for planning purposes the general factors contained in Attachment 1.
4. The frequency and intensity of inspections at the plant site are given in Part B of Attachment 1 and reflect the risk assessment of the Organisation conducted pursuant to paragraphs 18, 20 and 24 of Part VII of the Verification Annex.
5. The inspection team shall consist of no more than ____ persons.
6. The language(s) for communication between the inspection team and the inspected State Party during inspections shall be ____ (insert one or more of the languages of the Convention).

SECTION 2. HEALTH AND SAFETY

1. Health and safety matters are governed by the Convention, the OPCW Health and Safety Policy and Regulations and applicable national, local and plant site safety and environmental regulations. The specific arrangements for implementing the relevant provisions of the Convention and the OPCW Health and Safety Policy in relation to inspections at the plant site are contained in Attachment 2.
2. All applicable health and safety regulations relevant to the conduct of the inspection at the plant site are listed in Attachment 2 and shall be made available for use by the inspection team at the plant site.
3. In the course of the pre-inspection briefing the inspection team shall be briefed by the repre-

sentatives of the plant site on all health and safety matters which, in the view of those representatives, are relevant to the conduct of the inspection at the plant site, including:

(a) the health and safety measures at the Schedule 2 plants to be inspected and the likely risks that may be encountered during the inspection;

(b) any additional health and safety measures or regulations that need to be observed at the plant site;

(c) procedures to be followed in case of an accident or in case of other emergencies, including a briefing on emergency signals, routes and exits, and the location of emergency meeting points and facilities; and

(d) specific inspection activities which must be limited within particular areas at the plant site, and in particular within those Schedule 2 plants to be inspected under the inspection mandate, for reasons of health and safety.

Upon request, the inspection team shall certify receipt of any such information if it is provided in written form.

4. During the course of the inspection, the inspection team shall refrain from any action which by its nature could endanger the safety of the team, the plant site or its personnel or could cause harm to the environment. Should the inspected State Party refuse certain inspection activities, it may explain the circumstances and safety considerations involved, and shall provide alternative means for conducting the inspection activities.

5. In the case of emergency situations or accidents involving inspection team members while at the plant site, the inspection team shall comply with the plant site emergency procedures and the inspected State Party shall to the extent possible provide medical and other assistance in a timely and effective manner with due regard to the rules of medical ethics if medical assistance is requested. Information on medical services and facilities to be used for this purpose is contained in Part D of Attachment 2. If the Organisation undertakes other measures for medical support in regard to inspection team members involved in emergency situations or accidents, the inspected State Party will render assistance to such measures to the extent possible. The Organisation will be responsible for the consequences of such measures.

SECTION 3. CONFIDENTIALITY

1. Matters related to confidentiality are governed by the Convention, including its Confidentiality Annex, and the OPCW Policy on Confidentiality. The specific arrangements for implementing the provisions of the Convention and the OPCW Policy on Confidentiality in relation to the protection of confidential information at the plant site are contained in Attachment 3.

SECTION 4. MEDIA AND PUBLIC RELATIONS

1. Media and public relations are governed by the OPCW Media and Public Relations Policy. The specific arrangements for the inspection team's contacts with the media or the public, if any, in relation to inspections of the plant site are contained in Attachment 4.

SECTION 5. INSPECTION EQUIPMENT

1. As agreed between the inspected State Party and the Organisation, the approved equipment listed in Part A of Attachment 5 will, at the discretion of the Organisation and on a routine basis, be used specifically for the Schedule 2 inspection. The equipment will be used in accordance with the Convention, the relevant decisions taken by the Conference of the States Parties, and any agreed procedures contained in Attachment 5.

2. The provisions of paragraph 1 above are without prejudice to paragraphs 27 to 29 of Part II of the Verification Annex.

3. The items of equipment available on-site, not belonging to the Organisation which the inspected State Party has volunteered to provide to the inspection team upon its request for use on-site during the conduct of inspections together with any procedures for the use of such equipment, if required, any requested support which can be provided and conditions for the provision of equipment are listed in Part B of Attachment 5. Prior to any use of such equipment the inspection team may confirm that the performance characteristics of such equipment are consistent with those for similar OPCW approved equipment, or – with respect to items of equipment which are not on the list of OPCW approved equipment – are consistent with the intended purpose for using such equipment.

4. Requests from the inspection team for the inspected State Party during the inspection to provide equipment mentioned in paragraph 3 above, shall be made in writing by an authorised member of the inspection team using the form contained in Attachment 5. The same procedure will also apply to other requests of the inspection team in accordance with paragraph 30 of Part II of the Verification Annex.

5. Agreed procedures for the decontamination of any equipment are contained in Part C of Attachment 5.

SECTION 6. PRE-INSPECTION ACTIVITIES

1. The inspection team shall be given a pre-inspection briefing by the representatives of the plant site in accordance with Part II, paragraph 37 of the Verification Annex. The pre-inspection briefing shall include:
    (a) information on the plant site as described in Attachment 6;
    (b) health and safety specifications described in section 2 above and detailed in Attachment 2; and
    (c) any changes to the above-mentioned information since the last inspection.

2. Any information about the plant site that the inspected State Party has volunteered to provide to the inspection team during the pre-inspection briefing with indications as to which information may be transferred off-site is referenced in Part B of Attachment 6.

SECTION 7. CONDUCT OF THE INSPECTION

7.1 STANDING ARRANGEMENTS

1. The inspection period shall begin immediately upon completion of the pre-inspection briefing, unless agreed otherwise.

2. Arrangements for the conduct of a site tour, if any, are contained in Attachment 7.

3. The inspection team leader shall inform the representative of the inspected State Party during the inspection in a timely manner about each subsequent step to be taken by the inspection team in implementing the inspection plan. Without prejudice to paragraph 40 of Part II of the Verification Annex, this shall be done in time to allow the inspected State Party to arrange for the necessary measures to be taken to provide access and support to the inspection team as appropriate without causing unnecessary delay in the conduct of inspection activities.

4. The inspection team shall, upon the request of the inspected State Party, communicate with the personnel of the plant site only in the presence of or through a representative of the inspected State Party.

5. The inspected State Party shall, upon request, provide a securable workspace for the inspection team, including adequate space for the storage of equipment. The inspection team shall have the right to seal its workspace.

7.2 ACCESS TO AND INSPECTION OF AREAS, BUILDINGS AND STRUCTURES

1. The focus of the inspection shall be the declared Schedule 2 plant(s) within the declared plant

site as referenced in Attachment 8. If the inspection team requests access to other parts of the plant site, access to these areas shall be granted in accordance with the obligation to provide clarification pursuant to paragraph 51 of Part II and paragraph 25 of Part VII of the Verification Annex and in accordance with Attachment 8.

7.3 ACCESS TO AND INSPECTION OF DOCUMENTATION AND RECORDS

The agreed list of the documentation and records to be routinely made available for inspection purposes, mentioned in paragraph 26 of Part VII of the Verification Annex, to the inspection team by the inspected State Party during an inspection, as well as arrangements with regard to access to such records for the purpose of protecting confidential information, are contained in Attachment 9. Such documentation and records will be provided to the inspection team upon request.

7.4 SAMPLING AND ANALYSIS

Without prejudice to paragraphs 52 to 58 of Part II of the Verification Annex, procedures for sampling and analysis for verification purposes as mentioned in paragraph 27 of Part VII of the Verification Annex are contained in Attachment 10.

SECTION 8. DEBRIEFING AND PRELIMINARY FINDINGS

1. Before the conclusion of the debriefing, the inspected State Party may provide comments and clarifications to the inspection team on any issue related to the conduct of the inspection. The inspection team shall provide to the representative of the inspected State Party its preliminary findings in written form sufficiently prior to the conclusion of the debriefing to permit the inspected State Party to prepare any comments and clarifications. The inspected State Party's written comments and clarifications shall be attached to the document on preliminary findings.

SECTION 9. ADMINISTRATIVE ARRANGEMENTS

1. The inspected State Party shall provide or arrange for the provision of the amenities listed in detail in Attachment 11 to the inspection team in a timely manner throughout the duration of the inspection. The inspected State Party shall be reimbursed by the Organisation for such costs incurred by the inspection team, unless agreed otherwise.
2. Requests from the inspection team for the inspected State Party to provide or arrange amenities shall be made in writing by an authorised member of the inspection team[3] using the form contained in Attachment 11. Requests shall be made as soon as the need for amenities has been identified. The provision of such requested amenities shall be certified in writing by the authorised member of the inspection team. Copies of all such certified requests shall be kept by both Parties.
3. The inspection team has the right to refuse extra amenities that in its view are not needed for the conduct of the inspection.

SECTION 10. LIABILITIES

1. Any claim by the inspected State Party against the Organisation or by the Organisation against the inspected State Party in respect of any alleged damage or injury resulting from inspections at the plant site in accordance with this Agreement, without prejudice to paragraph

---

[3] The name of the authorised member(s) of the inspection team should be communicated to the inspected State Party no later than at the Point of Entry [footnote in original].

22 of the Confidentiality Annex, shall be settled in accordance with international law and, as appropriate, with the provisions of Article XIV of the Convention.

SECTION 11. STATUS OF ATTACHMENTS

1. The Attachments form an integral part of this Agreement. Any reference to the Agreement includes the Attachments. However, in case of any inconsistency between this Agreement and any Attachment, the sections of the Agreement shall prevail.

SECTION 12. AMENDMENTS, MODIFICATIONS AND UPDATES

1. Amendments to the sections of this Agreement may be proposed by either Party and shall be agreed to and enter into force under the same conditions as provided for under paragraph 1 of Section 14.
2. Modifications to the Attachments of this Agreement, other than Attachment 1 and Part B of Attachment 5 may be agreed upon at any time between the representative of the Organisation and the representative of the inspected State Party, each being specifically authorised to do so. The Director-General shall inform the Executive Council about any such modifications. Each Party to this Agreement may revoke its consent to a modification not later than four weeks after it had been agreed upon. After this time period the modification shall take effect.
3. The inspected State Party will update Part A of Attachment 1 and Part B of Attachment 5 as necessary for the effective conduct of inspections. The Organisation will update Part B of Attachment 1 as necessary for the effective conduct of inspections.

SECTION 13. SETTLEMENT OF DISPUTES

1. Any dispute between the Parties that may arise out of the application or interpretation of this Agreement shall be settled in accordance with Article XIV of the Convention.

SECTION 14. ENTRY INTO FORCE

1. This Agreement shall enter into force upon approval by the Executive Council and signature by the two Parties. If the inspected State Party has additional internal requirements, it shall so notify the Organisation in writing by the date of signature. In such cases, this Agreement shall enter into force on the date that the inspected State Party gives the Organisation written notification that its internal requirements for entry into force have been met.

SECTION 15. DURATION AND TERMINATION

1. This Agreement shall cease to be in force when the provisions of paragraph 12 of Part VII of the Verification Annex no longer apply to this plant site, except if the continuation of the Agreement is agreed by mutual consent of the Parties.

Done at ___ in ___ copies, in _____ language(s), each being equally authentic.

ATTACHMENTS
The following attachments shall be completed where applicable.

Attachment 1.   General factors for the conduct of inspections
Attachment 2.   Health and safety requirements and procedures
Attachment 3.   Specific arrangements in relation to the protection of confidential information at the plant site

ATTACHMENT 1. GENERAL FACTORS FOR THE CONDUCT OF INSPECTIONS

PART A. TO BE PROVIDED AND UPDATED BY THE INSPECTED STATE PARTY:
(a) plant site working hours: _____ hrs to _____ hrs (days)
(b) working days:
(c) holidays or other non-working days:
(d) Schedule 2 plant(s) working hours, if applicable: _____ hrs to _____ hrs (days)
(e) working days:
(f) holidays or other non-working days:
(g) inspection activities which could/could not[4] be supported during non-working hours with notation of times and activities:
(h) any other factors that could adversely effect the effective conduct of inspections:

PART B. TO BE PROVIDED AND UPDATED BY THE ORGANISATION:
Inspection Frequency:
(a) inspection frequency:
Inspection Intensity:
(b) maximum estimated period of inspection (for planning purposes): [5]
(c) approximate inspection team size:
(d) estimated volume and weight of equipment to be brought on-site:

ATTACHMENT 2. HEALTH AND SAFETY REQUIREMENTS AND PROCEDURES

A. BASIC PRINCIPLES
   1. Applicable health and safety regulations of the OPCW, with agreed variations from strict implementation, if any:
   2. Health and safety regulations applicable at the plant site:
   3. Health and safety requirements and regulations agreed between the inspected State Party and the Organisation:

B. DETECTION AND MONITORING
   1. Applicable specific safety standards for workspace chemical exposure limits and/or concentrations which should be observed during the inspection, if any:
   2. Procedures, if any, for detection and monitoring in accordance with the OPCW Health and Safety Policy, including data to be collected by, or provided to, the inspection team:

C. PROTECTION
   1. Protective equipment to be provided by the OPCW and agreed procedures for equipment certification and use, if required:

---

[4] Choose one option [footnote in original].
[5] Any figure indicated is without prejudice to paragraph 29 of Part VII of the Verification Annex [footnote in original].

2. Protective equipment to be provided by the inspected State Party, and agreed procedures, personnel training, and personnel qualification tests and certification required; and agreed procedures for use of the equipment:

D. MEDICAL REQUIREMENTS
    1. Applicable medical standards of the inspected State Party and, in particular, the inspected plant site:
    2. Medical screening procedures for members of the inspection team:
    3. Agreed medical assistance to be provided by the inspected State Party:
    4. Emergency medical evacuation procedures:
    5. Agreed additional medical measures to be taken by the inspection team:
    6. Procedures for emergency response to chemical casualties of the inspection team:

E. MODIFICATION OF INSPECTION ACTIVITIES DUE TO HEALTH AND SAFETY REASONS, AND AGREED ALTERNATIVES TO ACCOMPLISH THE INSPECTION GOALS:

ATTACHMENT 3. SPECIFIC ARRANGEMENTS IN RELATION TO THE PROTECTION OF CONFIDENTIAL INFORMATION AT THE PLANT SITE

1. Designation of the classification of the inspected State Party's documents provided to the inspection team:
2. Specific procedures for access by the inspection team to confidential areas or materials:
3. Procedures in relation to the certification by the inspection team of the receipt of any documents provided by the inspected plant site:
4. Storage of confidential documents at the inspected plant site (including, if applicable, procedures in relation to the use of a dual control container on site):
5. Procedures for the removal off site of any written information, data and other material gathered by the inspection team:
6. Procedures for providing the representatives of the inspected State Party with copies of written information, inspector's notebooks, data and other material gathered by the inspection team:
7. Other arrangements, if any:

ATTACHMENT 4. ARRANGEMENTS FOR THE INSPECTION TEAM'S CONTACTS WITH THE MEDIA OR THE PUBLIC

ATTACHMENT 5. INSPECTION EQUIPMENT

PART A. LIST OF EQUIPMENT:

Item of approved inspection equipment	Nature of restriction(s) (location, time periods, etc.), if any	Indication of reason(s) (safety, confidentiality, etc.)	Alternative for meeting inspection requirement(s), if so required by the inspection team

PART B. EQUIPMENT WHICH THE INSPECTED STATE PARTY HAS VOLUNTEERED TO PROVIDE:

Item of equipment	Procedures for use	Support to be provided, if required	Conditions (timing; cost, if any)

PART C. PROCEDURES FOR THE DECONTAMINATION OF EQUIPMENT:

REQUEST FOR AND CERTIFICATION OF EQUIPMENT AVAILABLE ON SITE TO BE PROVIDED IN ACCORDANCE WITH PARAGRAPH 3 OF SECTION 5

Date:
Plant Site:
Inspection number:
Name of the authorised member of the inspection team:
Type and number of item(s) of equipment requested:
Approval of the request by inspected State Party:
Comments on the request by the inspected State Party:
Indication of the costs , if any, for the use of the equipment requested/volunteered :
Certification of the authorised member of the inspection team that the requested item(s) of equipment have been provided:
Comments, if any, by the authorised member of the inspection team in regard to the equipment provided:
Name and signature of the authorised member of the inspection team:
Name and signature of the representative of the inspected State Party:

ATTACHMENT 6. INFORMATION ON THE PLANT SITE PROVIDED IN ACCORDANCE WITH SECTION 6

PART A. TOPICS OF INFORMATION FOR THE PRE-INSPECTION BRIEFING:

PART B. ANY INFORMATION ABOUT THE PLANT SITE THAT THE INSPECTED STATE PARTY VOLUNTEERS TO PROVIDE TO THE INSPECTION TEAM DURING THE PRE-INSPECTION BRIEFING AND WHICH MAY BE TRANSFERRED OFF-SITE:

ATTACHMENT 7. ARRANGEMENTS FOR SITE TOUR

The inspected State Party may provide a site tour at the request of the inspection team. Such tour shall take no more than 2 hours. The inspected State Party may provide explanations to the inspection team during the site tour.

ATTACHMENT 8. ACCESS TO THE PLANT SITE IN ACCORDANCE WITH SECT.7.2

PART A. AREAS OF THE DECLARED PLANT SITE TO WHICH INSPECTORS ARE GRANTED ACCESS:

PART B. ARRANGEMENTS WITH REGARD TO THE SCOPE OF THE INSPECTION EFFORT IN AGREED AREAS:

ATTACHMENT 9. RECORDS ROUTINELY MADE AVAILABLE TO THE INSPECTION TEAM AT THE PLANT SITE

ATTACHMENT 10. SAMPLING AND ANALYSIS FOR VERIFICATION PURPOSES

PART A. AGREED SAMPLING POINTS CHOSEN WITH DUE CONSIDERATION TO EXISTING SAMPLING POINTS USED BY THE PLANT(S) OPERATOR(S):

PART B. PROCEDURES FOR TAKING SAMPLES:

PART C. PROCEDURES FOR SAMPLE HANDLING AND SAMPLE SPLITTING:

PART D. PROCEDURES FOR SAMPLE ANALYSIS:

PART E. ARRANGEMENTS IN REGARD TO THE PAYMENT OF COSTS ASSOCIATED WITH THE DISPOSAL OR REMOVAL BY THE INSPECTED STATE PARTY OF HAZARDOUS WASTE GENERATED DURING SAMPLING AND ON-SITE ANALYSIS DURING THE INSPECTION:

ATTACHMENT 11. ADMINISTRATIVE ARRANGEMENTS

PART A. THE AMENITIES DETAILED BELOW SHALL BE PROVIDED TO THE INSPECTION TEAM BY THE INSPECTED STATE PARTY, SUBJECT TO PAYMENT AS INDICATED IN PART B BELOW:

1. International and local official communication (telephone, fax), including calls/faxes between site and headquarters:
2. Vehicles:
3. Working room, including adequate space for the storage of equipment:
4. Lodging:
5. Meals:
6. Medical care:
7. Interpretation services:
    (a) Number of interpreters
    (b) Estimated interpretation time:
    (c) Languages:
8. Other:

PART B. DISTRIBUTION OF COSTS FOR PROVISIONS OF AMENITIES BY THE INSPECTED STATE PARTY (TICK ONE OPTION FOR EACH AMENITY PROVIDED AS APPROPRIATE)

Paragraphs 1 to 8 in Part A above	To be paid directly by the OPCW after the inspection	To be paid by the inspection team on behalf of the OPCW during the in-country period	To be paid by the inspected State Party and subsequently reimbursed by the OPCW	To be paid by the inspected State Party

PART C. OTHER ARRANGEMENTS:

1. Number of sub-teams (consisting of no less than two inspectors per sub-team) to be accommodated:

REQUEST FOR AND CERTIFICATION OF AMENITIES TO BE PROVIDED OR ARRANGED

Date:
Facility:
Inspection number:
Category of amenities requested:
Description of amenities requested:
Approval of the request by inspected State Party:
Comments on the request by the inspected State Party:
Indication of the costs for the amenities requested:
Certification of the authorised member of the inspection team that the requested amenities have been provided:
Comments by the authorised member of the inspection team in regard to the quality of the amenities provided:
Name and signature of the authorised member of the inspection team:
Name and signature of the representative of the inspected State Party:

ANNEXES
Note: These Annexes, *inter alia*, can be attached if requested by the inspected State Party.

Annex 1. OPCW Media and Public Relations Policy

Annex 2. OPCW Health and Safety Policy and Regulations
Annex 3. OPCW Policy on Confidentiality
Annex 4. Plant Site Declaration
Annex 5. Preliminary and Final Inspection Report Formats

14.3 Model for CWSFs

C-IV/DEC.12 adopted by the Conference of the States Parties at its Fourth Session on 29 June 1999 and entitled "Model facility agreement for chemical weapons storage facilities"

The Conference

Recalling that, in accordance with paragraph 8 of Part III of the Verification Annex, facility agreements shall be based on models for such agreements;

Recalling that the issue of model facility agreements was referred by the Conference to the Committee of the Whole (C-I/2, dated 12 May 1997);

Further recalling its decision on the procedure for addressing unresolved issues during the third intersessional period (C-III/DEC.11, dated 20 November 1998);

Taking note of the decision taken by the Executive Council on the model agreement for chemical weapons storage facilities (EC-XIV/DEC.8, dated 5 February 1999;

Taking note of the report submitted to it by the Chairman of the Committee of the Whole on the results of the work on unresolved issues during the third intersessional period (this document will be allocated a reference number when made available to delegations);

Hereby:

Decides to adopt the model facility agreement for chemical weapons storage facilities as contained in the annex hereto;

Further decides to remove the issue of the model facility agreement for chemical weapons storage facilities from the list of unresolved issues.

ANNEX
MODEL FOR FACILITY AGREEMENTS FOR CHEMICAL WEAPONS
STORAGE FACILITIES

The Organisation for the Prohibition of Chemical Weapons, hereinafter referred to as the "OPCW", and the Government of ...., hereinafter referred to as the "inspected State Party", both constituting the Parties to this Agreement have agreed on the following arrangements in relation to the conduct of systematic verification in accordance with
Article IV of the Convention on the Prohibition of the Development, Production, Stockpiling and Use of Chemical Weapons and of their Destruction, hereinafter referred to as the "Convention", and Parts II, III, and IV(A) of its Annex on Implementation and Verification, hereinafter referred to as the "Verification Annex", at ...., Geographic coordinates: ...., declared under Article III, paragraph 1 (a)(ii) of the Convention and paragraph 1 (b) and (c) of Part IV(A) of the Verification Annex of the Convention, hereinafter referred to as the "facility":

SECTION 1. GENERAL PROVISIONS

1.   The purpose of this Agreement for a Chemical Weapons Storage Facility (CWSF), hereinafter referred to as this "Agreement," is to facilitate the implementation of the provisions of the Convention in relation to systematic verification conducted at the facility pursuant to paragraphs 3 and 4 of Article IV and the Verification Annex of the Convention and in accord-

ance with the respective obligations of the inspected State Party and the OPCW under the Convention.

2. Nothing in this Agreement shall be applied or interpreted in a way that is contradictory to the provisions of the Convention. In case of inconsistency between this Agreement and the Convention, the Convention shall prevail.

3. The Parties have agreed to apply for planning purposes the general factors contained in Attachment 1 to this Agreement.

4. In case of any development due to circumstances brought about by unforeseen events which could affect systematic verification, the inspected State Party shall notify the OPCW and the inspection team as soon as the development has occurred.

5. The language(s) for communication between the inspection team and the inspected State Party during inspections shall be _____ (insert one or more of the languages of the Convention).

6. In case of need for the urgent departure, emergency evacuation or urgent travel of inspector(s) from the territory of the inspected State Party the inspection team leader shall inform the inspected State Party of such a need. The inspected State Party shall arrange without undue delay such departure, evacuation or travel. In all cases the inspected State Party shall determine the means of transportation and routes to be taken. The costs of such departure, evacuation or travel of inspectors, if due to health or administrative reasons not related to the inspection, shall be borne by the OPCW.

7. Inspectors shall wear unique badges provided by the inspected State Party, or OPCW badges, which must be worn at all times while within the facility perimeter.

SECTION 2. HEALTH AND SAFETY

1. Procedures to ensure health and safety during inspections are governed by the Convention, the OPCW Health and Safety Policy and Regulations and applicable national, local and facility safety and environmental regulations. Attachment 2 contains agreements addressing operational conflicts between health and safety requirements, standards, and procedures of the OPCW and those in force at the facility at specific locations. It also contains agreed circumstances where the health and safety requirements and standards at the facility, being more stringent than those of the OPCW Health and Safety Policy, will take precedence. Also, the agreed conditions and procedures for on-site sampling and analysis for purposes of personal safety of the inspection team are contained in Attachment 2, Part B, paragraph 4.

2. In carrying out its activities, the inspection team shall, in accordance with paragraph 43 of Part II of the Verification Annex, observe applicable national safety and environmental regulations and safety and environmental regulations established at the inspected facility including regulations for the protection of controlled environments within the inspected facility and for personal safety, if applicable, as well as any additional safety requirements referred to in paragraph 3 of this Section, provided that these requirements and standards can be technically complied with. These documents shall be made available to the inspection team as necessary, as soon as practically possible upon the inspection team's request, but in any case no later than by the end of the pre-inspection briefing.

3. In the course of the pre-inspection briefing the inspection team shall be briefed by the representatives of the inspected State Party on all health and safety matters which, in the view of those representatives, are relevant to the conduct of the inspection at the facility, including:
   (a) full information on the health and safety requirements of the site identifying specific hazards and the likely risks associated with those hazards;
   (b) information on any additional health and safety measures or requirements not contained in this Agreement that should be observed during a particular inspection;
   (c) procedures to be followed in case of an accident or in case of other emergencies, includ-

ing a briefing on emergency signals, routes and exits, and the location of emergency meeting points and facilities; and

(d) information on any areas within the facility in which, for reasons of safety, specific inspection activities or access must be limited during a particular inspection, detailing reasons for limiting inspection activities or access and alternatives to access, if any. This is without prejudice to the obligations of the inspected State Party to provide access to the declared facility for the purpose of carrying out inspection activities, in accordance with the Convention.

Upon request, the inspection team shall certify receipt of any such information if it is provided in written form.

4. In the case of emergency situations or accidents involving inspection team members while at the facility, the inspection team shall comply with the facility emergency procedures and the inspected State Party shall to the extent possible provide medical and other assistance in a timely and effective manner with due regard to the rules of medical ethics if medical assistance is requested. Information on medical services and facilities to be used for this purpose is contained in Part D of Attachment 2 and in Part A of Attachment 13. If the Organisation undertakes other measures for medical support in regard to inspection team members involved in emergency situations or accidents, the inspected State Party will render assistance to such measures to the extent possible. The Organisation will be responsible for the consequences of such measures.

5. The inspection team shall refrain from any action during the course of an inspection which by its nature could endanger the safety of the team, the facility, its personnel, or cause harm to the environment. The inspected State Party may decline to conduct certain inspection activities, requested to be performed by the inspection team, if the inspected State Party considers that such activities could endanger the safety of the facility, its personnel, or the inspection team. In such cases, the inspected State Party shall explain the circumstances and safety considerations involved, and provide alternative means for accomplishing the inspection activities. This is without prejudice to the obligations of the inspected State Party to provide access to the declared facility for the purpose of carrying out inspection activities, in accordance with the Convention. The inspection team shall record any refusal of inspection activity, as well as inspection team comments and the inspected State Party's explanation, in the document on preliminary findings.

6. In accordance with the OPCW Health and Safety Policy, the inspected State Party may provide available data based on detection and monitoring, to the agreed extent necessary to satisfy concerns that may exist regarding the health and safety of the inspection team.

7. The inspected State Party shall have the opportunity to familiarise itself with the OPCW approved equipment, including the equipment listed in Part A of Attachment 7.

SECTION 3. CONFIDENTIALITY

Matters related to confidentiality for the Organisation relating to information collected during the conduct of inspections, are governed by the Convention, including its Confidentiality Annex, and the OPCW Policy on Confidentiality. The specific arrangements for implementing the provisions of the Convention and the OPCW Policy on Confidentiality in relation to the protection of confidential information at the facility by the Organisation relating to information collected during the conduct of inspections, are contained in Attachment 3.

SECTION 4. MEDIA AND PUBLIC RELATIONS

The specific arrangements for the inspection team's contacts with the media or the public, if any, in relation to inspections of the facility are contained in Attachment 4.

SECTION 5. INSPECTION EQUIPMENT

1. As agreed between the inspected State Party and the Organisation, the approved equipment listed in Part A of Attachment 7, shall, at the discretion of the Organisation and on a routine basis, be used specifically for the inspection at the facility. The equipment will be used in accordance with the Convention, in particular with paragraph 40 of Part II of the Verification Annex, and the relevant decisions taken by the Conference of the States Parties, and any agreed procedures contained in Attachment 7.

2. The provisions of paragraph 1 above are without prejudice to paragraphs 27 to 29 of Part II of the Verification Annex.

3. The list of facility equipment to be provided as a matter of routine by the inspected State Party for use by the inspection team, or to be operated by the inspected State Party under the supervision of the inspection team is listed in Part B of Attachment 7 to this Agreement, with notation of the nature of and procedures for its operation and necessary support. Prior to any use of such equipment the inspection team may confirm that the equipment meets the technical requirements necessary to support the inspection task intended to be accomplished. With respect to personal protective equipment, the requirements specified in the OPCW Health and Safety Policy and Regulations apply. With respect to the use of equipment available on-site other than the equipment listed in Part B of Attachment 7, requests made by the inspection team in accordance with paragraph 30 of Part II of the Verification Annex shall be made in writing.

4. The existing monitoring instruments at the facility belonging to the inspected State Party that have been agreed by the Parties for use by the OPCW, if any, and agreed procedures for their installation, replacement, upgrades, modifications, use, calibration, maintenance and testing by the inspected State Party, as well as their tamper-proofing as required, are listed in Part B of Attachment 7 to this Agreement.

5. The agreed monitoring instruments, if any, belonging to the OPCW to be installed at the facility, the agreed locations and procedures for their installation, replacement, upgrades, modifications, use, calibration, maintenance, testing and tamper-proofing as required, with indication of the agreed support by the inspected State Party, are listed in Part C of Attachment 7 to this Agreement.

6. The items of OPCW approved inspection equipment or supplies that require special handling or storage for safety purposes (such as agent standards or radioisotopic sources) are listed in Part D of Attachment 7 to this Agreement, with specification of special handling requirements.

7. The items of approved inspection equipment which may be subject to specific safety requirements are listed in Part D of Attachment 7 to this Agreement, with notation of the specific restrictions and the reasons for the restrictions.

8. For the entire period of its stay at the inspected facility the inspection team shall have the right to store its equipment in a securable work space(s) provided for the inspection team in accordance with Section 14 of this Agreement.

9. The inspection team, in co-operation with the inspected State Party shall decontaminate its equipment and supplies that were contaminated during the course of the inspection, in accordance with OPCW regulations and the inspected State Party's national and local regulations covering such activity. The inspection team may request decontamination support from the inspected State Party, including preparation of decontamination means and conduct of decontamination procedures. Any support provided by the inspected State Party shall be conducted in the presence of the inspection team, unless otherwise agreed upon, and in accordance with the specific arrangements for decontamination of equipment contained in Part E of Attachment 7 to this Agreement.

SECTION 6. PRE-INSPECTION ACTIVITIES

1. Upon arrival at the facility and before commencement of an inspection, the inspection team shall, in accordance with paragraph 37 of Part II of the Verification Annex, be briefed by facility representatives on the facility. This briefing shall contain the following:

    (a) an overview of the information contained in Attachments 2 and 5 to this Agreement, with an emphasis on any changes to that information that have occurred since the most recent inspection;

    (b) specification of any health and safety measures or limitations required for conduct of inspection activities contained in Attachment 2 and as referred to in paragraph 4 of Section 2 of this Agreement with emphasis on measures or limitations changed since the most recent inspection; and

    (c) information on administrative, logistical, and communications arrangements necessary for the inspection, in addition to those contained in Attachment 13 of this Agreement.

2. Any information about the facility that the inspected State Party has volunteered to provide to the inspection team during the pre-inspection briefing with indications as to which information may be transferred off-site is referenced in Part C of Attachment 5 of this Agreement.

3. The time spent for the briefing shall not exceed 3 hours.

4. Upon conclusion of the pre-inspection briefing, the inspection team leader shall provide to the representative of the inspected State Party a tentative inspection plan to facilitate the conduct of the inspection. For the purpose of facilitating development of an inspection plan, and familiarising the inspection team with the general layout of the declared facility, the inspected State Party may provide to the inspection team a tour of the declared facility, if possible and agreed. The tour will be limited to a visual drive-by tour with general explanation of the physical layout of the declared facility. The conduct of any such tour will be without prejudice to the 3-hour time limit for pre-inspection activities.

SECTION 7. INFORMATION ON THE FACILITY

1. Information on the facility as declared by the inspected State Party in its initial declaration or updated is referenced in Part A of Attachment 5 to this Agreement and shall be made available to the inspection team.

2. The inspected State Party shall also provide, as referenced in Part B of Attachment 5 to this Agreement, a detailed site diagram of the facility, which shall be drawn to scale, clearly showing the facility perimeter delineated where possible by using man-made or natural features. It shall include all road and rail exits; location of each structure situated within the facility with structure purpose, number, or designation indicated for each; significant geographical relief features in the vicinity of the facility; if the facility is situated within a larger complex, specification of the exact location within the larger complex; geographic coordinates of a point within the facility specified to the nearest second; an arrow indicating the orientation of the facility relative to true north; and a legend identifying all symbols used on the diagram and the scale used.

3. In addition to the information referred to in paragraphs 1 and 2 of this Section, the inspection team shall be provided with the information about the facility referenced in Part C of Attachment 5 of this Agreement.

4. The inspected State Party shall, in case of change(s) to the information referred to in this Section, inform the inspection team arriving for subsequent inspection about such change(s) during the pre-inspection briefing.

SECTION 8. ACTIVITIES OF THE INSPECTED STATE PARTY AT THE FACILITY

1. The inspected State Party may continue standard maintenance activities at the facility, includ-
    ing those listed in paragraph 9 of Part IV(A) of the Verification Annex. In accordance with
    paragraph 11 of Part IV(A) of the Verification Annex all maintenance activities at the facility
    shall be subject to monitoring by the Technical Secretariat. The standard maintenance activi-
    ties being continued at the facility by the inspected State Party and arrangements for monitor-
    ing them are contained in Attachment 6 to this Agreement.
2. Activities specifically mentioned in paragraph 10 of Part IV(A) of the Verification Annex
    shall not be conducted at the facility.

SECTION 9. CONDUCT OF THE INSPECTION

9.1 GENERAL
1. The period of inspection shall begin immediately upon completion of the pre-inspection ac-
    tivities.
2. Before the commencement of inspection activities, the inspection team leader shall inform
    the representative of the inspected State Party about the initial steps to be taken in implement-
    ing the inspection plan, the plan to be adjusted by the inspection team as circumstances war-
    rant throughout the inspection process in consultation with the inspected State Party as to its
    implementability in regard to paragraph 40 of Part II of the Verification Annex. If requested,
    at the beginning of inspection activities, the inspected State Party may provide a tour of the
    facility.
3. The inspection team shall abide by paragraph 40 of Part II of the Verification Annex which
    reads: "The activities of the inspection team shall be so arranged as to ensure the timely and
    effective discharge of its functions and the least possible inconvenience to the inspected State
    Party or host State and disturbance to the facility or area inspected. The inspection team shall
    avoid unnecessarily hampering or delaying the operation of a facility and avoid affecting its
    safety. In particular, the inspection team shall not operate any facility. If inspectors consider
    that, to fulfil their mandate, particular operations should be carried out in the facility, it shall
    request the designated representative of the inspected facility to have them performed. The
    representative shall carry out the request to the extent possible."
4. The inspection team shall have the right to confirm the precise location of the facility, i.e., its
    declared geographic co-ordinates, utilising, as necessary, approved location-finding equip-
    ment or other suitable techniques.
5. The inspection team shall have the right to seal its workspace.
6. Pursuant to paragraph 45 of Part II, and 41 and 49 of Part IV(A) of the Verification Annex,
    the inspection team shall have the right to unimpeded access to the inspected facility includ-
    ing any munitions, devices, bulk containers, or other containers therein, as defined by the
    declared perimeter specified on the site diagram contained in Part B of Attachment 5 to this
    Agreement.
7. The inspection activities described in this Section shall be performed in accordance with
    paragraphs 14 to 16 of the Confidentiality Annex and the health and safety requirements
    specified in Section 2 and Attachment 2 to this Agreement.
8. While at the inspection site, inspectors shall be free to conduct: visual inspections, record
    checks, inventorying, measurements, sealing, tagging and marking, monitoring, and inter-
    views. The team shall also be free to have photographs or images taken, or conduct other
    checks and activities consistent with the Convention, in accordance with agreed procedures
    detailed in this Section and the applicable attachments to this Agreement.

9.2 ACCESS TO AND INSPECTION OF DOCUMENTATION AND RECORDS

1. In accordance with Paragraph 47 of Part II of the Verification Annex, inspection team members shall have the right to inspect documentation and records they deem relevant to the conduct of their mission.

2. Without prejudice to this right, the inspected State Party shall make available routinely to the inspection team upon request, as soon as possible, for the purpose of, *inter alia*, providing assurance that the status of the site is consistent with the declaration and that no activity prohibited under the Convention has occurred, the documentation and records, listed in Attachment 8 to this Agreement, that will be required for the conduct of verification. The information on the specific documentation and records that shall be available, as well as location and format of the records and other documentation is contained in Attachment 8 to this Agreement.

9.3 INTERVIEWS

The agreed procedures for interviews are contained in Attachment 9 of this Agreement.

9.4 COMMUNICATIONS

1. In accordance with paragraph 44 of Part II of the Verification Annex the inspection team shall have the right throughout the in-country period to communicate with the Headquarters of the Technical Secretariat. For this purpose they may use OPCW approved equipment. The procedures governing the use of such equipment are contained in Part A of Attachment 7 to this Agreement. In case the inspection team and the inspected State Party agree to use any of the inspected State Party's communications equipment the list of such equipment and the provisions for its use are contained in Part B of Attachment 7 to this Agreement. The provision of communications services to the inspection team by the inspected State Party shall be in accordance with Attachment 13 to this Agreement.

2. The agreed means of communication between inspection team sub groups are contained in Part F of Attachment 7 to this Agreement.

9.5 PHOTOGRAPHS

1. Photographs shall be taken in accordance with paragraph 48 of Part II of the Verification Annex. The procedures for photography are contained in Attachment 10 to this Agreement.

2. One camera of the instant development type furnished by the inspection team shall be used for taking two identical photographs in numerical sequence.

3. The representative of the inspected facility has the right to object to the use of photographic equipment in specific areas, buildings or structures, if such use would be incompatible with safety or fire regulations given the characteristics of the chemicals stored in the area in question. The relevant restrictions on use of photographic equipment at the inspected facility are contained in Part A of Attachment 7 to this Agreement. If the objection is raised due to safety concerns, the inspected State Party will, if possible, furnish photographic equipment that meets the regulations. If the use of photographic equipment is not permissible at all in specific areas, buildings or structures for the reasons stated above, the inspected State Party shall provide a written explanation of its objection to the inspection team leader and propose an alternative. The explanation, along with the inspection team leader's comments will be included in the inspection team's preliminary findings.

4. The inspection team shall also have the right to have a photographic record of seals and tags it employs during the conduct of the inspection.

9.6 INVENTORY

1. In accordance with paragraph 48 of Part IV (A) of the Verification Annex, in carrying out the inventory, within the time available, the inspectors shall have the right:
   (a) to use any of the following inspection techniques:

- inventory all the chemical weapons stored at the facility;
- inventory all the chemical weapons stored in specific buildings or locations at the facility, as chosen by the inspectors; or
- inventory all the chemical weapons of one or more specific types stored at the facility, as chosen by the inspectors; and

(b) to check all items inventoried against agreed records and against declarations included in Attachment 5 to this Agreement.

2. At the request of the inspection team, representatives of the inspected State Party shall open, for observation or counting, containers in which chemical munitions or devices are stored in buildings or locations that are being inspected at the facility. These provisions shall not apply to filled munitions which have been over packed because they are leaking or munitions that present a safety hazard due to the high probability of their leaking in their shipping/firing containers. The containers to be opened shall be selected by the inspectors. The procedures for this activity are detailed in Attachment 15 to this Agreement.

9.7 SEALS, MARKERS AND OTHER INVENTORY CONTROL DEVICES

1. In accordance with paragraph 39 of Part IV(A) of the Verification Annex, inspectors shall employ, as appropriate, agreed seals, markers, or other inventory control procedures to facilitate an accurate inventory of declared items. Procedures for installation of these agreed seals, markers, and other devices are contained in Attachment 12 to this Agreement. In accordance with paragraph 40 of Part IV (A) of the Verification Annex the inspectors shall install such agreed seals as may be necessary to clearly indicate if any stocks are removed, and to ensure the securing of the storage facility during the inventory. After completion of the inventory, such seals will be removed unless otherwise agreed.

2. The list of seals left in place at the conclusion of the inspection, as agreed and required under the provisions of Part IV(A) of the Verification Annex, shall be attached to the document on preliminary findings.

3. Seals, markers, and other inventory devices will only be applied, removed, and/or altered in the presence of representatives of the inspection team and inspected State Party.

9.8 MEASUREMENTS

1. Measurements taken in the course of carrying out the inspection by the inspection team or by the inspected State Party at the inspection team's request shall be recorded and signed by an inspector.

2. To help resolve potential ambiguities these measurements and data may be certified as accurate by the representative of the inspected State Party, at the discretion of the inspected State Party, immediately after they are gathered. In case of discrepancies both Parties shall make efforts to resolve discrepancies as soon as possible before the end of the inspection period. If necessary, the representative of the inspected State Party and the inspector shall each record the method(s) used and the final result(s). Such measurements shall be recorded in the document on preliminary findings.

9.9 SAMPLING AND ANALYSIS

Pursuant to paragraph 49 of Part IV(A), and paragraphs 52 to 58 of Part II, of the Verification Annex, procedures for sampling and analysis for verification purposes, as appropriate, are contained in Attachment 11 of this Agreement. Procedures for tagging munitions, devices or containers for subsequent sampling and analysis are contained in Attachment 12 of this Agreement.

9.10 MONITORING WITH ON-SITE INSTRUMENTS

1. Pursuant to paragraph 10, Part III of the Verification Annex (if applicable), the Technical Secretariat shall have the right of continuous monitoring with instruments or systems.

2. The list of agreed on-site monitoring instruments, as well as agreed conditions, procedures, installation points, and security measures to prevent tampering with such on-site monitoring instruments are contained in Parts B and C of Attachment 7 of this Agreement, as applicable.

3. The inspected State Party shall in accordance with paragraph 14 of Part III of the Verification Annex immediately notify the Technical Secretariat if an event occurs or may occur at the facility where the monitoring instruments are installed, which may have an impact on the monitoring system. The inspected State Party shall co-ordinate subsequent actions with the Technical Secretariat with a view to restoring the operation of the monitoring system and establishing interim measures, if necessary, as soon as possible.

SECTION 10. REPRESENTATIVES OF THE INSPECTED STATE PARTY

1. The inspection team shall, upon the request of the inspected State Party, communicate with the personnel of the facility only in the presence of or through a representative of the inspected State Party.

2. In keeping with the provisions of paragraph 41 of Part II of the Verification Annex, the inspected State Party shall ensure that its representative(s) can at all times be reached by the inspection team leader and designated members of the inspection team either in person or exceptionally by telephone. The inspected State Party shall provide the names and means of contact for its designated representative(s) to the inspection team leader.

SECTION 11. CLARIFICATIONS

In accordance with paragraph 51 of Part II of the Verification Annex inspectors shall have the right to request clarifications in connection with ambiguities that arise during an inspection. Such requests shall be made promptly through the representative of the inspected State Party. The representative of the inspected State Party shall expeditiously provide the inspection team, during the inspection, with such clarification as may be necessary to remove the ambiguity. If questions related to an object or a building located within the inspection site are not resolved, the object or building shall, if requested, be photographed for the purpose of clarifying its nature and function. The inspection team shall include in the document on preliminary findings compiled in accordance with Section 12 of this Agreement any such unresolved questions, relevant clarifications, and a copy of any photographs taken.

SECTION 12. DEBRIEFING AND PRELIMINARY FINDINGS

1. In accordance with paragraph 60 of Part II of the Verification Annex, "upon completion of an inspection the inspection team shall meet with representatives of the inspected State Party and the personnel responsible for the inspection site to review the preliminary findings of the inspection team and to clarify any ambiguities. The inspection team shall provide to the representatives of the inspected State Party its preliminary findings in written form according to a standardised format, together with a list of any samples and copies of written information and data gathered and other material to be taken off-site. The document shall be signed by the head of the inspection team. In order to indicate that he has taken notice of the contents of the document, the representative of the inspected State Party shall countersign the document. This meeting shall be completed not later than 24 hours after the completion of the inspection".

2. The document on preliminary findings shall also include, *inter alia*, the list of results of

analysis, if conducted on site, records of seals, results of inventories, copies of photographs to be retained by the inspection team, and results of certified measurements. It will be prepared in accordance with the standardised preliminary findings format referenced in Attachment 16, any substantive changes of which will be made only after consultation with the inspected State Party.

3.   Any documentation and records provided by the inspected State Party that are not attached to the document on preliminary findings may be taken off-site by the inspection team only with the specific authorisation of the inspected State Party.

4.   Before the conclusion of the meeting the inspected State Party may provide written comments and clarifications to the inspection team on any issue related to the conduct of the inspection. These written comments and clarifications shall be attached to the document on the preliminary findings.

SECTION 13. VISITS

1.   As a measure of systematic verification, visits to the facility may be required, in accordance with the relevant provisions set forth in Part III and IV(A) of the Verification Annex:

(a)   to perform any necessary maintenance or replacement of equipment, or to adjust the coverage of the monitoring system as required, in accordance with paragraph 15 of Part III;

(b)   to take action subsequent to an event that has occurred or may occur at the facility which may have an impact on the monitoring system, in accordance with paragraph 14 or 16 of Part III; and

(c)   to resolve urgent problems in accordance with paragraph 45 of Part IV(A).

2.   The size of the team conducting such a visit shall be limited to the number of personnel required to perform the specific tasks for which the visit is being conducted and shall not exceed the maximum size of team allowed for this type of facility inspection.

3.   The duration of the visit pursuant to subparagraphs (a) to (c) of paragraph 1 of this Section shall be limited to the minimum time required to perform the specific tasks for which the visit is being conducted and in any case shall not exceed the maximum duration allowed for this type of facility inspection. Access provided during the visit shall be limited to that required to perform the specific tasks for which the visit is being conducted, unless otherwise agreed to with the inspected State Party.

4.   Arrangements for such a visit shall be the same as for the conduct of an inspection.

SECTION 14. SERVICES TO BE PROVIDED

1.   The inspected State Party shall provide or arrange for the provision of the following services listed in detail in Part A of Attachment 13 to this Agreement to the inspection team throughout the duration of the inspection period:

(a)   interpretation

(b)   communication means;

(c)   transportation;

(d)   working space, including equipment storage space;

(e)   lodging;

(f)   meals;

(g)   medical care; and

(h)   equipment and utilities support, as detailed in the pertinent Sections of this Agreement.

2.   The inspected State Party shall also provide other services and support as identified in all pertinent Sections of this Agreement.

3.   Requests from the inspection team to the inspected State Party to provide or arrange services

in addition to those listed in paragraphs 1 and 2 above, shall be made in writing if requested by the inspected State Party by the inspection team's leader or designate, using the form contained in Part B of Attachment 13 to this Agreement, and which shall be signed by the inspected State Party upon receipt. Requests should normally be made as soon as the need for services has been identified. The provision of such services shall be acknowledged in writing by an authorised member of the inspection team. Copies of all such requests signed by both Parties with provision acknowledged shall be kept by both Parties.

4. The costs of providing the services to the inspection team shall be borne by the inspected State Party as specified in Attachment 13 to this Agreement.

SECTION 15. LIABILITIES

Any claim by the inspected State Party against the Organisation or by the Organisation against the inspected State Party in respect of any alleged damage or injury resulting from inspections at the facility in accordance with this Agreement, without prejudice to paragraph 22 of the Confidentiality Annex, shall be settled in accordance with international law and, as appropriate, with the provisions of Article XIV of the Convention.

SECTION 16. STATUS OF ATTACHMENTS

The Attachments form an integral part of this Agreement. Any reference to the Agreement includes the Attachments. However, in case of any inconsistency between this Agreement and any Attachment, the sections of the Agreement shall prevail.

SECTION 17. AMENDMENTS, MODIFICATIONS AND UPDATES

1. Amendments to the Sections of this Agreement may be proposed by either Party and shall be agreed to and enter into force under the same conditions as provided for under Section 19.
2. Modifications to the Attachments of this Agreement, other than Attachment 1 and Part B of Attachment 5 may be agreed upon at any time between the representative of the Organisation and the representative of the inspected State Party, each being specifically authorised to do so. The Director-General shall inform the Executive Council about any such modifications. Each Party to this Agreement may revoke its consent to a modification not later than four weeks after it had been agreed upon. After this time period the modification shall take effect.
3. The inspected State Party will update Part A of Attachment 1 and Part B of Attachment 5 as necessary for the effective conduct of inspections. The Organisation will update Part B of Attachment 1 as necessary for the effective conduct of inspections.

SECTION 18. SETTLEMENT OF DISPUTES

Any dispute between the Parties that may arise out of the application or interpretation of this Agreement shall be settled in accordance with Article XIV of the Convention.

SECTION 19. ENTRY INTO FORCE

This Agreement shall enter into force upon approval by the Executive Council and signature by the two Parties. If the inspected State Party has additional internal requirements, it shall so notify the Organisation in writing by the date of signature. In such cases, this Agreement shall enter into force on the date that the inspected State Party gives the Organisation written notification that its internal requirements for entry into force have been met.

SECTION 20. DURATION AND TERMINATION

This Agreement shall cease to be in force when the provisions of paragraph 43 of Part IV(A) of the Verification Annex no longer apply to this facility.

Done at _____ in ___ copies, in _____ language(s), each being equally authentic.

ATTACHMENTS

Attachment 1	Planning Data for Inspections
Part A	To Be Provided and Updated by the Inspected State Party
Part B	To Be Provided and Updated by the OPCW
Attachment 2	Health And Safety Requirements And Procedures
Part A	Basic Principles
Part B	Detection And Monitoring
Part C	Protection
Part D	Medical Requirements
Part E	Health and Safety Training
Part F	Modification Of Inspection Activities
Attachment 3	Specific Arrangements in Relation to the Protection of Confidential Information at the Facility
Part A	General
Part B	Information to be Kept in the Dual Control Container
Attachment 4	Arrangements for Inspection Teams' Contacts with the Media or Public
Attachment 5	Information on the Facility Provided by the Inspected State Party
Part A	Declaration of the Facility
Part B	Site Diagram
Part C	Additional Information on the Facility
Attachment 6	Standard Maintenance Activities And Monitoring Arrangements
Attachment 7	Inspection Equipment
Part A	Approved Equipment Belonging to the OPCW and Agreed Procedures for its Use
Part B	Facility Equipment To Be Provided by the Inspected State Party
Part C	Monitoring Instruments Systems To Be Installed and Maintained with the Support of the Inspected State Party
Part D	Special Handling Requirements for Equipment or Supplies
Part E	Procedures for the Decontamination Of Equipment
Part F	Procedures for Use of Inspection Team Communications Equipment
Attachment 8	Records to be Maintained by the Facility
Attachment 9	Agreed Procedures for Conducting Interviews
Attachment 10	Agreed Procedures for Photography
Attachment 11	Sampling and Analysis Procedures
Attachment 12	Sealing, Marking and Inventory Control Procedures
Part A	Sealing
Part B	Marking and other Inventory Control Procedures
Attachment 13	Services to be Provided by the Inspected State Party
Part A	Services to be Provided
Part B	Form - Request for Additional Services to be Provided
Attachment 14	Chemical Weapons Tagging Procedures
Attachment 15	Procedures For Opening Shipping/Storage Containers
Attachment 16	Standardised Preliminary Findings Format

ATTACHMENT 1. PLANNING DATA FOR INSPECTIONS

PART A. TO BE PROVIDED AND UPDATED BY THE INSPECTED STATE PARTY:
(a) site working hours:
(b) site working days:
(c) holidays or other non-working days:
(d) facility working hours:
(e) facility working days:
(f) physical and/or other potential constraints to inspection activities:
(g) Inspection activities which could be supported during non-working hours with notation of times and activities:

PART B. TO BE PROVIDED AND UPDATED BY THE OPCW:
(a) estimated period of inspection (for planning purposes):
(b) approximate inspection team size:
(c) number of sub-teams (consisting of no less than two inspection team members per sub-team) to be accommodated:
(d) estimated volume and weight of equipment to be brought on-site:

ATTACHMENT 2. HEALTH AND SAFETY REQUIREMENTS AND PROCEDURES

PART A. BASIC PRINCIPLES
1. Applicable health and safety regulations of the OPCW, with agreed variations from strict implementation if any:
2. Applicable health and safety regulations of the inspected State Party:
3. Medical regulations and requirements of the inspected State Party or the OPCW that take precedence as being the more stringent:

PART B: DETECTION AND MONITORING
1. Agreed hazard specific standards for workspace exposure limits and/or concentrations:
2. Procedures for detection and monitoring performed by the inspected State Party, using its own equipment, including data to be provided to the inspection team:
3. Agreed procedures for detection and monitoring performed by the inspection team in the least intrusive manner, including data to be collected, as applicable:
4. Agreed procedures for workspace sampling and analysis for purposes of personal safety of the inspection team:

PART C. PROTECTION
1. Protective equipment to be provided by the OPCW, and agreed procedures for equipment certification and use, if required:
2. Protective equipment to be provided by the inspected State Party, and agreed procedures, personnel training, and personnel qualification tests and certification required; and agreed procedures for use of the equipment are identified in Attachment 7 and will be further identified during the Pre-Inspection briefing.

PART D. MEDICAL REQUIREMENTS
1. Personnel medical standards of the inspected State Party to be applied to the members of the inspection team:
2. Medical screening procedures for members of the inspection team, including pre- and post-entry checks, if required:
3. Agreed medical assistance to be provided by the inspected State Party:

4.   Emergency medical evacuation procedures:
5.   Agreed additional medical measures to be taken by the inspection team:
6.   Procedures for emergency response to chemical casualties of the inspection team, if required:

PART E. HEALTH AND SAFETY TRAINING
Safety training to be provided by the inspected State Party to members of the inspection team:

PART F. MODIFICATION OF INSPECTION ACTIVITIES
Activities that cannot be carried out due to health and safety reasons, and agreed alternatives to accomplish the inspection goals:

ATTACHMENT 3. SPECIFIC ARRANGEMENTS IN RELATION TO THE PROTECTION OF CONFIDENTIAL INFORMATION AT THE FACILITY

PART A. GENERAL
PART B. INFORMATION DETERMINED TO BE KEPT IN THE CONTAINER UNDER DUAL CONTROL

ATTACHMENT 4. ARRANGEMENTS FOR INSPECTION TEAMS' CONTACTS WITH THE MEDIA OR PUBLIC

ATTACHMENT 5. INFORMATION ON THE FACILITY PROVIDED BY THE INSPECTED STATE PARTY

PART A. DECLARATION OF THE FACILITY
PART B. SITE DIAGRAM
PART C. ADDITIONAL INFORMATION ON THE FACILITY PROVIDED BY THE INSPECTED STATE PARTY

ATTACHMENT 6. STANDARD MAINTENANCE ACTIVITIES AND MONITORING AR-RANGEMENTS

1.   Standard Maintenance Activities
2.   Monitoring Arrangements

ATTACHMENT 7. INSPECTION EQUIPMENT

PART A: APPROVED EQUIPMENT BELONGING TO THE OPCW; AND AGREED PROCEDURES FOR THEIR USE

Equipment name and identification/ procedures for use	Areas where equipment shall not be used	Restriction(s) (nature, conditions, reasons, etc.):	Alternative- measures for accomplishing inspection objectives

PART B: FACILITY EQUIPMENT TO BE PROVIDED BY THE INSPECTED STATE PARTY

Equipment type and specification	Location and operator	Agreed use by the inspection team	Remarks

PART C: MONITORING INSTRUMENTS TO BE INSTALLED AND MAINTAINED WITH THE SUPPORT OF THE INSPECTED STATE PARTY.

Instrument	Installation point	Maintenance procedures	Remarks

PART D: SPECIAL HANDLING REQUIREMENTS FOR EQUIPMENT OR SUPPLIES

Item	Special handling/ Control procedures	Location of storage	Remarks

PART E: PROCEDURES FOR DECONTAMINATION OF EQUIPMENT

PART F: PROCEDURES FOR USE OF INSPECTION TEAM COMMUNICATIONS EQUIPMENT

ATTACHMENT 8. RECORDS TO BE MAINTAINED BY THE FACILITY

ATTACHMENT 9. AGREED PROCEDURES FOR CONDUCTING INTERVIEWS

ATTACHMENT 10. AGREED PROCEDURES FOR PHOTOGRAPHY

ATTACHMENT 11. SAMPLING AND ANALYSIS PROCEDURES

ATTACHMENT 12. SEALING, MARKING AND INVENTORY CONTROL PROCEDURES

PART A. SEALING

PART B. MARKING AND OTHER INVENTORY CONTROL PROCEDURES

ATTACHMENT 13. SERVICES TO BE PROVIDED BY THE INSPECTED STATE PARTY

PART A. SERVICES TO BE PROVIDED

1. Vehicles:
2. Workspace:
3. Lodging:
4. Meals:
5. Medical:
6. Use of on-site sampling and analytical equipment as detailed Attachment 2, Part B, and Attachment 11 to this Agreement.
7. Communications:
8. Inspected State Party utilities (electricity, water, etc.), inspection equipment and maintenance, and other technical and logistical support for inspection team equipment as detailed in Attachment 7 to this Agreement.
9. Other services and support as identified in all pertinent sections of this Agreement or as otherwise agreed between the inspected State Party and the IT.
10. Secure storage areas:

PART B. FORM - REQUEST FOR SERVICES TO BE PROVIDED

Date:

Location:

Inspection number:

Name of the authorised member of the inspection team:

Category of services requested:

Description of services requested:

Approval of the request by inspected State Party:

Comments on the request by the inspected State Party:

Certification of the authorised member of the inspection team that the requested services have been provided:

Comments by the authorised member of the inspection team in regard to the quality of the services provided:

[Signature of the authorised member of the inspection team]

ATTACHMENT 14. CHEMICAL WEAPONS TAGGING PROCEDURES

ATTACHMENT 15. PROCEDURES FOR OPENING SHIPPING/STORAGE CONTAINERS

ATTACHMENT 16. STANDARDISED PRELIMINARY FINDINGS FORMAT

14.4 Model for CWPFs

C-IV/DEC.13 adopted by the Conference of the States Parties at its Fourth Session on 29 June 1999 and entitled "Model facility agreement for chemical weapons production facilities"

The Conference

Recalling that, in accordance with paragraph 8 of Part III of the Verification Annex, facility agreements shall be based on models for such agreements;

Recalling that the issue of model facility agreements was referred by the Conference to the Committee of the Whole (C-I/2, dated 12 May 1997);

Further recalling its decision on the procedure for addressing unresolved issues during the third intersessional period (C-III/DEC.11, dated 20 November 1998);

Taking note of the decision taken by the Executive Council on the model agreement for chemical weapons production facilities (EC-XV/DEC.8, dated 29 April 1999);

Taking note of the report submitted to it by the Chairman of the Committee of the Whole on the results of the work on unresolved issues during the third intersessional period (this document will be allocated a reference number when it is made available to delegations);

Hereby:

Decides to adopt the model facility agreement for chemical weapons production facilities as contained in the annex hereto;

Further decides to remove the issue of the model facility agreement for chemical weapons production facilities from the list of unresolved issues.

Annex
MODEL FACILITY AGREEMENT FOR CHEMICAL WEAPONS
PRODUCTION FACILITIES[6]

The Organisation for the Prohibition of Chemical Weapons, hereinafter referred to as the "OPCW",

---

[6] This model agreement is also applicable to chemical weapons production facilities in the process of conversion [footnote in original].

and ...., hereinafter referred to as the "inspected State Party", both constituting the Parties to this Agreement have agreed on the following arrangements in relation to the conduct of systematic verification in accordance with Article V of the Convention on the Prohibition of the Development, Production, Stockpiling and Use of Chemical Weapons and of their Destruction, hereinafter referred to as the "Convention", and Parts II, III, and V of its Annex on Implementation and Verification, hereinafter referred to as the "Verification Annex", at the ....
..............., Geographic Co-ordinates: ...., declared under Article III, paragraph 1 (c)(ii), and paragraph 1 of Part V of the Verification Annex of the Convention, hereinafter referred to as the "facility":

SECTI0N 1. GENERAL PROVISIONS

1. The purpose of this Agreement is to facilitate the implementation of the provisions of the Convention in relation to systematic verification, especially on-site inspection conducted at the facility pursuant to paragraph 6 of Article V and paragraphs 48 to 57 [and 73 and 79 to 85][7] of Part V of the Verification Annex of the Convention and in accordance with the respective obligations of the inspected State Party and the OPCW under the Convention.
2. Nothing in this Agreement shall be applied or interpreted in a way that is contradictory to the provisions of the Convention. In case of inconsistency between this Agreement and the Convention, the Convention shall prevail.
3. The Parties have agreed to apply for planning purposes the general factors contained in Attachment 1 to this Agreement.
4. In case of any development due to circumstances brought about by unforeseen events which could affect the conduct of systematic verification, the inspected State Party shall notify the OPCW and the inspection team as soon as the development has occurred.
5. The language for communication between the inspection team and the inspected State Party during inspections shall be _____ (one or more of the languages of the Convention).
6. In case of need for the urgent departure, emergency evacuation or urgent travel of inspector(s) from the territory of the inspected State Party the inspection team leader shall inform the inspected State Party of such a need. . The inspected State Party shall arrange without undue delay such departure, evacuation or travel. In all cases the inspected State Party shall determine the means of transportation and routes to be taken. The costs of such departure, evacuation or travel of inspectors, if due to health or administrative reasons not related to the inspection, shall be borne by the OPCW.
7. Inspectors shall wear unique badges provided by _____, which must be worn at all times, as agreed, within the facility perimeter.

SECTION 2. HEALTH AND SAFETY

1. Procedures to ensure health and safety during inspections are governed by the Convention, the OPCW Health and Safety Policy and Regulations and applicable national, local and facility safety and environmental regulations. Attachment 2 contains agreements addressing operational conflicts between health and safety requirements, standards, and procedures of the OPCW and those in force at the facility at specific locations. It also contains agreed circumstances where the health and safety requirements and standards at the facility, being more stringent than those of the OPCW Health and Safety Policy, will take precedence. Also, the agreed conditions and procedures for on-site sampling and analysis for purposes of personal safety of the inspection team are contained in Attachment 2, Part B, paragraph 4.

---

[7] Include second part if required for facilities to be converted for purposes not prohibited under the Convention [footnote in original].

2. In carrying out its activities, the inspection team shall, in accordance with paragraph 43 of Part II of the Verification Annex, observe applicable national safety and environmental regulations and safety and environmental regulations established at the inspected facility including regulations for the protection of controlled environments within the inspected facility and for personal safety, if applicable, as well as any additional safety requirements referred to in paragraph 3 of this Section, provided that these requirements and standards can be technically complied with. These documents shall be made available to the inspection team as necessary, as soon as practically possible upon the inspection team's request, but in any case no later than by the end of the pre-inspection briefing.

3. In the course of the pre-inspection briefing the inspection team shall be briefed by the representatives of the inspected State Party on all health and safety matters which, in the view of those representatives, are relevant to the conduct of the inspection at the facility, including:

    (a) full information on the health and safety requirements of the site identifying specific hazards and the likely risks associated with those hazards;

    (b) information on any additional health and safety measures or requirements not contained in this Agreement that should be observed during a particular inspection;

    (c) procedures to be followed in case of an accident or in case of other emergencies, including a briefing on emergency signals, routes and exits, and the location of emergency meeting points and facilities; and

    (d) information on any areas within the facility in which, for reasons of safety, specific inspection activities or access must be limited during a particular inspection, detailing reasons for limiting inspection activities or access and alternatives to access, if any. This is without prejudice to the obligations of the inspected State Party to provide access to the declared facility for the purpose of carrying out inspection activities, in accordance with the Convention.

    Upon request, the inspection team shall certify receipt of any such information if it is provided in written form.

4. In the case of emergency situations or accidents involving inspection team members while at the facility, the inspection team shall comply with the facility emergency procedures and the inspected State Party shall to the extent possible provide medical and other assistance in a timely and effective manner with due regard to the rules of medical ethics if medical assistance is requested. Information on medical services and facilities to be used for this purpose is contained in Part D of Attachment 2 and in Part A of Attachment 13. If the Organisation undertakes other measures for medical support in regard to inspection team members involved in emergency situations or accidents, the inspected State Party will render assistance to such measures to the extent possible. The Organisation will be responsible for the consequences of such measures.

5. The inspection team shall refrain from any action during the course of an inspection which by its nature could endanger the safety of the team, the facility, its personnel, or cause harm to the environment. The inspected State Party may decline to conduct certain inspection activities, requested to be performed by the inspection team, if the inspected State Party considers that such activities could endanger the safety of the facility, its personnel, or the inspection team. In such cases, the inspected State Party shall explain the circumstances and safety considerations involved, and provide alternative means for accomplishing the inspection activities. This is without prejudice to the obligations of the inspected State Party to provide access to the declared facility for the purpose of carrying out inspection activities, in accordance with the Convention. The inspection team shall record any refusal of inspection activity, as well as inspection team comments and the inspected State Party's explanation, in the document on preliminary findings and in the final inspection report.

6. In accordance with the OPCW Health and Safety Policy, the inspected State Party may provide available data based on detection and monitoring, to the agreed extent necessary to

satisfy concerns that may exist regarding the health and safety of the inspection team.

7. The inspected State Party shall have the opportunity to familiarise itself with the OPCW approved equipment, including the equipment listed in Part A of Attachment 7.

SECTION 3. CONFIDENTIALITY

The confidentiality of information collected during the conduct of inspections is governed by the Convention, including its Confidentiality Annex, and the OPCW Policy on Confidentiality. The specific arrangements for implementing the provisions of the Convention and the OPCW Policy on Confidentiality in relation to the protection of confidential information at the facility by the Organisation relating to information collected during the conduct of inspections, are contained in Attachment 3.

SECTION 4. MEDIA AND PUBLIC AFFAIRS

The specific arrangements for the inspection team's contacts with the media or the public, if any, in relation to inspections of the facility are contained in Attachment 4.

SECTION 5. EQUIPMENT

1. As agreed between the inspected State Party and the Organisation, the approved equipment listed in Part A of Attachment 7, shall, at the discretion of the Organisation and on a routine basis, be used specifically for the inspection at the facility. The equipment will be used in accordance with the Convention, in particular with paragraph 40 of Part II of the Verification Annex, and the relevant decisions taken by the Conference of the States Parties, and any agreed procedures contained in Attachment 7.

2. The provisions of paragraph 1 above are without prejudice to paragraphs 27 to 29 of Part II of the Verification Annex.

3. The list of facility equipment to be provided as a matter of routine by the inspected State Party for use by the inspection team, or to be operated by the inspected State Party under the supervision of the inspection team is listed in Part B of Attachment 7 to this Agreement, with notation of the nature of and procedures for its operation and necessary support. Prior to any use of such equipment the inspection team may confirm that the equipment meets the technical requirements necessary to support the inspection task intended to be accomplished. With respect to personal protective equipment, the requirements specified in the OPCW Health and Safety Policy and Regulations apply. With respect to the use of equipment available on-site other than the equipment listed in Part B of Attachment 7, requests made by the inspection team in accordance with paragraph 30 of Part II of the Verification Annex shall be made in writing.

4. The existing monitoring instruments at the facility belonging to the inspected State Party that have been agreed by the Parties for use by the OPCW, if any, and agreed procedures for their installation, replacement, upgrades, modifications, use, calibration, maintenance and testing by the inspected State Party, as well as their tamper-proofing as required, are listed in Part B of Attachment 7 to this Agreement

5. The agreed monitoring instruments, if any, belonging to the OPCW to be installed at the facility, the agreed locations and procedures for their installation, replacement, upgrades, modifications, use, calibration, maintenance, testing and tamper-proofing as required, with indication of the agreed support by the inspected State Party, are listed in Part C of Attachment 7 to this Agreement.

6. The items of OPCW approved inspection equipment or supplies that require special handling or storage for safety purposes (such as agent standards or radioisotopic sources) are listed

in Part D of Attachment 7 to this Agreement, with specification of special handling requirements.

7. The items of approved inspection equipment which may be subject to specific safety requirements are listed in Part D of Attachment 7 to this Agreement, with notation of the specific restrictions and the reasons for the restrictions.

8. For the entire period of its stay at the inspected facility the inspection team shall have the right to store its equipment in a securable work space(s) provided for the inspection team in accordance with Section 16 of this Agreement.

9. The inspection team, in cooperation with the inspected State Party shall decontaminate its equipment and supplies that were contaminated during the course of the inspection, in accordance with OPCW regulations and the inspected State Party's national and local regulations covering such activity. The inspection team may request decontamination support from the inspected State Party, including preparation of decontamination means and conduct of decontamination procedures. Any support provided by the inspected State Party shall be conducted in the presence of the inspection team, unless otherwise agreed upon, and in accordance with the specific arrangements for decontamination of equipment contained in Part E of Attachment 7 to this Agreement.

SECTION 6. PRE-INSPECTION ACTIVITIES

1. Upon arrival at the facility and before commencement of an inspection, the inspection team shall, in accordance with paragraph 37 of Part II of the Verification Annex, be briefed by facility representatives on the facility. This briefing shall contain the following:
   (a) an overview of the information contained in Attachments 2 and 5 to this Agreement, to include, *inter alia*, status of closure measures, and, for monitoring of destruction, results or plans for destruction during the period of this inspection, as applicable, with an emphasis on any changes to that information that have occurred since the most recent inspection;
   (b) information on the activities which were carried out at the inspected facility pursuant to Section 6 and in accordance with Attachment 6 to this Agreement, that may have occurred since the last time the inspection team was present at the facility;
   (c) specification of any health and safety measures or limitations required for conduct of inspection activities contained in Attachment 2 and as referred to in paragraph 5 of Section 2 of this Agreement, and in Part B of Attachment 14 with emphasis on measures or limitations changed since the most recent inspection; and
   (d) information on administrative, logistical, and communications arrangements in addition to those contained in Attachment 13 of this Agreement

2. The briefing shall not exceed 3 hours.

3. Upon conclusion of the pre-inspection briefing, the inspection team leader shall provide to the representative of the inspected State Party a tentative inspection plan to facilitate the conduct of the inspection. For the purpose of facilitating development of an inspection plan, and familiarising the inspection team with the general layout of the declared facility, the inspected State Party may provide the inspection team a tour of the declared facility, if possible and agreed. The tour will be limited to a visual drive-by tour with general explanation of the physical layout of the declared facility. The conduct of any such tour will be without prejudice to the 3-hour time limit for pre-inspection activities.

4. When more than one facility is to be inspected under a single mandate, a separate pre-inspection briefing will be presented prior to inspection of each declared facility, but not earlier than conclusion of discussions of the preliminary findings by the inspected State Party and the inspection team in accordance with Part II, paragraph 60 of the Verification Annex, unless otherwise agreed by both Parties.

SECTION 7. INFORMATION ON THE FACILITY

1. Information on the facility as declared by the inspected State Party in its initial declaration or updated is referenced in Part A of Attachment 5 to this Agreement and shall be made available to the inspection team.
2. The inspected State Party shall also provide, as referenced in Part B of Attachment 5 to this Agreement, a detailed site diagram of the facility. The site diagram shall be drawn to scale, clearly showing the facility perimeter delineated where possible by using man-made or natural features; it shall include all road and rail exits; location of each structure situated within the facility with structure purpose, number, or designation indicated for each; significant geographical relief features in the vicinity of the facility; if the facility is situated within a larger complex, specification of the exact location within the larger complex; geographic co-ordinates of a point within the facility specified to the nearest second; an arrow indicating the orientation of the facility relative to true north; and a legend identifying all symbols used on the diagram and the scale used.
3. In addition to the information referred to in paragraphs 1 and 2 of this Section, the inspection team shall be provided with the information about the facility referenced in Part C of Attachment 5 of this Agreement.
4. The inspected State Party shall, in case of change(s) to the information referred to in this Section, inform the inspection team arriving for subsequent inspection about such change(s) during the pre-inspection briefing.

SECTION 8. MAINTENANCE AND OTHER ACTIVITIES OF THE INSPECTED STATE PARTY AT THE FACILITY[8]

1. The following activities may be carried out at the facility between the time of closure and time of destruction of the facility by personnel from the inspected State Party:
    (a) in accordance with paragraphs 15 to 17 of Part V of the Verification Annex, the standard maintenance activities contained in Part A of Attachment 6 to this Agreement; and
    (b) in accordance with paragraph 14 of Part V of the Verification Annex, safety and physical security activities contained in Part B of Attachment 6 to this Agreement.
2. The inspected State Party shall submit, as part of its general and detailed plans for destruction, its plans for conducting maintenance activities at the facility in accordance with paragraph 16 of Part V of the Verification Annex.
3. No other activities unrelated to closure and destruction [or conversion] of the facility shall be conducted at the facility by personnel from the inspected State Party, except those activities listed in Part C of Attachment 6 to this Agreement.
4. Each activity conducted at the facility shall be recorded by the inspected State Party in a log-book kept at the facility for that purpose. The format of such a log-book is contained in Part D of Attachment 6 to this Agreement.
5. The inspected State Party shall:
    (a) indicate entrance(s) that would be used for activities, as specified in Parts A, B and C of Attachment 6 to this Agreement;
    (b) keep the log book referred to in paragraph 4 of this Section;
    (c) specifically indicate in the log book each activity at the facility, which resulted in the intentional or non intentional breakage of seals, and attach an explanation of the reasons and circumstances leading to such actions;
    (d) secure the facility after having conducted the activity, including the building(s) within

---

[8] Not applicable to facilities whose conversion the Director-General has certified has been completed [footnote in original].

its declared perimeter or the existing perimeter within which the facility is located with lock and key. Key control shall be maintained by the facility and all entries shall be contained in the log-book to ensure no unauthorised access per Part D of Attachment 6 to this Agreement;

(e) inform the OPCW, within the shortest time possible, of any breakage of seals and of subsequent measures taken to secure the facility; and

(f) present the log book to the inspection team as a matter of routine during the pre inspection briefing.

6. If access to the facility becomes necessary for reasons of safety, physical security or to prevent a hazard resulting from events unforeseen when the annual destruction plan was submitted, the inspected State Party shall:

(a) have the right to, if necessary, break the existing seals, as appropriate;

(b) within the shortest time possible notify the OPCW about the breaking of seals, specifying which seals are to be or were broken and the reason for the immediate access to the facility;

(c) secure the facility and its declared perimeter or the facility and the existing perimeter of the production area within which the facility is located with lock and key and notify the OPCW about the measures taken to secure the facility. Key control shall be maintained by the facility to ensure no unauthorised access; and

(d) record the occurrence as under paragraph 5(c) of this Section.

SECTION 9. AGREED MEASURES FOR FACILITIES UNDER CONVERSION

1. Agreed measures for conversion, and agreed measures affecting the closure of the facility to ensure that there is no resumption of chemical weapons production, are contained in Attachment 15 to this Agreement. No other activities unrelated to conversion of the facility shall be conducted routinely at the facility by personnel from the inspected State Party except those referred to in Part C of Attachment 15 to this Agreement.

2. Attachment 15 to this Agreement applies to facilities planned for conversion or under the process of conversion, for purposes not prohibited under the Convention.

SECTION 10. AGREED MEASURES FOR CLOSURE

In accordance with paragraph 13 of Part V of the Verification Annex, agreed measures undertaken for closure of the facility and securing the measures for closure are contained in Attachment 16 to this Agreement. These measures shall not be reversed except as part of the destruction of the facility.

SECTION 11. CONDUCT OF THE INSPECTION.

11.1 GENERAL

1. The period of inspection shall begin immediately upon completion of the pre-inspection activities.

2. Before the commencement of inspection activities, the inspection team leader shall inform the representative of the inspected State Party about the initial steps to be taken in implementing the inspection plan, the plan to be adjusted by the inspection team as circumstances warrant throughout the inspection process in consultation with the inspected State Party as to its implementability in regard to paragraph 40 of Part II of the Verification Annex. If requested, at the beginning of inspection activities, the inspected State Party may provide a tour of the facility.

3. The inspection team shall abide by paragraph 40 of Part II of the Verification Annex which

reads: "The activities of the inspection team shall be so arranged as to ensure the timely and effective discharge of its functions and the least possible inconvenience to the inspected State Party or host State and disturbance to the facility or area inspected. The inspection team shall avoid unnecessarily hampering or delaying the operation of the facility and avoid affecting safety. In particular, the inspection team shall not operate the facility. If the inspection team considers that, to fulfil the mandate, particular operations should be carried out in the facility, it shall request the designated representative of the inspected facility to have them performed. The representative of the inspected State Party shall carry out the request to the extent possible."

4. The inspection team shall have the right to confirm the precise location of the facility, i.e., its declared geographic co-ordinates, utilising, as necessary, approved location-finding equipment or other suitable techniques.

5. The inspection team shall have the right to seal its workspace.

6. Pursuant to paragraph 45 of Part II, and paragraph 53 of Part V of the Verification Annex, the inspection team shall have the right to unimpeded access to the inspected facility including any munitions, devices, bulk containers, or other containers therein, as defined by the declared perimeter specified on the site diagram contained in Part B of Attachment 5 to this Agreement.

7. The inspection activities described in this Section shall be performed in accordance with paragraphs 14 to 16 of the Confidentiality Annex and the health and safety requirements specified in Section 2 and Attachment 2 to this Agreement.

8. While at the inspection site, inspectors shall be free to conduct: visual inspections, record checks, inventorying, measurements, sealing, tagging and marking, monitoring, and interviews. The team shall also be free to have photographs or images taken, or conduct other checks and activities consistent with the Convention, in accordance with agreed procedures detailed in this Section and the applicable attachments to this Agreement.

9. In accordance with Paragraph 47 of Part II of the Verification Annex, inspection team members shall have the right to inspect documentation and records they deem relevant to the conduct of their mission.

11.2 INSPECTIONS OF MEASURES FOR CLOSURE[9]

The inspection team shall have the right to check, during an inspection with regard to the agreed measures for closure, in accordance with paragraph 13 of Part V of the Verification Annex, *inter alia* for the following:

(a) absence of any personnel at the specialised buildings and at standard buildings of the facility, except for personnel carrying out agreed activities;

(b) equipment directly related to the production of chemical weapons, including, *inter alia*, process control equipment and utilities, remains disconnected;

(c) protective installations and equipment used exclusively for the safety of operations of the chemical weapons production facility have been decommissioned;

(d) blind flanges and other devices installed to prevent the addition of chemicals to, or the removal of chemicals from, any specialised process equipment for synthesis, separation or purification of chemicals defined as a chemical weapon, any storage tank, or any machine for filling chemical weapons, the heating, cooling, or supply of electrical or other forms of power to such equipment, storage tanks, or machines have not been tampered with; and

(e) rail, road and other access routes for heavy transport to the facility, except those required for agreed activities, have been interrupted

---

[9] Not applicable to facilities whose conversion the Director-General has certified has been completed [footnote in original].

11.3 CONFIRMATION OF DESTRUCTION

In accordance with paragraphs 27 and 56 of Part V of the Verification Annex and the detailed plan for the destruction, inspectors shall have the right to confirm that the chemical weapons production facility has been destroyed.

11.4 ACCESS TO AND INSPECTION OF THE FACILITY

1. Pursuant to paragraph 45 of Part II and paragraph 53, and as applicable, paragraph 85, of Part V of the Verification Annex, the inspection team shall have unimpeded access to the inspected facility as defined by the declared perimeter specified on the site diagram contained in Part B of Attachment 5 to this Agreement.

2. In those areas defined in paragraph 1 of this Section to which unimpeded access shall be granted, the inspection activities described in this Section shall be performed in accordance with paragraphs 14 to 16 of the Confidentiality Annex and the health and safety requirements specified in Section 2 and Attachment 2 to this Agreement. Specific areas in which, for reasons of safety, inspection activity must be limited are identified in Part B of Attachment 14 to this Agreement with notation of the specific inspection activity that must be limited and reasons for the limitation.

3. In accordance with paragraph 85 of Part V of the Verification Annex, the inspection team shall also have managed access to the area of the plant site within which the facility is located. Such area is described in detail in Part A of Attachment 14 to this Agreement.

4. Inspectors shall have the right to observe all areas, all activities, and all items of equipment at the facility, and, in particular, as applicable:
   (a) check information concerning destroyed structures, verify the destruction of such structures, and check information concerning equipment and its destruction;
   (b) check on the nature of each facility operating at the site;
   (c) verify the certification of the inspected State Party that no specialised equipment or specialised buildings are being used and that specialised equipment and specialised buildings have been rendered inactive;
   (d) verify the implementation of the measures and procedures agreed under Section 8 of this Agreement; and
   (e) verify that activities prohibited by the Convention are not carried out at this facility.

11.5 ACCESS TO AND INSPECTION OF DOCUMENTATION AND RECORDS

1. In accordance with Paragraph 47 of Part II of the Verification Annex, inspection team members shall have the right to inspect documentation and records they deem relevant to the conduct of their mission.

2. Without prejudice to this right, the inspected State Party shall make available to the inspection team upon request, as soon as possible, for the purpose of, *inter alia*, providing assurance that the status of the site is consistent with the declaration and that no activity prohibited under the Convention has occurred, the documentation and records, listed in Attachment 8 to this Agreement, that will be routinely required for the conduct of verification. Records on maintenance activities, as specified in Section 8 and in Attachment 6 to this Agreement shall also be made available on a routine basis. The information on the specific documentation and records that shall be available, as well as location and format of the records and other documentation is contained in Attachment 8 to this Agreement.

11.6 INTERVIEWS

The agreed procedures for interviews are contained in Attachment 9 of this Agreement.

11.7 COMMUNICATIONS

1. In accordance with paragraph 44 of Part II of the Verification Annex the inspection team

shall have the right throughout the in-country period to communicate with the Headquarters of the Technical Secretariat. For this purpose they may use OPCW approved equipment. The procedures governing the use of such equipment are contained in Part A of Attachment 7 to this Agreement. In case the inspection team and the inspected State Party agree to use any of the inspected State Party's communications equipment the list of such equipment and the provisions for its use are contained in Part B of Attachment 7 to this Agreement. The provision of communications services to the inspection team by the inspected State Party shall be in accordance with Attachment 13 to this Agreement.

2. The agreed means of communication between inspection team sub-groups are contained in Part F of Attachment 7 to this Agreement.

11.8 PHOTOGRAPHS

1. Photographs shall be taken in accordance with paragraph 48 of Part II of the Verification Annex. The procedures for photography are contained in Attachment 10 to this Agreement.
2. One camera of the instant development type furnished by the inspection team shall be used for taking two identical photographs in numerical sequence.
3. The representative of the inspected facility has the right to object to the use of photographic equipment in specific areas, buildings or structures, if such use would be incompatible with safety or fire regulations given the characteristics of the chemicals stored in the area in question. The relevant restrictions on use of photographic equipment at the inspected facility are contained in Part C of Attachment 7 to this Agreement. If the objection is raised due to safety concerns, the inspected State Party will, if possible, furnish photographic equipment that meets the regulations. If the use of photographic equipment is not permissible at all in specific areas, buildings or structures for the reasons stated above, the inspected State Party shall provide a written explanation of its objection to the inspection team leader and propose an alternative. The explanation, along with the inspection team leader's comments will be included in the inspection team's preliminary findings and in the final inspection report.
4. The inspection team shall also have the right to have a photographic record of seals and tags it employs during the conduct of the inspection.

11.9 SEALS, MARKERS AND OTHER INVENTORY CONTROL DEVICES

1. In accordance with paragraph 45 of Part V of the Verification Annex, inspectors shall employ, as appropriate, agreed seals, markers, or other inventory control procedures to facilitate an accurate inventory of declared items.
2. In accordance with paragraphs 44(a) and (c), 49(a), (b) and (e) and paragraph 50 of Part V of the Verification Annex, the inspectors shall employ, as appropriate, tamper-indicating seals to prevent undetected reactivation of the facility.
3. Procedures for installation of these agreed seals, markers, and other devices are contained in Attachment 12 to this Agreement.
4. The list of seals left in place at the conclusion of the inspection, as agreed and required under the provisions of Part V of the Verification Annex, shall be attached to the document on preliminary findings.
5. Without prejudice to paragraph 6 of Section 8 above, seals, markers, and other inventory devices will only be applied, removed, and/or altered in the presence of representatives of the inspection team and inspected State Party.

11.10 MEASUREMENTS

1. Measurements taken in the course of carrying out the inspection by the inspection team or by the inspected State Party at the inspection team's request shall be recorded and signed by an inspector.
2. To help resolve potential ambiguities these measurements and data may be certified as accu-

rate by the representative of the inspected State Party, at the discretion of the inspected State Party, immediately after they are gathered. In case of discrepancies both Parties shall make efforts to resolve discrepancies as soon as possible before the end of the inspection period. If necessary, the representative of the inspected State Party and the inspector shall each record the method(s) used and the final result(s). Such measurements shall be recorded in the document on preliminary findings.

11.11 SAMPLING AND ANALYSIS

Without prejudice to paragraphs 52 to 58 of Part II of the Verification Annex, procedures for sampling and analysis for verification purposes are contained in Attachment 11.

11.12 MONITORING WITH ON-SITE INSTRUMENTS

1.   The list of agreed on-site monitoring instruments, as well as agreed conditions, procedures, installation points, and security measures to prevent tampering with such on-site monitoring instruments are contained in Parts A and B of Attachment 7 of this Agreement, as applicable.
2.   Pursuant to paragraph 10, Part III of the Verification Annex (if applicable), the Technical Secretariat shall have the right of continuous monitoring with instruments or systems.
3.   The inspected State Party shall in accordance with paragraph 14 of Part III of the Verification Annex immediately notify the Technical Secretariat if an event occurs or may occur at the facility where the monitoring instruments are installed, which may have an impact on the monitoring system. The inspected State Party shall co-ordinate subsequent actions with the Technical Secretariat with a view to restoring the operation of the monitoring system and establishing interim measures, if necessary, as soon as possible. All such actions shall be recorded in the log-book referred to in Section 8 of this Agreement.

SECTION 12. REPRESENTATIVE OF THE INSPECTED STATE PARTY

1.   In discharging their functions, inspectors shall communicate with personnel of the facility only through the designated representative(s) of the inspected State Party.
2.   In keeping with the provisions of paragraph 41 of Part II of the Verification Annex, the inspected State Party shall ensure that its representative(s) may at all times be reached by the inspection team leader and designated members of the inspection team either in person or by telephone. The inspected State Party shall provide the names and means of contact for its designated representative(s) to the inspection team leader.

SECTION 13. CLARIFICATIONS

In accordance with paragraph 51 of Part II of the Verification Annex inspectors shall have the right to request clarifications in connection with ambiguities that arise during an inspection. Such requests shall be made promptly through the representative of the inspected State Party. The representative of the inspected State Party shall provide the inspection team, during the inspection, with such clarification as may be necessary to remove the ambiguity. If questions related to an object or a building located within the inspection site are not resolved, the object or building shall, if requested, be photographed for the purpose of clarifying its nature and function. The inspection team shall include in the document on preliminary findings compiled in accordance with Section 14 of this Agreement any such unresolved questions, relevant clarifications, and a copy of any photographs taken.

SECTION 14. DEBRIEFING AND PRELIMINARY FINDINGS

1.   In accordance with paragraph 60 of Part II of the Verification Annex, "upon completion of

an inspection the inspection team shall meet with representatives of the inspected State Party and the personnel responsible for the inspection site to review the preliminary findings of the inspection team and to clarify any ambiguities. The inspection team shall provide to the representatives of the inspected State Party its preliminary findings in written form according to a standardised format, together with a list of samples and copies of written information and data gathered and other material to be taken off-site. The document shall be signed by the inspection team leader. In order to indicate that he has taken notice of the content of this document, the representative of the inspected State Party shall countersign the document. This meeting shall be completed not later than 24 hours after the completion of the inspection".

2.   The document on preliminary findings shall also include, *inter alia*, the list of results of analysis, if conducted on site, records of seals, results of inventories, copies of photographs to be retained by the inspection team, and results of certified measurements. It will be prepared in accordance with the standardised preliminary findings format referenced in Attachment 17. Any substantive changes to this format will be made only after consultation with the inspected State Party.

3.   Any documentation and records provided by the inspected State Party that are not attached to the document on preliminary findings may be taken off-site by the inspection team only with the specific authorisation of the inspected State Party.

4.   Before the conclusion of the meeting the inspected State Party may provide written comments and clarifications to the inspection team on any issue related to the conduct of the inspection. These written comments and clarifications shall be attached to the document on the preliminary findings.

SECTION 15. VISITS

1.   As a measure of systematic verification, visits to the facility may be required, in accordance with the relevant provisions set forth in Part III and V of the Verification Annex:
   (a)   to perform any necessary maintenance or replacement of equipment, or to adjust the coverage of the monitoring system as required, in accordance with paragraph 15 of Part III;
   (b)   to take action subsequent to an event that has occurred or may occur at the facility which may have an impact on the monitoring system, in accordance with paragraph 14 or 16 of Part III; and
   (c)   to resolve urgent problems in accordance with paragraph 52 of Part V.

2.   The size of the team conducting such a visit shall be limited to the number of personnel required to perform the specific tasks for which the visit is being conducted and shall not exceed the maximum size of team allowed for this type of facility inspection.

3.   The duration of the visit pursuant to subparagraphs (a) to (c) of paragraph 1 of this Section shall be limited to the minimum time required to perform the specific tasks for which the visit is being conducted and in any case shall not exceed the maximum duration allowed for this type of facility inspection. Access provided during the visit shall be limited to that required to perform the specific tasks for which the visit is being conducted, unless otherwise agreed to with the inspected State Party.

4.   Arrangements for such a visit shall be the same as for the conduct of an inspection.

SECTION 16. SERVICES TO BE PROVIDED

1.   The inspected State Party shall provide or arrange for the provision of the following services listed in detail in Part A of Attachment 13 to this Agreement to the inspection team throughout the duration of the inspection:

    (a) interpretation

    (b) communication means;

    (c) transportation;

    (d) working space, including equipment storage space;

    (e) lodging;

    (f) meals;

    (g) medical care; and

    (h) equipment and utilities support, as detailed in the pertinent Sections of this Agreement.

2.   The inspected State Party shall also provide other services and support as identified in all pertinent Sections of this Agreement.

3.   Requests from the inspection team to the inspected State Party to provide or arrange services in addition to those listed in paragraphs 1 and 2 above, shall be made in writing if requested by the inspected State Party by the inspection team's leader or designate, using the form contained in Part B of Attachment 13 to this Agreement, and which shall be signed by the inspected State Party upon receipt. Requests should normally be made as soon as the need for services has been identified. The provision of such services shall be acknowledged in writing by an authorised member of the inspection team. Copies of all such requests signed by both Parties with provision acknowledged shall be kept by both Parties.

4.   The costs of providing the services to the inspection team shall be borne by the inspected State Party as specified in Attachment 13 to this Agreement

SECTION 17. LIABILITIES

Any claim by the inspected State Party against the Organisation or by the Organisation against the inspected State Party in respect of any alleged damage or injury resulting from inspections at the facility in accordance with this Agreement, without prejudice to paragraph 22 of the Confidentiality Annex, shall be settled in accordance with international law and, as appropriate, with the provisions of Article XIV of the Convention.

SECTION 18. STATUS OF ATTACHMENTS

The Attachments form an integral part of this Agreement. Any reference to the Agreement includes the Attachments. However, in case of any inconsistency between this Agreement and any Attachment, the sections of the Agreement shall prevail.

SECTION 19. AMENDMENTS, MODIFICATIONS AND UPDATES

1.   Amendments to this Agreement may be proposed by either Party and shall be agreed to and enter into force under the same conditions as provided for under Section 21 of this Agreement.

2.   Modifications to the Attachments to this Agreement, with the exception of Attachment 1, Attachment 5, and Part D of Attachment 7, may be agreed upon in writing at any time between the representative of the OPCW and the representative of the inspected State Party, provided that both are specifically authorised to do so. The Director-General shall inform the Executive Council about any such modifications. Each Party to this Agreement may revoke its consent to a modification not later than 30 days after the modification was agreed upon. After this time period has elapsed, the modification shall be considered as meeting the requirements of Section 21 of this Agreement.

3.   Updates to Part A of Attachment 1, Attachment 5, and Part D of Attachment 7 to this Agreement shall be made by the inspected State Party. Updates to Part B of Attachment 1 to this Agreement shall be made by the OPCW. The Party making the updates shall provide written

notification thereof to the other Party no less than 30 days before the updates are to take effect.

SECTION 20. SETTLEMENT OF DISPUTES

Any dispute between the Parties that may arise out of the application or interpretation of this Agreement shall be settled in accordance with Article XIV of the Convention.

SECTION 21. ENTRY INTO FORCE

This Agreement shall enter into force upon approval by the Executive Council and signature by the two Parties. If the inspected State Party has additional internal requirements, it shall so notify the Organisation in writing by the date of signature. In such cases, this Agreement shall enter into force on the date that the inspected State Party gives the Organisation written notification that its internal requirements for entry into force have been met.

SECTION 22. DURATION AND TERMINATION

[This Agreement shall cease to be in force when the provisions of paragraph 55 of Part V of the Verification Annex no longer apply to this facility at the date on which all of the requirements of paragraph 56 of that Part have been met.]

[This agreement shall cease to be in force as determined by the Executive Council in accordance with paragraph 85 of Part V of the Verification Annex.][10]

Done at _____ in ___ copies, in _____ language(s), each being equally authentic.

ATTACHMENTS

List of Attachments	
Attachment 1	Part A. To be provided and updated by the inspected State Party
Planning Data for Inspections	Part B. To be provided and updated by the OPCW
Attachment 2	Part A. Basic principles
Health and Safety Requirements and Procedures	Part B. Detection and monitoring
	Part C. Protection
	Part D. Medical requirements
	Part E. Health and safety training
	Part F. Modification of inspection activities
Attachment 3	Part A. General
Specific Arrangements in Relation to the Protection of Confidential Information at the Facility	Part B. Information determined to be kept in the container under dual control
Attachment 4	
Arrangements for the Inspection Team's Contacts with the Media or the Public Concerning Inspections at the Facility	

---

[10] Use this second formulation if the agreement concerns a facility converted for purposes not prohibited [footnote in original].

List of Attachments	
Attachment 5 Information on the Facility to be Provided by the Inspected State Party	Part A. Declaration of the facility
	Part B. Site diagram
	Part C. Additional information on the facility provided by the inspected State Party
Attachment 6 Maintenance and Other Activities of the Inspected State Party at the Facility	Part A. Standard maintenance activities
	Part B. Safety and physical security activities
	Part C. Other agreed activities
	Part D. Format of the log-book for recording activities
Attachment 7 Inspection Equipment	Part A. Approved equipment belonging to the OPCW and agreed procedures for their use
	Part B. Facility equipment to be provided by the inspected State Party
	Part C. Monitoring instruments to be installed and maintained with the support of the inspected State Party
	Part D. Special Handling requirements for equipment or supplies
	Part E. Procedures for decontamination of equipment
	Part F. Procedures for use of inspection team communications equipment
	Part G. Request form
Attachment 8 Records to be Maintained by the Facility	
Attachment 9 Agreed Procedures for Conducting Interviews	
Attachment 10 Agreed Procedures for Photography	
Attachment 11 Sampling and Analysis	Part A. Procedures for taking samples
	Part B. Sample storage equipment and conditions for its use
	Part C. Procedures for sample handling and splitting
	Part D. Procedure for sample analysis
	Part E. Procedures for the disposal of hazardous waste
Attachment 12 Sealing, Marking and Inventory Control Procedures	Part A. Agreed methods for taking inventory
	Part B. Inventory control procedures for markers and other inventory control devices
	Part C. Sealing procedures
Attachment 13 Services to be Provided by the Inspected State Party	Part A. Services to be provided
	Part B. Request Form
Attachment 14 Access	Part A. Areas within the installation but beyond the facility perimeter for which access shall be permitted
	Part B. Restriction of unimpeded access for reasons of health and safety

List of Attachments	
Attachment 15	Part A. Measures related to conversion
Agreed Measures For Facilities Under Conversion	Part B. Closure measures affected by the conversion process
	Part C. Facility measures to ensure no resumption of chemical weapons production
	Part D. Verification measures and procedures agreed to ensure no resumption of chemical weapons production
Attachment 16 Agreed Measures for Closure	
Attachment 17 Standardised Preliminary Findings Format	

ATTACHMENT 1. PLANNING DATA FOR INSPECTIONS

PART A. TO BE PROVIDED AND UPDATED BY THE INSPECTED STATE PARTY:
  (a) site working hours:
  (b) site working days:
  (c) holidays or other non-working days:
  (d) facility working hours:
  (e) facility working days:
  (f) physical and/or other potential constraints to inspection activities:
  (g) Inspection activities which could be supported during non-working hours with notation of times and activities:

PART B. TO BE PROVIDED AND UPDATED BY THE OPCW:
  (a) estimated period of inspection (for planning purposes):
  (b) approximate inspection team size:
  (c) number of sub teams (consisting of no less than two inspection team members per sub team) to be accommodated:
  (d) estimated volume and weight of equipment to be brought on-site:

ATTACHMENT 2. HEALTH AND SAFETY REQUIREMENTS AND PROCEDURES

PART A. BASIC PRINCIPLES
1. Applicable health and safety regulations of the OPCW, with agreed variations from strict implementation if any:
2. Applicable health and safety regulations of the inspected State Party:
3. Medical regulations and requirements of the inspected State Party or the OPCW that take precedence as being the more stringent:

PART B. DETECTION AND MONITORING
1. Agreed hazard specific standards for workspace exposure limits and/or concentrations:
2. Procedures for detection and monitoring performed by the inspected State Party, using its own equipment, including data to be provided to the inspection team:
3. Agreed procedures for detection and monitoring performed by the inspection team in the least intrusive manner, including data to be collected, as applicable:
4. Agreed procedures for workspace sampling and analysis for purposes of personal safety of the inspection team:

PART C. PROTECTION
1. Protective equipment to be provided by the OPCW, and agreed procedures for equipment certification and use, if required:
2. Protective equipment to be provided by the inspected State Party, and agreed procedures, personnel training, and personnel qualification tests and certification required; and agreed procedures for use of the equipment are identified in Attachment 7 and will be further identified during the Pre-Inspection briefing

PART D. MEDICAL REQUIREMENTS
1. Personnel medical standards of the inspected State Party to be applied to the members of the inspection team:
2. Medical screening procedures for members of the inspection team, including pre- and post-entry checks, if required:
3. Agreed medical assistance to be provided by the inspected State Party:
4. Emergency medical evacuation procedures:
5. Agreed additional medical measures to be taken by the inspection team:
6. Procedures for emergency response to chemical casualties of the inspection team, if required:

PART E. HEALTH AND SAFETY TRAINING
Safety training to be provided by the inspected State Party to members of the inspection team:

PART F. MODIFICATION OF INSPECTION ACTIVITIES
Activities that cannot be carried out due to health and safety reasons, and agreed alternatives to accomplish the inspection goals:

ATTACHMENT 3. SPECIFIC ARRANGEMENTS IN RELATION TO THE PROTECTION OF CONFIDENTIAL INFORMATION AT THE FACILITY

PART A. GENERAL
PART B. INFORMATION DETERMINED TO BE KEPT IN THE CONTAINER UNDER DUAL CONTROL

ATTACHMENT 4. ARRANGEMENTS FOR THE INSPECTION TEAM'S CONTACT WITH THE MEDIA OR THE PUBLIC CONCERNING INSPECTIONS AT THE FACILITY

ATTACHMENT 5. INFORMATION ON THE FACILITY TO BE PROVIDED BY THE IN-SPECTED STATE PARTY

PART A. DECLARATION OF THE FACILITY
PART B. SITE DIAGRAM
PART C. ADDITIONAL INFORMATION ON THE FACILITY PROVIDED BY THE INSPECTED STATE PARTY

ATTACHMENT 6. MAINTENANCE AND OTHER ACTIVITIES OF THE INSPECTED STATE PARTY AT THE FACILITY

PART A. STANDARD MAINTENANCE ACTIVITIES

Standard maintenance activity	Procedures for monitoring

PART B. SAFETY AND PHYSICAL SECURITY ACTIVITIES
PART C. OTHER AGREED ACTIVITIES

PART D. FORMAT OF THE LOG-BOOK FOR RECORDING ACTIVITIES

ATTACHMENT 7. INSPECTION EQUIPMENT

PART A: APPROVED EQUIPMENT BELONGING TO THE OPCW; AND AGREED PROCEDURES FOR THEIR USE

Equipment name and identification/ procedures for use	Areas where equipment shall not be used	Restriction(s) (nature, conditions, reasons, etc.):	Alternative- measures for accomplishing inspection objectives

PART B: FACILITY EQUIPMENT TO BE PROVIDED BY THE INSPECTED STATE PARTY

Equipment type and specification	Location and operator	Agreed use by the inspection team	Remarks

PART C: MONITORING INSTRUMENTS TO BE INSTALLED AND MAINTAINED WITH THE SUPPORT OF THE INSPECTED STATE PARTY.

Instrument	Installation point	Maintenance procedures	Remarks

PART D: SPECIAL HANDLING REQUIREMENTS FOR EQUIPMENT OR SUPPLIES

Item	Special handling/ Control procedures	Location of storage	Remarks

PART E: PROCEDURES FOR DECONTAMINATION OF EQUIPMENT
PART F: PROCEDURES FOR USE OF INSPECTION TEAM COMMUNICATIONS EQUIPMENT
PART G. REQUEST FOR EQUIPMENT AVAILABLE ON-SITE TO BE PROVIDED IN ACCORDANCE WITH PARAGRAPH 3 OF SECTION 5

Date:
Facility:
Inspection code number:
Type and number of item(s) of equipment requested:
Submission of the request by the inspection team (name and signature of the inspection team leader or designate:
Approval of the request by the inspected State Party (name, date and signature of the representative of the inspected State Party:
Comments on the request by the inspected State Party:
Confirmation of provision of the requested item(s) (name and signature of the inspection team leader or designate):
Comments, if any, by the inspection team leader or designate in regard to the equipment provided:

ATTACHMENT 8. RECORDS TO BE MAINTAINED BY THE FACILITY

1. The following records will be provided during the pre-inspection briefing:

2. To the extent necessary to clarify discrepancies in inventories, to explain changes in inventories that have occurred between inspections, or to clarify ambiguous situations, the following documents, as applicable, will be made available for review upon written request of inspectors:

3. Records requested by the inspection team that the inspected State Party makes available for review will be provided not later than 24 hours after the request. Review will be conducted with escort present.

ATTACHMENT 9. AGREED PROCEDURES FOR CONDUCTING INTERVIEWS

ATTACHMENT 10. AGREED PROCEDURES FOR PHOTOGRAPHY

ATTACHMENT 11. SAMPLING AND ANALYSIS PROCEDURES

ATTACHMENT 12. SEALING, MARKING AND INVENTORY CONTROL PROCEDURES

PART A. SEALING
PART B. MARKING AND OTHER INVENTORY CONTROL PROCEDURES

ATTACHMENT 13. SERVICES TO BE PROVIDED BY THE INSPECTED STATE PARTY

PART A. SERVICES TO BE PROVIDED
1. International and local official communication (telephone, fax), including calls/faxes between site and headquarters:
2. Vehicles:
3. Working room, including adequate space for the storage of equipment:
4. Lodging:
5. Meals:
6. Medical care:
7. Interpretation services:
   (a) Number of interpreters:
   (b) Estimated interpretation time:
   (c) Languages:
8.   Other:

PART B. FORM - REQUEST FOR SERVICES TO BE PROVIDED
Date:
Location:
Inspection number:
Name of the authorised member of the inspection team:
Category of services requested:
Description of services requested:
Approval of the request by inspected State Party:
Comments on the request by the inspected State Party:
Certification of the authorised member of the inspection team that the requested services have been provided:
Comments by the authorised member of the inspection team in regard to the quality of the services provided:
[Signature of the authorised member of the inspection team]

ATTACHMENT 14. ACCESS

PART A. AREAS WITHIN THE INSTALLATION BUT BEYOND THE FACILITY PERIMETER FOR WHICH AC-
         CESS SHALL BE PERMITTED
PART B. RESTRICTION OF UNIMPEDED ACCESS FOR REASONS OF HEALTH AND SAFETY

ATTACHMENT 15. AGREED MEASURES FOR FACILITIES UNDER CONVERSION

PART A. MEASURES RELATED TO CONVERSION
PART B. CLOSURE MEASURES AFFECTED BY THE CONVERSION PROCESS
PART C. FACILITY MEASURES TO ENSURE NO RESUMPTION OF CHEMICAL WEAPONS PRODUCTION
PART D. VERIFICATION MEASURES AND PROCEDURES AGREED TO ENSURE NO RESUMPTION OF CHEMI-
         CAL WEAPONS PRODUCTION

ATTACHMENT 16. AGREED MEASURES FOR CLOSURE

ATTACHMENT 17. STANDARDISED PRELIMINARY FINDING FORMAT

14.5 Model for CWDFs

C-V/DEC.23 adopted by the Conference of the States Parties at its Fifth Session on 19 May 2000 and entitled "Model facility agreement for chemical weapons destruction facilities"

The Conference
     Recalling that, in accordance with paragraph 8 of Part III of the Verification Annex, facility agreements shall be based on models for such agreements;
     Bearing in mind that, in accordance with paragraph 19 of Part I of the Verification Annex, model agreements specify the general form and content for an agreement concluded between a State Party and the Organisation;
     Further recalling that at its Fourth Session, the Conference took cognisance of the status of consultations on a draft decision on the model facility agreement for chemical weapons destruction facilities (C-IV/DEC/CRP.30, dated 2 July 1999), and recommended that the Council should consider this matter further with a view to reaching agreement on the text of the model facility agreement, and to elaborating a recommendation to the Fifth Conference for its adoption.

Hereby:
1. Adopts the model agreement for chemical weapons destruction facilities as annexed to this decision, for immediate implementation;
2. Decides that this model facility agreement will be applicable to facilities conducting continuous chemical weapons destruction operations and, with appropriate modifications to be negotiated on a case by case basis, to facilities not conducting continuous chemical weapons destruction operations;
3. Also decides that individual facility agreements will be negotiated with due consideration of the requirements of the State Party and the specifics of the facility concerned, and shall be concluded and implemented in an equal and non-discriminatory manner in accordance with the Convention;
4. Further decides to remove the issue of the model agreement for chemical weapons destruction facilities from the list of outstanding issues and issues under consideration by the OPCW Executive Council.

MODEL FACILITY AGREEMENT
FOR CHEMICAL WEAPONS DESTRUCTION FACILITIES[11]

The Organisation for the Prohibition of Chemical Weapons hereinafter referred to as the "OPCW", and the Government of................................., hereinafter referred to as the "inspected State Party," both constituting the Parties to this Agreement have agreed on the following arrangements in relation to the conduct of inspections in accordance with Article IV of the Convention on the Prohibition of the Development, Production, Stockpiling and Use of Chemical Weapons and on their Destruction, hereinafter referred to as "the Convention," and Parts II, III, and IV(A) of its Annex on Implementation and Verification, hereinafter referred to as the "Verification Annex," at ...., Geographic coordinates: .... declared under Article IV of the Convention, hereinafter referred to as the "facility":

SECTION 1. GENERAL PROVISIONS

1. The purpose of this Agreement for a Chemical Weapons Destruction Facility (CWDF), hereafter referred to as this "Agreement", is to facilitate the implementation of the provisions of the Convention in relation to inspections conducted at the facility pursuant to paragraph 5 of Article IV of the Convention and in accordance with the respective obligations undertaken by the inspected State Party and the OPCW under the Convention.

2. Nothing in this Agreement shall be applied or interpreted in a way that is contradictory to the provisions of the Convention. In case of inconsistency between this Agreement and the Convention, the Convention shall prevail.

3. The Parties have agreed to apply for planning purposes the general factors contained in Attachment 1 to this Agreement.

4. The notification referred to in paragraph 33 of Part IV(A) of the Verification Annex shall be provided by the inspected State Party to the OPCW, promptly, no less than ____days in advance of any development that could affect inspection activities at the facility. In case of any development due to circumstances brought about by unforeseen events other than those addressed in Section 9.7, the inspected State Party shall notify the OPCW and the inspection team as soon as the development has occurred.

5. The language(s) for communication between the inspection team and the inspected State Party during inspections shall be _____ (insert one or more of the languages of the Convention).

6. In case of the need for the urgent departure, emergency evacuation or urgent travel of inspector(s) from the territory of the inspected State Party the inspection team leader shall inform the inspected State Party of such a need. The inspected State Party shall arrange without undue delay such departure, evacuation or travel. In such emergency or urgent circumstances, the OPCW may replace inspectors who have left the facility with new inspectors on a one-by-one basis. Inspectors replaced due to emergency or urgent circumstances cannot themselves return to the facility before the next planned rotation of inspectors at the facility. Notification for such replacements shall be provided to the inspected State Party not less than 3 working days prior to the scheduled arrival of the replacement at the point of entry of the inspected State Party. In all cases the inspected State Party shall determine the means of transportation and routes to be taken. The costs of such departure, evacuation or travel and replacement of

---

[11] This model facility agreement is applicable to facilities conducting continuous chemical weapons destruction operations. It is, however, equally applicable, with appropriate modifications to be negotiated on a case by case basis, to facilities not conducting continuous chemical weapons destruction operations [footnote in original].

inspector(s), if due to health, administrative or other reasons not related to the inspection, shall be borne by the OPCW.

7. Inspectors shall wear unique badges provided by the inspected State Party, or OPCW badges, which must be worn at all times while within the facility perimeter.

SECTION 2. HEALTH AND SAFETY

1. Procedures to ensure health and safety during inspections are governed by the Convention, the OPCW Health and Safety Policy and Regulations and applicable national, local and facility safety and environmental regulations. Attachment 2 to this Agreement contains agreements addressing variations between health and safety requirements, standards, and procedures of the OPCW and those in force at the facility at specific locations. It also contains agreed circumstances where the health and safety requirements and standards at the facility, being more stringent than those of the OPCW Health and Safety Policy, will take precedence. Also, the agreed conditions, places, and procedures for sampling and analysis for purposes of personal safety of the inspection team are contained in Part B, paragraph 4 of Attachment 2 to this Agreement.

2. In carrying out its activities, the inspection team shall, in accordance with paragraph 43 of Part II of the Verification Annex, observe applicable national safety and environmental regulations and safety and environmental regulations established at the inspected facility including regulations for the protection of controlled environments within the inspected facility and for personal safety, if applicable, as well as any additional safety requirements referred to in paragraph 3 of this Section, provided that these requirements and standards can be technically complied with. These documents shall be made available to the inspection team as necessary, as soon as practically possible upon the inspection team's request.

3. In the course of the pre-inspection briefing the inspection team shall be briefed by the representatives of the inspected State Party on all health and safety matters which, in the view of those representatives, are relevant to the conduct of the inspection at the facility, including:
   (a) full information on the health and safety requirements of the site identifying specific hazards and the likely risks associated with those hazards;
   (b) information on any additional health and safety measures or requirements not contained in this Agreement that should be observed during a particular inspection;
   (c) procedures to be followed in case of an accident or in case of other emergencies, including a briefing on emergency signals, routes and exits, and the location of emergency meeting points and facilities; and
   (d) information on any areas within the facility in which, for reasons of safety, specific inspection activities or access must be limited during a particular inspection, detailing reasons for limiting inspection activities or access and alternatives to access, if any. This is without prejudice to the obligations of the inspected State Party to provide access to the declared facility for the purpose of carrying out inspection activities, in accordance with the Convention.
   Upon request, the inspection team shall certify receipt of any such information if it is provided in written form.

4. In the case of emergency situations or accidents involving inspection team members while at the facility, the inspection team shall comply with the facility emergency procedures and the inspected State Party shall to the extent possible provide medical and other assistance in a timely and effective manner with due regard to the rules of medical ethics if medical assistance is requested. Information on medical services and facilities to be used for this purpose is contained in Part D of Attachment 2 and in Part A of Attachment 10 to this Agreement. If the OPCW undertakes other measures for medical support in regard to inspection team members involved in emergency situations or accidents, the inspected State Party will render

assistance to such measures to the extent possible. The OPCW will be responsible for the consequences of such measures.

5.   The inspection team shall refrain from any action during the course of an inspection which by its nature could endanger the safety of the team, the facility, its personnel, or cause harm to the environment. The inspected State Party may decline to conduct certain inspection activities, requested to be performed by the inspection team, if the inspected State Party considers that such activities could endanger the safety of the facility, its personnel, or the inspection team. In such cases, the inspected State Party shall explain the circumstances and safety considerations involved, and provide alternative means for accomplishing the inspection activities. The inspection team shall record any refusal of inspection activity, as well as inspection team comments and the inspected State Party's explanation, in the document on preliminary findings and in the final inspection report.

6.   In accordance with the OPCW Health and Safety Policy and Regulations, the inspected State Party may provide available data based on detection and monitoring, to the agreed extent necessary to satisfy concerns that may exist regarding the health and safety of the inspection team.

7.   The inspected State Party shall have the opportunity to familiarise itself with the OPCW approved inspection equipment, including the equipment listed in Part A of Attachment 5 to this Agreement.

SECTION 3. CONFIDENTIALITY

The confidentiality of information collected during the conduct of inspections is governed by the Convention, including its Confidentiality Annex, and the OPCW Policy on Confidentiality. The specific arrangements for implementing the provisions of the Convention and the OPCW Policy on Confidentiality in relation to the protection of confidential information at the facility by the OPCW relating to information collected during the conduct of inspections, are contained in Attachment 3 to this Agreement.

SECTION 4. MEDIA AND PUBLIC RELATIONS

The specific arrangements for the inspection team's contacts with the media or the public, if any, in relation to inspections of the facility are contained in Attachment 4 to this Agreement.

SECTION 5. INSPECTION EQUIPMENT

1.   As agreed between the inspected State Party and the OPCW, the approved equipment listed in Part A of Attachment 5, shall, at the discretion of the OPCW and on a routine basis, be brought specifically for the inspection at the facility. The equipment will be used in accordance with the Convention, in particular with paragraph 40 of Part II of the Verification Annex, and the relevant decisions taken by the Conference of the States Parties, and any agreed procedures contained in Attachment 5 to this Agreement.

2.   The provisions of paragraph 1 above are without prejudice to paragraphs 27 to 29 of Part II of the Verification Annex.

3.   The list of facility equipment to be provided as a matter of routine by the inspected State Party for use by the inspection team, or to be operated by the inspected State Party under the supervision of the inspection team is listed in Part B of Attachment 5 to this Agreement, with notation of the nature of and procedures for its operation and necessary support. Prior to any use of such equipment the inspection team may confirm that the equipment meets the technical requirements necessary to support the inspection task intended to be accomplished. With respect to personal protective equipment, the requirements specified in the OPCW Health and

Safety Policy and Regulations apply. With respect to the use of equipment available on-site other than the equipment listed in Part B of Attachment 5, requests made by the inspection team in accordance with paragraph 30 of Part II of the Verification Annex shall be made in writing.

4. The existing monitoring instruments at the facility belonging to the inspected State Party that have been agreed by the Parties for use by the OPCW, if any, and agreed procedures for their installation, replacement, upgrades, modifications, use, calibration, maintenance and testing by the inspected State Party, as well as their tamper-proofing as required, are listed in Part B of Attachment 5 to this Agreement.

5. The agreed monitoring instruments, if any, belonging to the OPCW to be installed at the facility, the agreed locations and procedures for their installation, replacement, upgrades, modifications, use, calibration, maintenance, testing and tamper-proofing as required, with indication of the agreed support by the inspected State Party, are listed in Part C of Attachment 5 to this Agreement.

6. The items of OPCW approved inspection equipment or supplies that require special handling or storage for safety purposes (such as agent standards or radioisotopic sources), if any, are listed in Part D of Attachment 5 to this Agreement, with specification of special handling requirements.

7. The items of approved inspection equipment which may be subject to specific safety requirements are listed in Part D of Attachment 5 to this Agreement, with notation of the specific restrictions and the reasons for the restrictions.

8. For the entire period of its stay at the inspected facility the inspection team shall have the right to store its equipment in a securable work space(s) provided for the inspection team in accordance with Section 14 of this Agreement.

9. Agreed procedures for the decontamination of any equipment are contained in Part E of Attachment 5 to this Agreement.

SECTION 6. INFORMATION ON THE FACILITY

1. Information on the facility in the inspected State Party's formally submitted and declared General Plan for Destruction, Detailed Facility Information (DFI), Detailed Annual Plans and Annual Reports, as well as and where relevant Manuals, Plans and Permits, are referenced in Attachment 6 to this Agreement. All information contained in these documents, including any update formally submitted previous to or subsequent to approval to this Agreement, will by reference form a part of this Agreement.

2 The detailed site diagram for the facility as declared to the OPCW in accordance with paragraph 29(b) of Part IV(A) of the Verification Annex can be used as a reference document during the inspection.

SECTION 7. PREPARATION FOR SYSTEMATIC VERIFICATION
OF THE DESTRUCTION PROCESS

1. Notification containing the OPCW request for logistical support for continuous monitoring at the facility shall be provided to the inspected State Party no later than thirty days prior to the planned installation of continuous monitoring system equipment at the facility. The notification format is contained in Attachment 10 to this Agreement.

2. The list of OPCW and/or inspected State Party inspection equipment for continuous monitoring and locations for its installation are contained in Part C Attachment 5 to this Agreement. Provisions for installation and testing are contained in Attachment 7 to this Agreement.

3. When monitoring equipment has already been installed at the facility by the inspected State Party, the OPCW and the inspected State Party will review and agree on the use of such

equipment for the systematic verification of destruction of chemical weapons. The OPCW and the inspected State Party may agree to replace, upgrade, modify any such equipment, if necessary. The list of existing monitoring equipment at the facility that has been agreed for use by the OPCW, agreed procedures for its replacement, upgrades, modifications, or tamper proofing as required, as well as its testing and use are contained in Attachment 8 to this Agreement.

4.   The inspection team may carry out a final engineering review of the facility in accordance with paragraph 60 of Part IV(A) of the Verification Annex. This review may include, *inter alia*:

    (a)   confirming that the design of the destruction process at the facility is in conformity with the information provided to the OPCW;

    (b)   confirming that the installed monitoring equipment operates in a satisfactory manner;

    (c)   arranging, if applicable, requirements for additional monitoring equipment; and

    (d)   if necessary, updating arrangements for verification and maintenance for installed monitoring equipment.

5.   The inspection team shall have the right, subject to the agreement of the inspected State Party, to have its inspection equipment installed, if applicable, *inter alia*, in the temporary holding area, in the chemical weapons disassembly area, in the chemical destruction process area, in the munitions body destruction process area, and in the solid, liquid and gas waste destruction product areas. The inspection team shall have the right to use for their equipment tamper proof seals or, if agreed by the inspected State Party, have its equipment installed in tamper proof boxes. The inspection team shall have the right to test and inspect the equipment under the observation of the inspected State Party. The inspected State Party shall, at the request of the inspection team provide the following:

    (a)   all necessary utilities for the installation and operation of the inspection equipment, including electricity, water, fuel, heating and sewerage, as required; and

    (b)   the site preparation necessary to accommodate the installation of inspection equipment for monitoring the process areas of the facility.

6.   If the inspection team determines that installation of additional inspection equipment or replacement, upgrade or modification of the already installed facility monitoring equipment are required for satisfactory assurance of non-diversion and confirmation of parameters of the destruction process, the inspection team, subject to the agreement of the inspected State Party, shall have the right to do so during the period(s) of stoppage of the facility operations so long as this revision does not impact the resumption of destruction operations on the notified date. The inspected State Party, under the observation of the inspection team, shall install, replace, upgrade or modify such equipment. The inspection team shall have the right to test and inspect the equipment under the observation of the inspected State Party.

7.   The working space for the inspection team shall be equipped, if applicable, to monitor the functioning of inspection equipment and to register the data obtained from such equipment installed at the facility to facilitate the inspection team's monitoring of the destruction process.

SECTION 8. STAFFING ARRANGEMENTS FOR CONTINUOUS PRESENCE OF INSPEC-
TORS, INCLUDING SITE FAMILIARISATION, BRIEFINGS
AND TRAINING FOR NEWLY ARRIVED INSPECTORS

1.   Upon arrival of inspectors and before the commencement of inspection activity by them, they shall be briefed by the facility representatives. This briefing, conducted in accordance with paragraph 37 of Part II of the Verification Annex, shall cover the following:

    (a)   an overview of the information contained in Attachment 6 to this Agreement, with an emphasis on any changes to that information since the last time the inspection team was present at the facility;

(b) details of any health and safety information as contained in paragraph 3 of Section 2 of this Agreement; and

(c) information on administrative and logistic arrangements additional to those contained in Attachment 1 to this Agreement, if any, that will apply during the systematic verification, as contained in Section 13 of this Agreement.

2. Notification to the inspected State Party of the intention to replace inspectors at the facility shall be provided seven days in advance of the planned date of the arrival of the replacement inspectors at the point of entry. The notification format is contained in Attachment 9 to this Agreement. Rotation of inspectors shall be carried out not more than once per .... day period and the number of inspectors subject to rotation in each case shall be no less than .... percent of the number of inspectors on site.

3. The inspected State Party shall provide inspectors the training outlined in Attachment 11 to this Agreement.

4. Pre-inspection initial safety training if necessary for inspectors shall be conducted by the inspected State Party, as contained in Attachment 11 to this Agreement. Specific training requirements are contained in Part E of Attachment 2 to this Agreement. If it is determined that an inspector's training is incomplete or out of date, then this training will be required prior to the inspector leaving the inspector work spaces to inspect the facility. This training will be provided by the inspected State Party and must be completed within 72 hours of arrival at the facility. Upon completion of such training, each member of the inspection team shall be certified by the inspected State Party as having completed the training necessary for the safe execution of their responsibilities during systematic verification at the facility.

SECTION 9. PROCEDURES FOR ON-SITE VERIFICATION

9.1 GENERAL

1. After initial visit of the inspection team for continuous monitoring, the inspection period shall begin immediately upon completion of the pre-inspection activities. Once it begins, the inspection period shall be considered continuous and uninterrupted, except as provided for in Section 9.7 to this Agreement.

2. Throughout systematic verification at the facility the inspection team leader, in conformity with paragraph 40 of Part II of the Verification Annex, shall coordinate with the representative of the inspected State Party about verification activities that require participation or assistance of the inspected State Party. Thereby, the inspected State Party can arrange for the necessary measures to provide access and support to the inspection team as appropriate without delaying the conduct of inspection activities.

3. The inspection team shall abide by paragraph 40 of Part II of the Verification Annex which reads: "The activities of the inspection team shall be so arranged as to ensure the timely and effective discharge of its functions and the least possible inconvenience to the inspected State Party or Host State and disturbance to the facility or area inspected. The inspection team shall avoid unnecessarily hampering or delaying the operation of a facility and avoid affecting its safety. In particular, the inspection team shall not operate any facility. If inspectors consider that, to fulfil their mandate, particular operations should be carried out in a facility, they shall request the designated representative of the inspected facility to have them performed. The representative shall carry out the request to the extent possible."

4. The detailed procedures for shift operations of the inspection team during systematic verification are contained in Attachment 12 to this Agreement.

5. The inspectors shall have the right to seal their office premises, including the equipment storage area.

6   The inspected State Party shall ensure adequate working conditions for the inspection team to carry out systematic verification.

7   As applicable, the list of types of vehicles subject to inspection and the detailed procedures for inspecting those vehicles when exiting the destruction facility are contained in Attachment 13 to this Agreement.

8.   Pursuant to paragraph 45 of Part II, and 70(a) of Part IV(A) of the Verification Annex, the inspection team shall have the right to unimpeded access as agreed in the facility agreement to the inspected facility including any munitions, devices, bulk containers, or other containers therein, as defined by the declared perimeter specified on the site diagram contained in Part B of Attachment 6 to this Agreement.

9.   While at the inspection site, inspectors shall be free to conduct: visual inspections, record checks, inventorying, measurements, sealing, tagging and marking, monitoring, and interviews. The team shall also be free to have photographs or images taken, or conduct other checks and activities consistent with the Convention, in accordance with agreed procedures detailed in this Section and the applicable attachments to this Agreement.

9.2   ACCESS TO AND INSPECTION OF DOCUMENTATION AND RECORDS

1.   Without prejudice to the right of inspectors in accordance with paragraph 47 of Part II of the Verification Annex to inspect documentation and records they deem relevant to the conduct of their mandate, the inspected State Party shall make available to the inspectors upon request as soon as possible, but not later than 24 hours, records and documentation listed in Attachment 15 to this Agreement, that will be routinely required for the conduct of an inspection.

2.   The aforementioned records and other documentation shall be provided to the inspection team in their existing format at the facility.

9.3   ARRANGEMENTS FOR INTERVIEWS

The agreed arrangements for interviews are contained in Attachment 14 to this Agreement.

9.4   COMMUNICATIONS

1.   In accordance with paragraph 44 of Part II of the Verification Annex the inspectors shall have the right throughout the in-country period to communicate with the Headquarters of the Technical Secretariat. For this purpose they may use OPCW duly certified approved inspection equipment. The procedures governing the use of such equipment are contained in Part F of Attachment 5 to this Agreement. In case the inspection team and the inspected State Party agree to use any of the inspected State Party's communications equipment the list of such equipment and the provisions for its use are contained in Part B of Attachment 5 to this Agreement. The provision of communications services to the inspection team by the inspected State Party shall be in accordance with Attachment 10 to this Agreement.

2.   The agreed means of communication between inspection team sub-groups are contained in Part F of Attachment 5 to this Agreement.

9.5   PHOTOGRAPHS

1.   Photographs shall be taken in accordance with paragraph 48 of Part II of the Verification Annex. The procedures for photography are contained in Attachment 28 to this Agreement.

2.   One camera of the instant development type furnished by the inspection team shall be used for taking two identical photographs consecutively.

3.   The representative of the inspected facility has the right to object to the use of photographic equipment in specific areas, buildings or structures, if such use would be incompatible with safety or fire regulations given the characteristics of the chemicals stored in the area in question. The relevant restrictions on use of photographic equipment at the inspected facility are contained in Attachment 5 to this Agreement. If the objection is raised due to safety concerns, the inspected State Party will, if possible, furnish photographic equipment that meets the regulations. If the use of photographic equipment is not permissible at all in specific areas, buildings or structures for the reasons stated above, the inspected State Party shall provide a written explanation of its objection to the inspection team leader and propose an alternative. The explanation, along with the inspection team leader's comments will be included in the inspection team's preliminary findings and in the final inspection report.

4.   The inspection team shall also have the right to have a photographic record of seals and tags it employs during the conduct of the inspection.

9.6   MEASUREMENTS

1.   Measurements taken in the course of the inspection by the inspection team or by the inspected State Party at the inspection team's request shall be recorded and signed by an inspector.

2.   To help resolve potential ambiguities these measurements and data may be certified as accurate by the representative of the inspected State Party, at the discretion of the inspected State Party, immediately after they are gathered. In case of discrepancies both Parties shall make efforts to resolve discrepancies as soon as possible before the end of the inspection period. If necessary, the representative of the inspected State Party and the inspector shall each record the method(s) used and the final result(s). Such measurements shall be recorded in the document on preliminary findings (or interim report).

9.7   VERIFICATION ACTIVITIES DURING PLANNED PERIOD OF INACTIVITY

1.   The inspection team shall have the right to remain at the facility during the scheduled period(s) of inactivity, as set forth in the inspected State Party's detailed annual plan for destruction, unless the estimated duration of such period of inactivity at the inspected facility is more than ____ days. The facility, however, remains subject to systematic verification. The inspected State Party shall confirm in writing to the inspection team its intentions in regard to each planned period of inactivity declared in its detailed annual plan of destruction thirty days in advance of the date of the beginning of such a period.

2.   The confirmation referred to in paragraph 1 shall contain the following information:
    (a) the date of stoppage of destruction operations at the facility;
    (b) the estimated date of resumption of destruction operations at the facility;
    (c) the reasons for the stoppage of destruction operations at the facility; and
    (d) the list of modifications to be introduced at the facility during the scheduled period of inactivity, if any.

3.   During any planned period of inactivity at the facility which is less than the period indicated in paragraph 1 above the inspection team may at its discretion reduce the intensity of systematic verification and indicate to the inspected State Party, in a timely manner, its specific proposals in this regard.

4.   Following periods of inactivity at the facility in which the inspection team departs or reduces the intensity of its systematic verification, the inspected State Party will inform the OPCW at least 14 days in advance of the resumption of destruction operations that destruction operations will resume.

5.   The inspection team may during any planned period of inactivity at the facility request the inspected State Party to install additional equipment, and/or to replace or update

existing inspection equipment in case such actions are required to implement the inspection mandate. All requests to replace, modify or install additional equipment will comply with the facility permit requirements. The inspection team shall have the right to observe the implementation of these measures in regard to the inspected State Party's equipment and shall have the right to assist the inspected State Party in the installation, replacement or update of inspection equipment belonging to the inspection team. The inspected State Party, at the request of the inspection team, shall carry out all routine maintenance and calibration of installed inspection equipment which is integral to the destruction process under the observation of the inspection team. The inspection team shall have the right to test, or have tested in its presence, that this equipment is able to perform the functions claimed for it, and to determine whether such equipment is suitable for the task(s) in hand. The inspected State Party shall provide the inspection team, upon request, with the necessary assistance and relevant information to facilitate the accomplishment of these tasks. Such information may include, *inter alia*, the following:

(a) decontamination activities and procedures adopted by the inspected State Party;

(b) list of facility monitoring equipment which will be installed or replaced; and

(c) date and time of the resumption of destruction operations.

6. The inspection team shall have the right to observe the measures mentioned above or to take part in such measures, if agreed in advance. Fulfillment of such measures shall take into account provisions of Section 5 to this Agreement.

7 As a measure of systematic verification during periods of inactivity as designated in paragraph 2 of this section, visits to the facility are provided for in accordance with the relevant provisions set forth in the Verification Annex:

(a) to perform any necessary maintenance, replacement of equipment, or to adjust the coverage of the monitoring systems as required, in accordance with paragraph 15 of Part III of the Verification Annex;

(b) to take action if an event occurs or may occur at the facility which may have an impact on the monitoring system, in accordance with paragraphs 14 and 16 of Part III of the Verification Annex;

(c) to resolve urgent problems; and

(d) undertake these activities described in paragraph 5 of this Section.

8. Administrative arrangements for such a visit shall be the same as for the conduct of an inspection.

9.8 PROCEDURES FOR ACCESS FOR THE INSPECTION TEAM TO TEMPORARY HOLDING AREA(S)

1. The inspection team shall have unimpeded access to the temporary holding area(s) of the facility, consistent with safety requirements.

2. Procedures for the inspection team access into the temporary holding area(s) are contained in Attachment 18 to this Agreement.

9.9 VERIFICATION OF THE RECEIPT OF CHEMICAL WEAPONS AT THE FACILITY AND THEIR INVENTORYING

1. In accordance with paragraphs 62 and 66(a) and (b) of Part IV(A) of Verification Annex, the inspectors shall have the right to verify the inventory of chemical weapons delivered to and destroyed at the facility. The inspectors shall have the right to verify the arrival and receipt and storage of chemical weapons at the facility and the inventory of each shipment. Agreed procedures for conducting such inventories, consistent with facility safety regulations, shall include those for the employment, as appropriate, of agreed seals, markers, or other inventory control procedures to facilitate an accurate inventory of the chemical weapons prior to destruction. These procedures are described in Attachments 16 and 19 to this Agreement.

2.   If applicable, the inspection team shall have the right to apply security seals to transit containers in which chemical weapons arrive at the destruction facility. The inspected State Party shall provide to the inspection team the quantity, type(s) of agent fill, common military designator(s), size(s)/calibre(s) of munitions, sub-munitions, devices, equipment, contained in each sealed container which has arrived at the facility. These seals will be maintained in place until the container is opened, at which time the inspection team shall have the opportunity to verify the inventory of the shipment in accordance with paragraph 1 above. The number, type, and content of sealed transit containers, if applicable, must be provided in accordance with the format contained in Attachment 17 to this Agreement.

9.10   INSPECTION PROCEDURES FOR DESTRUCTION PROCESS

9.10.1 *Procedures for Access for Inspection Team to the Destruction Process*

1.   The inspection team shall have unimpeded access to the facility destruction process subject to the negotiated access restrictions due to health and safety hazards as detailed in Section 2, paragraph 3(d) and Attachment 2 to this Agreement.

2.   Procedures for the inspection team access to the destruction process are contained in Attachment 20 to this Agreement.

9.10.2 *Confirmation of the Specific Type and Quantity of Chemical Weapons being Destroyed*

1.   In accordance with paragraphs 59 and 66(c) of Part IV(A) of the Verification Annex the inspectors shall have the right to verify through continuous monitoring with on-site monitoring instruments and physical presence of inspectors the specific type and quantity of chemical weapons being destroyed. In particular, the inspection team shall have the right to verify, *inter alia*, the following:

        (a) the number and type of chemical munitions, devices or containers going into the destruction area;

        (b) the type and identity of chemicals contained in tagged munitions, devices or containers after such munitions or devices have been opened in the disassembly area, if applicable;

2.   The inspectors shall have the right in accordance with paragraph 67 of Part IV(A) of the Verification Annex to tag, for sampling, munitions, devices, or containers located in the temporary holding area(s). The inspectors shall employ for this purpose, as appropriate, agreed tags, described in Attachment 19 to this Agreement. Agreed tagging procedures are also contained in Attachment 19 to this Agreement.

9.10.3 *Verification of the Process of Destruction*

1.   In accordance with paragraph 66(d) of Part IV(A) of the Verification Annex, the inspection team shall have the right to verify through their physical presence and monitoring with on-site instruments the process of destruction of chemical weapons, including working parameters for all stages of the destruction process, *inter alia* pressure, temperature and concentration of solvents and reagents if applicable.

2.   In accordance with the procedures contained in Subsection 9.10.7 below the inspectors shall have the right to request that samples be taken from the agreed processing points for the confirmation of the specific type of chemicals being destroyed. A list of such points are contained in Attachment 22 to this Agreement.

9.10.4 *Verification of the End-Product of Destruction*

        In accordance with paragraph 66(e) of Part IV(A) of the Verification Annex, the inspectors shall have the right to verify through physical presence and monitoring with on-site instruments the end-product of destruction. The list of agreed types of end-product of the destruction process, methods for determination (identification) of the end-product and residual percentage content of toxic chemicals in the end-product are contained in Attachment 23 to this Agreement. The agreed procedures for identification (confirmation) of the end product of destruction also are contained in Attachment 23 to this Agreement.

9.10.5   *Verification of the Mutilation of Metal Parts*
In accordance with paragraph 66(f) of Part IV(A) of the Verification Annex, the inspection team shall have the right to verify through physical presence and monitoring with on-site instruments the mutilation of metal parts of chemical weapons after destruction of toxic chemical fill and detoxification of metal bodies. The agreed procedures for confirmation of the destruction of metal parts are contained in Attachment 24 to this Agreement.

9.10.6   *Verification of the Integrity of the Destruction Process and of the Facility as a Whole*
Inspectors shall have the right to periodically inspect the structures, processes, and area of the facility and, as required, without prejudice to paragraph 40 of Part II of the Verification Annex, install seals and tags at agreed points at the facility to ensure the integrity of destruction operations. The locations where these seals and tags shall be placed are listed in Attachment 25 to this Agreement. Procedures for the employment of tags and seals are detailed in Attachment 19 to this Agreement.

9.10.7   *Sampling and Analysis of Chemical Weapons Tagged (at CWSF or CWDF) for Verification Purposes*
Pursuant to paragraph 49 of Part IV(A), and paragraphs 52 to 58 of Part II, of the Verification Annex, procedures for sampling and analysis for verification purposes, as appropriate, are contained in Attachment 26 to this Agreement. Procedures for tagging munitions, devices, or other containers for subsequent sampling are contained in Attachment 19 to this Agreement.

SECTION 10. REPRESENTATIVE OF THE INSPECTED STATE PARTY

1.   In discharging their functions inspectors shall communicate with personnel of the facility only through the designated representative(s) of the inspected State Party.

2.   In keeping with the provisions of paragraph 41 of Part II of the Verification Annex, the inspected State Party shall ensure that its representative(s) can at all times be reached by the inspection team leader and designated members of the inspection team either in person or exceptionally by telephone. The inspected State Party shall provide the names and means of contact for its designated representative(s) to the inspection team leader.

SECTION 11. CLARIFICATIONS

In accordance with paragraph 51 of Part II of the Verification Annex inspectors shall have the right to request clarifications in connection with ambiguities that arise during an inspection. Such requests shall be made promptly through the representative of the inspected State Party. The representative of the inspected State Party shall provide the inspection team, during the inspection, with such clarification as may be necessary to remove the ambiguity. If questions relating to an object or a building located within the inspection site are not resolved, the object or building shall, if requested, be photographed for the purpose of clarifying its nature and function. The inspection team shall include in the document on preliminary findings compiled in accordance with Section 12 of this Agreement any such unresolved questions, relevant clarifications, and a copy of any photographs taken.

SECTION 12. DEBRIEFING AND PRELIMINARY FINDINGS

1.   In accordance with paragraph 60 of Part II of the Verification Annex, "Upon completion of an inspection the inspection team shall meet with representatives of the inspected State Party and the personnel responsible for the inspection site to review the preliminary findings of

the inspection team and to clarify any ambiguities. The inspection team shall provide to the representatives of the inspected State Party its preliminary findings in written form according to a standardised format, together with a list of any samples and copies of written information and data gathered and other material to be taken off site. The document shall be signed by the head of the inspection team. In order to indicate that he has taken notice of the contents of the document, the representative of the inspected State Party shall countersign the document. This meeting shall be completed not later than 24 hours after the completion of the inspection".

2. The document on preliminary findings (or interim report) shall also include, *inter alia*, the list of results of analysis, if conducted on site, records of seals, results of inventories, copies of photographs to be retained by the inspection team, and results of certified measurements. It will be prepared in accordance with the standardised format referenced in Attachment 27. Any substantive changes to this format will be made only after consultation with the inspected State Party.

3. Any documentation and records provided by the inspected State Party that are not attached to the document on preliminary findings may be taken off-site by the inspection team only with the specific authorisation of the inspected State Party.

4. Before the conclusion of the meeting the inspected State Party may provide written comments and clarifications to the inspection team on any issue related to the conduct of the inspection. These written comments and clarifications shall be attached to the document on the preliminary findings (or interim report).

SECTION 13. SERVICES TO BE PROVIDED

1. The inspected State Party shall provide or arrange for the provision of the following services listed in detail in Part A of Attachment 10 to this Agreement to the inspection team throughout the duration of the inspection:
   (a) interpretation
   (b) communication means;
   (c) transportation;
   (d) working space, including equipment storage space;
   (e) lodging;
   (f) meals;
   (g) medical care; and
   (h) equipment and utilities support, as detailed in the pertinent Sections to this Agreement.

2. The inspected State Party shall also provide other services and support as identified in all pertinent Sections of this Agreement.

3. Requests from the inspection team to the inspected State Party to provide or arrange services in addition to those listed in paragraphs 1 and 2 above, shall be made in writing if requested by the inspected State Party by the inspection team's leader or designate, using the form contained in Part B of Attachment 10 to this Agreement, and which shall be signed by the inspected State Party upon receipt. Requests should normally be made as soon as the need for services has been identified. The provision of such services shall be acknowledged in writing by an authorised member of the inspection team. Copies of all such requests signed by both Parties with provision acknowledged shall be kept by both Parties.

4. The costs of providing the services to the inspection team shall be borne by the inspected State Party as specified in Attachment 10 to this Agreement.

SECTION 14. LIABILITIES

Any claim by the inspected State Party against the OPCW or by the OPCW against the inspected

State Party in respect of any alleged damage or injury resulting from inspections at the facility in accordance with this Agreement, without prejudice to paragraph 22 of the Confidentiality Annex, shall be settled in accordance with international law and, as appropriate, with the provisions of Article XIV of the Convention.

SECTION 15. STATUS OF ATTACHMENTS

The Attachments form an integral part to this Agreement. Any reference to the Agreement includes the Attachments. However, in case of any inconsistency between this Agreement and any Attachment, the sections of the Agreement shall prevail.

SECTION 16. AMENDMENTS, MODIFICATIONS AND UPDATES

1. Amendments to this Agreement may be proposed by either Party and shall be agreed to and enter into force under the same conditions as provided for under Section 19 of this Agreement.
2. Modifications to the Attachments to this Agreement, with the exception of Attachment 1, Attachment 6, and Part D of Attachment 5, may be agreed upon in writing at any time between the representative of the OPCW and the representative of the inspected State Party, provided that both are specifically authorised to do so. The Director-General shall inform the Executive Council about any such modifications. Each Party to this Agreement may revoke its consent to a modification not later than 30 days after the modification was agreed upon. After this time period has elapsed, the modification shall be considered as meeting the requirements of Section 19 of this Agreement.
3. Updates to Part A of Attachment 1, Attachment 6, and Part D of Attachment 5 to this Agreement shall be made by the inspected State Party. Updates to Part B of Attachment 1 to this Agreement shall be made by the OPCW. The Party making the updates shall provide written notification thereof to the other Party no less than 30 days before the updates are to take effect.
4. Any planned change to the information contained in Part A of Attachment 1 to this Agreement which might impact on the planning for the systematic verification at the facility, shall be communicated to the OPCW by the inspected State Party as soon as possible, but normally no later than 30 days before it would take effect.
5. Any change to the information contained in Part B of Attachment 1 to this Agreement which might impact on the planning for the systematic verification at the facility, shall be communicated to the inspected State Party by the OPCW as soon as possible, but normally no later than 30 days before it would take effect.

SECTION 17. SETTLEMENT OF DISPUTES

Any dispute between the Parties that may arise out of the application or interpretation to this Agreement shall be settled in accordance with Article XIV of the Convention.

SECTION 18. ENTRY INTO FORCE

This Agreement shall enter into force upon approval by the Executive Council and signature by the two Parties. If the inspected State Party has additional internal requirements, it shall so notify the OPCW in writing by the date of signature. In such cases, this Agreement shall enter into force on the date that the inspected State Party gives the OPCW written notification that its internal requirements for entry into force have been met.

SECTION 19. DURATION AND TERMINATION

This Agreement shall cease to be in force no later than 30 days after the inspected State Party has submitted to the OPCW notification of the completion of chemical weapons destruction at the facility and when this has been confirmed by the Technical Secretariat within that 30 day period.

ATTACHMENTS

Attachment 1	Planning Data for Inspections
Attachment 2	Health and Safety Requirements and Procedures
Attachment 3	Specific Arrangements in Relation to the Protection of Confidential Information at the Facility
Attachment 4	Arrangements for the Inspection Teams' Contacts with the Media or the Public Concerning Inspections at the Facility
Attachment 5	Inspection Equipment
Attachment 6	Information on the Facility Provided by the Inspected State Party
Attachment 7	Arrangements for Installation and Testing of Inspection Equipment and Stopping Destruction Operations for this Purpose
Attachment 8	List of Monitoring Equipment Already Installed and Agreed for Use
Attachment 9	Staffing Arrangements for the Continuous Presence of Inspectors
Attachment 10	Services to be Provided by Inspected State Party
Attachment 11	Arrangements for Inspected State Party Training of Inspection Team
Attachment 12	Procedures for Inspection Team Shift Operations
Attachment 13	List of Types and Procedures for the Inspection of Vehicles Exiting Destruction Facility
Attachment 14	Arrangements for Interviews
Attachment 15	Records to be Maintained by Facility
Attachment 16	Procedures for the Conduct of Inventories
Attachment 17	Format for Notifying Munitions Movement
Attachment 18	Procedures for Inspection Team Access to Temporary Holding Area(s)
Attachment 19	Procedures for the Employment of Tags and Seals
Attachment 20	Procedures for Inspectors Access to Destruction Process
Attachment 21	List of the OPCW's On-Site Monitoring Instruments, Installation Points, Procedures for Tamper Security Measures
Attachment 22	List of Process Sampling Points
Attachment 23	Agreed Types of Destruction End Products, Methods of Destruction and Residual Percentage Contents
Attachment 24	Agreed Methods for the Confirmation of the Destruction of Metal Parts
Attachment 25	Agreed Points for Installation of Tags and Seals for the Purpose of Confirming Integrity of Destruction Process and Facility
Attachment 26	Sampling and Analysis Procedures
Attachment 27	Standardised Format for the Interim Report
Attachment 28	Agreed Procedures for Photography

ATTACHMENT 1. PLANNING DATA FOR INSPECTIONS

PART A. TO BE PROVIDED AND UPDATED BY THE INSPECTED STATE PARTY:
  (a) site working hours:
  (b) site working days:
  (c) holidays or other non-working days:
  (d) facility working hours:

(e) facility working days:

(f) physical and/or other potential constraints to inspection activities:

(g) Inspection activities which could be supported during non-working hours with notation of times and activities:

PART B. TO BE PROVIDED AND UPDATED BY THE OPCW:

(a) estimated period of inspection (for planning purposes):

(b) approximate inspection team size:

(c) number of sub-teams (consisting of no less than two inspection team members per sub-team) to be accommodated:

(d) estimated volume and weight of equipment to be brought on-site:

ATTACHMENT 2. HEALTH AND SAFETY REQUIREMENTS AND PROCEDURES

PART A. BASIC PRINCIPLES

1. Applicable health and safety regulations of the OPCW, with agreed variations from strict implementation if any:

2. Applicable health and safety regulations of the inspected State Party:

3. Medical regulations and requirements of the inspected State Party or the OPCW that take precedence as being the more stringent:

PART B: DETECTION AND MONITORING

1. Agreed hazard specific standards for workspace exposure limits and/or concentrations:

2. Procedures for detection and monitoring performed by the inspected State Party, using its own equipment, including data to be provided to the inspection team:

3. Agreed procedures for detection and monitoring performed by the inspection team in the least intrusive manner, including data to be collected, as applicable:

4. Agreed procedures for workspace sampling and analysis for purposes of personal safety of the inspection team:

PART C. PROTECTION

1. Protective equipment to be provided by the OPCW, and agreed procedures for equipment certification and use, if required:

2. Protective equipment to be provided by the inspected State Party, and agreed procedures, personnel training, and personnel qualification tests and certification required; and agreed procedures for use of the equipment are identified in Attachment 7 and will be further identified during the pre-inspection briefing.

PART D. MEDICAL REQUIREMENTS

1. Personnel medical standards of the inspected State Party to be applied to the members of the inspection team:

2. Medical screening procedures for members of the inspection team, including pre- and post-entry checks, if required:

3. Agreed medical assistance to be provided by the inspected State Party:

4. Emergency medical evacuation procedures:

5. Agreed additional medical measures to be taken by the inspection team:

6. Procedures for emergency response to chemical casualties of the inspection team, if required:

PART E. HEALTH AND SAFETY TRAINING

Health and Safety training to be provided by the inspected State Party to members of the inspection team:

PART F. MODIFICATION OF INSPECTION ACTIVITIES

Activities that cannot be carried out due to health and safety reasons, and agreed alternatives to accomplish the inspection goals:

ATTACHMENT 3. SPECIFIC ARRANGEMENTS IN RELATION TO THE PROTECTION OF CONFIDENTIAL INFORMATION AT THE FACILITY

PART A. GENERAL

PART B. INFORMATION DETERMINED TO BE KEPT IN THE CONTAINER UNDER DUAL CONTROL

ATTACHMENT 4. ARRANGEMENTS FOR THE INSPECTION TEAM'S CONTACTS WITH THE MEDIA OR THE PUBLIC CONCERNING INSPECTIONS AT THE FACILITY

ATTACHMENT 5. INSPECTION EQUIPMENT

PART A: APPROVED INSPECTION EQUIPMENT BELONGING TO THE OPCW; AND AGREED PROCEDURES FOR THEIR USE

Equipment name and identification/ procedures for use	Areas where equipment shall not be used	Restriction(s) (nature, conditions, reasons, etc.):	Alternative- measures for accomplishing inspection objectives

PART B: FACILITY EQUIPMENT TO BE PROVIDED BY THE INSPECTED STATE PARTY

Equipment type and specification	Location and operator	Agreed use by the inspection team	Remarks

PART C: MONITORING INSTRUMENTS TO BE INSTALLED AND MAINTAINED WITH THE SUPPORT OF THE INSPECTED STATE PARTY.

Instrument	Installation point	Maintenance procedures	Remarks

PART D: SPECIAL HANDLING REQUIREMENTS FOR INSPECTION EQUIPMENT OR SUPPLIES

Item	Special handling/ Control procedures	Location of storage	Remarks

PART E: PROCEDURES FOR DECONTAMINATION OF INSPECTION EQUIPMENT

PART F: PROCEDURES FOR USE OF INSPECTION TEAM COMMUNICATIONS EQUIPMENT

ATTACHMENT 6. INFORMATION ON THE FACILITY PROVIDED BY THE INSPECTED STATE PARTY

PART A. DECLARATION OF THE FACILITY

PART B. SITE DIAGRAM

PART C. ADDITIONAL INFORMATION ON THE FACILITY PROVIDED BY THE INSPECTED STATE PARTY

ATTACHMENT 7. ARRANGEMENTS FOR THE INSTALLATION AND TESTING OF IN-
SPECTION EQUIPMENT AND STOPPING DESTRUCTION OPERATIONS
FOR THIS PURPOSE

ATTACHMENT 8. LIST OF MONITORING EQUIPMENT ALREADY INSTALLED
AND AGREED FOR USE

ATTACHMENT 9. STAFFING ARRANGEMENTS FOR THE CONTINUOUS
PRESENCE OF INSPECTORS

ATTACHMENT 10. SERVICES TO BE PROVIDED BY THE INSPECTED STATE PARTY

PART A. SERVICES TO BE PROVIDED
1. Vehicles:
2. Workspace:
3. Lodging:
4. Meals:
5. Medical:
6. Use of on-site sampling and analytical equipment as detailed in Attachment 2, Part B and
    Attachment 11 to this Agreement.
7. Communications:
8. Inspected State Party utilities (electrical, water, etc.), inspection equipment and maintenance,
    and other technical and logistical support for inspection team equipment as detailed in At-
    tachment 7 to this Agreement.
9. Other services and support as identified in all pertinent sections of this Agreement or as oth-
    erwise agreed between the inspected State Party and the inspection team.
10. Secure storage areas:

PART B. FORM - REQUEST FOR SERVICES TO BE PROVIDED
Date:
Location:
Inspection number:
Name of the authorised member of the inspection team:
Category of services requested:
Description of services requested:
Approval of the request by the inspected State Party:
Comments on the request by the inspected State Party:
Certification of the authorised member of the inspection team that the requested services have
been provided:
Comments by the authorised member of the inspection team in regard to the quality of the services
provided:
        [Signature of the authorised member of the inspection team]

ATTACHMENT 11. ARRANGEMENTS FOR INSPECTED STATE PARTY TRAINING
OF INSPECTION TEAM

ATTACHMENT 12. PROCEDURES FOR INSPECTION TEAM SHIFT OPERATIONS

ATTACHMENT 13. LIST OF TYPES OF VEHICLES AND PROCEDURES FOR THE IN-
SPECTION OF VEHICLES EXITING THE DESTRUCTION FACILITY

ATTACHMENT 14. ARRANGEMENTS FOR INTERVIEWS

ATTACHMENT 15. RECORDS TO BE MAINTAINED BY FACILITY

ATTACHMENT 16. PROCEDURES FOR THE CONDUCT OF INVENTORIES

ATTACHMENT 17. FORMAT FOR NOTIFYING MUNITIONS MOVEMENT

ATTACHMENT 18. PROCEDURES FOR INSPECTION TEAM ACCESS TO
TEMPORARY HOLDING AREA(S)

ATTACHMENT 19. PROCEDURES FOR THE EMPLOYMENT OF TAGS AND SEALS

ATTACHMENT 20. PROCEDURES FOR INSPECTORS ACCESS TO DESTRUCTION
PROCESS

ATTACHMENT 21. LIST OF THE OPCW'S ON-SITE MONITORING INSTRUMENTS, IN-
STALLATION POINTS, PROCEDURES FOR TAMPER SECURITY MEASURES

ATTACHMENT 22. LIST OF PROCESS SAMPLING POINTS

ATTACHMENT 23. AGREED TYPES OF DESTRUCTION END PRODUCTS,
METHODS OF DESTRUCTION AND RESIDUAL PERCENTAGE CONTENTS

ATTACHMENT 24. AGREED METHODS FOR THE CONFIRMATION
OF THE DESTRUCTION OF METAL PARTS

ATTACHMENT 25. AGREED POINTS FOR INSTALLATION OF TAGS AND SEALS
FOR THE PURPOSE OF CONFIRMING INTEGRITY OF DESTRUCTION PROCESS
AND FACILITY

ATTACHMENT 26. SAMPLING AND ANALYSIS PROCEDURES

ATTACHMENT 27. STANDARDISED FORMAT FOR THE INTERIM REPORT

ATTACHMENT 28. AGREED PROCEDURES FOR PHOTOGRAPHY

15. NATIONAL IMPLEMENTATION MEASURES (ARTICLE VII)

Article VII, paragraph 1 of the Convention states that "Each State Party shall, in accordance with its constitutional processes, adopt the necessary measures to implement its obligations under this Convention."

Article VII, paragraph 5 states that "Each State Party shall inform the Organization of the legislative and administrative measures taken to implement the Convention."

Article VIII, paragraph 38, subparagraph (e) calls upon the Technical Secretariat to "Provide technical assistance and technical evaluation to States Parties in the implementation of the provisions of this Convention."

15.1 Checklist for the Legislator[1]

Measures required under Article VII, paragraph 1:

MEASURE	CONVENTION REFERENCE
Prohibitions:	
• to develop, produce, otherwise acquire, stockpile or retain chemical weapons, or transfer, directly or indirectly, chemical weapons to anyone	Article I(1)(a)
• to use chemical weapons	Article I(1)(b)
• to engage in any military preparations to use chemical weapons	Article I(1)(c)
• to assist encourage or induce, in any way, anyone to engage in any activity prohibited to a State Party under the Convention	Article I(1)(d)
• to use riot control agents as a method of warfare	Article I(5)
• to produce, acquire, retain or use Schedule 1 chemicals outside the territories of States Parties or transfer such chemicals outside the State Party's territory except to another State Party	Article VI(2) and VA VI A(1)
• to produce, acquire, retain, transfer or use Schedule 1 chemicals except for the purposes listed in VA VI (A)(2)(a)-(d)	Article VI(2) and VA VI(A)(2)
• to retransfer Schedule 1 chemicals	Article VI(2) and VA VI(B)(4)
• to transfer Schedule 1 chemicals outside the regime established by VA VI(B)(5) and VI(B)(5 bis)	Article VI(2) and VA VI(B)(5) and VI(B)(5bis)
• to produce Schedule 1 chemicals outside the regime established by VA VI(C)	Article VI(2) and VA VI(C)
• to transfer to or receive from States not Party Schedule 2 chemicals	VA VII(C)(31) and C-V/DEC.16
• to transfer to States not Party Schedule 3 chemicals without first receiving an end-user certificate from the competent government authority of the State not Party	VA VIII (C)(26); C-III/DEC.6 and 7; and C-VI/DEC.10
penal provisions	Article VII(1)(a)
extraterritorial application to nationals (natural persons)	Article VII(1)(c)

---

[1] As the legislator will notice in reviewing this checklist, the Convention may impact several areas of law, depending upon the State Party's legal system, for instance: constitutional law, civilian and military statutes and penal codes, customs, immigration and administrative law, civil and criminal procedure.

Other measures normally necessary:

MEASURE	CONVENTION REFERENCE
definition of chemical weapons	Article II(1)
definition of toxic chemicals	Article II(2)
definition of 'purposes not prohibited under this Convention'	Article II(9)
arrangements enabling legal assistance to other States Parties	Article VII(2)
designate or establish the National Authority	Article VII(4)
mandatory reporting by natural and legal persons of information to the National Authority needed for NA declarations and notifications • Initial declarations of scheduled chemicals and facilities • Annual declarations of scheduled chemicals and facilities	Article VI(7) + VA VI(D)(13), (17) [Schedule 1]; VA VII(A)(2)(a) & (4)(a) + C-8/DEC.7 [Schedule 2]; VA VIII(A)(2)(a) & 4(a) + C-8/DEC.7 [Schedule 3]; VA IX(A)(1) & (3) [OCPFs] Article VI(8) + VA VI (D)(15)-(16), (19)-(20) [Schedule 1]; VA VII(A)(2)(b) & 4(b)-(c) + C-8/DEC.7 [Schedule 2]; VA VIII(A)(2)(b) & 4(b)-(c) + C-8/DEC.7 [Schedule 3]; VA IX(A)(3) [OCPFs]
regime for scheduled chemicals: • regulation of Schedule 1 production/use • criteria for Schedule 2 declarations (thresholds, mixtures – low concentrations) • criteria for Schedule 3 declarations (thresholds, mixtures – low concentrations) • import/export controls	Article VI(3) + VA VI(A) & (C) VA VII(A)(5); C-V/DEC.19; C-7/DEC.14 VA VIII(A)(5); C-V/DEC.19; C-7/DEC.14 VA VI(B) [Schedule 1]; VA VII(C) [Schedule 2]; VA VIII(C) [Schedule 3]; Article XI(2)(c)-(e)
licensing of industry	Article VI; VA VI, VII, VIII, IX
access to facilities	Article VI (9); Article IX(11)(b); VA II(E)(45)-(48); VA VI(E)(22), (29); VA VII(B)(12); VA VIII(B)(12); VA IX(B)(9)
Respect for privileges and immunities: • of inspectors • of the OPCW, delegates and staff	VA II(B) Article VIII(E)(48)-(50)
protection of confidential information	Article VII(6); CA(A)(4)
mandate and enforcement powers of the National Authority	Article VII(4)
annual submission of information on national protective programmes	Article X(4)
primacy of the Convention	--
liability	--
enabling inspections (and penalties for interfering with the inspection process or falsifying info)	Article VI(9) + VA II(E) [general]; VA VII(B)(25)-(29) [Schedule 2]; VA VIII(B)(20)-(24) [Schedule 3]

Article VI(9) + VA II(E) [general]; VA VII(B)(25)-(29) [Schedule 2]; VA VIII(B)(20)-(24) [Schedule 3]

MEASURE	CONVENTION REFERENCE
ensuring the safety of people and protecting the environment, including site security (storage and destruction facilities)	CWs: Article IV(10) + VA IV (A)(A)6(e) [safety and emissions standards], IV(A)(B) [site security] CWPFs: Article V(11) + VA V(B)(33)(g) [destruction], V(D)(78)(g) [conversion]
CW, CWPF and OF declarations	Article III + VA IV(A)(A) [CWs]; VA IV(B) [OCWs and ACWs]; VA V(A) [CWPFs]
enabling inspections (and penalties for interfering with the inspection process or falsifying info)	CWs: Article IV(4) + VA II(E) + VA IV(A) (D)(44)-(49) CWDFs & SFs: Article IV (5) + VA II(E) + VA IV(A)(D)(65) CWPFs [destruction]: Article V(6), 7(b) + VA II(E) + VA V (C) CWPFs [conversion]: Article V(15) + VA II(E) + VA V (D)(85)

Existing legislation/regulations to be reviewed to prevent conflicts with the Convention:

MEASURE	CONVENTION REFERENCE
• recognition of the legal capacity, privileges and immunities referred to in Article VIII (50) • recognition of the privileges and immunities of the inspection team	Article VIII(50) VA II (B)
granting of multiple entry/exit/transit visas (valid for at least two years) to each inspector/inspection assistant	VA II (B)(10)
entry and exit of inspection equipment	VA II (B)(11)(d) , (12)
use of inspection equipment	VA II (C)(27)-(30)
custody and transfer of samples	VA II(E)(53), (55)
standing diplomatic clearance number for non-scheduled aircraft	VA II(C)(22)
trade in chemicals	Article XI(2)(c)–(e)
allocate funds to pay assessed contribution to OPCW budget	Article VIII(A)(7)

Upon completion, and each time legislation is amended or supplemented:

MEASURE	CONVENTION REFERENCE
inform the OPCW of the legislative and administrative measures taken to implement the Convention	Article VII(5)
provide the text of national implementing legislation	Report of the First Review Conference, subpara. 7.83(c) of RC-1/5

15.2 National Legislation Implementation Kit for the Chemical Weapons Convention[2]

1. Main CWC-related definitions

1.1 Definition of "chemical weapon"

"*Chemical weapon*" means the following, together or separately—

(a) Toxic chemicals and their precursors, except where intended for purposes not prohibited under the Convention, as long as the types and quantities are consistent with such purposes;

(b) Munitions and devices, specifically designed to cause death or other harm through the toxic properties of those toxic chemicals specified in subparagraph (a), which would be released as a result of the employment of such munitions and devices;

(c) Any equipment specifically designed for use directly in connection with the employment of munitions and devices specified in subparagraph (b).[3]

1.2 Definition of "toxic chemical"

(1) "*Toxic chemical*" means any chemical which through its chemical action on life processes can cause death, temporary incapacitation or permanent harm to humans or animals.

(2) The definition in paragraph (1) includes all such chemicals therein, regardless of their origin or of their method of production, and regardless of whether they are produced in facilities, in munitions or elsewhere.[4]

(3) Toxic chemicals which have been identified for the application of verification measures by the Organisation are listed in the Schedules contained in the Annex on Chemicals to [the Convention / this [Act, Statute, Ordinance, etc.]].

1.3 Definition of "precursor"

(1) "*Precursor*" means any chemical reactant which takes part at any stage in the production by whatever method of a toxic chemical. This includes any key component of a binary or multicomponent chemical system.[5]

(2) Precursors which have been identified for the application of verification measures by the Organisation are listed in the Schedules contained in the Annex on Chemicals to [the Convention / this [Act, Statute, Ordinance, etc.]].

1.4 Definition of "purposes not prohibited under the Convention"

"*Purposes not prohibited under the Convention*" means—

(a) Industrial, agricultural, research, medical, pharmaceutical, or other peaceful purposes;

(b) Protective purposes, namely those purposes directly related to protection against toxic chemicals and to protection against chemical weapons;

(c) Military purposes not connected with the use of chemical weapons and not dependent on the use of the toxic properties of chemicals as a method of warfare; and

(d) Law enforcement including domestic riot control purposes.[6]

---

[2] The aim of this document is to address issues possibly faced by all States Parties. Special considerations to be addressed by States Parties which have declared chemical weapons and are engaged in chemical weapons destruction activities are not covered here.

[3] As defined in Article II(1) of the Convention.

[4] As defined in Article II(2) of the Convention.

[5] As defined in Article II(3) of the Convention.

[6] As defined in Article II(9) of the Convention.

1.5   Definition of "riot control agent"

"Riot control agent" means any chemical not listed in Schedule 1, 2 or 3, which can produce rapidly in humans sensory irritation or disabling physical effects which disappear within a short time following termination of exposure.[7]

1.6   Definition of "chemical weapons production facility"

(1) *"Chemical weapons production facility"* means any equipment, as well as any building housing such equipment, that was designed, constructed or used at any time since 1 January 1946:

(a) As part of the stage in the production of chemicals ("final technological stage") where the material flows would contain, when the equipment is in operation:

(i) Any Schedule 1 chemical; or

(ii) Any other chemical that has no use, above 1 tonne per year on the territory of [State Party] or in any other place under the jurisdiction or control of [State Party], for purposes not prohibited under this Convention, but can be used for chemical weapons purposes;

or

(b) For filling chemical weapons, including, inter alia, the filling of Schedule 1 chemicals into munitions, devices or bulk storage containers; the filling of chemicals into containers that form part of assembled binary munitions and devices or into chemical submunitions that form part of assembled unitary munitions and devices, and the loading of the containers and chemical submunitions into the respective munitions and devices;

(2) As an exception to paragraph (1) the term "chemical weapons production facility" does not include:

(a) Any facility having a production capacity for synthesis of chemicals specified in paragraph (1) subparagraph (a) that is less than 1 tonne;

(b) Any facility in which a chemical specified in paragraph (1) subparagraph (a) is or was produced as an unavoidable by-product of activities for purposes not prohibited under the Convention, provided that the chemical does not exceed 3 per cent of the total product and that the facility is subject to declaration and inspection under the Verification Annex; or

(c) The single small-scale facility for production of Schedule 1 chemicals for purposes not prohibited under the Convention as referred to in Part VI of the Verification Annex.[8]

1.7   Definition of "Schedule 1, 2 and 3 chemicals"

"Schedule 1, 2 and 3 chemicals" means those chemicals listed respectively in Schedule 1, Schedule 2 and Schedule 3 of the Annex on Chemicals to [the Convention

---

[7] As defined in Article II(7) of the Convention. The use of riot control agents as a method of warfare is prohibited by Article I(5) of the Convention. Such prohibition is criminalized in provision 6.5 of this Implementation Kit. It is also recalled that pursuant to Article III of the Convention, "Each State Party shall submit to the Organization, not later than 30 days after this Convention enters into force for it, [...] declarations [...] (e) With respect to riot control agents [...].This declaration shall be updated not later than 30 days after any change becomes effective."

[8] As defined by Article II(8) of the Convention. Under Article III(1)(c), and Article I(4) of the Convention States Parties must declare and destroy any chemical weapons production facilities they own or possess, or that are located under their jurisdiction or control. These provisions are implemented in provisions 5.1 and 5.3 of this Implementation Kit. To prevent proliferation of chemical weapons, Article V(5) of the Convention also prohibits construction of any new chemical production facilities and modification of any existing facilities for the purpose of chemical weapons production. Such prohibition is criminalized in provision 6.6 of this Implementation Kit.

/ this [Act, Statute, Ordinance, etc.]] regardless of whether the chemical is pure or contained in a mixture.

1.8   Definition of "discrete organic chemical"

"*Discrete organic chemical*" means any chemical belonging to the class of chemical compounds consisting of all compounds of carbon except for its oxides, sulfides and metal carbonates.[9]

1.9   Definition of "international inspection"

"*International inspection*" means inspections or visits carried out by International Inspectors in accordance with the Convention.

1.10   Definition of "international inspectors"

"*International inspectors*" means all individuals designated by the Organisation according to the procedures as set forth in Part II, Section A of the Verification Annex to carry out activities to verify compliance with obligations under the Convention, including its declaration requirements or to assist carrying out such activities.[10]

1.11   Definition of "inspection site"

"*Inspection site*" means any facility or area at which an international inspection is carried out and which is specifically defined in the respective facility agreement or inspection request or mandate or inspection request as expanded by the alternative or final perimeter.

1.12   Definition of "Convention"

"*Convention*" means the Convention on the Prohibition of the Development, Production, Stockpiling and Use of Chemical Weapons and on their Destruction, adopted on 13 January 1993[11], and includes any amendments to that Convention or the Annexes that are, or will become, binding on [State Party].

1.13   Definition of "Verification Annex"

"*Verification Annex*" means the Annex on Implementation and Verification to the Convention.

1.14   Definition of "Organisation"

"*Organisation*" means the Organisation for the Prohibition of Chemical Weapons established pursuant to Article VIII of the Convention.

1.15   Definition of "State Party"

"*State Party*" means a State which has consented to be bound by the Convention and for which the Convention is in force.[12]

1.16   Specifications and other definitions in the Convention

(1) The definitions shall be interpreted in light of the Convention, including its Annexes, and the decisions adopted thereunder. Such specifications can be laid down by regulations.

(2) Terms and expressions used and not defined in this [Act, Statute, Ordinance, etc.] but defined in the Convention shall, unless the context otherwise requires, have the same meaning as in the Convention.

2.   National Authority

(1) The [competent authority] shall by means of regulations designate or establish a National Authority to serve as the national focal point for effective liaison with the

---

[9] As defined by paragraph 4 of Part I of the Verification Annex.

[10] The proposed definition comes from paragraphs 13 and 18 of Part I of the Verification Annex, and aims at covering both inspectors and inspection assistants designated to carry out international inspections.

[11] States Parties may wish to consider adding references to the ratification instrument of the Convention by the State Party and, if applicable, to the Official Gazette that published the Convention.

[12] The model language reflects the language used in the 1969 Vienna Convention on the Law of Treaties.

Organisation and other States Parties and for coordination of all national measures to be taken to fully and effectively implement the Convention.

(2) In these regulations the [competent authority] shall direct or assign to the National Authority such powers and budget as may be necessary to coordinate the implementation and enforcement of the Convention, this law and its implementing regulations.

(3) The [competent authority] may designate or establish further authorities to which it may assign specific duties with regard to the implementation of the Convention, this law and its implementing regulations.[13]

3.   Control regime for scheduled chemicals and discrete organic chemicals

3.1   Control regimes for categories of chemicals[14]

3.1.1   Control regime for Schedule 1 chemicals

(1) The acquisition, retention, in-country-transfer, import, export and the use of Schedule 1 chemicals are prohibited unless the chemicals are exclusively applied to research, medical, pharmaceutical or protective purposes[15] and the types and quantities of chemicals are strictly limited to those which can be justified for such purposes. These activities are subject to prior declaration in accordance with regulations established under this [Act, Statute, Ordinance, etc.].[16]

If the prior declaration shows that the activity reported would conflict with the obligations of [State Party] under the Convention,[17] the [competent authority] shall prohibit or limit the activity.[18]

(2) The production of Schedule 1 chemicals is prohibited unless carried out for research, medical, pharmaceutical or protective purposes and in a facility licensed by the [competent authority] in accordance with regulations established under this [Act, Statute, Ordinance, etc.].[19]

Exemptions from this licensing requirement may be granted in the regulations under

---

[13] Such authorities may include a licensing authority and an advisory committee. Specific duties to be assigned may include the inspection of facilities or transferred goods.

[14] In addition to provisions 3.1.1 to 3.1.4 it is suggested considering the following provision:
Trade in toxic chemicals and their precursors
Traders of chemicals shall inform the National Authority when they have doubts of whether a purchaser of toxic chemicals or their precursors intends to use these chemicals for purposes not prohibited under the Convention. An indication of such intent is that it is improbable that the purchaser will use the full quantity of the purchased types of toxic chemicals and their precursors for purposes not prohibited under the Convention.

[15] It can be noted that these purposes are more restrictive than the purposes not prohibited as defined by provision 1.4 of this Implementation Kit, as far as Schedule 1 chemicals are concerned.

[16] The establishment of a prior declaration regime, as suggested in this provision, aims at allowing States Parties to ensure that the activities referred to in this provision will be conducted in compliance with the prohibitions and restrictions set out in Part VI of the Verification Annex, and allowing them to fulfil their obligation to make the prior notification of transfers of Schedule 1 chemicals as required by paragraph 5 of Part VI of the Verification Annex.

[17] One such case could be for example that the aggregate amount of Schedule 1 chemicals imported into the territory of the State Party or acquired by it in the year would exceed the 1 tonne limit set out in paragraph 2(c) and (d) of Part VI of the Verification Annex.

[18] States Parties may also wish to consider issuing clearance certificates, so as to ensure legal certainty for concerned natural and legal persons.

[19] In developing the licensing regime for Schedule 1 chemicals production facilities, States Parties shall take into consideration the specifications and restrictions found in paragraphs 8 to 12 of Part VI of the Verification Annex.

this [Act, Statute, Ordinance, etc.] in strict accordance with the Convention.[20] Further activities regarding Schedule 1 chemicals that shall only be carried out in licensed facilities may be identified in regulations established under this [Act, Statute, Ordinance, etc.] in strict accordance with the Convention.[21]

(3) The export and the import of Schedule 1 chemicals to or from a State not Party to the Convention, including transit through such State, are prohibited.[22]

(4) Any person having performed any activity that is covered by this section, or having operated a facility in which such activity was carried out, or anticipating carrying out such an activity in the future shall make declarations in accordance with the regime established in the regulations issued under this [Act, Statute, Ordinance, etc.].[23]

(5) Any person carrying out any activity that is covered by this provision shall adopt measures to physically secure the chemicals from access of unauthorised persons,[24] to ensure the safety of people and to protect the environment. Such appropriate measures may be identified in regulations under this [Act, Statute, Ordinance, etc.].

3.1.2   Control regime for Schedule 2 chemicals[25]

(1) Any person having performed an activity involving the production, processing or consumption of Schedule 2 chemicals, or having operated a facility in which such activity was carried out, or anticipating carrying out such an activity in the future shall make declarations in accordance with the regime established in the regulations issued under this [Act, Statute, Ordinance, etc.].[26]

(2) The export and the import of Schedule 2 chemicals to or from the territory of a State Party to the Convention shall be declared in accordance with the regime established in the regulations issued under this [Act, Statute, Ordinance, etc.].[27]

(3) The export and the import of Schedule 2 chemicals to or from the territory of a State not party to the Convention, including transit through such State, are prohibited[28] unless an exemption that is provided for in regulations is applicable;[29] in case such an exemption is applicable, the export and the import shall be subject to declaration in accordance with the regime established in the regulations under this [Act, Statute, Ordinance, etc.].

---

[20] States parties may consider granting such exemption to laboratories producing by synthesis Schedule 1 chemicals for research, medical or pharmaceutical purposes in aggregate quantities less than 100 g per year per facility in accordance with paragraph 12 of Part VI of the Verification Annex.

[21] See operative paragraph (b) of C-I/DEC.43, dated 16 May 1997.

[22] As prescribed by paragraph 3 of Part VI of the Verification Annex.

[23] This provision aims at ensuring that States Parties will be in a position to comply with their reporting obligations with respect to Schedule 1 chemicals. See Article VI(2) and (8) of the Convention and paragraph 6 of Part VI(B) and Part VI(D) of the Verification Annex.

[24] While not explicitly mentioned in the Convention the requirement to physically protect Schedule 1 chemicals aims at implementing the obligation of Article VI(2) of the Convention to ensure that activities relating to toxic chemicals and their precursors be carried out for purposes not prohibited under the Convention.

[25] States Parties may consider establishing a licensing regime for Schedule 2 chemicals.

[26] See Article VI(2), (4) and (8) of the Convention and Part VII(A) of the Verification Annex.

[27] This provision aims at allowing States Parties to collect the information and data required to comply with its obligation to declare aggregate national data as prescribed by paragraph 1 of Part VII of the Verification Annex. States Parties may also wish to require reporting before the import respectively export, so as to be in a position to issue a clearance certificate, which would facilitate the procedures at customs.

[28] As provided for in paragraph 31 of Part VII of the Verification Annex.

[29] States Parties may consider exempting from this prohibition the export and import to States not party of products containing low concentration of Schedule 2 chemicals to the extent allowed by C-V/DEC.16, dated 17 May 2000.

3.1.3   Control regime for Schedule 3 chemicals

(1) Any person who has produced Schedule 3 chemicals, or who operates a facility in which such an activity was carried out, or who anticipates carrying out this activity in the future shall make declarations in accordance with the regime established in the regulations under this [Act, Statute, Ordinance, etc.].[30]

(2) The export and the import of Schedule 3 chemicals shall be declared in accordance with the regime established in regulations issued under this [Act Statute, Ordinance, etc.].[31]

(3) Without prejudice of the requirement set out in paragraph (2) above, and except when exempted by regulations,[32] the export of Schedule 3 chemicals to the territory of a State not Party is prohibited unless licensed by the [competent authority] in accordance with regulations established under this [Act, Statute, Ordinance, etc.]. The license may only be granted after it has been ensured that the transferred chemicals shall only be used for purposes not prohibited under the Convention. No license shall be granted without first having received an end-use certificate from the competent authorities of the recipient State.

3.1.4   Control regime for unscheduled discrete organic chemicals

Any person operating a facility producing unscheduled discrete organic chemicals shall make declarations in accordance with the regime established in the regulations issued under this [Act, Statute, Ordinance, etc.].[33]

3.1.5   Record-keeping

Any person carrying out an activity referred to in provisions 3.1.1 to 3.1.4 above, or operating a facility where such activity is carried out, shall keep records in accordance with regulations established under this [Act, Statute, Ordinance, etc.].

3.1.6   Loss, theft or discovery of scheduled chemicals

(1) Any person carrying out an activity referred to in provisions 3.1.1 to 3.1.3 above, or operating a facility where such activity is carried out, shall report without delay any loss or theft of scheduled chemicals to the National Authority.

(2) Any person discovering scheduled chemicals on the territory of [State Party] shall inform without delay the [competent authority[34] which shall inform the National Authority].

3.2   Other relevant activities and facts

(1) The [competent authority] may in regulations identify further declarable past or anticipated activities and facts relevant to the Convention.

---

[30] See Article VI(2), (5) and (8) of the Convention and Part VIII(A) of the Verification Annex.

[31] This provision aims at allowing States Parties to collect the information and data required to comply with their obligation to declare aggregate national data as prescribed by paragraph 1 of Part VIII of the Verification Annex. States Parties may also wish to require reporting before the import respectively export, so as to be in a position to issue a clearance certificate, which would facilitate the procedures at customs.

[32] States Parties may consider exempting from restrictions applying to transfers of Schedule 3 chemicals to States not party those products containing low concentration of Schedule 3 chemicals to the extent allowed by C-VI/DEC.10, dated 17 May 2001.

[33] See Article VI(2), (6) and (8) of the Convention and Part IX(A) of the Verification Annex.

In C-I/DEC.39 dated 16 May 1997 the Conference of the States Parties has adopted the understanding that discrete organic chemicals are not covered by the definition, when:

a)   they are an oligomer or polymer, whether or not they contain phosphorus, sulphur or fluorine; or

b)   they contain only carbon and metal.

Instead of changing the national definition of discrete organic chemicals, States Parties may – in the regulations – simply not require the making of declarations from natural and legal persons, when the unscheduled discrete organic chemicals fulfil the conditions of paragraphs a) and b) above.

[34] E.g., the police.

(2) In the event that the [competent authority] has reason to believe that any natural or legal person has information that is relevant for a declaration required to be made by [State Party] to the Organisation, or that is relevant for the implementation of the Convention or for the enforcement of this [Act, Statute, Ordinance, etc.], it may by notice require the person to provide such information.

3.3 Basis for implementing regulations[35]

3.3.1 Legal basis for establishing a licensing regime

(1) The [competent authority] shall make regulations establishing a licensing regime for all licenses to be granted under this chapter.

(2) The regulations on licenses shall, *inter alia*,

    (a) provide for different types of licenses with different requirements;

    (b) prescribe procedures for applying for licenses;

    (c) establish procedures for processing the applications for licenses;

    (d) establish procedures for the granting or refusal of licenses;

    (e) prescribe terms and conditions for the grant of licenses;

    (f) provide for a regime according to which granted licenses may be suspended, revoked, extended, renewed, transferred, or replaced;

    (g) establish fees payable by applicants for or holders of licences; and

    (h) prescribe a record-keeping regime for licence applicants or holders.

(3) In case the licensed activity is not or only partially carried out, the [competent authority] shall be informed without delay.

3.3.2 Legal basis for establishing a declaration regime

(1) The [competent authority] shall make regulations establishing a declaration regime for all declarations to be made under this chapter.

(2) The Regulations on declarations shall, inter alia,

    (a) specify which past, present or anticipated activities and which relevant facts shall be declared;

    (b) prescribe procedures for making such declarations;

    (c) specify which documents shall be provided along with the declaration.

(3) The regulations may identify cases in which declarations are not required.

(4) The regulations shall prescribe a record-keeping regime for persons required to make declarations under this [Act, Statute, Ordinance, etc.].

3.3.3 Common rules for the licensing and the declaration regime

The regulations establishing a licensing and a declaration regime shall ensure that the [competent authority] is enabled to

    (a) prevent prohibited activities and comply with the requirements of the Convention;

    (b) gather all information as required under Article VI of the Convention; and

    (c) make all declarations to the Organisation under Article VI of the Convention in a comprehensive and timely manner.

---

[35] This chapter provides a list of issues that may need to be dealt with by such Regulations. In addition, since some legal systems may require that legislation implementing the Convention provides a legal basis for further implementing Regulations, this chapter also gives an example of how such a legal basis can be formulated.

4. International inspections[36]

4.1   General rule

(1) International inspections can be carried out in any place under the jurisdiction of [State Party] when required by the Convention.

(2) International inspections shall only be carried out in facilities that produced, processed or consumed scheduled chemicals or discrete organic chemicals in the past and facilities in which the production, processing or consumption of scheduled chemicals is anticipated unless the international inspection qualifies as a challenge inspection[37] or an investigation in a case of alleged use of chemical weapons,[38] or as part of the verification activities related to chemical weapons production facilities and their destruction[39] under the Convention.

(3) In performing their duties international inspectors have the powers, privileges and immunities as laid down in the Convention.

4.2   Escort team

(1) At each international inspection, the [competent authority] shall appoint an escort team, each member of which shall be authorised to act as an escort.

(2) Escorts shall meet the inspectors at the point of entry to the territory, be present during their operations and accompany them back to the point of exit from the territory.

(3) Escorts shall ensure that the international inspectors abide by the rules established in the Convention. They shall ensure that the inspected persons comply with their duties under this [Act, Statute, Ordinance, etc.] and the regulations to be established thereunder.

(4) The responsibility of the head of the escort team includes representing [State Party] vis-à-vis the head of the inspection team and the persons subject to international verification.

(5) Further rights and duties of the escort team and the head of the escort team shall be established in regulations to be established under this [Act, Statute, Ordinance, etc.].

4.3   Inspected persons and personnel

(1) Inspected persons and their personnel shall
   (a) facilitate the international inspection; and
   (b) cooperate with the international inspectors and the escort team during the preparation and performance of, and follow-up to the inspection.

(2) *Inter alia*, they shall –
   (a) grant access to the inspection site to the international inspectors and the escort team and – in case of a challenge inspection – to any observer;

---

[36] Most States Parties also establish a regime for national inspections. The rights and obligations of inspected persons and national inspectors in case of national inspections can be similar to the rights and obligations of inspected persons and international inspectors in international inspections.
However there are two major differences:
(1) While in international inspections there are three parties involved (i.e. the inspected person, the State Party and the Organisation) in national inspections only two parties are involved (the inspected person and the State Party). This will result in the absence of an escort team.
(2) National inspections can be more flexible in their planning than international inspections, which allows for an even more flexible approach with regard to the interests of the inspected person (in particular with regard to the timing of the inspection: appeals may have suspensive effect).

[37] As provided for in Article IX of the Convention and Part X of the Verification Annex.

[38] As provided for in Articles IX and X of the Convention and Part XI of the Verification Annex.

[39] As provided for in Article V of the Convention and Part V(C) of the Verification Annex.

(b) grant access to relevant records to the international inspectors and the escort team;

(c) provide all relevant information and data requested by the international inspectors;

(d) take and analyse samples [and/or] tolerate the taking and analysis of samples and the taking of photos in accordance with the Convention, this law and its implementing regulations;

(e) tolerate the installation and use of continuous monitoring instruments and systems and seals, and notify the National Authority immediately if an event occurs or may occur which may have an impact on the monitoring system.

(3) Further rights and duties of inspected persons and their personnel may be specified in regulations to be established under this [Act, Statute, Ordinance, etc.].

4.4   Procedures

(1) The [competent authority] shall notify the international inspection to the inspected person as soon as possible.

(2) The inspected person shall be assumed to have granted its consent, unless it informs the National Authority of the opposite within a timeline indicated in the notification in accordance with paragraph 1.

(3) In the event that the inspected person does not consent to the inspection, the National Authority shall apply for a search warrant on behalf of the international inspectors and the members of the escort team. The warrant shall be granted if the conditions for carrying out an international inspection under the Convention are fulfilled.

(4) An appeal by the inspected person against a search warrant shall not have suspensive effect on the carrying out of the international inspection.

5.   Further implementing provisions: forfeiture, confidentiality and legal assistance[40]

5.1   Declaration of chemical weapons production facilities

Any person holding any information that is related to a chemical weapons production facility in [State Party] or that is suspected to be related to such a facility shall inform without delay the [competent authority[41] which shall inform the National Authority].

5.2   Forfeiture of chemical weapons[42]

(1) If any chemical weapon, or old or abandoned chemical weapon is found in any place under the jurisdiction of [State Party], the weapon—

(a) is forfeited to the State; and

(b) may be seized without warrant by any [competent officer] of the State; and

(c) shall be stored pending disposal, and disposed of in a manner determined by [the competent authority] in accordance with the Convention.[43]

(2) Any chemical weapon discovered on the territory of [State Party] shall be reported to the Organisation by [competent authority] in accordance with the Convention.

(3) Any chemical that is being used in the development or production of a chemical weapon may be seized by the State.

---

[40] States Parties are required under Article VIII(50) of the Convention, to enter into a Privileges and Immunities Agreement with the Organisation that clearly delineates the scope of the privileges and immunities of the Organisation and its officials and experts. No legislation is required in this regard.

[41] E.g., the police.

[42] This Section closely relates to the Penal Provisions chapter. Accordingly some States Parties have included this provision in their penal implementing provisions.

[43] The relevant provisions are found in Article I(2) in conjunction with Article IV of the Convention and with Part IV(A) of the Verification Annex.

5.3   Seizure of a chemical weapons production facility

(1) If the [competent authority] has reasonable cause to believe that any equipment or
building is a chemical weapons production facility, or is being constructed or modified to be used as a chemical weapons production facility, the [competent authority]
shall:

(a) seize such equipment or building;

(b) as the case may be, order immediate suspension of all activities at the facility,
except safety and physical security activities at the facility.[44]

(2) Upon determination that the equipment or building is a chemical weapons production facility, or is being constructed or modified to be used as a chemical weapons
production facility—

(a) the facility shall be closed;

(b) cessation of all activities at the facility shall be ordered, except activities required for closure and safety and physical security activities at the facility;

(c) the facility shall be destroyed or converted in accordance with the Convention,[45]
and at the expense of [...].

(3) The [competent authority] shall declare the facility and report any other information
as may be required to the Organisation in accordance with the Convention.[46]

5.4   Protection of confidential information[47]

(1) All information and documents given to or obtained by [the National Authority]
pursuant to the Convention, this law or its implementing regulations shall be evaluated in order to establish whether they contain confidential information. Information
shall be considered confidential if it is so designated by the natural or legal person
to whom it relates or from whom it has been received. It shall also be considered
confidential if its disclosure could reasonably be expected to cause damage to the
person it relates to or from whom it has been received or to the mechanisms for
implementation of the Convention.

(2) All information and documents given to or obtained by any other person pursuant
to the Convention, this law or its implementing regulations shall be treated as confidential information, unless such information or document is publicly available.

(3) Disclosure of confidential information or documents is only allowed with the consent of the person to whose affairs it relates or for the purpose of—

(a) implementing the Convention;

(b) enforcing of this [Act, Statute, Ordinance, etc.]; or

(c) dealing with an emergency involving public safety.[48]

5.5   Enabling legal assistance to other States Parties

(1) Without prejudice to the confidentiality regime, the [competent authorities] for
crime prevention, criminal proceedings, and implementation of the Convention
may collaborate with competent authorities of other States and international organisations and entities, and coordinate their actions to the extent required by the
implementation of this [Act, Statute, Ordinance, etc.] or of the equivalent foreign
statute(s).

(2) The [competent authorities] may request other State authorities and international
organisations or entities, under paragraph (1), to provide relevant data or informa-

---

[44] See paragraph 14 of Part V of the Verification Annex.

[45] The relevant provisions are found in Article V and Part V(B) and (D) of the Verification Annex.

[46] The relevant provisions are found in Article III(1)(c) and Part V(A) of the Verification Annex.

[47] See Article VII(6) of the Convention and C-I/DEC.13/Rev.1 dated 2 February 2006, in particular section 2.1 of Chapter IV of its Annex.

[48] States Parties may consider that breach of confidentiality may cause financial damage and ensure that
its tort law provides for a legal basis for claiming compensation.

tion. The [competent authorities] are authorized to receive data or information concerning—

(a) the nature, quantity, and utilisation of scheduled chemicals and related technologies, and the places of consignment and consignees for such scheduled chemicals, and related technologies, or

(b) persons taking part in the production, delivery, or trade of the scheduled chemicals, or related technologies in subparagraph (a).

(3) If a State has entered into a reciprocity agreement with [State Party], the [competent authorities] may provide, on their own initiative or on request, the data or information described in paragraph (2) to that State so long as the competent authority of the other State provides assurances that such data or information shall—

(a) only be utilized for purposes consistent with this [Act, Statute, Ordinance, etc.] and

(b) only be used in criminal proceedings on the condition that they are obtained in accordance with those provisions governing international judicial cooperation.

(4) The [competent authorities of State Party] may provide the data or information described in paragraph (2) to international organisations or entities if the conditions set forth in paragraph (3) are fulfilled, in which case the requirement for a reciprocity agreement is waived.

6. Penal provisions

6.1 **Acquisition or possession of chemical weapons**

Any person[49] [level of intent][50] developing, producing, manufacturing, otherwise acquiring, possessing, stockpiling or retaining a chemical weapon, commits an offence and shall be punished upon conviction by [period of time] imprisonment [and/or] fined an amount ranging from [currency; amount] to [currency; amount].

6.2 **Transportation or transfer of chemical weapons**

Any person [level of intent] transporting, transiting, trans-shipping or transferring directly or indirectly a chemical weapon to any other person, commits an offence and shall be punished upon conviction by [period of time] imprisonment [and/or] fined an amount ranging from [currency; amount] to [currency; amount].

6.3 **Use of chemical weapons**

Any person [level of intent] using a chemical weapon, commits an offence and shall be punished upon conviction by [period of time] imprisonment [and/or] fined an amount ranging from [currency; amount] to [currency; amount].

6.4 **Engagement in military preparations to use of chemical weapons**

Any person [level of intent] engaging in any military preparations to use a chemical weapon, commits an offence and shall be punished upon conviction by [period of time] imprisonment [and/or] fined an amount ranging from [currency; amount] to [currency; amount].

6.5 **Use of riot control agents as a method of warfare**

Any person [level of intent] using riot control agents as a method of warfare commits an offence and shall be punished upon conviction by [period of time] imprisonment [and/or] fined an amount ranging from [currency; amount] to [currency; amount].

6.6 **Construction of new chemical weapons production facilities**

Any person [level of intent] owning or possessing a chemical weapons production facility, constructing any new chemical weapons production facility or modifying any

---

[49] States Parties should ensure that the term "person" includes natural and legal persons.

[50] E.g., "intentionally, knowingly, recklessly, or with gross negligence".

existing facility for the purpose of transforming it into a chemical weapons production facility commits an offence and shall be punished upon conviction by [period of time] imprisonment [and/or] fined an amount ranging from [currency; amount] to [currency; amount].

6.7   Producing, acquiring, retaining, using or in-country transferring Schedule 1 chemicals

Any person [level of intent]

(a) producing, otherwise acquiring, retaining, using or in-country transferring a Schedule 1 chemical in the territory of a State not Party to the Convention, commits an offence and shall be punished upon conviction by [period of time] imprisonment [and/or] fined an amount ranging from [currency; amount] to [currency; amount].

(b) illegally producing, otherwise acquiring, retaining, using or in-country transferring a Schedule 1 chemical commits an offence and shall be punished upon conviction by [period of time] imprisonment [and/or] fined an amount ranging from [currency; amount] to [currency; amount].

6.8   Re-exportation of Schedule 1 chemicals

Any person [level of intent] exporting a Schedule 1 chemical previously imported into [State Party] to a third state, commits an offence and shall be punished upon conviction by [period of time] imprisonment [and/or] fined an amount ranging from [currency; amount] to [currency; amount].

6.9   Export or import of Schedule 1 and 2 chemicals

Any person [level of intent] illegally exporting to, or importing from, a State not party to the Convention, a Schedule 1 or 2 chemical commits an offence and shall be punished upon conviction by [period of time] imprisonment [and/or] fined an amount ranging from [currency; amount] to [currency; amount].

6.10   Export of Schedule 3 chemicals

Any person [level of intent] illegally exporting a Schedule 3 chemical to a State not party to the Convention commits an offence and shall be punished upon conviction by [period of time] imprisonment [and/or] fined an amount ranging from [currency; amount] to [currency; amount].

6.11   Obstruction of verification and enforcement measures[51]

(1) Any person [level of intent] obstructing measures of verification or enforcement under the Convention [and/or] this law and its implementing regulations, commits an offence and shall be punished upon conviction by [period of time] imprisonment [and/or] fined an amount ranging from [currency; amount] to [currency; amount].

(2) Paragraph 1 does not apply to a person that has not granted its consent to the carrying out of the international inspection, unless a search warrant has been issued.

6.12   Failure to comply with the licensing or declaration regime[52]

Any person [level of intent] failing to comply with the licensing or the declaration regime including the record-keeping regime or any other requirement to provide information established by this law and its implementing regulations, commits an offence and shall be punished upon conviction by [period of time] imprisonment [and/or] fined an amount ranging from [currency; amount] to [currency; amount].

6.13   Failure to protect confidential information

Any person who [level of intent] fails to comply with the provision of this law and its

---

[51] This provision covers various kinds of behaviours and accordingly States Parties may wish to provide for a wide range of penal sanctions.

[52] Ibidem. While not explicitly mentioned, this provision for example covers the submission of false or misleading information in licensing and declaration.

implementing regulations to protect confidential information commits an offence and shall be punished upon conviction by imprisonment for a term of [period of time] [and/or] with a fine not exceeding [amount].

6.14   Accessory offence, conspiracy and attempt
Any person–
     (a) [level of intent] assisting, encouraging or inducing anyone to commit an offence under this [Act, Statute, Ordinance, etc.];
     (b) conspiring to commit an offence under this [Act, Statute, Ordinance, etc.]; or
     (c) attempting to commit an offence under this [Act, Statute, Ordinance, etc.]
shall be deemed to have committed the like offence.

6.15   Extraterritorial application
Any natural person who, in a place outside the jurisdiction of [State Party], commits an act or omission that would, if committed in a place under the jurisdiction of [State Party], constitute an offence under this [Act, Statute, Ordinance, etc.] is deemed to have committed it in a place under the jurisdiction of [State Party] if –
     (a) the person is a [State Party's] national; or
     (b) the place was under the control of [State Party].

7.   Final provisions

7.1   Primacy of the Convention
Where there is any inconsistency between any other law and this [Act, Statute, Ordinance, etc.] or the Convention, this [Act, Statute, Ordinance, etc.] and the Convention shall prevail.

7.2   Additional regulations
Further regulations shall be adopted as required for effective implementation of this [Act, Statute, Ordinance, etc.] and the Convention.

[7.3   Amendment of the Annex on Chemicals to this [Act, Statute, Ordinance, etc.]
In case the Annex on Chemicals to the Convention is amended the Annex on Chemicals to this [Act, Statute, Ordinance, etc.] shall be adjusted and for this purpose be amendable by regulations.]

15.3 Plan of Action regarding the implementation of Article VII obligations[53]

C-8/DEC.16 adopted by the Conference of the States Parties at its Eighth Session on 24 October 2003 and entitled "Plan of acting regarding the implementation of Article VII obligations"

The Conference
     Recalling the recommendations that the First Special Session of the Conference of the States Parties to Review the Operation of the Chemical Weapons Convention (First Review Conference) made on national implementation measures (as covered under agenda item 7(c)(v) of its report, subparagraphs 7.74 to 7.83 of RC-1/5, dated 9 May 2003), in particular the agreement in subparagraph 7.83(h) of that report to develop, at its next regular session, a plan of action based on a recommendation from the Executive Council (hereinafter "the Council") regarding the im-

---

[53] The Conference of the States Parties has subsequently adopted the following decisions on the follow up on the Action Plan regarding the implementation of Article VII obligations: C-9/DEC.4 dated 30 November 2004; C-10/DEC.16 dated 11 November 2005; C-11/DEC.4 dated 6 December 2006; C-12/DEC.9 dated 9 November 2007, C-13/DEC.7 dated 5 December 2008; and C-14/DEC.12 dated 4 December 2009.

plementation of obligations under Article VII of the Chemical Weapons Convention (hereinafter "the Convention"), with the objective of fostering the full, effective, and non-discriminatory implementation of the Convention by all States Parties;

Stressing the need to fully implement the recommendations of the First Review Conference on national implementation measures;

Recognising how important and how urgent it is that States Parties complete their obligations under Article VII to adopt, in accordance with their constitutional processes, the necessary measures to implement the Convention;

Convinced that the full and effective implementation of Article VII by all States Parties also contributes to universal adherence to the Convention;

Concerned that a large number of States Parties have not yet fulfilled the range of obligations under Article VII, and recognising that many of them may have difficulties in doing so; and

Taking note of the report by the Director-General to the Eighth Session of the Conference on national implementation measures (C-8/DG.5, dated 18 September 2003, and Add.1, dated 22 October 2003);

Having received the recommendation by the Council on the Plan of Action on national implementation measures (EC-M-23/DEC.2, dated 21 October 2003),

Hereby:

Identification and analysis of problems and needs (action items for the Technical Secretariat and States Parties)

1.   Requests the Technical Secretariat (hereinafter "the Secretariat") to intensify its work with those States Parties that have difficulties in adopting the measures required under Article VII, by further identifying, analysing, and addressing those difficulties;

2.   Further requests the Secretariat to submit to the Thirty-Sixth Session of the Council a report covering, *inter alia*, problems that have been identified, requirements of States Parties for support, the capabilities of the OPCW (that is, both of the Secretariat and of the States Parties) to provide implementation support, and any recommendations relevant to the implementation of the plan of action;

3.   Requests States Parties seeking assistance of any kind in meeting their national implementation obligations and that have not yet informed the Secretariat of what assistance they require, to do so preferably before 1 March 2004;

Resources for implementation support (action items for the Technical Secretariat and States Parties)

4.   Requests the Secretariat, within the parameters set by the OPCW Programme and Budget, to offer sustained technical support to States Parties that request it for the establishment and effective functioning of National Authorities, the enactment of national implementing legislation, and the adoption of any administrative measures required in accordance with Article VII;

5.   Welcomes voluntary contributions from States Parties towards the implementation of this plan of action, and requests the Secretariat to implement the plan of action within the resources approved for the OPCW Programme and Budget, together with any voluntary contributions received for national implementation, and in a cost-effective manner;

6.   Encourages States Parties to lend advice, upon request, to other States Parties in drafting and adopting national measures necessary to implement the Convention, *inter alia* to ensure that the laws reflect the comprehensive nature of the Convention by covering all activities that are to be prohibited or required in accordance with the Convention, and that involve the use of any toxic chemicals and their precursors; to cover the provision of annual declarations on past and anticipated activities; to ensure the implementation of the provisions related to transfers of scheduled chemicals; and to cover the annual submission of information on national

protective programmes in accordance with paragraph 4 of Article X;

7.   Requests States Parties able to provide assistance of any kind towards national implementation in other States Parties to inform the Secretariat, preferably before 1 March 2004, of what they can offer;

8.   Requests the Secretariat to further develop and improve its implementation support programme, including by mobilising States Parties' efforts so as to provide, upon request and within the limits on available resources, technical assistance and technical evaluations to States Parties in the implementation of the provisions of the Convention, in the areas identified in the section of the report of the First Review Conference on national implementation measures (subparagraph 7.74 to 7.83 of RC-1/5);

9.   Encourages the Secretariat to identify and, by mutual consent, engage with regional, subregional and other relevant groups of States Parties that can render support to the States Parties concerned in their implementation efforts;

10. Encourages the Secretariat and the States Parties to develop partnerships with relevant regional organisations and agencies that could render support to States Parties in their implementation work;

Overall time-frame, intermediate steps, and target date (action items for States Parties)

11. Without prejudice to the timelines set by the Convention, recalling States Parties' obligations under Article VII, and reminding them that it has been more than six years since the entry into force of the Convention, agrees that it is imperative that those States Parties that still need to do so take the necessary steps and set realistic target dates for these steps leading to the enactment of the necessary legislation, including penal legislation, and/or the adoption of administrative measures to implement the Convention no later than the Tenth Session of the Conference of the States Parties, scheduled for November 2005;

12. Calls upon those States Parties that still need to do so to make every effort to adhere to the overall time-frame established in paragraph 11 above, as well as to the steps and target dates they have established for themselves, and to maintain regular contact with the Secretariat about the implementation of these steps and target dates;

13. Encourages States Parties and the Secretariat to take measures to raise awareness of the prohibitions and requirements of the Convention, *inter alia* in their armed forces, in industry, and in their scientific and technological communities;

14. Underlines that the steps mentioned in paragraph 11 above should include:
   (a) designating or establishing a National Authority and notifying the Secretariat thereof in accordance with Article VII of the Convention, as soon as possible;
   (b) taking the steps necessary to enact the legislation, including penal legislation, and/or to adopt the administrative measures States Parties need in order to implement the Convention in accordance with their constitutional processes; and
   (c) providing the Secretariat with the full text of their national implementing legislation, including updates, or, in the case of States Parties with a monist legal system, with information on the specific measures they have taken to implement the Convention;

15. Urges States Parties that have not yet done so to review their existing regulations in the field of trade in chemicals in order to render them consistent with the object and purpose of the Convention;

Oversight by the Executive Council and the Conference of the States Parties (action items for States Parties and the Technical Secretariat)

16. Requests the Secretariat to report to the Ninth Session of the Conference and to every second session of the Council starting with the Thirty-Sixth, in March 2004, on the progress made in implementing this plan of action;

17. Further requests the Council to provide guidance to, and to coordinate with, the Secretariat as

necessary and to monitor the implementation of this plan of action;

18. Also requests States Parties that lend advice, upon request, to other States Parties on the drafting and adopting of national measures to implement the Convention, to keep the OPCW informed of their actions and the results they have achieved; and

19. Undertakes to review, at its Ninth Session, the progress made in implementing this plan of action, and to decide on any further action needed; and undertakes to review further, at its Tenth Session, the status of implementation of Article VII and to consider and decide on any appropriate measures to be taken, if necessary, in order to ensure compliance by all States Parties with Article VII.

16. PRIVILEGES AND IMMUNITIES
(ARTICLE VIII, SECTION E)

16.1 OPCW Headquarters Agreement

C-I/DEC.59 adopted by the Conference of the States Parties at its First Session on 14 May 1997 and entitled "OPCW Headquarters Agreement".[1] To facilitate the full implementation of the OPCW Headquarters Agreement, the Conference of the States Parties adopted at its Eleventh Session decision C-11/DEC.9 on the establishment of a Host Country Committee.

The Conference

Recalling that, in accordance with Article VIII, paragraph 50 of the Convention, the legal capacity, privileges and immunities referred to in Article VIII are to be defined in an agreement between the OPCW and the Host Country,

Recalling that the Commission, in PC-XV/25, paragraph 7.9, provisionally approved the Draft Agreement between the Organisation for the Prohibition of Chemical Weapons (OPCW) and the Kingdom of the Netherlands concerning the Headquarters of the OPCW, including the Separate Arrangement with respect to the Agreement between the Organisation for the Prohibition of Chemical Weapons and the Kingdom of the Netherlands Concerning the Headquarters of the OPCW ("OPCW Headquarters Agreement"), annexed to PC-XV/A/WP.10/Rev.1, and decided that this approval will become final if no objections from any delegation were received by the Secretariat by 10 January 1997 in The Hague,

Recalling further that no objection was received by the Secretariat by 10 January 1997 in The Hague and the Commission's provisional approval of the above-mentioned Draft OPCW Headquarters Agreement therefore became final,

Bearing in mind that the Commission recommended in paragraph 34.4 of its Final Report that the Conference approve the above-mentioned Draft OPCW Headquarters Agreement; that the Conference request the Director-General to sign the said agreement on behalf of the OPCW; and that the Conference further request the Director-General, following signature of the said agreement, to notify the Host Country in writing that the requirements for entry into force have been met,

Hereby:

1. Approves the OPCW Headquarters Agreement annexed hereto;
2. Requests the Director-General to sign the said agreement on behalf of the OPCW; and
3. Further requests the Director-General, following signature of the said agreement, to notify the Host Country in writing that the requirements for entry into force have been met.

---

[1] The Headquarters Agreement was signed on 22 May 1997, during the First Session of the Conference of the States Parties at a Signing Ceremony in the Netherlands Ministry of Foreign Affairs. It entered into force on 7 June 1997.

AGREEMENT BETWEEN THE ORGANISATION FOR THE PROHIBITION OF
CHEMICAL WEAPONS (OPCW) AND THE KINGDOM OF THE NETHERLANDS
CONCERNING THE HEADQUARTERS OF THE OPCW

The Organisation for the Prohibition of Chemical Weapons,
and
The Kingdom of the Netherlands,
    Whereas the Convention on the Prohibition of the Development, Production, Stockpiling and
Use of Chemical Weapons and on Their Destruction establishing the Organisation for the Prohibition of Chemical Weapons entered into force on 29 April, 1997,
    Whereas the seat of the headquarters of the Organisation for the Prohibition of Chemical
Weapons shall be The Hague, Kingdom of the Netherlands, pursuant to Article VIII, paragraph 3,
of the Convention,
    Having regard to the provisions set forth under the Convention, concerning the legal capacity
and the privileges and immunities of the Organisation for the Prohibition of Chemical Weapons
and its organs, as well as to the privileges and immunities of the Heads of Delegation, alternates
and advisers attached to Heads of Delegation, Permanent Representatives, members of the Permanent Missions, Delegates of States Parties, and the Director-General and the staff of the Organisation for the Prohibition of Chemical Weapons,
    Also having regard to the provisions set forth in Annexes 2 and 3 of the Resolution Establish-
ing the Preparatory Commission for the Organisation for the Prohibition of Chemical Weapons,
    Considering that the establishment of the seat of the headquarters of the Organisation for the
Prohibition of Chemical Weapons in the territory of the Kingdom of the Netherlands (The Hague)
requires the conclusion of an agreement,
    Have agreed as follows:

ARTICLE 1. DEFINITIONS

In this Agreement:
(a) "Convention" means the Convention on the Prohibition of the Development, Production,
     Stockpiling and Use of Chemical Weapons and on Their Destruction of 13 January 1993;
(b) "OPCW" means the Organisation for the Prohibition of Chemical Weapons;
(c) "Government" means the Government of the Kingdom of the Netherlands;
(d) "Appropriate authorities of the Kingdom of the Netherlands" means such state, municipal or
     other authorities of the Kingdom of the Netherlands as may be appropriate in the context of
     the relevant provisions of this Agreement and in accordance with the laws and customs ap-
     plicable in the Kingdom of the Netherlands;
(e) "Parties" means the OPCW and the Kingdom of the Netherlands;
(f) "Headquarters" means the area and any building, including any OPCW laboratory, equip-
     ment store, conference facilities, parts of buildings, land or facilities ancillary thereto, irre-
     spective of ownership, used by the OPCW on a permanent basis or from time to time, to carry
     out its official functions;
(g) "Director-General" means the Director-General referred to in Article VIII, paragraph 41, of
     the Convention;
(h) "State Party" means a State Party to the Convention;
(i) "Head of Delegation" means the accredited head of the delegation of a State Party to the
     Conference of the States Parties and/or to the Executive Council;
(j) "Alternates for and advisers attached to Heads of Delegation" means alternates for and advis-
     ers attached to Heads of Delegation;
(k) "Permanent Representative" means the principal representative of a State Party accredited to
     the OPCW;

(l) "Members of the Permanent Mission of a State Party" includes any staff member of the mission of the Permanent Representative to the OPCW;

(m) "Delegates of States Parties" means the designated representatives of States Parties and members of their delegations to any meeting of the OPCW which is not the Conference of the States Parties or the Executive Council;

(n) "Experts" means persons performing missions authorised by, serving on subsidiary bodies of, or in any way, at its request, consulting with the OPCW, provided that they are neither officials of the OPCW nor attached to Permanent Representatives;

(o) "Officials of the OPCW" means the Director-General and all members of the staff of the Technical Secretariat of the OPCW, except those who are locally recruited and remunerated on an hourly basis;

(p) "Inspectors on mission" means members of an inspection team as referred to in the Convention (Verification Annex, Part I, paragraph 17) who are in possession of an inspection mandate issued by the Director-General to conduct an inspection in accordance with the Convention;

(q) "Meetings convened by the OPCW" means any meeting of any of the organs or subsidiary organs of the OPCW, or any international conferences or other gatherings convened by the OPCW or under its sponsorship;

(r) "Property" means all property, assets and funds, belonging to the OPCW or held or administered by the OPCW in furtherance of its functions under the Convention and all income of the OPCW;

(s) "Samples" means samples as defined in the Convention;

(t) "Archives of the OPCW" means all records, correspondence, documents, manuscripts, computer and media data, photographs, films, video and sound recordings belonging to or held by the OPCW or any of its staff members in an official function, and any other material which the Director-General and the Government may agree shall form part of the archives of the OPCW;

(u) "The Vienna Convention" means the Vienna Convention on Diplomatic Relations of 18 April 1961.

ARTICLE 2. LEGAL PERSONALITY

The OPCW shall possess full legal personality. In particular, it shall have the capacity:

(a) to contract;

(b) to acquire and dispose of movable and immovable property;

(c) to institute and act in legal proceedings.

ARTICLE 3. FREEDOM OF ASSEMBLY

1. The Government recognises the right of the OPCW to convene meetings at its discretion within the headquarters in The Hague or, with the concurrence of the Government or of any appropriate authorities of the Kingdom of the Netherlands designated by the Government, elsewhere in the Kingdom of the Netherlands.

2. The Government guarantees to the OPCW full freedom of assembly, of discussion, and of decision. The Government shall take all proper steps to guarantee that no impediment is placed in the way of conducting the proceedings of any meeting convened by the OPCW.

ARTICLE 4. IMMUNITY FROM LEGAL PROCESS

1. Within the scope of its official activities the OPCW shall enjoy immunity from any form of legal process, except in the case of:

(a) civil action by a third party for damages arising out of an accident caused by a vehicle belonging to or operated on behalf of the OPCW where these damages are not recoverable from insurance;

(b) civil action relating to death or personal injury caused by an act or omission of the OPCW or officials of the OPCW in the Kingdom of the Netherlands.

2. Notwithstanding the provisions of paragraph 1 of this Article, the property, wherever located and by whomsoever held, shall be immune from search, foreclosure, seizure, all forms of attachment, injunction or other legal process except in so far as in any particular case the OPCW shall have expressly waived its immunity. It is, however, understood that no waiver of immunity shall extend to any measure of execution.

ARTICLE 5. IMMUNITY OF PROPERTY FROM OTHER ACTIONS, INVIOLABILITY OF THE ARCHIVES, SAMPLES, EQUIPMENT, AND OTHER MATERIAL

1. The property, wherever located and by whomsoever held, shall enjoy immunity from search, requisition, seizure, confiscation, expropriation and any other form of interference, whether by executive, administrative, judicial or legislative action.

2. The archives and samples of the OPCW, wherever located and by whomsoever held, shall be inviolable at any time.

3. The equipment and other material necessary for the OPCW's activities shall be inviolable at any time.

ARTICLE 6. THE HEADQUARTERS

The appropriate authorities of the Kingdom of the Netherlands shall take whatever action may be necessary to ensure that the OPCW shall not be dispossessed of all or any part of the headquarters.

ARTICLE 7. LAW AND AUTHORITY IN THE HEADQUARTERS

1. The Government recognises the inviolability at any time of the headquarters, which shall be under the control and authority of the OPCW as provided in this Agreement.

2. The OPCW shall have the power to make regulations, operative within the headquarters, for the purpose of establishing therein any conditions necessary for the full execution of its functions. No laws of the Kingdom of the Netherlands which are inconsistent with a regulation of the OPCW authorised by this Article shall, to the extent of such inconsistency, be applicable within the headquarters. Any dispute between the OPCW and the Kingdom of the Netherlands as to whether a regulation of the OPCW is authorised by this Article or as to whether a law of the Kingdom of the Netherlands is inconsistent with any regulation of the OPCW authorised by this Article, shall be promptly settled by the procedure set out in Article 26, paragraph 2, of this Agreement. Pending such settlement, the regulation of the OPCW shall apply and the law of the Kingdom of the Netherlands shall be inapplicable in the headquarters to the extent that the OPCW claims it to be inconsistent with the regulation of the OPCW.

3. The OPCW shall inform the Government of regulations made which fall within paragraph 2 of this Article.

4. Any person authorised to enter any place under any legal provision shall not exercise that authority in respect of the headquarters unless prior express permission to do so has been given by or on behalf of the Director-General. Any person who enters the headquarters with the permission of the Director-General shall, if so requested by or on behalf of the Director-General, leave the headquarters immediately.

5. This Article shall not prevent the reasonable application of fire protection regulations of the appropriate authorities of the Kingdom of the Netherlands. The consent of the Director-Gen-

eral to entry into the headquarters shall be presumed if he or his authorised representative cannot be reached in time.

6. Service of legal process may take place within the headquarters only with the prior consent of, and under conditions approved by, the Director-General.

7. The Director-General shall prevent the headquarters from being used to harbour persons who are avoiding arrest under any law of the Kingdom of the Netherlands, who are wanted by the Government for extradition to another country, or who are endeavouring to evade service of legal process.

ARTICLE 8. PROTECTION OF THE HEADQUARTERS

1. The appropriate authorities of the Kingdom of the Netherlands shall exercise due diligence to ensure that the security and tranquillity of the headquarters are not impaired by any person or group of persons attempting unauthorised entry into, or creating disturbances in, the immediate vicinity of the headquarters. As may be required for this purpose, the appropriate authorities shall provide adequate police protection on the boundaries and in the vicinity of the headquarters.

2. If so requested by the Director-General, the appropriate authorities of the Kingdom of the Netherlands shall provide a sufficient number of police for the preservation of law and order in the headquarters.

3. The appropriate authorities of the Kingdom of the Netherlands shall take all reasonable steps to ensure that the amenities of the headquarters are not prejudiced and that the purposes for which the headquarters are required are not obstructed by any use made of the land or buildings in the vicinity of the headquarters. The OPCW shall take all reasonable steps to ensure that the amenities of the land in the vicinity of the headquarters are not prejudiced by any use made of the land or buildings in the headquarters.

ARTICLE 9. PUBLIC SERVICES TO THE HEADQUARTERS

1. The appropriate authorities of the Kingdom of the Netherlands shall exercise, as far as it is within their competence, and to the extent requested by the Director-General, their respective powers to ensure that the headquarters shall be supplied, on fair conditions and on equitable terms, with the necessary services including, without limitation by reason of this enumeration, electricity, water, sewerage, gas, post, telephone, telegraph, any means of communication, local transportation, drainage, collection of refuse, fire protection and snow removal from public streets.

2. In case of any interruption or threatened interruption of any such services, the OPCW shall be accorded the priority given to essential agencies and organs of the Government, and the Government shall take steps accordingly to ensure that the work of the OPCW is not prejudiced.

3. The Director-General shall, upon request, make suitable arrangements to enable duly authorised representatives of the appropriate bodies to inspect, repair, maintain, reconstruct or relocate utilities, conduits, mains and sewers within the headquarters under conditions which shall not unreasonably disturb the carrying out of the functions of the OPCW. Underground work may be undertaken in the headquarters only in consultation with the Director-General or an official designated by him, and under conditions which shall not disturb the carrying out of the functions of the OPCW.

4. Where the services referred to in paragraph 1 of this Article are supplied by appropriate authorities of the Kingdom of the Netherlands, or where the prices thereof are under their control, the OPCW shall be supplied at tariffs which shall not exceed the lowest rates accorded to essential agencies and organs of the Government.

ARTICLE 10. FACILITIES AND IMMUNITIES IN RESPECT
OF COMMUNICATIONS AND PUBLICATIONS

1. The Government shall permit the OPCW to communicate, freely and without a need for spe-
    cial permission, for all official purposes, and shall protect the right of the OPCW to do so. The
    OPCW shall have the right to use codes and to dispatch and receive official correspondence
    and other official communications by courier or in sealed bags, which shall be subject to the
    same privileges and immunities as diplomatic couriers and bags.
2. The OPCW shall enjoy, as far as may be compatible with the International Telecommunica-
    tions Convention of 6 November 1982, for its official communications, treatment not less
    favourable than that accorded by the Government to any other organisation or government,
    including diplomatic missions of such other governments, in the matter of priorities and rates
    for mails, cables, telegrams, telexes, radiograms, television, telephone, fax, and other com-
    munications, and press rates for information to the press and radio.
3. The Government recognises the right of the OPCW to publish and broadcast freely within
    the Kingdom of the Netherlands for purposes specified in the Convention. All official com-
    munications directed to the OPCW and all outward official communications of the OPCW,
    by whatever means or whatever form transmitted, shall be inviolable. Such inviolability shall
    extend, without limitation by reason of this enumeration, to publications, still and moving
    pictures, videos, films, sound recordings and software.
4. The OPCW may install and use a wireless transmitter with the consent of the Government,
    which shall not be unreasonably withheld once the wave length has been agreed upon.
5. Nothing in paragraphs 3 and 4 in this Article shall be interpreted as exempting the OPCW
    from the application of any laws of the Kingdom of the Netherlands, or of any international
    conventions to which the Kingdom of the Netherlands is a party, relating to copyrights.

ARTICLE 11. EXEMPTION OF THE OPCW AND ITS PROPERTY
FROM TAXES AND DUTIES

1. Within the scope of its official activities, the OPCW, its assets, income and other property
    shall be exempt from all direct taxes, whether levied by national, provincial or local authori-
    ties.
2. Within the scope of its official activities, the OPCW shall be exempt from:
    (a) motor vehicle tax (*motorrijtuigenbelasting*);
    (b) tax on passenger motor vehicles and motorcycles (*BPM*);
    (c) value-added tax paid on all goods and services supplied on a recurring basis or involving
         considerable expenditure (*omzetbelasting*);
    (d) excise duty (*accijns*) included in the price of alcoholic beverages and hydrocarbons;
    (e) import (and export) taxes and duties (*belastingen bij invoer en uitvoer*);
    (f) insurance tax (*assurantiebelasting*);
    (g) real property transfer tax (*overdrachtsbelasting*);
    (h) any other taxes and duties of a substantially similar character to the taxes and duties
         provided for in this paragraph, imposed by the Netherlands subsequent to the date of
         signature of this Agreement.
3. The exemptions provided for in subparagraphs 2(c), 2(d), 2(f), 2(g) of this Article may be
    granted by way of a refund under conditions to be agreed upon by the OPCW and the Govern-
    ment.
4. Goods acquired or imported under the terms set out in paragraph 2 of this Article shall not be
    sold, given away or otherwise disposed of, except in accordance with conditions agreed upon
    with the Government.
5. The OPCW may establish a tax- and duty-free commissary for the sale of limited quantities

of certain articles for personal use or consumption and not for gift or sale, under conditions to be agreed upon by the Parties. This commissary will be open to officials of the OPCW, except for officials who are Netherlands citizens or permanently resident in the Kingdom of the Netherlands. It may also be open to Heads of Delegation, Permanent Representatives, alternates for and advisers attached to Heads of Delegation, and Members of the Permanent Missions and Delegates of States Parties who have diplomatic status.

ARTICLE 12. FREEDOM OF FINANCIAL ASSETS FROM RESTRICTIONS

1. Without being subject to any financial controls, regulations, notification requirements in respect of financial transactions, or moratoria of any kind, the OPCW may freely:
    (a) purchase any currencies through authorised channels and hold and dispose of them;
    (b) operate accounts in any currency;
    (c) purchase through authorised channels, hold and dispose of funds, securities and gold;
    (d) transfer its funds, securities, gold and currencies to or from the Kingdom of the Netherlands, to or from any other country, or within the Kingdom of the Netherlands and convert any currency held by it into any other currency; and
    (e) raise funds in any manner which it deems desirable, except that with respect to the raising of funds within the Kingdom of the Netherlands, the OPCW shall obtain the concurrence of the Government.

ARTICLE 13. EXEMPTION FROM IMPORT AND EXPORT RESTRICTIONS

Articles imported or exported by the OPCW for official purposes shall be exempt from all prohibitions and restrictions imposed by the Government on imports and exports.

ARTICLE 14. TRANSIT AND RESIDENCE

1. The Government shall take all necessary measures to facilitate and allow the entry into and sojourn in the territory of the Kingdom of the Netherlands and shall place no impediment in the way of the departure from the territory of the Kingdom of the Netherlands of the persons listed below, whatever their nationality, and shall ensure that no impediment is placed in the way of their transit to or from the headquarters and shall afford them any necessary protection in transit:
    (a) Heads of Delegation, alternates for and advisers attached to Heads of Delegation, Permanent Representatives and Members of the Permanent Missions of States Parties, their families and other members of their households, as well as administrative and technical staff attached to Heads of Delegation or Permanent Representatives and the spouses and dependent children of such personnel;
    (b) Delegates of States Parties, their spouses and dependent children, as well as administrative and technical staff attached to delegates of States Parties and the spouses and dependent children of such personnel;
    (c) officials of the OPCW, their families and dependent members of their households;
    (d) representatives and officials of international organisations with which the OPCW has concluded agreements or arrangements in accordance with the Convention, who have official business with the OPCW, and their spouses and dependent children;
    (e) experts and their spouses and dependent children.
2. This Article shall not apply in the case of general interruptions of transportation, which shall be dealt with as provided in Article 9, paragraph 2 of this Agreement, and shall not impair the effectiveness of generally applicable laws relating to the operation of means of transportation.

3. Visas which may be required for persons referred to in this Article shall be granted without charge. The Government shall take all necessary measures to ensure that visas are issued as promptly as possible in order to allow the timely conduct of official business with the OPCW.

4. No activity performed by any person referred to in this Article in his official capacity with respect to the OPCW as indicated in paragraph 1 of this Article shall constitute a reason for preventing his entry into or his departure from the territory of the Kingdom of the Netherlands or for requiring him to leave such territory.

5. No person referred to in paragraph 1(d) - (e) of this Article, except for officials of international organisations whose expulsion procedures are covered by special agreements to which the Kingdom of the Netherlands is a party, shall be required by the Government to leave the Kingdom of the Netherlands except in the event of an abuse of the right of residence. No proceeding shall be instituted to require any such person to leave the Kingdom of the Netherlands except with the prior approval of the Minister for Foreign Affairs of the Kingdom of the Netherlands. Such approval shall be given only in consultation with the Director-General. If expulsion proceedings are taken against any such person, the Director-General shall have the right to appear or to be represented in such proceedings on behalf of the person against whom such proceedings are instituted.

6. This Article shall not prevent the Government from requiring that persons claiming the rights granted by this Article comply with quarantine and health regulations.

7. The Director-General and the appropriate authorities of the Kingdom of the Netherlands shall, at the request of either of them, consult as to methods of facilitating entrance into the Kingdom of the Netherlands by persons coming from abroad who wish to visit the headquarters and who do not enjoy the privileges provided by this Article.

ARTICLE 15. PERMANENT MISSIONS TO THE OPCW

Permanent Missions of States Parties established in the Kingdom of the Netherlands, including their premises as defined in the Vienna Convention, shall enjoy the same privileges and immunities as are accorded to diplomatic missions established in the Kingdom of the Netherlands in accordance with the Vienna Convention.

ARTICLE 16. PRIVILEGES AND IMMUNITIES OF HEADS OF DELEGATION, PERMANENT REPRESENTATIVES TO THE OPCW AND STAFF MEMBERS OF PERMANENT MISSIONS

1. Each Head of Delegation and Permanent Representative shall be entitled, within the Kingdom of the Netherlands, to the same privileges and immunities as the Government accords to heads of diplomatic missions accredited to the Kingdom of the Netherlands in accordance with the Vienna Convention.

2. Staff members of Permanent Missions of States Parties shall be entitled to the same privileges and immunities as the Government accords to members, having comparable rank, of the staff of diplomatic missions established in the Kingdom of the Netherlands in accordance with the Vienna Convention.

3. The spouses, children and dependent members of the households of persons referred to in this Article shall enjoy the same privileges and immunities as the spouses, children and dependent members of the households of persons in diplomatic missions having comparable rank under the Vienna Convention.

ARTICLE 17. PRIVILEGES AND IMMUNITIES OF DELEGATES AND ALTERNATES FOR AND ADVISERS ATTACHED TO HEADS OF DELEGATION

1. Delegates of States Parties, and alternates for and advisers attached to Heads of Delegation, shall, without prejudice to any other privileges and immunities which they may enjoy while exercising their functions and during their journeys to and from the headquarters, enjoy within and with respect to the Kingdom of the Netherlands the following privileges and immunities:

   (a) immunity from personal arrest or detention;

   (b) immunity from legal process of any kind in respect of words spoken or written, and of all acts done by them, in the performance of their official functions; such immunity to continue although the persons concerned may no longer be engaged in the performance of such functions;

   (c) inviolability of all papers, documents and other official material;

   (d) the right to use codes and to dispatch or receive papers, correspondence or other official material by courier or in sealed bags;

   (e) exemption with respect to themselves, their spouses and their dependent children from immigration restrictions, alien registration and national service obligations;

   (f) the same protection and repatriation facilities as are accorded in time of international crisis to members, having comparable rank, of the staff of diplomatic missions established in the Kingdom of the Netherlands;

   (g) the same privileges with respect to currency and exchange restrictions as the Government accords to representatives of foreign governments on temporary official missions; and

   (h) the same immunities and facilities with respect to their personal and official baggage as the Government accords to members, having comparable rank, of the staff of diplomatic missions established in the Kingdom of the Netherlands.

2. Subparagraphs (e) - (h) of paragraph 1 of this Article shall not apply to Delegates of States Parties who are Netherlands citizens or permanently resident in the Kingdom of the Netherlands.

3. Where the incidence of any form of taxation depends upon residence, periods during which the persons designated in paragraph 1 of this Article may be present in the Kingdom of the Netherlands for the discharge of their duties shall not be considered as periods of residence. In particular, such persons shall be exempt from taxation on their salaries and emoluments during such periods of duty.

ARTICLE 18. PRIVILEGES AND IMMUNITIES OF THE DIRECTOR-GENERAL AND OTHER OFFICIALS OF THE OPCW

1. Officials of the OPCW shall enjoy within and with respect to the Kingdom of the Netherlands the following privileges and immunities:

   (a) immunity from arrest or detention and from inspection or seizure of their official baggage, to the extent provided under subparagraphs 2(c) and 2(d) of this Article;

   (b) immunity from legal process of any kind in respect of words spoken or written, and of acts performed by them, in their official capacity; such immunity to continue although the persons concerned may have ceased to be officials of the OPCW; in any event, such immunity, as well as any immunity provided under subparagraphs 2(c) and 2(d) of this Article, shall not extend to civil action by a third party for damage arising from an accident caused by a motor vehicle belonging to, driven by or operated on behalf of an official of the OPCW or in respect of a motor traffic offence involving such vehicle;

   (c) exemption from taxation in respect of the salaries, emoluments, pay and indemnities paid to them, directly or indirectly, in respect of their employment with the OPCW; the Government shall not take income so exempted into account when assessing the amount of tax to be applied to income from other sources;

(d) exemption, with respect to themselves, their spouses, their dependent relatives and other members of their households, from immigration restrictions and alien registration;

(e) exemption, with respect to themselves, their spouses, their dependent relatives and other members of their households, from national service obligations, provided that, with respect to citizens of the Kingdom of the Netherlands, such exemption shall be confined to officials whose names have, by reason of their duties, been placed upon a list compiled by the Director-General and approved by the Government; provided further that should officials other than those listed, who are citizens of the Kingdom of the Netherlands, be called up for national service, the Government shall, upon request of the Director-General, grant such temporary deferments in the call-up of such officials as may be necessary to avoid interruption of the essential work of the OPCW;

(f) freedom to acquire or maintain within the Kingdom of the Netherlands or elsewhere foreign securities, foreign currency accounts and other movable and, under the same conditions applicable to citizens of the Kingdom of the Netherlands, immovable property; and at the termination of their employment with the OPCW the right to take out of the Kingdom of the Netherlands through authorised channels without prohibition, or restriction, their funds;

(g) the same protection and repatriation facilities with respect to themselves, their spouses, their dependent relatives and other members of their households as are accorded in time of international crisis to members, having comparable rank, of the staff of diplomatic missions established in the Kingdom of the Netherlands.

2.   In addition to the privileges and immunities specified in paragraph 1 of this Article:

(a) the Director-General shall be accorded the privileges and immunities, exemptions and facilities accorded to heads of diplomatic missions accredited to the Government in accordance with the Vienna Convention;

(b) the Deputy Directors-General shall also be accorded the privileges and immunities, exemptions and facilities accorded to heads of diplomatic missions accredited to the Government in accordance with the Vienna Convention;

(c) officials having the professional grade of P-5 and above, and such additional categories of officials as may be designated, in agreement with the Government, by the Director-General, in consultation with the Executive Council, on the grounds of the responsibilities of their positions in the OPCW, shall be accorded the same privileges and immunities, exemptions and facilities as the Government accords to diplomatic agents of comparable rank of the diplomatic missions established in the Kingdom of the Netherlands, in conformity with the Vienna Convention;

(d) officials having the grade of P-4 and below shall be accorded the same privileges and immunities, exemption and facilities as the Government accords to members of the administrative and technical staff of the diplomatic missions established in the Kingdom of the Netherlands, in conformity with the Vienna Convention, provided that the immunity from criminal jurisdiction and personal inviolability shall not extend to acts performed outside the course of their official duties;

(e) inspectors on mission shall be permitted to leave and enter the territory of the Kingdom of the Netherlands, by whatsoever means of transportation, with their equipment and with samples. The appropriate authorities of the Kingdom of the Netherlands shall provide them, where appropriate, with priority treatment and priority luggage handling with regard to customs and security controls. The transport of toxic chemicals shall comply with the rules and regulations of the Kingdom of the Netherlands concerning the handling of such articles.

3.   Officials of the OPCW who are Netherlands citizens or permanently resident in the Kingdom of the Netherlands shall enjoy the privileges and immunities, exemptions and facilities accorded by this Agreement to the extent recognised by international law, provided, however, that Article 22, paragraph 1 and Article 18, subparagraph 1(a) regarding their official baggage, and subparagraphs 1(b), 1(c) and 1(e) of this Agreement, shall, in any event, apply to them.

ARTICLE 19. PRIVILEGES AND IMMUNITIES OF EXPERTS

1.   Experts shall enjoy, within and with respect to the Kingdom of the Netherlands, the following privileges and immunities so far as may be necessary for the effective exercise of their functions and during their journeys in connection with such functions and during attendance at the headquarters:
   (a)   immunity from personal arrest or detention and from inspection or seizure of their official baggage;
   (b)   immunity from legal process of any kind with respect to words spoken or written, and all acts done by them, in the performance of their official functions, such immunity to continue although the persons concerned may no longer be employed on missions for, serving on committees of, or acting as consultants for, the OPCW, or may no longer be present at the headquarters or attending meetings convened by the OPCW. In any event, such immunity shall not extend to civil action by a third party for damage arising from an accident caused by a motor vehicle belonging to, driven by or operated on behalf of the expert or in respect of a motor traffic offence involving such vehicle;
   (c)   inviolability of all papers, documents and other official material;
   (d)   the right, for the purpose of all communications with the OPCW, to use codes and to dispatch or receive papers, correspondence or other official material by courier or in sealed bags;
   (e)   exemption with respect to themselves and their spouses from immigration restrictions, alien registration and national service obligations;
   (f)   the same protection and repatriation facilities as are accorded in time of international crisis to members having comparable rank, of the staff of diplomatic missions established in the Kingdom of the Netherlands; and
   (g)   the same privileges with respect to currency and exchange restrictions as are accorded to representatives of foreign Governments on temporary official missions.
2.   Where the incidence of any form of taxation depends upon residence, periods during which the persons designated in paragraph 1 of this Article and who are not already residents of the Kingdom of the Netherlands, may be present in the Kingdom of the Netherlands for the discharge of their duties shall not be considered as periods of residence. In particular, such persons shall be exempt from taxation on their salaries and emoluments received from the OPCW during such periods of duty.
3.   Experts who are citizens of, or permanently resident in, the Kingdom of the Netherlands shall enjoy only the privileges and immunities, exemptions and facilities accorded by subparagraph 1(a) regarding their official baggage and subparagraphs 1(b), 1(c), 1(d) and 1(g) of this Article.

ARTICLE 20. REPRESENTATIVES AND OFFICIALS OF STATES NOT PARTY TO THE CONVENTION

The status of representatives and officials of States not Party to the Convention with which the OPCW has concluded agreements or arrangements in accordance with the Convention, who have official business with the OPCW, will be determined in such agreements or arrangements.

ARTICLE 21. NOTIFICATION

1. The OPCW shall promptly notify the Government of:
    (a) the list of Heads of Delegation, Permanent Representatives, Delegates of States Parties and other persons within the scope of Articles 16, 17 and 19 of this Agreement, and shall revise such list from time to time as may be necessary;
    (b) the appointment of the Director-General, the Deputy Directors-General, and other officials of the OPCW, their arrival and their final departure, or the termination of their functions with the OPCW;
    (c) the arrival and final departure of members of the families forming part of the households of the persons referred to in subparagraph 1(b) of this Article and, where appropriate, the fact that a person has ceased to form part of the household; and
    (d) the arrival and final departure of domestic employees of persons referred to in subparagraph 1(b) of this Article and, where appropriate, the fact that they are leaving the employ of such persons.
2. The Government shall issue to Heads of Delegation, Permanent Representatives, Delegates of States Parties, other persons within the scope of Articles 16, 17 and 19 of this Agreement and members of their families who form part of their households and domestic employees of persons referred to under subparagraph 1(a) of this Article an identity card bearing the photograph of the holder. This card shall serve to identify the holder in relation to all authorities of the Kingdom of the Netherlands.
3. The Government shall issue to the Director-General, the Deputy Directors-General and other officials of the OPCW and members of their families who form part of their households and domestic employees of persons referred to under subparagraph 1(b) of this Article an identity card bearing the photograph of the holder. This card shall serve to identify the holder in relation to all authorities of the Kingdom of the Netherlands.

ARTICLE 22. SOCIAL SECURITY

1. For the social security scheme established by or conducted under the authority of the OPCW, the OPCW and the officials of the OPCW to whom the above-mentioned scheme applies shall be exempt from all compulsory contributions to the social security organisations of the Kingdom of the Netherlands. Consequently, they shall not be covered by the social security regulations of the Kingdom of the Netherlands.
2. Any provident fund established by or conducted under the authority of the OPCW shall enjoy legal capacity in the Kingdom of the Netherlands if the OPCW so requests and shall enjoy the same exemptions, privileges and immunities as the OPCW itself.
3. The provisions of paragraph 1 of this Article shall apply, *mutatis mutandis*, to spouses and dependent relatives forming part of the households of the persons referred to in paragraph 1 of this Article, unless they are employed in the Kingdom of the Netherlands by an employer other than the OPCW or receive Netherlands social security benefit.

ARTICLE 23. EMPLOYMENT

Spouses and members of the family forming part of the households of officials of the OPCW shall be granted temporary working permits for the duration of the employment of those officials with the OPCW in the Kingdom of the Netherlands.

ARTICLE 24. ADDITIONAL PROVISIONS ON PRIVILEGES AND IMMUNITIES

1. The privileges and immunities granted under the provisions of this Agreement are conferred

in the interests of the OPCW and not for the personal benefit of the individuals themselves. It is the duty of the OPCW and all persons enjoying such privileges and immunities to observe in all other respects the laws and regulations of the Kingdom of the Netherlands.

2. This Agreement shall apply irrespective of whether the Government maintains or does not maintain diplomatic relations with the State concerned and irrespective of whether the State concerned grants a similar privilege or immunity to the diplomatic envoys or citizens of the Kingdom of the Netherlands.

3. The privileges and immunities granted to officials of the OPCW and experts under the provisions of this Agreement are granted on the understanding that the OPCW shall waive the immunity of the persons concerned in any circumstances in which the OPCW considers that such immunity would impede the course of justice, and whenever it can be waived without prejudice to the purpose for which it was granted.

4. The OPCW shall cooperate at all times with the appropriate authorities of the Kingdom of the Netherlands to facilitate the proper administration of justice and shall prevent any abuse of the privileges and immunities granted under the provisions of this Agreement by officials of the OPCW.

5. Should the Government consider that an abuse by an official of the OPCW or an expert of a privilege or immunity conferred by this Agreement has occurred, the Director-General shall, upon request, consult with the appropriate Netherlands authorities to determine whether any such abuse has occurred. If such consultations fail to achieve a result satisfactory to the Director-General and to the Government, the matter shall be determined in accordance with the procedure set out in Article 26, paragraph 2, of this Agreement.

6. The Director-General shall have the right and the duty to waive the immunity of any official of the OPCW or of an expert in cases when the immunity would impede the course of justice and can be waived without prejudice to the interests of the OPCW. In respect of the Director-General, the OPCW has a similar right and duty, which shall be performed by the Executive Council.

ARTICLE 25. INTERNATIONAL RESPONSIBILITY OF THE KINGDOM OF THE NETHERLANDS

The Kingdom of the Netherlands shall not incur by reason of the location of the headquarters of the OPCW within its territory any international responsibility for acts or omissions of the OPCW or of its officials acting or abstaining from acting within the scope of their functions, other than the international responsibility which the Kingdom of the Netherlands would incur on the same footing as other States Parties.

ARTICLE 26. SETTLEMENT OF DISPUTES

1. The OPCW shall make provision for appropriate methods of settlement of:
   (a) disputes arising out of contracts and disputes of a private law character to which the OPCW is a party; and
   (b) disputes involving an official of the OPCW or an expert who, by reason of his official position, enjoys immunity, if such immunity has not been waived by the OPCW.

2. Any dispute between the OPCW and the Government concerning the interpretation or application of this Agreement, or any question affecting the headquarters or the relationship between the OPCW and the Government, which is not settled amicably, shall be referred for final decision to a tribunal of three arbitrators, at the request of either Party to the dispute. Each Party shall appoint one arbitrator. The third, who shall be chairman of the tribunal, is to be chosen by the first two arbitrators.

3. If one of the Parties fails to appoint an arbitrator and has not taken steps to do so within two

months following a request from the other Party to make such an appointment, the other Party may request the President of the International Court of Justice to make such an appointment.

4.   Should the first two arbitrators fail to agree upon the third within two months following their appointment, either Party may request the President of the International Court of Justice to make such an appointment.

5.   The tribunal shall conduct its proceedings in accordance with the Permanent Court of Arbitration Optional Rules for Arbitration Involving International Organisations and States, as in force on the date of the signature of this Agreement.

6.   The tribunal shall reach its decision by a majority of votes. Such decision shall be final and binding on the Parties to the dispute.

ARTICLE 27. OPERATION OF THIS AGREEMENT

1.   This Agreement shall be construed in the light of its primary purpose of enabling the OPCW at its headquarters in the Kingdom of the Netherlands fully and efficiently to discharge its responsibilities and fulfil its purposes.

2.   Whenever this Agreement imposes obligations on the appropriate authorities of the Kingdom of the Netherlands, the ultimate responsibility for the fulfilment of such obligations shall rest with the Government.

ARTICLE 28. TERMINATION OF THE AGREEMENT

This Agreement shall cease to be in force by mutual consent of the OPCW and the Government.

ARTICLE 29. AMENDMENTS

1.   This Agreement may be amended at any time.

2.   Any such amendment shall be agreed by mutual consent and shall be effected by an Exchange of Notes.

3.   Consultations with respect to amendment of this Agreement may be entered into by the OPCW and the Government at the request of either Party.

ARTICLE 30. STATUS OF THE SEPARATE ARRANGEMENT

The Separate Arrangement concluded together with this Agreement forms an integral part thereof. Any reference to the Agreement includes the Separate Arrangement.

ARTICLE 31. ENTRY INTO FORCE

1.   This Agreement shall enter into force on the day after both Parties have notified each other in writing that the legal requirements for entry into force have been complied with.

2.   With respect to the Kingdom of the Netherlands, this Agreement shall apply to the part of the Kingdom in Europe only.

DONE at The Hague on .... 199... in two copies in Arabic, Chinese, English, French, Russian, Spanish and Dutch languages, each text being equally authentic.

SEPARATE ARRANGEMENT WITH RESPECT TO THE AGREEMENT BETWEEN
THE ORGANISATION FOR THE PROHIBITION OF CHEMICAL WEAPONS
AND THE KINGDOM OF THE NETHERLANDS CONCERNING
THE HEADQUARTERS OF THE OPCW

1. ARTICLE 11, PARAGRAPH 2(C): "CONSIDERABLE EXPENDITURE"
    For the purposes of exemption from value-added tax on any goods or services necessary
    for the OPCW's official activities involving considerable expenditure, "considerable
    expenditure" means, in accordance with the regulations in force, an amount above the
    threshold of Dfl. 500 per invoice.

2. ARTICLE 11, PARAGRAPH 4: "CONDITIONS AGREED WITH THE GOVERNMENT"
    The Government hereby sets forth the conditions under which goods acquired or im-
    ported under the terms set out in paragraph 4 of Article 11 may be sold, given away, or
    otherwise disposed of.
    (a) As a general principle, the Government grants the OPCW a fixed time period of five
         years for reducing to zero the value on sale/disposal, for the purpose of duties and
         tax exemptions, of all movable goods, except motor vehicles. After this five-year
         time period, goods may be sold free of taxes and duties. This "reduction" of all
         goods to zero value in a five-year period is accomplished in steps of 10% for each
         period of six months. However, if the local market value of the above-mentioned
         goods has declined to an amount lower than calculated above, this lower amount
         shall prevail.
    (b) It is also understood as a general principle that the OPCW has the right to sell any
         of its goods at any time to a person or entity who/which is entitled in the Kingdom
         of the Netherlands to an exemption from taxes and/or duties on those goods. At an
         appropriate time, the Government will provide information concerning the stand-
         ing procedure required to handle the exemption in those cases, not only for motor
         vehicles, but also for other goods.
    (c) In the case of motor vehicles, the Government grants the OPCW the following
         rights:
         (i)   motor vehicles imported tax-exempt from within the European Union may be
               sold two years after their acquisition on condition that those cars be sold to
               entrepreneurs who have to take into account the standing procedures in the
               Kingdom of the Netherlands with respect to VAT; and
         (ii) motor vehicles imported from outside the European Union exempt from du-
               ties and taxes may be sold two years after their acquisition on condition that
               those cars be sold to entrepreneurs who have to take into account the standing
               procedures in the Kingdom of the Netherlands with respect to VAT and import
               duties.
    (d) With respect to data processing and communications equipment, the Government
         grants the OPCW a fixed-term period of five years for reducing the value of the
         equipment to zero, as described in subparagraph 2(a) above. After a period of two
         years, the OPCW is also granted the right to sell the equipment to entrepreneurs
         who have to take into account the standing procedure in the Kingdom of the Neth-
         erlands with respect to VAT and/or import duties. If in practice certain equipment
         turns out to be no longer of use to the OPCW within a period shorter than two years,
         while it could still be sold to an entrepreneur, the Government is willing to favour a
         solution on an ad hoc basis. If the local market value of the above-mentioned goods
         has declined to an amount lower than calculated above, this lower amount shall
         prevail.
    (e) It is understood that the OPCW also has the right to dispose of exempt purchased

goods at any moment without payment or taxes and/or duties, through exportation to a country outside the European Union or by destroying them.

(f) The OPCW shall inform the Government of its disposal of exempt purchased goods. The procedure for informing the Government shall be effected in such a manner as to minimise the administrative burden.

3. OFFICIALS OF THE OPCW

(a) Subject to the provisions of Article 18 of the Headquarters Agreement, officials of the OPCW who are neither Netherlands citizens nor persons permanently resident in the Kingdom of the Netherlands shall, as far as the levying of Netherlands income tax is concerned, be taxed only on domestic income within the meaning of sections 48 and 49 of the 1964 Income Tax Act, received outside the OPCW function. As far as the levying of Netherlands wealth tax is concerned, only domestic wealth within the meaning of sections 12 and 13 of the 1964 Wealth Tax Act will be taxed. In this respect, the officials of the OPCW concerned are subject to the same treatment as members of diplomatic missions.

(b) Officials of the OPCW of grade P-5 and above shall be granted exemption from VAT, under article 33 in conjunction with article 36 of the Regulations implementing the 1959 State Taxes Act (*Algemene wet inzake rijksbelastingen*). The condition of reciprocity is not required.

(c) Officials of the OPCW who are eligible for the privileges and immunities laid down in the Vienna Convention shall be granted exemption from all taxes and duties if they import into or purchase within the European Union a motor vehicle intended for private use. After taxes and duties have been paid on the residual value of such a vehicle or after the car has been sold outside the European Union, another motor vehicle may be purchased tax-free. The exemption also applies to motor vehicle tax and excise duty on engine fuels. Officials of grade P-5 and above who live with their spouse shall also be granted exemption from all taxes related to a second motor vehicle in accordance with the regulations in force.

(d) Officials of the OPCW who are eligible for the privileges and immunities laid down in the Vienna Convention shall be granted diplomatic exemption from municipal taxes, including the user component of property tax.

(e) Officials of the OPCW shall, in accordance with the regulations in force, have relief from import duties, taxes, except payments for services, in respect of their furniture and personal effects and the right to export furniture and personal effects with relief from duty on termination of their duties in the Netherlands. Personal effects may include a reasonable number of cars that have been in use in the household and that are older than six months.

(f) If the regulations relating to diplomatic staff or international officials who are deemed to be of the same status as officials of the OPCW are amended, the regulations applicable to officials of the OPCW will also be amended.

4. ADDITIONAL PROVISION

(a) If and to the extent that the Government shall, in the future, enter into an agreement with any intergovernmental organisation containing terms or conditions more favourable to that organisation than comparable terms or conditions in this Agreement, the Government shall extend such more favourable terms or conditions to the OPCW or to any person entitled to privileges and immunities under this Agreement.

(b) The Government shall inform the OPCW of the office designated by the Ministry of Foreign Affairs to serve as official contact point and to be primarily responsible for all matters in relation to this Agreement. The OPCW shall be informed promptly about this designation and of any subsequent changes in this regard.

16.2 Privileges and Immunities Agreements between the OPCW and States Parties

C-8/DEC.12 adopted by the Conference of the States Parties at its Eight Session on 23 October 2003 and entitled "Privileges and Immunities Agreements between the Organisation for the Prohibition of Chemical Weapons and States Parties"

The Conference

Recalling that subparagraph 50 of Article VIII of the Chemical Weapons Convention (hereinafter "the Convention") specifies that the legal capacity, privileges, and immunities referred to in that Article shall be defined in agreements between the Organisation for the Prohibition of Chemical Weapons (OPCW) and the States Parties;

Recalling also that said privileges and immunities agreements are to be approved by the Conference of the States Parties (hereinafter "the Conference"); and

Recalling further that subparagraph 34(a) of Article VIII of the Convention provides that the Executive Council (hereinafter "the Council") shall conclude agreements or arrangements with States and international organisations on behalf of the OPCW, subject to prior approval by the Conference;

Hereby:

Calls upon all States Parties that have not yet negotiated their agreements with the OPCW on the matter of legal capacity, privileges, and immunities, to do so without delay;

Gives prior approval to the Council to conclude privileges and immunities agreements between the OPCW and States Parties; and

Requests the Council to notify the Conference, at the next regular session of the Conference following their conclusion, of the privileges and immunities agreements that have been concluded with States Parties by the Council on behalf of the OPCW.

16.3 Technical Secretariat's proposed text for bilateral Agreements on Privileges and Immunities under Article VIII, paragraph 50

AGREEMENT BETWEEN THE ORGANISATION FOR THE PROHIBITION OF CHEMICAL WEAPONS AND [THE STATE PARTY] ON THE PRIVILEGES AND IMMUNITIES OF THE OPCW

Whereas Article VIII, paragraph 48, of the Convention on the Prohibition of the Development, Production, Stockpiling and Use of Chemical Weapons and on Their Destruction provides that the OPCW shall enjoy on the territory and in any other place under the jurisdiction or control of a State Party such legal capacity and such privileges and immunities as are necessary for the exercise of its functions;

Whereas Article VIII, paragraph 49, of the Convention on the Prohibition of the Development, Production, Stockpiling and Use of Chemical Weapons and on Their Destruction provides that delegates of States Parties, together with their alternates and advisers, representatives appointed to the Executive Council together with their alternates and advisers, the Director-General and the staff of the Organisation shall enjoy such privileges and immunities as are necessary in the independent exercise of their functions in connection with the OPCW;

Whereas notwithstanding Article VIII, paragraphs 48 and 49 of the Convention on the Prohibition of the Development, Production, Stockpiling and Use of Chemical Weapons and on Their Destruction, the privileges and immunities enjoyed by the Director-General and the staff of the

Secretariat during the conduct of verification activities shall be those set forth in Part II, Section B, of the Verification Annex;

Whereas Article VIII, paragraph 50, of the Convention on the Prohibition of the Development, Production, Stockpiling and Use of Chemical Weapons and on Their Destruction specifies that such legal capacity, privileges and immunities are to be defined in agreements between the Organisation and the States Parties,

Now, therefore, the Organisation for the Prohibition of Chemical Weapons and [the State Party] have agreed as follows:

ARTICLE 1. DEFINITIONS

In this Agreement:
(a) "Convention" means the Convention on the Prohibition of the Development, Production, Stockpiling and Use of Chemical Weapons and on Their Destruction of 13 January 1993;
(b) "OPCW" means the Organisation for the Prohibition of Chemical Weapons established under Article VIII, paragraph 1, of the Convention;
(c) "Director-General" means the Director-General referred to in Article VIII, paragraph 41, of the Convention, or in his absence, the Acting Director-General;
(d) "Officials of the OPCW" means the Director-General and all members of the staff of the Secretariat of the OPCW;
(e) "State Party" means the State Party to this Agreement;
(f) "States Parties" means the States Parties to the Convention;
(g) "Representatives of States Parties" means the accredited heads of delegation of States Parties to the Conference of the States Parties and/or to the Executive Council or the Delegates to other meetings of the OPCW;
(h) "Experts" means persons who, in their personal capacity, are performing missions authorised by the OPCW, are serving on its organs, or who are, in any way, at its request, consulting with the OPCW;
(i) "Meetings convened by the OPCW" means any meeting of any of the organs or subsidiary organs of the OPCW, or any international conferences or other gatherings convened by the OPCW;
(j) "Property" means all property, assets and funds belonging to the OPCW or held or administered by the OPCW in furtherance of its functions under the Convention and all income of the OPCW;
(k) "Archives of the OPCW" means all records, correspondence, documents, manuscripts, computer and media data, photographs, films, video and sound recordings belonging to or held by the OPCW or any officials of the OPCW in an official function, and any other material which the Director-General and the State Party may agree shall form part of the archives of the OPCW;
(l) "Premises of the OPCW" are the buildings or parts of buildings, and the land ancillary thereto if applicable, used for the purposes of the OPCW, including those referred to in Part II, sub-paragraph 11(b), of the Verification Annex to the Convention.

ARTICLE 2. LEGAL PERSONALITY

The OPCW shall possess full legal personality. In particular, it shall have the capacity:
(a)   to contract;
(b) to acquire and dispose of movable and immovable property;
(c)   to institute and act in legal proceedings.

ARTICLE 3. PRIVILEGES AND IMMUNITIES OF THE OPCW

1. The OPCW and its property, wherever located and by whomsoever held, shall enjoy immunity from every form of legal process, except in so far as in any particular case the OPCW has expressly waived its immunity. It is, however, understood that no waiver of immunity shall extend to any measure of execution.
2. The premises of the OPCW shall be inviolable. The property of the OPCW, wherever located and by whomsoever held, shall be immune from search, requisition, confiscation, expropriation and any other form of interference, whether by executive, administrative, judicial or legislative action.
3. The archives of the OPCW shall be inviolable, wherever located.
4. Without being restricted by financial controls, regulations or moratoria of any kind:
    (a) the OPCW may hold funds, gold or currency of any kind and operate accounts in any currency;
    (b) the OPCW may freely transfer its funds, securities, gold and currencies to or from the State Party, to or from any other country, or within the State Party, and may convert any currency held by it into any other currency.
5. The OPCW shall, in exercising its rights under paragraph 4 of this Article, pay due regard to any representations made by the Government of the State Party in so far as it is considered that effect can be given to such representations without detriment to the interests of the OPCW.
6. The OPCW and its property shall be:
    (a) exempt from all direct taxes; it is understood, however, that the OPCW will not claim exemption from taxes which are, in fact, no more than charges for public utility services;
    (b) exempt from customs duties and prohibitions and restrictions on imports and exports in respect of articles imported or exported by the OPCW for its official use; it is understood, however, that articles imported under such exemption will not be sold in the State Party, except in accordance with conditions agreed upon with the State Party;
    (c) exempt from duties and prohibitions and restrictions on imports and exports in respect of its publications.
7. While the OPCW will not, as a general rule, claim exemption from excise duties and from taxes on the sale of movable and immovable property which form part of the price to be paid, nevertheless when the OPCW is making important purchases for official use of property on which such duties and taxes have been charged or are chargeable, the State Party will, whenever possible, make appropriate administrative arrangements for the remission or return of the amount of duty or tax.

ARTICLE 4. FACILITIES AND IMMUNITIES IN RESPECT OF COMMUNICATIONS AND PUBLICATIONS

1. For its official communications the OPCW shall enjoy, in the territory of the State Party and as far as may be compatible with any international conventions, regulations and arrangements to which the State Party adheres, treatment not less favourable than that accorded by the Government of the State Party to any other Government, including the latter's diplomatic mission, in the matter of priorities, rates and taxes for post and telecommunications, and press rates for information to the media.
2. No censorship shall be applied to the official correspondence and other official communications of the OPCW.
    The OPCW shall have the right to use codes and to dispatch and receive correspondence and other official communications by courier or in sealed bags, which shall have the same privileges and immunities as diplomatic couriers and bags.

Nothing in this paragraph shall be construed to preclude the adoption of appropriate security precautions to be determined by agreement between the State Party and the OPCW.

3.   The State Party recognises the right of the OPCW to publish and broadcast freely within the territory of the State Party for purposes specified in the Convention.

4.   All official communications directed to the OPCW and all outward official communications of the OPCW, by whatever means or whatever form transmitted, shall be inviolable. Such inviolability shall extend, without limitation by reason of this enumeration, to publications, still and moving pictures, videos, films, sound recordings and software.

ARTICLE 5. REPRESENTATIVES OF STATES PARTIES

1.   Representatives of States Parties, together with alternates, advisers, technical experts and secretaries of their delegations, at meetings convened by the OPCW, shall, without prejudice to any other privileges and immunities which they may enjoy, while exercising their functions and during their journeys to and from the place of the meeting, enjoy the following privileges and immunities:

(a)   immunity from personal arrest or detention;

(b)   immunity from legal process of any kind in respect of words spoken or written and all acts done by them, in their official capacity; such immunity shall continue to be accorded, notwithstanding that the persons concerned may no longer be engaged in the performance of such functions;

(c)   inviolability for all papers, documents and official material;

(d)   the right to use codes and to dispatch or receive papers, correspondence or official material by courier or in sealed bags;

(e)   exemption in respect of themselves and their spouses from immigration restrictions, alien registration or national service obligations while they are visiting or passing through the State Party in the exercise of their functions;

(f)   the same facilities with respect to currency or exchange restrictions as are accorded to representatives of foreign governments on temporary official missions;

(g)   the same immunities and facilities in respect of their personal baggage as are accorded to members of comparable rank of diplomatic missions.

2.   Where the incidence of any form of taxation depends upon residence, periods during which the persons designated in paragraph 1 of this Article may be present in the territory of the State Party for the discharge of their duties shall not be considered as periods of residence.

3.   The privileges and immunities are accorded to the persons designated in paragraph 1 of this Article in order to safeguard the independent exercise of their functions in connection with the OPCW and not for the personal benefit of the individuals themselves. It is the duty of all persons enjoying such privileges and immunities to observe in all other respects the laws and regulations of the State Party.

4.   The provisions of paragraphs 1 and 2 of this Article are not applicable in relation to a person who is a national of the State Party.

ARTICLE 6. OFFICIALS OF THE OPCW

1.   During the conduct of verification activities, the Director-General and the staff of the Secretariat, including qualified experts during investigations of alleged use of chemical weapons referred to in Part XI, paragraphs 7 and 8 of the Verification Annex to the Convention, enjoy, in accordance with Article VIII, paragraph 51, of the Convention, the privileges and immunities set forth in Part II, Section B, of the Verification Annex to the Convention or, when transiting the territory of non-inspected States Parties, the privileges and immunities referred to in Part II, paragraph 12, of the same Annex.

2. For other activities related to the object and purpose of the Convention, officials of the OPCW shall:

    (a) be immune from personal arrest or detention and from seizure of their personal baggage;
    (b) be immune from legal process in respect of words spoken or written and all acts performed by them in their official capacity;
    (c) enjoy inviolability for all papers, documents and official material, subject to the provisions of the Convention;
    (d) enjoy the same exemptions from taxation in respect of salaries and emoluments paid to them by the OPCW and on the same conditions as are enjoyed by officials of the United Nations;
    (e) be exempt, together with their spouses from immigration restrictions and alien registration;
    (f) be given, together with their spouses, the same repatriation facilities in time of international crises as officials of comparable rank of diplomatic missions;
    (g) be accorded the same privileges in respect of exchange facilities as are accorded to members of comparable rank of diplomatic missions.

3. The officials of the OPCW shall be exempt from national service obligations, provided that, in relation to nationals of the State Party, such exemption shall be confined to officials of the OPCW whose names have, by reason of their duties, been placed upon a list compiled by the Director-General of the OPCW and approved by the State Party. Should other officials of the OPCW be called up for national service by the State Party, the State Party shall, at the request of the OPCW, grant such temporary deferments in the call-up of such officials as may be necessary to avoid interruption in the continuation of essential work.

4. In addition to the privileges and immunities specified in paragraphs 1, 2 and 3 of this Article, the Director-General of the OPCW shall be accorded on behalf of himself and his spouse, the privileges and immunities, exemptions and facilities accorded to diplomatic agents on behalf of themselves and their spouses, in accordance with international law. The same privileges and immunities, exemptions and facilities shall also be accorded to a senior official of the OPCW acting on behalf of the Director-General.

5. Privileges and immunities are granted to officials of the OPCW in the interests of the OPCW, and not for the personal benefit of the individuals themselves. It is the duty of all persons enjoying such privileges and immunities to observe in all other respects the laws and regulations of the State Party. The OPCW shall have the right and the duty to waive the immunity of any official of the OPCW in any case where, in its opinion, the immunity would impede the course of justice and can be waived without prejudice to the interests of the OPCW.

6. The OPCW shall cooperate at all times with the appropriate authorities of the State Party to facilitate the proper administration of justice, and shall secure the observance of police regulations and prevent the occurrence of any abuse in connection with the privileges, immunities and facilities mentioned in this Article.

ARTICLE 7. EXPERTS

1. Experts shall be accorded the following privileges and immunities so far as is necessary for the effective exercise of their functions, including the time spent on journeys in connection with such functions.

    (a) immunity from personal arrest or detention and from seizure of their personal baggage;
    (b) in respect of words spoken or written or acts done by them in the performance of their official functions, immunity from legal process of every kind, such immunity to continue notwithstanding that the persons concerned are no longer performing official functions for the OPCW;
    (c) inviolability for all papers, documents and official material;

(d) for the purposes of their communications with the OPCW, the right to use codes and to receive papers or correspondence by courier or in sealed bags;

(e) the same facilities in respect of currency and exchange restrictions as are accorded to representatives of foreign Governments on temporary official missions;

(f) the same immunities and facilities in respect of their personal baggage as are accorded to members of comparable rank of diplomatic missions.

2. The privileges and immunities are accorded to experts in the interests of the OPCW and not for the personal benefit of the individuals themselves. It is the duty of all persons enjoying such privileges and immunities to observe in all other respects the laws and regulations of the State Party. The OPCW shall have the right and the duty to waive the immunity of any expert in any case where, in its opinion, the immunity would impede the course of justice and can be waived without prejudice to the interests of the OPCW.

ARTICLE 8. ABUSE OF PRIVILEGE

1. If the State Party considers that there has been an abuse of a privilege or immunity conferred by this Agreement, consultations shall be held between the State Party and the OPCW to determine whether any such abuse has occurred and, if so, to attempt to ensure that no repetition occurs. If such consultations fail to achieve a result satisfactory to the State Party and the OPCW, the question whether an abuse of a privilege or immunity has occurred shall be settled by a procedure in accordance with Article 10.

2. Persons included in one of the categories under Articles 6 and 7 shall not be required by the territorial authorities to leave the territory of the State Party on account of any activities by them in their official capacity. In the case, however, of abuse of privileges committed by any such person in activities outside official functions, the person may be required to leave by the Government of the State Party, provided that the order to leave the country has been issued by the territorial authorities with the approval of the Foreign Minister of the State Party. Such approval shall be given only in consultation with the Director-General of the OPCW. If expulsion proceedings are taken against the person, the Director-General of the OPCW shall have the right to appear in such proceedings on behalf of the person against whom they are instituted.

ARTICLE 9. TRAVEL DOCUMENTS AND VISAS

1. The State Party shall recognise and accept as valid the United Nations *laissez-passer* issued to the officials of the OPCW, in accordance with special OPCW arrangements, for the purpose of carrying out their tasks related to the Convention. The Director-General shall notify the State Party of the relevant OPCW arrangements.

2. The State Party shall take all necessary measures to facilitate the entry into and sojourn in its territory and shall place no impediment in the way of the departure from its territory of the persons included in one of the categories under Articles 5, 6 and 7 above, whatever their nationality, and shall ensure that no impediment is placed in the way of their transit to or from the place of their official duty or business and shall afford them any necessary protection in transit.

3. Applications for visas and transit visas, where required, from persons included in one of the categories under Articles 5, 6 and 7, when accompanied by a certificate that they are travelling in their official capacity, shall be dealt with as speedily as possible to allow those persons to effectively discharge their functions. In addition, such persons shall be granted facilities for speedy travel.

4. The Director-General, the Deputy Director(s)-General and other officials of the OPCW, travelling in their official capacity, shall be granted the same facilities for travel as are accorded

to members of comparable rank in diplomatic missions.

5.   For the conduct of verification activities visas are issued in accordance with paragraph 10 of Part II, Section B, of the Verification Annex to the Convention.

ARTICLE 10. SETTLEMENT OF DISPUTES

1.   The OPCW shall make provision for appropriate modes of settlement of:
     (a)   disputes arising out of contracts or other disputes of a private law character to which the OPCW is a party;
     (b)   disputes involving any official of the OPCW or expert who, by reason of his official position, enjoys immunity, if such immunity has not been waived in accordance with Article 6, paragraph 5, or Article 7, paragraph 2, of this Agreement.

2.   Any dispute concerning the interpretation or application of this Agreement, which is not settled amicably, shall be referred for final decision to a tribunal of three arbitrators, at the request of either party to the dispute. Each party shall appoint one arbitrator. The third, who shall be chairman of the tribunal, is to be chosen by the first two arbitrators.

3.   If one of the parties fails to appoint an arbitrator and has not taken steps to do so within two months following a request from the other party to make such an appointment, the other party may request the President of the International Court of Justice to make such an appointment.

4.   Should the first two arbitrators fail to agree upon the third within two months following their appointment, either party may request the President of the International Court of Justice to make such appointment.

5.   The tribunal shall conduct its proceedings in accordance with the Permanent Court of Arbitration Optional Rules for Arbitration Involving International Organisations and States, as in force on the date of entry into force of this Agreement.

6.   The tribunal shall reach its decision by a majority of votes. Such decision shall be final and binding on the parties to the dispute.

ARTICLE 11. INTERPRETATION

1.   The provisions of this Agreement shall be interpreted in the light of the functions which the Convention entrusts to the OPCW.

2.   The provisions of this Agreement shall in no way limit or prejudice the privileges and immunities accorded to members of the inspection team in Part II, Section B, of the Verification Annex to the Convention or the privileges and immunities accorded to the Director-General and the staff of the Secretariat of the OPCW in Article VIII, paragraph 51, of the Convention. The provisions of this Agreement shall not themselves operate so as to abrogate, or derogate from, any provisions of the Convention or any rights or obligations which the OPCW may otherwise have, acquire or assume.

ARTICLE 12. FINAL PROVISIONS

1.   This Agreement shall enter into force on the date of deposit with the Director-General of an instrument of ratification of the State Party. It is understood that, when an instrument of ratification is deposited by the State Party it will be in a position under its own law to give effect to the terms of this Agreement.

2.   This Agreement shall continue to be in force for so long as the State Party remains a State Party to the Convention.

3.   The OPCW and the State Party may enter into such supplemental agreements as may be necessary.

4.   Consultations with respect to amendment of this Agreement shall be entered into at the re-

quest of the OPCW or the State Party. Any such amendment shall be by mutual consent expressed in an agreement concluded by the OPCW and the State Party.

Done in The Hague in duplicate on _____, in [the] English [and .....] language [s, each text being equally authentic].

17. PROTECTION
(ARTICLE X)

17.1 OPCW data bank on protection against CWs

C-I/DEC.53 adopted by the Conference of the States Parties at its First Session on 16 May 1997 and entitled "Data bank on protection against chemical weapons to be established in accordance with Article X(5) of the Convention"

The Conference

Recalling that the Commission, in PC-V/12, paragraph 6.7(b), recommended that the data bank on protection against chemical weapons, to be established in accordance with Article X(5) of the Convention, be part of a library in the Technical Secretariat, and that this repository of information be indexed by a database which should be a standard commercially or otherwise available bibliographical programme allowing for the inclusion of data types such as those listed in Appendix 4 (Illustrative Format for Provision, by States Parties, of Information under Article X, paragraph 5) of the Chairman's Paper annexed to the Report of the Expert Group on Technical Cooperation and Assistance, as contained in PC-V/B/WP.16,

Recalling further that the Commission, in PC-VII/8, paragraph 6.5(b), adopted illustrative lists of some categories of information for the data bank on protection, as contained in Annex C to PC-VII/B/WP.6,

Bearing in mind that the Commission recommended in paragraph 61.3 of its Final Report that the Conference adopt the above-mentioned lists and requirements,

Hereby:
1. Decides that the above-mentioned data bank on protection against chemical weapons be established as part of a library in the Technical Secretariat, and that this repository of information be indexed by a database;
2. Decides that the database used for indexing the data bank on protection against chemical weapons should be a standard commercially or otherwise available bibliographical programme allowing for the inclusion of data types such as those indicated in Annex 1 hereto; and
3. Adopts the illustrative lists of some categories of information for the data bank on protection contained in Annex 2 hereto.

ANNEX 1
DATA TYPES TO BE INCLUDED IN THE INDEX OF THE DATA BANK
ON PROTECTION AGAINST CHEMICAL WEAPONS
based on the
ILLUSTRATIVE FORMAT FOR PROVISION, BY STATE PARTIES, OF INFORMATION
UNDER ARTICLE X, PARAGRAPH 5

A copy of this format must be filled out and attached to each document in which the information to be provided is contained. If the information is provided in a non-documentary form, e.g., as a video recording or a piece of equipment, the applicable parts of this format must be filled out and any other relevant data must be added.
1. Contributing State Party
2. Degree of confidentiality, if any, of the information
3. Author(s), name

4.   Author(s), address
5.   Point of contact for further information if different from author(s)
6.   Title of paper, report or book
7.   Language of publication
8.   Journal or report series where published
9.   Publication year (as listed in the publication)
10. Volume number of journal or serial number of report
11. First and last page of paper or number of pages of report or book
12. Publisher or issuing organisation
13. Organisation where work was performed
14. If only abstract supplied, indicate where publication is available
15. Brief abstract of publication

Annex 2

ILLUSTRATIVE LISTS

SOME CATEGORIES OF INFORMATION FOR THE DATA BANK ON PROTECTION

The following two lists contain categories of information on training and education and on available sources of information that could be included in the data bank on protection to be established according to Article X, paragraph 5. The lists are not intended to be limiting and every State Party is free to provide any information it deems appropriate.

List 1 - Categories of Information on Training and Education
1.   Name of the State Party
2.   Date of the provision or update of the information
3.   Local training
     3.1 Types of training or education offered
     3.2 Scope and basic contents of each course
     3.3 Number of courses and their duration
     3.4 Number of trainees accepted per course
     3.5 Qualifications required of trainees
     3.6 Facility requirements for courses
     3.7 Local personnel requirements for courses, including interpretation
     3.8 Local infrastructure requirements for courses
     3.9 Time required to set up courses
4.   Training in the country of the Assisting State Party
     4.1 Types of training or education offered
     4.2 Scope and basic contents of each course
     4.3 Number of courses and their duration
     4.4 Number of trainees accepted per course
     4.5 Provisions offered for trainees (transport, lodging, food, etc.)
     4.6 Qualifications required of trainees, including linguistic abilities
     4.7 Whether the courses occur regularly or are set up when required
5.   Point of contact for further technical information
     5.1 Organisation
     5.2 Name and function
     5.3 Telephone number
     5.4 Telefax number
     5.5 Telex number
     5.6 Office hours (note if in local time, CE or GMT)

6. Point of contact for request for urgent assistance
    6.1 Organisation
    6.2 Name and function
    6.3 Telephone number
    6.4 Telefax number
    6.5. Telex number
    6.6. Office hours (note if in local time, CE or GMT)

List 2 - Categories of Information on Information Sources
1. Name of the State Party
2. Date of the provision or update of the information
3. For databases
    3.1 Name of the database
    3.2 Types of data contained in the database
    3.3 Size of the database
    3.4 Conditions for and means of access to the database
    3.5 Technical requirements for access
    3.6 Availability of manuals
    3.7 Point of contact for further technical information
        3.7.1 Organisation
        3.7.2 Name and function
        3.7.3 Telephone number
        3.7.4 Telefax number
        3.7.5 Telex number
        3.7.6 Office hours (note if in local time, CE or GMT)
    3.8. Point of contact for request for urgent and immediate access
        3.8.1 Organisation
        3.8.2 Name and function
        3.8.3 Telephone number
        3.8.4 Telefax number
        3.8.5 Telex number
        3.8.6 Office hours (note if in local time, CE or GMT)
4. For specialised libraries and reference collections
    4.1 Name
    4.2 Type of material contained
    4.3 Size of the library or reference collection
    4.4 Accessibility for visits
    4.5 Mail, fax or phone requests for loans accepted?
    4.6 Photocopies of articles or papers provided by fax or mail?
    4.7 Point of contact for further technical information
        4.7.1 Organisation
        4.7.2 Name and function
        4.7.3 Telephone number
        4.7.4 Telefax number
        4.7.5 Telex number
        4.7.6 Office hours (note if in local time, CE or GMT)
    4.8 Point of contact for urgent and immediate requests for information
        4.8.1 Organisation
        4.8.2 Name and function
        4.8.3 Telephone number
        4.8.4 Telefax number

4.8.5   Telex number
4.8.6   Office hours (note if in local time, CE or GMT)
5.   For other information sources
   5.1   Type of information source
   5.2   Name of the information source
   5.3   Type of information contained in the source
   5.4   Size of the information contents of the source
   5.5   Availability of information from the source
   5.6   Technical requirements for obtaining or using information from the source
   5.7   Point of contact for further technical information
        5.7.1   Organisation
        5.7.2   Name and function
        5.7.3   Telephone number
        5.7.4   Telefax number
        5.7.5   Telex number
        5.7.6   Office hours (note if in local time, CE or GMT)
   5.8   Point of contact for urgent and immediate requests for information
        5.8.1   Organisation
        5.8.2   Name and function
        5.8.3   Telephone number
        5.8.4   Telefax number
        5.8.5   Telex number
        5.8.6   Office hours (note if in local time, CE or GMT)

17.2 Submission of information regarding national programmes related to protective purposes

C-9/DEC.10 adopted by the Conference of the States Parties at its Ninth Session on 20 November 2004 and entitled "Submission of information regarding national programmes related to protective purposes, pursuant to Article X, paragraph 4 of the Convention"

The Conference

Noting that paragraph 4 of Article X of the Chemical Weapons Convention (hereinafter "the Convention") requires each State Party, for the purposes of increasing the transparency of national programmes related to protective purposes, to provide annually to the Technical Secretariat (hereinafter "the Secretariat") information on its programme, in accordance with procedures to be considered and approved by the Conference of the States Parties (hereinafter "the Conference") pursuant to paragraph 21 (i) of Article VIII of the Convention;

Recalling that the First Special Session of the Conference of the States Parties to Review the Operation of the Chemical Weapons Convention (hereinafter "the First Review Conference") reaffirmed the continuing relevance and importance of the provisions of Article X of the Convention, and of the activities of the Organisation for the Prohibition of Chemical Weapons (hereinafter "the Organisation") in relation to assistance and protection against chemical weapons; and that these provisions and activities have gained additional relevance in today's security context (paragraph 7.92 of RC-1/5, dated 9 May 2003);

Recalling also that the First Review Conference declared that implementation of the requirement to submit information annually pursuant to paragraph 4 of Article X of the Convention would benefit from an early agreement on the procedures for such submissions, and further requested the Executive Council (hereinafter "the Council") to expeditiously develop and submit for adoption the procedures called for by the Convention (paragraph 7.94 of RC-1/5);

Noting that, pursuant to paragraph 2 of Article X of the Convention, nothing in the Convention shall be interpreted as impeding the right of any State Party to conduct research into, develop, produce, acquire, transfer or use means of protection against chemical weapons, for purposes not prohibited under the Convention;

Recognising that the Organisation should continue to strengthen its efforts to ensure the full implementation of Article X's provisions for assistance and protection against chemical weapons;

Stressing that all measures undertaken by States Parties to implement Article X of the Convention should assist in strengthening the ability of the Organisation better to co-ordinate and deliver to States Parties assistance and protection against chemical weapons; and

Having considered the recommendation of the Council regarding the submission of information regarding national programmes related to protective purposes, pursuant to Article X, paragraph 4 of the Convention (EC-M-24/DEC.6, dated 24 November 2004);

Hereby:

1. Adopts the attached format for States Parties to provide annually to the Secretariat information on national programmes for protective purposes, on the understanding that:
    (a) each State Party uses the attached format to provide the information relating to such activities for the previous calendar year, no later than 120 days after the end of that year;
    (b) the Secretariat makes available to States Parties, upon request, information provided by other States Parties; and any confidential information submitted is treated in accordance with the Confidentiality Annex of the Convention (Section A, paragraph 2); and

2. Agrees that this decision is without prejudice to the right of States Parties to protect sensitive information related to national programmes for protective purposes, and the right of States Parties to designate as confidential any sensitive information which they choose to provide to the Organisation in order to satisfy this reporting requirement.

ANNEX

FORMAT FOR THE ANNUAL REPORTING OF INFORMATION ON NATIONAL PROGRAMMES FOR PROTECTION AGAINST CHEMICAL WEAPONS, UNDER ARTICLE X OF THE CHEMICAL WEAPONS CONVENTION

Name of State Party providing the information:
1. Reporting period:
2. This report covers the calendar year:

INFORMATION ON THE EXISTENCE OF A NATIONAL PROGRAMME(S) RELATED TO PROTECTION AGAINST CHEMICAL WEAPONS
3. Does the State Party have a national programme(s) for the implementation of protective measures against CW?   YES ❑   NO ❑

    If Yes, do these cover:
    (a) protection of military personnel against attack from CW?   YES ❑   NO ❑

    (b) protection of the civilian population against attack from CW?   YES ❑   NO ❑

GENERAL INFORMATION ON THE MAIN ELEMENTS OF A NATIONAL
PROGRAMME(S) RELATED TO PROTECTIVE PURPOSES

4.   Summarise (in general terms) the national programme(s), and/or regional and local differences
     (as appropriate to and within the territory of the State Party), for the implementation of
     protective measures against CW attack against the State Party's armed forces or civilian
     population (continue on a separate sheet if necessary):

5.   List the main national government and/or regional and local bodies (as appropriate to the
     circumstances of the State Party) that have primary responsibility within the State Party for:
     (a) protection of armed forces:
     (b) protection of specialist personnel such as police, fire fighters, ambulance and medical
          personnel, or government officials:
     (c) protection of the general public:

6.   If protective equipment is provided for armed forces or civilians, is it:
     (a) developed from government-sponsored research and development? YES ❑   NO ❑

     (b) acquired commercially?   YES ❑   NO ❑

     (c) acquired from the governments of other States Parties?   YES ❑   NO ❑

7.   Has the State Party's government made an offer of assistance through
     the OPCW under Article X, paragraph 7 of the CWC?   YES ❑   NO ❑

INFORMATION ON THE MAIN ELEMENTS OF RESEARCH AND DEVELOPMENT AC-
TIVITIES RELATED TO PROTECTIVE PURPOSES

8.   Does the government of the State Party undertake research and
     development related to protection against CW, in the following fields:
     Respiratory protection   YES ❑   NO ❑

     Protective clothing   YES ❑   NO ❑

     Collective protection   YES ❑   NO ❑

     Decontamination technologies for area, personnel and materials   YES ❑   NO ❑

     Detection/identification of CW agents   YES ❑   NO ❑

     Laboratory analysis for CW agents   YES ❑   NO ❑

     Medical countermeasures   YES ❑   NO ❑

     Hazard modelling   YES ❑   NO ❑

INFORMATION ON THE EXISTENCE OF UNITS, ONE OF WHOSE PRINCIPAL
FUNCTIONS MAY BE PROTECTION AGAINST CHEMICAL WEAPONS

9.   Are there any military units one of whose principal functions is
     protection against CW?   YES ❑   NO ❑

10. If Yes, briefly state their main tasks (such as collective protection, decontamination, detection,
     and/or medical countermeasures). Continue on a separate sheet if necessary:

INFORMATION ON THE TRAINING PROGRAMME RELATED TO PROTECTIVE PUR-
POSES

11. Does the State Party conduct operational training for its armed forces
    using real CW agent or simulants?   YES ❑   NO ❑

12. Does the State Party train its military personnel in the following fields:
    (a) use of personal protection equipment?   YES ❑   NO ❑

    (b) decontamination?   YES ❑   NO ❑

    (c) detection?   YES ❑   NO ❑

    (d) medical aspects of protection?   YES ❑   NO ❑

13. Has the State Party's government provided, in the last year, training
    of foreign military or civilian personnel on protection from a possible
    CW attack?   YES ❑   NO ❑

INFORMATION ON PROTECTION OF THE CIVILIAN POPULATION

14. Does the programme for protection against CW provide for support to
    the civilian population in case of use or threat of use of CW? YES ❑   NO ❑

15. If Yes, indicate which of the following will provide the support:
    (a) Fire service?   YES ❑   NO ❑

    (b) Emergency medical personnel?   YES ❑   NO ❑

    (c) Police?   YES ❑   NO ❑

    (d) Military units?   YES ❑   NO ❑

    (e) Other contracted entities (e.g. private companies)?   YES ❑   NO ❑

16. If the answer to Question 14 is No, is there an objective for specialist
    personnel to provide such support in the future?   YES ❑   NO ❑

17. Are training exercises carried out which involve practising the
    response to CW attacks against the civilian population?   YES ❑   NO ❑

18. Is the general public provided with training to protect themselves
    against the effects of CW attack (excluding those involved in regular
    military training as part of compulsory national service)?   YES ❑   NO ❑

19. Is educational information available to the general public regarding
    protection against CW attack (e.g. leaflets, internet sites etc)? YES ❑   NO ❑

ADDITIONAL INFORMATION

20. Provide references (if available) to select, publicly available,
    scientific papers published in the reporting year related to national CW
    protective programmes:

18. INTERNATIONAL COOPERATION AND ASSISTANCE

18.1 Assistance format for the formulation, specification, or renewal of offers of assistance

C-10/DEC.8 adopted by the Conference of the States Parties at its Tenth Session on 10 November 2005 and entitled "Assistance format for the formulation, specification, or renewal of offers of assistance under subparagraph 7(c) of Article X"

The Conference of the States Parties,

Recalling that the First Special Session of the Conference of the States Parties to Review the Operation of the Chemical Weapons Convention (hereinafter "the First Review Conference") reaffirmed the continuing relevance and importance of the provisions of Article X of the Chemical Weapons Convention (hereinafter "the Convention"), and found that these provisions had gained additional relevance in today's security context (paragraph 7.92 of RC-1/5, dated 9 May 2003);

Recalling that at its Ninth Session it included "assistance and protection against chemical weapons, their use, or threat of use, in accordance with the provisions of Article X of the Convention", among the core objectives in the 2005 Programme and Budget (C-9/DEC.14, dated 2 December 2004);

Recalling also that, according to subparagraph 7(c) of Article X of the Convention, each State Party may, pursuant to its obligation under paragraph 7 to provide assistance to the OPCW, elect to declare, not later than 180 days after the Convention enters into force for it, the kind of assistance it might provide in response to an appeal by the OPCW;

Recalling further that the First Review Conference noted "the need for the Secretariat to evaluate the assistance offers made in accordance with subparagraph 7(c) of Article X, in order to identify gaps, redundancies, and incompatibilities, and to help minimise the resource requirements for the OPCW" (paragraph 7.98 of RC1/5);

Recalling further that at its Forty-First Session the Executive Council (hereinafter "the Council") noted the importance of the full implementation of Article X;

Noting with concern that, as at 31 October 2005, only 64 States Parties had fulfilled the requirement under paragraph 7 of Article X to elect one or more of the measures set out in that paragraph to provide assistance through the OPCW;

Having considered the guidance embodied in the assistance format annexed hereto; and

Noting the recommendation of the Council on this matter (EC-M-25/DEC.1, dated 9 November 2005);

Hereby:
1. Urges States Parties that have not yet done so to elect one or more measures of assistance pursuant to Article X, paragraph 7, of the Convention;
2. Recommends the assistance format annexed hereto as guidance for the submission of information concerning the kind of assistance made available in accordance with subparagraph 7(c) of Article X, on the understanding that:
    (a) use of the assistance format is voluntary and does not prejudice the right of States Parties to present this information in another format or to provide other assistance;
    (b) States Parties have the right to fulfil their obligation by electing other measures under paragraph 7 of Article X, such as contributions to the Voluntary Fund for Assistance and the conclusion of agreements with the OPCW concerning the provision of assistance; and

    (c) the Technical Secretariat (hereinafter "the Secretariat") will give the information sup-plied the level of classification requested by the State Party;

3. Encourages the Secretariat to assist States Parties upon request with the submission of their offers of assistance under subparagraph 7(c) of Article X; and

4. Requests the Secretariat to report to the Council on a regular basis on the status of implemen-tation of Article X.

ANNEX (English only)

GUIDANCE IN THE FORM OF A QUESTIONNAIRE: FORMAT FOR THE FORMULATION, SPECIFICATION, OR RENEWAL OF OFFERS OF ASSISTANCE UNDER ARTICLE X, SUBPARAGRAPH 7(C), OF THE CHEMICAL WEAPONS CONVENTION

GUIDANCE IN THE FORM OF A QUESTIONNAIRE[1]

FORMAT FOR THE FORMULATION, SPECIFICATION OR RENEWAL OF OFFERS OF ASSISTANCE UNDER ARTICLE X, SUBPARAGRAPH 7(C), OF THE CHEMICAL WEAPONS CONVENTION

OFFER OF EXPERTS, INSTRUCTORS, OR STAFF[2]

State Party			
Date of submission	Day:	Month:	Year:
EXPERTISE BEING OFFERED			
1. What type of expertise is being offered?	Analysis and assessment ☐	Chemical survey	☐
	Disaster management ☐	Detection and chemical reconnaissance	☐
	Decontamination ☐	Disposal of explosives	☐
	NBC[3] protection ☐	Medical doctors and experts	☐
	Medical treatment for exposure to chemical warfare agents ☐	Medical treatment of mass casualties	☐
	Search and rescue in contaminated areas ☐	Sampling and analysis	☐
	Urban search and rescue ☐	Water purification	☐
	Other (please specify)		
2. In which of the following languages are the experts referred to above proficient?	Arabic ☐	Chinese ☐	
	French ☐	English ☐	
	Russian ☐	Spanish ☐	
	Other (please specify):		
3. Are the experts referred to in 1 above familiar with civil-protection procedures?	Yes ☐	No ☐	

---

[1] This questionnaire has been prepared without prejudice to the rights of States Parties to conclude bi-lateral agreements with the OPCW in accordance with Article X, subparagraph 7(b) and to contribute to the Voluntary Fund for Assistance in accordance with Article X, subparagraph 7(a) [footnote in original].

[2] Please fill out a separate questionnaire for each offer of experts, instructors, and staff, and cross out items that are not relevant. If personnel will be taking equipment for distribution to an affected population, please also fill out the equipment questionnaire below [footnote in original].

[3] Nuclear, biological and chemical [footnote in original].

	FURTHER DETAILS ABOUT PERSONNEL				
4.	Name of expert[4]				
5.	Gender	Male ☐		Female ☐	
6.	Status	Civilian ☐		Military ☐	
7.	In the case of a team, please specify its general composition, including the number of experts and the number of team members overall.				
8.	Are any of the personnel members of the United Nations Disaster Assessment and Coordination team (UNDAC)?			Yes ☐	No ☐
9.	Have any of the personnel referred to in item 7 above been nominated to assist other international organisations?	Yes ☐ No ☐ If so, please specify to which one(s)			
10.	Please list any other relevant information about the personnel referred to in item 7, including as regards special requirements, that the OPCW should be aware of.				

	INSURANCE COVERAGE				
11.	Will all personnel be covered by insurance provided by the assisting State Party?[5]			Yes ☐	No ☐

	Logistics				
12.	Will the assisting State Party be transporting its own personnel?	Yes ☐		No ☐	
		If not, please indicate the point of exit from the assisting State Party.			
		If not, within how many hours of a request by the OPCW will personnel be available for pick-up?			
13.	Please list any factors that could delay the deployment of the personnel.				

---

[4] In the case of a team, please provide the name of the team leader here, and list the names of the other team members, along with relevant details for them, on an attached sheet [footnote in original].

[5] An offer of assistance should normally include insurance coverage for the personnel involved [footnote in original].

14. How will personnel be transported to the requesting State Party?			
15. Will any of the personnel be taking equipment with them?	Yes ☐		No ☐
	If so, please provide details.		
	Weight of equipment, in kilograms		
	Average per person:	Total for all personnel:	
	Volume of equipment, in cubic metres		
	Average per person:	Total for all personnel:	
16. Will any of the personnel be carrying hazardous materials?	Yes ☐		No ☐
	If so, please indicate the source of each hazard.		
	Radioactive source ☐		
	Explosives ☐		
	Chemicals ☐		
	Other (please specify)		
	Please list any applicable IATA[6] numbers.		

ON-SITE OPERATING CONDITIONS		
17. For how many days or hours will personnel be self-sufficient?[7] (Please indicate one or the other.)	Number of days	Number of hours
18. Please list the additional resources the personnel will need on-site.		
19. Please list any additional means of transport the personnel will need.[8]		
20. Please list any additional equipment the personnel will need.		
21. Please provide any other available information about on-site operations.		

---

[6] International Air Transport Association [footnote in original].

[7] Self-sufficiency means that the team does not need any support from the requesting State Party. Experts who are not routinely attached to a team are not expected to be self-sufficient [footnote in original].

[8] Only for personnel that usually deploy without their own means of transport [footnote in original].

ADDITIONAL SPECIFICATIONS[9]		
22. For each of the following operating parameters, please give an indication of the capabilities of the personnel.	Detection	
	Chemical reconnaissance	
	Sampling and analysis Number of samples per day:	
	Decontamination Number of persons per hour:	Number of m^2 per hour:
	Disposal of explosives Size of area that can be searched per day:	
	Urban search and rescue: Medical treatment—victims of chemical weapons attacks:	
	Medical treatment—other patients:	
	Water purification Number of litres per hour:	
	Other (please specify):	

CONTACT INFORMATION[10]	
23. Name of national contact person	
24. Function	
25. Organisation	
26. Office hours	
27. Address	

---

[9] Not all questions must be answered. The level of detail required will vary by State Party [footnote in original].

[10] Please provide more than one contact for this offer, if possible [footnote in original].

28. Office telephone[11]	
29. Mobile telephone	
30. Home telephone (optional)	
31. Fax	
32. E-mail address	

33. Can the above named person be telephoned or faxed 24 hours a day	Yes ☐	No ☐

34. Name of additional contact person	
35. Function	
36. Organisation	
37. Office hours	
38. Address	
39. Office telephone	
40. Mobile telephone	
41. Home telephone (optional)	
42. Fax	
43. E-mail address	

44. Can the above named person be telephoned or faxed 24 hours a day	Yes ☐	No ☐

GUIDANCE IN THE FORM OF A QUESTIONNAIRE

FORMAT FOR THE FORMULATION, SPECIFICATION OR RENEWAL OF OFFERS OF ASSISTANCE UNDER ARTICLE X, SUBPARAGRAPH 7(C), OF THE CHEMICAL WEAPONS CONVENTION

OFFER OF TRANSPORT[12]

State Party	
Date of submission	Day: Month: Year:

	TYPE OF EQUIPMENT BEING OFFERED	
1. What type of equipment is being offered?	Aircraft ☐	
	Road vehicle ☐	
	Ship ☐	
	Other (please specify)	
2. Please provide further details on the equipment being offered.[13]		

---

[11] Please include the country and city codes [footnote in original].

[12] Please fill out a separate questionnaire for each offer of transport [footnote in original].

[13] Please indicate, for example, for fixed wing aircraft makes such as Hercules 130 or Antonov 124 or the type of helicopter. For ships, please indicate the type of vessel, including tonnage. For road vehicles, please indicate, for example, "four-wheel drive, heave truck with three axles", and, in each case, the make and model, if possible [footnote in original].

3.	Status of operators	Civilian ☐		Military ☐

TECHNICAL SPECIFICATIONS				
4.	Loading capacity[14]	Cargo ☐		Passengers ☐
		Weight (in kilograms):		Number:
		Volume (in cubic metres):		
5.	Range, without refuelling			
6.	Average speed	Kilometres per hour:		Miles per hour:
7.	Fuel requirements	Type of fuel required:		
		Rate of consumption:		
8.	Loading and transhipment requirements			
9.	Other technical specifications			

ADMINISTRATIVE DETAILS			
10.	Is insurance coverage for the above means of transport provided?[15]	Yes ☐	No ☐

Logistics			
11.	Please indicate the point of exit.		
12.	Within how many hours of a request by the OPCW will the means of transport be available and operational?		
13.	Please specify any factors that could delay deployment.		
14.	Please indicate which international regulations, if any, are relevant to this offer.		
15.	Please indicate any relevant airport requirements.	Take-off:	Landing:

DETAILS REGARDING VEHICLE OPERATORS OR CREW			
16.	Please indicate the number of operators or crew members.		
17.	In which of the following languages are the crew or operators proficient?[16]	Arabic ☐	Chinese ☐
		French ☐	English ☐
		Russian ☐	Spanish ☐
		Other (please specify):	

---

[14] Please tick all that apply [footnote in original].

[15] An offer of assistance should normally include insurance coverage for the transport offered [footnote in original].

[16] At least one crew member should speak one of the six official languages of the OPCW. Please tick all that apply [footnote in original].

18. Please indicate any interoperability problems that might arise.	

CONTACT INFORMATION[17]

19. Name of national contact person	
20. Function	
21. Organisation	
22. Office hours	
23. Address	
24. Office telephone[18]	
25. Mobile telephone	
26. Home telephone (optional)	
27. Fax	
28. E-mail address	

29. Can the above-named person be telephoned or faxed 24 hours a day	Yes ☐	No ☐

30. Name of additional contact person	
31. Function	
32. Organisation	
33. Office hours	
34. Address	
35. Office telephone	
36. Mobile telephone	
37. Home telephone (optional)	
38. Fax	
39. E-mail address	

40. Can the above-named person be telephoned or faxed 24 hours a day?	Yes ☐	No ☐

---

[17] Please provide more than one contact for this offer, if possible [footnote in original].

[18] Please include the country and city codes [footnote in original].

GUIDANCE IN THE FORM OF A QUESTIONNAIRE

FORMAT FOR THE FORMULATION, SPECIFICATION OR RENEWAL OF OFFERS OF ASSISTANCE UNDER ARTICLE X, SUBPARAGRAPH 7(C), OF THE CHEMICAL WEAPONS CONVENTION

OFFER OF EQUIPMENT[19]

State Party		
Date of submission	Day: Month:	Year:
TYPE OF EQUIPMENT BEING OFFERED		
1. Please indicate what types of equipment are being offered. Please tick all that apply	Individual protection	Quantity
	Masks ☐	
	Suits ☐	
	Pairs of boots ☐	
	Pairs of gloves ☐	
	Sets (including all the above) ☐	
	Other (please specify)	
	Collective protection	Quantity
	Filter ventilation (FV) for stationary shelters ☐	
	FV for tents ☐	
	FV for mobile shelters ☐	
	Containers with built-in FV ☐	
	FV for vehicles ☐	
	Tents with built-in FV ☐	
	Other (please specify)	
	Decontamination	Quantity
	Individual decontamination kit ☐	
	Personnel decontamination kit ☐	
	Material decontamination kit ☐	
	Terrain decontamination kit ☐	
	Other (please specify)	
	Detection, and sampling and analysis	Quantity
	Hand-held detectors ☐	
	Portable analytical instruments ☐	
	Other means of detection (paper, tubes, pads, kits) ☐	
	Analytical instrument ☐ Please specify:	

[19] Please fill out a separate questionnaire for each offer of equipment. If sets of equipment are being offered, please fill out just the one questionnaire for each set [footnote in original].

(Type of equipment offered, continued)	Reconnaissance vehicle ☐	
	Sampling kit ☐	
	Other (please specify)	
	Medical	Quantity
	Antidote ☐	
	Medical equipment ☐ Please specify	
	Ambulance ☐	
	Other	Quantity
	Please specify	

	TECHNICAL INFORMATION	
2. For each item of equipment above, please provide the details requested. Please attach additional sheets if necessary.	Item:	
	Manufacturer:	
	Type:	
	Date of manufacture, if known:	
	Expiry date, if applicable	
	Other relevant details:	
	Item:	
	Manufacturer:	
	Type:	
	Date of manufacture, if known:	
	Expiry date, if applicable:	
	Other relevant details:	
	Item:	
	Manufacturer:	
	Type:	
	Date of manufacture, if known:	
	Expiry date, if applicable:	
	Other relevant details:	

3.	How many operators would be needed to run this equipment?		

TRAINING AND CERTIFICATION			
4.	Please indicate what training, if any, is required in order to run this equipment.		
5.	Please indicate what certification, if any, is required in order to run this equipment.		
6.	Please indicate what training, if any, can be included as part of the offer.		

7.	Are operating manuals included with the equipment?	Yes ☐	No ☐
		If so, in which languages?	
		Arabic ☐	Chinese ☐
		French ☐	English ☐
		Russian ☐	Spanish ☐
		Other (please specify):	

STORAGE AND PACKING		
8. Please indicate how the equipment should be stored.	In bulk ☐	
	In read-to-use packages	☐
	Specification:	

9. Will the equipment be packed on Europallets?	Yes ☐	No ☐
	If not, how will it be packed?	

10. Please list storage requirements for the equipment.	Toxic/chemical hazard	☐
	Radiation hazard	☐
	Explosion hazard	☐
	Fire hazard ☐	
	Other (please specify)	

11. Please list any required storage conditions.	Temperature range:
	Humidity range
	Light
	Other (please specify)

12. Please provide any other relevant details regarding storage.	

13. Please indicate the storage or exit point.					
14. Within how many hours of a request by the OPCW will the equipment be available at the storage or exit point?					
15. Is the assisting State Party willing to organise the transport of the equipment to the requesting State Party?		Yes ☐		No ☐	
16. Is the assisting State Party willing to cover the costs of transporting this equipment to the requesting State Party?		Yes ☐		No ☐	
17. Please list any requirements related to the transport of this equipment.	Please list any relevant IATA or ADR/ATP[20] regulations.				
18. Please indicate any hazards that may be posed by transporting this equipment.	Toxic/chemical hazard				☐
	Radiation hazard				☐
	Explosion hazard				☐
	Fire hazard ☐				
	Other (please specify)				
	Please list any relevant IATA or ADR numbers.				
19. Please list any requirements related to periodical maintenance or calibration of this equipment.	By an operator or technician ☐		By the manufacturer		☐
CONTACT INFORMATION[21]					
20. Name of national contact person					
21. Function					
22. Organisation					
23. Office hours					
24. Address					
25. Office telephone[22]					
26. Mobile telephone					
27. Home telephone (optional)					
28. Fax					

---

[20] European Agreement on the International Carriage of Dangerous Goods by Road/European Agreement on the International Carriage of Perishable Foodstuffs [footnote in original].

[21] Please provide more than one contact for this offer, if possible [footnote in original].

[22] Please include the country and city codes [footnote in original].

29. E-mail address			
30. Can the above-named person be telephoned or faxed 24 hours a day		Yes ☐	No ☐
31. Name of additional contact person			
32. Function			
33. Organisation			
34. Office hours			
35. Address			
36. Office telephone			
37. Mobile telephone			
38. Home telephone (optional)			
39. Fax			
40. E-mail address			
41. Can the above-named person be telephoned or faxed 24 hours a day?		Yes ☐	No ☐

GUIDANCE IN THE FORM OF A QUESTIONNAIRE

FORMAT FOR THE FORMULATION, SPECIFICATION OR RENEWAL OF OFFERS OF ASSISTANCE UNDER ARTICLE X, SUBPARAGRAPH 7(C), OF THE CHEMICAL WEAPONS CONVENTION

OFFER OF TECHNICAL ADVICE OR TRAINING[23]

State Party			
Date of submission	Day:	Month:	Year:
Nature of offer			
1. Please indicate the nature of the offer.	Training facility		☐
	Training course		☐
	Instructor ☐		
FOR AN OFFER INVOLVING A TRAINING FACILITY			
2. Facility name			
3. Location			
4. Status	Civilian ☐		Military ☐
5. Name of administering body			
6. Please indicate what types of training would be offered at this facility.			

---

[23] Training constitutes a vital part of any immediate response to a request for assistance, and an offer of training should form an integral part of an offer of emergency equipment such as individual protective equipment. In this context, emergency training is distinct from long-term training (see Article X, paragraph 5, of the Convention) [footnote in original].

7.	Please indicate what activities take place at the facility.		
8.	Please indicate what kind of infrastructure is available at the facility.		
9.	How many trainees can the facility accommodate?		
10.	What percentage of each gender?		% male % female

11.	Costs for which of the following are included in the offer?	Meals ☐
		Accommodation ☐
		Local transport ☐
		Other (please specify)

CONTACT INFORMATION FOR THE FACILITY

12.	Name of national contact person	
13.	Function	
14.	Organisation	
15.	Office hours	
16.	Address	
17.	Office telephone[24]	
18.	Mobile telephone	
19.	Home telephone (optional)	
20.	Fax	
21.	E-mail address	

FOR AN OFFER OF ONE OR MORE TRAINING COURSES

22.	Please indicate the nature of the course or courses. Please tick all that apply.	Chemical defence ☐	Medical—treatment of mass casualties ☐
		Decontamination ☐	Medical—treatment for exposure to chemical-warfare agents ☐
		Detection and chemical reconnaisance ☐	Sampling and analysis ☐
		Disaster management ☐	Testing of equipment ☐
		Emergency training (chemical weapons threat scenario) ☐	Urban search and rescue ☐
		Disposal of explosives ordnance ☐	Water purification ☐
		Other (please specify)	

---

[24] Please include the country and city codes [footnote in original].

COURSE INFORMATION		
23. For each course, please provide the details requested.	Title:	Number of trainees per session:
	Duration (in days):	Number of sessions a year
	Number of instructors provided in the requesting State Party:[25]	
	Title:	Number of trainees per session:
	Duration (in days):	Number of sessions a year
	Number of instructors provided in the requesting State Party:	
	Title:	Number of trainees per session:
	Duration (in days):	Number of sessions a year
	Number of instructors provided in the requesting State Party:	
	Title:	Number of trainees per session:
	Duration (in days):	Number of sessions a year
	Number of instructors provided in the requesting State Party:	
24. If the instructors are to travel to the requesting State Party, costs for which of the following are covered under this offer?	Meals ☐	
	Accommodation	☐
	Transport ☐	
	Other (please specify)	
25. In which of the following languages are the instructors proficient?	Arabic ☐	Chinese ☐
	French ☐	English ☐
	Russian ☐	Spanish ☐
	Other (please specify):	
26. Are course manuals included as part of the offer?	Yes ☐	No ☐
	If so, in which languages?	
	Arabic ☐	Chinese ☐
	French ☐	English ☐
	Russian ☐	Spanish ☐
	Other (please specify):	
CONTACT INFORMATION FOR THE COURSE OR COURSES		
27. Name of national contact person		
28. Function		
29. Organisation		
30. Office hours		
31. Address		

[25] If no instructors will be provided, write "None" [footnote in original].

32. Office telephone[26]	
33. Mobile telephone	
34. Home telephone (optional)	
35. Fax	
36. E-mail address	

18.2 Voluntary Fund for Assistance

C-I/DEC.52 adopted by the Conference of the States Parties at its First Session on May 1997 and entitled "Voluntary Fund for Assistance"

The Conference

Recalling that the Commission, as reflected in Article 6.10 of the [Draft] OPCW Financial Regulations, contained in PC-XIII/A/2 and Corr. 1, considered it appropriate that the Voluntary Fund for Assistance to be established in accordance with Article VIII(21)(j) and Article X(7)(a) of the Convention should be administered, unless otherwise provided by the Conference, in accordance with the applicable Financial Regulations,

Bearing in mind that the Commission recommended in paragraph 60.2 of its Final Report that the Conference adopt the same approach to the above-mentioned Voluntary Fund for Assistance,

Hereby:

Decides that the Voluntary Fund for Assistance shall be administered in accordance with the applicable OPCW Financial Regulations.

18.3 Guidelines for the use of the Voluntary Fund for Assistance

EC-XII/DEC.3 adopted by the Executive Council at its Thirteenth Session on 9 October 1997 and entitled "Guidelines for the use of resources of the Voluntary Fund for Assistance of the OPCW"

The Executive Council

Recalling that the Voluntary Fund for Assistance was established by the Conference of the States Parties at its First Session, in accordance with subparagraph 21(j) of Article VIII of the Chemical Weapons Convention (C-I/DEC.52, dated 16 May 1997);

Recalling further that the Executive Council, in subparagraph 16.8 of the Report of its Tenth Session (EC-X/2, dated 19 June 1998), requested the Technical Secretariat to convene an open-ended drafting group with experts of Member States to prepare draft guidelines for the operation of the Voluntary Fund for Assistance;

Having received and considered the Guidelines for the Use of Resources of the Voluntary Fund for Assistance of the OPCW submitted by the Technical Secretariat (annexed to this decision);

Hereby:

1. Adopts the Guidelines for the Use of the Resources of the Voluntary Fund for Assistance as annexed to this decision.

---

[26] Please include the country and city codes [footnote in original].

Annex
GUIDELINES FOR THE USE OF RESOURCES OF THE VOLUNTARY FUND FOR AS-SISTANCE OF THE OPCW

INTRODUCTION

1. The Voluntary Fund for Assistance was established by the Conference of the States Parties at its First Session, in accordance with subparagraph 21(j) of Article VIII of the Chemical Weapons Convention. The Fund is to be administered in accordance with subparagraph 39(c) of the same Article and with the applicable OPCW Financial Regulations (C-I/DEC.52, dated 16 May 1997).

THE SCOPE

2. The moneys of the Voluntary Fund are to be used to provide and deliver direct emergency or supplementary assistance and protection that may be needed in the case of the use or threat of use of chemical weapons. Such assistance to the recipient countries may take the form of the provision of experts, financing for individual or group training, and the provision of protection equipment and medical supplies. Paragraph 1 of Article X of the Convention defines "assistance" as "the coordination and delivery to States Parties of protection against chemical weapons, including, *inter alia*, the following: detection equipment and alarm systems; protective equipment; decontamination equipment and decontaminants; medical antidotes and treatments and advice on any of these protective measures".

ADMINISTRATION OF THE VOLUNTARY FUND FOR ASSISTANCE

3. The operations financed by the Voluntary Fund for Assistance shall be consistent with the objectives and procedures of the Organisation.
4. Administrative authority, the functional responsibilities within the Secretariat, the acceptance of contributions, and the implementation of financial controls, shall be consistent with the Organisation's Financial Regulations and Rules and other pertinent OPCW procedures.

ADMINISTRATIVE AUTHORITY

5. As set out in subparagraph 39(c) of Article VIII of the Convention, the Voluntary Fund is to be administered by the Secretariat, and in accordance with subparagraph 34(b) of the same article, is to be supervised by the Executive Council.

DECISIONS ON THE USE OF THE FUND

6. Decisions on the use of the Fund shall be taken by:
    (a) the Executive Council, in accordance with Article X, paragraph 10;
    (b) the Director-General, in accordance with Article X, paragraph 11.

REPORTING AND REVIEW

7. In addition to the reporting requirements under Article X, the Director-General shall, in accordance with the procedures of the Organisation, report annually on the administration, status and use of the Fund to the Conference of the States Parties through the Executive Council.

18.4 International Support Network for Victims of Chemical Weapons

C-16/DEC.13 adopted by the Conference of the States Parties at its Sixteenth Session on 2 December 2011 and entitled "The Establishment of the International Support Network for Victims of Chemical Weapons and the Establishment of a Voluntary Trust Fund for This Purpose"

The Conference of the States Parties,

Mindful that the States Parties to the Chemical Weapons Convention (hereinafter "the Convention") are determined for the sake of mankind, to exclude completely the possibility of the use of chemical weapons;

Mindful also that the States Parties to the Convention undertake never under any circumstances to use chemical weapons and to engage in any military preparations to use these weapons;

Recognising that chemical weapons have been used in the past, resulting in deaths and casualties, and that those injured in chemical warfare suffered from the effects the rest of their lives, and bearing in mind the commitment of the Organisation for the Prohibition of Chemical Weapons (OPCW) to eliminate the threat of chemical weapons completely;

Recalling that the Conference of the States Parties (hereinafter "the Conference") at its Tenth Session endorsed a proposal for the establishment of a Day of Remembrance for all victims of chemical warfare, and for the dedication in The Hague of a permanent memorial to them, and that it decided that the Day of Remembrance would be observed on 29 April each year— the date in 1997 on which the Convention entered into force;

Recalling further that the Executive Council (hereinafter "the Council") invited the Director-General, on behalf of the OPCW, to convey annually on 16 March to the authorities and inhabitants of the city of Halabja, Iraq, and on 28 June to the authorities and inhabitants of the city of Sardasht, the Islamic Republic of Iran, statements in memory of the chemical weapons attacks thereon, and to express sympathy for the victims;

Recalling that, at its Fifteenth Session, the Conference requested the Council to continue its deliberations, with a view to developing further measures for emergency assistance to Member States, including with regard to the victims of chemical weapons, taking into account all proposals from the States Parties relevant to this issue that were being brought forward to the Conference at its Fifteenth Session and/or the Council (paragraph 9.17 of C-15/5, dated 3 December 2010); and

Noting that, pursuant to Article VIII of the Convention, the Conference may make recommendations and take decisions on any questions, matters, or issues related to the Convention, raised by a State Party or brought to its attention by the Council, and that it shall act in order to promote the object and purpose of the Convention;

Hereby:
1. Decides, after a trust fund has been set up in accordance with paragraph 2 below, to establish the International Support Network for Victims of Chemical Weapons (hereinafter "the Network");
2. Decides that all activities undertaken in the context of the Network are to be financed solely from voluntary contributions, without any financial implications for the regular budget through the Trust Fund for the International Support Network for Victims of Chemical Weapons, to be established by the Director-General;
3. Requests the Technical Secretariat to:
    (a) administer a trust fund, without any financial implications for the regular budget, to fund the activities identified in this paragraph in accordance with the applicable Financial Regulations;
    (b) establish contacts, as appropriate, with international, regional, and non-governmental organisations (NGOs) relevant for the Network;

(c) establish links to appropriate sources of information relevant to the victims of chemical weapons, and establish and administer a subpage on the OPCW official website to contain information on the history of use of chemical weapons, details of relevant international and regional organisations, and of NGOs mandated to provide assistance to victims of chemical weapons, and information on international events to promote the Convention, at which victims of chemical weapons and representatives from relevant NGOs could participate; and

(d) establish a databank (on the website referred to in subparagraph (c) above) to include information on offers by Member States relevant to the victims of chemical weapons and information on needs of the victims of chemical weapons, as submitted by the Member States; and

4. Encourages the States Parties in a position to do so to actively support the Network, inter alia, by:

(a) providing financial contributions to the trust fund;

(b) providing medical treatment to victims of chemical weapons in their countries;

(c) organising events to raise awareness at the national level on victims of chemical weapons;

(d) exchanging information on experiences related to treatment of victims of chemical weapons, through e.g. providing research scholarships to the developing States Parties in the field of the treatment of victims of chemical weapons; and

(e) facilitating materials- and equipment-related assistance to States Parties to assist and support the victims of chemical weapons; and

5. Requests the Director-General to report every two years, through the Council, to the Conference at its regular sessions on the status of implementation of this decision.

18.5 Model bilateral Agreement on the Procurement of Assistance

C-I/DEC.54 adopted by the Conference of the States Parties at its First Session on 16 May 1997 and entitled "Model Bilateral Agreement concerning the Procurement of Assistance"

The Conference

Recalling that the Commission, in PC-VII/8, paragraph 6.4, adopted the Draft Model Bilateral Agreement Concerning the Procurement of Assistance, as contained in Annex A to PC-VII/B/WP.6,

Bearing in mind that the Commission recommended in paragraph 62.2 of its Final Report that the Conference adopt the above-mentioned Draft Model Bilateral Agreement Concerning the Procurement of Assistance,

Hereby:

1. Adopts the Model Bilateral Agreement Concerning the Procurement of Assistance annexed hereto.

ANNEX

MODEL AGREEMENT BETWEEN THE ORGANISATION FOR THE PROHIBITION OF CHEMICAL WEAPONS AND THE GOVERNMENT OF ....CONCERNING THE PROCUREMENT OF ASSISTANCE

The Organisation for the Prohibition of Chemical Weapons,
and
The Government of ....,

Recalling the undertaking of States Parties to the Convention on the Prohibition of the Development, Production, Stockpiling and Use of Chemical Weapons and On Their Destruction, to provide assistance through the Organisation for the Prohibition of Chemical Weapons as stipulated in Article X of the Convention;

Considering that it is desirable to conclude an agreement concerning the procurement, upon demand, of assistance in accordance with Article VIII, paragraph 34(b), and Article X, paragraph 7(b), of the same Convention;

Have agreed as follows:

ARTICLE I. DEFINITIONS

In this Agreement:
(a) "Assistance" means assistance as defined in Article X, paragraph 1, of the Convention on the Prohibition of the Development, Production, Stockpiling and Use of Chemical Weapons and On Their Destruction;
(b) "Assisting State Party" means the Government of ....;
(c) "Convention" means the Convention on the Prohibition of the Development, Production, Stockpiling and Use of Chemical Weapons and On Their Destruction;
(d) "Director-General" means the Director-General of the Technical Secretariat of the Organisation for the Prohibition of Chemical Weapons;
(e) "Parties" means the Assisting State Party and the Organisation for the Prohibition of Chemical Weapons.

ARTICLE II. OBLIGATIONS

1. The Assisting State Party undertakes to provide, upon request from the Director-General, assistance as contained in Annexes[27] A to .... of this Agreement. The Annexes constitute an integral part of this Agreement.[28]
2. The Assisting State Party shall immediately acknowledge the receipt of such a request.
3. Assistance shall be dispatched promptly to the State Party concerned. The dispatch of assistance designated as emergency or humanitarian assistance by the Assisting State Party shall be in accordance with the relevant provisions of Article X of the Convention and should be initiated not later than twelve (12) hours after receipt of the request by the Assisting State Party for such assistance from the Director-General.

ARTICLE III. AMENDMENTS

1. At the request of either Party, this Agreement may be amended by mutual consent at any time.
2. The Party submitting the request for amendment shall allow the other Party sixty (60) days to consider the request.
3. Consent to the amendment shall be effected through an Exchange of Notes.
4. The amendment shall enter into force upon completion of the Exchange of Notes.
5. The Annexes to this Agreement can be amended unilaterally by the Assisting State Party, which undertakes to amend the Annexes whenever any change occurs in the information

---

[27] The Annexes would consist of completed forms on items/equipment/personnel, selected as applicable from forms to be prepared on the basis of the lists contained in the Chairman's Paper (Appendix 2 of PC-V/B/WP.16) [footnote in original].

[28] In addition, the Parties may, as required, attach to this Agreement separate subsidiary arrangements regulating, e.g. transportation of equipment, cost-sharing if any, mode of use of the assistance, etc. Such attachments would be an integral part of this Agreement. Amendments of such attachments would follow the procedure set forth in Article III, paragraphs 1 to 4 [footnote in original].

contained therein and to inform the Director-General of the change no less than thirty (30) days prior to the change taking effect..

ARTICLE IV. SETTLEMENT OF DISPUTES

Any dispute arising under this Agreement shall be settled in accordance with Article XIV of the Convention. Notwithstanding any such dispute, the undertaking of the State Party to provide assistance shall be fulfilled to the extent possible in accordance with the requirements of Article II.

ARTICLE V. ENTRY INTO FORCE

This Agreement shall enter into force thirty (30) days after signature and shall be valid until terminated by one or both Parties in accordance with Article VI.

ARTICLE VI. TERMINATION

1. This Agreement may be terminated at any time by either Party.
2. A Party wishing to terminate this Agreement shall give a notice to that effect in writing to the other Party and the termination shall come into effect one-hundred eighty (180) days after the acknowledgement of receipt of the notice by the other Party. The Parties shall continue to fulfil their obligations under this Agreement pending its termination.

18.6 List of items to be stockpiled for emergency and humanitarian assistance

C-I/DEC.12 adopted by the Conference of the States Parties at its First Session on 16 May 1997 and entitled "Lists of items to be stockpiled for emergency and humanitarian assistance in accordance with Article VIII(39)(b) (Paris Resolution, subparagraph 12(b))"

The Conference
     Recalling that the Commission in its PC-VII/8, subparagraph 6.5(a), adopted the indicative lists of categories of information on assistance that could be made available by States Parties, as contained in Annex B to PC-VII/B/WP.6,
     Bearing in mind that the Commission recommended in paragraph 37.2 of its Final Report that the Conference adopt the above mentioned lists,

Hereby:
     Adopts the indicative lists of categories of information on assistance that could be made available by States Parties, annexed hereto.

ANNEX
INDICATIVE LISTS[29]

CATEGORIES OF INFORMATION ON ASSISTANCE THAT COULD BE MADE AVAILABLE BY STATES PARTIES

The purpose of the indicative lists is twofold. On the one hand they are intended to serve States Parties as a guideline when preparing information on the assistance being offered in accordance with Article X, subparagraphs 7(b) and (c), including the annexes to the Agreement in accordance

---

[29] Contained in PC-VII/B/WP.6, Annex B.

with subparagraph 7(b). On the other hand they define the categories of information to be included in the database on assistance which would enable the Technical Secretariat, whenever assistance is requested, to quickly determine what relevant assistance might be made available and the source of that assistance.

LIST 1 - CATEGORIES OF INFORMATION ON EQUIPMENT
1. Name of State Party.
2. Date of provision or update of the information.
3. Function of the equipment, described in terms used in the list of functions below.
4. Name, number or other designation of the equipment. Use if possible the standard nomenclature of the State Party or of the manufacturer.
5. Brief description of the purpose(s) for which the equipment can be used, including limitations on its use.
6. Number or quantity that can be made available.
7. Estimated remaining useful shelf-life in years. If several batches exist with differing remaining shelf-life, indicate for each batch or group of batches size and remaining shelf-life.
8. Time required for preparations before the equipment could be dispatched, provided that transportation was available.
9. Transportation information
   9.1 Number or quantity in each transportation unit package
   9.2 Size and weight of transportation unit package
   9.3 Requirements for international transportation if not provided by the Assisting State Party
   9.4 Special requirements for reception
   9.5 Special requirements for local transportation
10. Health or safety aspects to be observed
   10.1 Does the equipment contain toxic, corrosive, oxidising, inflammable or otherwise dangerous chemicals? If so, specify which chemical(s)
   10.2 Does the equipment contain any radioactive material or other source of ionising radiation? If so, specify type and strength of source
   10.3 Is use of the equipment physically so strenuous that it only can be used for short periods at a time in cold, normal or warm weather? If so, specify
   10.4 Does use of the equipment involve the generation of high temperatures or strong sound or light levels? If so, specify
   10.5 Are there other health or safety aspects to be observed? If so, specify
11. What training is required of a potential user before the equipment can be safely used?
12. Utility requirements. For each indicate requirements, if any, and if a self-supported source is included
   12.1 Electrical power
   12.2 Water
   12.3 Gas
   12.4 Compressed air
13. Expendable components
   13.1 Expendable components required
   13.2 Operational life of (each type of) expendable component
   13.3 Number of (each type of) expendable component provided
14. Point of contact for further technical information
   14.1 Organisation
   14.2 Name and function
   14.3 Telephone number
   14.4 Telefax number
   14.5 Telex number

14.6 Office hours (note if in local time, CE or GMT)
15. Point of contact for request of urgent delivery
    15.1 Organisation
    15.2 Name and function
    15.3 Telephone number
    15.4 Telefax number
    15.5 Telex number
    15.6 Office hours (note if in local time, CE or GMT)

List of categories of functions to be used under item 3 in the above format:
1. Personal protection
    1.1 Respiratory and eye protection
    1.2 Body protection
    1.3 Hand protection
    1.4 Foot protection
2. Collective protection
    2.1 Protection in buildings, shelters, and other permanent structures
    2.2 Protection in temporary structures
    2.3 Protection during normal evacuation from contaminated areas
    2.4 Protection during medical evacuation
3. Detection
    3.1 Manual detection
        3.1.1 Gas/aerosol clouds manual detection
        3.1.1.1 Nerve agents gas detection
        3.1.1.2 Mustard agent gas detection
        3.1.1.3 Other agents gas detection
        3.1.2 Liquid agents manual detection
        3.1.2.1 Nerve agents liquid detection
        3.1.2.2 Mustard agent liquid detection
        3.1.2.3 Other agents liquid detection
    3.2 Automatic detection
        3.2.1 Point sampling
        3.2.1.1 Gas/aerosol clouds automatic detection
        3.2.1.2 Liquid agents automatic detection
        3.2.2 Remote detection
4. Contamination control
    4.1 General decontamination
    4.2 Contamination-resistant materials and surfaces
    4.3 Personal decontamination
    4.4 Materiel and equipment decontamination
    4.5 Vehicle decontamination
    4.6 Terrain decontamination
5. Disposal of CW munitions
    5.1 CW munitions reconnaissance and identification
    5.2 CW munitions opening
    5.3 Chemical agent emergency disposal
6. Medical protection
    6.1 Personal prophylaxis
    6.2 Personal antidotes

LIST 2 - CATEGORIES OF INFORMATION ON MEDICAL ASSISTANCE

1. Name of the State Party
2. Date of the provision or update of the information
3. Medical emergency assistance team
   3.1 Size and composition of the team, including number of men and women
   3.2 Specialisation of the team
   3.3 Diseases for which the team members have been immunised
   3.4 Main equipment brought by the team
   3.5 Approximate treatment capacity of the team
   3.6 Preparation time required before dispatch of the team
   3.7 Minimum airfield requirements to receive team
   3.8 Local transportation requirements
   3.9 Local infrastructure requirements (water, electricity, etc.)
   3.10 Local requirements for food and housing for team members
4. Medical specialists
   4.1 Number of specialists and their specialisation
   4.2 Diseases for which they have been immunised
   4.3 Preparation time required before specialists can be dispatched
   4.4 Equipment, if any, brought by the specialists
   4.5 Local support personnel required by the medical specialists
   4.6 Local hospital support required by the medical specialists
   4.7 Local requirements for food and housing
5. Field hospitals
   5.1 Number and main type of field hospital(s)
   5.2 Number of personnel at each field hospital and their immunisations
   5.3 Approximate treatment capacity of each field hospital
   5.4 Minimum airfield requirements to receive a field hospital
   5.5 Local transportation requirements for a field hospital
   5.6 Minimum ground area and surface requirements for a field hospital
   5.7 Local infrastructure requirements (water, electricity, etc.)
   5.8 Local support personnel requirements
   5.9 Local requirements for food and housing for field hospital personnel
6. Treatment at Assisting State Party hospitals
   6.1 Type of treatment(s)
   6.2 Number of patients that can be received for each type of treatment
   6.3 Name and location of hospital(s) where patients are to be treated
   6.4 Preparation time required before patients can be accepted
   6.5 Transportation of patients:
       6.5.1 Type of transport that can be provided
       6.5.2 Preparation time required before transport can be dispatched
       6.5.3 Minimum airfield requirements
       6.5.4 Requirements for stabilisation of patients' conditions before transport
       6.5.5 Possibility for relatives to accompany a patient during transport
   6.6 Possibility for relatives to stay with a patient during treatment
7. Point of contact for further medical information
   7.1 Organisation
   7.2 Name and function
   7.3 Telephone number
   7.4 Telefax number
   7.5 Telex number
   7.6 Office hours (note if in local time, CE or GMT)

8. Point of contact for request for urgent assistance
    8.1 Organisation
    8.2 Name and function
    8.3 Telephone number
    8.4 Telefax number
    8.5 Telex number
    8.6 Office hours (note if in local time, CE or GMT)

LIST 3 - CATEGORIES OF INFORMATION ON OTHER SPECIALISED RESOURCES
1. Name of the State Party
2. Date of the provision or update of the information
3. Specialised assistance teams
    3.1 Size and composition of the teams, including number of men and women
    3.2 Specialisation of the teams
    3.3 Diseases for which the team members have been immunised
    3.4 Main equipment brought by the team
    3.5 Approximate capacity of the team
    3.6 Preparation time required before dispatch of the team
    3.7 Minimum airfield requirements to receive team
    3.8 Local transportation requirements
    3.9 Local infrastructure requirements (water, electricity, etc.)
    3.10 Local requirements for food and housing for team members
4. Training teams
    4.1 Types of training offered
    4.2 Scope and basic contents of each course
    4.3 Number of courses and their duration
    4.4 Number of trainees accepted per course
    4.5 Qualifications required of trainees
    4.6 Facility requirements for courses
    4.7 Local personnel requirements for courses, including interpretation
    4.8 Local infrastructure requirements for courses
    4.9 Time required to set up courses
5. Individual specialists
    5.1 Number of specialists and their specialisation
    5.2 Diseases for which they have been immunised
    5.3 Preparation time required before specialists can be dispatched
    5.4 Equipment, if any, brought by the specialists
    5.5 Local support personnel required by the specialists
    5.6 Local equipment support required by the specialists
    5.7 Local requirements for food and housing
6. Point of contact for further technical information
    6.1 Organisation
    6.2 Name and function
    6.3 Telephone number
    6.4 Telefax number
    6.5 Telex number
    6.6 Office hours (note if in local time, CE or GMT)
7. Point of contact for request of urgent assistance
    7.1 Organisation
    7.2 Name and function
    7.3 Telephone number

7.4 Telefax number

7.5 Telex number

7.6 Office hours (note if in local time, CE or GMT)

18.7 International financial assistance

C-V/DEC.15 adopted by the Conference of the States Parties at its Fifth Session on 17 May 2000 and entitled "International financial assistance to the Russian Federation for the destruction of its chemical weapons"

The Conference

Recognising that under Article 1 of the Chemical Weapons Convention each State Party undertakes to destroy chemical weapons its owns or possesses;

Also recognising that the Russian Federation's chemical weapons destruction programme is one of the most extensive programmes to be executed under the provisions of the convention;

Aware of the continuing grave financial and economic problems the Russian Federation encounters;

Also aware of the efforts made by the Russian Federation to develop its destruction programme within the limits of its economic constraints;

Taking into account the assistance already provided by a number of States Parties to the Russian Federation's destruction programme over the past years;

Noting that the Executive Council, at its Nineteenth Session, adopted a decision recommending that the Conference call upon States Parties to provide assistance to support the efforts of the Russian Federation (EC-XIX/DEX.7, dated 7 April 2000);

Hereby:

Decides to call upon all States Parties who are in a position to do so, to provide assistance to support the efforts of the Russian Federation for the destruction of its chemical weapons stockpile, and to call upon the Russian Federation to take additional possible measures to facilitate international assistance.

18.8 International cooperation for peaceful purposes in the field of chemical activities

C-10/DEC.14 adopted by the Conference of the States Parties at its Tenth Session on 11 November 2005 and entitled "Full implementation of Article XI"

The Conference

Recalling that at its Ninth Session it referred the matter of the full implementation of Article XI to the Executive Council (hereinafter "the Council"), with a view to the Council's forwarding a proposal to it at its Tenth Session for its consideration;

Stressing that economic and technological development through international cooperation in the field of chemical activities for purposes not prohibited under the Chemical Weapons Convention (hereinafter "the Convention"), in accordance with Article XI, is one of the core objectives of the OPCW;

Reaffirming the importance of the full, effective, and non-discriminatory implementation of Article XI, and bearing in mind its contribution to the promotion of the Convention and of its universality;

Recalling that, according to Article XI of the Convention, the provisions of the Convention shall be implemented in a manner which avoids hampering the economic or technological development of States Parties, and international cooperation in the field of chemical activities for purposes not prohibited under the Convention, including the international exchange of scientific and technical information and chemicals and equipment for the production, processing or use of chemicals for purposes not prohibited under the Convention;

Emphasising that the international-cooperation programmes of the OPCW should foster economic and technological development through international cooperation in the field of chemical activities for purposes not prohibited under the Convention, in accordance with the provisions of Article XI, and should in particular contribute to the development of States Parties' capacities to implement the Convention;

Bearing in mind the provisions on the implementation of Article XI in the report of the First Special Session of the Conference of the States Parties to Review the Operation of the Chemical Weapons Convention (RC-1/5, dated 9 May 2003);

Cognisant of the information contained in the Note by the Technical Secretariat (hereinafter "the Secretariat") on the implementation of international-cooperation programmes under Article XI (S/502/2005, dated 14 June 2005); and

Noting the recommendation of Council at its Twenty-Fifth Meeting on this matter (EC-M-25/DEC.8, dated 11 November 2005);

Hereby:
1. Reaffirms its determination to promote the full implementation of Article XI as it relates, *inter alia*, to the fullest possible exchange of chemicals, equipment, and scientific and technical information on the development and application of chemistry for purposes not prohibited under the Convention, subject to the provisions of the Convention and without prejudice to the principles and applicable rules of international law;
2. Resolves, as a step towards the full implementation of Article XI, to foster international cooperation for peaceful purposes in the field of chemical activities by:
   (a) requesting the Secretariat to:
      (i) maintain, for information purposes, lists of voluntary offers of cooperation from States Parties and of specific requests for cooperation, under the terms of Article XI;
      (ii) foster cooperation between the OPCW and the chemical industry through the States Parties concerned;
      (iii) develop and promote internship programmes for participants from States Parties;
      (iv) facilitate the provision of assistance with national capacity-building in the field of chemical activities for peaceful purposes;
      (v) continue to design, develop, enhance, and implement the OPCW's international-cooperation programmes, including with reference to the paragraph 3 below; and
      (vi) promote, and assist with, both the attendance by experts or trainees from States Parties at courses and workshops, and the organisation of international seminars in fields relevant to the Convention;
   (b) encouraging States Parties to:
      (i) develop cooperation projects in areas relevant to Article XI, with the Secretariat providing support upon request;
      (ii) exchange scientific and technical information, chemicals, and equipment for the production, processing, or use of chemicals for purposes not prohibited under the Convention, with the Secretariat providing support upon request; and
      (iii) continue to offer cooperation in terms of Article XI, either directly or through voluntary contributions to the OPCW, and without prejudice to the allocation of approved programme resources;
3. Requests the Secretariat to continue developing international-cooperation programmes:
   (a) that meet the needs of the States Parties for capacity-building and economic and techno-

logical development through international cooperation in the field of chemical activities for purposes not prohibited under the Convention, within the budgetary resources of the OPCW;

(b) that contribute to the effective and non-discriminatory implementation of the Convention;

(c) that focus on the specific competencies of the OPCW;

(d) that avoid duplicating the efforts of other international organisations; and

(e) whose high quality and cost-effectiveness are ensured through continuous evaluation by the Secretariat, in consultation with the States Parties.

4. Requests the Director-General to continue to report on the progress of implementation of all provisions of Article XI, including international-cooperation programmes and the status of implementation referred to in subparagraph 2(e) of Article XI.

5. Decides to remain seized of this issue, and to further review all the requirements of Article XI, including subparagraphs 2(c) and 2(e), and encourages States Parties to continue to address them constructively; and

6. Requests the Council to keep the issue under consideration and to report on the full implementation of Article XI to the Conference at each regular annual session.

C-16/DEC.10 adopted by the Conference of the States Parties at its Sixteenth Session on 1 December 2011 and entitled "Components of an Agreed Framework for the Full Implementation of Article XI"

The Conference of the States Parties,

Emphasising the importance of the provisions of Article XI of the Chemical Weapons Convention (hereinafter "the Convention") on the economic and technological development of States Parties and recalling that the full, effective and non-discriminatory implementation of Article XI is essential for the realisation of the object and purpose of the Convention;

Recalling that, in accordance with Article XI of the Convention, the provisions of the Convention shall be implemented in a manner which avoids hampering the economic or technological development of States Parties, and international cooperation in the field of chemical activities for purposes not prohibited under the Convention including the international exchange of scientific and technical information and chemicals and equipment for the production, processing or use of chemicals for purposes not prohibited under the Convention;

Recalling that the Conference of the States Parties (hereinafter "the Conference") at its Fourteenth Session requested the Technical Secretariat (hereinafter "the Secretariat") to organise in 2010 a workshop for the exchange of ideas among States Parties, and relevant stakeholders from States Parties, including inter alia, chemical industry associations, non-governmental organisations, regional and international institutions, which could assist, as appropriate, the policy-making organs of the OPCW to explore, identify and develop concrete measures on the full implementation of Article XI of the Convention (C-14/DEC.11, dated 4 December 2009); and

Recalling also that the Conference at its Fifteenth Session welcomed the holding of a workshop on Article XI of the Convention on 24 and 25 November 2010, and requested the Executive Council (hereinafter "the Council") to consider the outcome of the aforementioned workshop through the ongoing facilitation process on the full implementation of Article XI of the Convention, in order to develop concrete measures and recommendations within an agreed framework to ensure the full, effective, and non-discriminatory implementation of Article XI of the Convention (C-15/5, dated 3 December 2010);

Hereby:

1. Reaffirms its determination to promote the full, effective and non-discriminatory implemen-

tation of Article XI of the Convention as it relates, inter alia, to the fullest possible exchange of chemicals, equipment, and scientific and technical information on the development and application of chemistry for purposes not prohibited under the Convention, subject to the provisions of the Convention and without prejudice to the principles and applicable rules of international law;

2. Decides that the following concrete measures, which constitute, among others, components of an appropriate agreed framework, should be actively implemented by States Parties and the Secretariat, and included in the prioritisation of the activities of the Secretariat as guided by the Convention:

   (a) National capacity-building for the research, development, storage, production, and safe use of chemicals for purposes not prohibited under the Convention:

      (i)   to conduct, based on input from National Authorities and relevant stakeholders, a needs assessment on tools and guidance that would be helpful for promoting chemical safety and security; to assist, in cooperation with other relevant international organisations, National Authorities to develop chemical safety and security education and training programmes as well as outreach activities in the field of integrated chemical management; and, as appropriate, to provide financial support for electronic subscriptions to scientific journals relevant to the implementation of the Convention, as well as access to technical data, tools, guidance, and other references for departments of chemistry and other relevant institutions in developing countries;

      (ii) to cooperate with and advise National Authorities with a view to finding non-toxic chemical substitutes to reduce the risks associated with toxic chemicals as well as to promoting activities from a health, safety, anti-terrorism, and general security point of view;

      (iii) to organise workshops and training courses involving:

         a. border control and customs personnel, to promote the exchange of best practices for managing risks associated with the transfer of chemicals; and

         b. relevant governmental institutions, National Authorities, chemical industry and academic representatives, to promote the exchange of best practices, including on the improvement of chemical plant safety and safe transportation of toxic chemicals;

      (iv) to continue to facilitate States Parties in providing analytical equipment such as gas chromatography-mass spectrometry (GC/MS) and infrared (IR) equipment, including consumables and training, to appropriate institutions in developing countries. This might also extend to other laboratory equipment such as fume hoods, glassware, safety equipment, and personal computers. Training programmes could also be used to lay the basis for further development of the designated laboratory system by improving the analytical capabilities of laboratories in those parts of the world that do not currently possess a designated laboratory;

      (v)   to encourage voluntary funding and/or facilitate donations in providing assistance and facilitation regarding the provision of direct support on site to assist National Authorities with specific implementation tasks, whether bilaterally, regionally, or through or by the OPCW, and whether by experts from other States Parties or from the Secretariat;

   (b) Promoting networking and exchange among scientific communities, academic institutions, chemical-industry associations, non-governmental organisations, and regional and international institutions:

      (i)   to establish appropriate fora for promoting networking and exchange among stakeholders, and across national and regional organisations, on a need basis, and to facilitate links with academia on a national or regional basis. To this end, to provide funds to sponsor experts in the field of chemistry from developing countries to attend international scientific conferences with a view to promoting understanding of the Convention and promoting its implementation; and

(ii) to encourage the OPCW to continue to develop relations and partnerships as appropriate with relevant regional and international organisations, including international organisations related to chemical safety, chemical industry associations, the private sector, and civil society, in order to promote universality and awareness of the objectives and purposes of the Convention and, to this end, to improve the interactive environment in the OPCW for non-governmental organisations, the scientific community, and industry for their interaction, collaboration with and contribution to the work of the OPCW;

(c) Enhancing the effectiveness of current international-cooperation programmes of the OPCW:

(i) to request the Secretariat, in consultation with the States Parties, to improve the international cooperation programmes of the OPCW through evaluation of their effectiveness, with a view to ensuring that they are responsive to the needs of beneficiary States Parties, in order to optimise resource use and effectiveness, as well as to achieve a clear understanding of the competencies available, the needs of the States Parties, and the requirements of the Convention; to improve the evaluation process for training of National Authorities and to act on it; and, to this end, to request the Secretariat to develop, in consultation with States Parties, a formula for feedback and evaluation that assesses the real benefits;

(ii) to provide assistance to establishing an alumni association of the Associate Programme and to organise virtual annual meetings of the alumni association, in order to make full use of the lessons learned and experience gained; and

(iii) to establish a database of expertise from academia, industries, non-governmental organisations, civil society, and government, in order to facilitate regional and international links between those relevant stakeholders; and, in particular, to establish a clearing house function in the Secretariat, facilitating the exchange of needs and offers for equipment exchange and for matching offers with requests;

(d) Measures by States Parties and the OPCW to facilitate States Parties' participation in the fullest possible exchange of chemicals, equipment, and scientific and technical information relating to the development and application of chemistry, in accordance with the provisions of the Convention:

(i) to enhance communication among all relevant stakeholders of States Parties, through regional workshops or seminars; to enhance communication among all relevant stakeholders and raise awareness of the provisions of the Convention, including key outcomes and documents from international-cooperation programmes; as well as to adopt concrete measures to facilitate the participation of States Parties in the fullest possible exchange of chemicals, equipment, and scientific and technical information relating to the development and application of chemistry for purposes not prohibited under the Convention;

(ii) to call upon the States Parties and the OPCW to place an increased emphasis on greater fulfilment of Article XI objectives;

(iii) to organise, on a regular basis, workshops on Article XI for the exchange of ideas among States Parties and relevant stakeholders, with a view to assisting, as appropriate, the policy-making organs of the OPCW to further promote the full implementation of Article XI; and

(iv) to request the Council to mandate the ongoing facilitation process on Article XI to continue to deliberate and explore, as appropriate, additional measures within an agreed framework to ensure the full, effective and non-discriminatory implementation all provisions of Article XI;

3. Financial aspects

   (a) Decides that the implementation of the above-mentioned concrete measures be funded from within the resources of the annual programme and budget of the OPCW;

   (b) Encourages States Parties to provide additional funding on a voluntary basis for the implementation of the aforementioned concrete measures; and

4. Oversight by the Conference and the Council

   (a) Requests the Secretariat to report to each annual session of the Conference on the progress made in implementing this decision, and on the status of implementation of Article XI;

   (b) Requests the Council, as necessary, to provide guidance to and to coordinate with the Secretariat in monitoring and evaluating the implementation of this decision, as well as submitting, as appropriate, recommendations to further promote the full implementation of Article XI; and

   (c) Decides to review the status of the implementation of this decision at its Eighteenth Session, and to consider and take appropriate measures, if necessary, in order to promote the full implementation of Article XI.

19. UNIVERSALITY

19.1 Recommendation on ensuring the Universality of the Chemical Weapons Convention

C-7/DEC.15 adopted by the Conference of the States Parties at its Seventh Session on 10 October 2002 and entitled "Recommendation on ensuring the universality of the Chemical Weapons Convention"

The Conference

Recalling its previous recommendations on this subject, adopted by consensus (C-II/DEC.11, dated 5 December 1997, C-III/DEC.9, dated 20 November 1998, C-IV/DEC.22, dated 2 July 1999, C-V/DEC.21, dated 19 May 2000, and C-VI/DEC.11, dated 17 May 2001), which stressed the crucial importance of universality to all States Parties, especially to states with serious security concerns;

Recalling also resolutions of the United Nations General Assembly which stress the importance of achieving the universality of the Convention on the Prohibition of the Development, Production, Stockpiling and Use of Chemical Weapons and on Their Destruction (hereinafter the "Convention");

Welcoming the fact that, since the adoption of the recommendation on ensuring universality at the Sixth Session of the Conference of the States Parties, four additional states have ratified or acceded to the Convention;

Recognising that the effective universal achievement of the goals of the Convention would require the inclusion, amongst States Parties, of those states whose non-accession to the Convention causes serious concern;

Recognising that, among the common objectives of the Convention, the security assurances stipulated in the Convention and international cooperation in the field of chemical activities for purposes not prohibited under the Convention could facilitate and encourage further adherence to the Convention, thus realising the universality of the Convention;

Recognising that promotion of universal adherence to the Convention could contribute to the global anti-terrorist efforts;

Determined to achieve the full and effective implementation of the Convention;

Reaffirming also the vital and essential importance of universal adherence to the Convention for the realisation of its ultimate goal of a world free of chemical weapons;

Hereby:
1. Urges all states which have neither ratified nor acceded to the Convention to do so without delay;
2. Recommends that States Parties and the Director-General continue to make every effort to encourage all states, and in particular those states believed to possess chemical weapons which have neither ratified nor acceded to the Convention, to do so as soon as possible;
3. Encourages States Parties to promote the achievement of the common objectives of the Convention in order to enhance a cooperative atmosphere which could encourage other countries to join the Convention;
4. Requests the Director-General to submit a report on the implementation of the present recommendation to the Conference of the States Parties at its Eighth Session; and
5. Decides to include in the provisional agenda of its Eighth Session an agenda item entitled "Ensuring universality of the Convention".

19.2 Action Plan for Universality

EC-M-23/DEC.3 adopted by the Executive Council at its Twenty-Third Meeting on 29 October 2003 and entitled "Action plan for the universality of the Chemical Weapons Convention" at the recommendation of the First Special Session of the Conference to review the operation of the Chemical Weapons Convention and noted by the Conference of the States Parties at its Eighth Session

The Executive Council

Recalling that the First Special Session of the Conference of the States Parties to Review the Operation of the Chemical Weapons Convention (hereinafter "the First Review Conference") attached great importance to the attainment of universal adherence by States to the Chemical Weapons Convention (hereinafter "the Convention") and acting upon the recommendation of the First Review Conference that the Executive Council (hereinafter "the Council"), with the cooperation of the Technical Secretariat, develop and implement a plan of action to further encourage, in a systematic and coordinated manner, adherence to the Convention, and to assist States ready to join the Convention in their national preparations for its implementation;

Recalling also resolutions of the United Nations General Assembly which stress the importance of achieving the universality of the Convention;

Recalling that the Conference of the States Parties has reviewed annually the progress, and has repeatedly adopted decisions entitled "Recommendation on ensuring the universality of the Chemical Weapons Convention" which, *inter alia*, have urged all States that have neither ratified nor acceded to the Convention to do so without delay;

Firmly believing that universality of the Convention is fundamental to the full achievement of its object and purpose;

Welcoming the substantial progress made towards universality of the Convention since its entry into force;

Noting however that among the States not Party are some whose non-ratification or non-accession is a cause for serious concern;

Recognising the positive effects that every new accession or ratification has for international peace and security and for global stability;

Recalling the decision of the Council that the OPCW's contribution to global anti-terrorist efforts in the context of the Convention should focus, *inter alia*, on the promotion of universal adherence to the Convention;

Underlining the important political, economic, and security benefits of becoming a State Party to the Convention, recognising the positive effect of international cooperation (e.g. on Article XI) among the States Parties on universality, and convinced that the desire for increased security and the determination to participate fully in the global community are incentives for States not Party to adhere to the Convention;

Recalling that States that remain outside the Convention would not be able to take advantage of the benefits that the Convention offers the States Parties;

Encouraging States Parties to promote the achievement of the common objectives of the Convention in order to encourage other countries to join the Convention;

Conscious of the fact that States Parties can encourage States not Party to adhere to the Convention, and determined to take all appropriate steps to intensify bilateral and multilateral efforts towards universality of the Convention; and

Inspired by the objective of achieving universal adherence to the Convention ten years after its entry into force;

Hereby:

1. Urges the States Parties, in conjunction with the Council and the Technical Secretariat, to undertake further efforts to promote universality of the Convention, including initiatives to address specific regions, sub-regions, or States, and covering all States not Party, in particular those whose non-adherence is a cause of serious concern;

2. Strongly supports the designation of "points of contact" by States Parties, on a voluntary and informal basis, in all regions and sub-regions relevant for the effective promotion of universality, to assist regularly in the implementation of this Action Plan and for the purposes of effective coordination;

3. Recommends that the Director-General should designate an officer of the External Relations Division to act as the focal point within the Technical Secretariat for the implementation of this Action Plan and for the purposes of effective coordination;

4. Requests the Technical Secretariat, having consulted with States Parties, to prepare a comprehensive annual document on planned universality-related activities, and to provide information to the Council on proposed initiatives, including on potential synergies with States Parties willing and able to join in universality-related efforts. The document should contemplate and systematise activities in which the Technical Secretariat has traditionally engaged and, if deemed appropriate, formulate new universality-oriented projects. The document should set indicative targets for increased membership. In particular, the document could include:
   (a) measures envisaged by the Technical Secretariat to assist States ready to join the Convention in their national preparations for implementing it;
   (b) bilateral assistance visits;
   (c) bilateral meetings with States not Party not represented in The Hague, as well as those represented in The Hague, and other activities of participation support and outreach;
   (d) regional and sub-regional seminars and workshops;
   (e) international cooperation activities which might include States in the process of ratifying or acceding to the Convention;
   (f) measures to increase awareness of the Convention, and of the work of the OPCW, including publications in official languages, as well as measures to reach the appropriate audience in States not Party; and
   (g) attendance at meetings of, or joint activities with, relevant international and regional organisations;

5. Requests the Technical Secretariat, in support of the document of planned activities, to provide information containing up-to-date details regarding the status of States not Party *vis-à-vis* the Convention, their prospects for adherence, their participation in universality-related activities, any significant chemical industry and any other issues relevant to the provisions of the Convention;

6. Requests the Technical Secretariat to implement the document of planned activities within the resources approved for the Organisation's Programme and Budget, together with any voluntary contributions received for universality-related purposes, and in a cost-effective manner;

7. Strongly encourages States Parties to strengthen their efforts in the promotion of universality of the Convention, to actively pursue this objective, as appropriate, in their contacts with States not Party, and to seek the cooperation of relevant international and regional organisations;

8. Requests the Director-General to submit to the Conference at its regular sessions an annual report on the implementation of the Action Plan, and to keep the Council regularly informed, so that the Conference and the Council may review progress and monitor its implementation effectively;

9. Requests that this Action Plan be brought to the attention of the Conference at its Eighth regular session; and Recommends that the Conference decide to review, at its Tenth Session, the implementation of this Action Plan, and take any decisions deemed necessary.

C-10/DEC.11 adopted by the Conference of the States Parties at its Tenth Session on 10 November 2005 and entitled "Universality of the Chemical Weapons Convention and the implementation of the universality action plan"

The Conference

Recalling that at its Eighth Session it noted the action plan for the universality of the Chemical Weapons Convention (hereinafter "the Convention"), which the Executive Council (hereinafter "the Council") had adopted at its Twenty-Third Meeting (EC-M-23/DEC.3, dated 24 October 2003);

Noting with satisfaction the progress that has been achieved since the adoption of the action plan and the increase in the number of States Parties to the Convention to 175, and recognising that the number of States not Party has decreased from 40 to 19 since the action plan was launched;

Recognising also the contribution that every new ratification of and accession to the Convention makes to the fostering of international peace and security and of global stability;

Stressing that achieving the object and purpose of the Convention requires ratification or accession by all States not Party, in particular those whose non-adherence has given rise to serious concern;

Underlining the important political, economic, and security benefits of becoming a State Party;

Considering that efforts to raise awareness of the Convention contribute to its universality;

Recalling the decision of the Council that the OPCW's contribution to global anti-terrorist efforts in the context of the Convention should focus, *inter alia*, on the promotion of universal adherence of the Convention;

Welcoming the designation of points of contact (POCs), on a voluntary and informal basis, in all regions and subregions, with the aim of assisting with the implementation of the universality action plan;

Acknowledging the importance of advancing cooperation with relevant international and regional organisations for the purpose of further promoting the universality of the Convention, and also welcoming in this respect cooperation with a number of international, regional, and subregional organisations, including the United Nations and its regional disarmament bodies, the European Union, the African Union, the Organization of American States, the Organization of the Islamic Conference, the League of Arab States, the Organisation of Eastern Caribbean States, and the Pacific Islands Forum;

Recognising further the efforts of States Parties and the Technical Secretariat (hereinafter "the Secretariat") to promote the universality of the Convention;

Urging all remaining States not Party to join the Convention and to confirm thereby their commitment to disarmament and non-proliferation;

Hereby:

1. Calls upon all States not Party to join the Convention without delay, in particular those whose non-adherence is a cause for serious concern;
2. Urges all remaining States not Party to join the Convention and to confirm thereby their commitment to the object and purpose of the Convention as well as their commitment to global peace and security;
3. Emphasises that the universality of the Convention is fundamental to the achievement of its object and purpose;
4. Urges all States Parties and the Secretariat to intensify their universality-related efforts with a view to increasing the number of States Parties to at least 180 by the end of 2006 and to achieving the universality of the Convention 10 years after its entry into force;

5. Encourages the States Parties and the Secretariat to enhance their efforts to further encourage States not Party to advance the process of ratification of or accession to the Convention;

6. Also encourages the States Parties and the Secretariat to help States not Party that have officially expressed their readiness to join the Convention;

7. Strongly encourages States Parties to participate actively in universality-related activities planned by the Secretariat and to support the Secretariat's efforts in conducting bilateral-assistance visits to the remaining States not Party;

8. Requests the Secretariat to prepare a comprehensive annual document on planned universality-related activities, and to provide information to the Council on proposed initiatives, including on potential synergies with States Parties willing and able to join universality-related efforts;

9. Also requests the Secretariat to provide further up-to-date information regarding the status of States not Party vis-à-vis the Convention, their prospects for adherence, their participation in universality-related activities, any significant chemical-industry issue, and any other issues relevant to the Convention;

10. Further requests the Secretariat and States Parties to raise awareness of the Convention amongst States not Party, relevant international and regional organisations, non-governmental organisations, and the chemical industry, with a view to promoting the universality of the Convention;

11. Encourages the POCs who have been designated on a voluntary and informal basis, to continue to assist with the implementation of the action plan and for the purposes of effective coordination; and

12. Decides to continue with the action plan, and further decides that, at its Eleventh Session, it will review the results and progress of that plan, and that, at its Twelfth Session, 10 years after the entry into force of the Convention, it will review the implementation of the plan and take any decision it deems necessary, in particular addressing the status of those States not Party whose non-adherence to the Convention is a cause for serious concern.

C-11/DEC.8 adopted by the Conference of the States Parties at its Eleventh Session on 7 December 2006 and entitled "Universality of the Chemical Weapons Convention and the further implementation of the universality action plan"

The Conference

Recalling that at its Eighth Session it noted the action plan for the universality of the Chemical Weapons Convention (hereinafter "the Convention"), which the Executive Council (hereinafter "the Council") had adopted at its Twenty-Third Meeting (EC-M-23/DEC.3, dated 24 October 2003);

Recalling also that, at its Tenth Session, it decided, *inter alia*, to review, at its Eleventh Session, the results and progress of the action plan (C-10/DEC.11 dated 10 November 2005;

Reaffirming the priority it attaches to the universality of the Convention and the importance of the action plan, as reflected in C-10/DEC.11;

Noting the annual report on the implementation of the action plan from 11 November 2005 to 25 September 2006, submitted by the Director-General (EC-47/DG.5 C-11/DG.4, dated 29 September 2006);

Noting with satisfaction the progress that has been achieved since the adoption of the action plan, and the increase in the number of States Parties to the Convention to 181, thus leaving 14 States that have yet to join the Convention;

Stressing that achieving the object and purpose of the Convention requires ratification or accession by all States not Party, in particular those whose non-adherence has given rise to serious concern;

Recognising the efforts of States Parties and the Technical Secretariat (hereinafter "the Secretariat") to promote the universality of the Convention;

Welcoming Central African Republic, Comoros, Djibouti, Haiti, Liberia, and Montenegro, which have joined the Convention since the Tenth Session of the Conference of the States Parties (hereinafter "the Conference"); and

Bearing in mind the recommendations the Council has made in EC-M-26/DEC.3, dated 4 December 2006;

Hereby:
1. Reaffirms the importance of all the provisions of C-10/DEC.11;
2. Calls upon all remaining States not Party to join the Convention without further delay and to confirm thereby their commitment to the object and purpose of the Convention as well as their commitment to global peace and security;
3. Reconfirms that at its Twelfth Session, 10 years after the entry into force of the Convention, it will review the implementation of the plan and take any decision it deems necessary, in particular addressing the status of those States not Party whose non-adherence to the Convention is a cause for serious concern;
4. Requests all States Parties and the Secretariat to intensify their efforts and, as established in the action plan, to promote the universality of the Convention with a view to achieving universal adherence 10 years after the Convention's entry into force; and
5. Also requests the Secretariat to continue to provide information on activities related to promoting the universality of the Convention and the progress that is made thereon, including an annual report to the Conference at its Twelfth Session.

C-12/DEC.11 adopted by the Conference of the States Parties at its Twelfth Session on 9 November 2007 and entitled "Universality of the Chemical Weapons Convention and the further implementation of the universality action plan"

The Conference

Recognising the contribution that every new ratification of and accession to the Chemical Weapons Convention (hereinafter "the Convention") makes to the fostering of international peace and security and of global stability;

Reaffirming the priority it attaches to the attainment of the universality of the Convention and that the universality of the Convention is fundamental to the achievement of its object and purpose;

Recalling that, at its Eighth Session, the Conference of the States Parties (hereinafter "the Conference") noted the action plan for the universality of the Convention, which the Executive Council (hereinafter "the Council") adopted at its Twenty-Third Meeting (EC-M-23/DEC.3, dated 24 October 2003) at the recommendation of the First Special Session of the Conference of the States Parties to Review the Operation of the Chemical Weapons Convention (RC-1/5, dated 9 May 2003);

Reaffirming further the importance of all the provisions of the action plan and the measures identified therein for promoting the universality of the Convention, as well as the decisions adopted by the Conference at its Tenth (C-10/DEC.11, dated 10 November 2005) and Eleventh (C-11/DEC.8, dated 7 December 2006) Sessions;

Recalling also that, at its Tenth and Eleventh Sessions, the Conference decided, *inter alia*, to review, at its Twelfth Session, 10 years after the entry into force of the Convention, "the implementation of the plan and take any decision it deems necessary, in particular addressing the status of those States not Party whose non-adherence to the Convention is a cause for serious concern" (C-11/DEC.8);

Noting the annual report on the implementation of the action plan for the universality of the Convention during the period from 30 September 2006 to 31 August 2007, as submitted by the Director-General (EC-50/DG.14 C-12/DG.4, dated 14 September 2007);

Noting also with satisfaction that, as a result of the progress achieved since the adoption of the action plan, 27 States have become Parties to the Convention, and noting further that this reflects a total of 182 States Parties, with 13[1] States remaining to join the Convention;

Recognising the efforts of States Parties and the Technical Secretariat (hereinafter "the Secretariat") to promote the universality of the Convention; and

Recalling that States that remain outside the Convention would not be able to take advantage of the benefits that the Convention offers to States Parties;

Hereby:

1. Calls upon all the remaining States not Party to ratify or accede to the Convention without further delay, thereby confirming their commitment to global peace and security, disarmament, and non-proliferation;

2. Urges all States Parties and the Secretariat to continue to intensify their universality-related efforts with a view to increasing the number of States Parties;

3. Requests the Director-General to reinforce his contacts with the States not Party, encouraging them to join the Convention without further delay and to report on these contacts and the progress made thereon;

4. Requests the Secretariat to continue to utilise all available opportunities and resources, including diplomatic channels and international forums, to advance the objectives of the action plan in accordance with the mandate provided to it in the decisions on universality adopted by the Council and the Conference;

5. Decides to continue with the action plan, and further decides that, at its Fourteenth Session, it shall review the results and implementation of that plan and take any decision it deems necessary, in particular addressing the status of those States not Party whose non-adherence is a cause for serious concern; and

6. Also requests the Secretariat to continue to provide and keep current information on activities related to promoting the universality of the Convention and the progress being made thereon, including in an annual report to the Conference at its Thirteenth Session.

> **C-14/DEC.7 adopted by the Conference of the States Parties at its Fourteenth Session on 2 December 2009 and entitled "Universality of the Chemical Weapons Convention and the further implementation of the universality action plan"**

The Conference of the States Parties,

Recognising the contribution that every new ratification of and accession to the Chemical Weapons Convention (hereinafter "the Convention") makes to the fostering of international peace and security and of global stability;

Reaffirming the priority it attaches to the attainment of the universality of the Convention and that the universality of the Convention is fundamental to the achievement of its object and purpose;

Recalling that, at its Eighth Session, the Conference of the States Parties (hereinafter "the Conference") noted the action plan for the universality of the Convention, which the Executive Council (hereinafter "the Council") adopted at its Twenty-Third Meeting (EC-M-23/DEC.3, dated 24 October 2003) at the recommendation of the First Special Session of the Conference of the States Parties to Review the Operation of the Chemical Weapons Convention (RC-1/5, dated 9 May 2003);

---

[1] As indicated by the Director-General in his report [footnote in original].

Reaffirming also the importance of all the provisions of the action plan and the measures identified therein for promoting the universality of the Convention, as well as the decisions adopted by the Conference at its Third (C-III/DEC.9, dated 20 November 1998), Fourth (C-IV/DEC.22, dated 2 July 1999), Tenth (C-10/DEC.11, dated 10 November 2005), Eleventh (C 11/DEC.8, dated 7 December 2006), and Twelfth (C-12/DEC.11, dated 9 November 2007) Sessions;

Recalling that, at its Twelfth Session, the Conference decided to continue with the action plan and further decided that, at its Fourteenth Session, it would "review the results and implementation of that plan and take any decisions it deems necessary, in particular addressing the status of those States not Party whose non-adherence is a cause for serious concern" (C-12/DEC.11);

Recalling also that the Second Special Session of the Conference of the States Parties to Review the Operation of the Chemical Weapons Convention (hereinafter "the Second Review Conference") underlined the fact that the goal of universality shall be pursued by the Technical Secretariat (hereinafter "the Secretariat") as well as the States Parties as a matter of high priority, and acknowledged the efforts made by the States Parties, the policy-making organs, the Secretariat, and the Director-General to this end (paragraphs 9.12 and 9.13 of RC-2/4, dated 18 April 2008);

Recalling further that the Second Review Conference welcomed the decision by the Conference at its Twelfth Session to continue with the action plan for the universality of the Convention (C-12/DEC.11), and also called upon the Secretariat, the Director-General, the policy-making organs and all States Parties in a position to do so to intensify further their efforts with States not Party with a view to achieving full universality at the earliest possible date (paragraph 9.18 of RC-2/4);

Noting the annual report on the implementation of the action plan for the universality of the Convention during the period from 19 November 2008 to 11 September 2009, as submitted by the Director-General (EC-58/DG.9 C-14/DG.8, dated 29 September 2009);

Noting also with satisfaction that, as a result of the progress achieved since the adoption of the action plan, 33 States have become Party to the Convention, and noting further that this reflects a total of 188 States Parties, with seven States remaining to join the Convention, as indicated by the Director-General in EC-58/DG.9 C-14/DG.8;

Welcoming the fact that since the Conference met at its Thirteenth Session, four new States have become Party to the Convention, namely the Bahamas (21 May 2009), the Dominican Republic (26 April 2009), Iraq (12 February 2009), and Lebanon (20 December 2008);

Recognising the efforts of States Parties and the Secretariat to promote the universality of the Convention; and

Recalling that States that remain outside the Convention would not be able to take advantage of the benefits that the Convention offers to States Parties;

Hereby:
1. Calls upon all the remaining States not Party to ratify or accede to the Chemical Weapons Convention without further delay, thereby confirming their commitment to global peace and security, disarmament, and non-proliferation;
2. Urges all States Parties and the Secretariat to continue to intensify their universality-related efforts with a view to increasing the number of States Parties;
3. Requests the Director-General to continue his contacts with the States not Party, encouraging them to join the Convention without further delay and to report on these contacts and the progress made thereon;
4. Requests the Secretariat to continue to utilise all available opportunities and resources, including diplomatic channels and international forums, and relevant OPCW meetings and events to advance the objectives of the action plan in accordance with the mandate provided to it in the decisions on universality adopted by the Council and the Conference;
5. Decides to continue with the action plan, and further decides that, at its Sixteenth Session, it shall review the results and implementation of that plan and take any decision it deems

necessary, in particular addressing the status of those States not Party whose non-adherence is a cause for serious concern; and

6.   Requests the Secretariat to continue to provide and keep current information on activities related to promoting the universality of the Convention and the progress being made thereon, including in an annual report to the Conference at its Fifteenth Session.

C-16/DEC.16 adopted by the Conference of the States Parties at its Sixteenth Session on 2 December 2011 and entitled "Universality of the Chemical Weapons Convention and the further implementation of the universality action plan"

The Conference of the States Parties,

Recognising the contribution that every new ratification of and accession to the Chemical Weapons Convention (hereinafter "the Convention") makes to the fostering of international peace and security and of global stability;

Reaffirming the priority it attaches to the attainment of the universality of the Convention and that the universality of the Convention is fundamental to the achievement of its object and purpose;

Recalling that, at its Eighth Session (C-8/7, dated 24 October 2003), the Conference of the States Parties (hereinafter "the Conference") noted the action plan for the universality of the Convention, which the Executive Council (hereinafter "the Council") adopted at its Twenty-Third Meeting (EC-M-23/DEC.3, dated 24 October 2003) at the recommendation of the First Special Session of the Conference of the States Parties to Review the Operation of the Chemical Weapons Convention (RC-1/5, dated 9 May 2003);

Reaffirming also the importance of all the provisions of the action plan and the measures identified therein for promoting the universality of the Convention, as well as the decisions adopted by the Conference at its Third (C-III/DEC.9, dated 20 November 1998), Fourth (C-IV/DEC.22, dated 2 July 1999), Tenth (C-10/DEC.11, dated 10 November 2005), Eleventh (C-11/DEC.8, dated 7 December 2006), Twelfth (C-12/DEC.11, dated 9 November 2007), and Fourteenth (C-14/DEC.7, dated 2 December 2009) Sessions;

Recalling that, at its Fourteenth Session (C-14/DEC.7), the Conference decided to continue with the action plan and further decided that, at its Sixteenth Session, it shall review the results and implementation of that plan and take any decisions it deems necessary, in particular addressing the status of those States not Party whose non-adherence is a cause for serious concern;

Recalling also that the Second Special Session of the Conference of the States Parties to Review the Operation of the Chemical Weapons Convention (hereinafter "the Second Review Conference") underlined the fact that the goal of universality shall be pursued by the Technical Secretariat (hereinafter "the Secretariat"), as well as by the States Parties as a matter of high priority, and acknowledged the efforts made by the States Parties, the policy-making organs, the Secretariat, and the Director-General to this end (paragraphs 9.12 and 9.13 of RC-2/4, dated 18 April 2008);

Recalling further that the Second Review Conference welcomed the decision by the Conference at its Twelfth Session to continue with the action plan for the universality of the Convention (C-12/DEC.11), and also called upon the Secretariat, the Director-General, the policy-making organs, and all States Parties in a position to do so to intensify further their efforts with States not Party, with a view to achieving full universality at the earliest possible date (paragraph 9.18 of RC-2/4);

Noting the annual report on the implementation of the action plan for the universality of the Convention during the period from 16 September 2010 to 15 September 2011, as submitted by the Director-General (EC-66/DG.16 C-16/DG.15, dated 30 September 2011);

Noting also with satisfaction that, as a result of the progress achieved since the adoption of the action plan, 33 States have become Party to the Convention, and noting further that this reflects a total of 188 States Parties, with eight States remaining to join the Convention, as indicated by the Director-General in EC-66/DG.16 C-16/DG.15;

Recognising the efforts of States Parties and the Secretariat to promote the universality of the Convention; and

Recalling that States that remain outside the Convention would not be able to take advantage of any of the benefits that the Convention offers to States Parties;

Hereby:

1. Calls upon all the remaining States not Party to ratify or accede to the Convention as a matter of urgency and without preconditions, thereby confirming their commitment to global peace and security, and to disarmament, and non-proliferation;

2. Urges all States Parties and the Secretariat to continue to intensify their universality-related efforts with a view to increasing the number of States Parties to the Convention;

3. Requests the Director-General to continue his contacts with States not Party, encouraging them to join the Convention without further delay and to report on these contacts and the progress made thereon;

4. Requests the Secretariat to continue to utilise all available opportunities and resources, including diplomatic channels and international forums, and relevant OPCW meetings and events to advance the objectives of the action plan, in accordance with the mandate provided to it in the decisions on universality adopted by the Council and the Conference;

5. Decides to continue with the action plan, and further decides that, at its Eighteenth Session, it shall review the progress and implementation of that plan and take any decision it deems necessary, in particular addressing the status of those States not Party whose non-adherence is a cause for serious concern; and

6. Requests the Secretariat to continue to provide and keep current information on activities related to promoting the universality of the Convention and the progress being made thereon, including in an annual report to the Conference at its Seventeenth Session.

19.3 OPCW contribution to global anti-terrorist efforts

EC-XXVII/DEC.5 adopted by the Executive Council at its Twenty-Seventh Session on 7 December 2001 and entitled "The OPCW's contribution to global anti-terrorist efforts"

The Executive Council

Recalling the determination of the States Parties to the Chemical Weapons Convention for the sake of all mankind, to exclude completely the possibility of the use of chemical weapons, through the implementation of the provisions of this Convention, thereby complementing the obligations assumed under the Geneva Protocol of 1925;

Mindful of United Nations Security Council Resolutions 1373 (2001) and 1368 (2001) and United Nations General Assembly Resolution A/RES/56/1;

Recalling the statement by its Chairman on the terrorist attack which had taken place in the United States of America on 11 September 2001 (EC-XXVI/3, dated 28 September 2001);

Hereby:

1. Recognises that the full and effective implementation of all provisions of the Convention is in itself a contribution to global anti-terrorist efforts;

2. Stresses that, at this stage, the contribution to global anti-terrorist efforts in the context of the Chemical Weapons Convention should focus on the following main areas:

(a) promotion of universal adherence to the Convention;

(b) full implementation of the legislative measures required by Article VII;

(c) full implementation of the provisions of Articles IV and V related to the destruction of chemical weapons;

(d) full implementation of the provisions of Article VI related to activities not prohibited by the Convention; and

(e) ability of the OPCW to respond to the assistance and protection provisions under Article X.

3. Decides to establish an open-ended working group, chaired by the Chairman of the Council, to examine further the OPCW's contribution to global anti-terrorist efforts, with a view to presenting a recommendation to its Twenty-Eighth Session, including specific measures, taking into account resource implications.

20. TRAINING

20.1 Guidelines for the certification of training courses offered by Member States

C-I/DEC.49 adopted by the Conference of the States Parties at its First Session on 16 May 1997 and entitled "Guidelines for the certification of training courses offered by Member States as part of the General Training Scheme for any future inspector training activities by the OPCW"

The Conference

Recalling that The Commission, in its PC-VI/22, paragraph 6.5, adopted the Guidelines for the Certification of Training Courses Offered by Member States as Part of the General Training Scheme,

Bearing in mind that the Commission recommended in paragraph 55.2 of its Final Report that the Conference adopt the above-mentioned guidelines,

Hereby:
1. Adopts the Guidelines for the Certification of Training Courses Offered by Member States as Part of the General Training Scheme for any future inspector training activities by the OPCW, annexed hereto.

ANNEX
GUIDELINES FOR THE CERTIFICATION OF TRAINING COURSES
OFFERED BY MEMBER STATES AS PART OF THE GENERAL TRAINING SCHEME[1]

1. The Secretariat is responsible for the certification of training courses offered by Member States as part of the General Training Scheme (GTS). The process of certification is primarily intended to ensure the minimum quality standard for the GTS, with the procedure being applied to all training programmes developed to provide instruction for inspector/inspection assistant candidates. Each course needs to be certified individually in accordance with the guidelines and criteria set out in this Paper.

PROCEDURES
2. The certification process will begin in (dates to be determined based on future training requirements). The Secretariat will provide appropriate forms to Member States offering training course(s). Each training centre will have to provide information and course documentation to the Secretariat, according to the criteria listed in paragraphs 6 and 7 below.
3. The Secretariat will conduct an initial visit to national training centres (if applicable, during the pilot course) in order to check the administration, operations and resources of the course according to paragraph 8 below, as soon as possible after receiving the certification file (i.e. the request for certification and its supporting documentation).
4. The Secretariat will perform the certification process within two months of receiving the certification file.
5. The overall process shall be included in the period assigned to the certification of the approved module:
   - M 1 from (dates to be determined based on future training requirements)
   - M 2 from (dates to be determined based on future training requirements)

---

[1] Contained in Appendix 1 to PC-VI/B/WP.7.

CERTIFICATION CRITERIA

6. With regard to course design, Member States requesting certification should provide documentation according to the following principles:

(a) learning objectives match those approved by the Preparatory Commission;

(b) the training or teaching sequence provides the programme with the appropriate structure;

(c) primary training methods and didactic aids are designated for each objective;

(d) learning events or activities selected are based on the learning objectives;

(e) a process for the formal evaluation of student performance has been developed (see Enclosure to this Appendix entitled Guidelines for the Evaluation of Overall Student Performance). This should include, depending on the type of training:

  (i) evaluation of student participation, interaction, cooperation and demonstrated leadership skills by training centre staff/course managers;

  (ii) instruction block examinations, including as necessary practical exercises; and

  (iii) final course examination (final approval of the test questions rests with the Secretariat).

7. The Secretariat will review course development documentation sent to the Secretariat in order to ensure that:

(a) representative lesson plans and training support packages have been fully developed;

(b) the Programme of Instruction (POI) provides the appropriate number of instruction/practical exercise hours for each lesson block in accordance with the approved GTS outline;

(c) the POI identifies all facilities and other resources required to conduct the training;

(d) adequate information has been provided on the qualifications of each teacher/instructor.

8. Administration, operations, and resources. The following items will be checked by the Secretariat's representative(s) during the initial visit.

(a) Administration and Operations.

  (i) There is an effective internal evaluation programme to assess and maintain a high level of instructor performance and training.

  (ii) The following appropriate documentation will be maintained:

    (a) student performance records

    (b) course evaluations by the students

    (c) training staff/course manager student performance evaluation

    (d) instructor certificates

  (iii) The release of students from the training programme prior to completion of the course is carried out in accordance with established Secretariat staff policies.

  (iv) Student evaluations are used in the course evaluation process.

  (v) Training schedules are accurate and provide information and time to prepare for training. Changes are posted in a timely manner.

  (vi) Examination material is marked with appropriate control numbers; testing material is properly issued/accounted for, and examination procedures are in accordance with those prescribed by the Secretariat.

(b) Resources.

  (i) Classrooms, facilities, and equipment are adequate.

  (ii) Accommodations provide sufficient space and furnishings.

  (iii) The course receives adequate priority to ensure the availability of training areas in support of POI requirements.

  (iv) Required equipment is listed in the POI and appropriate action is taken to eliminate shortages.

    (a) Equipment tasking and scheduling procedures are adequate to ensure training objectives.

(b) Sufficient training aids are available and used to ensure effective training.

(c) Sufficient training support materials and references are on hand to train the prescribed number of students.

(v) Dining, mail, laundry, recreation (as appropriate) and other services/activities support training schedules and student needs.

PERIODICAL EVALUATION

9. The Secretariat will conduct site visit(s) while the courses are in progress in order to:

(a) observe instruction;

(b) conduct spot-checks of the course documentation;

(c) interview trainees;

(d) review items related to administration, operations and resources; and

(e) interview the training centre staff/course managers regarding overall student performance in the classroom and during practical exercises as such performance and conduct relate to individual suitability as inspector/inspection assistants as well as their potential for selection as team leaders.

At the conclusion of the visit, the Secretariat's representative(s) will submit a report concerning the site visit to the Director of the Verification Division. That report will be provided to the visited Member State and maintained on file as a matter of record.

ENCLOSURE

GUIDELINES FOR THE EVALUATION OF OVERALL STUDENT PERFORMANCE

1. The process for the formal evaluation of student performance should be developed for each module in order to confirm the ability of each student to fulfil his or her task as an inspector/inspector assistant. A final evaluation of student performance, based upon an overall assessment of all module evaluations and performance reports, will determine the final decision regarding the hiring of trainees into the OPCW and the selection of team leaders.

2. MODULE 1

(a) It is important that careful and precise evaluation processes are applied on a standardised basis during and at the end of Module 1. The overall evaluation of trainee performance should be conducted as follows:

(i) progress evaluation by training staff/course manager (e.g. use of case study and table-top exercises);

(ii) instruction block examinations (multiple choice or essay test questions prepared by the training centre); and

(iii) end of module examination: the format, preferably multiple choice, and the test questions will be selected by the Secretariat.

(b) Secretariat representatives must take the time to interview the training centre staff/course managers regarding the team leader selection process.

(c) At the conclusion of Module 1, each training centre will transmit all student performance evaluations to the Secretariat.

3. MODULE 2

(a) The objective of the student performance evaluation process differs from Module 1 in that specialist training will require continuous progress evaluation.

(b) Student performance evaluations should consist of training staff/course manager assessments of each student's abilities. Criteria for guiding student evaluations for M 2 training will be designed by the Secretariat and provided to this Expert Group for consideration at its next intersessional meeting.

(c) Secretariat representatives must take the time to interview the training centre staff/course managers regarding the team leader selection process.

(d) At the conclusion of Module 2, each training centre will send all student performance evaluations to the Secretariat.

4.   MODULE 3
Student performance evaluations should consist of training staff/course manager assessments of each student's abilities. Criteria for guiding student evaluations for M 3 on-site training will be designed by the Secretariat and provided to this Expert Group for consideration at its next intersessional meeting.

21. REVIEW OF OPERATION OF THE CONVENTION

21.1 The First Special Session of the Conference of the States Parties to Review the Operation of the Chemical Weapons Convention (First Review Conference; 28 April–9 May 2003)

RC-1/5 containing the Report of the First Special Session of the Conference of the States Parties adopted on 9 May 2003 and entitled "Report of the First Special Session of the Conference of the States Parties to review the operation of the Chemical Weapons Convention (First Review Conference)"

1.   AGENDA ITEM ONE – Opening of the First Review Conference

1.1 The First Special Session of the Conference of the States Parties to Review the Operation of the Chemical Weapons Convention (hereinafter "the First Review Conference") was opened at 10:35 on 28 April 2003 by its Chairman, Ambassador Nourreddine Djoudi of Algeria. It received a message from the Secretary-General of the United Nations (RC-1/4, dated 28 April 2003).

1.2 The following 113 States Parties participated in the First Review Conference: Albania, Algeria, Andorra, Argentina, Armenia, Australia, Austria, Azerbaijan, Bahrain, Bangladesh, Belarus, Belgium, Benin, Bolivia, Bosnia and Herzegovina, Botswana, Brazil, Brunei Darussalam, Bulgaria, Burkina Faso, Cameroon, Canada, Chile, China, Colombia, Costa Rica, Côte d'Ivoire, Croatia, Cuba, Cyprus, Czech Republic, Denmark, Ecuador, Eritrea, Estonia, Ethiopia, Finland, France, Gabon, Gambia, Georgia, Germany, Ghana, Greece, Holy See, Hungary, Iceland, India, Indonesia, Iran (Islamic Republic of), Ireland, Italy, Jamaica, Japan, Jordan, Kazakhstan, Kenya, Kuwait, Latvia, Lesotho, Lithuania, Luxembourg, Malaysia, Malta, Mexico, Monaco, Mongolia, Morocco, Namibia, Nepal, Netherlands, New Zealand, Nicaragua, Norway, Oman, Pakistan, Panama, Paraguay, Peru, Philippines, Poland, Portugal, Qatar, Republic of Korea, Republic of Moldova, Romania, Russian Federation, Saudi Arabia, Senegal, Serbia and Montenegro, Singapore, Slovakia, Slovenia, South Africa, Spain, Sri Lanka, Sudan, Sweden, Switzerland, Thailand, The former Yugoslav Republic of Macedonia, Togo, Tunisia, Turkey, Ukraine, United Arab Emirates, United Kingdom of Great Britain and Northern Ireland, United States of America, Uzbekistan, Venezuela, Viet Nam, Yemen, and Zambia.

1.3 In accordance with Rule 29 of the Rules of Procedure of the Conference of the States Parties (hereinafter "the Conference"), the following signatory States participated in the First Review Conference as observers: Haiti and Israel.

1.4 In accordance with Rule 30 of the Rules of Procedure of the Conference, and pursuant to decision RC-1/DEC.1/Rev.1, dated 8 May 2003, Angola and the Libyan Arab Jamahiriya were accorded observer status.

1.5 The First Review Conference, in decision RC-1/DEC.2, dated 28 April 2003, approved the participation of five international organisations and bodies in its Session.

1.6 The First Review Conference, in decision RC-1/DEC.3, dated 28 April 2003, approved the participation of 22 non-governmental organisations and six industry associations in its Session.

2.   AGENDA ITEM TWO – Adoption of the agenda

The First Review Conference adopted the following agenda:

AGENDA ITEM ONE – Opening of the First Review Conference
AGENDA ITEM TWO – Adoption of the agenda
AGENDA ITEM THREE – Organisation of work and establishment of subsidiary bodies
AGENDA ITEM FOUR – Statement by the Director-General
AGENDA ITEM FIVE – Report of the Chairman of the Executive Council on the preparations for the First Review Conference
AGENDA ITEM SIX – General debate
AGENDA ITEM SEVEN – Review of the operation of the Chemical Weapons Convention as provided for in paragraph 22 of Article VIII, taking into account any relevant scientific and technological developments, and as required by paragraph 26 of Part IX of the Verification Annex to the Chemical Weapons Convention:
    (a) The role of the Chemical Weapons Convention in enhancing international peace and security
    (b) Measures to ensure the universality of the Chemical Weapons Convention
    (c) Implementation of the provisions of the Chemical Weapons Convention relating to:
        (i)   General obligations and declarations related thereto
        (ii)   General provisions on verification
        (iii)   Chemical weapons and chemical weapons production facilities
        (iv)   Activities not prohibited under the Convention
        (v)   National implementation measures
        (vi)   Consultation, cooperation, and fact-finding
        (vii) Assistance and protection against chemical weapons
        (viii) Economic and technological development
        (ix)   Final clauses: Articles XII to XXIV
        (x)   The protection of confidential information
    (d) The functioning of the Organisation for the Prohibition of Chemical Weapons
AGENDA ITEM EIGHT – Reports of subsidiary bodies
AGENDA ITEM NINE – Any other business
AGENDA ITEM TEN – Adoption of the final documents of the First Review Conference
AGENDA ITEM ELEVEN – Closure

3.   AGENDA ITEM THREE – Organisation of work and establishment of subsidiary bodies

3.1 The First Review Conference adopted the recommendations of the General Committee reported to it in accordance with Rule 43 of the Rules of Procedure of the Conference.

3.2 The First Review Conference adopted the recommendation of the General Committee that it be closed on 9 May 2003.

4.   AGENDA ITEM FOUR – Statement by the Director-General

4.1 The First Review Conference noted the opening statement by the Director-General (RC-1/DG.3, dated 28 April 2003).

5.   AGENDA ITEM FIVE – Report of the Chairman of the Executive Council on the preparations for the First Review Conference

5.1 The Chairman of the Executive Council (hereinafter "the Council"), Ambassador Lionel Fernando of Sri Lanka, reported to the First Review Conference on the work of the Council in preparation for the First Review Conference. At his request, the Chairman of the open-ended working group on preparations for the First Review Conference, Ambassador Alberto Davérède of Argentina, reported to the First Review Conference on the results of the informal discussions he had held after the Thirty-Second Session of the Council prior to the First Review Conference, and submitted to the First Review Conference the consolidated Chairman's text for agenda item seven of the Provisional Agenda of the First Review Conference (RC-1/CRP.1, dated 17 April 2003), and the Chairman's text of the draft political declaration of the First Review Conference (RC-1/CRP.2, dated 25 April 2003).

6. AGENDA ITEM SIX – General debate

6.1 The following delegations made statements during the general debate: the Netherlands, the Russian Federation, the United States of America, Australia, Switzerland, Nigeria (on behalf of the African Group), the UN, the Islamic Republic of Iran (exercising the right of reply), Greece (on behalf of the European Union and acceding and associated countries, and of the European Free Trade Association countries Iceland and Norway), Canada, Norway, China, Slovakia, the Republic of Korea, Algeria, Singapore, Ecuador, Nepal, South Africa, Bangladesh, New Zealand, Ukraine, Saudi Arabia, the Philippines, Turkey, Cuba, Morocco, Brazil, Kuwait, Indonesia, France, the United Kingdom of Great Britain and Northern Ireland, Poland, Japan, Romania, India, Mexico, Bosnia and Herzegovina, Argentina, Gabon, the Czech Republic, The former Yugoslav Republic of Macedonia, the Islamic Republic of Iran, Pakistan, Qatar, the United Arab Emirates, Jamaica, the Sudan, Malaysia (on behalf of the Non-Aligned Movement and China), Thailand, Mongolia, Croatia, Ghana, and Panama.

7. AGENDA ITEM SEVEN – Review of the operation of the Chemical Weapons Convention as provided for in paragraph 22 of Article VIII, taking into account any relevant scientific and technological developments, and as required by paragraph 26 of Part IX of the Verification Annex to the Chemical Weapons Convention

AGENDA ITEM 7(A): THE ROLE OF THE CHEMICAL WEAPONS CONVENTION IN ENHANCING INTERNATIONAL PEACE AND SECURITY

7.1 The First Review Conference emphasised that the Chemical Weapons Convention (hereinafter "the Convention") is the first global and verifiable ban on a whole category of weapons of mass destruction. The complete and effective prohibition of the development, production, acquisition, stockpiling, retention, transfer, and use of chemical weapons, and their destruction are an essential safeguard against the future use of chemical weapons.

7.2 The First Review Conference noted with satisfaction that the Convention has been identified as one of the core treaties reflecting the fundamental purposes of the UN. It is an essential instrument for international peace and security. It is non-discriminatory in nature, and has set new standards for global disarmament under strict and effective international control, non-proliferation, assistance and protection against chemical weapons, and international cooperation in the chemical field for purposes not prohibited by the Convention.

7.3 The First Review Conference recognised, furthermore, the essential contribution that the Convention has made to confidence-building and cooperation among the States Parties, to international peace and security, and to the national security of the States Parties.

7.4 The First Review Conference stressed the important contribution of the Organisation for the Prohibition of Chemical Weapons (OPCW) to the global prohibition and elimination of chemical weapons.

7.5 The First Review Conference reaffirmed the commitment of all States Parties to comply with the Convention and to fully and effectively, and in a non-discriminatory manner, implement all its provisions. The Conference must continue to ensure that all States Parties comply fully with the obligations they have assumed under the Convention, as foreseen by the Convention. The Council, in keeping with its powers and functions, shall continue to promote compliance with the Convention.

7.6 The First Review Conference reiterated the importance of the obligation of the States Parties to declare their chemical weapons. The First Review Conference reiterated, furthermore, the importance of subjecting chemical weapons stockpiles to international verification by the OPCW, and of completing their destruction in accordance with the provisions of the Convention, including its time limits. The same applies to the destruction or conversion of chemical weapons production facilities. The First Review Conference welcomed the efforts made by the States Parties in respect to the timely destruction of their chemical weapons capabilities, as well as the efforts of the Technical Secretariat (hereinafter "the Secretariat") to further enhance the efficiency and cost-effectiveness of the verification measures applied to the chemical weapons stockpiles and chemical weapons production facilities and their elimination and conversion. The First Review Conference encouraged States Parties to provide assistance to others, upon request, in the destruction of chemical weapons.

7.7   The First Review Conference noted with satisfaction that the OPCW has established an effective verification system with a view to achieving the non-proliferation and confidence-building aims of the Convention. The further development of this regime should take account of relevant developments in science and technology, in accordance with the provisions of the Convention.

7.8   The First Review Conference, furthermore, recognised that the implementation of the Convention's provisions on assistance and protection against chemical weapons makes a significant contribution to countering the threats still associated with the possible use of chemical weapons. These measures to provide assistance should be implemented in cooperation with the State Party requesting assistance, and with other States Parties and relevant regional and international organisations.

7.9   The First Review Conference reaffirmed the importance that the Convention attaches to the fostering of international cooperation in the field of the peaceful chemical activities of the States Parties, and the objective of implementing the Convention in a manner that avoids hampering their economic and technological development and international cooperation in the field of chemical activities for purposes not prohibited by the Convention. The First Review Conference reaffirmed the right of the States Parties, subject to the provisions of the Convention and without prejudice to the principles and applicable rules of international law, to use chemicals for purposes not prohibited by the Convention, and their determination to undertake to facilitate the fullest possible exchange of chemicals, equipment, and scientific and technical information relating to the development and application of chemistry for purposes not prohibited by the Convention.

7.10 The First Review Conference noted with concern that, along with the continued threat of possible use of chemical weapons by States, the international community faces a growing danger of the use of chemical weapons by terrorists. The First Review Conference took cognisance of the request of the UN Security Council that international organisations evaluate ways in which they can enhance the effectiveness of their action against terrorism, in particular those organisations whose activities relate to the control of the use of or of access to chemical and other deadly materials.[1] The First Review Conference reaffirmed in this context the decision of the Council on the OPCW's contribution to the global struggle against terrorism, and noted that work was progressing in the Council's working group on terrorism.

AGENDA ITEM 7(B): MEASURES TO ENSURE THE UNIVERSALITY OF THE CHEMICAL WEAPONS CONVENTION

7.11   The First Review Conference stressed the importance of universal adherence by all States to the Convention, and of full compliance by all States Parties with all the provisions and requirements of the Convention. The First Review Conference was convinced that universality and full compliance by all States Parties with all the provisions of the Convention are

---

[1] SCR/RES/1456.

necessary to the achievement of the global ban on chemical weapons. Universal adherence to, and full implementation of, the Convention will contribute to the global anti-terrorist effort and strengthen the security of all states.

7.12   The First Review Conference recognised that the Convention has made considerable progress towards universality since its entry into force, with the number of States Parties now at 151. The First Review Conference noted with concern, however, that there remain a total of 43 States not Party to the Convention, including 25 signatory states and 18 non-signatory states. The First Review Conference recalled, in particular, that among the States not Party are some whose non-adherence to the Convention is a cause for serious concern. The First Review Conference recalled that it has reviewed progress towards universality at its past annual sessions, and repeatedly adopted decisions urging all states that have neither ratified nor acceded to the Convention to do so without delay.

7.13   The First Review Conference acknowledged the efforts made by the OPCW to promote universality, in the form, *inter alia*, of regional seminars, implementation workshops, and bilateral visits and discussions arranged by the Secretariat, with the cooperation and support of States Parties. The First Review Conference recognised that the efforts to achieve universality must coincide with the achievement of full implementation by all States Parties of their obligations under the Convention. The First Review Conference noted with particular concern information indicating that a large number of States Parties had not fulfilled, either in whole or in part, basic obligations associated with national implementation measures.

7.14   The First Review Conference was convinced that progress achieved towards universality is a reflection of the credibility and validity of, and of the global support for, the principles upon which the Convention is based.

7.15   The First Review Conference underlined that there are important political, economic, and security benefits of becoming a State Party to the Convention. The First Review Conference recognised the positive effect of international cooperation among the States Parties on universality. Furthermore, their desire for increased security and their determination to participate fully in the global community were incentives for them to adhere to the Convention. The First Review Conference also recalled that States that remain outside the Convention would not be able to take advantage of the benefits that the Convention offers the States Parties.

7.16   The First Review Conference urged all States that have neither ratified nor acceded to the Convention to do so without delay. The First Review Conference called upon the States Parties and the Director-General to continue to encourage all States not Party, and in particular those whose absence has given rise to particular concern, to ratify or accede to the Convention without delay. The First Review Conference encouraged States Parties to promote the achievement of the common objectives of the Convention in order to encourage other countries to join the Convention.

7.17   The First Review Conference considered that future universality efforts should be supported by the expansion of bilateral, regional, and appropriate measures on the part of States Parties and the Secretariat. These efforts should take into account factors for non-accession, in a manner that does not encourage delay.

7.18   The First Review Conference recommended that the Council, with the cooperation of the Secretariat, develop and implement a plan of action to further encourage, in a systematic and coordinated manner, adherence to the Convention and to assist States ready to join the Convention in their national preparations to implement it.

7.19   The First Review Conference also noted that more than one-fifth of States Parties had lost their voting privileges in the OPCW due to arrears in payment of their financial contributions. The First Review Conference urged States Parties and the Secretariat to consider all diplomatic measures to facilitate greater implementation and participation by all States Parties.

AGENDA ITEM 7(C)(I): GENERAL OBLIGATIONS AND DECLARATIONS RELATED THERETO

7.20   The First Review Conference reaffirmed the commitment of the States Parties to meet the obligations they have undertaken under Article I of the Convention.

7.21   The First Review Conference reaffirmed the continued relevance of the definitions contained in Article II of the Convention, which ensure the comprehensive nature of the prohibition of chemical weapons under the Convention.

7.22   The First Review Conference emphasised the importance of all States Parties ensuring that in implementing the Convention, all actions taken are consistent with all the provisions of the Convention.

7.23   The First Review Conference considered the impact of developments in science and technology on the Convention's prohibitions. The definitions contained in Article II, in particular of the terms "chemical weapons" and "chemical weapons production facility", were found to adequately cover these developments and to provide for the application of the Convention's prohibitions to any toxic chemical, except where such a chemical is intended for purposes not prohibited by the Convention, and as long as the types and quantities involved are consistent with such purposes. The First Review Conference noted, however, that science is rapidly advancing. New chemicals may have to be assessed in relation to their relevance to the Schedules of Chemicals of the Convention. The First Review Conference requested the Council to consider the developments in relation to additional chemicals that may be relevant to the Convention, and assess, *inter alia*, whether these compounds should be considered in the context of the Schedules of Chemicals.

7.24   The First Review Conference stressed the importance of the timely, complete, and accurate submission of the declarations required of each State Party under Article III. The First Review Conference noted with satisfaction that, by the end of 2002, all but two States Parties had submitted their declarations under Article III. The First Review Conference called upon the remaining States Parties that had yet to submit their Article III declarations to do so without any further delay, and called upon those states that had become States Parties in the meantime to submit their declarations under Article III when they are due. The First Review Conference encouraged the Secretariat to monitor progress in this respect, to offer assistance, including to states preparing to join the Convention in the future, and to keep the Council informed about the situation. The First Review Conference also encouraged States Parties that are able to do so, to provide assistance to other States Parties, if requested, in the preparation and submission of declarations and amendments and to inform the OPCW about such assistance.

7.25   The First Review Conference, noting the obligation of the States Parties to declare any former chemical weapons development facility (Article III, subparagraph 1(d)), and further noting that the infrastructure and personnel of these facilities may remain in place for activities not prohibited under the Convention, and that the Convention does not provide for routine verification of these facilities, called upon the Council to reach agreement on the declaration criteria for former chemical weapons development facilities (facilities designed, constructed, or used since 1 January 1946 primarily for the development of chemical weapons), with a view towards promoting confidence among States Parties.

AGENDA ITEM 7(C)(II): GENERAL PROVISIONS ON VERIFICATION OVERVIEW

7.26   The verification system is one of the most important provisions of the Convention. It provides for the monitoring of the elimination of chemical weapons and chemical weapons production facilities, contributes to achieving the non-proliferation objectives of the Convention, and provides assurances of compliance by the States Parties with the provisions of the Convention.

7.27 The First Review Conference noted with satisfaction that the OPCW has established a verification system that meets the requirements of the Convention. The OPCW has at its disposal a well-trained inspectorate, approved equipment and other technical capabilities, procedures to plan and conduct on-site inspections as required under the Convention, and a network of designated laboratories for off-site chemical analysis. There is, however, room for increased efficiency. The First Review Conference also noted that a number of procedures and guidelines that the Convention requires remain to be finalised and adopted. The Council has already included these in its work programme, and should resolve them as soon as possible.

7.28 The Secretariat and the States Parties have acquired considerable experience in the conduct of routine inspections, which they should bring to bear when identifying ways to further optimise the system, increase efficiency, and improve the conduct of inspections.

7.29 The First Review Conference noted that no challenge inspections or investigations of alleged use had been requested of the OPCW since the entry into force of the Convention.

7.30 The First Review Conference noted the Note by the Director-General conveying to the States Parties the observations of the Scientific Advisory Board (SAB) in relation to developments in science and technology that are relevant to the review of the operation of the Convention (RC-1/DG.2, dated 23 April 2003), together with his recommendations on these observations and findings. The First Review Conference requested the Council, assisted by the Secretariat and members of the SAB, as appropriate, to study these recommendations and observations with a view to preparing recommendations to the Conference on them.

Declarations

7.31 The timely and accurate submission of declarations is an important condition for the functioning of the verification system of the Convention. The First Review Conference noted the efforts made by the States Parties in collecting declaration data and submitting them to the OPCW. The First Review Conference took cognisance of improvements in the degree of standardisation of declaration data since the entry into force of the Convention, but stressed that there is a need for further improvement.

7.32 The First Review Conference noted the efforts made by the Secretariat to implement an effective system for receiving, handling, analysing, and protecting declarations, and for submitting declaration data to States Parties in accordance with the provisions of the Convention. In this context, the First Review Conference emphasised that the Secretariat and the States Parties concerned should make expeditious efforts to clarify any ambiguities and discrepancies in declarations submitted.

7.33 The First Review Conference noted the efforts of the Secretariat, consistent with its responsibilities under the Convention, to cooperate with the States Parties in ensuring that declarations submitted in accordance with the Convention were full and accurate, *inter alia* by clarifying ambiguities and discrepancies and by providing technical assistance and technical evaluation to States Parties in the implementation of the provisions of the Convention. The First Review Conference encouraged the Secretariat to continue these efforts, in close consultation with the States Parties and their National Authorities.

7.34 The First Review Conference noted the information provided by the Secretariat on the possibility of submitting declarations in electronic form. The First Review Conference noted the need to evaluate whether such a system could bring advantages to the Secretariat as well as to the States Parties. The First Review Conference welcomed the efforts made by some States Parties and by the Secretariat to develop software that could be used for the preparation, submission, and receipt of industry declaration data in electronic form. The First Review Conference requested the Director-General to further explore this possibility and to report to the Council, and recommended that an expert meeting open to all States

Parties be convened to study all aspects of the proposed submission of declarations in electronic form. The First Review Conference reiterated the need to ensure that confidential digital data is effectively protected at all times, in accordance with the requirements of the Convention.

Inspections

7.35   The implementation by all States Parties of the standing arrangements required by the Convention is important to the proper conduct of inspections. These arrangements include, *inter alia*, the designation of points of entry; the issuance to OPCW inspection team members of multiple entry/exit and/or transit visas valid for at least two years, and other such documents to enable them to enter and to remain on the territory of the State Party for the purpose of carrying out inspection activities; the according of privileges and immunities to inspection-team members as required by the Convention; the timely issuance of diplomatic clearance numbers for non-scheduled aircraft used by the Secretariat for inspection purposes; arrangements for the amenities needed by the inspection teams; the provision of access to inspected facilities as required by the Convention, and other arrangements necessary to the transportation, storage, and use of approved equipment by inspection teams. The First Review Conference urged all States Parties to implement these measures as required by the Convention.

7.36   The First Review Conference noted that a large part of the OPCW's verification resources have in the past been spent on the verification of chemical weapons destruction operations. The planned increase in chemical weapons destruction in coming years and any resource constraints will require a thorough review of the current verification methodology used for chemical weapons destruction verification, as part of the effort to optimise the verification regime of the Convention.

7.37   The First Review Conference requested the Council, assisted by the Secretariat, to intensify its study of how to further optimise the OPCW verification system, aiming at recommendations that should, if possible, take effect beginning in 2004. Such a study should take into account the findings of the SAB. The study should identify essential inspection tasks; assess how the different aspects of the inspection cycle, from planning to reporting, can be made more efficient; identify means that would further increase verification efficiency; and consider how best to meet the Convention's requirement in relation to sampling and analysis for verification purposes.

Reporting of verification results

7.38   The First Review Conference agreed that the reporting by the Secretariat to the Council and to the States Parties on verification results is an important matter, enabling States Parties to be assured of continued compliance with the Convention by other States Parties. This reporting includes the submission by the Secretariat to the States Parties of certain information to be provided in annual declarations, as well as general information that the Secretariat provides about the results of its verification activities, in accordance with the provisions of the Annex on the Protection of Confidential Information (hereinafter "the Confidentiality Annex").

Conclusions

7.39   The First Review Conference, in concluding its review of the general aspects of verification:

(a) called upon States Parties that have not yet done so to complete the national preparations required by the Convention for the receipt of inspections by the OPCW, and to afford full cooperation to OPCW inspection teams, in accordance with the provisions of the Convention;

(b) called upon all States Parties to submit declarations in a complete, accurate, and time-ly manner, and to amend them promptly as required;

(c) encouraged States Parties to avail themselves of their right to receive and examine declaration data from other States Parties, and to inform themselves about the results of the OPCW's verification activities, in accordance with the provisions of the Convention;

(d) recalled its previous decisions on the declaration of aggregate national data, called upon all States Parties to take the measures necessary to implement these decisions, and called upon the Council to review the progress of implementation, supported by reports by the Secretariat;

(e) called upon the States Parties to work with the Secretariat to clarify any ambiguities contained in their declarations;

(f) encouraged the Secretariat to more effectively apply information technology in the implementation of the verification regime, and encouraged the Secretariat and States Parties to continue cooperating toward the early implementation of a system that, while seeing to it that confidentiality is protected, would allow them, if they so decided, to submit their industry declarations, and to receive the information they are entitled under the Convention to receive from the Secretariat on a routine basis, in electronic form (for example on a CD-ROM);

(g) encouraged the Council and the Secretariat to work together to further improve the submission of information on verification results to the States Parties, *inter alia* by further improving the form and content of the Verification Implementation Report, consistent with the provisions of the Confidentiality Annex;

(h) stressed how important it is for the Secretariat to inform and consult with the Council, in coordination with the States Parties concerned, regarding any adaptation related to the practical implementation of verification measures previously approved by the Council;

(i) called upon the Secretariat to continue its efforts to optimise verification measures, and requested the Council to intensify its study of the issue of verification resource optimisation, aiming at recommendations that should, if possible, be phased in beginning in 2004; and

(j) requested the Council to resolve urgently the development of recommendations on the still-unresolved issues pertaining to the Convention's verification regime that the Convention requires it to adopt, and to submit draft decisions to the Conference as early as possible.

AGENDA ITEM 7(C)(III): CHEMICAL WEAPONS AND CHEMICAL WEAPONS PRODUCTION FACILITIES

7.40 The States Parties reaffirmed the obligation to destroy chemical weapons and to destroy or convert chemical weapons production facilities within the time limits provided for by the Convention. The possessor States Parties are fully committed to meeting their destruction obligations and the verification costs as required by the Convention. There has been progress in chemical weapons disarmament. However, there have been difficulties in the destruction of chemical weapons stockpiles, and the Conference has taken action on delays in some States Parties and granted extensions of destruction time limits, as provided for by the Convention.

7.41 The First Review Conference, whilst reaffirming that the destruction of chemical weapons is the responsibility of the possessor States Parties, called upon States Parties that are in a position to do so, to provide assistance to support the efforts of possessor States Parties that request such assistance in implementing their programmes of chemical weapons destruction.

7.42 The First Review Conference stressed how important it is that possessor States Parties implement appropriate measures to secure their storage facilities, and to prevent any movement of their chemical weapons out of the facilities, except their removal for destruction or, in accordance with the provisions of the Convention, the removal of Schedule 1 chemicals for use for research, medical, pharmaceutical, or protective purposes. The OPCW can serve as a forum for consultation and cooperation between the States Parties in this respect.

7.43   The First Review Conference requested the Council to continue exercising its important role in monitoring progress in the chemical weapons destruction activities. The First Review Conference urged possessor States Parties to provide realistic and required annual chemical weapons destruction plans, and to update these plans as may become necessary.

7.44   The First Review Conference noted that the declarations provided by the States Parties under Article III, which establish a baseline for measuring progress in the elimination of chemical weapons stockpiles, need to be comprehensive and accurate. The First Review Conference called upon the States Parties to ensure that their declarations under Article III are updated in a timely manner, if and when new information becomes available. The First Review Conference called upon the Secretariat to continue rendering technical assistance to the States Parties on the preparation of chemical weapons declarations, by mutual consent, and to submit proposals to the Council on any measures that may be necessary to maintain the technical competence of the Secretariat in this respect. The First Review Conference encouraged States Parties that are capable of doing so to assist other States Parties in the preparation and submission of declarations and amendments.

7.45   The First Review Conference reaffirmed that all chemical weapons shall be destroyed, under OPCW verification, in accordance with the provisions of Article IV and Part IV(A) of the Verification Annex to the Convention (hereinafter "the Verification Annex").

7.46   The First Review Conference stressed the importance of the effective verification of chemical weapons stockpiles as well as of their destruction. The First Review Conference recognised that this verification can be optimised and its efficiency increased. The Council has begun working on this issue, supported by the Secretariat. Reducing the manpower requirements for the verification of chemical weapons destruction operations was identified as the issue that could have the greatest impact on optimising verification resource use. Within the context of the discussions under agenda item 7(c)(ii), the First Review Conference recommended that the Secretariat continue working with the Council, with the appropriate involvement of the States Parties possessing chemical weapons stockpiles and destroying them, towards mutually agreeable solutions for optimising chemical weapons verification, whilst maintaining the effectiveness of verification activities. The First Review Conference requested the Council to oversee this work, and to submit to the Conference proposals for recommendations and decisions, with a view toward their implementation starting in 2004.

7.47   The First Review Conference noted that the Convention provides for States Parties to implement verification activities under bilateral or multilateral agreements, provided that such agreements are, *inter alia*, consistent with the verification provisions of the Convention (paragraphs 13 and 16, respectively, of Articles IV and V). The First Review Conference noted that States Parties, under the purview of the Council, can further examine possibilities for concluding bilateral or multilateral agreements in this regard.

7.48   The First Review Conference recalled the Conference's previous decisions on the mechanism for payment of verification costs by the inspected States Parties under Articles IV and V. The First Review Conference noted the efforts made by the States Parties concerned and by the Secretariat to effectively implement this mechanism. The First Review Conference called upon the Secretariat to ensure that invoices for relevant verification expenses under Articles IV and V are submitted to the possessor States Parties in a timely manner. The First Review Conference called upon the States Parties to pay Article IV and V verification costs in a timely manner, and called upon the Secretariat and the Council to monitor the efficacy of the steps taken to address problems related to the Article IV and V payment mechanism, and to implement any further measures to be agreed upon.

7.49   The First Review Conference reaffirmed the obligation to destroy or otherwise dispose of old chemical weapons, in accordance with the Convention, and noted the progress made in this regard.

7.50   The States Parties, furthermore, attached importance to the destruction of abandoned chemical weapons and to the cooperation that has developed between the Territorial and Abandoning States Parties. Such cooperation would also be necessary in regard to any abandoned chemical weapons discovered in the future.

7.51   The First Review Conference reviewed progress in relation to the destruction of chemical weapons production facilities, and noted with satisfaction that the elimination of CW production capabilities has progressed as required by Part V of the Verification Annex. The conversion of former chemical weapons production facilities for purposes not prohibited is permitted by the Convention, in exceptional cases of compelling need.

7.52   The First Review Conference reviewed the progress made in the field of conversion of former CW production facilities for purposes not prohibited by the Convention. The First Review Conference confirmed the States Parties' commitment to complete conversion as early as possible and to keep the Secretariat and the Council informed about the progress being made. The First Review Conference noted the intention of the Secretariat to inspect, soon after 29 April 2003, all chemical weapons production facilities that are subject to conversion for purposes not prohibited by the Convention, but that have not yet been certified as completely converted, and to report to the Council about the conversion status of each of these facilities.

7.53   The First Review Conference recalled that, after conversion of former chemical weapons production facilities for purposes not prohibited has been completed, these facilities remain liable to on-site inspection in accordance with paragraph 85 of Part V of the Verification Annex for a period of 10 years after the certification by the Director-General of their conversion. The First Review Conference also noted that, in accordance with the provisions of the Convention, these converted facilities shall be no more capable of being reconverted into a chemical weapons production facility than any other facility used for industrial, agricultural, research, medical, pharmaceutical, or other peaceful purposes not involving chemicals listed in Schedule 1 of the Annex on Chemicals. The First Review Conference recalled that the States Parties that have converted facilities are required to report annually on the activities at these facilities. Upon completion of the 10-year period following the completion of conversion, the Council shall decide on the nature of continued verification activities. The First Review Conference reaffirmed that future planning of verification measures needs to take account of these requirements for the verification of converted chemical weapons production facilities, and requested the Secretariat to submit a concept for these verification measures to the Council for consideration and to enable the Council to submit proposals for recommendations or decisions that may be needed to the Conference.

7.54   The First Review Conference recalled the need to adopt decisions on a number of unresolved issues related to chemical weapons, old chemical weapons produced after 1925, abandoned chemical weapons, and chemical weapons production facilities. It noted that the Council has included several urgent and long-standing issues in its work programme, and requested the Council to continue working towards an early resolution of these issues.

AGENDA ITEM 7(C)(IV): ACTIVITIES NOT PROHIBITED UNDER THE CHEMICAL WEAPONS CONVENTION
OVERVIEW

7.55   The First Review Conference reaffirmed the right of the States Parties, subject to the provisions of the Convention, to develop, produce, otherwise acquire, retain, transfer, and use toxic chemicals and their precursors for purposes not prohibited under the Convention.

The First Review Conference affirmed that the OPCW continues to provide a forum for discussing matters related to the observance of these rights among States Parties.

7.56   The First Review Conference reaffirmed that the provisions of the Convention related to activities not prohibited under it shall be implemented in a manner that avoids hampering the economic and technological development of the States Parties and international cooperation in the field of chemical activities not prohibited by the Convention, including the international exchange of information and chemicals and equipment for the production, processing or use of chemicals for purposes not prohibited by the Convention.

7.57   The First Review Conference reaffirmed the obligation of the States Parties to adopt the necessary measures to ensure that toxic chemicals and their precursors are developed, produced, otherwise acquired, retained, transferred, or used within their territories or in any other places under their jurisdiction or control, only for purposes not prohibited by the Convention.

7.58   The First Review Conference noted that progress has been made since the entry into force of the Convention in relation to the implementation of an effective verification regime in accordance with Article VI of the Convention. Major achievements in this connection include the submission of initial and annual declarations, and the conduct of on-site inspections by the Secretariat to verify that activities at declared chemical facilities were consistent with the obligations undertaken under the Convention, and consistent with the information to be provided in declarations.

7.59   The First Review Conference reaffirmed the importance of national implementation as an essential element of the implementation of the verification and other provisions of Article VI and Parts VI through IX of the Verification Annex. It addressed this issue in detail under agenda item 7(c)(v). The First Review Conference encouraged States Parties to share their experiences about the most effective ways to implement the Convention, and to cooperate in the resolution of issues they may encounter in the implementation of these provisions. The First Review Conference encouraged the Secretariat to continue providing technical assistance to States Parties, by mutual consent, in relation to the identification of declarable facilities, the submission of declarations under Article VI, the receipt of OPCW inspections and other technical questions that may arise in the implementation of the provisions related to activities not prohibited under the Convention.

Declarations

7.60   In relation to initial declarations, the First Review Conference recalled the serious concern it had, for several years after the entry into force of the Convention, about the level of implementation by all States Parties of this important provision, in particular in relation to the timeliness of submissions. The First Review Conference emphasised the importance of the timely submission of accurate and complete initial declarations by all States Parties, including by States joining the treaty in the future.

7.61   The First Review Conference noted that significant progress had been made since the entry into force of the Convention in relation to agreeing on common guidelines and criteria for the submission of declarations under Article VI. However, some important issues remain unresolved. The First Review Conference urged the Council to continue, with the support of the Secretariat, to work towards the early resolution of the unresolved Article VI declaration issues.

7.62   The First Review Conference stressed how important it is that all States Parties with facilities declarable under Article VI submit annual declarations in an accurate, complete, and timely manner. The same applies to the other declarations required under Article VI (aggregate national data, and notifications and declarations of transfers of Schedule 1 chemicals).

7.63   Furthermore, and recalling the decision taken by the Conference at its First Session on changes to annual declarations (C-I/DEC.38, dated 16 May 1997), the First Review Conference urged States Parties to implement, on a voluntary basis, the recommendation contained in paragraph 5 of the Annex to this decision to inform the Secretariat of cases when plants or plant sites that have been declared to undertake activities in relation to Schedule 2 or Schedule 3 chemicals cease to do so, and requested the Council to consider whether to require such submissions from States Parties.

Developments in science and technology
7.64   The First Review Conference considered scientific and technological developments in regard to activities not prohibited under the Convention, and recognised that the chemical industry is subject to change over time. The OPCW should therefore adapt its verification regime for the chemical industry so as to maintain its effectiveness and relevance, and its consistency with the inspection procedures established by the Convention.
7.65   The First Review Conference noted the Note of the Director-General submitting the Report of the Scientific Advisory Board to the First Review Conference (RC-1/DG.2, dated 23 April 2003), and recalled in this context its recommendation contained in paragraph 7.30 above.

Schedule 1 chemicals and facilities
7.66   In relation to the conduct of inspections at Schedule 1 facilities, the First Review Conference noted that all these facilities have been subjected to systematic inspections as required by the Convention. The First Review Conference recalled information submitted by the Secretariat indicating that only a small number of these facilities were at this moment involved with the production or storage of significant amounts of Schedule 1 chemicals. The provisions of the Convention on the number, intensity, duration, timing, and mode of inspections at Schedule 1 facilities are based on the quantities of Schedule 1 chemicals produced, the characteristics of the facilities, and the nature of the activities carried out there (paragraphs 23 and 30 of Part VI of the Verification Annex). Guidelines on this matter, however, have yet to be considered and approved by the Conference. The First Review Conference noted that these guidelines would assist in the future optimisation of the use of resources set aside for verification under Part VI of the Verification Annex, and requested the Council, assisted by the Secretariat, to prepare these guidelines for consideration and adoption as early as possible.
7.67   The First Review Conference also addressed transfers of Schedule 1 chemicals. In this context, it received a proposal to introduce a de minimis rule for the notification of transfers of Schedule 1 chemicals, and requested the Council to study this issue and, if agreed, to prepare a proposal for consideration by the Conference at one of its forthcoming annual sessions.

The verification regime in the chemical industry and the re-examination of Part IX of the Verification Annex
7.68   In relation to inspections of Schedule 2 facilities, the First Review Conference noted that almost all initial inspections had already been conducted, and that re-inspection had begun. Inspections of Schedule 3 facilities had been conducted at 100 facilities as at 31 December 2002 (23% of the inspectable facilities). Inspections of other chemical production facilities producing discrete organic chemicals, including PSF chemicals, commenced in 2000 as provided for by the Convention. Ninety-seven other chemical production facility inspections had been completed by 31 December 2002.
7.69   In accordance with the provisions of the Convention, inspections of other chemical production facilities commenced only in May 2000. The inspections conducted have indicated the usefulness of OCPF inspections and their value for increasing confidence in the chemical activities of the States Parties. At the same time, the current selection algorithm does not

use all the weighting factors provided for by the Convention and must be further improved. The First Review Conference also received the recommendations of the Director-General on the observations made by the SAB on the nature of other chemical production facilities (RC-1/DG.2, dated 23 April 2003). The First Review Conference agreed that there was a need to:

(a) fully implement all parts of the selection mechanism provided for in paragraph 11 of Part IX of the Verification Annex;

(b) reach early agreement on what basis (e.g., regional) proposals by States Parties for inspection should be presented to be taken into account as a weighting factor in the selection process specified in paragraph 11 of Part IX of the Verification Annex;

(c) take account of the other chemical production facilities declared by the States Parties, of their technical characteristics and activities, and of trends in science and technology that impact on these parameters, to increase the number of other chemical production facility inspections to the extent found appropriate as the budget process unfolds in ensuing years; and

(d) review the conduct of other chemical production facility inspections to ensure that they are conducted in a way that efficiently fulfils the inspection aims set out by the Convention.

The First Review Conference requested the Council to continue working on these issues, together with the Secretariat, and to prepare recommendations for the Conference's consideration at an early date.

7.70 In relation to the verification regime for the chemical industry as a whole, the First Review Conference confirmed the validity of the overall balance provided for in the Convention. The States Parties also affirmed the need to ensure the adequate frequency and intensity of inspections for each category of declared facilities under Article VI, taking into account, as relevant, all factors envisaged in the Convention, including risk to the object and purpose of the Convention, activities, characteristics, and equitable geographical distribution.

7.71 The First Review Conference concluded that the allocation of resources to the verification regime for the chemical industry needs to be further optimised, taking due account of the nature of the declared facilities, the inspection experience gathered, developments in science and technology, and the principles set out in Article VI. To this end, the First Review Conference encouraged the Council, assisted by the Secretariat, to work toward:

(a) resolving outstanding chemical industry cluster issues and submitting recommendations to the Conference at an early date;

(b) improving the submission and handling of industry declarations (including, *inter alia*, common criteria and standards, simplified declaration forms, and the submission of declaration data in electronic form);

(c) refining inspection conduct to improve consistency, efficiency and effectiveness (including, *inter alia*, a common approach to verifying the absence of Schedule 1 chemicals at inspected plant sites, the simplification of the format used to record preliminary findings, and sampling and analysis procedures);

(d) providing guidance to the Secretariat in respect to reporting on verification results in the chemical industry in order to increase the utility of the information provided to the States Parties; and

(e) studying the need for a recommendation about the future treatment of salts of Schedule 1 chemicals that are not explicitly mentioned in Schedule 1.

Transfer regulations

7.72 In relation to transfers of scheduled chemicals to or from States not Party, the First Review Conference recalled the prohibitions on any such transfers of Schedule 1 chemicals and, since 29 April 2000, of Schedule 2 chemicals. The First Review Conference urged all

States Parties to fully and effectively implement these prohibitions, including by enacting the necessary legislation, and to share experiences about the implementation of these provisions. The First Review Conference noted the impact that the full and effective implementation of these provisions can have on universality.

7.73   The question of whether there is a need for other measures in relation to transfers of Schedule 3 chemicals to States not Party remains under consideration in the Council. The First Review Conference reviewed this issue in the wider context of implementing effective transfer controls *vis-à-vis* States not Party. It concluded that all States Parties should take the necessary measures to ensure the full implementation of the Convention's requirement for end-use certification by recipient States not Party. This would be important for the consideration of potential non-proliferation benefits, the impact on universality, and the economic consequences of any other measures in relation to transfers of Schedule 3 chemicals. The First Review Conference requested the Council to continue working towards an early resolution of these issues, and to submit a recommendation on this matter to the next regular session of the Conference.

AGENDA ITEM 7(C)(V): NATIONAL IMPLEMENTATION MEASURES

7.74   The First Review Conference affirmed that national implementation is one of the essential conditions for the functioning of the Convention and for its full, effective, and non-discriminatory implementation.

7.75   National implementation is also important in relation to the ability of the Convention to respond to changes in the security environment or in science and technology that may affect the Convention. It contributes to meeting new challenges, including the possible use of toxic materials by non-state actors such as terrorists.

7.76   The First Review Conference noted that some progress had been made since the entry into force of the Convention in relation to the establishment or designation of National Authorities. One hundred and fifteen States Parties have now notified the OPCW of the establishment or designation of their National Authority. The First Review Conference noted with concern, however, that a large number of States Parties have yet to designate or establish a National Authority, and agreed that this situation needed urgent attention.

7.77   The adoption, in accordance with each State Party's constitutional process, of implementing legislation including penal legislation is an important State Party responsibility. The First Review Conference took note of the current status of national implementation measures. A major concern was the fact that a large number of States Parties had still not notified the OPCW of the legislative and administrative measures they had taken to implement the Convention, as required under paragraph 5 of Article VII. Furthermore, the information provided by the Secretariat indicates that an even larger number of States Parties have not adopted legislation covering all areas essential to adequate national enforcement of Convention obligations. Some States Parties may thus not be able to enforce the prohibitions required by the Convention, to provide legal cooperation to other States Parties, or to afford the appropriate form of legal assistance to facilitate the implementation of the obligations assumed under paragraph 1 of Article VII.

7.78   The First Review Conference noted that the Council had taken up the matter of implementing legislation, most recently in the context of its working group on terrorism. The First Review Conference noted that, while the threat of the use by terrorists of toxic chemicals has given added importance and urgency to the need to enact implementing legislation, the requirement that the States Parties adopt the necessary legislative and administrative measures to implement the Convention has its origin in the Convention itself.

7.79   The First Review Conference noted that a valuable aspect of national implementation measures involves ensuring that the chemical industry, the scientific and technological communities, the armed forces of the States Parties, and the public at large are aware of and knowledgeable about the prohibitions and requirements of the Convention.

7.80   The First Review Conference welcomed the efforts made by States Parties to assist each other in the development and enactment of implementing legislation, and in sharing experiences. The First Review Conference noted the value of both bilateral assistance, and networking within and among regions, especially for States Parties with limited resources.

7.81   The First Review Conference also noted that the Secretariat had developed a programme for implementation support aimed at providing technical assistance and technical evaluation in the implementation of the provisions of the Convention to States Parties, upon request. These include, *inter alia*, the provision of technical assistance and technical evaluation on-site, the training of National Authority personnel, the rendering of legal assistance, projects aimed at national capacity-building in areas relevant to the implementation of the Convention, support for regional networking among National Authorities, the development of tools and documentation to assist National Authorities, and other projects. The First Review Conference encouraged States Parties and the Secretariat to consult so as to further enhance the utility and effectiveness of these programmes.

7.82   The First Review Conference further agreed that the availability of effective support in the area of national implementation measures, rendered either by individual States Parties bilaterally or by the Secretariat, or in joint projects involving States Parties and the Secretariat, can help to promote the universality of the Convention.

7.83   The First Review Conference called upon States Parties that have not already done so to inform the OPCW by the next regular session of the Conference of the status of their adoption of the legislative and administrative measures necessary for or taken by them to implement the Convention, of any problems they have encountered, and of any assistance they require. Having considered the importance of national implementation measures for the proper functioning of the Convention, and having reviewed the activities undertaken by the States Parties as well as the Secretariat, the First Review Conference:

(a)   called upon States Parties that still have to designate or establish their National Authorities to do so as a matter of priority, and to notify the Secretariat accordingly;

(b)   called upon States Parties that have yet to prepare and enact implementing legislation, including penal legislation, and to adopt the required administrative and enforcement measures, either in whole or in part, to complete their internal preparations as soon as possible;

(c)   called upon States Parties to provide the OPCW with the full text of their national implementing legislation, including updates, or, in the case of States Parties with a monist legal system, with information on the specific measures they have taken to implement the Convention;

(d)   encouraged States Parties to take measures to raise awareness about the prohibitions and requirements of the Convention, *inter alia* in their armed forces, in industry, and in their scientific and technological communities;

(e)   encouraged States Parties to lend advice, upon request, to other States Parties in drafting and adopting national measures necessary to implement the Convention, *inter alia* to ensure that the laws reflect the comprehensive nature of the Convention by covering all activities that are to be prohibited or required in accordance with the Convention, and that involve the use of any toxic chemicals and their precursors; to cover the provision of annual declarations on past and anticipated activities; to ensure the implementation of the provisions related to transfers of scheduled chemicals; and to cover the annual submission of information on national protective programs in accordance with paragraph 4 of Article X;

(f)   encouraged the Secretariat to further develop and improve its implementation support programme, including by mobilising States Parties' efforts so as to provide, upon request and within the limits on available resources, technical assistance and technical evaluations to States Parties in the implementation of the provisions of the Convention, including in the areas identified in subparagraph 83(e) above;

(g)   urged States Parties that have not yet done so to review their existing regulations in the field of trade in chemicals in order to render them consistent with the object and purpose of the Convention;

(h)   agreed to develop, at its next regular session, a plan of action based on a recommendation from the Council regarding the implementation of Article VII obligations, with the objective of fostering the full and effective implementation of the Convention by all States Parties;

(i)   called upon the Council, in cooperation with the Secretariat, to closely monitor progress toward achieving effective implementation of Article VII obligations by all States Parties, and, at an appropriate time, to make suitable recommendations to the Conference regarding measures to ensure compliance with Article VII; and

(j)   encouraged the Secretariat as well as the States Parties to develop partnerships with relevant regional organisations and agencies that could render support to States Parties in their implementation work. Agenda item 7(c)(vi): Consultation, cooperation, and fact-finding

7.84   The First Review Conference reaffirmed the commitment of the States Parties to consult and cooperate, directly among themselves or through the OPCW, or by using other appropriate international procedures, including those within the framework of the UN and in accordance with its Charter, on any matter that may be raised relating to the object and purpose, or the implementation of the provisions of the Convention.

7.85   The First Review Conference recalled that, without prejudice to the right of any State Party to request a challenge inspection, States Parties should, whenever possible, first make every effort to clarify and resolve, through the exchange of information and consultation among themselves, any matter which may cause doubt about compliance with the Convention, or which gives rise to concerns about a related matter which may be considered ambiguous.

7.86   The First Review Conference noted that bilateral consultations to clarify issues had been used, and that this mechanism was valuable in ensuring compliance with the provisions of the Convention, and in clarifying and resolving concerns. The First Review Conference encouraged the States Parties to make full use of this bilateral-consultation mechanism.

7.87   The First Review Conference noted that the Council had received no clarification requests under paragraphs 3 to 7 of Article IX since entry into force. The First Review Conference reiterated that the Convention provides for all necessary arrangements to receive and expeditiously deal with any clarification request that a State Party may decide to submit in accordance with the applicable provisions of Article IX.

7.88   The First Review Conference noted that no challenge inspection had been requested since the entry into force of the Convention. The First Review Conference reaffirmed the right of each State Party to request an on-site challenge inspection, as provided for by the Convention, for the sole purpose of clarifying and resolving any questions concerning possible non-compliance with the provisions of the Convention. The First Review Conference also reaffirmed the right and obligation of each inspected State Party to make every reasonable effort to demonstrate its compliance, its obligation to provide access within the requested site for the sole purpose of establishing facts relevant to the compliance concern, and its right to take measures to protect sensitive installations and to prevent disclosure of confidential information and data not related to the Convention.

7.89   The First Review Conference recalled the provisions of the Convention intended to avoid abuse of the challenge inspection mechanism, and expressed its confidence that the States Parties will continue to uphold the value of the challenge inspection mechanism for compliance and compliance assurance, and at the same time keep any challenge inspection request within the scope of the Convention, and refrain from requests that are unfounded or abusive.

7.90   The First Review Conference noted that a number of issues related to challenge inspections are yet to be resolved. The First Review Conference requested the Council to continue its deliberations in order to expeditiously resolve them.

7.91   The First Review Conference took note of the preparations that the Secretariat had undertaken since entry into force in order to respond swiftly and effectively to any request for a challenge inspection. The First Review Conference noted the value, to the States Parties as well as the Secretariat, of challenge inspection exercises, and it recalled with appreciation the support provided by States Parties in this respect and invited them to continue to offer it in the future. The First Review Conference requested the Secretariat to continue maintaining a high standard of readiness to conduct a challenge inspection in accordance with the provisions of the Convention, to keep the Council informed about its readiness, and to report any problems that may arise in relation to maintaining the necessary level of readiness to conduct a challenge inspection.

AGENDA ITEM 7(C)(VII): ASSISTANCE AND PROTECTION AGAINST CHEMICAL WEAPONS

7.92   The First Review Conference reaffirmed the continuing relevance and importance of the provisions of Article X, and of the activities of the OPCW in relation to assistance and protection against chemical weapons. These have gained additional relevance in today's security context. The First Review Conference reaffirmed the rights of the States Parties to conduct research into, develop, produce, acquire, transfer, or use means of protection against chemical weapons, for purposes not prohibited under the Convention.

7.93   The First Review Conference also noted concerns related to the possibility that chemical facilities may become the object of attack, including by terrorists, which could lead to deliberate releases or theft of toxic chemicals. The First Review Conference was cognisant of the fact that some States Parties had taken measures to minimise these risks, and in this context recalled that the OPCW had been established as a forum for consultation and cooperation among the States Parties. States Parties could, if they so decided, make use of this framework to exchange experiences and to discuss issues related to this matter.

7.94   In relation to the annual provision by each State Party, for transparency purposes, of information on its national programme related to protective purposes, the First Review Conference noted that only 42 States Parties had submitted such information since the entry into force of the Convention. The First Review Conference reaffirmed the obligation of the States Parties to fully implement this requirement. The implementation of the requirement to submit this information annually would benefit from an early agreement on the procedures for such submissions. The First Review Conference requested the Council to expeditiously develop and submit for adoption the procedures called for by the Convention.

7.95   The First Review Conference requested the Secretariat to continue working on the OPCW data bank on protection, invited States Parties to contribute to the development of this data bank by submitting freely available information concerning various means of protection against chemical weapons and other relevant material for inclusion in the data bank, and encouraged States Parties to render support to the Secretariat in respect to the development, implementation, and maintenance of a database. The First Review Conference expressed concern about the hitherto slow progress in establishing this data bank.

7.96   In relation to the provision of expert advice by the Secretariat to States Parties that wish to further develop and improve their protective capacity, the First Review Conference noted the work of the OPCW protection network. The First Review Conference also noted that the number of requests for such expert advice received from States Parties recently exceeded the capacity of the Secretariat. The First Review Conference reiterated that the Secretariat must respond to such requests in an effective manner, within the limits on the resources available to it. Furthermore, States Parties should, on a voluntary basis, provide support to the OPCW so it can respond more effectively to requests for expert advice.

7.97   The First Review Conference noted with appreciation the measures elected by States Parties in relation to how they would provide assistance through the OPCW. It noted with concern, however, that only 63 States Parties had elected one or more such measures, and called upon the remaining States Parties to take the measures necessary to implement this requirement of the Convention.

7.98   The First Review Conference noted the need for the Secretariat to evaluate the assistance offers made in accordance with subparagraph 7(c) of Article X, in order to identify gaps, redundancies, and incompatibilities, and to help minimise the resource requirements for the OPCW. The First Review Conference requested the Secretariat to keep the policy-making organs informed about the status of assistance pledges by States Parties, and about any problems requiring attention and resolution.

7.99   In relation to a response to an assistance request in accordance with paragraph 8 of Article X, the First Review Conference noted that progress had been made in relation to the development and adoption of an operational concept of assistance. The First Review Conference noted in this context the OPCW's readiness for the delivery of assistance in the case of the use or threat of use of chemical weapons.

7.100   The First Review Conference stressed the importance of investigations of alleged use or threat of use of chemical weapons. For such situations, the OPCW must have the capacity, and be ready at all times, to investigate the need for follow-on action by the OPCW and by individual Member States, and to facilitate the delivery of assistance. The First Review Conference noted that the Secretariat had established the Assistance Coordination and Assessment Team (ACAT), the overall function of which had yet to be defined. This was an important and urgent matter. ACAT has been tested in assessment mode in exercises. The First Review Conference requested the Council to take up the possible function of the OPCW in facilitating the efficient delivery of assistance. In this context, the need was stressed for the OPCW to coordinate its activities in an assistance operation with other international agencies involved in an emergency response, in particular the UN Office for the Coordination of Humanitarian Affairs. Three principles were highlighted by the First Review Conference:

(a) the principle that the OPCW's role in such an emergency-response context should be firmly based on its mandate as provided by the Convention and on its particular experience and competence;

(b) the need to avoid duplication of efforts; and

(c) the need for coordination among all the agencies involved.

7.101   The First Review Conference encouraged the Secretariat to identify and engage relevant international organisations that are likely partners in situations where the OPCW needs to respond to an assistance request by a Member State, and to submit proposals to the policy-making organs.

7.102   The First Review Conference stressed the comprehensive nature of the definition of "Assistance" contained in paragraph 1 of Article X, and the right of any State Party to conduct research into, develop, produce, acquire, transfer, or use means of protection against chemical weapons for purposes not prohibited by the Convention.

7.103   The First Review Conference reaffirmed the undertaking of the States Parties to facilitate, and their right to participate in, the fullest possible exchange of equipment, material, and scientific and technological information concerning means of protection against chemical weapons.

AGENDA ITEM 7(C)(VIII): ECONOMIC AND TECHNOLOGICAL DEVELOPMENT

7.104   The First Review Conference reaffirmed the importance of the provisions of Article XI of the Convention relating to the economic and technological development of the States Parties. It recalled in this context that the full, effective, and non-discriminatory implementation of these provisions contributes to universality.

7.105 The First Review Conference reaffirmed the commitment of the States Parties to fully implement the provisions of the Convention on economic and technological development. It reaffirmed that the States Parties have the obligation to undertake to facilitate, and have the right to participate in, the fullest possible exchange of chemicals, equipment, and technical information relating to the development and application of chemistry for purposes not prohibited by the Convention. The First Review Conference stressed that the international cooperation programmes of the OPCW should also make a contribution to the development of States Parties' capacities required to implement the Convention.

7.106 The First Review Conference reaffirmed that the Convention shall be implemented in a manner that avoids hampering the economic or technological development of States Parties, and international cooperation in the field of chemical activities for purposes not prohibited by the Convention, including the international exchange of scientific and technical information, and chemicals and equipment for the production, processing, or use of chemicals for purposes not prohibited under the Convention.

7.107 The First Review Conference reaffirmed the provision of Article XI that the States Parties shall:

(a) not maintain among themselves any restrictions, including those in international agreements, incompatible with the obligations undertaken under the Convention, which would restrict or impede trade and the development and promotion of scientific and technological knowledge in the field of chemistry for industrial, agricultural, research, medical, pharmaceutical, and other peaceful purposes;

(b) not use the Convention as grounds for applying any measures other than those provided for, or permitted, under the Convention nor any other international agreement for pursuing an objective inconsistent with the Convention; and

(c) undertake to review their existing national regulations in the field of trade in chemicals in order to render them consistent with the object and purpose of the Convention. The First Review Conference called upon the States Parties to fully implement these provisions of the Convention. It also urged the Council to continue its facilitation efforts to reach early agreement on the issue of the full implementation of Article XI, taking into account earlier and recent proposals submitted.

7.108 The First Review Conference stressed the importance of international cooperation and its valuable contribution to the promotion of the Convention as a whole, including its universality, and in this context it:

(a) reaffirmed the commitment of the Conference to foster international cooperation for peaceful purposes in the field of chemical activities, and further reaffirmed its desire to promote international cooperation and exchange of scientific and technical information in the field of chemical activities;

(b) stressed the desirability of cooperation projects among States Parties in areas related to the peaceful uses of chemistry. The OPCW could facilitate the provision of expert advice on the peaceful uses of chemistry, as required and upon request, to and among States Parties;

(c) recognised the importance of assistance and national capacity-building in the field of chemical activities for peaceful purposes, particularly as it applies to the implementation of the Convention. An important component of these activities involves facilitating the provision of direct support on-site – bilaterally, regionally, or through or by the OPCW, for example, by experts from other States Parties or the Secretariat – to assist National Authorities with specific implementation tasks. The Secretariat should, in consultation with the States Parties, review and develop existing implementation support programmes;

(d) noted the relevance of the existing International Cooperation and Assistance Pro-
     grammes and recalled that all OPCW programmes should be improved through
     evaluation to optimise resource use and effectiveness, with consultations between
     the States Parties and the Secretariat aimed at achieving a clear understanding of the
     competencies available, the needs of the States Parties, and the requirements of the
     Convention;

(e) recognised the need for adequate resources, and concluded that decisions on ad-
     equate budgetary allocations for international cooperation should be based on the
     States Parties' needs, and how the programme addresses these needs, bearing in
     mind overall resource constraints;

(f) emphasised how important it is that the OPCW coordinate its activities with those
     of other relevant international and regional organisations, as appropriate, in order to
     build on existing competencies, develop synergies, and avoid duplication of efforts.
     The OPCW should further integrate itself as a partner in the establishment of inter-
     national programme-coordination mechanisms in the field of international coopera-
     tion, assistance, and capacity-building related to the peaceful uses of chemistry;

(g) encouraged the OPCW to continue to establish relations and partnerships, as appro-
     priate, with relevant regional and international organisations, including chemical
     industry associations and civil society, in order to promote universal adherence and
     awareness of the objectives and purposes of the Convention; and

(h) encouraged the OPCW to continue to develop its relationship with the private sector
     and in particular maintain, through the States Parties concerned, a productive and
     lasting partnership with the chemical industry, *inter alia* so that the industry the
     world over stays aware of the Convention and remains committed to its full imple-
     mentation.

7.109   The First Review Conference concluded that there was a need to develop guiding prin-
         ciples to be applied when determining international-cooperation programmes. These
         guiding principles should then be taken into account by the Secretariat when it is further
         developing proposals for such programmes. The Council should elaborate such guide-
         lines on international cooperation programmes, and apply them when evaluating both
         reports by the Secretariat on existing programmes, and proposals it makes for new ones.

AGENDA ITEM 7(C)(IX): FINAL CLAUSES: ARTICLES XII TO XXIV
7.110   The First Review Conference reaffirmed the continued relevance of the provisions of
         Articles XII through XXIV of the Convention.

AGENDA ITEM 7(C)(X): THE PROTECTION OF CONFIDENTIAL INFORMATION
7.111   The First Review Conference reiterated the importance that it attaches to the need for the
         OPCW to thoroughly protect confidential information, in accordance with the provisions
         of the Convention. The OPCW remains strongly committed to the principles and provi-
         sions set out in the Convention in relation to the protection of confidentiality, in particu-
         lar in the Confidentiality Annex. The First Review Conference recalled, in this context,
         the important role of the Director-General in ensuring the protection of confidential in-
         formation, as well as the responsibility of each staff member of the Secretariat to comply
         with all rules and regulations pertaining to the protection of confidential information.
7.112   The First Review Conference noted that the Secretariat continues to improve the im-
         plementation of the confidentiality regime in order to avoid breaches of confidentiality.
         There have been incidents, but these have not compromised the effectiveness of the
         OPCW's regime to protect confidentiality. The strict implementation of the OPCW's
         confidentiality procedures should, however, be further improved.

7.113　Proper conduct on the part of staff is essential to the effective implementation of a robust confidentiality regime, and the First Review Conference underlined the need for adequate training.

7.114　The First Review Conference stressed the importance of the procedures to be applied in cases of alleged breaches of confidentiality. The First Review Conference reaffirmed, furthermore, the important role of the Commission for the settlement of disputes related to confidentiality (hereinafter "the Confidentiality Commission") in settling any dispute related to breaches in confidentiality and involving both a State Party and the OPCW.

7.115　The First Review Conference noted that only 44 States Parties had, as required by the Confidentiality Annex, provided details, at the request of the OPCW, on their handling of information it had provided to them. The First Review Conference urged States Parties to provide that information expeditiously, as requested by the Secretariat.

7.116　The First Review Conference took cognisance of the fact that 85% of the information submitted to the Secretariat had been classified as confidential by the originating States Parties. The First Review Conference requested the Council, assisted by the Secretariat, to study the situation in relation to the classification of information held by the OPCW. The First Review Conference encouraged the Secretariat and the States Parties to review their respective practices in assigning levels of classification to such information, and if possible, and in accordance with the State Party's confidentiality procedures, to reduce the classification level they assign to such information, in order to increase work efficiency and ensure the smooth functioning of the system to protect confidentiality.

7.117　The First Review Conference recalled that, following an external security audit, the Secretariat was operating a Secure Critical Network (SCN) for the processing and storage of confidential information related to the verification activities of the OPCW. With the support of States Parties, and taking account of the advice rendered by the external security audit team, the Secretariat is continuing its work towards the development of a relational-database management system to be operated on the SCN to support verification activities. The First Review Conference noted the security audit team recommendation to adopt the ISO-17799 information-security management standard, and requested the Secretariat to evaluate what resources would be required to do this, and to inform the Council of its findings.

7.118　The First Review Conference noted that current confidentiality guidelines provide neither for the destruction of confidential documents and other data, including those kept on the Secretariat's SCN, nor for the downgrading of their classification levels over the long term. The First Review Conference encouraged the OPCW to take steps to reach agreement on developing and implementing guidelines regarding the long-term handling of confidential information.

7.119　The First Review Conference noted the need to ensure that the conditions in relation to the protection of confidentiality of information are met when the OPCW proceeds to the submission of declarations in electronic form (e.g., on CD-ROM; see also paragraph 7.39(f) above). Agenda item 7(d): The functioning of the Organisation for the Prohibition of Chemical Weapons

7.120　The States Parties have established the OPCW to achieve the object and purpose of the Convention, to ensure the implementation of its provisions, including those for international verification of compliance with it, and to provide a forum for consultation and cooperation among the States Parties. Its effective functioning has a direct impact on the operation of the Convention.

7.121　The work of the policy-making organs is an important aspect of the OPCW's effective functioning. They provide policy guidance to the OPCW, and the effectiveness of their work is essential to the involvement of all States Parties in the work of the OPCW. The First Review Conference called upon all States Parties to fully participate in the activities of the OPCW's policy-making organs.

7.122   The Council, as part of its powers and functions under the Convention, promotes the effective implementation of the Convention and compliance with it, supervises the activities of the Secretariat, cooperates with the National Authorities of the States Parties, facilitates consultation and cooperation among them, and reports to the Conference. It is therefore especially important that the Council function effectively. The First Review Conference noted how important it was for the Chairperson and Vice-Chairpersons of the Council to be engaged with the work of the facilitation groups. The First Review Conference also noted that focused agendas for both the formal meetings and the intersessional consultations of the Council were required in order for the Council to make decisions effectively.

7.123   The First Review Conference expressed concern about delays in the Council's implementation of Conference decisions on the resolution of unresolved issues. The First Review Conference noted that the Council had included important, long-standing, unresolved issues in its work programme, and urged it to increase momentum and strive to conclude all unresolved issues.

7.124   The First Review Conference reviewed the functioning of the subsidiary advisory bodies, and noted the following:

(a)   The Confidentiality Commission has been established in accordance with the Convention's Confidentiality Annex and the OPCW Policy on Confidentiality to consider any cases of disputes concerning breaches or alleged breaches of confidentiality involving both a State Party and the OPCW. No such disputes have been brought before the Confidentiality Commission since entry into force. The First Review Conference stressed the need for the Confidentiality Commission to be fully operational at all times, and requested the Secretariat to ensure that all necessary support is provided for this purpose.

(b)   The SAB was established by the Director-General following the direction given by the Conference on this matter, to enable him, in the performance of his functions, to render specialised advice in areas of science and technology relevant to the Convention, to the Conference, to the Council, or to the States Parties. The SAB has met in regular annual sessions since 1998, and its work has been supported by temporary working groups on a number of issues submitted to it for its consideration. The First Review Conference noted the advice rendered to the States Parties by the Director-General, following contributions made by the SAB, and recommended that the interaction between the SAB and delegations should continue and be further enhanced, in the context of the Council's facilitation process. The First Review Conference noted, furthermore, that the SAB had prepared a report to the First Review Conference on relevant scientific and technological developments that the States Parties should take into account in their review.

(c)   The Advisory Body for Administrative and Financial Matters (ABAF) has been established as a panel of experts of recognised standing to provide expert advice to the OPCW on administrative and financial matters. It has made valuable contributions to the work of the OPCW and prepared recommendations on financial and administrative matters on a regular basis.

7.125   The Secretariat assists the Conference and the Council in performing their functions, and carries out the verification measures provided for in the Convention, and other functions entrusted to it under the Convention, as well as those functions delegated to it by the Conference or the Council. The First Review Conference noted with satisfaction the dedication of Secretariat staff. The OPCW has at its disposal qualified and trained staff, and equipment and procedures fit for the tasks to be fulfilled under the Convention. Possible future improvements have been identified in the review by the First Review Conference of the operation of the Convention, and are recorded in different parts of this report.

7.126   The First Review Conference stressed the responsibility of the Director-General, as the head and chief administrative officer of the Secretariat, for the appointment of staff and for the organisation and functioning of the Secretariat. The First Review Conference, furthermore, recalled the provisions of paragraph 44 of Article VIII.

7.127   The First Review Conference considered the budgetary and financial mechanisms of the OPCW as they have evolved since entry into force. The First Review Conference stressed the need for the Council, with the support of the Secretariat, to continue monitoring and improving the implementation of these mechanisms. The First Review Conference underlined the importance of putting in place a more effective budgetary process, based on early consultations between the Secretariat and the States Parties, on thoughtful consideration and prioritisation of the programme objectives, and on regular assessments of whether these objectives are being met. The First Review Conference encouraged the Director-General to move ahead with the stepwise introduction of results-based budgeting. Furthermore, the First Review Conference noted the need for the Council to accelerate its deliberations on the outstanding issues in relation to the OPCW's Financial Rules.

7.128   The First Review Conference welcomed the decision by the Council on the effective starting date of tenure of staff, and recalled the Conference's decision at its Second Special Session on 30 April 2003 (C-SS-2/DEC.1, dated 30 April 2003). These decisions will now be implemented, and the First Review Conference stressed the need to monitor the implementation of the OPCW's tenure policy, and the need for regular reporting by the Director-General to the Council on its implementation, and in particular on the implementation of the guiding principles in effecting the turnover of staff. The First Review Conference also noted that the issue of the OPCW's Staff Rules and amendments to Staff Regulation 3.3, and the issue of the classification of posts, remain within the purview of the Council and should be resolved without delay.

7.129   The First Review Conference reaffirmed the importance to the effective functioning of the Secretariat of the principles set out in the Convention on the employment of staff. The First Review Conference reaffirmed that the paramount consideration in the employment of staff and in the determination of the conditions of service shall be the necessity of securing the highest standards of efficiency, competence, and integrity. Due regard shall be paid to the importance of recruiting staff on as wide a geographical basis as possible. Recruitment shall be guided by the principle that the staff shall be kept to the minimum necessary for the proper discharge of the responsibilities of the Secretariat.

7.130   The First Review Conference stressed that Secretariat staff, and in particular its inspectors, need to keep abreast with developments in science and technology in order to maintain professional excellence and to efficiently discharge their responsibilities. The First Review Conference requested that the Director-General bear these requirements in mind when identifying the future training needs of the Secretariat.

7.131   The First Review Conference stressed that the Secretariat should seek to apply information technology more efficiently to improve the functioning of the OPCW.

7.132   The First Review Conference also recalled the Conference's decision on the equal treatment of all official OPCW languages, and requested the Secretariat to continue its efforts to fully implement this decision.

7.133   The First Review Conference expressed its satisfaction at the excellent relations between the OPCW and the Host Country. The First Review Conference invited the Director-General to report to the Council, as appropriate, on this relationship.

7.134   The First Review Conference noted the evolving relationships between the OPCW and other international, regional, and sub-regional organisations, and in particular stressed the importance of the relationship with the UN, as provided for by the Agreement concerning the Relationship between the UN and the Organisation for the Prohibition of

Chemical Weapons (EC-MXI/DEC.1, dated 1 September 2000, and C-VI/DEC.5, dated 17 May 2001).

8.   AGENDA ITEM EIGHT – Reports of subsidiary bodies

COMMITTEE OF THE WHOLE

8.1 The First Review Conference noted the report of the Committee of the Whole on the results of its consideration of the agenda item referred to it on the recommendation of the General Committee (RC-1/CoW.1, dated 9 May 2003), and took action as required.

GENERAL COMMITTEE

8.2 The First Review Conference noted the reports of the General Committee, and took action as required. Credentials Committee

8.3 The report of the Credentials Committee (RC-1/2 dated 7 May 2003) was presented by its Chairwoman, Mrs Maria Dulce Silva Barros of Brazil. The Chairwoman orally reported that, following the close of the Credentials Committee meeting, formal credentials were received for the representatives of Albania, Costa Rica, Czech Republic, Italy, Jordan, Kenya and Mongolia, and faxes or copies of credentials in the form required by Rule 26 of the Rules of Procedure of the Conference were received from Namibia, Senegal and Tunisia. Formal credentials would be submitted for the latter in due course. The First Review Conference noted this additional information and approved the report. The First Review Conference also remarked on the number of Member States that had failed to submit credentials for their representatives on time, and urged adherence in future sessions to the requirements of Rule 26 of the Rules of Procedure of the Conference. Under that Rule, the Director-General should receive credentials preferably one week in advance of a given session.

CREDENTIALS COMMITTEE

8.4 The report of the Credentials Committee (RC-1/2 dated 7 May 2003) was presented by its Chairwoman, Mrs Maria Dulce Silva Barros of Brazil. The Chairwoman orally reported that, following the close of the Credentials Committee meeting, formal credentials were received for the representatives of Albania, Costa Rica, Czech Republic, Italy, Jordan, Kenya and Mongolia, and faxes or copies of credentials in the form required by Rule 26 of the Rules of Procedure of the Conference were received from Namibia, Senegal and Tunisia. Formal credentials would be submitted for the latter in due course. The First Review Conference noted this additional information and approved the report. The First Review Conference also remarked on the number of Member States that had failed to submit credentials for their representatives on time, and urged adherence in future sessions to the requirements of Rule 26 of the Rules of Procedure of the Conference. Under that Rule, the Director-General should receive credentials preferably one week in advance of a given session.

9.   AGENDA ITEM NINE – Any other business

10. AGENDA ITEM TEN – Adoption of the final documents of the First Review Conference

10.1 The First Review Conference adopted the Political Declaration of the First Review Conference (RC-1/3, dated 9 May 2003).

10.2 The First Review Conference considered and adopted the report of the First Review Conference.

11. AGENDA ITEM ELEVEN – Closure

The Chairman closed the First Review Conference at 23:33 on 9 May 2003.

21.2 The Second Special Session of the Conference of the States Parties to Review the Operation of the Chemical Weapons Convention (Second Review Conference; 7–18 April 2008)

RC-2/4 containing the Report of the Second Special Session of the Conference of the States Parties adopted on 18 April 2008 and entitled "Report of the Second Special Session of the Conference of the States Parties to review the operation of the Chemical Weapons Convention (Second Review Conference)"

1.   AGENDA ITEM ONE – Opening of the Second Review Conference

1.1   The Second Special Session of the Conference of the States Parties to Review the Operation of the Chemical Weapons Convention (hereinafter "the Second Review Conference") was opened at 15:12 on 7 April 2008 by the Chairperson of the Twelfth Session of the Conference of the States Parties (hereinafter "the Conference"), Ambassador Abuelgasim Abdelwahid Shiekh Idris of Sudan. It received a message from the Secretary-General of the United Nations (UN), delivered by his special representative, Mr Tim Caughley, Director of the Geneva Branch, Office for Disarmament Affairs and Deputy Secretary-General of the Conference on Disarmament (RC-2/2, dated 7 April 2008).

1.2   The following 114 States Parties participated in the Second Review Conference: Afghanistan, Algeria, Andorra, Argentina, Armenia, Australia, Austria, Azerbaijan, Bahrain, Bangladesh, Belarus, Belgium, Benin, Bolivia, Bosnia and Herzegovina, Brazil, Bulgaria, Burkina Faso, Cameroon, Canada, Chile, China, Colombia, Costa Rica, Côte d'Ivoire, Croatia, Cuba, Cyprus, Czech Republic, Denmark, Ecuador, El Salvador, Eritrea, Estonia, Finland, France, Gabon, Georgia, Germany, Ghana, Greece, Guatemala, Honduras, Hungary, Iceland, India, Indonesia, Iran (Islamic Republic of), Ireland, Italy, Jamaica, Japan, Jordan, Kazakhstan, Kenya, Kuwait, Kyrgyzstan, Latvia, Libyan Arab Jamahiriya, Lithuania, Luxembourg, Malaysia, Malta, Mexico, Monaco, Mongolia, Morocco, Mozambique, Namibia, Nepal, Netherlands, New Zealand, Nicaragua, Nigeria, Norway, Oman, Pakistan, Peru, Philippines, Poland, Portugal, Qatar, Republic of Korea, Republic of Moldova, Romania, Russian Federation, Rwanda, Saudi Arabia, Serbia, Singapore, Slovakia, Slovenia, South Africa, Spain, Sri Lanka, Sudan, Suriname, Sweden, Switzerland, Thailand, The former Yugoslav Republic of Macedonia, Tunisia, Turkey, Uganda, Ukraine, United Arab Emirates, United Kingdom of Great Britain and Northern Ireland, United States of America, Uruguay, Uzbekistan, Viet Nam, Yemen, Zambia, and Zimbabwe

1.3   In accordance with Rule 29 of the Rules of Procedure of the Conference, the following Signatory States participated in the Second Review Conference as observers: Guinea-Bissau and Israel.

1.4   In accordance with Rule 30 of the Rules of Procedure of the Conference, and pursuant to decision RC-2/DEC.1, dated 7 April 2008, Angola, Iraq, Lebanon were accorded observer status.

1.5   The Second Review Conference, in decision RC-2/DEC.2, dated 7 April 2008, approved the participation of five international organisations, specialised agencies, and other international bodies in its Session.

1.6   The Second Review Conference, in decision RC-2/DEC.3, dated 7 April 2008, approved the participation of 28 non-governmental organisations in its Session.

2.   AGENDA ITEM TWO – Election of the Chairperson

2.1   In accordance with Rule 8(b) of the Rules of Procedure of the Conference, the Second
         Review Conference, by acclamation, elected as its Chairperson Ambassador Waleed
         Ben Abdel Karim El Khereiji of Saudi Arabia.

3.   AGENDA ITEM THREE – Election of Vice-Chairpersons and other officers

3.1   In accordance with Rule 8(b) of the Rules of Procedure of the Conference, the Second
         Review Conference elected representatives of the following 10 States Parties as Vice-
         Chairpersons of the Conference: China, Costa Rica, Czech Republic, France, Iran (Is-
         lamic Republic of), Kenya, Nigeria, Russian Federation, United States of America, and
         Uruguay.
3.2   Also, in accordance with Rule 8(b) of the Rules of Procedure of the Conference, the
         Second Review Conference elected as Chairperson of the Committee of the Whole, Am-
         bassador Benchaâ Dani of Algeria.

4.   AGENDA ITEM FOUR – Adoption of the agenda

4.1   The provisional agenda for the Second Review Conference was circulated under cover
         of RC-2/1, dated 11 March 2008.
4.2   On the recommendation of the General Committee, the Second Review Conference
         adopted the following agenda:
AGENDA ITEM ONE – Opening of the Second Review Conference
AGENDA ITEM TWO – Election of the Chairperson
AGENDA ITEM THREE – Election of Vice-Chairpersons and other officers
AGENDA ITEM FOUR – Adoption of the agenda
AGENDA ITEM FIVE – Organisation of work and establishment of subsidiary bodies
AGENDA ITEM SIX – Statement by the Director-General
AGENDA ITEM SEVEN – Report of the Chairperson of the Executive Council on the preparations for
the Second Review Conference
AGENDA ITEM EIGHT – General debate
AGENDA ITEM NINE – Review of the operation of the Chemical Weapons Convention as provided
for in paragraph 22 of Article VIII, taking into account any relevant scientific and technological
developments:
     (a) the role of the Chemical Weapons Convention in enhancing international peace and
          security and in achieving the objectives as set forth in the preamble of the Convention;
     (b) ensuring the universality of the Chemical Weapons Convention;
     (c) implementation of the provisions of the Chemical Weapons Convention relating to:
          (i)   general obligations and declarations related thereto;
          (ii)   destruction of chemical weapons and destruction or conversion of chemical weap-
                 ons production facilities;
          (iii) verification activities of the OPCW;
          (iv)   activities not prohibited under the Chemical Weapons Convention;
          (v)   national implementation measures;
          (vi)   consultations, cooperation, and fact-finding;
          (vii) assistance and protection against chemical weapons;
          (viii) economic and technological development;
          (ix)   Articles XII to XV and final clauses; and
          (x)   the protection of confidential information;
     (d) the general functioning of the Organisation for the Prohibition of Chemical Weapons.

AGENDA ITEM TEN – Reports of subsidiary bodies
AGENDA ITEM ELEVEN – Any other business
AGENDA ITEM TWELVE – Adoption of the final documents of the Second Review Conference
AGENDA ITEM THIRTEEN – Closure

5.   AGENDA ITEM FIVE – Organisation of work and establishment of subsidiary bodies

5.1   The Second Review Conference considered and adopted the recommendations of the
         General Committee reported to it in accordance with Rule 43 of the Rules of Procedure
         of the Conference.
5.2   The Second Review Conference adopted the recommendation of the General Committee
         that it be closed on 18 April 2008.

APPOINTMENT OF THE CREDENTIALS COMMITTEE
5.3   In accordance with Rule 27 of the Rules of Procedure of the Conference, the Second Re-
         view Conference, on the recommendation of its Chairperson, appointed the following 10
         members of the Credentials Committee: Austria, Bolivia, Brazil, Bulgaria, Cameroon,
         Finland, Namibia, Poland, Sri Lanka, and Thailand.

6.   AGENDA ITEM SIX – Statement by the Director-General

6.1   The Second Review Conference noted the opening statement by the Director-General
         (RC-2/DG.2, dated 7 April 2008).

7.   AGENDA ITEM SEVEN – Report of the Chairperson of the Executive Council on the prepa-
     rations for the Second Review Conference

7.1   The Chairperson of the Executive Council (hereinafter "the Council"), Ambassador
         Romeo A. Arguelles of the Philippines, reported to the Second Review Conference
         on the work of the Council in preparation for the Second Review Conference. At his
         request, the Chairperson of the open-ended working group for the preparation of the
         Second Review Conference, Ambassador Lyn Parker of the United Kingdom of Great
         Britain and Northern Ireland, reported to the Second Review Conference on the work
         of the open-ended working group and submitted to the Second Review Conference the
         Chairperson's provisional text for agenda item nine of the Provisional Agenda of the
         Second Review Conference (RC-2/CRP.1, dated 31 March 2008).

8.   AGENDA ITEM EIGHT – General debate

8.1   The following delegations made statements during the general debate: Slovenia (on be-
         half of the European Union and associated countries), Netherlands, Cuba (on behalf of
         the Non-Aligned Movement and China), South Africa (on behalf of the African Group),
         Kyrgyzstan (on behalf of the Commonwealth of Independent States), United States of
         America, Saudi Arabia, China, Russian Federation, Singapore, Japan, Pakistan, Iran (Is-
         lamic Republic of), Serbia, Switzerland, Mexico, Algeria, Canada, New Zealand, South
         Africa (in its national capacity), Ukraine, Indonesia, Turkey, Bangladesh, Malaysia,
         Peru, Republic of Korea, Australia, Brazil, Tunisia, Yemen, Norway, Sudan, El Salva-
         dor, Mongolia, India, Colombia, Nigeria, Albania, Libyan Arab Jamahiriya, Thailand,
         Kuwait, United Arab Emirates, Qatar, Zambia, Uganda, Belarus, Morocco, China (Hong
         Kong Special Administrative Region), and Argentina.

9.   AGENDA ITEM NINE – Review of the operation of the Chemical Weapons Convention as
      provided for in paragraph 22 of Article VIII, taking into account any relevant scientific and
      technological developments:

AGENDA ITEM 9(A): THE ROLE OF THE CHEMICAL WEAPONS CONVENTION IN ENHANCING INTERNA-
TIONAL PEACE AND SECURITY AND IN ACHIEVING THE OBJECTIVES AS SET FORTH IN THE PREAMBLE OF
THE CONVENTION

9.1   The Second Review Conference welcomed the fact that eleven years after its entry into
          force, the Chemical Weapons Convention (hereinafter "the Convention") remains a
          unique multilateral agreement banning an entire category of weapons of mass destruc-
          tion in a non-discriminatory and verifiable manner under strict and effective interna-
          tional control. The Second Review Conference noted with satisfaction that implementa-
          tion of the Convention makes a major contribution to international peace and security
          through the elimination of existing stockpiles of chemical weapons, the prohibition of
          the acquisition or use of chemical weapons, and provides for assistance and protection
          in the event of use, or threat of use, of chemical weapons and for international coopera-
          tion for peaceful purposes in the field of chemical activities. The Convention sets new
          standards for global disarmament and non-proliferation through verification in a non-
          discriminatory and multilateral manner.

9.2   The Second Review Conference noted with satisfaction that since the First Review Con-
          ference in 2003 the total number of States Parties has risen from 151 to 183, leaving
          only 12 states still to join the Convention. This high level of participation signifies that
          an overwhelming majority of states consider chemical weapons and their use under any
          circumstances by any state, group or individual to be illegal and prohibited. The Sec-
          ond Review Conference categorically condemned the use of chemical weapons as de-
          fined in the Convention. The Second Review Conference reaffirmed the undertaking of
          States Parties not to use riot control agents as a method of warfare. The Second Review
          Conference also underlined the essential contribution that the Convention has made to
          confidence building and cooperation among States Parties, as well as to their national
          security.

9.3   The Second Review Conference strongly reaffirmed the commitment of all States Par-
          ties to comply with all obligations under the Convention, and the importance of this
          commitment in upholding the Convention's integrity and maximising its contribution
          to international peace and security. The Second Review Conference also stressed the
          important respective roles assigned by the Convention to the Council in promoting, and
          to the Conference in ensuring, that all States Parties comply with their obligations.

9.4   The Second Review Conference reaffirmed that complete destruction of chemical weap-
          ons, and conversion or complete destruction of chemical weapons production facilities
          (CWPFs), is essential for the realisation of the object and purpose of the Convention.
          The Second Review Conference also reaffirmed the importance of the obligation of the
          possessor States Parties to complete the destruction of their chemical weapons stock-
          piles within the final extended deadlines as established by the Conference at its Eleventh
          Session. The Second Review Conference welcomed the statements of possessor States
          Parties reiterating their commitment to meeting the final, extended deadlines established
          under the Convention by the Eleventh Session of the Conference. The Second Review
          Conference noted the significant progress made so far by possessor States Parties in the
          destruction of chemical weapons, as well as the recent completion by Albania of the
          destruction of its entire stockpile and commended the progress made by those States
          Parties which are close to achieving complete destruction of their stockpiles. The Sec-
          ond Review Conference noted that by 1 April 2008, over 38% of the total stockpiles of
          70,000 tonnes of Category 1 chemical weapons initially declared by States Parties had

been destroyed. However, the Second Review Conference expressed its concern that more than 60% of stockpiles still remained to be destroyed.

9.5 The Second Review Conference noted with satisfaction that the OPCW has established an effective verification system with a view to achieving the non-proliferation and confidence building aims of the Convention.

9.6 The Second Review Conference reaffirmed the right of the States Parties, subject to the provisions of the Convention and without prejudice to the principles and applicable norms of international law, to use chemicals for purposes not prohibited by the Convention. The Second Review Conference affirmed that the OPCW continues to provide a forum for consultation and cooperation related to the observance of this right among States Parties.

9.7 The Second Review Conference reaffirmed the importance that the Convention attaches to fostering international cooperation in the field of peaceful chemical activities of the States Parties, and the objective of implementing the Convention in a manner that avoids hampering their economic and technological development and international cooperation in the field of chemical activities for purposes not prohibited by the Convention. The Second Review Conference reaffirmed the right of the States Parties, subject to the provisions of the Convention and without prejudice to the principles and applicable rules of international law, to use chemicals for purposes not prohibited by the Convention, and their determination to undertake to facilitate the fullest possible exchange of chemicals, equipment, and scientific and technical information relating to the development and application of chemistry for purposes not prohibited by the Convention.

9.8 The Second Review Conference reaffirmed that the full and effective national implementation of the obligations under the Convention is essential for the realisation of the object and purpose of the Convention. It welcomed the considerable progress made in national implementation since the Conference at its Eighth Session adopted the plan of action for the implementation of Article VII obligations (C 8/DEC.16, dated 24 October 2003), while also recognising that there remain a sizeable number of States Parties that still need to take some or all of the necessary measures to implement their Article VII obligations, and that a number of these States Parties still require assistance and technical support.

9.9 The Second Review Conference reiterated that the implementation of the Convention's provisions on assistance and protection against chemical weapons makes a significant contribution to countering the threats associated with the possible use of chemical weapons. It stressed that, in a case of use of chemical weapons, the Convention makes provision for immediate assistance by the OPCW, subject to the requirements and procedures laid down in the Convention. For this purpose, the OPCW may cooperate with the requesting State Party and other States Parties and relevant international organisations. The Second Review Conference furthermore emphasised the need for the OPCW as well as the States Parties to achieve an effective capability to meet the requirements of Article X in order to provide timely and necessary assistance and protection against the use, or threat of use, of chemical weapons, and for the capacity building activities of the Technical Secretariat (hereinafter "the Secretariat").

9.10 The Second Review Conference noted with concern that, along with the continued threat of the possible use of chemical weapons by States under any circumstances, the international community also faces the increased danger of the use of chemical weapons by terrorists or other non-state actors. In this context, the Second Review Conference recalled the decision of the Council concerning the OPCW's contribution to global anti-terrorist efforts (EC-XXVII/DEC.5, dated 7 December 2001) and affirmed its continuing relevance.

9.11 The Second Review Conference noted the impact of scientific and technological progress on the effective implementation of the Convention and the importance for the OPCW and its policy-making organs of taking due account of such developments. In that context, it stressed that the Scientific Advisory Board should continue to play an objective and balanced role in advising the Director-General. The Second Review Conference reaffirmed the commitment by all States Parties to achieving the object and purpose of the Convention, as set out in its Preamble and provisions.

AGENDA ITEM 9(B): ENSURING THE UNIVERSALITY OF THE CHEMICAL WEAPONS CONVENTION

9.12   The Second Review Conference reiterated that the universality of the Convention is essential to achieve its object and purpose and enhance international peace and security. The Second Review Conference underlined that the goal of universality shall be pursued by the Secretariat as well as States Parties as a matter of high priority.

9.13   The Second Review Conference noted with satisfaction the substantial progress achieved since the adoption by the Council on 24 October 2003 of the Action Plan for the Universality of the Chemical Weapons Convention (EC-M-23/DEC.3, dated 24 October 2003) and subsequent decisions adopted by the Council and the Conference of the States Parties. It also acknowledged the efforts made collectively by the States Parties, the policy-making organs, the Secretariat, and the Director-General to this end. It welcomed the fact that, of the 40 States not Party when the Action Plan was adopted, more than two-thirds (including one possessor State) have since joined the Convention. However, it noted that there remain 12 States not Party to the Convention, including five signatory States and seven non-signatory States. It recalled in particular that among the States not Party there are some whose non-adherence is a matter of serious concern.

9.14   The Second Review Conference underlined the important political, economic, and security benefits of becoming a State Party to the Convention, recognised the positive contribution of cooperation among the States Parties and the OPCW to the achievement of universality, and recalled that States that remain outside the Convention are not able to take advantage of the benefits that it offers to States Parties.

9.15   The Second Review Conference underlined that the objectives of the Convention will not be fully realised as long as there remains even a single state not party that could possess or acquire such weapons. It stressed that the continued absence from the Convention of any country keeps open the risk that chemical weapons could be developed, acquired, transferred or used.

9.16   The Second Review Conference therefore strongly urged all 12 remaining States not Party to the Convention (Angola, the Bahamas, the Democratic People's Republic of Korea, the Dominican Republic, Egypt, Guinea-Bissau, Iraq, Israel, Lebanon, Myanmar, Somalia, and the Syrian Arab Republic) to ratify or accede to it as a matter of urgency and without preconditions, in the interests of enhancing their own national security as well as affirming their commitment to global peace and security and to the object and purpose of the Convention. In this connection, the Second Review Conference welcomed efforts by Guinea-Bissau, Iraq and Lebanon who are well advanced in the process of accession to the Convention, and requested the Secretariat to continue to support their ongoing efforts aimed at adherence.

9.17   The Second Review Conference expressed its conviction that universality matched by full implementation by all States Parties of their obligations under the Convention is essential to achieve the aims of the Convention.

9.18   The Second Review Conference called upon the Secretariat, the Director-General, policy-making organs and all States Parties in a position to do so to intensify further their efforts with States not Party with a view to achieving full universality at the earliest possible date. It encouraged them to make full use of all available opportunities and resources to pursue this goal at all levels. It welcomed the decision of the Twelfth Session of the Conference to continue with the Action Plan on Universality (C-12/DEC.11, dated 9 November 2007), and its intention to review the results and implementation of that plan at its Fourteenth Session and to take any decision it deems necessary addressing, in particular, the status of those States not Party whose non-adherence is a cause for serious concern.

AGENDA ITEM 9(C)(I): GENERAL OBLIGATIONS AND DECLARATIONS RELATED THERETO

9.19   The Second Review Conference reaffirmed the commitment of the States Parties to comply with the obligations that they have undertaken under Article I of the Convention.

9.20   The Second Review Conference underlined the obligations of all the States Parties to adopt in accordance with their constitutional processes the necessary measures to implement their obligations under the Convention, including the obligation to prohibit natural and legal persons within their territory and in any other place within their jurisdiction, from undertaking any activity prohibited to a State Party under the Convention.

9.21   The Second Review Conference also reaffirmed the continued relevance of the definitions contained in Article II of the Convention, which ensure the comprehensive nature of the prohibition of chemical weapons under the Convention.

9.22   The Second Review Conference considered the impact of developments in science and technology on the Convention's prohibitions. The definitions contained in Article II, in particular, of the terms "chemical weapons", "chemical weapons production facility", were found to adequately cover these developments and to provide for the application of the Convention's prohibitions to any toxic chemical, except where such a chemical is intended for purposes not prohibited by the Convention, and as long as the types and quantities involved are consistent with such purposes.

9.23   The Second Review Conference stressed the importance of the timely, complete, and accurate submission of the initial declarations required of each State Party under Article III. It noted that, by the end of 2007, all but 13 States Parties had submitted their initial declarations under Article III of the Convention. The Second Review Conference called upon those States Parties that had yet to submit their Article III declarations to do so as a matter of urgency. It requested the Secretariat to keep the Council informed of progress, and encouraged the Secretariat and the States Parties to provide assistance to present and future States Parties, if requested, in the preparation and submission of timely declarations and amendments.

9.24   The Second Review Conference reiterated the call of the First Review Conference upon the Council to reach agreement on the declaration criteria for former chemical weapons development facilities, required to be declared under the provisions of Article III, sub-paragraph 1(d), with a view towards promoting confidence among States Parties.

AGENDA ITEM 9(C)(II): DESTRUCTION OF CHEMICAL WEAPONS AND DESTRUCTION OR CONVERSION OF CHEMICAL WEAPONS PRODUCTION FACILITIES

9.25   The Second Review Conference reaffirmed that each State Party has undertaken to destroy chemical weapons it owns or possesses or which are located in any place under its jurisdiction or control and to destroy or convert any CWPFs in accordance with the provisions of the Convention.

9.26   The Second Review Conference reaffirmed that complete destruction of chemical weapons, and conversion or complete destruction of CWPFs, is essential for the realisation of the object and purpose of the Convention. The Second Review Conference also reaffirmed the importance of the obligation of the possessor States Parties to complete the destruction of their chemical weapons stockpiles within the final extended deadlines as established by the Conference at its Eleventh Session.

9.27   The Second Review Conference welcomed the statements of possessor States Parties reiterating their commitment to meeting the final, extended deadlines established under the Convention by the Eleventh Session of the Conference. The Second Review Conference noted the significant progress made so far by possessor States Parties in the destruction of chemical weapons, as well as the recent completion by Albania of the destruction of its entire stockpile and commended the progress made by those States Parties which are close to achieving complete destruction of their stockpiles.

9.28   The Second Review Conference noted that by 1 April 2008, over 38% of the total stockpiles of 70,000 tonnes of Category 1 chemical weapons initially declared by States Parties had been destroyed. However, the Second Review Conference expressed its concern that more than 60% of stockpiles still remained to be destroyed.

9.29   The Second Review Conference called upon the possessor States Parties to destroy their remaining chemical weapons within the extended final deadlines.

9.30   In this connection, the Second Review Conference noted that the obligation and responsibility for the destruction of chemical weapons lies solely with the possessor States Parties. At the same time it welcomed the assistance of other States Parties in providing support to destruction efforts, and reaffirmed the value of the continuation of such support offered by those States Parties that are in a position to do so.

9.31   The Second Review Conference underlined the responsibilities of the possessor States Parties to provide detailed annual chemical weapons destruction plans, updated as necessary, and of the policy-making organs to monitor their progress towards complete chemical weapons destruction in accordance with the provisions of the Convention, including their extended deadlines.

9.32   The Second Review Conference recalled the decision adopted by the Conference at its Eleventh Session on visits by representatives of the Council (C-11/DEC.20, dated 8 December 2006). In accordance with this decision, a visit to the Anniston chemical agent disposal facility in Alabama, United States, took place in October 2007 by the representatives of the Council. The Second Review Conference reaffirmed that nothing in visit reports shall in any way affect the obligation of possessor States Parties to destroy all their chemical weapons by the extended deadlines under the terms of the Convention.

9.33   The Second Review Conference recognised the decrease in the number of remaining Chemical Weapons storage facilities but reiterated the conclusion of the First Review Conference on the importance of possessor States Parties implementing appropriate measures to secure such storage facilities and to prevent movement of their chemical weapons out of the facilities, with the exception of removal for destruction or (in accordance with the provisions of the Convention) withdrawal of Schedule 1 chemicals for use for research, medical, pharmaceutical, or protective purposes.

9.34   The Second Review Conference also reaffirmed that declarations provided by States Parties under Article III, which establish a baseline for measuring progress in the elimination of chemical weapons stockpiles, need to be comprehensive and accurate. The Second Review Conference reminded States Parties to ensure that their declarations under Article III are updated in a timely manner, if and when new information becomes available. It called upon the Secretariat to continue rendering, when requested, technical assistance to States Parties on the preparation of declarations. The Second Review Conference also encouraged States Parties that are in a position to do so to assist other States Parties, at their request, in the preparation and submission of declarations and amendments.

9.35   The Second Review Conference reaffirmed the importance of the verification of chemical weapons stockpiles as well as of their destruction in accordance with the Convention. This is one of the main activities of the Secretariat and will remain so until stockpile destruction has been completed. It recalled the obligation of possessor States Parties to pay Article IV and V verification costs. It called on the relevant States Parties to pay assessed costs in full and without delay, and to avoid accumulating arrears in future.

9.36   The Second Review Conference reaffirmed the obligation to destroy or otherwise dispose of old chemical weapons in accordance with the Convention, and requested the Council, assisted by the Secretariat, to address the issue of new discoveries of old chemical weapons. It encouraged close cooperation among those States Parties concerned in relation to future discoveries of old or abandoned chemical weapons including over any necessary research and development to ensure the safe recovery and destruction of such weapons.

9.37   The Second Review Conference reaffirmed the undertaking of each State Party to destroy all chemical weapons it abandoned on the territory of another State Party in accordance with the provisions of the Convention. It welcomed the existing cooperation between territorial and abandoning States Parties, and noted with concern that a large amount of abandoned chemical weapons remain to be destroyed. The Second Review Conference called upon abandoning States Parties to make the fullest possible efforts to complete destruction as soon as possible with the appropriate cooperation provided by the territorial States Parties. It commended the active and positive role that has been played by the Secretariat in this process, and encouraged it to continue to play such a role in future.

9.38   The Second Review Conference reviewed progress in relation to the destruction or conversion of CWPFs as required by Part V of the Verification Annex. The Second Review Conference expressed its concern that full conversion or destruction of all facilities had not been completed within the deadlines set by the Convention. It also noted that additional CWPFs had been declared since the First Review Conference. The Second Review Conference urged all relevant States Parties to complete the destruction or conversion of such facilities as soon as possible, in accordance with the decisions of the Conference of the States Parties. The Second Review Conference requested the Council to continue to oversee completion of destruction or conversion.

9.39   The Second Review Conference recalled that, in accordance with the provisions of the Convention, converted facilities shall be no more capable of being reconverted into a CWPF than any other facility used for industrial, agricultural, research, medical, pharmaceutical, or other peaceful purposes. The Second Review Conference noted that States Parties with converted facilities are required to report annually on activities at those facilities and that converted facilities remain liable to on-site inspection, in accordance with paragraph 85 of Part V of the Verification Annex, for a period of 10 years after completion of certification by the Director-General of their conversion for purposes not prohibited.

9.40   Upon completion of the 10-year period following the completion of conversion, the Council shall decide on the nature of continued verification activities. The Second Review Conference reaffirmed that future planning of verification measures needs to take account of these requirements for the verification of converted CWPFs, and requested the Council to decide on the nature of continued verification at those facilities and to consider proposals for recommendations or decisions that may be needed.

AGENDA ITEM 9(C)(III): VERIFICATION ACTIVITIES OF THE OPCW

9.41   The verification system is one of the most important elements of the Convention. It provides for systematic verification with continuous on-site monitoring of the destruction of chemical weapons and systematic verification of the elimination of CWPFs. It also provides for the verification of activities not prohibited under the Convention.

9.42   The Second Review Conference noted with satisfaction that the OPCW has established a verification system that has been effective in meeting the requirements of the Convention and which continues to gain effectiveness and efficiency. It further noted that the verification system will need to continue to be improved in a manner consistent with the Convention in response to advances in science and technology. The Second Review Conference also recognised the continued need for the OPCW to have up-to-date verification technologies at its disposal.

9.43   The Second Review Conference noted that the Secretariat and the States Parties have acquired considerable experience with the conduct of more than 3000 inspections at over 1080 chemical weapons-related and industrial sites in 80 States Parties since the entry into force of the Convention. The Second Review Conference noted with satisfaction that no case of non-compliance had been brought to the attention of the Council.

9.44   The verification system of the Convention is based upon declarations from States Parties. The Second Review Conference therefore noted the importance of the timely and accurate submission of declarations in accordance with the Convention. The Second Review Conference noted the efforts made by the States Parties in collecting and updating declaration data and submitting this information to the Secretariat in accordance with Convention timelines, as well as continued improvements in the degree of standardisation of declaration data. It stressed that there is a need for further improvement in this area.

9.45   The Second Review Conference recognised the efforts of the Secretariat, consistent with its responsibilities under the Convention, to cooperate with the States Parties in ensuring that declarations submitted in accordance with the Convention are complete and accurate by, *inter alia*, clarifying ambiguities and discrepancies and providing technical assistance and technical evaluation to States Parties in the implementation of the provisions of the Convention. It encouraged the Secretariat to continue these efforts, in close consultation with the States Parties, and to provide appropriate assistance upon request to any State Party with a view to meeting its declaration obligations. The Second Review Conference also requested the Secretariat to ensure that the latest information provided by States Parties in their declarations is accurately captured, so that the most up to date information is used for planning inspections.

9.46   The Second Review Conference welcomed the progress made in introducing the Verification Information System, including the option of submitting declarations in electronic form. The Second Review Conference encouraged States Parties' National Authorities to avail themselves of this possibility. It requested the Secretariat to provide them, on request, with appropriate training and assistance. The Second Review Conference reiterated the need to ensure that confidential data is effectively protected at all times, in accordance with the requirements of the Convention.

9.47   The implementation by all States Parties of the standing arrangements required by the Convention for the conduct of inspections is important. Noting that some OPCW inspections still encountered difficulties in these areas, the Second Review Conference urged all States Parties to implement these measures without delay and in a manner fully consistent with the requirements of the Convention.

9.48   The Second Review Conference noted the progress made by the Secretariat in optimising verification procedures with the aim of increasing cost-effectiveness as well as the steps made by States Parties in this regard. It welcomed the constructive role that States Parties have played in this effort, and encouraged them to continue to cooperate with the Secretariat in identifying and implementing optimisation measures. It requested the Council to continue to monitor the optimisation process to ensure that the stringent verification requirements of the Convention are strictly preserved. It requested the Secretariat to continue to look for further improvements, particularly as additional chemical weapons destruction facilities come into operation in the years ahead, and also in light of the accumulated experience of the range of industrial inspections.

9.49   The Second Review Conference noted the experience gained as a result of the Secretariat's recent trial of sampling and analysis for verification purposes during Schedule 2 site inspections. The Second Review Conference welcomed the recent Note by the Director-General on this experience (S/688/2008, dated 10 April 2008), encouraged States Parties to review this carefully, and encouraged the Council to discuss this matter further, as appropriate.

9.50   The Second Review Conference requested the Council to resume, as a matter of priority, the consultations on the unresolved issues pertaining to the verification regime of the OPCW with the view of developing appropriate recommendations.

9.51   The Second Review Conference reaffirmed the importance of factual reporting by the Secretariat to the Council and the States Parties on verification results, in the interests of transparency and continued assurance of States Parties' compliance. It encouraged the Secretariat to continue its efforts to improve verification reporting and urged States Parties to avail themselves of this information, as well as availing themselves of their right to receive and examine declaration data from other States Parties, in accordance with the relevant provisions of the Convention.

AGENDA ITEM 9(C)(IV): ACTIVITIES NOT PROHIBITED UNDER THE CHEMICAL WEAPONS CONVENTION

9.52   The Second Review Conference reaffirmed the right of the States Parties, subject to the provisions of the Convention, to develop, produce, otherwise acquire, retain, transfer, and use toxic chemicals and their precursors for purposes not prohibited under the Convention. The provisions of Article VI shall be implemented in a manner which avoids hampering the economic or technological development of States Parties, and international cooperation in the field of chemical activities for purposes not prohibited under the Convention including the international exchange of scientific and technical information and chemicals and equipment for the production, processing or use of chemicals for purposes not prohibited under the Convention.

9.53   The Second Review Conference reaffirmed the obligation of the States Parties to adopt the necessary measures, including legislative and administrative steps, to ensure that toxic chemicals and their precursors are developed, produced, otherwise acquired, retained, transferred, or used within their territories or in any other places under their jurisdiction or control only for purposes not prohibited by the Convention.

9.54   The Second Review Conference noted that the Annex on Chemicals of the Convention clearly sets out the different levels of risk posed by scheduled chemicals to the Convention's object and purpose and the Verification Annex sets out distinctive verification regimes for different types of facilities. In this context, the Second Review Conference recalled that the selection of a particular facility or plant site for inspection shall take into account, besides the risk posed by the relevant chemical, *inter alia*, the characteristics of the facility and the nature of the activities carried out there. In this regard, the Second Review Conference further noted that:

(a)   Schedule 1 chemicals pose a high risk to the object and purpose of the Convention and Schedule 1 facilities shall be subject to systematic verification as required by paragraph 22 and paragraph 29 of Part VI of the Verification Annex.

(b)   Schedule 2 chemicals pose a significant risk to the object and purpose of the Convention and Schedule 2 facilities shall be subject to initial inspections and subsequent inspections as required by paragraph 14 of Part VII of the Verification Annex.

(c)   Schedule 3 chemicals poses otherwise a risk to the object and purpose of the Convention and Schedule 3 facilities shall be randomly selected for inspection as required by paragraph 14 of Part VIII of the Verification Annex.

(d)   Other Chemical Production Facilities shall be randomly selected for inspection as required by paragraph 11 of Part IX of the Verification Annex.

9.55   The Second Review Conference noted that between the entry into force of the Convention and 31 December 2007, the following inspections had been carried out:

(a) 182 Schedule 1 inspections were conducted, at an average frequency of 6.7 inspections per declared facility over a period of 10 years;

(b) 405 Schedule 2 inspections were conducted, at an average frequency of 2.5 inspections per facility over a period of 10 years;

(c) 218 Schedule 3 inspections were conducted, covering 50.2% of declared inspectable facilities; and

(d) in total, 521 other chemical production facilities (OCPFs) producing discrete organic chemicals (around 11.4% of the inspectable total) had been inspected after OCPF inspections commenced in 2000, as provided for by the Convention.

9.56   The Second Review Conference recalled the decision taken by the Council at its Twenty-Sixth Meeting to undertake discussions, under the industry cluster, in 2007, with the assistance of relevant experts of the Secretariat and States Parties, on the main issues related to the implementation of the verification regime established by Article VI of the Convention, including, *inter alia*, the frequency of inspections of the different categories of the facilities to be inspected as required by the Convention. The Second Review Conference urged States Parties to continue their ongoing discussions concerning the question of frequency of inspections of all plant sites.

9.57   The Second Review Conference underlined the need for comprehensive, effective, and efficient verification and recalled that such verification shall avoid undue intrusion into the States Parties chemical activities for purposes not prohibited under the Convention. The Second Review Conference noted that the Article VI verification system had been strengthened since the First Review Conference: the number of inspections of chemical industry facilities had been increased, further experience had been gathered in conducting such inspections effectively, and important decisions had been taken on industry declarations. The Second Review Conference stressed that there is still room for improvement and therefore efforts to strengthen the implementation of the Article VI verification system should continue, including increasing its efficiency and effectiveness.

9.58   The Second Review Conference noted that the Director-General, in his Note (WGRC-2/S/1, dated 27 November 2007 and Corr.1, dated 25 January 2008) refers to developments in science and technology since the First Review Conference and requested the Council to consider these issues.

9.59   The Second Review Conference encouraged States Parties to share their experiences about the most effective ways to implement the Convention, and to cooperate in the resolution of issues they may encounter in their implementation of these provisions and measures. It encouraged the Secretariat to continue to provide technical assistance to States Parties, on request, for the submission of Article VI declarations, the receipt of OPCW inspections, and other technical questions that may arise in the implementation of provisions related to activities not prohibited under the Convention. It also encouraged further development of existing fora, such as the annual, regional and subregional meetings of National Authorities, to facilitate exchanges on specific aspects of implementation including the early identification of annual themes.

9.60   The Second Review Conference stressed the importance of the timely submission of initial declarations and annual declarations in an accurate and complete manner by all States Parties under Article VI (facilities, aggregate national data, and notifications and declarations of transfers of Schedule 1 chemicals) in accordance with the timelines in the Convention. It encouraged the Secretariat to continue to provide support to States Parties in connection with the preparation and submission of declarations. It stressed the importance of the Secretariat's continuing to report to the Council in accordance with the decision of the Council (EC-51/DEC.1, dated 27 November 2007), with the aim of allowing the Secretariat to efficiently and effectively carry out its verification activities.

9.61   The Second Review Conference encouraged the Secretariat to continue to develop and periodically update existing databases on declarable chemicals, under the guidance of the Council, thus providing practical help to companies for identification of declarable chemicals. It noted the continued importance of providing practical help to States Parties and industry to enable them to identify all declarable facilities and activities. It also expressed appreciation for the ongoing project of the OPCW with the European Chemical Industry Council (CEFIC) aimed at extending the Chemical Abstracts Service (CAS) registry numbers to all declarable chemicals. It requested that, as recommended by the Scientific Advisory Board, the OPCW Declaration Handbook should provide references to the various CAS numbers corresponding to the entries in the Schedules.

9.62   The Second Review Conference recalled the decision of the First Conference of States Parties requesting States Parties to implement, on a voluntary basis, the recommendation of the Conference at its First Session (C-I/DEC. 38, dated 16 May 1997) that they inform the Secretariat when plants or plant sites that have been declared as undertaking activities in relation to Schedule 2 or Schedule 3 chemicals cease to do so. It further recalled that the First Review Conference had requested the Council to consider whether to require such submissions from States Parties, and noted that the Council had not yet taken up this issue. In this regard, the Second Review Conference requested the Secretariat to include, in the Declaration Handbook, a standard form for the submission of such notifications.

9.63   The Second Review Conference noted with concern that the issue of low concentrations in relation to Schedule 2A/2A* chemicals has not yet been resolved. It urged the Council to resume work promptly, with the support of the Secretariat, towards the earliest resolution of the issue in accordance with the requirements of the Convention (Verification Annex, Part VII, paragraph 5).

9.64   The Second Review Conference recalled that the Council had at its Fiftieth Session taken note of the modification announced by the Director-General to the Secretariat's OCPF site-selection methodology as reflected in the Note (S/641/2007, dated 25 May 2007, and Corr.1, dated 4 June 2007). The Council acknowledged that it will only be an interim measure. The Second Review Conference reiterated the request made by the Council for early resumption of consultations on the OCPF site selection methodology with a view to reaching a decision by States Parties, in accordance with Part IX, paragraphs 11 and 25, of the Verification Annex to the Convention. The Second Review Conference noted the Council's request to the Director-General to report to it on the performance of the modified methodology at the end of the first year of its implementation.

9.65   In relation to declaration and inspection of OCPFs (Part IX of Verification Annex of the Convention) the Second Review Conference noted the desirability of directing inspections towards facilities of greater relevance to the object and purpose of the Convention and of removing irrelevant facilities from the declarations and inspections. The Second Review Conference requested the Director-General to examine the options for achieving the above objectives without imposition of any additional declaration obligations and strictly in accordance with the relevant provisions of Part IX of the Verification Annex of the Convention and to submit his findings to the Council for its consideration.

9.66   The Second Review Conference noted the Director-General's view expressed in RC-2/S/1*, dated 31 March 2008, concerning the present level of assurance with respect to OCPFs. The Second Review Conference confirmed that any changes in the frequency of OCPF inspections, if required, should take into account any refinements to the OCPF inspection regime or improvements in site selection methodology, and should be based on a thorough discussion and a decision of the policy-making organs.

9.67   The Second Review Conference concluded that the allocation of resources to the verification regime for the chemical industry needed to be further optimised, taking due account of the nature of the declared facilities, the inspection experience gathered, developments in science and technology, and based on the principles set out in Article VI. To this end, it encouraged the Council and the Secretariat to work toward continued progress in those areas identified by paragraph 7.71 of the Report of the First Review Conference (RC-1/5, dated 9 May 2003), as well as:

(a) improving OPCW classified verification reporting by providing more information (consistent with confidentiality requirements) about sites inspected and issues that have arisen; through more precise classification of portions of text; and by making charts and tables available in spreadsheet form to facilitate analysis by States Parties;

(b) improving the submission and handling of industry declarations (in particular, through encouraging the submission of declaration data in electronic form). In this connection, the Second Review Conference encouraged States Parties to develop national projects that would allow the submission of declarations in electronic form and encouraged the Secretariat to explore what support it might be able to provide to States Parties wishing to move to electronic submissions; and

(c) consideration of the report to be produced by the Secretariat on the further development of the OCAD.

9.68   It also noted that an increasing number of States Parties had put in place the necessary measures on transfers of scheduled chemicals.

9.69   In relation to transfers of scheduled chemicals to or from States not Party, the Second Review Conference recalled the prohibitions on any such transfers of Schedule 1 chemicals and, from 29 April 2000, of Schedule 2 chemicals. It also noted that an increasing number of States Parties had put in place the necessary measures on transfers of scheduled chemicals. It urged all States Parties to implement the necessary legislative and administrative measures, and to share experiences about the implementation of these provisions.

9.70   The Second Review Conference considered the decision on measures regarding the transfers of Schedule 3 chemicals to States not Party to the Convention (EC-47/DEC.8, dated 8 November 2006) and reaffirmed this decision.

9.71   The Second Review Conference expressed concerns that the discrepancies between transfers declared by States Parties are of considerable magnitude and encouraged the continuing consultation efforts under the cluster of chemical industry and other Article VI issues. The Second Review Conference requested the Secretariat to continue working with the States Parties concerned on analysing persisting discrepancies between exporting and importing States Parties, with a view to identifying the factors that cause problems, and to recommend possible solutions.

AGENDA ITEM 9(C)(V): NATIONAL IMPLEMENTATION MEASURES

9.72   The Second Review Conference reaffirmed that the full and effective national implementation of the obligations under the Convention is essential for the realisation of the object and purpose of the Convention.

9.73   National implementation also contributes in an important manner to the Convention's ability to deal with changes in the security environment or in science and technology that may affect its operation. It contributes to meeting new challenges, including the threat or possible use of chemical weapons, as defined by the Convention, by non-state actors such as terrorists.

9.74   The Second Review Conference welcomed the significant progress made in the implementation of Article VII since the First Review Conference and commended the efforts of the States Parties, the Director-General, and the Secretariat in assisting with national implementation of the Convention through the Article VII Action Plan and follow-up decisions. The Second Review Conference encouraged the States Parties and the Secretariat to continue to support the implementation of the decision of the Conference (C-12/DEC.9, dated 9 November 2007) to achieve full implementation of Article VII obligations. In this connection, the Second Review Conference noted that seven States Parties have yet to designate or establish National Authorities. It reaffirmed the need to continue efforts, including encouragement and cooperation, to secure the designation or establishment of National Authorities by all States Parties without further delay.

9.75   The Second Review Conference highlighted the need for a comprehensive approach to the enactment of implementing legislation in line with each State Party's constitutional requirements, to filling gaps in legislation, and to ensuring that legislation reflects fully the Convention's prohibitions. The Second Review Conference expressed concern that 10% of submissions under Article VII, paragraph 5, are still outstanding. The Second Review Conference expressed concern that 101 States Parties, including over half of the original Parties to the Convention at its entry into force, have not yet fully enacted comprehensive implementing legislation. It recognised that 44 out of these 101 States Parties have informed the OPCW of some legislative or administrative measures taken to implement the Convention and that a further 45 States Parties have informed the OPCW that they are currently developing draft legislation.

9.76   The adoption of implementing legislation in accordance with each State Party's constitutional processes (including penal legislation, and other measures necessary to implement the Convention) is an important responsibility of each State Party. In light of the success of the Article VII Action Plan in assisting States Parties towards full implementation, the Second Review Conference recalled that the Conference at its Twelfth Session had requested the Council to submit to its next session a report to be prepared by the Secretariat along with its own recommendations, as appropriate, for consideration concerning those States Parties that have not submitted any information in accordance with paragraph 1 of that decision (C-12/DEC 9). The Second Review Conference recognised the distinctive characteristics of different States Parties' legislative processes in the context of the implementation of Article VII.

9.77   The Second Review Conference reaffirmed that raising the awareness of all stakeholders about the prohibitions and requirements of the Convention would benefit national implementation. The Second Review Conference noted that voluntary measures by relevant industry and scientific communities to promote responsible conduct can also help to guard against chemical weapons, as defined in the Convention, being used.

9.78   The Second Review Conference welcomed the efforts made by States Parties to assist each other upon request in their national implementation measures. It noted again the value of bilateral assistance and networking within and among regions, especially for States Parties with limited resources who may need particular assistance. It encouraged strengthened learning, communication, and mutual cooperation through further engagement by the Secretariat, by National Authorities, and as appropriate, with parliamentary representatives. The Second Review Conference encouraged the Director-General to make further recommendations in this regard to the Council as necessary.

9.79   The Second Review Conference noted with appreciation the ongoing programme for implementation support developed by the Secretariat, which provides technical assistance and technical evaluation in the implementation of the provisions of the Convention to States Parties upon request. The Second Review Conference encouraged States Parties and the Secretariat to continue to consult in order to enhance further the utility and effectiveness of these programmes, and it requested the Secretariat to evaluate the programme and report to the Council.

9.80   Having reviewed implementation of the Action Plan and subsequent decisions, in particular the decision of the Twelfth Session of the Conference (C-12/DEC.9), the Second Review Conference:

(a) Reaffirmed the approach contained in C-12/DEC.9 and called upon States Parties and the Secretariat to continue along those lines;

(b) Requested the Secretariat to keep current a progress report on the external server of the OPCW; and,

(c) Requested the Conference at its annual sessions to continue to review progress towards the full and effective national implementation of obligations under the Convention and to encourage further progress.

AGENDA ITEM 9(C)(VI): CONSULTATIONS, COOPERATION, AND FACT-FINDING

9.81 The Second Review Conference reaffirmed the commitment of the States Parties to consult and cooperate directly among themselves or through the OPCW, or by using other appropriate international procedures, including those within the framework of the United Nations and in accordance with its Charter, on any matter that may be raised relating to the object and purpose of the Convention or the implementation of its provisions in accordance with the Convention.

9.82 The Second Review Conference reaffirmed that, without prejudice to the right of any State Party to request a challenge inspection in line with Article IX of the Convention, States Parties should, whenever possible, first make every effort to clarify and resolve, through the exchange of information and consultation among themselves, any matter that might cause doubt about compliance with the Convention, or which gives rise to concerns about a related matter that may be considered ambiguous.

9.83 The Second Review Conference also emphasised the value and importance of bilateral consultations to clarify and to resolve issues regarding possible non-compliance with the provisions of the Convention. The Second Review Conference encouraged the States Parties to make full use of this bilateral consultation mechanism.

9.84 The Second Review Conference noted with satisfaction that the Council had received no clarification requests under paragraphs 3 to 7 of Article IX since entry into force. It reiterated the fact that the Convention provides for all necessary arrangements to receive and deal expeditiously with any clarification request that a State Party may decide to submit in accordance with the applicable provisions of Article IX.

9.85 The Second Review Conference also noted with satisfaction that no challenge inspection or investigation of alleged use had been requested since the entry into force of the Convention. It reaffirmed the right of any State Party to request an on-site challenge inspection, in accordance with the Convention, for the sole purpose of clarifying and resolving any questions concerning possible non-compliance with the provisions of the Convention.

9.86 The Second Review Conference also reaffirmed the right and obligation of any inspected State Party to make every reasonable effort to demonstrate its compliance, its obligation to provide access (in accordance with provisions of the Convention) within the requested site for the sole purpose of establishing facts relevant to possible non-compliance, and its right to take measures to protect sensitive installations and to prevent disclosure of confidential information and data not related to the Convention.

9.87 The Second Review Conference recalled the provisions of the Convention intended to avoid abuse of the mechanism for challenge inspections and expressed its confidence that the States Parties will continue to uphold the value of the challenge-inspection mechanism for compliance and compliance assurance, while at the same time, keeping any request for a challenge inspection by States Parties within the scope of the Convention. States Parties shall refrain from requests that are unfounded or abusive in order not to undermine the integrity of the Convention.

9.88 The Second Review Conference noted that a number of issues related to challenge inspections still remained to be resolved and that their resolution is important for challenge inspections. It requested the Council to continue its deliberations in order to resolve them expeditiously.

9.89   The Second Review Conference noted the preparations that the Secretariat had undertaken since entry into force in order to respond swiftly and effectively to any request for a challenge inspection or investigation of alleged use. It recalled with appreciation the support provided by States Parties for challenge inspection exercises.

9.90   The Second Review Conference requested the Secretariat to continue to maintain a high standard of readiness to conduct a challenge inspection or investigation of alleged use in accordance with the provisions of the Convention, *inter alia*, through the use of tabletop exercises and mock inspections, as well as keeping the Council informed about its readiness and reporting any problems that may arise in relation to maintaining the necessary level of readiness to conduct a challenge inspection. The Second Review Conference requested the Secretariat to maintain competence in the light of scientific and technological developments.

AGENDA ITEM 9(C)(VII): ASSISTANCE AND PROTECTION AGAINST CHEMICAL WEAPONS

9.91   The Second Review Conference re-emphasised the continuing relevance and importance of the provisions of Article X of the Convention and welcomed the activities of the OPCW in relation to assistance and protection against chemical weapons. It recognised that the assistance available under Article X could be a motivating factor for states to join the Convention. It recalled the definition of assistance contained in paragraph 1 of Article X and reaffirmed the right of States Parties to conduct research into, develop, produce, acquire, transfer, or use means of protection against chemical weapons for purposes not prohibited under the Convention.

9.92   The Second Review Conference also reaffirmed the undertaking of the States Parties to provide assistance through the OPCW and their undertaking to facilitate - as well as their right to participate in - the fullest possible exchange of equipment, material, and scientific and technological information concerning means of protection against chemical weapons. The Second Review Conference welcomed the progress that had been made on Article X since the First Review Conference but noted that there was scope for further efforts both by Member States and the Secretariat in order to achieve and maintain the high level of readiness of the OPCW.

9.93   The Second Review Conference appreciated the Secretariat's efforts in providing expert advice to States Parties that wish to establish or further develop their emergency-response capacity. The Second Review Conference also welcomed the effectiveness and efficiency of the increased focus on making full use of regional and subregional capacities and expertise, including taking advantage of training centres. The Second Review Conference called on the Secretariat to evaluate the effectiveness of current programmes undertaken under Article X and to assess to what extent and how efficiently they meet the current and future needs of States Parties.

9.94   The Second Review Conference reaffirmed concerns expressed at the First Review Conference that chemical facilities may become subject to attacks or other incidents that could lead to the release or theft of toxic chemicals. The Second Review Conference welcomed the fact that some States Parties had taken measures to minimise such risks and encouraged States Parties to exchange experiences and discuss related issues. It noted the value of Article X in this respect and the role of the OPCW as a forum for consultation and cooperation among the States Parties. The Second Review Conference recognised the need for close cooperation with other relevant international organisations and agencies active in this field.

9.95   The Second Review Conference, noting the possibility of the use of chemical weapons, as defined by the Convention, by non-state actors such as terrorists, the Second Review

Conference underlined the importance of the implementation of Article X in this regard by the States Parties and the Secretariat.

9.96   The Second Review Conference recalled that the Conference at its Ninth Session had adopted a format for States Parties to provide information to the Secretariat annually on national programmes for protective purposes in accordance with paragraph 4 of Article X (C-9/DEC.10, dated 30 November 2004). The Second Review Conference welcomed the progress made in this area but noted with concern that the number of submissions under paragraph 4 of Article X by States Parties since the entry into force of the Convention remained low. It noted that there were 75 such declarations in 2006 but only 62 in 2007.

9.97   Recalling States Parties' obligation to provide information on their national programmes for protective purposes, which is intended to increase transparency and build confidence among States Parties, and bearing in mind the potential relevance of such information for the coordination of assistance and protection among States Parties, the Second Review Conference urged all States Parties, particularly those that have not yet done so, to make their annual submissions of information in a timely fashion, and requested the Secretariat to assist States Parties with the timely completion of their submissions.

9.98   The Second Review Conference noted the progress made on setting up the OPCW data bank on protection and encouraged the Secretariat to update the information available on it regularly concerning assistance, protection equipment and knowledge offered by States Parties. The Second Review Conference requested the Secretariat to report periodically to the Council on the content of the data bank and its use.

9.99   The Second Review Conference requested the Secretariat to review and keep up to date its current lists of experts, both from within the Secretariat and from States Parties (including those in the Protection Network). This would enable it to ensure that it has a sufficient range of relevant expertise to call upon to provide advice and assist States Parties, upon request, in developing their protective capacity against chemical weapons, pursuant to Article X paragraph 5, and/or to participate in investigations of alleged use pursuant to the Verification Annex, Part XI, paragraph 7.

9.100   The Second Review Conference requested the Secretariat to make proposals to the Council on how to make best use of these resources, taking into account the options for assistance and protection made possible by advances in science and technology.

9.101   The Second Review Conference noted with appreciation the offers by States Parties, in accordance with paragraph 7 of Article X, of assistance in the event of the use or threat of use of chemical weapons, as well as national contributions to the voluntary fund for assistance, while also noting that the overall number of assistance offers, bilateral agreements, or contributions to the voluntary fund by States Parties still fall short of the requirements of Article X.

9.102   The Second Review Conference urged all States Parties that have yet to make offers of assistance to the OPCW to do so as required by paragraph 7 of Article X. The Second Review Conference also encouraged those States Parties that have made offers to ensure that they are up to date. It requested the Secretariat to evaluate the assistance offers already made in order to identify complementarities and synergies and to engage with States Parties to identify what further offers can be made to help optimise the use of OPCW resources.

9.103   The Second Review Conference requested the Secretariat to keep the policy-making organs informed about the status of pledges for assistance by States Parties and about any problems requiring attention and resolution. It also noted the necessity of regional coordination in speeding up response mechanisms and welcomed the Secretariat's efforts for capacity building at a regional and subregional level. In this connection, it welcomed the new focus on regional and subregional training programmes and encouraged the

Secretariat to build on the experience gained from such programmes as the three-year training project in Central Asia. It also encouraged the Secretariat to maintain the flexibility to address capacity building for public events where the consequence of chemical attack could be considerable for States Parties. It emphasised the usefulness of the annual report on the status of implementation of Article X in keeping the Council informed of progress, and encouraged greater follow-up to assess and build on the results of these efforts.

9.104   The Second Review Conference noted that at its Twelfth Session the Conference stressed the importance of achieving and maintaining a high level of readiness of the Secretariat, as well as States Parties, with respect to providing timely and needed assistance and protection against the use or threat of use of chemical weapons, and that it had requested the Council to conduct intensive deliberations to develop measures for emergency assistance to States Parties, including with regard to the victims of the use of chemical weapons, as provided for in Article X of the Convention.

9.105   The Second Review Conference stressed the importance of investigations of alleged use or threat of use of chemical weapons involving States Parties. For such situations, the OPCW must have the capacity and be ready at all times to investigate the need for follow-on action by the OPCW, as well as to facilitate the delivery of assistance. In this context, the Second Review Conference noted the Scientific Advisory Board's work on the analysis of bio-medical samples and requested the Director-General to present a proposal to develop this capability as foreseen by the Council at its Forty-Fourth Session (EC-44/2, dated 17 March 2006).

9.106   The Second Review Conference noted that, since the First Review Conference, the Secretariat had taken steps towards the implementation of the First Review Conference's recommendations with regard to an assistance response mechanism and requested the Council to monitor further development of an Assistance Response System to facilitate responses to requests for assistance and protection; had developed and trained the Assistance, Coordination, and Assessment Team (ACAT); and had participated in several field exercises with different international organisations. The Second Review Conference noted the importance of exercises to ensure effective coordination with States Parties and other international agencies in an emergency-response situation, and urged the Secretariat to apply the lessons learned from them and to keep the Council updated on this matter.

9.107   In this connection, the Second Review Conference reaffirmed three principles highlighted in paragraph 7.100 of the Report of the First Review Conference (RC-1/5, dated 9 May 2003).

9.108   The Second Review Conference requested the Conference of the States Parties to ensure the availability of adequate resources to be placed at the disposal of the Director-General to enable him to take emergency measures of assistance to victims of use of chemical weapons in accordance with paragraph 11 of Article X.

9.109   The Second Review Conference encouraged States Parties to make equipment related to the means of protection against the use of chemical weapons available, without undue restrictions, to other States Parties.

AGENDA ITEM 9(C)(VIII): ECONOMIC AND TECHNOLOGICAL DEVELOPMENT

9.110   The Second Review Conference re-emphasised the importance of the provisions of Article XI of the Convention on the economic and technological development of States Parties and recalled that the full, effective and non-discriminatory implementation of Article XI is essential for the realisation of the object and purpose of the Convention.

9.111   The Second Review Conference reaffirmed that the provisions of the Convention shall be implemented in a manner that avoids hampering the economic or technological development of States Parties and international cooperation in the field of chemical activities for purposes not prohibited under the Convention, including the international exchange of scientific and technical information, and chemicals and equipment for the production, processing, or use of chemicals for purposes not prohibited under the Convention.

9.112 The Second Review Conference reaffirmed that States Parties have the obligation, subject to the provisions of the Convention and without prejudice to the principles and applicable rules of international law, to facilitate, and have the right to participate in the fullest possible exchange of chemicals, equipment, and scientific and technical information relating to the development and application of chemistry for purposes not prohibited under the Convention.

9.113 The Second Review Conference reaffirmed the provision of Article XI that the States Parties shall, *inter alia*:

(a) not maintain among themselves any restrictions, including those in international agreements, incompatible with the obligations undertaken under the Convention, which would restrict or impede trade and the development and promotion of scientific and technological knowledge in the field of chemistry for industrial, agricultural, research, medical, pharmaceutical, and other peaceful purposes;

(b) not use the Convention as grounds for applying any measures other than those provided for, or permitted, under the Convention nor any other international agreement for pursuing an objective inconsistent with the Convention; and

(c) undertake to review their existing national regulations in the field of trade in chemicals in order to render them consistent with the object and purpose of the Convention.

9.114 The Second Review Conference called upon the States Parties to fully implement these provisions of the Convention. It also urged the Council to continue its facilitation efforts to reach early agreement on the issue of the full implementation of Article XI, taking into account earlier and recent proposals submitted.

9.115 The Second Review Conference stressed the importance of the international cooperation programmes of the OPCW. While noting the substantial strengthening of Article XI-related programmes and the growth in the budget of the International Cooperation and Assistance Division since the First Review Conference, it also noted the increase in the membership of the OPCW and the increase in demand of international cooperation and assistance programmes for capacity building. In this regard, the Second Review Conference also called for the adequate funding for the OPCW's international cooperation and assistance programmes, through the regular budget and voluntary funding.

9.116 The Second Review Conference stressed the importance of a focussed and well-evaluated programme of international cooperation and assistance to the promotion of the object and purpose of the Convention as a whole, including its contribution to universality. In this context, the Second Review Conference:

(a) underlined its commitment to promote international cooperation for purposes not prohibited in the field of chemical activities, and its desire to promote free trade in chemicals as well as international cooperation, and the fullest possible exchange of scientific and technical information in the field of chemical activities;

(b) stressed again the importance of cooperation projects among States Parties in areas related to the purposes not prohibited. The OPCW should continue to facilitate the provision, upon request, of expert advice on the peaceful uses of chemistry to and among States Parties;

(c) underlined the importance of assistance and national capacity building in the field of chemical activities for purposes not prohibited, particularly as it applies to the implementation of the Convention, and recalled that an important component of these activities involves facilitating the provision of direct support on-site to assist National Authorities with specific implementation tasks, whether bilaterally, regionally, or through or by the OPCW, and whether by experts from other States Parties or from the Secretariat. The Secretariat, in consultation with States Parties, is requested to continue to review and develop relevant programmes for requesting States Parties.

(d) noted the benefits of the existing International Cooperation and Assistance programmes, as well as programmes focussed on capacity building and transfer of skills, and recalled that all OPCW programmes should be improved through evaluation of their effectiveness with a view to ensuring that they are responsive to the needs of beneficiary States Parties, in order to optimise resource use and effectiveness. This should involve consultations between the States Parties and the Secretariat, aimed at achieving a clear understanding of the competencies available, the needs of the States Parties, and the requirements of the Convention. The Secretariat should develop further its own capacity to measure the quality and impact of all the OPCW's international cooperation and assistance programmes;

(e) recognised the need for ensuring the provision of adequate resources and concluded that decisions on budgetary allocations for international cooperation should be based on an objective assessment of States Parties' needs and how the programme addresses these needs, bearing in mind overall resource constraints;

(f) stressed the importance of coordination between the Secretariat and States Parties in a position to provide voluntary contributions, in terms of both financial and human resources. In this context, the Second Review Conference also welcomed the wide range of voluntary contributions by States Parties individually or collectively;

(g) emphasised how important it is that the OPCW coordinates its activities with those of other relevant international and regional organisations as appropriate, in order to build on existing competencies, develop synergies, and avoid duplication of efforts. The OPCW should further integrate itself as a partner in the establishment of international programme coordination mechanisms in the field of international cooperation, assistance, and capacity building related the peaceful uses of chemistry;

(h) encouraged the OPCW to continue to develop relations and partnerships as appropriate with relevant regional and international organisations including international organisations related to chemical safety, chemical industry associations, the private sector and civil society, in order to promote universality and awareness of the objectives and purposes of the Convention. The Second Review Conference welcomed the interest of such groups in the work of the OPCW, including the active engagement of chemical industry.

9.117 The Second Review Conference also recalled the decision of the Conference at its Twelfth Session (C-12/DEC.10, dated 9 November 2007) to request the States Parties and the Secretariat to continue actively to implement its previous decision at its Tenth Session (C-10/DEC.14, dated 11 November 2005) on the full implementation of Article XI, which identified steps towards the full implementation of Article XI to foster international cooperation for peaceful purposes in the field of chemical activities and requests and to request the Council to continue its intensive consultations at regular intervals to develop concrete measures within an agreed framework to ensure the full implementation of Article XI, and to report back to the Conference at its Thirteenth Session for consideration.

9.118 The Second Review Conference called upon States Parties, especially developed countries, to increase, their scientific and technological cooperation, with developing countries, in the peaceful uses of chemistry on a non-discriminatory basis.

AGENDA ITEM 9(C)(IX): ARTICLES XII TO XV AND FINAL CLAUSES

9.119   The Second Review Conference reaffirmed the continued relevance of the provisions of Articles XII to XV.

AGENDA ITEM 9(C)(X): THE PROTECTION OF CONFIDENTIAL INFORMATION

9.120   The Second Review Conference reiterated the importance of the protection of OPCW confidential information, in accordance with the provisions of the Convention in view of the fact that the verification provisions of the Convention require States Parties to disclose potentially sensitive information to the Secretariat. Confidence in the OPCW's ability to protect confidential information is thus essential. The Second Review Conference noted that the verification provisions of the Convention require States Parties to disclose potentially sensitive information to the Secretariat through declarations and inspections.

9.121   The Second Review Conference emphasised the important role of the Director-General in ensuring the protection of confidential information, as well as the responsibility of each staff member of the Secretariat to comply with all rules and regulations pertaining to the protection of confidential information. Proper conduct on the part of staff is essential to the effective implementation of a robust confidentiality regime, and the Second Review Conference underlined the need for encouraging staff awareness of relevant procedures, as well as adequate and sustained training within existing resources.

9.122   The Second Review Conference stressed the importance of the procedures to be applied in cases of alleged breaches of confidentiality. It reaffirmed the important role of the Confidentiality Commission in settling any dispute related to breaches or alleged breaches of confidentiality involving both a State Party and the OPCW, while noting with satisfaction that the Commission has had no such disputes brought before it since entry into force.

9.123   The Second Review Conference recalled that the First Review Conference had urged States Parties expeditiously to provide details of their handling of the information provided to them by the OPCW. The Second Review Conference noted a significant increase in the number of States Parties providing the details required since the First Review Conference but again urged all States Parties to provide this information expeditiously.

9.124   The First Review Conference encouraged the Secretariat and the States Parties to review their respective practices in assigning levels of classification to such information, and if possible, and in accordance with the States Party's confidentiality procedures, to adjust the classification level they assign to such information, in order to increase work efficiency and ensure the smooth functioning of the system to protect confidentiality. The Second Review Conference welcomed the improvements made in implementing the confidentiality regime since the First Review Conference, including the completion of the Confidentiality Supplement in 2006, which is to be issued with the next version of the Declarations Handbook, and the adoption of the latest version of the ISO information security management standard (ISO 27001).

9.125   The Second Review Conference noted that no agreement had yet been reached on the issue of developing and implementing guidelines regarding the long-term handling of confidential information. It recommended that the Secretariat make a report to the Council proposing solutions before the next Conference.

AGENDA ITEM 9(D): THE GENERAL FUNCTIONING OF THE ORGANISATION FOR THE PROHIBITION OF CHEMICAL WEAPONS

9.126   The Second Review Conference noted with satisfaction that the OPCW has matured in the 11 years since the Convention's entry into force and has developed into a well-established multilateral organisation for achieving the object and purpose of the Convention. The Second Review Conference reaffirmed that the work of the policy-making organs is important for the OPCW's effective functioning, which contributes directly to the aims of the Convention. The Second Review Conference welcomed the way in which the policy-making organs have developed a sustainable pattern of work since the First Review Conference and stressed again the need for all States Parties to participate fully in their activities.

9.127   The Second Review Conference reaffirmed that decision making by consensus by the policy-making organs plays an important role in achieving common goals and in ensuring strong support for and preserving the integrity of decisions. It noted the need for focussed agendas for both the formal meetings and intersessional consultations of the Council in order for it to take decisions effectively. The Second Review Conference reaffirmed the importance of the Chairperson and Vice-Chairpersons of the Council being engaged with the work of the facilitation groups. While noting improvements since the First Review Conference, the Second Review Conference also reaffirmed the importance of continued efforts by the Secretariat to provide documents in a timely fashion.

9.128   The Second Review Conference noted the Director-General's initiative regarding the OPCW Programme to Strengthen Cooperation with Africa with a view to assisting States Parties with their implementation of the Convention. It called upon the Secretariat to implement the Programme as soon as possible as well as to provide feedback on a regular basis on the activities and progress made in this regard.

9.129   The Second Review Conference underlined the importance for the OPCW of keeping abreast of the developments in science and technology in order to achieve the object and purpose of the Convention.

9.130   The Scientific Advisory Board continues to play a valuable role in enabling the Director-General to render specialised advice to the policy-making organs and the States Parties in areas of science and technology relevant to the Convention.

9.131   The Second Review Conference concluded that consideration should be given, through negotiations in the regular budget process, to meeting the cost of two meetings of the Scientific Advisory Board and two meetings of temporary working groups per year. It noted that, based on current activity levels, this would also still require additional funding through voluntary contributions to the Scientific Advisory Board trust fund.

9.132   The Second Review Conference encouraged States Parties generally to consider supporting the work of the Scientific Advisory Board by making voluntary contributions to the Scientific Advisory Board trust fund.

9.133   The Second Review Conference requested the Council, through a meeting of governmental experts open to all States Parties, to consider the report by the Scientific Advisory Board which the Director-General had forwarded to the Second Review Conference.

9.134   The Second Review Conference, in order to facilitate consideration of the specialised advice the Director-General provides to the policy-making organs and to States Parties on the basis of the advice he receives from the Scientific Advisory Board, invited the Director-General to provide considered advice to the Council on how to enhance the interaction between the Scientific Advisory Board and States Parties as well as the policy-making organs, making best use of governmental experts.

9.135   In reviewing the functioning of other subsidiary advisory bodies, the Second Review Conference noted the valuable contributions to the work of the OPCW made by the Advisory Body for Administrative and Financial Matters (ABAF) and stressed the importance of its membership, which comprises experts of recognised standing.

9.136   The Second Review Conference welcomed recent experience of interactions between National Authorities and other stakeholders in the OPCW from governments and the private sector. It underlined the importance of the involvement of all stakeholders, including the chemical industry and the scientific community in the promotion of the Convention's goals and in supporting national implementation. It encouraged the development of such cooperation, with due regard to the role and responsibilities of States Parties and their National Authorities, on the broadest possible geographical basis.

9.137   The Second Review Conference reaffirmed the autonomous and independent status of the OPCW and took cognisance of the resolutions of the United Nations on combating terrorism. The Second Review Conference, in this regard, invited States Parties to consult and cooperate both bilaterally and regionally on ways to prevent terrorists from acquiring and/or using chemical weapons. The Second Review Conference also took note of the work of the OPCW Open-Ended Working Group on Terrorism.

9.138   The Second Review Conference recognised the continued dedication, competence, and integrity of Secretariat staff under the leadership of the Director-General. It noted that the OPCW has at its disposal qualified and trained staff, equipment, and procedures fit for the tasks it must fulfil under the Convention. Cognisant of the implementation of the tenure policy, it reaffirmed that the paramount consideration in the employment of staff remains the necessity of securing the highest standards of efficiency, competence, and integrity, while paying due regard to the importance of recruiting on as wide a geographical basis as possible. The Second Review Conference requested the Director-General, in his recruitment of staff, to pay special attention to regions and countries that are under-represented. It also recognised the implementation of certain improvements for the operation of the Convention that were recommended by the First Review Conference.

9.139   The Second Review Conference welcomed, in particular, the fact that implementation of the tenure policy had proceeded as indicated by the First Review Conference. It requested the Director-General to continue to report regularly to the Council on the continued implementation of this policy, including the implications for the OPCW's effectiveness and efficiency and any limited exceptions to the normal policy that may be necessary on these grounds. The Second Review Conference noted the systematic approach to the amendment and updating of the Staff Regulations and Rules followed by the Director-General, in particular, the decision of the Conference at its Tenth Session (C-10/DEC.4, dated 8 November 2005). The Second Review Conference emphasised the importance of maintaining the high level of expertise of Secretariat staff, including the need to maintain professional knowledge.

9.140   The Second Review Conference noted that it will be important for the Secretariat to retain necessary chemical weapons-specific expertise in order to address issues related to the OPCW's activities. The Second Review Conference recommended that the Director-General take these considerations into account when assessing and developing future staffing plans.

9.141   The Second Review Conference noted that the OPCW had approved zero-nominal growth budgets for the previous three years. While underlining the need to maintain continued budgetary rigour, it also noted that such budgets may not always be sustainable given the objective demands on the organisation. The Second Review Conference welcomed the improvements to the budgetary process of the OPCW since the First Review Conference, including the streamlining of procedures and rules, completing the set of administrative measures needed, and step-by-step implementation of a results-based approach to budgeting.

9.142   The Second Review Conference noted that voluntary funds by States Parties contribute significantly to the work and programmes of the OPCW. The Second Review Conference recommended the Council to consider the possible development of guidelines for the offers and utilisation of voluntary funds contributed by individual States Parties and regional and other groups.

9.143   The Second Review Conference called on the Secretariat to continue to pursue results-based budgeting vigorously, with a view to completing its introduction as quickly as possible, while keeping the Council informed of progress on a regular basis, to use evaluation and internal and external audit mechanisms, and to continue to review the allocation of human and financial resources while ensuring that the resources available are sufficient to support the effective implementation of the Convention.

9.144   The Second Review Conference noted that a large number of assessed contributions have not been received on time or in full and urged all States Parties to regularise their payments without delay and in accordance with the Financial Rules in order to provide financial stability. The Second Review Conference also reaffirmed the need for the Council, with the support of the Secretariat, to continue the monitoring and assessment of budgetary mechanisms to ensure that objectives are being met.

9.145   The Second Review Conference reaffirmed the need for Secretariat staff, particularly its inspectors, to keep abreast of developments in science and technology in order to maintain professional excellence and to discharge their responsibilities efficiently. The Second Review Conference requested the Director-General to keep these requirements in mind when identifying the future training needs of the Secretariat.

9.146   The Second Review Conference requested the Secretariat to continue to seek to apply information technology more efficiently to improve the functioning of the OPCW, in particular, expanding the OPCW's use of internet-based communications to all sections of the Secretariat. It also recalled the decision of the Conference at its Sixth Session (C-VI/DEC.9, dated 17 May 2001) on the equal treatment of all official OPCW languages and called for further improvements, including regular updating of the website and sustaining the high level of translation and to continue meeting interpretation requirements at sessions of the Conference of the States Parties and the Council.

9.147   The Second Review Conference noted that it is essential for effective verification that the Secretariat's approved inspection equipment remains up to date and that the list of such equipment can be adjusted promptly as items become obsolete. It requested the Secretariat to review the operational requirements and technical specifications first approved by the Conference at its First Session (C-I/DEC.71 and Corr.1, both dated 23 May 1997), seeking the advice of the Scientific Advisory Board, and to submit a report to the Council.

9.148   The Second Review Conference again expressed its satisfaction at the relationship between the OPCW and the Host Country, including the role of the Director-General and the Council in promoting good relations with the Netherlands. The Second Review Conference welcomed the establishment of the Working Group on Relations with the Host Country in 2005, which was replaced by the Committee on Relations with the Host Country, established by a decision of the Conference at its Eleventh Session (C-11/DEC.9, dated 7 December 2006). It called on the Host Country to work towards resolving, as soon as possible, any outstanding issues relating to implementation of the Headquarters Agreement, in close cooperation with the Host Country Committee, and requested the Director-General to continue to report to the Council as appropriate on this relationship and the implementation of the Headquarters Agreement.

9.149   The Second Review Conference recognised that nothing in the concluding document of the Second Review Conference can, or intends to, modify any of the provisions of the Convention.

10. AGENDA ITEM TEN – Reports of subsidiary bodies

COMMITTEE OF THE WHOLE

10.1   The Second Review Conference noted the report of the Committee of the Whole on the results of its consideration of the agenda item referred to it on the recommendation of the

General Committee (RC-2/CoW.1, dated 18 April 2008), and took action as required.

GENERAL COMMITTEE
10.2   The Second Review Conference noted the reports of the General Committee, and took action as required.

CREDENTIALS COMMITTEE
10.3   The report of the Credentials Committee (RC-2/3 dated 16 April 2008) was presented by its Chairperson, Ambassador Wolfgang Paul of Austria. The Chairperson orally reported that, following the closure of the Credentials Committee meeting, formal credentials were received for the representatives of Cameroon, Colombia, Jamaica, Republic of Moldova and Uzbekistan, and faxes or copies of credentials in the form required by Rule 26 of the Rules of Procedure of the Conference were received from Benin. Formal credentials would be submitted for the latter in due course. The Second Review Conference noted this additional information and approved the report.

11. AGENDA ITEM ELEVEN – Any other business

12. AGENDA ITEM TWELVE – Adoption of the final documents of the Second Review Conference

The Second Review Conference considered and adopted the report of the Second Review Conference.

13. AGENDA ITEM THIRTEEN – Closure

The Chairperson closed the Second Review Conference on 18 April 2008.

21.3 The Third Special Session of the Conference of the States Parties to Review the Operation of the Chemical Weapons Convention (Third Review Conference; 8–19 April 2013)

RC-3/3* containing the Report of the Third Special Session of the Conference of the States Parties adopted on 19 April 2013 and entitled "Report of the Third Special Session of the Conference of the States Parties to review the operation of the Chemical Weapons Convention"

1. AGENDA ITEM ONE – Opening of the Third Review Conference

1.1   The Third Special Session of the Conference of the States Parties to Review the Operation of the Chemical Weapons Convention (hereinafter "the Third Review Conference") was opened at 10:07 on 8 April 2013 by the Chairperson of the Seventeenth Session of the Conference of the States Parties (hereinafter "the Conference"), Ambassador Peter Goosen of South Africa.
1.2   The following 122 States Parties participated in the Third Review Conference: Afghanistan, Albania, Algeria, Andorra, Antigua and Barbuda, Argentina, Armenia, Australia, Austria, Azerbaijan, Bahrain, Bangladesh, Belarus, Belgium, Benin, Bolivia, Bosnia and Herzegovina, Brazil, Bulgaria, Burkina Faso, Cameroon, Canada, Chile, China, Colombia, Costa Rica, Côte d'Ivoire, Croatia, Cuba, Cyprus, Czech Republic, Denmark, Dominican Republic, Ecuador, El Salvador, Estonia, Fiji, Finland, France, Gambia,

Georgia, Germany, Ghana, Greece, Guatemala, Holy See, Honduras, Hungary, Iceland, India, Indonesia, Iran (Islamic Republic of), Iraq, Ireland, Italy, Japan, Jordan, Kazakhstan, Kenya, Kuwait, Lao People's Democratic Republic, Latvia, Lebanon, Lesotho, Libya, Lithuania, Luxembourg, Malaysia, Malta, Mexico, Monaco, Mongolia, Morocco, Mozambique, Namibia, Netherlands, New Zealand, Nicaragua, Nigeria, Norway, Oman, Pakistan, Panama, Paraguay, Peru, Philippines, Poland, Portugal, Qatar, Republic of Korea, Republic of Moldova, Romania, Russian Federation, Saudi Arabia, Senegal, Serbia, Singapore, Slovakia, Slovenia, South Africa, Spain, Sri Lanka, Sudan, Suriname, Sweden, Switzerland, Tajikistan, Thailand, the former Yugoslav Republic of Macedonia, Togo, Tunisia, Turkey, Uganda, Ukraine, United Arab Emirates, United Kingdom of Great Britain and Northern Ireland, United States of America, Uruguay, Viet Nam, Yemen, Zambia, and Zimbabwe.

1.3   In accordance with Rule 29 of the Rules of Procedure of the Conference, the following Signatory States participated in the Third Review Conference as observers: Israel and Myanmar.

1.4   In accordance with Rule 30 of the Rules of Procedure of the Conference, and pursuant to decision RC-3/DEC.1, dated 8 April 2013, Angola was accorded observer status.

1.5   The Third Review Conference, in decision RC-3/DEC.4, dated 9 April 2013, approved the participation of eight international organisations, specialised agencies, and other international bodies in its Session.

1.6   The Third Review Conference considered and adopted a decision entitled "Amendment of Rule 33 of the Rules of Procedure of the Conference of the States Parties with Respect to Attendance of Non-Governmental Organisations at Meetings of Special Sessions of the Conference of the States Parties to Review the Operation of the Chemical Weapons Convention" (RC-3/DEC.2, dated 8 April 2013).

1.7   The Third Review Conference, in decision RC-3/DEC.3, dated 8 April 2013, approved the participation of 70 non-governmental organisations in its Session.

2.   AGENDA ITEM TWO – Election of the Chairperson

2.1   In accordance with Rule 8(b) of the Rules of Procedure of the Conference, the Third Review Conference, by acclamation, elected as its Chairperson Ambassador Krzysztof Paturej of Poland.

3.   AGENDA ITEM THREE – Election of Vice-Chairpersons and other officers

3.1   In accordance with Rule 8(b) of the Rules of Procedure of the Conference, the Third Review Conference elected representatives of the following 10 States Parties as Vice-Chairpersons of the Conference: Algeria, Guatemala, Iran (Islamic Republic of), Ireland, Japan, Russian Federation, Slovakia, South Africa, United States of America, and Uruguay.

3.2   Also, in accordance with Rule 8(b) of the Rules of Procedure of the Conference, the Third Review Conference elected as Chairperson of the Committee of the Whole, Ambassador Sa'ad Abdul Majeed Ibrahim Al-Ali of Iraq.

4.   AGENDA ITEM FOUR – Adoption of the agenda

4.1   The provisional agenda for the Third Review Conference was circulated under cover of RC-3/1, dated 21 February 2013.

4.2   On the recommendation of the General Committee, the Third Review Conference adopted the following agenda:

AGENDA ITEM ONE – Opening of the Third Review Conference

AGENDA ITEM TWO – Election of the Chairperson

AGENDA ITEM THREE – Election of Vice-Chairpersons and other officers

AGENDA ITEM FOUR – Adoption of the agenda

AGENDA ITEM FIVE – Organisation of work and establishment of subsidiary bodies

AGENDA ITEM SIX – Statement by the Director-General

AGENDA ITEM SEVEN – Report of the Chairperson of the Executive Council on the preparations for the Third Review Conference

AGENDA ITEM EIGHT – General debate

AGENDA ITEM NINE – Review of the operation of the Chemical Weapons Convention as provided for in paragraph 22 of Article VIII, taking into account any relevant scientific and technological developments:

    (a) the role of the Chemical Weapons Convention in enhancing international peace and security and in achieving the objectives as set forth in the preamble of the Convention;

    (b) ensuring the universality of the Chemical Weapons Convention;

    (c) implementation of the provisions of the Chemical Weapons Convention relating to:

        (i)   general obligations and declarations related thereto;

        (ii) reports by the Director-General on destruction-related issues;

        (iii) destruction of chemical weapons, including implementation of the Conference of the States Parties and Executive Council decisions on destruction-related issues;

        (iv) destruction or conversion of chemical weapons production facilities;

        (v) verification activities of the OPCW;

        (vi) activities not prohibited under the Chemical Weapons Convention;

        (vii) national implementation measures;

        (viii) consultations, cooperation, and fact-finding;

        (ix) assistance and protection against chemical weapons;

        (x) economic and technological development;

        (xi) Articles XII to XV and final clauses; and

        (xii) the protection of confidential information; and

    (d) the general functioning of the Organisation for the Prohibition of Chemical Weapons.

AGENDA ITEM TEN – Reports of subsidiary bodies

AGENDA ITEM ELEVEN – Any other business

AGENDA ITEM TWELVE – Adoption of the final documents of the Third Review Conference

AGENDA ITEM THIRTEEN – Closure

5.   AGENDA ITEM FIVE – Organisation of work and establishment of subsidiary bodies

5.1   The Third Review Conference considered and adopted the recommendations of the General Committee reported to it in accordance with Rule 43 of the Rules of Procedure of the Conference.

5.2   The Third Review Conference adopted the recommendation of the General Committee that it be closed on 19 April 2013.

APPOINTMENT OF THE CREDENTIALS COMMITTEE

5.3   In accordance with Rule 27 of the Rules of Procedure of the Conference, the Third Review Conference, on the proposal of its Chairperson, appointed the following 10 members of the Credentials Committee: Belgium, Croatia, Czech Republic, Nicaragua, Peru, Philippines, Portugal, Rwanda, Thailand, and Tunisia.

5.4   Subsequently, the Third Review Conference, at the request of the African Group and on the proposal of its Chairperson, appointed Senegal to replace Rwanda as a member of the Credentials Committee, due to unforeseen circumstances.

6.   AGENDA ITEM SIX – Statements by the Director-General of the OPCW, the Secretary-General of the United Nations, and ministers

6.1   The Third Review Conference noted the opening statement by the Director-General (RC-3/DG.4, dated 8 April 2013).

6.2   The Third Review Conference was addressed by the Secretary-General of the United Nations.

6.3   The Third Review Conference was also addressed by the Minister of Foreign Affairs of the Netherlands, on behalf of the Host Country, the Deputy Prime Minister of Luxembourg, and the Minister of Foreign Affairs of Turkey.

7.   AGENDA ITEM SEVEN – Report of the Chairperson of the Executive Council on the preparations for the Third Review Conference
      The Chairperson of the Executive Council (hereinafter "the Council"), Ambassador Bhaswati Mukherjee of India, reported to the Third Review Conference on the work of the Council in preparation for the Third Review Conference.

8.   AGENDA ITEM EIGHT – General debate

8.1   The following delegations made statements during the general debate: Iran (Islamic Republic of) (on behalf of the Non-Aligned Movement and China), Ireland (on behalf of the European Union and associated countries), Sudan (on behalf of the African Group), Saudi Arabia, Argentina, Iraq, Iran (Islamic Republic of) (in its national capacity), India, Norway, Singapore, China, Brazil, Qatar, Pakistan, Malaysia, Cuba, United Arab Emirates, Thailand, Chile, Peru, Sweden, Yemen, United Kingdom of Great Britain and Northern Ireland, Mexico, Philippines, Costa Rica, New Zealand, Switzerland, Belarus, Russian Federation, Tunisia, France, Algeria, Hungary, Republic of Korea, Lithuania, Oman, Belgium, Fiji, Ukraine, United States of America, Canada, Germany, Romania, Panama, Indonesia, Ecuador, Croatia, Slovakia, Lao People's Democratic Republic, Guatemala, Kenya, Zambia, Bolivia, Ireland, Australia, Zimbabwe, Uruguay, Japan, Sri Lanka, Paraguay, Senegal, Nigeria, Kazakhstan, Morocco, Afghanistan, Cameroon, and Mongolia.

8.2   The following international organisations made statements during the general debate: the International Committee of the Red Cross and the African Union.

8.3   In accordance with paragraph 3 of Annex of RC-3/DEC.2, the following non-governmental organisations gave presentations at the plenary meeting which was held following the general debate: Green Cross International, Colorado Citizens Advisory Commission, Society for Chemical Weapons Victims Support, Institute for Security Studies, Okan University, Centre for Non-Proliferation and Export Control Issues, International Campaign to Abolish Nuclear Weapons, VERTIC, International Centre for Chemical Safety and Security Tarnow, Green Cross Russia, Omega Research Foundation, PUC Institute of International Relations, Global Green USA, and NPS Global Foundation.

9.   AGENDA ITEM NINE – Review of the operation of the Chemical Weapons Convention as provided for in paragraph 22 of Article VIII, taking into account any relevant scientific and technological developments:

9.1   The Chairperson of the Open-Ended Working Group for the Preparation of the Third Review Conference, Ambassador Nassima Baghli of Algeria, reported to the Third Review Conference on the work of the open-ended working group and submitted to the Third Review Conference the Chairperson's provisional text for agenda item nine of the provisional agenda of the Third Review Conference (WGRC-3/1 RC-3/CRP.1, dated 28 March 2013).

Part A: Political Declaration of the Third Special Session of the Conference of States Parties to Review the Operation of the Chemical Weapons Convention

9.2   Having convened in The Hague from 8 to 19 April 2013 for the Third Review Conference and having undertaken their review of the Chemical Weapons Convention (hereinafter "the Convention") as agreed to in Part B below:
        The States Parties solemnly declared their:

9.3   *Unequivocal commitment* to achieving the object and purpose of the Convention as set out in its Preamble and its provisions;

9.4   *Conviction* that the provisions of the Convention are mutually reinforcing and that the full, effective, and non-discriminatory implementation of all of its provisions, taking into account relevant developments in science, technology and industry, is of critical importance;

9.5   *Conviction* that the Convention, sixteen years after its entry into force, has reinforced its role as the international norm against chemical weapons, and that it constitutes a major contribution to:
        (a) International peace and security;
        (b) Eliminating chemical weapons, noting that as 31 March 2013, 55,474.00 MTs (79.90%) of Category 1 chemical weapons have been destroyed, and in preventing their re-emergence;
        (c) The ultimate objective of general and complete disarmament under strict and effective international control;
        (d) Excluding completely, for the sake of all mankind, the possibility of the use of chemical weapons; and
        (e) Promoting international cooperation and exchange in scientific and technical information in the field of chemical activities among States Parties for peaceful purposes in order to enhance the economic and technological development of all States Parties; and

9.6   *Unqualified commitment* to achieve the universality of the Convention and urgently called upon all of the States not Party to join the Convention without delay and precondition.
        The States Parties also noted that the full, effective, and non-discriminatory implementation of key aspects of the Convention remains to be achieved and in this context expressed their:

9.7   *Concern* regarding the Director-General's statement in his report to the Sixty-Eighth Session of the Executive Council, provided in accordance with paragraph 2 of C-16/DEC.11, dated 1 December 2011, that "three possessor States Parties, namely Libya, the Russian Federation, and the United States of America, have been unable to fully meet the final extended deadline of 29 April 2012 for the destruction of their chemical weapons stockpiles" (EC-68/DG.9, dated 1 May 2012);

9.8   *Determination* that the destruction of all categories of chemical weapons shall be completed in the shortest time possible in accordance with the provisions of the Convention and its Annex on Implementation and Verification, and with the full application of the relevant decisions that have been taken;

9.9   *Recognition* that new challenges related to the Convention continue to arise and that its implementation may need to be improved to continue to achieve the object and purpose of the Convention and to stay abreast of developments in science and technology;

9.10   *Commitment* to adopt, in accordance with their constitutional processes, the necessary measures to fully implement their obligations under the Convention as a matter of priority, noting that 97 States Parties still need to adopt such measures, and to keep the effectiveness of these measures under review;

9.11   *Determination* to increase their efforts to guard against the possible hostile use of toxic chemicals by non-State actors such as terrorists; and

9.12   *Commitment* to foster, and to further develop and enhance actions for, international cooperation amongst States Parties in the peaceful uses of chemistry, and also to implement the provisions of the Convention in a manner which avoids hampering economic and technological development for purposes not prohibited under the Convention.

The States Parties furthermore underlined their:

9.13   *Intention* to continue providing the Organisation for the Prohibition of Chemical Weapons (OPCW) with the support that it requires in order to achieve the object and purpose of the Convention, to ensure the full, effective, and non-discriminatory implementation of its provisions and to deal more effectively with future opportunities and challenges;

9.14   *Commitment* that the OPCW remain the global repository of knowledge and expertise on the implementation of the Convention and their desire that the Technical Secretariat present proposals for ensuring continuity in its knowledge base and expertise;

9.15   *Determination* to maintain the Convention's role as a bulwark against chemical weapons; to that end to promote, inter alia, outreach, capacity building, education and public diplomacy;

9.16   *Desire* to improve interaction with chemical industry, the scientific community, academia, and civil society organisations engaged in issues relevant to the Convention, and cooperate as appropriate with other relevant international and regional organisations, in promoting the goals of the Convention; and

9.17   *Intention* to keep the above mentioned declarations under review at each regular session of the Conference of the States Parties.

The States Parties also:

9.18   Recalling the Thirty-Second Meeting of the Executive Council, *reiterated* their deep concern that chemical weapons may have been used in the Syrian Arab Republic and underlined that the use of chemical weapons by anyone under any circumstances would be reprehensible and completely contrary to the legal norms and standards of the international community.

9.19   Recalling the expertise in the OPCW for the investigation of alleged use of chemical weapons, the States Parties *expressed* their support for the close cooperation, in accordance with paragraph 27 of Part XI of the Verification Annex of the Convention, between the Director-General of the OPCW and the Secretary-General of the United Nations in this regard.

Part B: Review of the operation of the Chemical Weapons Convention as provided for in paragraph 22 of Article VIII, taking into account any relevant scientific and technological developments

<u>The role of the Chemical Weapons Convention in enhancing international peace and security and in achieving the objectives as set forth in the Preamble of the Convention</u>

9.20   The Third Review Conference recalled that the Convention is a unique multilateral agreement banning an entire category of weapons of mass destruction in a non-discriminatory and verifiable manner under strict and effective international control, and noted with satisfaction that the Convention continues to be a remarkable success and an example of effective multilateralism.

9.21   The Third Review Conference noted with satisfaction that implementation of the Convention makes a major contribution to international peace and security.

9.22   The Third Review Conference reaffirmed the commitment by all States Parties to achieving the object and purpose of the Convention, as set out in its Preamble and provisions.

9.23   The Third Review Conference reaffirmed that the obligation of the States Parties to complete the destruction of chemical weapons stockpiles as well as the destruction or conversion of chemical weapons production facilities (CWPFs) in accordance with the provisions of the Convention and its Verification Annex, and under verification by the Technical Secretariat (hereinafter "the Secretariat"), is essential for the realisation of the object and purpose of the Convention.

9.24   The Third Review Conference stressed that the destruction of all categories of chemical weapons is a fundamental objective of the Organisation.

9.25   The Third Review Conference reiterated the obligation to destroy or otherwise dispose of old chemical weapons.

9.26   The Third Review Conference reaffirmed the obligation to complete the destruction of abandoned chemical weapons in accordance with the provisions of the Convention, and the decision taken by the Council at its Sixty-Seventh Session (EC-67/DEC.6, dated 15 February 2012).

9.27   The Third Review Conference noted with concern that, along with the threat of the possible production, acquisition and use of chemical weapons by States, the international community also faces the danger of the production, acquisition and use of chemical weapons by non-State actors including terrorists. These concerns have highlighted the necessity of achieving universal adherence to the Convention, as well as the high level of OPCW readiness.

9.28   The Third Review Conference reaffirmed that the full, effective, and non-discriminatory implementation of all Articles of the Convention makes a major contribution to international peace and security, through the elimination of existing stockpiles of chemical weapons and prohibition of their acquisition and use, and provides for assistance and protection in the event of use, or threat of use, of chemical weapons and for international cooperation for peaceful purposes in the field of chemical activities.

9.29   The Third Review Conference noted the importance of adequate funding from the regular budget for the full, effective, and non-discriminatory implementation of all Articles of the Convention, while also noting with appreciation the voluntary contributions made to support its implementation, including for verification and international cooperation and assistance.

9.30   The Third Review Conference noted with concern that, although the number of States Parties has risen from 183 in 2008 to 188 in 2013, eight States have still to join the Convention, including some whose non-adherence is a cause for serious concern.

9.31   The Third Review Conference recalled that in terms of Article XIII of the Convention "nothing in this Convention shall be interpreted as in any way limiting or detracting from the obligations assumed by any State under the Protocol for the Prohibition of the Use in War of Asphyxiating, Poisonous or Other Gases, and of Bacteriological Methods of Warfare, signed at Geneva on 17 June 1925". The Third Review Conference also recalled that the Convention excludes completely the possibility of the use of chemical weapons thereby complementing the obligations assumed under the 1925 Geneva Protocol. It appealed to all High Contracting Parties to the 1925 Geneva Protocol to observe strictly its principles and objectives and called upon those States Parties that continue to maintain reservations to the 1925 Geneva Protocol related to the Convention to withdraw them and to notify the Depositary of the 1925 Geneva Protocol accordingly. The Third Review Conference invited States Parties to inform the next regular session of the Conference when a reservation to the 1925 Geneva Protocol is withdrawn.

9.32   The Third Review Conference noted the impact of scientific and technological progress on the effective implementation of the Convention and the importance for the OPCW and its policy-making organs of taking due account of such developments. In that context, it stressed that the Scientific Advisory Board (SAB) should continue its role in advising the Director-General and expressed appreciation for the report of the SAB prepared for the Third Review Conference that identifies a number of issues relevant to the operation of the Convention (RC-3/DG.1, dated 29 October 2012).

Ensuring the universality of the Chemical Weapons Convention

9.33   The Third Review Conference reiterated that the universality of the Convention is essential to achieving its object and purpose and to enhancing the security of States Parties, as well as international peace and security. The Third Review Conference underlined that the objectives of the Convention will not be fully realised as long as there remains even a single State not Party that could possess or acquire such weapons.

9.34   The Third Review Conference called for the adequate funding for the OPCW's universality activities, through the regular budget and voluntary funding.

9.35   The Third Review Conference welcomed the fact that five additional States (the Bahamas, the Dominican Republic, Guinea Bissau, Iraq, and Lebanon) had joined the Convention since the Second Special Session of the Conference of the States Parties to Review the Chemical Weapons Convention (hereinafter "the Second Review Conference").

9.36   The Third Review Conference noted that there remain eight States not Party to the Convention, including some whose non-adherence is a cause for serious concern.

9.37   The Third Review Conference reaffirmed the importance of the Action Plan on Universality (EC-M-23/DEC.3, dated 24 October 2003) and the subsequent decisions of the Conference to regularly review the results and implementation of it and to take any decision it deems necessary addressing, in particular, the status of those States not Party whose non-adherence is a cause for serious concern. It also recalled that States that remain outside the Convention are not able to take advantage of the benefits that it offers to States Parties.

9.38   The Third Review Conference noted that the proposal for the establishment of a zone free of nuclear weapons and all other weapons of mass destruction in the Middle East is consistent with the objective of universality of the Convention. The Third Review Conference regretted that an international conference was not convened in 2012 and expressed the hope that an international conference will be convened for this purpose at an early date. In this context, it welcomed the provision of background information by the Director-General that highlighted the achievements of the Convention as a model disarmament treaty.

9.39   The Third Review Conference, having reviewed developments in the field of universality:

(a) Strongly urged all eight remaining States not Party to the Convention (Angola, the Democratic People's Republic of Korea, Egypt, Israel, Myanmar, Somalia, South Sudan, and the Syrian Arab Republic) to ratify or accede to it as a matter of urgency and without preconditions, in the interests of enhancing their own national security as well as contributing to global peace and security;

(b) Requested the States Parties to intensify further their efforts with all States not Party to encourage them to ratify or accede to the Convention at the earliest, with a view to achieving full universality;

(c) Requested the Secretariat and the Director-General to make full use of all available opportunities and resources including new mechanisms such as special envoys, as and when considered appropriate by the Director-General, to pursue this goal at all levels, including in close cooperation with other international, regional, and subregional organisations; and

(d) Request the policy-making organs to continue to annually review ongoing efforts to achieve universality.

General obligations and declarations related thereto

9.40   The Third Review Conference reaffirmed that full, effective, and non-discriminatory implementation of Articles I, II and III is essential for the realisation of the object and purpose of the Convention.

9.41   The Third Review Conference reaffirmed the continued relevance of the definitions contained in Article II of the Convention, which ensure the comprehensive nature of the prohibition of chemical weapons under the Convention. The definitions contained in Article II, in particular, of the terms "chemical weapons" and "chemical weapons production facility", were found to adequately cover the impact of developments in science and technology on the Convention's prohibitions and to provide for the application of these prohibitions to any toxic chemical, except where such a chemical is intended for purposes not prohibited by the Convention, and as long as the types and quantities involved are consistent with such purposes.

9.4   The Third Review Conference stressed the importance of the full and timely implementation by States Parties of all declaration obligations under Article III.

9.43   The Third Review Conference reaffirmed that declarations provided by States Parties under Article III, which establish a baseline for measuring progress in the elimination of all categories of chemical weapons, as well as CWPFs, need to be comprehensive and accurate.

9.44   The Third Review Conference, having reviewed the subject of general obligations and declarations under Article III:
(a) Called upon those States Parties that had yet to submit their initial declarations to do so as a matter of urgency;
(b) Requested the Secretariat to deploy continued efforts in support of those States Parties and to keep the Council informed of progress in the preparation and submission of initial declarations;
(c) Called upon States Parties to ensure that their declarations under Article III are updated in a timely manner, if and when new information becomes available; and
(d) Called upon the Secretariat to continue rendering, when requested, technical assistance to States Parties on the preparation and submission of declarations and amendments.

Destruction of chemical weapons, including implementation of the Conference of the States Parties and Executive Council decisions on destruction-related issues

9.45   The Third Review Conference reaffirmed that full, effective, and non-discriminatory implementation of Article IV is essential for the realisation of the object and purpose of the Convention.

9.46   The Third Review Conference reaffirmed that each State Party has undertaken to destroy chemical weapons it owns or possesses or which are located in any place under its jurisdiction or control, and to destroy or convert any CWPFs in accordance with the provisions of the Convention. The Third Review Conference reaffirmed that complete destruction of chemical weapons and conversion or complete destruction of CWPFs are essential for the realisation of the object and purpose of the Convention.

9.47   The Third Review Conference welcomed the completion of the full destruction of the chemical weapons that had been owned or possessed by A State Party, Albania, and India, in accordance with the provisions of the Convention.

9.48   The Third Review Conference noted that, as at 31 March 2013, 55,474.00 MTs (79.90%) of declared Category 1 chemical weapons had been destroyed under strict verification by the Secretariat and noted with concern that, as at the same date, 20.10% of them remained to be destroyed.

9.49 The Third Review Conference noted that the Conference at its Sixteenth Session had adopted a decision regarding the final extended deadline of 29 April 2012 (C-16/DEC.11). Further to this decision, the Third Review Conference conducted a comprehensive review of the implementation of this decision at a specially designated meeting.

9.50 The Third Review Conference expressed its concern regarding the Director-General's statement in his report to the Council at its Sixty-Eighth Session, provided in accordance with paragraph 2 of C-16/DEC.11, that "three possessor States Parties, namely Libya, the Russian Federation, and the United States of America, have been unable to fully meet the final extended deadline of 29 April 2012 for the destruction of their chemical weapons stockpiles" (EC-68/DG.9, dated 1 May 2012).

9.51 The Third Review Conference noted further that the measures that had been identified in paragraph 3 of the decision (C-16/DEC.11) were now being implemented.

9.52 The Third Review Conference further noted the statements and comments made by States Parties on the destruction of the remaining chemical weapons by possessor States, recalling the relevant Convention obligations and relevant decisions by the Conference and the Council. The Third Review Conference recalled that the destruction of the remaining chemical weapons by possessor States Parties should continue in accordance with the provisions of the Convention and its Annex on Implementation and Verification and with the application of the measures contained in decision C-16/DEC.11.

9.53 Further to the aforementioned decision by the Conference at its Sixteenth Session (subparagraph 3(h)(ii) of C-16/DEC.11), the Director-General provided a written report (RC-3/DG.3/Rev.1, dated 11 April 2013) at a specially designated meeting of the Third Review Conference, based on the independent information received by the Secretariat from the Organisation's inspectors undertaking verification in accordance with Part IV(A) D of the Verification Annex, which included information on:
(a) The progress achieved to meet the planned completion date(s); and
(b) The effectiveness of any specific measures that have been undertaken to overcome problems in the destruction programmes.

9.54 The Third Review Conference noted the statements and comments made by States Parties on the Report by the Director-General.

9.55 The Third Review Conference noted the Report by the Director-General on the overall progress with respect to the destruction of the remaining chemical weapons stockpiles in which he stated that he "is in the position to confirm that the three possessor States, namely Libya, the Russian Federation and the United States of America, have taken the necessary measures to meet the planned completion dates for their destruction activities" (RC-3/DG.3/Rev.1).

9.56 Further to the same decision by the Conference at its Sixteenth Session (subparagraph 3(h)(i) of C-16/DEC.11), Libya provided a report at a specially designated meeting of the Third Review Conference on the progress achieved to meet the planned completion date, including on any specific measures undertaken to overcome problems in the destruction programmes and information on the projected schedule for destruction activities to meet the planned destruction date, which was considered and noted by the Third Review Conference, along with comments on the issue as mentioned above.

9.57 Further to the same decision by the Conference at its Sixteenth Session (subparagraph 3(h)(i) of C-16/DEC.11), the Russian Federation provided a report at a specially designated meeting of the Third Review Conference on the progress achieved to meet the planned completion date, including on any specific measures undertaken to overcome problems in the destruction programmes and information on the projected schedule for destruction activities to meet the planned destruction date, which was considered and noted by the Third Review Conference, along with comments on the issue as mentioned above.

9.58   Further to the same decision by the Conference at its Sixteenth Session (subparagraph 3(h)(i) of C-16/DEC.11), the United States of America provided a report at a specially designated meeting of the Third Review Conference on the progress achieved to meet the planned completion date, including on any specific measures undertaken to overcome problems in the destruction programmes and information on the projected schedule for destruction activities to meet the planned destruction date, which was considered and noted by the Third Review Conference, along with comments on the issue as mentioned above.

9.59   The Third Review Conference stressed that the provisions of Article IV and the detailed procedures for its implementation shall apply to all chemical weapons owned or possessed by a State Party, or that are located in any place under its jurisdiction or control.

9.60   The Third Review Conference reaffirmed the importance of the destruction of all abandoned chemical weapons in accordance with the provisions of the Convention and the decision taken by the Council at its Sixty-Seventh Session (EC-67/DEC.6). The Third Review Conference, while recalling concerns noted by the Council that the extended deadline of 29 April 2012 would not be fully met, welcomed the Council's decision EC-67/DEC.6. The Third Review Conference noted that, in implementing the relevant decision, the relevant States Parties have conducted a number of technical coordinations among relevant States Parties and have addressed challenges including ensuring the safety of people and protecting the environment. While noting that, in 2012, the destruction progress was less than expected in the destruction plan attached to the relevant decision, the Third Review Conference recognised efforts by the relevant States Parties and the achievement of the destruction of 35,931 items of abandoned chemical weapons by the end of 2012. The Third Review Conference welcomed the close cooperation between relevant States Parties. The Third Review Conference noted that the relevant States Parties welcome visits of the Chairperson of the Council, the Director-General and a delegation representing the Council to destruction facilities to obtain an overview of the destruction of the abandoned chemical weapons. The Third Review Conference reaffirmed the role of the Council, the Conference and the Review Conference with regard to the abandoned chemical weapons destruction related issues as defined in the provisions of the Convention and in the Council's decision EC-67/DEC.6.

9.61   The Third Review Conference reaffirmed the obligation to destroy or otherwise dispose of old chemical weapons in accordance with the Convention.

9.62   The Third Review Conference, having reviewed the destruction of chemical weapons:
(a) Reaffirmed the decision that the destruction of the remaining chemical weapons in the possessor States concerned shall be completed in the shortest time possible in accordance with the provisions of the Convention and its Annex on Implementation and Verification and with the full application of all the measures contained in decision C-16/DEC.11 on the final extended deadline of 29 April 2012;
(b) Requested the Conference and the Council to continue to keep under review and oversee the completion of destruction of chemical weapons stockpiles and, in this regard, underlined the importance of continuing to receive the Director-General's confirmation that the necessary measures are being undertaken by the possessor States concerned to meet the planned completion dates for their destruction activities;
(c) Encouraged the Director-General to continue consulting with the possessor States concerned in order to continue improving the reporting that is required from the States Parties concerned in the application of the decision C-16/DEC.11, and requested that future reporting by the possessor States concerned, on the basis of

C-16/DEC.11, continue to contain information on the progress achieved to meet the planned completion date by which the destruction of the remaining chemical weapons is to be completed;

(d) Requested the Director-General to continue to provide a written report to the Council and the Conference as per their relevant decisions;

(e) Encouraged States Parties to continue addressing the issues related to new discoveries of old chemical weapons and of abandoned chemical weapons within the provisions of the Convention; and

(f) Urged the relevant States Parties to continue to make the fullest possible efforts to complete destruction of abandoned chemical weapons as soon as possible in accordance with the Council decision (EC-67/DEC.6) and encouraged continued cooperation between relevant States Parties to that effect.

Destruction or conversion of chemical weapons production facilities

9.63   The Third Review Conference reaffirmed that full, effective, and non discriminatory implementation of Article V is essential for the realisation of the object and purpose of the Convention.

9.64   The Third Review Conference noted progress in relation to the destruction or conversion of CWPFs as required by Part V of the Verification Annex. The Third Review Conference also noted that full conversion or destruction of all facilities had not been completed within the deadlines set by the Convention. It also noted that additional CWPFs had been declared since the Second Review Conference.

9.65   The Third Review Conference noted that States Parties with converted CWPFs are required to report annually on activities at those facilities and that converted facilities remain liable to on-site inspection, in accordance with paragraph 85 of Part V of the Verification Annex, for a period of ten years after certification by the Director-General of completion of their conversion for purposes not prohibited under the Convention.

9.66   The Third Review Conference noted the decision by the Council (EC-67/DEC.7, dated 16 February 2012) that established the nature of continued verification measures at converted facilities for which 10 years have elapsed after the Director-General's certification of their conversion, and emphasised that the decision ensures that any verification measures applied to facilities converted over 10 years previously are consistent with the non-discriminatory and effective implementation of the Convention.

9.67   The Third Review Conference, having reviewed the destruction or conversion of CWPFs:

(a) Urged all relevant States Parties to complete the destruction or conversion of such facilities as soon as possible; and

(b) Requested the Council to continue to keep under review and oversee completion of destruction or conversion of CWPFs.

Verification activities of the OPCW

9.68   The Third Review Conference reaffirmed that full, effective, and non-discriminatory implementation of Article VI is essential for the realisation of the object and purpose of the Convention.

9.69   The Third Review Conference called for the adequate funding for the OPCW's verification activities, through the regular budget and voluntary funding.

9.70   The Third Review Conference noted that the verification system is an important element of the Convention. It provides for systematic verification with continuous on-site monitoring of the destruction of chemical weapons and systematic verification of the elimination of CWPFs. It also provides for the verification of activities not prohibited under the Convention.

9.71   The Third Review Conference noted that the OPCW has established a verification system that meets the requirements of the Convention. It further noted that the verification system should continue to be improved in a manner consistent with the Convention in response to advances in science and technology, taking into consideration, as appropriate, the SAB's advice to the Director-General, as circulated to the Council. The Third Review Conference also recognised the continued need for the OPCW to have up-to-date verification technologies at its disposal, and encouraged the Secretariat to continue to work with States Parties that wish to familiarise themselves with approved verification equipment.

9.72   The Third Review Conference recalled the obligation for all States Parties to submit timely, accurate and complete declarations consistent with the provisions of the Convention under Article VI. The Third Review Conference reiterated that declarations provided by States Parties are the cornerstone of the verification regime of the Convention.

9.73   The Third Review Conference took note of the need for the Secretariat to conduct the approved number of inspections under Article VI in accordance with the agreed guidelines (EC-66/DEC.10, dated 7 October 2011) which are to be reviewed after three years of implementation. The Third Review Conference noted the results of the analysis of the performance of the site-selection methodology for other chemical production facilities (OCPFs) in accordance with S/962/2011 (dated 8 September 2011) in 2012. The Third Review Conference requested the Secretariat to continue engaging States Parties in demonstrating the site-selection random processes and procedures in an effort to increase transparency and confidence.

9.74   The Third Review Conference welcomed the continued progress since the Second Review Conference in maintaining the Verification Information System, including the option of submitting declarations in electronic form.

9.75   The Third Review Conference noted that the verification system had been strengthened since the Second Review Conference and noted that the efforts made by States Parties in the standardisation of declaration data, the increase in the number of inspections of chemical industry facilities, the reduction of the size of inspection teams, and the introduction of a new interim OCPF site-selection methodology had contributed to increasing the effectiveness and efficiency of the verification system.

9.76   The Third Review Conference urged all States Parties to implement the standing arrangements required by the Convention without delay and in a manner fully consistent with the requirements of the Convention and its Verification Annex.

9.77   The Third Review Conference welcomed the benefit gained as a result of the Secretariat's practices related to sampling and analysis for verification purposes during Schedule 2 site inspections, and emphasised the importance of adequate and up-to-date analytical tools for the efficient, effective, and accurate conduct of on-site sampling and analysis.

9.78   The Third Review Conference noted that the Secretariat has experience in cooperating with States Parties, upon request, in fulfilling declaration obligations.

9.79   The Third Review Conference, having reviewed the verification activities of the OPCW:
        (a) Requested the Secretariat to assist National Authorities, upon request, in building up and improving their capacity to fulfil their obligations under the verification regime, including in fulfilling their declaration obligations;
        (b) Encouraged States Parties' National Authorities in a position to do so, to submit declarations in an electronic form, and further requested the Secretariat to continue providing States Parties with appropriate training and assistance;
        (c) Stressed the importance for the Secretariat to maintain verification expertise relating to chemical weapons and requested the policy-making organs to support this objective;
        (d) Encouraged the Secretariat to maintain and further develop, update and improve its

practices in regard to its capability to perform sampling and analysis under the different scenarios envisaged in the Convention with a view to ensuring the efficiency and effectiveness of verification without creating new obligations for States Parties, and in this context to maintain its efforts to keep updated the OPCW Central Analytical Database and to continue to submit proposed updates in this regard to the Council for its approval;

(e) Encouraged the Secretariat through the National Authorities to continue to strengthen relations with respective national chemical industry. The Secretariat is also encouraged to strengthen its relationship with regional and international chemical industry associations; and

(f) Encouraged the Director-General to continue to render specialised advice to the policy-making organs and States Parties in the areas of science and technology relevant to the Convention on the basis of advice from the SAB; and encouraged greater participation and involvement by States Parties in the information sessions organised by the SAB.

Activities not prohibited under the Chemical Weapons Convention

9.80   The Third Review Conference reaffirmed that full, effective, and non-discriminatory implementation of Article VI is essential for the realisation of the object and purpose of the Convention.

9.81   The Third Review Conference called for the adequate funding for the OPCW's verification activities under Article VI, through the regular budget and voluntary funding.

9.82   The Third Review Conference reaffirmed the right of each State Party, subject to the provisions of the Convention, to develop, produce, otherwise acquire, retain, transfer, and use toxic chemicals and their precursors for purposes not prohibited under the Convention.

9.83   The Third Review Conference emphasised that the full implementation of the provisions of the Convention at a national level, including the timely submission of accurate and complete declarations in accordance with the provisions of the Convention, and updates to those declarations, is essential to ensuring the efficiency and effectiveness of the Convention regime.

9.84   The Third Review Conference, while noting that some States Parties have not yet submitted their initial declarations, recognised the need for a tailor-made assistance approach to improve the status of submission of declarations.

9.85   The Third Review Conference reviewed progress made in the implementation of the Conference decision on guidelines regarding low-concentration limits for declarations of Schedule 2A and 2A* chemicals (C-14/DEC.4, dated 2 December 2009) and called for fuller implementation of the Conference decision at the domestic level.

9.86   The Third Review Conference also noted the continued importance of providing practical help to States Parties to enable them to identify all declarable facilities and activities, thereby ensuring that these are effectively brought under the purview of the Convention's industry verification regime. The Third Review Conference noted with satisfaction that in November 2008, the Secretariat released a major revision of the Declarations Handbook and stressed that any further revision of the Declarations Handbook should take into account the views of States Parties.

9.87   In relation to the declaration and inspection of OCPFs, the Third Review Conference noted the desirability of directing inspections towards facilities of greater relevance to the object and purpose of the Convention and of removing irrelevant facilities from the declarations and inspections.

9.88   The Third Review Conference recalled that the Annex on Chemicals of the Convention clearly sets out the different levels of risk posed by scheduled chemicals to the Convention's object and purpose and the Verification Annex sets out distinctive verification regimes for different types of facilities. In this context, the Third Review Conference recalled that the selection of a particular facility or plant site for inspection shall take into account, besides the risk posed by the relevant chemical, inter alia, the characteristics of the facility and the nature of the activities carried out there.

9.89 The Third Review Conference welcomed the decision adopted by the Council on policy guidelines for determining the number of Article VI inspections (EC-66/DEC.10). 9.90

9.90 The Third Review Conference noted that the Article VI verification system could be improved, taking into account any relevant changes in science and technology.

9.91 In relation to transfers of scheduled chemicals to or from States not Party, the Third Review Conference recalled the prohibitions on any such transfers of Schedule 1 and Schedule 2 chemicals. It also noted that an increasing number of States Parties had put in place the necessary measures in that regard.

9.92 The Third Review Conference recalled the decision of the Council on measures regarding the transfer of Schedule 3 chemicals to States not Party to the Convention (EC-47/DEC.8, dated 8 November 2006) and noted the matter remains an issue under consideration of the Council. It encouraged the Council to continue with its work in this regard.

9.93 The Third Review Conference noted that discrepancies in transfers declared by States Parties continue, and encouraged the cluster on chemical-industry and other Article VI issues to consult on the ways to reconcile such discrepancies.

9.94 The Third Review Conference noted the utility of consultations in the cluster on chemical-industry and other Article VI issues, which has provided solutions that contribute to improving the verification regime.

9.95 The Third Review Conference, having reviewed activities not prohibited under the Convention:

(a) Called upon those States Parties that have not yet submitted their initial declarations to do so as soon as possible;

(b) Called upon States Parties that have not yet implemented the decision on guidelines regarding low-concentration limits for declarations of Schedule 2A and 2A* chemicals to take necessary measures to expedite its implementation;

(c) Urged States Parties to ensure that declarations are submitted in a timely, complete and accurate manner, consistent with the provisions of the Convention, making use of the Secretariat's resources, as appropriate;

(d) Encouraged the Secretariat to continue to provide technical assistance to States Parties for the receipt of OPCW inspections, and other technical questions that may arise in the implementation of provisions related to activities not prohibited under the Convention;

(e) Encouraged the Secretariat to continue to develop and periodically update existing databases on declarable chemicals, which facilitate the identification of such chemicals;

(f) Encouraged the Secretariat, in close cooperation with States Parties, to continue to make efforts to increase the effectiveness and efficiency of the verification system;

(g) Called upon States Parties and the Secretariat to continue working to identify the causes of discrepancies related to Article VI declarations, such as those relating to aggregate national data for Schedule 2 and 3 transfers, as well as OCPF declarations, and recommend possible solutions and alternatives to the policy-making organs;

(h) In view of advances in science and technology, the development of the chemical industry, and the growth in the trade of chemicals, encouraged the Secretariat to continue to strengthen its relations with regional and international chemical industry associations; and

(i) Called upon States Parties to continue to use the cluster established by the Council on chemical-industry and other Article VI issues and to develop ways to improve the implementation of the industry verification regime.

National implementation measures

9.96   The Third Review Conference reaffirmed that full, effective, and non-discriminatory implementation of Article VII is essential for the realisation of the object and purpose of the Convention.

9.97   The Third Review Conference called for the adequate funding for the OPCW's national implementation programmes, through the regular budget and voluntary funding.

9.98   The Third Review Conference reaffirmed that the effective contribution of the Convention to international and regional peace and security can be enhanced through its full and effective implementation.

9.99   The Third Review Conference acknowledged that some progress has been made in the implementation of Article VII since the adoption of the action plan by the Conference at its Eighth Session (C-8/DEC.16, dated 24 October 2003). The Third Review Conference welcomed the fact that since the Second Review Conference an additional nine States Parties have adopted legislation to fully implement the provisions of the Convention. The Third Review Conference noted the challenges ahead, and further noted that only 91 States Parties have fully enacted legislation and/or adopted administrative measures to fully meet these obligations under the Convention. The Third Review Conference noted the commitment of States Parties to adopt, in accordance with constitutional processes, the necessary measures to fully implement their obligations under the Convention as a matter of priority, and to keep the effectiveness of these measures under review.

9.100   The Third Review Conference highlighted the need for a comprehensive approach to national implementation in line with each State Party's constitutional requirements, to filling gaps in national implementation, and to ensuring that national implementation measures are consistent with the provisions of the Convention.

9.101   The Third Review Conference acknowledged the role of education, outreach and awareness-raising as a relevant activity for the national implementation of the Convention, including awareness among academia and relevant scientific communities of the provisions of the Convention, the domestic laws and regulations relevant to the Convention. Accordingly, the Third Review Conference welcomed the establishment of the SAB temporary working group on education and outreach.

9.102   The Third Review Conference, while acknowledging the challenges still faced by certain States Parties, commended the efforts of States Parties and the Secretariat in assisting with national implementation measures. It noted again the value of bilateral assistance and networking within and among regions, especially for States Parties that may need particular assistance.

9.103   The Third Review Conference, having reviewed national implementation measures:

(a) Called upon all States Parties to adopt, in accordance with constitutional processes, the necessary measures to fully implement their obligations under the Convention in line with the commitment reflected in paragraph 9.99;

(b) Encouraged the States Parties which are yet to fulfil their obligations under Article VII to engage with the Secretariat on the steps that need to be undertaken for the national implementation of the Convention;

(c) Encouraged the Secretariat to explore innovative methods of providing assistance on tailor-made approaches as a potential means to further advance the implementation of Article VII;

(d) Called upon all States Parties to keep the effectiveness of national implementation measures under review so as to ensure at all times that the provisions of the Convention are implemented within their territory or in any other place under their respective jurisdiction;

(e) Encouraged the Secretariat, in concert with the SAB temporary working group on education and outreach, to assist States Parties, upon request, in implementing education and outreach activities, including by disseminating materials, conducting workshops and regional meetings;

(f) Encouraged the Secretariat to develop, within existing resources, activities that will enhance South-South, regional, and subregional cooperation, as well as special programmes towards the full implementation of Article VII;

(g) Encouraged States Parties and the Secretariat to continue to consult in order to enhance further the utility and effectiveness of all implementation-support programmes, and requested the Secretariat to evaluate these programmes and report to the Council;

(h) Requested the Secretariat to continue to submit its annual report on the implementation of Article VII to the Conference, and requested the Conference at its annual sessions to continue to review progress towards the full and effective national implementation of obligations under the Convention and to encourage further progress. The Secretariat is further requested to include an assessment in this report, for consideration by the policy-making organs, containing a comprehensive and objective analysis of the current status of national implementation, with a view to tracking the progress made and formulation of focused assistance programmes;

(i) Encouraged the Secretariat to expand the use of contemporary technological developments to assist and promote its training methods, including further development of e-learning modules; and

(j) Encouraged States Parties in a position to do so to continue to enhance their practical support for the implementation of Article VII obligations by those States Parties so requested.

Consultations, cooperation, and fact-finding

9.104   The Third Review Conference reaffirmed that, without prejudice to the right of any State Party to request a challenge inspection in line with Article IX of the Convention, States Parties should, whenever possible, first make every effort to clarify and resolve, through the exchange of information and consultation among themselves, any matter that might cause doubt about compliance with the Convention, or which gives rise to concerns about a related matter that may be considered ambiguous.

9.105   The Third Review Conference noted that the Council had received no clarification requests under paragraphs 3 to 7 of Article IX since entry into force of the Convention.

9.106   The Third Review Conference also noted that no challenge inspection or investigation of alleged use in a State Party had been requested since entry into force.

9.107   The Third Review Conference recalled that in case of any abuse the provisions of paragraph 23 of Article IX of the Convention shall apply.

9.108   The Third Review Conference stressed the importance of investigations of alleged use or threat of use of chemical weapons involving States Parties. For such situations, the OPCW must have the capacity and be ready at all times to investigate such matters and identify any necessary follow-on action by the OPCW, as well as to facilitate the delivery of assistance in cooperation with relevant international organisations and the United Nations.

9.109   The Third Review Conference noted with satisfaction the preparations that the Secretariat had undertaken since entry into force in order to respond swiftly and effectively to any request for a challenge inspection or investigation of alleged use and underlined the importance of the Secretariat maintaining and further developing the technical capabilities, expertise, and necessary preparedness. It recalled with appreciation the support provided by States Parties for challenge inspection and investigation of alleged use exercises.

9.110   The Third Review Conference welcomed the Supplementary Arrangement that the OPCW concluded with the United Nations in 2012 related to investigations of alleged use involving States not Party, and noted that in case the provisions of paragraph 27 of Part XI of the Verification Annex to the Convention or any other document related thereto and concluded between the OPCW and the United Nations are invoked, the Director-General will promptly inform the Council and all States Parties of the request and of the actions that the Secretariat is undertaking to respond to the request.

9.111   The Third Review Conference, having reviewed the implementation of the provisions of the Convention on consultations, cooperation, and fact-finding:

(a)   Encouraged States Parties to make further use, as appropriate, of the bilateral consultation mechanism provided by Article IX;

(b)   Requested the Secretariat to continue to improve the standard of readiness to conduct a challenge inspection or an investigation of alleged use in accordance with the provisions of the Convention. To this end, it could continue to conduct table-top exercises and mock inspections;

(c)   Requested the Secretariat to keep the Council informed about its readiness and to report any problems that may arise in relation to maintaining the necessary level of readiness to conduct a challenge inspection or an investigation of alleged use;

(d)   Encouraged States Parties in a position to do so to further assist the Secretariat in maintaining a high standard of readiness through, inter alia, the conduct of challenge inspection exercises; and

(e)   Noted that a number of issues related to challenge inspections still remained to be resolved and that their resolution is important for challenge inspections, and requested the Council to continue its deliberations in order to resolve them expeditiously.

Assistance and protection against chemical weapons

9.112   The Third Review Conference reaffirmed that full, effective, and non-discriminatory implementation of Article X is essential for the realisation of the object and purpose of the Convention.

9.113   The Third Review Conference called for the adequate funding for the OPCW's assistance and protection programmes, through the regular budget and voluntary funding.

9.114   The Third Review Conference welcomed the activities of the OPCW in relation to assistance and protection against chemical weapons and supported further efforts both by States Parties and the Secretariat to promote a high level of readiness to respond to chemical weapons threats as articulated in Article X, and also welcomed the effectiveness and efficiency of the increased focus on making full use of regional and subregional capacities and expertise, including taking advantage of established training centres.

9.115   The Third Review Conference, in the light of the possibility of the use of chemical weapons against States Parties to the Convention through threat by actions or activities of any State as described by paragraph 8 of Article X as well as the threat of the possibility of the use of chemical weapons by non-State actors including terrorists, welcomed the measures taken by the Secretariat to strengthen its ability to respond promptly to requests for assistance made under Article X and to investigate the alleged use of chemical weapons.

9.116   The Third Review Conference acknowledged with appreciation the establishment of the International Support Network for Victims of Chemical Weapons and the establishment of a voluntary trust fund for that purpose.

9.117   The Third Review Conference encouraged States Parties to make equipment related to the means of protection against the use of chemical weapons available, without undue restrictions, to other States Parties.

9.118   The Third Review Conference, having reviewed the assistance and protection against chemical weapons:

(a) Encouraged the Secretariat to take measures to further strengthen its capacity to respond promptly to requests for assistance under Article X and to investigate the alleged use of chemical weapons, including developing capabilities to undertake biomedical sampling and analysis;

(b) Encouraged the Secretariat to engage in more active cooperation with relevant regional and subregional organisations as well as international organisations that have mandates relevant to assistance and protection against chemical weapons. Such cooperation could include joint exercises and training including by the use of e-learning modules;

(c) Encouraged the Secretariat to continue its efforts for capacity building at the regional and subregional level and to make better use of regional and subregional capacities and expertise for providing assistance to States Parties upon request; and called on States Parties in the regions and subregions concerned to cooperate closely and to participate in joint exercises and training programmes;

(d) Encouraged the Secretariat to improve coordination in the selection of its regional assistance and protection activities with the States Parties in each region;

(e) Urged all States Parties, particularly those that have not yet done so, to make their annual submissions of information on their national programmes related to protective purposes in a timely fashion, and requested the Secretariat to assist States Parties with the timely completion of their submissions;

(f) Urged all States Parties that have yet to make offers of assistance to the OPCW to do so as required by Article X;

(g) Requested the Secretariat to continue evaluating the offers of technical assistance and donation of equipment and keep States Parties informed about how these can be optimised and about any problems requiring attention;

(h) Requested the Secretariat to review and keep up to date the OPCW data bank on protection, its current lists of experts, both within the Secretariat and from States Parties (including those listed in paragraph 7 of Part XI of the Verification Annex and those in the Protection Network);

(i) Encouraged States Parties to facilitate and make materials and equipment-related assistance available to other States Parties to assist and support the victims of chemical weapons, without undue restrictions;

(j) Encouraged States Parties to contribute to the voluntary fund regarding the International Support Network for Victims of Chemical Weapons in order to enhance the humanitarian aims of the network;

(k) Encouraged the OPCW to engage in more active involvement and participation of relevant civil society organisations and chemical industry associations in the assistance and protection programmes; and

(l) Encouraged the Secretariat to include in its annual report on the status of implementation of Article X an evaluation of the results of its programmes under Article X.

Economic and technological development

9.119   The Third Review Conference reaffirmed that full, effective, and non-discriminatory implementation of Article XI is essential for the realisation of object and purpose of the Convention.

9.120   The Third Review Conference commended the decision entitled "Components of an

Agreed Framework for the Full Implementation of Article XI" adopted by the Conference at its Sixteenth Session (C-16/DEC.10, dated 1 December 2011). It recognised that the decision provides guidance for the full, effective, and non-discriminatory implementation of Article XI, as well as identifying avenues for further work that would advance its objectives.

9.121   The Third Review Conference called for the adequate funding for the OPCW's international cooperation and assistance programmes, through the regular budget and voluntary funding.

9.122   While noting States Parties' scientific and technological cooperation in the peaceful uses of chemistry on a non-discriminatory basis, the Third Review Conference called upon all States Parties to facilitate and enhance such cooperation.

9.123   The Third Review Conference underlined that the comprehensive implementation of Article XI reinforces capacity building in each State Party and in doing so reinforces the ability of States Parties to fully implement the Convention. In this context, it underlined the importance of assistance and national capacity building in the field of chemical activities for purposes not prohibited under the Convention. The Third Review Conference welcomed national and regional efforts in this area.

9.124   The Third Review Conference commended the Secretariat for its efforts in the implementation of Article XI.

9.125   The Third Review Conference recognised that recent plans and activities on the implementation of Article XI showed valuable examples of South-South cooperation.

9.126   The Third Review Conference recalled that chemical safety and security, while being two distinct processes, are the prime responsibilities of States Parties. It encouraged the promotion of a safety and security culture regarding chemical facilities and of transportation of toxic chemicals. It noted that capacity-building activities in these fields are one of the elements of the decision on components of an agreed framework for the full implementation of Article XI adopted by the Conference at its Sixteenth Session (C-16/DEC.10).

9.127   The Third Review Conference noted the initiatives taken by States Parties and the Secretariat to promote activities in the areas of chemical safety and security, and welcomed the role of the OPCW as a platform for voluntary consultations and cooperation among the States Parties and the relevant stakeholders, including the private sector and academia, to promote a global chemical safety and security culture.

9.128   The Third Review Conference welcomed the establishment by States Parties of national and international resource centres and centres of excellence to offer expertise, training, and best-practice exchanges in the areas of international cooperation and assistance.

9.129   The Third Review Conference reaffirmed the provision of Article XI that the States Parties shall not use the Convention as grounds for applying any measures other than those provided for or permitted under the Convention, nor any other international agreement for pursuing an objective inconsistent with the Convention.

9.130   The Third Review Conference reaffirmed that the provisions of the Convention shall be implemented in a manner that avoids hampering the economic or technological development of States Parties and international cooperation in the field of chemical activities for purposes not prohibited under the Convention, including the international exchange of scientific and technical information, and chemicals and equipment for the production, processing, or use of chemicals for purposes not prohibited under the Convention.

9.131   The Third Review Conference, having reviewed economic and technological development:

(a) Commending the decision entitled "Components of an Agreed Framework for the Full Implementation of Article XI" adopted by the Conference at its Sixteenth Session (C-16/DEC.10), it recognised that the decision provides guidance for the full,

effective, and non-discriminatory implementation of Article XI and allows for consideration of additional proposals to further develop and enhance actions for the
advancement of its objectives;

(b) Called upon States Parties to fully implement the provisions of Article XI, and encouraged States Parties to continue supporting the activities under Article XI, including through voluntary contributions;

(c) Encouraged the Council to continue the ongoing facilitation process in order to
deliberate and explore, as appropriate, additional measures within an agreed framework to ensure the full, effective, and non-discriminatory implementation of all
provisions of Article XI;

(d) Requested the Secretariat to prepare and submit, on a regular basis, concrete programmes and actions relevant for States Parties related to the implementation of
Article XI, as well as to report to the Conference on the progress made in the implementation of the decision on the components of an agreed framework for the full
implementation of Article XI (C-16/DEC.10);

(e) Noting that the decision on the components of an agreed framework for the full
implementation of Article XI (C-16/DEC.10) identified concrete measures to be
implemented by States Parties and the Secretariat, reiterated the importance of national capacity-building for the research, development, storage, production, and
safe use of chemicals for purposes not prohibited under the Convention;

(f) Recommended that all OPCW programmes relating to Article XI should be improved through evaluation of their effectiveness, with a view to ensuring that they
are responsive to the needs of beneficiary States Parties, in order to optimise resource use and effectiveness. This should involve consultations between States Parties and the Secretariat, aimed at achieving a clear understanding of the competencies available, the needs of States Parties, and the requirements of the Convention;

(g) Encouraged the Secretariat and States Parties to consider augmenting programmes
to assist States Parties, upon request, in maintaining and developing their analytical
skills and laboratory capabilities in support of National Authorities;

(h) Requested the Secretariat to continue facilitating and promoting the provision, upon
request, of expert advice on the peaceful uses of chemistry to and among States Parties, including supporting cooperation projects among States Parties;

(i) While taking into account the independent and autonomous nature of the Organisation, encouraged the Secretariat to coordinate its activities with those of other
relevant international and regional organisations as appropriate, in order to build on
existing competencies, develop synergies, and avoid duplication of efforts;

(j) Encouraged the Secretariat to continue to develop relationships and partnerships
with other relevant bodies, national and international, that are working to promote
the peaceful and responsible use of chemistry, including capacity building;

(k) Encouraged the States Parties and the Secretariat to promote the OPCW's role as
a platform for voluntary consultation and cooperation among States Parties in the
areas of chemical safety and security, including through the exchanges of information and best practices, and to support national capacity building, upon request;

(l) Encouraged the Secretariat to continue to develop relations and partnerships as appropriate with relevant regional and international organisations, as well as chemical
industry associations, the private sector, academia, and civil society, in order to raise
awareness of the activities of the OPCW;

(m) Requested the Secretariat to make the information relevant to international cooperation activities available to the National Authorities in a timely fashion on the
external server, as well as to make the above information more widely publicised;

(n) Called upon the Secretariat to continue implementing the OPCW Programme to

Strengthen Cooperation with Africa on the Chemical Weapons Convention, and other appropriate programmes, as well as to provide feedback on a regular basis on the activities and progress made in this regard and, while emphasising the importance of regular budgetary funding for these programmes, encouraged States Parties to make further voluntary contributions to support them;

(o) Encouraged the Secretariat to maintain an alumni association of the Associate Programme and other capacity-building programmes in order to preserve lessons learned and experience gained;

(p) Encouraged the Secretariat to expand the use of e-learning as one of the means for capacity-building and outreach activities; and

(q) Undertake to review their existing national regulations in the field of trade in chemicals in order to render them consistent with the object and purpose of the Convention.

Articles XII to XV and final clauses

9.132   The Third Review Conference reaffirmed the continued relevance of the provisions of Articles XII to XV.

The protection of confidential information

9.133   The Third Review Conference reiterated the need to ensure that confidential data, including the information collected from the chemical industry, is effectively protected at all times, in accordance with the requirements of the Convention. In this context, it emphasised the role of the Director-General in ensuring the protection of confidential information, as well as the responsibility of each staff member of the Secretariat to comply with all rules and regulations pertaining to the protection of confidential information.

9.134   The Third Review Conference stressed the importance of the procedures to be applied in cases of alleged breaches of confidentiality and noted with satisfaction that the Confidentiality Commission has had no disputes relating to such breaches of confidentiality brought before it since entry into force.

9.135   The Third Review Conference welcomed the improvements made in implementing the confidentiality regime since the Second Review Conference, including new initiatives by the Secretariat in relation to the implementation of the confidentiality regime of the OPCW.

9.136   The Third Review Conference, having reviewed the protection of confidential information:

(a) While noting an increase in the number of States Parties that have provided the details of their handling of the information provided to them by the OPCW, urged the remaining States Parties to provide them expeditiously;

(b) Encouraged States Parties to review their practices in assigning levels of classification to confidential information, particularly that related to chemical weapons destruction, and if possible, and in accordance with the States Parties' confidentiality procedures, to adjust the classification level they assign to such information, in order to increase work efficiency and ensure the smooth functioning of the system to protect confidentiality;

(c) Called on the Secretariat to continue assisting States Parties in improving their handling of confidential information; and

(d) While noting the Note (EC-61/S/3, dated 21 May 2010) on the issue of developing and implementing guidelines regarding the long-term handling of confidential information, encouraged the Secretariat and the Council to complete the ongoing work in this regard.

The general functioning of the Organisation for the Prohibition of Chemical Weapons

9.137   The Third Review Conference reaffirmed that full, effective, and non-discriminatory implementation of Article VIII is essential for the realisation of object and purpose of the Convention.

9.138   The Third Review Conference called for the adequate funding for the functioning of the Organisation, through the regular budget and voluntary funding.

9.139   The Third Review Conference recognised the important role and function of the policy-making organs in ensuring the implementation of the Convention. It noted with satisfaction the prevailing practice of and the commitment by the States Parties to adopting decisions by consensus, which had played an important role towards the achievement of common goals and had strengthened the authority of the Convention.

9.140   The Third Review Conference recognised the important contribution made by the Council in advancing and furthering the work of the OPCW. It noted the efforts made with regard to improving its methodology of work and appreciated in this connection the commitment and dedication of the Chairperson of the Council in the context of improving its methodology and enhancing its effectiveness and efficiency.

9.141   The Third Review Conference recognised the valuable role of the SAB and noted that this role will be of increasing importance in the future as scientific and technological changes continue apace. The Third Review Conference further noted the SAB report (RC-3/DG.1) and the response by the Director-General thereto (RC-3/DG.2, dated 31 January 2013). It requested the Director-General and the Council to take into account the recommendations made therein.

9.142   The Third Review Conference noted the increasing convergence of chemistry and biology, and welcomed the establishment of the SAB temporary working group on the convergence of chemistry and biology to explore and consider the potential implications of these advances to the Convention.

9.143   The Third Review Conference noted the valuable contribution to the work of the OPCW made by the Advisory Body for Administrative and Financial Matters.

9.144   The Third Review Conference noted the importance of the contribution to the goals of the Convention that is made by the chemical industry, the scientific community, academia, and civil society organisations engaged with issues relevant to the Convention.

9.145   The Third Review Conference, while reaffirming the autonomous and independent status of the OPCW, while bearing in mind that the OPCW is not an anti-terrorism organisation, took cognisance of the relevant resolutions of the United Nations on combating terrorism and, with a view to enabling States Parties that seek international cooperation in the context of their national, regional, and subregional efforts, underscored the need to explore further cooperation on this issue and build on existing work with relevant international organisations and international bodies that deal with the potential threats of chemical terrorism.

9.146   The Third Review Conference took note of the work of the OPCW Open-Ended Working Group on Terrorism (OEWG) and expressed appreciation for the personal contributions made to its activities by successive Chairpersons. The Third Review Conference noted the relevance of the Council decision of 2001 (EC-XXVII/DEC.5, dated 7 December 2001). The Third Review Conference further encouraged the OEWG to continue to fulfil its mandate.

9.147   The Third Review Conference noted the United Nations General Assembly resolution "Cooperative measures to assess and increase awareness of environmental effects related to waste originating from chemical munitions dumped at sea", adopted at its 65th session by consensus, and invited States Parties to support voluntary sharing of information, raising awareness and cooperation on this issue.

9.148   The Third Review Conference recognised the continued dedication, competence, and integrity of Secretariat staff under the able leadership of the Director-General. It noted the importance of the OPCW continuing to have at its disposal qualified and trained staff, equipment, and procedures fit for the tasks it must fulfil under the Convention, and reaffirmed the importance of recruiting staff in full adherence to the provisions of the Convention.

9.149   The Third Review Conference welcomed the improvements to the budgetary process of the OPCW since the Second Review Conference. It commended the initiatives undertaken by the Secretariat, such as the adoption of International Public Sector Accounting Standards (IPSAS) and the ongoing implementation of results-based management (RBM). The Third Review Conference also reaffirmed the need for the Council, with the support of the Secretariat, to continue the monitoring and assessment of budgetary mechanisms, to ensure that objectives are being met.

9.150   The Third Review Conference noted with concern that many assessed contributions have not been received on time or in full and encouraged States Parties that are in arrears to enter into a payment plan in this regard.

9.151   The Third Review Conference noted that voluntary contributions by States Parties and regional organisations contribute significantly to the work and programmes of the OPCW.

9.152   The Third Review Conference recalled the decision of the Conference at its Sixth Session (C-VI/DEC.9, dated 17 May 2001) on the equal treatment of all official OPCW languages and called for further improvements, including regular updating of the website, sustaining the high level of translation, and continuing to meet the interpretation requirements at sessions of the Conference and the Council.

9.153   The Third Review Conference commended the Secretariat for its efforts in achieving more effective, efficient, and transparent working practices to support the work of the policy-making organs. The Third Review Conference once again pointed out that in order to guarantee good results of the policy-making organs, it is necessary to ensure prompt and timely production of documents. In this context, the Third Review Conference stressed that more openness and transparency will serve the multilateral effectiveness of the Organisation.

9.154   The Third Review Conference expressed its satisfaction with the relationship between the OPCW and the Host Country, including the role of the Director-General, the Council, and the Host Country Committee in promoting good relations with the Netherlands. While noting the goodwill on the part of the Host Country, the Third Review Conference urged continued consultations to make progress on outstanding issues related to the implementation of the Headquarters Agreement.

9.155   The Third Review Conference, having reviewed the general functioning of the OPCW:
         (a) Called upon the Secretariat to ensure prompt and timely production of documents related to the policy-making organs, and to enhance efficiency and effectiveness in this regard;
         (b) Encouraged States Parties to consider supporting the work of the SAB by making voluntary contributions to its trust fund and to consider a greater involvement and participation of States Parties in the information sessions organised by the SAB;
         (c) Encouraged States Parties and the Secretariat to continue to keep the convergence of chemistry and biology under review, including through the SAB temporary working group on the convergence of chemistry and biology, and encouraged greater interaction between relevant experts;
         (d) Called upon States Parties and the Secretariat, as part of efforts to promote the ethical norms of the Convention, to encourage and promote efforts by the appropriate national and international professional bodies to inculcate awareness amongst

scientists and engineers at an early stage in their training that the knowledge and technologies used for beneficial purposes should only be used for purposes not prohibited under this Convention;

(e) Urged all States Parties, particularly those that are two or more years in arrears, to regularise their payments, related to their assessed contributions, without delay and in accordance with the Financial Regulations and Rules;

(f) Requested the Director-General to continue to report regularly to the Council on the continued implementation of the tenure policy, including the implications for the OPCW's effectiveness and efficiency and any limited exceptions to the normal policy that may be necessary on these grounds;

(g) Emphasised the importance of continuing to have an open and transparent policy for recruiting staff and underlined the need for maintaining within the Secretariat chemical weapons-specific expertise and paying due consideration to geographical and gender balance;

(h) Stressed that the OPCW should remain the global repository of knowledge and expertise with regard to chemical weapons disarmament, the verification of their non-possession and non-use, and their destruction, and requested the Secretariat to identify and implement ways of ensuring continuity in its knowledge base and expertise in these areas;

(i) Requested the Director-General to keep in view developments in science and technology when identifying the future training needs of the Secretariat;

(j) Called upon the Secretariat to continue to vigorously pursue initiatives such as IPSAS, and encouraged the Secretariat to further improve the budgetary process of the OPCW and the implementation of RBM;

(k) Encouraged the Secretariat to continue its efforts to be more compact, flexible, and efficient, optimising its use of human and financial resources while ensuring that sufficient resources are available to support the effective implementation of the Convention, and to keep the Council regularly informed of progress via the annual Budget process;

(l) Encouraged the Secretariat to continue to improve the effectiveness and efficiency of its work;

(m) Encouraged the Director-General to review the current situation related to the administrative costs of the Organisation in order to secure its proper functioning, as well as the possibilities for cost-reduction measures; and

(n) Encouraged the Secretariat and the States Parties to improve interaction with the chemical industry, the scientific community, academia, and civil society organisations engaged in issues relevant to the Convention, and encouraged the Secretariat and States Parties to develop a more open approach, in conformity with the Rules of Procedure of the policy-making organs with regard to such interaction.

10. AGENDA ITEM TEN – Reports of subsidiary bodies

COMMITTEE OF THE WHOLE

10.1   The Third Review Conference noted the report of the Committee of the Whole on the results of its consideration of the agenda item referred to it on the recommendation of the General Committee (RC-3/CoW.1, dated 19 April 2013), and approved the report.

GENERAL COMMITTEE

10.2   The Third Review Conference noted the reports of the General Committee, and approved the reports.

CREDENTIALS COMMITTEE

10.3   The report of the Credentials Committee (RC-3/2, dated 17 April 2013) was presented by its Chairperson, Ambassador Mohamed Karim Ben Bécher of Tunisia. The Chairperson orally reported that, following the closure of the Credentials Committee meeting, formal credentials were received for the representative of Cameroon. The Third Review Conference noted this additional information and approved the report.

11. AGENDA ITEM ELEVEN – Any other business

The Third Review Conference welcomed the announcement by Somalia about its decision to accede to the Convention, as reported by the Director-General.

12. AGENDA ITEM TWELVE – Adoption of the final documents of the Third Review Conference

The Third Review Conference considered and adopted the report of the Third Review Conference.

13. AGENDA ITEM THIRTEEN – Closure

The Chairperson closed the Third Review Conference at 23:58 on 19 April 2013.

21.4 OPCW Academic Forum and Industry and Protection Forum

S/674/2008 containing a Note by the Technical Secretariat dated 1 February 2008 and entitled "The 2007 OPCW Academic Forum and the Industry and Protection Forum: in support of comprehensive implementation of the Chemical Weapons Convention"

INTRODUCTION

1. As part of the celebrations of the tenth anniversary of the entry into force of the Chemical Weapons Convention (hereinafter "the Convention"), the Technical Secretariat (hereinafter "the Secretariat"), together with representatives of the chemical industry and a number of prestigious academic institutions, organised the OPCW Academic Forum (held on 18 and 19 September 2007) and the OPCW Industry and Protection Forum (held on 1 and 2 November 2007).

2. Both forums provided a platform for discussion amongst the Organisation for the Prohibition of Chemical Weapons (OPCW) and other key stakeholders in the Convention, such as the National Authorities, the chemical industry, the scientific community, and other international organisations. A wide range of topics was considered, including a review of the accomplishments of the OPCW, the progress made in national implementation, and the political and technical challenges that will confront the Organisation in the future. Specifically, participants had the opportunity to discuss how the OPCW can adapt to the new security environment and to the changes that are occurring in science, technology, and the chemical industry, especially in regard to new chemicals and processes.

3. These two forums were organised in recognition of the multi-stakeholder nature of the Convention and the need to involve all relevant sectors of society in its implementation. The overall goal involved enhancing cooperation amongst the chemical industry, National Authorities, and other parties interested in full implementation.

4. The proceedings of both forums will be published in due course. Given that the recommendations and conclusions of both forums are relevant to the objectives of the upcoming Second

Special Session of the Conference of the States Parties to Review the Operation of the Chemical Weapons Convention, the Secretariat has prepared this Note to inform the States Parties in a timely fashion of the discussions that took place and the observations that emerged.

5. No funding had been allocated for the forums in the 2007 Programme and Budget, and financial support came in the form of contributions by the Government of the Netherlands as well as by the European Union (EU).

THE ACADEMIC FORUM

6. The Academic Forum was organised in association with the Netherlands Institute for International Relations "Clingendael" ("Instituut Clingendael") and the Netherlands Organisation for Applied Scientific Research or TNO ("Nederlandse Organisatie voor Toegepast Natuurwetenschappelijk Onderzoek"). It brought together leading academics, scientists, diplomats, military officers, and policy-makers involved in shaping and implementing disarmament and non-proliferation policies, in particular those related to the prohibition of chemical weapons.

7. The forum was opened by the Director-General of the OPCW, Ambassador Rogelio Pfirter, who also chaired the meeting. Welcome addresses were delivered by Dr Ph. de Heer, Secretary-General of the Dutch Ministry of Foreign Affairs, and Admiral (ret.) Cees van Duyvendijk from the TNO. Statements at the opening plenary were made by the representatives of the United Nations (UN), the World Health Organization (WHO), the United Nations Training and Research Institute (UNITAR), and the Clingendael Institute. The keynote presentation was given by Ambassador Rolf Ekeus, Chairman of the Governing Board of the Stockholm International Peace Research Institute (SIPRI) who, from 1991 and 1997, was Chairman of the UN Special Commission on Iraq (UNSCOM).

8. Parallel workshops on four broad themes took place, and covered the following topics: the destruction of chemical weapons stockpiles, the non-proliferation of chemical weapons, the impact of science and technology on the Convention, and the role of the Convention in a world that is essentially free of chemical weapons. In addition, a multilateral game formed part of the programme. This game simulated some of the scenarios that might unfold and the negotiation-related challenges the OPCW would have to face in relation to future implementation of the Convention.

ISSUES RELATED TO CHEMICAL WEAPONS AND THEIR DESTRUCTION

9. The workshop participants noted that all possessor States Parties had at times experienced significant difficulties and delays in destroying their chemical weapons stockpiles. Determined to complete their destruction operations as soon as possible, States Parties are aware that they must do so observing stringent requirements with regard to the safety of people and the environment. So far, no deaths have taken place that are directly related to the implementation of chemical weapons destruction operations, although some injuries have occurred. This is noteworthy, given the intrinsic risks involved in the storage, handling, transportation, and destruction of chemical weapons, and especially given the fact that stockpiles are aging. The workshop stressed the need for adequate and timely funding of the destruction programmes and of the provision of assistance where it is needed and requested.

10. The workshop also considered the challenges related to the destruction of old and abandoned chemical weapons (OACWs), an issue that will undoubtedly become more important in the future. At this stage, three countries have declared abandoned chemical weapons (ACWs), and 13 countries have declared old chemical weapons (OCWs). However, it is known that there are many other sites where training with chemical weapons was conducted in the past, or where military operations took place, with chemical weapons forming part of the armoury of the belligerents. One should therefore still expect more – potentially many more – declarations of OACWs in the future.

11. The workshop participants noted that little was known about what changes have ensued to the chemical weapons that had been disposed of by dumping at sea, during a period long before the negotiations of the Convention had been completed. For all practical purposes, given that States Parties have discretion as to whether to declare chemical weapons disposed of in this manner and whether to destroy them in accordance with the Convention, this issue remains outside the purview of this disarmament treaty. It remains to be seen how States Parties proceed in relation to this matter, and what the involvement, if any, of the OPCW would be in terms of any future recovery and destruction operations in regard to these chemical weapons.

12. On a more general note, the workshop concluded that, although destruction deadlines cannot always be met, they are important. Deadlines help to focus the efforts of States Parties and ensure that sufficient funding for the destruction of chemical weapons is provided. Because of the potential danger to the public involved in the destruction of chemical weapons, which can have a major environmental and health impact on the communities concerned, most speakers stressed the importance of public outreach and information, given that this is a topic of public interest. In addition, the Convention points out that the protection of human health and of the environment is an essential precondition for the conduct of chemical weapons destruction operations.

ISSUES RELATED TO THE NON-PROLIFERATION OF CHEMICAL WEAPONS

13. There was recognition by the workshop participants that the concept of chemical weapons non-proliferation has evolved over the years. Today, it is considered that the use of chemical weapons lacks legitimacy, and the main object of concern is the possibility that some States outside the Convention or non-State actors could acquire chemical weapons covertly.

14. The workshop participants made the observation that, given their regional and political contexts, countries have different reasons for joining the Convention. This has an impact on how they prioritise the responsibilities related to implementation, and underlines the fact that measures in regard to national implementation ought to be country-specific and must take into account the prevailing historical, legal, regulatory, economic (including trade), security and other factors and conditions. No one-size solution fits all conditions and requirements.

15. In terms of implementation of the Convention, there is also a need to find the right balance between prohibitions related to chemical weapons, and free access to chemicals and to chemical equipment and technology.

16. Participants also stressed that effective national implementation remains an essential condition for providing reliable non-proliferation assurances. There is a need to move from a quantitative approach that focuses simply on numbers of States Parties and National Authorities (and calculations on how many of them have drafted the required implementing legislation) to a more qualitative approach that concentrates on improving the effectiveness of implementation and enforcement measures. Capacity building by the OPCW remains an important tool for improving the situation.

17. National implementation was seen as vital in terms of countering the possible terrorist use of toxic materials. But the Convention's routine verification regime was originally formulated with militarily significant quantities of chemical agents/precursors in mind.

18. The workshop participants were of the view that the comprehensive scope of the Convention – the "General Purpose Criterion" – needs to be preserved and restated, so as to maintain the relevance of the Convention in the light of scientific, technological, and political developments.

19 The conclusion was reached that the Convention needed to be embedded in the scientific community through education, the discussion of ethics, and the raising of the awareness of dual-use issues. It was noted, however, that there are divergent ministerial/departmental responsibilities amongst States Parties, and National Authorities need to persuade and advise other stakeholders in government and society to take action to this end.

20. The workshop raised a number of longer-term issues that may require future consideration and action by the OPCW. These included the following:
    (a) Should there be a broader implementation concept of the Convention, allowing the Secretariat to consider longer-term strategic issues?
    (b) It may be useful to learn from the evolution of the Organisation for Economic Cooperation and Development (OECD), which was originally a technical agency, but which now follows a "knowledge-based" model, and which provides policy support at the same time.
    (c) Are there lessons to be learned from the intersessional process of the Biological and Toxin Weapons Convention, such as the conduct of thematic meetings of States Parties (at expert and diplomatic levels) on key subjects?
    (d) Is there room for a joint approach with other international organisations in terms of developing a policy on the management of chemicals, and could that be a significant incentive in persuading States Parties to adopt and implement their own plans in terms of national implementation?

ADVANCES IN SCIENCE AND TECHNOLOGY

21. The starting point for discussions during the third workshop was that the Convention is science-based; in other words, the drafters of the Convention had recognised that advances in sciences and technology could have an impact on the definition of what actually constitutes chemical warfare, on what agents could be produced and by what means, and on how these developments could have an impact on the verification of compliance.

22. The workshop took account of the rapid developments in the life sciences, including the increasing convergence of chemical and biological sciences, the advances in combinatorial chemistry and nanotechnology, the changing nature of chemical-production processes (including the use of micro-reactors), and the globalisation of chemical production and trade. These developments will bring major benefits to humankind (for example in terms of sustainable development, improved public health, better food production, and enhanced international cooperation in the peaceful uses of chemistry). They may also help to provide better protective measures against chemical weapons (detection, protection, medical counter-measures, forensic analysis, and decontamination).

23. However, there was a recognition that the rapid advances in science and technology, including in chemistry and related sciences, also present a number of challenges to the Convention. These include the following:
    (a) *chemicals of biological origin* (CBOs) – developments in this field could lead to the design or discovery of novel chemical weapons agents;
    (b) *databanks of many thousands of novel synthetic chemicals* – their existence and enlargement could lead to a future generation of chemical weapons agents;
    (c) *targeted delivery* – developments in this area could result in a more efficient dissemination of chemical weapons agents; and
    (d) *incapacitants* – advances in science and technology, it was observed, could well add to the existing problems that had been inherited from the original negotiations that took place in regard to the Convention.

24. Concerns were expressed in relation to the fact that, given the way the OPCW is structured and the processes by which decisions are taken, the Organisation simply does not have the flexibility it needs to respond quickly and effectively to developments in science and technology that necessitate changes to the implementation process.

25. At the same time, it should be borne in mind that advances in science and technology create new opportunities for international cooperation between States Parties in the peaceful uses of chemistry. The workshop participants acknowledged the achievements of the OPCW in this field, and also recognised the following:

(a) the importance of ensuring that international-cooperation projects correspond to the needs of the States Parties;

(b) the importance of developing synergies between the OPCW and other international organisations involved in international cooperation and development projects; and

(c) the usefulness of academic collaboration projects between developed and developing countries, in that these endeavours support the objectives of the Convention; these projects would also benefit from being linked to the OPCW's International Cooperation Programme.

THE CONVENTION IN A CHEMICAL-WEAPONS-FREE WORLD

26. The participants acknowledged that the Convention has been successful in reducing the likelihood of State-to-State use of chemical weapons. The military use of chemical weapons is much less likely today than when the Convention was first drafted. The possibility of chemical agents falling into the hands of terrorists, on the other hand, constitutes a potential problem.

27. During discussions, questions were raised as to whether the OPCW needed to take an integrated approach towards regulating toxic chemicals and what its role should be with regard to non-State actors (participants, however, acknowledged that the Convention was not an anti-terrorism instrument). The specific and important question was raised as to whether the Convention was able to deal with the threats that lie ahead. Some argued that there now was a need for a global governance scheme for science and technology, and posed the question as to whether the OPCW was capable of adjusting its mandate to deal with these emerging issues.

28. For example, participants asked whether the present categorisation of chemicals in the schedules of chemicals will remain useful in the future, and whether there is any utility remaining in regard to challenge-inspection schemes. Some stated that there was an enormous role to be played by non-governmental organisations (NGOs) and professional organisations, and argued for the further extension of the OPCW's relationships with other international and regional organisations.

29. In any event, participants concluded that the Convention will have to undergo a functional shift after the destruction of chemical weapons has been completed, thus requiring changes to the processes by which it is implemented. It was suggested that a governance approach might be adopted, but to follow such an approach, more stakeholders would need to be involved and allowed to actively participate in comprehensive implementation.

30. To ensure continued success for the Convention in the post-destruction environment, three areas require consideration, that is, whether:

(a) to establish networks to assist in reviewing the impact on the verification regime of advances in science and technology; and

(b) to facilitate a greater involvement by stakeholders (such as other international organisations, regional organisations and NGOs).

31. Looking beyond the challenges of chemical warfare in the traditional sense, the workshop observed that the Convention now faces new challenges, such as the potential use of toxic industrial chemicals (for example, by non-State actors). This may require States Parties to look again at the assistance-and-protection provisions in the Convention, and some participants argued it would be necessary to reconsider the definition of what constitutes a chemical weapon.

32. The medical aspects of current and emerging threats were discussed, and the need was highlighted for effective collaboration and coordination with international organisations such as the WHO, regional non-governmental scientific and/or medical organisations, as well as national organisations (such as societies of chemistry and toxicology, others involved in the safe use of toxins and poisons, and groups working on the development of codes of ethics). It was agreed that more training and exercises simulating chemical exposure should be offered to

first responders, so that medical-response systems can be improved. The workshop also noted that there was a need for more participation on the part of the chemical industry.

33. The observation was made that the Convention as it is constituted is a delicate balance of rights and prohibitions, making this treaty unique and offering an incentive for countries to join. If that balance is disturbed, then the attractiveness of the Convention may be reduced. It was noted that the OPCW does not simply deal with chemical weapons, but also with the safe use and management of chemicals. Consequently, participants stated that an integrated approach should be formulated, and that the OPCW would be well advised to further develop its partnerships with other treaties or treaty organisations involved in the issue of chemical safety. An integrated framework needed to be developed, and the OPCW should play a part in this.

FINAL OBSERVATIONS

34. The discussions of the Academic Forum highlighted a key point: The world has changed since the Convention was negotiated. The Convention has been successful in reducing the threat of State-to-State use of chemical weapons. But as the global context changes, so must the OPCW. For this to take effect, interaction between the OPCW and society, including the academic world and the chemical industry, is becoming ever more vital.

35. The eventual completion of the destruction of chemical weapons stockpiles will shift the global focus from chemical weapons disarmament to the prevention of the acquisition of chemical weapons. The transition of the verification regime from a focus primarily on disarmament to one which concentrates on non-proliferation, cooperation, and assistance will call for adjustments in the mandates given to the OPCW by its Member States, and for a conceptual rethinking of some of the Organisation's programmes and approaches.

36. The Academic Forum recognised the value of academic input to the OPCW and the processes by which it implements the Convention. Although a range of mechanisms already exist to enable such interaction, there was a sense that it would be beneficial if this dialogue and cooperation were enhanced.

The Industry and Protection Forum

37. With the financial support of the EU, the Industry and Protection Forum was organised in association with the International Council of Chemical Associations (ICCA) and the European Chemistry Council (CEFIC). It brought together representatives from the chemical industry, government, international organisations, National Authorities, national laboratories and agencies, academia, and other institutions that work in the different fields (verification, assistance and protection, and the safety and security of chemical weapons) that formed the focus of this Forum.

38. A non-commercial exhibition that demonstrated solutions for how the different requirements of the Convention can be met was also organised.

39. The Forum was opened by the Director-General of the OPCW, Ambassador Rogelio Pfirter. Welcome addresses were delivered by Mr René van Sloten, Executive Director for Industrial Policy of the CEFIC, and Ms Ana Gomes, Vice-President of the Committee for Security and Defence of the European Parliament. The Director-General delivered a second statement at a joint plenary session attended by Forum participants and National Authority representatives. This was followed by a statement by Mr Jack Gerard, Chief Executive Officer of the American Chemistry Council (ACC) and Secretary of the International Council of Chemical Associations (ICCA), speaking on behalf of the latter organisation.

40. Three parallel workshops were organised on the following subject areas: issues surrounding verification and implementation of the Convention that are of relevance to the chemical industry (including sampling and analysis), assistance and protection, and the safety and security of chemical plants.

Verification and implementation in the chemical industry (including sampling and analysis during industry inspections)

41. The workshop started with the discussion of the idea that the chemical industry, since entry into force of the Convention, considers implementation-related processes as a normal part of their day-to-day activities. Of course, there are issues that still need to be addressed. The complexities inherent in the definitions, terms, and regulations of the Convention can create difficulties. Also, there remain differences in relation to national regulations, the nomenclature used by various countries/associations, the declaration of transfers, and the declaration of mixtures containing scheduled chemicals. In all these areas, the chemical industry needs clarity and consistency in order to implement requirements and to ensure that equitable and similar standards are applied to all States Parties. The adjustments made in the selection methodology for inspection of other chemical production facilities (OCPFs) were seen as a way of devising a fairer distribution in terms of this type of inspection.

42. It was noted that it remains important for the Organisation to provide practical help to countries and companies in order to enable them to identify all declarable facilities and/or activities. A joint CEFIC-OPCW project has made progress on updating a spreadsheet that identifies scheduled chemicals. This update should be made available to States Parties and to companies involved in the chemical industry by April 2008.

43. The workshop recognised that the knowledge that chemical companies have of how the requirements of the Convention are to be implemented needs to be maintained. Preserving awareness and transferring knowledge within and between companies was an important responsibility of chemical-industry associations. In addition, it was important that the National Authorities remain engaged with the chemical industry as partners and advisors in the implementation process.

44. The workshop reviewed the progress that the OPCW had made with regard to the use of sampling and analysis as an inspection method in the chemical industry, and discussed the results of the trial phase of sampling and analysis during Schedule 2 inspections.

45. One conclusion that emerged during the discussions was that National Authorities should educate facilities about, and prepare them for, the use of sampling and analysis in industry inspections. It was pointed out that the conditions on-site are checked. Regulations may also exist in States Parties that may affect the transportation or use of the equipment and chemicals carried by OPCW inspection teams for on-site analysis.

46. The issue of performing on-site analysis in open or "blinded" mode was analysed. The Secretariat explained that any issues related to this should be resolved during the course of an inspection. It is known that false positives can occur. If the analytical equipment is operated in "blinded" mode, a resolution of any difficulties requires the setting-up of the instrument from scratch and beginning the analysis once again. It was noted, in this context, that operating the instrument in open mode must not be confused with undertaking a full analysis – significant protections exist in open mode to ensure that the sample composition will not be disclosed, except with regard to the confirmation that no scheduled chemicals are present.

47. Concerns were raised in relation to the possibility that, during on-site analysis, small quantities of scheduled chemicals might be detected (for example, unknown impurities). This appears unlikely, however, given the detection limits that are applied. It would be desirable to fill the gaps in the OPCW Central Analytical Database (OCAD) so as to avoid false positives.

48. There were a number of practical issues that the pilot phase had highlighted, such as the option for inspectors to use a facility for on-site analysis that is in close proximity but outside the perimeters of the inspected facility (in other words, "in-country off-site") to obtain supplies needed for analysis from local sources, or to shift the check of inspection equipment from the point of entry to the inspection site.

49. To summarise, the workshop noted that sampling and analysis in industry inspections has been demonstrated to work well, and that the necessity to protect confidentiality can be met

with the existing equipment, software, databases, and procedures. Whilst it places an extra burden both on the facility to be inspected and on the OPCW, some participants stressed that it was a requirement under the Convention, and the only means of providing scientific proof of the absence of scheduled chemicals.

ASSISTANCE AND PROTECTION

50. The workshop came to the conclusion that the submission of information by States Parties on their national protective programmes under paragraph 4 of Article X is important, in that not only does it provide transparency, but it also enables States Parties capable of providing assistance to be identified, as well as those in need of it.
51. The observation was also made that States Parties are fully supportive of, and recognise the need to meet, the requirements of Article X of the Convention. Despite the newly adopted formats for the annual submission of information on national protective programmes, only 76 declarations about protective programmes were submitted in 2006 (and, by the time of the Forum, only 50 in 2007).
52. As for the assistance offers made by States Parties, the workshop noted a number of examples of what they had offered, which included international or regional training courses, or national-assistance offers (including procedures, and equipment for detection, protection, and decontamination). Forty-four assistance offers had been received from States Parties by the time of the Forum.
53. The workshop also recalled that, by the end of 2007, the databank on protection required under Article X would be made available (by means of a password-controlled network) to the National Authorities and to the Permanent Representatives outside the OPCW headquarters.
54 The provision of expert advice to States Parties that wish to enhance their protective capacity has become an important implementation issue. Whilst in the early years after entry into force, the focus of such measures was on national capacity building, that focus has shifted since 2004 to regional (and subregional) capacity building.
55. States Parties' contributions under subparagraph 7(a) of Article X remains limited, and stands at EUR 1.3 million, well short of what would be required to fund any large-scale operation. The workshop was informed about the exercises conducted in Croatia (in 2002) and in Ukraine (in 2005), and about the efforts to improve cooperation and coordination with other relevant international organisations.
56. The Secretariat reviewed its standard operating procedures and its work instructions so as to take account of the practical experiences gained in the various exercises that had been conducted. The lessons learned also extended to identifying what equipment most suitable for the delivery of assistance and investigations of the alleged use of chemical weapons needed to be procured, what training needed to be provided, and what training concepts needed to be developed.
57 The participants of the workshop raised a number of issues that they considered deserved further consideration. These included:
   (a) whether attacks on chemical facilities with conventional weapons should be considered a violation of the Convention, and whether a State Party so attacked would be able to request assistance;
   (b) what methods needed to be developed in relation to developing the coordination between the different international agencies and units that would respond to a request for assistance (this included such issues as different languages involved, communications systems, standard operating procedures, equipment, tactics, and so on);
   (c) whether States Parties should focus on building up regional capacity (for example by setting up regional training centres) and whether, consequently, assistance offers could be made on a regional basis;
   (d) how the Organisation could ensure that the right people attended the training courses; and

    (e)   what would constitute an appropriate level of chemical defence once chemical weapons stockpiles had been destroyed.

58. The participants recognised the wide range of possible scenarios for assistance operations and what the requirements for such activities would be, and also the need for more information on what the States Parties' assistance offers actually included. There were only limited resources for the building-up of regional networks and for "train the trainers" events. States Parties needed to be better prepared to receive any assistance that was needed; this included enhanced coordination between all organisations involved in an emergency response.

SAFETY AND SECURITY AT CHEMICAL PLANTS

59. This workshop began with the premise that the Convention was neither a counter-terrorism nor a chemical-safety treaty. However, an analysis of its effectiveness indicated that it had helped to make it more difficult for malicious acts involving the use of toxic chemicals to occur. Given that the deadlines for the completion of chemical weapons disarmament are approaching, the view was expressed that new perspectives in terms of implementation need to be formulated, and that more attention should be paid to issues related to the chemical industry.

60. The workshop participants identified a number of challenges that potentially loom ahead:
    (a)   the fact that it would take only one incident for trust in the Convention to be lost;
    (b)   the recognition that attacks on chemical facilities or the theft of toxic chemicals would constitute only the beginning of a chain of events that would subsequently start to unfold, and therefore there was a need to consider how to manage all the consequences of such an incident;
    (c)   there remained a lack of clear and internationally agreed definitions of what constitutes terrorism and how to define "criminal acts"; and
    (d)   issues involving safety and/or security needed attention in regard to the entire chain of the existence of chemicals, from their production to their eventual disposal.

61. There were a number of balances that needed to be struck: The provision of enhanced security could help catalyse the development of innovations in industry, but could also become a hindrance. There was also a need to raise awareness about safety and security issues, but also an inherent danger of creating hysteria by doing so. The need also existed to make information available to the public on possible chemical hazards, but such information could also be useful to malicious actors. Finally, there needed to be an assessment as to what the responsibilities and activities of industry, government, and international bodies were.

62. At the international level, the workshop recognised the need for synchronised action of all stakeholders in the Convention. The chemical industry needs to participate in the efforts being made to enhance safety and security, and these efforts must be inclusive. There was a need to create a level playing field for the chemical industry with regard to security costs. Lessons can be learned from the International Atomic Energy Agency (IAEA) and the WHO in terms of promoting safety and disseminating best practices in the field of safety and security.

63. The workshop recalled that the OPCW has been established by the Convention as a forum for consultation and cooperation between the States Parties, which could include the exchange of ideas and the discussion of best practices in such areas as chemical safety and security. This may, in fact, increase the attractiveness of the OPCW framework for States not yet Party, and may help to improve national implementation by exploiting the synergisms between national implementation of the Convention and measures to ensure the safety and security of activities related to chemicals.

64. The workshop also recognised the relevance of the provisions of Articles X and XI, and that opportunities existed to more fully meet the objectives of these provisions by raising chemical safety and security issues in the context of the OPCW.

FINAL OBSERVATIONS

65. The Industry and Protection Forum highlighted the fact that, the chemical industry, like any other modern enterprise, is continuing to evolve, while the Convention's verification mechanism remains relatively stable. The increasing overlaps between chemical and biological sciences, the integration of chemical engineering into the life sciences, and the fusion between these and information technology are factors that are having a significant impact on the Convention.

66. The Forum, at this stage, focused much of its attention on sampling and analysis in industry inspections. There will be a need to broaden this agenda in the future and to continue to address other issues related to the effective and consistent implementation of the Convention in the chemical industry. This would have to include many of the issues that were also discussed at the Academic Forum.

67. Other challenges to non-proliferation are emerging as a result of changes to the security environment. Risks include actions by non-State actors, such as criminals and terrorists, to produce or acquire chemical weapons. There is a need for especial vigilance in establishing and maintaining controls on the manufacturing, transfer, and use of dual-use materials through national and international regulatory mechanisms, as well as through effective self-governance in industry and by scientific and teaching institutions.

68. It is crucial that the OPCW be able to adapt to the changing realities so that the verification and implementation regimes of the Convention can continue to prevent the proliferation of chemical weapons and the materials for making them, and in a manner that does not impede legitimate developments in the chemical industry. Non-State actors must not be allowed to gain access to toxic chemicals or to the means for producing them.

69. In this ever-changing world, the smooth interaction between the National Authorities and other stakeholders in the Convention, both from the government and private sectors, is of the essence. There is a need to focus more on the quality of implementation, the involvement at the national level of other agencies, and the coordination of national-implementation measures between all the agencies involved. Such an integrated approach at the national-implementation level can lead to the increased adoption and implementation of non-proliferation and safety-and-security regulations, and of UN Security Council Resolution 1540.

NEXT STEPS

70. The Academic Form and the Industry and Protection Forum confirmed that, for the Convention to be comprehensively implemented, it is vital that all stakeholders, including the chemical industry and the scientific community, become involved in the promotion of its goals, especially in relation to national implementation, assistance and protection against chemical weapons, and the achievement of universality. In this context, these forums reaffirmed the need for the continuing interaction between the OPCW and all parties that are interested in achieving full implementation of this crucial disarmament treaty.

71. The Conference of the States Parties, at its Twelfth Session (which took place from 5 to 9 November 2007), took note of both forums and encouraged participation on the broadest possible geographical basis of all stakeholders in such events in the future. The overall objective is the continuation of the discussions and interchanges that had been initiated at the forums, especially in terms of promoting national implementation, international cooperation, and universality.

72. The continuation of the forums will provide a useful platform for the active engagement of OPCW stakeholders in promoting and/or supporting comprehensive implementation of the Convention, especially in relation to Articles VI, VII, X, and XI.

73. This dialogue between the multiple stakeholders of the Convention could, for example, in-

volve more detailed studies of specific issues by small project groups, specialised workshops on topics relevant to the Convention and that require broad involvement from a variety of parties (including from the chemical industry), and the use of the worldwide web as a platform for raising and discussing issues.

74. The support of the Member States of the OPCW is essential to ensuring the success of the emerging platform for cooperation and dialogue, and thus the Secretariat would like to encourage Member States and their institutions to do all they can to foster its continuing development.

75. No funds will be allocated in the OPCW Programme and Budget for any activities associated with the follow-up process, and thus any such activities would rely on funding through voluntary contributions.

Procedures and Mandates of the OPCW

22. CONFERENCE OF THE STATES PARTIES (ARTICLE VIII(B))

22.1 Rules of Procedure of the Conference of the States Parties

C-I/3/Rev.2 adopted by the Conference of the States Parties at its First Session on 12 May 1997 (paragraph 5 of the Report of the Conference of States Parties, document C-I/9), as amended by the Conference of States Parties at its Third Special Session (C-SS-3/DEC.1, dated 7 April 2008) and by the Third Special Session of the Conference of the States Parties to Review the Operation of the Chemical Weapons Convention (RC-3/DEC.2, dated 8 April 2013)

RULES OF PROCEDURE OF THE CONFERENCE OF THE STATES PARTIES

I. *SESSIONS*

A. REGULAR SESSIONS

RULE 1   DATE OF SESSIONS
The Conference of the States Parties (hereinafter called "the Conference") of the Organisation for the Prohibition of Chemical Weapons (hereinafter called "the Organisation") shall meet in regular sessions which shall be held annually unless it decides otherwise.[1] The session shall be convened on a date set by the Conference at its previous regular session.

RULE 2   NOTIFICATION OF SESSIONS [2]
The Director-General shall notify all Members of the Organisation at least 90 days in advance of each regular session, of the opening date, place and expected duration thereof.

B. SPECIAL SESSIONS

RULE 3   HOLDING OF SPECIAL SESSIONS
Special sessions of the Conference shall be convened in accordance with Article VIII, paragraph 12 of the Convention.

RULE 4   SUMMONING BY THE CONFERENCE
Special sessions of the Conference shall be convened when decided by the Conference.[3]

RULE 5   SUMMONING AT THE REQUEST OF THE EXECUTIVE COUNCIL
Special sessions of the Conference shall be convened not later than 30 days after the receipt by the Director-General of a request for such a session from the Executive Council, unless specified otherwise in the request.[4]

RULE 6   SUMMONING AT THE REQUEST OF MEMBERS
Any Member of the Organisation may request the Director-General to convene a special ses-

---

[1] Article VIII, paragraph 11.
[2] For the First Session of the Conference the notification was issued by the Secretary-General of the United Nations in his capacity as the depositary of the Convention [footnote in original].
[3] Article VIII, subparagraph 12(a).
[4] Article VIII, subparagraph 12(b).

sion of the Conference. The Director-General shall immediately inform the other Members of the Organisation of the request and inquire whether they concur with it. If one third of the Members concur with the request, a special session of the Conference shall be convened by the Director-General not later than 30 days after the receipt by him or her of such request.[5]

RULE 7   NOTIFICATIONS OF SPECIAL SESSIONS
The Director-General shall notify all Members of the Organisation at least 21 days in advance of each special session, of the opening date, place and expected duration thereof.

C. SPECIAL SESSIONS TO REVIEW THE OPERATION OF THE CONVENTION

RULE 8   CONVENING OF SPECIAL REVIEW SESSIONS [6]
(a) The Conference shall not later than one year after the expiry of the fifth and the tenth year after the entry into force of the Convention, and at such other times within that time period as may be decided upon, convene in special sessions to undertake reviews of the operation of the Convention. Such reviews shall take into account any relevant scientific and technological developments. At intervals of five years thereafter, unless otherwise decided upon, further sessions of the Conference shall be convened with the same objective.[7]
(b) Each Special Review Session shall elect a Chairman and ten Vice-Chairmen and such other officers as it may decide, having due regard to the principle of equitable geographical representation. They shall hold office solely for the purpose of the Special Review Session. Their rights, duties, and functions are identical to those ascribed by the present rules to the Chairman and Vice-Chairmen of the Conference of the States Parties, notwithstanding the provisions of Rule 35 below.

D. REGULAR AND SPECIAL SESSIONS

GENERAL PROVISIONS

RULE 9   PLACE OF SESSIONS
Sessions of the Conference shall take place at the seat of the Organisation unless the Conference decides otherwise.[8]

RULE 10   DURATION OF SESSIONS
On the recommendation of the General Committee, the Conference shall, at the beginning of each session, fix a closing date for the session.

RULE 11   TEMPORARY ADJOURNMENT OF SESSIONS
The Conference may decide at any session to adjourn temporarily and resume its meetings at a later date.

---

[5] Article VIII, subparagraph 12(c).
[6] Article VIII, paragraph 22.
[7] The Conference may also be convened in the form of an Amendment Conference in accordance with Article XV, paragraph 2. In this case these Rules would apply as appropriate [footnote in original].
[8] Article VIII, paragraph 14.

II. *AGENDA*

A. REGULAR SESSIONS

RULE 12 PREPARATION OF PROVISIONAL AGENDA

The provisional agenda for all regular sessions of the Conference shall be drawn up by the Executive Council[9] and sent by the Director-General to all Members of the Organisation not later than 60 days in advance of the session.

RULE 13 CONTENTS OF PROVISIONAL AGENDA

The provisional agenda for each regular session shall include:

(a) All items the inclusion of which has been decided by the Conference at a previous session;

(b) All items proposed by the Executive Council;

(c) All items proposed by any Member of the Organisation;[10]

(d) All resolutions and all agenda items which the United Nations has referred or proposed to the Organisation, as well as any item proposed by a specialised agency, and which the Executive Council submits to the Conference in accordance with the agreement establishing the relationship between the Organisation and the United Nations and the Organisation and a specialised agency;

(e) Election of Members to membership of the Executive Council;

(f) The annual draft report of the Organisation on the implementation of the Convention, the annual report of the Executive Council and such other reports as the Executive Council deems necessary or which the Conference may request;

(g) Fostering of international cooperation for peaceful purposes in the field of chemical activities;

(h) The programme and budget of the Organisation, submitted by the Executive Council, for the ensuing financial period and all items pertaining to this budget;[11]

(i) The External Auditor's report on the audited financial statements of the Organisation as forwarded by the Executive Council;[12]

(j) The scale of assessments to be paid by States Parties;[13]

(k) Any issue to be brought to the attention of the United Nations requiring approval by the Conference in accordance with Article XII of the Convention;[14]

(l) The opening date and anticipated duration of the next regular session of the Conference;

(m) All items which the Director-General, in consultation with and following agreement from the Executive Council, deems necessary to put before the Conference; and

(n) Other items required by the Convention.

RULE 14 SUPPLEMENTARY ITEMS

A Member of the Organisation, the Executive Council, the Director-General, in agreement with the Executive Council or the United Nations, may, not later than 30 days before the date set for the opening of any regular session, request the inclusion of supplementary items in the agenda. Such items shall be placed on a supplementary list, which shall be communicated to Members at least 21 days before the opening of the session.

---

[9] Article VIII, subparagraph 32(c).

[10] Article VIII, paragraph 19.

[11] Article VIII, subparagraph 32(a) and the Draft Financial Regulations of the OPCW, Article 3.

[12] Draft Financial Regulations of the OPCW, Articles 13.10 and 13.11.

[13] Article VIII, subparagraph 21(b).

[14] Article XII, paragraph 4.

RULE 15 APPROVAL OF THE AGENDA

The provisional agenda for each regular session, and the supplementary list, if applicable, together with the report thereon of the General Committee, shall be submitted to the Conference for approval as soon as possible after the opening of the session by a simple majority of Members present and voting.

RULE 16 ADDITIONAL ITEMS

Any items of an important and urgent character, proposed by a Member, the Executive Council or the United Nations, which have not been placed on the provisional agenda pursuant to Rule 13 of these Rules or on the supplementary list pursuant to Rule 14 of these Rules, shall be referred to the General Committee, which shall report promptly thereon to the Conference. Such items may be placed on the agenda if the Conference so decides by a simple majority of Members present and voting. No additional item may be considered until seven days after it is placed on the agenda, unless the Conference, by a two thirds majority of Members present and voting, decides otherwise.

B. SPECIAL SESSIONS

RULE 17 PROVISIONAL AGENDA

The provisional agenda for all special sessions of the Conference shall be drawn up by the Executive Council and sent by the Director-General to all Members of the Organisation not later than nine days after the receipt of any decision or a request to convene such a special session.

RULE 18 CONTENTS OF PROVISIONAL AGENDA

The provisional agenda for each special session shall consist only of those items proposed for consideration in the decision by the Conference to convene such a session or in the request for the holding of the session by the Executive Council or a Member of the Organisation. The contents of the provisional agenda for the special sessions to review the operation of the Convention shall be drafted by the Executive Council in accordance with Article VIII, paragraph 22, of the Convention.

RULE 19 APPROVAL OF THE AGENDA

The provisional agenda for each special session, together with the report thereon of the General Committee, shall be submitted to the Conference for approval as soon as possible after the opening of the session by a simple majority of the Members present and voting.

RULE 20 ADDITIONAL ITEMS

Any items of an important and urgent character, proposed by a Member, the Executive Council or the United Nations, which have not been placed on the provisional agenda pursuant to Rule 16 of these Rules, shall be referred to the General Committee, which shall report promptly thereon to the Conference. Such items may be placed on the agenda, if the Conference so decides, by a two-thirds majority of the Members present and voting. No additional item may be considered until two days after it is placed on the agenda, unless the Conference, by a two-thirds majority of Members present and voting, decides otherwise.

C. REGULAR AND SPECIAL SESSIONS

GENERAL PROVISIONS

RULE 21 EXPLANATORY MEMORANDA

Each item proposed for inclusion in the agenda, except an item proposed by the Executive Council, shall be accompanied by an explanatory memorandum and, if possible, by basic documents or by a draft decision.

RULE 22 AMENDMENT AND DELETION OF ITEMS
Items on the agenda may be amended or deleted from the agenda of the Conference by a simple majority of the Members present and voting except for items placed on the agenda in accordance with Rule 20 of these Rules for which a two-thirds majority of Members present and voting is required.

III. *REPRESENTATION OF MEMBERS*

RULE 23 COMPOSITION OF DELEGATIONS
Each Member of the Organisation shall be represented at the Conference by one representative, who may be accompanied by as many alternates and advisers as may be required by the delegation.[15] The representative and all such alternates and advisers shall constitute the Member's delegation to the Conference.

RULE 24 ALTERNATES
Each representative may designate any alternate in his or her delegation to act in his or her place during the Conference.

RULE 25 REPRESENTATION ON COMMITTEES AND OTHER SUBSIDIARY BODIES OF THE CONFERENCE
Each representative may designate any alternate or any adviser in his or her delegation to act for his or her delegation on any committee or other subsidiary body of the Conference on which his or her delegation is represented.

IV. *CREDENTIALS*

RULE 26 SUBMISSION OF CREDENTIALS
The credentials of each representative and the names of the persons constituting the Member's delegation shall be submitted to the Director-General[16] if possible not less than seven days in advance of the session which the delegation will attend. The credentials shall be issued either by the Head of State or Government or by the Minister of Foreign Affairs of the Member concerned or any other authority acting on their behalf.

RULE 27 EXAMINATION OF CREDENTIALS
A Credentials Committee shall be appointed at the beginning of each session. It shall consist of ten members, which shall be appointed by the Conference on the proposal of the Chairman. The Committee shall elect its own officers. It shall examine the credentials of all representatives and report without delay to the Conference.

RULE 28 PROVISIONAL ADMISSION TO A SESSION
Pending a decision of the Committee upon their credentials, representatives shall be entitled to participate provisionally in the session. Any representative to whose admission a Member has made objection shall be seated provisionally with the same rights as other representatives until the Credentials Committee has reported and the Conference has given its decision.

---

[15] Article VIII, paragraph 9.

[16] For the First Session of the Conference credentials shall be addressed to the UN Secretary General and deposited with the Provisional Technical Secretariat of the Preparatory Commission [footnote in original].

V. *PARTICIPATION OF SIGNATORY STATES, OBSERVER STATES, AND OTHER OBSERVERS*

RULE 29 SIGNATORY STATES

Any State signatory to the Convention which has not yet deposited its instrument of ratification in accordance with Article XXI, paragraph 2, of the Convention shall be entitled, subject to prior written notification to the Director-General,[17] to participate, without taking part in the adoption of decisions, whether by consensus or by vote, in the deliberations of the Conference. This means that Signatory States shall be entitled to appoint observers to attend plenary meetings of the Conference other than those designated private meetings; to deliver statements at such meetings; to receive the documents of the Conference and to submit its views in writing to delegations.

RULE 30 OBSERVER STATES

Any other State which, in accordance with Article XX of the Convention, may accede to it may apply to the Director-General[18] for observer status, which will be accorded on the decision of the Conference. Such a State shall be entitled to appoint an observer to attend and participate without the right to vote in the plenary meetings of the Conference other than those designated private meetings and to receive documents of the Conference.

RULE 31 REPRESENTATIVES OF THE UNITED NATIONS AND OF THE SPECIALISED AGENCIES

The Secretary-General of the United Nations or his or her representative and the representatives of the specialised agencies shall be entitled to attend and participate without vote in sessions of the Conference on matters of common interest between them and the Organisation in accordance with their respective relationship agreements or subject to the approval of the Conference.

RULE 32 REPRESENTATIVES OF OTHER INTERNATIONAL ORGANISATIONS

Representatives of international organisations, other than the United Nations and the specialised agencies shall be entitled to attend and participate without vote in plenary meetings of the Conference on matters of common interest between them and the Organisation in accordance with their respective relationship agreements or subject to the approval of the Conference.

RULE 33 NON-GOVERNMENTAL ORGANISATIONS

Representatives of non-governmental organisations may attend the plenary sessions of the Conference, and participate in the activities of review conferences, in accordance with such rules or guidelines as the Conference has approved.

VI. *CHAIRMAN, VICE-CHAIRMEN AND CHAIRMAN OF THE COMMITTEE OF THE WHOLE*

RULE 34 ELECTION OF CHAIRMAN, VICE-CHAIRMEN AND CHAIRMAN OF THE COMMITTEE OF THE WHOLE

The Conference shall elect a Chairman, ten Vice-Chairmen, the Chairman of the Committee of the Whole and such other officers as it may decide, having due regard to equitable geographical representation.

RULE 35 PERIOD OF OFFICE

The Chairman, the Vice-Chairmen, the Chairman of the Committee of the Whole and other officers shall hold office until their successors are elected at the next regular session.

---

[17] For the First Session of the Conference notifications shall be addressed to the UN Secretary General and deposited with the Provisional Technical Secretariat of the Preparatory Commission [footnote in original].

[18] See footnote above.

RULE 36 ACTING CHAIRMAN
If the Chairman is absent during a meeting or any part thereof, he or she shall appoint one of the Vice-Chairmen to take his or her place, who, while acting as Chairman, shall have the same powers and duties as the Chairman.

RULE 37 REPLACEMENT OF THE CHAIRMAN
Notwithstanding Rule 35, if the Chairman is unable to continue his or her functions, a new Chairman shall be elected by the Conference for the unexpired term of office of the Chairman.

VII. *SECRETARIAT*

RULE 38 THE ROLE OF THE DIRECTOR-GENERAL
The Director-General shall act in that capacity at all meetings of the Conference and of its committees and other subsidiary bodies, or he or she may designate a member of his or her staff to represent him or her at any such meetings. The Director-General or his or her representative may, with the approval of the presiding officer, make oral or written statements to such meetings.

RULE 39 DIRECTION OF STAFF
The Director-General shall provide and direct the staff required by the Conference, its committees and other subsidiary bodies and shall be responsible for all the necessary arrangements for the meetings of the Conference, its committees and other subsidiary bodies.

RULE 40 DUTIES OF THE SECRETARIAT
Under the direction of the Director-General, the Secretariat shall receive, translate, reproduce and distribute documents of the Conference, its committees and other subsidiary bodies; interpret speeches made at meetings; have custody of documents of the Conference in the archives of the Organisation; publish the reports of the meetings of the Conference; distribute all documents of the Conference to the Members of the Organisation; and generally perform all other work which the Conference, its committees or other subsidiary bodies may require.

VIII. *COMMITTEES OF THE CONFERENCE*

A. GENERAL COMMITTEE

RULE 41 GENERAL COMMITTEE
At each session the Conference shall appoint a General Committee which shall consist of the Chairman of the Conference, who shall serve as Chairman, the ten Vice-Chairmen and the Chairman of the Committee of the Whole. If the Chairman of the Conference is absent during a meeting of the General Committee or any part thereof, he or she shall appoint one of the Vice-Chairmen to preside. If any other member of the General Committee is absent from the meeting of the General Committee, he or she may designate a member of his or her delegation to take his or her place. No two members of the General Committee shall be members of the same delegation, and it shall be so constituted as to ensure its representative character.

RULE 42 REPRESENTATION IN THE GENERAL COMMITTEE OF BODIES OTHER THAN THE COMMITTEE OF THE WHOLE
The Chairman of the Executive Council and the Chairmen of committees of the Conference other than the Committee of the Whole may participate without vote in the meetings of the General Committee. The Chairman of the Executive Council and the Chairmen of any such committee of the Conference may designate a Vice-Chairman of the body concerned to represent him or her in the General Committee.

RULE 43 FUNCTIONS OF THE GENERAL COMMITTEE

(a) The General Committee shall at the beginning of each session of the Conference consider the provisional agenda, together with any supplementary list, and shall report thereon to the Conference. It shall consider requests, made pursuant to Rules 14 and 20 of these Rules, for the inclusion of additional items and shall report thereon to the Conference. In considering matters relating to the agenda of the Conference, the General Committee shall not discuss the substance of any item, except insofar as this bears upon the question whether the General Committee should recommend the inclusion of the item in the agenda, the rejection of the request for inclusion or the inclusion of the item in the provisional agenda of a future session, and what priority should be accorded to an item the inclusion of which has been recommended.

(b) The General Committee shall propose to the Conference the allocation of agenda items to committees and the establishment of any additional committees which it considers necessary. It shall make recommendations to the Conference concerning the closing date of the session. It shall assist the Chairman of the Conference in conducting and coordinating the work of the Conference.

RULE 44 PARTICIPATION BY MEMBERS REQUESTING THE INCLUSION OF ITEMS IN THE AGENDA

A Member of the Organisation which has no representative in the General Committee and which has requested the inclusion of an item in the agenda shall be entitled to attend any meeting of the General Committee at which its request is discussed, and to participate, without vote, in the discussion of that item.

B. MAIN AND OTHER COMMITTEES

RULE 45 MAIN COMMITTEE

The main committee of the Conference shall be the Committee of the Whole, which shall consider and report on any item referred to it by the Conference under these Rules.

RULE 46 CREATION OF OTHER COMMITTEES

The Conference may set up such other committees as it deems necessary for the performance of its functions.

RULE 47 OFFICERS AND SUBCOMMITTEES

Except as provided in Rules 34 and 41, each committee of the Conference shall elect its own Chairman and other officers. These officers shall be elected on the basis of equitable geographical representation, experience and personal competence. Each committee may set up subcommittees or other subsidiary organs, which shall elect their own officers.

RULE 48 REFERENCE OF AGENDA ITEMS TO COMMITTEES

Agenda items relating to the same category of subjects shall be referred to the committee or committees dealing with that category of subjects. Committees shall not introduce new items on their own initiative.

IX. *CONDUCT OF BUSINESS AT PLENARY MEETINGS OF THE CONFERENCE*

RULE 49 THE PRESIDING OFFICER

The Chairman of the Conference, or, in his or her absence, a Vice-Chairman appointed by him or her to take his or her place shall be the presiding officer of the Conference.

RULE 50 GENERAL POWERS OF THE PRESIDING OFFICER

In addition to exercising the powers which are conferred upon him or her by these Rules, the presiding officer shall declare the opening and closing of each meeting of the Conference, shall direct its discussions, ensure observance of these Rules, accord the right to speak, put questions and announce decisions. He or she shall rule on points of order and, subject to these Rules, shall have control of the proceedings of the Conference and over the maintenance of order at its meetings. The presiding officer may propose to the Conference the limitation of the time to be allowed to speakers, the limitation of the number of times each representative may speak on any question, the closure of the list of speakers or the closure of the debate. He or she may propose the suspension or adjournment of the meeting or the adjournment of the debate on the item under discussion. The presiding officer, in the exercise of his or her functions, shall remain under the authority of the Conference.

RULE 51 VOTING

The presiding officer shall not vote, but may appoint another member of his or her delegation to vote in his or her place.

RULE 52 PUBLIC AND PRIVATE MEETINGS

Plenary meetings of the Conference shall be held in public unless declared private. Meetings of subsidiary bodies, including committees, shall be held in private unless designated otherwise. All decisions of the Conference taken at a private meeting shall be announced at an early public meeting. At the close of each private meeting of committees and other subsidiary bodies, the presiding officer may issue a communiqué through the Director-General.

RULE 53 QUORUM

A majority of the Members of the Organisation shall constitute a quorum at the plenary meetings of the Conference.[19]

RULE 54 SPEECHES

No representative may address the Conference without having previously obtained the permission of the presiding officer. Subject to Rule 55 of these Rules, the presiding officer shall call upon speakers in the order they signify their desire to speak. The presiding officer may call a speaker to order if his or her remarks are not relevant to the subject under discussion.

RULE 55 PRECEDENCE

The presiding officer may accord precedence to the Chairman of the Executive Council and to the Chairman or other officer of a committee or any other subsidiary body of the Conference, for the purpose of explaining a report or recommendations submitted to the Conference. He or she may also accord precedence to the Director-General or his or her representative.

RULE 56 POINTS OF ORDER

During the discussion of any matter, a representative may rise to a point of order, and the point of order shall be immediately decided by the presiding officer in accordance with these Rules. A representative may appeal against the ruling of the presiding officer. The appeal shall be immediately put to the vote and the presiding officer's ruling shall stand unless overruled by a majority of the Members present and voting. A representative rising to a point of order may not speak on the substance of the matter under discussion.

---

[19] Article VIII, paragraph 16.

RULE 57 TIME-LIMIT ON SPEECHES
The Conference may limit the time to be allowed to each speaker and the number of times each representative may speak on any question. When debate is limited and a representative has spoken his or her allotted time, the presiding officer shall call him or her to order without delay.

RULE 58 CLOSING OF LIST OF SPEAKERS AND RIGHT OF REPLY
During the course of a debate the presiding officer may announce a list of speakers and, with the consent of the Conference, declare the list closed. He or she may, however, accord the right of reply to any representative if a speech delivered after the list has been closed makes this desirable.

RULE 59 ADJOURNMENT OF DEBATE
During the discussion of any matter, a representative may move the adjournment of the debate on the item under discussion. Permission to speak on the motion shall be accorded only to two representatives in favour of and to two opposing the adjournment, after which the motion shall be immediately decided. The presiding officer may limit the time to be allowed to speakers under this Rule.

RULE 60 CLOSURE OF DEBATE
A representative may at any time move the closure of the debate on the item under discussion, whether or not any other representative has signified his or her wish to speak. Permission to speak on the motion shall be accorded only to two representatives opposing the closure, after which the motion shall be immediately decided. If the Conference is in favour of the closure, the presiding officer shall declare the closure of the debate. The presiding officer may limit the time to be allowed to speakers under this Rule.

RULE 61 SUSPENSION OR ADJOURNMENT OF THE MEETING
A representative may at any time move the suspension or the adjournment of the meeting. The presiding officer may limit the time to be allowed to the speaker moving the suspension or adjournment of the meeting. No discussion on such motions shall be permitted and they shall be immediately decided.

RULE 62 ORDER OF PROCEDURAL MOTIONS
Subject to Rule 56 of these Rules, the following motions shall have precedence in the following order over all proposals or motions before the meetings:
(a) To suspend the meeting;
(b) To adjourn the meeting;
(c) To adjourn the debate on the item under discussion; and
(d) To close the debate on the item under discussion.

RULE 63 PROPOSALS AND AMENDMENTS
Proposals and amendments shall normally be submitted in writing to the Director-General who shall circulate copies to all delegations. Unless the Conference decides otherwise, proposals shall not be discussed or considered for decision until the day after copies thereof have been circulated. The presiding officer may, however, permit the discussion and consideration of amendments, or of motions as to procedure, even though these amendments or motions have not been distributed or have been distributed the same day.

RULE 64 DECISIONS ON COMPETENCE
Subject to Rule 62 of these Rules, any motion calling for a decision on the competence of the Conference to adopt a proposal submitted to it shall be decided upon before a decision is taken on the proposal in question.

RULE 65 WITHDRAWAL OF PROPOSALS AND MOTIONS

Any proposal or a motion may be withdrawn by its proposer at any time before voting on it has commenced, provided that it has not been amended by decision of the Conference. A proposal or a motion thus withdrawn may be reintroduced by any representative.

RULE 66 RECONSIDERATION OF PROPOSALS AND AMENDMENTS

When a proposal or amendment has been adopted or rejected, it shall not be reconsidered at the same session unless the Conference, by a two-thirds majority of the Members present and voting, so decides. Permission to speak on a motion to reconsider shall be accorded only to two speakers opposing reconsideration, after which the motion shall be immediately put to the vote.

X. DECISION MAKING

RULE 67 VOTING RIGHTS

Each Member of the Organisation shall have one vote.[20] A Member of the Organisation which is in arrears in the payment of its financial contribution to the Organisation shall have no vote in the Organisation if the amount of its arrears equals or exceeds the amount of the contribution due from it for the preceding two full years. The Conference may, nevertheless, permit such a Member to vote if it is satisfied that the failure to pay is due to conditions beyond the control of the Member.[21]

RULE 68 DECISIONS ON QUESTIONS OF PROCEDURE

The Conference shall take decisions on questions of procedure, including those pursuant to Rules 56 to 61, by a simple majority of the Members present and voting.[22]

RULE 69 DECISIONS ON MATTERS OF SUBSTANCE

Decisions on matters of substance should be taken as far as possible by consensus. If consensus is not attainable when an issue comes up for decision, the presiding officer shall defer any vote for 24 hours and during this period of deferment shall make every effort to facilitate achievement of consensus, and shall report to the Conference before the end of this period. If consensus is not possible at the end of 24 hours, the Conference shall take the decision by a two-thirds majority of the Members present and voting unless specified otherwise in the Convention.[23]

RULE 70 DECISION WHETHER THE QUESTION IS ONE OF SUBSTANCE OR NOT

When the issue arises as to whether the question is one of substance or not, that question shall be treated as a matter of substance unless otherwise decided by the Conference by the majority required for a decision on matters of substance.[24]

RULE 71 MEANING OF THE PHRASE "MEMBERS PRESENT AND VOTING"

For the purpose of these Rules, the phrase "Members present and voting" means Members casting a valid affirmative or negative vote. Members who abstain from voting shall be regarded as not voting.

RULE 72 METHODS OF VOTING

Except in elections to the Executive Council, the normal method of voting shall be by show of hands. Any representative may request a roll-call, which shall then be taken in the English alpha-

---

[20] Article VIII, paragraph 17.
[21] Article VIII, paragraph 8.
[22] Article VIII, paragraph 18.
[23] Article VIII, paragraph 18.
[24] Article VIII, paragraph 18.

betical order of the names of the Members of the Organisation, beginning with the Member whose name is drawn by lot by the presiding officer. The name of each Member shall be called in all roll-calls, and its representative shall reply "yes", "no" or "abstention". The result of the vote shall be inserted in the record of the meeting.

RULE 73 CONDUCT DURING VOTING
After the presiding officer has announced the commencement of a vote, the voting shall not be interrupted until the result has been announced, except on a point of order in connection with the actual conduct of the voting.

RULE 74 EXPLANATION OF VOTE
Representatives may make brief statements consisting solely of explanations of a vote, before the voting has commenced or after the voting has been completed. Similarly, explanatory statements of position may be made in connection with a decision taken without a vote. The presiding officer may limit the time to be allowed for such explanations. The presiding officer shall not permit the proposer of a proposal or of an amendment to explain his or her vote on his or her own proposal or amendment.

RULE 75 DIVISION OF PROPOSALS AND AMENDMENTS
A representative may move that parts of a proposal or of an amendment shall be voted on separately. If objection is made to the request for division, the motion for division shall be first voted upon. Permission to speak on the motion for division shall be accorded only to two representatives in favour and two representatives against. If the motion for division is carried, those parts of the proposal or of the amendment which are subsequently approved shall be put to the vote as a whole. If all operative parts of the proposal or of the amendment have been rejected, the proposal or the amendment shall be considered to have been rejected as a whole.

RULE 76 VOTING ON AMENDMENTS
(a) When an amendment to a proposal is moved, the amendment shall be voted first. When two or more amendments are moved to a proposal, the Conference shall first vote on the amendment deemed by the presiding officer to be furthest removed in substance from the original proposal and then on the amendment next furthest removed therefrom, and so on, until all the amendments have been put to the vote. Where, however, the adoption of one amendment necessarily implies the rejection of another amendment, the latter amendment shall not be put to the vote. If one or more amendments are adopted, the amended proposal shall then be voted upon.
(b) A motion shall be considered an amendment to a proposal if it merely adds to, deletes from or revises part of that proposal.

RULE 77 VOTING ON PROPOSALS
If two or more proposals relate to the same question, the Conference shall, unless it decides otherwise, vote on the proposals in the order in which they have been submitted. The Conference may, after each vote on a proposal, decide whether to vote on the next proposal.

RULE 78 EQUALLY DIVIDED VOTES
If a vote is equally divided in voting other than elections, the presiding officer will give additional time for reconsideration of the issue before the proposal is once again put to vote. In case the vote is still equally divided, the proposal voted upon shall be considered as not adopted.

XI. *ELECTIONS*

A. GENERAL PROVISIONS

RULE 79 SECRET BALLOT

Members of the Executive Council shall be elected by acclamation by the Conference upon designation by a regional group. In case a regional group has been unable to agree on a complete slate, the Conference shall fill the seats pertaining to that group which have not been agreed upon within the group, by secret ballot, by a simple majority of Members present and voting. Other elections shall be by secret ballot if ten or more Members so request.

RULE 80 ELECTIONS TO FILL ONE ELECTIVE PLACE

When only one elective place is to be filled and no candidate obtains in the first ballot a majority required, a second ballot shall be taken which shall be restricted to the two candidates who obtained the largest number of votes in the first ballot. If in the second ballot the votes are equally divided, the presiding officer shall decide between the candidates by drawing lots.

RULE 81 ELECTIONS TO FILL TWO OR MORE ELECTIVE PLACES

When two or more elective places are to be filled at one time under the same conditions, those candidates obtaining in the first ballot the majority required shall be elected. If the number of candidates obtaining the majority required is less than the number of elective places to be filled, there shall be no more than two ballots in respect of each elective place remaining to be filled. If in the first ballot for an unfilled elective place no candidate obtains the majority required, a second ballot shall be taken which shall be restricted to the two candidates who obtained the largest number of votes in the first ballot for that elective place. If in the second ballot for that elective place the votes are equally divided, the presiding officer shall decide between the candidates by drawing lots.

RULE 82 APPOINTMENT OF THE DIRECTOR-GENERAL

The Director-General shall be appointed by the Conference upon the recommendation of the Executive Council for a term of four years, renewable for one further term, but not thereafter.

B. ELECTIONS TO THE EXECUTIVE COUNCIL [25]

RULE 83 ELECTIVE PLACES TO BE FILLED

Before the Conference at each regular session proceeds to elections to the Executive Council, the presiding officer shall indicate to the Conference those elective places on the Executive Council which must be filled so as to ensure that after the end of that session the Executive Council will be constituted in accordance with Article VIII, paragraph 23, of the Convention.[26]

RULE 84 BALLOT PAPERS

There shall be a single ballot in respect of all the elective places to be filled. The ballot paper shall specify elective places which are to be designated by each regional group in the order that these groups are referred to in Article VIII, paragraph 23, of the Convention.

RULE 85 INVALID VOTES

In elections to the Executive Council invalid votes shall include those cast for a Member of the Organisation:

---

[25] Article VIII, paragraphs 23 and 24.

[26] In accordance with Article VIII, paragraph 24, for the first election of the Executive Council 20 members out of 41 shall be elected for a term of one year [footnote in original].

(a) Which is not in that group referred to in Article VIII, paragraph 23, of the Convention;
(b) Whose term of office as an elected Member will not expire at the end of the session in which the election is being held.

A ballot paper containing more names from the relevant group than the number of seats assigned to it will be declared invalid.

XII. *CONDUCT OF MEETINGS OF COMMITTEES AND OTHER SUBSIDIARY BODIES*

RULE 86 APPLICATION OF THESE RULES TO COMMITTEES AND OTHER SUBSIDIARY BODIES
Subject to any decision of the Conference and subject to these Rules, procedures governing the conduct of business in committees and other subsidiary bodies of the Conference shall conform as far as it is appropriate to the rules governing the conduct of business at plenary meetings of the Conference.

XIII. *LANGUAGES AND DOCUMENTATION*

RULE 87 OFFICIAL LANGUAGES
Arabic, Chinese, English, French, Russian and Spanish shall be the official languages of the Conference.

RULE 88 INTERPRETATION FROM OTHER LANGUAGES
Any representative may make a speech in a language other than the official language provided that if he or she does so he or she shall himself or herself provide for interpretation into one of the official languages. In such cases, interpretation into the other official languages by the interpreters of the Secretariat may be based on the interpretation provided by the representative.

RULE 89 DOCUMENTS SUBMITTED BY MEMBERS
All documents submitted by a Member to the Secretariat shall be in one of the official languages of the Conference.

RULE 90 RECOMMENDATIONS AND DECISIONS
All recommendations, decisions and other important documents of the Conference shall be published in the official languages of the Conference and shall be distributed by the Secretariat to all Members of the Organisation as soon as possible.

RULE 91 REPORTS
(a) Reports of plenary sessions of the Conference shall be issued by the Secretariat in the official languages of the Conference and shall contain the text of all recommendations and decisions of the Conference adopted at that session.
(b) Reports of meetings of subsidiary bodies of the Conference and their recommendations shall be issued by the Secretariat, unless the Conference decides otherwise. Reports containing recommendations to, or otherwise requesting action or a decision to be taken by the Conference shall be issued in the official languages of the Conference.

RULE 92 OFFICIAL RECORDS
A set of official records shall be maintained by the Secretariat in the official languages of the Conference, containing the text of all recommendations and decisions of the Conference, and recommendations of subsidiary bodies to plenary sessions of the Conference, as well as a complete list of all conference documents and reports.

XIV. *AMENDMENT, SUSPENSION AND INTERPRETATION OF RULES*

RULE 93 AMENDMENT OF RULES

These Rules may be amended by the Conference, subject to the provisions of the Convention, in accordance with the procedures for decisions on matters of substance as set forth in Rule 69 of these Rules and provided that the Conference has received a report on such amendment from an appropriate committee.

RULE 94 SUSPENSION OF RULES

Any of these Rules may be suspended, subject to the provisions of the Convention, by a decision of the Conference taken in accordance with the procedures for decisions on matters of substance as set forth in Rule 69 of these Rules.

RULE 95 INTERPRETATION OF RULES

The description of these Rules in the table of contents and the description prefixed to each Rule shall be disregarded in the interpretation of these Rules.

22.2 Official Languages of the OPCW

C-VI/DEC.9 adopted by the Conference of the States Parties at its Sixth Session on 17 May 2001 and entitled "Official Languages of the OPCW"

The Conference of the States Parties,

Bearing in mind Article XXIV of the Convention, Rules 87 to 92 of the Rules of Procedure of the Conference of the States Parties (hereinafter the "Conference"), as well as Rules 15, 17 and 19, and 51 to 55 of the Rules of Procedure of the Executive Council (hereinafter the "Council"), and in accordance with previous decisions of the Conference and the Council on the distribution of documents,

Taking note of the difficulties experienced by Member States, and especially by their National Authorities, owing to the late translation of official documents or to the lack of translation of specialised documents necessary for the implementation of the Convention,

Considering that the effective use of all official languages, on an equal basis, is coherent with the principle of universality of the Convention and essential for its equal implementation,

Noting with appreciation the efforts made by the Technical Secretariat (hereinafter the "Secretariat"), to improve the accuracy of translation and interpretation, and encouraging the Secretariat to continue to enhance the quality of such services,

Upon recommendation of the Council at its Twenty-Fourth Session,

Hereby:

Requests the Secretariat to ensure respect for equal treatment of the six official languages of the OPCW, as well as to promote the appropriate linguistic balance in the dissemination of information within the Organisation;

Further requests the Secretariat to strongly endeavour, in particular, to simultaneously distribute in the six official languages the documents mentioned by the Rules of Procedure of the Conference and the Council, as well as all documents related to the decision-making process, including notes by the Director-General or the Secretariat and National papers, with due regard to the time frames established in the Rules of Procedure, by the Conference or by the Council.

22.3 Guidelines for future attendance and participation by non-governmental organisations

Annex to RC-3/DEC.2 adopted by the Third Review Conference on 8 April 2013 and entitled "Amendment of Rule 33 of the Rules of Procedure of the Conference of the States Parties With Respect to Attendance of Non-Governmental Organisations at Meetings of Special Sessions of the Conference of the States Parties to Review the Operation of the Chemical Weapons Convention"

ANNEX
GUIDELINES FOR FUTURE ATTENDANCE AND PARTICIPATION BY NON-GOVERN- MENTAL ORGANISATIONS

1. Attendance of non-governmental organisations

1.1 Representatives of non-governmental organisations (NGOs), whose activities/interests are demonstrably relevant to the object and purpose of the Chemical Weapons Convention (hereinafter "the Convention"), will be allowed to:

(a) attend plenary sessions of the Conference of the States Parties (hereinafter "the Conference"), other than those sessions or meetings during sessions that are designated as closed;

(b) be seated in the public gallery;

(c) receive documents of the Conferences, other than those that are classified as confidential information in accordance with the Convention; and

(d) at their own expense, make written material available to the participants at the Conference, as provided for in paragraph 4 below.

1.2 In its application to the Technical Secretariat (hereinafter "the Secretariat") to attend a session of the Conference, and in order to be eligible for such attendance, each NGO must clearly demonstrate how its activities/interests are relevant to the object and purpose of the Convention.

1.3 After vetting by States Parties through the General Committee, and on its recommendation, the Secretariat is to submit a list of those eligible NGOs that have not previously been approved for attendance at a review conference, for approval by the review conference and for accreditation to its future sessions. The members of the General Committee will keep the regional groups informed of the process and will keep the General Committee informed of inputs from the regional groups.

1.4 The Secretariat will, as appropriate, inform or inform on a tentative basis, the NGO of its eligibility to attend the Conference, once it is satisfied that:

(a) the NGO has been previously approved, or has been recommended for approval by the General Committee, for attendance of a session of the Conference; and

(b) the activities/interests of the NGO demonstrably relevant to the object and purpose of the Convention.

1.5 The NGO will be solely responsible for any travel arrangements, visas, expenses, and other arrangements necessary for the attendance of their representatives at sessions of the Conference.

2. Coordination between non-governmental organisations

NGOs are to designate a coordinator ("NGO Coordinator") from amongst their own ranks, who is to be responsible for liaising with the Secretariat and the Chairperson of the Conference on issues related to NGO participation.

3. Participation by non-governmental organisations

Without prejudice to a decision by the States Parties as to the programme of work of the

Conference session, a plenary meeting for presentations by NGOs will be held at each session of the Conference in the period following the general debate. NGOs will coordinate among themselves in deciding which representatives will address the Conference during such a meeting. The NGO Coordinator will provide a confirmed list of speakers, as well as a set of 15 copies of each presentation (for interpretation purposes), to the Secretariat prior to the commencement of such a meeting.

4. **Facilities for non-governmental organisations**

In order to facilitate their participation in the sessions of the Conference, a meeting room will be made available for use by all accredited NGOs. The need for any technical equipment and services that may be required should be communicated in advance by the NGO Coordinator to the Secretariat, and will be supplied on a reimbursable basis. In the event that a meeting room is not available at the Conference venue, a meeting room will be made available at the OPCW Headquarters building.

5. **Documentation**

NGOs may be allowed to display documents and other information materials that are relevant to the object and purpose of the Convention on a designated table, which will be outside the plenary room. One copy of each document should be provided in advance to the Secretariat through the NGO Coordinator.

6. **Side events and exhibits of non-governmental organisations**

The availability of space for side events during the session is limited. Side events held by NGOs will be accommodated, if meeting room space and any necessary technical equipment or services are available for the time requested. Limited space will also be available for exhibits. Any technical equipment and services that may be required should be communicated in advance by the NGO Coordinator to the Secretariat, and will be supplied on a reimbursable basis.

23. EXECUTIVE COUNCIL
(ARTICLE VIII(C))

23.1 Rules of Procedure of the Executive Council

C-I/DEC.72 adopted by the Conference of the States Parties at its First Session on 23 May 1997 and entitled "Rules of Procedure of the Executive Council"

I. REPRESENTATION OF MEMBERS

RULE 1   REPRESENTATIVES
Each member of the Executive Council (hereinafter referred to as "the Council") shall designate one person as its Representative. Each Representative may be accompanied by alternates and advisers. The Representative and all such alternates and advisers shall constitute the member's delegation to the Council.

RULE 2   ALTERNATES
Alternates shall be empowered to act in place of their Representative if so required.

RULE 3   SUBMISSION OF CREDENTIALS
The credentials of Representatives on the Executive Council shall be submitted to the Director-General not less than twenty-four hours before the first meeting which they are to attend. The credentials shall be issued either by the Head of State or Government, or by the Minister of Foreign Affairs of the member concerned, or by any other authority acting on their behalf. They shall remain valid for the whole period for which that member was elected unless they are withdrawn or replaced by new credentials. Representatives shall notify the Director-General of the names of the alternates and advisers in their delegations in writing.

RULE 4   EXAMINATION OF CREDENTIALS
The credentials of each Representative shall be examined by the Director-General, who shall submit a report thereon to the Council for approval.

RULE 5   PROVISIONAL ADMISSION TO THE MEETINGS
Pending the approval of the credentials of a Representative on the Council in accordance with Rule 4 of these Rules, such Representative shall be seated provisionally with the same rights as other Representatives.

II. OFFICERS OF THE COUNCIL

RULE 6   CHAIRMAN AND VICE-CHAIRMEN
The Chairman and four Vice-Chairmen shall be elected from among the accredited Representatives and shall hold office for a period of one year. The new officers shall be elected at the regular Council meeting closest to the conclusion of the one year period of office. The chairmanship of the Council shall rotate among Representatives from the five regional groups specified in Article VIII, paragraph 23 of the Convention. The Vice-Chairmen shall be elected upon the designation of the respective groups with the exception of the group which provides the Chairman.

RULE 7   PRESIDING OFFICER
The Chairman shall preside at all meetings of the Council. If the Chairman is absent during a meeting or any part thereof, or whenever he or she deems that for the proper fulfilment of the

responsibilities of the chairmanship he or she should not preside over the Council during the consideration of a particular question, he or she shall appoint one of the Vice-Chairmen to take his or her place, who, while acting as Chairman, shall have the same powers and duties as the Chairman. The Chairman and the Vice-Chairmen may at all times participate in the discussions of the Council as representatives and may also vote in that capacity. Alternatively the Chairman or a Vice-Chairman acting as Chairman may designate another member of his or her delegation to participate in the discussion and vote in his or her place.

RULE 8   REPLACEMENT OF THE CHAIRMAN OR THE VICE-CHAIRMEN
If the Chairman or one of the Vice-Chairmen is unable to continue his or her functions, the Council shall elect a new Chairman or Vice-Chairman for the unexpired term of office.

III. THE TECHNICAL SECRETARIAT

RULE 9   DUTIES OF THE DIRECTOR-GENERAL
(a) The Director-General shall perform his or her duties in accordance with the provisions of the Convention as well as carrying out those functions delegated to the Technical Secretariat by the Conference and the Executive Council.
(b) The Director-General shall act in that capacity at all meetings of the Council, its committees and other subsidiary bodies but shall not have the right to vote. He or she may designate a member of his or her staff to represent him at any such meeting. The Director-General or his or her Representative may at any time, with the approval of the presiding officer, make oral or written statements to any such meeting.

RULE 10   DIRECTION OF THE STAFF
The Director-General shall provide and direct the staff required by the Council, its committees and other subsidiary bodies, and shall be responsible for the arrangements required for all meetings of the Council, its committees and other subsidiary bodies.

RULE 11   DUTIES OF THE SECRETARIAT
Under the direction of the Director-General, the Secretariat shall provide administrative and technical support to the Council in the performance of its functions. In particular it shall receive, translate, reproduce and distribute documents of the Council, its committees and other subsidiary bodies; prepare and circulate reports of meetings, decisions adopted by the Council and any other documentation required; provide language interpretation at meetings; have custody of documents of the Council in the archives of the Organisation; and generally perform all other work which the Council, its committees and other subsidiary bodies may require.

IV. MEETINGS OF THE COUNCIL

RULE 12   MEETINGS OF THE COUNCIL
The Council shall meet for regular sessions. Between regular sessions it shall meet as often as may be required for the fulfilment of its powers and functions. For this purpose, each member of the Council should be prepared, at short notice, to attend meetings of the Council. In particular:
(a) the Council shall meet without delay to consider any issue or matter within its competence affecting the Convention and its implementation, including concerns regarding compliance, and cases of non-compliance. The Council shall be convened immediately after having received a challenge inspection request and in any case within the twelve hour period referred to in Article IX, paragraph 17;
(b) the Council shall meet at the request of the Chairman, or any member of the Council, or of the Director-General; and

(c) the Council shall meet at the request of any member of the Organisation to assist in clarifying any situation which may be considered ambiguous or which gives rise to a concern about the possible non-compliance of another State Party with the Convention or to obtain clarification from another State Party on any situation which may be considered ambiguous or which gives rise to a concern about its possible non-compliance with the Convention.

RULE 13 PLACE OF MEETINGS

Meetings shall normally be held at the seat of the Organisation unless the Council decides otherwise.

RULE 14 NOTICE OF MEETINGS

No advance notice of the calling of a meeting shall be required when the date and time have been decided by the Council at an earlier meeting. The Director-General shall notify each Representative as far in advance as possible and in any case not less than seventy-two hours in advance of the calling of other meetings unless shorter notification timelines are required by the Convention.

V. AGENDA OF THE COUNCIL

RULE 15 LIST OF MATTERS WHICH ARE UNDER CONSIDERATION BY THE COUNCIL

The Director-General with the approval of the Council shall regularly communicate to all members of the Organisation a list of matters of general interest which may be under consideration by the Council.

RULE 16 PROVISIONAL AGENDA The Director-General shall prepare, in consultation with the Chairman, the provisional agenda for meetings of the Council. The provisional agenda shall include:
(a) all items which the Council has previously decided to include in the provisional agenda;
(b) all items referred to the Council by the Conference;
(c) all items the inclusion of which is requested by any member of the Organisation in accordance with the provisions of the Convention;
(d) all items which may be referred to the Council through the Director-General in accordance with the relationship agreement between the Organisation and the United Nations, or with a relationship agreement between the Organisation and the States or international organisations;
(e) reports of the Director-General, including reports concerning action taken on decisions and recommendations of the Council;
(f) such other items as the Director-General shall consider it necessary to include, after consultation with the Chairman; and
(g) any other item which, in the view of the Director-General, requires the urgent attention of the Executive Council.

RULE 17 CIRCULATION OF THE PROVISIONAL AGENDA

Except as provided for in Rule 14 of these Rules, the provisional agenda for meetings and important supporting documents shall be sent in the language(s) which the member has chosen as its language(s) of communication with the Organisation to each Representative as far in advance as possible, and in any case not less than seventy-two hours before the meeting unless shorter timelines are required under the Convention. The provisional agenda shall be sent to other Member States as far in advance as possible accompanied by a list of supporting documents, which will be made available upon request. The provisional agenda shall also be sent as far in advance as possible to the United Nations and to any States and international organisations with which the Organisation has a relationship agreement which so requires.

RULE 18 EXPLANATORY MEMORANDA
Each matter brought to the attention of the Council by the Director-General or proposed for inclusion in the agenda by any member of the Organisation, the United Nations or a State or an international organisation with which the Organisation has a relationship agreement shall be accompanied by an explanatory memorandum and, if possible, by basic documents or by a draft decision or recommendation.

RULE 19 CIRCULATION OF DOCUMENTS OF PARTICULAR IMPORTANCE
Documents of particular importance, such as drafts of the reports, programme and budget of the Organisation and of the Council's annual report to the Conference shall be sent, in the language(s) which the member has chosen as its language(s) of communication with the Organisation, to each Representative and to other Member States as far in advance as possible, and in any case not less than eight weeks prior to the date fixed for the meeting of the Council at which they are to be considered.

RULE 20 ADOPTION OF THE AGENDA
The Council shall normally adopt the agenda for a meeting at the beginning of that meeting. However, the Council may at any time decide in advance upon its agenda for a subsequent meeting or meetings, in which case no provisional agenda shall be laid before that meeting or those meetings for adoption.

RULE 21 REVISION OF THE AGENDA
During any meetings other than meetings called pursuant to Article IX, paragraph 17 of the Convention, the Council may revise its agenda by adding, deleting, deferring or amending any item.

VI. CONDUCT OF BUSINESS AT MEETINGS

RULE 22 OPEN AND CLOSED MEETINGS OF THE COUNCIL
The Council may decide to hold open or closed meetings. Meetings of the Council shall be open unless the Council decides that a meeting shall be closed. By a closed meeting is meant a meeting reserved for members of the Council. By an open meeting is meant a meeting that is also open to the attendance as an observer of a delegate of a member of the Organisation which is not a member of the Council. Upon their request, the Chairman may with the concurrence of the Council invite observers to present their views, without a role in the decision-taking, when the Council is considering matters of interest to them.

RULE 23 FUNCTIONS OF THE PRESIDING OFFICER
(a) The presiding officer shall declare the opening and closing of each meeting of the Council, direct the discussions, ensure observance of these Rules, accord the right to speak, put questions and announce decisions. He or she shall rule on points of order and, subject to these Rules, have control of the proceedings of the Council and over the maintenance of order at its meetings.
(b) The presiding officer may propose to the Council the limitation of the time to be allowed to speakers, the limitation of the number of times each Representative may speak on any question, the closure of the list of speakers or the closure of the debate. He or she may also propose the suspension or adjournment of the meeting or the adjournment of the debate on the item under discussion.
(c) The presiding officer shall, in exercising his or her functions, remain under the authority of the Council.
(d) No Representative may address the Council without having previously obtained the permission of the presiding officer. The presiding officer shall call upon speakers in the order in

which they signify their desire to speak. The presiding officer may call a speaker to order if his or her remarks are not relevant to the subject under discussion.

RULE 24 POINTS OF ORDER

During the course of debate, a Representative may rise to a point of order and the point of order shall be immediately decided by the presiding officer in accordance with these Rules. A Representative may appeal against the ruling of the presiding officer. The appeal shall be immediately put to the vote and the presiding officer's ruling shall stand unless overruled. A Representative rising to a point of order shall not speak on the substance of the matter under discussion.

RULE 25 TIME-LIMIT ON SPEECHES

The amount of time to be allowed to each speaker and the number of times each Representative may speak on any question may at any time be limited. When debate is so limited and a Representative has spoken his or her allotted time, the presiding officer shall call him or her to order without delay.

RULE 26 ADJOURNMENT OF THE DEBATE

During the debate on any matter, a Representative may move the adjournment of the debate on the item under discussion. In addition to the proposer of the motion, two Representatives may speak in favour of and two against the motion, after which it shall be immediately voted upon. If the Council is in favour of the adjournment, the presiding officer shall declare the adjournment of the debate. The presiding officer may limit the time to be allowed to speakers under this Rule.

RULE 27 CLOSURE OF THE DEBATE

A Representative may at any time move the closure of the debate on the item under discussion whether or not any other Representative has signified his or her wish to speak. Permission to speak on the motion shall be accorded only to two Representatives opposing the closure, after which the motion shall be immediately put to the vote. If the Council is in favour of the closure, the presiding officer shall declare the closure of the debate. The presiding officer may limit the time to be allowed to speakers under this Rule.

RULE 28 SUSPENSION OR ADJOURNMENT OF MEETINGS

During the debate on any matter, a Representative may move the suspension or the adjournment of the meeting. Such motions shall not be debated but shall be immediately voted upon.

RULE 29 ORDER OF PROCEDURAL MOTIONS

The following motions shall have precedence in the following order over all other proposals or motions before the meeting except points of order:
(a) to suspend the meeting;
(b) to adjourn the meeting;
(c) to adjourn the debate on the item under discussion;
(d) to postpone until a later fixed date a decision on the substance of any proposal; and
(e) for the closure of the debate on the item under discussion.

RULE 30 DECISION ON COMPETENCE

Subject to Rule 29 of these Rules, any motion calling for a decision on the competence of the Council to adopt a proposal before it shall be voted upon before a vote is taken on such a proposal.

RULE 31 PROPOSALS AND AMENDMENTS

Proposals and amendments shall normally be introduced in writing and handed to the Director-General, who shall circulate copies to all the Representatives. As a general rule, no proposal shall be discussed or put to the vote unless it has been circulated to all the Representatives not later than the day preceding the meeting unless shorter timelines are required by the Convention. The presiding officer may, however, permit the discussion and consideration of amendments or of motions as to procedure even though such amendments or motions have not been circulated or have only been circulated the same day.

RULE 32 WITHDRAWAL OF PROPOSALS

A proposal may be withdrawn by its proposer at any time before voting on it has commenced, provided that it has not been amended by decision of the Council. A proposal which has thus been withdrawn may be reintroduced by any Representative.

RULE 33 RECONSIDERATION OF PROPOSALS OR AMENDMENTS

(a) When a proposal or an amendment has been adopted or rejected, it may not be reconsidered within four months unless the Council, by a two-thirds majority of all Representatives so decides. Permission to speak on a motion to reconsider shall be accorded only to two speakers opposing the motion, after which it shall be immediately voted upon.

(b) After the lapse of four months a proposal or amendment which has been previously adopted or rejected may be reconsidered at any meeting provided that a proposal for reconsideration has been placed on the agenda of that meeting.

RULE 34 PROPOSALS INVOLVING FINANCIAL IMPLICATIONS

Without prejudice to the timelines established in the Convention, a proposal involving financial implications for the Organisation shall not be voted upon in the absence of a report from the Director-General on the financial, administrative and programme and budget implications of the proposal.

VII. VOTING

RULE 35 VOTING RIGHTS

Each member of the Council shall have one vote. A member of the Council which is in arrears in the payment of its financial contribution to the Organisation shall have no vote in the Council if the amount of its arrears equals or exceeds the amount of the contribution due from it for the preceding two full years unless the Conference permits such a member to vote in accordance with Article VIII, paragraph 8 of the Convention.

RULE 36 DECISIONS ON MATTERS OF SUBSTANCE

Subject to Rules 37 through 39 of these Rules, decisions of the Council on matters of substance shall be made by a two-thirds majority of all its members.

RULE 37 DECISIONS UNDER ARTICLE X, PARAGRAPH 10 OF THE CONVENTION

In accordance with Article X, paragraph 10 of the Convention, decisions of the Council to provide supplementary assistance shall be made by a simple majority of all its members.

RULE 38 DECISION AGAINST CARRYING OUT A CHALLENGE INSPECTION

In accordance with Article IX paragraph 17 of the Convention, decisions of the Council against carrying out a challenge inspection shall be made by a three-quarters majority of all its members.

RULE 39 DECISIONS ON QUESTIONS OF PROCEDURE

Decisions of the Council on questions of procedure, including those under Rules 24 to 28 of these Rules, shall be made by a simple majority of all its members.

RULE 40 DECISIONS ON WHETHER THE QUESTION IS ONE OF SUBSTANCE OR NOT

When the issue arises as to whether the question is one of substance or not, that question shall be treated as a matter of substance unless otherwise decided by the Council by the majority required for a decision on matters of substance.

RULE 41 METHOD OF ELECTION

Where voting is necessary elections shall be held by secret ballot.

RULE 42 METHOD OF VOTING

(a) Voting on all matters other than elections shall as a rule be by show of hands.

(b) Whenever a roll-call vote has been requested, it shall be taken in the English alphabetical order of the names of the members of the Council, beginning with the member of the Council whose name is drawn by lot by the presiding officer. Each Representative shall reply "yes", "no" or "abstention". The vote of each member of the Council participating in a roll-call vote shall be inserted in the record.

RULE 43 CONDUCT DURING VOTING

After the voting has begun, no Representative shall interrupt the voting except on a point of order in connection with the actual conduct of the voting.

RULE 44 EXPLANATION OF VOTE

The presiding officer may permit Representatives to explain their votes, either before or after the voting, except when the vote is taken by secret ballot. The presiding officer may limit the time to be allowed for such explanations. The presiding officer shall not permit the proposer of a proposal or of an amendment to explain his or her vote on his or her own proposal or amendment.

RULE 45 DIVISION OF PROPOSALS AND AMENDMENTS

A Representative may move that parts of a proposal or an amendment shall be voted on separately. If objection is made to the request for division, the motion for division shall be voted upon. Permission to speak on the motion for division shall be given only to two speakers in favour and two speakers against. If the motion for division is carried out, those parts of the proposal or amendment that are subsequently approved shall be put to the vote as a whole. If all the operative parts of the proposal or amendment have been rejected, the proposal or amendment shall be considered to have been rejected as a whole.

RULE 46 VOTING ON AMENDMENTS

(a) When an amendment is moved to a proposal, the amendment shall be voted on first. When two or more amendments are moved to a proposal, the Council shall first vote on the amendment deemed by the presiding officer to be the furthest removed in substance from the original proposal, and then on the amendment next furthest removed therefrom, and so on, until all the amendments have been put to the vote. Where, however, the adoption of one amendment necessarily implies the rejection of another amendment, the latter amendment shall not be put to the vote. If one or more amendments are adopted, the amended proposal shall then be voted upon.

(b) A motion shall be considered an amendment to a proposal if it merely adds to, deletes from or revises part of that proposal.

RULE 47 VOTING ON PROPOSALS

If two or more proposals relate to the same subject, the Council shall, unless it decides otherwise, vote on the proposals in the order in which they were submitted. The Council may, after voting on each proposal, decide whether to vote on the next proposal.

VIII. RECOMMENDATION ON THE APPOINTMENT OF THE DIRECTOR-GENERAL

RULE 48 RECOMMENDATION ON THE APPOINTMENT OF THE DIRECTOR-GENERAL
The Director-General shall be appointed by the Conference upon the recommendation of the Council.

IX. PARTICIPATION OF THE UNITED NATIONS, ORGANISATIONS, AND INDIVIDUALS

RULE 49 PARTICIPATION OF THE UNITED NATIONS
The Secretary-General of the United Nations, or a Representative designated by him or her, shall be invited by the Chairman of the Council to attend meetings while matters of common interest to the Organisation and the United Nations are being discussed.

RULE 50 PARTICIPATION OF STATES, ORGANISATIONS AND INDIVIDUALS
The Council may, without prejudice to the Convention or to Rule 22, invite any Member State which is not a member of the Council to attend any meeting without a role in decision-taking. The Council may also invite any State which is not a member of the Organisation, any specialised agency or other international organisation to attend any meeting of the Council without a role in decision-taking. The Council may, on a case by case basis, invite any non-governmental organisation or any individual to be represented at or to attend a meeting of the Council if the consideration of a particular agenda item at the meeting so requires.

X. LANGUAGES AND RECORDS

RULE 51 OFFICIAL LANGUAGES
Arabic, Chinese, English, French, Russian and Spanish shall be the official languages of the Council.

RULE 52 INTERPRETATION FROM OTHER LANGUAGES
Any Representative may make a speech in a language other than an official language provided, however, that such a Representative shall provide for interpretation into one of the official languages. In such a case, interpretation into the official languages by the interpreters of the Secretariat may be based on the interpretation provided by the Representative.

RULE 53 LANGUAGES OF DOCUMENTS AND NOTIFICATIONS
Reports of Council meetings shall be made available in the official languages. Other important documents, as referred to, *inter alia* , in Rules 15, 17 and 19, as well as notifications, shall be sent in the official language(s) which the member has chosen as its language(s) of communication with the Organisation.

RULE 54 RECORDS OF MEETINGS
Reports of meetings of the Council shall be issued by the Secretariat and distributed to Member States as soon as possible.

RULE 55 RECORDS OF MEETINGS OF COMMITTEES AND OTHER SUBSIDIARY BODIES
Reports of meetings of committees and other subsidiary bodies of the Council shall be issued by the Secretariat when requested by the Council and distributed to Member States.

XI. COMMITTEES AND OTHER SUBSIDIARY BODIES

RULE 56 ESTABLISHMENT OF COMMITTEES AND OTHER SUBSIDIARY BODIES
The Council may establish such committees and other subsidiary bodies and may appoint such rapporteurs as it may deem desirable.

RULE 57 CONDUCT OF BUSINESS IN COMMITTEES AND OTHER SUBSIDIARY BODIES
Subject to any decision of the Council and subject to these Rules, the conduct of business in committees and other subsidiary bodies shall conform as far as is appropriate to these Rules.

XII. AMENDMENT, SUSPENSION AND INTERPRETATION OF RULES

RULE 58 AMENDMENT OF RULES
These Rules may be amended, subject to the provisions of the Convention, by a decision of a two-thirds majority of all members of the Council.

RULE 59 SUSPENSION OF RULES
Any of these Rules may be suspended, subject to the provisions of the Convention, by a decision of a two-thirds majority of all members of the Council.

RULE 60 INTERPRETATION OF RULES
The description of these Rules in the table of contents and the description prefixed to each Rule shall be disregarded in the interpretation of these Rules.

RULE 61 CONFIDENTIALITY
Nothing in these rules may be implemented or interpreted in any way which would prejudice the OPCW policy on confidentiality.

24. TECHNICAL SECRETARIAT
(ARTICLE VIII(D))

24.1 Secrecy Agreement[1]

In accordance with paragraph 9 of the Confidentiality Annex to the Convention and Interim Staff Rule 1.6.02, staff members of the Technical Secretariat are required to enter into individual secrecy agreements with the Secretariat covering their period of employment and a period of five years after it is terminated. The standard text of the agreement is the following:

SECRECY AGREEMENT

between

The undersigned ....[staff member].. ('the Signatory')

and

The Technical Secretariat of the Organisation for the Prohibition of Chemical Weapons ('OPCW Secretariat')

1. I, the Signatory, confirm that I have familiarised myself with the Staff Regulations, Staff Rules, the Confidentiality Annex of the Convention on the Prohibition of the Development, Production, Stockpiling and Use of Chemical Weapons and on their Destruction ('the Convention'), the OPCW Policy on Confidentiality, and the administrative directives which support it.

2. As a condition for employment with the OPCW Secretariat, I hereby undertake to comply with the letter and spirit of the OPCW Policy on Confidentiality and the administrative directives which support that Policy.

3. In view of my obligation to carry out faithfully and conscientiously the professional duties entrusted to me during my employment with the OPCW Secretariat, and my position as an international officer, I further undertake that for the duration of that employment, I shall:
    — restrict any use I make of OPCW confidential information, both within the OPCW Secretariat and outside the OPCW Secretariat, to the proper execution of my duties;
    — respect and apply the procedures established under the OPCW Policy on Confidentiality and under the administrative directives which support that Policy, for the protection, handling, dissemination and release of confidential information;
    — refrain from disclosing information, to which I have had access in the course of my employment to persons not authorised to receive such information; and
    — refrain from any unauthorised use of information to which I have had access in the course of my employment, including any unauthorised use which seeks to serve the interests of myself or any third party, or which may damage the interests of any party.

4. Without limiting the foregoing, I undertake that at all times following my separation from the service of the OPCW Secretariat, I shall refrain from any use, disclosure or dissemination of confidential information to which I have had access in the course of my employment with the OPCW Secretariat, except as explicitly authorised by the Director-General, and take no action that may lead to such information being disclosed or exploited to the detriment of the OPCW Secretariat, a State Party to the Convention, or a person or commercial entity of a State Party.

5. I confirm that I am aware:

---

[1] In accordance with the Convention, Annex on Confidentiality, paragraph 9.

– that the OPCW Secretariat has the right to institute disciplinary measures or other sanctions against me under the Staff Regulations and Staff Rules, should I breach any provision of the OPCW Policy on Confidentiality, the administrative directives which support that Policy, or my undertakings under this Agreement; and

– that a breach of the above mentioned provisions or of the undertakings of this secrecy agreement during or after my service with the OPCW Secretariat may result in a waiver of immunity and consequent penal prosecution or civil action under the jurisdiction of a State Party of the Convention which could result in severe penalties or liability for damages.

SIGNATORY

Signature   Full name   Date

Done in two copies at (The Hague, Kingdom of the Netherlands) in (a Convention language)

UNDERTAKING AND ACCEPTANCE BY THE OPCW SECRETARIAT

I confirm that, as the responsible representative of the OPCW Secretariat, I have accepted this agreement with the Signatory; that I made available to the Signatory the OPCW Policy on Confidentiality and other documentation relating to confidentiality obligations of the staff of the OPCW Secretariat; that I have briefed the Signatory on the obligations relating to confidentiality incurred in undertaking employment with the OPCW Secretariat; that throughout his/her term of employment, the OPCW Secretariat will continue actively to promote the Signatory's understanding of all applicable obligations, policy and procedures relating to confidentiality, including any updates and amendments to the Policy on Confidentiality, or to the administrative directives which support that Policy; and that the OPCW Secretariat will provide briefing on such obligations upon request at any time following the Signatory's separation from the service of the OPCW Secretariat.

Signature   Full name   Date

WITNESS: The execution of this agreement was witnessed by the undersigned

Signature   Full name   Date

CONFIRMATION: On my separation from the service of the OPCW Secretariat, I confirm my understanding that the obligations relating to confidentiality continue to apply without time limitation in the future.

SIGNATORY

Signature   Full name   Date

24.2 OPCW Staff Regulations and Interim Staff Rules

The OPCW Staff Regulations were adopted by the Conference of the States Parties at its Fourth Session (C-IV/DEC.25 dated 2 July 1999). Subsequently, the Staff Regulations were amended by the Conference at its Tenth Session (C-10/DEC.4 dated 8 November 2005), at its Twelfth Session (C-12/DEC.8 dated 7 November 2007) and at its Seventeenth Session (C-17/DEC.7 dated 27 November 2012).

The Interim Staff Rules were promulgated as document OPCW-S/DGB/4 by the Director-General on 15 November 1999 in order to implement the Staff Regulations approved by the Conference. Subsequently the Interim Staff Rules were amended by the Director-General by documents OPCW-S/DGB/5 dated 21 November 2000, OPCW-S/DGB/6 dated 10 September 2001, OPCW-S/DGB/7 dated 26 September 2001, OPCW-S/DGB/12 dated 20 July 2007 and OPCW-S/DGB/16 dated 27 October 2010.

The following is the consolidated text of the Staff Regulations, approved by the Conference of States Parties at its Fourth Session and amended at its Tenth, Twelfth and Seventeenth Sessions, and the Interim Staff Rules, as amended by the Director-General, and as promulgated by the Director-General by OPCW-S/DGB/19 of 30 March 2012. It also reflects the amendment of Interim Staff Rule 4.1.05 as approved by the Executive Council at its Forty-Third Meeting on 24 July 2014 (EC-76/DEC.6, dated 24 July 2014).

STAFF REGULATIONS AND INTERIM STAFF RULES
OF THE TECHNICAL SECRETARIAT OF THE
ORGANISATION FOR THE PROHIBITION OF CHEMICAL WEAPONS

SCOPE AND PURPOSE OF THE STAFF REGULATIONS
The staff regulations (hereinafter referred to as the "Staff Regulations") contain fundamental conditions of service and basic rights, duties and obligations of the Technical Secretariat (hereinafter referred to as the "Secretariat") of the Organisation for the Prohibition of Chemical Weapons (hereinafter referred to as "Organisation"). These Staff Regulations embody the broad principles of personnel policy for the staffing and administration of the Secretariat.

Rule 0.0.1   Applicability

These staff rules (hereinafter referred to as the "Staff Rules") are applicable to all staff members appointed by the Director-General.

ARTICLE I
DUTIES, OBLIGATIONS AND PRIVILEGES

Regulation 1.1
Staff members of the Secretariat are international civil servants. As such, their responsibilities are not national but exclusively international. By accepting appointment, they pledge to discharge their functions and to regulate their conduct with the interests of the Organisation only in view.

Rule 1.1.01   Loyalty

The interests of the Organisation and the loyalty that staff members owe to it shall always take precedence over their other interests or ties. Staff members shall act in such a manner as to ensure their independence of any person, entity or authority outside the Organisation.

Regulation 1.2

Staff members are subject to the authority of the Director-General and to assignment by him to any of the activities or offices of the Organisation. They are responsible to the Director-General in the exercise of their functions. The whole time of staff members shall be at the disposal of the Director-General. The Director-General shall establish a normal working week.

Rule 1.2.01   Obligation to supply information

(a) Staff members shall be responsible on appointment to supply the Director-General with whatever information may be required for the purpose of determining their status under the Staff Regulations and Rules or of completing administrative arrangements in connection with their appointments.

(b) Staff members shall also be responsible for promptly notifying the Director-General, in writing, of any subsequent changes affecting their status under the Staff Regulations and Rules.

(c) A staff member may at any time be required by the Director-General to supply information concerning facts anterior to his or her appointment and relevant to his or her suitability, or concerning facts relevant to his or her integrity, conduct and service as a staff member.

Rule 1.2.02   Hours of work

(a) The Director-General shall determine in an Administrative Directive the normal working hours within a normal working week of 40 hours as well as any exceptions thereto required by the needs of service.

(b) A staff member shall be required to work beyond the normal working hours whenever required to do so on the terms and conditions to be determined by the Director-General in an Administrative Directive.

(c) Staff members in the General Service category who are to work in excess of the normal working hours shall receive additional payments or shall be given compensatory time off under terms and conditions determined by the Director-General in an Administrative Directive.

(d) Staff members may be placed on standby duty and shall receive a standby duty rate of compensation as determined by the Director-General in an Administrative Directive.

Rule 1.2.03   Official holidays

The Director-General shall set a maximum of 10 official holidays annually.

Regulation 1.3

All Secretariat documents shall be issued on the responsibility of the Director-General.

Rule 1.3.01   Secretariat documents

The Director-General shall issue an Administrative Directive setting out internal controls over the issuance of Secretariat documents in such a way as to ensure consistency and accountability.

Regulation 1.4

(a) In the performance of their duties, staff members of the Secretariat shall neither seek nor accept instructions from any Government or from any other authority external to the Organisation.

(b) Any staff member who in the performance of his or her duties is confronted with any attempt by a Government or by a third party external to the Organisation to induce him or her to violate his or her obligations of loyalty shall promptly inform the Director-General thereof.

Regulation 1.5

(a) Staff members of the Secretariat shall conduct themselves at all times in a manner befitting their status as international civil servants. They shall not engage in any activity that is incompatible with the proper discharge of their duties with the Organisation. They shall avoid any action, and in particular any kind of public pronouncement, which may adversely reflect on their status or on the integrity, independence and impartiality which are required by that status. While staff members are not expected to give up their national sentiments or their political and religious convictions, they shall at all times bear in mind the reserve and tact incumbent upon them by reason of their international status.

(b) No staff member shall be actively associated with the management of or hold a financial interest in any business concern if his or her official position with the Secretariat would make it possible for him or her to promote the interest of that concern or to derive additional benefits from his or her participation in that concern. Any staff member who deals in his or her official capacity with any matter involving a business concern in which he or she holds a financial interest shall at once disclose the nature and extent of that interest to the Director-General.

Rule 1.5.01   Incompatible activities

Staff members shall not, except in the normal course of official duties and with the prior approval of the Director-General or other officer duly authorised by the Director-General, perform any one of the following acts, if such an act relates to the purpose, activities or interests of the Organisation:

(a) issue statements to the press, radio or other agencies of public information;

(b) accept speaking engagements;

(c) take part in film, photo, theatre, radio or television productions;

(d) submit articles, books or other material for publication.

Rule 1.5.02   Discriminatory Conduct

The Director-General shall take all appropriate measures to ensure that, consistent with the Staff Regulations and Rules, within the Secretariat no discrimination or other inappropriate conduct based on grounds such as age, race, religion, gender, disability, sexual orientation, language and national or social origin will be tolerated. The Director-General will take disciplinary action against any staff member demonstrating unsatisfactory conduct in this regard.

Rule 1.5.03   Outside activities and interests

(a) Staff members shall not engage in any continuous or recurring outside occupation or employment without the prior approval of the Director-General.

(b) A staff member who has occasion to deal in his or her official capacity with any matter involving a business concern in which he or she holds a financial interest shall disclose the measure of that interest to the Director-General.

(c) The mere holding of shares in a company or other similar holding in a commercial entity shall not constitute a financial interest within the meaning of this Rule unless such holding constitutes a substantial control.

Regulation 1.6

(a) Staff members shall exercise the utmost discretion in regard to all matters of official business. They shall not communicate even after termination of their functions to any person, organisation or other entity any information known to them by reason of their official position which has not been made public, except by authorisation of the Director-General in the performance of their duties. They shall not at any time use such information to private advantage and they shall not at any time publish anything based thereon except with the written approval of the Director-General.

(b) Staff members of the Secretariat shall not disclose even after termination of their functions to any unauthorised person, organisation or other entity any confidential information coming to their knowledge in the performance of their official duties. They shall also not communicate to any State, organisation or person outside the Secretariat any information, to which they have access in connection with their activities, in relation to any State Party.

Rule 1.6.01   Confidential information

(a) The Director-General shall, in conformity with the Annex on the Protection of Confidential Information to the Convention ("Confidentiality Annex") and the OPCW Policy on Confidentiality, promulgate an Administrative Directive containing procedures for the receipt, handling, reproduction, despatch, storage, destruction and/or release of confidential information.

(b) If a staff member is cleared for access to confidential information, the scope of such access shall be specified at the time of such clearance in accordance with the Administrative Directive referred to in sub-paragraph (a) above.

(c) In evaluating job performance, specific attention shall, in accordance with paragraph 12 of the Confidentiality Annex, be given to the staff member's record regarding the protection of confidential information.

Rule 1.6.02   Secrecy Agreement

Staff members are required to enter into individual secrecy agreements with the Secretariat, in accordance with paragraph 9 of the Confidentiality Annex.

Regulation 1.7

No staff member shall accept any honour, decoration, favour, gift or remuneration from any Government or any other source external to the Organisation, without first obtaining the approval of the Director-General. Approval shall be granted only in exceptional cases and where such acceptance is not incompatible with the terms of these Staff Regulations and with the individual's status as an international civil servant.

Rule 1.7.01

The provisions of Staff Regulation 1.7 do not preclude approval of the acceptance by staff members of academic awards and other tokens of a commemorative character.

Regulation 1.8
Staff members may exercise the right to vote but shall not engage in any political activity which is inconsistent with, or might reflect upon, the independence and impartiality required by their status as international civil servants.

Rule 1.8.01   Membership of political parties and participation in political activities

(a) Membership of a political party is permitted provided that such membership does not entail action, or obligation to action, contrary to Staff Regulation 1.8. The payment of normal financial contributions shall not be construed as an activity contrary to Staff Regulation 1.8.
(b) In any case of doubt as to the interpretation or application of Staff Regulation 1.8 and the present Rule, the staff member concerned shall request a ruling from the Director-General.

Regulation 1.9
Any privileges and immunities enjoyed by the Organisation and by its staff members are conferred in the interests of the Organisation, and such privileges and immunities furnish no excuse to the staff who enjoy them for non-performance of their private obligations or failure to observe laws and regulations. In any case where a question of these privileges and immunities arises, the staff member concerned shall immediately report to the Director-General who shall decide, in consultation with the Executive Council where appropriate, whether they shall be waived.[2]

Rule 1.9.01   Supply of information

A staff member who is arrested, charged with an offence other than a minor traffic violation, or summoned before a court as a defendant in a criminal proceeding, or convicted, fined or imprisoned for any offence other than a minor traffic violation shall immediately report the fact to the Director-General.

Regulation 1.10
Staff members shall subscribe to the following oath or declaration
"I solemnly swear (undertake, affirm, promise) to exercise in all loyalty, discretion and conscience the functions entrusted to me as an international civil servant of the Organisation for the Prohibition of Chemical Weapons, to discharge these functions and regulate my conduct with the interests of the Organisation only in view, and not to seek or accept instructions in regard to the performance of my duties from any Government or authority external to the Organisation."

---

[2] It is understood that privileges and immunities provided by the Host Country in the Headquarters Agreement do not form part of the terms and conditions of employment.

> **Regulation 1.11**
> The oath or declaration shall be made orally by the Director-General at a session of the Conference of the States Parties. All staff members of the Organisation shall make the oath or declaration before the Director-General or his authorised representative or in writing.

ARTICLE II
CLASSIFICATION OF POSTS

> **Regulation 2**
> In conformity with principles laid down by the Conference of the States Parties, with due regard to the Programme of Work and Budget and the OPCW Financial Regulations and Rules, and taking into consideration the master standards of job classification as developed by the International Civil Service Commission (hereinafter the "ICSC"), the Director-General shall prepare and submit to the Executive Council for its consideration and approval, proposals for the classification of posts according to the nature of the duties and responsibilities required.

ARTICLE III
SALARIES AND RELATED ALLOWANCES

> **Regulation 3.1**
> Salaries of staff shall be fixed by the Director-General, and shall be adjusted in accordance with the levels authorised by the United Nations General Assembly for staff in the Professional and higher category and by the ICSC for staff in the General Service category, with due regard to the Programme of Work and Budget approved by the Conference of the States Parties and having due regard to the financial situation of the Organisation. The salaries of staff shall be determined in accordance with Annex I to the present Staff Regulations.

Rule 3.1.01   Post adjustment

(a) Post adjustment, in terms of paragraph 5 of Annex I to the Staff Regulations, shall be applied in accordance with paragraph (b) below in the case of staff members in the Professional and higher category.

(b) (i) The amount of post adjustment for each level and step of the Professional and higher category shall be determined by applying the post adjustment multiplier for The Hague, as published by the International Civil Service Commission, to the corresponding net base salary rates.

     (ii) A staff member who is entitled to salary at the dependency rate shall be paid post adjustment calculated on the basis of such salary regardless of where the staff member's dependants reside.

(c) While the salary of a staff member is normally subject to the post adjustment for The Hague during an assignment for one year or more, the Director-General may decide, if a staff member is assigned to The Hague for less than one year to either:

     (i) apply the post adjustment applicable to The Hague and, if appropriate, to pay an assignment grant under Staff Rule 7.1.13 and the non-removal allowance under Staff Rule 7.2.03; or

(ii) in lieu of the above, to authorise payment of the subsistence allowance.

(d) Internationally recruited staff members who rent housing accommodation in The Hague may be paid a rental subsidy under terms and conditions determined by the Director-General in an Administrative Directive based on the thresholds and maximum amounts applied by the United Nations common system.

Rule 3.1.02 Salary increments

(a) Salary increments shall be awarded in accordance with Annex I to the Staff Regulations.

(b) The normal qualifying period for in-grade movement between consecutive steps is one year, except as provided in paragraph 2 of Annex I to the Staff Regulations, for which a two-year period at the preceding step is required.

(c) Satisfactory service for the purpose of awarding a salary increment shall be defined, unless otherwise decided by the Director-General in any particular case, as satisfactory performance and conduct of staff members in their assignments as evaluated by their supervisors.

(d) Salary increments shall be effective on the first day of the pay period in which service requirements are completed.

Rule 3.1.03 Salary policy on step and level changes

(a) If a staff member whose service has not been satisfactory is demoted, the staff member's eligibility for salary increment at the lower level will be based on satisfactory service at the lower level.

(b) If a staff member whose service has been outstanding is promoted to a higher level, he or she shall be placed at the lowest step in the level to which he or she is promoted that provides an increase in net base salary equal to at least the amount that would have resulted from the granting of two steps at the lower level.

(c) If the advancement is effective on the month in which an increment at the lower level is due, such increment will be included in the salary at the lower level, to which two steps will then be added to determine the staff member's salary after such advancement in accordance with paragraph (b) above.

(d) The date of the first salary increment at the higher level shall be the anniversary date of the advancement, except that in the case of those increments that require two years of satisfactory service, the first increment at the higher level will become due two years from the date of the advancement.

(e) Where the total net remuneration before promotion of a staff member in the General Service category exceeds that at the Professional level after promotion, a personal transitional allowance in an amount sufficient to meet the requirements in accordance with the methodology applied by the United Nations common system will be paid until such time as it is overtaken by increases in remuneration at the Professional level.

Rule 3.1.04 Special post allowance

(a) Staff members shall be expected to assume temporarily, as a normal part of their customary work and without extra compensation, the duties and responsibilities of higher level posts.

(b) A staff member who is called upon to assume the full duties and responsibilities of a post at a level clearly recognisable as higher than his or her own for a temporary period exceeding three months may, in exceptional cases, be granted a special post allowance from the beginning of the fourth month of service at the higher level, which allowance shall not be taken into account in calculating the contributable remuneration for purposes of the Provident Fund.

(c) In the event that a staff member in the General Service category is required to serve in a higher level post in the Professional category, or when a staff member in any category is required to serve in a post which is classified more than one level above his or her level, the allowance may be paid from the date upon which the staff member assumes the higher duties and responsibilities.

(d) The amount of the special post allowance shall be equivalent to the salary increase (including post adjustment and dependency allowances, if any) which the staff member would have received had the staff member been promoted to the next higher level.

Rule 3.1.05   Salary advances

(a) Salary advances may be made to staff members:
  (i)   upon departure for extended official travel or for approved leave involving absence from duty for a minimum period of 17 days including one pay day, in the amount that would fall due for payment during the anticipated period of absence;
  (ii) in cases where staff members do not receive their regular salary payment through no fault of their own, in the amount due;
  (iii) upon separation from service, where final settlement of pay accounts cannot be made at the time of departure, subject to the advance not exceeding 80 per cent of the estimated final net payments due;
  (iv) in cases where new staff members arrive without sufficient funds, in such amount as the Director-General may deem appropriate.

(b) The Director-General may, in exceptional and compelling circumstances, and if the request of the staff member is supported by a detailed justification in writing, authorise an advance for any reason other than those enumerated above.

(c) Salary advances other than those referred to in subparagraphs (a)(i), (ii) and (iii) above shall be liquidated at a constant rate as determined at the time the advance is authorised, in consecutive pay periods, commencing not later than the period following that in which the advance is made.

Rule 3.1.06   Retroactivity of payments

A staff member who has not been receiving an allowance, grant or other payment to which he or she is entitled shall not receive retroactively such allowance, grant or payment unless the staff member has made a written claim:

(a) in the case of the cancellation or modification of the Staff Rule governing eligibility, within three months following the date of such cancellation or modification;

(b) in every other case, within one year following the date on which the staff member would have been entitled to the initial payment.

Rule 3.1.07   Deductions and contributions

(a) Staff assessment and staff contributions to the Provident Fund shall be deducted each pay period from the total payments due to each staff member.

(b) Deductions from salaries and other emoluments may also be made for the following purposes:
  (i)   for contributions, other than to the Provident Fund, for which provision is made under these Staff Rules;
  (ii) for indebtedness to the Organisation;
  (iii) for indebtedness to third parties when any deduction for this purpose is authorised by the Director-General;
  (iv) for lodging provided by the Organisation, by a Government or by a related institution;

(v) for contributions to the Staff Representative Body established pursuant to Staff Regulation 8, provided that each staff member has the opportunity to withhold his or her consent to, or at any time to discontinue, such deduction, by notice to the Director-General.

Regulation 3.2

(a) The Director-General shall establish terms and conditions under which an education grant shall be available to an internationally recruited staff member serving outside his or her recognised home country whose dependent child is in full-time attendance at a school, university, or similar educational institution of a type that will, in the opinion of the Director-General, facilitate the child's re-assimilation in the staff member's recognised home country. The grant shall be payable in respect of the child up to the end of the fourth year of post-secondary studies, but in any case not exceeding the age of 25. The amount of the grant per scholastic year for each child shall be 75 per cent of the admissible educational expenses actually incurred, subject to a maximum amount as approved by the United Nations General Assembly for the United Nations common system and endorsed by the Executive Council.

(b) The Director-General shall also establish terms and conditions under which an education grant, not in excess of levels authorised for the United Nations, shall be available to a staff member serving in a country whose language is different from his own and who is obliged to pay tuition for the teaching of the mother tongue to a dependent child attending a local school in which the instruction is given in a language other than his or her own.

(c) The Director-General shall also establish terms and conditions under which an education grant shall be available to a staff member whose child is unable, by reason of physical or mental disability, to attend a normal educational institution and therefore requires special teaching or training, or while attending a normal educational institution, requires special teaching or training to assist him or her in overcoming the disability. The amount of this grant per year for each disabled child shall be equal to 100 per cent of the educational expenses actually incurred, up to a maximum amount approved by the United Nations General Assembly for the United Nations common system and endorsed by the Executive Council.

(d) Travel costs of each child covered by the education grant or the special-education grant may be paid for an outward and return journey once in each scholastic year between the educational institution and The Hague.

Rule 3.2.01   Education grant

Definitions
(a) For the purposes of the Staff Rules:
   (i) "child" means a child of a staff member who is dependent upon the staff member for main and continuing support;
   (ii) "disabled child" means a child who is unable, by reason of physical or mental disability, to attend a normal educational institution and therefore requires special teaching or training to prepare him or her for full integration into society or, while attending a normal educational institution, requires special teaching or training to assist him or her in overcoming the disability;
   (iii) "home country" means the country of home leave of the staff member under Staff Rule 5.2.01. If both parents are eligible staff members, "home country" means the country of home leave of either parent;
   (iv) "The Hague" means the municipality of The Hague or the area within commuting distance as determined by the Director-General in an Administrative Directive.

Eligibility for education grant

(b) A fixed-term staff member who is regarded as an international recruit under Staff Rule 4.1.04 and who is serving outside his or her home country shall be entitled to an education grant in respect of each child in full-time attendance at a school, university or similar educational institution, at or outside The Hague, in accordance with the provisions of Staff Regulation 3.2.

(c) The grant shall not, however, be payable in respect of:

    (i)   attendance at a kindergarten or nursery school at the pre-primary level;

    (ii) attendance at a free school or one charging only nominal fees;

    (iii) correspondence courses, except those which in the opinion of the Director-General are the best available substitute for full-time attendance at a school of a type not available in The Hague;

    (iv) private tuition, except tuition in a language of the home country if satisfactory school facilities for learning that language are not available in The Hague;

    (v)   vocational training or apprenticeship which does not involve full-time schooling and in which the child receives payment for services rendered.

(d) The grant will not normally be payable beyond the school year in which the child reaches the age of 25 years. If the child's education is interrupted for at least one school year by national service, illness, or other compelling reasons, the period of eligibility shall be extended by the period of interruption.

(e) Where attendance is for less than two thirds of the scholastic year, the amount of the grant for that year shall be that proportion of the grant otherwise payable which the period of attendance bears to the full scholastic year.

(f) Where the period of service of the staff member does not cover the full scholastic year, the amount of the grant for that year shall normally be proportionally adjusted.

Travel expenses related to the education grant

(g) Travel expenses payable in terms of Staff Regulation 3.2 shall not be paid if the requested journey is unreasonable, either because of its timing in relation to other authorised travel of the staff member or his or her eligible family members or because of the brevity of the visit in relation to the expense involved.

(h) Where attendance is for less than two-thirds of the school year, travel expenses shall not normally be payable.

(i) Transportation expenses shall not exceed the cost of a journey between the staff member's home country and The Hague.

Claims for the education grant

(j) Claims for the education grant shall be submitted in writing and supported by evidence satisfactory to the Director-General.

Establishment of the education grant in local currency

(k) When educational expenses are incurred outside the Netherlands, the amounts shall be established in local currency.

Rule 3.2.02   Mother tongue tuition

The Director-General will decide in each case whether the education grant shall be paid for tuition of the mother tongue under Staff Regulation 3.2(b).

Rule 3.2.03 Special education grant for disabled children

(a) A special education grant for disabled children shall be available to all fixed-term staff members of all categories, regardless of whether or not they are serving in their home country.

(b) The amount of the grant shall be as provided for in Staff Regulation 3.2(c). "Educational expenses" reimbursable under the special education grant shall comprise the expenses incurred to provide an educational programme designed to meet the needs of the disabled child in order that he or she may attain the highest possible level of functional ability.

(c) The grant shall be computed on the basis of the calendar year if the child is unable to attend a normal educational institution, or on the basis of the school year if the child is in full-time attendance at a normal educational institution while receiving special teaching or training. The grant shall be payable in respect of any disabled child from the date on which the special teaching or training is required up to the end of the school year or the calendar year, as appropriate, in which the child reaches the age of 25 years. In exceptional cases, the age limit may be extended up to the end of the school year or the calendar year, as appropriate, in which the child reaches the age of 28 years.

(d) Where the period of service does not cover the full school year or calendar year, the amount of the grant shall be that proportion of the annual grant which the period of service bears to the full school or calendar year.

(e) Claims for the grant shall be submitted annually in writing and supported by medical evidence satisfactory to the Director-General regarding the child's disability. The staff member shall also be required to provide evidence that he or she has exhausted all other sources of benefits that may be available for the education and training of the child. The amount of educational expenses used as the basis for the calculation of the special education grant shall be reduced by the amount of any benefits so received or receivable by the staff member.

(f) The provisions of Staff Rule 3.2.01(k) above shall also apply to the computation and payment of the special education grant for disabled children.

(g) Where the disabled child attends an educational institution away from The Hague, travel costs may be paid for up to two round trips per school year between the educational institution and The Hague , provided the Director-General is satisfied that the needs of the disabled child require attendance at the educational institution. In very exceptional circumstances, travel may also be reimbursed for the person accompanying the disabled child.

Regulation 3.3
(a) In the event a staff member is subject to national income taxation with respect to the net salaries and emoluments paid by the Organisation to staff members, the Director-General is authorised to refund to him or her the amount of those taxes paid. The Director-General will make arrangements with the States Parties concerned for the reimbursement to the Organisation.
(b) If taxes are levied by States Parties on the salaries and emoluments paid by the Organisation to staff members who are citizens of those States Parties, the Organisation shall, however, only refund the amounts of taxes to the extent that such amounts are reimbursed to the Organisation by the States Parties concerned.

Rule 3.3.01 Staff assessment

Staff assessment is an amount consisting of the difference between the net and gross salary as it appears in the salary scale for staff members as contained in Annex I of the Staff Regulations.

Regulation 3.4

(a) Staff members in the Professional and higher category shall be entitled to receive dependency allowances as follows:

   (i) For each dependent child an annual amount equal to the amount approved by the United Nations General Assembly for the United Nations common system, except that the allowance shall not be paid in respect of the first dependent child if a staff member has no dependent spouse, in which case the staff member shall be entitled to the dependency rate of staff assessment;

   (ii) For each disabled child an annual amount equal to the amount approved by the United Nations General Assembly for the United Nations common system. However, if the staff member has no dependent spouse and is entitled to the dependency rate of staff assessment in respect of a disabled child, that allowance will be limited to an amount equal to the amount provided for in subparagraph (a)(ii) of Regulation 3.4 of the United Nations Staff Regulations;

   (iii) Where there is no dependent spouse, a single annual amount equal to the amount approved by the United Nations General Assembly for the United Nations common system for either a dependent parent, a dependent brother or a dependent sister.

(b) If both husband and wife are staff members, one may claim for dependent children under subparagraphs (a)(i) and (ii) above, in which case the other may claim only under subparagraph (a)(iii) above, if otherwise entitled.

(c) With a view to avoiding duplication of benefits and in order to achieve equality between staff members who receive dependency benefits under applicable laws in the form of governmental grants and staff members who do not receive such dependency benefits, the Director-General shall prescribe conditions under which the dependency allowance for a child specified in subparagraph (a)(i) above shall be payable only to the extent that the dependency benefits enjoyed by the staff member or his or her spouse under applicable laws amount to less than such a dependency allowance.

(d) Staff members whose salary rates are set by the Director-General under paragraph 3 of Annex I to the present Staff Regulations shall be entitled to receive dependency allowance at rates and under conditions determined by the Director-General, due regard being given to the circumstances in The Hague.

(e) Claims for dependency allowances shall be submitted in writing and supported by evidence satisfactory to the Director-General. A separate claim for dependency allowance shall be made each year.

Rule 3.4.01   Dependency allowances

(a) All staff members whose salary rates are set by the Director-General under paragraph 1 of Annex I to the Staff Regulations shall be entitled to receive a dependency allowance. The terms, conditions and rates of the dependency allowances shall be as determined by the Director-General in an Administrative Directive and based on the rates applied by the United Nations common system.

(b) Where the staff member or his or her spouse receives a direct governmental grant in respect of a child, the dependency allowance payable under this Rule for such a child shall be the approximate amount by which the governmental grant is less than such a dependency allowance. In no case shall the sum of the two payments be less than the rate set out under the Staff Regulations and Rules or in the event that the governmental grant equals or exceeds the dependency allowance payable under this Rule, no such allowance will be payable to the staff member concerned.

(c) Staff members shall be responsible for notifying the Director-General in writing of claims for a dependency allowance and may be required to support such claims by documentary evidence satisfactory to the Director-General. They shall be responsible for reporting to the Director-General any change in the status of a dependant affecting the payment of this allowance.

(d) A dependency allowance shall be paid in respect of not more than one dependent parent, brother or sister qualifying as a secondary dependant, and such payment shall not be made when a payment is being made for a dependent spouse.

Rule 3.4.02 Definition of dependency

For the purposes of the Staff Regulations and Rules:

(a) A "dependent spouse" shall be a spouse whose occupational earnings, if any, do not exceed the lowest entry level of the General Service category's gross salary scales in force on 1 January of the year concerned at the UN duty station in the country of the spouse's place of work, provided that for the spouse of a staff member in the Professional and higher category the amount of such entry level shall not be less than the equivalent of the lowest entry level at the base of the salary system (GS-2, step I, for New York).

(b) A "dependent child" shall be:
(i)   a staff member's natural or legally adopted child;
(ii) a staff member's stepchild, if residing with the staff member; or
(iii) any other child as may be determined by the Director-General under special conditions set out in an administrative directive,
so long as the child is under the age of 18 years or, if the child is in full-time attendance at a school or university (or similar educational institution), under the age of 21 years, and the staff member provides main and continuing support for the child. In the case of a child over the age of 18 years who is physically or mentally incapacitated for substantial gainful employment, either permanently or for a period expected to be of long duration, the requirements as to school attendance and age shall be waived.

(c) A staff member claiming a child as dependent must certify that he or she provides main and continuing support for the child. This certificate must be supported by documentary evidence satisfactory to the Director-General, if a child:
(i)   does not reside with the staff member because of divorce or legal separation of the staff member;
(ii) is married; or
(iii) is regarded as a dependant under the special conditions referred to above.

(d) A "secondary dependant" shall be the father, mother, brother, or sister of whose financial support the staff member provides one half or more, and in any case at least twice the amount of the dependency allowance, provided that the brother or sister fulfils the same age and school attendance requirements established for a dependent child. If the brother or sister is physically or mentally incapacitated for substantial gainful employment, either permanently or for a period expected to be of long duration, the requirements as to school attendance and age shall be waived.

ARTICLE IV
APPOINTMENT

Regulation 4.1

(a) The power of appointment of staff rests with the Director-General. Upon appointment each staff member shall receive a letter of appointment in accordance with the provisions of Annex II to the present Staff Regulations and signed by the Director-General or by an official in the name of the Director-General.

(b) Only citizens of States Parties shall be appointed or employed by the Organisation as staff members or engaged in any form of special services agreement.

Rule 4.1.01   Letter of appointment

The letter of appointment granted to every staff member contains expressly or by reference all the terms and conditions of employment. All contractual entitlements of staff members are strictly limited to those contained expressly or by reference in their letter of appointment.

Rule 4.1.02   Effective date of appointment

(a) The appointment of every locally recruited staff member shall take effect from the date on which the staff member starts to perform his or her duties.

(b) The appointment of every internationally recruited staff member shall take effect from the date on which the staff member enters into official travel status to assume his or her duties or, if no official travel is involved, from the date on which the staff member starts to perform his or her duties.

Rule 4.1.03   Local recruitment

(a) The conditions under which staff members shall be regarded as local recruits for the purpose of these Staff Rules shall be as determined by the Director-General in an Administrative Directive.

(b) A staff member regarded as having been locally recruited shall not be eligible for the allowances or benefits indicated in Staff Rule 4.1.04(a).

Rule 4.1.04   International recruitment

(a) Staff members other than those regarded under Staff Rule 4.1.03 as having been locally recruited shall be considered as having been internationally recruited. The allowances and benefits in general available to internationally recruited fixed-term staff members include: payment of travel expenses upon initial appointment and on separation for themselves and their spouses and dependent children, removal of household goods or shipment of personal effects, assignment grant, home leave where applicable, education grant and repatriation grant as detailed in the relevant Staff Rules.

(b) A staff member who has changed his or her residential status in such a way that he or she may, in the opinion of the Director-General, be deemed to be a permanent resident of any country other than that of his or her nationality may lose entitlement to the allowances referred to in paragraph (a) above, if the Director-General considers that the continuation of such entitlement would be contrary to the purposes for which such allowances were created.

Rule 4.1.05 Retirement

Staff members shall not normally be retained in service beyond the age of sixty-five years. The Director-General may in the interest of the OPCW extend this age limit in individual cases.

Rule 4.1.06 Citizenship

(a) In the application of Staff Regulations and Rules, the Director-General shall, in the event a staff member holds citizenship of more than one State Party, only recognise one citizenship for that staff member.

(b) When a staff member has been legally accorded citizenship by more than one State Party, the staff member's citizenship for the purposes of the Staff Regulations and Rules shall be the citizenship stated in the staff member's letter of appointment.

(c) The application for recruitment by the OPCW shall contain a declaration by the applicant of all citizenships he or she possesses. The Director-General has the right to verify, by every possible means, this information as well as all other data provided by the candidate.

Rule 4.1.07 Change of residence or citizenship

A staff member who intends to acquire permanent residence status in any country other than that of his or her citizenship or who intends to change his or her citizenship shall notify the Director-General of that intention before the change in residence status or in citizenship takes place.

Regulation 4.2

The paramount consideration in the appointment, transfer and promotion of staff shall be the necessity of securing the highest standards of efficiency, professional competence and integrity. Due regard shall be paid to the importance of recruiting the staff on as wide a geographical basis as possible. Recruitment shall be guided by the principle that the staff shall be kept to a minimum necessary for the proper discharge of the responsibilities of the Secretariat.

Regulation 4.3

Selection of staff shall be made without distinction as to race, gender or religion. So far as practicable, selection shall be made on a competitive basis. Selection and appointment of candidates shall also be done in a manner that ensures transparency of the process and consistency with the principles contained in Staff Regulation 4.2, as well as with decisions taken by the Conference of the States Parties or the Executive Council.

Rule 4.3.01 Family relationships

(a) Except where another person equally well qualified cannot be recruited, appointment shall not be granted to a person who is the father, mother, son, daughter, brother or sister of a staff member.

(b) The spouse of a staff member may be appointed provided that he or she is fully qualified for the post for which he or she is being considered and that the spouse is not given any preference by virtue of the relationship to the staff member.

(c) A staff member who bears to another staff member any of the relationships specified in (a) and (b) above:

    (i) shall not be assigned to serve in a post which is superior or subordinate in the line of authority to the staff member to whom he or she is related;

    (ii) shall disqualify himself or herself from participating in the process of reaching or reviewing an administrative decision affecting the recruitment, status or entitlements of the staff member to whom he or she is related.

(d) The marriage of one staff member to another shall not affect the contractual status of either staff member but their entitlements and other benefits shall be modified as provided in the Staff Regulations and Rules.

Regulation 4.4

(a) The OPCW is a non-career organisation. This means that no permanent contracts shall be granted. Staff members shall be granted one of the following types of temporary appointments: short-term or fixed-term. The initial contract period shall not normally exceed three years. Contract extensions are possible; however, contracts, including extensions, carry no expectation of renewal or re-employment. Contract extension will become progressively more difficult, and shall be assessed upon, inter alia, the staff member's performance measured in accordance with a rigorous performance appraisal system. Any contract extension will be based on a continuing need on the part of the Organisation for the specific skill and knowledge of the staff member.

(b) The total length of service of Secretariat staff shall be seven years unless otherwise specified below:

    (i)   The Director-General may exclude locally recruited General Service staff from the maximum length of service requirement on the basis of the needs of the Organisation, and may grant these staff members additional fixed-term contracts.

    (ii)   The Director-General may also exclude linguist staff from these requirements on the basis of the needs of the Organisation and, in consultation with States Parties concerning options for improving linguistic services, may grant these staff members additional fixed-term contracts. Each such extension shall be subject to the same procedure.

(c) Staff members shall be required to serve a probationary period of six months. In individual cases, especially for short-term and part-time appointments, the Director-General may, in the best interest of the Organisation, adjust the terms and conditions of the probationary period.

(d) For the top structure positions spelled out in Annex V, the initial contract period will be three years, with up to four one-year extensions.

Rule 4.4.01   Appointments

Staff members may be granted one of the following types of appointments: short-term appointment or fixed-term appointment.

(a) Short-term appointment

    (i)   A short-term appointment may be granted where the total period of service is expected to be less than one year.

    (ii) A short-term appointment does not carry any expectation of renewal of appointment or of conversion to any other type of appointment.

    (iii) Short-term appointments shall be granted on the terms and conditions determined by the Director-General in an Administrative Directive and based on the Staff Regulations and Rules.

(b) Fixed-term appointment

    (i)   A fixed-term appointment, having an expiration date specified in the letter of appointment, may be granted for such period or periods as the Director-General determines in light of the provisions of Staff Regulation 4.4.

(ii) A fixed-term appointment does not carry any expectation of renewal or of conversion to any other type of appointment.

Rule 4.4.02 Expiration of appointments

(a) All appointments shall expire automatically and without prior notice on the expiration date specified in the letter of appointment.

(b) Separation as a result of the expiration of an appointment shall not be regarded as a termination within the meaning of the Staff Regulations and Rules.

Regulation 4.5
The Director-General shall establish appropriate medical standards which staff shall be required to meet before appointment.

Rule 4.5.01 Medical report

All offers of fixed-term appointments shall be made subject to a satisfactory report from the Organisation's medical officer. The report will be based on the results of a medical examination conducted by the Organisation's medical officer or a designated alternate physician. Should the result of the examination be unfavourable, the Director-General may cancel the offer of appointment or amend its terms.

ARTICLE V
ANNUAL LEAVE AND SPECIAL LEAVE

Regulation 5.1
Staff shall be allowed appropriate annual leave, as provided in the Staff Rules.

Rule 5.1.01 Annual leave

(a) Staff members shall accrue annual leave while in full pay status at the rate of 30 working days a year, subject to the provisions of Staff Rule 5.3.01(c). No leave shall accrue while a staff member is receiving compensation equivalent to salary and allowances under Staff Rule 6.2.03.

(b) (i) Annual leave may be taken in units of days and half-days.

(ii) Leave may be taken only when authorised. If a staff member is absent from work without authorisation, payment of salary and allowances shall cease for the period of unauthorised absence. However, if, in the opinion of the Director-General, the absence was caused by reasons beyond the staff member's control, and the staff member has accrued annual leave, the absence will be charged to that leave.

(iii) All arrangements as to leave shall be subject to the exigencies of the service, which may require that leave be taken by a staff member during a period designated by the Director-General. The personal circumstances and preferences of the individual staff member shall, as far as possible, be considered.

(c) Annual leave may be accumulated, provided that not more than 30 working days of such leave shall be carried forward beyond 1 January of any year without the prior approval of the Director-General.

(d) Notwithstanding paragraph (c) above, a staff member appointed before 1 January 2011 who has accumulated more than 30 days of annual leave as of 31 December 2010, may carry forward:
    (i)   60 days as of 1 January 2011;
    (ii) 50 days as of 1 January 2012;
    (iii) 40 days as of 1 January 2013; and
    (iv) 30 days as of 1 January 2014.

(e) A staff member may, in exceptional circumstances, be granted advance annual leave up to a maximum of 10 working days, provided his or her service is expected to continue for a period beyond that necessary to accrue the leave so advanced.

Regulation 5.2
Eligible staff shall be granted home leave once in every two years subject to the Staff Rules.

Rule 5.2.01   Home leave

(a) Fixed term staff members regarded as international recruits under Staff Rule 4.1.04 and not excluded from home leave under Staff Rule 4.1.04(b), who are serving outside their home country and who are otherwise eligible, shall be entitled, along with their eligible family members, once in every two years of qualifying service, to visit their home country at the Organisation's expense for the purpose of spending in that country a substantial period of annual leave. Leave taken for this purpose shall be under the terms and conditions determined by the Director-General in an Administrative Directive.

(b) A staff member shall be eligible for home leave provided his or her service is expected by the Director-General to continue:
    (i)   at least six months beyond the date of his or her return from any proposed home leave; and
    (ii) in the case of the first home leave, at least six months beyond the date on which the staff member will have completed two years of qualifying service.

(c) The home country shall be the country of the staff member's nationality, subject to the following terms, conditions, and exceptions:
    (i)   the place of home leave of the staff member within his or her home country shall be, for purposes of travel and transportation entitlements, the place with which the staff member had the closest residential tie during the period of his or her most recent residence in the home country. In exceptional circumstances, a change in the place in the country of home leave may be authorised, under conditions established by the Director-General;
    (ii) a staff member who has served with another public international organisation immediately preceding his or her appointment shall have the place of home leave determined as though his or her entire previous service with the other international organisation had been with the Organisation;
    (iii) the Director-General, in exceptional and compelling circumstances, may authorise:
        (aa) a country other than the country of nationality as the home country, for the purposes of this Rule. A staff member requesting such authorisation will be required to satisfy the Director-General that the staff member maintained normal residence in such other country for a prolonged period preceding his or her appointment, that the staff member continues to have close family and personal ties in that country and that the staff member's taking home leave there would not be inconsistent with the purposes and intent of Staff Regulation 5.2;

(bb) travel in a particular home leave year to a country other than the home country, subject to conditions established by the Director-General. In such a case, the travel expenses borne by the Organisation shall not exceed the cost of travel to the home country.

(d) (i) A staff member's first home leave shall fall due in the calendar year in which the staff member completes two years of qualifying service.

(ii) Home leave may be taken, subject to the exigencies of the service and to the provisions in subparagraph (i) above any time during the calendar year in which it falls due.

(e) If both spouses are staff members who are eligible for home leave, and taking into account Staff Rule 4.3.01(d), each staff member shall have the choice either of exercising his or her own home leave entitlement or of accompanying the spouse. A staff member who chooses to accompany his or her spouse shall be granted travel time appropriate to the travel involved. Dependent children whose parents are staff members, each of whom is entitled to home leave, may accompany either parent. The frequency of travel shall not exceed the established periodicity of the home leave both with regard to staff members and to their dependent children, if any.

(f) If a staff member delays taking his or her home leave beyond the calendar year in which it falls due, such delayed leave may be taken without altering the time of his or her next and succeeding home leave entitlements, provided that normally not less than twelve months of qualifying service elapse between the date of the staff member's return from the delayed home leave and the date of his or her next home leave departure.

(g) In exceptional circumstances, a staff member may be granted advance home leave, provided that, normally, not less than 12 months of qualifying service have been completed or that not less than 12 months of qualifying service have elapsed since the date of the staff member's return from home leave. The granting of advance home leave shall not advance the calendar year in which the next home leave falls due. The granting of advance home leave shall be subject to the conditions for the entitlement subsequently being met. If these conditions are not met, the staff member will be required to reimburse the costs paid by the Organisation for the advance home leave.

(h) A staff member may be required to take his or her home leave in conjunction with travel on official business, due regard being paid to the interests of the staff member and his or her family.

(i) A staff member shall be entitled to claim, in respect of authorised travel on home leave, travel time and expenses for himself or herself and eligible family members for the outward and return journeys between The Hague and the place of home leave.

(j) Travel of eligible family members shall be in conjunction with the approved home leave of the staff member, provided that exceptions may be granted if the exigencies of the service or other special circumstances prevent the staff member and his or her family members from travelling together.

(k) A staff member travelling on home leave shall be required to spend a substantial period of leave in his or her home country. The Director General may request a staff member, on his or her return from home leave, to furnish satisfactory evidence that this requirement has been fully met.

Regulation 5.3
Special leave may be authorised by the Director-General in exceptional cases, and normally without pay, in accordance with the Staff Rules.

Rule 5.3.01   Special leave

(a) Special leave may be granted, normally without pay, for advanced study or research in the interest of the Organisation, in cases of extended illness, for child care, or for other important reasons for such period and on such conditions as the Director-General may determine in an Administrative Directive in accordance with the relevant United Nations rules. In exceptional cases, the Director-General may, at his or her own initiative, place a staff member on special leave with partial or full pay if he or she considers such leave to be in the interest of the Organisation.

(b) A staff member who is called upon to serve in the armed forces of the State of which the staff member is a national, whether for training or active duty, may be granted special leave without pay for the duration of such military service, in accordance with terms and conditions determined by the Director-General in an Administrative Directive based on the relevant United Nations rules to the extent possible.

(c) Staff members shall not accrue service credits towards sick, annual and home leave, salary increment, seniority, termination indemnity and repatriation grant during periods of special leave with partial pay or without pay. Periods of less than one full month of such leave shall not affect the ordinary rates of accrual. Continuity of service shall not be considered broken by periods of special leave.

ARTICLE VI
SOCIAL SECURITY

Regulation 6.1

Provision shall be made for the participation of staff members in a Provident Fund funded by staff members and the Organisation. The Director-General shall establish the rules needed to govern this fund. The Director-General shall submit the rules governing the Provident Fund to the Executive Council for approval.

Rule 6.1.01   Participation in the Provident Fund

(a) Participation in the Provident Fund of staff members with fixed-term appointments is compulsory. The Director-General may exempt a staff member with a fixed term appointment from participation by his or her letter of appointment when the Director-General has determined that such a staff member is participating in another fund of a government or of an international organisation in the United Nations common system that affords coverage similar to that provided by the Provident Fund.

(b) The contributable remuneration of staff members in the Professional and higher category for purposes of the Provident Fund shall be the scale of pensionable remuneration as established in the United Nations common system.

(c) The contributable remuneration of staff in the General Service category for purposes of the Provident Fund shall be the gross remuneration according to the salary scales contained in Annex I to the Staff Regulations.

(d) Contributions to the Provident Fund shall be calculated as determined by the Director-General in an Administrative Directive and shall be in accordance with the principles generally applied by the United Nations common system.

(e) The Provident Fund shall be administered in terms of its charter and the administrative rules thereunder.

Regulation 6.2
The Director-General shall establish a cost-effective and administratively efficient scheme of social security for the staff, which includes adequate provisions for health protection, sick leave and maternity leave and reasonable compensation in the event of illness, accident or death attributable to the performance of official duties on behalf of the Organisation.

Rule 6.2.01   Sick leave

(a) Staff members who are incapacitated from the performance of their duties by illness or injury or whose attendance at work is prevented by public health requirements will be granted sick leave in accordance with the terms and conditions to be determined by the Director-General in an Administrative Directive, at the rates set out below:

   (i) A staff member holding a short-term appointment shall be granted sick leave credit at the rate of two working days per full month of service;

   (ii) A staff member holding a fixed-term appointment of one year or longer but less than three years shall be granted sick-leave for up to three months on full salary and three months on half salary in any period of twelve consecutive months;

   (iii) A staff member holding a fixed-term appointment of three years or longer or who has completed three years of continuous service shall be granted sick leave up to nine months on full salary and nine months on half salary in any period of four consecutive years.

(b) When sickness of more than three consecutive working days occurs within a period of annual leave, including home leave, sick leave may be approved on production of an appropriate medical certificate or other satisfactory evidence.

(c) A staff member shall immediately notify the Organisation's senior medical officer of any case of contagious disease occurring in his or her household or of any quarantine order affecting the household. In such a case, or in the case of any other condition which may affect the health of others, a staff member may be directed not to attend the office. He or she shall receive full salary and other emoluments for the period of authorised absence.

(d) In cases of family emergency, a staff member may use part of his or her sick leave entitlements, without medical certification or consultation but with the approval of the Director-General, to attend to such emergency. All sick leave entitlements shall lapse on the last day for pay purposes.

Rule 6.2.02   Maternity and paternity leave

(a) A staff member shall be entitled to maternity or paternity leave in accordance with the terms and conditions determined by the Director-General in an Administrative Directive in accordance with the relevant United Nations rules.

(b) Annual leave shall accrue during the period of maternity or paternity leave, provided that the staff member returns to service for at least six months after the completion of maternity or paternity leave.

Rule 6.2.03   Compensation for death, injury or illness attributable to service

Staff members or their beneficiaries, as appropriate, shall be entitled to compensation in the event of death, injury or illness attributable to the performance of official duties on behalf of the Organisation, in accordance with the terms and conditions determined by the Director-General in an Administrative Directive based on the relevant United Nations rules.

Rule 6.2.04   Compensation for loss or damage to personal effects attributable to service

Staff members shall be entitled, within the limits and under terms and conditions determined by the Director-General in an Administrative Directive in accordance with the relevant United Nations rules, to reasonable compensation in the event of loss or damage to their personal effects determined to be directly attributable to the performance of official duties on behalf of the Organisation.

Rule 6.2.05   Medical insurance

(a) Staff members shall participate in the Organisation's medical insurance scheme under the terms and conditions determined by the Director-General in an Administrative Directive.
(b) The amount of contributions to such medical insurance scheme shall be as determined by the Director-General in an Administrative Directive in accordance with the amounts applied by the United Nations common system.

ARTICLE VII
TRAVEL AND REMOVAL EXPENSES

Regulation 7.1
(a) Subject to the conditions and definitions prescribed in the Staff Rules promulgated by the Director-General, the Director-General shall in appropriate cases, in accordance with the Staff Rules issued under this Regulation, pay the travel expenses of staff members, their spouses and dependent children bearing in mind the need for maximum economy.
(b) For official travel by air by inspectors for the purpose of conducting inspections the standard of accommodation may, at the discretion of the Director-General, exceed economy class, but remain below first class, for official travel of more than ten hours duration without stopover. Except for special cases, such as challenge inspections and investigations of alleged use where a stopover would be inconsistent with the short time lines involved, the less expensive of a stopover or business class travel by air shall be used.

Rule 7.1.01   Official travel of staff members

(a) Subject to the conditions laid down in these Rules and determined by the Director-General in an Administrative Directive, the Organisation shall pay the travel expenses of a staff member under the following circumstances:
  (i)   on initial appointment, provided that the staff member is considered to have been internationally recruited under Staff Rule 4.1.04 for service outside his or her home country;
  (ii) when required to travel on official business;
  (iii) on home leave, in accordance with the provisions of Staff Rule 5.2.01;
  (iv) on separation from service, in accordance with the provisions of Article IX of the Staff Regulations and Rules;
  (v)   on travel authorised for medical or security reasons or in other appropriate cases, when, in the opinion of the Director-General, there are compelling reasons for paying such expenses.
(b) Should a staff member, on separation, wish to go to any place other than the place of recruitment or the place of home leave, the travel expenses borne by the Organisation shall not exceed the maximum amount that would have been payable on the basis of return transportation to the place of recruitment or home leave.

Rule 7.1.02   Official travel of family members

(a) Subject to the conditions laid down in these Staff Rules and determined by the Director-General in an Administrative Directive, the Organisation shall pay the travel expenses of a staff member's eligible family members under the following circumstances:

   (i) on the initial fixed-term appointment of a staff member who is considered to have been internationally recruited under the provisions of Staff Rule 4.1.04, , provided the staff member's services are expected by the Director-General to continue for more than six months beyond the date on which travel of his or her family members commences;

   (ii) following completion by the staff member of not less than one year of continuous service, provided his or her services are expected by the Director-General to continue for more than six months beyond the date on which travel of his or her family members commences;

   (iii) on home leave, in accordance with the provisions of Staff Rule 5.2.01;

   (iv) on separation of a staff member from service, provided the staff member's appointment was for a period of one year or longer or the staff member had completed not less than one year of continuous service;

   (v) on journeys approved in connection with the education of a staff member's child;

   (vi) on travel authorised for medical or in other appropriate cases, when, in the opinion of the Director-General, there are compelling reasons for paying such expenses.

(b) Under subparagraphs (a)(i) and (ii) above, the Organisation shall pay the travel expenses of a staff member's eligible family members either from the place of recruitment or from the place of home leave. Should a staff member wish to bring any eligible family member to The Hague from any other place, the travel expenses borne by the Organisation shall not exceed the maximum amount that would have been payable on the basis of travel from the place of recruitment or home leave.

(c) Under subparagraph (a)(iv) above, the Organisation shall pay the travel expenses of a staff member's eligible family members from The Hague to the place to which the staff member is entitled to be returned in accordance with the provisions of Staff Rule 7.1.01. Where both spouses are staff members and either or both are entitled to the payment of travel expenses on separation from service, and taking into account Staff Rule 4.3.01(d), travel expenses shall be paid for each of them only upon their own separation from service. Where both spouses are entitled to return travel expenses, each staff member shall have the choice either of exercising his or her own entitlement or of accompanying the other spouse, provided that in no case shall such expenses be paid for a staff member while he or she remains in the service of the Organisation.

Rule 7.1.03   Loss of entitlement to return transportation

(a) A staff member who resigns before completing one year of service or within three months following the date of his or her return from travel on home leave shall not be entitled to payment of return travel expenses for himself or herself and family members unless, in the opinion of the Director-General, there are compelling reasons for authorising such payment.

(b) Entitlement to return travel expenses shall cease if travel has not commenced within six months after the date of separation. However, where both spouses are staff members and the spouse who separates first is entitled to return travel expenses, and taking into account Staff Rule 4.3.01(d), his or her entitlement shall not cease until six months after the date of separation of the other spouse.

Rule 7.1.04   Eligible family members

(a) Eligible family members, for the purposes of official travel, shall be deemed to comprise the staff member's spouse and those children recognised as dependent under Staff Rule 3.4.02(b). In addition, children in respect of whom an education grant is payable, even though they are no longer recognised as dependent under Staff Rule 3.4.02(b), shall be eligible for education grant travel.

(b) The Director-General may authorise payment of the travel expenses of a child for one trip either to The Hague or to his or her home country beyond the age when the dependency status of the child would otherwise cease under the relevant Staff Regulations and Rules, either within one year of the time that the child is no longer considered a dependent or upon completion of the child's continuous full-time attendance at a university, when the attendance at the university commenced during the period of recognised dependency status.

(c) Notwithstanding Staff Rule 7.1.02(a)(iv), the Director-General may also authorise payment of the travel expenses for repatriation purposes of a former spouse.

Rule 7.1.05   Authority for travel

Travel shall be authorised in writing before it is undertaken. In exceptional cases, staff members may be authorised to travel on oral orders, but such oral authorisation shall require written confirmation. A staff member shall be personally responsible for ascertaining that he or she has the proper authorisation before commencing travel.

Rule 7.1.06   Reimbursement of expenses

For all official travel to or from The Hague, a staff member may claim reimbursement of expenses incurred on the terms and conditions and at the rates determined by the Director-General in an Administrative Directive and based on the terms, conditions and rates generally applied by the United Nations common system.

Rule 7.1.07   Travel expenses

(a) Travel expenses that shall be paid or reimbursed by the Organisation under the relevant provisions of these Staff Rules include:
   (i)   transportation expenses (i.e., carrier fare);
   (ii) terminal expenses;
   (iii) transit expenses;
   (iv) travel subsistence allowance;
   (v)   necessary additional expenses incurred during travel.

(b) Staff members shall exercise the same care in incurring expenses that a prudent person would exercise if travelling on personal business.

Rule 7.1.08   Route and mode of transportation

Official travel shall, in all instances, be by a route and mode of transportation as determined by the Director-General to be the most economical and efficient.

Rule 7.1.09   Standard of accommodation

(a) For all official travel by air by staff members and their eligible family members the standard of accommodation shall not exceed full fare economy class for trips of less than 14 hours duration. For trips of more than 14 hours duration the Director-General will authorise a stop over.

(b) Air travel accommodation under paragraph (a) above shall be provided at the most economical rate appropriate. Children under two years of age travelling by air shall be provided with a ticket giving entitlement to a seat.

(c) For all official travel by sea approved by the Director-General in exceptional cases, staff members and their family members shall be provided with the standard of accommodation which is, in the opinion of the Director-General, appropriate to the circumstances of the case.

(d) For official travel by train approved by the Director-General, staff members and their family members shall be provided with regular first class or equivalent accommodation, including sleeper and other facilities, as appropriate.

(e) A higher standard of accommodation may be approved when, in the opinion of the Director-General, exceptional and special circumstances warrant it.

(f) If a staff member or family member travels by more economical accommodations than the approved standard, the Organisation shall only pay for the standard of accommodations actually used by the traveller.

Rule 7.1.10   Travel by automobile

Staff members who are authorised to travel by automobile shall be reimbursed by the Organisation at rates and under conditions determined by the Director-General in an Administrative Directive in accordance with the relevant United Nations rules.

Rule 7.1.11   Purchase of tickets

(a) Unless the staff member concerned is specifically authorised to make other arrangements, all tickets for transportation involving official travel of staff members and eligible family members shall be purchased by the Organisation in advance of actual travel or, where circumstances so require, shall be secured by the staff member. The Director-General shall endeavour to negotiate contract fare rates especially for the most frequently travelled routes.

(b) When a staff member, for reasons of personal preference or convenience, requests a standard of accommodation in excess of his or her entitlement or requests travel by other than the approved route or mode or transportation, the staff member shall be required to reimburse the Organisation for any additional costs thus incurred before the Organisation provides him or her with the necessary tickets.

Rule 7.1.12   Travel subsistence allowance

A staff member authorised to travel at the Organisation's expense shall receive an appropriate daily subsistence allowance on the terms and conditions and at the rates determined by the Director-General in an Administrative Directive and based on the terms, conditions and rates generally applied by the United Nations common system.

Rule 7.1.13   Assignment grant

(a) A staff member who travels at the Organisation's expense to The Hague for an assignment expected to be of at least one year's duration shall be paid an assignment grant, subject to the conditions set forth below in accordance with the relevant United Nations rules.

(b) The amount of the assignment grant shall be equivalent to:

(i) 30 days of subsistence allowance at the daily rate applicable under subparagraph (c)(i) below; and

(ii) 30 days of subsistence allowance at half such daily rate in respect of each family member for whom travel expenses have been paid by the Organisation under Staff Rule 7.1.02 (a) (i) or (ii).

The above-mentioned amounts shall be calculated on the basis of the rate prevailing on the date of arrival at The Hague of the staff member or of the staff member's family member, as appropriate.

(c) (i) The Director-General may establish special rates of subsistence allowance for the purposes of the assignment grant for specific categories of staff and publish such rates in an Administrative Directive.

(ii) Under conditions determined by the Director-General, the limit of 30 days provided in paragraph (b) above may be extended to a maximum of 90 days. The amount of the grant during the extended period shall be up to 60 per cent of the appropriate prevailing rate.

(d) In addition to any amount of grant paid under paragraph (b) above, a lump sum equal to one month of the staff member's net base salary and, where appropriate, post adjustment at The Hague may be paid under conditions determined by the Director-General. The lump sum shall only be payable if the staff member is not entitled to removal costs under Staff Rule 7.2.01.

(e) Where both spouses are staff members who are travelling at the Organisation's expense to The Hague, and taking into account Staff Rule 4.3.01(d), the daily subsistence allowance portion of the assignment shall be paid each in respect of himself or herself. If they have a dependent child or children, the assignment grant in respect of such child or children shall be paid to the staff member on whom the child is recognised to be dependent.

(f) If both spouses would otherwise qualify for the lump sum portion of the grant, such lump sum shall be paid only to the spouse whose lump sum portion yields the higher amount.

(g) In cases where the staff member has not completed one year of service, the grant shall be adjusted proportionately and recovery made under conditions determined by the Director-General who, in exceptional circumstances, may decide to waive recovery for reasons to be recorded in writing.

(h) The Director-General may, in appropriate cases, authorise payment of all or part of the assignment grant where the Organisation has not been required to pay travel expenses upon the appointment of a staff member regarded as internationally recruited under Staff Rule 4.1.04.

Rule 7.1.14   Excess baggage and unaccompanied shipments

(a) For the purposes of these Staff Rules "excess baggage" shall mean baggage in excess of the weight or volume carried without extra charge by transportation companies, and "personal effects and household goods" shall be as defined in Staff Rule 7.2.01(e).

(b) Staff members travelling at the Organisation's expense shall be entitled to payment of excess baggage for themselves and their eligible family members to the extent determined by the Director-General in an Administrative Directive in accordance with the relevant United Nations rules.

(c) When the authorised travel is by air or by land, charges for unaccompanied shipment of personal baggage relating to travel on home leave or education grant may be reimbursed to the extent determined by the Director-General in an Administrative Directive in accordance with the relevant United Nations rules.

(d) For travel on appointment or assignment for one year or more, on transfer or on separation from service in the case of an appointment for one year or more, where no entitlement to removal costs exists under Staff Rule 7.2.01, a staff member shall be paid expenses incurred in transporting personal effects and household goods by the most economical means up to a maximum as determined by the Director-General in an Administrative Directive in accordance with the relevant United Nations rules.

(e) For travel on appointment or separation from service, where entitlement to removal costs does exist under Staff Rule 7.2.01, a staff member shall be paid expenses incurred in transporting, as an unaccompanied shipment, a reasonable amount of personal effects and household goods as an advance removal shipment, by the most economical means on the terms and conditions determined by the Director-General in an Administrative Directive in accordance with the relevant United Nations rules.

Rule 7.1.15   Insurance

(a) Staff members shall not be reimbursed for the cost of personal accident insurance or insurance of accompanied personal baggage. However, compensation may be paid in respect of loss or damage to accompanied personal baggage, in accordance with such arrangements as may be in force pursuant to Staff Rule 6.2.04.
(b) In the case of unaccompanied shipments, such insurance coverage will be provided by the Organisation as determined by the Director-General in an Administrative Directive and based on the general practice followed in the United Nations common system.

Rule 7.1.16   Travel advances

Staff members authorised to travel shall provide themselves with sufficient funds for all current expenses by securing an advance of funds if necessary. A reasonable advance of funds against the estimated reimbursable travel expenses may be made to a staff member or his or her family members for authorised expenses in accordance with the terms and conditions determined by the Director-General in an Administrative Directive.

Rule 7.1.17   Illness or accident during travel

The Organisation shall pay or reimburse reasonable hospital and medical expenses, in so far as these are not covered by other arrangements, which may be incurred by staff members who become ill or are injured while in travel status on official business.

Rule 7.1.18   Transportation of decedents

Upon the death of a staff member or of his or her spouse or dependent child, the Organisation shall pay the expenses of transportation of the body from The Hague, or in the event of death having occurred while in travel status, from the place of death, to a place to which the deceased was entitled to return transportation under Staff Rules 7.1.01 or 7.1.02. These expenses shall include reasonable costs for preparation of the body. If local interment is elected, reasonable expenses incurred for the interment may be reimbursed.

Regulation 7.2
Subject to the conditions and definitions prescribed in the Staff Rules promulgated by the Director-General, staff members shall be entitled to removal costs. Where, however, the Director-General considers that it is in the interest of the Organisation to do so, having regard to the cost of removal and the probable period of appointment or transfer, the Director-General may elect not to offer to pay the cost of removal of household goods and to pay instead for the shipment of personal effects and a non-removal element of the relevant allowance at the rate established for the United Nations common system.

Rule 7.2.01 Removal cost

(a) When an internationally recruited staff member who is serving outside his or her home country is to serve for a continuous period that is expected to be one year or longer, the Director-General shall decide whether to pay the non-removal allowance under Staff Rule 7.2.03 or to pay the costs for the removal of the staff member's personal effects and household goods under the following circumstances:

(i)   on initial appointment for a period of one year or longer;

(ii) upon completion of one year of continuous service;

(iii) upon separation from service, provided that the staff member had an appointment for a period of one year or longer or had completed not less than one year of continuous service and had been granted removal to The Hague.

(b) Under subparagraphs (a)(i) and (ii) above, the Organisation shall pay the expenses of removing a staff member's personal effects and household goods either from the place of recruitment or from the place of home leave under Staff Rule 5.2.01, provided that the effects and goods were in the staff member's possession at the time of appointment and are being transported for his or her own use. Payment of removal expenses from a place other than one of those specified above may be authorised by the Director-General in exceptional cases, on such terms and conditions as the Director-General deems appropriate. No expenses shall be paid for removing a staff member's personal effects and household goods from one residence to another in The Hague or within commutable distance thereof.

(c) Under subparagraph (a)(iii) above, the Organisation shall pay the expenses of removing a staff member's personal effects and household goods from The Hague to any one place to which the staff member is entitled to be returned in accordance with the provisions of Staff Rule 7.1.01 or any other one place authorised by the Director-General in exceptional cases on such terms and conditions as the Director-General deems appropriate, provided that the effects and goods were in the staff member's possession at the time of separation from service and are being transported for his or her own use.

(d) Payment by the Organisation of removal expenses shall be subject to such further terms and conditions as determined by the Director-General in an Administrative Directive and based on the terms and conditions normally applied by the United Nations common system, including reasonable limits on the weight and volume of personal effects and household goods which are covered.

(e) For the purposes of unaccompanied shipments and removal, personal effects and household goods shall include all effects and goods normally required for personal or household use, provided that animals, boats, automobiles, motorcycles, trailers and other power-assisted conveyances shall in no case be considered as such effects and goods.

(f) Where both spouses are staff members and each is entitled to removal of personal effects and household goods or to unaccompanied shipment under Staff Rule 7.1.14(d), and taking into account Staff Rule 4.3.01(d), the maximum weight or volume that may be removed at the Organisation's expense for both of them shall be that provided for a staff member with a spouse or dependent child(ren) residing at The Hague.

(g) When a staff member is internationally recruited and the non-removal allowance is authorised, the Organisation shall pay the cost of the storage of personal effects and household goods and other pertinent charges, including the cost of insurance, on such terms and conditions as are determined by the Director-General in an Administrative Directive and based on the terms and conditions generally applied by the United Nations common system.

Rule 7.2.02 Insurance of removal

The cost of insurance of personal objects and household goods in transit under Rule 7.2.01 shall be reimbursed up to a maximum valuation as determined by the Director-General in an Administrative Directive and based on the valuation generally applied by the United Nations common system.

Rule 7.2.03 Non-removal allowance

(a) Where the appointment is for one year or more, full removal costs will normally be paid.
(b) In cases where the Director-General elects not to offer to pay the full removal cost, a non-removal allowance will be paid to compensate for the absence of an entitlement to removal of household goods to The Hague. It accounts for three percentage points at the net salary at P-4 level, step VI at the dependency rate. The resulting annual amounts of the allowance are applicable to staff at level P-4 and P-5. For staff at the D-1 and D-2 levels, the amounts are increased by 13 percent; for those at the P-1 to P-3 levels, the amounts are reduced by 13 percent. These are the dependency rates for the different levels. The single rates are 75 percent of the dependency rates.
(c) The non-removal allowance is not payable to staff on initial appointment in the home country, where such appointment does not give rise to a right to removal costs as provided for by Staff Rule 7.2.01.

Rule 7.2.04 Loss of entitlement to unaccompanied shipment or removal expenses

(a) A staff member who resigns before completing one year of service shall not normally be entitled to payment of removal expenses under Staff Rule 7.2.01 above.
(b) Entitlement to removal expenses under Staff Rule 7.2.01(a)(i) and (ii) shall normally cease if removal has not commenced within one year after the date on which the staff member became entitled to removal expenses or if the staff member's services are not expected to continue for more than six months beyond the proposed date of arrival of the personal effects and household goods.
(c) Upon separation from service, entitlement to unaccompanied shipment expenses under Staff Rule 7.1.14(d) or removal expenses under Staff Rule 7.2.01 shall cease if the shipment or removal has not commenced within six months or one year, respectively, after the date of separation. However, where both spouses are staff members and the spouse who separates first is entitled to unaccompanied shipment or removal expenses, and taking into account Staff Rule 4.3.01(d), his or her entitlement shall not cease until six months or one year, as the case may be, after the date of separation of the other spouse.

ARTICLE VIII
STAFF RELATIONS

Regulation 8
(a) The Director-General shall establish and maintain continuous contacts and communication with staff in order to ensure their effective participation in identifying, examining and resolving issues relating to conditions of work.
(b) A staff representative body shall be established and shall be entitled to initiate proposals to the Director-General for the purpose set forth in paragraph (a) above. It shall be organised in such a way as to afford equitable representation to all staff.
(c) The Director-General shall establish joint staff/management machinery to advise him regarding personnel policies and general questions of staff welfare and to make to him such proposals as it may desire for amendment of the Staff Regulations and Rules.

Rule 8.1.01   Staff Council

(a) A staff representative body (hereinafter the "Staff Council") elected by the staff members shall be established for the purpose of ensuring continuous contact between the staff members and the Director-General.

(b) The Staff Council shall be composed in such a way as to afford equitable representation to all levels of staff.

(c) Election of the Staff Council shall take place once every year under regulations drawn up by the Staff Council and agreed to by the Director-General. Each staff member on a fixed-term appointment may participate in such elections and shall be eligible for election.

(d) The Staff Council shall be consulted on questions relating to conditions of work and shall be entitled to make proposals to the Director-General on behalf of the staff on such questions.

(e) Except for instruction to meet emergency situations, general administrative instructions or directives on questions within the scope of paragraph (d) above shall be transmitted in advance to the Staff Council for its consideration and comments.

Rule 8.1.02   Joint Advisory Board

(a) A "Joint Advisory Board" shall be established.

(b) The Joint Advisory Board shall advise the Director-General on:
    (i)   the Secretariat's personnel policies;
    (ii)   general questions of staff administration and welfare; and
    (iii) amendment of the Staff Regulations, Rules and Administrative Directives.

(c) The Joint Advisory Board shall be composed of three members and three alternate members designated by the Director-General and three members and three alternate members designated by the Staff Council.

(d) The Joint Advisory Board shall determine its own rules of procedure and shall elect its own chairperson and alternate chairperson.

(e) The agenda of the Joint Advisory Board shall consist of items requested by the Director-General or by the Staff Council.

ARTICLE IX
SEPARATION FROM SERVICE

Regulation 9.1
  (a) The Director-General may terminate the appointment of a staff member prior to the expiration date of his or her contract if the necessities for the service require abolition of the post or reduction of the staff; if the services of the individual concerned prove unsatisfactory; if the conduct of a staff member indicates that he/she does not meet the highest standards of integrity required by the Organisation; if the staff member is, for reasons of health, incapacitated for further service, or if facts anterior to the appointment of the staff member and relevant to his or her suitability come to light that, if they had been known at the time of appointment, should, under the standards established under these Staff Regulations, have precluded his or her appointment.

  (b) No termination under subparagraph (a) shall take place until the matter has been considered and reported on by a special advisory board appointed for that purpose by the Director-General.

  (c) The Director-General shall terminate the appointment of a staff member in case the State Party of which the staff member is a citizen ceases to be a member of the Organisation.

Rule 9.1.01   Consideration of termination of appointment and definition of termination

(a)   Special Advisory Boards
      The special advisory board(s) referred to in Staff Regulation 9.1(b) shall be composed of representatives of both staff and management. The Director-General shall set out the specific composition of such boards, as well as their terms of reference, in an Administrative Directive.

(b)   Definition of termination
      A termination within the meaning of the Staff Regulations and Rules is any separation from service initiated by the Director-General other than the expiration of a contract, non-confirmation of a contract at the end of probation, retirement at the age of 62 years or more or summary dismissal for serious misconduct.

Regulation 9.2
Staff members may resign from the Secretariat upon giving the Director-General the notice required under the terms of their appointments.

Rule 9.2.01   Resignation

(a)   A resignation, within the meaning of the Staff Regulations and Rules, is a separation initiated by a staff member.

(b)   Unless otherwise specified in their letters of appointment, 60 days' written notice of resignation shall be given by staff members having a fixed-term appointment and five days' written notice of resignation by those having short-term appointments. The Director-General may, however, accept resignations on shorter notice.

(c)   The Director-General may require the resignation to be submitted by the staff member in person in order to be acceptable.

Regulation 9.3
If the Director-General terminates an appointment, the staff member shall be given such notice and such indemnity payment as may be applicable under these Staff Regulations. Payments of termination indemnity shall be made by the Director-General in accordance with the rates and conditions established by the United Nations General Assembly for the United Nations common system and specified in Annex III to the present Staff Regulations.

Rule 9.3.01   Notice of termination

(a)   If the fixed-term appointment of a staff member is to be terminated, such staff member shall be given not less than 60 days' written notice of such termination.

(b)   A staff member whose short-term appointment is to be terminated shall be given not less than five working days' written notice for contracts of three months or less and not less than ten working days' written notice for contracts with a duration longer than three months.

(c)   The notice of termination shall state the reasons for the termination.

(d)   In lieu of these notice periods, the Director-General may authorise compensation calculated on the basis of the salary and allowances which the staff member would have received had the date of termination been at the end of the notice period.

Rule 9.3.02   Termination indemnity

(a) Payment of termination indemnity under Staff Regulation 9.3 and Annex III to the Staff Regulations shall be calculated:
   (i) for staff in the Professional and higher category, on the basis of the staff member's gross salary less staff assessment in accordance with Annex I to the Staff Regulations;
   (ii) for staff in the General Service category, on the basis of the staff member's gross remuneration less staff assessment in accordance with Annex I to the Staff Regulations.
(b) Length of service shall be deemed to comprise the total period of a staff member's full-time continuous service with the Secretariat, regardless of types of appointment. Continuity of such service shall not be considered as broken by periods of special leave. However, service credits shall not accrue during periods of special leave with partial pay or without pay of one full month or more.

Regulation 9.4
The Staff Rules shall establish a scheme for the payment of repatriation grants to defray expenses associated with repatriation upon separation from service. In principle, the repatriation grant shall be payable to staff members whom the Organisation is obliged to repatriate. The repatriation grant shall not, however, be paid to staff members who are summarily dismissed. Staff members shall be entitled to a repatriation grant only upon relocation outside the Netherlands. The amount of the grant shall be determined in accordance with the relevant Staff Rules. Detailed conditions relating to eligibility and requisite evidence of relocation shall be determined by the Director-General.

Rule 9.4.01   Repatriation grant

Payment of repatriation grants under Staff Regulation 9.4 and Annex IV to the Staff Regulations shall be subject to the following conditions and definitions:
(a) "Obligation to repatriate", as used in Annex IV to the Staff Regulations, shall mean the obligation to return a staff member and his or her spouse and dependent children, upon separation, at the expense of the Organisation, to a place outside the Netherlands.
(b) "Home country" shall mean the country of home leave under Staff Rule 5.2.01 or such other country as the Director-General may determine.
(c) If at any time a staff member was considered to have acquired permanent residence in the Netherlands and subsequently changed from such status, the staff member's continuous service will be deemed to have commenced at the time the change was made. Continuity of such service shall not be considered as broken by periods of special leave. However, for the purpose of calculating the amount of the grant payable, service credit shall not accrue during periods of special leave with partial pay or without pay of one full month or more.
(d) Payment of the repatriation grant shall be subject to the provision by the staff member of documentary evidence of relocation away from the Netherlands.
(e) Entitlement to repatriation grant shall cease if no claim for payment of the grant has been submitted within two years after the effective date of separation. However, where both spouses are staff members and the spouse who separates first is entitled to repatriation grant, his or her entitlement to repatriation grant shall cease if no claim for payment of the grant has been submitted within two years after the date of separation of the other spouse.
(f) Payment of the repatriation grant shall be calculated:
   (i) for staff in the Professional and higher category, on the basis of the staff member's gross salary, less staff assessment in accordance with Annex I to the Staff Regulations;

(ii) for staff in the General Service category, on the basis of the staff member's gross remuneration, including a language allowance, if any, less staff assessment in accordance with Annex I to the Staff Regulations.

(g) Payment shall be at the rates specified in Annex IV to the Staff Regulations.

(h) No payments shall be made to any staff member who abandons his or her post or to any staff member who is residing at the time of separation in his or her home country while performing official duties.

(i) A dependent child, for the purpose of a repatriation grant, shall mean a child recognised as dependent under Staff Rule 3.4.02(b) at the time of the staff member's separation from service. The repatriation grant shall be paid at the rate for a staff member with a spouse or dependent child to eligible staff members regardless of the place of residence of the spouse or dependent child.

(j) Where both spouses are staff members and each is entitled, on separation, to payment of a repatriation grant, and taking into account Staff Rule 4.3.01(d), payment shall be made to each at single rates, according to their respective entitlements. In cases where dependent children are recognised, the first parent to be separated may claim payment at the rate applicable to a staff member with a spouse or dependent child. In this event, the second parent, on separation, may claim payment at the single rate for the whole period of qualifying service, or, if eligible, at the rate applicable to a staff member with a spouse or dependent child for the whole period of his or her qualifying service, from which shall normally be deducted the amount of the difference between the dependency rate and the single rate of the repatriation grant paid to the first parent.

(k) Loss of entitlement to payment of return travel expenses under Staff Rule 7.1.03 shall not affect a staff member's eligibility for payment of the repatriation grant.

(l) In the event of the death of an eligible staff member, no payment shall be made unless there is a surviving spouse or one or more dependent children whom the Organisation is obligated to return to their home country. Payment shall be subject to proof of relocation. If there is one such survivor, payment shall be made at the single rate; if there are two or more such survivors, payment shall be made at the rate applicable to a staff member with a spouse or dependent child.

Rule 9.4.02 Commutation of accrued annual leave

(a) If, upon separation from service, a staff member has accrued annual leave, the staff member shall be paid a sum of money in commutation of the period of such accrued leave up to a maximum of 30 working days.

(b) Notwithstanding paragraph (a) above, a staff member appointed before 1 January 2011 who has accrued more than 30 days of annual leave as of 31 December 2010, shall be paid a sum of money in commutation of the period of such accrued leave up to a maximum of:
(i) 60 days, if the staff member separates between 1 January 2011 and 31 December 2011;
(ii) 50 days, if the staff member separates between 1 January 2012 and 31 December 2012;
(iii) 40 days, if the staff member separates between 1 January 2013 and 31 December 2013; and
(iv) 30 days, if the staff member separates after 31 December 2013.

(c) The payment in commutation of the period of accrued annual leave shall be calculated:
(i) for staff in the Professional and higher category, on the basis of the staff member's net base salary plus post adjustment; and
(ii) for staff in the General Service category, on the basis of the staff member's gross remuneration less staff assessment, in accordance with Annex I to the Staff Regulations.

Rule 9.4.03   Restitution of advance annual and sick leave

Upon separation, a staff member who has taken advance annual or sick leave beyond that which he or she has subsequently accrued shall make restitution for such advance leave by means of a cash refund or an offset against moneys due to the staff member from the Organisation, equivalent to the remuneration received, including allowances and other payments, in respect of the advance leave period. The Director-General may waive this requirement if in the opinion of the Director-General there are exceptional or compelling reasons for so doing.

Rule 9.4.04   Last day for pay purposes

(a) When a staff member is separated from service, the date on which entitlement to salary, allowances and benefits shall cease (i.e., the last day for pay purposes) shall be determined according to the following provisions:

  (i)   upon resignation, the last day for pay purposes shall be either the date of expiration of the notice period under Staff Rule 9.2.01 or such other date as accepted by the Director-General. Staff members will be expected to perform their duties during the notice period, except when the resignation takes effect upon the completion of maternity leave or following sick or special leave;

  (ii) upon expiration of a fixed-term appointment, the last day for pay purposes shall be the date specified in the letter of appointment;

  (iii) upon termination, the last day for pay purposes shall be the date provided in the notice of termination;

  (iv) in case of summary dismissal, the last day for pay purposes shall be the date of dismissal;

  (v)   in case of death, the last day for pay purposes shall be the date of death, unless there is a surviving spouse or dependent child. In this event, the last day for pay purposes shall be extended beyond the date of death by one month for each completed year of service, with a minimum of three months.

  (vi) payment related to the period of extension beyond the date of death may be made in a lump sum as soon as the pay accounts and related matters can be closed. Such payment shall be made only to the surviving spouse and dependent children. For staff in the Professional and higher category, the payment shall be calculated on the basis of the staff member's gross salary, less staff assessment in accordance with Annex I to the Staff Regulations. For staff in the General Service category, the payment shall be calculated on the basis of the staff member's gross remuneration, including language allowance if any, less staff assessment in accordance with Annex I to the Staff Regulations.

(b) When an internationally recruited staff member is exercising an entitlement to return travel, the last day for pay purposes shall be the date established under subparagraphs (a)(i), (ii), or (iii) above or the estimated date of arrival at the place of entitlement, whichever is later. The estimated date of arrival shall be determined on the basis of the time it would take to travel without interruption by an approved route and mode of direct travel from The Hague to the place of entitlement, the travel commencing no later than the day following the date established under paragraph (a).

Rule 9.4.05   Certification of service

Any staff member who so requests shall, on leaving the service of the Organisation, be given a statement relating to the nature of his or her duties and the length of service. On the staff member's written request, the statement shall also refer to the quality of his or her work and his or her official conduct.

ARTICLE X
DISCIPLINARY MEASURES AND PROCEDURES

Regulation 10.1

The Director-General shall establish an administrative body which will advise him or her in disciplinary cases.

Rule 10.1.01   Joint Disciplinary Committee

A Joint Disciplinary Committee shall be established and shall be available to advise the Director-General in disciplinary matters.

Rule 10.1.02   Composition of Joint Disciplinary Committee

(a) The Joint Disciplinary Committee shall be composed of:
   (i) a chairperson, appointed by the Director-General from among a list presented by the Joint Advisory Board;
   (ii) one member appointed by the Director-General;
   (iii) one member elected by the staff.
(b) An alternate for each person in paragraph (a) shall be selected at any time in the same manner as indicated in that paragraph.
(c) The chairperson and members of the Joint Disciplinary Committee shall be appointed or elected for two years, shall be eligible for reappointment or re-election, and shall remain in office until their successors are appointed or elected, as long as they are staff members.
(d) The chairperson may be removed from the Joint Disciplinary Committee by the Director-General after consultation with the Joint Advisory Board. The member appointed by the Director-General may be removed by him. The member elected by the staff may be recalled by a majority vote of the staff, taken at the initiative of the Staff Council.
(e) The Director-General may, at the request of either party, disqualify the chairperson or any member from consideration of a specific case if, in the opinion of the Director-General, the action is warranted by the relation of that Committee-member to the staff member whose case is to be considered or by any possible conflict of interest. The Director-General may also excuse any member from consideration of a specific case at that member's request. A person so disqualified or excused will be replaced by an alternate referred to in paragraph (b) above.

Rule 10.1.03   Joint Disciplinary Committee procedure

(a) In considering a case, the Joint Disciplinary Committee shall act with maximum dispatch and shall make every effort to provide its advice to the Director-General within four weeks after the case has been submitted to it.
(b) Proceedings before the Joint Disciplinary Committee shall normally be limited to the original written presentation of the case, together with brief statements and rebuttals, which may be made orally or in writing, but without delay. If the Committee considers that it requires the testimony of the staff member concerned or of other witnesses, it may, at its sole discretion, obtain such testimony by written deposition, by personal appearance before the Committee, before one of its members or before another staff member acting as a special master, or by telephone or other means of communication.

(c) The Joint Disciplinary Committee shall adopt its own rules of procedure which shall be con-sistent with these Staff Rules and with any applicable administrative instructions, as well as with the requirements of due process.
(d) The Joint Disciplinary Committee shall permit a staff member to arrange to have his or her case presented before it by any other staff member or former staff member of the Organisation or by any other person who is a staff member or retired staff member within the context of the United Nations common system.

Regulation 10.2
The Director-General may impose disciplinary measures on staff whose conduct is unsatisfactory.

Rule 10.2.01   Unsatisfactory Conduct

Failure by a staff member to comply with his or her obligations under the Staff Regulations and Rules, the Financial Regulations and Rules, or an Administrative Directive may amount to unsat-isfactory conduct within the meaning of Staff Regulation 10.2. The Director-General may impose such disciplinary measures as are in the Director-General's opinion appropriate on staff members whose conduct is unsatisfactory.

Rule 10.2.02   Disciplinary measures

(a) Disciplinary measures under Staff Regulation 10.2 may take one or more of the following forms:
    (i)   written censure by the Director-General;
    (ii) loss of one or more steps-in-grade;
    (iii) deferment, for a specified period, of eligibility for within-grade increment;
    (iv) suspension without pay;
    (vi) demotion;
    (vii)termination of appointment, with or without notice or compensation in lieu thereof, not withstanding Staff Rule 9.3.01.
(b) The following measures shall not be considered to be disciplinary measures, within the mean-ing of this Rule:
    (i)   reprimand, written or oral, by a supervisory official;
    (ii) recovery of moneys owed to the Organisation;
    (iii) suspension pursuant to Staff Rule 10.3.02.

Rule 10.2.03   Due process

(a) No disciplinary proceedings may be instituted against a staff member unless he or she has been notified of the allegations against him or her, as well as of the right to seek the assistance in his or her defence of another staff member or former staff member of the Organisation or of any other person who is a staff member or retired staff member within the context of the United Nations system, and has been given a reasonable opportunity to respond to those al-legations.
(b) No staff member shall be subject to disciplinary measures until the matter has been referred to the Joint Disciplinary Committee for advice as to what measures, if any, are appropriate, except that no such advice shall be required:
    (i)   if referral to the Joint Disciplinary Committee is waived by mutual agreement of the staff member concerned and the Director-General;

    (ii) in respect of summary dismissal imposed by the Director-General in cases where the seriousness of the misconduct warrants immediate separation from service.

(c) An appeal in respect of a disciplinary measure considered by a Joint Disciplinary Committee pursuant to either paragraph (b) above or pursuant to Staff Rule 10.3.01(c) may be submitted to the Appeals Council.

Regulation 10.3
The Director-General may summarily dismiss staff for serious misconduct. In such cases no termination indemnity shall be payable.

Rule 10.3.01   Summary dismissal for serious misconduct

(a) A serious breach, as determined by the Director-General, of the OPCW Policy on Confidentiality, will be considered serious misconduct.

(b) Summary dismissal of a staff member for serious misconduct does not prejudge such staff member's right to due process as provided for in Staff Rule 10.2.03.

(c) In cases of summary dismissal imposed without prior submission of the case to a Joint Disciplinary Committee in accordance with subparagraphs (b)(i) and (ii) of Staff Rule 10.2.03, the staff member or former staff member concerned may, within two months of having received written notification of the measure, request that the measure be reviewed by the Joint Disciplinary Committee. A request shall not have the effect of suspending the measure. After the advice of the Committee has been received, the Director-General shall decide as soon as possible what action to take in respect thereof.

Rule 10.3.02   Suspension during investigation and disciplinary proceedings

(a) If the Director-General considers that there is <u>prima facie</u> evidence of a breach of the OPCW Policy on Confidentiality or other serious misconduct by a staff member, the Director-General may suspend the staff member from duty, pending investigation. Such suspension shall be for a period which should normally not exceed three months and shall be with pay unless, in exceptional circumstances, the Director-General decides that suspension without pay is appropriate. Suspension pending investigation shall not be considered a disciplinary measure and shall be without prejudice to the rights of the staff member if the evidence of serious misconduct is not sustained.

(b) If a staff member, following investigation, is not summarily dismissed, he or she shall be paid for any period of suspension without pay as if he or she had not been suspended. In the event of summary dismissal, the dismissal may be made effective from the date of suspension; in that case no entitlements shall accrue during the period of suspension without pay.

(c) A staff member suspended pursuant to paragraph (a) shall be given a written statement of the reason for the suspension and its probable duration.

ARTICLE XI
APPEALS

Regulation 11.1
Staff members have the right of appeal against any administrative decision alleging non-observance of the terms of appointment, including relevant Staff Regulations and Rules, and against disciplinary action.

> **Regulation 11.2**
> The Director-General shall establish an administrative body to advise him or her in case of any appeal by a staff member.

Rule 11.2.01   Appeals Council

(a) An "Appeals Council" shall be established to consider and advise the Director-General on appeals filed under the terms of Staff Regulation 11.1.

(b) The Appeals Council shall be composed of:
   (i) a chairperson appointed by the Director-General from among a list presented by the Joint Advisory Board;
   (ii) one member appointed by the Director-General;
   (iii) one member elected by the staff.

(c) An alternate for each person in paragraph (b) shall be selected in the same manner as indicated in that paragraph.

(d) The chairperson and members of the Appeals Council shall be appointed or elected for one year, shall be eligible for reappointment or re-election, and shall remain in office until their successors are appointed or elected.

(e) The chairperson of the Appeals Council may be removed by the Director-General upon the recommendation of the Joint Advisory Board. The member appointed by the Director-General may be removed by the Director-General. The member elected by the staff may be recalled by a majority vote of the staff, taken at the initiative of the Staff Council.

(f) The Appeals Council shall establish its own rules of procedure.

(g) The Appeals Council may, by a majority vote of its members, recommend to the Director-General changes in the present chapter of these Rules.

(h) The secretariat of the Appeals Council shall consist of a Secretary and such other staff as may be required for its proper functioning.

Rule 11.2.02   Objections in respect of administrative decisions

(a) A staff member wishing to appeal an administrative decision pursuant to Staff Regulation 11.1 shall, as a first step, address a letter to the Director-General, requesting that the administrative decision be reviewed; such a letter must be sent within two months from the date the staff member received notification of the decision in writing.
   (i) If the Director-General replies to the staff member's letter, the staff member may appeal against the answer within one month of the receipt of such reply;
   (ii) if the Director-General does not reply to the letter within one month, the staff member may appeal against the original administrative decision within one month of the expiration of the time-limit specified in this subparagraph for the Director-General's reply.

(b) The Director-General, in reviewing the administrative decision in question, may, with the consent of the staff member or at the latter's request, seek the assistance of the chairperson, a member or an alternate of the Appeals Council, to be designated by its presiding officer, with a view to reaching a conciliatory conclusion of the matter. This procedure is without prejudice to the right of the staff member to pursue an appeal under the provisions of this Rule.

(c) Neither a request for administrative review under paragraph (a) above nor the filing of an appeal under Staff Rule 11.2.03(a) shall have the effect of suspending action on the contested decision.

(i) However, the staff member concerned may request a suspension of action on such a decision by writing to the Secretary of the Appeals Council. The request shall set forth the relevant facts and indicate how implementation would directly and irreparably injure the staff member's rights.

(ii) Upon receipt of such a request, the Appeals Council shall be promptly constituted, and shall act expeditiously. If after considering the views of both parties, the Appeals Council determines that the decision has not been implemented and that its implementation would result in irreparable injury to the appellant, it may recommend to the Director-General the suspension of action on that decision until the time-limits specified in paragraph (a)(i) or (ii) above have passed without an appeal having been filed or if an appeal is filed, until a decision on the appeal is taken.

(iii) The Director-General's decision on such a recommendation is not subject to appeal.

Rule 11.2.03   Appeal Procedures

(a) An appeal against the Director-General's decision on disciplinary action shall be filed with the Secretary of the Appeals Council within two months from the time the staff member received notification of the decision in writing.

(b) An appeal pursuant to paragraph (a) above shall be filed with the Secretary of the Appeals Council.

(c) No person who has assisted the Director-General in a conciliation procedure referred to in Staff Rule 11.2.02(b) shall serve on the Appeals Council for an appeal relating to the same case.

(d) The Director-General may, at the request of either party, disqualify the chairperson or a member if, in the opinion of the Director-General, such action is warranted to ensure impartiality. The Director-General may also excuse the chairperson or a member from serving on the Appeals Council.

(e) Any person disqualified or excused in terms of paragraph (d) above shall be replaced by an alternate.

(f) An appeal shall not be receivable unless the time-limits specified in Staff Rule 11.2.02(a) or paragraph (a) above have been complied with or have been waived, in exceptional circumstances, by the Appeals Council.

(g) Proceedings before the Appeals Council shall normally be limited to the original written presentation of the case, together with brief statements and rebuttals, which may be made orally or in writing.

(h) A staff member may arrange to have his or her appeal presented to the Appeals Council on his or her behalf by another staff member or former staff member or by any other person who is a staff member or retired staff member in the context of the United Nations common system. The staff member may not, however, be represented before the Appeals Council by any other person.

(i) The Appeals Council shall decide its own competence.

(j) In case of termination or other action on grounds of inefficiency or relative efficiency, the Appeals Council shall not consider the substantive question of efficiency but only evidence that the decision was motivated by prejudice or by some other extraneous factor.

(k) The Appeals Council shall have the authority to call members of the Secretariat who may be able to provide information concerning the issues before it and shall have access to all documents pertinent to the case. Notwithstanding the preceding sentence, should the Appeals Council wish to have information or documents relating to the proceedings of the Management Board, it shall request such information or documents from the Director-General, who shall decide on the Appeals Council's request, taking into account the interests of confidentiality. This decision of the Director-General is not subject to appeal. The chairperson of the

Appeals Council shall determine which documents are to be transmitted to all members of the Appeals Council and the parties.

(l) In considering an appeal, the Appeals Council shall act with the maximum dispatch consistent with a fair review of the issues before it.

(m) Within one month of the date on which the consideration of an appeal has been completed, the Appeals Council shall, by majority vote, adopt and submit a report to the Director-General. The report shall be considered as constituting a record of the proceedings in the appeal and may include a summary of the matter as well as all recommendations that the Appeals Council considers appropriate. Votes on the recommendations shall be recorded and any member of the Appeals Council may have his or her dissenting opinion included in the report.

(n) The final decision on the appeal will normally be taken by the Director-General within one month after the Appeals Council has forwarded its report, and shall be communicated to the staff member, together with a copy of the Appeals Council's report. The Director-General's decision and a copy of the Appeals Council's report shall also be transmitted to a designated officer of the Staff Council, unless the staff member objects.

Regulation 11.3
Arrangements shall be made for the hearing by the Administrative Tribunal of the International Labour Organisation of appeals by staff members against the administrative decisions referred to in Staff Regulation 11.1. These arrangements shall fully respect the Annex on the Protection of Confidential Information of the Convention and the OPCW Policy on Confidentiality.

Rule 11.3.01   Administrative Tribunal

(a) Staff members shall have the right to appeal to the Administrative Tribunal of the International Labour Organisation, in accordance with the provisions of the Statute of that Tribunal, against administrative decisions and disciplinary actions taken, after reference to the Appeals Council.

(b) A staff member may, in agreement with the Director-General, waive the jurisdiction of the Appeals Council and appeal directly to the Administrative Tribunal of the International Labour Organisation, in accordance with the provisions of the Statute of that Tribunal.

ARTICLE XII
GENERAL PROVISIONS

Rule 12.0.01   Financial responsibility

Any staff member may be required to reimburse the Organisation either partially or in full for any financial loss suffered by the Organisation as a result of the staff member's negligence or of his or her having violated any regulation, rule or administrative directive.

Rule 12.0.02   Performance appraisal

The service and conduct of all staff members shall be the subject of performance reports made from time to time by the staff member's supervisors. Such reports, which shall be shown to the staff member, shall form a part of his or her permanent cumulative record.

Rule 12.0.03   Proprietary rights

All rights, including title, copyright and patent rights, in any work performed by a staff member as part of his or her official duties shall be vested in the Organisation.

Rule 12.0.04   Liability insurance

Staff members who own or drive motor vehicles shall carry public liability and property damage insurance in an amount adequate to insure them against claims arising from injury or death to other persons or from damage to the property of others caused by their motor vehicles.

Regulation 12.1
The present Staff Regulations may be supplemented or amended by the Conference of the States Parties, without prejudice to the existing contracts of staff members.

Regulation 12.2
The Director-General may make Interim Staff Rules to implement the present Staff Regulations. The Interim Staff Rules shall be provisionally applied until the requirements of Staff Regulations 12.3 and 12.4 below have been met.

Rule 12.2.01   Amendment of, and exceptions to, Staff Rules

(a) Subject to Staff Regulations 12.1, 12.2, 12.3, 12.4 and 12.5, these Staff Rules may be amended by the Director-General in a manner consistent with the Staff Regulations.
(b) Exceptions to the Staff Rules may be made by the Director-General, provided that such exceptions are not inconsistent with any Staff Regulation or other decision of the Conference of the States Parties or of the Executive Council and provided further that it is agreed to by the staff member directly affected and is, in the opinion of the Director-General, not prejudicial to the interests of any other staff member or group of staff members.

Regulation 12.3
The Interim Staff Rules shall be reported by the Director-General to the Executive Council. The Interim Staff Rules shall be approved by the Executive Council.

Regulation 12.4
The Interim Staff Rules reported by the Director-General shall enter into force as Staff Rules on the first day of the month following the month in which they are approved by the Executive Council.

Rule 12.4.01   Effective date of Staff Rules

Except as otherwise indicated and subject always to the provisions of Staff Regulations 12.2, 12.3, 12.4 and 12.5 these Staff Rules shall enter into full force on 15 November 1999.

> **Regulation 12.5**
> Interim Staff Rules promulgated by the Director-General under Staff Regulation 12.2 shall not give rise to acquired rights while they are interim within the meaning of Staff Regulation 12.2.

ANNEX I
SALARY SCALES AND RELATED PROVISIONS

1. Except as provided in paragraph 3 of the present annex, the salary scales for staff shall be fixed in accordance with the provisions of Staff Regulation 3.1.
2. Subject to satisfactory service, salary increments in accordance with the salary scales set forth in Annex I to the Staff Regulations of the United Nations, and published in information circulars at the OPCW, shall be awarded annually, except that any increments to step XII of the P-2 level, steps XIV and XV of the P-3 level, steps XIII, XIV and XV of the P-4 level, steps XI, XII and XIII of the P-5 level, above step IV of the D-1 level, and above step I of the D-2 level, shall be preceded by two years at the previous step.
3. The Director-General shall determine the salary rates to be paid to personnel specifically engaged for conferences and other short-term services, to consultants, and to technical assistance experts.
4. No salary shall be paid to staff in respect of periods of unauthorised absence from work unless such absence was caused by reasons beyond their control or duly certified medical reasons.
5. The net base salaries referred to in paragraph 1 of the present annex shall be adjusted by application of a post adjustment the amount of which shall be determined in accordance with the terms and conditions promulgated by the ICSC.

ANNEX II
LETTERS OF APPOINTMENT

(a) The letter of appointment shall state:
   (i) that the appointment is subject to the provisions of the Staff Regulations and Rules and to changes that may be made thereto from time to time;
   (ii) the nature of the appointment;
   (iii) the date at which the staff member is required to enter upon duty;
   (iv) the period of appointment, the notice required to terminate it and period of probation, if any;
   (v) the category, level, commencing rate of salary and, if increments are allowable, the scale of increments, and the maximum attainable;
   (vi) any special conditions that may be applicable.
(b) A copy of the Staff Regulations and Rules shall be transmitted to a staff member with the letter of appointment. In accepting appointment the staff member shall state that he or she has been made acquainted with and accepts the conditions laid down in the Staff Regulations and Rules.

ANNEX III
TERMINATION INDEMNITY

Staff members whose appointments are terminated shall be paid an indemnity in accordance with the schedule of payments as outlined in Annex III of the United Nations Staff Regulations. The Secretariat shall publish the schedule of payments applied at the United Nations, and any amendments, in information circulars.

ANNEX IV
REPATRIATION GRANT

In principle, the repatriation grant shall be payable to staff members whom the Organisation is obliged to repatriate. The repatriation grant shall not, however, be paid to staff members who are summarily dismissed. Staff members shall be entitled to a repatriation grant only upon relocation outside the Netherlands. Detailed conditions and definitions relating to eligibility and requisite evidence of relocation shall be determined by the Director-General. The amount of the grant shall be proportional to the length of service with the Organisation and in accordance with the relevant United Nations scale as contained in Annex IV of the United Nations Staff Regulations. The Secretariat shall publish that scale, and any amendments thereto, in information circulars.

ANNEX V
OPCW TOP STRUCTURE

Deputy Director-General
Director of the Office of Special Projects
Director of the Office of Internal Oversight
Director of the Office of the Legal Adviser
Director of the Secretariat for the Policy Making Organs
Director of the Verification Division
Director of the Inspectorate Division
Director of the Administration Division
Director of the External Relations Division
Director of the International Co-operation and Assistance Division

24.3 OPCW Tenure Policy

C-SS-2/DEC.1 adopted by the Conference of the States Parties at its Second Special Session on 30 April 2003 and entitled "Tenure policy of the OPCW"

The Conference

Recalling that, in a decision of 2 July 1999 (C-IV/DEC.25), the Fourth Session of the Conference of the States Parties (hereinafter "the Conference") adopted Staff Regulation 4.4, which provides that the OPCW is a non-career organisation and that the total length of service for the OPCW Technical Secretariat (hereinafter "the Secretariat") staff is seven years except as otherwise specified;

Recalling that the Conference at its Fourth Session (Report C-IV/6 of 2 July 1999) requested the Executive Council (hereinafter "the Council") to decide on the effective starting date for the seven-year total length of service of the Secretariat staff;

Mindful that the Director-General, in implementing the decisions of both the Conference and the Council regarding the seven-year total length of Service of the Secretariat staff and its starting date, will have to be guided by the need to maintain the continued financial stability and effectiveness of the OPCW;

Further recalling the provisions contained in Article VIII Paragraph 44 of the Convention, including *inter alia* that "the paramount consideration in the employment of the staff and in the determination of the conditions of service shall be the necessity of securing the highest standards of efficiency, competence and integrity" and that "due regard shall be paid to the importance of recruiting staff on as wide a geographical basis as possible";

Recalling also the requirement in Staff Regulation 4.4(a), for contract extensions to be assessed upon, *inter alia*, the Secretariat staff member's performance measured in accordance with a rigorous performance appraisal system, and noting the Director-General's stated intention to maintain and continuously improve the Performance Management Appraisal System;

Taking into account the decision of the Council (EC-M-22/DEC.1, dated 28 March 2003):

Hereby:
1. Decides that:
   (a) the average rate of turnover beginning with the calendar year 2003 with respect to turnover of Secretariat staff subject to tenure, other than those falling under the provisions of Staff Regulation 4.4(b) (i) and (ii), shall be one-seventh per year;
   (b) as an exceptional measure so as not to compromise the financial stability and operational effectiveness of the Organisation, the Director-General shall be authorised to grant contract extensions or renewals which would result in a total length of service in excess of the seven-year limit provided for in Staff Regulation 4.4(b); and
   (c) this exceptional authority of the Director-General to grant contract extensions or renewals beyond the seven-year total length of service provided for in Staff Regulation 4.4(b) shall expire effective 1 January 2009. At that time, not more than 10% of the number of staff subject to tenure that were incumbent on 2 July 1999, other than those falling under the provisions of Staff Regulation 4.4(b) (i) and (ii), may remain on staff, and by 31 December 2009, no member of Secretariat staff, other than those falling under the provisions of Staff Regulation 4.4(b) (i) and (ii), who has served more than seven years shall remain on staff.
2. Reaffirms that:
   (a) the nature of the OPCW as a non-career organisation with limited staff tenure, and the Staff Regulations, in particular Staff Regulation 4.4, require the Director–General, when considering contract extensions or renewals, to take fully into account the need for decisions on contracts to contribute to, and be consistent with, the faithful implementation of overall tenure policy; and,
   (b) when implementing the Staff Regulations and the decisions of the Council and the Conference in this matter, the Director-General's authority includes at any time to extend or renew or not to extend or renew contracts for Secretariat staff who have served less than seven years.

C-11/DEC.7 adopted by the Conference of the States Parties at its Eleventh Session on 7 December 2006 and entitled "Future implementation of the Tenure Policy"

The Conference

Having considered a recommendation by the Executive Council on the future implementation of the OPCW policy on tenure (EC-47/DEC.14, dated 8 November 2006);

Hereby:

Amends subparagraph 1(c) of C-SS-2/DEC.1, dated 30 April 2003, to read as follows:

"as a one-time measure, which does not set a precedent for the future, this exceptional authority of the Director-General to grant contract extensions or renewals beyond the seven-year total length of service provided for in Staff Regulation 4.4(b) shall expire effective 29 April 2012. At that time, no staff subject to tenure with a total length of service in excess of seven years, other than those falling under the provisions of Staff Regulation 4.4(b) (i) and (ii), may remain on staff."

C-16/DEC.9 adopted by the Conference of the States Parties at its Sixteenth Session on 30 November 2011 and entitled "Future implementation of the Tenure Policy of the OPCW"

The Conference of the States Parties,

Having considered the decision by the Executive Council (hereinafter "the Council") at its Thirty-First Meeting (on 23 and 24 November 2011) concerning the future implementation of the tenure policy of the OPCW;

Hereby:

1. Modifies the decision taken by the Conference of the States Parties at its Eleventh Session (C-11/DEC.7 (dated 7 December 2006)), which amended subparagraph 1(c) of C-SS-2/DEC.1 (dated 30 April 2003), to read as follows:

   "(c) as a one-time measure, which does not set a precedent for the future, this exceptional authority of the Director-General to grant contract extensions or renewals beyond the seven-year total length of service provided for in Staff Regulation 4.4(b) shall expire effective 29 April 2016. This exceptional authority shall apply to the operational requirements of verification and inspection of destruction-related activities. At that time, no staff subject to tenure with a total length of service in excess of seven years, other than those falling under the provisions of Staff Regulation 4.4(b) (i) and (ii), may remain on staff";

2. Decides that no staff member who receives an exceptional extension in service pursuant to subparagraph 1(c) above may remain on staff for a total length of service in excess of ten years;

3. Decides that the Council may explore at a later stage possible options, so as to ensure the Organisation has staff with the requisite skills and expertise to meet its operational requirements; and

4. Requests the Director-General to provide an annual report on the implementation of this decision to the Council at its third regular session every year. This report will include information on the posts for which extensions have been granted. The first such report will be submitted to the Council at its Sixty-Ninth Session.

24.4 Appointment of the Director-General

Extracts of C-SS-1/DEC.4 adopted by the Conference of the States Parties at its First Special Session on 25 July 2002 and entitled "Terms of Appointment of the Director-General"[3]

The Conference

Recalling the decision of the Conference of the States Parties (hereinafter the "Conference") on the terms of appointment of the Director-General (C-II/DEC.4, dated 5 December 1997);

Recalling further the decision of the Executive Council (hereinafter the "Council") on the terms of appointment of the Director-General (EC-VIII/DEC.1, dated 30 January 1998); and

Recalling also that the Director-General was appointed by the Conference at its First Special Session for a term of four years beginning on 25 July 2002, and ending on 24 July 2006 (C-SS-1/DEC.3, dated 25 July 2002);

---

[3] The Conference of the States Parties had adopted decision C-II/DEC.4 at its Second Session on 5 December 1997, having similar provisions to those in C-SS-1/DEC.4.

Hereby:

Decides to establish the following terms of appointment for the Director-General, equivalent to the terms of appointment of other executive heads within the United Nations system who are ungraded officials:

...

Decides further that the terms of appointment of the Director-General as provided for above shall be subject to adjustments by the Executive Council, after consultation with the Director-General, to keep them in line with those of other executive heads within the United Nations system or of members of the staff of the Technical Secretariat, as the case may be.

24.5 OPCW Financial Regulations and Financial Rules

The Conference of the States Parties adopted the OPCW's Financial Regulations at its First Session (C-I/DEC.3, dated 14 May 1997) and amended them (C-I/DEC.3/Rev.1, dated 2 December 2004) at its Eighth, Ninth, Eleventh, Fifteenth, Sixteenth and Seventeenth Sessions (C-8/DEC.4, dated 22 October 2003, C-9/DEC.11, C-9/DEC.12, both dated 2 December 2004, C-11/DEC.6, dated 7 December 2006, C-15/DEC.5, dated 1 December 2010, C-16/DEC.7, dated 30 November 2011, and C-17/DEC.6, dated 26 November 2012).

At its Forty-Sixth Session, the Executive Council approved the Financial Rules of the OPCW in accordance with Financial Regulation 16.2 (EC-46/DEC.6*, dated 5 July 2006) and amended at its Sixty-First Session (EC-61/DEC.7, dated 1 July 2010).

The following is the consolidated text of the OPCW Financial Regulations and Financial Rules as approved at its First Session and amended by the Conference of the States Parties at its Eighth, Ninth, Eleventh Fifteenth, Sixteenth and Seventeenth Sessions and the Executive Council, respectively, and as set forth in document OPCW-S/DGB/22, dated 14 December 2012.[4]

FINANCIAL REGULATIONS AND RULES OF THE
ORGANISATION FOR THE PROHIBITION OF CHEMICAL WEAPONS

ARTICLE 1
APPLICABILITY

Regulation 1.1
These Regulations shall govern the financial administration of the Organisation for the Prohibition of Chemical Weapons, hereinafter "the OPCW".

Rule 1.1.01
Authority and applicability

These Rules are prepared by the Director-General and approved by the Executive Council to implement, as appropriate, the Financial Regulations. They shall govern, together with the Financial Regulations, Directives and any other instructions as may be issued by or on behalf of the Director-General, the financial administration of the OPCW, except as may otherwise be provided by the Conference of the States Parties.

---

[4] The OPCW General Terms and Conditions for the supply of goods and service, which routinely form part of all agreements concluded by the OPCW, are available at http://www.opcw.org.

Rule 1.1.02
Authority of the Principal Financial Officer

The Director-General shall designate a staff member as the Principal Financial Officer of the OPCW. In accordance with Financial Regulation 14.2, the Director-General may delegate to the Principal Financial Officer such authority as he considers necessary for the efficient and effective implementation of the Financial Regulations, Rules and Directives. The Director-General shall duly notify the Executive Council of the designated Principal Financial Officer.

Rule 1.1.03
Personal responsibility/liability

All staff members of the OPCW are responsible to the Director-General for the actions taken by them in the course of their official duties. Any staff member who contravenes the Financial Regulations or Rules or corresponding administrative instructions may be held personally accountable and financially liable for his or her action.

ARTICLE 2
DEFINITIONS

Regulation 2.1
The OPCW's financial period for both budgetary and financial accounting shall be the calendar year.

Regulation 2.2
For the purpose of these Financial Regulations and any Financial Rules and Directives issued hereunder, the definitions set out below shall apply.

Appropriations shall mean the aggregate of the expenditure authorisations approved by the Conference of the States Parties for the regular budget of the OPCW for a financial period against which obligations may be incurred for the purposes specified by the Conference of the States Parties.

Arrears of Contributions shall mean contributions unpaid by the date on which they are due in accordance with Regulation 5.4.

Budget Appropriations Resolution shall mean the resolution of the Conference of the States Parties in which appropriations for a programme and budget are approved.

Budget Chapter shall mean either: that part of the budget relating to administrative and other costs; or that part of the budget relating to verification costs.

Budget Programme shall mean a subsidiary of the budget chapter which represents a group of activities having a common objective in the programme and budget.

Budget Subprogramme shall mean a subsidiary of the budget programme, grouping together activities with common detailed objectives in the programme and budget.

Budgetary Accounting shall mean the recording and reporting of financial information on a modified cash basis, the same basis as that followed for appropriations for the regular budget or for other funds governed by other agreements, in a manner that is consistent with the Financial Regulations and Rules, with Financial Directives, and with any other instructions as may be issued by or on behalf of the Director-General for their administration.

Cash Surplus shall mean the excess of cash receipts over cash disbursements for a given financial period.

Commitment shall mean entering into a contractual agreement involving a liability against the resources of future years, for which expenditure authority has not yet been given by the Conference of the States Parties.

Conference of the States Parties shall mean the body established pursuant to Article VIII (B) of the Convention.

Contributions shall mean those amounts payable by States Parties under the provisions of Articles IV, V and VIII of the Convention in order to finance the cost of the OPCW's activities for a given financial period.[5]

Contingency Margin shall mean that portion of the budget appropriations for which the Director-General shall not authorise expenditures until and to the extent that it is determined that the income received will be adequate to meet the full needs of the appropriations in a given financial period.

Convention shall mean the Convention on the Prohibition of the Development, Production, Stockpiling and Use of Chemical Weapons and on their Destruction.

Disbursement shall mean an amount actually paid.

Executive Council shall mean the body established pursuant to Article VIII (C) of the Convention.

***Ex Gratia* Payment** shall mean a payment for which there is no legal liability but where the underlying circumstances indicate that payment is justifiable.

Expenditure shall mean the sum of disbursements and unliquidated obligations.

Financial Accounting shall mean the recording and reporting of financial information on an accrual basis, in accordance with the International Public Sector Accounting Standards, and all definitions shall be in accordance with those found in the most recent version of the International Federation of Accountants' Handbook of International Public Sector Accounting Pronouncements.

Funds shall mean an independent accounting entity established pursuant to these Regulations for a specified purpose.

Obligation shall mean entering into a contractual agreement or other transaction involving a liability against which authority has been given.

---

[5] Explanatory note: Under this definition, "contributions" means (a) amounts assessed on States Parties under the provisions of Article VIII of the Convention, and (b) payments by States Parties of verification costs based on invoices issued by the Secretariat subsequent to the verification activities undertaken under the provisions of Articles IV and V of the Convention.

Object of Expenditure shall mean a uniform classification identifying proposed or actual expenditure by the types of goods or services, without regard to the purposes for which they are used.

Programme and Budget shall mean that document which sets out the OPCW's activities, objectives, and aims - together with the resource requirements - for a defined financial period.

Regular Budget Fund shall mean that fund established in accordance with Article VIII of the Chemical Weapons Convention to finance the OPCW's verification, administrative and other costs from the financial contributions of States Parties.

Short-Term Investments are investments for a period not exceeding 12 months.

Special Fund shall mean a fund established for a particular project, programme or activity which shall be financed in a manner as recommended by the Executive Council and subsequently approved by the Conference of the States Parties

Trust Fund shall mean a fund for monies administered by the OPCW on behalf of, and for activities specified by, a donor of voluntary contributions.

Transfer shall mean an increase in a budget chapter, a budget programme or a budget subprogramme within a budget programme offset by decreasing by the same total amount another budget chapter, budget programme or budget subprogramme within a budget programme.

Unforeseen and Extraordinary Expenditure shall mean the entering into a contractual agreement involving a liability not covered by existing appropriations, but in relation to which expenditure authority has been given to the Director-General to cover an unusual event.

Unliquidated Obligation shall mean that part of an obligation which has not been disbursed.

Voluntary Contributions shall mean those resources, whether in cash or in kind, provided by donors to fund either the Voluntary Fund for Assistance or activities specified by the donor.

Working Capital Fund shall mean a fund designed to meet short-term liquidity problems.

Rule 2.2.01
Interpretation of the Financial Rules

In case of a doubt as to the interpretation of any of the Financial Rules, the Director-General shall provisionally rule thereon and shall notify the Executive Council of the interpretation applied. The Executive Council may amend the Financial Rule in doubt in order to clarify or revise the Director-General's interpretation.

Rule 2.2.02
Glossary of definitions

Additional definitions relevant to the understanding of these Financial Rules are set out below.

Approving Officer shall mean a staff member of the budget and finance function (but not the Principal Financial Officer or the Treasury Officer) designated by the Director-General as being responsible for examining proposed obligations before these are established in the accounting records to ensure the following: that obligations have been authorised by the appropriate Certifying Officer; that vouchers and other documents passed by Certifying Officers for payment are properly supported by evidence that goods or services have been received in accordance with the contractual agreement establishing the obligation; that the documents comprise duly certified original vouchers; that payment has not previously been made, and that the supporting documents do not have irregularities which might indicate that the payment is not properly due. The Approving Officer can never be a Certifying Officer.

Certifying Officer[6] shall mean a staff member designated by the Director-General in accordance with Financial Regulation 14.2 as being responsible for the delivery of one or more specific programme or subprogramme activities as are required under the Convention, and as set out in the approved programme and budget. The Certifying Officer shall be responsible for examining all obligations proposed by requestors to ensure that appropriate funds are available and have been allotted, and that the proposed expenditure is consistent with the purpose for which the relevant appropriation was intended.

Principal Financial Officer shall mean a staff member designated by the Director-General as being responsible for the oversight of the OPCW's financial resources, including the implementation of the OPCW's Financial Regulations and Rules and Directives and the promulgation of such additional guidance as may be necessary on financial management matters. This staff member shall perform functions in accordance with the Financial Rules and in particular Rules 1.1.02 and 11.1.01.

Treasury Officer shall mean a staff member of the budget and finance function designated by the Principal Financial Officer as being responsible for the proper management and custody of the OPCW's cash assets, including investments. The Treasury Officer can never be the Principal Financial Officer.

Imprest Fund shall mean a fund or account established in a fixed amount and maintained at the level by periodic replenishments (normally monthly) of the sums disbursed.

Officials shall mean the Director-General and all members of the staff of the Technical Secretariat of the OPCW.

ARTICLE 3
PROGRAMME AND BUDGET

Regulation 3.1
The Director-General shall prepare a draft programme and budget (hereinafter "the budget") for each financial period.

Regulation 3.2
The draft budget shall cover income and expenditure for the financial period to which such income and expenditure relate. The budget shall be presented in Euros.

---

[6] Explanatory note: Under this definition, the "Certifying Officer" is also the programme manager.

Rule 3.2.01
Preparation of the draft budget

The draft budget, both for expenditures and income, shall be prepared on a gross basis.

Regulation 3.3

Pursuant to paragraph 7 of Article VIII (A) of the Convention the budget shall comprise two separate chapters, one relating to administrative and other costs, and one relating to verification costs. Each chapter shall be divided into programmes, and, as appropriate, each programme shall be divided into subprogrammes. The budget shall include any information annexes and explanatory statements requested by, or on behalf of, the Conference of the States Parties or the Executive Council. It shall also include such further information as the Director-General may deem necessary and useful. As a minimum, the budget shall contain:

(a) an overview and introduction, describing:
   - the objectives identified for the work to be financed by the budget;
   - the basic assumptions having budgetary implications;
   - the detailed assumptions having budgetary implications; and
   - overall budgetary growth proposed (real and nominal) together with a brief explanatory statement;

(b) a breakdown of each budget chapter by programme, providing for each programme:
   - an overview statement;
   - a statement of responsibilities;
   - a statement of objectives;
   - the proposed activities to be performed, listed in order of priority and divided by sub-programme, where appropriate, with a brief description;
   - the appropriations required, by subprogramme and by main object of expenditure; and
   - comparison between the budgets of the current and previous financial periods;

(c) supporting tables, as appropriate, for the budget as a whole and for each chapter, programme and subprogramme, showing:
   - organisation charts;
   - post requirements;
   - resource requirements;
   - resource requirements by main object of expenditure; and
   - budgetary growth proposed (real and nominal); and

(d) as separately identified and suitably detailed items, programme and budget proposals for verification in accordance with the following provisions of the Annex on Implementation and Verification to the Convention:
   - paragraph 13 of Part VII;
   - paragraph 13 of Part VIII; and
   - paragraph 10 of Part IX.

Rule 3.3.01
Tasks of the Certifying Officer

(a) Certifying Officers shall prepare the respective draft budget proposals, that is, the programme content and resource allocation, for the following financial period at such times and in such detail as the Director-General may prescribe in a Financial Directive and in accordance with the Financial Regulations and Rules. The budget proposals shall be detailed by chapter, programme and subprogramme, and by object of expenditure within each programme and subprogramme.

(b) Detailed guidelines for preparing budget estimates shall be issued to the Division Directors by the Director of the Administration Division, in consultation with the Director-General. The proposals of the Division Directors shall be submitted simultaneously to the Director of the Administration Division and to the Head of the Budget, Planning and Control Branch for consolidation.

Rule 3.3.02
Content and resource allocation

After review of the draft budget proposals, the Director-General shall decide on the final programme content and resource allocation of the draft budget to be submitted through the Executive Council to the Conference of the States Parties for approval.

Regulation 3.4

The Director-General shall submit the draft budget for the ensuing financial period to the Executive Council. The submission of the draft budget to the Executive Council shall take place at least eight weeks prior to the date fixed for the meeting of the Executive Council at which the draft budget is to be considered. The draft budget and the comments and recommendations of the Executive Council shall be transmitted to States Parties at least four weeks prior to the opening of the regular session of the Conference of the States Parties at which the draft budget is to be considered.

Regulation 3.5

The Director-General may, in exceptional cases, submit supplementary budgetary proposals to the Conference of the States Parties through the Executive Council. Such supplementary budgetary proposals shall be prepared in a format consistent with that used for the budget. The applicable time limit for the submission of the document may be waived by the Executive Council with respect to the submission of supplementary budgetary proposals.

Rule 3.5.01
Supplementary budgetary proposals

Certifying Officers shall, where necessary, prepare supplementary budgetary proposals in such detail as the Director-General may prescribe. Such supplementary proposals shall be prepared in a format consistent with that used for the budget.

Regulation 3.6

The Conference of the States Parties shall:
(a) consider and adopt at its regular session the programme and budget of the OPCW, submitted by the Executive Council;
(b) decide on the scale of assessments to be paid by States Parties; and
(c) vote budget appropriations by chapter and in total for the financial period to which they relate.

Regulation 3.7
The draft budget submitted to the Executive Council and to the Conference of the States Parties under Regulation 3.4 shall be accompanied by corresponding preliminary estimates for the following financial period.

Rule 3.7.01
Basis for preparing the preliminary estimates

The preliminary estimates for the following financial period shall be submitted at the same time as the draft budget. These estimates shall include proposed allocations by programme, subprogramme and object of expenditure, to the extent possible.

Regulation 3.8
The draft budget and preliminary estimates submitted to the Executive Council under Regulations 3.4 and 3.7 shall be accompanied by a medium-term plan. Such a plan would give an overview of the aims and programme priorities of the next few years, to be adjusted annually as necessary. The medium-term plan should not prejudge coming budgets. It should also be a concise document.

ARTICLE 4
AUTHORITY TO INCUR EXPENDITURE

Regulation 4.1
The appropriations approved by the Conference of the States Parties under Regulation 3.6 shall constitute an authorisation for the Director-General to incur obligations and make payments for the purposes for which the appropriations were voted and up to the amounts so voted, subject to any transfers under Regulation 4.5 and the provisions of Regulation 4.7.

Rule 4.1.01
Financial plan and issue of allotments

(a) Financial plan: At the end of the year, a detailed financial plan based on the approved appropriations shall be prepared for the following financial year by the Principal Financial Officer in cooperation with all the Certifying Officers, and approved by the Director-General. The financial plan shall be established in such format and for such purposes as the Director-General may prescribe.

(b) Review of financial plan: The estimate in the financial plan shall be revalued every month. Actual expenditures shall be monitored by the Principal Financial Officer against the revalued financial plan on a cumulative basis. The financial plan shall be reviewed whenever necessary, but in any event after the first six months of the financial year, and revised as necessary. All revisions of the financial plan shall be subject to approval by the Director-General.

(c) Allotments: Under the authority of the Director-General, the Principal Financial Officer shall issue allotments to Certifying Officers in accordance with the appropriate budget appropriation resolution and other relevant resolutions or decisions of the Executive Council and the Conference of the States Parties. An allotment constitutes the authority for the Certifying

Officer to request the incurring of obligations up to the amount and for the purposes stated in the allotment advice, and in accordance with applicable directives and procedures.

Rule 4.1.02
Basis of obligations

(a) Obligations for goods and services shall be based on a contractual agreement entered into under the responsibility of the Director-General on behalf of the OPCW. All such obligations shall be supported by appropriate obligating documents. The obligation shall be carried as an unliquidated obligation during the period set forth in Regulation 4.3, unless liquidated prior thereto.

(b) All commitments, obligations and expenditures require at least two authorising signatures, in either conventional or electronic form. All commitments, obligations and expenditures must first be signed (certified) by a duly designated Certifying Officer. Following certification, duly designated Approving Officers (Financial Rule 10.1.04) must then sign to approve the establishment of obligations, the recording of expenditures in the accounts, and the processing of payments. Expenditures recorded against an established, certified obligation do not require additional certification, provided that they do not exceed the amount obligated by more than EUR 2,500. The aggregate amount exceeded on a pre-encumbrance and obligation may not be more than EUR 2,500.

Regulation 4.2

Appropriations shall be available for obligation during the financial period for which they were made, in accordance with the provisions of the budget appropriations resolution.

Regulation 4.3

Appropriations shall remain available for the twelve months following the end of the financial period to which they relate, to the extent that they are required to liquidate any outstanding legal obligation of that financial period.

Regulation 4.4

At the end of the twelve-month period referred to in Regulation 4.3, the remaining balance of any appropriations retained shall lapse. Any unliquidated obligations of the financial period in question shall at that time be cancelled, unless the obligation remains a valid charge, in which case the obligation shall be transferred as an obligation against appropriations for the current financial period.

Rule 4.4.01
Obligations which cannot be liquidated

In those cases where the obligation cannot be liquidated within the time period set forth in Financial Regulation 4.3, the procedure under Financial Regulation 4.4 shall be followed. This procedure requires the examination of each such obligation in accordance with Financial Rule 10.3.06 before it is cancelled or reobligated against appropriations of the current financial period.

Regulation 4.5
Subject to any provisions set out in the budget appropriations resolution, the Director-General may transfer appropriated funds between programmes within a budget chapter. The total of all such transfers shall not exceed 10 percent of the original appropriation for the programme to which the transfer is made. The Director-General shall notify the Executive Council of any such transfer(s). Transfers in excess of the 10 percent limit shall be made only with the prior concurrence of the Executive Council. All transfers between budget programmes shall be reported to the Conference of the States Parties.

Rule 4.5.01
Transfers of funds

(a) In the event that transfers of funds in accordance with Regulations 4.5 to 4.7 become necessary, the Certifying Officer proposing the transfers shall provide the required justification and shall make proposals, through the Principal Financial Officer, to the Director-General.

(b) Requests for transfers of appropriated funds between approved budget programmes and/or between budget subprogrammes in accordance with Financial Regulations 4.5 and 4.6, but within the scope of objectives approved for the year in the annual programme and budget, shall be submitted by the designated Certifying Officer, through the Principal Financial Officer, to the Director-General for decision. These requests shall contain a description of the activity giving rise to the funding-transfer requirement, a justification for its urgency and estimated cost, and alternative sources of funding.

Regulation 4.6
Subject to any provisions set out in the programme budget appropriations resolution, the Director-General may transfer appropriated funds between subprogrammes within a budget programme. The total of all such transfers shall not exceed 15 percent of the original appropriation for the budget subprogramme to which transfers are made. The Director-General shall notify the Executive Council of any such transfers. Transfers in excess of the 15 percent limit shall be made only with the prior concurrence of the Executive Council.

Regulation 4.7
The Director-General shall prudently manage the appropriations voted for a financial period to ensure that expenditures can be met from the funds available for such a period, keeping in view the income received, the availability of cash balances and the application to the approved appropriations of a contingency margin as provided for in the Financial Rules.

Rule 4.7.01
Contingency margin

The Director-General shall determine the percentage for the contingency margin, having regard to the average collection rate for assessed contributions over the last three years. The Director-General may authorise the allotment and obligation of funds up to the level of the approved budget appropriations less this contingency margin. Further authorisations for allotment and obligation shall only be permitted when and to the extent that adequate contributions have been received. The application of a contingency margin shall ensure that expenditure does not exceed the available funds in any given financial period.

Regulation 4.8

The Director-General shall incur unforeseen and extraordinary expenditures only in accordance with the conditions and procedures determined by the Conference of the States Parties.

Regulation 4.9

No draft decision involving financial implications shall be presented to the Conference of the States Parties unless it is accompanied by an estimate of expenditure and a report on the financial, administrative and programme and budget implications, prepared by the Director-General, and the Executive Council's recommendations thereon.

Regulation 4.10

No subsidiary body of the Conference of the States Parties shall take a decision involving a new commitment of funds unless it has before it a report from the Director-General on the financial, administrative and programme and budget implications of the proposal; no expenditure shall be incurred without a decision by the Conference of the States Parties.

Regulation 4.11

With the prior concurrence of the Conference of the States Parties, the Director-General may, if necessary, enter into commitments for future financial periods, provided that such commitments relate to work authorised in the current budget and concern: (a) administrative requirements of a continuing nature; (b) contracts where longer lead times are required for purchases of goods or services; or (c) purchases for which payment is to be made over several years.

    The commitments mentioned above shall be annexed to the budget document(s) submitted to the Conference of the States Parties for approval on their first occurrence. In the following periods, they shall be recorded in a table annexed to the budget document(s) submitted to the Conference of the States Parties.

Rule 4.11.01
Deferred charge account

Commitments entered into under Financial Regulation 4.11 shall be charged to a deferred charge account. The deferred charge shall, in turn, be transferred to the appropriate account when the necessary appropriation or funds become available (see also Rule 4.11.02 with respect to commitments for future years).

Rule 4.11.02
Commitments for future years

Obligations resulting from commitments against resources for future years in accordance with Regulation 4.11 shall initially be charged to a deferred charge account for subsequent transfer to the appropriate allotment for the financial year to which the obligation refers once the relevant appropriation is approved by the Conference of the States Parties.

Regulation 4.12

With respect to the reimbursement of States Parties for expenses incurred by them on authorisation of the OPCW in accordance with paragraph 26 of Part II of the Annex on Implementation and Verification to the Convention, the Director-General shall effect such reimbursements in accordance with these Regulations, and as provided for in the Financial Rules issued under this Regulation.

Rule 4.12.01
Reimbursement of States Parties

In accordance with Part II paragraphs 25 and 26 of the Annex on Implementation and Verification to the Convention, States Parties shall be reimbursed for specific expenses incurred by them in relation to provision of necessary amenities. The following procedures shall apply for reimbursement of States Parties:

(a) In cases where the State Party is providing directly an amenity or service, the Secretariat shall reimburse to the State Party the actual cost of the service or amenity. However, where established United Nations rates exist (*e.g.,* travel, accommodation, meals, and other services), reimbursement shall not exceed the relevant United Nations rate unless, in exceptional cases and after prior authorisation by the Director-General, such services or amenities would be essential for the conduct of the inspection. In cases where the State Party simply arranges for services or amenities, the inspection team shall not accept services or amenities in excess of established United Nations rates without prior authorisation.

(b) Reimbursement to a State Party shall take place on the basis of an itemised list of services provided by the Inspected State Party to the Team Leader. The Team Leader shall sign and date the list for services received and shall retain a copy for the Technical Secretariat.

(c) The invoice for reimbursement of the cost of the services shall be prepared on the basis of the original list of services signed for acceptance by the Team Leader. In cases where facilities or areas of an Inspected State Party are located on the territory of a Host State Party, claims for reimbursement of expenses incurred by the Host State Party shall be submitted and paid through the Inspected State Party, unless otherwise agreed between the Host State Party and the Inspected State Party.

(d) The invoice shall be sufficiently detailed by each type of expenditure and shall be made out in local currency. If the local currency is not convertible, the invoice shall be prepared in Euros.

(e) The invoice together with the original list of services received and signed by the Team Leader shall generally be forwarded by the State Party to the Technical Secretariat for reimbursement within 60 days from the completion date of the inspection.

(f) The invoice, after being checked and certified for correctness, shall be paid by the Technical Secretariat not later than 30 days after receipt from the State Party.

ARTICLE 5
CONTRIBUTIONS AND ADVANCES

Regulation 5.1

The costs of the OPCW's activities shall be paid by States Parties in accordance with the United Nations scale of assessments adjusted to take into account differences in membership between the United Nations and the OPCW, and subject to the provisions of Articles IV and V of the Convention. The contributions from States Parties shall finance the appropriations approved by the Conference of the States Parties. Assessed contributions shall be subject to the adjustments effected in accordance with the provisions of Regulation 5.2. Pending the receipt of such contributions, the appropriations may be financed from the Working Capital Fund.

Regulation 5.2

The assessed contributions of States Parties shall be assessed for each financial period, taking into account adjustments for:

(a) supplementary appropriations for which States Parties have not previously been assessed;

(b) estimated contributions made under the provisions of Articles IV and V of the Convention for the financial period with respect to which the assessment of contributions is being made;

(c) estimated miscellaneous income for the financial period with respect to which the assessment of contributions is being made;

(d) contributions resulting from the assessment of new States Parties under the provisions of Regulation 5.7; and

(e) allocation of the cash surplus in accordance with Regulation 6.3.

Regulation 5.3

After the Conference of the States Parties has adopted the budget, determined the amount of the Working Capital Fund and decided on the scale of assessments for both, the Director-General shall:

(a) transmit the relevant documents to States Parties;

(b) inform States Parties of their commitments in respect of their assessed contributions to the budget and advances to the Working Capital Fund; and

(c) request States Parties to remit their assessed contributions and advances.

Rule 5.3.01
Receipt of contributions and advances

Contributions to the Regular Budget Fund and advances to the Working Capital Fund shall be credited to the debtor account of a particular State Party on the date when the OPCW receives a cheque from the State Party concerned or, in the case of transfers, when the OPCW's bank account receives credits for these funds. Bank charges applied by the paying bank shall be borne by the State Party concerned.

Regulation 5.4

Assessed contributions to the budget and advances to the Working Capital Fund shall be due and payable in full within 30 days of the receipt of the communications referred to in Regulation 5.3 above, or on the first day of the financial period to which they relate, whichever is later.

Contributions subject to the provisions of Articles IV and V of the Convention shall be due and payable in full within 90 days of receipt of the invoice, subject to the Financial Rules under this Regulation.

Rule 5.4.01
Contributions under Articles IV and V of the Convention

(a) Contributions subject to the provisions of Articles IV and V of the Convention shall, where the State Party concerned concurs with the invoice in its entirety, be paid in full to the OPCW by the State Party within 90 days of receipt of the invoice. Where the State Party concerned is in a position to concur initially with only part of the invoice, that part with which it agrees shall likewise be paid in full within 90 days of receipt of the invoice.

(b) Where the State Party concerned challenges either an entire invoice or part of an invoice for technical reasons, or seeks further clarification from the Technical Secretariat, the following procedures will apply with respect to those amounts in the invoice—and only those amounts—that are contested or for which clarification is sought:

(i) A State Party that contests the whole or any part of an Article IV or V invoice issued by the Technical Secretariat shall, within 30 days of receipt of the invoice, inform the Technical Secretariat in writing of its specific concerns, indicating in detail the specific amount or amounts which it is questioning, and the reason(s) why.

(ii) The Technical Secretariat shall, within 60 days of the State Party's receipt of the invoice, reply in writing to the State Party's written challenge or query, providing either a detailed clarification or, in the event of agreement concerning a contested amount, a revised invoice containing the revised amount or amounts for those parts of the initial invoice that had been challenged.

(iii) The Technical Secretariat and the State Party concerned shall make every effort to settle any differences with regard to invoices or parts of invoices within 90 days of the State Party's receipt of the initial invoice. Resolution of differences within the 90-day period should be considered the norm; and lack of agreement, an exceptional circumstance.

(iv) The State Party concerned shall, within 120 days of receipt of the initial invoice, pay in full any amount(s) that had been contested and on which agreement had been reached during the 90-day period referred to in Financial Rule 5.4.01(b)(iii).

(v) In the exceptional circumstance that no agreement is reached during the 90-day period following receipt of the invoice, the Director-General shall, in his monthly report to the Executive Council on OPCW income and expenditures, include a report on unresolved differences concerning Article IV and V invoices, listing the amounts involved and explaining the nature and duration of the dispute.

Regulation 5.5
Contributions to the budget and advances to the Working Capital Fund shall be assessed and paid in Euros.

Regulation 5.6
(a) Payments made by a State Party, other than contributions under Articles IV and V of the Convention shall be credited first to the Working Capital Fund and then to the assessed contribution(s) due, in the order in which those contributions were assessed.

(b) Payments made by a State Party pursuant to Articles IV and V of the Convention shall be credited to the specific invoice(s) referenced by the State Party.

Regulation 5.7
New States Parties shall be required to make an assessed contribution to the budget for the financial period in which they become members, and to provide their proportional share of the total advances to the Working Capital Fund at rates to be determined by the Conference of the States Parties. The assessed contribution of a new State Party for the financial period in which it joins the OPCW shall be based on the number of full months remaining in the financial period after the date on which the new State Party has deposited its instrument of ratification of, or accession to, the Convention. A new State Party's assessed contribution to the budget and its advances to

the Working Capital Fund shall be due and payable within 30 days of receiving notice from the Director-General of the assessments made by the Conference of the States Parties.

Regulation 5.8

The Director-General shall submit to each regular session of the Conference of the States Parties, through the Executive Council, a report on the collection of contributions to the budget and advances to the Working Capital Fund, drawing attention to the provisions of Article VIII, paragraph 8 of the Convention as appropriate.

Regulation 5.9

A State Party which withdraws from the Convention on the Prohibition of the Development, Production, Stockpiling and Use of Chemical Weapons and on Their Destruction, under Article XVI of the Convention, and thus ceases to be a member of the OPCW, shall not be entitled to reimbursement of contributions.

ARTICLE 6
FUNDS

Regulation 6.1

A Regular Budget Fund shall be established for the purpose of accounting for the OPCW's income and expenditure. All contributions received from States Parties under Regulation 5.1, irrespective of whether such contributions are for the current financial period, a future financial period, or are arrears from a previous financial period, shall be credited to the Regular Budget Fund. Miscellaneous income and transfers from the Working Capital Fund shall also be credited to the Regular Budget Fund. All of the OPCW's expenditures for appropriations authorised under Regulation 4.1 shall be made from the Regular Budget Fund. Reimbursements to the Working Capital Fund under Regulation 6.6 shall also be made from the Regular Budget Fund.

Regulation 6.2

At the end of each financial period the provisional cash balance for the financial period shall be determined by establishing the balance between the following credits and charges to the Regular Budget Fund:
(a) credits:
     – contributions actually received for the financial period from States Parties; and
     – miscellaneous income received for the financial period;
(b) charges:
     – all disbursements against the appropriation for that financial period;
     – provisions for unliquidated obligations to be charged against the appropriations for that financial period; and
     – transfers to special funds as authorised by the Conference of the States Parties.
The provisional cash balance shall be retained in the Regular Budget Fund for the next twelve months.

Regulation 6.3

Cash surplus:

(a) at the end of the twelve-month period referred to in Regulation 6.2 the cash surplus for the financial period shall be determined by crediting to the provisional cash balance:
  - any arrears of prior years' contributions received during that period;
  - any savings from the provisions made for unliquidated obligations pursuant to Regulation 6.2(b); and
  - any receipts of miscellaneous income relating to prior years.

(b) after the final audit by the External Auditor of the accounts for the twelve-month period referred to in Regulation 6.2 has been completed, the cash surplus shall be allocated among States Parties in accordance with the scale of assessments for the financial period to which the surplus relates; and

(c) the individual allocations to those States Parties which have paid their assessed contributions in full for the financial period to which the surplus relates shall be applied to liquidate, in the following manner:
  - any outstanding advances to the Working Capital Fund;
  - any arrears of assessed contributions;
  - any arrears of contributions subject to the provisions of Articles IV and V of the Convention, provided the amounts concerned are not contested; and
  - assessed contributions for the current and following financial period.

Regulation 6.4

A Working Capital Fund shall be established in an amount and for the purposes to be determined from time to time by the Conference of the States Parties. It should not exceed two-twelfths of the budget provision for that financial period, subject to the provisions of Regulation 6.5. The Working Capital Fund shall be funded by advances from States Parties made in accordance with the scale of assessments as determined by the Conference of the States Parties for the apportionment of the OPCW's approved budget. Advances shall be carried to the credit of the States Parties which make them.

Regulation 6.5

On joining the OPCW, every new State Party shall make an advance to the Working Capital Fund in accordance with the scale of assessments applicable to the budget of the year of its ratification or accession. The level of the Working Capital Fund shall be increased by the amounts that new States Parties are required to pay until the Conference of the States Parties establishes a new level for the fund.

Regulation 6.6

All transfers of funds made from the Working Capital Fund to finance budgetary appropriations shall be reimbursed as soon as feasible, but in any case within the financial period which follows the period in which they are made.

Regulation 6.7

Income derived from Working Capital Fund investments shall be credited to miscellaneous income.

Regulation 6.8

To account for voluntary contributions, trust funds may be established by the Conference of the States Parties for clearly defined activities of the OPCW. Such funds may also be established by the Director-General, on which he shall report through the Executive Council to the Conference of the States Parties. Trust funds shall be administered in accordance with the applicable Financial Regulations, unless otherwise provided for by the Conference of the States Parties.

Regulation 6.9

Special funds may be established by the Conference of the States Parties for clearly defined activities which are consistent with the object and purpose of the OPCW as defined in the Convention. Any special funds which are established shall be financed in a manner determined by the Conference of the States Parties. Special funds shall be administered in accordance with the applicable Financial Regulations, unless otherwise provided for by the Conference of the States Parties.

Regulation 6.10

All receipts from voluntary contributions to the Voluntary Fund for Assistance established in accordance with Article X(7)(a) of the Convention shall be credited to that Fund. Unless otherwise provided by the Conference of the States Parties, this Fund shall be administered in accordance with the applicable Financial Regulations, and as provided for in the Financial Rules issued under this Regulation.

Rule 6.10.01
Objective of the Voluntary Fund for Assistance

The objective of the Voluntary Fund for Assistance shall be to coordinate and deliver assistance, in terms of Article X of the Convention, to a State Party when requested. The Technical Secretariat shall ensure that assistance can be provided in an appropriate manner.

Rule 6.10.02
Application of the Voluntary Fund for Assistance

To fulfil the objective set out in Financial Rule 6.10.01, the Voluntary Fund for Assistance shall be applied as follows:
(a) to contribute to the creation, maintenance and periodic replenishment of the stockpile for emergency assistance to be maintained by the OPCW; and
(b) to ensure that the OPCW has continued availability of means to provide assistance under Article X of the Convention.

Rule 6.10.03
Contributions to the Voluntary Fund for Assistance

The Voluntary Fund for Assistance shall be credited with voluntary contributions from States Parties, which shall be made in convertible currencies to the OPCW. The Director-General may accept contributions for credit to the Voluntary Fund for Assistance from other sources, inter alia non-governmental organisations, institutions, private parties or individuals. The Director-General is authorised to accept contributions to the Voluntary Fund for Assistance under the following conditions:

(a) There shall be no limit, upper or lower, on the amount(s) contributed to the Voluntary Fund for Assistance.

(b) No donor may place any restrictions on the use to which the OPCW may apply contributions to the Voluntary Fund for Assistance, except where the Conference of the States Parties or, acting on its behalf, the Executive Council has determined that the Director-General may accept such contributions.

Rule 6.10.04
Reporting to the Executive Council

The Director-General shall administer the Voluntary Fund for Assistance under the supervision of the Executive Council. At least once a year, the Director-General shall report to the Executive Council, for its review, on the status of the Voluntary Fund for Assistance. Such a review will cover the uses to which contributions have been applied and the adequacy of resources available.

Rule 6.10.05
Replenishment of the Voluntary Fund for Assistance

Acting under the direction of the Executive Council, the Director-General shall take appropriate measures to encourage contributions to the Voluntary Fund for Assistance, including, from time to time, its replenishment.

ARTICLE 7
OTHER INCOME

Regulation 7.1

All other income shall be classified as miscellaneous income and credited to the Regular Budget Fund, except:

(a) contributions to the budget under Regulation 5.1;

(b) advances to the Working Capital Fund under Regulation 6.4;

(c) direct refunds of expenditures made during the financial period;

(d) advances, deposits or voluntary contributions to trust funds or special funds established by the Conference of the States Parties under Regulation 6.8; and

(e) contributions to the Voluntary Fund for Assistance.

Rule 7.1.01
Miscellaneous income

Miscellaneous income shall include the assessed contributions required of new States Parties under Regulation 5.7. Where such membership comes after the adoption of the scale of assessments for the following year, the new State Party's assessment for that year shall also be credited to miscellaneous income.

Rule 7.1.02
Proceeds from loans

Proceeds from the reimbursable loans of staff members or from other services rendered shall be credited as miscellaneous income.

Rule 7.1.03
Refunds of expenditure

Refunds of expenditure which had been charged in the same financial period against the budgetary accounts shall be credited against the same accounts, but refunds of expenditure from prior financial periods shall be credited to miscellaneous income.

Rule 7.1.04
Adjustments to special funds and trust funds

Adjustments which arise subsequent to the closing of special or trust funds shall be charged or credited to miscellaneous income of the appropriate account.

Regulation 7.2
Voluntary contributions that are consistent with the policies, aims and activities of the OPCW for the implementation of the Convention may be accepted by the Director-General in accordance with the relevant provisions of these Regulations and the criteria laid down by the Executive Council and confirmed by the Conference of the States Parties.

Rule 7.2.01
Voluntary contributions involving financial liability

Voluntary contributions which directly or indirectly involve a current or future financial liability for the OPCW shall be accepted by the Director-General only with the prior approval of the Conference of the States Parties on the basis of a recommendation from the Executive Council. In submitting such cases for the approval of the Conference of the States Parties, the financial liability shall be indicated separately and suitably detailed.

Regulation 7.3
Monies accepted under Regulation 7.2 for purposes specified by the donor, except contributions to the Voluntary Fund for Assistance, shall be treated as trust funds under Regulation 6.8.

Regulation 7.4
Monies accepted under Regulation 7.2 for which no purpose is specified shall be treated as miscellaneous income and reported as "gifts" in the OPCW's financial statements.

Regulation 7.5
The accounting policy for determining the monetary value of voluntary contributions in kind shall be determined by the Executive Council, in accordance with Financial Regulation 11.1 and Financial Rule 11.1.03.

ARTICLE 8
CUSTODY OF FUNDS

Regulation 8.1

The Director-General shall designate the banks or other financial institutions in which the OPCW's funds shall be kept.

Rule 8.1.01
Bank accounts

The Director-General shall establish such official bank accounts as may be required for the transaction of OPCW business and shall designate signatories to operate these accounts. On behalf of the Director-General, the Principal Financial Officer may, with appropriate notification to the bank, amend the list of authorised signatories.

Regulation 8.2

In designating such banks or other financial institutions, the Director-General shall have regard for the security of the OPCW's cash assets. In particular, the Director-General shall select only banks or other financial institutions that have a high credit rating and financial standing in the financial community.

Rule 8.2.01
Selection of banks or other financial institutions in which OPCW's funds shall be kept

The Principal Financial Officer shall advise the Director-General on the selection of banks or other financial institutions in which the OPCW's funds shall be kept. The Principal Financial Officer shall introduce appropriate procedures to ensure that the status of designated banks or other financial institutions is regularly reviewed.

ARTICLE 9
INVESTMENTS

Regulation 9.1

The Director-General may make short-term investments of monies that are not needed to pay for the OPCW's immediate requirements. In making such investments, the Director-General shall take all necessary steps to ensure that the OPCW has sufficient liquid funds for its day-to-day operations; that undue currency risks are avoided; and that a reasonable rate of return is earned on investments, without jeopardising the security of the OPCW's assets. The Executive Council may request the Director-General to establish an Investment Advisory Group to provide advice on short- and long-term investments.

Rule 9.1.01
Investment of funds

(a) Acting on behalf of the Director-General, the Principal Financial Officer may make short-term investments of monies not needed to pay for the OPCW's immediate requirements, and may make investments on account of the Regular Budget Fund, trust funds, special funds and other funds, subject always to the provisions of the appropriate regulations, rules, terms or conditions relating to such funds.

(b) The Principal Financial Officer shall ensure, including by establishing appropriate guidelines, that funds are invested in such a way as to place primary emphasis on minimising the risk to principal funds and ensuring the liquidity necessary to meet the Organisation's cash flow requirements. In addition to these criteria, investments shall be selected on the basis of achieving the highest reasonable rate of return and shall accord with the principles of the OPCW. A summary statement of the investment activities of the OPCW shall be provided to the External Auditor at the time of audit.

Rule 9.1.02
Limit on investments with one institution

The Director-General shall ensure that no more than 25% of the OPCW's total cash assets are normally invested in one institution, subject to a maximum of EUR 12 million. The Director-General shall report any exceptions to this Rule to the Executive Council.

Rule 9.1.03
Investments ledger

Investments shall be registered in an investments ledger which shall show relevant details for each investment, including the face value, cost, date and place of deposit, date of maturity, proceeds of sale and income earned.

Rule 9.1.04
Investment Advisory Group

Subject to the concurrence of the Executive Council on the composition of the Investment Advisory Group, membership of the Group shall normally be restricted to experts of recognised standing on investment management.

Regulation 9.2
The Director-General may, after approval by the Executive Council, make long-term investments of monies standing to the credit of trust funds and special funds.

Regulation 9.3
Income derived from investments shall be credited to the fund from which it was derived, unless otherwise provided for by the Conference of the States Parties.

Rule 9.3.01
Income from investments

(a) Income derived from investments of the Regular Budget Fund and of the Working Capital Fund shall be taken into account as miscellaneous income. Income from investments of trust funds and special funds shall include amounts from investments and other income attributable to such funds and shall be credited to the trust funds or special funds concerned.

(b) Any investment losses must be reported at once by the Principal Financial Officer to the Director-General. The Director-General shall prepare a detailed report concerning these losses and any required follow-up action. This report shall be provided immediately to the External Auditor, as well as reported to Member States through existing reporting mechanisms.

(c) Investment losses shall be borne by the fund, trust fund, or reserve or special account from which the principal amounts were obtained.

Regulation 9.4

The Director-General shall report at least annually to the Executive Council on the status of investments made.

ARTICLE 10
INTERNAL CONTROL

Regulation 10.1

The Director-General shall:

(a) establish detailed financial rules and procedures to ensure: effective financial administration; the exercise of economy; the efficient use of resources; and the proper custody of the OPCW's physical assets;

(b) maintain necessary accounting records, in accordance with Financial Regulation 11.1 and Financial Rule 11.1.03, and in sufficient detail to form the basis of the OPCW's financial statements;

(c) maintain separate accounting records, for both budgetary and financial accounting of the General Fund, whereby financial accounts shall be in accordance with Financial Regulation 11.1 and Financial Rule 11.1.03;

(d) maintain separate financial accounting records for all trust funds, special funds, and the Voluntary Fund for Assistance, in accordance with Financial Regulation 11.1 and Financial Rule 11.1.03;

(e) cause all disbursements to be made on the basis of supporting vouchers and other documents that ensure that the services or goods have been received and that payment has not previously been made;

(f) designate a strictly limited number of officers who may receive monies, incur obligations, and make payments on behalf of the OPCW; and

(g) maintain internal financial controls that provide for effective ongoing examinations and/or reviews of financial transactions to ensure:

   (i) the regularity of the receipt, custody, and disposal of the OPCW's funds and other financial resources;

   (ii) that the OPCW's obligations and expenditures are in conformity with the appropriations and other financial provisions approved and adopted by the Conference of the States Parties and, as appropriate, with the purposes and rules relating to trust funds, special funds, and the Voluntary Fund for Assistance; and

   (iii) that the OPCW's resources are used economically.

Rule 10.1.01
Basis for payment of salaries and related entitlements

The basis for payment of salaries and related entitlements to staff members shall be the letters of appointment and the salary scales and other entitlements as set out in the Staff Regulations, Rules and Directives. For payments to individuals other than staff members, such as consultants, lecturers at OPCW meetings, inspector trainees and holders of fellowships, the payment of entitlements shall be based on the terms of the contractual agreement or other equivalent document setting out the emoluments applicable.

Rule 10.1.02
Basis for payment of entitlements related to official travel

For payments related to official travel by staff members and their dependants, entitlements shall be based on the Staff Regulations, Rules and Directives. For travel by other individuals, payments shall be based on the terms of the contractual agreement or other equivalent document setting out the payments applicable.

Rule 10.1.03
Basis for payment for goods and services

Subject to the provisions of Financial Rules 10.1.09 and 10.1.11 on advance and progress payments, payment for goods and services shall be made in accordance with the terms of the relevant contractual agreement.

Rule 10.1.04
Approving Officer

(a) The Director-General shall designate the Approving Officers and their alternates in a Financial Directive. To ensure segregation of duties, the Principal Financial Officer and the Treasury Officer shall not act as an Approving Officer.

(b) Approving authority and responsibility is assigned on a personal basis and cannot be delegated. An Approving Officer cannot exercise certifying functions or bank signatory functions.

(c) Approving Officers must maintain detailed records of the obligations they approve, and must be prepared to submit any supporting documents, explanations and justifications that might be requested by the Director-General.

Rule 10.1.05
Approval of obligations

An Approving Officer shall be responsible for examining proposed obligations to ensure that the appropriate Certifying Officer has authorised the obligation because, as a general principle, no obligation shall be established without prior certification by a Certifying Officer.

Rule 10.1.06
Approval of payments

An Approving Officer shall be responsible for ensuring that vouchers and other documents passed by Certifying Officers for payment are properly supported by evidence that goods or services have been received in accordance with the contractual agreement establishing the obligation; that the documentation comprises duly certified original vouchers; that payment has not previously been made; and that the supporting documents do not have irregularities which might indicate that the payment is not properly due.

Rule 10.1.07
Certification of supporting documents

For payments which are directly related to, and not in excess of, a recorded obligation whose establishment has previously been certified by a Certifying Officer, certification of the invoice shall not be required. For payments of EUR 2,500 and below, where no funds were reserved in advance by the recording of an obligation under the authority of Rule 10.3.02, the supporting documentation indicating that a payment is due must be certified by a Certifying Officer before the payment may be approved.

Rule 10.1.08
Discounts

Every effort shall be made to benefit from discounts offered by a supplier or contractor for timely payment provided that prompt payments do not jeopardise the solvency of any account portfolio by resulting in negative balances.

Rule 10.1.09
Advance payments

(a) When standard commercial practices or the interest of the OPCW so requires, contractual agreements may exceptionally be issued to provide for payment or deposits in advance of the receipt of goods or the performance of services or the submission of shipping documents.

(b) Advance payments may also be made in respect of entitlements of staff members as set forth in the Staff Regulations and Rules, expenditures related to official travel, expenditures related to meetings, including training courses, held by the OPCW, and imprest funds. Such advance payments shall be settled at the earliest opportunity, which shall not be later than one month unless, in exceptional cases, the Director-General approves a longer settlement period.

(c) All advance payments shall be authorised by the Principal Financial Officer or by other officials designated by the Principal Financial Officer and shall be accompanied by appropriate safeguards. In addition, the Principal Financial Officer may authorise such other advances as may be approved by the Director-General.

(d) Whenever an advance payment is agreed to, the reasons for the advance shall be documented in the underlying accounting records, in accordance with Financial Regulation 11.1 and Financial Rule 11.1.03.

Rule 10.1.10
Imprest funds

On behalf of the Director-General, the Principal Financial Officer may establish imprest funds when, in the opinion of the Principal Financial Officer, it would improve the efficiency of the OPCW's operations to do so, for example when the OPCW cannot make timely payment by following standard procedures. Such funds may be used only for the purposes specified, and payment made from them shall not exceed the limits authorised. The levels of the imprest funds should be established in line with operational requirements. The Principal Financial Officer shall establish procedures for the operation of imprest funds. The procedure shall be spelled out in a Financial Directive.

Rule 10.1.11
Receipt of income

Only the Principal Financial Officer, the Treasury Officer, and other officials designated by the Director-General shall be authorised to receive monies and to issue official receipts on behalf of the OPCW if so required by a State Party, donor or other contributor. Each receipt of money shall be recorded in the OPCW's accounting records by means of a receipt voucher as of the day of receipt and not later than the next business day.

Rule 10.1.12
Notification of income receipt

On receipt of advances to the Working Capital Fund, contributions to the Regular Budget Fund or voluntary contributions, an official letter of receipt signed by the Principal Financial Officer or other authorised staff member shall be transmitted promptly to the State Party concerned or to the donor.

Rule 10.1.13
Deposit of monies

The Treasury Officer shall ensure that all monies received are deposited in an official bank account of the OPCW not later than the next business day following the day of receipt.

Rule 10.1.14
Currency conversion

Except in case of investment transactions or for other purposes authorised by the Principal Financial Officer, staff members responsible for the operation of OPCW bank accounts or for holding OPCW cash or negotiable instruments shall not be authorised to exchange one currency for another, except to the extent necessary for the transaction of official business.

Rule 10.1.15
Payments

The Principal Financial Officer, the Treasury Officer and other officials as designated by the Director-General are authorised to make payments which have been approved by an Approving Officer. Payments shall normally be made by written bank instruction, except for cash payments made from imprest funds. A payment shall be recorded on the accounts as of the date when the payment is processed. For the purpose of this Rule, written bank instructions shall include the following: cheques, transfer orders, letters of credit, payment orders, and cables and other electronically transmitted instructions that are duly authenticated with the pertinent confidential code and of which a hard copy is retained.

Rule 10.1.16
Bank signatories

Written bank instructions shall be signed by two staff members designated by the Director-General pursuant to Rule 10.1.15. When satisfied that adequate safeguards are provided, the Director-General may authorise the signature of cheques by one signatory only or may authorise the use of facsimile or stamp signatures. Cables and other electronically transmitted instructions may be despatched only by staff members authorised by the Principal Financial Officer. To provide adequate internal control, Approving Officers shall not be authorised to issue written bank instructions.

Rule 10.1.17
Accounting records

The Principal Financial Officer shall ensure that, for both budgetary and financial accounting, appropriate accounting records are maintained, showing all payments made and receipts received, and that adequate evidence supporting payment or receipt is obtained for all transactions.

Regulation 10.2
The Director-General shall establish rules and procedures for the storage and protection of all materials, supplies, instruments and equipment in the possession of the OPCW.

Rule 10.2.01
Accounting for non-expendable property

The Principal Financial Officer shall ensure that complete and accurate records are maintained for all OPCW non-expendable property with a purchase or acquisition value of EUR 1,000 or more per unit and with a serviceable life of more than one year. Subject to these conditions, non-expendable property includes inspection and laboratory equipment, information systems equipment, furniture, motor vehicles, and other tangible assets as may be purchased by the OPCW. The records shall document the value of equipment and other property purchased, and the projected serviceable life span of each asset. Attractive non-expendable items with a value below EUR 1,000 per unit shall also be subject to similar control. Financial accounting for non-expendable property will be in accordance with Financial Regulation 11.1 and Financial Rule 11.1.03.

Rule 10.2.02
Responsibility for the non-expendable-property records

Responsibility for the non-expendable-property records shall rest with the Principal Financial Officer, who shall designate the staff member(s) responsible for maintaining the property records, the staff member(s) accountable for the property records, and the staff member(s) accountable for the property. Non-expendable property shall be assigned to the receiving programme, and the Division Director concerned shall be responsible and accountable for the property. Where non-expendable property items are transferred from one programme to another programme, the property records shall be adjusted accordingly.

Rule 10.2.03
Verification of non-expendable property

The Principal Financial Officer shall ensure that the existence, ownership and condition of non-expendable property are periodically verified. This physical verification shall take place at such intervals as deemed necessary by the Principal Financial Officer, but at least once each year.

Rule 10.2.04
Inventories

The Principal Financial Officer shall establish appropriate accounting and physical controls to ensure the proper custody and management of inventories.

Rule 10.2.05
Receipt of supplies and equipment

All supplies, equipment or other property received by the OPCW shall be inspected to ensure that their condition is satisfactory and in accordance with the terms of the related contractual agreement. A receiving report shall be issued for all items received and shall be entered into the appropriate property records.

Rule 10.2.06
Supporting documentation

All transactions related to supplies, equipment or other property shall be recorded, and these records shall be supported by appropriate vouchers or evidence of receipt and issue, except for such items where the maintenance of detailed records is deemed by the Principal Financial Officer to be uneconomical or impractical.

Rule 10.2.07
Property Survey Board

The Director-General may establish a Property Survey Board to provide advice on the management of the OPCW's non-expendable property. The composition of the Board and its terms of reference shall be determined by the Director-General and announced in a Financial Directive.

Rule 10.2.08
Sale or disposal of non-expendable property

The Principal Financial Officer may arrange for the sale of non-expendable property declared surplus or unserviceable. Such sales shall normally be by competitive bidding. However, competitive bidding is not necessary when:
(a) the estimated sales value is, in the opinion of the Principal Financial Officer, less than EUR 2,500;
(b) the best interest of the OPCW will be served by sale at fixed unit prices recommended by the Principal Financial Officer and approved by the Director-General;
(c) the exchange of property in partial or full payment for replacement equipment will, in the opinion of the Director-General, be in the interest of the OPCW; and
(d) the destruction of the surplus or of unserviceable items will be more economical or is required by law or by the nature of the property.

Rule 10.2.09
Removal of assets from the non-expendable property records

Property which has been lost, sold or disposed of shall be removed from the records of non-expendable property. Removal of such items from the records shall require the prior authorisation of the Principal Financial Officer.

Rule 10.2.10
Sales on a cash basis

Sales of OPCW property shall be on a basis of cash payments on or before delivery, except as provided for in Rules 10.2.08(c) and 10.2.08(d).

Rule 10.2.11
Accounting for proceeds from sales

The proceeds from the sale of property shall be credited as miscellaneous income to the Regular Budget Fund, trust funds, or special funds, and financial accounting for these sales shall be in accordance with Financial Regulation 11.1 and Financial Rule 11.1.03.

Rule 10.2.12
Intangible Assets

The Principal Financial Officer shall establish appropriate accounting and controls to ensure the proper custody and management of intangible assets.

Regulation 10.3
No obligations shall be incurred until allotments or other appropriate authorisations have been made in writing by the Director-General.

Rule 10.3.01
Responsibility for allotments

The Certifying Officers to whom allotments are issued are responsible to the Director-General for the correct use of such allotments.

Rule 10.3.02
Expenditure items requiring obligation documents

Certifying Officers shall ensure that funds are reserved in the appropriate allotment account through the recording of an obligation before a commitment is entered into from any contract, agreement, or undertaking of any nature and which exceeds EUR 2,500. Obligations for salaries, common staff costs, temporary assistance, overtime, and travel shall require reservation of funds in the appropriate allotment accounts before a commitment is entered into, irrespective of the amount involved.

Rule 10.3.03
Proposals to incur obligations

(a) Certifying Officers shall ensure that proposals to incur obligations against allotments under their responsibility are fully documented. The proposals shall indicate the purpose of the proposed expenditure and the specific allotment to be charged.
(b) Designated Certifying Officers are responsible for managing the utilisation of resources, including posts, in accordance with the purposes for which those resources were approved, the principles of efficiency and effectiveness, and the Financial Regulations and Rules of the OPCW. Certifying Officers must maintain detailed records of all obligations and expenditures against the funding objects for which they have been delegated responsibility. They must be prepared to submit any supporting documents, explanations, and justifications requested by the Director-General.

Rule 10.3.04
Certifying Officers

(a) The Director-General shall designate in a Financial Directive the individual Certifying Officers and their alternates, notwithstanding that the Principal Financial Officer shall have authority to act as Certifying Officer for obligations under all allotments. Certifying Officers shall be responsible for examining the proposed obligations to ensure that funds are available and have been allotted, and that the proposed expenditure is in accordance with the purpose for which the relevant appropriation was intended. The authority granted and responsibility assigned to Certifying Officers is a personal one and can be delegated only to the alternates as designated by the Director-General in the Financial Directive.

(b) One or more officials shall be designated by the Director-General as the Certifying Officer(s) for the funding object(s) pertaining to a Chapter, programme or subprogramme of an approved budget.

(c) Certifying Officers are responsible for ensuring that the proposed utilisation of resources, including posts, is in accordance with the purposes for which those resources were approved and with the Financial Regulations and Rules of the OPCW. Certifying Officers must maintain detailed records of all obligations against the funding objects for which they have been delegated certifying responsibility. They must be prepared to submit any supporting documents, explanations and justifications requested by the Director-General.

Rule 10.3.05
Increase and decrease in obligations

Increases in obligations incurred or proposed shall be subject to the same procedures that apply to the incurring of original obligations. Certifying Officers shall have the responsibility for notifying the Approving Officer when an obligation is increased, decreased (other than by payment) or cancelled, so that the accounting records may be adjusted accordingly.

Rule 10.3.06
Review of outstanding obligations

Certifying Officers shall be responsible for reviewing periodically the outstanding obligations retained against appropriations of the previous financial period in accordance with Regulation 4.3. Obligations reflected in the accounts which are no longer valid shall be cancelled from the accounts forthwith, and the resulting credit surrendered. If the obligation is determined to be valid, it shall be reobligated against the appropriations of the current financial period.

Regulation 10.4

The Director-General may make such *ex gratia* payments as he deems to be necessary in the interest of the OPCW, up to such limits as may be determined by the Executive Council and as may be approved by the Conference of the States Parties. The Director-General shall, in the OPCW's audited financial statements, submit a statement of such payments to the Executive Council and the Conference of the States Parties.

Rule 10.4.01
Ex gratia payments

The Director-General may make *ex gratia* payments up to such limits as determined by the Executive Council from time to time in cases when, although in the opinion of the Legal Adviser there is no legal liability on the OPCW, the moral obligation is such as to make payment desirable in the interest of the OPCW. The personal approval of the Director-General is required for *ex gratia* payments when:
(a) the amount exceeds EUR 5,000; or
(b) the recipient is a staff member of the OPCW receiving a salary equivalent to, or higher than, that of the lowest level and step of the professional category.
In other cases the Director-General may delegate authority for approval of *ex gratia* payments to the Principal Financial Officer.

Regulation 10.5
The Director-General shall, after full investigation, and subject to the recommendations of the Executive Council and approval of the Conference of the States Parties, write off losses of cash, stores, and other assets. Notwithstanding the above, the Director-General shall, after full investigation and acting on his own authority and without prior consideration by the Executive Council and the Conference of the States Parties, authorise the write-off of losses of funds, stores, equipment, and other assets (other than arrears of assessed contributions and the payment of verification costs under Articles IV and V of the Convention) to an amount not exceeding EUR 500 per item and not exceeding a total amount of EUR 10,000 in a given financial period.

For arrears of assessed contributions and the payment of verification costs under Articles IV and V of the Convention, the Director-General shall, after a full investigation and for the purposes of IPSAS-compliant reporting, write down the amounts that are outstanding. This write-down in no way constitutes a legal discharge of the arrears to the OPCW. Only the Conference of the States Parties, on the recommendation of the Executive Council, will have the authority to legally discharge Member States from the arrears of assessed contributions and from verification costs that are outstanding.

A statement of all write-offs and write-downs during each financial period shall be submitted to the External Auditor as part of the financial statements prepared under Regulation 11.1.

Rule 10.5.01
Writing-off of losses of cash, stores and assets

Any loss of cash, stores and other assets must be reported by the Principal Financial Officer to the Director-General and, subsequently, to the External Auditor. No amount due to the OPCW may be waived without the prior written authorisation of the Director-General. The investigation referred to in Regulation 10.5 shall, in each case, fix the responsibility, if any, attaching to any staff member of the OPCW for the loss. Such staff member may be requested by the Director-General to reimburse the loss, either partially or in full.

Rule 10.5.02
Write-down of arrears of assessed contributions and payment of verification costs

The Principal Financial Officer, on a yearly basis, shall recommend to the Director-General the amounts to be provided for or written down with respect to arrears of assessed contributions and payment of verification costs for the purposes of IPSAS-compliant financial reporting. Under no circumstance will this write-down constitute a legal discharge of the arrears or amounts owed to the OPCW.

Regulation 10.6

<u>General principles</u>: Procurement functions include all actions necessary for the acquisition, by purchase, rental or lease, of property, including products and real property, and of services, including works. The following general principles shall be given due consideration when exercising the procurement functions of the OPCW:
(a) best value for money;
(b) fairness, integrity, and transparency;
(c) effective international competition; and
(d) the interests of the OPCW.

Rule 10.6.01
Contractual agreements, authorised officials, and directives

(a) Contractual agreements for the purchase, rental, or sale of goods or services, including professional services in the form of consultancies, but excluding staff contracts, shall be entered into on behalf of the OPCW only by officials duly authorised by the Director-General, as laid down in a Financial Directive. Purchasing, renting, or selling activities shall include, in addition to entering into contractual agreements, the calling for tenders, quotations, or proposals and the negotiation with potential suppliers or purchasers on the basis of detailed specifications.

(b) The Director-General shall establish a Financial Directive outlining the internal procurement procedures to be followed to ensure adherence to these Financial Rules. The Financial Directive shall include procedures for the selection of professional services as described in this Rule.

(c) The Director-General shall establish a Committee on Contracts to render written advice on procurement actions, leading to the award or amendment of procurement contracts, which for the purposes of these Regulations and Rules includes the agreements or other written instruments, such as purchase orders and contracts. The Director-General shall establish the composition and the terms of reference of such a committee, which shall include the types and monetary values of the proposed procurement actions which are subject to review.

Rule 10.6.02
Requests for procurement

Requests for procurement shall be made in writing and shall include full particulars and detailed specifications relating to the request. Such requests shall be authorised by the Certifying Officer concerned or a duly authorised delegated official and submitted to officials authorised pursuant to Rule 10.6.01 subject to availability of funds in accordance with Rule 10.3.04.

Rule 10.6.03
Calls for tenders, quotations, or proposals

(a) Except as provided in Rule 10.6.04, contractual agreements for the purchase or rental of goods or services shall be let after calling for tenders, quotations, or proposals.

(b) Tenders shall be required for procurement requests of over EUR 35,000 and shall be invited by advertising through publication or distribution of formal invitations to tender on as wide an international basis as possible, taking into account the existence of possible sources of procurement.

(c) All calls for tenders, quotations, and proposals issued for inspection equipment will carry the stipulation that procurement of items of equipment will be subject to the commercial availability of all such items to States Parties.

(d) Invitations to tender shall provide all information necessary for a potential supplier to prepare a tender for the goods or services to be provided. Criteria that will be used to determine the award (such as cost, technical acceptability, and time for completion) and the relative importance of such criteria shall be specifically described in the invitation.

(e) Where the nature of the work involved precludes invitations to tender and where proposals are called, a comparative analysis of such proposals shall be kept on record.

(f) Quotations shall be required for procurement requests of EUR 2,500 to EUR 35,000 and shall be invited by the distribution of at least three requests to quote. Supporting documentation shall be kept on record.

(g) A list of authorised suppliers may be kept in accordance with Financial Directives to be issued by the Director-General. Inclusion in this list shall not be construed as a prerequisite for submitting a valid tender where no pre-qualification criteria have been established. Such a list shall periodically be made available to States Parties.

(h) For more complex projects, including orders for custom-designed technology, pre-qualification criteria shall be established to ensure that only those suppliers assessed as capable of performing the work incur the cost of submitting a tender. Such pre-qualification criteria shall be made public well in advance of any project.

(i) The Director-General shall, in accordance with the Financial Regulations and Rules, seek to provide a full and fair competitive opportunity to all potential suppliers, whilst also ensuring a transparent and competitive procurement procedure.

Rule 10.6.04
Exceptions to calling for tenders, quotations, or proposals

Contractual agreements may be awarded without calling for tenders, quotations, or proposals, provided that such agreements are in compliance with Rule 10.6.03(c) and when:

(a) the proposed contractual agreement involves commitments of under EUR 2,500;

(b) the proposed contractual agreement involves a sole available supplier of a particular good or service;

(c) the prices or rates are fixed pursuant to national legislation or by regulatory bodies;

(d) the goods or services are available only from a particular supplier for reasons of standardisation and because of the need for compatibility with existing goods or services; or

(e) in extreme cases, the exigencies of the OPCW do not permit the delay attendant upon calling for tenders, quotations or proposals.

(f) the goods or services are on the list of authorised suppliers or are standardised equipment for inspection that is subject to familiarisation by the States Parties.

Rule 10.6.05
Opening of tenders

A tender-opening procedure shall be established by the Director-General in a Financial Directive. The Directive shall also define the composition and terms of reference of the tender-opening panel.

Rule 10.6.06
Award of contractual agreements

(a) Following receipt and opening of tenders, quotations, or proposals, they shall be evaluated both technically and commercially. In the case of a pass-or-fail evaluation, the lowest technically acceptable tender, quotation, or proposal shall be considered for award. In the case of a qualifying evaluation, the tender, quotation, or proposal providing the best value for money shall be considered for award, taking into account other criteria, such as suppliers' financial soundness, and the capacity of the supplier to deliver the goods, perform the services within the time required, and provide the necessary maintenance. When the lowest technically acceptable tender, quotation, or proposal is not selected for award of contractual agreement, a written record giving reasons for this shall be prepared. A comparative analysis of the technical and commercial evaluation shall also be kept on record.

(b) Suppliers shall not be permitted to alter their tenders or quotations after the deadline for receipt.

(c) When tenders, quotations or proposals relate to a group of items, the contractual agreement may be awarded to the supplier who has submitted the lowest aggregate tender, quotation or proposal.

(d) Contractual agreements shall be awarded to the supplier who has submitted the tender, quotation, or proposal providing the best value for money, provided that the other necessary criteria are met. Where the interests of the OPCW so require, all offers may be rejected. In that event, the responsible official authorised under Rule 10.6.01 shall determine whether new competitive tenders, quotations, or proposals shall be invited. In the latter event, the reasons for this shall be recorded in writing and shall be available to interested States Parties upon request. Upon request, unsuccessful bidders/offerors shall be provided with the reasons of rejection of their offer.

(e) All contractual agreement awards shall be made available to States Parties on request.

Rule 10.6.07
Purchases to be made in writing

(a) Contractual agreements for goods and services shall be established, as appropriate, for every purchase from a supplier in the aggregate amount of EUR 1,000 or more. Contractual agreements shall be in writing.

(b) Contractual agreements shall specify:
   (i) in the case of supplies or equipment, the exact description of the goods, the quantity required, the price of each article, the conditions of delivery and the terms of payment;
   (ii) in the case of services, the nature of the services, the period covered, the conditions of fulfilment, the cost and the terms of payment.

(c) The Director of Administration may waive the requirements of any part of this Financial Rule in certain cases, such as requests for partial deliveries of supplies for the maintenance of buildings, where one blanket purchase order might be issued covering a variety of items. In the event of such a waiver, a written record shall be established to ensure that:
   (i) the supplier and purchaser are in agreement as to what is being purchased;
   (ii) an itemised record of sale and receipt is prepared at the time of delivery; and
   (iii) payment is based on the itemised record of sale and receipt referred to in (ii) above.

Rule 10.6.08
Written findings

Each determination or decision required of an authorised officer by the provisions of these Rules shall be supported by the written findings of such officer. These written findings shall be placed in the appropriate case file maintained by the responsible office, and shall accompany the related obligating documents submitted for approval and recording in the accounts. The information to be kept on record documenting each tender or proposal and its outcome shall be established in a Financial Directive.

Rule 10.6.09
Interested parties

A Financial Directive shall include details on the information to be provided to interested parties upon request after the award of a contractual agreement.

ARTICLE 11
FINCANCIAL REPORTING

Regulation 11.1

The Director-General shall submit annually financial statements prepared in accordance with the International Public Sector Accounting Standards for the financial period to which they relate.

The financial statements and the notes to the financial statements, including significant accounting policies, shall include all funds, where such funds include, amongst other things, the Regular Budget Fund, the Working Capital Fund and the Voluntary Fund for Assistance. The account(s) shall provide comparative figures for the financial period prior to that being reported on.

In addition, the Director-General shall submit the following information:

(a) a statement of the Director-General's responsibilities and approval of the financial statements;

(b) a statement for the status of appropriations, including:
   – the original budget appropriations;
   – the appropriations as modified by any transfers of funds;
   – credits, if any, other than appropriations approved by the Conference of the States Parties;
   – the amounts charged against the appropriations and/or other credits; and
   – an unobligated balance of appropriations;

(c) a statement on the investments held at 31 December;

(d) such notes, other statements, and schedules, as are required to provide a fair presentation of the financial statements and the results of the OPCW's operations for the financial period; and

(e) a statement of all losses.

Rule 11.1.01
Responsibility for maintaining the accounts

Acting on the advice of the Principal Financial Officer, the Director-General shall designate the staff members responsible for performing significant financial duties. On behalf of the Director-General, the Principal Financial Officer shall prescribe and maintain the financial records, review for the Director-General's approval all financial systems and the major financial procedures of the OPCW and ensure that these financial statements are properly implemented and carried out.

Rule 11.1.02
Preparation of financial statements

The financial statements for the financial period shall be prepared under the direction of the Principal Financial Officer as at 31 December of the financial period. The financial statements shall, after approval by the Director-General, be submitted to the External Auditor not later than three months following the end of the financial year, together with such statements as may be required.

Rule 11.1.03
Basis of accounting

The financial accounting records of the OPCW shall be maintained and financial statements prepared on an accrual basis, in accordance with the International Public Sector Accounting Standards. The basis of budgetary accounts shall be on a modified cash basis.

Rule 11.1.04
Subsidiary accounts

The Principal Financial Officer may establish subsidiary accounting records, including accountability records for non-expendable property and stocks of consumable supplies, which shall be subject to such control accounts as the Principal Financial Officer may deem necessary in the circumstances.

Rule 11.1.05
Retention and destruction of records

The Principal Financial Officer shall ensure that accounting and other financial and property records and all supporting documents are retained for five years or other period(s) as may be agreed with the External Auditor, after which, on the authority of the Director-General, such records and documents may be destroyed. The retention periods shall be spelled out in a Financial Directive.

Regulation 11.2
The financial statements enumerated in Regulation 11.1 shall constitute the core financial statements as submitted for, and subject to, examination by the External Auditor. The Conference of the States Parties or the Executive Council acting on its behalf may, from time to time, request the Director-General to submit additional financial or other information. Such information should be submitted in an informational annex accompanying, but not part of, the core financial statements.

Regulation 11.3
The OPCW's annual financial statements shall be presented in Euros. The underlying accounting records may, however, be kept in such currency or currencies, as the Director-General deems necessary. Accounting rates of exchange shall be determined by the Director-General according to the rates of exchange promulgated by the United Nations.

Rule 11.3.01
Currency of accounts

The accounts of the OPCW shall be maintained in Euros. Unless otherwise authorised, where cash is held in a currency other than the currency in which the accounts are kept, the amount shall be recorded both in local currency and the equivalent in Euros converted at the rate of exchange established under Rule 11.3.02.

Rule 11.3.02
Exchange of currencies

The Principal Financial Officer shall maintain a record of the operational rates of exchange between the Euro and other currencies as published by the United Nations which shall be used for the recording of all OPCW transactions. In accordance with Regulation 5.5, assessed contributions shall be paid in Euros.

Rule 11.3.03
Conversion of currencies

Where there is a conversion of currencies, the actual amounts obtained shall be taken into account; any difference between that amount and the amount which would have been obtained at the official rate of exchange shall be accounted for in accordance with Financial Rule 11.1.03.

Rule 11.3.04
Loss or gain on exchange on the closing of accounts

For the purposes of budgetary accounting, on the closing of the accounts for the financial period, the balance in the account for "loss or gain on exchange" shall be debited to the appropriate expenditure account, if there is a net loss; in case of a net gain, the gain shall be credited to miscellaneous income. Financial accounting for losses or gains on foreign exchanges on the closing of accounts shall be undertaken in accordance with Financial Rule 11.1.03.

Regulation 11.4
The financial statements shall be submitted by the Director-General to the External Auditor not later than 31 March following the end of the financial period to which they relate.

ARTICLE 12
INTERNAL OVERSIGHT

Regulation 12.1
The Director-General shall establish an internal-oversight mechanism which includes internal audit. This mechanism will assist the Director-General in the management of the OPCW's resources, through internal audit, inspection, evaluation, investigation and monitoring in order to enhance the efficiency, and economy of the operations of the OPCW. The internal-oversight mechanism shall exercise operational independence in the conduct of its duties under the authority of the Director-General. The Head of the internal-oversight mechanism may be removed by the Director-General only for cause and with the prior approval of the Executive Council.

Rule 12.1.01
The internal-oversight mechanism

The internal-oversight mechanism shall be a functional unit within the Technical Secretariat designed to carry out the functions of internal audit, inspection, evaluation and investigation.

Regulation 12.2

The purpose of internal oversight audits shall be to review, evaluate and report on the soundness, adequacy and application of systems, procedures and related internal controls. The audits shall, on a regular basis, address the following:

(a) compliance - a review of financial transactions to determine whether they are in compliance with decisions of the Conference of the States Parties, these Regulations and any Rules and Directives issued hereunder, and the Staff Regulations, Rules and Directives;

(b) economy and efficiency - an appraisal of the operational efficiency and economy with which the OPCW's financial, physical and human resources are utilised; and

(c) effectiveness - a review of programmes and activities to compare programme delivery with the commitments set out in the programme narratives in the approved budget.

The Office of Internal Oversight shall also carry out oversight audits covering confidentiality and quality assurance. The latter shall be conducted in accordance with current ISO auditing standards.

Rule 12.2.01
Inspections and evaluation

Inspection, evaluation and monitoring are procedures to review the efficiency and effectiveness of the implementation of programmes and mandates of the OPCW, and to allow for corrective action, if needed. Such a mechanism shall give particular attention to the most effective way of accomplishing the aims of the programmes and mandates. The operational efficiency of the OPCW, including its internal system of security and confidentiality, shall be assessed annually, and a report thereon shall be submitted to the Conference of the States Parties through the Executive Council, along with any comments of the Director-General. An assessment of the analytical network, including the OPCW quality-assurance/quality-control programme for on-site analysis, the OPCW laboratory, together with the designated and other laboratories' performances shall likewise be submitted. Evaluation may also cover individual staff performance in instances where such performance has a major impact on the efficiency and effectiveness of a programme. The primary responsibility for monitoring rests with the management of the Technical Secretariat. The role of the Office of Internal Oversight as regards the monitoring function is to assist in improving it, initially through the issuance of policies and guidelines and routinely through regular assessments of the quality of management reports on monitoring activities.

Rule 12.2.02
Investigations

The mechanism may investigate alleged violations of OPCW Financial Regulations, Rules and Directives issued thereunder, and the relevant Staff Regulations, Rules and Directives. It may also conduct enquiries into issues of waste, fraud and mismanagement that come to its attention.

Regulation 12.3

The internal-oversight mechanism shall have:

(a) the operational independence, objectivity, and authority to conduct internal audits, inspections, evaluations, investigations and monitoring;

(b) access to all records and officials of the OPCW relevant to the purposes listed in subparagraph 12.2 above;

(c) the right, if necessary, to request the Director-General to instruct Division Directors to provide such information or assistance as is reasonably required to conduct the work of the OPCW;

(d) procedures in place that provide for: direct confidential access of staff members to the internal-oversight mechanism for the purposes of suggesting improvements for programme delivery or for reporting perceived cases of misconduct; protection against repercussions; due process for all parties concerned; and fairness during any investigation; and

(e) procedures for a prompt, effective follow-through on recommendations in, or derived from, its reports.

Rule 12.3.01
Operational independence

The internal-oversight mechanism shall have the operational independence to develop its own tasks and audit plans under the authority of the Director-General, consistent with the approved programme of work and budget. In addition, the Director-General has the right to request the internal-oversight mechanism to address specific issues and concerns within its mandate.

Rule 12.3.02
Protection of sources

The Director-General shall issue a Financial Directive establishing procedures to protect the identity of, and to prevent reprisals against, any staff member making a complaint or disclosing information to, or cooperating in any audit, investigation or inspection by, the internal-oversight mechanism. The Financial Directive shall also provide for procedures to protect individual rights, the anonymity of staff members, due process for all parties concerned, and fairness during any investigations. It shall provide further that falsely accused staff members are fully cleared and that disciplinary or other proceedings are initiated without undue delay in cases where the Director-General considers it justified.

Rule 12.3.03
Protection from disclosure to third parties

The internal-oversight mechanism shall submit to the Director-General procedures which complement those prepared under Rule 12.3.02. The mechanism shall be responsible for safeguarding suggestions and reports it receives from unauthorised disclosure to third parties. It will also ensure that the identity of the staff members and others who have submitted reports to the mechanism is not disclosed, as provided for in the Financial Directive under Rule 12.3.02.

Rule 12.3.04
Implementation of recommendations

Recommendations contained in the internal-audit, inspection, and investigation reports prepared by the internal-oversight mechanism shall be submitted to the Director-General for appropriate action. An initial written response to all recommendations is due from the appropriate responsible official to the Director-General one month after formal receipt of the report and its accompanying recommendations. This response shall include information on the timing of implementation of the recommendations. In the event that the responsible official believes that any recommendation should not be implemented or should be modified, the reasons for this shall be provided in detail. When the Director-General has taken a final decision on the recommendation of the internal-oversight mechanism, the Director-General shall ensure that the relevant Division Director acts in an appropriate manner on this recommendation. Decisions shall be implemented without delay, and compliance shall be evaluated by the internal-oversight mechanism, in accordance with Rule 12.3.05.

Rule 12.3.05
Compliance implementation

The internal-oversight mechanism shall establish procedures to track compliance and the implementation of recommendations originating from it and with relevant decisions by the Director-General. The mechanism shall also establish either a systematic review of responses to determine whether implementation is satisfactory, or, in the event that compliance is unsatisfactory and non-compliance is not sufficiently justified, a follow-through procedure, including a direct referral of the issue to the Director-General for resolution.

Regulation 12.4
Reports on each separate audit, inspection, evaluation, investigation, and monitoring activity shall be submitted to the Director-General. For each report, the relevant Division Director shall be afforded adequate opportunity to consider and comment upon the observations and draft recommendations. Copies of all reports and accompanying comments by the Director-General shall be provided to the External Auditor.

Rule 12.4.01
Reports

The internal-oversight mechanism shall provide a copy of the draft report to the Technical Secretariat element most directly concerned in the audit, inspection, evaluation, or investigation. Following discussions and review with the Division Director, the report shall then be put into final form and be forwarded to the Director-General. Copies of all reports and accompanying comments by the Director-General shall be provided to the External Auditor. If requested, copies shall also be provided to the Advisory Body on Administrative and Financial Matters (in accordance with subparagraph (f) of Regulation 15.1).

Regulation 12.5
For each calendar year the Head of internal oversight shall prepare a summary report on the internal oversight activities for that year including the status of implementation. This report shall be transmitted through the Executive Council to the Conference of the States Parties by the Director-General together with such comments as the Director-General and the Executive Council may deem appropriate.

Rule 12.5.01
Summary report of the internal-oversight mechanism

The summary report shall be an annual analytical and summary report on the internal-oversight activities of the internal-oversight mechanism of that year, including the status of implementation. The report may contain the following:

(a) a description of the scope of the mechanism's activities;

(b) a description of significant problems, abuses and deficiencies relating to the administration of a programme or operation disclosed during the period;

(c) a description of all final recommendations for corrective action made by the internal-oversight mechanism during the reporting period relative to the significant problems, or deficiencies identified;

(d) a description of all recommendations not approved by the Director-General and his/her reasons for not doing so;

(e) identification of each significant recommendation in previous reports on which corrective action has not been completed;

(f) a description and explanation of reasons for any significant revised management decision made during the reporting period;

(g) information about any "significant management decision" not in accordance with policies, regulations or rules or not cost-efficient oriented;

(h) a summary of any instance when information or assistance requested by the mechanism was refused; and

(i) the value and cost savings or recovered amounts resulting from recommendations and corrective action.

Rule 12.5.02
Additional reports

Where the Head of internal oversight deems a matter to be of particular significance or urgency requiring the prompt attention of Member States, or where the Head of internal oversight wishes to bring any additional reports on significant internal-oversight or investigative findings to the attention of Member States, such reports shall be transmitted to the Executive Council or the Conference of the States Parties in accordance with Regulation 12.5.

Regulation 12.6
Internal oversight activities shall be conducted in accordance with best professional practice and, in the case of internal audits, in accordance with the auditing standards promulgated by the Institute of Internal Auditors.

ARTICLE 13
EXTERNAL AUDIT

Regulation 13.1
An External Auditor, who shall be the Auditor-General (or an officer holding an equivalent title) of a State Party, shall be appointed in the manner and for the period determined by the Conference of the States Parties and for a single period of not less than two years, but not exceeding six years.

Regulation 13.2

If the External Auditor ceases to hold office as Auditor-General in his own country, his appointment as External Auditor of the OPCW shall terminate forthwith and he shall be succeeded as External Auditor by the person who succeeds him as Auditor-General in his home country. The External Auditor may not otherwise be removed during the tenure of his appointment, except by the Conference of the States Parties.

Regulation 13.3

The External Auditor shall conduct annual audits of the OPCW's financial statements in accordance with the auditing standards promulgated by the International Organisation of Supreme Audit Institutions (INTOSAI) and other generally accepted international auditing standards. Such annual audits shall include "management" or "value for money" examinations, the results of which shall be included in the External Auditor's annual report. Subject to any special directions issued by the Executive Council or the Conference of the States Parties, the audit shall be conducted in conformity with the additional terms of reference set out in the Annex to these Regulations, which forms an integral part of these Regulations.

Regulation 13.4

The External Auditor may make observations with respect to the regularity and efficiency of the OPCW's financial procedures, the accounting system, the internal financial controls and, in general, the administration and management of the OPCW.

Regulation 13.5

The External Auditor shall be completely independent and shall be solely responsible for the conduct of audits.

Regulation 13.6

The Conference of the States Parties may request the External Auditor to perform special examinations and to issue separate reports on the results thereof. Acting under the authority of the Conference, the Executive Council may do likewise.

Regulation 13.7

The Director-General shall provide the External Auditor with the facilities he may require to perform audits.

Regulation 13.8

For the purpose of making local or special examinations or of reducing the costs of audits, the External Auditor may engage the services of any national Auditor-General (or officer holding an equivalent post), commercial public auditors of known repute or any other person or firm who, in the opinion of the External Auditor, is technically qualified to conduct audits.

Regulation 13.9

The External Auditor shall issue a report and opinion on his audits of the OPCW's financial statements, which shall include such information as he deems necessary in regard to matters referred to in Regulation 13.4 and in the additional terms of reference set forth in the Annex to these Regulations.

Regulation 13.10

The External Auditor shall transmit his report and opinion and the audited financial statements, in accordance with any directions given by the Conference of the States Parties, to the Executive Council. The Executive Council shall examine the audited financial statements and the External Auditor's report and opinion, and shall forward them to the Conference of the States Parties with such comments as it deems appropriate. The External Auditor's report and opinion and the audited financial statements shall be submitted to the Executive Council preferably not later than 31 May following the end of the financial period to which they relate.

Rule 13.10.01
Implementation of the recommendations of the External Auditor

The Director-General shall report semi-annually to the Conference of the States Parties, through the Executive Council, on the implementation of the recommendations of the External Auditor as contained in the External Auditor's Report on the financial statements of the OPCW and as endorsed by the Conference of the States Parties.

Regulation 13.11

The External Auditor or his representative shall be present when the External Auditor's report and opinion is first considered by the Executive Council. In addition, the External Auditor or his representative may present his report and opinion to the Conference of the States Parties if he considers this necessary, or may be present during subsequent consideration of the External Auditor's report and opinion by the Executive Council or the Conference of the States Parties, if so requested by the Council or by the Conference of the States Parties.

ARTICLE 14
DELEGATION OF AUTHORITY

Regulation 14.1

The Director-General shall establish a transparent and effective system of accountability and responsibility.

Regulation 14.2

The Director-General may delegate to other staff members of the OPCW such authority as he considers necessary for the efficient and effective implementation of these Regulations and any Rules and Directives issued hereunder. Such delegations shall be communicated and documented in Financial Directives issued under the Financial Rules.

Rule 14.2.01
Delegation of authority

The Director-General may delegate his authority to implement the Financial Regulations, Rules and Directives, subject to any limitations set forth elsewhere in these Rules. Such delegations of authority shall be made in writing. Staff members to whom the Director-General has delegated authority for the implementation of the Financial Regulations, Rules and Directives are responsible for the correct and proper exercise of such authority. Any staff member who takes any action contrary to the Financial Regulations or Rules and Directives issued in connection therewith may be subject to disciplinary proceedings in accordance with the Staff Regulations and Rules. Delegations of authority to other staff members does not relieve the Director-General from his overall responsibility.

ARTICLE 15
ADVISORY BODY ON ADMINISTRATIVE AND FINANCIAL MATTERS

Regulation 15.1
The Executive Council may establish a body to advise it on administrative and financial matters. This body shall consist of experts of recognised standing from States Parties and shall:
(a) examine and report on the draft programme and budget submitted by the Director-General under Regulation 3.4;
(b) examine and report on the preliminary estimates submitted by the Director-General under Regulation 3.7;
(c) examine and report on any supplementary budgetary proposals submitted by the Director-General under Regulation 3.5;
(d) when feasible, consider and comment on any budgetary transfers submitted by the Director-General under Regulations 4.5 and 4.6;
(e) if appropriate examine and comment on the status of the OPCW's investments, submitted by the Director-General under Regulation 9.4;
(f) where appropriate, examine and comment on the internal-oversight/audit reports;
(g) examine and report on the OPCW's audited financial statements, including the External Auditor's report and opinion thereon;
(h) examine and report on the financial regulations, rules and amendments thereto, as submitted by the Director-General; and
(i) advise and comment on any other administrative and financial matters when appropriate.

ARTICLE 16
GENERAL PROVISIONS

Regulation 16.1
These Regulations shall be effective as of the date of their approval by the Conference of the States Parties and may be amended only by the Conference. Any proposed amendments to these Regulations, whether initiated by a State Party or the Director-General, shall be submitted by the Director-General, through the Executive Council, to the Conference of the States Parties.

Regulation 16.2

The Director-General shall prepare Financial Rules to implement and enforce these Regulations. The Financial Rules, and any subsequent amendments thereto, shall be submitted to the Executive Council for approval.

Rule 16.2.01
Effective date of the Financial
Rules

These Rules shall be effective as of the date of their approval by the Executive Council.

Regulation 16.3

The Director-General shall issue such Financial Directives as he considers necessary to assist in the interpretation and application of the Financial Regulations and Rules.

ANNEX
ADDITIONAL TERMS OF REFERENCE GOVERNING EXTERNAL AUDIT

1. The External Auditor shall examine and check the OPCW's books of accounts and records, including the books and records of all trust and special funds, as he deems necessary to enable him to report whether:

    (a) the OPCW's financial statements are in accord with its books and records;

    (b) the financial transactions reflected in the OPCW's financial statements complied with these Regulations and any Rules and Directives issued hereunder, as well as with budgetary provisions and other applicable directives;

    (c) the securities and monies on deposit and on hand have been verified by certificates received directly from the OPCW's depositories or by actual count;

    (d) the OPCW's internal controls, including the internal audit, are adequate in the light of the reliance placed thereon; and

    (e) procedures satisfactory to the External Auditor have been applied to the recording of all assets, liabilities, surpluses and deficits.

2. The External Auditor shall be the sole judge of whether to accept, in whole or in part, the Director-General's certifications and representations and may make such detailed examination and verification as he chooses of all financial records, including those relating to supplies and equipment.

3. The External Auditor and his staff shall have free access at all convenient times to all books, records and other documentation which are necessary for the performance of an audit. The External Auditor and his staff shall respect the confidential nature of any classified information provided and shall not make use of it except in direct connection with the performance of audits. The External Auditor may draw to the attention of the Conference of the States Parties any denial of information classified as confidential which was required for an audit. Without prejudice to his duty to report to the Conference of the States Parties, the External Auditor and his staff shall comply with the OPCW Policy on Confidentiality.

4. The External Auditor shall not have the authority to disallow items in the OPCW's accounts. However, the External Auditor shall draw to the Director-General's attention for appropriate action any transaction concerning whose legality or propriety the External Auditor entertains any doubt. Audit objections to transactions shall be immediately communicated to the Director-General.

5. The External Auditor shall express an opinion on the audited financial statements which shall be signed and dated. The form and content of the External Auditor's opinion shall follow the audit in Financial Regulation 13.3.

6. The External Auditor shall report in writing to the Conference of the States Parties on the financial operations of the period. The External Auditor's report should include:

    (a) a description of the nature and scope of his examination and any restrictions on it;

    (b) any matters affecting the completeness or accuracy of the accounts, including, where appropriate:

        (i)   information necessary for the correct interpretation of the accounts;

        (ii) any amounts which ought to have been received but which have not been included in the accounts;

        (iii) any amounts for which a legal or contingent obligation exists and which have not been recorded or reflected in the financial statements;

        (iv) expenditures not properly substantiated; and

        (v)   the extent to which the presentation of statements deviates materially from internationally accepted accounting principles applied on a consistent basis;

    (c) other matters that should be brought to the notice of the Conference of the States Parties including:

        (i)   cases of fraud or suspected fraud;

        (ii) wasteful or improper expenditure of the OPCW's money or other assets (notwithstanding that the accounting for the transaction may be correct);

        (iii) expenditure likely to commit the OPCW to further outlay on a large scale;

        (iv) any defect in the general system or detailed regulations and/or rules governing the control of receipts and disbursements or of supplies and equipment;

        (v)   expenditure not in accordance with the intention of the OPCW after making allowance for duly authorised transfers within the budget;

        (vi) expenditure in excess of appropriations as amended by duly authorised transfers within the budget; and

        (vii) expenditure not in conformity with the authority governing it;

    (d) the accuracy or otherwise of the supplies and equipment records as determined by stock-taking and examination of the records; and

    (e) transactions accounted for in a previous financial period concerning which further information has been obtained or transactions in a later financial period with respect to which the External Auditor believes the OPCW should be informed.

7. The External Auditor may make such observations on the findings resulting from his audit and such comments on the Director-General's financial report as he deems appropriate to the Conference of the States Parties, its subsidiary organs or the Director-General.

8. Whenever the scope of the External Auditor's audit is restricted or he is unable to obtain sufficient evidence, he shall note the matter in his opinion and report, making clear in the report the reasons for his comments, and the effect of any restrictions or lack of evidence on the financial position and the financial transactions recorded.

9. The External Auditor shall not include any criticism in his opinion and report unless he has first afforded the Director-General adequate opportunity to explain the matter in question.

10. The External Auditor is not required to mention any matter referred to in the foregoing provisions which, in his opinion, is neither material to the financial position presented by the annual financial statements nor significant to the financial affairs of the OPCW.

24.6 International Public Sector Accounting Standards (IPSAS)

C-14/DEC.5 adopted by the Conference of the States Parties at its Fourteenth Session on 2 December 2009 and entitled "Adoption of the International Public Sector Accounting Standards"

The Conference of the States Parties,

Recalling that, pursuant to OPCW Financial Regulation 11.1 and OPCW Financial Rule 11.1.03, the annual financial statements of the OPCW shall be prepared in accordance with the United Nations common accounting standards and that the accounting records of the OPCW shall be maintained in accordance with the United Nations System Accounting Standards (UNSAS), as noted by the United Nations General Assembly in document A/48/530, dated 29 October 1993, and subsequently revised;

Noting that, by its resolution A/RES/60/283, adopted on 7 July 2006, the United Nations General Assembly approved the adoption by the United Nations of the International Public Sector Accounting Standards (IPSAS);

Noting also the information provided in two Notes by the Director-General on IPSAS (EC-57/DG.12, dated 19 June 2009 and EC-58/DG.3, dated 2 September 2009), including an outline of the potential impact of IPSAS adoption for the OPCW, the resources required as specified in paragraph 19 of EC-58/DG.3, and the widely acknowledged benefits of the adoption of IPSAS as specified in paragraph 7 of EC-57/DG.12; and

Noting further the recommendations made on this matter by the Executive Council (hereinafter "the Council") at its Fifty-Eighth Session (EC-58/DEC.2, dated 15 October 2009);

Hereby:

1. Approves the adoption of IPSAS by the OPCW, for its financial statements for the reporting period beginning 1 January 2011;
2. Requests the Technical Secretariat (hereinafter "the Secretariat") to provide updates on the status of implementation of IPSAS to the Council at each of its sessions during 2010 and to the Conference of the States Parties (hereinafter "the Conference") at its Fifteenth Session;
3. Requests the Director-General to submit proposed amendments to the Financial Regulations to the Council for consideration and subsequent submission, along with the recommendations of the Council, as appropriate, to the Conference at its Fifteenth Session, in accordance with Financial Regulation 16.1;
4. Requests the Secretariat to submit a report to the Council on amendments to the Financial Rules, which may consequently be required to be approved by the Council in accordance with Financial Regulation 16.2; and
5. Further requests the Director-General and the Secretariat to submit the proposed amendments to the Financial Regulations, as well as the report on the amendments to the Financial Rules, referred to in paragraphs 3 and 4 above, in a time frame that would enable the Council to refer these matters to the Advisory Body on Administrative and Financial Matters for advice and comments.

25. SCIENTIFIC ADVISORY BOARD
(ARTICLE VIII, SUBPARAGRAPHS 21(H) AND 45)

25.1 Terms of Reference of the Scientific Advisory Board

C-II/DEC.10/Rev.1 adopted by the Conference of the States Parties at its Ninth Session on 2 December 2004 and entitled "Scientific Advisory Board", amending C-II/DEC.10/Rev.1 adopted by the Conference at its Second Session on 5 November 1997

The Conference

Referring to Article VIII, paragraphs 21(h) and 45 of the Convention concerning the establishment of a Scientific Advisory Board composed of independent experts appointed in accordance with terms of reference adopted by the Conference,

Recalling that the terms of reference of the Scientific Advisory Board were listed in the Final Report of the Preparatory Commission for the OPCW to the First Session of the Conference as an unresolved issue (paragraph 81 of PC-XVI/37),

Considering the results of the informal consultations undertaken by the facilitator during the first intersessional period in accordance with the procedure for addressing unresolved issues adopted by the Conference (C-I/DEC.70, dated 22 May 1997),

Hereby:

1. Directs the Director-General to establish a Scientific Advisory Board to enable him, in the performance of his functions, to render specialised advice in areas of science and technology relevant to the Convention, to the Conference, the Executive Council or States Parties;
2. Adopts the Terms of Reference of the Scientific Advisory Board annexed hereto[1] and
3. Decides that the budget of the OPCW, starting from 1998, shall contain resources adequate for travel and per diem costs associated with the annual meeting of the Scientific Advisory Board, and that any other meetings of the Scientific Advisory Board shall be held at no cost to the OPCW.

ANNEX

TERMS OF REFERENCE OF THE SCIENTIFIC ADVISORY BOARD

INTRODUCTION

1. As directed by the Conference of the States Parties, and in accordance with Article VIII, paragraphs 21(h) and 45 of the Convention, the Director-General shall establish the Scientific Advisory Board (hereinafter referred to as "the Board") pursuant to these Terms of Reference of the Scientific Advisory Board.

ROLE AND FUNCTIONS

2. The role of the Board shall be to enable the Director-General, in the performance of his functions, to render specialised advice to the Conference, Executive Council or States Parties in areas of science and technology relevant to the Convention. Consistent with the provisions of the Convention, the functions of the Board include the following:

---

[1] The Terms of Reference of the Scientific Advisory Board were amended by the Conference of the States Parties at its Ninth Session (C-9/DEC.13, dated 2 December 2004). These amendments have been incorporated into the text of the Terms of Reference of the Scientific Advisory Board annexed to this revised decision, which consequently supersedes all previous versions [footnote in original].

(a) assess and report to the Director-General developments in scientific and technological fields relevant to the Convention;

(b) as necessary, provide advice on proposed changes to the Annex on Chemicals originated by States Parties in accordance with Article XV of the Convention;

(c) co-ordinate the efforts of the working groups temporarily established in accordance with paragraph 9 below;

(d) as necessary, provide scientific and technological advice relevant to the Convention, including advice on technical matters related to co-operation and assistance, to the Technical Secretariat upon request;

(e) upon the request of the Director-General, assess the scientific and technological merit of a present, or proposed, methodology for use by the Technical Secretariat in verification under the Convention;

(f) when directed by the Conference acting in accordance with paragraph 22 of Article VIII, provide advice and make recommendations taking into account any relevant scientific and technological developments for the purpose of assisting the Conference in its review of the operation of the Convention;

(g) assess and report on emerging technologies and new equipment which could be used on verification activities.

COMPOSITION

3. The Board shall consist of 25 members appointed by the Director-General in consultation with States Parties from a list of nominees put forward by the States Parties. The members of the Board shall serve in their individual capacity as independent experts.

4. The members of the Board shall be appointed from eminent persons active at such institutions as research institutions, universities, chemical industry companies, defence and military organisations, on the basis of their expertise in the particular scientific fields relevant to the implementation of the Convention. The members of the Board shall be selected based on their qualifications and experience, taking into account their publications, scientific, academic or professional activities, distinctions and international experience with due regard to the area of speciality. Preference shall be given to persons who are knowledgeable about the relevant scientific and technological developments, and who are familiar with the implementation of the Convention. Efforts shall be made to maintain a balance between the areas of research, development and applications.

5. Each State Party may present to the Director-General one or more experts available and qualified to serve on the Board. The 25 members shall be appointed by the Director-General through a process of consultations with States Parties. These consultations shall take into account the need for a comprehensive spread of relevant fields of scientific and technological expertise, and result in a fair distribution of appointments from the regions. Only citizens of States Parties are eligible to serve as members of the board.

6. The term of office of members of the Board shall be three years. A Board member may serve for two consecutive terms.

7. The Director-General, in consultation with States Parties, shall appoint persons to replace members who are for any reason prevented from taking part in the work of the Board for the remainder of their term in office. The Director-General shall report the replacement and the reason thereof in his annual report to the Conference.

RULES OF PROCEDURE

8. The Director-General shall provide Rules of Procedure, after notification of the Executive Council, for the organisation and functioning of the Board, which shall include the following:

(a) rules for the convening and conduct of meetings, consistent with paragraphs 13 and 14 below, and for the adoption of its reports, assessments or recommendations;

   (b) rules for the election of the Chair by the Board by annual election from amongst its members ;

   (c) rules regarding the protection of confidential information;

   (d) rules to ensure that a Board member shall disclose to the Director-General any activity which may affect the individual's impartiality or appearance of impartiality;

   (e) rules regarding communication, through the Technical Secretariat, with States Parties;

   (f) procedure for the dismissal of any member of the Board for just cause and for reporting such dismissal to the Conference, as appropriate.

WORKING GROUPS

9.   In consultation with members of the Board, the Director-General may establish temporary working groups of scientific experts to provide recommendations within a specific time-frame on specific issues, in accordance with Article VIII, paragraph 45 of the Convention.

10. Each working group shall be chaired by a member of the Board appointed for that purpose by the Chair with the approval of the Director-General. The Director-General may appoint to the working group such experts from the lists provided by States Parties or as suggested by the Board or its members. Only citizens of States Parties are eligible to serve as members of a working group.

11. In consultation with the Chair and after notification of the Executive Council, the Director-General shall provide Rules of Procedure for the organisation and functioning of the working groups, which shall include the following:

   (a) rules for the convening and conduct of meetings;

   (b) rules regarding the protection of confidential information;

   (c) rules to ensure that a working group member shall disclose to the Director-General any activity which may affect the individual's impartiality or appearance of impartiality;

   (d) rules to ensure that all communication, information-sharing and co-operation with States Parties, other relevant international agencies and the scientific community shall be with the approval of the Director-General.

RELATIONSHIP WITH THE TECHNICAL SECRETARIAT

12. The Director-General shall provide through the Technical Secretariat appropriate support for the preparation, organisation and implementation of the Board's activities and that of the temporary working groups referred to in paragraph 9.

MEETINGS

13. The Board shall meet annually prior to or in conjunction with the session of the Executive Council which immediately precedes the annual session of the Conference, at a time and place in The Hague to be designated by the Director General, in order to provide a report of its activities, including an account of its contributions during the previous year, to the Director-General.

14. On the Director-General's own behalf or at the request of the Executive Council or of the Conference, the Director-General may, in consultation with the Chair of the Board, convene ad hoc meetings of the Board in The Hague.

S/563/2006 containing a Note by the Technical Secretariat dated 13 April 2006 and entitled "Establishment of a trust fund for the Scientific Advisory Board"

1.   The Director-General wishes to inform the States Parties of the Organisation for the Prohibition of Chemical Weapons (OPCW) that he has established a new trust fund, the Trust Fund for the Scientific Advisory Board (hereinafter "the Trust Fund"). The purpose of this Trust

Fund is to support those activities of the Scientific Advisory Board (SAB) for which no funding is allocated in the Programme and Budget, such as the work of the SAB's temporary working groups.

2.   In this context, the Secretariat wishes to recall that, in its decision on the terms of reference of the SAB, the Conference of the States Parties (hereinafter "the Conference") decided that "the budget of the OPCW, starting from 1998, shall contain resources adequate for travel and *per diem* costs associated with the annual meeting of the Scientific Advisory Board, and that any other meetings of the Scientific Advisory Board shall be held at no cost to the OPCW" (operative paragraph 3 of C-II/DEC.10, dated 5 December 1997).

3.   In practice, these restrictions have made it difficult for the SAB to carry out its programme of work effectively, particularly in terms of the following:

(a)   Restrictions in funding have essentially limited the SAB to meeting only once a year, meaning that it is unable systematically to handle all the issues it needs to consider.

(b)   The lack of additional funds has meant that not all the members of the SAB's temporary working groups can attend group meetings and directly contribute to the work they carry out.

(c)   Insufficient funding has also meant that the SAB finds its work hampered as it seeks to implement the recommendation of the First Special Session of the Conference of the States Parties to Review the Operation of the Chemical Weapons Convention that the interaction between the SAB and the delegations continue and be further enhanced, in the context of facilitations in the Executive Council (hereinafter "the Council") (paragraph 7.124(b) of RC-1/5, dated 9 May 2003). This increased interchange may be of particular relevance to any issues the Council decides to pass on to the SAB for review. At present, there is no budgetary allocation for the travel that is required for such interaction to take place, and any such travel expenses must be covered from other budget allocations.

4.   Experience has shown that the SAB needs to meet more than once a year. Many of the matters on which it is asked for advice require careful collective study by its members, and cannot simply be resolved "on the spot" during its regular annual sessions. Holding just one session annually makes it difficult for the SAB to provide timely and well-researched scientific and technical advice.

5.   The same applies to the work of the SAB's temporary working groups. Under the applicable rules, the SAB initially defines the precise terms of reference for each of these groups. Once it has received and reviewed a report from such a working group, the SAB passes its observations and recommendations on it to the Director-General. Only then can the Director-General, in turn, submit his recommendations for action to the States Parties or to the policy-making organs, or to both. Because the SAB must meet before it can pass its recommendations to the Director-General, and, because it now meets just once a year, recommendations from these working groups often reach the policy-making organs only after a considerable length of time. It would be in the OPCW's interest to minimise such delays in order to make the SAB's scientific and technical advice more effective and timely.

6.   It has also become apparent that the effectiveness and quality of the work of the SAB may suffer because certain members of the temporary groups who are not funded by their own institutions or governments are not able to attend group meetings. The sole contributions these individuals can make to the SAB's work are in the form of written communications – a restriction that is not conducive to the discussion that is often required. Additional funding for meetings of the temporary working groups would therefore be of considerable value.

7.   The Trust Fund will enable the Director-General to allocate funding for that part of the SAB's work that is associated with activities for which no provision is currently made in the OPCW's annual Programme and Budget. The Trust Fund will be operated in accordance with the Financial Regulations and Draft Financial Rules of the OPCW. The guidelines and the rules for this fund are annexed hereto.

8. The Trust Fund is ready to receive contributions from interested States Parties in the form of voluntary contributions or, for instance, of the return of any cash surplus to be distributed to the States Parties in accordance with Financial Regulation 6.3. States Parties are invited to consider making such contributions in support of the SAB's work.

9. States Parties that wish to make a voluntary contribution to the Trust Fund are invited to transfer their monies into the account specified in paragraph 1 of the Annex to this Note.

10. As noted in the guidelines, and as required by Financial Regulation 6.8, the Director-General shall administer the Trust Fund and shall report, on an annual basis, on its use through the Council to the Conference. Such a review will cover the uses to which contributions have been applied and the adequacy of resources available. The Trust Fund will be subject to examination by the External Auditor and will otherwise be operated in accordance with the relevant Financial Regulations and Draft Financial Rules.

11. The financial operations of the Trust Fund will also be reflected in the Technical Secretariat's quarterly income-and-expenditure reports to the Council and in the annual financial statements of the OPCW.

ANNEX
OPERATING RULES FOR THE TRUST FUND
FOR THE SCIENTIFIC ADVISORY BOARD

1. The Director-General has established the Trust Fund for the SAB in accordance with the procedure set out in Financial Regulation 6.8. States Parties wishing to make a contribution to this Trust Fund are invited to transfer funds to the following account:
    BENEFICIARY: OPCW Trust Fund Scientific Board
    ACCOUNT NUMBER: 42 67 17 767
    BANK NAME: ABN AMRO Bank, the Netherlands
    IBAN NUMBER: NL46 ABNA 0426 7177 67
    BIC/SWIFT CODE: ABNANL2A

2. The purpose of the Trust Fund is to support those activities of the SAB that are not covered in the annual Programme and Budget, including the work of its temporary working groups.[2]

3. The Trust Fund shall be administered in accordance with the applicable Financial Regulations and Draft Financial Rules of the OPCW.

4. The Trust Fund shall be credited with voluntary contributions, which shall be made in convertible currencies to the OPCW. The Director-General may accept contributions for credit to the Trust Fund from other sources, including non-governmental organisations, institutions, or private donors. The Director-General is authorised to accept contributions to the Trust Fund under the following conditions:
    (a) There shall be no upper or lower limit on the amount or amounts that can be contributed to the Trust Fund.
    (b) No donor may place any restrictions on how the OPCW uses contributions to this fund.

5. Pursuant to the objective set out in paragraph 2 above, monies from the Trust Fund will be used to cover:
    (a) those travel expenses that are incurred by SAB members, as well as by members of its temporary working groups, to attend SAB meetings other than its regular annual session, to the extent that those expenses are not covered by any other institution; and
    (b) any other expenses directly related to such meetings.

---

[2] Note that operative paragraph 3 of C-II/DEC.10, which includes the terms of reference of the SAB, stipulates that "the budget of the OPCW, starting from 1998, shall contain resources adequate for travel and per diem costs associated with the annual meeting of the Scientific Advisory Board, and that any other meetings of the Scientific Advisory Board shall be held at no cost to the OPCW" [footnote in original].

6. The status of the Trust Fund will be included in the quarterly income-and-expenditure statements submitted by the Director-General to the Council.
7. The Trust Fund shall make financial statements for each year in which it operates. These statements are subject to audit by the External Auditor.
8. The Director-General shall administer the Trust Fund and shall report, on an annual basis, on its use through the Council to the Conference, as required under Financial Regulation 6.8. Such a review shall cover the uses to which contributions have been applied and the adequacy of resources available.
9. The Director-General shall take appropriate measures to encourage contributions to the Trust Fund, including those made to replenish it.

25.2 Rules of Procedure of the Scientific Advisory Board

Annex to the Note by the Director-General on Rules of Procedure of the Scientific Advisory Board and Temporary Working Groups of Scientific Experts (document EC-XIII/DG.2 dated 28 October 1998), of which the Executive Council took cognisance by subparagraph 12.6 of the Report of the Thirteenth Session of the Executive Council (document EC-XIII/2 of 11 December 1998)

Pursuant to paragraphs 21(h) and 45 of Article VIII of the Convention and Conference decision C-II/DEC.10, the Director-General established the Scientific Advisory Board on 22 July 1998 (S/62/98).

In accordance with paragraph 8 of the Terms of Reference of the Scientific Advisory Board adopted by the Conference of the States Parties in decision C-II/DEC.10, the Director-General was to provide, after notification of the Executive Council, the rules of procedure for the organisation and the functioning of the Scientific Advisory Board and the temporary working groups of scientific experts.

RULES OF PROCEDURE FOR THE SCIENTIFIC ADVISORY BOARD AND TEMPORARY WORKING GROUPS OF SCIENTIFIC EXPERTS

PREAMBLE

The Scientific Advisory Board has been established by the Director-General of the OPCW to carry out the functions ascribed to it in paragraphs 21(h) and 45 of Article VIII of the Convention on the Prohibition of the Development, Production, Stockpiling and Use of Chemical Weapons and on Their Destruction (hereinafter referred to as "the Convention"). The terms of reference for the Board were adopted by the Conference of the States Parties (C-II/DEC.10, dated 5 December 1997).

In consultation with the members of the Scientific Advisory Board, the Director-General may establish temporary working groups of scientific experts to provide recommendations on specific issues within a specific time frame, in accordance with paragraph 45 of Article VIII of the Convention.

RULE 1. MODE OF OPERATION

The Scientific Advisory Board
1.1 The Scientific Advisory Board shall appoint by consensus a Chair and a Vice-Chair by annual election from among its members.
1.2 The Director-General, in consultation with the Chair of the Scientific Advisory Board, shall notify each member of the Board of a planned meeting, stating the purpose, the venue, the opening date and the expected duration of the meeting, as far in advance as possible, but at

least 30 days before the opening day of the meeting. The period of advance notification may be shorter if an emergency meeting is required. The provisional agenda (see Rule 1.4 below) shall be transmitted together with the notice of the meeting. Such notification shall be given in writing and dispatched by an appropriate means of communication.

1.3 Meetings of the Scientific Advisory Board shall be held at the headquarters of the OPCW in The Hague.

1.4 A provisional agenda for each meeting of the Scientific Advisory Board shall be prepared by the Chair of the Board, in consultation with the Director-General of the OPCW. The Board shall adopt an agenda for each of its meetings on the basis of the provisional agenda submitted by the Chair. The provisional agenda may be revised, as necessary, by deferring, deleting or amending items on the agenda.

1.5 The Director-General may include in the agenda of the Scientific Advisory Board any item related to its terms of reference which he or she wishes to have discussed by the Board.

TEMPORARY WORKING GROUPS

1.6 A temporary working group shall be chaired by a member of the Scientific Advisory Board appointed for that purpose by the Chair of the Board, with the approval of the Director-General.

1.7 The Director-General shall transmit to the Chair of each temporary working group a mandate setting out: (a) the specific issue to be addressed, and (b) the time limit within which the working group must report on the issue.

1.8 The Chair of the temporary working group may convene meetings of the group. For this purpose, the Chair shall notify each member of a planned meeting, stating the purpose, the venue, the opening date and the expected duration of the meeting, at least 15 days before the opening day of the meeting. Such notification shall be given in writing, and dispatched by an appropriate means of communication.

1.9 Meetings of the temporary working groups shall normally be held at the headquarters of the OPCW in The Hague.

RULE 2. OBSERVERS

Unless prior written approval has been obtained from the Director-General, observers will not be permitted to attend meetings of the Scientific Advisory Board, nor of the temporary working groups. Any observers who do participate, shall do so without cost to the OPCW.

RULE 3. SECRETARIAL SUPPORT

The Director-General shall provide, through the Technical Secretariat, administrative and technical support for the preparation, organisation and implementation of activities of the Scientific Advisory Board. The same support shall be provided to the temporary working groups.

RULE 4. LANGUAGE

4.1 The official languages of the Scientific Advisory Board shall be Arabic, Chinese, English, French, Russian and Spanish. The working language shall be English. Interpretation shall be provided by the interpreters of the Technical Secretariat upon request..

4.2 At any meeting of the Scientific Advisory Board or of a temporary working group, a member may make a presentation in a language other than one of the official languages, provided that he or she also provides a written version of the text in English. In such cases, interpretation into the official languages by the linguists of the Technical Secretariat will be based on the English text provided by the member of the Board or temporary working group.

RULE 5. COMMUNICATION

5.1 Any formal communication by the members of the Scientific Advisory Board acting in that capacity, or by members of the temporary working groups acting in that capacity with States Parties shall be made through the Technical Secretariat of the OPCW.

5.2 For any formal communication other than that referred to under the above rule, the prior approval of the Director-General shall be required.

RULE 6. REPORTS

SCIENTIFIC ADVISORY BOARD

6.1 The Scientific Advisory Board shall provide to the Director-General an annual report of its activities, including an account of its contributions during the previous year. The report shall include the reports of the temporary working groups covering the same period. The report of the Scientific Advisory Board shall be adopted by consensus. The conclusions and recommendations of the reports of the Scientific Advisory Board shall be developed through a consensus process. If consensus on the conclusions and recommendations can not be achieved, the report of the Scientific Advisory Board shall reflect any minority view(s), as appropriate.

TEMPORARY WORKING GROUPS

6.2 Within the time limit provided in the Director-General's mandate, in accordance with Rule 1.7 above, each temporary working group will provide a report to the Chair of the Scientific Advisory Board, with a copy to the Director-General, on the results of its research into and analysis of the issue in question. The reports of each temporary working group will be reviewed by the Scientific Advisory Board. Any comments resulting from this review will be forwarded to the Director-General as soon as possible, to allow him or her to take action based on the report of the temporary working group and the comments on that report provided by the Scientific Advisory Board. Any report of a temporary working group shall be attached, without modification, to the annual report of the Scientific Advisory Board.

RULE 7. CONFLICT OF INTEREST

7.1 Each member of the Scientific Advisory Board or of a temporary working group shall immediately disclose to the Director-General any activity in which he or she is involved that could affect his or her impartiality or appearance of impartiality. The Director-General shall then inform all other members of the Scientific Advisory Board of any such disclosure. In such cases, if the Director-General considers it appropriate, the member concerned shall be requested either to refrain from that specific activity, or to cease participation in all activities relating to the Scientific Advisory Board or temporary working group.

7.2 If any member of the Scientific Advisory Board or of a temporary working group is aware of any activity of another member of the Board or working group that could affect his or her impartiality or appearance of impartiality, he or she shall notify such activity to the Director-General.

RULE 8. CODE OF CONDUCT

8.1 The purpose of this Code of Conduct is to enhance confidence in the integrity of the members of the Scientific Advisory Board and of the temporary working groups as independent experts serving in their individual capacity.

8.2 In carrying out their duties, all members of the Scientific Advisory Board and the temporary working groups shall:

(a) perform their official duties and arrange their private affairs in such a manner that public confidence and trust in the integrity, objectivity and impartiality of the members are conserved and enhanced;

(b) act in good faith for the best interest of the scientific advisory process;

(c) disclose annually to the Director-General all sources of funding for attendance at ad hoc meetings of the Scientific Advisory Board or the meetings of the temporary working group(s);

(d) not give preferential treatment to any person or any interest in any official manner related to the Scientific Advisory Board or the temporary working groups.

RULE 9. CONFIDENTIALITY

9.1 Without prejudice to Rule 2 above, the deliberations of the Scientific Advisory Board and the temporary working groups shall take place in closed sessions.

9.2 Members of the Scientific Advisory Board and the temporary working groups shall be bound by the provisions of the Confidentiality Annex to the Convention, and of the OPCW Policy on Confidentiality, and shall, when using confidential documents, apply the OPCW Manual of Confidentiality Procedure, mutatis mutandis.

9.3 The Director-General shall ensure that meetings of the Scientific Advisory Board and temporary working groups in which confidential information is considered receive support only from those staff members of the Technical Secretariat who have been specifically cleared by the Director-General.

9.4 The members of the Scientific Advisory Board and the temporary working groups shall enter into individual secrecy agreements with the Director-General, using the format set out in the attachment hereto.

9.5 Nothing in these rules may be implemented or interpreted in any way that would prejudice the OPCW Policy on Confidentiality.

RULE 10. DISMISSAL OF BOARD MEMBERS

The Director-General may dismiss any member of the Scientific Advisory Board for just cause, such as a breach of confidentiality, or a gross breach of the code of conduct detailed in Rule 8 above. In case of dismissal, the Director-General shall communicate in writing the reasons for the dismissal to the Board members, including the Board member concerned. Thereafter, the Director-General will report any such dismissal to the Conference of the States Parties, as appropriate.

RULE 11. AMENDMENT OF RULES

The Scientific Advisory Board may make recommendations to the Director-General to amend these Rules of Procedure.

ATTACHMENT:
SECRECY AGREEMENT

between

The undersigned .... ("the Signatory")

and

The Director-General of the Organisation for the Prohibition of Chemical Weapons

1. I, the Signatory, confirm that I have read and understood the Confidentiality Annex of the Convention on the Prohibition of the Development, Production, Stockpiling and Use of Chemical Weapons and on their Destruction ("the Convention"), and the OPCW Policy on Confidentiality.

2. As a condition for my appointment to the OPCW Scientific Advisory Board or to a temporary working group, I hereby undertake to comply with the letter and spirit of the OPCW Policy on Confidentiality.

3. In view of my obligation to carry out faithfully and conscientiously the tasks entrusted to me during my term (or terms) as a member of the Scientific Advisory Board or as a member of a temporary working group, I further undertake that for the duration of that term (or terms), I shall:
    -   restrict any use I make of OPCW confidential information, both within the Organisation and outside the Organisation, to the proper execution of my tasks;
    -   respect and apply the procedures established under the OPCW Policy on Confidentiality and under the administrative directives which support that Policy, for the protection, handling, dissemination and release of confidential information;
    -   refrain from disclosing information to which I have had access by virtue of my membership in the Scientific Advisory Board or by virtue of my membership in a temporary working group; and
    -   refrain from any unauthorised use of information to which I have had access as a member of the Scientific Advisory Board or as a member of a temporary working group, including any unauthorised use which seeks to serve the interests of myself or any third party, or which may damage the interests of any party.
4. Without limiting the foregoing, I undertake that at all times following the expiry of my term (or terms) as member of the Scientific Advisory Board or as a member of a temporary working group, I shall refrain from any use, disclosure or dissemination of confidential information to which I have had access in the course of my term (or terms) as member of the Scientific Advisory Board or as a member of a temporary working group, and I shall take no action that may lead to such information being disclosed or exploited to the detriment of the OPCW, a State Party to the Convention, or a person or commercial entity of a State Party.
5. I confirm that I am aware that a breach, as determined by the Conference of the States Parties, of these provisions and undertakings during or after my term (or terms) as member of the Scientific Advisory Board or as a member of a temporary working group may result in penal prosecution or civil action under the jurisdiction of a State Party to the Convention which could result in severe penalties or liability for damages.

SIGNATORY

Signature   Full name   Date

Done in triplicate at The Hague, Kingdom of the Netherlands in (a Convention language)

....

UNDERTAKING AND ACCEPTANCE BY THE DIRECTOR-GENERAL ON BEHALF OF THE OPCW

I confirm that I have accepted this agreement with the Signatory; that I made available to the Signatory the OPCW Policy on Confidentiality and the OPCW Manual of Confidentiality Procedure; that I have briefed the Signatory on the obligations relating to confidentiality incurred in accepting appointment to the Scientific Advisory Board or to a temporary working group; that throughout his/her term (or terms) of membership on the Scientific Advisory Board or on a temporary working group, the OPCW Secretariat will continue actively to promote the Signatory's understanding of all applicable obligations, policy and procedures relating to confidentiality, including any updates and amendments to the Policy on Confidentiality, or to the administrative directives which support that Policy.

Signature   Full name   Date

WITNESS: The execution of this agreement was witnessed by the undersigned

Signature   Full name   Date

CONFIRMATION: On the expiration of my term or consecutive terms as member of the OPCW Scientific Advisory Board or member of a temporary working group, I confirm my understanding that the obligations relating to confidentiality continue to apply without time limitation in the future.

Signature   Full name   Date

26. CONFIDENTIALITY COMMISSION
(CONFIDENTIALITY ANNEX, PARAGRAPH 23)

26.1 Operating Procedures of the Confidentiality Commission

C-III/DEC.10/Rev.2 adopted by the Conference of the States Parties at its Ninth Session on 4 December 2013 entitled "Operating Procedures of the Confidentiality Commission". The rules governing the Confidentiality Commission are contained in Part IX.2 of the OPCW Policy on Confidentiality.

The Conference

Recalling that Rule 3 of the Rules Governing the Commission for the Settlement of Disputes related to Confidentiality, set out in Part IX.2 of the OPCW Policy on Confidentiality, provides for the establishment of rules governing the detailed operating procedures for the Confidentiality Commission which are to be approved by the Conference;

Hereby:

Approves the Operating Procedures of the Confidentiality Commission as annexed hereto[1].

ANNEX
[table of contents omitted]
OPERATING PROCEDURES OF THE CONFIDENTIALITY COMMISSION

I. INTRODUCTION

RULE 1 APPLICATION OF OPERATING PROCEDURES

(a) These Operating Procedures of the Confidentiality Commission are a set of rules governing the proceedings of the Commission for the Settlement of Disputes Related to Confidentiality (hereinafter referred to as the "Confidentiality Commission"), established by the Conference of the States Parties (hereinafter referred to as the "Conference") of the Organisation for the Prohibition of Chemical Weapons (hereinafter referred to as the "OPCW") pursuant to paragraph 23 of the Annex on the Protection of Confidential Information (hereinafter referred to as the "Confidentiality Annex") to the Convention on the Prohibition of the Development, Production, Stockpiling and Use of Chemical Weapons and on Their Destruction (hereinafter referred to as the "Convention").

(b) The parties to disputes relating to confidentiality shall cooperate in good faith with the Confidentiality Commission in accordance with these Operating Procedures.

(c) In assisting the parties in an independent and impartial manner in their attempt to reach an amicable settlement of their dispute pursuant to these Operating Procedures, the Confidentiality Commission shall be guided by principles of objectivity, fairness and justice, giving consideration to, among other things, the rights and obligations of the parties and the circumstances surrounding the dispute.

---

[1] The Operating Procedures of the Confidentiality Commission have been amended by the Conference of the States Parties at its Ninth Session (C-9/DEC.16, dated 2 December 2004) and at its Eighteenth Session (C-18/DEC.5, dated 4 December 2013). These amendments have been incorporated into the text of the Operating Procedures of the Confidentiality Commission annexed to this revised decision, which consequently supersedes the previous version [footnote in original].

II. COMPOSITION

RULE 2 APPOINTMENT OF MEMBERS

(a) After expiration of the terms of appointment of the members of the first Confidentiality Commission in accordance with the Rules governing the Commission for the Settlement of Disputes related to Confidentiality (hereinafter referred to as the "Confidentiality Policy Rules") as set out in Part IX.2 of the OPCW Policy on Confidentiality (document C-I/DEC.13, dated 16 May 1997, hereinafter referred to as the "Confidentiality Policy"), the members of the Confidentiality Commission shall be appointed by the Conference in accordance with the procedure set out below.

(b) In accordance with Confidentiality Policy Rules 1.1 and 1.2, the States Parties belonging to each of the five regions specified in paragraph 23 of Article VIII of the Convention (hereinafter referred to as the "regional groups") shall select four candidates from among the persons nominated by the States Parties in their region, to serve in a personal capacity. The States Parties in each of the regional groups shall do their utmost, through the process of consultation, to reach consensus on their selection. A list of 20 candidates reflecting the selection of the regional groups shall be submitted to the Conference for appointment. The decision on appointment shall be taken by the Conference as a matter of substance, in accordance with paragraph 18 of Article VIII of the Convention.

(c) If the States Parties of a region cannot achieve consensus on the candidates to be submitted to the Conference, the list submitted to the Conference shall include the names of all persons nominated by the States Parties from that region. The Conference shall elect the Confidentiality Commission members from that region by a ballot on all nominees from the region. The four nominees who obtain the most votes shall be the candidates from the region. In the event of a tie, the Conference shall elect the member by a further ballot on the tied nominees.

RULE 3 TERM OF OFFICE

After expiration of the terms of appointment of the members of the first Confidentiality Commission in accordance with the Confidentiality Policy Rules, the members of the Confidentiality Commission shall be appointed by the Conference every two years at its regular annual session. Members shall take up their appointment for a period of two years starting from 1 May in the year immediately following the session of the Conference at which they were appointed. A person who has completed three consecutive terms as a member of the Confidentiality Commission shall not be eligible for immediate re-appointment.

RULE 4 VACANCY

In the event of a vacancy on the Confidentiality Commission prior to the expiration of the term of office of a member, the Chair of the Conference, after consultation with the regional group concerned, shall appoint a person from that regional group who meets the qualifications set forth in Confidentiality Policy Rule 1.3, to fill the vacancy for the remainder of the term of office concerned.

RULE 5 EXTENSION OF APPOINTMENTS FOR CONTINUING PROCEEDINGS

In cases where the term of office of a member of the Confidentiality Commission expires while proceedings in a case under consideration in which he or she is involved are continuing, the member's participation in the Confidentiality Commission's hearing of that case shall be extended until the termination of the proceedings. The outgoing member shall participate only in the Confidentiality Commission's consideration of the case in question.

III. DECISION-MAKING

RULE 6 QUORUM

(a)   Fourteen of the members of the Confidentiality Commission shall constitute a quorum.

(b)   In the event that 14 members are not present during the regular annual meetings of the Confidentiality Commission, 12 of the members of the Confidentiality Commission shall constitute a quorum, provided that all regional groups are represented.

RULE 7 DECISION-MAKING

(a) In respect of any decision or recommendation before the Confidentiality Commission, the Chair of the Confidentiality Commission shall seek consensus.

(b) If consensus cannot be reached on a recommendation or a decision on a matter of substance, the Confidentiality Commission shall resolve the matter by a two-thirds majority of its members present and voting.

(c) The Confidentiality Commission shall take decisions on questions of procedure by a simple majority of its members present and voting.

(d) When the issue arises as to whether the question is one of substance or not, that question shall be treated as a matter of substance unless otherwise decided by the Confidentiality Commission by a two-thirds majority of its members present and voting.

IV. OFFICERS OF THE CONFIDENTIALITY COMMISSION

RULE 8 ELECTION OF CHAIR AND VICE-CHAIRS

The Chair and four Vice-Chairs shall be elected by consensus from among the members of the Confidentiality Commission at each of its regular annual meetings, in accordance with Rule 9. If the Chair is absent or unable to exercise his or her functions as Chair, these shall be exercised by one of the four Vice-Chairs. The order of precedence of the Vice-Chairs shall be by English alphabetical order of regional group, starting with the regional group following that which provided the Chair.

RULE 9 REGIONAL DISTRIBUTION OF OFFICERS

The Chair shall rotate annually among members from the regional groups. The Vice-Chairs shall be elected upon the recommendation of the Confidentiality Commission's regional groups, with the exception of the regional group which provides the Chair. On completion of their terms of office, the Chair and the Vice-Chairs shall not be eligible for re-election to the same posts for the following term of office.

V. CONFLICT OF INTEREST

RULE 10 PROVISION OF INFORMATION TO THE CHAIR

A party to a dispute under consideration by the Confidentiality Commission which is aware of circumstances believed to give rise to justifiable doubts as to the impartiality or independence of a member of the Confidentiality Commission may bring such circumstances to the attention of the Chair. If the conflict of interest involves the Chair, a Vice-Chair shall be entrusted with the Chair's functions as provided for under Rule 11.

RULE 11 DISCLOSURE

Each member of the Confidentiality Commission shall, as soon as he or she is informed of a dispute, disclose to the Chair any circumstances likely to give rise to justifiable doubts as to his or her impartiality or independence in regard to the case. The Chair shall inform all members of the Confidentiality Commission of any such disclosure and, if the Confidentiality Commission considers it appropriate, such a member shall either refrain from specific activities relating to the case or from any participation in the consideration of the case. If the Chair has an apparent conflict of interest, he or she shall entrust to one of the Vice-Chairs the functions which are affected by such conflict.

VI. TYPES OF DISPUTE

RULE 12 DISPUTES CONSIDERED PURSUANT TO PARAGRAPH 23 OF THE CONFIDENTIALITY ANNEX
Consideration of a dispute by the Confidentiality Commission pursuant to paragraph 23 of the Confidentiality Annex shall be initiated either by the Director-General on behalf of the Organisation or by one or more States Parties. A request for the initiation of proceedings shall be addressed to the Chair of the Confidentiality Commission through the Registry as appointed in Rule 21.

RULE 13 DISPUTES CONSIDERED PURSUANT TO PARAGRAPH 4 OF ARTICLE XIV OF THE CONVENTION
Where, pursuant to paragraph 4 of Article XIV of the Convention, the Conference entrusts the Confidentiality Commission with a dispute relating to confidentiality other than a dispute of the type identified in Rules 12 and 14, the Confidentiality Commission's proceedings shall be initiated by the Conference by means of a request addressed to the Chair of the Confidentiality Commission.

RULE 14 DISPUTES CONSIDERED PURSUANT TO PARAGRAPH 2 OF ARTICLE XIV OF THE CONVENTION
Where, pursuant to paragraph 2 of Article XIV of the Convention, the Confidentiality Commission is chosen to consider a dispute over a matter of confidentiality as a means of resolving their dispute, the parties shall initiate such proceedings by a request addressed to the Chair of the Confidentiality Commission through the Registry.

VII. GENERAL RULES FOR PROCEEDINGS OF THE CONFIDENTIALITY COMMISSION

RULE 15 FORM OF REQUEST FOR INITIATION OF PROCEEDINGS
All requests for the initiation of proceedings shall be accompanied by a statement of claim in accordance with Rule 22 below.

RULE 16 MEETINGS OF THE CONFIDENTIALITY COMMISSION
The Confidentiality Commission shall meet at the headquarters of the Organisation, unless the Confidentiality Commission decides otherwise for a specific case. The Confidentiality Commission's meetings and hearings shall be private.

RULE 17 LANGUAGE OF PROCEEDINGS
The proceedings of the Confidentiality Commission shall be conducted in one of the Convention's official languages, which shall be chosen by the Confidentiality Commission on a case by case basis. At the request of any of the parties or a member of the Confidentiality Commission, interpretation of the proceedings into any of the official languages of the Convention shall be provided, and official translations into any of the official languages of the Convention shall be made of the written submissions of the parties, the Confidentiality Commission's report and any other documents issued by the Confidentiality Commission.

RULE 18 DELIBERATIONS
When all parties to the dispute have completed their presentations, including any rebuttals requested by the Confidentiality Commission, the Chair of the Confidentiality Commission shall

declare the hearings closed and the Confidentiality Commission shall deliberate in private.

RULE 19 CONFIDENTIALITY

(a) The deliberations of the Confidentiality Commission shall be confidential, and the documents considered at such meetings shall, when deemed necessary, be assigned the appropriate classification level in accordance with the Confidentiality Policy.

(b) No information submitted by a member of the Confidentiality Commission, a party to the dispute, an interested third party or any other person shall be disclosed by any person present at the deliberations of the Confidentiality Commission. This shall not preclude a party to the dispute from disclosing statements of its own position in a manner which fully takes into account the provisions of the Confidentiality Annex, the Confidentiality Policy, and the OPCW Media and Public Affairs Policy. Parties providing written submissions to the Confidentiality Commission may be asked by it to provide non-confidential summaries of these submissions that may be disclosed to the States Parties.

(c) Members of the Confidentiality Commission shall be bound by the provisions of the Confidentiality Annex and of the Confidentiality Policy and shall, when using confidential documents, apply the OPCW Manual of Confidentiality Procedure, *mutatis mutandis*.

(d) The Director-General shall ensure that meetings of the Confidentiality Commission at which confidential information is considered receive support only from those staff members of the Technical Secretariat who have been specifically cleared by the Director-General and proposed to the parties to the dispute, as far as possible at least ten days before the staff members are cleared, for access to confidential information pertaining to the dispute under consideration in accordance with paragraph 11 of the Confidentiality Annex.

(e) The Chair of the Confidentiality Commission shall ensure that its meetings are attended only by persons whose functions require them to deal with the issues under consideration and that those persons will have access to relevant confidential information only on the basis of a "need-to-know" principle governing access to confidential information.

(f) The members of the Confidentiality Commission shall enter into individual secrecy agreements with the Conference, using the format set out in the annex hereto.

RULE 20 TIME LIMITS

The parties shall comply with the time limits fixed in these Operating Procedures. After initiating proceedings, a party may make a written request for changes to the time limits applicable to those proceedings.

RULE 21 ASSISTANCE TO THE CONFIDENTIALITY COMMISSION AND APPOINTMENT OF A REGISTRY

(a) The Technical Secretariat shall, upon request, render administrative and technical assistance to the Confidentiality Commission.

(b) The Conference shall appoint a Registry.

VIII. RULES FOR PROCEEDINGS

RULE 22 STATEMENT OF CLAIM

(a) In requesting the initiation of proceedings pursuant to Rules 12, 13 and 14, the initiator shall submit a statement of claim which shall be a concise statement of the facts supporting the request and which shall include, *inter alia*, the following particulars:

   (i) the name and address of the representative of the initiator and the name and address of the respondent;

   (ii) a description of the alleged infringement of obligations concerning the protection of confidential information;

   (iii) the circumstances under which the alleged infringement occurred, by which activities under the Convention or by which violation of its provisions the confidential information was obtained;

(iv) an assessment of the nature and amount of actual or potential damage, if any, to the interests of any party(ies) concerned; and

(v) the relief or remedy sought.

(b) Relevant documents or other evidence may be annexed to the statement of claim.

(c) The Registry shall serve the statement of claim on the respondent forthwith.

RULE 23 INITIAL CONSIDERATION OF THE DISPUTE

(a) Upon receiving a statement of claim, the Chair shall immediately forward it to all members of the Confidentiality Commission and shall, in consultation with the Vice-Chairs, make written recommendations to the members on the following matters:

(i) the convening of a meeting of the Confidentiality Commission;

(ii) the appointment of a mediator, if relevant, as one of the means of dispute resolution appropriate to the case. The mediator shall be one or more of the members of the Confidentiality Commission;

(iii) a tentative timetable for the dispute settlement process;

(iv) other modes of dispute settlement.

(b) The recommendation of the Chair shall be accepted and implemented by the Confidentiality Commission unless at least 11 members inform the Chair otherwise within the time limit specified in the recommendation.

(c) A meeting of the Confidentiality Commission shall be convened upon the request of 11 of its members if the Chair does not recommend that it be convened.

(d) If a meeting of the Confidentiality Commission is to be convened, it shall be held no later than 21 days from the date of receipt of the statement of defence.

RULE 24 MODES OF DISPUTE SETTLEMENT

The modes of dispute settlement applied shall be in accordance with relevant provisions of the Convention and in conformity with paragraph 1 of Article 33 of the Charter of the United Nations.

RULE 25 STATEMENT OF DEFENCE

The respondent shall submit a statement of defence within 30 days from the date of service of the statement of claim, which shall reply to the allegations of the statement of claim and may contain such other facts or arguments as the respondent deems pertinent. Relevant documents or other evidence referred to in the reply to the statement of claim may be annexed to the statement of defence.

A. MEDIATION

RULE 26 MEDIATION

(a) As soon as practicable after the proceedings have been initiated, but no later than 21 days after the date of service of the statement of defence, mediation shall immediately be offered to the parties by the Chair. On acceptance of mediation by the parties to the dispute, the mediator appointed pursuant to Rule 23 shall formulate proposals on a mediation process in accordance with the principles set out in Confidentiality Policy Rules 3.2 and 3.3. Such proposals shall be communicated to the parties to the dispute, each of which shall inform the mediator of whether or not it agrees with the proposals.

(b) The mediator shall convene a meeting with the parties no later than fifteen days after their acceptance of the proposals in Rule 26(a).

(c) The mediator shall attempt to gather information concerning the dispute and to identify the issues involved, shall explore the respective interests of the parties underlying the positions that they maintain in respect of the dispute, shall develop options that might satisfy the respective interests of the parties, and shall evaluate options that exist for settling the dispute in the light of the parties' respective interests and each party's alternatives to settlement in accordance with one of the options.

RULE 27 REPORTING TO MEMBERS OF THE CONFIDENTIALITY COMMISSION
(a) The mediator shall periodically inform all members of the Confidentiality Commission on the progress and results of the mediation process.
(b) If mediation proceedings are terminated or if only a partial settlement is achieved, the mediator shall report in detail to the Confidentiality Commission on the discussions that have been held, on the positions taken by the parties, and on any conclusions and recommendations. Any additional documentation pertaining to the matter shall be annexed to the report of the mediator.

RULE 28 SETTLEMENT
(a) If the parties agree to a settlement or partial settlement of a dispute, they shall draw up and sign a written settlement or partial settlement agreement. The mediator may, if requested, assist in drawing up such an agreement.
(b) The settlement or partial settlement agreement shall be submitted to the Confidentiality Commission as soon as practicable, but no later than 20 days after signature by the parties. The Confidentiality Commission shall ascertain whether the parties have agreed to the settlement or partial settlement agreement and, if so satisfied, shall certify it.
(c) All certified settlement agreements shall be listed in the record book maintained by the Registry. The Registry shall also maintain the originals of certified settlement agreements and shall provide copies to the parties to the dispute.

RULE 29 TERMINATION OF MEDIATION PROCEEDINGS
(a) Mediation proceedings shall be terminated:
   (i)   when the dispute has been successfully settled in accordance with Rule 28;
   (ii) when the mediator declares, in writing, and in consultation with, or on written notification by, any of the parties, that further efforts at mediation are no longer justified;
   (iii) when the time period for mediation efforts under the time-table set by the Confidentiality Commission has elapsed and no party or the mediator has requested an extension of the time period.
(b) If mediation proceedings are terminated without a settlement of the dispute or with only a partial settlement achieved, the Confidentiality Commission, if it considers this necessary, shall set the terms for fact-finding pursuant to Rule 30, or shall appoint the conciliation panel with the consent of the parties pursuant to Rule 33. This provision shall not apply if the parties have agreed to arbitration pursuant to Rules 38 to 40.
(c) Mediation proceedings and, in particular, positions taken by the parties to the dispute during these proceedings, shall be confidential, and the documents considered during these proceedings shall, when deemed necessary, be assigned the appropriate classification level, without prejudice to the rights of any party in any further proceedings before the Confidentiality Commission.

B. FACT-FINDING

RULE 30 FACT-FINDING
(a) When mediation proceedings are terminated without settlement of the dispute or with only a partial settlement achieved, the Confidentiality Commission, if it considers this necessary, shall forthwith hold a hearing in accordance with Rule 31 in order to clarify any points or to

obtain any additional facts which may lead to a resolution of the dispute.

(b) If the Confidentiality Commission considers it necessary to hold a hearing, it may appoint a panel of five members to undertake this task. In appointing the panel, the Confidentiality Commission shall consider regional distribution and the expertise available.

(c) Alternatively, the Confidentiality Commission may use the services of an expert as contemplated in Rule 45 to clarify any points or to obtain additional facts which may lead to a resolution of the dispute.

RULE 31 PROCEDURE FOR THE HEARING

(a) The claimant shall present its case and the respondent shall present its defence. The Confidentiality Commission or the panel may, at any time during the hearing, put questions to the parties. They may ask the parties to provide explanations either in the course of the hearing or subsequently in writing.

(b) The parties to the dispute shall make available to the Confidentiality Commission or to the panel a written version of their oral statements.

(c) Each party shall have the burden of proving the facts relied on to support its claim or defence.

RULE 32 REPORTING

The panel shall report to the Confidentiality Commission on its proceedings. Its report shall include conclusions.

C. CONCILIATION

RULE 33 PANELS

(a) Where the parties have agreed to conciliation, the Confidentiality Commission shall appoint a panel from amongst its members. Each party may nominate one member and the Confidentiality Commission shall appoint the remainder to a total of five, taking into account such factors as regional distribution and the expertise available. The Confidentiality Commission shall appoint the Chair of the panel.

(b) Vacancies

    (i) In case of vacancy on the panel because of death, incapacitation or resignation of a member, the Confidentiality Commission shall immediately appoint a replacement from among the members of the Confidentiality Commission in consultation with the parties, taking into account such factors as regional distribution and the expertise available.

    (ii) Upon notification to the Confidentiality Commission of a vacancy on the panel, the proceedings shall be or shall remain suspended until the vacancy has been filled.

    (iii) If any panel member is replaced, prior hearings may be repeated at the discretion of the panel.

(c) The panel shall take the documents submitted to the Confidentiality Commission under these Rules, and as directed by the Confidentiality Commission, as its point of departure.

(d) Sittings of the panel

    (i) The Chair of the panel shall conduct its hearings and preside over its deliberations.

    (ii) The presence of a majority of the members of the panel shall be required at its sittings.

    (iii) The Chair of the panel shall fix the date and hour of its sittings.

(e) Decisions of the panel

    (i) Decisions of the panel shall be taken by a majority of the votes of all its members. Abstention shall count as a negative vote.

    (ii) Except as otherwise provided by these rules or decided by the Confidentiality Commission, the panel may take any decision by correspondence among its members, provided that all of them are consulted. Decisions so taken shall be certified by the Chair of the panel.

(iii) The panel shall report on its proceedings to the Confidentiality Commission. The report shall include final recommendations.

RULE 34 PANEL MODE OF OPERATION

(a) In order to bring about agreement between the parties, the panel may, from time to time at any stage of the proceedings, make, orally or in writing, recommendations to the parties. It may recommend that the parties accept specific terms of settlement or that they refrain, while it seeks to bring about agreement between them, from specific acts that might aggravate the dispute; it shall point out to the parties the arguments in favour of its recommendations. It may fix time limits within which each party shall inform the panel of its decision concerning the recommendations made.

(b) The panel shall decide cases in accordance with the Permanent Court of Arbitration Optional Conciliation Rules. Articles 6, 9(1), 10, 12, 13(2), 13(3) and 15 of those Rules shall be applied *mutatis mutandis*.

RULE 35 CONFIRMATION OF PANEL REPORTS

All panel reports shall be submitted to the Confidentiality Commission as a whole for confirmation. A panel report shall be considered confirmed unless two-thirds of the members of the Confidentiality Commission present and voting vote against confirmation. If the Confidentiality Commission refuses to confirm a panel report, the former shall, in consultation with the parties, consider the case itself.

D. REPORTING PROCEDURE FOR FACT-FINDING AND CONCILIATION

RULE 36 FINAL REPORT OF THE CONFIDENTIALITY COMMISSION

(a) Within 30 days of the end of the fact-finding or the conciliation hearing, the Confidentiality Commission shall issue the final report on its findings and recommendations, which shall include, in accordance with Confidentiality Policy Rule 3.5:

(i)   a description of facts relating to the dispute;

(ii) the findings and conclusions with respect to the dispute, as reflected in the panel report if confirmed, including: whether a breach of confidentiality has occurred; the responsibility for that breach; the nature and amount of the damage caused by the breach; observations on reasons and circumstances which led to the occurrence of the breach; and

(iii) recommendations concerning the remedy for the situation and the prevention of the occurrence of similar events, as well as time limits within which each party shall inform the Confidentiality Commission of its decision concerning the recommendations made.

(b) The final report shall not contain confidential information. The Confidentiality Commission may, however, include in a special annex to its final report such confidential details as it deems necessary for the implementation of conclusions contained in the report. The annex shall be classified and shall be made available only in accordance with the Confidentiality Policy.

RULE 37 RELEASE OF REPORTS

All Confidentiality Commission reports shall be listed in the record book maintained by the Registry. The Registry shall maintain the originals of the Confidentiality Commission's report and shall provide copies of the report to the parties to the dispute. The Confidentiality Commission may also instruct the Registry to provide copies of the report to the Executive Council if the Confidentiality Commission considers that the gravity or urgency of the case requires such action.

E. ARBITRATION

RULE 38 PANELS

(a) If the parties have agreed to arbitration, the Confidentiality Commission shall appoint a panel from amongst its members. Each party may nominate one member and the Confidentiality Commission shall appoint the remainder to a total of five, taking into account such factors as regional distribution and the expertise available. The Confidentiality Commission shall appoint the Chair of the panel.

(b) Vacancies

    (i) In case of vacancy on the panel because of death, incapacitation or resignation of a member, the Confidentiality Commission shall immediately appoint a replacement from among the members of the Confidentiality Commission in consultation with the parties, taking into account such factors as regional distribution and the expertise available.

    (ii) Upon notification to the Confidentiality Commission of a vacancy on the panel, the proceedings shall be or shall remain suspended until the vacancy has been filled.

    (iii) If any panel member is replaced, prior hearings may be repeated at the discretion of the panel.

(c) The panel shall take as its point of departure the documents submitted to the Confidentiality Commission pursuant to these rules and as directed by the Confidentiality Commission.

(d) Sittings of the panel

    (i) The Chair of the panel shall conduct its hearings and shall preside at its deliberations.

    (ii) The presence of a majority of the members of the panel shall be required at its sittings.

    (iii) The Chair of the panel shall fix the date and hour of its sittings.

(e) Decisions of the panel

    (i) Decisions of the panel shall be taken by a majority of the votes of all its members. Abstention shall count as a negative vote.

    (ii) Except as otherwise provided by these rules or as decided by the Confidentiality Commission, the panel may take any decision by correspondence among its members, provided that all of them are consulted. Decisions so taken shall be certified by the Chair of the panel.

    (iii) The panel shall report on its proceedings to the Confidentiality Commission. The report shall include the panel's decision.

RULE 39 PANEL PROCEDURE

The panel shall decide cases in accordance with the Permanent Court of Arbitration Optional Rules for Arbitration involving International Organisations and States or the Permanent Court of Arbitration Optional Rules for Arbitrating Disputes between two States, as appropriate. Articles 15, 24, 25, 28, 29, 30, 32 and 34 of the Permanent Court of Arbitration Optional Rules for Arbitration involving International Organisations and Articles 15, 24, 25, 28, 29, 30, 32 and 34 of the Permanent Court of Arbitration Optional Rules for Arbitrating Disputes between two States shall be applied *mutatis mutandis*.

RULE 40 CERTIFICATION OF PANEL DECISIONS

All decisions of the panel shall be submitted to the Confidentiality Commission for certification, after which they shall be listed in the record book by the Registry.

F. GENERAL PROVISIONS APPLICABLE TO CONCILIATION, FACT-FINDING AND ARBITRATION

RULE 41 DOCUMENTS AND OTHER EVIDENCE

(a) The parties may submit to the Confidentiality Commission documents or other evidence to support their positions.

(b) At any time during its proceedings the Confidentiality Commission may require the parties to produce documents or other evidence within such a time as the Confidentiality Commission shall determine.

RULE 42 ADDITIONAL SUBMISSIONS
(a) Statements of rebuttal may be submitted by any of the parties in accordance with the timetable set for the matter.
(b) During its proceedings the Confidentiality Commission may require the parties to submit further written statements, as necessary.

RULE 43 THIRD PARTIES
If the Confidentiality Commission is of the opinion that a third party has a substantial interest in a matter under consideration by the Confidentiality Commission, the Confidentiality Commission may decide to provide the third party with an opportunity to make written and/or oral submissions. These submissions shall be provided to the parties to the dispute and may, if the Confidentiality Commission considers it appropriate, be reflected in the Confidentiality Commission's report.

RULE 44 INVESTIGATION BY THE DIRECTOR-GENERAL
(a) The Director-General shall submit to the Confidentiality Commission the report of investigations carried out pursuant to paragraph 19 of the Confidentiality Annex, if such investigations are related to a case under consideration by the Confidentiality Commission.
(b) The Confidentiality Commission may require the Director-General to initiate an investigation pursuant to paragraph 19 of the Confidentiality Annex or to supplement a previous investigation by investigating additional issues.

RULE 45 EXPERTS
(a) The Confidentiality Commission may appoint one or more independent experts to report to it in writing on specific issues relating to a case pending before the Confidentiality Commission. The experts shall be bound by the relevant provisions of the Confidentiality Annex and the Confidentiality Policy and shall be required to enter into an individual secrecy agreement with the Conference, using the format set out in the annex hereto. The experts shall, when using confidential information, apply the OPCW Manual of Confidentiality Procedure, *mutatis mutandis*.
(b) If the issues to be considered by an expert appointed by the Confidentiality Commission relate to confidential information of one of the parties, the expert shall be appointed with the consent of the party concerned. In such cases, the Confidentiality Commission shall inform all parties through the Registry, of the name, qualifications and nationality of a person proposed for appointment as an expert. The party whose confidential information is to be considered by the expert shall inform the Registry, within seven days of receiving the notice, of whether it consents to the appointment of the expert. If the party does not indicate its rejection of the proposed expert within this time, it shall be deemed to have consented to the appointment of the proposed expert.

RULE 46 PROVISIONAL MEASURES TO PROTECT EVIDENCE AT AN INSPECTION SITE
A party to a dispute before the Confidentiality Commission may request it to order provisional measures to protect evidence at an inspection site or elsewhere. The Confidentiality Commission shall, in consultation with the parties, order such provisional measures as it considers necessary to protect evidence relevant to a dispute pending before it. The Confidentiality Commission shall request the Director-General to take such provisional measures as it considers necessary.

IX. MISCELLANEOUS

RULE 47 AMENDMENTS

Proposals for amendment of these procedures may be made by any member of the Confidentiality Commission for consideration at its regular annual meeting. Such proposals shall be notified to the Secretariat at least 45 days prior to the meeting and, to the members of the Confidentiality Commission, not less than 21 days prior to the meeting. Decisions on proposals for amendments shall be treated as decisions on matters of substance. Proposals agreed to shall be recommended to the Conference for adoption.

RULE 48 RECORD BOOK

The Registry shall keep a record book which shall list, subject to the provisions of the Convention related to confidentiality, all the filings and hearings in each matter brought before the Confidentiality Commission.

RULE 49 ANNUAL REPORTING TO THE CONFERENCE

At its regular annual meeting, the Confidentiality Commission shall report to the Conference on its activities in the preceding year. In accordance with Confidentiality Policy Rules 3.8 and 3.11(b), its annual report shall include the categories of disputes considered, the outcomes reached, and details of the outcomes consistent with the continuing protection of confidentiality. In accordance with Confidentiality Policy Rules 3.8, 3.11(c) and 3.12(j), the report shall also include a review of the efficiency of the Confidentiality Commission's operations, taking into account factors such as the number of disputes brought to it, the number of disputes resolved by mediation, conciliation or arbitration, and the length of time taken to issue its reports. On the basis of this review, the Confidentiality Commission may, if it deems this necessary, recommend measures for the improvement of efficiency.

RULE 50 COSTS

For each case submitted to the Confidentiality Commission, the costs shall be borne by the parties to the dispute pursuant to Articles 38 to 40 of the Permanent Court of Arbitration Optional Rules for Arbitration involving International Organisations and States and Articles 38 to 40 of the Permanent Court of Arbitration Optional Rules for Arbitrating Disputes between Two States, applied *mutatis mutandis*.

ANNEX
ORGANISATION FOR THE PROHIBITION OF CHEMICAL WEAPONS
SECRECY AGREEMENT

between

THE UNDERSIGNED .... ('THE SIGNATORY')

and

THE CONFERENCE OF THE STATES PARTIES OF THE ORGANISATION FOR THE PROHIBITION OF CHEMICAL WEAPONS

1. I, the Signatory, confirm that I have read and understood the Confidentiality Annex of the Convention on the Prohibition of the Development, Production, Stockpiling and Use of Chemical Weapons and on their Destruction ("the Convention"), and the OPCW Policy on Confidentiality.
2. As a condition for my appointment to the OPCW Commission for the Settlement of Disputes Related to Confidentiality ("Confidentiality Commission"), I hereby undertake to comply with the letter and spirit of the OPCW Policy on Confidentiality.

3. In view of my obligation to carry out faithfully and conscientiously the tasks entrusted to me during my term (or terms) as a member of the Confidentiality Commission, I further undertake that for the duration of that term (or terms), I shall:
   - restrict any use I make of OPCW confidential information, both within the Organisation and outside the Organisation, to the proper execution of my tasks;
   - respect and apply the procedures established under the OPCW Policy on Confidentiality and under the administrative directives which support that Policy, for the protection, handling, dissemination and release of confidential information;
   - refrain from disclosing information to which I have had access by virtue of my membership in the Confidentiality Commission; and
   - refrain from any unauthorised use of information to which I have had access as a member of the Confidentiality Commission, including any unauthorised use which seeks to serve the interests of myself or any third party, or which may damage the interests of any party.

4. Without limiting the foregoing, I undertake that at all times following the expiry of my term (or terms) as member of the Confidentiality Commission, I shall refrain from any use, disclosure or dissemination of confidential information to which I have had access in the course of my term (or terms) as member of the Confidentiality Commission, and I shall take no action that may lead to such information being disclosed or exploited to the detriment of the OPCW, a State Party to the Convention, or a person or commercial entity of a State Party.

5. I confirm that I am aware that a breach, as determined by the Conference of the States Parties, of these provisions and undertakings during or after my term (or terms) as member of the Confidentiality Commission may result in penal prosecution or civil action under the jurisdiction of a State Party to the Convention which could result in severe penalties or liability for damages.

SIGNATORY
SIGNATURE   FULL NAME   DATE

Done in triplicate at The Hague, Kingdom of the Netherlands in (a Convention language)
………………………………….. .

UNDERTAKING AND ACCEPTANCE ON BEHALF OF THE CONFERENCE OF THE STATES PARTIES OF THE OPCW.
I confirm that, as elected Chair of the Conference of the States Parties of the OPCW, I have accepted this agreement with the Signatory; that I made available to the Signatory the OPCW Policy on Confidentiality and the OPCW Manual of Confidentiality Procedure; that I have briefed the Signatory on the obligations relating to confidentiality incurred in accepting appointment to the Confidentiality Commission; that throughout his/her term (or terms) of membership on the Confidentiality Commission, the OPCW Secretariat will continue actively to promote the Signatory's understanding of all applicable obligations, policy and procedures relating to confidentiality, including any updates and amendments to the Policy on Confidentiality, or to the administrative directives which support that Policy; and that the OPCW Secretariat will provide briefing on such obligations upon request at any time following the expiration of the Signatory's term (or terms) as member of the Confidentiality Commission.

SIGNATURE   FULL NAME   DATE

WITNESS: The execution of this agreement was witnessed by the undersigned

SIGNATURE   FULL NAME   DATE

CONFIRMATION: On the expiration of my term or consecutive terms as member of the OPCW Confidentiality Commission, I confirm my understanding that the obligations relating to confidentiality continue to apply without time limitation in the future.

SIGNATURE   FULL NAME   DATE

26.2 Registry of the Confidentiality Commission: International Bureau of the Permanent Court of Arbitration

C-II/DEC.14 adopted by the Conference of the States Parties at its Second Session on 5 December 1997 and entitled "Operating procedures of the Confidentiality Commission". The Registry Agreement between the Organisation for the Prohibition of Chemical Weapons and the Permanent Court of Arbitration was approved by the Executive Council in its decision EC-XII/DEC.6 dated 9 October 1998 and signed on 9 December 1998.

The Conference,

…

Hereby:

…

4.   Appoints the International Bureau of the Permanent Court of Arbitration in The Hague to serve as Registry of the Confidentiality Commission, subject to the conclusion of an agreement between the OPCW and the International Bureau of the Permanent Court of Arbitration, which shall include provisions on measures to ensure that the Registry acts in accordance with the OPCW confidentiality regime, and in this regard;

5.   Directs the Executive Council to negotiate and conclude an agreement with the International Bureau of the Permanent Court of Arbitration, in accordance with paragraphs 30 and 34(a) of Article VIII of the Convention; …

27. ADVISORY BODY ON ADMINISTRATIVE AND FINANCIAL MATTERS

27.1 Establishment of the Advisory Body on Administrative and Financial Matters

EC-II/DEC.1 adopted by the Executive Council at its Second Session on 30 June 1997 and entitled "Establishment of an advisory body on administrative and financial matters"[1]

The Executive Council

Recalling that the Conference of the States Parties at its First Session approved the Financial Regulations of the OPCW (C-I/DEC.3),

Whereas Regulation 15.1 of the Financial Regulations states that the Executive Council may establish a body to advise it on administrative and financial matters and that this body shall consist of experts of recognised standing from States Parties with functions as specified in that Regulation,

Hereby:

Provisionally decides to establish an Advisory Body on Administrative and Financial Matters to fulfil the functions as specified in Regulation 15.1 of the Financial Regulations. This body shall be open-ended and without decision making powers;

Requests the Director-General to circulate a note inviting States Parties to appoint experts of recognised standing in the financial and administrative fields to serve on the Advisory Body. These experts shall be provided at no cost to the Organisation.

The Council will review the operation of this body after some experience of its functioning has been gained. This Decision will become final if no objection from any Member of the Council is received by the Secretariat by 4 July 1997 in The Hague.

27.2 Rules of Procedure of the Advisory Body on Administrative and Financial Matters

Annex 2 to the Report of the Twenty-Seventh Session of the Administrative Body on Administrative and Financial Matters (document ABAF-27/1, dated 3 September 2009), contains the Rules of Procedure of ABAF. The Executive Council noted at its Fifty-Eighth Session the Rules of Procedure (paragraph 9.1 of EC-59/9, dated 16 October 2009).

ANNEX 2

RULES OF PROCEDURE FOR THE ADVISORY BODY ON ADMINISTRATIVE AND FINANCIAL MATTERS

I. MEMBERS OF THE ADVISORY BODY

RULE 1 MEMBERS
The Advisory Body on Administrative and Financial Matters, hereinafter "Advisory Body", shall

---

[1] The Advisory Body on Administrative and Financial Matters is established under Regulation 15.1 of the OPCW Financial Regulations.

consist of experts of recognised standing from the States Parties. Members of the Advisory Body shall be nominated by States Parties and appointed by the Executive Council for a three-year renewable term of office. Members shall serve in their personal capacity.

RULE 2 ATTENDANCE OF MEMBERS OF THE ADVISORY BODY
Each member of the Advisory Body shall attend all of its sessions. In case of absence, a member may, with the prior approval of the Chairperson, designate an alternate expert to attend a session on his/her behalf.

RULE 3 ATTENDANCE OF PERSONS OTHER THAN MEMBERS OF THE ADVISORY BODY
The Chairperson may invite members of the Secretariat and any other individuals who can contribute to the activities of the Advisory Body to attend sessions or part sessions of the Advisory Body.

II. OFFICERS OF THE ADVISORY BODY

RULE 4 OFFICERS
(a) The Chairperson of the Advisory Body shall be chosen by its members.
(b) The Advisory Body shall also choose a Vice-Chairperson.
(c) Both the Chairperson and the Vice-Chairperson shall be chosen for a one-year renewable term of office.
(d) If the Chairperson is absent from a session or any part thereof, or is temporarily unable to perform his or her functions, the Vice-Chairperson shall act in his or her place. When the Vice-Chairperson chairs a session or part session under such circumstances, he/she shall have the same powers and functions as the Chairperson. In the absence of both the Chairperson and the Vice-Chairperson, the members of the Advisory Body shall choose an acting chairperson.

III. TECHNICAL SECRETARIAT

RULE 5 FUNCTIONS
The Secretariat of the OPCW shall provide the Advisory Body with all information and all administrative support which it may require for the proper implementation of its mandate, and shall exercise such functions as the Advisory Body may determine.

IV. SESSIONS OF THE ADVISORY BODY

RULE 6 SESSIONS OF THE ADVISORY BODY
(a) The Executive Council may, at its discretion, convene sessions of the Advisory Body. Otherwise, the Advisory Body may itself determine the frequency and times of its own sessions.
(b) The work of the Advisory Body shall be conducted in plenary sessions in accordance with these rules of procedure.
(c) The Advisory Body may, at its own discretion, meet in informal sessions and may set up working groups.

V. AGENDA OF THE ADVISORY BODY

RULE 7 DETERMINATION OF AGENDA
The Advisory Body shall determine its own agenda, on the basis, *inter alia*, of Regulation 15.1 of the OPCW Financial Regulations (C-I/DEC.3, dated 14 May 1997).

RULE 8 REQUESTS FOR ADVICE
In accordance with Regulation 15.1, subparagraph (i) of the Financial Regulations, requests for advice shall normally be submitted in writing to the Chairperson of the Advisory Body, who shall circulate copies of such requests to all members of the Advisory Body for their consideration. If a request is made when the Advisory Body is not in session, the Secretariat shall provide copies of it to the Chairperson and members of the Advisory Body as soon as possible.

VI. CONDUCT OF BUSINESS

RULE 9 QUORUM
One-third of the members of the Advisory Body shall constitute a quorum.

RULE 10 GENERAL POWERS AND FUNCTIONS OF THE CHAIRPERSON
(a) In addition to exercising the powers conferred upon the Chairperson elsewhere in these rules, the Chairperson shall convene and preside at the plenary sessions of the Advisory Body.
(b) If the Chairperson resigns or is permanently unable to perform his/her functions, a new Chairperson shall be chosen by the Advisory Body from amongst its own members.
(c) The Chairperson, or the Vice-Chairperson acting in the capacity of Chairperson, shall act as experts in their own right.

RULE 11 DECISIONS
(a) All decisions and recommendations of the Advisory Body may be taken by consensus of all members present.
(b) On procedural matters, decisions may be taken by the majority of members present and voting. In case of a tie, the Chairperson may cast the deciding vote..

VII. LANGUAGE

RULE 12 LANGUAGE
As a matter of economy, the Advisory Body shall use English as its working language.

VIII. AMENDMENT OF RULES

RULE 13 AMENDMENTS
These rules of procedure may be amended by consensus.

IX. ATTACHMENT

Regulation 15 of the OPCW Financial Regulations is reproduced in the annex to these rules of procedure.

28. COMMITTEE ON RELATIONS WITH THE HOST COUNTRY

28.1 Establishment of the Committee on Relations with the Host Country

C-11/DEC.9 adopted by the Conference of the States Parties at its Eleventh Session on 7 December 2006 and entitled "Establishment of a committee on relations with the host country"

The Conference

Recalling the provisions on the legal capacity and the privileges and immunities of the Organisation for the Prohibition of Chemical Weapons (OPCW) and its organs, as well as on the privileges and immunities of the Heads of Delegation, alternates and advisers attached to Heads of Delegation, Permanent Representatives, members of the Permanent Missions, Delegates of States Parties, and the Director-General and the staff of the OPCW – provisions set forth in the Agreement between the OPCW and the Kingdom of the Netherlands concerning the Headquarters of the OPCW;

Recognising that resolving in a constructive and timely fashion any issues that may arise in connection with the interpretation and implementation of the Headquarters Agreement is of interest to the Member States of the OPCW, including the Host Country, as well as to the Director-General;

Bearing in mind that at its Tenth Session it requested the Executive Council (hereinafter "the Council") to submit to it at its Eleventh Session a recommendation to establish a Host Country Committee; and

Having considered the recommendation the Council has submitted (EC-47/DEC.10, dated 8 November 2006);

Hereby:
1. Establishes a Committee on Relations with the Host Country, composed of the following members:
    (a) the Chairperson of the Council;
    (b) two representatives of each regional group;
    (c) a representative of the Host Country, to be appointed by that State Party; and
    (d) the Director-General.
2. Instructs the Committee to address the privileges and immunities referred to above, as well as all categories of issues that were considered by the Working Group that the Chairperson of the Council established pursuant to a mandate of the Council at its Fortieth Session, and by the Contact Group that was subsequently established to find, together with the Secretariat and the Host Country, mutually satisfying solutions to pending matters regarding the full implementation of the Headquarters Agreement;
3. Authorises the Committee to convene periodically and whenever it is convoked by its Chairperson at the request of any Member State or the Director-General;
4. Requests the Committee to report to it at its Twelfth Session, through the Council, on the progress it has made;
5. Requests the Director-General to provide the Committee with all necessary assistance, and to bring to its attention issues of concern relating to the implementation of the Headquarters Agreement; and
6. Requests the Host Country to assist the Committee in its work by encouraging the participation and cooperation, as and when appropriate, of those of its national institutions that are relevant to the work of the Committee.

Relationship with
Other International Organisations

29. RELATIONSHIP WITH THE UNITED NATIONS

29.1 Relationship Agreement between the United Nations and the OPCW

Annex to EC-MXI/DEC.1 adopted by the Executive Council at its Eleventh Session on 1 September 2000 and entitled "Relationship Agreement between the United Nations and the OPCW"[1]

AGREEMENT CONCERNING THE RELATIONSHIP
between
THE UNITED NATIONS
and
THE ORGANISATION FOR THE PROHIBITION OF CHEMICAL WEAPONS

The United Nations and the Organisation for the Prohibition of Chemical Weapons,

Bearing in mind the relevant provisions of the Charter of the United Nations (hereinafter the "Charter") and of the Convention on the Prohibition of the Development, Production, Stockpiling and Use of Chemical Weapons and on Their Destruction (hereinafter the "Convention");

Bearing in mind that, in accordance with the Charter, the United Nations is the principal organisation dealing with matters relating to the maintenance of international peace and security, and acts as a centre for harmonising the actions of nations in the attainment of the goals set out in the Charter;

Considering that the Organisation for the Prohibition of Chemical Weapons (hereinafter the "OPCW") shares the purposes and principles of the Charter, and that its activities performed pursuant to the provisions of the Convention contribute to the realisation of the purposes and principles of the Charter;

Desiring to make provision for a mutually beneficial relationship, to avoid unnecessary duplication of their activities and services, to facilitate the discharge of the respective responsibilities of both organisations,

Noting General Assembly resolution 51/230 of 22 May 1997 and the relevant decision of the Conference of the States Parties at its Fourth Session (C-IV/DEC.4, dated 2 July 1999), calling for the conclusion of a relationship agreement between the United Nations and the OPCW;

Have agreed as follows:

ARTICLE I
GENERAL

1. The United Nations recognises the OPCW as the organisation, in relationship to the United Nations as specified in this agreement, responsible for activities to achieve the comprehensive prohibition of chemical weapons in accordance with the Convention.
2. The United Nations recognises that the OPCW, by virtue of the Convention, shall function as an independent, autonomous international organisation in the working relationship with the United Nations established by this Agreement.
3. The OPCW recognises the responsibilities of the United Nations, in accordance with its Charter, in particular in the fields of international peace and security and economic, social, cultural and humanitarian development, protection and preservation of the environment and

---

[1] The Relationship Agreement was approved by the CSP by way of decision C-VI/DEC.5 on 17 May 2001 and entered into force in 2001.

peaceful settlement of disputes.

4. The OPCW undertakes to conduct its activities in accordance with the purposes and princi-ples of the Charter to promote peace, disarmament and international cooperation and with due regard to the policies of the United Nations furthering safeguarded worldwide disarma-ment.

ARTICLE II
COOPERATION

1. The United Nations and the OPCW, recognising the need to work jointly to achieve mutual objectives, and with a view to facilitating the effective exercise of their responsibilities, agree to cooperate closely within their respective mandates and to consult on matters of mutual in-terest and concern. To that end, the United Nations and the OPCW shall cooperate with each other in accordance with the provisions of their respective constituent instruments.

2. Cooperation between the United Nations and the OPCW, in particular, shall require that:

   (a) cases of particular gravity and urgency which, in accordance with paragraph 36 of Ar-ticle VIII of the Convention, shall, including relevant information and conclusions, be brought directly to the attention of the General Assembly and the Security Council by the Executive Council, through the Secretary-General in accordance with the existing United Nations procedures;

   (b) cases of particular gravity which, in accordance with paragraph 4 of Article XII of the Convention, shall, including relevant information and conclusions, be brought to the attention of the General Assembly and the Security Council by the Conference of the States Parties through the Secretary-General in accordance with the existing United Na-tions procedures;

   (c) the OPCW shall, in accordance with paragraph 27 of Part XI of the Verification Annex, closely cooperate with the Secretary-General in cases of the alleged use of chemical weapons involving a State not party to the Convention or in a territory not controlled by a State Party to the Convention and, if so requested, shall in such cases place its re-sources at the disposal of the Secretary-General;

   (d) the OPCW and the United Nations shall, in accordance with their respective mandates, explore possibilities for cooperation in the provision of assistance to States concerned in cases of the use or serious threat of use of chemical weapons, as provided for in para-graph 10 of Article X of the Convention;

   (e) the OPCW and the United Nations shall, insofar as covered by their respective mandates, in the context of economic and technological development in their Member States, co-operate to foster international cooperation for peaceful purposes in the field of chemical activities and facilitating the exchange of chemicals, equipment and scientific and tech-nical information relating to the development and application of chemistry for purposes not prohibited under the Convention; and

   (f) the United Nations and the OPCW shall cooperate on any matter that may relate to the object and purpose of the Convention, or which may arise in connection with its imple-mentation.

3. The OPCW, within its competence and in accordance with the provisions of the Convention, shall cooperate with the General Assembly and the Security Council by furnishing them, at the request of either, such information and assistance as may be required in the exercise of their respective responsibilities under the United Nations Charter.

4. The United Nations and the OPCW shall cooperate in the field of public information and shall arrange, upon request, for the exchange of information, publications and reports of mutual interest and for the furnishing of special reports and studies and information.

5. The Secretariat of the United Nations and the Technical Secretariat of the OPCW shall main-

tain a close working relationship in accordance with such arrangements as may be agreed between the Secretary-General and the Director-General.

ARTICLE III
COORDINATION

The United Nations and OPCW recognize the necessity of achieving, where applicable, effective coordination of the activities and services of OPCW and of the United Nations, and of avoiding unnecessary duplication of their activities and services.

ARTICLE IV
REPORTING

1. The Director-General will keep the United Nations informed of the OPCW's routine activities, and will report on a regular basis, as appropriate and as duly mandated by the Executive Council, through the Secretary-General to the General Assembly and the Security Council.
2. If the Executive Council takes a decision to provide, pursuant to Article X of the Convention, supplementary assistance to a State Party to the Convention requesting such assistance in connection with the use or threat of use of chemical weapons, the Director-General (representing the OPCW, as specified in this Agreement) shall transmit to the Secretary-General (representing the United Nations, as specified in this Agreement) the above-mentioned decision of the Executive Council, together with the investigation report prepared by the Technical Secretariat in connection with the request for such assistance.
3. Whenever decisions are taken by the Conference of the States Parties, pursuant to Article XII of the Convention, on measures, including collective measures recommended to States Parties, to ensure compliance with the Convention and to redress and remedy any situation which contravenes the provisions of the Convention, the Director-General, upon instructions from the Conference, shall inform the General Assembly and the Security Council accordingly, through the Secretary-General.
4. Should the Secretary-General report to the United Nations on the common activities of the United Nations and the OPCW or on the development of relations between them, any such report shall be promptly transmitted by the Secretary-General to the OPCW.
5. Should the Director-General report to the OPCW on the common activities of the OPCW and the United Nations or on the development of relations between them, any such report shall be promptly transmitted by the Director-General to the United Nations.

ARTICLE V
RECIPROCAL REPRESENTATION

1. The Secretary-General shall be entitled to attend and to participate in relation to matters of common interest, without vote and in accordance with the relevant rules of procedure, in sessions of the Conference of the States Parties and in sessions of the Executive Council of the OPCW. The Secretary-General shall also be invited as appropriate to attend and to participate without vote in such other meetings as the OPCW may convene at which matters of interest to the United Nations are under consideration. The Secretary-General may, for the purposes of this paragraph, designate any person as his/her representative.
2. The Director-General shall be entitled to attend plenary meetings of the General Assembly of the United Nations for the purpose of consultations. The Director-General shall be entitled to attend and to participate without vote in the meetings of the Committees of the General Assembly, and in meetings of the Economic and Social Council and, as appropriate, of any subsidiary organs of these bodies and the General Assembly. The Director-General may, at

the invitation of the Security Council, attend its meetings to supply the Council, as duly mandated by the Executive Council, with information or give other assistance with regard to matters within the competence of the OPCW. The Director-General may, for the purposes of this paragraph, designate any person as his/her representative.

3. Written statements presented by the United Nations to the OPCW for distribution shall be distributed by the Technical Secretariat of the OPCW to all members of the appropriate organ(s) or subsidiary organ(s) of the OPCW. Written statements presented by the OPCW to the United Nations for distribution shall be distributed by the Secretariat of the United Nations to all members of the appropriate organ(s) or subsidiary organ(s) of the United Nations.

ARTICLE VI
AGENDA ITEMS

1. The United Nations may propose agenda items for consideration by the OPCW. In such cases, the United Nations shall notify the Director-General of the agenda item or items concerned, and the Director-General shall, in accordance with his/her authority and the relevant rules of procedure, bring any such agenda item or items to the attention of the Conference of the States Parties, the Executive Council or such other organ(s) of the OPCW as may be appropriate.

2. The OPCW may propose agenda items for consideration by the United Nations. In such cases, the OPCW shall notify the Secretary-General of the agenda item or items concerned, and the Secretary-General shall, in accordance with his/her authority, bring any such item or items to the attention of the General Assembly, the Security Council, the Economic and Social Council or such other organ(s) of the United Nations as may be appropriate.

ARTICLE VII
INTERNATIONAL COURT OF JUSTICE

1. The United Nations takes note of Article XIV, paragraph 5, of the Convention, which empowers the Conference of the States Parties or the Executive Council of the OPCW, subject to authorisation from the General Assembly of the United Nations, to request the International Court of Justice to give an advisory opinion on any legal question(s) arising from within the scope of activities of the OPCW, apart from any question(s) concerning the mutual relationship between the OPCW and the United Nations.

2. The United Nations and the OPCW agree that each such request for an advisory opinion shall first be submitted to the General Assembly, which will decide upon the request in accordance with Article 96 of the Charter.

3. When seeking an advisory opinion as referred to in paragraph 1 of this Article, the OPCW agrees to furnish, in accordance with the Confidentiality Annex to the Convention and the OPCW Policy on Confidentiality, any such information as may be required by the International Court of Justice in accordance with the Statute of the International Court of Justice.

ARTICLE VIII
RESOLUTIONS OF THE UNITED NATIONS

The Secretary-General shall transmit to the Director-General resolutions of the General Assembly or the Security Council pertaining to issues relevant to the Convention. Upon receipt thereof, the Director-General will bring the resolutions concerned to the attention of the relevant organs of the OPCW, and will report back to the Secretary-General on any action taken by the OPCW, as appropriate.

ARTICLE IX
UNITED NATIONS LAISSEZ-PASSER

Officials of OPCW shall be entitled, in accordance with such administrative arrangements as may be concluded between the Secretary-General and the Director-General, to use the laissez-passer of the United Nations as a valid travel document where such use is recognized by States Parties in the applicable instruments defining the privileges and immunities of OPCW and its officials. The administrative arrangements will take into account, to the extent possible, the special requirements of OPCW arising from its verification activities under the Convention.

ARTICLE X
PERSONNEL ARRANGEMENTS

1. The United Nations and the OPCW agree to consult whenever necessary concerning matters of common interest relating to the terms and conditions of employment of staff.
2. The United Nations and the OPCW agree to cooperate regarding the exchange of personnel, bearing in mind the nationality of Member States of the OPCW, and to determine conditions of such cooperation in supplementary arrangements to be concluded for that purpose in accordance with Article XIV of this Agreement.

ARTICLE XI
BUDGETARY AND FINANCIAL MATTERS

1. OPCW recognizes the desirability of establishing budgetary and financial cooperation with the United Nations in order that OPCW may benefit from the experience of the United Nations in this field and in order to ensure, as far as may be practicable, the consistency of the administrative operations of the two organizations in this field.
2. The United Nations may arrange for studies to be undertaken concerning budgetary and financial matters of interest to OPCW with a view, as far as may be practicable, to achieving coordination and securing consistency in such matters.
3. OPCW agrees to follow, as far as may be practicable, the standard budgetary and financial practices and forms used by the United Nations.

ARTICLE XII
EXPENSES

Expenses resulting from any cooperation or provision of services pursuant to this Agreement shall be subject to separate arrangements between OPCW and the United Nations.

ARTICLE XIII
PROTECTION OF CONFIDENTIALITY

1. Subject to paragraphs 1 and 3 of Article II, nothing in this Agreement shall be so construed as to require either the United Nations or the OPCW to furnish any material, data and information whose disclosure could in its judgement require it to violate its obligation under its constituent instrument or policy on confidentiality, to protect such information.
2. The United Nations and the OPCW shall ensure the appropriate protection, in accordance with their constituent instruments and policies on confidentiality, in respect to such information.

ARTICLE XIV
IMPLEMENTATION OF THE AGREEMENT

The Secretary-General and the Director-General may enter into such supplementary arrangements and develop such practical measures for the implementation of this Agreement as may be found desirable.

ARTICLE XV
AMENDMENTS

1. This Agreement shall enter into force on the date on which the United Nations and the OPCW have exchanged written notifications that their internal requirements for entry into force have been met.
2. This agreement shall be applied provisionally by the United Nations and the OPCW upon signature.

ARTICLE XVI
ENTRY INTO FORCE

1. This Agreement shall enter into force on the date on which the United Nations and OPCW have exchanged written notifications that their internal requirements for entry into force have been met.
2. This Agreement shall be applied provisionally by the United Nations and OPCW upon signature.

IN WITNESS THEREOF the undersigned, being duly authorised representatives of the United Nations and the OPCW, have signed the present agreement.

Signed, this 17th day of October 2000 at New York in two originals in the English language.

FOR THE UNITED NATIONS
Louise Fréchette
Deputy Secretary-General

FOR THE ORGANISATION FOR THE PROHIBITION OF CHEMICAL WEAPONS
José M. Bustani
Director-General

C-VI/DEC.5 adopted by the Conference of the States Parties at its Sixth Session on 17 May 2001 and entitled "Relationship Agreement between the United Nations and the OPCW"

The Conference,

    Recalling that Article VIII, subparagraph 34(a) of the Convention provides that the Executive Council shall conclude agreements or arrangements with States and international organisations on behalf of the OPCW, subject to prior approval by the Conference of the States Parties;

    Noting with satisfaction the decision of the Executive Council which: (a) recommended the draft Relationship Agreement as contained in the Annex to that decision; and (b) authorised the Director-General, pending approval by the United Nations General Assembly and the Conference, to sign the agreement for provisional application (EC-MXI/DEC.1, dated 1 September 2000);

    Welcoming the signature of the Agreement concerning the Relationship between the United Nations and the Organisation for the Prohibition of Chemical Weapons in New York on 17

October 2000 and the outcome of the commencement of provisional application of the agreement (paragraphs 48 to 51 of EC-XXII/DG.12, dated 5 December 2000);

Hereby:
1. Approves the Agreement concerning the Relationship between the United Nations and the OPCW as annexed to the decision of the Executive Council (Annex to EC-MXI/DEC.1, dated 1 September 2000);
2. Requests the Director-General to send written notification to the United Nations that the internal requirements of the OPCW for entry into force of the Agreement have been met; and
3. Further requests the Director-General to inform the Member States of the outcome of the United Nations General Assembly's consideration of the Agreement and the date of entry into force of the Agreement.

Resolution A/RES/55/283 adopted by the General Assembly at its 111th plenary meeting on 7 September 2001 and entitled "55/283. Cooperation between the United Nations and the Organization for the Prohibition of Chemical Weapons"

The General Assembly,

Recalling its resolution 51/230 of 22 May 1997, by which it invited the Secretary-General to take steps to conclude with the Director-General of the Technical Secretariat of the Organization for the Prohibition of Chemical Weapons an agreement between the United Nations and the Organization to regulate the relationship between the two organizations, and to present the negotiated draft relationship agreement to the General Assembly for its approval,

Noting the decision of the Conference of the States Parties to the Chemical Weapons Convention of 17 May 2001 to approve the Agreement concerning the Relationship between the United Nations and the Organization for the Prohibition of Chemical Weapons,[2]

Having considered the Agreement concerning the Relationship between the United Nations and the Organization for the Prohibition of Chemical Weapons,
1. Approves the Agreement concerning the Relationship between the United Nations and the Organization for the Prohibition of Chemical Weapons, the text of which is annexed to the present resolution;
2. Decides to include in the provisional agenda of its fifty-sixth and subsequent sessions the item entitled "Cooperation between the United Nations and the Organization for the Prohibition of Chemical Weapons".

29.2 United Nations Security Council Resolutions

Resolution S/RES/1540 (2004) adopted by the Security Council at its 4956th meeting on 28 April 2004 concerning non-proliferation of weapons of mass destruction. The Security Council, by resolutions 1673 (2006), 1810 (2008) and 1977 (2011), extended the mandate of the Committee established pursuant to resolution 1540 (2004) and reiterated the objectives of that resolution.[3]

The Security Council

Affirming that proliferation of nuclear, chemical and biological weapons, as well as their

---

[2] See A/55/988.

[3] See also decision EC-XXVII/DEC.5, adopted by the Executive Council at its Twenty-Seventh Session on 7 December 2001 on "OPCW's contribution to global anti-terrorism efforts", Section 19.3.

means of delivery,[4] constitutes a threat to international peace and security,

Reaffirming, in this context, the Statement of its President adopted at the Council's meeting at the level of Heads of State and Government on 31 January 1992 (S/23500), including the need for all Member States to fulfil their obligations in relation to arms control and disarmament and to prevent proliferation in all its aspects of all weapons of mass destruction,

Recalling also that the Statement underlined the need for all Member States to resolve peacefully in accordance with the Charter any problems in that context threatening or disrupting the maintenance of regional and global stability,

Affirming its resolve to take appropriate and effective actions against any threat to international peace and security caused by the proliferation of nuclear, chemical and biological weapons and their means of delivery, in conformity with its primary responsibilities, as provided for in the United Nations Charter,

Affirming its support for the multilateral treaties whose aim is to eliminate or prevent the proliferation of nuclear, chemical or biological weapons and the importance for all States parties to these treaties to implement them fully in order to promote international stability,

Welcoming efforts in this context by multilateral arrangements which contribute to non-proliferation,

Affirming that prevention of proliferation of nuclear, chemical and biological weapons should not hamper international cooperation in materials, equipment and technology for peaceful purposes while goals of peaceful utilization should not be used as a cover for proliferation,

Gravely concerned by the threat of terrorism and the risk that non-State actors[4] such as those identified in the United Nations list established and maintained by the Committee established under Security Council resolution 1267 and those to whom resolution 1373 applies, may acquire, develop, traffic in or use nuclear, chemical and biological weapons and their means of delivery,

Gravely concerned by the threat of illicit trafficking in nuclear, chemical, or biological weapons and their means of delivery, and related materials,[4] which adds a new dimension to the issue of proliferation of such weapons and also poses a threat to international peace and security,

Recognizing the need to enhance coordination of efforts on national, subregional, regional and international levels in order to strengthen a global response to this serious challenge and threat to international security,

Recognizing that most States have undertaken binding legal obligations under treaties to which they are parties, or have made other commitments aimed at preventing the proliferation of nuclear, chemical or biological weapons, and have taken effective measures to account for, secure and physically protect sensitive materials, such as those required by the Convention on the Physical Protection of Nuclear Materials and those recommended by the IAEA Code of Conduct on the Safety and Security of Radioactive Sources,

Recognizing further the urgent need for all States to take additional effective measures to prevent the proliferation of nuclear, chemical or biological weapons and their means of delivery,

Encouraging all Member States to implement fully the disarmament treaties and agreements to which they are party,

Reaffirming the need to combat by all means, in accordance with the Charter of the United Nations, threats to international peace and security caused by terrorist acts,

---

[4] Definitions for the purpose of this resolution only:
Means of delivery: missiles, rockets and other unmanned systems capable of delivering nuclear, chemical, or biological weapons, that are specially designed for such use.
Non-State actor: individual or entity, not acting under the lawful authority of any State in conducting activities which come within the scope of this resolution.
Related materials: materials, equipment and technology covered by relevant multilateral treaties and arrangements, or included on national control lists, which could be used for the design, development, production or use of nuclear, chemical and biological weapons and their means of delivery [footnote in original].

Determined to facilitate henceforth an effective response to global threats in the area of non-proliferation,

Acting under Chapter VII of the Charter of the United Nations,

1. Decides that all States shall refrain from providing any form of support to non-State actors that attempt to develop, acquire, manufacture, possess, transport, transfer or use nuclear, chemical or biological weapons and their means of delivery;

2. Decides also that all States, in accordance with their national procedures, shall adopt and enforce appropriate effective laws which prohibit any non-State actor to manufacture, acquire, possess, develop, transport, transfer or use nuclear, chemical or biological weapons and their means of delivery, in particular for terrorist purposes, as well as attempts to engage in any of the foregoing activities, participate in them as an accomplice, assist or finance them;

3. Decides also that all States shall take and enforce effective measures to establish domestic controls to prevent the proliferation of nuclear, chemical, or biological weapons and their means of delivery, including by establishing appropriate controls over related materials and to this end shall:

    (a) Develop and maintain appropriate effective measures to account for and secure such items in production, use, storage or transport;

    (b) Develop and maintain appropriate effective physical protection measures;

    (c) Develop and maintain appropriate effective border controls and law enforcement efforts to detect, deter, prevent and combat, including through international cooperation when necessary, the illicit trafficking and brokering in such items in accordance with their national legal authorities and legislation and consistent with international law;

    (d) Establish, develop, review and maintain appropriate effective national export and trans-shipment controls over such items, including appropriate laws and regulations to control export, transit, trans-shipment and re-export and controls on providing funds and services related to such export and trans-shipment such as financing, and transporting that would contribute to proliferation, as well as establishing end-user controls; and establishing and enforcing appropriate criminal or civil penalties for violations of such export control laws and regulations;

4. Decides to establish, in accordance with rule 28 of its provisional rules of procedure, for a period of no longer than two years, a Committee of the Security Council, consisting of all members of the Council, which will, calling as appropriate on other expertise, report to the Security Council for its examination, on the implementation of this resolution, and to this end calls upon States to present a first report no later than six months from the adoption of this resolution to the Committee on steps they have taken or intend to take to implement this resolution;

5. Decides that none of the obligations set forth in this resolution shall be interpreted so as to conflict with or alter the rights and obligations of State Parties to the Nuclear Non-Proliferation Treaty, the Chemical Weapons Convention and the Biological and Toxin Weapons Convention or alter the responsibilities of the International Atomic Energy Agency or the Organization for the Prohibition of Chemical Weapons;

6. Recognizes the utility in implementing this resolution of effective national control lists and calls upon all Member States, when necessary, to pursue at the earliest opportunity the development of such lists;

7. Recognizes that some States may require assistance in implementing the provisions of this resolution within their territories and invites States in a position to do so to offer assistance as appropriate in response to specific requests to the States lacking the legal and regulatory infrastructure, implementation experience and/or resources for fulfilling the above provisions;

8. Calls upon all States:

    (a) To promote the universal adoption and full implementation, and, where necessary, strengthening of multilateral treaties to which they are parties, whose aim is to prevent the proliferation of nuclear, biological or chemical weapons;

(b) To adopt national rules and regulations, where it has not yet been done, to ensure compliance with their commitments under the key multilateral nonproliferation treaties;

(c) To renew and fulfil their commitment to multilateral cooperation, in particular within the framework of the International Atomic Energy Agency, the Organization for the Prohibition of Chemical Weapons and the Biological and Toxin Weapons Convention, as important means of pursuing and achieving their common objectives in the area of nonproliferation and of promoting international cooperation for peaceful purposes;

(d) To develop appropriate ways to work with and inform industry and the public regarding their obligations under such laws;

9. Calls upon all States to promote dialogue and cooperation on nonproliferation so as to address the threat posed by proliferation of nuclear, chemical, or biological weapons, and their means of delivery;

10. Further to counter that threat, calls upon all States, in accordance with their national legal authorities and legislation and consistent with international law, to take cooperative action to prevent illicit trafficking in nuclear, chemical or biological weapons, their means of delivery, and related materials;

11. Expresses its intention to monitor closely the implementation of this resolution and, at the appropriate level, to take further decisions which may be required to this end;

12. Decides to remain seized of the matter.

29.3 United Nations General Assembly Resolutions

Resolution A/RES/68/45 adopted by the United Nations General Assembly at its Sixtieth Plenary Meeting on 10 December 2013 and entitled "68/45. Implementation of the Convention on the Prohibition of the Development, Production, Stockpiling and Use of Chemical Weapons and on Their Destruction". The General Assembly has adopted a number of similar resolutions on the implementation of the Chemical Weapons Convention (see resolutions 55/33 H (2000), 56/24 K (2001), 57/82 (2002), 58/52 (2003), 59/72 (2004), 60/67 (2005), 61/68 (2006), 62/23 (2007), 63/48 (2008), 64/46 (2009), 65/57 (2010), 66/35 (2011), and 67/54 (2012)).

The General Assembly,

Recalling its previous resolutions on the subject of chemical weapons, in particular resolution 67/54 of 3 December 2012, adopted without a vote, in which the General Assembly noted with appreciation the ongoing work to achieve the object and purpose of the Convention on the Prohibition of the Development, Production, Stockpiling and Use of Chemical Weapons and on Their Destruction,[5]

Determined to achieve the effective prohibition of the development, production, acquisition, transfer, stockpiling and use of chemical weapons and their destruction,

Noting that, since the adoption of resolution 67/54, two additional States have acceded to the Convention, namely, Somalia and the Syrian Arab Republic, bringing the total number of States parties to the Convention to 190,

Taking note of the report of the United Nations Mission to Investigate Allegations of the Use of Chemical Weapons in the Syrian Arab Republic on the alleged use of chemical weapons in the Ghouta area of Damascus on 21 August 2013,[6] in which the Mission concludes that chemical

---

[5] United Nations, Treaty Series, vol. 1974, No. 33757.

[6] A/67/997-S/2013/553.

weapons have been used in the ongoing conflict between the parties in the Syrian Arab Republic, as well as against civilians, including children, on a relatively large scale,

Condemning in the strongest possible terms the use of chemical weapons,

Taking note of decision EC-M-33/DEC.1 of 27 September 2013 of the Executive Council of the Organization for the Prohibition of Chemical Weapons and of Security Council Resolution 2118 (2013) of the same date,

Reaffirming the importance of the outcome of the Third Special Session of the Conference of the States Parties to Review the Operation of the Chemical Weapons Convention, held in The Hague from 8 to 19 April 2013 (the Third Review Conference), including its consensus final report, in which the Conference addressed all aspects of the Convention and made important recommendations on its continued implementation,

Emphasizing that the Third Review Conference welcomed the fact that the Convention is a unique multilateral agreement banning an entire category of weapons of mass destruction in a non-discriminatory and verifiable manner under strict and effective international control and noted with satisfaction that the Convention continues to be a remarkable success and an example of effective multilateralism,

Convinced that the Convention, 16 years after its entry into force, has reinforced its role as the international norm against chemical weapons, and that it constitutes a major contribution to:

(*a*) International peace and security,

(*b*) Eliminating chemical weapons and preventing their re-emergence,

(*c*) The ultimate objective of general and complete disarmament under strict and effective international control,

(*d*) Excluding completely, for the sake of all mankind, the possibility of the use of chemical weapons,

(*e*) Promoting international cooperation and exchange in scientific and technical information in the field of chemical activities among States parties for peaceful purposes in order to enhance the economic and technological development of all States parties,

1. *Emphasizes* that the universality of the Convention on the Prohibition of the Development, Production, Stockpiling and Use of Chemical Weapons and on Their Destruction1 is essential to achieving its object and purpose and to enhancing the security of States parties, as well as to international peace and security, underlines that the objectives of the Convention will not be fully realized as long as there remains even a single State not party to the Convention that could possess or acquire such weapons, and calls upon all States that have not yet done so to become parties to the Convention without delay;

2. *Underlines* that the full, effective and non-discriminatory implementation of all articles of the Convention makes a major contribution to international peace and security through the elimination of existing stockpiles of chemical weapons and the prohibition of their acquisition and use, and provides for assistance and protection in the event of use or threat of use of chemical weapons and for international cooperation for peaceful purposes in the field of chemical activities;

3. *Notes* the impact of scientific and technological progress on the effective implementation of the Convention and the importance for the Organization for the Prohibition of Chemical Weapons and its policymaking organs of taking due account of such developments;

4. *Reaffirms* that the obligation of the States parties to complete the destruction of chemical weapons stockpiles and the destruction or conversion of chemical weapons production facilities in accordance with the provisions of the Convention and the Annex on Implementation and Verification (Verification Annex) and under the verification of the Technical Secretariat of the Organization for the Prohibition of Chemical Weapons is essential for the realization of the object and purpose of the Convention;

5. *Stresses* the importance to the Convention that all possessors of chemical weapons, chemical weapons production facilities or chemical weapons development facilities, including previ-

ously declared possessor States, should be among the States parties to the Convention, and welcomes progress to that end;

6. *Recalls* that the Third Special Session of the Conference of the States Parties to Review the Operation of the Chemical Weapons Convention, held in The Hague from 8 to 19 April 2013 (the Third Review Conference) expressed concern regarding the statement made by the Director-General of the Organization for the Prohibition of Chemical Weapons in his report to the Executive Council of the Organization at its sixty-eighth session, provided in accordance with paragraph 2 of decision C-16/DEC.11 of 1 December 2011 adopted by the Conference of the States Parties at its sixteenth session, that three possessor States parties, namely, Libya, the Russian Federation and the United States of America, had been unable to fully meet the final extended deadline of 29 April 2012 for the destruction of their chemical weapons stockpiles, and also expressed determination that the destruction of all categories of chemical weapons should be completed in the shortest time possible in accordance with the provisions of the Convention and the Verification Annex, and with the full application of the relevant decisions that have been taken;

7. *Notes with concern* that, along with the threat of the possible production, acquisition and use of chemical weapons by States, the international community also faces the danger of the production, acquisition and use of chemical weapons by non-State actors, including terrorists, concerns which have highlighted the necessity of achieving universal adherence to the Convention, as well as the high level of readiness of the Organization for the Prohibition of Chemical Weapons, and stresses that the full and effective implementation of all provisions of the Convention, including those on national implementation (article VII) and assistance and protection (article X), constitutes an important contribution to the efforts of the United Nations in the global fight against terrorism in all its forms and manifestations;

8. *Emphasizes* that the full implementation of the provisions of the Convention at the national level, including the timely submission of accurate and complete declarations in accordance with the provisions of the Convention, and updates to those declarations, is essential to ensuring the efficiency and effectiveness of the Convention regime;

9. *Notes* that the effective application of the verification system builds confidence in compliance with the Convention by States parties;

10. *Stresses* the importance of the Organization for the Prohibition of Chemical Weapons in verifying compliance with the provisions of the Convention as well as in promoting the timely and efficient accomplishment of all its objectives;

11. *Urges* all States parties to the Convention to meet in full and on time their obligations under the Convention and to support the Organization for the Prohibition of Chemical Weapons in its implementation activities;

12. *Welcomes* progress made in the national implementation of article VII obligations, commends the States parties and the Technical Secretariat for assisting other States parties, on request, with the implementation of the follow-up to the plan of action regarding article VII obligations, urges States parties that have not fulfilled their obligations under article VII to do so without further delay, in accordance with their constitutional processes, and notes that the Third Review Conference noted the commitment of States parties to adopt, in accordance with constitutional processes, the measures necessary to fully implement their obligations under the Convention as a matter of priority and to keep the effectiveness of these measures under review;

13. *Emphasizes* the continuing relevance and importance of the provisions of article X of the Convention, welcomes the activities of the Organization for the Prohibition of Chemical Weapons in relation to assistance and protection against chemical weapons, supports further efforts by both States parties and the Technical Secretariat to promote a high level of readiness to respond to chemical weapons threats as articulated in article X, and welcomes the effectiveness and efficiency of the increased focus on making full use of regional and subre-

gional capacities and expertise, including taking advantage of established training centres;

14. *Acknowledges with appreciation* the establishment of the International Support Network for Victims of Chemical Weapons and of a voluntary trust fund for that purpose;

15. *Reaffirms* that the provisions of the Convention shall be implemented in a manner that avoids hampering the economic or technological development of States parties and international co-operation in the field of chemical activities for purposes not prohibited under the Convention, including the international exchange of scientific and technical information, and chemicals and equipment for the production, processing or use of chemicals for purposes not prohibited under the Convention;

16. *Underlines* that the comprehensive implementation of article XI of the Convention reinforces capacity-building in each State party and, in doing so, reinforces the ability of States parties to fully implement the Convention, and in this context also underlines the importance of assistance and national capacity-building in the field of chemical activities for purposes not prohibited under the Convention;

17. *Commends* the adoption of decision C-16/DEC.10 of 1 December 2011 on the components of an agreed framework for the full implementation of article XI by the Conference of the States Parties at its sixteenth session, and recognizes that the decision provides guidance for the full, effective and non-discriminatory implementation of article XI and identifies avenues for further work that would advance its objectives;

18. *Notes with appreciation* the ongoing work of the Organization for the Prohibition of Chemical Weapons to achieve the object and purpose of the Convention, to ensure the full implementation of its provisions, including those for international verification of compliance with it, and to provide a forum for consultation and cooperation among States parties;

19. *Commends* the desire expressed at the Third Review Conference to improve interaction with the chemical industry, the scientific community, academia and civil society organizations engaged in issues relevant to the Convention, and to cooperate as appropriate with other relevant international and regional organizations, in promoting the goals of the Convention;

20. *Welcomes* the cooperation between the United Nations and the Organization for the Prohibition of Chemical Weapons within the framework of the relationship agreement between the United Nations and the Organization,[7] in accordance with the provisions of the Convention;

21. *Also welcomes* the awarding of the Nobel Peace Prize for 2013 to the Organization for the Prohibition of Chemical Weapons for its extensive efforts to eliminate chemical weapons;

22. *Decides* to include in the provisional agenda of its sixty-ninth session, under the item entitled "General and complete disarmament", the sub-item entitled "Implementation of the Convention on the Prohibition of the Development, Production, Stockpiling and Use of Chemical Weapons and on Their Destruction".

60th plenary meeting
5 December 2013

---

[7] United Nations, Treaty Series, vol. 2160, No. 1240.

30. RELATIONSHIP WITH OTHER INTERNATIONAL ORGANISATIONS

30.1 Cooperation with international organisations

C-VI/DEC.15 adopted by the Conference of the States Parties at its Sixth Session on 17 May 2001 and entitled "Cooperation with International Organisations"

The Conference

Recalling that Article VIII, subparagraph 34(a) of the Convention provides that the Executive Council shall conclude agreements or arrangements with States and international organisations on behalf of the OPCW, subject to prior approval by the Conference of the States Parties;

Recognising that the effective implementation of the Convention can be facilitated by cooperation between the OPCW and other international organisations;

Hereby:

Gives its approval that the Executive Council consider and conclude the negotiated texts of cooperation agreements between the OPCW and other international organisations, as may be required for the effective implementation of the Convention.

30.2 1986 Vienna Convention on the Law of Treaties between States and International Organisations or between International Organisations

C-V/DEC.7 adopted by the Conference of the States Parties at its Fifth Session on 17 May 2000 and entitled "1986 Vienna Convention on the Law of Treaties between States and International Organisations or between International Organisations"

The Conference

Recalling that the Vienna Convention on the Law of Treaties between States and International Organisations or between International Organisations of 21 March 1986 (as contained in the annex to EC XV/DEC/CRP.6, dated 12 April 1999, hereinafter the "1986 Vienna Convention") is one of the conventions codifying the law of treaties which has been adopted under the aegis of the United Nations;

Considering that the codification of the practice of treaties concluded between States and international organisations or between international organisations promotes acceptance of and respect for the principles of international law;

Having considered the Note by the Director-General on the 1986 Vienna Convention on the Law of Treaties between States and International Organisations or between International Organisations (EC-XV/DG.11 and Add.1, dated 9 April and 29 July 1999, respectively);

Noting that the OPCW is entitled to accede to the 1986 Vienna Convention under Article 84, paragraph 1 of that Convention;

Noting further the recommendation of the Executive Council set out in EC-XVI/DEC.1, dated 24 September 1999,

Hereby:

Authorises the Director-General, on behalf of the Organisation for the Prohibition of Chemical Weapons, to deposit with the Secretary-General of the United Nations as Depositary for the 1986 Vienna Convention the instrument of accession of the OPCW to the 1986 Vienna Convention on the Law of Treaties between States and International Organisations or between International Organisations.

History

31. PROTOCOL FOR THE PROHIBITION OF THE USE IN WAR OF ASPHYXIATING, POISONOUS OR OTHER GASES, AND OF BACTERIOLOGICAL METHODS OF WARFARE[1], 1925 (GENEVA PROTOCOL OF 1925)

Protocol for the Prohibition of the Use in War of Asphyxiating, Poisonous or Other Gases, and of Bacteriological Methods of Warfare signed in Geneva on 17 June 1925

The undersigned Plenipotentiaries, in the name of their respective governments:

Whereas the use in war of asphyxiating, poisonous or other gases, and of all analogous liquids, materials or devices, has been justly condemned by the general opinion of the civilised world; and

Whereas the prohibition of such use has been declared in Treaties to which the majority of Powers of the world are Parties; and

To the end that this prohibition shall be universally accepted as a part of International Law, binding alike the conscience and the practice of nations;

Declare:

1. That the High Contracting Parties, so far as they are not already Parties to Treaties prohibiting such use, accept this prohibition, agree to extend this prohibition to the use of bacteriological methods of warfare and agree to be bound as between themselves according to the terms of this declaration.
2. The High Contracting Parties will exert every effort to induce other States to accede to the present Protocol. Such accession will be notified to the Government of the French Republic, and by the latter to all signatories and acceding Powers, and will take effect on the date of the notification by the Government of the French Republic.
3. The present Protocol, of which the English and French texts are both authentic, shall be ratified as soon as possible. It shall bear to-day's date.
4. The ratifications of the present Protocol shall be addressed to the Government of the French Republic, which will at once notify the deposit of such ratification to each of the signatory and acceding Powers.
5. The instruments of ratification of and accession to the present Protocol will remain deposited in the archives of the Government of the French Republic.
6. The present Protocol will come into force for each signatory Power as from the date of deposit of its ratification, and, from that moment, each Power will be bound as regards other Powers which have already deposited their ratifications.

In witness whereof the Plenipotentiaries have signed the present Protocol.

Done at Geneva in a single copy, the seventeenth day of June, One Thousand Nine Hundred and Twenty-Five.

---

[1] Employing asphyxiating, poisonous or other gases, and all analogous liquids, materials or devices is defined as a war crime as per Article 8, paragraph b(xviii) of the Rome Statute.

32. UN GENERAL ASSEMBLY RESOLUTIONS

32.1 United Nations General Assembly Resolution 42/37 (1987)

Resolution A/RES/42/37 adopted by the United Nations General Assembly at its Eighty Fourth Plenary Meeting on 30 November 1987 and entitled "Chemical and bacteriological (biological) weapons"

A.
CHEMICAL AND BACTERIOLOGICAL (BIOLOGICAL) WEAPONS

The General Assembly,

Recalling its previous resolution relating to the complete and effective prohibition of the development, production and stockpiling of all chemical weapons and to their destruction,

Reaffirming the urgent necessity of strict observance by all States of the principles and objectives of the Protocol for the Prohibition of the Use in War of Asphyxiating, Poisonous or Other Gases, and of Bacteriological Methods of Warfare signed at Geneva on 17 June 1925[1] and of the adherence by all States to the Convention on the Prohibition of the Development, Production and Stockpiling of Bacteriological (Biological) and Toxin Weapons and on Their Destruction, signed in London, Moscow and Washington on 10 April 1972,[2]

Taking note of the Final Document of the Second Review Conference of the Parties to the Convention on the Prohibition of the Development, Production and Stockpiling of Bacteriological (Biological) and Toxin Weapons and on Their Destruction, adopted by consensus on 26 September 1986,[3] and in particular of article IX of the Final Declaration of the Conference,[4]

Having considered the report of the Conference on Disarmament,[5] which incorporates, inter alia, the report of its Ad Hoc Committee on Chemical Weapons,[6] and noting that following the precedents set over the past three years, consultations are continuing during the intersessional period, thus increasing the time devoted to negotiations,

Convinced of the necessity that all efforts be exerted for the continuation and successful conclusion of negotiations on the prohibition of the development, production, stockpiling and use of all chemical weapons and on their destruction,

Noting the bilateral and other discussions, including the ongoing exchange of views between the Union of Soviet Socialist Republics and United States of America in the framework of the multilateral negotiations, on issues related to the prohibition of chemical weapons,

Noting further with appreciation the efforts made at all levels by States to facilitate the earliest conclusion of a Convention and, in particular, the concrete steps designed to promote confidence and to contribute directly to that goal,

Wishing to encourage Member States to take further initiatives to promote confidence and openness in the negotiations and to provide further information to facilitate prompt resolution of outstanding issues, thus contributing to an early agreement on the Convention on the prohibition of the development, production, stockpiling and use of all chemical weapons and on their destruction,

---

[1] League of Nations, *Treaty Series*, vol. XCIV (1929), N° 2138.
[2] Resolution 2826 (XXVI), annex.
[3] BWC/CONF.II/13.
[4] *Ibid.*, part II.
[5] *Official Records of the General Assembly, Forty-second Session, Supplement N° 27* (A/42/27).
[6] *Ibid.*, para. 79.

1. Taking note with satisfaction of the work of the Conference on Disarmament during its 1987 session regarding the prohibition of chemical weapons, and in particular appreciates the progress in the work of its Ad Hoc Committee on Chemical Weapons on that question and the tangible results recorded in its report;

2. Expresses again none the less its regret and concern that notwithstanding the progress made in 1987, a Convention on the complete and effective prohibition of the development, production, stockpiling and use of all chemical weapons and on their destruction has not yet been elaborated;

3. Urges again the Conference on Disarmament, as a matter of high priority, to intensify, during its 1988 session, the negotiations on such a Convention and to reinforce further its efforts by, *inter alia*, increasing the time during the year that it devotes to such negotiations, taking into account all existing proposals and future initiatives, with a view to the final elaboration of a Convention at the earliest possible date, and to re-establish its Ad Hoc Committee on Chemical Weapons for this purpose with the mandate to be agreed upon by the Conference at the beginning of its 1988 session;

4. Requests the Conference on Disarmament to report to the General Assembly at its forty-third session on the results of its negotiations.

84th plenary meeting
30 November 1987

B.

SECOND REVIEW CONFERENCE OF THE PARTIES TO THE CONVENTION
ON THE PROHIBITION OF THE DEVELOPMENT, PRODUCTION AND
STOCKPILING OF BACTERIOLOGICAL (BIOLOGICAL) AND TOXIN WEAPONS
AND ON THEIR DESTRUCTION

The General Assembly,

Recalling its resolution 2826 (XXVI) of 16 December 1971, in which it commended the Convention on the Prohibition of the Development, Production and Stockpiling of Bacteriological (Biological) and Toxin Weapons and on Their Destruction and expressed the hope for the widest possible adherence to the Convention,

Recalling its resolution 39/65 D of 12 December 1984, in which it noted that, at the request of a majority of States parties to the Convention, a second Review Conference of the Parties to the Convention would be held in 1986,

Recalling that the States parties to the Convention met at Geneva from 8 to 26 September 1986 to review the operation of the Convention with a view to assuring that the purposes of the preamble to and the provisions of the Convention, including the provisions concerning negotiations on chemical weapons, were being realized,

Recalling also its resolution 41/58 A of 3 December 1986, in which it, *inter alia*, noted with appreciation on that on 26 September 1986, the Second Review Conference of the Parties to the Convention on the Prohibition of the Development, Production and Stockpiling of Bacteriological (Biological) and Toxin Weapons and on Their Destruction adopted by consensus a Final Declaration,[4]

Noting with satisfaction that, at the time of the Second Review Conference of the Parties to the Convention, there were more than a hundred States parties to the Convention, including all the permanent members of the Security Council,

1. Notes with appreciation that, in accordance with the Final Declaration of the Second Review Conference of the Parties to the Convention on the Prohibition of the Development, Production and Stockpiling of Bacteriological (Biological) and Toxin Weapons and on Their Destruction, an Ad Hoc Meeting of Scientific and Technical Experts from States parties to the

Convention was held at Geneva from 31 March to 15 April 1987, which adopted by consensus a report[7] finalizing the modalities for the exchange of information and data agreed to in the Final Declaration, thus enabling States parties to follow a standardized procedure;

2.   Notes that the Ad Hoc Meeting of Scientific and Technical Experts from States parties to the Convention agreed in its report that the first exchange of information and data should take place not later than 15 October 1987 and that thereafter information to be given on an annual basis should be provided through the Department for Disarmament Affairs of the Secretariat not later than 15 April;

3.   Notes with satisfaction that the first such exchange of information and data has commenced;

4.   Requests the Secretary-General to render the necessary assistance and to provide such services as may be required for the implementation of the relevant parts of the Final Declaration;

5.   Calls upon all signatory States that have not ratified or acceded to the Convention to do so without delay, and also calls upon those States which have not yet signed the Convention to join the States parties thereto at an early date, thus contributing to the achievement of universal adherence to the Convention and to international confidence.

84th plenary meeting
30 November 1987

C.
MEASURES TO UPHOLD THE AUTHORITY OF THE 1925 GENEVA PROTOCOL AND TO SUPPORT THE CONCLUSION OF A CHEMICAL WEAPONS CONVENTION

The General Assembly,

Recalling the provisions of the Protocol for the Prohibition of the Use in War of Asphyxiating, Poisonous or Other Gases, and of Bacteriological Methods of Warfare, signed at Geneva on 17 June 1925[1], and other relevant rules of customary international law,

Recalling also the necessity of the adherence by all States to the Convention on the Prohibition of the Development, Production and Stockpiling of Bacteriological (Biological) and Toxin Weapons and on Their Destruction, signed in London, Moscow and Washington on 10 April 1972,[2]

Reiterating its concern about reports that chemical weapons have been used and over indications of their emergence in an increasing number of national arsenals, as well as about the growing risk that they may be used again,

Noting with satisfaction that the Conference on Disarmament is actively engaged in negotiating a Convention on the prohibition of the development, production, stockpiling and use of all chemical weapons and on their destruction,[8] including detailed provisions for the on-site verification of compliance with the Convention, and expressing its support for the early and successful conclusion of those negotiations,

Noting also that prompt and impartial investigation of reports of possible use of chemical and bacteriological weapons would further enhance the authority of the 1925 Geneva Protocol,

Expressing its appreciation for the work of the Secretary-General, and noting the procedures available to him in support of the principles and objectives of the 1925 Geneva Protocol,

1.   Renews its call to all States to observe strictly the principles and objectives of the 1925 Protocol for the Prohibition of the Use in War of Asphyxiating, Poisonous or Other Gases, and of Bacteriological Methods of Warfare, and condemns all actions that violate this obligation;

2.   Urges all States to be guided in their national policies by the need to curb the spread of chemical weapons;

---

[7]   BWC/CONF.II/EX/2.

[8]   See *Official Records of the General Assembly, Forty-second Session, Supplement N° 27* (A/42/27) sect. III.D.

3.   Recognizes the need, upon the entry into force of a chemical weapons Convention, to review the modalities available to the Secretary-General for the investigation of reports of the possible use of chemical weapons;

4.   Requests the Secretary-General to carry out investigations in response to reports that may be brought to his attention by any Member State concerning the possible use of chemical and bacteriological (biological) or toxin weapons that may constitute a violation of the 1925 Geneva Protocol or other relevant rules of customary international law in order to ascertain the facts of the matter and to report promptly the results of any such investigation to all Member States;

5.   Requests the Secretary-General, with the assistance of qualified experts provided by interested Member States to develop further technical guidelines and procedures available to him for the timely and efficient investigation of such reports of the possible use of chemical and bacteriological (biological) or toxin weapons;

6.   Also requests the Secretary-General, in meeting the objectives set forth in paragraph 4 above, to compile and maintain lists of qualified experts provided by Member States whose services could be made available at short note to undertake such investigations, and of laboratories with the capability to undertake testing for the presence of agents the use of which is prohibited;

7.   Further requests the Secretary-General, in meeting the objectives of paragraph 4 above:
     (a) To appoint experts to undertake investigation of the reported activities;
     (b) Where appropriate, to make the necessary arrangements for experts to collect and examine evidence and to undertake such testing as may be required;
     (c) To seek, in any such investigation, assistance as appropriate from Member States and the relevant international organizations;

8.   Requests Member States and the relevant international organizations to co-operate fully with the Secretary-General in the above-mentioned work;

9.   Requests the Secretary-General to submit a report to the General Assembly at its forty-third session on the implementation of the present resolution.

84th plenary meeting
30 November 1987

32.2 United Nations General Assembly Resolution 47/39 (1992)

Resolution A/RES/47/39 adopted by the United Nations General Assembly at its Seventy Fourth Plenary Meeting on 30 November 1992 and entitled "47/39. Convention on the Prohibition of the Development, Production, Stockpiling and Use of Chemical Weapons and on Their Destruction" based on the report of the First Committee (A/47/690)

The General Assembly

Recalling the long-standing determination of the international community to achieve the effective prohibition of the development, production, stockpiling and use of chemical weapons, and their destruction, as well as the continuing support for measures to uphold the authority of the Protocol for the Prohibition of the Use in War of Asphyxiating, Poisonous or Other Gases, and of Bacteriological Methods of Warfare, signed at Geneva on 17 June 1925,[9] as expressed by consensus in many previous resolutions,

Recalling in particular its resolution 46/35 C of 6 December 1991, in which the Assembly strongly urged the Conference on Disarmament, as a matter of the highest priority, to resolve

---

[9] League of Nations, *Treaty Series*, vol. XCIV (1929), No. 2138.

outstanding issues so as to achieve a final agreement on a Convention on the prohibition of the development, production, stockpiling and use of chemical weapons and on their destruction during its 1992 session,

Bearing in mind the Final Declaration of the Conference of States Parties to the 1925 Geneva Protocol and Other Interested States,[10] held in Paris from 7 to 11 January 1989, in which participating States stressed their determination to prevent any recourse to chemical weapons by completely eliminating them,

Determined to make progress towards general and complete disarmament under strict and effective international control, including the prohibition and elimination of all types of weapons of mass destruction,

Convinced, therefore, of the urgent necessity of a total ban on chemical weapons, so as to abolish an entire category of weapons of mass destruction, and thus to eliminate the risk to mankind of renewed use of these inhumane weapons,

Welcoming the draft Convention on the Prohibition of the Development, Production, Stockpiling and Use of Chemical Weapons and on Their Destruction,[11] adopted by the Conference on Disarmament and contained in its report, the result of many years of intensive negotiations, which constitutes an historic achievement in the field of arms control and disarmament,

Also convinced that the Convention, particularly as adherence to it approaches universality, will contribute to the maintenance of international peace and improve the security of all States and that it therefore merits the strong support of the entire international community,

Further convinced that the implementation of the Convention should promote expanded international trade, technological development and economic cooperation in the chemical sector, in order to enhance the economic and technological development of all States parties,

Determined to ensure the efficient and cost-effective implementation of the Convention,

Recalling the support for the prohibition of chemical weapons expressed in the declaration by representatives of the world's chemical industry at the Government-Industry Conference against Chemical Weapons, held at Canberra from 18 to 22 September 1989,[12]

Bearing in mind the relevant references to the Convention in the final documents of the Tenth Conference of Heads of State or Government of Non-Aligned Countries, held at Jakarta from 1 to 6 September 1992,[13]

Welcoming the invitation of the President of the French Republic to participate in a ceremony to sign the Convention in Paris on 13 January 1993,

1. Commends the Convention on the Prohibition of the Development, Production, Stockpiling and Use of Chemical Weapons and on Their Destruction, as contained in the report of the Conference on Disarmament;

2. Requests the Secretary-General, as depositary of the Convention, to open it for signature in Paris on 13 January 1993;

3. Calls upon all States to sign and, thereafter, according to their respective constitutional processes, to become parties to the Convention at the earliest possible date, thus contributing to its rapid entry into force and to the early achievement of universal adherence;

4. Also calls upon all States to ensure the effective implementation of this unprecedented, global, comprehensive and verifiable multilateral disarmament agreement, thereby enhancing cooperative multilateralism as a basis for international peace and security;

5. Also requests the Secretary-General to provide such services as may be requested by the signatory States to initiate the work of the Preparatory Commission for the Organization on the Prohibition of Chemical Weapons;

---

[10] A/44/88, annex.

[11] *Official Records of the General Assembly, Forty-seventh Session, Supplement No. 27* (A/47/27), appendix I.

[12] See A/C.1/44/4.

[13] See A/47/675-S/24816, annex.

6. Further requests the Secretary-General, as depositary of the Convention, to report to the General Assembly at its forty-eighth session on the status of signatures and ratifications of the Convention.

74th plenary meeting
30 November 1992

33. PARIS RESOLUTION ESTABLISHING THE PREPARATORY COMMISSION FOR THE OPCW AND RELATED UNDERSTANDINGS

Paris Resolution Adopted by the Signatory States to the Convention at the Signing Ceremony in Paris, 13 to 15 January 1993

RESOLUTION ESTABLISHING THE PREPARATORY COMMISSION FOR THE ORGANISATION FOR THE PROHIBITION OF CHEMICAL WEAPONS

The States signatories of the Convention on the Prohibition of the Development, Production, Stockpiling and Use of Chemical Weapons and on Their Destruction, adopted by the Conference on Disarmament at Geneva on 3 September 1992,

Having decided to take all necessary measures to ensure the rapid and effective establishment of the future Organisation for the Prohibition of Chemical Weapons,

Having decided to this end to establish a Preparatory Commission,

1. Approve the Text on the Establishment of a Preparatory Commission, as annexed to the present resolution;

2. Request the Secretary-General, in accordance with paragraph 5 of resolution A/RES/47/39, adopted by the General Assembly on 30 November 1992, on the Convention on the Prohibition of the Development, Production, Stockpiling and Use of Chemical Weapons and on Their Destruction, to provide the services required to initiate the work of the Preparatory Commission for the Organisation for the Prohibition of Chemical Weapons.

TEXT ON THE ESTABLISHMENT OF A PREPARATORY COMMISSION

1. There is hereby established the Preparatory Commission for the Organisation for the Prohibition of Chemical Weapons (hereinafter referred to as "the Commission") for the purpose of carrying out the necessary preparations for the effective implementation of the Convention on the Prohibition of the Development, Production, Stockpiling and Use of Chemical Weapons and on their Destruction, and for preparing for the first session of the Conference of the States Parties to that Convention.

2. The Secretary-General of the United Nations shall convene the Commission for its first session at The Hague, Kingdom of the Netherlands, not later than 30 days after the Convention has been signed by 50 States.

3. The Seat of the Commission shall be The Hague, Kingdom of the Netherlands.

4. The Commission shall be composed of all States which sign the Convention. Each signatory State shall have one representative in the Commission, who may be accompanied by alternates and advisers.

5. The expenses of the Commission, including those of the Provisional Technical Secretariat, shall be met by the States signatories to the Convention, participating in the Commission, in accordance with the United Nations scale of assessment, adjusted to take into account differences between the United Nations membership and the participation of States signatories in the Commission and timing of signature. The Commission and the Provisional Technical Secretariat may also benefit from voluntary contributions.

6. All decisions of the Commission should be taken by consensus. If, notwithstanding the efforts of representatives to achieve consensus, an issue comes up for voting, the Chairman of the Commission shall defer the vote for 24 hours and during this period of deferment shall make every effort to facilitate achievement of consensus, and shall report to the Commission

before the end of the period. If consensus is not possible at the end of 24 hours, the Commission shall take decisions on questions of procedure by a simple majority of the members present and voting. Decisions on matters of substance shall be taken by two-thirds majority of the members present and voting. When the issue arises as to whether the question is one of substance or not, that question shall be treated as a matter of substance unless otherwise decided by the Commission by the majority required for decisions on matters of substance.

7. The Commission shall have such legal capacity as necessary for the exercise of its functions and the fulfilment of its purposes.

8. The Commission shall:

a.   Elect its Chairman and other officers, adopt its rules of procedure, meet as often as necessary and establish such committees as it deems useful;

b.   Appoint its Executive Secretary;

c.   Establish a Provisional Technical Secretariat to assist the Commission in its activity and to exercise such functions as the Commission may determine, and appoint the necessary staff in charge of preparatory work concerning the main activities to be carried out by the Technical Secretariat to be established by the Convention. Only nationals of signatory States shall be appointed to the Provisional Technical Secretariat;

d.   Establish administrative and financial regulations in respect of its own expenditure and accounts.

9. The Commission shall make arrangements for the first session of the Conference of the States Parties, including the preparation of a draft agenda and draft rules of procedure.

10. The Commission shall undertake, *inter alia*, the following tasks concerning the organisation and work of the Technical Secretariat and requiring immediate attention after entry into force of the Convention:

a.   Elaboration of a detailed staffing pattern of the Technical Secretariat, including decision-making flow charts;

b.   Assessments of personnel requirements;

c.   Staff rules for recruitment and service conditions;

d.   Recruitment and training of technical personnel and support staff;

e.   Organisation of office and administrative services;

f.   Preparation of administrative and financial regulations;

g.   Purchase and standardisation of equipment.

11. The Commission shall undertake, *inter alia*, the following tasks on matters of the Organisation requiring immediate attention after the entry into force of the Convention:

a.   Preparation of programme of work and budget of the first year of activities of the Organisation;

b.   Preparation of detailed budgetary provisions for the Organisation taking into account that the budget shall comprise two separate chapters, one relating to administrative and other costs, and one relating to verification costs;

c.   Preparation of the scale of financial contributions to the Organisation;

d.   Preparation of administrative and financial regulations for the Organisation providing for, *inter alia*:

i.   Proper financial control and accounting by the Organisation;

ii.   Preparation and approval of periodic financial statements by the Organisation;

iii. Independent audit of the Organisation's financial statements;

iv.   Annual presentation of the audited financial statements to a regular session of the Conference of the States Parties for formal acceptance;

e.   Development of arrangements to facilitate the election of 20 members for a term of one year for the first election of the Executive Council.

12. The Commission shall develop, *inter alia*, the following draft agreements, provisions and guidelines for consideration and approval by the Conference of the States Parties pursuant to Article VIII, paragraph 21 (i) of the Convention:

a. Guidelines on detailed procedures for verification and for the conduct of inspections, in accordance with *inter alia*, Part II, paragraph 42, of the Verification Annex;

b. Lists of items to be stockpiled for emergency and humanitarian assistance in accordance with Article VIII, paragraph 39 (b);

c. Agreements between the Organisation and the States Parties in accordance with Article VIII, paragraph 50;

d. Procedures for the provision of information by States Parties on their programmes related to protective purposes, in accordance with Article X, paragraph 4;

e. A list of approved equipment, in accordance with Part II, paragraph 27, of the Verification Annex;

f. Procedures for the inspection of equipment, in accordance with Part II, paragraph 29, of the Verification Annex;

g. Procedures concerning the implementation of safety requirements for activities of inspectors and inspection assistants, in accordance with Part II, paragraph 43, of the Verification Annex;

h. Procedures for inclusion in the inspection manual concerning the security, integrity and preservation of samples and for ensuring the protection of the confidentiality of samples transferred for analysis off-site, in accordance with Part II, paragraph 56, of the Verification Annex;

i. Models for facility agreements in accordance with Part III, paragraph 8, of the Verification Annex;

j. Appropriate detailed procedures to implement Part III, paragraph 11 and 12 of the Verification Annex, in accordance with paragraph 13 of that Part;

k. Deadlines for submission of the information specified in Part IV (A), paragraphs 30 to 32 of the Verification Annex, in accordance with paragraph 34 of that Part;

l. Recommendations for determining the frequency of systematic on-site inspections of storage facilities, in accordance with Part IV (A), paragraph 44, of the Verification Annex;

m. Recommendations for guidelines for transitional verification arrangements, in accordance with Part IV (A), paragraph 51, of the Verification Annex;

n. Guidelines to determine the usability of chemical weapons produced between 1925 and 1946, in accordance with Part IV (B), paragraph 5, of the Verification Annex;

o. Guidelines for determining the frequency of systematic on-site inspections of chemical weapons production facilities, in accordance with Part V, paragraph 54, of the Verification Annex;

p. Criteria for toxicity, corrosiveness and, if applicable, other technical factors, in accordance with Part V, paragraph 71 (b), of the Verification Annex;

q. Guidelines to assess the risk to the object and purpose of the Convention posed by the relevant chemicals, the characteristics of the facility and the nature of the activities carried out there, in accordance with Part VI, paragraph 23, of the Verification Annex;

r. Models for facility agreements covering detailed inspection procedures, in accordance with Part VI, paragraph 27, of the Verification Annex;

s. Guidelines to assess the risk to the object and purpose of the Convention posed by the quantities of chemicals produced, the characteristics of the facility and the nature of the activities carried out there, in accordance with Part VI, paragraph 30, of the Verification Annex;

t. Guidelines for provisions regarding scheduled chemicals in low concentrations, including in mixtures, in accordance with Part VII, paragraph 5, and Part VIII, paragraph 5, of the Verification Annex;

u. Guidelines for procedures on the release of classified information by the Organisation, in accordance with paragraph 2 (c) (iii) of the Confidentiality Annex;

v.   A classification system for levels of sensitivity of confidential data and documents, taking into account relevant work undertaken in the preparation of the Convention, in accordance with paragraph 2 (d) of the Confidentiality Annex;

w.   Recommendations for procedures to be followed in case of breaches or alleged breaches of confidentiality, in accordance with paragraph 18 of the Confidentiality Annex.

13. Pursuant to Article VIII, paragraph 50, of the Convention, the Commission shall develop the Headquarters Agreement with the Host Country, based, *inter alia*, on the privileges, immunities and practical arrangements as specified in Annex 2 to this text.

14. The Commission shall:

a.   Facilitate the exchange of information between signatory States concerning legal and administrative measures for the implementation of the Convention and, if requested, give advice to signatory States on these matters;

b.   Prepare such studies, reports and records as it deems necessary.

15. The Commission shall prepare a final report on all matters within its mandate for the first session of the Conference of the States Parties and the first meeting of the Executive Council.

16. The property, functions and recommendations of the Commission shall be transferred to the Organisation at the first session of the Conference of the States Parties. The Commission shall make recommendations to the Conference of the States Parties on this matter.

17. The Commission shall remain in existence until the conclusion of the first session of the Conference of the States Parties.

18. The Host Country undertakes to accord the Commission, its staff, as well as the delegates of signatory States such legal status, privileges and immunities as are necessary for the independent exercise of their functions in connection with the Commission and the fulfilment of its object and purpose, as outlined in Annex 1 to this text.

ANNEX 1
PRIVILEGES, IMMUNITIES AND PRACTICAL ARRANGEMENTS
IN CONNECTION WITH THE HOSTING OF THE PREPARATORY COMMISSION

1.   The Government of the Netherlands is prepared to grant to the delegates to the Preparatory Commission, who have been notified as such by the sending State, and who reside in The Hague, privileges and immunities similar to those granted by the Government of the Netherlands to diplomats of comparable rank of diplomatic missions accredited to the Netherlands.

2.   The Government of the Netherlands is prepared to apply Article V of the Convention on the Privileges and Immunities of the Specialised Agencies of 21 November 1947 to non-residing delegates to the Preparatory Commission while exercising their functions and during their journeys to and from the place of meeting.

3.   The Government of the Netherlands is prepared to grant to the Executive Secretary and staff members of the Preparatory Commission privileges and immunities similar to those which the Government of the Netherlands has undertaken to grant to the Director-General and staff members of the Organisation for the Prohibition of Chemical Weapons, as set out under Annex 3, "Privileges and Immunities", points 1, 2 and 3, "Social Security", point 13, and "Employment", points 14 and 15.

4.   It is understood that the above will be elaborated in an agreement to be concluded with the Government of the Netherlands.

5.   The practical arrangements for the hosting for the Preparatory Commission shall be based on the information submitted and commitments undertaken by the Netherlands and by the City of The Hague as contained in Annex 3 on the Netherlands bid, under "Building and Equipment".

Annex 2
PRIVILEGES, IMMUNITIES AND PRACTICAL ARRANGEMENTS
TO BE LAID DOWN IN THE HEADQUARTERS AGREEMENT

1. The Headquarters Agreement between the Organisation and the Netherlands, where the seat
    of the Organisation is located, shall be based on the information submitted and commitments
    undertaken by the Netherlands and by the City of The Hague as contained in Annex 3 on the
    Netherlands bid.
2. In order to ensure the effective functioning of the Organisation, the privileges and immunities
    to be laid down in the Headquarters Agreement shall be in conformity with the regime of the
    Convention on the Privileges and Immunities of the Specialised Agencies of 21 November
    1947 (United Nations General Assembly Resolution 179/II).
3. In order to ensure the effective functioning of the Organisation, the Headquarters Agreement
    shall also include provisions for:
    3.1 the granting to Heads of Delegations to the Organisation of ambassadorial rank the title
         of Permanent Representative and the privileges and immunities to which Ambassadors
         to the Netherlands are entitled;
    3.2 the establishment of a tax-free commissary for the officials of the Organisation entitled
         to duty free privileges;
    3.3 the exemption from tax on or in respect of salaries and emoluments paid by the Organi-
         sation; the Host Country shall not take into account the salaries and emoluments thus
         exempted when assessing the amount of tax to be applied to income from other sources.

Annex 3
INFORMATION SUBMITTED AND COMMITMENTS
UNDERTAKEN BY THE NETHERLANDS AND BY THE CITY OF THE HAGUE

1. The following information is given and commitments are undertaken by the Netherlands and
    by the City of The Hague with respect to arrangements for the hosting of the Preparatory
    Commission as well as for the Headquarters Agreement. These are reflected in:
    –   the Annex to Paper No. 1 of 28 April 1992 of the "Friend of the Chair on the Seat of the
        Organisation";
    –   the Bidbook of 18 May 1992 presented by the Netherlands;
    –   the statement of 2 June 1992, made by Mr. Martini, Acting Burgomaster of The Hague,
        to the Ad Hoc Committee on Chemical Weapons;
    –   the statement of 2 June 1992 made by Mr. M. van Zelm, Programme Director of the
        Prins Maurits Laboratory, to the Ad Hoc Committee on Chemical Weapons.
2. These documents are filed with the Secretariat of the Conference on Disarmament in Geneva.
3. Other aspects may be included in the Headquarters Agreement by mutual agreement.

PRIVILEGES AND IMMUNITIES

1. Full diplomatic privileges will be granted to those staff members of the Organisation and
    their dependants who qualify under the relevant provisions of the Agreement. Pursuant to
    Annex l, the Netherlands is prepared to extend diplomatic privileges to personnel with ranks
    comparable to P-5 and above in conformity with the regime of the Convention on the Privi-
    leges and Immunities of the Specialised Agencies of 21 November 1947 (United Nations
    General Assembly Resolution 179/II).
2. Other staff members will enjoy:
    a.   immunity from legal proceedings of any kind with respect to words spoken or written
         and all acts performed by them in their official capacity;
    b.   in any event, immunity shall not extend to a civil action by a third party for damage aris-

ing from an accident caused by a motor vehicle belonging to, driven by or operated on behalf of a staff member or in respect of a traffic offence involving such a vehicle;

c.   inviolability of all their official papers and documents;

d.   immunity from inspection of official baggage;

e.   exemption from Netherlands income tax on salaries and emoluments paid to them by the Organisation.

Moreover, staff members who do not have the Dutch nationality will:

f.   enjoy exemption with respect to themselves and members of their families who are part of their households from all measures restricting entry and alien registration. Any visas which may be required shall be issued without charge as promptly as possible;

g.   be given the same repatriation facilities in time of international crisis as officials of diplomatic missions, together with members of their families who form part of their households;

h.   not require a work permit for their official duties with the Organisation;

i.   in accordance with the regulations in force, have relief from import duties and taxes, except payment for services, in respect of their furniture and personal effects and the right to export furniture and personal effects with relief from duty on termination of their duties in the Netherlands. Personal effects may include a reasonable number of cars that have been in use in the household and are older than six months.

3.   In addition, persons who have lived outside the Netherlands for at least 12 months before taking up a position with the Organisation will be allowed to import one motor vehicle tax-free. The vehicle should be imported within 12 months after they take up their position and can be sold tax-free after 12 months.

4.   Pursuant to Annex 2, the Netherlands is furthermore prepared to grant to the Heads of Delegation with ambassadorial rank, accredited to the Organisation for the Prohibition of Chemical Weapons, the title of Permanent Representatives and the privileges and immunities to which Ambassadors to the Netherlands are entitled.

BUILDING AND EQUIPMENT

5.   An office building of 3,300 square metres will be supplied free of charge during the preparatory phase (maximum of five years). The building is located at the centre of The Hague near the Peace Palace and several embassies. The Netherlands Congress Centre is 1 km away. The modern office building was built in 1986 and consists of 3,300 square metres of office space divided over five floors. Office space can be made available immediately as soon as the Organisation begins working in The Hague. The building offers sufficient flexibility to allow the Organisation to grow in stages up to a maximum of 200 people. The Hague and the Netherlands will pay for the rent of the office space, parking places for the Organisation, maintenance costs of the building and the installations, energy costs (heating, cooling, electricity, water) and turnkey costs (carpeting, partitioning) during the preparatory phase.

6.   Before the full implementation phase, office space with a maximum of 18,000 square metres is foreseen to be made available for the Organisation in a new purpose-built office building, to be known as the "Peace Tower". Construction can be started as soon as the Organisation can specify the required volume and further details. The building is expected to be completed two and a half years later. The Tower will be situated in the city centre business district next to Central Station[1]

---

[1] [In 1993 the Preparatory Commission expressed its concerns about the security of the Koningen Julianaplein site and requested the Host Country to locate a suitable alternative site. The Host Country agreed and offered the Catsheuvel site on Johan de Wittlaan (see subparagraph 12.5 of the Final Report of the Preparatory Commission, PC-XVI/37).]

For a period of 3 years during the full implementation phase, The Hague and the Netherlands will pay for the rent of the office space, 110 parking places for the Organisation inside the building, maintenance costs of the building and the installations, energy costs (heating, cooling, electricity, water) and turnkey costs (carpeting, partitioning).

The building is flexible enough to allow space to be made available to the Organisation in proportion to the number of staff, up to a maximum of 18,000 square metres. After the period in which the Netherlands Government will pay for the office space as described above, office space can be leased by the Organisation at a guaranteed price of US$ 250 per square metre (indexed on the basis of the 1992 price level, basic rent).

If required expansion needs of the Organisation are known before the end of 1993, the building can be expanded to a maximum of 22,000 square metres. This expansion can be leased by the Organisation at a guaranteed price of US$ 250 per square metre (indexed on the basis of 1992 price levels, basic rent).

7.   When needed, a conference room for approximately 170 delegations will be made available, free of charge, during the maximum eight year period of the Netherlands bid at the nearby Peace Palace or Netherlands Congress Centre.

8.   Subject to the promise that all office supplies, service contracts and other office materials for which the Organisation will pay, shall be purchased at the normal going rates from a supplier designated by The Hague, the Netherlands offer during the preparatory phase (maximum of five years) includes:
   –   providing all necessary office furniture according to official European standards, free of charge;
   –   providing all the reasonably necessary office equipment, free of charge;
   During the preparatory phase (maximum of five years) the Netherlands offer also includes:
   –   providing a fully integrated digital telephone switchboard, telephones on every desk and 10 fax machines free of charge.

9.   After the preparatory phase during a period of three years office furniture (according to official European standards) and reasonably necessary office equipment will be supplied free of charge on a one-time basis, provided that all office supplies, service contracts and other office materials for which the Organisation will pay, shall be purchased at the normal going rates from a supplier designated by The Hague.[2]

LABORATORY/TRAINING

10.   The Prins Maurits Laboratory (PML) of the Netherlands Organisation for Applied Scientific Research (TNO), a fully independent not-for-profit research organisation, will grant the Organisation access to its database with analytical chemical data, free of charge. This database contains spectrometric and chromatographic data of a large number of compounds relevant to the Convention.

11.   PML is also prepared to provide a technical training programme for 100-150 candidate inspectors of the future Organisation drawn from developing countries mainly. The training programme will be free of charge for the participants.

12.   Finally PML, if needed in co-operation with other TNO institutes, could carry out a number of technical functions of the Organisation, such as analyses of samples, development of analytical chemical methods, synthesis of reference compounds, calibration and development of verification equipment, advice on and development of detection and protection equipment, sampling equipment, seals and markers, etc., at a price determined by the integral costs of its activities.

---

2 [In December 1998, the relationship with the sole supplier was terminated. See subparagraphs 19.4 and 19.5 of C-III/4 and EC-XIII/DEC.2.]

SOCIAL SECURITY

13. If the Organisation establishes its own social security system with comparable coverage to Dutch schemes, the Netherlands Government will exempt the Organisation, its Director and staff members/personnel from compulsory insurance under national social security schemes. The exemption rules will be laid down in the Headquarters Agreement. For persons who are not exempt, compulsory insurance schemes will apply and the Organisation will be responsible for paying contributions.

EMPLOYMENT

14. Non-Dutch employees of international organisations in the Netherlands who do not carry diplomatic status, will be -as a matter of routine- granted work and residence permits for the duration of their employment in the Netherlands.
15. Family members of persons working at the Organisation who have the nationality of one of the member States of the European Community may take up employment in the Netherlands. Members of the family who do not have the nationality of one of the member States of the European Community may take up employment subject to the requirements of the labour market.

GENERAL CONDITIONS RELATING TO THE NETHERLANDS BID

16. The Dutch bid applies if the Organisation is to remain in The Hague throughout its existence.
17. Property, furniture, equipment and other items that are made available will remain the property of the supplier and/or the Netherlands.

Understandings and Supplementary Understandings concluded between the Preparatory Commission and the Host Country in relation to implementation of certain aspects of the Paris Resolution. The Understandings and Supplementary Understandings are contained in the annexes to Conference decision C-I/DEC.5 adopted by the Conference at its First Session on 6 May 1997, entitled "(Preliminary) Tenancy Agreement and related Understandings and Supplementary Understandings", by which the conference confirmed the Understandings.

UNDERSTANDINGS BETWEEN THE HOST COUNTRY AND THE
PREPARATORY COMMISSION FOR THE OPCW
CONCERNING THE IMPLEMENTATION OF
PARAGRAPHS 6, 7, 9 AND 11 OF ANNEX 3 OF THE PARIS RESOLUTION[3]

The Preparatory Commission for the Organisation for the Prohibition of Chemical Weapons (hereinafter called the 'Commission') and the Government of the Kingdom of the Netherlands and the Municipality of The Hague (hereinafter called the 'Host Country'), have reached the following understandings which will form the basis for their future actions with regard to the implementation of paragraphs 6, 7, 9 and 11 of Annex 3 of the Paris Resolution.

---

[3] The Understandings were approved by the Preparatory Commission at its Ninth Session (subparagraph 9.3(b) of PC-IX/11; adopted on 16 January 1995 (subparagraph 9.2 of PC-X/23); and duly incorporated by an Exchange of Letters between the Chairman and Executive Secretary of the Preparatory Commission and the Minister for Foreign Affairs of the Host Country, on 31 January 1995 and 9 March 1995 respectively (subparagraph 9.3 of PC-X/23).

I

1. The Paris Resolution is the basic legal framework in any negotiations between the Commission and the Host Country concerning the OPCW accommodation as well as any other matters part of the Netherlands Bid. The Host Country will remain responsible for the implementation of Annex 3 of the Paris Resolution.

2. The Commission recognises the financial constraints under which the Host Country must function. The Host Country also recognises the constraints under which the Commission must operate. The Commission and the Host Country are therefore willing to cooperate in keeping expenses related to the implementation of paragraphs 6, 7, 9 and 11 of Annex 3 of the Paris Resolution predictable to the greatest extent possible.

3. The Host Country guarantees that as long as the Commission and the OPCW remain in the tailor-made building on the Catsheuvel site, the Commission and the OPCW will never under any circumstances have to pay any compensation whatsoever to anyone for the use of the site. This guarantee applies regardless of whether the Commission and the OPCW rent, lease or buy the tailor-made building, now or in the future from whatever owner.

II

4. The Host Country, in close consultation with the Commission, will conclude a development agreement with the property developer for the construction of the new purpose built office building. The development agreement shall stipulate that the building will be fully ready for occupancy 30 months after signature of the development agreement, provided that the Commission meets the planning deadlines set out in an addendum to the development agreement. The Commission will enter into a preliminary tenancy agreement with the property developer, to be confirmed by the Conference of the States Parties at its First Session, to rent, lease, or buy the new building.

5. In case that the Host Country is not obliged to rent the office building at Laan van Meerdervoort 51 for the full maximum period of 5 years as mentioned in Annex 3, paragraph 5 of the Paris Resolution, the amount of money which would be needed to pay the rent for the remaining period until the end of this period of maximum 5 years, will be used to contribute to the actual rental cost for interim-accommodation for the Commission and/or the OPCW. This contribution will be paid after the mentioned period of 5 years.

6. The Commission undertakes to formally recommend to the Conference of States Parties at its First Session that the OPCW rent or lease, based upon conditions agreed in the above mentioned preliminary agreement, for 15 years (including the three years to be paid by the Host Country in terms specified in paragraph 7 and 8 hereof) the tailor-made building which will be built on the Catsheuvel site. Alternatively, as specified in paragraph 10, the Commission may also recommend to the Conference of States Parties to purchase the building.

7. The Host Country will reimburse the OPCW for the annual rental costs of the building (110 parking places included) and the annual cost of the depreciation of its fit-up (turn key cost) and maintenance costs for a period of three years beginning on the date when the OPCW rents or leases the building. Such reimbursement will amount to the actual costs incurred by the OPCW, as agreed in the tenancy agreement and the development agreement, which are quoted for by PROVAST at Dfl. 5,249,710 per year, indexed to 1997 price levels. In addition to the annual rental costs, for the same period of three years the Host Country will pay the energy costs (heating, cooling, electricity, water).

8. The Host Country will reimburse, additionally, the OPCW for extra costs during the same three year period which may arise out of decisions taken during the design phase, the development phase or the construction phase of the new building, provided that any such decisions have prior approval from the Host Country. The total extra reimbursement of costs mentioned

above in this paragraph will never exceed Dfl. 400,000 per year (indexed as from 1997). Therefore, the total payments of the Host Country specified in paragraphs 7 and 8 hereof shall not exceed the amount of Dfl. 5,700,000 per year (indexed to 1997 price levels).

9. During the balance of 12 years, the cost to the OPCW for the rental of the building will not exceed Dfl. 5,700,000 (indexed to 1997 price levels), provided that any changes in the Programme of Requirements initiated and approved by the Commission (PC-VI/A/4) do not exceed the level specified in paragraph 8 above.

10. Should the Commission or the OPCW decide to purchase the building, the Host Country undertakes to make the same annual financial contribution to the purchase price of the OPCW building as stated in paragraphs 7 and 8 hereof.

11. Security outside the OPCW premises as defined in the OPCW Headquarters Agreement will be provided by the Netherlands at no cost to the OPCW. Internal security within those premises will be the responsibility of the OPCW.

12. The Host Country will provide the OPCW with the conference accommodation and facilities for the First Session of the Conference of the States Parties as well as for the sessions of the Conference of the States Parties during the first two years after entry into force (this does not necessarily imply calendar years).

13. The Host Country will thereafter provide the OPCW with accommodation and facilities for one session of the Conference of the States Parties per year up to 8 February 2001 and for any special sessions when needed during the same period. The accommodation and facilities will be provided to the OPCW for a period requested by the OPCW, with a maximum of 9 days per session as follows:
    – 2 days preparation for the session of the Conference of the States Parties;
    – 5 days for the actual session;
    – 1 day extra;
    – 1 day dismantling of the facilities.

14. The conference accommodation and facilities mentioned in paragraphs 12 and 13 will be in the Netherlands Congress Centre in The Hague, and will consist of the following:
    – 1 fully equipped meeting room with 7 interpreters' booths and debating installation for approximately 140 delegations consisting of 6 persons;
    – Carel Willink Hall and associated rooms as rented by the Commission in June 1993;
    – Frans Hals room, Mesdag 1 & 2 rooms and Maris 1 & 2 rooms, or equivalent space as well as partitioning and curtains necessary to create auxiliary rooms as used during the Sessions of the Commission;
    – For Special Sessions the conference facilities will be limited to the Carel Willink Hall and the associated rooms as rented by the Commission in June 1993, plus the Frans Hals room, Mesdag 1 & 2 rooms and Maris 1 & 2 rooms or equivalent space as well as partitioning and curtains necessary to create auxiliary rooms as used during the Sessions of the Commission;
    – In all cases, additional areas agreed by the OPCW and the Host Country necessary to ensure security.

15. The Host Country will, for a period of three years, reimburse the OPCW for the actual annual cost of the rent or lease of a laboratory and the equipment storage facilities in the Netherlands as well as the turn key cost (carpeting, partitioning) and maintenance costs up to a maximum of Dfl. 250,000 per year (indexed to the prices of the first year of occupation). In addition, during the same period the Host Country will also pay for the energy costs (heating, cooling, electricity, water) with respect to the laboratory and equipment storage facilities. The Commission or the OPCW may itself determine the beginning of the three-year period in question. The Commission or the OPCW can decide to purchase the laboratory and equipment storage facilities in which case the Host Country undertakes to make the same annual financial contribution to the purchase price of the OPCW laboratory and equipment storage facilities.

16. The further implementation of the Netherlands Bid with regard to the supply of office furniture, office equipment, telephones and fax machines will proceed in the same way as at
present.

17. The Host Country will pay the actual costs of certified Module 1 training programme for 135
inspectors, on the condition that any such training programmes will take place in the Netherlands, and will be organised by or under the responsibility of the TNO. The Preparatory
Commission will reimburse the Host Country for accommodation and meals up to Dfl. 700
per week per student.

18. The above paragraphs represent an agreed interpretation of all aspects of paragraphs 6, 7, 9
and 11, including the costs of discharging the Host Country's undertakings, as at November
1994. If circumstances arise in the future, which could not have been foreseen at the moment
of adoption of these understandings and which could affect these interpretations, the Host
Country and the Commission will consult to seek solutions in good faith and in the spirit of
the Paris Resolution.

SUPPLEMENTARY UNDERSTANDINGS BETWEEN THE
PREPARATORY COMMISSION FOR THE OPCW AND THE HOST COUNTRY
RELATING TO THE PRELIMINARY TENANCY AGREEMENT
FOR THE NEW PURPOSE-BUILT OFFICE BUILDING[4]

The Preparatory Commission for the Organisation for the Prohibition of Chemical Weapons (hereinafter called the 'Commission') and the Government of the Kingdom of the Netherlands and
the Municipality of The Hague (hereinafter called the 'Host Country'), further to paragraphs 4,
6, 7 and 8 of the Understandings, which set out the legal and financial arrangements for the new
purpose-built office building, and
        Recalling the Commission's decision (subparagraph 9.6(a) of PC-X/23) that the three-
year period when the rent for the new purpose-built office building will be paid by the Host
Country shall commence on the date of delivery of that building, have reached the following Supplementary Understandings.

1. The Commission will sign with the property developer a Preliminary Tenancy Agreement
which will enter into force after its confirmation by the Conference of the States Parties at its
First Session and will terminate 15 years from the date of delivery of the new purpose-built
office building.

2. If, on the date of delivery of the building, the OPCW does not yet exist, the Secretariat of the
Commission will move into the new building. From that date the OPCW Foundation, acting
as agent for the Host Country, will be the lessee of the building for a maximum term of three
years. The legal relationship between the Commission and the OPCW Foundation during this
period will be arranged in a separate agreement. If the Convention enters into force during
the three-year period, the OPCW will become the lessee and the OPCW Foundation will pay
for the rent for the balance of the three-year period.

3. If the OPCW still does not exist three years after delivery of the building, the Secretariat of
the Commission will have the option to remain in the building on the same terms and conditions. In that case, the Commission will take over from the OPCW Foundation the Tenancy
Agreement as the tenant for a period of one year or until the Commission ceases to exist,
whichever comes earlier. As long as the Commission exists, it will decide on an annual basis
whether to prolong the Tenancy Agreement.

---

[4] The Supplementary Understandings were authorized by the Preparatory Commission at its Eleventh
Session (subparagraph 9.6 of PC-XI/17); approved by the Committee on Relations with the Host Country
on 1 September 1995 (subparagraph 2.1 of PC-XII/HC/7); and duly incorporated in an Exchange of Letters
between the Chairman and the Executive Secretary of the Preparatory Commission and the Minister for
Foreign Affairs a.i. of the Host Country, on 1 September and 28 September 1995 respectively.

4. If the Commission decides not to take over or to prolong the Tenancy Agreement as mentioned under paragraph 3 above, the Secretariat of the Commission will vacate the building. As long as there is no new tenant, the Host Country will assume the necessary guarantees towards the lessor. The lessor and the Host Country will then both have the right and the obligation to look for a new tenant as soon as possible or otherwise to dispose of the building.

5. If the Conference of the States Parties at its First Session does not confirm the Preliminary Tenancy Agreement signed by the Executive Secretary and the property developer, the Host Country will assume the necessary guarantees towards the lessor. The lessor and the Host Country will then both have the right and the obligation to look for a new tenant as soon as possible. In that case the OPCW has the option to remain in the building until the end of the three-year period as mentioned above, at which time it shall either take over the tenancy or vacate the building.

34. PROTOCOL REGARDING THE TRANSFER OF ASSETS, LIABILITIES, RECORDS AND FUNCTIONS FROM THE PREPARATORY COMMISSION TO THE OPCW

C-I/DEC.4 adopted by the Conference of the States Parties at its First Session on 14 May 1997 and entitled "Matters related to the transfer of property, functions and recommendations of the Commission to the OPCW"[1]

The Conference

Recalling that, in accordance with the Paris Resolution, paragraph 16, the property and functions of the Commission shall be transferred to the OPCW and that the legal instrument drawn up to accomplish this is the Draft Protocol Regarding the Transfer of Assets, Liabilities, Records and Functions from the Preparatory Commission for the Organisation for the Prohibition of Chemical Weapons to the Organisation for the Prohibition of Chemical Weapons ("Transfer Protocol"),

Recalling further that, in accordance with the authority delegated to it by the Commission in PC-XV/25, paragraph 7.2, Working Group A, in PC-XVI/A/4, paragraph 3.1, finally approved the Transfer Protocol, annexed to PC-XV/A/WP.11, as amended, on the understanding that all letters referred to in its Annexes 2 and 4 be made available to delegations and that no objections be received in The Hague by the Secretariat within seven days after circulation of the said letters,

Recalling further that the said letters were circulated on 17 March 1997, that no objection was received by the Secretariat in The Hague within seven days thereafter (26 March 1997) and that the approval of the above-mentioned Draft Transfer Protocol therefore became final,

Aware that, in accordance with the Paris Resolution, paragraph 10(g) the Commission undertook, in PC-VIII/A/WP.7, Annex, to purchase equipment required for training of inspectors and evaluation purposes and that at present approximately 15,000 items of equipment have been purchased. Equipment standardisation, as required, was accomplished by ensuring that all equipment items procured were checked prior to the placement of orders against the operational requirements and technical specifications for such equipment developed and approved by the relevant bodies of the Commission (PC-VI/B/WP.4, PC-VII/B/WP.5, PC-VIII/B/WP.2 and Corr. 1, PC-VIII/B/WP.12, PC-IX/B/WP.3, PC-XI/B/WP.1, PC-XI/B/WP.6, PC-XII/B/WP.6, PC-XIII/B/WP.5, PC-XIV/B/WP.5 and Corr. 1 PC-XV/B/WP.9 and Corr.1, PC-XVI/B/WP.6). Major items of equipment were also evaluated for compliance with the approved specifications by a number of Member States which had offered to provide these services to the Secretariat (PC-XV/B/WP.9 and PC-XVI/B/WP.6.). Seventy-five percent of this equipment is currently being used by inspector trainees in the course of the General Training Scheme. All equipment which is not being used is stored at the OPCW Equipment Store in Rijswijk, a city close to The Hague. The facility in Rijswijk also houses the OPCW Laboratory equipped with the most modern analytical and other laboratory equipment.

Bearing in mind that the Commission recommended in paragraph 33.6 of its Final Report that the Conference note the above-mentioned activities regarding the purchase and standardisation of equipment undertaken by the Commission; that the Conference approve the above-mentioned Draft Transfer Protocol; and that the Conference authorise the Director-General to sign the Transfer Protocol on behalf of the OPCW and act as Depositary for the Transfer Protocol upon its signature by the Executive Secretary of the Commission,

---

[1] The Transfer Protocol was signed on 21 May 1997 by the Executive Secretary of the Preparatory Commission, Mr Ian Kenyon, and the Director-General of the OPCW, Mr José M. Bustani, during the First Session of the Conference of the States Parties.

Hereby:

1. Notes the activities regarding the purchase and standardisation of equipment undertaken by the Commission,
2. Adopts the Transfer Protocol annexed hereto, and
3. Authorises the Director-General to sign the Transfer Protocol on behalf of the OPCW and, upon signature by the Executive Secretary of the Commission, to act as Depositary for the Transfer Protocol.

ANNEX

PROTOCOL REGARDING THE TRANSFER OF ASSETS, LIABILITIES, RECORDS AND FUNCTIONS FROM THE PREPARATORY COMMISSION FOR THE ORGANISATION FOR THE PROHIBITION OF CHEMICAL WEAPONS TO THE ORGANISATION FOR THE PROHIBITION OF CHEMICAL WEAPONS

The Preparatory Commission for the Organisation for the Prohibition of Chemical Weapons ("Commission")
and
the Organisation for the Prohibition of Chemical Weapons ("OPCW"),

Noting that:

Paragraph 17 of the Text attached to the Resolution Establishing the Preparatory Commission for the Organisation for the Prohibition of Chemical Weapons ("Paris Resolution"), adopted by signatory States to the Convention on the Prohibition of the Development, Production, Stockpiling and Use of Chemical Weapons and on Their Destruction ("Convention") at the Signing Ceremony on 13-15 January 1993, provides that the Commission shall remain in existence until the conclusion of the First Session of the Conference of the States Parties of the OPCW;

Paragraph 16 of the same Text provides, *inter alia*, that the property and functions of the Commission shall be transferred to the OPCW at the First Session of the Conference of the States Parties;

Desiring that:

The details of the transfer be determined;

Agree as follows:

ARTICLE 1. TRANSFER OF ASSETS AND LIABILITIES

1.1 All assets and liabilities of the Commission shall be transferred to the OPCW by the conclusion of the First Session of the Conference of the States Parties. The assets and liabilities of the Commission shall include the assets held, including all transferable rights, and the liabilities incurred, in the name of the Commission.

1.2 The transfer shall include the rights in respect of movable, immovable and intellectual property.

1.3 The movable property shall be listed in an inventory drawn up by the Commission, as on the date of the entry into force of the Convention, and accepted by the OPCW at the time of the transfer. The Inventory shall be annexed to this Protocol as Annex 1.

1.4 The transfer of rights and obligations with respect to the office furniture and office equipment supplied free of charge to the Commission by the supplier designated by The Hague under paragraph 8 of Annex 3 of the Text attached to the Paris Resolution, shall be in accordance with the Exchange of Letters between the Executive Secretary of the Commission and the Director of the OPCW Foundation. This Exchange of Letters is contained in Annex 2 to this

Protocol. The inventory, as on the date of entry into force of the Convention, of such office furniture and office equipment is contained in Annex 3 to this Protocol.

1.5   The transfer of rights and obligations with respect to the office furniture and office equipment supplied free of charge to the Commission on behalf of the OPCW by the supplier designated by The Hague under paragraph 9 of Annex 3 to the Text attached to the Paris Resolution, shall be in accordance with the Exchange of Letters between the Executive Secretary of the Commission and the Representative of the Host Country. The Exchange of Letters is contained in Annex 4 to this Protocol. The current inventory of such office furniture and office equipment is contained in Annex 5 to this Protocol.

1.6   The transfer of assets shall include an eventual audited cash surplus, if any, which will be reflected in the final audited financial statements of the Commission. The transfer of assets shall not include Capital Advance payments made by Member States to the Commission, since these funds shall be reimbursed to Member States in accordance with Commission Financial Regulation 6.2, taking into account Financial Regulation 6.3. After the final audit of the Commission's account is completed, any cash surplus shall be reimbursed to the Member States of the Commission in accordance with Commission Financial Regulation 6.1(b), unless a Member State decides to temporarily credit this amount to the OPCW until it becomes a State Party. Cash surpluses of those Member States which are also States Parties of the OPCW shall be treated in accordance with OPCW Financial Regulation 6.3(c).

1.7   It is understood that gifts presented to the Commission by Governments, public bodies or private individuals, whether they have become part of the buildings or whether they have retained the character of movable property, shall be transferred to the OPCW on the same terms as those on which the said gifts were presented.

ARTICLE 2. SUCCESSION TO CONTRACTS

2.1   The terms and conditions under which the OPCW may succeed to contracts entered into by the Commission are specified in said contracts.

2.2   All contracts concluded by the Commission have foreseen the dissolution of the Commission and, where appropriate and feasible, have provided for succession by the OPCW, without prejudice to the OPCW's right not to succeed to these contracts.

2.3   While not in written contract form, appropriate bank accounts and signature cards will be prepared by the Commission to facilitate the transfer of cash to the OPCW, and the deposit of OPCW contributions as received.

2.4   A list of the contracts specified in 2.2 above is attached to this Protocol as Annex 6.

ARTICLE 3. TRANSFER OF FUNCTIONS

1.   As of the date of the conclusion of the First Session of the Conference of the States Parties, the remaining relevant functions of the Commission shall be transferred to the OPCW.

ARTICLE 4. ACCRUED BENEFITS OF STAFF MEMBERS

4.1   The OPCW shall recognise the accrued benefits of those staff members of the Provisional Technical Secretariat of the Commission who are appointed by the Director-General to the Technical Secretariat of the OPCW. The accrued benefits shall be specified in the Letter of Appointment.

4.2   If the Conference of the States Parties decides to establish a Provident Fund for the staff members of the Technical Secretariat of the OPCW, the staff members of the Provisional Technical Secretariat who are subsequently appointed by the Director-General to the Technical Secretariat shall be offered the option of having their Commission Provident Fund credits transferred directly to the OPCW Provident Fund and will be fully credited accordingly for the deposit.

ARTICLE 5. OFFICE OF THE LIQUIDATOR

5.1 Immediately after the conclusion of the First Session of the Conference of the States Parties, the Office of the Liquidator for the Commission shall be established. The Liquidator shall be appointed by the Director-General at the same time. The Executive Secretary of the Commission shall initially undertake the liquidation of the Commission until his contract expires.

5.2 The Liquidator shall act under the supervision of the Director-General. The Liquidator is hereby fully empowered to complete the final closure of the Commission's accounts in accordance with the Financial Regulations and Rules of the Commission and to carry out the liquidation of the Commission as specified in Article 5.3 below. As necessary to complete the liquidation, the Liquidator is empowered to assume the duties of "the Executive Secretary" and "the Director of Administration" specified in the Financial Regulations and Rules of the Commission.

5.3 The mandate of the Liquidator shall be:
  (a) to take full account of the financial assets and liabilities of the Commission; to collect all receivables and obligations owing to the Commission and to otherwise enforce any claims of the Commission; to pay, discharge and satisfy or otherwise provide for all known liabilities and obligations of the Commission; to set aside a portion of the Commission's financial assets as a reserve for the payment of contingent liabilities and obligations, such reserve to be established over such time and from such assets as the Conference of the States Parties may deem advisable;
  (b) to take authority for the preparation of the final financial statements of the Commission and to submit them to the External Auditor not later than 31 March following the end of the current calendar year;
  (c) to cooperate with the External Auditor as he may require in the performance of the audit;
  (d) to be present when the final audited financial statements are presented to the Executive Council and the Conference of the States Parties and to respond to requests by those organs in this connection;
  (e) to disburse to each Member State its share of the Capital Advance credited to its account by the Commission in accordance with Financial Regulation 6.2, once the Conference of the States Parties has noted the final audited financial statements of the Commission;
  (f) to transfer to the OPCW an eventual audited cash surplus, if any, identified in the final audited financial statements of the Commission in accordance with paragraph 1.6 of this Protocol;
  (g) to perform any other actions necessary or advisable in order to carry out the liquidation of the Commission.

5.4 For the duration of the liquidation process, the books and accounts of the Commission shall be kept separately from those of the OPCW.

5.5 The services of the Liquidator shall be provided by the OPCW. The OPCW will also provide, clerical and administrative support and supplies to the Liquidator as are deemed necessary to complete the liquidation. The services of the Liquidator, the clerical and administrative support and the supplies mentioned in this paragraph shall be borne by the OPCW budget. All other costs related to the liquidation shall be charged to the Commission's account.

5.6 The Conference of the States Parties shall expeditiously terminate the Office of the Liquidator and shall, at its next regular session after the submission of the financial statements as provided for in subparagraph 5.3(b), dissolve the residual legal entity after the conclusion of the liquidation process.

ARTICLE 6. ENTRY INTO FORCE; TERMINATION

1.   This Protocol shall enter into force on the date on which it is signed by the Executive Secretary of the Commission and the Director-General of the OPCW. The Protocol shall apply in perpetuity.

ARTICLE 7. ANNEXES

The Annexes to this Protocol constitute an integral part of this Protocol. The Annexes are:

Annex 1:   Inventory of movable property being transferred by the Commission to the OPCW

Annex 2:   Exchange of Letters between the Executive Secretary of the Commission and the Director of the OPCW Foundation related to paragraph 8 of Annex 3 to the Text attached to the Paris Resolution

Annex 3:   Inventory of office equipment and office furniture supplied to the Commission and which are the property of the supplier designated by The Hague under the Paris Resolution

Annex 4:   Exchange of Letters between the Executive Secretary of the Commission and the Director of the OPCW Foundation related to paragraph 9 of Annex 3 to the Text attached to the Paris Resolution

Annex 5:   Inventory of office equipment and office furniture supplied to the Commission on behalf of the OPCW and which are the property of the supplier designated by The Hague under the Paris Resolution

Annex 6:   List of contracts entered into by the Commission

The text of this Protocol, done in a single copy, in the Arabic, Chinese, English, French, Russian and Spanish languages, each text being authentic, shall be deposited with the Director-General of the OPCW.

DONE at The Hague this ...... day of .... one thousand nine hundred and ninety-seven.

On behalf of the Preparatory Commission   On behalf of the Organisation for the
for the Organisation for the Prohibition of   Prohibition of Chemical Weapons
Chemical Weapons

[Ian R. Kenyon]   [José M. Bustani]

Executive Secretary   Director-General

35. EMBLEM OF THE OPCW

35.1 Emblem of the OPCW

C-II/8 containing the Report of the Second Session of the Conference of the States Parties adopted on 5 December 1997, Subparagraph 11.2(d)

...

11.2 The Conference took the following action on the basis of recommendations and decisions of the Executive Council: ...

   (d) OPCW LOGO

      in accordance with the recommendation of the Executive Council at its Fourth Session, and on the basis of the revised design contained in the annex to EC-IV/DG.7/Add.2, dated 3 September 1997, the Conference considered and adopted this revised design for the OPCW logo for use by the OPCW;

...

INDEX

Printing: Ten Brink, Meppel, The Netherlands
Binding: Stürtz, Würzburg, Germany